January 1–May 15, 1776

Paul H. Smith, Editor

Gerard W. Gawalt, Rosemary Fry Plakas, Eugene R. Sheridan
Assistant Editors

LIBRARY OF CONGRESS   WASHINGTON   1978

This volume is printed on permanent/durable paper.

Library of Congress Cataloging in Publication Data (Revised)

Main entry under title:

Letters of delegates to Congress, 1774–1789.

   Includes bibliographical references and indexes.
   CONTENTS: v.1. August 1774–August 1775.—v.2.
September–December 1775.—v.3. Jan. 1–May 15,
1776.

   1. United States. Continental Congress—History—
Sources—Collected works. I. Smith, Paul Hubert,
1931–
JK1033.L47   328.73′09′033   76–2592
ISBN 0–8444–0177–3

ISBN for complete set: 0–8444–0177–3
ISBN for this volume: 0–8444–0259–1

For sale by the Superintendent of Documents, U.S. Government Printing Office
Washington, D.C. 20402

Stock No. 030-000-00083-8

Foreword

Well before the signing on July 4, 1966, of Public Law 89–491, establishing a national American Revolution Bicentennial Commission, the Library of Congress began considering how it could contribute to the celebration of the Bicentennial of the American Revolution. In 1968 Congress approved the Library's general plan and subsequently authorized the addition to the Library's staff of several historians, all specialists in early American history. The Library took as the theme for its Bicentennial program "Liberty and Learning" from James Madison, who asked: "What spectacle can be more edifying or more seasonable, than that of Liberty & Learning, each leaning on the other for their mutual and surest support." Reflecting the Library's unparalleled resources for the study of the revolutionary era, its Bicentennial program ranges widely: from the presentation of symposia to the publication of facsimiles and the texts of rare or unique material to the recording of American folk music and the compilation of bibliographies and guides.

In preparing one of those guides, *Manuscript Sources in the Library of Congress for Research on the American Revolution* (Washington: Library of Congress, 1975), the staff of the Bicentennial Office discovered large numbers of letters, written by members of the Continental Congresses, which had not been published in Edmund C. Burnett's magisterial 8-volume edition of *Letters of Members of the Continental Congress* (Washington: Carnegie Institution, 1921–36). Initially, it appeared that these letters might be published as a supplement to Burnett's work, but as additional unpublished letters of delegates turned up and as a cursory survey of other repositories suggested that even more unpublished letters were available, the Library decided that a new, expanded edition would be a valuable and appropriate Bicentennial project.

The present edition has benefited immensely from Burnett's pathfinding work, of course, and from the generous cooperation of the editors of several other documentary publications that have a common focus on the era of the American Revolution. From them the Library has borrowed heavily and to them it owes a debt that it can never adequately acknowledge. It is, therefore, a pleasure to give special thanks to the editors of *The Adams Papers*, *The Papers of Benjamin Franklin*, *The Papers of Thomas Jefferson*, *The Papers of Henry Laurens*, *The Papers of James Madison*, and *The Papers of George Washington* for their assistance and counsel.

Thanks are also due to the Library's Advisory Committee on its American Revolution Bicentennial Program for support and encouragement. To the Ford Foundation, which supplied a generous grant to help underwrite the project, we gratefully record our indebtedness. And, finally, we are beholden to the Congress of the United States, which appropriates funds for the publication of these volumes of the

papers of its distinguished predecessors and has, with great understanding, supported the Library's Bicentennial program.

Elizabeth Hamer Kegan
Assistant Librarian of Congress
for American and Library Studies

Editorial Method and Apparatus

In its treatment of documents this edition of delegate letters strives to achieve a middle ground between facsimile reproduction and thorough modernization. The original spelling and grammar are allowed to stand except in cases where editorial changes or insertions are required to make the text intelligible. For example, when a badly misspelled word is misleading, the correct spelling is inserted in roman type in brackets after the word. Moreover, words omitted through oversight have been supplied at appropriate places in italic type in brackets. Obvious slips of the pen and inadvertent repetitions are usually silently corrected. Capitalization and punctuation have been standardized according to certain conventions. Each sentence begins with a capital letter, as do all proper and geographic names as well as days of the week and months of the year. Doubtful cases have been resolved in favor of modern usage; otherwise the usage of the original texts has been followed. Generally, abbreviations, contractions, and monetary signs are preserved as they appear in manuscript except when they are ambiguous or misleading. On the other hand, the thorn and the tilde are consistently expanded. "Ye" always appears as "The," for instance, and "recvd" as "received." Likewise, "pr." and "℣" are always expanded to "per," "pre," or "pro," as the case demands. Finally, superscript letters are always lowered to the line.

Gaps in the text are indicated by ellipses in brackets for missing words and by blank spaces in brackets for missing numbers. Conjectural readings are supplied in roman type in brackets, and editorial insertions in italic type in brackets. Material canceled in manuscript but restored to the printed text is included in italic type in angle brackets ("square parentheses"). Marginalia in letters are treated as postscripts, and postscripts which appear without explicit designation are supplied with a *P.S.* in brackets. Documents are arranged chronologically, with more than one document of the same date being arranged alphabetically according to writer. Documents dated only by the month or by the year are placed at the end of the respective month or year. Place-and-date lines always appear on the same line with the salutation regardless of their position in the manuscript.

A descriptive note at the foot of each entry provides abbreviations indicating the nature and location of the document when it was copied for this project, except for privately owned manuscripts whose ownership is fully explained. The descriptive note also contains information on the document's authorship if explanation is necessary, and endorsements or addresses are quoted when they contain more than routine information. Other editorial practices employed in this work are explained in the sections on editorial apparatus which follow.

The following devices will be used in this work to clarify the text.

[. . .], [. . . .]	One or two words missing and not conjecturable.
[. . .]¹, [. . . .]¹	More than two words missing; subjoined footnote estimates amount of material missing.
[ ]	Number or part of a number missing or illegible.
[ ]¹	Blank space in manuscript; explanation in subjoined footnote.
[roman]	Conjectural reading for missing or illegible matter; question mark inserted if reading is doubtful.
[*italic*]	Editorial insertion in the text.
⟨*italic*⟩	Matter crossed out in manuscript but restored.

The following symbols are used in this work to describe the kinds of documents drawn upon. When more than one symbol is used in the descriptive note, the first to appear is that from which the main text is taken.

RC	recipient's copy
FC	file copy
LB	letterbook copy
MS	manuscript
Tr	transcript (used to designate not only contemporary and later handwritten copies of manuscripts, but also printed documents)

The following symbols, denoting institutions holding the manuscripts printed in the present volume, are taken from *Symbols of American Libraries*, 11th ed. (Washington: Library of Congress, 1976).

CSmH	Henry E. Huntington Library, San Marino, Calif.
Ct	Connecticut State Library, Hartford
CtHi	Connecticut Historical Society, Hartford
CtNlHi	New London Historical Society, New London, Conn.
CtY	Yale University, New Haven, Conn.
DFo	Folger Shakespeare Library, Washington, D.C.
DLC	Library of Congress
DNA	National Archives
InU	Indiana University, Bloomington
MA	Amherst College, Amherst, Mass.

M–Ar	Massachusetts Archives, Boston
MH	Harvard University, Cambridge, Mass.
MHi	Massachusetts Historical Society, Boston
MWA	American Antiquarian Society, Worcester, Mass.
MdAA	Maryland Hall of Records, Annapolis
MdAn	U.S. Naval Academy, Annapolis
MdBJ–G	John Work Garrett Library, Johns Hopkins University, Baltimore, Md.
MdHi	Maryland Historical Society, Baltimore
MeHi	Maine Historical Society, Portland
MiU–C	William L. Clements Library, University of Michigan, Ann Arbor
N	New York State Library, Albany
NBLiHi	Long Island Historical Society, Brooklyn, N.Y.
NHi	New-York Historical Society, New York
NHpR	Franklin D. Roosevelt Library, Hyde Park, N.Y.
NN	New York Public Library, New York
NNC	Columbia University, New York
NNPM	Pierpont Morgan Library, New York
NSchU	Union College, Schenectady, N.Y.
Nc–Ar	North Carolina State Department of Archives and History, Raleigh
NcD	Duke University, Durham, N.C.
NcU	University of North Carolina, Chapel Hill
Nh	New Hampshire State Library, Concord
Nh–Ar	New Hampshire Division of Archives and Records Management, Concord
NhD	Dartmouth College, Hanover, N.H.
NhHi	New Hampshire Historical Society, Concord
NjHi	New Jersey Historical Society, Newark
NjMoHP	Morristown National Historical Park, Morristown, N.J.
NjP	Princeton University, Princeton, N.J.
NjR	Rutgers University, New Brunswick, N.J.
OClWHi	Western Reserve Historical Society, Cleveland, Ohio
PHC	Haverford College, Haverford, Pa.
PHarH	Pennsylvania Historical and Museum Commission, Harrisburg, Pa.
PHi	Historical Society of Pennsylvania, Philadelphia
PP	Free Library of Philadelphia
PPAmP	American Philosophical Society, Philadelphia
PPRF	Rosenbach Foundation, Philadelphia
PU	University of Pennsylvania, Philadelphia
R–Ar	Rhode Island State Archives, Providence
RHi	Rhode Island Historical Society, Providence
RPJCB	John Carter Brown Library, Providence

Vi	Virginia State Library, Richmond
ViHi	Virginia Historical Society, Richmond
ViU	University of Virginia, Charlottesville
ViW	College of William and Mary, Williamsburg, Va.
WHi	State Historical Society of Wisconsin, Madison

ABBREVIATIONS AND SHORT TITLES

Abbreviations and short titles frequently cited in the present volume are identified below.

Adams, *Diary* (Butterfield)
   Adams, John. *Diary and Autobiography of John Adams.* Edited by Lyman H. Butterfield et al. 4 vols. Cambridge: Harvard University Press, Belknap Press, 1961.
Adams, *Family Correspondence* (Butterfield)
   Butterfield, Lyman H., et al., eds. *Adams Family Correspondence.* Cambridge: Harvard University Press, Belknap Press, 1963–.
Adams, *Works* (Adams)
   Adams, John. *The Works of John Adams, Second President of the United States. . . .* Edited by Charles Francis Adams. 10 vols. Boston: Charles C. Little and James Brown, 1850–56.
T. R. Adams, *American Independence*
   Adams, Thomas R. *American Independence: The Growth of an Idea.* Providence: Brown University Press, 1965.
Am. Archives
   Force, Peter, ed. *American Archives: Consisting of a Collection of Authentick Records, State Papers, Debates, and Letters and Other Notices of Publick Affairs.* 4th series, 6 vols. 5th series, 3 vols. Washington: U.S. Government Printing Office, 1837–53.
Austin, *Life of Gerry*
   Austin, James T. *The Life of Elbridge Gerry, with Contemporary Letters to the Close of the American Revolution.* 2 vols. Boston: Wells and Lilly, 1828–29.
Bio. Dir. Cong.
   U.S. Congress. *Biographical Directory of the American Congress, 1774–1971.* Washington: U.S. Government Printing Office, 1971.
Burnett, *Letters*
   Burnett, Edmund C., ed. *Letters of Members of the Continental Congress.* 8 vols. Washington: Carnegie Institution of Washington, 1921–36.
Clark, *Naval Documents*
   Clark, William Bell, et al., eds. *Naval Documents of the American Revolution.* Washington: Department of the Navy, 1964–.

DAB

    Dictionary of American Biography. Edited by Allen Johnson and Dumas Malone.

Jay, *Papers (Morris)*

    Jay, John. *John Jay, the Making of a Revolutionary: Unpublished Papers, 1745–1780.* Edited by Richard B. Morris et al. New York: Harper & Row, 1975–.

JCC

    U.S. Continental Congress. *Journals of the Continental Congress, 1774–1789.* 34 vols. Edited by Worthington C. Ford et al. Washington: Library of Congress, 1904–37.

Jefferson, *Papers* (Boyd)

    Jefferson, Thomas. *The Papers of Thomas Jefferson.* Edited by Julian P. Boyd et al. Princeton: Princeton University Press, 1950–.

Journal of Charles Carroll

    Carroll, Charles. *Journal of Charles Carroll of Carrollton, during His Visit to Canada in 1776, as One of the Commissioners from Congress.* Edited by Brantz Mayer. Baltimore: Maryland Historical Society, 1876.

Journals of N.Y. Prov. Cong.

    New York. *Journals of the Provincial Congress, Provincial Convention, Committee of Safety and Council of Safety of the State of New York, 1775–1777.* 2 vols. Albany: T. Weed, 1842.

Md. Archives

    Archives of Maryland. Edited by William H. Browne et al. Baltimore: Maryland Historical Society, 1883–.

N.C. Colonial Records

    North Carolina. *The Colonial Records of North Carolina.* Edited by William L. Saunders. 10 vols. Raleigh and Goldsboro, N.C.: P.M. Hale et al., 1886–90.

N.H. Provincial Papers

    New Hampshire. *Provincial and State Papers.* 40 vols. Concord, 1867–1943.

NYHS Collections

    Collections of the New-York Historical Society.

Pa. Archives

    Pennsylvania Archives. 9 series, 119 vols. in 120. Philadelphia: J. Severns & Co., 1852–56; Harrisburg: State printer, 1874–1935.

PCC

    Papers of the Continental Congress. National Archives and Records Service. Washington, D.C.

PMHB

    Pennsylvania Magazine of History and Biography.

PRO

    Public Record Office. London.

Rodney, *Letters* (Ryden)
Rodney, Caesar. *Letters to and from Caesar Rodney, 1756–1784.* Edited by George H. Ryden. Philadelphia: University of Pennsylvania Press, 1933.
Shipton, *Harvard Graduates*
Shipton, Clifford K. *Biographical Sketches of Those Who Attended Harvard College.* Sibley's Harvard Graduates. Boston: Massachusetts Historical Society, 1873–.
Susquehannah Co. Papers
Boyd, Julian P., and Taylor, Robert J., eds. *The Susquehannah Company Papers.* 11 vols. Ithaca, N.Y.: Cornell University Press, 1962–71.
Ward, *Correspondence* (Knollenberg)
Ward, Samuel. *Correspondence of Governor Samuel Ward, May 1775– March 1776, with a Biographical Introduction Based Chiefly on the Ward Papers covering the period 1725–1776, and Genealogy of the Ward Family, Thomas Ward, Son of John, of Newport and Some of His Descendants.* Edited by Bernhard Knollenberg and compiled by Clifford P. Monahon. Providence: Rhode Island Historical Society, 1952.
Warren-Adams Letters
Warren-Adams Letters, Being Chiefly a Correspondence among John Adams, Samuel Adams, and James Warren. 2 vols. Massachusetts Historical Society Collections, vols. 72–73. Boston: Massachusetts Historical Society, 1917–25.
Washington, *Writings* (Fitzpatrick)
Washington, George. *The Writings of George Washington.* Edited by John C. Fitzpatrick. 39 vols. Washington: U.S. Government Printing Office, 1931–44.

Acknowledgments

To the Library of Congress, the Congress of the United States, and the Ford Foundation this edition owes its existence. It is fitting, therefore, that we take this opportunity to acknowledge the foresight of the Library's administration in planning a timely and comprehensive observation of the American Revolution Bicentennial, of the Congress in funding a Bicentennial Office in the Library, and of the Ford Foundation in making a generous grant in support of this project as a scholarly contribution to the celebration of the Bicentennial era. It is with the most profound gratitude that the editors acknowledge their appreciation to all those who bore responsibility for the decisions that made possible these contributions. Our appreciation is also extended to the innumerable persons who have contributed to enriching the holdings of the Library of Congress to make it the premier institution for conducting research on the American Revolution.

The photocopies of the more than twenty thousand documents that have been collected for this project have been assembled through the cooperation of several hundred institutions and private persons devoted to preserving the documentary record upon which the history and traditions of the American people rest, and it is to their work that a documentary publication of this nature should ultimately be dedicated. Unfortunately, the many individual contributors to this collecting effort cannot be adequately recognized, but for permission to print documents appearing in the present volume, we are especially grateful to the following institutions: the American Antiquarian Society, American Philosophical Society, Amherst College, John Carter Brown Library, William L. Clements Library, Columbia University, Connecticut Historical Society, Connecticut State Library, Dartmouth College, Duke University, Folger Shakespeare Library, John Work Garrett Library, Harvard University, Haverford College, Henry E. Huntington Library, Indiana University, Long Island Historical Society, Maine Historical Society, Maryland Hall of Records, Maryland Historical Society, Massachusetts Archives Division, Massachusetts Historical Society, Pierpont Morgan Library, Morristown National Historical Park, National Archives and Records Service, New Hampshire Division of Archives and Records Management, New Hampshire Historical Society, New Hampshire State Library, New Jersey Historical Society, The New London County Historical Society, New-York Historical Society, New York Public Library, New York State Library, North Carolina State Department of Archives and History, University of North Carolina, Pennsylvania Historical and Museum Commission, Historical Society of Pennsylvania, University of Pennsylvania, Free Library of Philadelphia, Princeton University, Public Record Office (London), Rhode Island Historical Society, Rhode Island State Archives, Franklin D.

Roosevelt Library, Rosenbach Foundation, Rutgers University, Scottish Record Office, Union College, United States Naval Academy, Virginia Historical Society, Virginia State Library, University of Virginia, Western Reserve Historical Society, College of William and Mary, The Royal Archives (Windsor Castle), State Historical Society of Wisconsin, and Yale University. And in addition we express our thanks and appreciation to the following persons: The Earl of Ancaster, Mr. Sol. Feinstone, Mrs. John Frazer, Mr. Ronald von Klaussen, Mr. J. Woodward Redmond, Mrs. Elsie O. Sang and Mr. Philip D. Sang, Capt. J. G. M. Stone, Mr. Robert J. Sudderth, Jr., Mr. Paul Francis Webster, and Mrs. John G. Wood. Finally we owe thanks to the historians who have served on the Advisory Committee on the Library's American Revolution Bicentennial Program, and especially to Mr. Julian P. Boyd, Mr. Lyman H. Butterfield, and Mr. Merrill Jensen, who generously act as an advisory committee for the *Letters* project.

Chronology of Congress

January 1	Recommends "the reduction of St. Augustine."
January 3	Recommends a quarantine of Queens County, N.Y., for refusal to send deputies to the New York Convention.
January 6	Adopts regulations for the division of marine prizes.
January 8	Orders reinforcements to Canada; receives news of the king's speech from the throne (October 27, 1775) and of the destruction of Norfolk, Va.
January 11	Resolves that any person refusing to accept Continental currency "shall be . . . treated as an enemy of his country."
January 16	Limits black recruitment to the reenlistment of "free negroes who have served faithfully in the army at Cambridge."
January 17	Receives news of General Montgomery's defeat at Quebec; appoints a committee to prepare regulations for opening American ports on March 1, 1776.
January 19	Orders additional reinforcements to Canada in response to General Montgomery's defeat.
January 24	Orders publication of a public statement on the repulse at Quebec and of a new "Letter to the Inhabitants of the Province of Canada."
January 25	Orders preparation of a monument and delivery of a funeral oration in tribute to the memory of General Montgomery.
January 26	Appoints a committee "to repair to New York, to consult and advise . . . respecting the immediate defence of the said city."
January 27	Directs the Secret Committee to import goods for use of the commissioners of Indian affairs "in order to preserve the friendship and confidence of the Indians."
January 31	Forbids enlistment of prisoners of war.
February 5	Recommends that additional efforts be made to instruct and convert the Indians.
February 13	Exempts intercolonial trade in naval stores from general trade restrictions; tables draft "address to the inhabitants of these Colonies."
February 15	Appoints a committee to proceed to Canada to promote support for the American cause.
February 17	Appoints the Treasury Committee; resolves to emit additional $4 million; appoints Gen. Charles Lee to the Canadian command.

February 23   Appoints committees to promote the manufacture of firearms and the production of saltpetre, sulphur, and powder.

February 26   Prohibits sailing of vessels loaded for Great Britain, Ireland, or the British West Indies.

February 27   Establishes separate military departments for the middle and southern colonies.

February 29   Receives General Washington's letter on Lord Drummond's peace mission.

March 1   Appoints Gen. Charles Lee to command of the southern department.

March 2   Committee of Secret Correspondence appoints Silas Deane agent to France to transact business "commercial and political."

March 4   Removes the sailing ban on vessels loaded for Great Britain, Ireland, or the British West Indies and desiring to import arms and ammunition.

March 6   Appoints Gen. John Thomas to the Canadian command.

March 9   Appoints a committee to study the "state of the colonies in the southern department"; denies military officers authority to impose test oaths.

March 14   Adopts resolves on defending New York and disarming the "notoriously disaffected" in all the colonies.

March 16   Declares May 17 "a day of humiliation, fasting, and prayer."

March 20   Adopts instructions for the commissioners appointed to go to Canada.

March 23   Adopts a declaration and resolutions on privateering, subjecting British ships to seizure as lawful prizes.

March 25   Adopts a report on augmenting the defenses of the southern department.

March 27   Attends the funeral of Samuel Ward.

April 1   Establishes the Treasury Office.

April 2   Commends General Washington and his troops for conducting the successful siege and forcing the evacuation of Boston.

April 3   Adopts "Instructions" for privateers.

April 6   Opens the trade of the colonies "to any parts of the world which are not under the dominion of the [King of Great Britain]"; prohibits the importation of slaves.

April 11   Delivers a speech to Captain White Eyes of the Delaware Indians.

April 15   Urges cultivation of harmony between the Connecticut and Pennsylvania settlers in the Wyoming Valley.

April 16   Requests the Maryland Council of Safety to arrest Gov.
              William Eden.
April 23   Appoints Continental "agents for prizes in the several
              colonies"; instructs the commissioners to Canada "to
              publish an Address to the people of Canada."
April 29   Instructs a committee "to prepare a plan of an expedi-
              tion against Fort Detroit."
April 30   Appoints the Indian Affairs Committee.
May 6   Postpones prescribing procedures for receiving peace
              commissioners rumored to be en route to America; re-
              solves to raise $10 million "for the purpose of carrying
              on the war for the current year" and appoints a "ways
              and means" committee.
May 9   Resolves to emit an additional $5 million.
May 10   Recommends that the colonies "adopt such government
              as shall, in the opinion of the representatives of the
              people, best conduce to the happiness and safety of
              their constituents."
May 15   Adopts a preamble to its May 10 resolution on estab-
              lishing new governments, asserting the necessity of
              suppressing "the exercise of every kind of authority"
              under the British crown.

List of Delegates to Congress

This section lists both the dates on which delegates were elected to terms falling within the period covered by this volume and the inclusive dates of their attendance. The former are generally ascertainable from contemporary state records, but the latter are often elusive bits of information derived from the journals of Congress or extrapolated from references contained in the delegates' correspondence, and in such cases the "facts" are inevitably conjectural. It is not possible to determine interruptions in the attendance of many delegates, and no attempt has been made to record interruptions in service caused by illness or brief trips home, especially of delegates from New Jersey, Delaware, Maryland, and Pennsylvania living within easy access of Philadelphia. For occasional references to such periods of intermittent service as survive in the correspondence and notes of various delegates, see the index under individual delegates. Until fuller information is provided in a consolidated summary of delegate attendance in the final volume of this series, the reader is advised to consult Burnett, *Letters*, 1:xli–lxvi, for additional information on conjectural dates of attendance. Brief biographical sketches of all the delegates are available in the *Biographical Directory of the American Congress, 1774–1971*, and fuller sketches of more than half of the delegates can be found in the *Dictionary of American Biography*.

CONNECTICUT

Silas Deane
  Elected: November 3, 1774
  Attended: January 1–16, 1776
Eliphalet Dyer
  Elected: November 3, 1774
  Attended: January 1–16, 1776
Titus Hosmer
  Elected: November 3, 1774; October 12, 1775
  Did not attend in 1776
Samuel Huntington
  Elected: October 12, 1775
  Attended: January 16 to May 15, 1776
Roger Sherman
  Elected: November 3, 1774; October 12, 1775
  Attended: January 1 to March 19?; April 10 to May 15, 1776
Jonathan Sturges
  Elected: November 3, 1774
  Did not attend in 1776

William Williams
 Elected: October 12, 1775
 Did not attend before May 15, 1776
Oliver Wolcott
 Elected: October 12, 1775
 Attended: January 16 to May 15, 1776

DELAWARE

Thomas McKean
 Elected: October 21, 1775
 Attended: January 1 to May 15, 1776
George Read
 Elected: October 21, 1775
 Attended: January 22 to March 7; April 11? to 27, 1776
Caesar Rodney
 Elected: October 21, 1775
 Attended: January 22 to February 4?; April 27 to May 15, 1776

GEORGIA

 Georgia was not represented during the period January 1 to May 15, 1776. On July 7, 1775, the Georgia Provincial Congress had elected Archibald Bulloch, Lyman Hall, John Houstoun, Noble Wimberly Jones, and John Joachim Zubly to Congress, all of whom—except Jones, who did not attend Congress until 1781—had returned home before the end of 1775. Bulloch, Hall, and Houstoun were reelected on February 2, 1776, at which time Button Gwinnett and George Walton were elected to replace Jones and Zubly, but it was not until May 20, 1776, that Gwinnett and Hall reached Philadelphia to restore Georgia's representation in Congress.

MARYLAND

Robert Alexander
 Elected: December 9, 1775; January 15, 1776
 Attended: January 3 to May 15, 1776
Samuel Chase
 Elected: August 14, 1775; January 15, 1776
 Attended: February ? to May 15, 1776 (traveled as commissioner to Canada, March 25 to June 11)
Robert Goldsborough
 Elected: August 14, 1775; January 15, 1776
 Attended: April 29? to —— 1776
Thomas Johnson
 Elected: August 14, 1775; January 15, 1776
 Attended: March 7? to May —, 1776

William Paca
  Elected: August 14, 1775; January 15, 1776
  Attended: January 17 to April 13?, 1776
John Rogers
  Elected: December 9, 1775; January 15, 1776
  Attended: January 1 to February 27?; May 3?–15, 1776
Thomas Stone
  Elected: August 14, 1775; January 15, 1776
  Attended: April 2? to May 15, 1776
Matthew Tilghman
  Elected: August 14, 1775; January 15, 1776
  Attended: March 4–16?; April 25? to May 15, 1776

MASSACHUSETTS

John Adams
  Elected: November 10, 1775; January 18, 1776
  Attended: February 9 to May 15, 1776
Samuel Adams
  Elected: November 10, 1775; January 18, 1776
  Attended: January 1 to May 15, 1776
Thomas Cushing
  Elected: November 10, 1775
  Attended: January 1–2, 1776
Elbridge Gerry
  Elected: January 18, 1776
  Attended: February 9 to May 15, 1776
John Hancock
  Elected: November 10, 1775; January 18, 1776
  Attended: January 1 to May 15, 1776
Robert Treat Paine
  Elected: November 10, 1775; January 18, 1776
  Attended: January 1 to May 15, 1776

NEW HAMPSHIRE

Josiah Bartlett
  Elected: August 23, 1775; January 23, 1776
  Attended: January 1 to March 18, 1776
John Langdon
  Elected: January 25, 1775; January 23, 1776
  Attended: January 1–2, 1776
William Whipple
  Elected: January 23, 1776
  Attended: February 29 to May 15, 1776

NEW JERSEY

John Cooper
  Elected: February 14, 1776
  Did not attend Congress
Stephen Crane
  Elected: January 24, 1775
  Attended: February 6?–20, 1776
John DeHart
  Elected: January 24, 1775; February 14, 1776
  Attended: March 30 to April —; April — to May 15, 1776
William Livingston
  Elected: January 24, 1775; February 14, 1776
  Attended: January 1 to March 16?; April 30? to May 15, 1776
Jonathan Dickinson Sergeant
  Elected: February 14, 1776
  Attended: February 20 to April 5; April 23 to May 15, 1776
Richard Smith
  Elected: January 24, 1775; February 14, 1776
  Attended: January 1 to March 30, 1776

NEW YORK

John Alsop
  Elected: April 21, 1775
  Attended: February 11 to April 24?, 1776
George Clinton
  Elected: April 21, 1775
  Attended: April 11? to ante May 4, 1776
James Duane
  Elected: April 21, 1775
  Attended: January 1 to May 15, 1776
William Floyd
  Elected: April 21, 1775
  Attended: January 1 to February 11?; April 23 to May 15, 1776
John Jay
  Elected: April 21, 1775
  Attended: January 1–7?; March 3 to May 3, 1776
Francis Lewis
  Elected: April 21, 1775
  Attended: February 2 to March 3?, 1776
Philip Livingston
  Elected: April 21, 1775
  Attended: January 1–12?; February 20? to March 1?; March 17 to
  April 9, 1776
Robert R. Livingston
  Elected: April 21, 1775
  Attended: May 12?–15, 1776

Lewis Morris
  Elected: April 21, 1775
  Attended: January 16?–30; February 15? to March 19; April 11 to
  May 15, 1776
Henry Wisner
  Elected: April 21, 1775
  Attended: January 1 to February —, 1776

NORTH CAROLINA

Joseph Hewes
  Elected: September 2, 1775
  Attended: January 1 to May 15, 1776
William Hooper
  Elected: September 2, 1775
  Attended: January 1 to February 5?; March 6–27?, 1776
John Penn
  Elected: September 8, 1775
  Attended: January 1 to March 27, 1776

PENNSYLVANIA

Andrew Allen
  Elected: November 4, 1775
  Attended: January 1 to May 15, 1776 (traveled on mission to New
  York City, January 26 to February 11)
Edward Biddle
  Elected: November 4, 1775
  Did not attend in 1776
John Dickinson
  Elected: November 4, 1775
  Attended: January 1 to May 15, 1776
Benjamin Franklin
  Elected: November 4, 1775
  Attended: January 1 to May 15, 1776 (traveled as commissioner to
  Canada, March 25 to May 31)
Charles Humphreys
  Elected: November 4, 1775
  Attended: February 23? to May 15, 1776
Robert Morris
  Elected: November 4, 1775
  Attended: January 1 to May 15, 1776
John Morton
  Elected: November 4, 1776
  Attended: January 29? to February 12; April 6? to May 15, 1776

Thomas Willing
  Elected: November 4, 1775
  Attended: January 1 to May 15, 1776
James Wilson
  Elected: November 4, 1775
  Attended: January 1 to May 15, 1776

RHODE ISLAND

William Ellery
  Elected: May 4, 1776
  Attended: May 14?–15, 1776
Stephen Hopkins
  Elected: December 9, 1774; May 3, 1776
  Attended: January 1 to May 15, 1776
Samuel Ward
  Elected: December 9, 1774
  Attended: January 1 to March 13, 1776 (died March 26, 1776)

SOUTH CAROLINA

Christopher Gadsden
  Elected: November 29, 1775
  Attended: January 1–17, 1776
Thomas Heyward
  Elected: February 16, 1776
  Attended: April 24? to May 15, 1776
Thomas Lynch, Sr.
  Elected: November 29, 1775; February 16, 1776
  Attended: January 1 to February 18?, 1776 (traveled on mission to
  New York City, January 26 to February 11)
Thomas Lynch, Jr.
  Elected: March 23, 1776
  Attended: April 24? to May 15, 1776
Arthur Middleton
  Elected: February 16, 1776
  Attended: April 24? to May 15, 1776
Henry Middleton
  Elected: November 29, 1775
  Did not attend in 1776
Edward Rutledge
  Elected: November 29, 1775; February 16, 1776
  Attended: January 1 to May 15, 1776
John Rutledge
  Elected: November 29, 1775; February 16, 1776
  Did not attend in 1776

VIRGINIA

Carter Braxton
  Elected: December 15, 1775
  Attended: February 23 to May 15, 1776
Benjamin Harrison
  Elected: August 11, 1775
  Attended: January 1 to May 15, 1776 (traveled on mission to New
  York City, January 26 to February 11)
Thomas Jefferson
  Elected: August 11, 1775
  Attended: May 14–15, 1776
Francis Lightfoot Lee
  Elected: August 15, 1775
  Attended: January 1 to May 15, 1776
Richard Henry Lee
  Elected: August 11, 1775
  Attended: March 11 to May 15, 1776
Thomas Nelson
  Elected: August 11, 1775
  Attended: January 1 to February 23?, 1776
George Wythe
  Elected: August 11, 1775
  Attended: January 1 to May 15, 1776

Illustrations

"An East Prospect of the City of Philadelphia; taken by George Heap from the Jersey Shore, under the Direction of Nicholas Scull Surveyor General of the Province of Pennsylvania." This detail is from an engraving by Thomas Jefferys based on an etching of the city published in Thomas Jefferys, *A General Topography of North America and the West Indies. Being a Collection of All the Maps, Charts, Plans, and Particular Surveys, That Have Been Published of That Part of the World, Either in Europe or America* (London: R. Sayer, 1768).

Livingston, a member of a powerful New York family, had moved to New Jersey a few years before the Revolution and there enjoyed a long and distinguished career as a delegate to Congress, brigadier general of militia, and the state's first governor, from 1776 until his death in 1790. Earlier his political writings had earned him an enviable reputation that led to several important committee appointments during the early days of Congress, and his family ties and territorial connections led Lord Drummond to consider him as one of the conciliatory leaders to consult during his effort to launch negotiations with the colonies. Drummond's conclusion that Livingston sympathized with his plans is open to question, since it was Livingston who on March 5 offered a motion designed to curb Drummond's activities by calling him to account before Congress.

Etching by Albert Rosenthal, Philadelphia, 1888.

A New Castle lawyer, Read had resigned his post as Delaware attorney general during the First Continental Congress, but he continued to play a prominent role in Continental affairs during the early years of the Revolution. Politically close to his friend John Dickinson, Read was among those who early in 1776 actively fought against the mounting tide of independence that was stimulated by the king's recent denunciation of the colonies in an address to Parliament and by the publication of *Common Sense*. Although he opposed the independence resolution adopted by Congress on July 2, 1776, Read subsequently signed the Declaration and remained politically active throughout the revolutionary era, capping his long public career with a term in the United States Senate and an appointment as chief justice of Delaware.

Engraving by Samuel Sartain. *Magazine of American History* (April 1885).

Aux habitants de la province du Canada 147

Congress' efforts to bring Canada into the protest movement against Britain—which had included sending "letters to Quebec" in October 1774 and May 1775, dispatching the Montgomery and Arnold expeditions into Canada, and appointing a "committee to the northward" during the autumn of 1775—had received a severe setback when Montgomery's assault on Quebec was repulsed on December 31, 1775. Ultimately this led Congress to appoint three commissioners to undertake a sensitive· mission to Canada, but in the meantime Congress resolved on January 24 to publish both a public explanation of the "unsuccessful attempt made to gain possession of Quebec" and a third "Letter to the Inhabitants of the Province of Canada." The latter was immediately translated into French and distributed as the broadside shown here.

Papers of the Continental Congress, National Archives and Records Service.

Andrew Allen 197

On January 26, 1776, Pennsylvania delegate Allen was appointed with Benjamin Harrison and Thomas Lynch to a committee to confer with Gen. Charles Lee and the New York Committee of Safety about the defense of New York City. Fears that the impetuous Lee might order an attack on the British men-of-war in New York Harbor and trigger a naval bombardment of the city had spread panic before the committee arrived, and the nearly simultaneous appearance of Gen. Henry Clinton with troops from Boston en route to the Carolinas only heightened the tension, which Allen described in a February 5 letter to his wife Sarah.

While in New York Allen also found time to reopen talks with Lord Drummond, with whom he had conferred in Philadelphia the previous month on prospects for a reconciliation with Britain. Yet by spring it was clear to Allen that there was little prospect for reconciliation, and he apparently quit attending Congress in mid-May. Adamantly opposed to independence, he was not reelected to Congress when the Pennsylvania Convention selected a new slate of delegates in July. In December Allen threw in his lot with Britain, joining General Howe's army at Trenton. He thereby became one of five delegates who ultimately declared themselves loyalists, joining Joseph Galloway, Isaac Low, and John J. Zubly, who had become estranged from the American cause in 1775, and Robert Alexander, whose withdrawal from active politics coincided with Allen's.

Etching by Albert Rosenthal.

Letter of February 5, 1776, from Thomas Lynch, Sr.
to George Washington   202

An "oppulent Planter," South Carolinian Thomas Lynch was "highly esteemed" by his fellow delegates, not only as an early advocate of strong measures against Britain but also because he had appeared at the First Continental Congress in American homespun. "Plain, Sensible, above Ceremony," Silas Deane had reported; "of great Understanding and Integrity and the best affections to our Country and Cause," John Adams noted. Notwithstanding his sterling reputation and the confidence reposed in him by even the more outspoken New Englanders, Lynch showed a clear willingness early in 1776 to promote Lord Drummond's peace mission. In this letter he asked Washington to forward to British general James Robertson Drummond's request for safe passage for congressional negotiators who might be sent to London. Lynch suffered a serious stroke just two weeks later, however, and was too ill to participate in the congressional debates that took place when Washington forwarded Drummond's letter to President Hancock for action. Although he recovered slightly in the spring, Lynch never resumed his duties in Congress, and he died in Maryland while on his way home later in the year.
George Washington Papers, Library of Congress.

William Smith's *Oration in Memory of General Montgomery*   279

On January 25, 1776, Congress resolved to pay tribute to Richard Montgomery by erecting a monument to his memory and requesting William Smith "to prepare and deliver a funeral oration in honor of General Montgomery, and of those officers and soldiers, who so magnanimously fought and fell with him in maintaining the principles of American Liberty." Smith's performance proved to be a disappointment to many delegates, however, who believed that the orator—an Anglican minister and provost of the College of Philadelphia—had taken advantage of the occasion to publicize tory principles and emphasize America's dependence on Britain. Therefore when William Livingston proposed that Congress formally thank Smith and arrange publication of the oration, the motion was denounced, and Livingston accordingly withdrew it. "The orator then printed it himself," John Adams later explained, "after leaving out or altering some offensive Passages."
Rare Book and Special Collections Division, Library of Congress.

William Hooper   370

Hooper, a Wilmington lawyer who was Boston born, Harvard educated, and trained to the law by James Otis, reflected the political ambivalence of many Americans when, early in 1776, he wrote, "My

first wish is to be free, My second to be reconciled to Great Britain."
He subsequently concluded that reconciliation could only be achieved
at the expense of American liberties and became a reluctant supporter
of independence. Although primarily concerned with the interests of
his North Carolina constituents, who four times elected him to Congress,
Hooper retained his interest in New England affairs through his correspondence with former acquaintances, such as the Trumbulls of
Connecticut, and his efforts to keep informed of his mother's plight
during the British occupation of Boston. He was regarded by one of his
colleagues in Congress as "a sensible, sprightly young lawyer, and a
rapid, but correct speaker."

Enlargement of a detail from John Trumbull's painting *The Declaration of Independence, 4 July 1776* in the Capitol rotunda. Courtesy of
the Architect of the Capitol.

John Adams' *Thoughts on Government*   401

As Americans became increasingly interested in independence and
creating new governments of their own making, several delegates
turned their minds to the forms new state constitutions might take. In
the spring of 1776 several colonies made preparations to convene constitutional conventions, and when North Carolina delegates William
Hooper and John Penn prepared to return home in March to attend
such a convention, John Adams was asked to systematize his political
views for their examination and study. In response Adams wrote a
brief essay which other delegates soon asked to peruse and which, with
some revisions, was published a few weeks later in pamphlet form as
*Thoughts on Government: Applicable to the Present State of the American Colonies.
In a Letter from a Gentleman to His Friend.* One of the earliest versions of
Adams' essay was the letter he wrote for John Penn which is printed in
this volume under the date March 19–27. His letter of April 20, 1776,
to James Warren contains his fullest explanation of the genesis and
production of the tract. The title page shown here is from the copy of
the pamphlet owned by Thomas Jefferson.

Rare Book and Special Collections Division, Library of Congress.

Francis Lewis   418

The congressional career of New York merchant Francis Lewis
generally reflected his mercantile background. As a member of several
committees concerned primarily with supplying American land and
naval forces, Lewis was often preoccupied with matters involving procurement of arms, production of gunpowder, and construction of ships,
rather than with constitutional or political questions. His practical
sagacity and administrative experience led to his appointment to the
Admiralty Board in 1779, after he had served more than four years in

Congress. He was appropriately described by Benjamin Rush as a "moderate Whig, but a very honest man, and very useful in executive business."

Engraving by Charles Cushing Wright, 1825. In John Sanderson, ed., *Biography of the Signers to the Declaration of Independence*, vol. 6, ed. Robert Waln, Jr. (Philadelphia: R. W. Pomeroy, 1824).

Although Congress decided in committee of the whole on March 19 to permit privateering against British trade, resolutions on the subject were not formally adopted until an acceptable preamble was approved on March 23, 1776. This momentous step was widely regarded as a milestone on the road to American independence, preceding by less than three weeks the even more significant decision of April 6 to open American ports to foreign trade.

George Washington Papers, Library of Congress.

The conditions under which American privateers were permitted to arm were set forth in an April 3 resolve of Congress and incorporated into printed commissions. The blank commissions were then signed by President Hancock and sent "to the general assemblies, conventions, and councils or committees of safety of the United Colonies" for delivery "to the persons intending to fit out such private ships of war, for making captures of British vessels and cargoes." In addition to these commissions, Congress also simultaneously issued lengthy "instructions" for commanders of privateers, which were both widely published in American newspapers and disseminated in broadside form.

Rare Book and Special Collections Division, Library of Congress.

Carter Braxton, who sat in Congress from February to August 1776, was one of the more conservative delegates to represent Virginia during the movement for American independence. Often politically estranged from his fellow delegates, Braxton shared his apprehensions about America's drift toward independence with his uncle Landon Carter, to whom in April he expressed his fear that once the New England colonies had thrown off their subjection to Britain they would "embrace their darling Democracy." It is not surprising, therefore, that when John Adams' *Thoughts on Government* appeared in the spring of 1776, Braxton attempted to win support for more conservative constitutional principles by publishing *An Address to the Convention of the Colony and Ancient Dominion of Virginia* on the eve of the convening of the Virginia constitutional convention in Williamsburg. The *Address*, Adams explained to a friend, was published "as an antidote to the popular poison in 'Thoughts on Government'."

The Library Company of Philadelphia.

Samuel Chase   610

Chase, an Annapolis lawyer, was one of the earliest and most outspoken opponents of parliamentary authority in the colonies and was often regarded as one of the more radical American leaders before the summer of 1776. With the achievement of independence, however, he became increasingly alarmed at the activities of popular leaders demanding greater democratization of the government of Maryland, a concern eventually reflected in the cooling of his relation with John Adams and his growing affinity for the political principles of John Dickinson. His congressional career came to an unpleasant end in 1778 when he was discredited after becoming enmeshed in a speculative scheme involving privileged congressional information on the procurement of flour for the French navy. Although Chase never returned to Congress after 1778, he nevertheless enjoyed a long public career, and his name ultimately became a familiar one in American history after his impeachment by the United States House of Representatives in 1804 when a justice of the Supreme Court.

Chase's repeated advocacy of vigorous Canadian measures made him a logical appointee when commissioners (Chase, Franklin, and Charles Carroll of Carrollton) were selected in February 1776 to undertake a mission to restore American prestige among the inhabitants of Canada and revive morale among the American forces remaining in Quebec. More than two dozen of the commissioners' letters written during their trip to Canada appear in this and the following volume of delegate correspondence.

Engraving by J. B. Forrest from a drawing by James B. Longacre after an original portrait by John Wesley Jarvis. In James Herring and James B. Longacre, eds., *The National Portrait Gallery of Distinguished Americans*, vol. 4 (Philadelphia: James B. Longacre; New York: James Herring, 1839).

Resolve on New Governments, May 10 and 15, 1776   677

Congress' May 10 resolve recommending creation of new state governments, and the May 15 "preamble" explaining its necessity, climaxed months of effort by those who believed that the colonies were moving too timidly. Conservatives such as James Duane, John Adams later declared, denounced the resolve as "a Machine to fabricate independence"; and James Wilson asserted that passage of the preamble would produce "an immediate Dissolution of every Kind of Authority" in his province of Pennsylvania. Adams himself conceded as much when he explained that "it was indeed on all hands considered by Men of Understanding as equivalent to a declaration of Independence, tho a formal declaration of it was still opposed."

The May 10 resolution was the product of extended debate in the committee of the whole. The preamble was undoubtedly the work of Adams, who with Richard Henry Lee and Edward Rutledge was appointed to a committee expressly charged with preparing such a preamble.

The Library Company of Philadelphia.

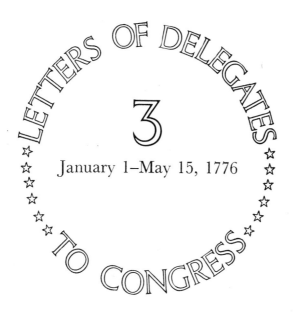

LETTERS OF DELEGATES

3

January 1–May 15, 1776

TO CONGRESS

Josiah Bartlett to Mary Bartlett

Philadelphia January first 1776. "This will be Delivered you by Gideon George, who I have Consented should return home without me. Capt Langdon & his man returns with him, so that I shall be now here without any body from New Hampshire. I was, till lately in hopes I should be able to return with him; but to my great Disappointment I now find Publick Business will not permit me to leave this place till our New Hampshire Convention appoint & send another Delegate to take my place here. I shall write to our Convention for that purpose."[1] Concludes with lengthy discussion of his personal affairs.

RC (NhHi).
[1] For Bartlett's further explication of the need for an additional delegate to Congress, see Bartlett to the New Hampshire Committee of Safety, January 20, 1776.

Committee of Congress to Philip Schuyler

Sir.   Philadelphia January 1st. 1776.

By the Extract from the Journal of the Congress and the Copies of two Depositions, inclosed herewith, you will percieve the purport of this application to you.[1] We have been informed by a certain John Conner whom we now send to you, that 53 Chests containing 25 Stands of Arms each, together with a Ton of powder were hid by him and certain Samuel Sutton, Arthur Redman, Robert Picken, Jas. McDonald (a Captain in his Majesty's Service) and Sir John Johnston, about 500 Yards from Sir John's House, on the 25th October last, and where we apprehend they still remain. It is the wish of the Congress that these arms and ammunition as well as all other arms & Indian Blankets at Sir John's, which belong to the Crown or may be likely to be used to the Injury of the Americans, may be immediately secured for the Use of the Continent, and that all such persons as you may find too dangerous to go at large be apprehended & imprisoned and all Scotch Roman Catholic Soldiers inlisted by Captn. McDonald, or other Tories in the Neighbourhood of Sir John, be disarmed.

We rest assured, you will exert every prudent & necessary Step immediately to accomplish the above, and with the utmost Secrecy collect as many Men as may be sufficient for the purpose. We are Sir with great Regard, Your most obedient, humble Servant.

                   Thomas McKean

                   Thomas Lynch

                   John Jay

Tr (NN).
[1] See *JCC*, 3:464, 466–67.

Eliphalet Dyer to Joseph Trumbull

Dear Sr   Philadelphia Jany. 1st 1776
    I Sincerely Wish you & the Gentlemen of the Army a happy New
Year. God Grant it may be a Year of American deliverance from the
Tyrrany, Oppression, Lawless & Hostile power, of Great Britain & May
Success Attend all our Counsells & opperations for that purpose. I have
just recievd yours of the 19th & 17th Ultmo. Am Oblidgd to you for
every part of Intelligence. Have Nothing New from this part of the
World. The Congress are taking every Method of defence from North
to south. I would mention some particulars but fear my letter might
possibly be Intercepted. I wrote to you a few days agoe wherein I
Informed you it might be well for you to get the General in some of his
letters to Mention how Inadequate your pay is to your services &
expences Which would give the best opening for Application here for an
Advance.[1] I should think the best way would be by a small Commission
which would goe down much best with the Multitude but I expect every
day to be Superseded by the comming of Messr Wolcott & Huntington.
They will come & Mr. Dean & my self depart in a most Critical season
especially for our Colony but hope all will be well. Am Very glad for
my self I may return tho I think the Colony might have been a little
more Complaisant in our dismission.
    How could the cask of Rhubarb which was sent by order of Congress &
was then extreamly wanted in the Hospital lye by to this time.[2] After
you came away I wrote to Daniel Brown to see it delivered. You Need
say Nothing about either price or pay as it is brot in with a large quantity
of Other druggs I was Employed to furnish the Army with by Congress,
& is setled here with the other Account. You Mention not a word of
Capt Thos.[3] I hear he has raised a Company & gone to the Army.
Suppose now all will be quiet when the rest have Absconded. I dare
say you will be his friend. By every friendly advice & Assistance I hope
he will behave well & with Spirit & rise Superior to his Enemys. If any
thing should open for him better & he is deserving you & your friends
I have no doubt will give a helping hand. I hope Gray Stays behind;[4]
really wish something may be done for him. As to Field officers the
Congress mean to have the appointment, as they say the army will not
yield to Provincial appointments but then they will be ready to receive
and much Attend to any Provincial recommendations or from the genll
officers in the Army where they can be had they will be Very Sure.
This is favored by Capt Langdon a Delegate from New Hampshire to
whom your Civilitys will be very Acceptable. He will Acquaint you with
our Naval preparations &c of which I could not write for reason above.
I may possibly be here a Month longer; if not you will hear from me
from Windham. Regards to Friends and believe me Sincerely yours,
                                                    Elipht Dyer

[*P.S.*] Mr. Dean presents his Compliments to you. He is Confoundedly Chagrind at his recall. He is really Very Usefull here & much esteemd in Congress.

RC (CtHi).
  [1] See Dyer to Joseph Trumbull, December 26, 1775, and January 15, 1776.
  [2] See Dyer to Joseph Trumbull, September 15, 1775.
  [3] Dyer's son Thomas.
  [4] Probably Ebenezer Gray, who had served with Dyer's son Thomas in the Third Connecticut Regiment. Captain Dyer and Lieutenant Gray joined the Twentieth Continental Infantry on January 1, 1776, and Gray became regimental quartermaster. F. B. Heitman, *Historical Register of Officers of the Continental Army* . . . (Washington [Baltimore]: Press of Nichols, Killam & Maffit, 1893), pp. 162, 197.

Thomas Lynch to John Morgan

Dear Sir   January 1. 1776
  I have for some time been wishing for an hour to answer your Favour, upon your arrival at Camp, but seeing no probability of it, I take this Method of writing during long Speeches in Congress.
  I am very glad to find the Camp so agreable to Mrs. Morgan and that you are so well settled as I find from Mr. Duché you are.
  I have mentioned your wants to Congress,[1] but there are so much before them that no determination has been had on that Head, in the Mean Time the Hour approaches in which these things will be necessary. I hope the Scotch Prize will furnish you actual Necessaries, and your own Ingenuity be exerted to supply deficiences.
  Capt Manly has done singular Service to the Southern Colonies, by taking Kirkland and his Papers.[2] He has my hearty thanks for this and his many other Services to the Continent.
  I hear with concern that our Friend Mifflin continues running himself into unnecessary Dangers, I wish he woud consider that he has no right to have our Quarter Master Genl. knocked in the Head.
  I have nothing of any Consequence to tell you but beg a happy New Year to you all & my best wishes & Respects to the General, to Genls. Lee, Putnam, Gates, Thomas, Green & Sullivan, to Mr Mifflin and my other Friends, add Mrs. & Miss Lynchs to Mrs. Morgan & Mrs. Mifflin.
  Dear Sir yours sincerely & affecly.   Tho Lynch

[*P.S.*] Do ask Gates if he remembers his promise to send a Deserter Drummer and Fifer, my very Affectionate Regards to Moyland, I hear with pleasure of his Services & of the Esteem he is held in, none better deserves it. I shall write to him soon.

RC (PHi). Addressed: "To Doctor John Morgan, M. D., Head Quarters, Cambridge. By Favour of Mr Cushing."

¹ For an indication of some of the problems confronting Dr. Morgan at this time, see his letter to Washington of December 12, 1775, in *Am. Archives*, 4th ser. 4:263.
² See Richard Smith's Diary, December 30, 1775.

Massachusetts Delegates to the
Massachusetts Assembly

Honble Gentlemen,   Philadelphia Jany. 1st. 1776
    We have had the Honor to receive the Memorial of the General Court to the Congress and the Accounts Accompanying the Same, which we immediately laid before the Congress.¹ They were referred to a Committee but could not be passed upon as the vouchers did not Come with them, however they have Voted to advance to the Colony in part of their Accounts the sum of Four hundred and forty Three Thousand three hundred & thirty three Dollars & one Third of a dollar which we have receivd & have hired a light Waggon to Convey it to Watertown, under the Care of Mr Cushing. Inclosed you have an Invoice of the same which we wish safe to hand.
    We are with great respect, Your Honours, Most obedient humble servts,   John Hancock   Samuel Adams

                                Thomas Cushing   Rob Treat Paine

RC (M-Ar). Written by Cushing and signed by Adams, Cushing, Hancock, and Paine.
    ¹ See John Hancock to the Massachusetts Assembly, December 2, 1775, note 2.

Robert Treat Paine to Joseph Hawley

                                                        Philada. Jany 1. 1776
    I arrived here the 28th of this Mo. & found one of our delegates Viz J A returned home. Many are the conjectures here of the occasion, tho to argue from Circumstantial Evidence I can discern a Cause: I understand that the last years Delegation is lengthend to the End of Jany. Currt. I suppose a new sett in part at least will be chosen, to this I shd. acquiese if conductd in a generous political plan, but to be undermined, discarded & displaced by the Secret machinations, Slanders & Tyranny of a Faction & representd as unfit for or unfaithful in the Service, must give Vexation its keenest Edge; it is exceeding melancholly that in a Scituation like that of ours who have put our Selves in the fore front of the Battle we shd have Occasion, or what is worse, be necessarily driven to Observations like this, but so it is. In Addition to the cold, haughty, disrespectful behaviour of the two Adams towards

me & their other Brethren for a long time past, since my return I have come at the Sight of an Extract of a Letter wrote by James Warren to the honble J A in which I am treated in such a manner as I flatter my self I deserve from no body, I am sure I dont from him. This Added to the Information I had of his Conduct respecting me at the Election of Councellors, satisfys me, that there are a set of men among us who set up their own Opinion as the Standard of Political Rectitude & who will Stick at no measure, to break every thing that will not bend to their despotic determination.[1] Dispositions of this kind are not uncommon toward different & clearly determined partys, but that the Defenders of Life, Liberty & property should practice a faction which must Stabb the vitals of this defence; that they shd. machinate & Traduce for the Bearskin when it is uncertain whether it will be saved is to me more astonishing than Sleeping on the top of a mast, & must shew a disposition so dangerous as to require immediate restraint; when I see seeds of so noxious a nature so early shooting their Roots in our new Admin it gives me the most alarming prospects & I am ready to cry out in the words of the Spanish Proverb "Good Lord deliver us from our Selves." What a Scituation am I in, to expose my Life & fortune & the happiness of my family, & at the best to waste my Estate in Exertions for my Countrys Safety & at the same time to be Slandered & degraded by those with whom I thought I was struggling [*side by*] side in the Common Cause.

You may remember when I was with you in the Summer that I expressed an uneasiness that Mr. J A was ranked above me at the Council Board. I never could discover any reason but the Sovereign good Will of his Freinds; since my Return here I have rec'd from the Dpty Secy a notification of the appointmt. of a set of Judges of the Supr. Court & that J A is Cheif Justice. I want exceedingly to know whether any besides himself has Accepted, & how the matter is relished by Judges Cushing & Read. This Mr. Adams is youngest man & youngest Lawyer at the Barr save Mr. Serjent. Mr. C. has been a Judge of the Supr. Ct. to good Acceptance & Mr Read has been a Lawyer of long standing & Reputation & many years as Judge of the Common pleas; if we were not qualified for the Post why were we Chosen, if we were why had we not our Rank. How these observations will affect you I dont know, but I think the Cause of them bodes no good, for my part when I consider my reasonable pretensions of Rank & how much I have exposed my Self when that Gentn. was out of Sight, or without drawing any Comparison to his Seeming disadvantage in this matter I will say that when I consider that from the beginning of this Controversy I have advanced my self in the most exposed scituations that have fallen in my way, I am much alarmd to find my self disgraced from my just Rank in my Profession & this alone if I had no other Reason would be sufficient to induce me to give my answer in the negative.[2]

Excuse me sr. that I write thus freely to you, I feel a Satisfaction to unbosom my mind to a person in whom I can place Confidence, I have no desire to irritate you against persons but if you think their measures are wrong you will conduct accordingly & give me that Support you may think I deserve. Inclosed I send you a Copy of the Extract referred to, it came to light in this manner, Mr J A on his way home met the person who had it for him & after reading it delivered it unsealed to the Bearer & directed him (as the Bearer Said) to deliver it to our Delegates, we suppose the order was to Mr. S A. The Bearer not finding Mr. S A delivered it to another of the Delegates saying Mr J A ordered him so to do, this Delegate finding it unsealed Concluded it Contained some news & Read it & finding the Contents Carefully copyed this Extract which we have reason to think is but a specimen of many more of the same kind. If you think any good may arise you will shew this Extract & my observations to any persons. For my part I am sure I have nothing in view but to promote the good of our Common Cause but while I am doing that I think I may defend my Self. I have wrote Coll Palmer on the same Subject but have not time to Copy the Extract for him. Wishing you Health & all kind of happiness I [remain].

FC (MHi).

¹ The simmering conflict within the Massachusetts delegation became an open rupture when Paine gained access to a James Warren letter disparaging Paine's journey to Canada and his work in Congress. This further breakdown of unanimity in the Bay Province's popular party is discussed in Stephen E. Patterson, *Political Parties in Revolutionary Massachusetts* (Madison: University of Wisconsin Press, 1973), pp. 134–35; and Shipton, *Harvard Graduates*, 12:474–76. Warren's critical letter of December 3, 1775, is in *Warren-Adams Letters*, 1:187–90. See also Paine's letters to Joseph Palmer and to James Warren, this date.
² See Robert Treat Paine to the Massachusetts Council, this date. According to James Warren, Paine's appointment was secured by Hawley and Joseph Palmer over his opposition. James Warren to John Adams, October 20 and November 5, 1775, *Warren-Adams Letters*, 1:149–55, 175-79.

Robert Treat Paine to
the Massachusetts Council

May it please your Honors   Philadelphia Jany 1, 1776
I arrived at this place the 28th Ultimo where I found a Letter ¹ from Mr Morton, Deputy Secy, wrote by the direction of the major part of the honorable Council of the Province of the Massachusetts Bay, by which I am acquainted that they have honored me with an appointment as one of the Justices of the Superior Court of Judicature &c for that Province. I am also favoured with a list of the other Gentlemen appointed to the Superior Bench and of our Arrangement in Rank. I am

also requested to signify to the honorable Board as soon as may be my acceptance or refusal in writing.[2]

That my answer has been so long delayed from the arrival of this Letter, has been intirely owing to my absence on a Commission to the Northward, so that I have really been notified but a few days of my appointment to that important office, & have not had that time and opportunity to consider the matter which I could have wished; but as your Honors have thought it expedient that a Superior Court should be appointed, & the appointment is of so long standing, I think it necessary to give my answer by this first opportunity, least the matter remaining any longer undetermined, might prevent the Accomplishment of your Honors determination.[3] After expressing my sincere thanks for the honor you have conferred upon me by this appointment, I find myself constrained to decline accepting it, & without troubling your Honors with a detail of reasons which are not required, I beg leave to observe, that I have the highest sense of the importance of that office, and am satisfied that if sufficiently qualified, I could not attend to the due execution of it, while the attacks made by our Enemys in every thing we hold dear, appear to me to demand our constant attention. I heartily wish the establishment of peace & the due administration of Justice in our Province, success to your Honors endeavours to effect these valuable purposes & happiness to your Persons, and am with unfeigned respect, your Honors most obedient & obliged humble Servant.

Robt. Treat Paine

Tr (M-Ar). FC (MHi).
[1] Paine wrote "of Octr 28" in his FC.
[2] Paine was not reconciled to the appointment of John Adams as chief justice of the Massachusetts Superior Court of Judicature. See Paine's letters to Joseph Hawley and to Joseph Palmer, this date. He later accepted appointment to the Massachusetts Supreme Judicial Court in 1790. Shipton, *Harvard Graduates*, 12:480. For John Adams' professed concern about being elevated above senior members of the legal profession, see Adams to Perez Morton, November 24, 1775.
[3] Paine lined out the following sentence in his FC. "Knowing that however indulgent & candid your Honr. might be if I Should take Some further time to Consider of it, there are not those wanting in our Province to put injurious Construction on it."

Robert Treat Paine to Joseph Palmer

My Dear Freind   Philada Jany 1. 1776
I arrived here the 28th ulto from my Journey as far as Ticonderoga. We proceeded no farther, as we had some expectation when we set out, partly because the Season was too late to pass Safely by Water & too early to pass on the Ice & also because the Object of our Commission of most immediate importance could be determined at Ticonderoga,

but a very great Reason was also because the Military Scituation of Canada would not admit of our receiving that assistance from Genl. Montgomery wch was necessary to promote the chief purpose of our going there.

At Albany we attended a treaty with the Six Nations & it appeared to be very serviceable to the Cause that a Cmttee from the Grand Council Fire at Philada. attended it. The Indians were much elated & behaved with every mark of Freindship, their Speech contains matters of importance & I suppose will be published as soon as the Report arrives from Albany to the Congress.

You write in low Spirits about Salt petre making among you but as yr. Letter is of old date, I hope your Spirits have been since raised by the production of considerable quantitys and in diverse places. We are informed here that you have got into the right method & that you make considerable quantitys, pray use your influence to have people in different parts set up small works; this will spread & encrease it & the Works will always be enlarged in proportion to the Success. They make it here at this time in the City Works from Earth taken from the bottom of Cellars where Wood & Vegetables have lain & they have good success; it is Spreading also in the Family Way. I intended to enlarge on this Subject, but have not been here long enough to digest matters; at present my mind is much agitated on the discovery of a malicious & Slanderous Correspondence between James Warren & John Adams respecting Mr. Cushing & my Self, & on comparing what is written with the behaviour of some of my brother Delegates, it appears to me that while I have been exerting my Self to the utmost in supporting the Common Defense of all that is valuable & by that means exposing my Self to the vengeance of Administration if I should fall into their hands, Some particular persons whom I considered as Struggling with & Supporting me in the same Cause, to my astonishment are undermining my importance, happiness & Safety, so that not only if our true Enemy conquers me shall I be made miserable but if our struggles are crowned with sucess, I am then to be crushed & rendered unhappy by the very men I have been endeavoring to Support at the risque of every thing that is valuable.[1]

I have recd. a notification of my Appointment as one of the Judges of the Supr. Court & a list of the whole Set with the Rank, of wch. the honble J. Adams is Chief Justice. By this Opportunity I have Sent my Answer in the negative & have assigned one Reason which I think of itself sufficient.[2] I have had but little time to consider the matter & could have wished to know how the other Gentlemen like their Rank & whether they have accepted; I am far from thinking that the honble. Board had the least intention of disparaging the Merit of any Gentleman, but when we consider that the proposed Chief Justice ranks the last but one in Age & as a Lawyer at the Barr, it looks to me as if some imperceptible

Influence had regulated the Appointment of a Chief Justice upon political or *other* principles than what are usual in such cases; if I was not worthy of such a Trust (as my former freind Col Warren suggests) why was I appointed; if I am defective either in Law, Knowledge, Integrity, or Political Rectitude, it certainly was wrong to appoint me; but if supposed sufficiently qualified in these Respects, why am I degraded? I mourn the Appearance of these things & some other matters that are coming to light. I fear they Spring from a fountain that will embitter the Administration of our publick Affairs.

Excuse my writing thus freely to you but it is to no purpose to disguise some sorts of uneasiness; if a Junto of 2, 3, or 4 men are able to combine together, settle a Test of political Rectitude, & distroy every one who will not Comply with their mode of Conduct, I must confess things are like to take a turn very different from what I expected.

Inclosed is the Extract, but I have not time to explain the manner in which it came to light, but I have wrote to Majr. Hawley who will explain the matter to you.

I have no desire to incence you against particular persons, but if you think such Conduct is wrong you will behave accordingly & give me that Support you may think I deserve. Wishing the promotion of our Common happiness & a deliverance from the Perils of public Enemys & also false Brethren I am with great Esteem, yr freind & hble Servt

R T Paine

RC (NjR: Elsie O. and Philip D. Sang deposit).
[1] See Paine's letters to Joseph Hawley and to James Warren, this date.
[2] Robert Treat Paine to the Massachusetts Council, this date.

Robert Treat Paine to James Warren

Sr,   Philada Jany. 1. 1776
I wrote you last from Hackinsac dated Novr. 15 [1] that I had put my Trunk on board a Waggon bound for Cambridge & had directed it to yr. Care. This Letter I think I sent by the Post, but the Waggon & Trunk Never set out from Philada. By this means you are saved any further trouble & I the burthen of being under any further Obligation to you. How far your malevolent disposition towards me would have Suffered you to have kept up the External appearance of good Offices I know not, tho' I believe another disposition would have prompted you to it. I dare say by this time you are trying to pretend to yr Self a Surprize at this Kind of Expression from a person whom you Supposed Considered you as his best Friend, but I dare appeal to Conscience which will at Some time do the Strictest Justice, that you deserve Severe Censure from me. However it is not my design to take notice of yr. Conduct towards me in any other way than Expostulation & call back yr mind to the first

principles of our Common Opposition from wch. it seems to me you
are widely Straying. Union is undoubtedly the Platform of our Opposition. Upon this we set out & when ever we depart from it there is an
End of our Defence. Whoever directly or indirectly doth any thing to
break this union is so far an Enemy to American Liberty, whoever
abuses, disparages or discourages fellow Labourers is so far an Enemy
to the Cause; without enlarging in this strain to which there could be no
End, I must referr yr Contemplations to a Letter you sent to Mr John
Adams dated Decr. 3d. 1775.[2] Mr. Adams met this Letter on the Road
home & forgetting what distruction the discovery of traducing Letters
has brought on some others & how necessary it is that such a correspondence be kept secret in order to answer the vile purposes of it Sent
it open to his brother Delegates; I can not describe the Astonishment,
Grief & vexation' I felt when I read it. If possible explain to me wherein
I deserve such Treatment from you. In the close Acquaintance of 15 yrs.
& more did you ever find me unfaithful, was I not Watchfully observant
of yr. Interest, Reputation & happiness, has any person been more
attentive to the Interest & Welfare of the Family with wch. you are
Connected, your *dulce Decus & presidium*, & that at a time when my
Interest & promotion would have been much advanced by Contrary
Conduct? I mention not these matters to upbraid but to give you an
Idea of the Reflections with wch. yr. Conduct agitate my mind. I know
not what principle to derive yr. Treatment of me from unless it be that
to the opposing of which in other Persons you owe all yr. Glory, could
you not have "perticular friends" without Calumniating, ridiculing &
degrading your other Friends. "Paine I hear is gone to gratify his
Curiosity in Canada." Did you hear this from any of yr. perticular
freinds, Alass I fear what you call "freindship" has for its object a very
Contracted monopolizing System for the support of wch. many in-
cumbrances must be cleared off. "A good Journey to him, he may
possibly do as much good there as at Philada." What apprehensions
have you of the little good I do at Philada. unless from the intimation
of yr. perticular freinds & pray sr. what good do you do at Watertown
or Cambridge? Do you consider how far & to what subjects such enquiry
may be extended? & do you know as well as I do what the answer might
be? "Tho I find some people here would not have pitched on him for
the business we suppose he is gone on & perhaps there are Some who
would not have done it for any." By all accts. if your machinations had
Succeeded I had not been chosen into the Council & I could clearly
percieve when there last that the influence of one of your Party in favour
of one of yr. particular friends degraded me in point of Rank; & what
other Plotts you have laid against me you well know. Pray sr. do you
really think that when such important matters were to be Consulted &
determined respecting our Expeditions in the North, that I took that
fatiguing journey in such a season to gratify my Curiosity. If you knew

how I spent all the time I was abroad in this Journey & what Report the Committee made you would not think that Curiosity either prompted or engaged any pursuit.[3] I certainly took great pains to be excused from the Service but was urged to it by one of yr perticular freinds. If I have not Acquitted my self well in this & all other political undertakings let my deficiency be pointed out to me that I may amend.

That there are some in our Colony who would not have chosen me to this or any other business may be true, but if you were not one of them wherefore this insidious Clandestine way of spreading the knowldge of it. Who these people are & how many of them owe their Sentiments to yr influence you do not say. Are there any or how many do you think there are who have the same Opinion of you. Do you really think I have done & do no good here, do you know how I have spent & do spend my time? I could sett this matter in a light that would sufficiently account for some things but I have affairs of more importance to attend to. That you are my Enemy & have been laboring my disgrace I am Satisfied; that finding yr. self discovered your implacable Temper will urge you on to execute your ill will I have so much Reason to think that I must necessarily take care of my Self.

FC (MHi). Tr (MHi).
    [1] Date supplied from Tr.
    [2] This letter is printed in *Warren-Adams Letters*, 1:187–90. See also Paine to Joseph Hawley, this date.
    [3] For the activities of this committee, see Committee to the Northward Minutes of Proceedings, November 30, 1775; and *JCC*, 3:446–52.

Richard Smith's Diary

                                                    Monday 1 January 1776
    We finished reading the Journal & sundry Passages were marked, according to Custom as improper for present Publication. Some Letters read. An Expedition agt. St. Augustine recommended to the Colonies of S. & N. Carolina & Georgia if the ruling Powers there shall deem it practicable. Report from the Comee. on Ld. Stirlings Letters partly agreed to, 1000 Dollars & 400 Weight of Powder was allowed, and partly disagreed to & recommitted. Much was said upon that Part of it relative to disarming & securing the Tories in N Jersey & in Case persons ordered to be secured by Authority would not surrender, then to put them to Death. During this Debate Wilson moved that all Persons in the 13 United Colonies who would not sign the Association should be disarmed and several written Propositions were made about disarming, securing & destroying such Tories as resisted an Arrest ordered by the present Authority.[1] 2 Companies of Ld. Stirlings Regt. are to go to the New Fort on the North River in the Highlands. The Report on Capt

Sellicks affair confirmed. An order passed to commission the Officers
of the Battalions raised in N. Carolina. Motion by Dyer to pay a Gentle-
mans Expences who accompanied the 2 Frenchmen from Gen. Washns.
Camp, was postponed.[2] Motion by Langdon & Bartlett to take One
Battalion of the New Hampshire Troops into Continental Pay was
opposed by Jay & others & the Matter adjorned. A printed Copy of
Mr. Rittenhouse's Oration was presented to each Delegate by the
Philosophical Society of Philada. & in Novr. preceeding Messrs. Norman
& Bell dedicated to & furnished the Members with a neat American
Edition of Swan's Designs in Architecture.[3] A former Article or Order
respecting Deserters was ordered to be published in the Papers. An
Adjutant chosen by Ballot for Col Bulls Battalion.

MS (DLC).
 [1] For Congress' final action on January 2 on the report of this committee, which
had been appointed on December 26 to consider letters from Col. William Alexander
to Hancock of December 3, 6, 14, and 19, 1775, see *JCC*, 4:17–22; Smith's Diary,
January 2, 1776; and *Am. Archives*, 4th ser. 4:164–65, 202–3, 354–55. See also *JCC*,
3:406, 413, 417, 443, 445, 460, 465.
 [2] On January 2 Congress decided to pay Judah Allen $50 for escorting Messrs.
Penet and de Pliarne from Cambridge to Philadelphia. *JCC*, 4:16; and Smith's
Diary, December 30, 1775, note 3.
 [3] David Rittenhouse, *An Oration, Delivered February 24, 1775, before the American
Philosophical Society* . . . (Philadelphia: John Dunlap, 1775); and Abraham Swan,
*A Collection of Designs in Architecture, Containing New Plans and Elevations of Houses, for
General Use* . . . (Philadelphia: R. Bell, 1775).

Samuel Adams to Elbridge Gerry

My dear Sir   Philade Jany 2 1776
    Your very acceptable Letter of the 13th of Decr is now before me.[1]
Our opinions of the Necessity of keeping the military Power under the
Direction & Controul of the legislative I always thought were alike. It
was far from my Intention in my Letter to you on the Subject, to attempt
the correcting any imagined Error in your Judgment, but rather,
shortly to express my own Apprehensions at this time, when it is become
necessary to tollerate that Power, which is always formidable, & has so
often provd fatal to the Liberties of mankind.
    It gives me great Satisfaction to be informd, that the Members of the
House of Representatives are possessd of so warm a Spirit of Patriotism,
as that "an Enemy to America may as well attempt to scale the Regions
of Bliss, as to insinuate himself into their favor." Whatever kind of Men
may be denominated Enemies to their Country, certainly he is a very
injudicious Friend to it, who gives his Suffrage for any Man to fill a
publick office, merely because he is *rich*; and yet you tell me there are
recent Instances of this in our Government. I confess it mortifies me

greatly. The giving such a Preference to Riches is both dishonorable and dangerous to a Government. It is indeed equally dangerous to promote a Man to a Place of publick Trust only because he wants Bread, but I think it is not so dishonorable; for Men may be influenced to the latter from the Feelings of Humanity, but the other argues a base, degenerate, servile Temper of Mind. I hope our Country will never see the Time, when either Riches or the Want of them will be the leading Considerations in the Choice of publick officers. Whenever Riches shall be deemd a necessary Qualification, Ambition as well as Avarice will prompt men most ardently to thirst for them, and it will be commonly said as in ancient times of Degeneracy

      quæren dapecunia primum est

Virtus post Numenos

"Get Money, Money still

And then let Virtue follow if she will"

    I am greatly honord if my late Letter has been acceptable to the House.[2] I hope the Militia Bill, to which that Letter referrd, is compleated to the Satisfaction of both Houses of the Assembly.

    The Account you give me of the Success our People meet with in the Manufacture of Salt petre is highly pleasing to me. I procurd of a Gentleman in the Colony of New York[3] the Plan of a Powder Mill, which I lately sent to Mr Revere. I hope it may be of some Use.

    I have time at present only to request you to write to me by the Post, and to assure you that I am, Your affectionate Friend,

S A

RC (PPRF).

  [1] This letter is printed in Austin, *Life of Gerry*, 1:122–24.

  [2] See Samuel Adams to Elbridge Gerry, October 29, and to James Otis, Sr., November 23, 1775.

  [3] Henry Wisner. See Wisner to Benjamin Towne, December 21, 1775, note 3.

Silas Deane to Thomas Mumford

Dear Sir   Philadelphia Jany 2d 1776

    I have not as yet received Col. Latimers Acct. so can say Nothing on that head. Mr B Marshall has sent You the Invoice of the Flour shipp'd you on which is a ball[ance] which I will if You direct it discharge out of the Five Hundred Dollrs. in my hands over what I D[elivere]d Col. Latimer. The Sloop with Your Flour had the Misfortune to be Cast away,[1] & I fear will make near a Totall Loss of Vessel, & Cargo; hope you insured your Interest. A Man came up from Warner to Mr Marshall, who Consulted Me on the subject, & on the Whole We sent him back, to do the best he could. When he left the Vessel She was sunk in the sand to her bends as he says, They got about Twenty barrels out, & he tho't the upper Tier was not damaged, but the Lower would be lost. The place is somewhere near Cape May where She now lies, & the Moment I receive any further intelligence shall forward it you. News we have none of any Consequence, I hear Nothing of Our Successors though they ought to have been here some Days since. I hear that the Lettr. wrote by Col. Dyer & self gave Offence.[2] We meant only to inform the Assembly that We were not insensible. I am sorry I could not have been at Our Assembly at thier last Session, not meerly to justify my Conduct but to make some proposals which I think must have been greatly for the Advantage of the Colony whose true Interests always have, & I trust ever shall be my Constant study. The Complemts of the Season to Your Family, I am Sir Yours &c,   Silas Deane

RC (Robert J. Sudderth, Jr., Lookout Mountain, Tenn., 1973).
   [1] The Secret Committee had contracted with Mumford to export flour in order to procure gunpowder. See Secret Committee Minutes of Proceedings, November 28, 1775; and Deane to Mumford, January 25, 1776.
   [2] See Connecticut Delegates to Jonathan Trumbull, December 5; and Deane to Elizabeth Deane, December 15, 1775.

John Hancock to the Massachusetts Assembly

Honble Gentlemen,   Philadelphia 2d Januy. 1776
   I have the Honour to Transmitt you severall Resolutions pass'd in Congress, to which beg leave to Refer you.[1] The Money order'd in consequence of the Accotts. you were pleas'd to Transmitt to your Delegates, sets off this Day, of which Mr. Cushing is so kind as to Take Charge. I hope it will Arrive safe, and that the Conduct of your Delegates in this instance will meet your Approbation.[2]
   As I am now Call'd upon to attend publick Business, I beg Leave to Refer you to Mr Cushing for further particulars.[3]
   Wishing you the Compliments of the Season, I have the honour to be, Gentn. Your most Obedt servt.,   John Hancock Presidt.

RC (M-Ar).
   [1] Probably the resolves passed this date for neutralizing the loyalists and requesting copies of all provincial petitions submitted to Britain since 1762. *JCC*, 4:18–22.
   [2] See Massachusetts Delegates to the Massachusetts Assembly, January 1, 1776. Perez Morton's letter to Congress of October 25, 1775, and the enclosed accounts are in PCC, item 65, 1:59–67; and *Am. Archives*, 4th ser. 3:1182–83.
   [3] Robert Treat Paine noted in his diary for this date: "Fine day. Mr. Cushing Satt out for home." MHi.

John Hancock to Philip Schuyler

Sir   Philadelphia Jany. 2d. 1776.

I have the Honor to inform you that it is the Desire of Congress, you would immediately on Receipt of this take effectual Measures to have Brigadier General Prescot secured in safe and close Custody, till further Orders from Congress.[1]

The Reasons which induced the Congress to give these Orders, are the Information recd. through you from Genl. Montgomery & from the intercepted Letters, by which it appears there is but too just Grounds to believe the General has been a principal Cause of Allen's being put in Irons. But were he innocent in that Matter, Justice & Reason and a Regard for those who risque their Lives in this Cause make it necessary to use the Law of Retaliation, in Order if possible to put a Stop to the Inhumanity of our Enemies.

By this Conveyance you will receive a Sum of Silver & Gold, a further Sum will be transmitted you when collected. The affairs of your Department are under Consideration, when the Congress have come to a Determination, I shall do myself the pleasure of transmitting it to you.[2] In the mean Time I am Sir, Your most obedt. Servt.

                                        John Hancock President

Tr (NN).

[1] See *JCC*, 4:16.

[2] The "Committee on General Schuyler's letters" reported to Congress on January 8, and Congress passed a series of related resolves on that and the following day. *JCC*, 4:38–40, 43–45.

Thomas Lynch to Philip Schuyler

Dear Sir   January 2d. 1776

I wish I had any good News to write you, thank God there is none bad. Carolina has had the good luck to have one Kirkland who has done much Mischief among the Back Settlers there, taken by the fortunate and gallant Manly with all the Plans, Letters & papers of our Enemies.[1]

Give me leave to introduce the Bearer Mr. Bingham a young Gentleman of this City to your Acquaintance and good Offices.

I hope you have been successful in recruiting the York Forces that poor gallant Montgomery may be supported. Our best Respects attend you and the Ladies.

[I] am [Sir your] most Obedt   Tho Lynch

RC (MH).

[1] For the "Letters & papers" referred to here, see Richard Smith's Diary, December 30, 1775, note 1.

North Carolina Delegates
to Samuel Johnston

My dear Sir   Philad January 2 1776
The unexpected detention of the Express which carries this gives me
an opportunity to drop a few lines to you. They contain nothing new,
they are the testimonial of that unaltered esteem and affection which
I entertain for you—take them merely as such. Politicks at present are
at a Stand. We impatiently wait to know the fate of Quebec. Montgomery
and Arnold are now before Quebec & if Courage and Perseverance can
give success, I know of None who have better pretensions to it than
these brave Officers. Arnolds Expedition has been marked with such
scenes of misery, that it requires a stretch of faith to believe that human
nature was equal to them. Subsisting upon dead dogs, devouring their
Shoes & the leather of their Cartouch Boxes are but part of that Catalogue of woe which attended the expedition. Heaven seems to have
interposed in preserving almost miraculously what still remains of the
brave little Army, & placing them in health & spirits to compleat the
grand work of the subduction of Canada.
    Washington is before Boston, His army in good order, Howe pent
within the Walls of the town, Burgoygne gone to England, some armed
Vessels with troops gone to the Southward whither We know not,
perhaps to Virginia—possibly to Carolina. I hope they will find you
watching.
    The State of Virginia & South Carolina point out the necessity of
embodying the two battalions in North Carolina. I hear with particular
pleasure the promptitude they discovered in marching to the Assistance
of Virginia, & we (from some Information we have got) with insulting
triumph tell the So. Carolinians that 4 or 500 of our Men are engaged
in defence of that province.[1] No. Carolina rises & be assured that with
a tolerable show of Merit, in Hewes & Myself she will not want pane-
g[y]rists to do ample justice to all her Worth. You talk of the impropriety
of raising troops without being able to arm them. Men may be dis-
ciplined without musquets, We follow in this the example of our
Northern Friends. Pray stimulate the Industry of our Countrymen, to
imitate their expedition in removing the objection you feel.
    We hear with sincere regret of the death of Mr Knox, Upon your
Account I lament the loss of him. I lament it upon the publick score,
his Zeal in this Cause & his influence with others made him a very
useful Member of Society. May he rest in peace, May his Slumbers be
the slumbers of the just.
    You perhaps have heard that Lowther has been seized by the Man
of War (the Phoenix) at New York, his Vessell probably sent to Boston.
Your Letters to Hewes are in Capt Parkers possession. Pray write us

only by land opportunities, & when you scribble what Tyrants call Treason, do not sign your Name. We well know your Scribble, without a nominal Index.

By Goddard We send you the different processes for making Salt petre. Pray try it in your family, encourage your Neighbours to it. It is attempted with great success in private families here, the making is as simple, as making Hominie. Adieu. I want materials to go on, & sure I am Your patience is at an end. Remember me with respect to your Lady, Affectionately to my worthy f[rien]d Iredell & believe me to be With sincere esteem, Your Friend,   Wm Hooper

[*P.S.*] Hewes adds as follows

In a Letter from Lowther dated New York Per 22d Decr. he says, "I left Edenton the 26th of Nov. and arived at Sandy Hook the 16th instt. where I was stopt & detained by Capt. Parker of his Majestys ship Phoenix and all our Chests Searched for Letters. I happened to have a great number which were all taken & Carried on board the Man of War, about one half of them were opened when they were returned to me next day, one only was detained which was from Mr. Johnston for you. The Capt told me it gave a very particular account of the usage Mr Pollok met with at Edenten & that he was resolved to shew it to Govr. Tryon as he understood Mr Pollok was in the Circle of his acquaintance, that it did honour to Mr Johnston and he hoped would be of Service to him at a future day.[2] They still detain my Sloop & Cargo and the Capt. says she must be sent to Boston."[3] Mr Hewes desires his Complemt. to Mr Johnstons Family & Connections,————.

RC (PHi). Body of letter written and signed by Hooper; postscript in the hand of Joseph Hewes.

[1] In the middle of December 1775, Col. Robert Howe had arrived in Norfolk with more than four hundred soldiers of the Second North Carolina Regiment to help Virginians to defend this town against Lord Dunmore. Hugh F. Rankin, *The North Carolina Continentals* (Chapel Hill: University of North Carolina Press, 1971), pp. 23–25.

[2] For further details on the "usage" of Cullen Pollok, a resident of Edenton, N.C., who had incurred the wrath of the local revolutionary committee by an incautious remark which he had made about the dispute between America and Great Britain, see Clark, *Naval Documents*, 3:563; and *N. C. Colonial Records*, 10:1027–32.

[3] The full text of Capt. William Lowther's letter to Hewes is in Clark, *Naval Documents*, 3:207.

Robert Treat Paine to Philip Schuyler

My dear General   Philada Jany. 2d. 1776
I did desert, because I found that was my only method of getting from Albany. I should have taken my Leave of your most agreable family, but the Urgency of my Journey would not admitt of it, pray

make my Excuses & present my Compliments to yr. Lady (whose Welfare I should gladly hear of) & also to the young Ladys yr. Daughters.

I had a fatiguing Journey here, but don't find myself the worse for it. We want much to have the Report of the Cmssrs of the Indian Treaty. The Report of the Cmttee I was upon is Committed, & I hope will soon be reported, I shall press the matter;[1] I find the Time of my Delegation is Extended to the Last of the month after which it is uncertain whether I shall be here.

Inclosed I send a Newspaper containing a simple & I think very intelligeable method of making Salt petre, as also the result of the Cmttee you were upon which I am sure never was dispersed in the manner it ought to have been. I am sure you will extend the knowledge & practice of this most essential manufacture as far as you possibly can. I assure you it becomes more & more necessary to encrease it.

My Compliments to Mr. Dough [Volkert P. Douw?], Col Tenbroek & others with whom I had the pleasure of any Acquaintance.

Hoping you health & best happiness, I rest yr most hble Sevt.,

R T Paine

P.S. I also send you a Resolve of Congress occasioned by the Kings Proclamation.[2]

They have got to make Salt petre in large quantitys in many places, & to that degree in Massa. that the Government are about Setting up two powder Mills. Pray don't be behind the best of us.

There is no news here, except that the River is broke up here & I expect 2 ships of 30 guns & 2 Briggs of 18 or 20 will sail soon on a Cruise.[3]

RC (MdBJ-G).
[1] Congress passed a series of resolves dealing with the military situation in New York and Canada on January 8–9. *JCC*, 4:38–40, 42–45.
[2] Congress' resolution of December 6, 1775, which was subsequently printed as a broadside by John Dunlap. *JCC*, 3:409–12, 513.
[3] The following day Paine wrote a brief letter to Schuyler introducing Maj. Thomas Hanson of Maryland. Paine to Philip Schuyler, January 3, 1776, PHi.

Richard Smith's Diary

Tuesday 2 Jany. [1776]

Before Congress met I attended the Comee. of Claims. Some Accots. of Capt. Mott, Egbert Dumond and others for Subsistance and travelling Expences of the Prisoners from St. Johns, were adjusted, these Expences run very high.

Yesterdays Minutes read. Agreed to write to Gen Schuyler ordering Him to confine Brig. Gen. Prescot now at Kingston in Ulster County, till further Order, acquaintg. Him, Schuyler, of the reason viz the ill

Usage of Col. Ethan Allen. We did not order the Prisoner into Irons because it is not quite certain how Allen is treated. Some Accots. were reported by Mr. Willing Chairman of the Comee. of Claims which were passed. Gadsden moved to add a Friend of his to John Rutledge & Middleton now in S. Carolina to whom the Dispatches of Congress relative to the Attack on St. Augustine are to be directed, & he further moved for Leave to repair to S. Carolina he being Commander in Chief of the Militia there where an Attack is apprehended.[1] These Motions were opposed by his Colleagues Lynch & E. Rutledge & others and were carried in the Negative. Bartlett & S. Adams were added to the Comee. of Claims. The Comee. on Ld. Stirlings Letters again made Report which being discussed & amended was passed & that Part of it concerning the future Treatment of the Tories was directed to be published in the News Papers. The Report from the Comee. on Capt. Coffin & Capt. Paddocks Petition whereby they allowed Nantucket to import 7000 Barrels of Flour per Annum, there being on that Island about 7000 People, was objected to & at length rejected. It is said We have no less than 51 Battalions now raised or ordered so to be in the 13 United Colonies. A thin Congress today, not more than 30 Members.

MS (DLC).
[1] For Gadsden's return to South Carolina, see Christopher Gadsden to Esek Hopkins, January 15, 1776.

Samuel Ward to Deborah Ward

Philadelphia 2nd Jany. 1776. Gives directions about taking care of his children and his farm. Cautions against concluding from his failure to correspond regularly that he is unwell, "for if you knew how much I am engaged you would wonder that I write half so much rather than that I miss some opportunities. I am not like to get time to be Inoculated and there is very little of the Small Pox now in the city." [1] Regrets neglecting the education of his children, but bids them all to cultivate virtuous lives.[2]

Abstracted from Ward, *Correspondence* (Knollenberg), pp. 163–65.
[1] Ward died of smallpox in Philadelphia on March 26, 1776.
[2] Ward also wrote this day to his daughter Mary, reminding her that she had to rely on herself while he was in Congress and expressing apprehension at not having heard lately from her brother Samuel. Ward, *Correspondence* (Knollenberg), p. 163.

Lord Drummond's Notes

[January 3–9? 1776]
Left New York on Thursday, reached E[lizabeth] Town that Evg.,

reached Trentown Friday Night—and Pa. on Saturday.[1]

One of the first Circums[tance]s that reached them was the Acct. of Adams having moved that Mr. E[lliot] & Ld. D[rummon]d should be put under Confine[men]t—which was averted by a Majority of 8 to 3 C[olonie]s—that Lynch in particular was of the Majority and had opposed the Motion with grt. Warmth. Mr. Morris in particular exerted his Influence in behalf of Mr. Elliot and amongst other arguments used the Unpopularity of the Step from Mr. Elliots standing so very high in Esteem with the Quakers—as well as the People at Large. Mr. Morris mentiond his Apprehension at one time for Ld. D[rummon]d but that the Gentlemen of the Southern Colos. had opposed the Motion generally. That their friends in the Congress had advised that a Deputation from the Comme. of Safety shoud for the purpose of quieting the more violent Part of them, be sent to take a Parole from them and which shoud be conceived in Terms calculated not to interfere with any Negotiation either in its Present or any other Stage & that as Acquaint[ance]s Mr. Jn. Cadwallader, Jos. Reed and Mr. Wilcock waited on them, and apologizing for the Liberty of making the Request, received the Parole.

Had some Convers[atio]n with Mr. Lynch on Pol[itica]l Sub[ject]s and found him unreserved and noways distant.

Told by Mr. E[lliot] that he had been on the Subjt. of Politicks with A[ndrew] A[llen], that he found him firm, at same time well Disposed—that he seemed anxious to know whether there was Likelyhood of any Overtures from the other Side the Water in Consequence of the Petion by Mr. P[enn].[2]

Mr. Duane in all his Conv[ersatio]ns Shewed uncommon Anxiety—dwelt much on the Sincerity of their Intentions expressd in the Petition: and hinged the future fate of A[meric]a on its Reception or Rejection.

What had been suggested to Mr. E[lliot] by A[ndrew] A[llen] confirmd by Mr. D[uane] that tho none of the Gent. in the Congs. confided in each other so far as to communicate their Views or Opinions, at least the Extent of them to each other—that a Similarity of Views had classed them into two Partys. That they formed Conjecture of each others Opinions from those they herded with. That the Northern Colonies kept detached from the Middle and Southern ones (Virginia excepted who attached themselves to the Northern Colonies).

Mr. D[uane] told L. D[rummon]d that he didnt immagine any one Man coud pronounce (from his Knowledge) on the decisive Part any two Men beyond himself woud take in a Negotiation. From this General diffidence that No Assembly was more disjointed nor Influence more Confined.

D[uane] being asked if [. . .] Popularity extended to that Ass[embl]y answered in the Negative & this confirmed by People in Genl.

D[uane] pointed at Mr. Lynch as having more Genl. Influence than any other Member especially as to the Southern Colos.—talkd of him as moderate in his Views at same time manly. This Opinion confirmed by the Gentn. of Pensylvania.

D[ua]ne advised D[rummon]d to sound his Disposition towards accommodation. In the Course of Conversation found willing to be undeceived as to the Character of Ministers.

Livingstone [3] from Rel[igio]n, Connections & Abilitys was a Cha[racte]r of great Moment at this Juncture. From the Set of People he associated with—From his being on no footing of Intimacy with the Northern Delegats—from the Tenor of his Conversation in his Careless Moments he was considerd as much averse from Independency, but this, not so much on Principles either of Loyalty to the present, or any King but that he foresees that this Species of Govt. (Which he had perhaps a natural Bias to) woud be attended with numberless immediate Evils to that Part of the Cont. where his Property [and] every thing Connected with him lay.

Jay had been sent to the Congs. rather by the Suffrages of the more moderate Men as being a Man who had shown himself possessd of good Abilities, and ambitious at many times of distinguishing them, a Church Man and one who they thought might prove some Check to the violent Measures. He had in the Course of the former session renderd himself much considerd in that Assembly by his Readiness in Debate as well as in Composition. How far his Connection (by Marriage) with Mr Wm Livingstone might influence his Condt. was problematical. Duane who was the Man the most likely to have attended to his Political Conduct ranked him as much inclined to Reconciliation. The Business at large was communicated to him and his Opinions gave Encouragement to it. As Mr. J[ay] had very lately appeard as one of a Deputn. to the Assembly of Jersey for the Purpose of Staying an Address to the Crown on the Subject of Accommodation, his Disposn. had become suspected. [4] His friends however accounted for this that he only took a warm Part in this Deputn. from an Opinion that such an address might carry the appearance of W[an]t of Unanimity and that he only prayd their awaiting the Answer from the Crown.

The More secret Facts were from this Cause opend to him with some Reserve. He urged this same argts. of want of Propriety in taking any fresh Steps on any Business of this sort While a Petition as yet unanswered lay before the King. On Ld. D[rummon]d removing that Difficulty by alledging the Intention of the Ministers to transmit an Answer & even anticipating its Purport He enterd readily into Disquisitions with Regard to the Terms now communicated to them. As Mr. J[ay] & the other Branches of his own family have large Landed Property Mr. E[lliot] urged in particular the immediate Danger all Lands in N. York Colony run from the N. E[nglan]d Provinces. As his Secret Ambition lay in procuring himself a Seat in the Assembly Mr E[lliot] held up to him the Popularity with a Commericial People of again Establishing their Trade and with Extentions which they were hitherto Strangers to.

Jay seemd at first to think that the Article proposing the Perpetual Grant might alarm, but when he came to view the Compensations on the other hand in their fullest Extent his Apprehensions subsided. He saw the salutary Effect that woud be produced from the Removal of the Dread of Taxation: and at same time saw the extensive Consequences that were comprehended under the last Article.

MS (Scottish Record Office: Drummond Castle Papers).

[1] Saturday, December 30, 1775. Thomas Lundin, Lord Drummond (1742–80), was the central figure in what one historian has called "the last effort before the Declaration of Independence to reconcile the American colonies with Great Britain and prevent the disruption of the empire." Milton M. Klein, "Failure of a Mission: The Drummond Peace Proposal of 1775," *Huntington Library Quarterly* 35 (August 1972): 343. Born in Scotland, Drummond, whose father claimed the title of 10th earl of Perth, came to America in 1768 to oversee family lands in East Jersey. In America Drummond acquired many friends among the New York and New Jersey aristocracies and developed a sympathy for colonial grievances over the Townshend, Tea, and Coercive Acts. In the autumn of 1774, after adjournment of the First Continental Congress, he offered to present to the British government the views of certain moderate delegates who had expressed to him "their Readiness to contribute towards the general Support [*of the empire*] shoud such a mode be devised for the Completion of this Purpose as woud give a Security against any further Invasion of their Property by Parliament." Drummond never identified the delegates to whom he volunteered his services, but the views which he ascribed to them were remarkably similar to those expressed by James Duane. See Drummond to Lord North?, March 24, 1776; and "Narrative of Lord Drummond's Proceedings on Going to America," ca. July 1779, Scottish Record Office: Drummond Castle Papers, Nj microfilm; James Duane's Propositions before the Committee on Rights, September 7–22, 1774; and Klein, "Failure of a Mission," pp. 347–52.

Drummond arrived in England in December 1774 and soon entered into conversations with Lord North and Lord Dartmouth. In March 1775 he drew up a "Plan of Accommodation" listing six points as bases for negotiations between America and Great Britain (and printed in full in Klein, pp. 377–80). In brief, Drummond's "Plan" called for colonial assemblies to provide the crown with "a perpetual Grant" of revenue derived from taxes on "such Articles . . . as they shall deem most likely to keep pace with the *Growth* or *Decline* of the said Colonies." In return for this concession, he proposed that Parliament formally relinquish "all future Claim of Taxation" over the colonies and agree to apply revenue from American trade to "the Expenses of Collection," with surpluses "to be subject to the disposal of the respective Houses of Assembly." According to Drummond, this "Plan" was approved not only by North and Dartmouth but also by Chief Justice Mansfield and Sir Gilbert Elliot, the latter a Scottish MP who had been instrumental in persuading a skeptical House of Commons to pass North's Conciliatory Resolve of February 20, 1775. At first Drummond intended to send a copy of the "Plan" to friends in America, but he was dissuaded by Elliot, who convinced him that negotiations were more likely to succeed if they were represented as originating in America. As a result Drummond left England in September 1775 and returned to America in the capacity of a private subject purporting unofficially to represent the views of the North ministry. "Narrative of Lord Drummond's Proceedings on Going to America," ca. July 1779, Scottish Record Office: Drummond Castle Papers, Nj microfilm; John Graves Simcoe, "Memo of Conversation with Ch. Justice [William] Smith," March 3, 1792, DLC; Francis Lightfoot Lee to Richard Henry Lee, January 8? 1776; and Charles R.

Ritcheson, *British Politics before the American Revolution* (Norman: University of Oklahoma Press, 1954), pp. 186–88.

Late in December 1775 Drummond came to Philadelphia in the company of Andrew Elliot, the royal collector in New York and brother of Sir Gilbert. The Pennsylvania Committee of Safety was suspicious of their designs and asked Congress on January 3 if they should not be arrested. When Congress decided against this step, the committee exacted an oath from them not to reveal any information about Philadelphia's defenses. Thereafter Drummond and Elliot began a series of conversations lasting through January 14 with a group of moderate delegates, chief among whom were Andrew Allen, James Duane, John Jay, William Livingston, and Thomas Lynch. They are also known to have spoken with Silas Deane, James Wilson, and Edward Rutledge, and to have been in indirect contact with John Hancock. In all this Drummond was careful to disclaim any official authorization from the British government, and the delegates made it clear that they were not treating in behalf of Congress.

During preliminary conversations Drummond sought to convince the delegates of the good intentions of the British government and in the process concluded that "the old Point of Taxation was still the Hinge on which the state of America was likely to turn." He then informed them of his "Plan of Accommodation." Initially the delegates were reluctant to assent to his proposal for a colonial grant of a perpetual revenue to the crown, but at length he overcame their doubts. Once agreement had been reached on this issue, the range of the talks broadened considerably, in the course of which the delegates agreed not to press their complaints about vice-admiralty court jurisdiction, the Statute of Treason passed during the reign of Henry VIII, or the Declaratory and Quebec Acts. These conversations also led to the formulation of a list of negotiating positions in which the delegates demanded such concessions as relinquishment of Parliament's claim to a right to tax the colonies; freedom to manufacture and consume finished products made from colonial raw materials; inclusion of Canada "in the Indemnification;" appointment of provincial supreme court justices during good behavior; and the revision of the Navigation Acts. In return, they pledged to observe the Acts of Trade, to grant Great Britain a perpetual revenue, and to provide her with naval and military supplies, when "calld upon in Cases of Urgency." Finally, agreement was reached on a compromise plan for the government of Massachusetts, which, according to Drummond, was shown to and approved by John Hancock. Specific details about this plan are lacking, but Thomas Lynch insinuated that it envisioned either the return of the Bay Colony's 1691 charter or concessions to the province in the form of an amendment to the Massachusetts Government Act of 1774.

The next problem was how to initiate formal negotiations between America and Great Britain. At first the delegates wanted Drummond and Elliot to open talks with the North ministry, but Drummond insisted that the cause of peace would be served best if Congress sent an official deputation. Although the delegates were cool to this idea, pointing out that they were subject to arrest for treason in the mother country, they agreed to a congressional peace delegation when Drummond consented to remain in America as a hostage.

Drummond subsequently maintained that at the conclusion of his talks with the delegates around January 14, "a very decided Majority of the Members of the Congress, representing not less than seven different Provinces," favored negotiations along the lines described above. Whatever the accuracy of this claim, however, owing to a variety of circumstances Congress never formally took up the question of sending a delegation to England. Thomas Lynch was on the verge of introducing this issue in Congress when news arrived on January 17 of the American defeat at Quebec on New Year's Eve, which, combined with earlier intelligence about Lord Dunmore's New Year's Day attack on Norfolk, left Congress in no mood for conciliation. Early the next month Lynch and Andrew Allen took advantage of their appointment to a committee to confer with the New York Committee of Safety about the activities of Gen. Charles Lee to meet again with Drummond, who meanwhile had returned to New York to promote peace negotiations. As a result of their conversation on February 5, Drummond wrote a letter to British Gen. James Robertson in Boston, asking him to arrange passports for a congressional peace delegation. Lynch, in turn, sent Drummond's letter to Washington, requesting the general to forward it to Robertson. Instead of complying with this request, however, Washington sent both Drummond's and Lynch's letters to Congress, where they arrived on February 29 and were considered in a committee of the whole on March 5.

Washington's action could scarcely have come at a worse time for the proponents of reconciliation. Lynch was incapacitated by a stroke; Duane was compromised by the revelation of the treachery of his valet, James Brattle; and Jay was absent from Congress until March 2. In addition, the cause of reconciliation had been dealt a stunning blow by the arrival in Philadelphia on February 27 of news of the Prohibitory Act, which at one time both declared war on American commerce and held out the prospect of a royal peace commission. Even so, the delegates' response to the intelligence from Washington revealed surprising support in Congress for negotiations, for although they commended Washington's action, they simultaneously rejected motions by George Wythe to forbid anyone "other than the Congress or the People at large . . . to treat for Peace" and by William Livingston to bring Drummond to Philadelphia "to explain his Conduct."

Nevertheless, the events of March 5 marked the effective end of the Drummond peace mission. For several months moderates continued to hope that Britain would send commissioners to America empowered to conclude terms similar to those promised by Drummond. Unfortunately for this hope, the Howe brothers' commission did not become operative until two weeks after the Declaration of Independence, and its terms were disappointing. Unidentified Correspondent to Drummond, Philadelphia, April 8, 1776, Scottish Record Office: Drummond Castle Papers, Nj microfilm; and Ira D. Gruber, *The Howe Brothers and the American Revolution* (New York: Atheneum, 1972), pp. 72–78, 89–97.

Several imponderables make it difficult to assess the significance of Drummond's mission. Although it seems clear that influential members of the North ministry approved his original "Plan of Accommodation," it is far less certain—and much more unlikely—that they would have approved terms he and the delegates agreed on in Philadelphia. It is also unclear to what extent Allen, Duane, Jay, Livingston, and Lynch represented the views of a larger element in Congress. In sum, the Drummond mission indicates that powerful elements on both sides of the Atlantic favored reconciliation early in 1776, but it fails to demonstrate that their expectations were sufficiently similar to permit the opening of formal negotiations.

For further references in this volume to Drummond's activities, see—in addition to Drummond's own minutes and notes of January 5, 6, 9, 10, 14, and February 5— Richard Smith's Diary, January 3, February 29, and March 5; Joseph Hewes to Samuel Johnston, January 6; Thomas Lynch's letters to Washington of January 16 and February 5 and to Philip Schuyler of January 20; and John Hancock to Washington, March 6, 1776. For additional information on Drummond's peacemaking activities, see William Smith, *The Candid Retrospect; or the American War Examined, by Whig Principles* (Charleston: Robert Wells & Sons?, 1780); *Royal Gazette* (New York), September 8, 1781; and Herbert A. Meistrich, "Lord Drummond and Reconciliation," *Proceedings of the New Jersey Historical Society* 81 (October 1963): 256–77. See also John Dickinson's Proposed Instructions for Commissioners to Negotiate with Great Britain, January 9–24? 1776.

The provenance of Drummond's various minutes and notes is not clear. Some appear to be strictly contemporary rough notes, others more finished copies of earlier rough notes made sometime after Drummond returned to England late in 1778. The present entry has been assigned the date January 3–9? 1776, on the assumption that it was written after Drummond's encounter with the Pennsylvania Committee of Safety on January 3 but before he began exchanging proposals with the delegates on January 9.

² A reference to the Olive Branch Petition of July 8, 1775. *JCC*, 2:158–62.

³ William Livingston. Klein, "Failure of a Mission," p. 358, mistakenly identifies him as Robert R. Livingston, who at this time was still at home at Clermont, New York. See John Jay to Robert R. Livingston, January 6, 1776, note 2.

⁴ See Notes on Delegates' Remarks to the New Jersey Assembly, December 5, 1775, note 1.

John Hancock to William Alexander

Sir,   Philada Jany. 3. 1775 [*i.e.* 1776]
Your several letters of the 3, 5, 6, 14, 17 & 19th of December with the enclosures being duly received were laid before Congress.¹ The multiplicity of important business, which engaged their attention prevented them from paying an earlier attention to the matters therein contained.

The enclosed resolutions,² which I have the honor of transmitting you, will serve to shew the sense of Congress in answer to your letters, to which, from your zeal and attachment to the cause of your country, the Congress have the firmest confidence you will pay all due Regard.

I have the honor to be, Sr, Your obedt. humble Servt.,
                                  John Hancock Presidt

RC (NN). Written by Charles Thomson and signed by Hancock.

¹ These letters with enclosures are in PCC, item 162, fols. 329–57, and *Am. Archives*, 4th ser. 4:164–67, 184, 202–3, 294–96, 354–55.

² For these resolves of January 2, see *JCC*, 4:17–18.

Richard Smith's Diary

                                  [January 3, 1776]
Wednesday 3d. I was on the Comee. of Claims. Sundry Accots. were there adjusted as Capt. Motts, the Signers of the first 3 Millions of Dollars whose Accot. came to £437-2-8 1/2 Pennsa. Cur. and some others. In Congress the Report on the State of New York was considered. Col. Nat Heard of the Minute Men at Woodbridge & Col. Warterbury of Connecticut are ordered to take each a large Body of their Men & meet at a Day agreed on, in Queens County Long Island, & there disarm the Tories & secure the Ringleaders who it is said are provided with Arms & Ammunition from the Asia Man of War,¹ & other Parts of the Report agreed to as was a Report from the Secret Comee. implying that a large Quantity of Produce shall be exported for a Supply of Sail Cloth, other Cloth, Blankets, Needles, Military Stores & other Necessaries to fit out our Fleet and Army. A Report recommendg. to send

out Produce to the Amount of 160,000 Dollars for the Importation of
Gold and Silver, was rejected after thoro Discussion. Mr. Alexander
from Maryland took his Seat. Reports of Accounts from the Comee.
of Claims confirmed. A Letter was recieved from Mr. Hanson Chairman
of a Comee. in Maryland with Conolly & Cameron Two Prisoners—
Smith made his Escape.[2] The Comee. of Safety here were desired to
secure & take the Examination of these Criminals & a Letter was
directed to be sent to the Comee. of Frederick County to search a certain
Saddle for Conollys Instructions. Intelligence of this Saddle had been
recd. from Gen. Washn. from whom a Letter was now recd. inclosg.
a Copy of Gen. Howe's Answer to our Generals spirited Requisition
about Allen.[3] An Answer was made up & sealed to Ld. Stirling inclosing
Copies of the necessary Papers. Application was made from the Comee.
of Philada. asking Advice Whether to secure Ld. Drummond and
Andrew Elliot now in Philada. Some Members gave them good political
Characters & they remained unhurt.[4] 4 Colonels were ballotted for
to command the 4 Battalions now raising in Pennsa. These Officers
were chosen as the Delegates of that Province recommended viz 1.
Arthur St. Clair who ranks next to Col. Bull, 2. John Shee, 3. Anthony
Wayne, 4. Robert Magaw. They had been ballotted for with 4 others
in the Comee. of Safety & had the highest Votes.

MS (DLC).
[1] Congress took this action in response to a request for assistance from the New
York Provincial Congress conveyed in a letter to the New York delegates dated
December 21, 1775. See *Am. Archives*, 4th ser. 4:435; and Bernard Mason, *The Road
to Independence: The Revolutionary Movement in New York, 1773–1777* (Lexington: University of Kentucky Press, 1967), pp. 197–98.
[2] For the Frederick County Committee's letter to Hancock of December 30, 1775,
see *Am. Archives*, 4th ser. 4:479–80.
[3] For Washington's letter to Hancock of December 25, 1775, and enclosures, see
PCC, item 152, 1:373–80; and *Am. Archives*, 4th ser. 4:453–54.
[4] On this point, see Lord Drummond's Notes, January 3–9? 1776, note 1; and
Am. Archives, 4th ser. 4:509.

Joseph Hewes to Samuel Johnston

Dear Sir   Philadelphia 4th Jany. 1776
   The Congress at our request have agreed to send two Clergymen to
North Carolina to explain to the Highlanders and regulators the nature
of the dispute between Great Britain and the Colonies, and left the
appointment to us. We applied to Mr. Elihu Spencer and Mr. Alexander
McWhorter two eminent divines of the Presbyterian religion who have
undertaken the Service.[1] They are strongly attached to our cause and
I hope will render it essential Service. They intend to go first to Halifax
and are the bearers of this Letter. If they should fall in your way I doubt

not you will Shew them proper Civility. If by giving them any Letters to your friends in the West you can contribute to make their Journey more agreable to them it will oblige them and me. No Letter from you had got to my hands except that of the 5th of Novr. by Captain Fell. Hooper wrote to you two days ago from the Congress room. At the Bottom of his Letter I wrote an extract of a Letter from Mr Lowther to me by which you will find he was taken by a Man of War, his Letters opened but all returned to him except one from you to me, his Vessel was to be sent to Boston. Hooper sent his Letter by an express sent to South Carolina by the delegates of that province. I wrote you a letter by Mr Hogg & put it under cover to Mr Miller of Halifax, another by Mr Houston one of the Georgia Delegates, another by an express that left this City early in December, I hope you have recd. them all.[2] I expect our express will return here in a day or two and that then I shall have the pleasure of hearing from you. I shall write again by Mr Goddard who will set out in two or three days.

Our Troops had not got hold of Quebec on the 23d of Nov. which is the latest acco. from them. My Complemts to Mrs. Johnston & Family. I am Dear Sir, yours affectionately,   Joseph Hewes

RC (PU).
[1] See North Carolina Delegates to Elihu Spencer, December 8, 1775, note 2. Hewes, William Hooper, and John Penn also wrote a letter on January 4 to Richard Bennehan, at Little River, Orange County, N.C., introducing Spencer and Mc-Whorter. "We have such a regard for them as Clergymen, Gentlemen & Patriots," they explained, "that we wish to interest you & all our friends in making their Tour agreeable to them." Nc-Ar.
[2] Hewes might be referring to his letters to Samuel Johnston of November 1 and 26 and December 1, 1775.

John Jay to James Jay

Philadelphia. 4 January 1776.

As to Politick's I can say little, nor do I desire that Your Letters should say anything on that Subject.[1] Thus much I can say in general that Everything with us is in a good Way, and, tho' We desire Reconciliation, are well prepared for contrary Measures. This is an unnatural Quarrel, & God only knows why the British Empire should be torn to Pieces by unjust Attempts to subjugate us. Some say a great Number of Foreign Troops are coming over, but I think it somewhat uncertain whose Battles they will fight. Adieu Dr Brother.   J. Jay.

Tr (PRO: C.O. 5, 40:113). Endorsed "Extract. To Sr. James Jay, at Bath, under Cover to Henry Cruger, Junr Esq."
[1] Sir James Jay (1732–1815), physician and elder brother of John Jay. Sir James, who had been knighted by George III in 1763 for his fundraising activities in behalf of King's College, New York, was in England when this letter was written and did not return to America until 1778. DAB.

Thomas Nelson, Jr., to Mann Page

My Dear Page   Philada Jany 4th 1776

Jefferson having left us a few days ago, I shall take the whole of your last Letter to myself. I wish, with you, most sincerely that we were better prepared for our Enemies upon the Water not only to act defensively, but offensively. By land I do not fear them, but their Maritime Force is formidable, & as far as their Cannon can reach, Devastation will be spread. I was much pleas'd to hear that our Troops had got possession of Norfolk, but that pleasure would have been hightend almost to Frenzy, to have been inform'd that Lord Dunmore had [fallen] into our hands. Untill that is done, I fear there will be no peace in Virginia. He is lying still at present, only to project some Diabolical scheme, for our destruction; but I am not without hopes that you will be able to counterplot him. Vigorous & decisive measures must be pursued. We have only two Months, if that to guard against the whole power of Great Britain for be assured, early in the spring, they will begin their operations & in my opinion, the fate of America depends altogether upon the next Summers Campaign. If so, have we a single moment to spare? Every attempt should be made, every [power] should be strain'd, to supply us with the [needful article?]. With a sufficiency of that, we may be certain of success; without it, America will be lost.

I thought before I receivd your Letter that Capt Leslie's retreat might have [been] cutt off, which would have effectually check'd Ld Dunmores career, at least for some time. However I do not mean to censure Colo Woodford's conduct upon that occasion.[1] He may perhaps have good reasons for not attempting that, or demanding a surrender of the Fort; which you seem to think, circumstanced as Capt Leslie was, must have been comply'd with. Our obtaining Victories with so little, or I may say without any loss at all, is certainly a proof of our being under the immediate protection of Providence & while we have so just a cause & humanity marks the conduct of our Commanders after Victory, we need not fear success.

The Postcript of your Letter was very acceptable to me as it gave me the first information of our doing anything upon the Water. I give you joy of our success in that [. . . .][2] The Terror of their [Landing? . . .][3] did of our Oyster Boats. There was a Report in this City last night that Capt Manley had taken another Vessel with a large quantity of Gun powder, but I fear it wants confirmation.

Lieutenant Colo Connelly, Commandant, of her Majestys own Loyal American Regiment, was brought to Phila yesterday afternoon & will probably spend this Summer in a fine [secure] jail just finished for his reception. Doctor Smith, by the carelessness of the guard, made his escape. Pray give my Compts to your good Lady &c & believe me to be, Dr Page, Your sincere friend.   Thos Nelson jr

RC (Ronald von Klaussen, State of Florida, 1975).

[1] On December 9, 1775, Col. William Woodford's Virginia troops had successfully repulsed an attack at Great Bridge by British regulars under Capt. Samuel Leslie. The British forces subsequently abandoned Fort Murray and retreated first to Norfolk and finally to Dunmore's ships. For Woodford's account of the victory, see *Am. Archives*, 4th ser. 4:228–29, 233.

[2] MS damaged; approximately five words missing.

[3] MS damaged; approximately three words missing.

Richard Smith's Diary

Thursday 4 Jany. [1776]

Comee. of Claims allowed the Accots. for keeping Conolly & his Associates & bringing them from Maryland to Philada. Congress agreed to raise a Sixth Battalion in Pennsa. and in the Counties of Cumberland & York, the People there offering their Service, & that one Compy in each of the Six Battalions shall consist of Riflemen. The Lieut. Cols. to the 4 Pennsa. Battals. were now appointed & an Order entered for settling the Rank of Officers chosen in one Day viz. as they are entered on our Journals & their Commissions are to be numbered. The said Lt. Cols. are 1. Lambart Cadwallader, 2. Wm. Allen Junr., 3. Francis Johnston, 4. Joseph Penrose. Reports from the Comee. of Claims allowed. Debates on the Report of the State of N York, great Fault found with the Fort now constructing in the Highlands under the Auspices of Bernard Romans the Engineer, as too large and expensive and ill calculated to annoy the Enemy. Maps produced and Proceedings of the N York Convention thereon read. Mr. Palmer attending on their Behalf, ordered that he be heard Tomorrow Morng. A Vessel or Two of War are now fitting out in Maryland on Accot. of the Congress. I recd. from the Continental Treasury the 1000 Dollars lately advanced to our Comee. of Safety for purchasing Arms for the use of the Continental Troops raised here. I wrote to Samuel Tucker Esqr., Presidt. of the Comee. of Safety & forwarded the Dispatches and Articles of War to Ld. Stirling.[1] The Majors of the 4 Pennsa. Battalions were appointed viz. 1. Jos. Wood, 2. Geo. Nagle, 3. Henry Bicker, 4. Nicholas Hausaker. A Commissary ordered for the 3 companies gone to Accomac. (They were afterwards recalled.) Major Preston allowed the Liberty of other Captive Officers. A report made on the Allowance proper for Officers Prisoners.

MS (DLC).

[1] See Richard Smith to Samuel Tucker, this date.

Richard Smith to Samuel Tucker

Dr. Sir   Philadelphia Jany. 4. 1776.

I am desired by Congress to transmit You the inclosed Extracts from their Proceedings, the whole of which, relative to that Subject, I have sent to Lord Stirling by this Post, together with 6 Dozen Copies of the Articles of War. The 1000 Dollars mentioned in the Extract, I have received from the Continental Treasury, and they wait your Commands.[1]

The Congress wish to know in what Manner the Prisoners of War at Trenton live, who supplies them, and upon what Terms. The Reason of the Inquiry is that very extravagant Claims are made on this Head from other Quarters, and We aim to render the Public Burthens as light as possible. You will, as soon as it is convenient, afford me the necessary Information.[2] I am, Your affectionate faithful Servt.,

                                                           Richd. Smith

RC (NN).

[1] Smith sent Tucker, the president of the New Jersey Committee of Safety, resolves of January 2 about the provision of barracks for Colonel Alexander's troops and the appropriation of $1,000 by Congress to enable New Jersey to pay for arms it had received from New York. *JCC*, 4:17–18; and *Am. Archives*, 4th ser. 4:662.

[2] No reply to Smith from Tucker has been found, but see Smith's Diary for January 12, 1776, as well as the letters to Hancock from the New Jersey Committee of Safety of January 19 and 23, 1776, in PCC, item 68, fols. 35–46; and *Am. Archives*, 4th ser. 4:772, 815.

Lord Drummond's Minutes

(Secret.)   Philadelphia Jan 5th. 1776.

Some of the Gentlemen from the Southern Colonies being apprehensive that the Northern Delegates from a determind purpose of defeating all Accommodation (when they were not to be made the *Necessary Men*) might in Opposition to the present plan[1] urge the former Resolution of *hearkning to no Terms* till the Repeal of the *Port Bill*, &c. and that in Support of this they might alledge even the Honor of the whole Delegates as Individuals being pledged; it was proposed that Ld. D[rummon]d and Mr. [Jay][2] shoud meet next Morning to consider of this Subject and to endeavor to remove the Difficulty under which they seemd to have laid themselves.

In Consequence of an Interview with [Jay] on this Head this Morng. at Mr [Duane] the following Expedient was suggested and approved as the Means of absolving them from any Ties private as well as publick which might be alledged on this Head.

"That on the Supposition that such Terms of accommodation shoud be acceded to on the Part of England as shoud be deemd by a *Majority* of the American Representatives to be worthy of the Justice of England and beneficial to the Colonies in General, but that such Terms shoud nevertheless be rejected on the Part of any *particular* Colonies, that in such Case the Commissioners on the Part of America conceiving the Question before them to be of such Magnitude shall *adjourn* for the Purpose of taking the Sense of their Respective Colonies and that this *Adjournment* and the Object of it shall be made publick by Proclamation." The Conclusions drawn by Mr. [Jay] were that on such an Event so soon as they the Southern Delegates shoud come to hold up to the People at large in the middle and Southern Colonies, the Reestablishment of a *Peace* founded on such Liberal terms on one hand, and to contrast with it all the Horrors of a civil War on the other, & which they were to plunge themselves into merely to humour a Set of People who were obnoxious to them, that the Question of *receiving*, or *Rejecting* the terms woud not bear a Moments Hesitation with the People.

MS (Scottish Record Office: Drummond Castle Papers). Endorsed by Drummond: "To be shewn to Mr. Lynch and Mr. Allen only."

¹ For Drummond's "Plan of Accommodation," see Drummond's Notes, January 3–9? 1776, note 1.

² When Drummond drafted these and various other minutes and memoranda pertaining to his activities in Philadelphia and New York, he omitted the names of the delegates he met. However, after he returned to England in November 1778 he wrote most of the omitted names in the margins of his notes—here and below. This he apparently did no earlier than January 1779, for in his minutes for January 6, 1776, he wrote "Jay now President," and Jay's appointment as president of Congress in December 1778 could not have been known to him before that date.

James Duane to Robert Livingston

My dear and honored Sir   Philad 5 January 1776

I expected by this time to have been on my Journey to the Manour but if it was possible in this wet Season to travel, which is hardly the Case, the Situation of publick affairs is too critical to justify my leaving the Congress without permission of our Convention which will not assemble till the beginning of next month. To speak Candidly I expect important Intelligence from England which will fix the Fate of America. If Parliament shoud offer [reasonable?] Terms of Conciliation I shoud never forgive myself for being absent on so great and interesting an Occasion. I am not without some Hopes of a Just and honourable Peace. The ministry can expect no Success without the aid of foreign Troops. Will the Nation trust the King with the Command of 20 or 30000 mercenaries? Will these mercenaries Conquer for Britain, or like all other Barbarians set up their own Empire on the Ruins of Americans? These are serious Reflections which if the nation is not quite infatuated must have a serious Operation. I do not however judge on mere Conjecture. Lord Drummond who left England in September is arrived here; full of the opinion that matters may be accommodated. He has had the best opportunity of Information; is sensible, Candid, and his all—a proprietary Right of East Jersey, is at Stake. I cannot descend into particulars—even this is in Confidence. But I do not think the Conditions which he supposes woud be granted ought to be disagreeable to Americans.[1]

However when we consider the Conduct of Administration we must be discouraged from placing much faith in their professions. A few weeks will probably give us the means of Judging decisively; and in the mean time however irksome and distressing I *must* be reconciled to this tedious Separation from my Wife, my Children and my Friends.

I sincerely condole with you on the sudden Death of our worthy and respected Friend Judge Livingston. He is a great Loss both to his Family and his Country and I very sensibly partake in the misfortune.

The Governour I learn has dissolved the assembly and issued new writs. If it is not for the sake of Form and to have a House ready to do Business when peace shall be restored I cannot even guess at his Excellency's motives. The Whiggs I suppose will prevail and send their Friends from all the Counties except Queen's and Richmond unless they [. . .] fall out among themselves in a squabble for the office. So many have a claim on the score of merit in the great Contest, that it will be difficult to fix the preferences. I am well pleased to be out of the way, and shall not interfere even by a Hint in favour or to the prejudice of any Competitor.

Be pleased to present my dutiful Regards to Mamma and accept the same yourself; and to my Brothers, Sisters and Children my cordial affections. I remain Dear & honurd sir Your ever dutiful Son & faithful Servant.   Jas. Duane

[*P.S.*] I am in a Quaker Town. No body has wished me the Compliments of the Season, & I forgot to pay you that Respect. May God grant you and all you love many happy years. May this be the last in which our dear Country shall experience the Horror of War & Desolation!

RC (NHi).
[1] For further details on Drummond, see Lord Drummond's Notes, January 3–9? 1776, note 1.

Naval Committee to Esek Hopkins

In the Naval Committee
Jany. 5th 1776.
Orders and Directions for the Commander in Chief of the Fleet of the United Colonies.[1]

You are to take care that proper discipline, good order and peace be preserved amongst all the Ships, and their companies, under your command.

You are to direct the several Captains to make out and deliver monthly or oftner, an exact return of the officers, seamen and marines on board of each respective vessel noteing their particular condition and circumstance—also the quantity and quality of provisions and stores of every kind together with the state of the respective ships—which returns or copies of them you are to transmit to Congress, or a Committee by them appointed, to receive such returns, as often as opportunity offers.

You are by every means in your power to keep up an exact correspondence with the Congress or Committee of Congress aforesaid, and with the Commander in chief of the Continental forces in America.

As by your instructions you are impowered to equip Such Vessels as may fall into your power, and to appoint officers for such Vessels, As often as this shall happen you are by the very first opportunity to transmit to Congress or the Committee aforesaid, the burthen, force and manner of equipment of such vessels, together with an exact list of such officers as you may appoint, in order that their appointment may be confirmed by Congress or others be appointed in their Stead.

You will be particularly careful to give such orders and instructions, in writing, to the Officers under your Command as the good of the service may in every case require—to devise or adopt and give out to the Commanding Officer of every Ship, such signals and other marks and distinctions as may be necessary for their direction.

You are to take very particular care that all the men under your command be properly fed and taken care of when they are in health, as well as when they are sick or wounded. You will also very carefully attend to all the just complaints which may be made by any of the people under your command and see that they are speedily and effectually redressed—for on a careful attention to these important subjects the good of the service essentially depends.

You are always to be exceedingly careful that your Arms, as well great as small, be kept in the very best condition for service and that all your cartridges, powder, shott and every accoutrement whatsoever belonging to them be kept in the most exact order: always fit for immediate service.

You will carefully attend to such prisoners as may fall into your hands—see that they be well and humanely treated. You may also send your Prisoners on shore in such convenient places where they may be delivered to the Conventions, Committee's of Safety or inspection in order to their being taken care of and properly provided for.

You will also give proper orders and directions to the Captains or Commanders of the ships or Vessels under your command in case they should be seperated by stress of weather or any other accident in what manner [2] and at what places they shall again join the Fleet. [3]

Step Hopkins   Silas Deane

Christ Gadsden   Joseph Hewes

RC (RHi). In a clerical hand.

[1] In addition to these general orders for the management of the fleet, the Naval Committee supplied Hopkins with specific cruising orders, also dated January 5, 1776, which are printed in *JCC*, 4:335–36. The following day the committee issued instructions to Abraham Whipple, captain of the ship *Columbus*, to Nicholas Biddle of the *Andrew Doria*, to Dudley Saltonstall of the *Alfred*, to John Burroughs Hopkins of the *Cabot*, and to John Hazard of the *Providence* to put themselves under Hopkins' command. See Clark, *Naval Documents*, 3:657–58.

[2] Remainder of MS missing, but it is printed in full in ibid., pp. 636–37.

[3] For two brief documents containing additional information on decisions reached by the Naval Committee on January 4, see also ibid., pp. 612–13.

New York Delegates to
the New York Provincial Convention

Gentlemen: Philadelphia, 5th January 1776

The Congress has been so much incumbered With Business that it has not till now been in our power to write to you Decisively on the Subject of your Several Favours. Indeed the Appointment of an Officer to Command in the Highlands Still Remains undetermined; tho' we Doubt not the Recommendation communicated in your Letter of the 8th of December will have its Due weight. [1]

We highly applaud the Spirited and at the Same time, Respectful manner, in which you have Supported the Dignity and Independancy of our Colony, and demanded Reparation, on the Subject of the Connecticut inroad. An Interposition so rash, Officious, and violent, gave us great Anxiety, as it was not only a high Insult to your authority; but had a Direct Tendency to confirm that fatal Spirit of Jealousy and Distrust of our Eastern Brethren, which has done so much Injury to our Cause, and which every wise and virtuous patriot Should Study to Suppress.

The Government of Connecticut we are perswaded will, not only Do you the Justice which you have required, But adopt Effectual means to Restrain their Inhabitants from Similar Attempts in future. In this Expectation we shall take the Liberty to defer the Application to Congress which you Direct, untill we are favoured with a Copy of Governour Trumbles answer to your Letter. [2]

The enclosed Resolution of Congress Respecting the Loan of £45000 on the Credit of our Colony will We hope be no Disappointment. It is in our Opinion founded on good Reasons. The Precedent would have Justified every other Colony in Soliciting the like Indulgence which Could not without gross Partiality have Been Refused. The Faith of *all* must in Every Instance have been pledged to Secure the Repayment and Consequently *all* exposed to the Effects of Mismanagement and want of Oeconomy in each Separate Government. The Quantity of paper money would not have been Diminished. The Sums thus Borrowed must in the Course of the present Contest have become Ennormous. These Objections, among others, operated so Strongly against the measure that if we had thought ourselves at Liberty to Exercise Discression, in the Case of a positive Instruction, We Should have Declined an application to which, in our Judgment, we could not wish Success. [3]

The Deputation from your Convention Respecting the Fortification in the Highlands was very proper and Seasonable. They have Confered with a Committee of Congress and been heard by the House, and will inform you of Every thing which Occurred; so that it is needless for us to be explicit.

A Copy of the Resolution of the Congress will be Delivered to you by your Deputies to which we have nothing to add. [4]

Mr. Secretary McKesson has furnished us with a Copy of your Resolutions Respecting your Delegates. [5] This Arrangement, or Something Similar, we had much at heart, as the Constant Attendance of so large a Quoram as five would naturally be precarious especially when only that Number were in town.

The Defection of Queen's and Richmond is much to be Lamented, a committee of Congress has that Subject now under Consideration and it will not be long before their Resolutions on that head will be Communicated to you.

We have the Honor to be, with Great Respect Gent., your Most obdt. & humble Servants,   Phil. Livingston   Henry Wisner

Jas. Duane   Wm. Floyd

John Jay

P.S. You have likewise inclosed a Resolution of Congress respecting the Enlistment of Soldiers. [6]

RC (RPJCB). Written by Floyd, with postscript by Duane, and signed by Duane, Floyd, Jay, Livingston, and Wisner. *Journals of N. Y. Prov. Cong.*, 2:142. Salutation, place, and dateline taken from Tr.

[1] On December 8, 1775, in response to repeated requests from the New York delegates, the New York Provincial Congress submitted the names of four nominees for the office of commander of the fortifications in the Highlands, but Congress, for reasons that remain obscure, failed to act on any of them. In the meantime Col. Isaac Nicoll, a New York militia officer, remained in charge of these strategic posts until June 1776, when he was replaced by Lt. Col. Henry Beekman Livingston, whom Washington had appointed the previous month to take command in the Highlands. See New York Delegates to the New York Provincial Congress, November 9; James

Duane to the New York Provincial Congress, November 28, 1775; Washington, *Writings* (Fitzpatrick), 5:10–11; and *Am. Archives*, 4th ser. 4:392, 6:445–46, 510, 673, 818.

² On December 18, 1775, in reaction to the recent raid on loyalist printer James Rivington by Isaac Sears and a band of Connecticut men, the provincial congress asked the New York delegates to secure congressional approval of a regulation "to prevent those jealousies which the introduction of parties of armed men from any neighbouring Colony, unless properly requested, will naturally beget." *Am. Archives*, 4th ser. 4:422–23; and John-Jay to Nathaniel Woodhull, November 26, 1775, note 3.

³ On December 23, 1775, Congress turned down a request from the provincial congress for a loan of £45,000. *JCC*, 3:452; and *Am. Archives*, 4th ser. 4:397.

⁴ See *JCC*, 4:34.

⁵ See *JCC*, 4:14.

⁶ A resolution adopted by Congress on December 27, 1775. *JCC*, 3:459–60; and *Am. Archives*, 4th ser. 4:1034–35.

Richard Smith's Diary

[January 5, 1776]

Friday 5. On my Motion it was resolved that 10,000 Dols. shall be struc to exchange ragged & torn Bills, under the Inspection of the Persons now forwarding the last 3 Millions and of the same Denomins. A Collection of Money was made among the Delegates for Mr. Lovell now in Boston Goal & a Requisition agreed to be made through Washington to Howe, to exchange that Gentn. for Major Skeene Senr. It had been proposed to present Him with 100 or 200 Doll[ar]s but that was dropt as a bad Precedent. Mr. Palmer & Capt. [John Grenell] from New York called in & examined as to the Fortifications to be built on Hudsons River, this Affair took up several Hours & was at last, after passing a Resoln. to abandon the Works at Martilers Rock with Romans the Projector of them & to fortify at Poplopens Kill, referred back to the N. York Convention or Comee. of Safety to execute this Resolve as they may think fit. The Delegates of N Jersey and Connectt. were desired to take the proper Steps for carryg. into Execution the Resolves of Yesterday about disarming and seizing the Tories on Long Island. Some Accots. passed & the New York Report agreed to. A long Memorial from the Town of Newport was presented prayg. Leave to continue to supply the British Men of War with Provisions, otherwise they fear immediate Destruction, this was postponed.¹ The Comee. of Phila. prayed Directions about selling & drinking Tea, which was deferred. Benja. Davies eldest Lieut. in Col. Bulls Battalion was chosen by Ballot a Captain vice Wm Allen Junior promoted to a Lt. Col. ship. An Application from the Wife of Lieut. Tylee of Connect. now a Prisoner on Board of the Men of War near N York requesting Means may be used for exchanging Him, Deferred. Our Secret Comee. have sent to Europe for some able Engineers much wanted now in America.² It is said a Specimen of the

Saltpetre Rock in Virginia was sometime past produced in Congress. Quaere Whether it answers Expectation.

MS (DLC).
¹ Congress referred this memorial to the Rhode Island Assembly on January 6. *JCC*, 4:36.
² Pursuant to a resolution of Congress of December 2, 1775. *JCC*, 3:400–401.

Lord Drummond's Minutes

Philad. 6th Jany. [1776]
At an Interview with Mr. [Jay]¹ in the Night [Jay] informed Ld. D[rummon]d that he had to sollicit his immediate Return to England for the purpose of charging himself with Overtures from the Colonies on the Subject of an Accommodation. He added that undeceived as they now were with Regard to the Misrepresentations from the other Side of the Water they were satisfied they Coud not embrace too early an Opportunity of availing themselves of the present disposition of Adminn. in England as described by Ld. D[rummon]d. He added that he had to sollicit his good Offices with Mr. Elliot in endeavouring to prevail on him to accompany him to Engd. as one who was more Master of the Commercial Interests between the two Countries than any Man on either Side of the Water.²

Mr. [Jay now President] then signifyd to him the handsome Intentions of the Congress towards him and Mr. Elliot shoud they undertake the Management of this Business. Mr. [Jay] on this occasion dwelt much on the unfortunate fate of their *Petition* which went by Mr. Penn—and the Triumph which the Northern Colonies had gained over the Southern Colonies from its receiving no Answer. He condemned the Terms in which this Petition had been conceivd, but trusted that Adminn. woud by Means of their Secret Information have been Masters of the real history attending it. This he said had made any further Petition very uphill Work with them.

Ld. Drumd. urged on the other hand the many advantages that woud arise from their sending a *Deputation from their own Body* instead of himself, as the most certain Road to enforce a Belief with the People on the other Side the Water of the Sincerity of their Intentions. He pressd them at same time to hasten the departure of their Deputation as he conceived many advantages woud arise to America were the Advances to be made on their Part. That before their Departure shoud Commissioners from Britain arrive, and they shoud on the Part of the Crown make a Demand of the last Terms which Coud possibly be accepted, this woud necessarily involve in it a preclusion of all future Concession on the Part of England. Whereas were Overtures to be made on the part of America, such Advances might be accompanied with Instructions to those deputed for the Management of the Accommodation so as to enable them to enter upon Discussions as points might arise; such Modifications still to be left open for the final Ratification of the Colonies.

10 oClock forenoon

Mr. Elliot has just informed Ld. Drumd. that at a Meeting with Mr. [Govr. Livingston] he has had a Conversation on the same Subject—and that his Sollicitations had been accompanied with his throwing out Expectations of a handsome Appointment on the Part of the Colonies.

Mr. Elliot likewise mentiond that in Consequence of [Abel James] [3] having been employed in sounding the Leaders of the Quakers on the Subject of this Plan he found them universally satisfyd with the terms and anxious to have an Opportunity of affording every Support to the Plan proposed.

He likewise mentions the Report made to him by [Nixon & Nesbitt] [4] who had sounded the Mercantile Interest particularly the Irish Merchants who form a powerful Influence in the middle Cols.

MS (Scottish Record Office: Drummond Castle Papers).

[1] For an explanation of the names inserted in brackets here and below, see Drummond's Minutes, January 5, 1776, note 2.

[2] See Drummond's Notes, January 3–9? 1776, note 1.

[3] Abel James, Philadelphia merchant and partner in the mercantile firm of James and Drinker. "Effect of the 'Non-Importation Agreement' in Philadelphia, 1769–1770," *PMHB* 14 (April 1890): 41–45.

[4] John Maxwell Nesbitt (ca. 1730–1802) and John Nixon (1733–1808) were both Philadelphia merchants who were prominent in the revolutionary movement in Pennsylvania. Nesbitt was currently serving as paymaster of the Pennsylvania navy and Nixon as sometime president of the Pennsylvania Committee of Safety. *DAB.*

John Hancock to George Washington

Sir,   Philada. Jany. 6. 1776

I have the honor of enclosing you sundry resolutions passed yesterday respecting Mr Lovell. [1]

The Congress are desirous to know your opinion what rank it would be proper the aide de camp of the general Officers ought to hold in the army and on this head I am directed to write to you & request yr. answer. [2]

Just after the receipt of your letter Conolly & Cameron were brought to town. By some mismanagement, Smith one of the associates was suffered to escape from Frederic where they were confined. Orders were given to have the saddles examined, but nothing is discovered. There is reason to believe he must have found means to withdraw his

William Livingston

papers, as we find by an account from Frederic that his saddle was mended there.[3]

The French gentlemen are arrived and referred to the secret committee.[4]

The Congress have given orders to general Schuyler[5] immediately to secure and keep in safe and close custody Brigr. general Prescot until further orders.[6]

RC (DLC). Written by Charles Thomson and signed by Hancock.

[1] Congress authorized Washington to exchange Philip Skene for James Lovell and his family, and urged Washington to provide Lovell a job. *JCC*, 4:32–33. Lovell (1737–1814), Boston schoolmaster and political ally of John Hancock, had been arrested in June 1775 for sending military information from Boston to the provincial convention. Despite the congressional offer, Lovell was not exchanged until November, 1776, whereupon he was immediately elected to the Continental Congress. Shipton, *Harvard Graduates*, 14:31–48.

[2] See *JCC*, 4:33–34. Washington's response is contained in his January 30 letter to Hancock. Washington, *Writings* (Fitzpatrick), 4:287.

[3] See *JCC*, 3:394, 415, 445, 4:29.

[4] Pierre Penet and Emmanuel de Pliarne, who had arrived in Philadelphia with a letter of introduction from Washington. See *JCC*, 3:466; and Richard Smith's Diary, December 30, 1775, note 3, and January 9, 1776.

[5] See John Hancock to Philip Schuyler, January 2, 1776.

[6] For the continuation of this letter, see Hancock to Washington, January 16, 1776.

Joseph Hewes to Samuel Johnston

Dear Sir   Philadelphia 6th Jany 1776.

I wrote to you two days ago by two Ministers of the Gospel who are sent by order of Congress to the Western parts of North Carolina, where some of the inhabitants we are told are pursuing measures hostile to the friends of America; they are to endeavour to prevail on those people by reason and Argument to become Active in support of those rights and privileges which belong to them in common with the rest of the Inhabitants. I hope their well meant endeavours will be usefull to our Province.

In your favour of the 5th of November[1] the only one I have received from you I observe the plan you Adopted to get Arms and Amunition and your wish that the general Association had not been infringed. I have often wished the same thing, the Congress having adopted and pursued a Similar mode and on a much larger Scale. However, altho we have not yet reaped much advantage from it I have altered my mind on that subject and am now perfectly reconciled to it, from a Conviction that our utmost efforts in every way will barely furnish us with a Sufficient quantity of those Necessary Articles.

Some of the Zealous City politicians are alarmed at the Arival of a Lord Drummond who came to Town a few days ago. It seems he is son to the Earl of Perth, has lived several years in New York Government, is possessed of a landed Estate in New Jersey, went to England in Novemr 1774, came out to Boston in a Man of War in August last, from thence in the same conveyance soon after, to New York. Had he left the Title of Lord behind him he might have walked the Streets of this City a long time unnoticed, now the Eyes of all are upon him and consider him as a Suspicious Character. In private company I am told he says he was several months in London and frequently in company with Lord North, that the ministry are heartily tired of the controversy between Great Britain and the Colonies, but the pride of the people of England will not suffer them to relax. He thinks the matter might be easily setled. If America would consent to give a very small sum Annually so as to save appearances, England would repeal all the obnoxious acts and give up more than we ask. He says Lord North was astonished at the Union and Strength of the Colonies, declared he did not think it was possible for such things to be brought about, that he had no idea of such resistance. Some people think this Lord is employed to make Overtures to the Congress, others imagine he is only to sound some of the leading Members & indeavour to find out the whole scope, design and Views of the Congress. Certain it is he has had private conferences with several Characters of the first distinction Among us. I dont find he has yet Closeted any of the wise men of the East, however I am not certain of it, my indisposition has kept me from Congress for two days past in which time I have seen very few members.[2]

A report prevails this day in Town that by some late Advices received to the eastward from England the Ministry are determined to send a large Army to America early in the Spring and land it in this Province in order to subdue it at all events considering it the most Active in the present Rebellion. This like many other reports, the talk of a day, wants confirmation, tho all Accounts Agree (except what comes from the Lord above mentioned) that Administration will make one grand effort in the Spring to subdue the Colonies, therefore it becomes Necessary for us to provide for the event. We have Fifty three Regiments raised and raising each to consist of 728 men officers included.[3] To this Strength you may add twice the number of Regiments of well regulated Militia. Some of our Regiments are in Canada and more must be sent there. I will trespass no longer upon your patience than to request you to present my Compliments to Mrs. Johnston and family.

I am Dear Sir, your mo. Obedt. hume Servt.,   Joseph Hewes

Januy 7th. 1775 [*i.e.* 1776][4]

Postscript,

Since writing the foregoing several Vessels have arived from the foreign Islands and brought in Seven Tons of powder. The master of one of them informs that he left a number of Vessels all waiting for the same Article, that they were assured one hundred & Fifty Tons were hourly expected at those Islands which had been sent for to supply the injured Americans. Another Vessel is Just arived in the River from Old France with near Sixty Tons of Salt Petre on board. A Letter from Gen. Montgomery of the 6th of Decemr. informs us he had sat down before Quebec and was in hopes he should be in possession of it in a few days.[5]

I am &c.   J.H.

RC (Nc-Ar). FC (NcU: Hayes Collection microfilm).

[1] For Johnston's letter to Hewes of November 5, 1775, see Clark, *Naval Documents*, 2:898–99.

[2] For further information on Drummond, see Lord Drummond's Notes, January 3–9? 1776, note 1.

[3] In place of this sentence Hewes had originally written in his FC: "Our Establishment at present stands thus:

1 Regiment now raising in Georgia
3 do . . . . South Carolina
2 do . . . . North Caro . . . . already raising
6 do . . . . Virginia
1 do . . . . Delaware Counties
7 do . . . . Pensylvania including 1 Regt. of Rifle men now at Cambridge
2 do . . . . New Jersey
4 do . . . . New York
26 do . . . . Eastern Govermts. at Boston
1 do . . . . Canadians."

[4] Although this postscript is located in the Joseph Hewes Papers, NcU, it is apparently the continuation of Hewes' January 6 letter to Johnston.

[5] Hewes must be referring to Montgomery's letter to Schuyler of December 5, 1775. *Am. Archives*, 4th ser. 4:188–90.

William Hooper to James Iredell

My dear Friend   Philadelphia January 6th 1776
    So great has been my proportion of scribbling publick letters, that I have not had an opportunity to pay that respect to my private connections to which they have so just a Claim, to you to whom I owe it as a duty, as well as a testimony of Sincere reciprocal esteem.
    That day, I hope, is not at a great distance, when retired from the bustle of publick life, I shall enjoy all the sweets of domestick retirement & private friendship. I am weary of politicks, it is a study that corrupts the human heart, degrades the Idea of human nature, and drives men to expedients that morality must condemn. Deep stratagems, dark disguise, Fiction, falsehood, are but the fair side of the picture of a perfect, politician—a Machiavel—a Hobbs—a Richlieu—a North. No, my Friend, the Science of politicks is not to be learned in the principles

of the laws of nature and Nations, it is wrote only in the recesses of the mind of princes, and Vice assumes another name, when it ministers to the strength and importance of the state. The black part of the Character is ascribed to this and Virtues if any there are, are the personal property of the prince. Hide the picture! 'tis a horrid one.

We have met with nothing of much importance lately from the Continental Armies. A scarcity of Gunpowder has for some time past kept them inactive, that Want is now plentifully supplied, and I suppose e'er long we shall hear of the happy effects. To what are we reduced, that we can hear of bloodshed without remorse; and amidst the horror of this unnatural War derive consolation from a conquest sealed with the blood of our fellow subjects. Yes, Britain, It is the Criterion of thy existence; thy greatness totters. Luxury & Wealth with every vice in their train, are hurrying thee down the precipice, & liberty shuddering at thy fate is seeking an Asylum westward. Oh Heaven still check her approaching Ruin, restore her to reason, restore her to the Affection of her American Subjects. May she long flourish the guardian of freedom and when that Change comes and come it must, that America must become the seat of Empire, may Britain gently verge down the decline of life, and sink away in the Arms of her American Sons. A Fleet is begun here at the Continental Expense, Should it's success be great it will much exceed my expectations. It has a formidable power to cope with, the luxury of Britain has not yet enervated its seamen. However if this War continues, which God forbid, A Navy we must have. That of the United Provinces was trifling in its commencement, its increase and importance shewed the propriety of it. Some small armed Vessels about Boston have made some valuable acquisitions.

This City scarce feels the interruption of trade. The Manufacturers, Mechanicks & Seamen find employment in the publick works. And the Merchants find means to dispose of their Commodities which are necessary to procure *the means of Offence & defence*. The Eastern Colonies furnish Soldiers and the necessaries for subsisting them, so that much of the Continental money will center with them. Their poor are employed and none left for clamor. The Southern Colonies will feel it first. The American Army raised & immediately to be raised is as follows, In Massachussetts 27 battalions. (i.e. New England.) In New York 4. In Canada 1. (Canadians) In Jersey 2. In Philadelphia 6. In Delawar Counties 1. In Virginia 6. In North Carolina 2. In So. Carolina 3. Georgia 1—besides the provincial establishment in each province. Philadelphia is to be made the seat of action early in the spring, so say private letters.

I am extremely sorry that Polluck has been made the mark of publick vengeance, I am told that he was examined and acquitted by the Committee of Safety. Is it true! Oh the licentiousness of the times. Surely persecution never begot Converts, such Violence hurts the cause.

Remember me most respectfully to your Lady & the family. I wrote
Mr. Johnston via Virginia—by an Express. By a Vessel which sails
tomorrow for Wilmington, I wish to hear from him. Compls to Mr.
Smith, Mr. Jas. Charlton & all friends. I have only room to add what
I do with great truth & sincerity, that I am your sincere friend,

Will Hooper

RC (NcD).

John Jay to James Duane

Sir   Philadelphia 6 Jany 1776
    As I intend to leave this City Tomorrow I take the Liberty of sending
you the inclosed. I have just recd. a Letter from H. B. Livingston and
his Brother John. Harry informs me that his Major had quitted the
Service and that his Collo. has also resigned. These Places being vacant
I think Harry should be made a Lieut-Coll immediately, for as the
Lieut-Collo continues in the Service he certainly ought to have the
Regiment.[1] John it seems has heard that the Congress were about
employing a Person to purchase Goods at Montreal, and is desirous of
that Appointment.[2]
    By attending to these matters you will have the Satisfaction of obliging
a worthy Family as well as your &c   J.J.

FC (DLC).
    [1] This day Jay wrote a brief letter to Henry Beekman Livingston, assuring him
"It gives me Pleasure to be informed that the Congress have now an Opportunity
of conferring upon you a further Mark of their Esteem, and you may rest assured,
that my Endeavours shall upon no occasion be wanting to promote every Measure
calculated to reward Merit and advance your Prosperity." Robert R. Livingston
Papers, DLC. Livingston's January 2 letter to Jay informing him "that there is a
Vacant Majority for me, in the Regiment to which I belong, if I think proper to
accept it," is in Jay, *Papers* (Morris), pp. 220–21. Livingston, then a captain in the
Fourth New York Regiment, eventually became colonel of this regiment in Novem-
ber 1776, but even before then Congress appointed him lieutenant colonel of the
Second New York Regiment, upon the recommendation of the New York Provincial
Congress. See *JCC*, 4:190; and *Am. Archives*, 4th ser. 4:1531.
    [2] Jay also wrote a brief letter this day to John R. Livingston, explaining that
"The Report of the Congress intending to send a Person to Montreal to purchase
Goods, is, I believe, without foundation. Should such a measure be adopted, I will
take the Liberty of recommending you to the Congress for that appointmt." Robert
R. Livingston Papers, DLC. Although unsuccessful in his quest for a position as a
contractor for the Continental Army, Livingston was engaged by the New York
Provincial Congress in October 1776 to procure clothing for soldiers raised in that
province. *Am. Archives*, 5th ser. 3:218.

John Jay to Robert R. Livingston

Dear Robert   Philadelphia 6 Jany. 1776
Your Letter & those from your Brothers were delivered to me this afternoon just as I was about setting off for Elizabeth Town.[1] I shall leave this Place in the morning & probably be absent near a month.

Amidst the various Sources of Consolation in Seasons of poignant Distress, which the wise have long amused themselves & the World with, the little Share of Observation & Experience which has fallen to my Lott, convinces me that Resignation to the Dispensations of a benevolent as well as omnipotent Being, can alone administer Relief.[2]

The Sensations which the first Paragraph of your Letter has occasioned, mock the Force of Philosophy; & I confess has rendered me the sport of Feelings which you can more easily concieve than I express. Grief, if a weakness, is nevertheless on certain occasions amiable, and recommends itself by being in the Train of Passions which follow Virtue.

But remember my Friend that your Country bleeds, and calls for your Exertions. The Fate of those very Friends, whose Misfortune so justly affects you, is linked with the common Cause, and cannot have a separate Issue. Rouse therefore, and after vigorously discharging the Duties you owe your Country, return to your peaceful Shade, and supply the Place of your former Joys, by the Reflection, that they are only removed to a more kindred Soil, like Flowers from a thorny Wilderness by a friendly Florist; under whose care they will flourish & bloom and court your Embraces forever.

Accept my warmest Thanks for the Ardor with which you wish a Continuance of & Increase of that Friendship to which I have long been much indebted. Be assured that its Duration will always be among the first objects of my Care, and let us unite in proving by our Example that the Rule which declares juvenile Friendships, like vernal Flowers, to be of short Continuance, is not without Exceptions even in our degenerate Days.

I wish something could be done for John—at present I know of nothing, except in the military Line. The first Opportunity of serving him in some other Department which offers, shall engage my Attention. Mr. Deane has this Moment come in, so that must conclude, as I hope to conclude every Letter to you, with an assurance That I am your affct. Friend   J.J.

P.S. 50 Tons of Salt Petre arrived this Day.

FC (DLC). John Jay, *The Correspondence and Public Papers of John Jay*, ed. Henry P. Johnston, 4 vols. (New York: G. P. Putnam's Sons, 1890–93), 1:42–43. FC damaged; missing words supplied from Tr.

[1] See Jay to James Duane, this date.

[2] Robert R. Livingston, who was still at his Clermont estate in New York mourning the recent death of his father and striving to put the family's affairs in order, did not return to Congress until after May 11, 1776. Burnett, *Letters*, 1:lvi; and George Dangerfield, *Chancellor Robert R. Livingston of New York, 1746–1813* (New York: Harcourt, Brace and Co., 1960), pp. 66–67.

Naval Committee to Samuel Purviance, Jr.

Sir,[1]   Philadelphia 6th January 1776

By Coll Harrison, Coll Lee & many other Gentlemen we are abundantly informed how much the American Cause owes to your Zeal & Activity in General, & particularly to your Assistance in fitting out the two armed Vessels at Baltimore, for this we cannot but beg you will accept the Thanks of this Committee.

Coll Lee acquaints us that a second Leiutt. was necessary for the Hornet, a Commission for one we now inclose you & shall be oblig'd to you to fill up the Blank with the name of a Person as well qualifyd for that Station as you can get & present it to him. We likewise inclose you blank Warrants for the Master, Boatswain, Gunner & Carpenter of the Hornet & also one for the Master of the Wasp wch. we desire may be filled up with the names of those persons that were appointed by Coll. Harrison or in Case of Accidents, with such persons as you think proper to supply their places.

We approve of your Appointment of a Carpenter, Cooper & Armourer, for the former we send you the Warrant already mentioned, to the other two or to a Capts. Clerk, tis not usual to give warrants, it will be sufficient for them & all of their rank wch. are called petty Officers to have their names enter'd in the Sloops books with the Title Capts. Clerk, Cooper, Armourer &c. annexed thereto. This will be sufficient to entitle them to their pay & prize Money, as such the Comee. have thought proper to allow a Capts. Clerk & two Midshipman to the Sloop fitted out here & desire you will order the like for the Hornet.

The Comee. were induced on this first Cruize (by no means to be made use of as a precedent hereafter) to allow the Capts. of the Ships at the Continental Expence a Qr. Cask of better rum than that laid in for the Ships Company & another of Wine with a proportionable quantity of Sugar & a little Coffee. This we desire may be allowed to Capt. Stone as near as you can adjust or guess the matter, a little more or less, as this Practice is by no means to be continued, will be of no great Consequence.

As for Cabbin Stores we have consented to pay for such as are usually provided here by owners of Ships for Masters of Vessels sailing out of this Port all in the most frugal manner & have left the Matter under such [. . .] to two Sea Capts. of Repute that have long saild out of this Port, & whatever you may do in this respect you may depend on our being perfectly satisfy'd with. We are apprehensive that a Letter we sent to Capt. Stone the middle of last Month has Miscarried or been intercepted. We now inclose you a Copy thereof, together with Copy of the Rations allowed for the Sea Service by the Congress, also our Letter to Capt. Stone wch. we have left open for your perusal. This done, we shall be obliged to you to seal & forward it to him. We shall be farther obliged to you to tell Capt. Stone & the Commandg. Officer of the Wasp that they are to look upon themselves as under the Command of Esek Hopkins Esqr. appointed by Congress as Commandr. in Chief of the Fleet of the united Colonies, & that it is expected that they obey with all possible punctuality & Expedition all such Orders as they may from time to time receive from him.

Such Orders I make no doubt they will receive soon, perhaps by this Conveyance, as Mr. Hopkins expects to leave town to Morrow Morning & we have not above an hours business more to transact with him. The Ships & Briggs fell down the day before Yesterday, the Sloop yesterday. We are Sir, yr. most hble servts., Step Hopkins

Chris Gadsden

Silas Deane

Joseph Hewes

RC (MeHi). In an unidentified hand and signed by Hopkins, Gadsden, Deane, and Hewes.
[1] Probably Samuel Purviance, Jr. A letter from Purviance to the Naval Committee dated January 13, 1776, which is apparently his response to this letter from the committee, is in Clark, *Naval Documents*, 3:773-74.

Robert Treat Paine's Diary

[January 6, 1776]
Fine day. News Came of the Reelection of all the Massa Delegates for 12 mo. save Elbridge Gerry Esqr in the room of Mr. Cushing.[1]

MS (MHi).
[1] For additional information on the election of the new Massachusetts delegation, which revealed the cleavages that had developed in Massachusetts' revolutionary party and among her delegates to Congress, see Paine to Joseph Hawley, January 1, note 1, and John Hancock to Thomas Cushing, January 17, 1776, note 1.

Richard Smith's Diary

Saturday 6 Jany [1776]
Minutes of yesterday read & Letters informing of a considerable

Quantity of Powder just arrived at Egg Harbor, some of it consigned to the Congress by Jonathan Parsons, some consigned to Pelatiah Webster & some to another Person in Philada. Congress agreed to purchase the whole & the Secret Comee. are desired to have it brought here under a Guard commanded by a Lieut. A Letter of Thanks directed to be sent to Mr. Parsons for his Attention to the Public Welfare. I sent off the Dispatches to Cols. Waterbury & Heard by Mr. Palmer of N York province. A Letter was recieved from a French or Swiss Officer at Lisbon offering his Service & another or Two from other Foreign Officers, these were committed to the Secret Comee.[1] The Memorial from the Town of Newport was agitated for several Hours & at last referred generally to the Assembly of Rhode Island. Mr. Gadsden from the Naval Comee. reported the Rules for Distribution of the Prize Money which were confirmed with one Alteration viz, That the Rewards for extraordinary Exertions shall not be paid out of the Continental Share of the Captures. Letters just recd. from Gens. Schuyler, Montgomery and Wooster pressing for an immediate Supply of hard Money & for more Troops otherwise they fear all will be lost in that Quarter.[2] Montgomery was before Quebec on the 16th of Decr. with 8 or 900 effective Men & some Canadians and had planted by Way of Feint a Battery of Cannon agt. the Lower Town but intended his chief Efforts by Way of Storm agt. the Upper Town. Monday Morng. was assigned to consider this Business & Nothing else to interfere, the Delegates to be upon Honor to meet punctually at 10 oCloc. A Report respecting Canada was produced.[3] Dr. Franklin shewed me to day a Pattern Paper containing 6 or 8 Sorts of Cloths lately manufactured at one or both of the Company Manufactories of Philada.[4] Cols. Heard & Waterbury are to disarm the Tories of Queens County on Oath that they have delivered up all their Arms & ammunitn. and to imprison all that refuse the Oath, these Tories are not to quit their County without a Pass certifying that they are well disposed to the American Cause—all to be considered as Tories who voted agt. sending Delegates to the Present N York Convention. No Lawyer may bring an Action for them. Quære Whether People are not forbid to trade with these Tories. The Cols. are also to seize certain Persons named in a List & Confine them till further Order of Congress. 500 Doll[ar]s and 200 Lb. of Powder allowed for the Expedition (which was afterwards well executed by the Jersey Militia only those of Connectt. being countermanded).

MS (DLC).

[1] See *JCC*, 4:35.

[2] General Schuyler's letter to Hancock of December 31, 1775 (misdated in the journals as December 30), and General Wooster's letter to Schuyler of December 18 are in PCC, item 153, 1:374–78; and *Am. Archives*, 4th ser. 4:310, 480. General Montgomery's letter to Wooster of December 16, which was enclosed in Schuyler's

letter to Hancock, is in *Am. Archives*, 4th ser. 4:288–89.
[3] Burnett thought that this might refer to a report Congress approved on November 29, 1776, but it seems certain that it actually was the report of the committee on General Schuyler's letters which Congress adopted on January 8, 1776. See *JCC*, 4:37–40, 6:990–91; Smith's Diary, January 8, 1776; and Burnett, *Letters*, 1:300n.5.
[4] The remainder of this entry concerns actions taken by Congress on January 3. *JCC*, 4:25–27.

Samuel Adams to James Warren

My dear Sir,　　　　　　　　　　　　Philade Jany 7 1776

I verily believe the Letters I write to you are three, to one I receive from you. However I consider the Multiplicity of Affairs you must attend to in your various Departments, and am willing to make due Allowance.

Your last is dated the 19th of December. It contains a List of very important Matters lying before the General Assembly. I am much pleasd to find that there is an End put to the Contest between the two Houses concerning the Establishment of a Militia, and that you are in hopes of making an effectual Law for that Purpose.[1] It is certainly of the last Consequence to a free Country, that the Militia which is its natural Strength, should be kept upon the most advantageous Footing. A standing Army, however necessary it may be at some times, is always dangerous to the Liberties of the People. Soldiers are apt to consider themselves as a Body distinct from the rest of the Citizens. They have their Arms always in their hands. Their Rules and their Discipline is severe. They soon become attachd to their officers and disposd to yeild implicit Obedience to their Commands. Such a Power should be watchd with a jealouse Eye. I have a good Opinion of the principal officers of our Army. I esteem them as Patriots as well as Soldiers. But if this War continues, as it may for years yet to come, we know not who may succeed them. Men who have been long governd by military Laws, and inurd to military Customs and Habits, may lose the Spirit and Feeling of Citizens. And even Citizens, having been used to admire the Heroism which the Commanders of their own Armies have displayd, and to look up to them as their Saviours, may be prevaild upon to surrender to them those Rights, for the Protection of which against an Invader, they had employd & paid them. We have seen too much of such a Disposition among some of our Countrymen. The Militia is composd of free Citizens. There is therefore no Danger of their making Use of their Power to the Destruction of their own Rights, or suffering others to invade them. I earnestly wish that young Gentlemen of a military Genius, and many such I am satisfied there are in our Colony, might be instructed in the Art of War, and taught at the same time the

Principles of a free Government, and deeply impressd with a Sense of that indespensible Obligation which every Individual is under to the whole Society. These might in Time be fit for officers in the Militia; and being thoroughly acquainted with the Duties of Citizens as well as Soldiers, might be intrusted with a Share in the Command of our Army, at such Times as Necessity might require so dangerous a Body to exist.

I am glad that your Attention is turnd so much to the Importation of Powder, & that the Manufacture of Salt petre is in so flourishing a Way. I cannot think you are restraind by the Resolve of Congress, from exporting Fish to Spain.[2] I will make my self more certain, by recurring to our Records tomorrow when the Secretary returns; he being at this time (6 o'Clock P M) at his House three Miles from Town. And I will inform you by a Postscript to this Letter, or by another Letter by the Post. I have the Pleasure to acquaint you that a Vessel with five Tons of Powder *certainly* arrivd at Egg Harbour the Night before last, besides two Tons in this River. A Part of it is consignd to the Congress. The Rest is the Property, partly of Mr ⟨*Thomas Boylston*⟩[3] and partly of a Gentleman in this City. Congress has orderd the whole to be purchasd for publick Use. We are also informd that Six Tons more arrivd a few days ago in New York, which I believe to be true. But better still, A Vessel is *certainly* arrivd in this River with between fifty and Sixty Tons of Salt petre. This I suppose will give you more Satisfaction for the present, than telling you Congress News, as you request. You ask me, "When you are to hear of our Confederation"?[4] I answer, when some Gentlemen (to use an Expression of a Tory) shall "feel more bold." You know it was formerly a Complaint in our Colony, that there was a timid kind of Men, who perpetually hinderd the Progress of those who would fain run in the Path of Virtue and Glory. I find, wherever I am, that Mankind are alike variously classed. I can discern the Magnanimity of the Lyon, the Generosity of the Horse, the Fearfulness of the Deer, and the *Cunning of the Fox*—I had almost overlookd the *Fidelity* of the Dog. But I forbear to indulge my rambling Pen is this Way, lest I should be thought chargeable, with a Design to degrade the *Dignity* of our Nature by comparing Men with Beasts. Let me just observe to you, that I have mentioned only the more excellent Properties that are to be found among Quadrupeds. Had I suggested an Idea of the *Vanity* of the Ape, the *Tameness* of the ox, or the *stupid Servility* of the Ass, I might have been lyable to Censure.

Are you sollicitous to hear of our Confederation? I will tell you, It is not dead but sleepeth. A Gentleman of this City told me the other day, that he could not believe the People without Doors would follow the Congress passibus æquis, if such Measures as *some* called spirited, were pursued. I was of a different opinion. It put me in Mind of a Fable of the high mettled horse and the dull horse. My excellent Colleague Mr J A can repeat to you the Fable; and if the Improvement had been made of it, which our very valuable Friend Coll M[ifflin] proposd,[5] you would have seen that Confederation compleated long before this time. I do not despair of it, since our Enemies themselves are hastening it. While I am writing an Express arrives from Baltimore in Maryland, with the Deposition of Capt Horn of the Snow Bird belonging to Providence. The Deponent says, that on Monday the 1st Instant he being at Hampton in Virginia heard a constant firing of Cannon—that he was informd a Messenger had been sent to inquire where the firing was, who reported that the Ships of War were cannonading the Town of Norfolk—that about the Middle of the Afternoon they saw the Smoke ascending from Norfolk as they supposd—that he saild from Hampton the Evening of the same day, and the firing continued till the next day. This will prevail more than a long Train of Reasoning to accomplish a Confederation, and other Matters which I know your heart as well as mine is much set upon.

I forgot to tell you that a Vessel is arrivd in Maryland having, as part of her Cargo four thousand Yards of Sail Cloth—An Article which I hope will be much in Demand in America. Adieu my Friend,

S A

RC (MHi). FC (NN).

[1] The Massachusetts Council had informed the House that it would concede the right to appoint militia officers, reserving the power of veto. The first officers were appointed on January 23, 1776. James Warren to Samuel Adams, December 19, 1775, *Warren-Adams Letters*, 2:429–30; and *Am. Archives*, 4th ser. 4:1413. See also Samuel Adams to James Otis, Sr., November 23, 1775.

[2] See *JCC*, 3:308, 314, and Samuel Adams to James Warren, January 10, 1776.

[3] Adams wrote "Thos. Boylston" in the FC, but the name is inked out in the RC.

[4] Confederation was being considered by members of Congress both in- and out-of-doors, but there is no mention in the journals of the subject between Benjamin Franklin's introduction of his draft Articles of Confederation on July 21, 1775, and June 7, 1776, except that on December 24, 1775, it was included in a list of unfinished business. *JCC*, 2:195–201, 3:456, 5:425–26. See also Richard Smith's Diary, January 16, 1776.

[5] For confirmation that the reference is to Mifflin, see Samuel Ward to Henry Ward, January 8? 1776.

Samuel Ward to Nicholas Cooke

Sir,   Philadelphia 7th Jany. 1776

We have the Honor of your Letter of 26th last Month, the Marine Service is of such vast Importance that We doubt not of your utmost Attention to it in all its Branches.

The Ravages committed by the armed Vessels & the continual Alarms raised by them must be very distressing to the Colony but what would not a wise Man do or suffer to preserve his Liberty, the alone Source of human Happiness and only Security for the permanent

Enjoyment of it. The Colony has bravely defended Itself and supported the common Cause of America. The next Campaign of our Enemies will make every possible Effort against Us [and] will probably require still greater Exertions. We are therefore clearly in Opinion with You that a Regiment ought to be raised & kept up in the Colony at the continental Expence & shall embrace the first favourable Opportunity of applying for one. If by the divine Blessing We succeed next Campaign, the Burthen of the War will be over & the Reestablishment of our just Rights and Privileges will be the glorious Reward of this arduous Struggle.

The Removal of the Stock is of great Importance & We are happy to find that proper Measures are adopted for that Purpose.

We lament that any Persons should be so lost to Virtue & the Love of their Country as to attempt to divide Us when our Union is essential to our Preservation but We hope that the wise & temperate & yet spirited Conduct of the general Assembly will prevent the intended Mischief & preserve Union in the Colony.

We are concerned for the Uneasiness occasioned by the different Constructions of the Resolve of 15th July last. We lately gave our Opinion upon it, but horned Cattle, Sheep, hogs & poultry cannot be exported by it, our extreme Want of Powder occasioned that Resolve.[1] No Man ought to take the Advantages of the Necessities of his Country to demand exorbitant Prices for what she stands in Need of, nor to abuse a License given by her to her Injury or should an instance of that kind happen others ought by no Means to violate her Resolves for if once the Resolutions of Congress are trampled upon there will be no common Bond of Union left, no adequate Power to collect & exert the united Strength of the Colonies, Confusion and certain Destruction would soon follow. A moments Reflection must satisfy any Man of this & induce him as he values everything dear to human Nature religiously to support the Resolves of Congress.

We are with great Regard Sir Your most obedient very humble Servants   Sam Ward

P.S. Mr. Hopkins is so engaged he could not attend to look over the letters & desired me to sign & forward them myself, for important news refer you to my Letter to the Govr. & Com[pan]y.[2]

This Moment an Express from N. York has brought the Kings Speech at the Opening of Parliament which I have enclosed;[3] It is decisive; Every Man must now be convinced that under God our Safety depends wholly upon a brave, wise and determined Resistance. May infinite Wisdom direct all your measures to the Preservation of America in general and the Happiness of the Colony in particular.

S. Ward

RC (RHi). Ward, *Correspondence* (Knollenberg), pp. 171–72.

¹ On July 15, 1775, Congress approved the exportation of American "produce" in exchange for certain war materials. Then, on October 26, it ordered copies of this resolve distributed throughout Europe and the West Indies, with the term "provisions" replaced by the phrase "the produce of these colonies," and passed another resolve permitting American exports to the foreign West Indies "except horned cattle, sheep, hogs, and poultry." *JCC*, 2:184–85, 3:306, 308. For an indication of the confusion caused by these apparently conflicting resolves, see Ward to Nathaniel Shaw, Jr., December 13, 1775.
² Not found.
³ See John Dickinson's Proposed Resolutions on a Petition to the King, January 9–24, 1776, note.

John Adams to Samuel Adams

Braintree Jany. 8. 1776. Reports on his efforts to gain support for the fledgling American navy during his recent journey to Massachusetts. "In my Return, I had an opportunity of dining at Mr. Shermans in New Haven with a Number of Members of the Assembly then Sitting in that Place, and of Seeing Captain Saltonstall, and consulting with him and others concerning Measures for engaging Seamen to go to Philadelphia to man our Fleet. From N. Haven I went to Providence and had the Honour of an Interview with Governor Cooke, Mr. H. Marchant, and some Members of their assembly which was then sitting in that Place. I proposed the same Thing to them, and as I am now informed with some success, for the Govr laid it before the Assembly who instantly voted that all seamen who were in the service of the Colony in their Army who inclined to go to Philadelphia, should have leave and accordingly sixty of them, inlisted immediately and are gone." Approves Congress' decision to build 13 ships and hopes for an easing of restrictions on American trade, explains recent political developments at home and his desire for stronger executive authority in Massachusetts, and asks rhetorically "if they [Britain] make Treaties against Us is it not lawfull for Us to make Treaties [against] them?" ¹

RC (NN).
¹ On this same day, Adams wrote a letter to Mercy Otis Warren discussing the advantages of a republican form of government. *Warren-Adams Letters*, 1:201–3.

Josiah Bartlett to John Langdon

Sir,   Philadelphia Jan 8th 1776.
The Congress have ordered the Secret Committee to purchase and bring in for the use of the Navy and Army sundry articles which were under consideration before you left the Congress.¹ At my request, the Committee have directed me to inform you, that they are willing one

vessel should be sent from our Colony for that purpose if a proper trading for the European market, such as fish, potash, bee's wax &c can be purchased reasonable.[2]

If you think it will answer and agree to send, you may charter a vessel and procure a loading, and forthwith inform the Committee that they may direct what goods and the quantities you are to send for, and remit you the money to pay for the cargo. This will be of the same nature of your former contract.

Your friend Wharton tells me he has some money in the hands of Mr Tracy of Newburyport, for which he is willing to draw and receive the money here, which will save some expense of conveyance. I think seven or eight hundred pounds L.M.

You will see the necessity of this Committee's being informed of your determination on this affair as speedily as possible.

Last Saturday Major Patton's brig arrived with above fifty tons of salt petre, and a few days before another vessel brought 3 tons and a half of powder.

Our fleet fell down the river the latter end of the week.

Please to inform me of the present situation of our Colony affairs and don't forget to put our Convention in mind to send somebody here to relieve me as soon as convenient.[3]

I am your friend and Servt,   Josiah Bartlett

January 9th.

I have now a proper agreement drawn which I now enclose; if you like it, you will sign it and forward it back as soon as possible. You will give orders concerning the money to be remitted to you.

Your's ut Supra,   J.B.

N.B. 23 tons of powder arrived at New York.

Tr (DLC).
[1] By resolution of January 3, 1776. *JCC*, 4:24–25.
[2] On February 20 the Secret Committee entered into a contract with John Langdon to import "such woollen or other goods as the sd. Com[mitte]e shall direct" for which he was advanced $10,000. Secret Committee Minutes of Proceedings, February 20, 1776.
[3] In a letter written this day to his wife, Bartlett noted: "I have wrote to our Convention to Send another Delegate here in my Stead, as soon as he comes here I shall prepare to return home. You will know who is appointed & when he Sets out and by that means know when I can return home as I must tarry here till another Delegate arrives." Bartlett to Mary Bartlett, January 8, 1776, NhHi. Bartlett, John Langdon, and William Whipple were appointed delegates to Congress on January 23, 1776. Langdon had left Philadelphia for home on January 2, and Whipple did not arrive in Philadelphia until February 29. *N.H. Provincial Papers*, 8:51; and Richard Smith's Diary, January 1 and February 29, 1776.

Joseph Hewes to Robert Smith

Dr Sir   [January 8? 1776] [1]
I have not been favoured with a line from you since I left Edenton.
The reason is plain: I have not wrote to you, therefore you are not
obliged to know that I ever arived here, I wish you had forgiven me
and been less Ceremonious.
  I find by Mr. Johnstons Letter the mode you adopted in Council
to get the one thing Necessary; we have done the same here on a much
larger Scale. [2] Necessity, dire Necessity induced us to make that infring-
ment of one of our own Laws. I cannot say I approved of it my self at
first but I have altered my opinion of the matter and am now perfectly
satisfied we are right. Our utmost exertions in every way we could
devise have hitherto proved insufficient to furnish the Necessary Supplies
of powder, consequently some of our movements have gone on heavily,
I thank God the prospect now brightens a little. Two Vessels arived
yesterday from the Foreign West India Islands with each one Ton of
Powder, and last night another came into the River with Six Tons
more from the same quarter. The Captain of the latter says he left
fifteen Vessels behind all waiting for the same precious article, that they
had the fullest assurance 150 Tons of it were hourly expected at those
places which had been sent for in Order to supply the distressed
Americans. Another Vessel is also Arived in the River from old France
with near 60 Tons of Salt Petre on board and I have the pleasure to
inform you there is Sulpher enough in this City to work it all up.
  On Thursday and Fryday Last the following Vessels fitted out for the
protection of the United Colonies sailed from this City on a Cruise to
witt

Ship Alfred, Captain Saltinstoll   28 Guns
Ship Columbus   Whipple   26 do
Brigg Cabot   Hopkins   16 do
Brigg Andrea Doria Biddle   14
Sloop Providence   Hazard   12
    now ready in a Neighbouring port on the same acco.
Sloop Hornet   Stone   10
Schooner Wasp   4

These Vessels will all be well manned and I hope get to sea in a few
days.
  It is currently reported that Great Britain intends to make one grand
effort in the Spring to reduce the Colonies for which purpose they are
to land a very large Army in this province and subdue it first considering
it as foremost in Rebellion. As they mean to give the land of the Rebels
to the Soldiers it will be prudent to begin here where land is best
improved and most Valuable. Seven Vessels of War of different denominations are already fitted out for the Protection & defence of the United

Colonies, thirteen more are ordered to be built to vary from 24 to 32
Guns, all the Artificers that can be found are employed in making
Arms [and gunpowder], & salt petre is dayly coming into this and
[. . .] other ports so that in all probabil[it]y we shall be able to look
danger in the face, and in all these Circumstances if we do not defend
ourselves, our Country, no our most Sacred rights & priveleges, we
ought to be made hewers of wood & drawers of water and consigned to
everlasting infamy.

I send you A news paper enclosed. You will observe a Letter in it
from an Officer under Col. Arnold dated the 21st of November giving
an Acco. of the March of that Little Army to Canada. The Letter is
genuine and may be depended on, that extraordinary March is thought
to equal Hanibals over the Alps. By an express arived yesterday we
have Letters from Gen. Mongomery of the 6t December. As he had
found Arnold with a Body of troops from Montreal, [he] had invested
the City of Qu[e]bec and expected to be in possession of it in a few days.
He is a brave officer and I hope his attack on this Fortress will be
Crowned with Success. If so the whole Province of Canada is our own.

A few days ago Mr. Spencer & Mr. McWhorter, two Presbyterian
Clergymen, set out for the Western parts of North Car. in order to
prevail on the Regulators & highlanders to become active in support
of our common cause. If they should fall in your way I beg your friendly
attention to them as ministers of the Gospel, Gentlemen, friends to
liberty and our cause. They have the warmest recommendation.

FC (NcU: Hayes Collection microfilm).
[1] Hewes' references to the arrival "yesterday" of vessels from the West Indies and
to General Montgomery's letter indicate that he wrote this letter on this date. See
Hewes to Samuel Johnston, January 6, 1776, and its postscript of January 7.
[2] In October 1775 the North Carolina Provincial Council had sent ships to the
foreign West Indies to trade for arms and ammunition—a policy which Congress
formally adopted on October 26, 1775. *JCC*, 3:308; and Clark, *Naval Documents*,
2:898–99.

Francis Lightfoot Lee to Richard Henry Lee

[January 8? 1776] [1]
[   ] [2] being so full as other ways I shou'd. You have seen the Kings
speech, which you wou'd suppose must convince everybody of the
bloody intentions of the King & ministry, but it is far from being the
case in this City; for there is a certain Ld. Drummond who persuades
the tools who are gaping after a reconciliation, that he is in the secrets
of the inner Cabinet, that the sincere wish is to make up with America,
upon her own terms, that even Ld. Mansfield is a warm friend to our
Cause. All this is so absurd, that you will say none but rank tories can

pretend to beleive it & so shoud I did I not find the contrary, for you
may be assured that many friends & well meaning people are taken in &
wish loudly for Congress to send deputies home. Indeed I am not
without my fears, that Congress may be somewhat affected.[3] This day
a motion was made to [. . . .][4] from this measure, by myself & some
others. You shoud be here as soon as possible,[5] I mean with tolerable
convenience to yourself, for I see no prospect of the Congress adjourning.
Nine batallions are order'd for Canada to march as quickly as they can
be raised. Bull's & Maxwell's are two of them who go off directly.[6]
Montgomeries last Letter informs us of his being before Quebec, &
confident of success. We have recd. 57 tons of saltpetre & 30 tons of
powder; & have intelligence of a vessell with 15 tons & 2000 stand of
arms which is every day expected. Yr. fleet is not yet out of the River
but I believe they have Now No obstruction, Tho Virga. I believe will
not receive any benefit as the pilots are sent home.[7] Norfolk we hear is
destroyd, but we are anxious to know the fate of the troops there.[8] God
bless you. Farewell,   F. L. Lee

RC (ViU).
[1] The date and the recipient of this letter have been conjectured from the content
of Lee's remarks.
[2] The top portion of this letter is missing.
[3] See Lord Drummond's Notes, January 3–9? 1776, note 1.
[4] MS damaged; several lines missing.
[5] Richard Henry Lee, the probable recipient of this letter, did not return to
Congress until early March. See *JCC*, 4:196; and Richard Henry Lee to George
Washington, March 13, 1776.
[6] See the resolutions of January 8, 1776, *JCC*, 4:39.
[7] See Benjamin Harrison to Wilson Miles Cary, December 10, 1775.
[8] On January 1 Norfolk was cannonaded by Dunmore's ships, and a landing party
set fire to the warehouses along the wharf. The heaviest destruction, however, was
apparently the result of fires set by Virginia troops. See Clark, *Naval Documents*,
3:563–65, 579–80, 617–18; and Thomas J. Wertenbaker, *Norfolk, Historic Southern
Port* (Durham, N.C.: Duke University Press, 1931), pp. 67–68.

Secret Committee Minutes of Proceedings

Philada. Comee. C[hamber] Jany. 8th. 1776[1]
At a meeting of the Commee. of Secrecy present Saml. Ward, Benjn.
Franklin, Tho. McKean, Josiah Bartlett & Robt. Morris. A Contract
was enterd into between Phil. Livingston of the State of N. York &
the said C[ommittee]. That the Sum of 20,000 dlls Contl. Money shall
be now advancd & paid by the sd. Come. of S[ecrecy] to the sd. P. L.
to be laid out by him in flour & other produce of these Colonies & shippd
on board a vessel or vessels to be by him charterd for that purpose, to
some proper port, or ports in Europe & there disposd of on the best
terms. And the nett proceeds of the sd. Cargoe to be laid out in such

woolen & other goods as the sd. Comee. shall direct & shippd for the sd. Colonies.

MS (MH).
¹ On this day the committee appointed Andrew Sterett to be their clerk. Journal of the Secret Committee, fol. 22, MH.

Richard Smith's Diary

Monday 8 January [1776]
Votes of Saturday read as were Letters from Gens. Schuyler and Montgomery.¹ The latter, it seems, was before Quebec the 5th of Decr. & expects Success in his intended Storm, he demands 10,000 Men to defend Canada. A Report consisting of several Articles about that Country was agreed to, then it was voted, after much Consideration that 9 Battalions shall be destined for the Service in Canada including the Canadian Regiment there which is intended to consist of 1000 Men under Col. James Livingston. A Battalion consists of about 726 Officers & Men. One of these Battalions is to be raised in New Hampshire, One in Connectt., One in N York. Col. Maxwells to be sent out of N Jersey, Col Bulls to be sent out of Pennsa. & a new One to be raised there, Two to be reinlisted from the Corps under Montgy. & Arnold. This Business took up the whole Day but previous to its coming on & after the Letters were read, Gadsden moved and was seconded by me that Col. Arnold may be made a Brigadier Gen. and recieve the Thanks of the Congress for his extraordinary March from Cambridge to Quebec & for his other spirited Exertions, this was debated & put off till Tomorrow.² The Kings Speech of the 27th of October (1775) arrived to day³ as did a Report that a large Fleet was seen at Sea with 500 Troops on Board, but some think this premature. An Express came with Letters from Baltimore informg. that Ld. Dunmore has destroyed the Town of Norfolk in Virginia.⁴ 300 Barrels of Powder just arrived in New York as did 8 Ton the Week before. 50 or 60 Tons of Saltpetre arrived here at Phila. in Masons Vessel. The 3 Comps. under Lt. Col. Irwin of Bulls Battaln. gone to Accomac are to return soon and be replaced by Minute men from Maryland.

MS (DLC).
¹ General Schuyler's letter to Hancock of December 26, 1775, is in PCC, item 153, 1:370–73, and *Am. Archives*, 4th ser. 4:463–64. General Montgomery's letter to Schuyler of December 5, 1775, is in *Am. Archives*, 4th ser. 4:188–90.
² Congress promoted Arnold to the rank of brigadier general on January 10. See *JCC*, 4:47.
³ Robert Treat Paine had also noted in his diary for this date: "The kings Speech of Octr. 27th arrived here." MHi.
⁴ See the letter and enclosure of January 5, 1776, from Samuel Purviance, Jr.,

chairman of the Baltimore Committee, to Hancock in PCC, item 78, 18:21–25, and *Am. Archives*, 4th ser. 4:578.

Samuel Ward to His Daughter

My Dearest   Philadela. 8th Jany. 1776
I have only Time to let you know that I am very well especially considering that I am incessantly employed in Attention to Business & have no Exercise & not even Time for proper Relaxation. The enclosed Papers give you all the News except that the Kings Speech to Parliament opened 27th [i.e. 26th] Octr. is come to hand. He calls all Rebels, charges us with endeavouring to amuse the Nation by Professing of Affection to them & loyalty to him & meaning only to gain Time to make our Preparations for a general Revolt in Order to sett up an independent Empire, says he has greatly augmented his naval & land Forces, determines to be decisive, has the offer of foreign assistance if necessary & the strongest assurances that his Operations in America will not be interrupted by any foreign Disturbances. Thus you see my Love your Daddy's Sentiments are confirmed that the savage ever meant to make himself an absolute despotic Tyrant. May the Reward of his Hands & wicked Heart be given him. Every Idea of Peace is now over & all possible Exertions are to be made for the common Defence, the Vessel that brings this met a Fleet of Men of War & Transports with five thousand Soldiers on Board coming to Boston. By an Express from Maryland the Men of War have cannonaded Norfolk in Virginia 2 1/2 Days & probably destroyed it. 50 Tons of salt petre & 6 Tons of Powder arrived here a day or two ago & 8 Tons Powder at New York. The Express waits. God preserve my dear little Tribe, Friends & Family & also all my dearest Country. Proper Regards to all your Aunts &c. Your very affec. Father

RC (RHi). In Ward's hand, though not signed.

Samuel Ward to Henry Ward

[January 8? 1776] [1]
I am entirely of your Opinion that We shall be undone unless the most spirited Measures are pursued. You may recollect the Fable of the strong spirited Horse & the lean one which I mentioned to you when at home. We are eternally plagued with that dull Horse, sometimes he pricks up his Ears and goes a little Way & with Spirit, then flaggs & is a dead Weight upon his Mate. I think however we shall make him useful upon the whole, if not let him in Mifflin's spirited language be

given to the Dogs, the strong One I am sure is able to perform the Journey tho' a severe one.

The fitting out Privateers, a Treaty &c many of Us have in Contemplation & as soon as we can prepare others shall carry into Execution. I have no Time to correct much less copy & am almost worn out with continual Application of Mind & no Exercise. Give Me in your next a particular Acct. of the Proceedings of Assembly & every thing important.

I recd. a Letter from Messr. Clarke & Nightingale which does not require an Answer, but I would notwithstanding have wrote to them to let them know that if they or any other Merchts. in Providence capable of the Business had a Mind to enter into a Contract with the secret Comee. to import such things as Congress has order'd I could serve them if I knew their Intentions very soon & any Persons here to contract & receive the Money. You may let Mr. John Brown [know] that I have recd. his Letter inclosing his Brothers & that he may prepare to execute a Contract to the Amount he mentions.[2] He must direct to whom the Money is to be paid & with whom the contract is to [be] entered into. Tobacco is an Article that I think will do vastly well & several ship loads may be had from our Colony, in shiping Produce We ought to avoid as much as possible all Provisions for I think we are in a fair Way of reducing them by famine.

50 Tons of Salt petre & 6 Tons of Powder have arrived here in a few Days & 8 Tons Powder at New York. The manufacturing salt Petre goes on finely. I will write Messrs. Brown the first Opportunity; I want the Express should arrive at Providence whilst the Assembly is setting & therefore conclude abruptly. Yours most affectionately,

                                                                    Sam Ward

P.S. My Friend Mr. Adams begs the Favor of You to forward his Letter to Colo. Warren by first Post.

RC (RHi).
    [1] Ward's letter has been assigned this date on the supposition that the letter referred to in the postscript is that of Samuel Adams to James Warren, January 7, 1776.
    [2] See Ward to Henry Ward, December 12, 1775, note 2.

Josiah Bartlett to
the New Hampshire Convention

Gentm   Philadelphia Janry 9th 1776
    The Enclosed Resolves of Congress I am Directed to transmit to you.[1]
    I Beg leave to inform the Colony that it will be necessary on many

accounts that I should return to New Hampshire as soon as conveniently may be: that there is no prospect that the Congress can rise this winter. Whenever it rises they have resolved that a Committee Consisting of one Delegate from Each Colony Should Remain to transact Business in the recess.[2] I therefore hope that our Colony will appoint one or more Delegates immediately to repair here and that I may have leave to return to New Hampshire.

I should be very glad to be informed what Cost our Colony is at for its own Defence as also what value in paper Bills they have Emitted.

I am, your Most Obedient, Humble, Servant,   Josiah Bartlett

RC (DLC). Addressed: "To the President of the Convention or Committee of Safety, Exeter, New Hampshire."
[1] Probably the resolves passed January 8 dealing with military affairs in New York and Canada and calling on New Hampshire for more troops. *JCC*, 4:38–40.
[2] See *JCC*, 3:426–27, 430–31, 454.

John Dickinson's Proposed Resolutions
on a Petition to the King

[January 9–24? 1776] [1]

1. That an humble & dutiful Petition be presented to his Majesty, expressing the deep Affliction with which the Inhabitants of these Colonies, perceive by his Majesty's late speech to Parliament, that his Majesty apprehends, We are contending for Empire & Independance— to assure his Majesty that he is misinform'd concerning the Intentions of his faithful subjects in America, and repeating our former supplications, that his Majesty will point out some Mode for terminating the present unhappy Differences by a mutually beneficial Accommodation.

2. That   or more Delegates Members of this Congress be appointed to present this Petition—to conferr   to mention some terms.

MS (PHi). In the hand of John Dickinson.
[1] On January 8 the text of George III's speech from the throne of October 26, 1775, reached Philadelphia, and almost immediately several delegates began a move in Congress to secure passage of a resolution denying the king's charge that the colonies were waging a rebellious war "for the purpose of establishing an independent Empire." A motion to disavow that charge introduced by James Wilson the following day was postponed to January 12, and then delayed until the 24th, when a committee was appointed to prepare an address for that purpose. However, the committee's report, in the form of an address in Wilson's hand, was tabled when it was brought in on February 13, and the issue was permitted to die. As Richard Smith noted, the address "was very long, badly written and full against Independency (Wilson percieving the Majority did not relish his Address and Doctrine never thought fit to stir it again.)" A succession of events that followed quickly upon arrival of the king's speech ultimately undermined any hope that men of Wilson's principles

might have had to put Congress on record against independence. January 8 was also the very day Thomas Paine's *Common Sense* was published in Philadelphia, and only the evening before letters had been received from Virginia bearing news of Lord Dunmore's devastating attack on Norfolk on January 1. And when Congress learned on January 17 of Montgomery's repulse at Quebec, the mood of the delegates changed decisively, ensuring the eventual defeat of Wilson's motion. See *Am. Archives*, 4th ser. 6:1–3; Richard Smith's Diary, January 8, 9, and 24, and February 13, 1776; and *JCC*, 4:87, 134–46. See also John Jay's Essay on Congress and Independence, January ? 1776.

Nevertheless, the discussions begun a few days earlier by Lord Drummond with delegates known to be sympathetic to negotiating with Britain had already reawakened interest in exploring paths leading to reconciliation, and in the face of these developments it is not surprising that John Dickinson was moved by "his Majesty's late speech to Parliament" to call for an official avowal of the colonies' desire for "a mutually beneficial Accommodation." It is not known when Dickinson drafted the proposed resolutions and instructions printed here and below, or what use was actually made of them. It seems clear, however, that Dickinson was one of the supporters of Wilson's motion on January 9 and may have written them in anticipation of the resumption of debate on the subject that he originally expected to take place on January 12. No evidence survives to indicate that Dickinson ever met with Lord Drummond, but there are striking similarities between Dickinson's proposed instructions for commissioners to Britain and various measures discussed by the delegates who met with Drummond, and considering Dickinson's views and prominence it is difficult to believe that he did not know of the progress of those talks.

For additional information on Dickinson's efforts in conjunction with James Wilson and others to obtain a congressional denial of the charge that Americans desired independence, see John Dickinson's Notes for a Speech in Congress, January 24?; and John Dickinson's Draft Address to the Inhabitants of America, January 24? 1776.

The entry printed here appears on the verso of the MS containing the proposed resolutions printed in the following entry.

John Dickinson's Proposed Resolutions for Negotiating with Great Britain

[January 9–24? 1776][1]

That two or more Delegates Members of this Congress be immediately sent to Great Britain.

1. That they use their utmost Endeavours to convince his Majesty, that these Colonies do not wish to change or alter the Forms of Government subsisting in them at the Commencement of the present unhappy Controversy.

2. To assure his Majesty, that they are sent for the express purpose of removing, if it be possible, all apprehensions from his royal Mind, of such Intentions on the part of the Colonies.

3. That by removing those apprehensions, his Majesty's Clemency may be moved to hear with Favor the humble supplications of his faithful Colonists, and graciously inclined to institute some Method, that

may have a Tendency to bring the present Contest to a perfect and lasting Accommodation.

4. That for effecting this Event so ardently desired by his Majesty's dutiful subjects in America, they most humbly beg Leave to represent, that his Majesty's Orders to his Governors on this Continent to assent to Acts of Assembly in the several Colonies, appointing Commissioners to meet for the purpose of conferring with persons nominated by his Majesty, will be a Measure likely to produce the salutary purposes intended by the good People of the Colonies.

5. If a Repeal of the Duty Acts complain'd of by last Congress cannot be otherwise obtain'd, then to conferr concerning Revenue by way of Commutation for the Duties—The Mode of Collection to be confirmed by perpetual Acts of the several Assemblies.

Cessation of Hostilities—in the Meantime—

To treat but not conclude on the following Points. Regulation. Renunciation of the Power of Taxation. Tea. Charters established. Money emitted by the Colonies. Indemnities to officers &c. Redress of Grievances. Pardon & indemnity to Inhabitants of Canada. Establishment of the Commerce of the Colonies on permanent Foundation. Correcting Errors & removing Fears & Jealousies for the future. A Return of all prisoners.

The Delegates to be instructed, to avail themselves of the Situation of Affairs & the Disposition of Administration, upon their Arrival in Great Britain—and to enlarge or restrain the Expectations they give to Administration of the Concessions the Colonies may be probably induc'd to make, according to the Urgency of Circumstances, never exceeding these Limits undermentioned.

1st. If they find the Forces sent or sending out to be such, that in their opinion, these Colonies can resist the same so far as to stand their Ground without Danger of any imminent Calamity during the next Campaign, in such Case, to confine themselves in their Conferences with Administration wholly to the first four Articles above mentioned.

2dly. If they find the forces sent or sending out to be so formidable that in their Opinion, these Colonies cannot so far resist the same as to stand their Ground without Danger of some imminent Calamity during the next Campaign, in such Case, to conferr with Administration on the Subject of the several Articles mentioned after the first four above mentioned.

3dly. Tho they find such a formidable force sent out or sending out, as is last mentioned, yet, if they are assured, that any Measures are taken by Administration, as prove a sincere Intention on their part of treating with the Colonies in Junction, and not separately, then even in that Case, to confine themselves in the Conferences with Administration to the four first Articles above mentioned.

MS (PHi). In the hand of John Dickinson.
[1] For a discussion of the circumstances surrounding the drafting of these proposals, see the preceding entry.

John Dickinson's Proposed Instructions for Commissioners to Negotiate with Great Britain

[January 9–24? 1776] [1]

That   Delegates, Members of this Congress be immediately sent to Great Britain.

Instructions

1. You shall most humbly and dutifully represent to his Majesty, that his faithful Subjects of these Colonies, observing with the deepest affliction in his late Speech to both Houses of Parliament, that his Majesty charges them with a Design of establishing an independant Empire, have deputed You in their Behalf for the express Purpose of laying them humbly at his Majesty's Feet, and in the strongest Terms assuring him, that they do not wish to change or alter the respective Forms of Government subsisting in these Colonies at the Commencement of the present unhappy Controversy.

2. You shall represent, that it is the sincere & fervent Desire of the Colonists, and the Intention of your Delegations, that these Apprehensions being removed from his Majesty's Mind, his royal Clemency may be graciously inclined to hear with Favor the humble supplication of his faithful American People, and to direct some Measures that may tend to bring the present Contest to a perfect and lasting Accommodation.

3. You shall earnestly beseech his Majesty to direct some such Measure, as by his Wisdom shall be best approved.

4. If no other Method equally expedient shall be proposed or will be admitted, You shall humbly beg Leave to represent as the Sense of the Colonists that the appointment of Commissioners by Acts of Assembly in the several Colonies with the assent of their Governors, to meet together and conferr with persons nominated by his Majesty will be a Measure likely to produce a Settlement of the Differences now subsisting.

5. If on your Arrival in Great Britain, You shall find the Forces sent and sending out to America to be such, that in your Judgment, these Colonies will be able to resist the same so far as not to be in imminent Danger of suffering any great Calamity in the Course of the next Campaign, likely to have a decisive Influence on the Event of the war, in such Case You shall confine Yourselves in your Conferences with his Majesty's Ministers, solely to the articles before mentioned. Quære— if this may not be more ascertained, by mentioning the number of troops & Men of War?

6. If on your Arrival, You shall find the Forces sent and sending out to be so formidable, that in your Judgment, these Colonies will not be able to resist the same, so far as not to be in Danger of suffering any great Calamity in the Course of the next Campaign, likely to have a decisive Influence on the Event of the War, in such Case, You shall make the following Representations, under this Restriction—to wit—that You shall pay the strictest Attention to important Circumstances that may happen or that You are assured will happen, and which will have an evident Influence on the Affairs of America—such as the Death of Princes, Declarations of War, Quarrels between Sovereigns, Disturbances in Great Britain or any other parts of the British Dominions, the Force of opposition in Great Britain to the present Ministry, or Changes in the Ministry; in any of which Cases, You shall offer to Administration or suppress such of the following proposals, as in your Judgment shall most conduce to the Safety and Happiness of these Colonies.

7. You shall declare, that on a Repeal of the Statutes & parts of Statutes complain'd of in the Petition to the King from the late Congress and of the Statute relating to any Colony or Colonies in America, past in the first Session of the present Parliament—a Settlement of the Quartering of Troops on such a permanent Footing as may be consistent with the Safety and Peace of these Colonies—Acts of Assembly being past with the Assent of the several Governors and duely confirmed, for sinking the Monies emitted by the Colonies or any of them during the present Contest,—a Transfer by Act of Parliament to the Colonies respectively of all Duties payable within them by any other Statutes now declared to be in Force or that may hereafter be made [and] a Renunciation by Parliament of the Right of taxing these Colonies—these Colonies respectively will settle a certain perpetual Revenue upon the King & his Successors to be disposed of by Parliament to the full Amount of such Duties at present after the Charges of Collection are deducted, and in such a Manner, that the said Revenue shall increase with the increasing Wealth of the Colonies—and will confirm, if it be required, by perpetual Acts of their several Legislatures the Acts commonly called The Acts of Navigation & the said Acts by which such Duties are to arise.[2]

Quære. If here should not be added—A permanent & unalterable Estabt. of the most important Branches of our Commerce nearly on the Footing of 1763—Judges Commissions during good Behaviour, Election of Jurors in criminal & civil cases by Lott—nearly as in England, by a late act of parlt. in civil Cases—Renunciation of the Power of Parliament to interfere in our Internal Police—Mutual Commerce of these Colonies with each other & Indians?

8. If this Declaration is not satisfactory to Administration & the prosecution of the War in the Manner before mentioned cannot otherwise be avoided, You shall make the same Declaration even tho a Repeal

of the Statutes & parts of Statutes imposing Duties payable in these Colonies & mentioned in the Petition to the King from the late Congress, cannot be obtained; provided the Duties thereby imposed are transferrd to the Colonies in the Manner above mentioned, in which Case, the Revenue to be granted to the Crown will be proportionally increased.

9. If this Declaration is rendered inadmissible, by insisting on the Renunciation aforesaid, and the prosecution of the war in the Manner before mentioned cannot otherwise be avoided, You are to recede from that proposal.

10. If this Declaration is rendered inadmissible in the Manner before mentioned, by insisting on a Repeal of the 35th of Henry the 8th & of the 12th of the present King so far as it relates to the Colonies, You are not farther to insist on the said Repeal.

11. If this Declaration is rendered inadmissible in the Manner before mentioned, by insisting on a Settlement of the Quartering of Troops on a permanent footing, You are to recede from that proposal, provided that there shall be a total & immediate Cessation of all Attempts to carry into Execution by Force of Arms any Acts of Parliament for laying Taxes in America; for enforcing the Collection of those Taxes; and for altering and changing the Constitution & internal Police of some of the Colonies—& all Danger of such Attempts being renewed shall be removed.

12. If this Declaration is rendered inadmissible in the Manner before mentioned by insisting on a Transferr of Duties, You are to recede from that proposal and finally and solely insist on a Repeal of the Statutes relating to any Colony or Colonies past in the last Session of the late Parliament and in the first Session of the present Parliament— Acts of Assembly being past with the Assent of the several Governors and duely confirmed, for sinking the Monies emitted by the Colonies or any of them during the present Contest—a total and immediate Cessation of all attempts to carry into Execution by Force of Arms any acts of Parliament for levying Taxes in America & for enforcing the Collection of those Taxes; and that all Danger of such Attempts being renewed, shall be removed &c &c &c &c

Pardons & Indemnities to all the Inhabitants of Canada.

Return of Prisoners, &c &c.

MS (PHi). In the hand of John Dickinson.

[1] For a discussion of the circumstances surrounding the drafting of these proposals, see Dickinson's Proposed Resolutions on a Petition to the King, this date.

[2] The following "Quaere" appears in the margin of the MS beside Dickinson's seventh instruction.

Lord Drummond's Notes

Philadelphia Jany 9th. 1776

Of the different preliminaries which appear on the Minutes taken from the Interviews and Discussions on political points between the Gentlemen of the Congress, and Lord Drummond and Mr. Elliot up to this day the following are the principal.[1]

It is stipulated that the Remonstrance (in the Bill of Rights of 1774) against the Extending the Act of Henry the Eight to America[2] be withdrawn on the Conditions that America is to be left to understand that no further Explanatory Act is to be passed on the Part of England to call it into future Exercise.

As it appears that the Grievances complained of in the Extension of the Powers of the Admiralty Courts will be left in the Effects to be produced by the last Article in the plan proposed (and contained in Ld. Norths Propositions) and particularly that *Trials* by *Jury* woud take place in future against the illicit trader who woud henceforth become An Offender against the particular Colony where the Trespass is committed—that therefore their Complaint on this head shall no longer remain a Part of those Grievances on which Redress is to be sollicited.[3]

As the present Plan of Accommodation is founded on *Compact* and the System containd therein must supersede every further Pretension against the Colonies, that the Declaratory Act shall therefore be No longer enumerated amongst American Grievances.

That the Remonstrance against the Quebec Bill shall be totally withdrawn.

No. I. Propositions on the Part of the Colonies—

deliverd to Ld. Drummond

1st. It is understood that Great Britain shall in open Parliament declare a Relinquishment of Taxation over her Colonies, and shall withold from interfering with their internal Polity.

2d. That Great Britain shall not suppress their manufactoring for their own Consumption such Materials as these Colonies produce, and that they shall not be restrained from transporting from one Colony to another such Materials or manufactures.

3d. That Troops shall not be introduced into these Colonies without the Consent of their Legislatures.

4th. That Canada shall be included in the Pacification.

5th. In Consequence of the Colonies having experienced very fatal Effects from improper Men being appointed to preside in their Courts of Justice, it is recommended that some Mode be adopted that woud tend to secure them against the Apointment of such Men as are not qualified for the Discharge of this important Office—and that these Judges shall as in England hold their Offices during good Behaviour.

6th.   That the Navigation Act shall remain inviolate, but nevertheless if on Investigation any Restrictions or Regulations shall be found to be injurious to the Trade of the Colonies, without affording any apparent advantages to the Mother Country, it is expected that such Restrictions or Regulations will on proper Representation be taken into Consideration and amended or withdrawn.

7th.   That towards the common Exigency of the State, these Colonies shall by perpetual Grant as in the Plan annexed give such annual Aid or Supply as shall be deemd consistent with the abilities of the respective Colonies.

No. II. Answers—to the foregoing Propositions
delivered to Mr. L[ynch] by Ld. Drummond.
1st.   The first Clause in this Article is fully answerd by the fifth Article of the Plan annexed.[4] To the subsequent Claim it is necessary that some further Definition shoud be given, and that the Object of the Request shoud be specifyd, before any Discussion can be enterd into with Precision.

2d.   As nothing short of the Elapse of some Centuries can produce so close a Population in America as to establish Manufactories to any Extent, at least such as to resist a Competition from the Mother Country, it is not probable that she will withold her Consent to this Request.

With Regard to the Transportation of Materials or Manufactures from one Colony to another, there are but two Instances that now fall within our Recollection when there is any Prohibition.

3d.   The Subject of this Requisition does not fall within the Controul of Parliament, but is Part of the Prerogative of the Crown, and has at all times been exercised as such—neither does it fall within the Extent of the Wishes of America *of being restord to the golden Æra of 1763.*

4th.   As far as this Article is meant to extend to the Canadians any Act of Indemnification that may be granted on the Part of the King—it is not probable that any particular Exception woud be made to the People of Canada. In alleging these general Distinctions his Majesty possesses Notions much too elevated to stoop to Resentments against Individuals for their past political Delusions.

5th.   On the Conditions of the Colonies making suitable and permanent Establishments for their Júdges, these apointments will become an Object with Men of Reputation and Abilities in their Profession. It is therefore suggested to the Colonies that they submit to his Majesty and Ministers, whether it might not be advisable that such Gentlemen as are proposd to fill the Office of Chief Justice in future shoud, previous to their Apointment, undergo an Examination by the twelve Judges of England—and receive their Approbation.

6th.   So very inseperable are the Interests of the Mother Country from those of her Colonies, that it must ever be against all Policy in Great Britain to perpetuate Evils that are to affect their Joint Welfare.

7th. The Subject of this Article cannot fail to be considerd by his Majesty and Ministers, as the Basis on which to found an immediate Reestablishment of Union, and as an Earnest of their future Claim to the Affections of the Colonies.

MS (Scottish Record Office: Drummond Castle Papers).

[1] For the background of these "Interviews and Discussions," see Drummond's Notes, January 3–9? 1776, note 1.

[2] See Congress' declaration of rights and grievances, October 14, 1774, in *JCC*, 1:65.

[3] Lord North's Conciliatory Resolve of February 20 and Drummond's "Plan of Accommodation" of March 1775 both provided that any revenues arising from parliamentary statutes regulating trade were to be placed at the disposal of the colonies. In a conversation on January 22, 1776, with William Smith, the New York historian and provincial councillor, Drummond attempted to explain the relationship between this proposal and the problem of admiralty court jurisdiction in the colonies. "That Lord North wished to conclude an Agreement that should put it out of the Power of any Successor to renew the Controversy by securing a Revenue from the Colonies for the common Defence without which the landed Interest would never be satisfied—That his Project for this purpose was to perswade every Colony to name a Duty which would at this Day raise a Contribution it could bear & put it upon some Import or Export increasing with the growth of the Colony. That then Parliament should cease to tax and give all Duties for the Regulation of Trade to the Colonies, who are to maintain their own internal Polity and Government [to] ask extraordinary Aids in the old Course of Requisition. In this Way all Disputes about the Admiralty Courts would subside & the Coercive Laws lately passed to be repealed as unnecessary." William Smith, *Historical Memoirs from 16 March 1763 to 9 July 1776 of William Smith*, ed. William H. W. Sabine (New York: Colburn and Tegg, 1956), p. 257.

[4] The fifth article of Drummond's March 1775 "Plan of Accommodation" stipulated that Great Britain should renounce its claim to a right to tax the colonies. See Milton M. Klein, "Failure of a Mission: The Drummond Peace Proposal of 1775," *Huntington Library Quarterly* 35 (August 1972): 379.

Richard Smith's Diary

Tuesday Jan. 9. [1776]

The Votes read & some Letters, one of them from Matthew Tilghman Esqr. President of the Convention in Maryland desiring our Two small armed Vessels the Hornet and Viper at Baltimore may convoy to the Capes of Virginia some Vessels going with Provisions on Accot. of the Congress, to get Necessaries for our Fleet and Army.[1] This was agreed to & Directions are to be given to Admiral Hopkins to meet them. A Letter from Ld. Stirling inclosing a Packet which he caused to be intercepted near Elizabeth Town containing 1. A Letter from Gov. Franklin to Lord Dartmouth inimical to the Americans which inclosed a printed Journal of Congress, and Extract from the Votes of the Jersey Convention, a paper from New England, a Copy of a Petition to our Assembly against Independency, the Manuscript Votes of last Session, with his messages & the Councils and some News papers as also some Notes of the Speeches made in our Assembly by John Dickinson, John Jay and Geo. Wyth when they lately attended there from the Congress & prevailed with the Assembly to drop their Petition to the King, there was likewise a Copy of John De Harts Resignation. Divers of these papers were in the Hand Writing of Cortland Skinner Speaker of the Assembly who immediately upon this Discovery fled on Board of the Ship Dutchess of Gordon, those copied by Him were the Extract, the paper from N England, the Notes & the resignation, the Petition was in Danl. Ellis's Hand. 2. A Letter from Cortland Skinner to his Bror. Wm. full of strong Toryism. Some Letters were in the Packet directed to Mrs. Gage which Ld. Stirling opened & sent forward.[2]

After going thro other Business the Congress directed that the Presidt. shall write to Ld. Stirling to seize Cortland Skinner and to keep Him confined till further Order from hence and that he be examined before the Comee. of Safety in N Jersey who are to have a Copy of his Letter & his Examinn. is to be transmitted to this Congress. Nothing was done respecting Gov. Franklin. The Comee. of Claims reported some Accots. for Cartage of Powder, to Cambridge & Accounts of Abrm. Hunt and others which brought on a Discourse of the extravagant Living of the Captive Officers at Trenton, a Motion was made that they be notifyed that it shall be at their own Expence which was committed to Wm. Livingston, Floyd & Dyer. The Report on Gen. Schuylers Letters was taken up, some of the Articles agreed to and some recommitted. Capt. Lamb of the Artillery was rewarded with the rank of Major and to be allowed 50 Dollars per Month from the 1st of January Instant & to be Commandant of the Artillery in Canada, the pay master with Schuylers Army to be allowed Two Deputies. John MacPherson aid du Camp to Montgy. promoted to be a Major, a Conductor of Artillery appointed, distinct from the Commandant. The Promotion of Arnold was again moved and deferred till Tomorrow. Wilson moved & was strongly supported that the Congress may expressly declare to their Constituents and the World their present Intentions respecting an Independency, observing that the Kings Speech directly charged Us with that Design, he was opposed but Friday was fixed for going into that Affair.[3] Several Members said that if a Foreign Force shall be sent here, they are willing to declare the Colonies in a State of Independent Sovereignty.

M. Pliant [de Pliarne] one of the Two Frenchmen in Treaty with our Secret Comee. offers to supply the Continent from France with all Sorts of Goods & Military Stores at the price common in France & hints that our Ships may trade to that Kingdom by Connivance & that they are willing to send their Bottoms here, he treats apparently in Behalf of a Company at Paris & he stays here till his Partner returns from thence. The Militia ordered to be discharged from the Fort at the Highlands on Hudsons River. 500,000 Dollars voted to be sent to Gen Washington thro the Pennsa. Delegates. The President desired to write to Gen. Schuyler inter alia requiring Him to try Lieut. Halsey at a Court Martial.[4] Col. Van Schaick, Lt Col. Yates & Major Gansevoort are to be continued in the Service and appointed to that Battaln. now to be raised in N York. A Communication is to be opened between Skeenesborough and Fort Anne & Wood Creek to be cleared out.

MS (DLC).

[1] Matthew Tilghman's letter to Hancock of January 5 is in PCC, item 78, 22:5, 8; and *Am. Archives*, 4th ser. 4:575–76.

[2] Colonel Alexander's letter to Hancock of January 6 is in PCC, item 162, 2:359; and *Am. Archives*, 4th ser. 4:586–87. Many of the enclosures listed here by Smith are in *N. J. Archives*, 10:676–98.

[3] On this point, see Samuel Adams to John Adams, January 15; Thomas McKean to George Read, January 19, note 2; and Smith's Diary, January 24, February 13, 1776.

[4] See John Hancock to Philip Schuyler, January 10, 1776.

Samuel Adams to James Warren

My dear Sir,   Philadelphia January 10 1776

I wrote to you the 7th Instant by Mr Anthony by the Way of Providence, and should not so soon have troubled you with another Letter but to inform you, that upon looking over the Journals of Congress I find that the Recommendation of the 26th of Octobr to export Produce for a certain Purpose, is confind to the foreign West Indies—and the Resolution to stop all Trade till the first of March is subsequent to it. This last Resolution prevents your exporting your Merchantable Fish to Spain for the purpose mentioned; which I am satisfied was not intended, because I am very certain the Congress means to encourage the Importation of those necessary Articles, under the Direction of proper Persons, from every Part of the World. I design to propose to my Colleagues to joyn with me in a Motion to extend the Recommendation so as to admit of exporting Fish to any Place besides the foreign West Indies.[1]

A few days ago, being one of a Committee to consider General Washingtons last Letter to Congress, I proposd to the Committee and they readily consented to report the inclosd Resolutions, which were unanimously agreed to in Congress. The Committee also reported that a certain Sum should be paid to Mr Lovel out of the military Chest towards enabling him to remove himself and his Family from Boston, but the Precedent was objected to and the last Resolve was substituted in its stead.[2] The Gentlemen present however contributed and put into my hands Eighty two Dollars for the Benefit of Mr Lovell, which I shall remit either in Cash or a good Bill. I hope I shall soon be so happy as to hear that he is releasd from Bondage. I feel very tenderly for the Rest of my fellow Citizens who are detaind in that worst of Prisons. Methinks there is one Way speedily to release them all.

This day Congress have appointed General Fry a Brigadier General of the Army at Cambridge and Coll Arnold a Brigadr General for the Army in Canada.[3]

Another sum of Money is orderd to be sent to you for the Use of the Army.[4]

RC (MHi).

[1] See Samuel Adams to James Warren, January 7, 1776, note 2.

[2] Congress agreed to the exchange of Philip Skene for James Lovell and his family on January 5. *JCC*, 4:32-34. Samuel Adams' draft of the committee report on Lovell is in the Signers Collection, MA. For more information on the release of Lovell, see John Hancock to George Washington, January 6, 1776, note 1.

[3] See *JCC*, 4:47.

[4] For the continuation of this letter, see Adams to Warren, January 13, 1776.

Lord Drummond's Minutes

Minute   Philadelphia Jany. 10th 1776.

As the foregoing paper which was deliverd to the Gentlemen of the Colonies by Ld. Dr[ummon]d contained Objections to several Material Points in the Propositions on the Part of America,[1] These Propositions were superseded by a new Set as contained in No. III.

These however still holding up some Objectionable Points several Conversations were held in Consequence with particular Members, which terminated in the Propositions again undergoing some Amendments and which appear included within the *Lines* in No. III.[2]

The Import of the Clause in the first Article with Respect to *internal Polity* seemd not fully understood by Mr. Lynch who deliverd Lord D[rummon]d the Paper. In a Conversn. with Mr. L[ivingston] & Mr. [Allen][3] who had not been present at the drawing up of the Articles, they seemd to think it alluded to the alledged Innovation by Great Britain in Cancelling the Massachusets Bay Charter, that if it meant anything further it meant too much, for that in the disputes which must arise hereafter between the different Colonies, nothing but the Interposition of the Parent Country coud effect a Settlement as being placed beyond the Reach of an American Invasion.[4]

With regard to the last Clause, in the Second Article Mr. [Gov. Livingston] and Mr. Duane were of Opinion that this shoud not be insisted on. That with Regard to the Article of Wool in particular England shoud by no Means be interfered with.

The third Article on the Subject of *Troops* which was the Point by much the most contended for by the most Southern as well as New

Engd. Colonies was at last struck out. The Arguments used to effect this were not stated in Writing—as containing too dangerous a Doctrine.

Propositions by America,
as amended.   Recd. 11th Jany 76.
                              No. III.
1st.   It is understood that Great Britain shall in open Parliament declare a Relinquishment of Taxation over her Colonies [5] and shall withold from interfering with their internal Polity.
2d.   That Great Britain shall not suppress their Manufactoring for their own Consumption such Materials as these Colonies produce and that they shall not be restrained from transporting from one Colony to another such Materials or Manufactory.
3d.   ⟨That Troops shall not be introduced into these Colonies without the Consent of their Legislatures.⟩
4th.   That Canada shall be included in the Indemnification.
5th.   That the Colonies shall fix suitable and permanent Establishments for the Office of Chief Justice and the Judges of their Supreme Courts. That the chief Judges hereafter to be apointed shall previously undergo an Examination by the twelve Judges of England and be recommended by them to such apointment. And that when so apointed they shall as in England hold their Offices during good Behaviour.
6th.   That the Navigation Act shall remain inviolate but nevertheless if on Investigation, any Restriction or Regulation shall be found to be injurious to the Trade of the Colonies without affording any advantages to the Mother Country, it is expected that such Restrictions or Regulations will on proper Representation be taken into Consideration and amended or withdrawn.
7th.   That towards the common Exigency of the State the Colonies shall by perpetual Grant as in the Plan annexed give such annual Aid or Supply as shall be deemd consistent with the abilities of the respective Colonies.
8th.   That as a further Demonstration of their Loyalty to the Crown and their Affection to the Mother Country they shall notwithstanding the above perpetual Grant, hold themselves subject to be calld upon in Cases of Urgency for Supplies of naval and Military Stores.

MS (Scottish Record Office: Drummond Castle Papers).
   [1] See Drummond's Notes, January 9, 1776.
   [2] See note 5 below.
   [3] For an explanation of the insertion of names in brackets here and below, see Drummond's Minutes, January 5, 1776, note 2.
   [4] Elsewhere Drummond observed of his discussions with the delegates about Parliament's right to interfere in internal colonial affairs: "This Subject bore a Deal of Argument on both Sides. Mr. Elliot and myself contended, I had almost said Concluded with them, that as the Infraction of the Massachusetts Bay Charter was the single Instance in which themselves coud charge England with having improperly exercised this Power, so we must of course confine the Reparation lookd

for, to that single Point—besides that any further Controul did not fall within the Extent of their favorite Wish of being placed as in the golden Æra of [17]63." Drummond to Lord North?, March 24, 1776, Scottish Record Office: Drummond Castle Papers, Nj microfilm.

⁵ In the MS Drummond drew lines around the remainder of this paragraph for reasons he explained in the second paragraph of this document.

Christopher Gadsden to Esek Hopkins

Dr. sir,   Philada. 10th Janry 1776

Inclosed is Copy of an Order from the Committee to Capt. Stone sent by Directions of Congress on an Application from Maryland wch. it is necessary you shou'd have.¹

I also take the Liberty to send you a List of the Field Officers & Captains of two Regiments of Foot & three Companies of Artillery all Provincials station'd in Charles Town So. Carolina.² Shou'd you go there, upon your Arrival off the Bar the Pilot will informe You what Officer is at Fort Johnson or any of the nearest Batteries to You, from whom you may depend on all the Assistance they can give. They are most of them Gentlemen of considerable Fortunes with us who have enter'd into the service merely from Principle & to promote & give Credit to the Cause, they take it by Turns to be at the Fort, & the Zeal & Activity of all of them are such that you can't happen amiss let who will be there.

In Charles Town my particular Friends Mr Lowndes, Mr. Ferguson, Coll Powell, Mr. Benja Elliott, Coll Pinckney, Mr. Drayton, Mr. Timothy & the Revd. Mr. Tennant, a Countryman of yours, will introduce you to many others, who will all be glad to have an Opportunity of obliging you & promoting the Service. I wrote Yesterday to Mr. Ferguson one of the Gentn just mention'd by Way of Georgia, by a Gentleman I can depend on who will destroy my Letter shou'd he be taken; in this Letter I have hinted to look out for you, & be ready to assist you at a Moment's Warning. The two large Ships seen off of Virginia the 29th of last Month we are told were not bound there, however you will know more certainly by the Time you get out of the Capes I make no doubt. I hope you will be able to effect that Service, but whether you may or not, sooner or later I flatter myself we shall have your Assistance at Carolina, where you may depend on an easy Conquest, or at least be able to know without Loss of Time when off our Bar the Strength of the Enemy, & shou'd it be too much for you prudently to encounter, wch. I hardly think probable if soon attempted wth. the Assistance to be depended on from us, you may in such Case Retreat with great Ease, Safety & Expedition.³

Wishing you every Success you can possibly wish yourself, I am, Dr. sir, yr. most hble serv.,   Christ Gadsden

P. S. Pray make my Complimts. to Capt Saltenstall & the Rest of your Captains, & shall be obliged to you if you go to Carolina to introduce them to any or all the Gentlemen I have mention'd who I am sure will be glad to shew them every Civility in their Power. I hope Capt. Whipple is better.

One of the Maryland Gentn. Mr. Alexander a Delegate of that Colony tells me there is a very good ship of about 20 Guns there easily fitted out wch. he is in hopes will join you with the Hornet & Wasp, & that he shou'd press it to be done. This I mention by the by.

RC (RHi). Addressed: "To The Honble Esek Hopkins Esqr. Commander in Chief of the Fleet of The United Colonies."
[1] See the letter of this date from the Naval Committee, of which Gadsden was a member, to William Stone.
[2] This "List" is printed in Clark, *Naval Documents*, 3:721.
[3] For additional information on Hopkins' mission, see the cruising orders contained in the Naval Committee's letter to him of January 5, 1776, printed in *JCC*, 4:335–36.

John Hancock to William Alexander

My Lord   Philadelphia Jany 10,1776
I have it in charge from Congress to order Col Maxwell to put his Regimt in a State of Readiness to march to Albany,[1] which you will please to Direct immediately, & as soon as Ready pray inform me, that the particular orders of Congress may be Transmitted for his proceedings.

I am, Your most obed Ser,   John Hancock President

Tr (DLC).
[1] See *JCC*, 4:39.

John Hancock to Philip Schuyler

Sir,   Philada. Jany. 10th. 1776.
I had the Pleasure of transmitting you some Days ago a Letter of Thanks for your eminent Services in the Cause of your Country.[1]

The several Letters you mention in your last came safe to Hand, and were laid before Congress.[2]

The Distresses of this Great Continent thrown into Convulsions by an unnatural War, the unprepared State we were in, when unjustly attacked, the Enemies that have arisen up against us in different Quarters, and the horrid Attempts of the Southern Governors to excite domestic Insurrections, and bring the Savages to desolate our Frontiers, the Necessity of providing armed Vessels, to prevent, if possible, the

Desolation threatned our Sea-Coasts; these and other Matters of the highest Importance, which you can easily conceive, must apologize for your Letters not having an earlier Answer. Besides, the Congress flattered themselves from the steps they had taken and from the Orders & Instructions given to their Committee, who were sent to confer with you, that your Army would have reinlisted, and your Difficulties, in other Respects, have been relieved.

After the Return of their Committee, the Congress took into Consideraration your several Letters, and the Report of the Committee, and thereupon came to sundry Resolutions, which I have the Honor to enclose.[3]

Phelps has thrown in a Petition praying to be heard in his Justification; but as Matters of higher Moment engage the Attention of the Congress, *that* is suffered to lie over.[4]

The Congress resent the Conduct of Lieut. Halsey, & are of opinion you should proceed to have his Conduct inquired into by a Court Martial, giving him previous Notice to appear in his own Defence, and that such Sentence should be passed on him, as the Court Martial shall think just: and should he decline to submit his Conduct to such Examination and Sentence, in that Case, all Arrears due to him, ought to be stopped.[5]

I cannot sufficiently express the Confidence the Congress have in your Attention to the Public Interest, and their Reliance that you will give to the proper officers in your Department, such Orders as will procure Indemnification to the Public for any Embezzlement or Waste of its Stores or Monies.

Desirous of giving every reasonable Encouragement and Indulgence to Men who have risqued their Lives in the Cause of their Country, they have given you Power to grant Discharges to such officers as find themselves under a Necessity of quitting the Service, and to remit to such of the Troops raised in the Colony of New York as may reinlist, any Right the Congress might have to stop Wages for the under Cloathes delivered to them.

I must not omit to inform you of the grateful Sense the Congress have of the friendly Offices Mr. Price has done to Genl. Montgomery for the Support of the American Cause. You will therefore be pleased to embrace the first Opportunity of returning him their Thanks for the same, and assure him, immediate Measures shall be taken for replacing the Monies he has advanced. You will also be pleased to notify to Col. Easton their approbation of his Services, and that they will retain in their Minds a just Sense of them.

The Conduct, Spirit, and Resolution shewn both by the Officers and Men who have penetrated Canada, have induced the Congress in Testimony of their Approbation, to reserve the raising of two Regiments out of the Forces now there, for the Defence and Protection of that

Country, which their Valour has rescued from Slavery. The Regiments in Pennsylvania and New Jersey, are under Orders to march and join them, and the other Regiments destined for that Service, will be ordered to march as fast as raised. The enclosed Resolutions of Congress are so full & explicit, that I need not enlarge.

I shall be happy to hear of your perfect Recovery, being with much Esteem, Sir &c   J H Prest.

LB (DNA: PCC, item 12A).
[1] Probably Hancock to Schuyler, November 30, 1775.
[2] See *JCC*, 4:37–38.
[3] See *JCC*, 4:38–40, 43–45.
[4] Elisha Phelps, deputy commissary in the northern department, presented a petition to Congress which was read on December 11, 1775. *JCC*, 3:418–19, 423. For related documents, see *Am. Archives*, 4th ser. 3:1520–29.
[5] Notwithstanding the complaints of embezzlement lodged against him, Congress eventually resolved that Lt. Jeremiah Halsey "ought to receive the arrears of his pay, and that the resolution of Congress, of the ninth of January last, be repealed." *JCC*, 4:43, 5:736, 745–46.

Naval Committee to William Stone

Sir   Philadelphia 10th January 1776
We are orderd by Congress to signify to you, that you are with the Hornet & Wasp under your Command to take under your Convoy such Vessels as are ready for the Sea as shall be committed to your Care by the Comee. of Safety at Maryland, & see them safe through the Capes of Virginia & without a Moments Loss of Time after this Service is done you are to go to the Capes of Delaware & proceed upwards till you join the Fleet, or in Case of its having Sailed receive such Orders as may be left for you by Esek Hopkins Esqr. Commander in Chief of the Fleet of the United Colonies—wch. Orders you are to Obey.[1]

Stephen Hopkins   Silas Deane

Christr. Gadsden   Joseph Hewes

Tr (RHi). Addressed: "To Willm. Stone Esqr., Commander of the Sloop Hornet, In the Service of The United Colonies." Enclosed in Christopher Gadsden to Esek Hopkins, this date.
[1] Although the Naval Committee had previously planned to have Stone drop down from Baltimore to harrass Dunmore's forces in Chesapeake Bay and to join Esek Hopkins' fleet when it arrived off Virginia, it is clear that by January 10 Dunmore was no longer the primary objective of the Continental Navy and that the *Hornet* and *Wasp* were now expected to participate in operations elsewhere. This change in Stone's orders was the result of a letter of January 5 to Congress from the Maryland Council conveying recent intelligence on the strength of British naval forces in the Chesapeake and expressing concern for the safety of several vessels

nearly ready to embark from Baltimore for the foreign West Indies. See Naval Committee to William Stone, December ? 1775; *JCC*, 4:41; and *Am. Archives*, 4th ser. 4:575–78.

Richard Smith's Diary

Wednesday 10 Jany. [1776]

The Votes of Yesterday read. 35000 Dollars allowed to Thomas Lowrey the Jersey Commissary in Addition to what he has had, for fitting out Ld. Stirlings and Maxwells Troops. The Comee. of Safety in Pennsa. desired to fit out with Necessaries their 6 Battalions. A Third Battalion ordered to be raised in N Jersey on the same Terms with the other Two, this was on Motion of W. Livingston. Duane moved that 4 more Battalions may be raised in N York, after Discussion it was referred to a Comee. of 5 now named to consider what Force is necessary to be raised in the 13 United Colonies.[1] The Two vacant Brigadierships were now filled up, the Pennsa. Delegates, Wilson in particular, contended strenuously for Col. Thompson but Major Gen. Fry of the Massachusetts was elected 9 Colonies to 3. Benedict Arnold Esqr. was unanimously elected the other Brigr. The Field Officers of the 6th Pennsa. Battalion were fixed, viz Wm. Irvin Col., Thos. Hartley Lt. Col. & James Dunlap Major. The Resolution for subduing the Tories on Queens County was now altered so that no Troops are to go from Connectt. but Heard is to call on Ld. Stirling for 3 of his Companies. I sent the Dispatches to Col. Heard by Capt. Morris. Hooper read Two Letters from North Carolina[2] informing of Commotions there between the Whigs and Tories of the back Parts. Foreign Goods begin now to come in, I bought some Linnen from St. Eustatia at 4/ per Yard. A Report passed concerng. the proper Necessaries for Maxwells Battalion about to march to Canada who are to have the same pay, 50/ per Month for the Privates, as the Northern Forces, to commence from the Time they set off. The Comee. of Claims reported some Accots. & among them Commissary Lowreys.

MS (DLC).

[1] Congress approved the raising of four new battalions in New York on January 19. See *JCC*, 4:69; and Smith's Diary, January 16, 19, 1776.

[2] Not found.

John Hancock to
Michael Hillegas and George Clymer

Gentlemen: Philadelphia, January 11, 1776.

Please to pay to the Committee of Safety of Pennsylvania, six thousand dollars for the use of the Battalion in this City, the said Committee to be accountable for the expenditure of said sum.[1]

I am gentlemen, your most obedient servant,

John Hancock, President.

MS not found; reprinted from *Am. Archives*, 4th ser. 4:516.

[1] See *JCC*, 4:50.

New York Delegates to
the New York Committee of Safety

Gentlemen   Philad 11th Januy 1776

We are honour'd with your favour of the 4th Instant requesting the Permission of Congress to export a quantity of Flaxseed to Ireland, for the purpose you mention.[1] However important the object we are perfectly satisfied that it will be in vain to expect an Indulgence so repugnant [to] the Non-exportation System, and, particularly, to the motives of this Article of our commercial Restriction which were thought to be very cogent. Not relying entirely on our own Judgement, we have consulted several of the members, and find them so averse to the Proposition that we despair of it's being seconded by a single Colony. We think it bad Policy, and an Humiliation of our respectable Constituents, to ask, in their Names, for what we foresee *must* be rejected. Upon these Considerations we shall take the Liberty to defer any Application, 'till informed of our Apprehensions. We shall be favour'd with your further Commands. If you should still incline to hazard the Attempt we shall most chearfully obey your directions.

We enclose you two Resolutions of this Congress which respect our Colony,[2] and a third for the exchange of Lieut Tyley [Edward Tilley] of General Wooster's Regimt. now a prisoner on board the Asia.[3]

We are with the highest Regard, Gentlemen, Your most Obedient & very humble Servants,   Jas. Duane

Wm Floyd

Henry Wisner

P.S. We also inclose you several Resolutions of Congress which passed the 8t Instant which we are directed to communicate since we closed the preceding Letter.[4]

RC (N). Written by Duane and signed by Duane, Floyd, and Wisner. *Journals of N.Y. Prov. Cong.*, 2:141. RC damaged; missing words supplied from Tr.

[1] The Committee of Safety had written to Hancock on January 4, asking permission to ship flaxseed to Ireland in exchange for gunpowder. *Am. Archives*, 4th ser. 4:1021. In PRO: C.O. 5, 1107, there is a letter with the place and dateline "Philadelphia Jany. ye 6th 1776" and bearing the endorsement "The above Letter Sent

by the Continental Congress to the Provincial Congress of New York." However, the evidence of this place and dateline and endorsement to the contrary notwithstanding, this letter is in reality an abstract of the Committee of Safety's letter to Hancock of January 4.

[2] These were probably resolutions of January 9 discharging certain New York militia units from further service in the Highlands and appointing officers for a battalion that was to be raised in New York for service in Canada. *JCC*, 4:42–43; and *Am. Archives*, 4th ser. 4:1046.

[3] See *JCC*, 4:49.

[4] These resolves, which dealt with a variety of issues relating to the reinforcement and supply of General Schuyler's army, are in *JCC*, 4:38–40.

Secret Committee Minutes of Proceedings

Philade. Jany. 11th. 1776

At a meeting of the Come. of Secy. Present, Saml. Ward, Benjamn. Franklin, Silas Deane, Thos. McKean & Josiah Bartlett. Mr. Robert Morris of this City Mercht. was impowerd by sd. Come. to engage nine ships or vessels for exportg. the produce of these Colonies for the benifit of the 13 U[nited] C[olonies].[1]

At a meeting of the Comee. of Secy. Present Saml. Ward, Benjn Franklin, Robt. Morris, Josiah Bartlett, & Ths McKean. A Contract was enterd into between Silas Deane & Barnabas Deane of the Colony of Connecticut & the sd. Come. that the sum of thirty thousand dlls Contl. Money now advanced & paid by the sd. Come. of Secy. to the sd. Silas Deane & Barnabas Deane shall be laid out by them in the produce of these Colonies & shipd. on board proper vessels to be by them charterd for that purpose to some proper ports in the foreign West Indies & Europe & there disposd of on the best terms; & the nett proceeds of such Cargoes laid out in the purchase of such goods, wares or merchandises as the sd. Come. of Secy. shall direct & shippd for the sd U[nited] C[olonies].[2]

At a meeting of the C[ommitt]ee. Present Saml. Ward, Ths. McKean, Silas Deane, B. Franklin & Robt Morris.

A Contract was enterd into between Oswell Eve & George Losch both of the County of Phila. & the sd. Come. for manufacturg. Saltpetre.[3]

MS (MH).

[1] On January 10 Morris had received from the Secret Committee "an order on the Treasurer for the Sum of 80,000 dlls for the service of the United Colonies." Journal of the Secret Committee, fol. 23, MH.

[2] A list of goods to be imported by the Deanes was agreed to on February 16. Journal of the Secret Committee, fol. 36, MH. For other transactions pertinent to this contract, see Clark, *Naval Documents*, 4:614.

[3] See *JCC*, 4:40. By this agreement Eve and Losch were to "manufacture all the Salt Petre which shall be delivered to them severally for one year from this date by the Committee of Secrecy aforesaid, into good Gun Powder, and furnish all the

Sulphur and charcoal, &c., necessary for that purpose, at their own costs and charges, and also refine the said Salt Petre, and carry the same to their respective Powder Mills, and redeliver the powder at such place in the city of Philadelphia, as shall be assigned by sd Committee," and the committee was to pay eight dollars per hundred weight of powder. *Pa. Archives*, 1st ser. 4:696. On January 19 a similar agreement was made with G. Hubner of Northampton County, Pa. Journal of the Secret Committee, fol. 25, MH.

Richard Smith's Diary

Thursday 11 Jany. [1776]

The Comee. of Claims settled the Accots. of the Commissioners of the Northern Department of Indians, the whole Expence of the late Treaty at Albany was about £3300. In Congress a Recommendation was directed to the New York Convention to release by Exchange Lieut. Tylee [Edward Tilley] of Connecticut now a Prisoner on Board of the Asia. A Comee. was appointed to give proper Instructions to the Officers on the recruiting Service.[1] A Report from the Comee. on the Paper Currency was ably argued for 4 Hours, the Report recommended that the present 6 Millions of Dollars be called in and large Notes issued to that Amount bearing Interest, with sundry other Particulars, but a proposition of Duane's took Place implying that all who refuse to take the Continental Curr[enc]y shall be treated as Enemies to their Country. A subsequent Resolution was voted out importing that the several Assemblies, Conventions & Committees of Safety shall take Care to put this resolve in Execution.[2] A Letter from Owen Jones Provincial Treasurer here to a County Treasurer was read desiring as little Congress Money might be sent to Him as possible for that he could not change it into Province Bills and a Letter from another Person fearing a Depreciation. Something was said about preventing Counterfeits.

MS (DLC).
[1] For the resolves adopted on January 17 in response to the report of this committee, see *JCC*, 4:63–64.
[2] The committee on paper currency had been appointed on November 23, 1775, in response to the reception of documents from the Philadelphia Committee showing that certain Philadelphians had refused "to receive the Continental Bills in the Course of their Business." *JCC*, 3:367, 4:49–50; PCC, item 69, fols. 25–26; and *Am. Archives*, 4th ser. 3:1388–89.

Samuel Adams to John Pitts

My dear sir   Philade Jany 12 1776

It is a long time since I had the pleasure of receiving a Letter from you.[1] I flatter my self that you still place me among your Friends. I am not conscious of having done any thing to forfeit your Regards for me and therefore I will attribute your omission not to a designd Neglect, but to a more probable Cause, the constant Attention you are called upon to give to the publick Affairs of our Colony. It is for this Reason that I make my self easy, though one post arrives and one Express after another without a Line from you; assuring my self that your Time is employd to much better purpose than writing to or thinking of me. I speak Truth when I tell you, that I shall be exceedingly gratified in receiving your Favors, whenever your Leisure may admit of your suspending your Attention to Matters of greater Importance. I will add that your Letters will certainly be profitable to me; for I shall gain that Intelligence and Instruction from them which will enable me the better to serve the Publick in the Station I am placed in here. Give me Leave to tell you therefore, that I think it is a part of the Duty you owe to our Country to write to me as often as you can.

You have seen the *most gracious* Speech [2]—Most Gracious! How strangely will the Tools of a Tyrant pervert the plain Meaning of Words! It discovers, to be sure, the most *benevolent & humane* Feelings of its Author. I have heard that he is his own Minister—that he follows the Dictates of his own Heart. If so, why should we cast the odium of distressing Mankind upon his Minions & Flatterers only. Guilt must lie at his Door. Divine Vengeance will fall on his head; for all-gracious Heaven cannot be an indifferent Spectator of the virtuous Struggles of this people.

In a former Letter I desired you to acquaint me of your Fathers health and the Circumstances of the Family. I have a very great Regard for them and repeat the Request. Adieu,   S.A.

FC (NN).
   [1] John Pitts (1737–1815), Boston merchant and selectman, was a member of the Massachusetts Provincial Congress in 1775 and subsequently served in both the House and the Council of the General Court. Shipton, *Harvard Graduates*, 14:197–201.
   [2] The king's speech to Parliament of October 26, 1775.

Samuel Adams to John Sullivan

My dear sir   Philade Jany 12 1776
   Your very acceptable Letter of the 3d Inst duly came to hand. I thank you heartily for the favor and shall be much obligd to you if you will write to me as often as your Leisure will admit of it.

It gave me pain to be informd by you, that by an unlucky Circumstance you were prevented from executing a plan, the Success of which would have afforded you Laurels, and probably in its immediate Effects turnd the present Crisis in favor of our Country. We are indebted to you for your laudable Endeavor; Another Tryal will, I hope, crown your utmost Wish.

I have seen the Speech which is falsly & shamefully called *most gracious*. It breathes the most malevolent Spirit, wantonly proposes Measures calculated to distress Mankind, and determines my opinion of the Author of it as a Man of a wicked Heart. What a pity it is, that Men are become so degenerate and servile, as to bestow Epithets which can be appropriated to the supreme Being alone, upon Speeches & actions which will hereafter be read & spoken of by every Man who shall profess to have a spark of Virtue & Honor, with the utmost Contempt and Detestation. What have we to expect from Britain, but Chains & Slavery? I hope we shall act the part which the great Law of Nature points out. It is high time that we should assume that Character, which I am sorry to find the Capital of your Colony has publickly and expressly disavowd.[1] It is my most fervent prayer to Almighty God, that he would direct and prosper the Councils of America, inspire her Armies with true Courage, shield them in every Instance of Danger and lead them on to Victory & Tryumph. I am yr affectionate Friend,

S.A.

FC (NN).
[1] The city of Portsmouth had instructed its representatives to the New Hampshire Convention not to seek the formation of a new government for New Hampshire. *N.H. Provincial Papers*, 7:701–2.

John Hancock to Jonathan Trumbull, Sr.

Sir   Philadelphia 12th Jany. 1776 [1]

By the last advices from Canada we are flattered with the hopes of a fortunate issue of the Campaign in that quarter.

As our Enemie laid great stress on the succours they expected from that Province, and the fond expectations, that by means of the Canadians and Indians, they would be enabled to execute their execrable designs of reducing us to slavery & spreading desolation through the New England Colonies; and as there is reason to believe, from the steps taken by Govr Carleton that our enemies will endeavour, among their first attempts in the Spring, to regain possession of that Country, as well to retrieve their honor as to effect their wicked purposes, the Congress have determined to support, this year, nine battalions for its defence.[2]

One of these is to be composed of Canadians, under the Command of Colo. James Livingston who has so signally exerted himself in the Cause of America.

Two are to be composed out of the troops now serving there, the Congress deeming it an indispensible duty which, in testimony of their

approbation, they owed to those brave men, to give them an opportunity of reaping the fruits of their labours and defending a Country
which their resolution and valour, favored by the smiles of Providence,
has rescued from slavery. Two battalions, one from Pensylvania, the
other from New Jersey, which are now raised, armed and equipped, are
ordered to march immediately for that Country, and another is to be
raised in Pensylvania and sent after with all expedition. The remaining
three, as you will perceive by the inclosed resolutions, are to be raised
to the Eastward (viz) one in your Colony, one in New Hampshire and
one in New York.

As the arrival of the troops in due time will greatly conduce to the
preservation of that Country and baffling the designs of our enemies;
and as the month of February, which is fast approaching, is the best and
indeed the only time before the Summer, of crossing the lakes, the
Congress rely that you will, according to your usual zeal, exert your
utmost influence to have the battalion from your Colony raised and sent
forward with all possible expedition.

The battalion is to consist of eight companies, each company to consist
of one Captain, two Lieutenants, one Ensign, 4 Serjeants, 4 Corporals,
a Drum, a Fife and 76 Privates, the Staff Officers, a Chaplain, Adjutant,
Quartermaster and Surgeon.

I am, with great esteem and respect, Sir, Your humble Servant,

John Hancock Presidt.

Tr (Ct).
[1] Hancock wrote similar letters this day to the New Hampshire Committee of
Safety and to the New York Convention. Nh-Ar, and *Am. Archives*, 4th ser. 4:654–55;
N, and *Am. Archives*, 4th ser. 4:1073.
[2] For contemporary congressional action in regard to the northern army, see
JCC, 4:38–40, 43–47; and Hancock to Philip Schuyler, January 10, 1776.

Richard Smith's Diary

[January 12, 1776]
Friday 12. The Minutes read. The Comee. of Claims made some
Reports of Accounts. Mr. Wm. Livingston made a Report on the Mode
of maintaining the Captive Officers at Trenton which being amended
was passed, they are to pay their own Expences, to be removed to some
other Place and be allowed 15/ per Week which they are to repay
having already had Leave to draw Bills of Exchange for their Subsistance. In Grand Comee. Govr. Ward in the Chair, the point was Whether
to open Trade to Foreign Countries on the First of March next, wherein
much Ability was displayed for several Hours and at last it was postponed for a Week.[1] Then the Comee. went on the Affair of allowing the
Sale of what Tea is on Hand which was strongly advocated by McKean

and others and as strongly opposed by Dr. Franklin, Lynch &c & the
Result Delayed till Tomorrow.[2]

MS (DLC).
  [1] For the progress of this issue in Congress, culminating in the adoption on April 6
of a momentous series of resolves opening American ports, with certain restrictions,
to trade with any country not part of the British empire, see *JCC*, 4:62, 113, 148,
153, 154, 178, 256–59; Smith's Diary, January 17, February 16, 26, 29; Oliver
Wolcott to Samuel Lyman, February 3, 19; John Adams' Notes of Debates, February 16; John Adams to James Warren, March 21, and to Horatio Gates, March 23;
and Elbridge Gerry to James Warren, March 26, April 6, 1776.
  [2] The Maryland delegates raised this issue in Congress in response to a December
23, 1775, resolution of the Maryland Convention directing them to persuade Congress to allow the sale of tea imported into America before March 1, 1775, excepting
"any Teas imported for, or on account of, the English East-India Company, or
imported from Great Britain contrary to the Continental Association." Congress
rejected this proposal on January 15, 1776, but several months later, on April 13,
reversed itself and decided to permit the sale of all teas imported before December 1,
1774, except such as came from the East India Company. See *JCC*, 4:277–78;
Am. Archives, 4th ser. 4:723; Smith's Diary, January 15; and Robert Alexander to
the Maryland Council of Safety, January 30, 1776.

Samuel Adams to James Warren

Jany 13 [1776]
    I have Sent to Mrs Adams a Pamphlet which made its first Appearance
a few days ago.[1] It has fretted some folks here more than a little. I
recommend it to your Perusal and wish you would borrow it of her.
Dont be displeasd with me if you find the Spirit of it totally repugnant
with your Ideas of Government. Read it without Prejudice and give me
your impartial Sentiments of it when you may be at Leisure. Your
Friend   S A

RC (MHi). A continuation of Adams to James Warren, January 10, 1776.
  [1] Probably Thomas Paine's *Common Sense*, which was first advertised for sale on
January 9. Richard Gimbel, *Thomas Paine: A Bibliographical Check List of Common
Sense, with an Account of Its Publication* (New Haven: Yale University Press, 1956), p. 21.

Josiah Bartlett to John Langdon

Sir,   Philadelphia Jany 13th 1776.
    I wrote you 9th inst per post informing you of a contract for importing
goods for the use of the Army to the amount of ten thousand dollars
which the Secret Committee are willing to make with you which letter
I hope will come safe to your hands, and that you will answer it as
soon as may be.[1]

Last evening the draughts of the several ships of war were laid before the Marine Committee and approved of; and they have ordered one for each of the Contractors to be forthwith made out. But it is so large I know not how to send it to you; it cannot be sent in a letter and what other way to contrive I know not, but will do the best I can as soon as I can procure it.[2]

This morning I see in the newspaper (which by the way is almost the only way I hear from our Colony) that Portsmouth had appointed Messrs Cutts, Sherburne and Long, to represent that town in Provincial Convention, and by the Instructions I find the town is very much afraid of the idea conveyed by the frightful word *Independence*! This week a pamphlet on that Subject was printed here, and greedily bought up and read by all ranks of people.[3] I shall send you one of them, which you will please to lend round to the people; perhaps on consideration there may not appear any thing so terrible in that thought as they might at first apprehend, if Britain should force us to break off all connections with her. Give my compliments to Col Whipple who I see is left out by the Town in their choice of Delegates for the Provincial Convention.

I am Sir your friend and servt,   Josiah Bartlett

P.S. The 57 tons of Salt petre which arrived here last week was this day by order of Congress purchased by the Secret Committee for the use of the Continent and three tons of powder this day arrived here from the Jersies.   J.B.

Pray write me a full account of our affairs and don't forget to put the Colony in mind to send Delegates here as soon as may be that I may return to my family.

Tr (DLC).
    [1] See Bartlett to John Langdon, January 8, 1776, note 2.
    [2] For a discussion of the designing and building of the frigate *Raleigh*, under the direction of Langdon, see M. V. Brewington, "The Designs of Our First Frigates," *American Neptune* 8 (January 1948): 13, 16–19, with plates 5 and 6.
    [3] Thomas Paine's *Common Sense*.

Josiah Bartlett to
the New Hampshire Convention

Gentlemen: Philadelphia, January 13, 1776.
    In order that General *Schuyler* may be properly informed what pay the officers and soldiers, who served in the expedition to *Canada* last year, have received from their respective Colonies, the Congress passed the enclosed resolve, which they have ordered me to transmit to you.[1] An order of Congress, for raising a regiment in the western parts of our

Province, for *Canada*, will be sent you by the President.[2]
I am, gentlemen, your most humble servant,

Josiah Bartlett.

MS not found; reprinted from *Am. Archives*, 4th ser. 4:658. Addressed: "To the Convention, or the Committee of Safety of New Hampshire."
[1] See *JCC*, 4:39.
[2] On January 8, Congress called for the raising of one battalion in New Hampshire. *JCC*, 4:40. See also John Hancock to Jonathan Trumbull, January 12, 1776, note 1.

Silas Deane to Elizabeth Deane

My Dear   Philadelphia Jany. 13th 1776
I have to acknowledge the Receipt of yours per my Brother, & one since by the post, and that I have been promising myself to write you a Long Lettr. by him when he returned, which shall be unable to perform. Col. Dyers Treatment at Norwich & Windham is truly infamous, & has that mark of WitchCraft upon it which must forever attend ingratitude, for with all his other Foibles, one has been his constantly standing up, & disputing on all Occasions in favor of them very people. He goes home rather heavily, the more so, as I shall not accompany him. It is not in my power, though I hope to leave This in about a FortNight after the Arrival of my Successors for whom I am now most impatiently looking out, & am happy that the Assembly did not Continue Us, in Our present Station. You know the dismission never fretted Me, indelicate as it was, & I have every Day had less & less cause to be uneasy on Account of it. As to those who meant to humble Me or Mortify my Vanity by that Measure, they have only given Me an Opportunity of knowing myself, by experience, & of shewing the World, how much I was their Superior, by letting them & others know that my Character stands above the reach of their Malice, though a fair Object for their Envy.

My Love & Congratulations to Sister Hannah Buck, & the whole Family, which includes Sally whose first Boy I expect will be called after Me. Remember Me to all Freinds in the Neighborhood, who remember Me, and tell Jesse he must write Me again. I long to see You all. Is Sister Molly with you? I hope so, & therefore pray to be remembered to her. Barny must inform you how Govr. Ward & Mrs. House *Cheese* together, & of twenty other little Matters which I cannot Write at this late hour, Now past Two oClock at Night, but will only wish, & pray Your Sleeping & Waking hours may be forever happy. Good Night.

(Saturday Morning) I received a few Days since, from before Quebec, Two Long Lettrs. from my brave Freind Col. Arnold, which I improved in his favor, and the other Day he was unanimously chosen a Brigadier

General, for the Army in Canada, but I suppose this will be urged against Me by some as a Crime equall to my recommending *Putnam* on a former Occasion.[1] I may not add, but am your's Affectionately,

Silas Deane

RC (CtHi).
[1] See *JCC*, 4:47; and Deane to Elizabeth Deane, July 15, 1775.

Richard Smith's Diary

Saturday 13 Jany. [1776]

The Votes read & Letters from Gen. Washn., Governor Trumbull and others.[1] An Application from Connectt. for more Money was objected to because no Accounts have been exhibited and the Motion was withdrawn.[2] Some Amendts. proposed by Duane to the resolutions of Thursday concerning the Credit of the Continental Bills, were lost on a Vote. Several Petitions were presented desiring a new Arrangement of some Officers in Bulls Battalion & that Morgan may be preferred to the first Lieutenancy, this last was agreed to but the other discountenanced. Debates Whether Bernard Romans shall be called in and examined about his Fortifications on Hudsons River were terminated in a Reference to 5 Members.

MS (DLC).
[1] This day Congress received letters to Hancock of January 3 from the New York Committee of Safety and of January 4 from Washington. See PCC, item 67, 1:145–48, item 152, 1:407–10; *Am. Archives*, 4th ser. 4:562; and Washington, *Writings* (Fitzpatrick), 4:208–10. There is no indication in PCC or the journals that any letter from Connecticut governor Jonathan Trumbull arrived this day, but for a Trumbull letter which Congress received two days later, see Smith's Diary, January 15, 1776, note 1.
[2] There is no mention in the journals of this "Application," but it was probably related to the request made by Governor Trumbull in a letter to Hancock of December 20, 1775, for a grant of £60,000 to enable Connecticut to pay for a number of "expenses incurred by this Colony in the general service of the United Colonies." Not until March 7, 1776, however, did Congress agree to provide Connecticut with $100,000 for this purpose. *JCC*, 4:188; PCC, item 66, 1:45–46; and *Am. Archives*, 4th ser. 4:365. See also Oliver Wolcott to Ezekiel Williams, February 10, note 3, and Wolcott to Thomas Seymour, April 16, 1776, note 2.

Henry Wisner to John McKesson

Sir,   [January 13? 1776] [1]

I have only to ask the favor of you to read this pamphlet, consulting Mr. Scott and such of the Committee of Safety as you think proper, particularly Orange and Ulster, and let me know their and your opinion of the general spirit of it. I would have wrote a letter on the subject, but the bearer is waiting.

Reprinted from Franklin Burdge, *A Second Memorial of Henry Wisner* (New York: Privately printed, 1898), p. 23.

[1] According to Burdge, this brief letter was written "on the margin of the first page" of "a copy of the first edition" of Thomas Paine, *Common Sense: Addressed to the Inhabitants of America* . . . (Philadelphia: R. Bell, 1776). Since this edition was first advertised on January 9, and since the first mention of it in the correspondence of other delegates occurs on January 13, Wisner's letter has been arbitrarily assigned the latter date. For other evidence of the early dissemination of Paine's classic by the delegates, see the letters of this date from Samuel Adams to James Warren and from Josiah Bartlett to John Langdon.

Lord Drummond's Minutes

(Minute)   Philada. Jany 14 [1776] 12 at Night.
     A Plan of Compromise having been struck out for the Government of Masachusets Bay,[1] this Plan, excepting in the Article of adopting the mode used in S. Carolina for the forming their Juries (by Ballot instead of leaving it to the *Management* of the Sherriffs nominated by the King) difers so but very little from the new modelld Govt., which is generally approved by the Southern Delegates, it was agreed between Mr. [Lynch?][2] and Ld. Drummond that this shoud be communicatd to [Hancock][3] as introductory to the Genl. Plan.
     Mr. [Hancock] has accordingly signifyed his approb[a]t[ion] of the M[assachusetts] B[ay] p[la]n and promises every Sup[por]t in carry[ing] the whole into Ex[e]c[utio]n.

MS (Scottish Record Office: Drummond Castle Papers).

[1] There is no known extant copy of this "Plan of Compromise," although Thomas Lynch insinuated that it provided for the restoration of Massachusetts' 1691 charter or the alteration of the Massachusetts Government Act of 1774. See Drummond's Minutes, February 5, 1776, note 2. Drummond's remarks on this subject were more guarded. Of all the issues which he had discussed with the delegates in Philadelphia, he later observed, "the Boston Charter remains but the single Point in Contest. I'm very far from thinking a Mode might not be falln on that woud give satisfaction to both Parties. I suggested two Different Propositions. One of them I found was most unacceptable to some of the *Leading* Men of that Colony—and durst I commit it to writing, which Im affraid of doing by this Conveyance, I flatter myself your Lordship would not disapprove it." Drummond to Lord North?, March 24, 1776, Scottish Record Office: Drummond Castle Papers, Nj microfilm.

[2] Blank in the MS, but probably Thomas Lynch.

[3] For an explanation of the insertion of names in brackets here and below, see Drummond's Minutes, January 5, 1776, note 2.

Lord Drummond's Minutes

Minute   Philada. Jany. [14? 1776] [1]
    The American Delegates having come to a Resolution of sending a
Deputation from the Cols. to England they found themselves under some
difficulty with respect to the Persons to be nominated.[2] Aware of the
Intrigues of the Northern Gentlemen, and of the sudden turns to which
Popular Assemblies are ever liable they forsaw the Disadvantages that
might attend the Absence of any of the Leading Men amongst them. To
others again of a different Description they coud not entrust their
Affairs. Under these Difficulties it was suggested that Mr. [Silas Deane] [3]
of Connecticut might not be an improper Man. That they coud confide
at least in his Resentment against the two [Adams] by whose Intrigues
he had lost his Seat in the Congress on Account of his Moderation and
Disposition towards Accommodation. It was contrived that Lord Drumd.
shoud have an Opportunity of forming some Judgement of him by
meeting him at the Corner House in Markt. Street for the Discussion
of a particular Point in Commerce. L[ord] D[rummond] found him
plausible and to appearance moderate, but did not think him enough
a Man of the world for this Business besides his being subjected to those
Prejudices that must always attend every Man from his Part of the
Continent in the Eye of the other American Colonies. This Idea was
accordingly laid aside.
    A Difficulty had arisen with Respect to the Danger that woud attend
any of the Members of the Congress being of this proposed Deputation,
as they woud on their arrival in England expose themselves to immediate
trial for high treason. To remedy this the following Expedient was
submitted to Ld. Drumd. whether for the Guaranteeing the Safety of
any such Members as shoud be of this Deputation to England, he woud
pledge Himself as a Hostage to the Congress, and subject his Person
to be held responsible in all Respects for the fate of such Members.
    An Engagement agreeable to this was accordingly formed. The fixing
their Choice for this Deputation became the next Object when the
general Voice seemd for Mr. [Lynch] to be accompanied or not, as
shoud afterwards be determind, by Mr. [Allen] or Mr. [Jay].

MS (Scottish Record Office: Drummond Castle Papers).
    [1] This date has been assigned on the supposition that talks in Philadelphia between
the delegates and Lord Drummond came to an end around January 14. See Drummond's Notes, January 3–9? 1776, note 1.
    [2] Later Drummond described more fully the delegates' decision to send a peace
delegation to England, once "their thoughts were . . . turned towards setting on
foot a Negotiation. They cast their Eyes on Mr Elliot and myself and press'd us
much to go immediately to England, mistaking us I suppose for Men of much
greater Influence than we were. In this I was too proud to undeceive them, but as
the shortest Road to make known their Disposition at home, as well as to remove
all Suspicions of Insincerity, we urged their sending home a Deputation of their own

Number, and for whose Safety I proposed myself as a Pledge. A Day was accordingly fixed for agitating the Proposition in Congress but before its arrival Accounts were brought them of their Loss before Quebec. This occasioned a short Delay, which was unfortunately succeeded by another in the Burning of Norfolk—which heated the minds of those who 'twas suspected might oppose the Measure." See Drummond to Lord North?, March 24, 1776, Scottish Record Office: Drummond Castle Papers, Nj microfilm. Drummond's assertion in this letter that Congress learned of the British burning of Norfolk after learning of the American defeat at Quebec is erroneous.

³ For an explanation of the insertion of names in brackets here and below, see Drummond's Minutes, January 5, 1776, note 2.

Samuel Adams to John Adams

My dear sir   Philad Jany 15 1776
Altho I have at present but little Leisure, I cannot omit writing you a few Lines by this Express.

I have seen certain Instructions which were given by the Capital of the Colony of New Hampshire to its Delegates in their provincial convention the Spirit of which I am not alltogether pleasd with. There is one part of them at least, which I think discovers a Timidity which is unbecoming a People oppressd and insulted as they are, and who at their own request have been advisd & authorizd by Congress to set up and exercise Government in such form as they should judge most conducive to their own Happiness.[1] It is easy to understand what they mean when they speak of "perfecting a form of Govt *stable* and *permanent.*" They indeed explain themselves, by saying that they *"should prefer the Govt of Congress* (their provincial Convention) till quieter times." The Reason they assign for it, I fear, will be considerd as showing a readiness to condescend to the Humours of their Enemies, and their publickly, expressly, & totally disavowing Independency either in the nation, or the *Man* who insolently & perseveringly demands the surrender of their Liberties with the Bayonet pointed at their Breasts may be construed to argue a Servility & Baseness of Soul for which Language doth not afford an Epithet. It is by indiscrete Resolutions and Publications that the Friends of America have too often given occasion to their Enemies to injure her Cause. I hope however that the Town of Portsmouth doth not in this Instance speak the Sense of that Colony. I wish, if it be not too late, that you would write your Sentiments of the Subject to our worthy Friend, Mr. L——,[2] who I suppose is now in Portsmouth. If that Colony should take a wrong Step I fear it would wholly defeat a Design which I confess, I have much at heart.

A Motion was made in Congress the other day to the following purpose—that whereas we had been chargd with aiming at Independency, a Comte should be appointed to explain to the People at large the Principles & Grounds of our opposition &c.[3] The Motion alarmd me.

I thought Congress had already been explicit enough, & was apprehensive that we might get our selves upon dangerous Ground. Some of
us prevaild so far as to have the Matter postpond but could not prevent
the assigning a day to consider it. I may perhaps have been wrong in
opposing this Motion, and I ought the rather to suspect it, because the
Majority of your Colony as well as of the Congress were of a different
opinion.[4]

I had lately some free Conversation with an eminent Gentleman
whom you well know, and whom your Portia, in one of her Letters,
admired, if I recollect right, for his *expressive Silence*,[5] about a Confederation—A Matter which our much valued Freind Coll W——,[6] is very
sollicitous to have compleated. We agreed that it must soon be brought
on, & that if all the Colonies could not come into it, it had better be
done by those of them that inclind to it. I told him that I would endeavor
to unite the New England Colonies in confederating, if *none* of the rest
would joyn in it. He approvd of it, and said, if I succeeded, he would
cast in his Lot among us. Adieu.

Jan. 16th
As this Express did not sett off yesterday according to my Expectation,
I have the opportunity of acquainting you that Congress has just
receivd a Letter from General Washington inclosing the Copy of an
Application of our General Assembly to him to order Payment to four
Companies stationd at Braintree, Weymouth, & Hingham. The General
says they were never regimented, & he cannot comply with the Request
of the Assembly without the Direction of Congress. A Com[mitte]e is
appointed to consider the Letter of which I am one. I fear there will be
a Difficulty and therefore I shall endeavor to prevent a Report on this
part of the Letter, unless I shall see a prospect of Justice being done to
the Colony, till I can receive from you authentick Evidence of those
Companies having been actually employed by the continental officers,
as I conceive they have been, in the Service of the Continent.[7] I wish
you wd inform me whether the two Companies stationd at Chelsea &
Malden were paid out of the Continents Chest. I suppose they were,
and if so, I cannot see Reason for any Hesitation about the paymt of
these. I wish also to know how many Men our Colony is at the Expence
of maintaining for the Defence of its Sea Coasts. Pray let me have some
Intelligence from you, of the Colony which we represent. You are
sensible of the Danger it has frequently been in of suffering greatly for
want of regular Information.

RC (MHi). In Adams' hand, though not signed.
[1] Instructions of the town of Portsmouth to its representatives in the provincial
congress. *Am. Archives,* 4th ser. 4:459–60.
[2] John Langdon.
[3] James Wilson's motion of January 9. See Richard Smith's Diary, January 9, 1776.
[4] Notwithstanding his feigned diffidence, Samuel Adams apparently soon entered

the campaign for men's minds outside of Congress, turning his pen to the cause of independence and against those who argued for new efforts at reconciliation. According to his biographer Wells, Adams was the author of two newspaper essays exploiting these themes which appeared under the pseudonyms of "Candidus" and "Sincerus" in the *Pennsylvania Evening Post* on February 3 and 12, 1776. William V. Wells, *The Life and Public Services of Samuel Adams*, 3 vols. (Boston: Little, Brown and Co., 1865), 2:349–52, 360–63.

⁵ Benjamin Franklin, who first proposed his plan for confederation on July 21, 1775. *JCC*, 2:195–201.

⁶ Although Charles Francis Adams had conjectured that the reference was to George Wythe—an assumption that Burnett later endorsed—it seems clear that the reference is to James Warren, particularly since Samuel Adams had explicitly discussed this issue in his recent January 7 letter to Warren. See Adams, *Works* (Adams), 9:373; Burnett, *Letters*, 1:311; and Samuel Adams to James Warren, January 7, 1776.

⁷ George Washington to John Hancock, December 31, 1775. Washington refused to pay for the companies without express authority from Congress, a decision he explained in a letter to the Massachusetts General Court, December 29, 1775. See Washington, *Writings* (Fitzpatrick), 4:192–99. Although Congress acted on most of the letter's contents on January 16, Adams apparently succeeded in postponing action on the guard companies. *JCC*, 4:54, 60–61.

Eliphalet Dyer to Joseph Trumbull

Dear Sr.   Philadelphia Jany. 15th 1776
    I have been Impatiently expecting an Answer to one or two letters I sent you since your Arrival at Cambridge but have recievd None tho one or two posts beside as many expresses have arrived here since. Your apprehensions that I should have left Philadelphia before this time I Imagine to be the reason, but Unhappily for me the Gentn. appointed to Supersede Mr Dean & my self have not yet Arrived. I have hitherto Neglected making Application to Congress for some further Allowance for your services than your monthly Wages (which I believe all are Convinced are not Adequate) but before such application thot it proper to be possessd with the best Materials by which I might most likely Succeed in my Application. I was Advised that it would be of Consequence for you to procure some favourable representation & recommendation from Genll Washington & other Genll. Officers which might be of great service but before you receive this I really wish & expect to be on my return to my family, & hope the Colony will have delegates here to represent them, whose Zeal & Ardor for their Countrys Service & particularly for the Colony to which we belong (who often Stand in Need of the Warmest Advocates, or their Interest & those employd therefrom may much Suffer) will much exceed mine. From the Appearence of the Kings Speech All hopes of Reconciliation seem at an end; therefore Nothing remains on our part but the most Vigorous preparation & Exertions. The Congress are Augmenting their forces in every Quarter. Several Battalions are Ordered for Canada, two or 3

from Pensylvania, one from the Jerseys, One from New York & one to be Immediately raised in Connecticutt. Regiments are raising in every Province Southward, but we still fear for the Grand Army before Boston for The Congress having broke Up the New England plan of raising an Army there, I allways thot would be attended with Consequences the most unfavourable & would much Impede the raising an Army there equal to our Wishes but hope I may be Mistaken. Have not heard one word from my son since his Arrival at the Camp. Incourage him to do well, & friendly tell him when & where he fails. I a little fear he will not be Carefull enough about the Company he keeps & that he will be apt rather to decline those above him when he has oppertunity, or at least to be Sociable where he may with propriety, & tho I dont like to see a Gentn too fond of dress, yet I think his fault has been the Contrary. I hope you will see that he appears with propriety. He will much mind & Depend on your advice. There is just arrived in this City about 60 Tons Salt Petre & Several Tons of Powder. Fifteen Tons of Powder is ordered from New York for your Camp part of a larger quantity arrived there. I hope in Mercy Boston will be made too hot for the Savage Unclean Beasts who Inhabit there & am with respects, regards &c to all those proper, Yours,   Elipht Dyer

[*P.S.*] Please to deliver the Inclosed to my son. I have recievd pay for the Cask Rhubarb therefore need say Nothing about it.

Since I wrote this day our new Delegates arrived and I am myself happily relieved in a Most important critical Situation of Congress.[1] Colony a/c [account] unseteled.[2]   ED

RC (CtHi).
[1] Dyer left Philadelphia on January 20. See Silas Deane to Elizabeth Deane, January 21, 1776.
[2] See Richard Smith's Diary, January 13, 1776, note 2.

Christopher Gadsden to Esek Hopkins

Sir,   Philada. 15th Janry 1776
I last Night received my Orders to go to Carolina[1] & expect to set out a Thursday morng. for one of our Pilot Boats now at New Castle in which I shall take my Chance. Shou'd you come our Way if you think proper to let me know to morrow or next day what Signal you will shew when off our Bar, you may depend on my keeping a good Look-Out for You, & to let no Body know the Signal but where it is necessary.

I am Sr., yr most hble servt.,   Christ. Gadsden

RC (RHi). Addressed: "To the Honble Esek Hopkins Esqr. Commander in Chief of the Fleet Of the united Colonies."

¹ Gadsden, the colonel of the First South Carolina Regiment of Foot, is presumably referring to an order issued by the South Carolina Council of Safety on October 2, 1775, directing him to return to his native colony in order to assume command of the provincial forces there. John Drayton, ed., *Memoirs of the American Revolution, from its Commencement to the Year 1776, inclusive; as relating to the State of South-Carolina and occasionally referring to the states of North-Carolina and Georgia*, 2 vols. (Charleston: A. E. Miller, 1821), 2:171–72. Why this order took so long to reach Philadelphia is unknown, but his compliance with it shortly after this letter was written took Gadsden away from Congress, never to return.

New York Delegates to John Hancock

Sir   New York 15th Jany. 1776
Mr. Livingston Arived here on Saturday and Immediately Communicatd. to us Your Letters desireg us to purchase a Quantity of powder &c.¹ We Accordingly made a particular Inquiry how much of that Article is now in this Province, & find there is not, nor has there been any since last April but what has been in the hands of the Committe here, of which we send an Account Inclosed,² whereby it appears that there is now in the Public Store 6350 lb which with what is due from the Continent to this Province, is all the Stock they have. 462 Quartr. Casks was all the Powder that was brought from Curacoa, tho' it was said that it was to the Amo. of 300 Bbls & that Several Other Vessels which Arived About the same time had Also brought Powder which was without foundation. A report prevails Here that a Fleet of 18 Transports, 3 Ships of War & a Bomb Ketch have Saild from Boston, that Genl. Lee has desired Govr. Trumbal to Gett 1500 Men in Readiness with all dispatch, that he intended to March with a small body of Men from Cambridge to Connecticut & with the Troops to be raised in Conecticut to March to this place, but as it is probable You have Information from the Genl. it will be Needless for us to Enlarge.
The Asia & Phenix are both in this Harbour, and the Viper at Sandy Hook.³ We are Sr. Your Most Humbe. Servts.   Phil. Livingston

John Alsop

Frans Lewis

RC (DNA: PCC, item 78). Written by Alsop and signed by Alsop, Lewis, and Livingston.
¹ On January 8, in response to news that 15 tons of gunpowder had recently arrived in New York, Congress directed Alsop, John Jay, Lewis, and Philip Livingston to purchase this gunpowder and forward it to Washington's army at Cambridge. See *JCC*, 4:40, 62. The letters from Hancock to the New York delegates have not been found.
² This "account" was in the form of a letter of January 15 from Alexander McDougall to Philip Livingston. *Am. Archives*, 4th ser. 4:681–82.
³ In reality H.M.S. *Viper* was at Antigua at this time. Clark, *Naval Documents*, 3:802n.3.

Richard Smith's Diary

[January 15, 1776]

Monday 15. Letters from Washington, Montgomery, Arnold and others.[1] 3 Letters from Ld. Stirling inclosing Letters between Govr. Franklin and Lieut. Col. Winds,[2] they were on the Point of removing the Govr. to genteel Lodgings at Eliza. Town till the Pleasure of Congress is known, this Business was referred to Wm. Livingston & 4 others, & a Comee. of 3 appointed on Washns. Letters. Then the House went into Grand Comee. Govr. Ward in the Chair, on the permission to sell & use what Tea is in the Country. It was battled for divers Hours with much Heat & much Oratory & at length it was carried agt. granting any Permission by 7 Colonies to 4. (However the Advocates for this Measure carried their point in March or April following.)[3] A Paragraph of a Letter from Peter Timothy was read whereby it appears that any Two of the S. Carolina Gentn. are constituted a Quorum.[4] A Comee. was appointed of which Wisner was Head, to provide for Casting Cannon for the Land and Sea Service. I wrote to Mr. Kinsey this Eveng. inclosing Copies of Govr. Franklins and Cortland Skinners intercepted Letters.[5] It was recommended to the Comee. of Safety of Pennsa. to discharge such Privates as they pleased that were lately cast away on Board of the Transport at Egg Harbor. In the Morning the Comee. of Claims settled several Accots. as Hiltzheimers for Expresses and others, Expences run very high.

MS (DLC).

[1] Washington's letter to Hancock of December 31, 1775, and enclosures are in PCC, item 152, 1:381–406, and Am. Archives, 4th ser. 4:485–94. For letters and enclosures received this day from Connecticut governor Jonathan Trumbull to Hancock of January 6 and from the New York Committee of Safety to the New York delegates of January 11, see PCC, item 66, 1:55–66; and Am. Archives, 4th ser. 4:590–91, 1038. There is no mention in the journals of the reception this day of letters from Arnold or Montgomery, nor have any such been found in PCC.

[2] Although the journals for this date only record the arrival of letters from Colonel Alexander of January 8 and 11, Congress also received a letter from him this day of January 10, together with enclosures of correspondence concerning New Jersey governor William Franklin. See PCC, item 162, 2:360–72; and Am. Archives, 4th ser. 4:596, 621–22, 627.

[3] See Smith's Diary, January 12, 1776, note 2.

[4] See JCC, 4:54; and Am. Archives, 4th ser. 4:74.

[5] Smith's letter to Kinsey has not been found. For the letters of Franklin and Skinner referred to here, see Smith's Diary, January 9, 1776.

John Hancock to George Washington

Jany. 16 [1776]

Your letters of the 25 and 30 of December & 4th of January have been duly received and laid before Congress.[1] By the enclosed resolutions you will perceive that the Congress, in providing for the defence of Canada, have directed that two batallions be formed out of the troops now serving there.[2] This they did in testimony of their approbation of the services of those brave men, apprehending at the same time, that it would be agreeable both to the officers and men to have the honor of defending a country which their valour had rescued from slavery. And the Congress have a firm confidence that general Montgomery, who has a warm and just sense of their merit and services, will cheerfully embrace this opportunity of continuing and promoting the officers of that corps, and as far as in his power, of rewarding with offices and commands in those batallions such voluntiers and others, as have distinguished themselves.

The committee to whom your letters were referred brought a report on part, whereupon the Congress came to'certain resolutions which you will see in the enclosed extracts.[3] I am just to acquaint you, it is expected when the paymaster general draws any bills on me he will observe to make them payable a few days after sight Say 3 or 4. The committee have desired leave to sit again which is granted. When they have compleated their report and the Congress have come to a determination thereon I shall do myself the pleasure of transmitting it to you.

The money just voted is now ready and will I expect be sent forward tomorrow.

I have the pleasure to inform you the secret Committee have purchased the salt petre and have agreed with the owners of Mills to manufacture it into powder. One of the Mills, it is expected, will make near a ton per week and another near half a ton. I hope you will soon receive the powder ordered to be purchased at New York. There were besides eight tons imported in the same vessel for the use of that Colony.

The public papers will inform you, that Lord Dunmore has endeavoured to exercise the same barbarity against the defenceless town of Norfolk, as was exercised against Falmouth. By these repeated instances of inhumanity so contrary to the rules of war and so long exploded by all civilized nations, it would seem as if the rancorous ministry, despairing of their measures to conquer and enslave, had determined to glut their revenge with destruction & devastation.

For my part I shall not be surprized to hear that, in the frenzy of rage and to effect their dark purposes, they proceed under form of law to murder those prisoners, whom the tools of their vengeance have chanced to take, and whom with officious zeal they have so hastily & industriously sent to England.

As it is now apparent that our enemies mean to exert their whole force against us next summer, the Congress are taking measures for putting the middle and southern colonies in a posture of defence.

We shall, doubtless, in this great struggle suffer much, but I trust no losses or sufferings will induce us to give over the defence of our liberty, and that cost what it may, we will persevere with unremitting vigour to maintain that inestimable jewel which we have received from our ancestors and transmit the same with unsullied lustre to our posterity.

The committee to whom your letter of the 31st of December was referred desire to be informed whether the companies stationed at Chelsea and Malden are regimented and whether, if those at Hingham, Weymouth & Braintree were withdrawn,[4] it would be necessary to replace them out of the continental Army.[5]

RC (DLC). A continuation of Hancock to Washington, January 6, 1776.

[1] These letters are in PCC, item 152, 1:373–410; and Washington, *Writings* (Fitzpatrick), 4:181–83, 194–99, 208–10.

[2] For the resolutions of January 8 and 9, adopted in response to the report of the "Committee on General Schuyler's letters," see *JCC*, 4:38–40, 43–45.

[3] See *JCC*, 4:60–61.

[4] See Samuel Adams to John Adams, January 15, 1776, note 7.

[5] For the continuation of this letter, see Hancock to Washington, January 18, 1776.

Thomas Lynch to George Washington

Dear Sir   Phila Jany 16. 1776

I am happy to be at last able to write you that every thing you desired me to get done is accomplished, for the present. Our President assures me he has sent you the determination of Congress concerning the Trial of Captures;[1] Courts of Admiralty have been appointed in the Colony for that purpose. Colo Frye has been appointed Brigadier in your Army (Mr. Arnold preceeds him in that at Quebec) and I inclose Copies of the Resolutions for the direction of the Post Master, relative to Letters of Officers & Soldiers in our Service.[2]

The delays in procuring the money has given me much concern, being sensible of the injury occasioned thereby to the Service, but the Calls for money from every Quarter, so far outrun the diligence of the Signers, that my reiterated solicitations coud get the sum no sooner.

We have resolved to raise exclusive of your Army, in New Hampshire 1 Batn, in Connecticut one, in N. York one, in Jersey three, in Pensilvania five, in the Lower Counties one, in Virginia six, in North Carolina three, & South Carolina three, in Georgia 1, & in Canada two, exclusive of Canadians. Besides these, I have no doubt New York will have four more & Maryland two, which with the Regiments of Artillery will be 62 or 3 Battalions & the Expence not less than ten Millions of Dollars. How quick a transfer of property from the Rich to the Poor, such an Expenditure must produce, you are well able to Judge. The Prospect is far from receiving light when tis considered how each Colony lavishes away its private Treasure at the same Time, or when we view the amazing and unaccountable supiness of all our Governments. Not a single [one] anywhere in civil Department, seems to consider himself as interested in public matters, unless he can get money by them; the Idea of all the paper being mortgages on their private Estates is totally lost and forgotten.

In this State of things, I have, besides my Dependance on the Continuance of the Favour of Heaven, Trust in two Supports alone, the one, on your Vigorous Exertions, the other on the Weakness of our Enemies. Shoud they lose footing in America this winter, I shoud despise their thirty thousand Russians, scattered by Storms, arriving one Transport after another, fatigued & debilitated by the Fatal Effects of long Voyages, without a Spot to collect and recruit themselves for the Field & depending for every Necessary on Supplies from a Country 3000 miles distant.

Do not the Speeches of the King and his Minister hold very different Language from those of the last year! America is no longer the abject, cowardly and defenceless Wretch she was then, now his Lordship woud have dispised had they not bravely supported their Rights, seems to approve their vigorous support of them & offers the terms of 1763. A gentleman well known to Moyland, Ld Drummond just from England, assures me he will give much more. He tells me that he has had many Conversations with Ministry on the Subject & Shewed me a Paper approved by all of them & which he is sure will be supported in both Houses. The Substance of it is America to be declared free in point of Taxation & internal Police, Judges to be approvd by the Judges of England and commissioned during good Behaviour, upon stated & sufficient support be statedly assigned them by the Colonies, all Charters to be held Sacred, that of Boston restored, Britain to regulate Trade sub modo, all Duties laid for the purpose of Regulation be paid into the Colony Treasury where they arise, applicable to its uses by its own Legislature, in Lieu of which America shall, by Duties on such Articles as will probably keep pace in its Consumption with the Rise or declention of the Colony, laid by each Legislature by permanent Act of Assembly, Grant towards the general Support of the Empire, annual Sums in proportion to £5000 Sterling for this Colony.[3] As this sum is little more than half of what did arise by Duties heretofore paid in this place, I doubted his information, but was assured that Ministry wanted nothing but a shew of Reve[nue] to hold up to Parliament, as they are affraid [to] propose Reconciliation, without saving what the[ir] stiff old Englishmen call the Honor of the Nation. His Lordship came hither thro' Hallifax, Boston, & York, where I fancy he saw what induced him to hint once or twice at beginning with a Suspention of Arms, to which I turned a very deaf Ear, well knowing that the Season winter is ours, and that much may be done by April next. I sincerely wish I had your sentiments on these heads, I shall propose them to the Consideration of

Congress, as soon as the most urgent affairs are over. I think the[y]
merit it.

Congress has Ordered you 15 ton of Gun Powder from New York &
we have Salt Petre enough here, to make 80 Ton more so that I hope
we shall not soon want again. [4] Large Quantities are every day expected.
I beg you'l make our Compliments to your Lady and to the rest of your
Family, and all my Friends, Dr Sir your most Obedt

                                                        Tho Lynch

[*P.S.*] We have just heard from Charles Town that they have mounted
on the Batteries there above 160 Cannon from 12 to 42 Pounders & 70
more in different parts of the Province, that the Party raised by Kirkland
& his gang are totally suppressd, he is come but I have not yet seen him.

RC (DLC).
   [1] For Congress' resolutions on the disposition of prize ships, adopted on January 6,
see *JCC*, 4:36–37.
   [2] Although this day Congress extended the privilege of free postage to "any letters
to or from private soldiers, while engaged in defense of the United Colonies," according to a report submitted to Congress on February 16, 1776, a similar privilege had
yet to be bestowed on officers. See *JCC*, 4:43, 155.
   [3] A paper entitled "Articles proposed as Objects for the Imposition of Taxes,"
which Drummond apparently drew up early in January 1776 in order to specify
the sources of revenue for this permanent "Grant," is in the Drummond Castle
Papers, Scottish Record Office. In this paper Drummond called for import duties
on wine, tea, sugar, and coffee. He also envisioned export duties on rice and indigo
from Georgia and South Carolina; rice and tobacco from North Carolina; tobacco
and flour from Maryland and Virginia; and flour, wheat, biscuits, and flaxseed
from Delaware, Pennsylvania, New Jersey, and New York. Whether Lynch or the
other delegates with whom he conferred ever saw this paper is not known. See also
Lord Drummond's Notes, January 3–9? 1776, note 1.
   [4] See New York Delegates to John Hancock, January 15, 1776.

Richard Smith's Diary

                                             Tuesday 16 January [1776]
   Messrs. Wolcott and Huntington from Connecticut took their Seats.
A Report passed from the Comee. on Gen. Washns. Letters, to allow the
Paymaster at Cambridge to draw upon the Continental Treasurers for
any Sum not exceeding a Months Pay of that Army, to allow Him to
reinlist the free Negroes, to continue Col Gridley as Chief Engineer,
to appoint a Chaplain to every 2 Battalions & the Pay of such Chaplain
fixed at 33 1/3 Dollars per Month &c. A Tender was asked for &
allowed to our Naval Armament under Admiral Hopkins. Duane &
E. Rutledge were desired to rectify a Mistake in the Journals now
printing, as to the Date of the Bills of Credit. The Report was made
from the Comee. on the Number of Troops necessary, they recommend

4 new Battalions to be raised in New York & one in N Carolina, the latter was confirmed & a day named to consider the former.[1] Considerable Arguments on the Point Whether a Day shall be fixed for considering the Instrument of Confederation formerly brought in by a Comee. It was carried in the Negative. Dr. Franklin exerted Himself in Favor of the Confederation as did Hooper, Dickinson and others agt. it.[2] Two Applications from French or other Foreigners for Employ in our Service, were referred to the Comee. for nominating fit persons for Officers.[3] A French Vessel just arrived here with Powder. It is reported that they are fitting out 4 or 5 Privateers or other Vessels of War in So. Carolina & their Agent is now in this City on his Way to New England to engage 500 Seamen. He is empowered to offer such high Terms that the S. Carolina Delegates acquainted Congress with it least it should prejudice our Service and a Comee. was chosen to consider the Matter.[4] A Vessel is about to sail from Philada. with Produce for Bermudas to procure Powder and if it belongs to the King to seize it by Force; if there is none there She is to go to New Orleans, Carthagena or to a noted Port near Carthagena or elsewhere and if She cannot get Ammunition the Captain is to obtain hard Money. The Secretary was desired to make out a List of all Committees & their Business and leave it on the Table. Col Kirkland with his little Son is brought here & secured in Goal. He was offered the Choice of having his Son with him or that the Boy should be put to Colledge, he chose the former. A Petition was presented from Benjamin Randolph of Chesnut Street praying Leave to raise a Troop of Light Horse for Continental Service, it was opposed by E. Rutledge and neglected or rejected.

MS (DLC).

[1] See Smith's Diary, January 10, 1776, note 1.

[2] See Silas Deane's Proposals to Congress, November? 1775, note 1.

[3] One of these applicants has not been identified, but the other was Dohickey Arundel, who was brought to Congress' attention by Francis Lewis and appointed on March 19, 1776, as a captain of artillery under Gen. Charles Lee. *JCC*, 4:58, 111–12, 120, 211–12, 241, 243; and André Lasseray, *Les Français sous les treize étoiles (1775–1783)*, 2 vols. (Macon and Paris: Imprimerie Protat Frères, 1935), 1:119–20.

[4] On January 19 Congress approved resolves raising the bounties and lowering the wages which Capt. Robert Cochran had been authorized by the South Carolina Council of Safety to offer to New England seamen who agreed to enlist in that province's navy. *JCC*, 4:67–68; and Clark, *Naval Documents*, 3:326–28. For additional information on Cochran's recruiting efforts, see Clark, *Naval Documents*, 3:647, 1316, 1333.

Samuel Ward to Nicholas Cooke

Sir   Philadela. 16th Jany.1776

Our Seamen arrived here the Day before yesterday, those concerned in the naval Department are highly pleased with them, their Arrival gives fresh Spirits to the whole Fleet.

Your Favor of the 4th we recd.[1] I would wish to have the Instructions of the Genl. Assembly relative to the Regiment or any other colonial affairs as soon as may be.

The Letters of Govr. Franklin & the Speaker of the assembly of New Jersey's were intercepted, an Order of Congress was issued for seizing the latter but he escaped on Board the Asia, the Govr. is under a continental Guard in his own House until Order from Congress may be issued.[2]

I enclose the Resolves of Congress ord[ered] to the several Colonies.[3] Time only permits Me to add that I am With most sincere Regard Sir Your most obedient humble Servant   Sam Ward

P.S. I recd. a Letter from Messrs. Clarke & Nightingale relative to the contract entered into by Admiral Hopkins.[4] As I have not time to write them beg your Honor to let them know that I think the public Service requires that the Voyage should proceed with all Dispatch.

RC (R-Ar).
    [1] For Cooke's letter of December 4, 1775, see Ward, *Correspondence* (Knollenberg), pp. 135–37.
    [2] See Richard Smith's Diary, January 9, 1776.
    [3] These resolves cannot be identified precisely, but they probably included those of January 2 and 11 on the treatment of tories and of persons who refused to accept Continental bills of credit. *JCC*, 4:18–22, 49–50.
    [4] See Secret Committee Minutes of Proceedings, December 11, 1775.

John Hancock to Thomas Cushing

Dear Sir   Philadelphia Januy. 17th. 1776
    Your favr. from Milford I duly Rec'd, and thank you for it. Your observations respectg. the Conduct of the Merchts. of New York as to Remittances is very just, and I think with you that those Sums could & ought to be improv'd here for much better purposes. I am much oblig'd for your trouble in Calling upon my Aunt. I hope this will find you safe arriv'd & in the Enjoyment of Domestick Ease & happiness, that you found all your particular Connections well, & not Destitute of many Friends, altho' some would gladly have it thought that you are totally deserted, but by no means, My Good Friend, let the Circumstance of the Election Discourage you from the Noble pursuit in which you are Engaged, your Cause is just, and I am Confident your Conscience will Acquit you. I can tell you for a truth that you have left in Congress many who are peculiarly friendly to you, & who, had they a Suspicion that you would not have Return'd soon to Congress, would

have given you many Expressions of their Friendship previous to your Departure. I never Flatter, but shall ever in future unbosom my self to you, & write freely, in Confidence that I can Rely on your Friendship, & from a Conviction that you are Deserving of the Esteem I have for you, & I shall ever feel a pleasure in doing any thing that can Contribute to your Ease or Reputation, as I must Say I have Reason to think Endeavours have been made to Disturb both, & which I will not let pass over unnotic'd, for it may Operate further & be the means of Stirring up Jealousies & Animosities which had better be nipt in the Bud, of wch. more in my next.[1]

Severall Members of Congress have mention'd to me the Desire they have to Establish you in that Agreeable point of light which your Conduct in their Estimation merits. For that purpose they are framing a Letter to you, to be made such use of as you think best, to be Sign'd by a number of them, as they have some how an opinion that undue Methods have been practic'd which have Operated to your Disadvantage in the late Election.[2] They are very sanguine in this matter, and I assure you that you are mention'd by Respectable Members in the most Advantagious & Agreeable Light, & you may Rely I do not throw any Contradictory Strokes in the way; of this more in my next. As I did not Expect to be able to write you a Line by this, you must Excuse my not being more Explicit, having ever since your Departure been exceeding ill, my Cold brought on a Fever, & much Affected one of my Eyes, that I have, & still do, suffer greatly, I hope by next oppory. to be able to write you more fully.

With Respect to the Ships, I must Beg you will set the Wheels in Motion; Money & particular Instructions shall come by next as I am now unable to Compleat what I intended. The whole Conduct of these Ships I Submit to you. Pray be Expeditious in setting forward the work, & let me hear from you.

South Carolina have Authoriz'd Mr. Lynch & Rutlidge to Act, & have sent for Mr. Gadsden home, who Departs by water tomorrow. We have this Day rec'd disagreeable Accotts. from Canada, poor Montgomery & severall officers kill'd, Arnold Wounded &c. We have Agreed to have Nine Battalions in Canada, I now Send this Express, to have one Rais'd in N. Hampshire, one in Connecticutt &c. I fear for the Defection of New York, the Spring will open before we are Ready, however we must bestir ourselves. I hope in my next to Send you a good Accott. of a little Expedition order'd, which is now Executing, but I am under injunction &c. Intercepted Letters from Gov. Franklin & the Speaker of the Jersey Assembly Mr Skinner have been Read in Congress, their Contents I can't mention.[3] Gov. Franklin is under Guard, & Skinner gone on board the Asia.

I inclose you a pamphlet which makes much Talk here, said to be wrote by an English Gentleman Resident here by the name of Paine,

& I believe him the Author, I Send it for your and Friend's Amusement.

The Inclos'd Letters I Return you having Rec'd them since your Departure.

I shall Look on you as a stated friendly Correspondent, I make offers of sincere Attachment & Friendship to you, & wish for a Return of yours, & you may Rely on every Service in my power, & that I am totally undisguis'd, & beg that our friendly Correspondence may continue, I will Give you every thing from hence, both in & out Doors, that I consistently can, & pray write me every Occurrence with you, by every Post, omitt no Oppor[tunitie]s. For a very particular Reason do send me the State of the late Election of members for Congress, Number of Votes &c Candidates &c what is the Assembly about. I have Rec'd no orders to Remain here, we know nothing of the Election but by the News papers. Give me all news, & by every Oppory. I shall Send your Letters always under Cover to the General.

Mrs. Hancock Joines me in best Complimts. to you & Lady & Family. Do Tell Mrs. Cushing when I See her I shall use friendly Freedoms more than ever & shall not look upon her as a Stranger, & would not be so thought by her. I shall give her your history.

I am with Real Esteem, My Good Friend, Yours without Reserve,

John Hancock

[*P.S.*] How goes on the militia matters in assembly; am I to be notic'd in the appointment of officers.

RC (MHi).
¹ Hancock's alienation from his more radical colleagues is discussed in Herbert S. Allan, *John Hancock, Patriot in Purple* (New York: MacMillan Co., 1948), pp. 199–202, 212–15. Cushing later reported to Hancock that "Soon after I arrived here I found You as well as myself had been placed in a disagreable light and measures taken to hurt our Influence, I instantly endeavoured to remove every Impression of this kind. . . . It is true I am Informed some few, whom it is needless to mention, as you are well acquainted with their names & characters, have Endeavor'd by their little, low, Dirty & sly Insinuating Actes & Machinations to distroy my Influence among the new Members of the House. . . . The State of the Election you have Inclosed, They Struck also at Mr Paine & had he not been upon a Committee in Canada, he would, I am told, have been left out of the delegation." Thomas Cushing to John Hancock, January 30, 1776, MHi.
² Only a fragment of this testimonial letter has survived. "Your sudden Departure not giving most of us an Opportunity of taking our Leave of you, we take this method of expressing our Concern at parting with a Gentleman we so greatly esteem'd & of most cordially bidding you *Farewell*. The Consciousness of your long & faithful Services to your Country will doubtless afford you the most heart-felt satisfaction amidst all the gloomy scenes in which the arbitrary Measures of the Ministry have involved us. . . ." James Duane, Stephen Hopkins, William Hooper, John Morton, and George Read to Thomas Cushing, [January 17, 1776], Bigelow Papers, MHi. For Samuel Adams' disparaging remarks on this testimonial, see Adams to James Warren, March 8, 1776.
³ See Richard Smith's Diary, January 15, 1776.

Benjamin Harrison to Robert Carter Nicholas

Dr Sir,   Philada Jany. 17th. 1776
I have your Favor of the sixth Instant, as also that of the 26th ulto. inclosing the Bills of Exchg. of which I inform'd you [1] by the Return of Page who I hope will get down before Mr Braxton leaves Town, in which case you will have an oppy. of geting an order on Willing & Morris from my Son for what money you may want in this Place. He has an order from those Gentn. for about a thousand Pounds but as that will not be near the Sum he will have occasion for to Execute his Commission, you may enlarge it to double or treble the sum as you shall see cause. I have used every endeavour in my Power to fall on some mode of transacting money matters betwixt this Place and ours, without laying you under the Disagreeable necessity of Drawing Bills, but find it is not to be done, as all intercourse of Trade betwixt the two Countries is at an end, if Ben succeeds in his Business perhaps it may be more easy hereafter.

The Person you furnish'd with an order on Duval is not the Capt. I mention'd to you. Mr Morris has seen your Letter and gave for answer that he would pay his Drafts when presented, the other is for a Sum not exceeding sixty Pounds, which he is also to pay, but perhaps it may never be Presented to you as the order is to you, or any Committee that it may be presented to. Some Sailors it seems rose on the Poor man, took his Vessel from him, set him on shore and went off, he expected to Virga. He is in pursuit of them and being in want of money is furnish'd with our order at Morris's request, I think it Probable the Villains are with our Devil of a Governour.

I have an order in my Possession Drawn by Mr Thos Mathews on you for three hundred thirty three and a third Dollars, advanced to him by Gen. Washington. The Congress have Desired us to have it negotiated, if you think fit to pay it, you may give the money to Ben and take his Rect. and I will have it Settled here. I did not think it safe to trust the original but have Inclosed you a Copy. Mathews and Robinson are here and will set off for Virga. in two or three Days.[2]

Our Devil of a Governor goes on at a Devil of a rate indeed, but I hope Providence in its good time will bring him to acct. for all his missdoings.

We have no late News from Canada. I wish that matter may go on well, an excellent officer Commands there but he is Weak. I sent the Kings Speech & the proceedings of the Parlit. on it by the last Post from which you will see we have nothing to expect but Fire and Sword. I am Dr Sir, your most obedt Servt,   Benj Harrison

P.S. Fifteen Ream of Paper are come in, we shall have the rest we are told next Week, as soon as it comes we will Dispatch a Waggon immediately with it.   B H

RC (MHi).
[1] See Harrison to Nicholas, December 30, 1775.
[2] Mathews and Robinson had been taken prisoner by Lord Dunmore and sent to Boston. In order to enable them to return to Virginia, Washington had advanced them £100. See *JCC*, 4:54, 56; and Washington, *Writings* (Fitzpatrick), 4:197–98.

New York Delegates to Philip Schuyler

Dear Sir,   New York. 17th January. 1776
    The Continental Congress having directed that Two Ships be built in this Colonie for the Public Service, the bearers of this are two Master Builders,[1] with whom we have agreed for the Expediting that work, and Poughkeepsy being the place destined for that business where we imagine they may frequently want necessary Articles, and assistance from Albany.
    We therefore have taken the liberty of recommending them to your Patronage, well knowing that under your Influence they can procure every assistance they may want. We have the Honor to be, Sir, Your Most obedt Humble Servts.,   Frans. Lewis

                                                                        John Alsop

RC (InU). Written by Lewis and signed by Alsop and Lewis.
[1] Not identified.

Richard Smith's Diary

                                                        Wednesday 17 Jany. [1776]
    The Votes read, as was a Petition from Dr. Benjamin Church in Jail in Connecticut setting forth his piteous Situation, asserting his Innocence & prayg. a Release, this was referred to a Comee.[1]
    In Grand Comee. on the Propriety of opening Trade after 1 March next it was concluded to trade to the Foreign West India Islands & to open the Trade under certain regulations to be fixed by a Comee. now chosen.[2] While we were in the midst of this Business a Packet of Letters [3] came from Gens. Schuyler, Wooster and Arnold, Col. Donald Campbell and others with the unfortunate News that Gen. Montgomery had attempted before Day Break of the [31st] of Decr. to storm Quebec but this gallant Soldier and amiable Man was killed with the first Fire, Brig. Arnold wounded in the Leg and carried off to a Hospital whereby the Command devolved on Col. Campbell who retreated, not being able to make his Men advance. Major MacPherson Aid duCamp to Mr. Montgomery was killed with Capt. Cheeseman and a few more and on the other Side of the City, Arnolds Detachment to the Number

of between 3 & 400 Hundred including Major Lamb and his Artillery had made a Lodgment in the Lower Town but was obliged to surrender after 3 Hours Resistance.

A Report from the Comee. about a French Artillery Officer who offers his Service and brought a Certificate from the Military School at Strasburgh and Two Commissions of Lieutenancy from the King of France, was referred to Dr. Franklin and Col. St. Clair to examine his Abilities.[4] 400 Dollars were advanced to a Canadian Prisoner for his Maintenance, he to give his Draught upon the Kings Paymaster at Quebec. A Petition was exhibited from sundry Captains, Lieuts. & Ensigns of Col Bull's Battalion charging their Colonel with Extortion & haughty Behavior & a Comee. was instituted to hear both Parties & report thereon.[5] The Commissions for these Gentn. were ordered to be signed and delivered. A Comee. reported Instructions for the recruiting Officers which were accepted. The pay of a Regimental Surgeon is 25 Dollars per Month.

MS (DLC).

[1] Dr. Benjamin Church's petition to Congress of January 1, 1776, is in PCC, item 41, 2:5–8, and *Am. Archives*, 4th ser. 4:531–32. Congress responded to it on January 18 by denying Church's request to be released from jail in Norwich, Conn., to return to his family in Taunton, Mass., while directing Gov. Jonathan Trumbull to move Church to a more commodious place of confinement and to allow him more freedom to exercise. *JCC*, 4:65.

[2] See Smith's Diary, January 12, 1776, note 1.

[3] See *JCC*, 4:64; and *Am. Archives*, 4th ser. 4:480–82, 666–71.

[4] See Smith's Diary, January 16, 1776, note 3.

[5] These complaints led to Col. John Bull's resignation as commander of the First Pennsylvania Battalion on January 20 and his replacement two days later by Col. John Philip De Haas. *JCC*, 4:72–73, 78; and *Am. Archives*, 4th ser. 4:785.

Oliver Wolcott to Laura Wolcott

My Dear   Philidelphia 17t Janry 1776

I arrived here the 15t with Mr. Huntington Well and by the Blessing of God am so Now. We had much delay by the Ferrys and found the Roads bad. We have put up at a House in third street with one Mr. Duncan. Mr. Sherman, Who will soon come to live with us provided our Lodgings and I think they are good, and where We shall not have too much company. I yesterday attended Congress and perceive the members have a hard service. There has been bro't in here about sixty Tons of Salt Petre. Our fleet are yet in the River by Reason of Ice. You will hear of the Destruction of Norfolke. No News in special. Have paid Mr. Saml. Bowne sixty four pounds York Currency and have his Recet. Take Care of your Health and may the Blessing of the almighty attend you and the Family. I shall Write to you as I have oppertunity. This goes by Col Dyer. Mr. Dean will go soon. There is no probability of a Recess of Congress, at least not soon. I am with the tenderest affection your,   Oliver Wolcott

[*P.S.*] (in hast), My Regards to my Freinds.

RC (CtHi).

Andrew Allen to
the Pennsylvania Committee of Safety

Sr: Jan'y 18th, 1776.
   The Congress having understood that there has been some Dispute about the classing the field-Officers of the Battalions lately raised, have determined to leave that matter altogether to the Comm'ee of Safety, & desired me to signify to them their Resolutions on that Head.[1] They also desire that the Comm'ee would examine the Prisoners taking with Capt. Campbell, and if there appear no material Reasons for detaining them in Prison that they may be discharged, as the Expence of maintaining them runs high.[2] I would have attended the Board this morning for these Purposes, but am obliged to be present at an Examination of Col. Bull, upon some Charges exhibited agst him by his officers.
   I am with Regard, Your most obedt Servt.,   And'w Allen.

MS not found; reprinted from *Pa. Archives*, 1st ser. 4:702. Addressed: "To John Nixon, Esqr., Chairman of the Committee of Safety for Pennsylvania."
   [1] This decision was apparently reached in the "Committee on the Qualifications of officers," of which Allen was a member. There is no mention of "Resolutions on that Head" in the journals of Congress, but see *JCC*, 4:23–24, 29–30, 50, 53, 58–59.
   [2] A reference to the men recruited by Capt. Duncan Campbell of the Royal Highland Emigrants taken prisoner in October 1775 when their ship the *Rebecca and Frances* ran aground on the New Jersey coast. See *JCC*, 3:305, 4:56.

John Hancock to George Washington

Jany. 18 [1776]
   Since writing the above we have received a letter from Messrs. P. Livingston, Alsop & Lewis by which to our mortification we are informed that we were deceived in the account of powder and that there were only 462 quarter casks imported for the colony of New York, which they have in part distributed among several counties.
   Before this reaches you, I doubt not you will hear the disagreeable news from Quebec, on which sincerely condole with you. The express

arrived yesterday evening;[1] The Congress I presume will take it up this morning.[2]

I have the Honour to be with the utmost Esteem, Sir, Your most Obedt hume servt,   John Hancock Prest

Jany 21st.

The foregoing was design'd to have been forwarded by Express earlier but Congress directed a Delay, for further Resolutions, for which I refer you to my other Letter by this Express.[3]

RC (DLC). A continuation of Hancock to Washington, January 16, 1776. Postscript in the hand of John Hancock.

[1] General Schuyler's dispatch was read in Congress on January 17. *JCC*, 4:64.

[2] Hancock wrote another brief letter to Washington on January 18 which indicates that he expected to dispatch this long, continuing letter this date. "The bearer Captn. F[rancis] Gurney has the Charge of conducting 500,000 dollars for the use of the army under your command. I wish it safe to hand. I shall this evening dispatch an express to you with sundry matters of importance." Washington Papers, DLC.

[3] See Hancock to Washington, January 20, 1776.

Naval Committee to Esek Hopkins

Sir,   Philadelphia January 18. 1776

As this perhaps may be the last opportunity we may have to write to you before you go to sea, we thought it necessary to give you every intelligence that is come to our knowledge. We shall first give you the disagreable intelligence brought hither by an Express from Quebec of an unsuccessful attack that was made to storm that city on the 31st of December in the morning in which General Montgomery, his Aid de Camp Capt. Macpherson, and Capt Cheesman, both by his side were all shott instantly dead by the Grapeshott of one Cannon—upon which his party rather deserted their duty. Coll. Arnold who conducted a different attack proceeded a while successfully but upon his receiving a Wound and falling after he had entered the city, altho the party were afterward commanded and behaved with great bravery, by the other attack failing were overpowered and surrounded by numbers and after a most gallant defence of four hours were obliged to surrender themselves prisoners of war, and we hear are very kindly used by General Charlton. This is the substance of what we have heard from thence. We have just received a report from New York, that three men of War and eighteen transports had sailed from Boston, to what place not known, but supposed to be for Newport, New York, or Virginia. Thus much of the report is certain, that the Asia and Phoenix are laying in the East River in New York and that the Viper is laying at Sandy Hook.

From Virginia we have heard nothing material but what you are well acquainted with. From the Carolinas, we are informed that Lord

William Campbell with the Tamar Sloop and Cherokee Cutter had departed from Charles Town road. That Govr. Martin in the Scorpion Sloop of War had also departed from Cape Fear. It is supposed that both these are gone to Savanna in Georgia, in order to seduce that province, if it is in their power, from the Union of the Colonies, and to get provisions, if they can, to subsist on. Should it be your fate to go Southward as far as Savanna it is very probable you may have three Governors to dine with you on board your own ship—and increase your Naval Strength by the Tamar, Scorpion & Cherokee.

The Congress have determined to erect a splendid Monument to the memory of the Gallant Montgomery and to every other commanding officer bravely fighting and falling in his countrys cause. We wish you a successful Cruize and are, Your sincere friends,   Step Hopkins

Joseph Hewes

Silas Deane [1]

RC (RHi). In a clerical hand and signed by Deane, Hewes, and Hopkins.
[1] Although Deane last attended Congress on January 16, he remained in Philadelphia another seven weeks during which he devoted a considerable portion of his time to Naval Committee affairs. See Deane to Elizabeth Deane, January 21; and John Alsop et al. to Silas Deane, March 1, 1776, note 2.

Richard Smith's Diary

Thursday 18 Jany. [1776]
The Proceedings read as usual. A Report was made on Dr. Church. It was opposed and voted out and a Resolve passed that He shall be confined in a more convenient Room and have Liberty to ride out under a Guard.[1] Dr. Smith an Associate to Connolley was brought in Prisoner from Maryland, some of Connolleys Letters written since his Confinement were found on Smith & read & the Prisoner consigned to the Comee. of Safety here. Myself & several of the New Members signed the Engagement, heretofore entered into while I was absent, not to divulge any Thing while under Consideration or any Thing the Congress agrees to keep secret, on Pain of Expulsion.[2] The Letters recd. Yesterday concerng. the Storm of Quebec were again read [3] and Mr. Antill, Son of the late Hon. Mr. Antill of N Jersey, who brought the Packet, was called in & examined for 2 Hours, he gave a very clear Account of every Circumstance, he was with Gen. Montgy. when he fell. Before this Gentn. came in, Hooper moved in a florid Speech that the Delegates may wear Mourning (a Crape round the left Arm) for One Month for Montgomery & that Mr. Duché be desired to preach a Sermon, to which Lynch added that a Public Monument be erected to his Memory, the Motions were objected to by Govr. Ward and others on the Ground that no Mourning is ever worn by any Courts on

such Accounts & that the General is already embalmed in the Heart of every good American and that such Proceeding may cause too much alarm at such a critical Juncture. These reasons had their intended Weight. A Comee. of 5 was chosen to report their Opinion what is best to be done in Respect to the Affairs of Canada.[4] Mr. Burr Son of the late President of Princeton Colledge behaved well, as they say, in the Affair at Quebec, Our Troops have made a Stand about 3 Miles from that City, Antill recommends Capt. Hazen to command a Regiment of Canadians & says these are between Hawk and Buzzard but will generally join our Side if we send a strong Force there immediately.

MS (DLC).
[1] See Smith's Diary, January 17, 1776, note 1.
[2] Congress had adopted a secrecy resolution on November 9, 1775. *JCC*, 3:342–43.
[3] See Smith's Diary, January 17, 1776, note 3.
[4] This committee brought in a report on January 19, which was the basis of an extensive series of resolves adopted by Congress on that and the following day. *JCC*, 4:70–76.

Andrew Allen to
the Pennsylvania Committee of Safety

Sir,   Jany. 19th 1776
    The Committee of Congress appointed to fill up the vacant Offices in the respective Battalions on this Continent find themselves at a Loss how to determine the Merits of the Applicants. There are six vacant Ensigncy's in Col. Bulls Battalion and only four have applied. They desire therefore that the Committee of Safety would be pleased to recommend to them six Gentlemen for the above Vacancies.[1]
    I am Sr. Your most Obedt. Servt.,   Andw Allen

RC (NN). Addressed: "To John Nixon Esqr., Chairman of Commee. of Safety."
[1] For the various appointments in Colonel Bull's battalion that Congress made this date, see *JCC*, 4:69–70.

Samuel Huntington to Jabez Huntington

Philadelphia 19th January 1776. "I arrived at this place the last Monday Morning after a Comfortable Journey Considering the Season. Have nothing remarkable to Communicate at present; as I Suppose before this you will receive the disagreeable News of the Death of the Brave General Montgomery in the unsuccessful attempt to Scale the City of Quebec it is needless to give the particulars."

RC (MH).

George Read

Thomas McKean to George Read

Dear Sir,   Philadelphia Jany. 19th. 1776
I embraced the first opportunity of moving the Congress, after your favor of the 17th came to hand to appoint the Field Officers in the Delaware Battalion and they have accordingly been just now elected by ballot, to wit, John Haslet, Esquire Colonel and Gunning Bedford Esquire as Lieutenant Colonel.[1] Poor Mcpherson is no more—he died like a hero—Colonel Gadsden must tell you the rest. You must fall on some way of recommending a Major or rather two as the Committee of Safety here have done that in every instance lately.

I shall refer you to Colonel Gadsden for all the news, as I dont like to communicate bad news.

My dear Sir you must come up here as soon as you possibly can, for I am almost wore down, being upon Four standing Committees besides occasional ones and owing to the multiplicity of business.[2]

This I write in the Congress and Father Shurman is speaking. Present my best compliments to Mrs. Read and my love to Mr. Thompson's & Mr. O[we]n Leuvenigh's families when you see them. If Mrs. McKean should have gone to Newcastle, be so Kind as to acquaint her I am well. Colonel Gadsden will deliver you the two Commissions, which please to forward.

I am dear Sir, Your most obedt. Servant,   Thos. McKean

Tr (MH). Endorsed: "22 Jany. attended."
[1] See JCC, 4:68–69.
[2] George Read told Caesar Rodney in a letter of this date: "I have just received letters from Messers Andrew Allen and William Hooper requesting your attendance and mine immediately at Congress as there is business of the last importance depending, particularly a Motion the general tenor of which is to declare the Principles on which America had hitherto acted and those which they are disposed still to proceed on. They are extremely pressing, and I totally unprovided as to my business here have determined to be at Philada. this evening and shou'd be glad you wou'd come up immediately." *Parke-Bernet Galleries Catalog*, no. 2569 (May 16, 1967), item 46.

Roger Sherman to Zebulon Butler

Sir,   Philadelphia Jan. 19th. 1776
The enclosed Paper contains several resolutions of the Congress and an Act of the Assembly of Connecticut,[1] Colo. Dyer informs me that he Sent Copies of the Resolves of Congress immediately after they were passed to you and to the Magistrates in the County of Northumberland. We have had an Account of an attack on our people by Some of the Pennsylvanians who were repulsed with the loss of two men killed,[2] but have heard nothing from the Connecticut people relative to that Action

or whether they Sustained any loss. There is a report here that your people have given Some disturbance to the Settlers under Pennsylvania, I Should be Glad of a particular account from you of the Situation of affairs relative to that unhappy controversy which tends to weaken the Union of the Colonies at the present alarming Crisis. I hope you will do all in your power to prevent any disturbance being given to the Settlers under Pennsylvania by our people and that the resolutions of the Congress be duly observed.[3] You will observe that the Assembly of Connecticut have Shortened the western limit of Westmoreland. I would advise that no Jurisdiction be exercised over the Settlers under Pennsylvania with in the limits of P. Town if any be contrary to their mind. Colo. Dyer and Mr. Dean have left Congress, the time they were appointed for being expired, and Oliver Wolcot and Saml. Huntington Esqrs. are now attending in their Stead. You will observe that the Congress have recommended that all the effects taken and detained from any persons on the Controverted lands be restored, it will be proper to [4] apply to the Magistrates who took Cognizance of that matter for restitution or to the Sheriff who had the Goods in Custody, and if they are not restored that the Case be represented to the Congress and if any thing hath been taken from the people of Pennsylvania by the Connecticut people that the same be restored. I am sir with due regards, Your humble Servant,   Roger Sherman

RC (*Parke-Bernet Galleries Catalog*, no. 2569, May 16, 1967, item 53). Tr (DLC). RC incomplete; missing words supplied from Tr.

[1] The congressional resolutions of November 4 and December 20 and 23, 1775, concerned with the territorial dispute between Connecticut and Pennsylvania and the Connecticut act "for altering and further ascertaining the Bounds and limits of the Town of Westmoreland in this Colony," were printed in the *Pennsylvania Journal; and the Weekly Advertiser*, January 3, 1776. For earlier references to the dispute, see Eliphalet Dyer to William Judd, July 23; and Connecticut Delegates' Proposed Resolution, October 17? 1775.

[2] On December 21–22, 1775, Butler's men had defeated an armed expedition under William Plunket that had been ordered by Governor Penn to reestablish Pennsylvania law in the Wyoming Valley. See *Susquehannah Co. Papers*, 5:1–1ii.

[3] A draft "narrative" that Sherman probably wrote about this time, outlining the claims of Connecticut and Pennsylvania to the disputed Wyoming territory and summarizing the disturbances occurring there since July 1775, is printed in *Susquehannah Co. Papers*, 7:28–32.

[4] Remainder supplied from Tr.

Richard Smith's Diary

[January 19, 1776]

Friday 19. The Votes read. A Report made of some Accounts. 5 New Members added to the Comee. of Claims in the Room of so many now absent. 10,000 Dollars advanced to the Commissioners of the Southern

Indian Department. A Report agreed to relative to the procuring of Sailors for South Carolina.[1] The Report for raising 4 new Battals. in N York was confirmed and the Yorkers are desired to recommend at least Two persons for each Office that Congress may take a Choice. A report made from the Comee. on Canadian Affairs, it is resolved to forward the new Levies immedy. & that Gen. Washn. be desired to send a Battalion from his Camp, that another Battaln be raised in Canada, and other parts of the Report were recommitted after an Opinion of Mr. Antills on this Subject had been read. The Papers concerning the Complaint agt. Col Bull were laid on the Table by the Committee who declined making any Report, the Matter was argued and postponed till Tomorrow.[2] The Col. John Haslett, & Lieut. Col. Gunning Bedford of the Lower Counties Battalion were elected. The Comee of this Place are to be requested to assist Mr. Mease in getting Blankets by desiring the Housekeepers to spare each one or Two. Col. St. Clairs Battalion is destined for Canada when compleated. A Motion that the new Troops be inlisted for 3 Years or as long as the War shall continue was opposed by the Northern Colonies & carried in the Negative.[3]

MS (DLC).

[1] See Smith's Diary, January 16, 1776, note 4.

[2] Ibid., January 17, 1776, note 5.

[3] There is no mention of this motion in the journals for this date, nor did Congress subsequently approve military enlistments for the duration of the war until September 16, 1776. *JCC*, 5:762.

Josiah Bartlett to
the New Hampshire Committee of Safety

Gentlemen   Philadelphia Janry 20th 1776

The Congress on the 8th Inst voted to raise one Regiment in the western parts of our Province for the Service in Canada.[1] The news of the Misfortune at Quebeck arriving here last Thursday, They voted yesterday to give the men a Bounty of forty Shillings and one months pay advance, to Encourage the speedy inlisting & Sending forward Said Regiment,[2] and I hope you will do every thing in your power to hasten it, as the taking & Securing Canada this winter or Early in the Spring before the arrival of Brittish troops, will be of almost Infinite advantage to the Continent, more Especially to New England and to our Colony in particular.

One Regiment will begin to march from this place for Canada in a few Days, and one Regiment from New Jersey in 8 or ten Days; orders are also given to raise as Soon as possible for the Same Service (Beside those in New Hampshire) one more Regiment in Pennsylvania, one Do.

New Jersey, one Do. on the western parts of New York, and one Do. in Conectticut, and this Day I Expect one will be ordered to be raised in Massachusetts, for the Same purpose. No Cost or pains must be Spared to Secure the important Province of Canada.

I Beg leave to renew my request, that Delegates may be appointed & Sent here as Soon as may be, as in my opinion the Representation of a Colony at this important Crisis is too weighty and important to be intrusted to any one person. That you may see the necessity of a larger Representation of our colony, I would inform you, that Beside Committees for Special purposes that are frequently Chosen, there are four or five Standing Committees appointed, Some for Secrecy, Some for Dispatch, Some of which Committees are Entrusted with large powers and that there may be no Cause of Complaint, those Committees consist of one Delegate from Each Colony; Sometimes two, Sometimes 3, of those Committees Set at the Same time So that tho' I attend Some one of the Committees almost Every night & morning before & after Congress yet some Business of Consequence is transacted by them without our Colony being Represented, and Sometimes the Committees Set while the Congress is Seting so that our Colony must be unrepresented in one of them, while Every other Colony may be represented in Both.

I have been here almost five months, great part of the time without a Coleague. I really find that I never knew what Confinement with Business was before; and that I want more Exercise of Body & less of mind, at least for Some time; I please my Self with hopes I Shall Soon See Delegates here from our Colony and that I may return to my family, and with my Domestick affairs relax and unbend my fatigued mind.

The Sum of 12500 Dollars which the Congress ordered to be Sent to you, to be used in raising our Regiment for Canada, I shall Send forward as soon as I Can.[3] Please to acquaint me with the Publick affairs of our Colony as often as Convenient, and in particular of your Success from time to time in raising the Regiment. As the Congress have Entrusted you with appointing the officers, I know you will do the best you Can to appoint proper persons, and hope you will be so fortunate as [to] Give General Satisfaction. I am Gentln your most obedient Servant,   Josiah Bartlett

RC (Nh-Ar).

[1] See *JCC*, 4:40.
[2] See *JCC*, 4:71.
[3] See Bartlett to the New Hampshire Committee of Safety, January 24, 1776.

James Duane to Philip Schuyler

Dear Sir   Philad. 20t Jany 1776
Mr Hare of this Town whose Porter and Person you are acquainted

with requests me to procure the necessary accomodations for his Brother's [1] passing from Canada to pay him a Visit.

The young gentleman having an Inclination to see America was advised to embark for Quebec as a place exempt from the Confusions of War. But he had not long been there before it was invested. He retired to some part of the Country where he now remains waiting for Letters from his Brother. I beg leave to enclose you a Note I this moment receivd from Mr Hare on the subject, in Consequence of which I take the Liberty to request you to procure him such a Reception at the different posts as will make his Journey agreeable.

Everybody here feels for the Fate of our brave and worthy Friend Montgomerie. It is deplored as the greatest publick Loss, and you may be assured that Congress will do every honour to his memory which his most sanguine Friends can wish. I have no Time to enlarge on this melancholy Theme which on many Accounts distresses me beyond Expression.

The Express brings you dispatches from Congress to which I refer.

I am with great Respect, Dear Sir, your most Obedient, humble Servant,   Jas Duane

RC (NN).
[1] Richard Hare. See Thomas Lynch to Richard Montgomery, November 14, 1775.

John Hancock to
Michael Hillegas and George Clymer

Philadelphia, January 20, 1776. "Please to pay to the Committee of Safety of Pennsylvania, fifteen thousand Dollars, for the use of the Battalions in Pennsylvania; the said Committee to account for the expenditure of the same." [1]

MS not found; reprinted from *Am. Archives*, 4th ser. 4:523.
[1] See *JCC*, 4:72.

John Hancock to
the New Hampshire Convention

Gentlemen   Philada. January 20th. 1776 [1]

In addition to the resolutions of Congress passed the 8th Inst for the defence of Canada, I have now to add sundry others which the advices lately received, and the repulse our troops met with in their attempt on Quebec, render absolutely necessary to be carried into execution with all possible expedition.[2]

There is every reason to hope that a timely reinforcement will not only secure our Friends and retrieve our losses, but put us in possession of Quebec before succours can reach our enemies.

I am therefore directed most earnestly to press you with all possible expedition to levy & forward the batallion ordered to be raised in your colony. And as you lie the most contiguous I trust from your wonted zeal you will be the first to carry relief & succour.

You will easily conceive what life, spirit and confidence the arrival of but one company will give our friends there, especially when they understand it is quickly to be followed by more forces. You will therefore with the utmost dispatch forward the first that can be got ready.

To prevent any delay, I send inclosed by order of Congress blank commissions for the field officers, captains & subalterns, which you will please to fill up with such gentlemen as you shall judge best qualifyed & proper for the service.

The money for defraying the expence of the batallion will be forwarded by your delegate with all dispatch. The encouragement given to the men, will, I hope, facilitate your business, and I trust your zeal will not be wanting in the defence of our common liberties.

Time will not permit me to enlarge. I must therefore beg leave for other matters to refer you to the enclosed extracts, only reminding you that the batallion is to consist of eight companies, each company of a captain, two lieutenants, one ensign, four sergeants, four corporals, a drum and fife, & 76 Privates. The staff officers, a surgeon, a quarter master, an adjutant, & *a chaplain for every two batallions* with the pay of 33 1/3 dollars.

I have the honour to be, Gentlemen, Your most Obedt Servt,

John Hancock Presidt

RC (Nh-Ar). In a clerical hand and signed by Hancock.

[1] Hancock wrote a similar letter, omitting the last paragraph, to Gov. Jonathan Trumbull of Connecticut on this date. PCC, item 12A; and *Am. Archives,* 4th ser. 4:782.

[2] For the enclosed resolves of Congress, dated January 19 and 20, see *JCC,* 4:70–71, 73–76. In a February 8 letter, Meshech Weare reported the success of New Hampshire in raising the troops. "We hear some companies have marched, and expect the whole battalion, consisting of the number desired, will follow them in a few days." Weare to John Hancock, February 8, 1776, PCC, item 64, fols. 5–6; and *Am. Archives,* 4th ser. 4:964.

John Hancock to
the New Jersey Committee of Safety

Gentlemen   Philadelphia January 20th. 1776.

I am directed by Congress to forward to you the enclosed resolutions,[1] by which you will perceive it is their earnest desire that you should exert your utmost endeavours in forwarding the march of the batallion to Canada.

As another batallion is ordered to be raised in your colony, it is expected you will pursue the most effectual measures for levying the same with all possible expedition, and supplying them with arms, accoutrements and other necessaries. That there may be no delay I am directed to request you to send the names of such gentlemen as you judge best qualifyed at least two for each command out of whom the Congress may elect Field officers for said batallion.[2] Blank commissions will be sent you to fill up with the names of such as you shall please to appoint for officers under the rank of a Major.

I must not omit pressing the necessity of attending to the collecting of Specie an article so necessary just at this juncture, that the safety of America depends upon it. For without it an army cannot at this time be kept up in Canada And the loss of Canada will in all probability involve us in an Indian war.

I am Gentlemen, Your most Obedt servt.,

John Hancock Presidt

[*P.S.*] Please to Deliver the Inclos'd to Lieut Hamar, it carries him the Approbation of Congress to Reside at Strawberry Hill.[3]

RC (NN). In the hand of Timothy Matlack, with signature and postscript by Hancock.

[1] *JCC*, 4:70–71, 73–76.

[2] New Jersey's recommendations for field officers were received and approved by Congress on February 9. *JCC*, 4:123.

[3] See *JCC*, 4:62. See also John Jay to Ibbetson Hamar, November 22, 1775.

John Hancock to
the New York Provincial Convention

Gentlemen,   Jany 20th. 1776.

I have the Honor of enclosing you sundry Resolutions passed by Congress as well for the Defence of your Colony, as for repairing the loss lately sustained in Canada, and succouring our Friends there.[1]

The shortness of the time will not permit me to enlarge. I must therefore beg leave to refer you to the enclosed extracts, and just inform you the Congress rely with Confidence on your zeal for the cause, that you will exert your utmost Endeavours to hasten the march of the troops ordered to Canada, and to raise those destined for the defence of your colony. Herewith I send you blank commissions for the officers under the Rank of majors which you will please to fill up. On the Recommendation of general Schuyler the Congress have continued

Col. V. Schaick, Lieut. colonel Yates and major Gansevoort in the service of the united colonies, and appointed them to the command of the batallion to be raised in your colony for the defence of Canada.[2] And they have directed me agreeable to an established rule to request you would please as soon as possible to Transmitt the names of a Number of gentlemen, whom you shall judge duly qualifyed, at least two for each command out of whom they may elect field officers for the other batallions.[3]

I am Gent[lemen] Your [. . . .]   Joh[n Hancock]

[*P.S.*] I inclose you the Commiss[ion]s for the officers under the Rank of a Major for the Canada Battalion, those for your other Battalions shall follow, as I am pinch'd for time.

RC (N). In the hand of Timothy Matlack, with signature and postscript by Hancock. LB (DNA: PCC, item 12A). RC damaged; missing words supplied from LB.
[1] Apparently the resolves passed January 19 and 20. *JCC*, 4:69–71, 73–76.
[2] Congress made these appointments on January 9, 1776. *JCC*, 4:43.
[3] *JCC*, 4:69. The New York Convention sent its recommendations in a February 28 letter, from which Congress made its selection on March 8. Nathaniel Woodhull to John Hancock, February 28, 1776, PCC, item 67, fols. 180–86; *Am. Archives*, 4th ser. 4:1530–32; and *JCC*, 4:190.

John Hancock to Philip Schuyler

Sir   Philadelphia. Jany. 20t. 1776
On Wednesday Evening Mr. Antill arrived with your Dispatches of the 13t Inst. which were immediately communicated.[1] The Congress sincerely condole with you on the Loss of your amiable Friend, their gallant and much esteemed General.

Having conferred with Mr. Antill and duely deliberated on the Situation of our Affairs in that Quarter, they have come to sundry Resolutions, which I have the Honour to inclose, and which you will please to communicate with the utmost Dispatch to General Wooster as far as they relate to the Defence of Canada or are necessary for his Direction.[2]

The Congress rely with Confidence that he will exert his best Endeavors to keep up the Spirit of his Troops especially when you assure him that every Means will be used with all possible Expedition to succour and support him.

The Batallions from Pennsylvania and New Jersey which were under marching Orders will set forward the Beginning of next Week, and Dispatches are sent to General Washington and to the Colonies of Connecticut and New Hampshire to hasten up Troops from thence.

Enclosed are a Number of Commissions for the Batallions to be raised in Canada, which you will cause to be filled up with the Names of such as you shall deem most suitable. As General Montgomery to whom it was left to recommend proper persons is now no more, you will endeavor to find out the most accomplished and suitable Men for the Canadian Regiments, and such as have an Influence in that Country and are best attached to our Cause. I am with the utmost Respect Sir, Your obedient humble Servant, John Hancock president

Jany 21st. The Companies of the Pennsylvania Batallions will begin their March to Morrow to you.

Tr (NN).
¹ See *JCC*, 4:64. Schuyler's letter is in PCC, item 153, 1:396–98; and *Am. Archives*, 4th ser. 4:666–67.
² See *JCC*, 4:70–71, 73–76.

John Hancock to George Washington

Sir, Philadelphia January 20th. 1776

In my former letter I mentioned the disagreeable news we received from Canada. The Congress have taken that matter under consideration and having examined Mr. Antil and duly deliberated on the situation of our affairs in that quarter they have come to sundry resolutions, which I have the honor to inclose.¹

. I would just observe that by Mr. Antil's examination it appears our loss is greater than what is set forth in the dispatches he brought, a copy of which was transmitted to you. Almost the whole of General Arnolds gallant detachment are taken prisoners having after four hours resistance been obliged to surrender at discretion. However we have the satisfaction to hear that the prisoners are treated with humanity.

The Congress are anxious as well from motives of policy as of justice and humanity to repair our losses in that quarter and if possible to gain possession of Quebec and drive our enemies out of that Country before they can be reinforced in the spring.

An active able general is wanted to take the command there and if such a one can be spared from the service at Cambridge it is their desire you should send one.

The batallion from Pennsylvania and that from New Jersey will set forward the beginning of next week.

As it is of great importance as well for the security and relief of our Friends as for confirming the wavering that speedy succours should arrive, I am directed to request you to detach from the Camp at Cambridge one batallion if the service there will permit you to spare one with orders to march with the greatest expedition possible to Canada.²

If this cannot be done you will at least use your utmost endeavours in stimulating the governor of Connecticut and the convention of New

Hampshire to whom I write by this opportunity to forward with the utmost dispatch the very first that can be raised in those colonies. You can easily conceive what effect the arrival of even one company will have on the minds of our Friends especially when they shall be satisfied that they will soon be followed by more.

The Colony of South Carolina has been so fortunate as to oblige Lord W. Campbell with the armed Vessel to quit their harbour. Being earnestly desirous of providing for their defence they have resolved to fit out some armed vessels but not having seamen among themselves they have dispatched capn Cockran to the Northward to inlist a number of seamen for the service of that Colony.

Lest the offers he was empowered to make might prejudice the service the Congress have chalked out a plan for him to go by, as you will see in the enclosed extracts and I am directed to desire you will please to forward this service.[3]

Yesterday doctor Smith who made his escape from Frederic was brought to this town. He was taken at the little meadows on his way to Detroit & had with him letters from Conolly to the commanding officer there.[4]

I hinted to you in my former letter that the Congress were taking measures for the defence of the middle and southern Colonies. For this purpose over and above those destined for Canada they have ordered four batallions to be raised in New York, two in New Jersey, four in Pennsylvania, one in the counties on Delaware, six in Virginia, three in North Carolina, three in South Carolina, and one in Georgia, each to consist of 728 men including officers making in the whole with those for Canada 34 batallions.

I have the honour to be with the greatest Respect, Sir Your most Obedt. hume servt.,   John Hancock President

[*P.S.*] This Express is Charg'd with a large Packett of Importance for the Colony of New Hampshire, I Request you will please to order it to that Colony by a fresh Express.[5]

I have Taken the Freedom to put under your Cover a Letter for Mr Cushing, respectg. the Buildg Two Ships of Force, I must beg you to Send it him by a safe hand.

Will you be so obliging as when you Send into Boston about Mr Lovell, to suffer the Two Letters from Mr Webster to go in.

Inclos'd is a Commission for Brigr Genl Frye.

RC (DLC). In the hand of Timothy Matlack, with signature and postscript by Hancock.

[1] See *JCC*, 4:70–71, 73–76.

[2] Washington had already ordered the raising of three regiments of militia for Canadian service. Washington to Hancock, January 19 and 30, 1776, PCC, item 152, 1:419–22, 447–54; and Washington, *Writings* (Fitzpatrick), 4:258–61, 286–93.

[3] See *JCC*, 4:59–60, 64, 67–68. Capt. Robert Cochran received permission from

the Massachusetts General Court on February 16 to enlist seamen in that province. *Am. Archives*, 4th ser. 4:1307–8. See also Richard Smith's Diary, January 16, 1776, note 4.

⁴ See *JCC*, 4:72.

⁵ See the letters of Hancock to the New Hampshire Convention and Josiah Bartlett to the New Hampshire Committee of Safety, this date.

Thomas Lynch to Philip Schuyler

Dear Sir   Phila Jany. 20. 1776

Never was any City so universally Struck with grief, as this was on hearing of the Loss of Montgomery. Every lady's Eye was filled with Tears. I happened to have Company at Dinner but none had Inclination for any other Food than sorrow or Resentment. Poor gallant Fellow: if a Martyr's sufferings merit a Martyr's Reward his claim is indisputable. I am sure from the time he left Ticonderoga to the Moment of his release by Death his Suffering had no Interval. He now rests from his Labour and his Works can't but follow him.

The gentlemen who carry this will be able to inform you of the Steps taken for the Relief of Canada & to compleat its reduction, at least what relates to their Canadian Battalions. Two Regiments under excellent & experienced Colonels go from hence, Sinclair & Dehaus, who served all last War in America. The other officers are said to be mostly Gentlemen. Will your Battalion raising for that Service be well officerd. As you have had an opertunity of knowing them by the Test of Experience I don't doubt it will.

Besides the above, 1 Battalion is ordered to be raised & marched directly for that service by New Hampshire & another from Connecticut and a Company of Artillery from each Colony that sends a Battalion thither and two Regiments to be raised in Canada out of the Fragments now there. As you must have been informed, the whole Number is Eight Battalions of Provincials, Livingstons and the New Corps of Canadians, besides those which may be sent from Cambridge.

Congress has ordered the Genl there to send one immediately with a good general if they can be spared. We have just heard from him that he had sent Lee with 700 towards New York for its Defense against an Embarkation of Troops lately from Boston tis said of of 2 Regiments convoyed by 2 twenty gun ships of War. Perhaps they are gone to Charles Town where if they dont Dress them properly it will be their own Faults, having I am assured 160 Cannon mounted from 12 to 42 Pounders.

I had before we heard of our Misfortune resolved to move for a Mode of application for Peace, being assured by Ld. Drummond that Ministry were very desirous of it on very generous Terms, such indeed as I woud have dictated had I them, as they wished to have us, that is at their

Feet. It must wait a little; we cool & Set ourselves on a Footing in Canada.[1]

I have not been able as yet to send you a Committee, as you wish. I will be at them till tis done, unless I have as bad luck as I had on my repeated Motions for Supplies for poor Mongomery with which I as constantly attended Congress as ever Nurse did her Patient with a Bolus, till abt a Month ago when, in Despair, I assured them I shoud never mention it more. Business now goes on Swimmingly: for Why? My Coll[e]ague Gadsden is gone home to Command our Troops, God Save them.

Your Stay will I doubt not return a Triumphant Care with Tories dragged behind to attend your Oration at least if the Prayers of Some honest Whiggs of the Name you have been so kind as to honor can avail any thing. You have our hearty acknowledgements for the Favour. Were the distance not so great one of my Family woud ask the further Favour of being allowed to be God Mother.

We heartily Congratulate you & your Lady on her safe delivery & desire our best Respects to you both and to the young Ladies.

Dear Sir you most affect hume Servt.   Thos Lynch

RC (NN).
[1] See Lord Drummond's Notes, January 3–9? 1776, note 1.

Richard Smith's Diary

Saturday 20 Jany. [1776]

The Remainder of the Report about Canada was agreed to, Washington is to detach a General Officer there, the ruling Powers in every Colony are to collect all the Gold and Silver they can for the Service in Canada and 6 or 7 other Articles.[1] Blank Commissions for the New Regiments are ordered to New Hampshire & Connectt. for the greater Dispatch. Report of Sundry Accots. liquidated by the Comee. of Claims, this Comee. reminded the Congress of Leonard Snowden who was imprisoned here for being concerned with Dr. Kearsley & others in traiterous Practices & he, Snowden, was ordered to be released. A Petition was brought in from Capt. Duncan Campbell praying to be discharged from Jail on his Parole, it was not attended to. Some Powder was ordered for those Companies of Maxwell's who are ready to march to Canada & Tim. Matlack was directed to furnish them with Ball & Flints.[2] Tim. is a Commissary & Clerk in Chief to our Comee. of Claims (this Person who it is said was once a Quaker Preacher is now Col. of the Battalion of Rifle Rangers at Philadelphia). Col. Bull now thought proper to resign his Commission by Writing addressed to the Congress. An Express was ordered to Gen. Wooster at Montreal with Copies of our Votes & to inform of the immediate Succors intended, and the same Express to call on the Comee. of Safety in Jersey.

Sunday [January 21] I went to Burlington.[3]

MS (DLC).

[1] See Smith's Diary, January 18, 1776, note 4.

[2] This day Timothy Matlack sent Hancock a brief note saying that he did not have in his possession the "quantity of ball or lead proportioned to 300 wt of Powder" which Congress had directed him to forward to the New Jersey delegates for the use of Colonel Maxwell's battalion. At the foot of this note Hancock wrote Matlack the following reply: "Mr. Matlack, The Congress desire you would please to purchase a sufficiency of Ball, wch. it was said was to be Sold in this City, & your Bill shall be immediately paid. They look on you as their Commis[sar]y. Yours, J. Hancock." New Jersey Letters, NjR. Matlack (1736–1829), Pennsylvania merchant, militia officer, and assistant to Secretary Thomson, subsequently was a delegate to Congress in 1780. *DAB;* and *Bio. Dir. Cong.*

[3] Smith was in Burlington January 21–23.

Silas Deane to Elizabeth Deane

Philadelphia Jany 21st. 1776. "I wrote Yesterday by Col. Dyer, which you will probably not receive before This comes to hand, he set off in a Violent hurry Yesterday morning & my Boy with him, as farr as Newark, in my Phaeton, from whence he agreed, to shift for himself.

"I have not sat in Congress since last Tuesday when with pleasure, I gave place to my Successor of whom as Our Neighbor says, *I say Nothing.* But of my Old Colleague, Sh——n[1] suffice it to say, that if the order of Jesuits is extinct, their practises are not out of fashion, even among *modern New Light Saints,* or some of them, for I will never particularize any Sect."

Comments on Connecticut politics and continues: "Col. Dyer plead, scolded, fretted, & even threatened Me to make me set out for home with him, & finally parted rather in an ill humour with Me because I would not give him, all the reasons for my tarrying, conclude it will occasion some Speculation and almost wish to know what reasons he assigns for my tarrying behind. The ostensible reason, and a very good one Too, is the Necessity of my tarrying to close the Naval Accts., and assist in getting forward the preparations for the Fleet in the coming Season."

RC (CtHi). *Collections of the Connecticut Historical Society,* 2 (1870): 349–51.

[1] Roger Sherman.

Samuel Ward to Anna Ward

My dearest [1]   Philadelpa. 21st Jany. 1776
    Blessed be God your dear Bror. of whom I never heard one Word
from the Time he left Fort Weston until last Thursday is alive, and
well and hath behaved well. Here is a Gentn. who saw him the Day
before the Attack upon Quebec. He had been very ill with the yellow
Jaundice but one Capt. McClean formerly of Boston took him home &
cured him & this Gentn. tells me he was happy to go upon that Service.
General Montgomerie was killed & his Troops immediately retired
which left the whole Force of the Enemy to attack your Kinsman
Lt. Colo. Greene [2] who upon Arnolds being wounded & carried off
led the Detachment on nobly. They carried two Barriers, attacked the
third & fought gloriously with much superior Forces under Cover also.
Four Hours after being overpowered with Numbers they were compelled to surrender Prisoners of War & are very kindly treated. I have
wrote by Express to your Bror. & shall send him some Money. [3] Call
upon all that owe us for some, I shall want it much.
    Write immediately to Colo. Greene's Wife that he is well & treated
with great Humanity, he has acquired vast Honor in the Service and
I doubt not will soon be exchanged. In the mean time I have wrote
Sammy to let him know that his Family is well and that if he wants
any Money he may draw upon me & I will punctually pay it.
    Why have I had no Letters for a long while from home. Surely some
of you might write every week. See that it is done & let Me know
every thing of Importance. [4] God bless you all. Your affece. Father,
                                                          Sam Ward

P.S. In Colo Greenes Detachment there were 120 killed & wounded,
near half killed. Troops begin their March from here to Morrow to
reinforce our Army in Canada.

RC (MWA).
    [1] The recipient of this letter is incorrectly identified as Catherine Greene in Ward,
Correspondence (Knollenberg), pp. 177–78, where the text is taken from a Tr made
in 1842, although curiously enough a deleted endorsement on this Tr specifically
states: "*The original was addressed to Miss Nancy Ward, Westerly R. Island.*"
    [2] Christopher Greene, Ward's son-in-law, was lieutenant colonel of the First
Rhode Island Regiment in which Samuel Ward, Jr., served as a captain. Greene
and Ward, Jr., both had volunteered for service with Col. Benedict Arnold's Canadian expeditionary force. Ibid., p. 35. See also Ward to Catherine Greene, November 13, 1775, note 1.
    [3] Ward's letter of this date to Samuel Ward, Jr., is in Ward, *Correspondence* (Knollen-
berg), pp. 175–77.
    [4] Ward wrote another letter to Anna on January 24, in which he simply repeated
much of the information about Samuel, Jr., contained in this letter. NjMoHP.

John Hancock to the Trenton Committee

Gentlemen   Philadelphia Jany 22d. 1776
   Your Letter of 19th Inst. Sign'd by your Honl President being duly
receiv'd, was laid before Congress, and is Referr'd for Consideration to
a Committee.[1] When the Congress have Come to a Determination
thereon, I shall take the earliest Opportunity of Communicating the
same to you. I inclose the two Blank Commissions mention'd in your
Letter.
   Coll. Wyncoop having reported to Congress that he had Escorted a
Number of officers who are Prisoners to Trenton, among whom are
Brigadr General Prescott, and a Capt Chace who lately Commanded
the Gaspy Arm'd Vessell in Canada, I am Directed by Congress to
Desire you will immediately Send those two Gentn. under a proper &
sufficient Guard to this City for the further order of Congress.[2] This
you will please to Effect in such a manner that no previous Notice of
your Design may Reach the Gentlemen mention'd, so as to prevent the
wish of Congress being Carried into Execution.
   I have the honour to be with Esteem, Gentlemen, Your most Obedt
sevt.,   John Hancock Presidt.

RC (NBLiHi).
   [1] This letter, containing a request made by British prisoners quartered at Trenton,
is in PCC, item 68, fols. 35–38, and *Am.. Archives*, 4th ser. 4:772. For Congress'
response to this request, see *JCC*, 4:77, 115–16, 213, 220.
   [2] Richard Prescott and Robert Chase arrived in Philadelphia on January 25, and
on January 29 Congress ordered Prescott imprisoned in Philadelphia and Chase
remanded to Trenton. *JCC*, 4:89, 101. See also Samuel Tucker to John Hancock,
January 23, 1776. PCC, item 68, fol. 47; and *Am. Archives*, 4th ser. 4:814.

Francis Lightfoot Lee to Landon Carter

My dear Col.   Philadelphia Jan 22d 1776
   Having very little to communicate except our unfortunate attempt
upon Quebec; a particular Account of which I have given to our mutual
friend Col. Tayloe; I shou'd not now Trouble you, but to convince you
that our correspondence shall not be broken off on my pàrt. I hope
Ld. Dunmore has left you spirits enough, Still to enjoy a little Xmas
mirth, and to give him a warm reception, if he shoud venture up Rapa.
A few days agoe, a plan was formed in our Army at Cambridge, to
burn about a dozen houses, the remains of Charles Town, beyond
the Enemies fortifications on Bunker's Hill which they used as barracks for part of their troops. It was effected in the night, & 7 prisoners
taken. The Enemy was thrown into the greatest confusion & a universal
firing, from all quarters, on every side & in the Air, continued a considerable time, to the great entertainment of our men, who came off

unhurt.[1] We have not yet got powder to effect any thing considerable in that quarter; And I fear the proper season will be over, before we shall. The French & Spaniards do not seem inclined to furnish us with military stores. Their politics plainly tend to drive us to extremity, that we may be forced to break off all connection with G. B. and join with them, which they know nothing but hard necessity can ever effect. Indeed the Ministry appear determined to leave us no alternative, but absolute submission, or foreign assistance. Which will be your choice my friend? Will it not be wise, in time to leave a people who are so corrupt, that their ruin must be inevitable?

I wish all happiness to Sabine Hall and [remain?] at all times my dear Colonel's afft. Respectfull Servant,   Francis Lightfoot Lee

RC (NjR: Elsie O. and Philip D. Sang deposit).

[1] Washington had included an account of this incident in his January 11 letter to President Hancock, which was read in Congress on January 22. See *JCC*, 4:77; and Washington, *Writings* (Fitzpatrick), 4:229–30.

Oliver Wolcott to Philip Schuyler

Sir   Philadelphia 22d Janry 1776
Your Letter to Congress respecting the unfortunate Death of General Montgomery and the Disaster of his Troops peirced every Heart. I sincerely Sympathize with you the Loss of that brave officer. I know your affliction must be great for in him you have lost a most Valuable Freind and an officer in whom you deservedly put the greatest Confidence—but Such is Heavens Will, and let us Acquiesce in the Divine Providence. What Aid Congress Mean to give the Northern Army you have. I hope a steady Attention will be given to that important Affair. We have no special News. The Congress are Very Busy and like to continue So. Sundry Members call on Me for the Journal of Our last Indian Negotiation. Your busy Attention to Other Matters, I can easily believe occasion its not being sent, but Wish it might be forwarded to me so that it might be laid before Congress, as soon as conveniently might be, together with an Acco. of Expenditures.[1] I suppose a Representation and Evidence how the Susquehannah affair came to be introduced into the August Treaty will be Transmitted to Congress.[2] Whatever Commands you shall give me at Philadelphia shall cheerfully comply with. Wishing you Sir the Establishment of Health, I Am sir, your most obediant, humble Servt.,   Oliver Wolcott

RC (NN).

[1] Schuyler's response was contained in his letter to President Hancock of March 19, 1776. PCC, item 153, 2:57–60; and *Am. Archives*, 4th ser. 5:415–16.

[2] Wolcott was probably referring to a letter to Congress that his fellow Indian

commissioners for the Northern Department had drafted at their December 1775 meeting, in which they charged that Turbutt Francis, one of the commissioners, was responsible for introducing the Susquehannah issue into the treaty negotiations with the Indians at Albany in August 1775. Apparently this letter was not included with the papers related to Indian affairs that Schuyler enclosed in his March 19 letter to Congress, and there is no evidence that it was ever formally presented to Congress. A petition from Francis was referred to a committee in June, but the committee failed to gain the cooperation of the Indians and was subsequently discharged. *JCC*, 4:240, 415, 5:458. The commissioners' draft letter was included in an extract of their proceedings, which is printed in *Susquehannah Co. Papers*, 6:416–20. See also Turbutt Francis' letter of April 23, 1776, to Schuyler and Volkert P. Douw, ibid., 7:11–12; and Wolcott to Timothy Edwards, November 29, 1776.

Josiah Bartlett to Mary Bartlett

My Dear   Philadelphia Janry 24th 1776
    Yours of the 6th Inst. I Received the 22nd & as I had not Received any letter from you Since yours of the 7th of December, it gave me great pleasure to hear you & my family were well the 6th of this month; I hope you & they Still Continue So. I am by the favor of kind providence in health at this time. I have been lately a little troubled with a pain in my head, owing I Suppose to my being So long Confined without any Bodily Exercise. As the Days grow longer I Design Every Day before or after Congress to ride or walk an hour or two; I have 2 or 3 Days this week, after the Congress rose walked from 5 to 6 of the Clock. At four the Congress Comonly rise, Dine by 5, walk till Six, then on a Committee till 8, 9 or 10: this is Comonly my Business Every Day.
    I have wrote to our Convention at Exeter to request them to Send Delegates here, which I hope they will Comply with; as soon as they arrive here, I shall prepare to return home. Remember me to All the Children, to Col Greely, Mr Procter, and all friends. I hope Capt Calef has hired me a good faithful hand. Give my Kind regards to him and tell him I am glad to hear he has Success in making Salt petre.
    Tell Polly and Lois I Recd their letter and shall write to Mr Sweat about the powder mill. I am, yours &c,   Josiah Bartlett

P.S. The Express is going So Soon I Can't write to Samuel Sweat but will Endeavor to next week.

RC (NhHi).

Josiah Bartlett to
the New Hampshire Committee of Safety

Gentm   Philadelphia Janry 24th 1776
    The Congress ordered me to Send you the Sum of Twelve Thousand

five hundred Dollars for the use of the Regiment to be raised for Canada.[1] I have agreed with Mr. Wheat of Conecticut (who Carries the Same Sum to Conecticut) to Deliver it to you or to Col Gilman the treasurer at Exeter for which he is to have thirty Six Dollars, which you will please to pay him & take his Recept which Recept you will Enclose to me that I may Receive the Same out of the Continental treasurer, as the money is to be Sent on the Cost of the Continent. I am Gentm yours   Josiah Bartlett

P.S. As I was not Certain whither the president had Sent you the Resolves of Congress of the 17th I have Enclosed them.[2] The ten Shillings mentioned is this Currency, Equal to Eight Shillings L[awful] M[oney].   J. B.

RC (Nh-Ar). Addressed: "The Provincial Committee of Safety or to Nicholas Gilman, Esq., Colony Treasurer."
  [1] See *JCC*, 4:74.
  [2] See *JCC*, 4:63.

John Dickinson's Notes for a Speech in Congress

[January 24? 1776] [1]
Some Authority of the Parent State over Colonies from the Nature of Things. E.g. Justice. What is it—Original Circumstance to be recover'd. Settlement under *Permission—protection—*on *Lands according to the then prevailing Notions of publick Law the property of Mother Country*.
    1. Permission. Discovered by English Subjects Cabot & Hudson. Every Colony settled under Grant; from English Crown. It is said Massachusetts Bay was not—Nay, that they settled *against* the Consent of the King & People of England. Denied—settled under the Plymouth Company. See Hutchinson [2] & W. Logan's Pamphlet.[3] The Evidence indisputable, proved by the Series of Transactions from that Day to this. But suppose Massachusetts Bay was settled against Consent. It is the Case of a single Colony. This is a Common Cause. We must assume principles suited to *all*. What was the Case of *all* the other Colonies? Unquestionably under the permission of the Mother Country.
    2. Protection. The History of every Colony proves this protection was always looked up to—Always in Effect—sometimes in Act. Can it be imagined We should have been so little disturbed by other powers— if it had not been for the Claims & Fear of the English. Remember the Case of the French on one side—the Dutch on the other—how extensive. What prevented those Claims from being extended—& those of the Dutch being at Length extinguished very early in the Course of our Settlement & thereby gave Relief from that Quarter a Century ago to the New England Colonies? The Power & Protection of England.

3. On Lands then the supposed property of England. A Question has been made What Right European Nations took by Discovery by their Subjects or Persons navigating under their Authority & the Extention of that Right into the Country. That is one Question not necessary to be discussed on the present Occasion. I incline to think no European Nation took any Right whatever by such Discoveries. If the Objects held up by the European Nations of spreading the Light of the Gospel among the ignorant Natives had been the Principle of those Discoveries & the consequent possession—& if that grand Object could not [have] been attempted without the European Nations obtaining a property in part of the Country—there might more be said in Favor of their Right. But that was not the *Cause*. It was only a *Patina*. Ambition & Love of Gain were the Causes—& so far from [instructing?] in Truth or improving in Morality, We have only super[added?] European [bias?] on [Indian?] Errors.

Whether this Question be determined on one side or the other is immaterial on the present Occasion. It is no more to the Point than whether the Title of the great Mogul is Cousin to the Sun or Brother to the Moon & Stars. The true Question is—What was the Idea of an European Right at the Time of Emigration & Settlement between the Emigrants & the Country from which they emigrated, for as all legal Government is founded on express or implied Compact, no [. . .] can lead us so plainly to the knowledge of that Compact where not express, as those Ideas manifested by both Parties at that Time.

I say then, that at that Time, the Emigrants believed they were settling on Lands then reputed to belong to the Crown of England. They settled under that Idea, with express permission of that Kingdom, under her expected & afterward frequently requested & sometimes actually obtained Protection. There was then some Tie, some Bond, some Connection springing ex Visceribus of the Transaction. And whatever that Tie or Bond or Connection was it must remain in Force, untill it be utterly dissolv'd by some absolute Necessity that by superior Power—either of hostile Interference, or the great first Law of self preservation. As to the last—However unhappy our Situation—I believe this Assembly does not chuse at present to determine that the Connection is thus dissolv'd. As to the first—it has not taken Place. Things must therefore be considered upon the Ground of the Original Connection.

I would explain this Idea, by comparing to a Case of our municipal Law, which will shew, that Things standing as they did at first, the Obligation between the Parties continued whatever Errors either or both of them were under at the Time of Compact. The principle is sufficient for Elucidation tho it may run on all four.

Lease by Trade—by a Man who has not a legal Title—good between them unless Lessor enters or the Lessee be ejected by him who has the Title.

We at this Day enjoy the Grant—in part disolv'd indeed, but We will not say the Lease is entirely broken. And I think it will do no Credit to our Cause at this Time of Day, to pry for Flaws into the Title of our Lessors, and upon the pretence to withhold those Rents which We & our Ancestors have ever been accustomed to pay.

This Ground of the American Cause is not tenable. We must be driven from it. Let us retreat to another position & see if We can make a stand there. A Stand has been made there. I wish it had not.

If We settled under any Permission and Protection & on Lands belonging to any European Power, It was with the Permission under the Protection & on Lands belonging to the King [4]—not to the Crown of England—it will be said.

A very extraordinary Doctrine indeed.

These Colonies settled chiefly under the Stuarts before the Union of England & Scotland. Did the King at any Time grant Permission or Charter as King of Scotland. Did he or any Man living at that Time suppose he had any pretence of Right or Claim as King of Scotland? Suppose England & Scotland had continued during all that Period of Emigration & Settlement distinct Kingdoms under different Monarchs, would the King of Scotland [have] made the least pretence to Right on the Coast of These Colonies? No. The Kings of G. B. had Officers of State for both Kingdoms. Did those of Scotland interfere at any Time in the slightest Manner with the Affairs of America? No. All past thro the Hands of the officers of the Realm of England.

But it may be said—he had the Right such as it was as King in his own person. This is to Me incomprehensible. If he had it as King he had it in a Capacity relative to some People or Country of which he was *King*. If he had it in his own person, abstractly, so to speak, he had it not *as King*—He had it as James Stuart or Charles Stuart. It will not be said expressly he had it thus, tho the Consequences deduced from the premises, demonstrate, that those [Premises?] mean this, or they mean nothing.

The Rights of a King can be no more than what are assigned to him in the Constitution of that State of which he is King. He is part of that Constitution of Government. He is the highest Magestrate—or rather servant of the State. When the King is spoken of, ex vi terminis he is intended in that relative Capacity. This is the Doctrine of Locke, Blackstone, & every distinguished English Author, who has written on Government. Quotations might be [summoned?]. They are needless here.

Gentlemen seem not to be aware of the Consequences of this Doctrine. It strikes at the Foundation of all legal Government which must be founded on express or implied Compact—as is now acknowledged by British Subjects—and formed for the Welfare of the People. By· inevietable Deduction the kingly Office can be considered solely as an Institution for Promoting that Welfare—as a Member of the Constitu-

tion. To consider him as vested with Rights *as King* not assigned him
by the Constitution, is to unhinge that Constitution form'd on its broad
& solid Basis of public Wellfare. It is to overset it. It is to establish a
new & inconsistent Principle of Authority—taken from what source I
know not. For if all the Rights of a King are not assigned him by the
Constitution for the purpose intended by Divine Providence of promoting the Good of his Creatures by the Establishment of Governments,
From whence does he derive his Rights? Are they inherent in his person
jure divino? The notion is exploded. *Who* bestowed any other Rights
upon him or *when* did he obtain them? James 1st was King of Scotland
before he was King of England. Had he these extraordinary Rights
then? No. He past the Tweed on the Death of Elizabeth. Did he get
them then? Yes. And do these Rights, by some Inchantment of Nature
only grow in those soils, where Thistles cannot grow? This is a kind of
Magic with which I am utterly unacquainted. It is common sense, & I
can understand very well, that he had Rights as Monarch of England
which he had not as Monarch of Scotland. But how his legal Succession
to the Crown of England could give him Rights not referrable to &
derived from the Crown of England I cannot understand, No more
than I can form an Idea of a Man, "without Stature, Feature, Colour,
Hands, Head, Feet, or any Body." I can compare it to nothing but
the Phantom raised by Juno to save her favorite Turnus—"tenuem
sine viribus umbram," "sine mente sonum." [5]

Sir, I repeat the Question *when* were these extraordinary Rights annexed to the King, of contracting *as King* with English Subjects & yet
not as King of England. Sir, this new Doctrine strikes not only at the
Foundation of all legal Government as mentioned but it is a two edged
Sword that cuts against the Constitutions of these Colonies directly &
immediately. It destroys all those Evidences of· English Rights—contained in every Grant, Charter, Constitution & Recognition of those
Rights from the Beginning of Colonization to this Day—so much relied
on as vouchered by all these Colonies. If the Right universally admitted
in those first Days of Colonization that the King of England had no
Right to grant these Lands, notwithstanding the general opinion—We
give the [. . .] & most decisive Judgment against ourselves to the Objection that the King by his Grant of Charters at that Time, could not
grant Us Charters that should be valid against the Claims of Parliament
notwithstanding the universally acknowledged and undisputed Prerogative of the Crown at that Time to grant such Charters. Let us take the
First of Charles 1st—who granted the first Charter to the Massachusetts
Bay—& go back to that Instant of Time when Application was made
to him for a Grant to settle in that Colony—The Application of the
Brownists in Holland offering a settlement on Hudson's River. He was
then prior to that Grant, King of England. The appliers were English
Subjects—the Land applied for descended to the King from his Father.

His Father came to the legal possession of it a few years before—in Consequence of his Succession to the English Crown, for it had been vested in the *English Crown* several Ages *before* that Succession took Place.

Here was a Contract to be formed by an English King with English Subjects for English Lands—Yet had all this Transaction no Reference to the *Crown of England?* It is incredible. The Appliers were then Subjects of the *English Crown*. Their Design was not to change their Sovereignty. They dared not to have Proposed to the King, to dissolve the then subsisting Allegiance to him as King of England & substitute another Allegiance to him as King of the Territory of the Plymouth Company—without any other Connection with the Realm of England than they had with Scotland, that is, having the same King.

Their Colony was not *then* settled. They could not *then* say—"Your Majesty *is* the King of our Colony—by Virtue simply of the Blood royal that flows in your veins." They could not *then* say—"We *are not* Subjects of the English Crown, and the Allegiance We owe You *is not* due from Us as Englishmen." They could not *then* say—"The Lands We petition to have granted to Us, *at this Instant*, so absolutely belong to the imperial House of Stuart, that your Majesty may grant them to Us English Subjects unfettered by any Regard for the English Laws, Constitution, & in such Manner if You think Proper, as may tend to the Injury or even Destruction of that Kingdom."

Sir, They were under the indisputable Obligation of Ties & Truths, that at that Time, must have closed their Lips in profound silence on those Points. They applied to the King of England or they applied to no King. They applied as English Subjects owing Allegiance to the King of England or they applied as no Relation whatever to him. And how the Execution of the Contract could wholly annihilate those Ties & Truths instantaneously preexistent to its Completion I cannot apprehend. They took their Grant under the great Seal of England & constantly applied afterwards to the Company in England.

Sir, I have heard this Distinction supposed by the Exploitation of that Pretense for excusing Treason by a difference between the person & political Capacity of the King. The Case applies not. It Proves only that the *Crime* of Treason cannot be committed against the King without being committed against his Person. They are so mixt that as to Offences against him they cannot be distinguished & therefore the Pretense failed for Cause. The Case of Acts against the King is different from the Case of Acts by the King. The distinction was futile. But the Question here is in what Capacity the King acted & how he could act unless as King of England. It was said in Calvin's Case that Allegiance was due to the King's natural Body. It was a wise saying—it was calculated to avoid the same Question which Englishmen avoid—That Resistance to the King is justifiable. Our Law does not expressly authorize yet our Constitution admits it—And to shew that the Notion is just is to be thus qualified. I would instance the Revolution—Was Allegiance due to James 2d after that Period? Some will say it was—then Allegiance is due not strictly to the natural Body of the King. It is a Doctrine if thus strictly applied, that is destructive of the Constitution. It is best answered by the Case of the poor Peasant who saw an Arch Bishop in Arms as a General &c.

I have heard the Case of Crown Lands compar'd to this Case & an Inference drawn, that because the King could alienate them he may alienate these Colonies. *Answer*—I acknowledge the Constitution allowed him as King of England to alienate Crown Lands if the Alienations were valid.

I have heard that these Colonies are so vested in the King, that he might legally alienate any of them, without Consent of Parliament—& therefore they belong to him personally. Answer—If he could so alienate as King of England it is because the Constitution of England allow'd him so to do—if legally the Laws of England declare it so—if by the Word "legally" be not meant the Laws of England the Question is shifted & We embrace a Cloud. It is like many other Cases where the King may exercise his Prerogative without Consent of Parliament. If the King could alienate them on the Conclusion of a war Does it follow he could alienate them any other way. If he could to England [still?] does it follow he could alienate them to others? If only to them, as is the Case, it was still as Sovereign of England. &c.

But We never have been so alienated. We cannot be. All Pacifications now approv'd by Parliament. To regard the several Grants or Charters under which We have settled as such *absolute Alienations*, is begging the Question.

I am perfectly astonished to find that Gentlemen of such surpassing Abilities & most respectable & indisputable worth, should so strongly confide in Propositions so subversive of the Principles of legal Government—and so utterly inconsistent with that grand Principle on which this important Constroversy has been always conducted. To be attributed to oppression & Resentment. It is the Excess of their Virtue has carried them such Lengths.

We have from one End of the Continent to the other repeatedly & solemnly declared, that We derive our Blood from the Blood of Englishmen—that our political Connection is with the people of that Kingdom—that between them & us subsists that Bond of Union which We wish may never be dissolv'd. We look to that Body at this Time for Relief, when all the Formal Power of the Constitution & Government are inimical. We resort to the Original Source of all Power in England and in these Colonies—the People of England—& yet hold it an essential of our political Creed—that We have no other Constitutional Connection with that People but that We happen to have the same King—that is—than We have with the Hanoverians or than formerly subsisted between the People of England & the Dutchy of Aquitaine? Some *other* Connection there must be in Common Sense, Justice & Equity.

Sir, I know the Dread Gentlemen entertain of admitting Parliamentary Authority in a single Instance because it inferrs a Supreme Authority or Sovereignty. I utterly deny the Consequence. The supreme Legislation of Parliament I also deny. The Right of Regulation I admit. They differ as much as the old & new Testaments. The one may be said to contain the Fall of Man—the other his Salvation.

MS (PHi). In the hand of John Dickinson. Endorsed: "Arguments in Congress to prove the Dependance of the Cols. on G.B." These notes are strikingly cryptic and are strewn with abbreviations which have been expanded without brackets in this text.

[1] The arrival in Philadelphia on January 8 of the text of the king's speech from the throne of October 26, 1775, accusing Americans of aiming at independence, was a fresh blow to conservatives struggling to curb the spread of support for independence. In response, several delegates supported a motion offered by James Wilson on January 9 formally denying the king's charge, but opponents succeeded in having action postponed to January 12 and subsequently to the 24th, when the subject was apparently debated at length and a committee—consisting of Robert Alexander, John Dickinson, James Duane, William Hooper, and James Wilson— was appointed "to prepare an address to the inhabitants of the United Colonies." *JCC*, 4:87.

In addition to the diary of Richard Smith—the chief source of information pertaining to these developments—letters of Samuel Adams and George Read also reveal that the resumption of debate on Wilson's motion was regarded as a crucial test and perhaps the last opportunity to secure congressional endorsement of an explicit statement affirming American dependence on the crown and desire for reconciliation. Adams believed that Congress had already been explicit enough in stating its goals, and was "apprehensive we might get ourselves upon dangerous ground" explaining "the principles & grounds of our opposition." Others, however, thought that the issue was one "of the last importance"; and since Read had returned home to Delaware, Andrew Allen and William Hooper urged him to return to Philadelphia before the debate resumed. See Richard Smith's Diary, January 9 and 24; Samuel Adams to John Adams, January 15; and Thomas McKean to George Read, January 19, 1776, note 2.

The substance of these notes suggests that Dickinson drafted them for the delivery of a speech given on January 24, when according to Smith "much was said about Independency and the Mode and Propriety of stating our Dependance on the King." It also seems clear that this was the occasion of one of Dickinson's least effective performances and represented another milestone in the decline of his influence in Congress. From an early date some delegates believed that he was prone to lecture them and often became "lengthy" in developing elaborate and overly subtle arguments concerning tangential issues. Surely few delegates could have believed that at this late date Americans were interested in an excessively legalistic review of the nature of colonial dependency or that the position Dickinson herein developed could become the basis for a congressional statement defending American rights. It does nevertheless reveal many of the elements of his thought and the limited appeal of the position that he was attempting to defend at this relatively late date in the dispute with Britain.

For further information on Dickinson's activities early in 1776 in behalf of reconciliation, see also his proposed "Resolutions" and "Instructions" which have been

printed above under the date January 9–24? 1776, and his Draft Address to the
Inhabitants of America which follows the present entry.

[2] Apparently a reference to Thomas Hutchinson's work *The History of the Colony
of Massachusets-Bay, from the First Settlement Thereof in 1628, until its Incorporation with
the Colony of Plimouth, Province of Main. &c., by the Charter of King William and Queen
Mary, in 1691* (Boston: Thomas & John Fleet, 1764), in which a discussion of Massachusetts' origins and relationship to the "Plymouth Company" is found on pp. 5–13.

[3] Efforts to determine the meaning of this reference have been unsuccessful.

[4] In the margin opposite this passage in the MS, Dickinson wrote "nor Bond with
the People."

[5] "Tenuem sine viribus umbram" (a powerless and insubstantial shade), Virgil
Aeneid 10.636; "sine mente sonum" (a mindless sound), ibid. 10.640.

John Dickinson's Draft Address
to the Inhabitants of America

[January 24? 1776] [1]
How far We have discharged it with skill, must be determined by
You, who are our Principals and Judges, to whom We esteem it our
Duty as faithful Servants, to render an Account of our Conduct, our
Motives, the situation of our Affairs, and the Ends We have kept and
still keep in View. [2]

We think it unnecessary to recapitulate all the Circumstances of the
present unhappy Controversy with G B, previous to our appointment.
They have been so frequently and fully [discussed?] in several Publications, that we shall content ourselves with recommending to your
Perusal for particular Information on that subject, the Address made
to You by the late Congress.

In brief, the Sentence of universal Slavery has gone forth against
You, declaring, "that his Majesty in Parliament hath a *Right* to bind
You by Statutes & Laws *in all Cases whatsoever*." Your Fortunes, your
Liberties, your Lives—every Thing that can render You or your
Posterity happy—all are the Objects of Laws: all must be enjoyed,
impaired, or destroyed, as the Laws direct. From this monstrous &
detestable position just [. . .] Parliament inferrs, that You are a miserable People, the lowest Class of Wretches in human shapè, who have
nothing, that *of Right* You *can* or *ought* to call *your own*. All the Bounties
of Nature, all the Blessings of Providence, your Health, your Strength,
the Fertility of your Country, the Commerce of your ports, the Riches
of your Seas & Rivers, the Profits of your Industry, Prudence & Virtue,
all these they contend, were not design'd for your own Use, but for the
use of those, [3] who by some inexplicable Mistery of Politics, in opposition
to all Reason, Equity & Humanity, hold an unbounded & superriding
Authority over your persons and consequently over every possession
You have accustomed to consider as *belonging* to Your persons. The

Acts of Parliament for *taxing* You against your Consent, for *shutting up* the Port of Boston, *indemnifying the "Murderers"* of the Inhabitants of the *Massachusetts Bay* and [altering?] their *chartered* Constitution of Government, for altering the Government of *Quebec*, thereby depriving the People of an Assembly, trials by Jury and the English Laws, and extending the Limits of that province so as to comprehend those vast Regions that lye adjoining to the northernly & westernly Boundaries of these Colonies, are all parts of the grand System of Operations lately concerted for carrying that direful Sentence into Execution with full Effect.

Before We assembled in last *May*, and while You were waiting patiently for the Result of his Majesty's Determinations in Parliament on the humble & dutiful Petition from the late Congress, which one of the principal Secretaries of State told our Agents, "was a decent one & had been graciously received," the answer was unexpectedly written in Letters of Blood at *Lexington* and *Concord* by the unprovoked Murder of our brave Fellow Citizens.

War having been thus wantonly and cruelly begun by our Enemies, We met together at *Philadelphia*.

Immediately taking the State of these Colonies into our most serious Consideration, and having no other Objects in View, than their *Defence* and *Preservation* against the *Force actually employed* for executing the destructive System before mentioned, and the Restoration of the former Harmony with G.B., these Resolutions were formed. (Here insert the Resolutions beginning with these Words, *"Resolved unanimously"* inclusively in pa. 62 to the Words "the King" in pa. 64—inclusively.)

Knowing, that we represented a People who preferr'd Death to servitude, a People whose Loyalty to their Sovereign and whose Affection to their British Fellow subjects on the other side of the Atlantic, all the Outrages of Administration had not extinguished, We endeavoured to combine their magnanimous and generous Sentiments in our Determinations.

In order to render your Resistance successful as to the objects of the war already pointed out, and also to defend You as much as possible from Suffering in the Course of it, we not only employed a large Army in the Colony of *Massachusetts Bay*, then actually invaded by your Enemies, and a smaller one in the Colony of New York, which we expected to be soon invaded; but have used our utmost Industry to put the Militia of all the Colonies upon the best footing, to import arms and military Stores from foreign Countries & to promote the Manufactory of those Articles on this Continent. We can with Truth, and with a Pleasure of which every worthy American may be sensible, inform You, that our Counsels have been prosecuted with such spirit & Prudence by all Ranks of People, but more especially by the several Assemblies, Conventions, Councils of Safety & Committees of Observation, whose Zeal & Wisdom merit the highest Applauses from all Lovers of their Country, that these Colonies are now put into a respectable State of Defence, which will in a short Time certainly receive great Additions by the Accomplishments of some well founded Measures, of which we have not the least Reason to doubt.

These Efforts were soon attended with such Effect, that the British Army still confined within the Town of *Boston* & its Environs, and the Fleet sent to cooperate with it, finding the Fruits of their plundering our seacoasts too precarious and dangerous, Ships of war began to seize our vessels, carry them to *Boston* & take out their Cargos of provisions. It therefore became expedient to make some Regulations to prevent their receiving such supplies, which have been effectual.

The war being thus prosecuted against these Colonies by Sea as well as by Land, Several armed vessels have been fitted out by us, and many considerable Captures have been made of Transports loaded with warlike Stores and Provisions for the army in Boston.

Upon this same Principle of self preservation, founded on the Laws of Nature, and justified by the Laws of Nations, We approved of an Expedition into *Canada*, against the British Forces in that Province. With such a dangerous Caution did We proceed in this important Measure, that when the proposal was first made in Congress, it was rejected: But sometime after, receiving undoubted Intelligence that Governor *Carleton* was by every Artifice exciting our fellow subjects in *Canada* & the *Indians* to commence Hostilities, and that Administration entertained Designs and Expectations of putting these Colonies between two Fires, and even of carrying on the War by the worst of Assassinations, even those of Women & Children, in letting loose & enflaming the Tribes of Barbarians, with whom Mercy is a Reproach, We judged, that We should be impardonably criminal with Regard to You, who had put your Lives into our Hands, if We hesitated any longer to frustrate as much as We could the cruel Machinations of your Enemies.

We knew Governor *Carleton's* Forces were not great, but We also knew the Power vested in him by the late act of Parliament for changing the Government of that Province to be so exorbitant, that there was Reason to fear, that, if he was allowed time to strengthen himself in quiet, by using all the advantages his authority or art could give him, he would quickly grow formidable. Besides, We were convinc'd 'that if he requested Assistance from G.B. it would be sent to him early in the Spring; and that whenever he was fully prepared, the Storm would burst with its greatest Fury by the Way of the Lakes on the Colonies of *New York*, *Connecticut* & *New Hampshire*, and if the first of those Colonies should at the same Time be attacked from the Sea, he might make a very considerable Impression. Influenced by these Reasons, We directed the army in the Colony of *New York*, where its Reserve was not so immediately necessary, to march into *Canada*. You are now in Possession of the whole Province except *Quebec*. All the success We could expect has attended your Arms; but great as it has been, We almost regret advantages purchased at so high a Price as the Life of General *Montgomery*.

Several large Reinforcements are now marching into that Country, and others will soon follow them. The Inhabitants are well affected to your Cause.

The *Indians* in the northern, middle & southern Departments, have entered into Treaties of Friendship with You.

It seems needless to us, to give a more particular Detail of our Transactions, and the Events that have happened in Consequence of them, because they have been so regularly communicated to You in the public Prints.

Upon the whole, the situation of your Affairs at present appears to us to be so favorable, that We can look in the Face the Trials preparing for Us next spring without Terror. The Justice of your Cause is a perpetual Source of Comfort to us. We humbly hope, that the all wise and all gracious Ruler of the Universe, will bless the Means afforded you by his Goodness, and employed for the purpose of preserving the Innocent from the Fury of their unprovoked Foes. He hath declared, that he "will be a Refuge for the oppressed in Times of Trouble," and We trust in his sacred promise. But, beloved Brethren, We most earnestly beseech You, that You will not confide too much in the Injustice of your Adversaries, for a Recommendation of yourselves to the Divine protection. Let every Individual entering into a strict Examination of himself, & renouncing and repenting of his Offences, cultivate such Affections, and observe such a Tenor of Conduct for the Future, as he knows will be pleasing to the Allmighty, & may thro his infinite Mercys procure Favor to this distressed Land. We entreat You also in your applications to the Throne of Grace, to remember us, on whom You have devolved Duties so important and so difficult, and fervently to pray, that We may be endued with wisdom to conduct your Affairs in the most advantageous Manner amidst the Convulsions that now shake the British Empire to its deepest Foundations.

Upon a Review of our whole Conduct We do not recollect a single Step We have taken that appear'd so likely to draw down upon Us the Censure of our Constituents, as our Petition to the King. After so many Petitions from assemblies had been treated by Administration with such Uniformity of Contempt; after the Petition from the late Congress had been not only treated in the same Manner, but had been immediately succeeded by Fleets & Armies sent to invade Us, by the Slaughter of our Countrymen and by the Burning of *Charlestown*, petitioning seem'd not only to be useless, but even dangerous, as that Mode of proceeding had so recently produced additional Rage and fresh Violences on the Part of our Enemies.

However, so passionate was our Desire to stop the Effusion of British

Blood by British Hands, and to bind up the wounds of this unnatural War, that We resolved once more to lay his American People in all Humility at his Majesty's Feet, and to strive, if it were possible, to frame our address in such a manner, as might procure some Degree of Attention to our Supplications. We had been well inform'd that all the Petitions from *America* for several Years past, had been rejected, because they insisted on Claims said to be derogatory of the Dignity and Authority of the British Crown & Parliament. We therefore determined to make an Attempt hitherto untried on this Continent, and thro the Representatives of so many united Colonies, to use a Language, which no single Colony had ever condescended to employ. Sincerely aiming at Peace & Reconciliation, We avoided every Expression, that might raise any Obstruction to the attainment of those desired Objects, by irritating Minds, however causelessly, which We wish'd to sooth into a Temper equally amicable with our own. Accordingly waving even the slightest mention of every *Right* & every *Grievance*, We confined ourselves to the measured, & even in the opinion of our Enemies, respectful Terms, of praying for "Relief from our Fears & Jealousies," and "that his Majesty would be pleased to direct some Mode, by which the united applications of his faithful Colonists, in Pursuance of their Common Councils, might be improved into a happy & permanent Reconciliation."

Thus, the injured made the first Advance for promoting Peace, which perhaps might have been made more consistently with the Character of a magnanimous Nation, by the Aggressors; and in making this proposal, tho a cruel War was then levied against Us in his Majesty's Name, yet we carried our Reverence for the royal Character so far, that sufficiently declaring our Meaning, yet We forbore using the Word *Treaty*, least the Term should appear too harsh, when offered by subjects to their sovereign. Nor could we devise a more dutiful and unexceptionable Method of conveying our ardent and loyal Wishes to his Majesty, than by relying on his "wisdom" for "the Direction of a Mode" that might improve the Requests of his American subjects into a perfect accommodation. It appeared to us too, a fortunate Circumstance, that our Petition would be delivered to his Majesty by so respectable a Gentleman as the honorable *Richard Penn* Esquire late Governor of *Pennsylvania*, who had taken no Part in the present unhappy Dispute.

Having in this Manner guarded aginst every Objection to the gracious Reception of our Petition, We flattered ourselves that it would produce the desired Effect. The Exception taken by some persons against the Reception of the former Petition, because a Congress is a Body not known to the Constitution, we considered as too frivolous to damp our Expectations. We all individually signed the Petition, "in behalf of ourselves and the Inhabitants of these Colonies," and our President

signed as a Common Member, without the Addition of his Office. So
that tho We mentioned a Matter of Fact, that the Inhabitants of these
Colonies had deputed us to represent them "in general Congress," yet
that Circumstance could not deprive us of the Right of petitioning,
which is so solemnly recognized & established by the Bill of Rights.
This Right is the same, whether the Petition be that of one or of many.
The very Reason alledged in the Exception, is a Reason for receiving a
Petition from a Number of his subjects, even tho they stiled their
Meeting a Congress, which indeed is convertible Terms with the other:
For if a Congress is a "Body not known to the Constitution," the Reception of a Petition from a Congress, is not an Acknowledgment
express or implied, of any Powers, Authority or Priveledges as attended
or annexed to such a Body: Whereas, on the other side, if the Framers
of a Petition usurp or unjustly assume the Name or Title of a Body
known to the Constitution, the general Reception of their Address
might involve in it in some Degree an Acknowledgment that the
Powers, Authority or Priviledges attach'd by the Constitution to such
a Body, were vested in the Petitioners. Let the advocates for the mistaken Dignity of the British Government point out the constitutional
Principles that warranted the Assembly of the Barons at *Runnamede*
when *Magna Charta* was granted, the *Convention Parliament*, that *restored
Charles* the second, and the *Convention* of Lords & Commons that placed
William on the Throne at the *Revolution*. When they have done this,
We shall perhaps be able to apply their Principles to prove the propriety
& Legality of a Congress.[4]

As our Enemies well knew, that We were vested with the highest
Trust & Power, which the Freemen of their united Colonies could
delegate, and acted in pursuance of that Trust & Power for them, We
were perswaded administration could not neglect a Petition in every
Respect so unexceptionable, and containing such Grounds for an
honourable and advantageous Accommodation with G.B. unless they
were resolved to reduce Us to the unconditional submission heretofore
dictated to Us, by the Edge of the Sword. This Conduct, as We had by
the last Measure exhausted all peacable Modes of obtaining Redress,
We were assured, would convince every Man of Sense upon the Continent, that these Colonies could only rely, in an humble Dependance
on Divine Providence, upon their own virtuous & vigorous Exertions
for Relief. Contrary[5]

MS (PHi). In the hand of John Dickinson.
[1] The committee appointed by Congress on January 24 "to prepare an address
to the inhabitants of the United Colonies" consisted of Robert Alexander, John
Dickinson, James Duane, William Hooper, and James Wilson, five of the most
conspicuously conservative delegates in Congress. Since committees responsible for
stating positions upon which Congress was to take a public stand were normally
balanced to represent several points of view, the composition of this committee
suggests that the majority of delegates did not expect to endorse its work. During

the two weeks that had elapsed since Wilson originally introduced the motion calling for its appointment, several developments had sharply altered the chances that
its report would be received favorably. The reception accorded *Common Sense*, which
was published only the day before Wilson first offered his motion, and the nearly
simultaneous dissemination throughout the colonies of reports of Lord Dunmore's
attack on Norfolk and General Montgomery's repulse at Quebec virtually ensured
that the committee would be ignored. In any event, when the committee's report
was submitted and read on February 13, it sparked little comment and was quietly
tabled. In the words of Richard Smith, it "was very long, badly written and full
against Independency (Wilson percieving the Majority did not relish his Address
and Doctrine never thought fit to stir it again)."
    Because the journals contain little information on the subject, recording nothing
beyond the appointment of the committee and the submission of its report, almost
everything that is known about the circumstances that led to its appointment and
the delegates' reaction to its work rests upon a few references contained in the
writings of a handful of delegates, although the committee's report, in the hand of
James Wilson, is in the PCC and was published with the journals by Worthington C.
Ford in 1906. See Richard Smith's Diary, January 9, 24, and February 13; Samuel
Adams to John Adams, January 15; and Thomas McKean to George Read, January 19, 1776, note 2. See also John Dickinson's Proposed Resolutions on a Petition
to the King, January 9–24? 1776, and Notes for a Speech in Congress, January 24?
1776.
    But the opening of the R. R. Logan Collection of Dickinson's papers at PHi in
1969 made available two additional documents bearing upon this episode. The
longer of these is a draft in Wilson's hand of the committee's address that is essentially
the same as the document Ford printed in 1906 and was undoubtedly prepared for
the perusal of other committee members. It contains suggested alterations in Dickinson's hand and was endorsed by him: "Amendments of a Draft made in Congress
by Mr. W. in order to prevent People inclining to a total separation from G.B."
Because Wilson ignored nearly all of Dickinson's suggested deletions and incorporated fewer than half of his minor and chiefly verbal substitutions into the final
report, the MS confirms that the committee's report was primarily Wilson's work.
It also contains a few minor suggestions in another, unidentified hand, indicating
that Wilson may have circulated it among other delegates as well but that they too
contributed only slightly to the final product.
    The second document, entirely in Dickinson's hand and printed here for the first
time, is apparently a major fragment of an earlier draft prepared for the committee.
Because little of it survives in the final report, however, its influence on Wilson's
work remains obscure. Nor is it apparent why or at what stage Dickinson prepared
it. There is little in the text to support the conclusion that Dickinson was asked to
make the committee's first draft, and considering his eminence as a writer it seems
unlikely that he would have been assigned a duty of this nature that was subsequently
reassigned to another. It seems more likely that he simply committed his thoughts
to paper and passed them on to Wilson to use as he pleased. Although a few passages (designated in the notes below) survive nearly verbatim in Wilson's draft,
these do not indicate that Dickinson's contribution was a major one. The document
contains few passages adding significantly to what we know about Dickinson's
views through other products of his pen, but it does represent a conservative's
review of the course of events of the preceding year and the steps Congress had taken
to preserve American rights in the struggle with Britain. Cast in the form of a report
to the delegates' constituents who are acknowledged to be the final judges of Congress' conduct, it also suggests that Dickinson hoped thereby to appeal to the American people to check a congressional majority who appeared to him to be taking
needless risks and courting a confrontation that might yet be avoided if officials on
both sides of the Atlantic would only recognize the merits of reconciliation.

² See *JCC*, 4:134–35.
³ See *JCC*, 4:136.
⁴ See *JCC*, 4:137.
⁵ Remainder of MS missing.

John Hancock to Philip Schuyler

Sir   Philadelphia Jany. 24t. 1776

I had the Honor of addressing you by Letter on the 20th of this Month to which I beg Leave to refer you. The Return of the Military Stores that were at Ticonderoga Landing & Crown Point mentioned to be inclosed in your Letter of the 21st of December is by some Means mislaid. I am therefore directed to desire you will send to Congress as soon as possible a Return of all the Cannon and Artillery at Crown Point & Ticonderoga exclusive of those taken by Colo. Knox for General Washington.[1]

I have the pleasure to inform you the first Company of the Pennsylvania Battalion begun their March Yesterday. Another set out to Day and the rest will follow at the Distance of one Day. They are to be provided with provisions by the Commissary who attends them till they reach Albany, after which you will please to order the Commissary General of the Northern Department to make provision for them afterwards.

I have just to inform you that the Congress have appointed Mr. Moses Hazen Colonel Commandant of the second Canadian Regiment and Mr. Edward Antill Lieutenant Colonel.[2]

The Appointment of the Majors, Captains and Subalterns as well as Staff Officers is left to the Commander in Chief in Canada, with the advice of the General Officers in that Country, Col. Hazen and Col. Antill & Mr. Price.

Mr. Hazen & Antill will wait on you and take your Instructions & Directions.

Such part of the inclosed Resolves as respect Mr. Hazen & Antill you will communicate to them for their future proceeding & forward by Letter to the Commander in Canada the necessary Directions in every Respect in Consequence of the Resolutions of Congress.

I have paid Mr. Hazen and Antill one thousand pounds this Currency in Specie towards the Expence of raising the Canadian Battalion. I have also paid Mr. Antill two hundred Dollars on account of his Expences, and to Mr. Hazen 533⅓ Dollars on Account of the Loss he has sustained, all which Sums are to be accounted for.[3] I have heretofore sent you —— Commissions, but least you should be in Want I have sent a few more, you will deliver what are necessary to Mr. Hazen. I have sent addresses of Congress to the Canadians,[4] which you will please to forward by Mr. Hazen.

459

A U X
HABITANTS
DE LA PROVINCE DU CANADA.

AMIS ET COMPATRIOTES;

NOTRE Précédente Adreffe vous a démontré nos Droits, nos Griefs & les Moyens que nous avons en notre pouvoir, & dont nous fommes autorifés par les CONSTITU-TIONS BRITANNIQUES, à faire ufage pour maintenir les uns, & obtenir juftice des autres.

Nous vous avons auffi expliqué, que votre Liberté, votre Honneur & votre Bonheur, font effentiellement & néceffairement liés à l'Affaire malheureufe que nous avons été forcé d'entreprendre, pour le foutien de nos Priviléges.

Nous voyons avec joie, combien vous avez été touché, par les remontrances juftes & équitables de vos Amis & Compatriotes, qui n'ont d'autres vues que celles de fortifier & d'établir la caufe de la Liberté : les fervices que vous avez déjà rendus à cette caufe commune, méritent notre reconnoiffance ; & nous fentons l'obligation où nous fommes, de vous rendre le reciproque.

Les meilleures caufes font fujettes aux évènements, les contre-temps font inévitables, tel eft le fort de l'humanité ; mais les ames genereufes, qui font éclairées & échauffées par le feu facré de la Liberté, ne feront pas découragées par de tels échecs, & furmonteront tous les obftacles qui pourront fe trouver entr'eux & l'objet précieux de leurs vœux.

Nous ne vous laifferons pas expofé à la fureur de vos ennemis & des nôtres ; deux Bataillons ont reçu ordre de marcher au Canada, dont une partie eft déjà en route ; on leve fix autres Bataillons dans les Colonies unies pour le même fervice, qui partiront pour votre Province auffi-tôt qu'il fera poffible ; & probablement ils arriveront en Canada, avant que les Troupes du Miniftere, fous le Général Carleton, puiffent recevoir des fecours : en outre, nous avons fait expédier les ordres néceffaires pour faire lever deux Bataillons chez vous. Votre affiftance pour le foutien & la confervation de la Liberté Américaine, nous caufera la plus grande fatisfaction ; & nous nous flattons que vous faifirez avec zèle & empreffement, l'inftant favorable de co-opérer au fuccès d'une entreprife auffi glorieufe. Si des forces plus confidérables font requifes, elles vous feront envoyées.

Apréfent, vous devez être convaincus, que rien n'eft plus propre à affurer nos intérêts & nos libertés, que de prendre des méfures efficaces, pour combiner nos forces mutuelles, afin que par cette réunion de fecours & de confeils, nous puiffions éviter les efforts & l'artifice d'un ennemi qui cherche à nous affoiblir en nous divifant : pour cet effet, nous vous confeillons & vous exhortons, d'établir chez vous des Affociations en vos différentes Paroiffes, de la même nature que celles qui ont été fi falutaires aux Colonies unies ; d'élire des Députés pour former une Affemblée Provinciale chez vous, & que cette Affemblée nomme des Délegués, pour vous repréfenter en ce Congrès.

Nous nous flattons de toucher à l'heureux moment, de voir difparoître de deffus cette terre, l'Etendard de la Tyrannie, & nous efpérons qu'il ne trouvera aucune place en l'Amérique Septentrionale.

Signé au Nom & par l'Ordre du Congrès : JOHN HANCOCK, *Préfident.*

A Philadelphie, le 24 Janvier 1776.

Aux habitants de la province du Canada

We are collecting Specie, hope soon to send some forward.

I most sincerely wish your perfect Recovery and am with the greatest Esteem, Sir, Your most humble Servant,

John Hancock President

[*P.S.*] I am in great Hurry. You will please to note the Resolve respecting Ticonderoga.[5]

Tr (NN).
[1] *JCC*, 4:84.
[2] Congress took this action on January 22. *JCC*, 4:78.
[3] See *JCC*, 4:87.
[4] The "Letter to the Inhabitants of the Province of Canada," which Congress approved and ordered to be translated this day. *JCC*, 4:85–86.
[5] Probably the congressional resolve passed January 25, "that the fortress at Ticonderoga be repaired and made defensible." *JCC*, 4:91.

Richard Smith's Diary

Wednesday 24 January [1776]

I was in Congress. A State of the late Action at Quebec was laid before the House and ordered to be published.[1] 1000 Dollars advanced to Carpenter Wharton the Commissary who goes with the Troops to Albany. A Motion was made by Edwd. Rutledge to appoint a War Office and its Business defined, which was argued and a Comee. of 7 chosen to consider the Plan.[2] Most of the Day was spent on a proposal to address the People of America our Constituents deducing the Controversy ab Initio and informing them of our Transactions and of the present State of Affairs, much was said about Independency and the Mode and Propriety of stating our Dependance on the King, a Comee. was appointed to draw the Address.[3] W Livingston reported an Address to the Canadians which was agreed to with Some Alteration and ordered to be translated into French and printed. Edwd. Antill (made Lt. Col. to Hazens Regiment) was desired to take £1000 in hard Money with Him to the Gen. in Canada. It was agreed to advance to Mr. Hazen £200 to be deducted from the Amount of his Losses, & to allow something to Him and Antill for their Expences in coming down & going back. Brig. Prescott being expected in Town to night an Order passed to keep Him under Guard till Tomorrow. Col. De Haas who supplies the Place of Bull in the first Pennsa. Battalion made Return of what Arms are wanting for his Men whereupon it was recommended to the City Comee. to procure all the Arms they can for the Soldiers about to march to Canada. Govr. Ward shewed me a Recommendatory Letter from a Canadian Seigneur, a Captive here, in Favor of the Govrs. Son now a Prisoner in Quebec.

MS (DLC).
¹ For the text of this statement, see *JCC*, 4:82–84.

² This committee submitted its report to Congress on April 18, and Congress approved it on June 12, 1776, leading to the creation of the Board of War. *JCC*, 4:85, 215, 293, 5:434–35.

³ On this point, see also Smith's Diary, January 9, 1776, note 3.

Oliver Wolcott to Laura Wolcott

Philadelphia 24 Janry. 1776. "The News of a Repulse at Quebec seems to be unhappy, but perhaps needfull to give us a proper sense of our Dependence, and to stimulate us to make better Provision for that Department, than would otherwise have been done. One Battalion is ordered to be raised in Connecticut for that Service.¹ Mr. Burr escaped unhurt tho extremely exposed at the Quebec Attack, and has acquired much Reputation by his good Conduct, and I understand is made an Aide de Camp. No foreingn News. Preparations are making for the spring Service—which I hope may be effectual to disappoint our Enimies. . . . I have sent you enclosed to Mr. Lyman the Journols of Congress—together with a Phamplet lately published in this City intituled common Sence. It has had a great Sale—and has been Variously Animadverted upon. Said to be Wrote by one Mr. Payn."

RC (CtHi).
¹ In order to expedite the recruiting of this battalion, the Connecticut delegates received on January 20 an advance of $12,500, which they transmitted in the care of Capts. Samuel Wheat and Jared Tracy. An order to pay $16 to Wheat and Tracy for this service, directed to Connecticut treasurer John Lawrence at Hartford and signed by Samuel Huntington, Roger Sherman, and Wolcott, is in the Autograph File, MH. See also *JCC*, 4:74–75; and J. H. Trumbull and Charles J. Hoadly, eds., *The Public Records of the Colony of Connecticut* . . ., 15 vols. (Hartford: Case, Lockwood & Brainard Co., 1850–90), 15:231.

Committee of Congress
Report on General Montgomery's Memorial

[January 25, 1776]

That it is the opinion. of this committee ¹ that in consideration of the many signal and important services which with the greatest valour and conduct have been rendered to these Colonies by their late General Richard Montgomery who after a series of successes obtained under amazing difficulties at length fell in a gallant attack upon Quebec the Capital of Canada ——— as a tribute of Justice to the memory of that valiant officer, that his Patriotism, Conduct, Boldness of Enterprize &

⟨scorn of danger and fearlessness⟩ Contempt of danger & of death may stand recorded to posterity exhibiting an Example truly worthy of imitation.

Resolved that a Monument be procured from Paris or any other part of France, and erected in that Room of the State House in Philadelphia in which the Continental Congress now sit, & that it bear an Inscription sacred to the memory of Genl Richard Montgomery & best calculated to perpetuate his fame,[2] & that the Continental Treasurer be directed to advance a Sum not exceeding 300 £ Stirling to the order of ⟨*Doctor Franklin*⟩ who shall be appointed & shall undertake to see this Resolution duly executed in order to pay the expence thereof.

Resolved that a funeral Oration be delivered by the Reverend Dr W Smith in honor of that deceased General & those officers and soldiers who so magnanimously fought & fell with him in maintaining the principles of American Liberty & from an heroick Love to their Country.

MS (PHi). In the hand of William Hooper.

[1] The committee "to consider of a proper method of paying a just tribute of gratitude to the memory of General Montgomery," which was appointed on January 22 and reported on the 25th. See *JCC*, 4:78, 89–90.

[2] The following inscription, in the hand of Charles Thomson, was apparently intended for the monument. "This monument is erected by the Order of Congress 25 Jany 1776 to transmit to posterity a grateful remembrance of the patriotism, conduct, enterprize, perserverance ⟨*and contempt of Danger*⟩ of Maj. Genl Richard Montgomery who after a series of successes amidst the most discouraging difficulties fell in the Attack on Quebec. 31 Decr. 1775. Age 39 yrs." Chamberlain Collection, MB.

Silas Deane to Thomas Mumford

Dear Sir   Philadelphia Jany. 25th. 1776

I wrote you the 23d per Mr Wheat in answer to yours of the 10th[1] and therein dismiss'd my Opposers in Connecticut with all the Grace they merit at my hands, and shall hereafter labor to 'think no more of them, than of Nonentities, for while I cannot think favorably of any one, I choose to forget him intirely. Inclosed is Mr. Marshalls Acct. Ball[ance]s £24.17.10 or Sixty Six & 1/3d Dollars which I paid, like true Christians they deducted their Commissions. This Morning I settled with Mr. Latimer, and send you his Acct. Ballance £127.0.9 L[awful] or Three Hundred Thirty Eight & 2/3d Dollars. The Five Barrels deducted he is confident is on board, if it prove so I promised that you would remit the Money to Mr. Marshall for him, on your receiving the Acct. from the West Indies.[2] You left with Me—10,500 Dollars out of which I pd.

Mr Latimer   10.338 2/3
Mr Marshall   66 1/3
                ────────
                10.405   leaves in my hands Ninety five Dollars
                    95
                ────────
                10.500

The Flour will cost the Continent at least Three hundred pounds more than if it had been laid in at this City but I shewed the Accts. to Mr. Morriss who was buying large Quantities at the same place for the public who told Me he gave the same price. The reason is that at this Season, vessels can often get to Sea from there when this port is shut by the Ice. Our Fleet is still detained below by the Ice. Hinman will undoubtedly arrive in season. I had the pleasure of helping forward my Freind *Arnold*, before I left the Congress. He and *Putnam* are the only Two Officers by Land that can be charged to My influence for advancing, and for them I dare to be responsible. The River is excessive full of Ice and We have no Communication with any thing below this, so that I know nothing of Captn. Saltonstall since we parted.

I wish in Answer to this you would send Me a breif Estimate of the Cargoes you may have shipped for Martineco and To whom Addressed. My reasons are, a thought of adventuring that Way on the public Acct.,[3] and should not be willing to interfere with any other. My Complimts. to your Brother. I recd. his Letter and thank him for it but have not Time to reply by this Opportunity for though out of Congress I am still employed, & shall be for some little Time.[4] I am with respects to your Lady & Family, Dear sir, Your very Huml servt.,

                                              Silas Deane

RC (Robert J. Sudderth, Jr., Lookout Mountain, Tenn., 1973).

[1] Mumford's letter of January 10 is printed in *NYHS Collections* 23 (1890): 551–52.

[2] See Deane to Thomas Mumford, January 2, 1776.

[3] Silas and Barnabas Deane had recently obtained a contract with the Secret Committee to procure needed goods. See Secret Committee Minutes of Proceedings, January 11, 1776.

[4] Three days later Deane sent another letter to Mumford explaining his plans for the immediate future. "It is Now a Week since I sat in Congress, but can tell you Thus much that the ports will certainly be opened on the 1st. of March, but the particular Regulations are not all agreed upon as yet. I shall leave this City in Ten Days on a Tour to the Southward, which will delay my return untill Spring. It is my Freind no Tour of pleasure I assure you, but of Business & that of a public and important Nature. I should hold myself highly criminal should I indulge myself in taking my pleasure abroad, when the Storm was thickening so fast over My Country, but it is certainly a point of Duty to go where I can do the greatest Service, & by that only am I directed in my present measures for I am Confident that I should be of little Significancy in a Colony which has censured Me by implication, in the Face of the whole Continent, and refused even to hear Me, in my Justification, but at the same Time my Life, & all that is dear in possession, or prospect are at the service of my Country. You will oblige Me by Continuing Your Letters though you must not expect any return suddenly. Inclose your Letters under Cover To Messrs Willing & Morris Merchts. & Members of Congress. They will know where to send them." Deane to Thomas Mumford, January 28, 1776, Robert J. Sudderth, Jr., Collection.

John Hancock to Thomas Lowrey

Sir,   Philada. Jany. 25th. 1776

On the 11th Inst there was a Draught on the Treasury in your Favour, for 35,000 Dollars, out of which you were directed to provide sundry Articles wanting for second New Jersey Batallion which was ordered to March to Canada.[1]

By a. Letter this Day recd. from Col. Maxwell the Congress are informed that the Articles are not yet provided.[2] The Necessity of the Service requires that the Batallion should march with all possible Expedition, I am therefore directed to press you to exert your utmost Endeavours to provide the Articles, and facilitate the March of the Companies as fast as they can be got ready by all the Means in your Power. I am &c,   J H Pt.

LB (DNA: PCC, item 12A).

[1] Thomas Lowrey (1737–1806), Flemington, N.J., grain merchant and commissary, had been authorized by Congress to supply the New Jersey troops. See *JCC*, 3:360, 4:46–47, 89; and Henry Race, *Historico-Genealogical Sketch of Col. Thomas Lowrey, and Esther Fleming, His Wife* (Flemington, N.J.: H. E. Deats, 1892), pp. 3–8.

[2] William Maxwell's January 23 letter to Hancock is in *Am. Archives*, 4th ser. 4:813–14.

John Hancock to William Maxwell

Sir,   Philada. Jany. 25th. 1776

When the Congress on the 8th Inst. ordered your Batallion to march to Canada, they appointed a Come. to inquire what was wanting to fit them for the March.[1]

The Come. having taken Time to make the necessary Enquiry made Report on the 10th "That before your Batallion could be fit to march the following Articles ought to be provided viz 688 Haversacks, 688 Cartouch Boxes, and Cross Belts, 688 Tomhawks 64 pitching Axes, and nine Baggage Waggons."[2] No Notice being taken of Arms, Blanketts, or Cloathing, it was presumed your Troops were properly supplied with these Articles. In Order therefore that the Articles wanting might be provided, they immediately ordered a very considerable Sum to be put into the Hands of Mr. Lowry with Orders to purchase the same, and to pay the Men up to the first of February, deducting out of their Pay the Price of the Articles furnished the Men more than what was allowed in Lieu of Bounty.

By these Means the Congress expected your Batallion would have been properly equipped, and that the first Company that could be got ready, would be immediately ordered to set out on their March.

The Urgency of the Service requires that your Batallion should begin their March with all possible Expedition. It will be vain to send Men without Arms. But as the Come. of Trenton have informed Congress that Arms can be purchased, I have by this opportunity transmitted to them by order of Congress 4000 Dollars for the Purchase of suitable Arms, and have desired them to take Measures for supplying you with Blanketts.

I hope I need not use arguments to stimulate you in this Matter. I would only observe, and have you take Notice that it is the Desire of Congress that you would send forward the first Company that can be got ready; and that it be followed by the other Companies, one at a Time, as fast as they can be provided with Necessaries without waiting till the whole are equipped.
I am, &c,   J H Pt.

LB (DNA: PCC, item 12A).
 [1] See *JCC*, 4:39–40.
 [2] *JCC*, 4:46–47.

John Hancock to the Trenton Committee

Gentlemen,   Philada Jany 25. 1776
Your letter of the 23d being received was communicated to Congress.[1]
The necessity of the service requires that Col Maxwell's regiment should march as soon as possible. When the orders were first given for their march, enquiry was made what articles were wanting and a considerable sum of money was lodged in the hands of Mr Lowry for that purpose. But as arms and blankets were not then mentioned, the Congress have ordered a draught in your favour for the sum of 4000 dollars in order to purchase arms, which you say may be procured for money for such as want them.[2]

I would just observe that in order to supply the batallion ordered to march from Pensylvania the committee of inspection for the city and liberties of Philadelphia went round from house to house & procured blankets of the inhabitants. I trust your zeal & that of the inhabitants of your colony will not be behind your neighbours. The owners of the blankets will be allowed the value according to your estimation.

I have wrote to Colonel Maxwell to stimulate him and I rely you will give him all the aid in your power.

I am with Respect, Gentlemen, Your most obedt servt.,
                                        John Hancock Presidt.

[*P.S.*] I am Directed by the Congress to Desire you will be pleas'd to give Directions for the obtaining Waggons to Transport the Baggage of the Prisoners which is at Walpack in the Jerseys to Lancaster in this province. This you will please to order effected in the most Expeditious

& Cheap manner.

The Money will be forwarded this day.

RC (DLC). In the hand of Charles Thomson, with signature and postscript by Hancock.

[1] Samuel Tucker wrote two letters on January 23 for the Trenton Committee informing Hancock of the disposition of the two prisoners, General Prescott and Captain Chase. See *JCC*, 4:82, 87; Hancock to the Trenton Committee, January 22, 1776, note 2; and *Am. Archives*, 4th ser. 4:814–15.

[2] *JCC*, 4:89.

Richard Smith's Diary

Thursday 25 Jany. [1776]

The Votes of Yesterday read. 4000 Dollars ordered to be sent by the Return of Prescott's Guard, to the Comee. of Safety of our Colony for purchasing Arms for Maxwells Men. Letters were recd. from Lancaster, Gen. Washington and others, some of them committed to a Comee.[1] A Petition was read from Matthias Aspden for Permission to loan a French Vessel with Produce, it was referred to a Comee.[2] A Comee. was elected for and reported a Conference with Gen. Prescott & Capt. Chase relative to Prescotts Cruelty to Col. Ethan Allen & others, he pleads the Commands of Carlton his Superior Officer. The same Comee. enquired of Col. Antill who charges Prescott with great Malevolence & bad Behavior to our People, the Matter is to be further sifted.[3] A Comee. was appointed for and reported a Conversation with Col. Hazen about his Parole of not serving agt. the King, this from the Circumstances of it, was thot. void and Hazen reappointed Col. & Edwd. Antill Lt. Col. of the 2d Battalion of Canadians. James Mease was chosen a Commissary to the Troops raised and to be raised in Pennsa. for the Continental Service. Gen. Washn. inclosed some late English Newspapers in his Letter and informs of the British Troops meeting a Storm and putting back to Milford Haven. His own Army is much in Want of Money and Powder and other Military Stores. 10,000 Dollars voted on Account, to the Troops in North Carolina. 2 or 3 Ships of War are fitting out there for our Service accordg to Report.[4] The Comee. of Safety in N Jersey are desired to forward the Captive Officers Baggage from Walpack to Lancaster. A Report from a Comee. was agreed to purporting that Dr. Franklin shall procure from France or elsewhere a Monument to the Value of £300, this Cur[renc]y, for Gen. Montgomery and that Dr. Wm. Smith Provost of the College be desired to compose an Oration in Praise of the Gen. to be delivered in Presence of the Congress.

MS (DLC).

[1] Washington's letter to Hancock of January 14 is in PCC, item 152, 1:415–17, and Washington, *Writings* (Fitzpatrick), 4:237–39.

[2] There is no mention of this subject in the journals for this date. However, on February 2 Congress approved a resolve which granted Aspden permission to ship to Port-au-Prince certain articles "to the amount of 1800 pounds Pensylvania currency," but warned that this action should "not be drawn into precedent." *JCC*, 4:108.

[3] On January 29 Congress ordered Prescott confined to a Philadelphia jail, pending further consideration of his case. *JCC*, 4:101.

[4] In reality, these three ships were intended for service in the North Carolina rather than the Continental Navy. Clark, *Naval Documents*, 3:201, 980n.2.

Samuel Ward to Henry Ward

Dear Bror.   Philadelpa. 25th Jany. 1776
My very worthy Friend Colo. Gadsden recommended Capt. Cochran to Me. He is a very reputable Sea Captain (in the last War of a Privateer). His Business is to get Seamen for So. Carolina. I beg Leave to Introduce him to you; I have told him that such is the State of our Colony that I imagine there is no Prospect of his Success with Us; any Services which you can do him consistently I shall take as a Favor.[1]
I have not had the Pleasure of a Letter from the Govr. or from you a long Time. I promised myself several before now. For news I refer you to the inclosed Paper. By the Testimony inclosed You may see the Politics of some here, they appear to Me to have taken their Part. I hope every Possible Exertion will be made in all the N. E. Colonies for their own Defence; every Man must be a Soldier.
One Company marched from here yesterday for Canada; others from the Jerseys & here also will follow in a Day or two. Sammy is well; he was with Colo. Greene & taken Prisoner with the rest of the Party.[2] They are well and Majr. [*i.e.* Brigadier General] Prescot arrived here yesterday. He is charged with having put Colo Allen in Irons &c. I was one of a Comee. appointed to examine him. He is at present at a Tavern under Guard; to Morrow he will be disposed of I believe. Make my most respectful Compliments to the Govr. & due Regards to all Friends. I am, Your very Affecte. Bror.,   Sam Ward

RC (RHi).
[1] For additional information on Capt. Robert Cochran, see Richard Smith's Diary, January 16, 1776, note 4.
[2] On this point, see Ward to Anna Ward, January 21, 1776.

John Hancock to Charles Lee

Sir   Philadelphia Jany. 26. 1776
This Morning I was favour'd with your Letter by Express which I laid before Congress in consequence of which they have appointed a

Committee of three of their Members vizt. Coll Harrison, Mr Lynch & Mr Allen immediately to repair to New York and confer with you and the Committee of Safety of that Colony, on the Subject of your Letter which supercedes the necessity of my being particular, as I must refer you to those Gentlemen.[1]

I have only to add my best wishes for your Health, and that success may attend your important exertions.

I have the honor to be with Esteem, Sir, Your most obedt. humble Servt.,   John Hancock Presidt.

Tr (DLC).

[1] General Lee's letter dated January 22, asking advice on the handling of New York tories, was read in Congress this day. The committee appointed in response to the general's letter met with the New York Committee of Safety on February 1 to discuss the entrance of Lee's forces into the province of New York. PCC, item 158, 1:1–12; *Am. Archives*, 4th ser. 4:805–8, 1100; and *JCC*, 4:92, 94. See also the New York Delegates to the New York Committee of Safety, January 27, 1776; and John R. Alden, *General Charles Lee: Traitor or Patriot?* (Baton Rouge: Louisiana State University Press, 1951), pp. 95–103. For John Adams' opinion on the advisability of General Lee's move into New York, which was solicited by General Washington in consequence of Lee's letter of January 5 to Washington, see Adams' letter to Washington of January 6, 1776, dated at Watertown, Mass., in Adams, *Works* (Adams), 9:370–71.

Robert Treat Paine to Robert R. Livingston

My Dear Sr.   Philada. Jany. 26th 1776

I received yrs. addressed to Mr. Langdon & my Self after he was Sett out for home,[1] & I must now assure you it was not for want of respect that I did not visit you in my return. Mr. Langdon being on horseback Set out before me & I followed him on the west side of the River & crossed the Country from Esopus. I am Sorry.to find we are not like to have yr. Company here Soon, & most sincerely condole with you & yr. Respected family the very melancholly occasion of your sudden departure from Albany & absence from Congress; had I wrote you some time ago as I intended I Should have found my mind over-charged to express to you my Sympathy with you in your Loss of the best of Parents & bewail with you the Loss of a Father of his Country in the Death of Judge Livingston; but how shall I now adress you! In vain do I seek Expression Suitable to my Grief when I attempt to lament your reiterated loss in the brave, the amiable Montgomery. Nor is there any thing that in the least can divert my Greif for you unless it be the sense I have of my own Affliction in Common with America. Excuse me if my freedom should cause yr wounds to bleed afresh. I write not for ceremonious Compliment. You may not monopolize the Loss tho yr endeared Connection may cause the deepest wounds; The

Congress deeply impressed with the merits of their deceased General after mature consideration of the most respectful mode of doing Honour to his Memory have directed an Oration to be Pronounced by Dr. Smith & a Monument to be erected with some suitable inscription. America recognizes his Worth, America will establish his memory, & Posterity will hand down his Fame when Statues are mouldered into Dust.[2]

Pray make my Sincere Compliments of respect & Condolence to yr. Amiable & afflicted family.[3]

We have no foreign news here but what you will soon have in yr. York Papers. 57 Ton of Salt petre arrived here some time past from abroad. I send inclosed a paper Containing an Art[icle]. Powder mills are wanted, I hope yr affairs will not prevent your [*putting*] in Execution yr fathers intention of rebuilding the Mill.

The plot thickens fast. A few more struggles & then the birth day of American Liberty. Adieu my friend. May heaven bless you & all yr. Connections & soon grant us a happy meeting is the sincere wish of yr., &c.

FC (MHi).
[1] See Robert R. Livingston to Robert Treat Paine and John Langdon, December 19, 1775.
[2] See *JCC*, 4:89–90.
[3] John Jay also wrote a letter of condolence to Livingston this day from Elizabethtown, N.J., where he had gone to be with his wife (who was "the Day before Yesterday delivered of a Boy") and where he expected to remain "for 3 weeks yet to come." John Jay to Robert R. Livingston, January 26, 1776, Jay, *Papers* (Morris), 1:223.

Richard Smith's Diary

Friday 26 Jany. [1776]
The Votes read. 1000 Dollars advanced to the Indian Commissioners of the Middle Department. A Comee. chosen to examine Commissary Lowrey & Mease's Fees of One and a Quarter per Cent it being suggested to be extravagant.[1] A Petition from some Citizens of Philada. praying that no Apprentices may be inlisted without Consent of the Masters was neglected.[2] A Letter was read from Gen. Lee Dated from Connect[icut] setting forth that he is on his Way for the Defence of N York and has gathered a large Body of Connecticut Militia and inclosing a Letter to him from the Comee. of Safety at N York disapproving of his Proceedgs. This occasioned a Motion from E. Rutledge & Duane that a Comee. may be appointed to repair to New York forthwith and agree with the Comee. of Safety there and with Gen. Lee upon the proper Measures of Defence. After an Argument of 4 or 5 Hours Harrison, Lynch & Allen were fixed upon to proceed to N York

accordingly. Some Letters from Pittsburg about Indian Affairs were postponed.[3]

MS (DLC).

[1] There is no mention of this matter in the journals, nor has any report by this committee been found.

[2] Congress appointed a committee to consider this issue on January 27, and approved its report in favor of granting the prayer of this petition on January 30. *JCC*, 4:94, 96, 103–4.

[3] Not found, but see *JCC*, 4:94.

William Livingston to Samuel Tucker

Dr Sir   Phil. 27 Jany 1776

I just now received yours of the 25 Instant, & am obliged to you for your favourable opinion of my Son. Mr Walton White who Was last Summer at the Camp where general Washington entertain'd a high opinion of his merit, but could find no opening to promote him in the service, & for whom many Gentlemen of this Congress have a great Regard, would probably be glad of some honourable Post in our third Battalion. I mention this not in the least to give any Directions respecting the Recommendation of your Congress, but only to put you in mind of that young Gentleman, that in Case your Convention should really think him a proper person for a Major they may act accordingly. He is certainly of a respectable Family, & of a military turn.[1] The Congress has voted the 4000 Dollars, & Mr Smith will send the money by Capt Scot.[2]

I am afraid Collo Maxwell does not truly apprehend his marching orders. It is not the Intention of the Congress that his Regiment shall be compleat before it marches to Canada by Companies, but that the first company that is ready shall march. And if the matter can be managed no otherwise, I think the Company that is best provided with arms should compleat themselves with the arms of another, & then march & so for the second. The Expedition to Quebec requires the utmost Dispatch, & if no Company is detached till the whole Battalion be compleately equippd, it may take some weeks before any of them march.

A Committee of Congress waited on General Prescot, & examined him about some particulars respecting Allen's Confinement. He behaved very modestly, but his fate is not yet determined. I am Sir, your most humble Svt.   Wil. Livingston

RC (NN).

[1] On February 6 the New Jersey Provincial Congress recommended Anthony Walton White's appointment as lieutenant colonel of the Third New Jersey Battalion, and on February 9 Congress elected him to this position. *Am. Archives*, 4th

ser. 4:1586; and *JCC*, 4:123.

² On January 25, in response to a January 23 letter from Col. William Maxwell describing his battalion's equipment shortages, Congress provided the Trenton Committee, of which Tucker was president, with $4,000 to purchase the needed articles. *JCC*, 4:89; PCC, item 78, 15:3–6; and *Am. Archives*, 4th ser. 4:813–14.

New York Delegates to
the New York Committee of Safety

Gentlemen   Philad. 27th Januy 1776

The Congress this day ¹ received a Letter from General Lee apprizing us of his intended march into New York, in obedience to orders from General Washington: favouring us at the same time, with a Copy of your Letter to him on this Subject.

As we perceiv'd it was General Lee's Intention immediately to proceed to your City; and that you thought such a Measure dangerous to the Lives of the Inhabitants and, in other Respects, unseasonable; we thought it our Duty to apply for a Committee of Congress to examine into the Expediency of the Expedition and to give such Directions as upon Consulting you and the General, might appear most prudent and Adviseable.

Col. Harrison, Mr. Lynch, and Mr. Allen are entrusted with this important business, a choice which we approve, having the highest sentiments of their Humanity, Patriotism and judgment!² We are well satisfied that every mark of Respect will be shewn to them by your Body, as well as by Individuals, not only on account of their great Merit, but because the Employment in which they are now engaged immediately regards the Safety and Preservation of the Capital of our own Colony.

We acknowledge the Receipt of your Favour, this day, respecting the Scheme of protecting the navigation by Cruizers at the continental Expence.³ When you are made acquainted that this, and other Colonies, have engagd in a similar Plan at their own provincial Charge, you will perceive the proposition to be attended with difficulty, as proceeding from Us. The Deputation from Congress will however give you an oppertunity of representing the Propriety of such a Measure as is calculated to prevent the supply of provisions to the Fleet & Army employed for the Enslaving these Colonies; and the Necessity of Stationing some of the continental Cruizers in the places you may suggest. This will bring on the Enquiry where such Vessells can most conveniently be had? and your purposes may be answered very effectually, as we are confident that every thing which they recommend will have the greatest weight with the Congress.

The several Matters communicated in your Letter by Mr Foster will be answered by that Gentleman when he returns which will not be till the beginning of next week.[4]

We have the Honour to be with great Respect Gentlemen, your most obedient, humble Servants,   Jas Duane

Wm Floyd

Henry Wisner

RC (N). Written by Duane and signed by Duane, Floyd, and Wisner. *Journals of N. Y. Prov. Cong.*, 2:138. RC damaged; missing words supplied from Tr.

[1] Although Duane dated this letter January 27, he undoubtedly drafted it on the 26th, the day Congress received the letters from General Lee and the committee of safety referred to in the first paragraph. *JCC*, 4:92.

[2] Andrew Allen and Thomas Lynch took advantage of their appointment to this committee to resume their negotiations with Lord Drummond, who had returned to New York City at the conclusion of their talks earlier in the month. See Lord Drummond's Notes, January 3–9? 1776.

[3] In a letter to the New York delegates of January 22, the committee of safety proposed that Congress pay the expenses of outfitting four vessels to prevent the shipment of supplies from New York City to the British Army in Boston and to harass British shipping in the waters off New York and New Jersey. *Am. Archives*, 4th ser. 4:1066–67.

[4] For the committee of safety's letter to the New York delegates of January 20, which was brought to Philadelphia by John Foster, see ibid., pp. 1060–62. For the delegates' reply, see New York Delegates to the New York Committee of Safety, January 30, 1776.

New York Delegates to
the New York Committee of Safety

Gent   Philadelphia Jan. 27. 1776

We Send you by favour of the Committee who are going to New York 12500 Dollars for the Raising a Regiment Destined for Canada.[1] The other is for Mr Lewis from the marine Committee[2] which be pleased to Deliver to him and you'l oblige your very humble Servts

Wm Floyd

Henry Wisner

[*P.S.*] Also 129 Dollars and four Tenths to be Disposed of by Mr Lewis.[3]

RC (N). Written by Floyd and signed by Floyd and Wisner. Addressed: "Pierre V. Cortlandt Esqr. Chairman of the Committee [of] Safety, New York."

[1] On January 20 Congress agreed to provide $12,500 to each of the colonies required to raise reinforcements for the American army in Canada. *JCC*, 4:39–40, 74, 75.

[2] See William Floyd to Francis Lewis, January 29, 1776.

[3] See *JCC*, 4:80.

Richard Smith's Diary

Saturday 27 January [1776]
Letters from Gen. Washington, Ld. Stirling and others, my Lord has
taken a Transport at Sandy Hook and 2 more Vessels are taken by one
of the Massachusetts armed Ships.

On Motion of Wilson (an Indian Commissioner for the Middle
Department) One of the Indian Chiefs was constituted a Colonel & is
to be presented with a Gorget. The Matter of inlisting Apprentices and
small Debtors was committed to McKean, Paine & myself.[1]
A Petition was produced from the Debtors in Philada. Goal praying
that the several Colony Assemblies may be directed to devise Methods
to free all Prisoners for Debt. This Petition was not read the President
thinking it coram non Judice. A Petn. was read & Committed, from
Keppele & Steinmetz prayg. Recompense for a Ship & Cargo carried
into Boston to the Value of £5000 & upwards.[2] Mr. Juge of Maryland
permitted to export Produce from that Colony in Return for Canvass
imported.

Duane from a Comee. reported on the Indian Treaty at Albany &
it was accepted & the Secret Comee. directed to import a large Quantity
of Indian Goods for that & the other Two Departments.[3]

The Indian Treaty at Pittsburg and Proceedings as returned by the
Middle Commissioners were consigned to a Committee of 5. The Comee
of Claims reported a Settlement of Lt. Col. Wynkoops Accounts for
bringing down Prisoners from Albany, it appearing that the Officers
have lived very extravagantly a resolve passed that the Comee. at
Kingston in Ulster County shall settle the Rates of maintaining the
Captives there. McKean moved on Behalf of Col. Hazen that he may
have the rank of first Col. in Canada otherwise he declines the Service.
This was opposed and a Comee. of 2. appointed to confer with Hazen
on the Subject.[4]

MS (DLC).
[1] See Smith's Diary, January 26, 1776, note 2.
[2] On February 2 Congress rejected Henry Kepple's and John Steinmetz's petition
for compensation for the loss of their ship, the *Charming Peggy*, which had been seized
by the British in August 1775 while on a voyage from Philadelphia to Lisbon. *JCC*,
4:108–9; and Clark, *Naval Documents*, 3:1103n.3.
[3] This committee, which Congress appointed on November 23, 1775, drew up
plans for the shipment of Indian trade goods from France to America and for congressional regulation of trade with the Ohio Indians, copies of which were sent to
New York governor William Tryon early in December by James Brattle, a British
spy employed ʲas a valet by committee member James Duane. *JCC*, 3:366, 456;
PRO: C.O. 5, 1107:125–26; and New York Delegates to the New York Provincial
Congress, November 9, 1775, note 2. These plans, although by no means identical
to the resolves which Congress adopted this day on the procurement of Indian
trade goods from Europe and the regulation of trade with Indians in the northern,
middle, and southern departments, are nevertheless sufficiently similar to them to

be regarded as their forerunners. *JCC*, 4:96–98.
⁴ See Smith's Diary, January 29, 1776.

William Floyd to Francis Lewis

Dear Sr.   Philadelphia January 29th. 1776
The members of your Marine Committee gave me an order on the
Treasurer for Forty thousand Dollars, to be transmitted to you.¹ I Recd.
the Same and for which I gave my Receipt, and Sent it with twelve
thousand five hundred dollars by Mr. Lynch and Mr. Allen to the
Committee of Safety at New York. There was also one hundred 29 and
4 tenths dollars for the Accounts you Sent to our Committee of Claimes
all which I hope will come Safe to your hand.²
I am with great Respect, Sr. your Most humble Servt.
                                                              Wm. Floyd

P.S. The 12500 dollars are to raise and forward the Regiment which
our Convention is to send to Canada.

FC (MH).
¹ Lewis, who had been appointed to a committee to outfit vessels for the Continental Navy, was in New York City at this time on committee business. *JCC*, 3:427–
28; and *Am. Archives*, 4th ser. 4:1055, 1078.
² See New York Delegates to the New York Committee of Safety, January 27,
1776.

John Hancock to the Massachusetts Assembly

Gentlemen   Philadelphia January 29th. 1776.
The Congress highly approve the prudence and zeal of the general
in applying to you and the other colonies to raise forces for the service
of Canada in the present exigency and at the same time highly commend
the ready attention you have shewn to his application and the alacrity
with which you undertook and the expedition with which you proceed
in the business.¹ These they consider as additional proofs of your meritorious attachment to the common cause, and may produce signal advantages.
There is the greatest reason to hope that the speedy arrival of troops
in Canada will not only repair the losses our troops have met with there
but in all probability put us in possession of Quebec, before our enemies
can send reinforcements.
It is easy to perceive how much this will advance our cause and
disappoint our enemies. It is therefore the earnest desire of the Congress
that you would continue to exert your utmost endeavour with all

possible expedition to raise and forward both the Regiment and matrosses. That no time may be lost I am directed to forward you blank commissions and to inform you that 12500 Dollars is drawn for and will be sent you for defraying the expences or raising, equiping and paying the men which you will please to dispatch by Companies as fast as they can be got ready.[2]

The Congress have adopted the recommendation of your house to the general respecting the arms of the Soldiers as you will perceive by the enclosed resolutions.[3]

I would just observe that important as the service in Canada is, it cannot be carried on without specie, it is therefore earnestly recommended to the Several legislatures on the continent to collect what silver and Gold they can and inform the Congress thereof, that they may send continental bills in exchange for it. In this business I trust your zeal will not be wanting.

I have the honour to be with the highest Sentiments of Esteem, Gentlemen, Your most Obedt huml servt.,

John Hancock Presidt

[*P.S.*] I have Sent the Money, Say, 12,500 Dollars by Mr Fessenden the Express, agreeable to the Inclos'd Invoice.

I have also Sent by him the Blank Com[missions] which you will please to fill up with the Names of the Gentlemen you shall Appoint.

Our Time of Delegation expires to morrow,[4] as we have not had the honour of any Advice from you, we cannot presume to Set in Congress beyond that time.[5]

RC (M-Ar). In a clerical hand, with signature and postscript by Hancock.
[1] See Hancock to George Washington, this date.
[2] See *JCC*, 4:99.
[3] Congress resolved that the provincial governments should reimburse the troops for damage to or the loss of their firearms in the line of duty. *JCC*, 4:100.
[4] See *JCC*, 4:106.
[5] For the continuation of this letter, see Hancock to the Massachusetts Assembly, January 31, 1776.

John Hancock to George Washington

Sir   Philadelphia January 29th 1776

The Congress have received your Letter of the 19th Instant,[1] and highly commend your prudence and zeal in applying to the Governments of New Hampshire, Massachusetts Bay and Connecticut to raise forces for the service of Canada at this exigency. They have fond hopes by the zeal and alacrity of these Colonies troops will be forwarded with such expedition as will not only succour our friends, but in some measure retrieve our loss and put us in possesion of Quebec before our enemies can receive reinforcements.

The Congress have agreed to add the Massachusetts regiment to the forces they at first destined for Canada; This is the more Necessary as it is now uncertain whether two battalions as was expected, can be raised out of the troops in that country. But they do not by this mean to weaken your Army. They have therefore ordered that the three regiments you applied for from Massachusetts Bay, New Hampshire and Connecticut shall be exclusive of the thirteen wanted for the army at Cambridge.[2]

By the latest advices from England it appears that administration are determined to exert themselves and to send a considerable force against us next Spring, though at the same time they pretend to say that they will offer terms of accommodation and mean only by their armament to enforce their terms.

It behoves us therefore to be ready to receive them. For should an accommodation take place the terms will be severe or favourable in proportion to our ability to resist.

The Congress highly approve your sending general Lee to the assistance of New York as a measure judicious and necessary and have also appointed three of their body to repair to New York and confer with General Lee and the committee of Safety of New York on the subject of putting that colony in a posture of defence.[3]

General Prescot arrived here last Thursday and is this day ordered into close confinement in the goal of this city.[4]

I must beg leave to Refer you to the Inclos'd Resolutions.[5] I Send by this Express Commiss[ion]s for the Massachs. Battalion, & the Money order'd, to the Assembly.[6]

I have the honour to be with the greatest Esteem, Sir, Your most Obedt hume sevt.,   John Hancock Presidt.

RC (DLC). In the hand of Timothy Matlack, with the last two paragraphs and signature by Hancock.

[1] This letter was read in Congress on January 27 and can be found in PCC, item 152, fols. 419–34, and Washington, *Writings* (Fitzpatrick), 4:258–61.

[2] See *JCC*, 4:99–100.

[3] See Hancock to Charles Lee, January 26, 1776.

[4] *JCC*, 4:101. See also Hancock to the Trenton Committee, January 22, 1776, note 2.

[5] Hancock enclosed several resolutions of January 29 and two resolutions adopted on January 30 in response to Washington's letter of January 14. *JCC*, 4:99–100, 102–3.

[6] See Hancock to the Massachusetts Assembly, January 29, 1776.

Joseph Hewes to Samuel Purviance, Jr.

Dear Sir   Philadelphia 29th Jany. 1776

I received your favour of the 20th instt. informing me of M Lux's resignation. The Marine Commee. met the day after your Letter got here, a majority of whom were of Opinion that a Letter should be wrote to M Lux to request him to Act in his Appointment and Mr. Morris was requested to write in behalf of the Committee to him on that Subject. They were also of Opinion in case M Lux should refuse, that the business should go on under the direction of yourself, Mr. Chase & Mr. Stewart.[1] I should have been very glad to have had your Brother put on that Service in M Lux's room, but the Commee. in general thought it unnecessary to add another, seeing two good Men had Agreed to Join Mr Chase in the service. As Mr Chase is entirely unacquainted with Ship Building I do not expect you will be much assisted by him. I wish you had been mentioned at first on this business that no time might have been lost, however I make no doubt but that you will have your Ship ready before some of them that are building to the Northward.

You have enclosed Mr. McGackins receipt for a quantity of shingles, please to settle the matter with him if you possibly can. The Shingles were the property of one Chantrell in No. Carolina who died some time ago and left me his Executor. I understood the Quantity left was about thirty thousd. but of this I am not certain. I shall be glad to have a line from you when any thing Occurs and am with Compliments to your Brother.

Dear Sir, your most obed hum Servt,   Joseph Hewes

RC (MdHi).
[1] Hewes is referring here to the construction at Baltimore of the Continental frigate *Virginia*, in accordance with a congressional resolution of December 13, 1775. *JCC*, 3:425–26; and Clark, *Naval Documents*, 3:1038n. Hewes and Samuel Chase, as members of the marine committee, had a particular interest in the successful completion of this project. *JCC*, 3:427–28, 4:90n. Purviance and William Lux, both of whom were merchants and members of the Baltimore Committee of Observation, had been involved in outfitting the sloop *Hornet* and schooner *Wasp* for Continental service in December 1775. Apparently they were also involved in the initial stages of the building of the *Virginia*, as that seems to be the project to which "Lux's resignation" is related. Clark, *Naval Documents*, 3:218, 260, 607, 773–74; and Benjamin Harrison to Wilson Miles Cary, December 10, 1775.

New York Delegates to Philip Schuyler

Dear Sir,   Philadelphia Jan. 29th 1776
It has given us much Concern to hear of the unsuccessful attempt of General Montgomery on Quebeck, But Congress is Determined to get possession of Canada this winter if possible, and for that purpose they have ordered Seven Battalions from the Colonies and two in Canada;[1] the troops are Dayly marching in Companies from this place, and we hope they will be Soon on their march from the other Colonies.

We take the Liberty to Recommend the Bearer Mr Robert Allison

to your Notice. He is Nephew to our Worthy and Reverend friend
Doctor Allison of this City.

He was well Recommended to the Congress as a young Gentleman
of Merrit which Induced them to appoint him to the office of Ensign
in the first Battalion Raised in this Collony.[2]

We are [with?] Esteem Sr your Humble Servts,

Henry Wisner

William Floyd

RC (facsimile, *Parke-Bernet Galleries Catalog*, no. 2569, May 16, 1967, item 10).
Written by Floyd and signed by Floyd and Wisner.
[1] See *JCC*, 4:39–40.
[2] See *JCC*, 4:69.

Secret Committee to
the Rhode Island Committee of Safety

Philad. Jany 29th. 1776

Agreeable to a Resolutn of the Contl Congress, We the Subscribers,
by them appointed as a Come of Secrecy do hereby authorize & empower
Nathl. Greene & Co. Merchts. Rhode Isld. to load a vessel or vessels
with the produce of these Col[onie]s (horned Cattle, Sheep, hogs, &
poultry ex[cepte]d) agreeable to the resolves of C[ongress] to the amount
of 10,000 dlls.[1] The sd. vessel or Vessels not to sail 'till further orders from
this Comee.

Saml. Ward	Thos. McKean
R. Alexander	Jo. Hewes
Josiah Bartlett	Robt. Morris

Tr (MH).
[1] According to the Secret Committee's accounts, Nathanael Greene & Co. were
advanced $10,000 on February 6, 1776. An order on the treasurers to pay the
company $10,000 "agreable to a Contract made with them 6th. Feby. last" was
recorded in the June 19 entry of the committee journal, but the contract was not
mentioned in the February 6 entry. On February 28, 1776, the Connecticut Council
of Safety agreed to permit the company to purchase three cargoes of Connecticut
produce. See Secret Committee Account, September 27, 1775–August 26, 1776;
Journal of the Secret Committee, fol. 77, MH; and J. H. Trumbull and Charles J.
Hoadly, eds., *The Public Records of the Colony of Connecticut . . .*, 15 vols. (Hartford:
Case, Lockwood & Brainard Co., 1850–90), 15:246.

Richard Smith's Diary

Monday 29 Jany. [1776]

The Votes read and Two English News papers of the 8th of November. A Report was made on the Inlistment of Apprentices & Debtors, objected to and recommitted.[1] Report made on Gen Prescott & that Gentleman ordered to be confined in the Common Jail of Philada. by a Vote of 8 Colonies to 2. Capt. Chase is to go out on his Parole. Capt. Nelsons Compy. of Riflemen from the back Parts of Pennsa. was taken into Pay and a Comee. of 3 nominated to agree with him on the Terms & Road of Marching. Wyth made report on Gen Washingtons, Gen Schuylers & Ld. Stirling's Letters.[2] Letters were recd. from Govr. Trumbull and others.[3] Comee. reported that Hazen accepts the Command as offered to Him and desires to be recommended to the Generals in Canada. A Petition presented from Dr. Wheelock for more money for his Indian College at Dartmouth in New Hampshire referred to a Comee.[4]

MS (DLC).

[1] See Smith's Diary, January 26, 1776, note 2.

[2] See *JCC*, 4:105.

[3] Connecticut governor Jonathan Trumbull's letter to Hancock of January 20 is in PCC, item 66, 1:67–68; and *Am. Archives*, 4th ser. 4:789–90. The journals fail to mention the arrival of any other letters on this day.

[4] Eleazar Wheelock's petition is in Washington Papers, DLC. Congress rejected his request for financial assistance on April 10, but after reconsidering the matter it approved the payment of $500 for the upkeep of Wheelock's Indian college on September 19, 1776. *JCC*, 4:267, 5:787.

Robert Alexander to the Maryland Council of Safety

Gent.   Phila 30 Janry 1776.

You have inclosed two Resolutions of Congress, one respecting the Collection of Gold & Silver for the Pay of the Troops in Canada, the other on the Case of Mr Juge, referred to Congress by the Convention of your Province.[1] In Consequence of the Resolve of the Convention, We made Application to Congress to grant permission to consume the Tea imported before the first of Feby last; the Application was referred to a Committee of the whole House, where the Subject was debated for two Days, & over ruled by a Majority 7 Colonies to 5, the last N. York, Jersy, Pensa., Delaware & Maryland, and a Report made by the Chairman, that it was inexpedient to alter the Association, this Report now lies on the Table.[2] The Loss of Genl. Montgomery with the

particulars of his unfortunate Attack on Quebeck, you will have heard.
Measures are now taken by Congress, which I trust will reduce Carlton
& his few Troops before the End of February. Had one third of the
Succours been sent Montgomery, in all human probability, the Life of
that brave & gallant Officer had been saved & Quebec long e'er this
in our Possession. The Instructions of the Convention are come to
Hand, but not as yet laid before Congress. I am much pleased with
them, they intirely coincide with my Judgment & that Line of Conduct
which I had determined to persue. The Farmer and some others to
whom in Confidence they were shewn, say they breathe that Spirit,
which ought to govern all publick Bodies, Firmness tempered with
Moderation. [3]

I am Gent with Respect, Yr Hble servant,   Robt. Alexander

RC (MdAA).
[1] See *JCC*, 4:59, 73, 96. For the council's response to these resolutions, see *Md.
Archives*, 11:131–33.
[2] The Maryland Convention's resolution of December 23, 1775, is in *Am. Archives*,
4th ser. 4:723. The journals of Congress contain no record of deliberations within
the committee of the whole, but for the action referred to by Alexander, see Richard
Smith's Diary, January 12 and 15, 1776; and *JCC*, 4:62.
[3] On January 11–12 the Maryland Convention resolved to send its delegates to
Congress conditional instructions "that you do not, without the previous knowledge
and approbation of the Convention of this Province, assent to any proposition to
declare these Colonies independent of the Crown of Great Britain, nor to any proposition for making or entering into alliance with any foreign Power, nor to any union
or confederation of these Colonies, which may necessarily lead to a separation from
the mother country." *Am. Archives*, 4th ser. 4:739.

Francis Lightfoot Lee to John Page

My Dear Page   Philada Jany 30th, 1776
    I received yours of the 20th Instant last night. I will deliver any
Letter you may send to Mr. Rittenhouse, tho' my acquaintance with
him is but slight.
    A very critical time is approaching. It is expected that administration
will make some advances towards an accomodation. There are English
Papers in this City brought by a Ship from Dunkirk, that mention
Mr Penn, who carried the last Petition to the King, being examined
before the House of Lords. His answers were short and clearer and
seem'd to have weight with some of that Body, who had before been
kept in the Dark. The expression is that he had made several of them
Quakers. The Duke of Grafton, the Archbishop of Canterbury, and
the bishop of Peterborough have espous'd the American cause. The
bolus begins to operate & I think some of them will quake er'e it be long.
    Administration have demanded 25,000 Men for the American service,

which is ridicul'd by those in opposition, as entirely insufficient, after having been told by Mr Penn that the province of Pennsylvania singly, was 60,000 strong. They were call'd upon to speak out at once and declare what would be demanded, but that they did not chuse to do, until they had sounded and found how the Land laid. I have endeavoured to procure a paper for you, but being in the hands of the Printers, who do not chuse to part with them, I am disappointed & must therefore refer you to Purdies, who will have the News from his Brother Printers of this City. A Battallion of the Devonshire Militia have petitioned the King to send them over to America to thrash the Rebels. This petition was attack'd in the House of Commons by the Friends of Liberty as dangerous & highly improper; & the Minister condemn'd for suffering such an one to be presented to his Majesty: He was also accus'd of altering several parts of it himself & suiting it to his own purpose, after it had been taken out of the hands of the Petitioners. Thus have I given you all the News I can recollect, tho' in a very imperfect manner, having never seen the Paper.

I am much concerned to find Bullit & Innes neglected by the Convention. I will consult my colleagues whether it will be proper to move for the former to have rank as a Colo. I think it would, & if they will join me it may be done. What we can do for Innes I do not know unless, provided a General be appointed, we can prevail on him to make him his Aid de Camp, a post that I think would suit him well, but there his rank would be only that of Major, whether he would like this or not I can not tell.[1] Adieu   [Francis Lightfoot Lee]

Reprinted from Lawrence H. Leder, ed., *The Genesis of American Freedom, 1765–1795* (Waltham, Mass.: Brandeis University, 1961), p. 21.

[1] On March 6, 1776, Thomas Bullit was appointed deputy adjutant general in the southern department with the rank of lieutenant colonel. James Innis became a major on August 13, 1776. *JCC*, 4:187, 5:649.

Thomas McKean to Philip Schuyler

Sir,   Philadelphia January 30th 1776

A certain Duncan Campbell, Captain in the Royal Scotch Emigrants and now a Prisoner here, in a conversation yesterday with Capt. Wade of the Militia of this City, who is a relation of Sir John Johnston, so far forgot himself, as to mention to him that there were two hundred of that regiment in the neighbourhood of Sir John.

These Soldiers are supposed to be the McDonalds & highlanders settled on the lands of Sir John.

I am desired by the Congress to communicate this information to you, that these Soldiers and their Officers may be apprehended and detained as prisoners of war and not considered merely as Tories.[1] If they are

Soldiers and can be secured, they may possibly be exchanged for the like number of our friends in Quebec.

I wish you a quick restoration of your [health], and am, Sr, with the utmost regard, Your most obedient humble Servant,

Thos McKean

RC (NN). Burnett, *Letters*, 1:335–36. RC damaged; missing words supplied from Tr.

[1] Although there is no mention of this episode in the journals, see Richard Smith's Diary, this date. General Schuyler, acting on similar intelligence, had already led a formidable force to Johnstown, and on January 20 had forced Sir John Johnson and his tenants to surrender their arms and ammunition. Barbara Graymont, *The Iroquois in the American Revolution* (Syracuse: Syracuse University Press, 1972), pp. 81–85; and Benson J. Lossing, *The Life and Times of Philip Schuyler*, 2 vols. (New York: Sheldon & Co., 1872–73), 2:17–21.

Robert Morris to Samuel Inglis

Dear sir   Philada. Jany 30th. 1776

Your letters of the 31st Decr., 6 & 7th Inst. have given me infinite Concern.[1] Before the receipt of them I was prepared to hear of your suffering a Considerable loss of property by the operations at Norfolk, but still had hopes it woud not be so great as to approach any thing near that point you mention. I sincerely Sympathize with you for the miserable situation of those you are Connected with & lament that they took part with those whom it was & is disgracefull to side with. For my part I considered this Subject early & fixed on principle the part I shoud take in the unhappy Contest. I sided with this Country because their claims are founded in Justice and I wish every Friend to the American Cause may act on the same principle that every Tory wou'd consider it well before they act against it, but I doubt your Friends have only thought the Power of Great Britain insurmountable & founded their Conduct on that belief. This I believe to be the case with most of the Tories in America.

I not only lament your situation but woud willingly help you out of it, therefore I beg you will keep up your Spirits & Collect your affairs into the best Posture you can. That done, inform me how you stand & tell me what can be done to serve you; every thing in my power that can be exerted in your service Consistently shall be done. I also wish you to send up soon as possible W[illing] M[orris] & Cos. Virginia Account Current which remains unsettled in Our Books. I expect to suffer a good deal in Virginia, South Carolina & other places, however, if this plan does but stand its ground as I hope it will, I must be Content to suffer heavily otherwise. I am in haste, Dr Sir, Your affectionate Hble Servt.,   Robt Morris

RC (MH).

¹ These three letters are in the Robert Morris Papers, DLC, the second of which is also printed in Clark, *Naval Documents*, 3:662–63. Inglis (d. 1783), a member of the firm Willing, Morris & Co., operating out of Norfolk, had written from Northampton County, Va., on December 31 suggesting that Morris obtain his appointment as paymaster or commissary to the troops Congress had recently authorized for Virginia. On January 6 he wrote from Williamsburg to report his heavy losses in Dunmore's January 1 attack on Norfolk, and the following day he asked Morris to ignore his previous request for an appointment in view of the condition of his affairs in the aftermath of Dunmore's disastrous attack.

New York Delegates to
the New York Committee of Safety

Gentlemen,   Phila. 30th Jany 1776.

We had the Honour of writing to you yesterday by Mr Lynch. We now set down to say a Word or two respecting the Case of Mr Foster.¹

Sorry as we are that the priviledge granted by our Convention to that Gentleman has led him into Inconveniences, Yet the Restraint upon exporting Live stock is grounded upon such solid Reasons, and appeared so essential to Congress, that we are perswaded it will be in vain to ask for a Relaxation in this or any Instance. We have consulted some of our Congress Friends who are of the same Opinion; and have satisfied Mr Foster that it will be to no purpose to make the proposition.

We hope however you may think of some method of putting it in his power in another way to make up his Losses, which will give us particular Pleasure.

The other matters containd in that Dispatch we shall consider and act upon with all Diligence.

We have the Honour to be with the greatest Respect, Gentlemen, Your most Obedient, humble Servant,   Jas. Duane

                                          Henry Wisner

                                          Wm. Floyd

RC (N). Written by Duane and signed by Duane, Floyd, and Wisner. *Journals of N.Y. Prov. Cong.*, 2:137. RC damaged; missing words supplied from Tr.

¹ On August 5, 1775, the New York Provincial Congress agreed to allow John Foster, then a member of this body from Suffolk County, to ship a cargo of livestock to the West Indies in exchange for "military stores for the benefit of this Colony." Clark, *Naval Documents*, 1:1071. Before Foster was ready to send a ship to the West Indies, however, Congress decided on November 1 to forbid the exportation of livestock from the colonies. *JCC*, 3:315. When, therefore, Foster was finally ready for this voyage early in January 1776, he asked the New York Committee of Safety to allow him to take advantage of the permission to ship livestock which he had received from the provincial congress several months before. The committee of safety refused to do this and instead referred the issue to the New York delegates, who apparently refrained from bringing it before Congress. *Am. Archives*, 4th ser. 4:1059–60.

Richard Smith's Diary

Tuesday Jany. 30 [1776]
A Petition was read from a Serjeant in Capt. (now Lt. Col.) Wm.
Allens Compy. prayg. Pay or some Recompence from his Capt., it
was ordered to lie on the Table. A Report on Apprentices, Small
Debtors and Infants inlisting was a second Time made, altered, passed &
ordd. to be published.¹ A Comee. of 5 was chosen to consider the Representation from the Convention of N York.² Rob. Morris was added
to Dr. Franklin & Dickinson the secret Comee. of Correspondence. Mr.
President laid before Us a Desire of some Persons that Gen Prescott
may be discharged from Goal on Account of an old Wound & his ill
state of Health, the Drs. Cadwallader & Shippen Junr. are requested
to visit Him & make Report.³ Dr. Wm. Smith had Leave to inspect the
Letters relative to Gen. Montgomys Death, the Dr. being to pronounce
an Oration on the Occasion. McKean informed Congress that 200 and
odd Men in Tryon County are inlisted in the Kings Regiment of Royal
Emigrants, Mr. McKean was desired to acquaint Gen Schuyler of it
by Letter.⁴ Dr. Franklin from a Comee. reported inter alia in Favor of
the Application from Dr. Huddleston for Release alledging the Custom
of Armies to set free all Surgeons taken Prisoners, it was objected to
and postponed.⁵ A Bill of Exchange from Cambridge on the Continental
Treasurers for 1000 Dollars, was ordered to be honored. The Report for
granting a Bounty for Inlistment in the New England Army was agitated
and postponed because Virginia and So. Carolina are not fully represented. Morton reported on Capt. Nelsons Company of Riflemen
which was agreed to. A Letter was recd. by the Jersey Delegates from
Mr. Faesch offering to cast Cannon for the American Service.⁶ Yesterday
I went with some of the Delegates to view the Boom Chain, Fire Rafts
and Two Men of War on the Stocks One of 32 & the other of 28 Guns
at Kensington. 30,000 Dollars voted on Account to the Comee for
Building the 13 new Men of War. On the 24th Instt. an Order passed
for allowg the Pay master or Captains to retain Part of the Soldiers Pay
with their Consent, to sustain their Wives and Children.

MS (DLC).
¹ See Smith's Diary, January 26, 1776, note 2.
² The New York Committee of Safety's "Representation" has not been identified,
nor has any committee report on it been found. See *JCC*, 4:104.
³ On February 1 Congress agreed to allow Brigadier General Prescott to be attended in jail by his servant and a physician. *JCC*, 4:107.
⁴ See Thomas McKean to Philip Schuyler, this date.
⁵ Huddleston's "application" had been received on January 25. See *JCC*, 4:87–88.
⁶ This letter to the New Jersey delegates from John Jacob Faesch (1729–99),
ironmaster and government contractor, has not been found. Faesch, a native of
Basel, Switzerland, who emigrated to New Jersey in 1764, owned the Mount Hope
furnace in Bergen County, where he subsequently manufactured shot and shell for

the American army with the assistance of several hundred Hessian prisoners of war. *DAB*. See also *JCC*, 5:608; and Smith's Diary, February 15, 1776.

James Duane to Robert R. Livingston

My dear Sir   Philad. Jany 31st 1776.

Much as I feel for you, our Family, our Country, and myself, on the death of our generous and heroic Friend; I shall make no Reflections on the fatal Event. Every Tongue is loud in celebrating his Praises, and lamenting his Fate; and on every Breast his distinguished merit is written in Characters indelible. Among the first Patriots and Heros, the faithful Page of History will perpetuate the name of Montgomerie to the latest Posterity for their Example and Admiration!

The Congress impressed with the highest Sense of Gratitude to their favourite General for his eminent Services, have unanimously resolved to erect a monument sacred to his memory, which is to be finished in the most elegant manner in France under the Direction of Doctor Franklin.[1] The place where it is to be erected is not determined, your Friends Wishing to know your Opinion in this particular, which will I believe have great weight.

The Congress have also desird Doctor Smith to prepare and deliver a funeral Oration in Honour of their Heroe. No time is yet appointed for this Solemnity. Indeed the Doctor is at a Loss for the Circumst[ance]s of his birth, Education, and general Outlines of his Life, previous to this short but glorious Race which he has run in the Service and for the preservation of our distressed Country. Nor am I, to whom he has applied, sufficiently informd to instruct Him. Will you then, my dear Sir, Supply what is so requisite by the earliest Opportunity?[2] enlarging his amiable Character with every Circumstance which may serve to adorn a performance which will probably be read with avidity not only in America but Europe. Smith has Taste, Elegance and ambition, and I look for an extraordinary production from his masterly Pen.

Our Friend Hooper with that refined Sensibility, and generous Friendship for which he is justly distinguished took the Lead on this occasion. I have not time to send you a Copy of the Resolution, which conveys a most honourable Testimonial of our Departed Friends uncommon Merit, but shall not neglect it when another Opportunity offers. This comes by Express.

Poor Mrs. Montgomerie! How I feel for her Distress! But I quit a Subject of which I cannot think without real Pain.

Adieu my dear Sir and ever believe me to be with the utmost Regard, your Affectionate Kinsman,[3] & most Obed hume Servant,

Jas Duane

RC (NHpR: Livingston-Redmond Collection deposit).

¹ See *JCC*, 4:89–90.

² General Montgomery had been married to Livingston's older sister, Janet. George Dangerfield, *Chancellor Robert R. Livingston of New York, 1746–1813* (New York: Harcourt, Brace and Co., 1960), genealogical chart facing p. 516. Although a note survives in the Edmund C. Burnett Collection, DLC, indicating that Thomas Lynch also wrote a letter to Robert R. Livingston this date, recent efforts to locate this document have failed. "To express my own feelings is impossible," Lynch wrote. "The whole city of Philadelphia was in tears. Every person seemed to have lost his nearest relative and heart friend." Lynch then continued with a request for information concerning Montgomery's life that might be used by William Smith in preparing his funeral oration for the fallen general. Livingston's response to Lynch included the following pertinent passage: "I am extremely sorry that by some accident (what I know not) your favor of the 31st ult did not reach me till yesterday so that no accounts that I can send will be with you in time to be of any service to Doctor Smith." Bancroft transcript, dated "February 1776," NN.

³ Duane's wife, Mary, and Robert R. Livingston were distant cousins. Ibid.

John Hancock to the Massachusetts Assembly

Januy. 31 [1776]

On moving to Congress our Scituation and my proposing to Resign in Consequence of the Expiration of our Authority from you; the Congress apprehending your intention to be that Massachusetts should be constantly Represented, & a Newspaper being produc'd wherein mention was made of a New Delegation they directed the paper to be put on File, and Desir'd us to attend as usual in Congress untill we could be honour'd with your further Directions.¹

RC (M-Ar). A continuation of Hancock to the Massachusetts Assembly, January 29, 1776.

¹ The Massachusetts Assembly had formally elected delegates on January 18, although official word of this did not reach Congress until John Adams and Elbridge Gerry arrived and presented their credentials on February 9, 1776. Actually the assembly had made a preliminary selection of delegates for 1776 on December 15, 1775, and, according to Robert Treat Paine, word of this action reached Philadelphia as early as January 6. See *JCC*, 4:122; *Am. Archives*, 4th ser. 4:1235–36, 1339; and Robert Treat Paine's Diary, January 6, 1776.

Richard Smith's Diary

Wednesday Jany. 31. [1776]

Votes read & Letters from Ld. Stirling, Col. Maxwell & others.¹ Maxwell attendg., Paine & Wisner were named to confer with Him & they made a Report & we furnished the Col with Copies of that & a former Order. Capt Dempster of the Blue Mountain Valley lately taken by Ld. Stirling having a private Property on Board, the same was now restored to Him by Congress at the Request of his Lordship,

Quaere Whether the Mates Adventure was not also allowed to Him.
Wyth reported on the Remainder of Washns., Schuylers & Ld Stirlings
Letters, part of it about the Captive Officers travelling Expences was
recommitted.[2] The Powers of the Massas. Delegates expiring this day
they seemed to be of Opinion that they could not attend again till their
new Delegations arrived but the Appointments published in Two News
Papers being read, Congress was unanimous to accept them. The Affair
of Prescotts Confinement was agitated and postponed after the Physicians' Opinion had been read. Something done about the Indians of the
Middle Departmt. McKean moved to reconsider the resolution of
Yesterday about small Debtors, Apprentices & Infants inlisting, he was
oppugned & withdrew his Motion.

MS (DLC).
[1] See *JCC*, 4:104–5.
[2] See *JCC*, 4:94–95, 99–100, 105.

John Jay's Essay on Congress and Independence

[January? 1776][1]
It has long been the Art of the Enemies of America to sow the seeds
of Dissentions among us and thereby weaken that Union on which our
Salvation from Tyranny depends. For this Purpose Jealousies have been
endeavoured to be excited, and false Reports, wicked Slanders and
insidious misrepresentations industriously formed and propagated.

Well knowing that while the People reposed Confidence in the
Congress, the Designs of the Ministry would probably be frustrated no
Pains have been spared to traduce that respectable Assembly and
misrepresent their Designs and actions.

Among other aspersions cast upon them, is an ungenerous & ground-
less Charge of their aiming at Independence, or a total Separation from
G. Britain.

Whoever will be at the Trouble of reviewing their Journal will find
ample Testimony against this accusation, and for the sake of those who
may not have either Leisure or Opportunity to peruse it, I have selected
the following Paragraphs which abundantly prove the Malice and falsity
of such a Charge.[2]

Page 59. The Congress in giving orders for securing the Stores taken
at Crown Point & Ticonderogah direct "That an Exact Inventory be
taken of all such Cannon and Stores, in order that they may be safely
returned, *when the Restoration of the former Harmony between Great Britain &*
these Colonies, so ardently wished for by the latter shall render it prudent and
consistent with the *over-ruling Law of self Preservation*."

Page 63. The Congress after resolving that the Colonies ought to be put in a State of Defence, thus proceed unanimously. "But as *we most ardently wish* for a *Restoration of the Harmony* formerly subsisting between our Mother Country and these Colonies, the Interruption of which must, at all Events be exceedingly injurious to both Countries, *that with a sincere Design of contributing by all the Means in our Power,* (not incompatible with a just Regard for the undoubted Rights and true Interests of these Colonies) *to the Promotion of this most desireable Reconciliation,* an humble and dutiful Petition be presented to his Majesty. Resolved that *measures be entered into for opening a negotiation, in order to accommodate the unhappy disputes subsisting between Great Britain and these Colonies,* and that *this* be made a *Part* of the *Petition to the King.*"

Page 64. The Congress recommend to the Convention of New York "to persevere the more vigorously in preparing for their Defence, as it is very uncertain whether *the earnest Endeavours of the Congress to accommodate the unhappy Differences between Great Britain and the Colonies, by conciliatory Measures, will be successful.*"

Page 84. The Congress in order to rescue the Province of Massachusetts Bay from Anarchy, advise that their "Assembly or Council exercise the Powers of Government *until a Governor of his Majestys Appointment* will consent *to govern the Colony according to its Charter.*"

Page 87. The Congress in their vote for a general Fast recommend that we should "offer up our joint Supplications to the all wise, omnipotent & merciful Disposer of all Events (among other Things) [3] *to bless our rightful Sovereign King George the Third,* that *a speedy End* may be put to the civil *Discord between Great Britain and the American Colonies* without further Effusion of Blood." "And that all America may soon behold a gracious Interposition of Heaven for the Redress of her many Grievances, the Restoration of her invaded Rights, *a Reconciliation with the parent State on Terms consitutional and honorable to both.*"

Page 149. The Congress after declaring the Reasons which compelled them to recur to Arms, thus express themselves—"Lest this Declaration should disquiet the Minds of our Friends & Fellow Subjects in any Part of the Empire, we assure them that *we mean not to dissolve that Union which has so long & so happily subsisted between us,* and which we *sincerely wish* to see *restored. Necessity* has not yet *driven* us into that *desperate* Measure, or induced us to excite any other nation to War against them. We *have not* raised Armies *with ambitious Designs of separating from Great Britain, and establishing independent States.*"

[*Page*] 150. "We most humbly [4] implore the divine Goodness *to dispose our Adversaries to Reconciliation on reasonable Terms.*"

Page 155. In the Petition to the King, every Line of which breaths affection for his Majesty & Great Britain, are these remarkable Sentences.

"Attached to your Majestys Person, Family & Government, with all the Devotion that Principle & Affection can inspire, *connected with Great*

Britain by the strongest Ties that can unite Societies, and *deploring every Event* that tends in *any Degree* to *weaken* them, we *solemnly assure* your Majesty, that we not only *most ardently desire* the former *Harmony* between her and these Colonies may be *restored,* but that a *Concord* may be *established between them* upon so *firm a Basis* as to perpetuate its Blessings uninterrupted *by any future Dissentions to succeeding Generations in both Countries.*" "We beg Leave further to assure your Majesty that notwithstanding the *Sufferings* of your loyal Colonists during the Course of this present Controversey our Breasts retain *too tender a Regard for the Kingdom from which we derive our origin,* to request such a Reconciliation as might in *any Manner be inconsistent with her Dignity or Welfare.*"

Page 163. In the last Address of the Congress to the People of Great Britain are the following Passages.

"*We are accused of aiming at Independence;* but *how* is this accusation *supported?* By the *Allegations* of your *Ministers* not by *our Actions. Abused, insulted & contemned what steps have we pursued to obtain Redress? We have carried our dutiful Petitions to the Throne. We have applied to your Justice for Relief.*"

Page 165. "Give us Leave most solemnly to assure you, *that we have not yet lost Sight of the Object we have ever had in View, a Reconciliation with you on constitutional Principles, and a Restoration of that friendly Intercourse which to the Advantage of both, we till lately maintained.*"

Page 172. In the Address of the Congress to the Lord Mayor, Aldermen and Livery of London, there is this Paragraph vizt.

"*North America* My Lord! *wishes most ardently for a lasting connection with Great Britain on Terms of just and equal Liberty.*"

From these testimonies it appears extremely evident that to charge the Congress with aiming at a Separation of these Colonies from Great Britain is to charge them falsely and without a single Spark of Evidence to support the accusation.

Many other Passages in their Journal might be mentioned, but as that would exceed the Limits of this Paper, I shall reserve them for some future Publication.[5]

It is much to be wished that People would read the Proceedings of the Congress and consult their own judgments, and not suffer themselves to be *duped by Men who are paid for decieving them.*

MS (NNC photocopy). In Jay's hand and endorsed by him, apparently at a much later date: "Proofs that the colonies do not aim at independence. Probably in 1775."

[1] Aside from Jay's noncontemporary and somewhat tentative endorsement, there is no direct evidence available about the provenance and date of this essay. It seems likely that Jay was moved to compose it in response to the arrival in Philadelphia early in January 1776 of news of George III's October 26, 1775, address to Parliament accusing the colonists of waging "rebellious war . . . for the purpose of establishing an independent Empire" and in conjunction with his own efforts at this time, in negotiations with Lord Drummond, to achieve a reconciliation between America and Great Britain. Jay's participation in the talks with Drummond may well explain

his failure to mention the king's speech in this essay, believing, in his zeal to bridge
the widening gap between the colonies and mother country, that it was preferable
to criticize the monarch's advisers instead of the monarch himself. In any case,
Jay's direct quotations in this essay from an edition of the journals of Congress
which was not available to the public until December 11, 1775, suggest that he
could not have written it before then; and the rapidly changing mood in Philadelphia toward independence in January 1776, after the publication of *Common Sense*
and the arrival of word of Dunmore's attack on Norfolk, makes it unlikely that he
wrote it later in the year. See *JCC*, 3:514; *Am. Archives*, 4th ser. 6:1–3; and Lord
Drummond's Notes, January 3–9? 1776.

Apparently John Dickinson was also considering a response to the king's charges
at about this time. Among a group of Dickinson MSS in the Gratz Collection, PHi,
is the following notation, in Dickinson's hand, on a fragment of a page: "Proofs
that the Colonies do not aim at an Independant Empire. See pa. 49 of the first
Journal—61—69—75—91—142. 2d Journal—63, 64, 111, 112, 149, 156, 163, 164,
165, 166." For the "first Journal," see *JCC*, 1:136; and for the "2d Journal," see
below, note 2.

² All quotations cited by Jay refer to actions of Congress from May 18 through
July 8, 1775, and are taken from *Journal of the Proceedings of the Congress, held at
Philadelphia; May 10, 1775* (Philadelphia: William and Thomas Brandford, 1775),
which was originally advertised for sale on December 11, 1775. *JCC*, 3:514. For the
same citations from a more accessible edition of the journals, see *JCC*, 2:56, 64–66,
84, 87–88, 155–57, 160, 166, 167, 171.

³ Parenthetical remark inserted by Jay.

⁴ "Devoutly" in journals.

⁵ No contemporary printing of this essay has been found, nor has any sequel to
it been discovered.

Robert R. Livingston to Thomas Lynch

Dear Sir   [January? 1776] ¹

I have long wished to write to you & mention some matters which
struck me as important because I was well satisfied that if you saw them
in the same light you would endeavour to enforce them; if otherwise
that would excuse any trouble that a desire to serve a cause which you
have so warmly & ably espoused created [*for*] you.

When the expedition agt. Canada was first projected I opposed it
for reasons which have been too often reiterated to make any mention of
them necessary & our success has not changed my sentiments but
whether the loss which I have sustained by the death of my very worthy
friend a relation may not have confirmed me in (what is possible) an
error I will not pretend to determine. However it is indisputable that the
possession of Canada will drain us of our specie, disapate without ading
to our strength, for it is most evident that the Canadians are not to be
relied on & that they will always side with the stronger power & it is
more than probable that if we should at any time be unfortunate when
our enemies had an army in the country that their perfidy may be the
total destruction of any troops we have sent there. It is true indeed that

if our enemies returned that country it might lay us under a necessity of defending an extensive frontier not only from the incursions of such of the inhabitants of Canada as chose to take up arms but against the Indians who would in such case be very much under their influence.

If therefore an expediant could be fall'n upon which would at once free us from this danger & the expence of defending that province I can not help thinking that it should be readily adopted however daring it may seem for it is much too late to deliberate about the arms we shall use when the enimy are at the door. I must own that I can not help entertaining a thought which may perhaps be too visionary to realize yet I submit it to your judgment; if it should happen to coincide with your sentiments I shall be strongly confirmed in my opinion.

We are told from pretty good authority that the French have lately sent 7000 men to Hispaniola.[2] This in all probability is with a view to take advantage of the troubles in America. If so, large discretionary power must be vested in their commander. I can not help thinking that an offer of the quiet possession of Canada & the solemn assurinces & plighted faith of America that we will at no time even in case of a reconciliation with G. Britain lend them our aid in any designs that they may form against the French West Indies would be an aluring bait & at the same time cost us nothing. If the commander of the French troops should be an enterprizing man he will run the risque of the attempt in the hopes of its being approved by [his?] court—or if disavowed he might be flattered with the sovereignty of the country allowing to the Canadians as much freedom as the genious of their people would make them desire in which case it would not be difficult to maintain that province against all the power of Great Britain or if our partizans were driven out of it they would greatly increase our strength.

It may indeed be objected that this would not be treating the Canadians as we promised them. But it should be remembered that our promises were founded upon their accession to the union & confederacy of these colonies with which they have never yet complied & I dare say it would be infinitly more agreeable to the few real friends we have in that country to have any security [than] to be left to the uncertain contingency of our being able to defend them. These are only loose hints on which if you think them worthy of notice you will doubtless improve.

Our enimies have Set us the example of calling in foreign aid.[3] I know none that can so easily assist us as France nor any thing more inviting that we can offer than what I have proposed. Our trade indeed would be a valuable object but the offer of that excludes all hope of an accomodation with Great Britain as it must end in their total ruin. Besides that, the offer must be precarious & founded only upon a supposition that we shall succeed—whereas here is a present good which does not depend upon particular contingencies.

I always had it very much at Heart that the Congress should set at Albany or some other place nearer the scene of Action than Philadelphia & I am most firmly persuaded that we should not have met with the late mortifying check at Quebec had that been the case. The officers & soldiers being more immediately under their inspection would have been ashamed to desert their duty in the manner they have done or at least some remedy would have been applied to the evil. I believe from what I can learn that not above one third of the troops raised for this department were ever at any one time in actual service so that instead of 40/ a month we may without exageration assert that every soldier in Canada cost us £6—an expence this which it is utterly impossible we should be able to bear long. I wish that you would think of some meathod of puting a stop to this mischief which must end in our ruin.

Genl. Schuyler shewed me your resolve with respect to the fortification in the highlands.[4] I was much pleased to find that you had sent a committee to examine the place & fixed on a spot down the river but I must confess that desisting from the work at Martilars Rock after so much money had been layd out upon it surprized me.[5] The finishing only one bastion would make it extreamly formidable and indeed impassible unless the enemy were very much favoured by the wind nor could the expence be very great after what has been already done. It is true it is commanded by the west point but a hundred men there would prevent the enimies possessing themselves of it even without any further expence than a palisade in the water of about 50 yards long near the only place where an enemy could land. There is a natural intrenchment in the rocks within musket shot of every vessel that passes, besides that booms may be thrown across at this place more conveniently than in any other part of the river. But if the finishing this bastion should be thought too expensive at least let an battery be erected at some little distance from the fort to the eastward which may be made of earth by the soldiers & commands the whole reach below & must of necessity prove very troublesome to shiping coming up. I could have wished instead of leaving this matter to the Provincial Congress certain persons had been appointed to superintend the works & the congress requested to afford them any assistance they might require. I am the more anxious on this head because I am firmly of Opinion that our country is only accessable by water. If an army should march from New York there is a pass in the highlands which I am persuaded 1000 men could guard agt. ten times that number & the retreat of the enemy cut off by a deep [. . .] 40 miles from New York which they would be obliged to repass & which the militia of Connecticut, Long Island & New Jersey who would naturally being on their rear could easily prevent. If they should attempt to penetrate Connecticut by the way of New York their frontier is likewise defended by a river & the whole force of our province & New Jersey would cut off their retreat & render it impossible for them to receive supplies. But if they should be able to pass our fortifications on Hudsons River they may not only ravage our whole province without any difficulty but penetrate into New Jersey & Pennsilvania on their northern frontiers where the [. . .] naturally weak & at the same time keep up an uninterupted communication with the Indians who lay [along?] the rear of all the southern governments or they [might?] enter three of the New England Governments without any danger of being hemmd in by two armies—so that the fortifiing strongly Hudsons River is an object of the last importance [to] all the Continent. It was Genl. Montgomerries opinion that fort was of little avail without a boom. [He] wrote to me on the subject but ten days before his death. I wish some Engineer could be found to take the charge of this matter at any price. I dread the leaving the whole management to the provincial convention who have frequent recesses & are at best but slow in their operations. I ought to appologize for having taken up so much of your time but the present situation of our family from the death of my father, Grandfather & brother in law preventing my attendance on Congress I thought it proper to throw out hints which if worthy of Attention you will not fail to improve; if otherwise suppress. Be pleased Sir to present my best Compts. to your own family & Messrs. Rutledge & Middleton if they are still with you. I am &c

FC (N).
  [1] Although the precise date of this letter cannot be determined, the fact that Livingston, who apparently wrote it from his home at Clermont, refers to several topics that were discussed in the correspondence of other delegates writing from Philadelphia during the first half of January suggests that it was written during the latter half of this month.
  [2] A rumor to this effect, based upon "a Letter of authority from the Island of Hispaniola dated the 23d of November," was current in New York early in January 1776. Clark, *Naval Documents*, 3:654, 942.
  [3] Perhaps Livingston is referring to the king's revelation in his October 26, 1775, speech to Parliament that "I have also the satisfaction to inform you, that I have received the most friendly offers of foreign assistance; and if I shall make any treaties in consequence thereof, they shall be laid before you." *Am. Archives*, 4th ser. 6:2.
  [4] See the resolution on this subject adopted by Congress on January 5, in *JCC*, 4:34.
  [5] See Committee to the Northward to John Hancock, November 23, 1775.

Committee of Congress to
the New York Committee of Safety

New York, February 1, 1776
  Messrs. Harrison, Lynch, and Allen,[1] present their compliments to the Committee of Safety of this Colony. They have received the order of their Board, but are under a necessity of informing them that they cannot undertake that the troops commanded by General Lee shall be

under the entire direction of the Committee or Provincial Congress, as
that would be to exceed any powers lodged in them by the Continental
Congress. They cannot see the propriety of this order, after the conference had by them with Colonel McDougall and Mr. Scott, and the
assurances given those gentlemen this morning.[2]

MS not found; reprinted from *Am. Archives*, 4th ser. 4:1098.
  [1] For the background of this congressional committee, see *JCC*, 4:92, 94; and
John Hancock to Charles Lee, January 26, 1776.
  [2] For the minutes of the conference this day between Alexander McDougall and
John Morin Scott of the committee of safety and the members of the committee
of Congress, see *Am. Archives*, 4th ser. 4:1096. The committee of safety rescinded
its order placing General Lee's troops under its "direction" after a conference with
the delegates later this day at which the delegates successfully argued that this
authority had been vested in them by Congress. Ibid., p. 1100. For subsequent
deliberations between the committee of safety and the committee of Congress, see
ibid., pp. 1106–10.

John Hancock to Thomas Cushing

Dear Sir,   Philadelphia, Feby. 1st. 1776
  I Rec'd your favor Dated at Head Quarters, am Glad to hear of your
safe Arrival there; since which none of your favors. I wrote you a long
Letter by an Express under Cover to the General. The Letter I then
mention'd to be Signing by the Delegates will be Deliver'd you by
Mr. Hooper [1] who has Leave of Absence and is now on his way to the
Camp. Make a proper use of that Letter, and of some other Circumstances you are Acquainted with. Not having heard any thing from our
Assembly with respect to a new Delegation, and our Time Expiring
yesterday, we mention'd it to Congress, and I proposed to Resign my
place, not looking upon ourselves Authorized to appear in Congress
again; the Congress apprehending it was not the intention of Massachusetts to be unrepresented and a News paper being produc'd wherein
mention was made of a new Appointment they order'd the paper to be
put on file, and Desir'd us to Attend in Congress as usual, untill we
Rec'd the further Directions of our Assembly. How can it happen that
no Account was forwarded, the Secretary ought to know his Duty. I
cannot Reconcile it, but ———[2]
  We go on as usual. I have been much hurried, in giving out Commissions, etc., very little time to my self. I have sent Cash and Commissions for the Battalion Raising in our province for Canada to the
Assembly. Lord Stirling with some of his Troops has Taken a large
Transport Ship bound with Necessaries to Boston, and she is now
unloading in Elizabeth Town point. We are Disarming the Tories in
New York Government. Schuyler we hear has Attack'd John Johnson
with 700 Tories, Vanquish'd them and Taken 700 Arms. The Philadelphia Battalion is march'd to Canada, the New Jersey Battalion

follows in a day or two. Col. St. Clair's Battalion in a few days will follow. This St. Clair was a Regular Officer, he married Mr. Bayard's Daughter of Boston, and a fine fellow he is. I hope the General will send a General Officer to Command in Canada, we have wrote him to that Effect.[3] We have sent a Committee to New York to Confer with Genl. Lee and the New York Committee about that City.

I inclose you a Minute respecting the Conduct here as to the Ships. You will peruse it, and I leave it entirely to you to Determine matters as you think best, and do give me a particular Account in your next and at all times how you go on. The plans and Drafts will be Ready to morrow, and shall be immediately sent. I cannot make them go on faster; do let me know as soon as you can the exact purchases you can make and the Articles, and I must desire you will immediately Dispatch to me a person in whom you can Confide to Carry you the Money, it is Ready, and the Committee think it best you should Dispatch a Man on purpose, as we cannot have a safe Opportunity otherwise, this you will do directly, order the Man to travell fast. Pray hurry the Builders, etc. They must do as well as they can till the plans Come. Let me know what Article cannot be purchas'd with you. The Iron cannot be got down, the River is froze, you must get the best you can. Be particular in your next, pray use Dispatch. Tell the people they shall have their pay Regularly, it only wants fetching. Do write me all News, Assembly matters and everything. Do be a faithful Correspondent. Send me what I wrote for in my last. Let me know every movement with you. I send you the Inclos'd Memo. only for your Guide, you will Conform as Circumstances require, but do the best you can in all matters. I Leave it with you, only use the utmost Dispatch, and by all means let ours be as forward as any, do not suffer Massachusetts to be behind any Colonies.

Give us always every Occurrence, write every Post, send your Man for the Money, and do the Needfull in all matters. Adieu. I am sincerely your Friend and Hum. Servt.   John Hancock.

[*P.S.*] If my Man Mr. Spriggs should apply to you for a little Money, I shall be oblig'd to you to supply him. I will Repay you with Thanks.

Our Marine Committee meets this Evening, the plans shall follow this.

MS not found; reprinted from *Proceedings of the Massachusetts Historical Society* 60 (January 1927): 100–102.

[1] See the letter of James Duane, William Hooper, George Read, Stephen Hopkins, and John Morton to Thomas Cushing extracted in John Hancock to Thomas Cushing, January 17, 1776, note 2.

[2] See *JCC*, 4:106. Although the Massachusetts delegation had been elected on January 18, 1776, the credentials were not presented to Congress until February 9, when Elbridge Gerry and John Adams arrived at Philadelphia. *JCC*, 4:122.

[3] See John Hancock to George Washington, January 29, 1776. Congress appointed Charles Lee as commander in Canada on February 17, but before he could depart Lee was replaced by John Thomas. *JCC*, 4:157, 186.

Secret Committee Contract

February 1, 1776

This Charter Party made the first day of February[1] in the year of our Lord one thousand seven hundred and seventy six Between James King and Joseph Harper of the City of Philadelphia Merchants and owners of the Brigantine Cornelia of the burthen of one hundred Tonns or thereabouts whereof Thomas Genn is Master of the one part & Samuel Ward, Benjamin Franklin, Thomas McKean, Joseph Hewes, Josiah Bartlett and Robert Morris Esquires a secret Committee appointed by the Honoble. the Continental Congress of the other part. Witnesseth that the said James King and Joseph Harper for the considerations hereinafter mentioned have hired and let to freight and by these presents do hire and let to freight the said Brigantine unto the said secret Committee afsd. for a voyage to be by her performed in the service of the United American Colonies, from this port of Philadelphia to any port or place that may be ordered in South Carolina,[2] there to receive on board such cargo of rice, indigo or other merchandize, as the Agents or factors of said Committee may put on board to the full loading of said Brigantine with which she is to depart & sail for the port of Nantz in France there delivering the said Cargo agreeable to bills of lading and then receiving on board again all such goods, wares & merchandizes as the Agents or Factors of the said Committee may choose to put on board wherewith said Brigantine is to return back to this Coast and making the first good harbour between Virginia and New Hampshire consistant with the Instructions given the Master of the said Brigantine. He is then to deliver the said goods & merchandize to the order of the said Committee. The said James King and Joseph Harper do further agree that the said Brigantine shall be tight, stiff, strong, and staunch, well and sufficiently fitted, found, victualled & manned for this voyage; and that they will pay all charges and expences arising or accruing on said Brigantine during this voyage, also; That the Master, Mate & Mariners shall at every port & place give the Customary assistance in taking in or discharging goods and otherways perform their duties of their respective stations with proper diligence and dispatch.

In consideration whereof the said Samuel Ward, Benjamin Franklin, Thomas McKean, Joseph Hewes, Josiah Bartlett, and Robert Morris Esquires do in behalf of the United Colonies covenant & agree that they will pay or cause to be paid unto the said James King & Joseph Harper their heirs or assigns the monthly hire or freight of one hundred and twenty pounds Pennsylvania Currency for every month the said Brigantine shall be employed in this voyage which said hire shall commence on the day of the date hereof and shall continue until the day after said Brigantine returns to this port of Philadelphia, unless the said Brigantine shall happen to be lost, sunk, taken, seized or destroyed before such arrival and in that case the monthly hire shall cease on the day such loss, sinking, taking, seizure or destroying happens.[3]

It is also mutually agreed that said Brigantine with all her tackle & apparel, Boats &c. shall be valued and she is hereby valued at the sum of six hundred & fifty pounds Pennsylvania currency which sum the said Committee do hereby insure to the said Owners against any capture or seizure of said Brigantine that may be made by the Enemy of the said United Colonies, agreeing to pay them over and above the said monthly hire the said sum of six hundred & fifty pounds if it shall so happen that said Brigantine is seized or taken by the Enemy. For the true performance of all and singular the convenants and agreements aforesaid, the said parties do mutually bind themselves each to the other in the penal sum of two thousand pounds Pennsylvania Currency to be paid by the party defaulting to the party complying.

In Witness whereof we have hereunto set our hands and seals the day and year first above written.

Witness.   Sam. Ward   James King
                      B Franklin   Joseph Harper
                      Tho McKean
                      Josiah Bartlett
                      Robt Morris
                      Joseph Hewes

MS (PPRF). In a clerical hand, signed by Bartlett, Franklin, Hewes, McKean, Morris, and Ward for the committee, and by Joseph Harper and James King.

[1] The MS originally read "seventeenth day of January."

[2] An order authorizing "Mr. John Dorsius of S. Carolina, Merchant, to load the Brigantine Cornelia, Thomas Genn Master, with the produce of that Colony" was recorded in the committee journal for January 29, 1776. Journal of the Secret Committee, fols. 27–28, MH.

[3] On June 13 the Secret Committee made a final settlement with the owners of the *Cornelia*, which was captured by the British on March 15. See Secret Committee Minutes of Proceedings, June 13, 1776; and Clark, *Naval Documents*, 4:517, 558.

Richard Smith's Diary

Thursday 1 Feb. 1776.

The Votes of Yesterday read accordg to Custom. Gen. Prescott allowed a Servant and Physicians to see Him in Gaol, after a Proposition to allow Him the Liberty of the Hall & Yard and to see his Friends had been voted out by a small Majority. The Report taken up and spoken to about fixing the Price of Expresses & their Stages from hence to Cambridge; it was postponed till Dr. Franklin the Postmaster has consulted his Deputies. S. Adams was added to the Comee. for Stating Expences. Having little Business today the House broke up at 2 oCloc which is much earlier than usual.

MS (DLC).

John Hancock to William Alexander

My Lord   Philadelphia, Feb. 2. 1776
I have the pleasure of Communicating to you the sense of Congress on your alertness, activity and good conduct, and on the readiness and Spirit of the gentlemen and others from Elizabeth Town who voluntarily assisted you in taking the ship Blue Mountain Valley.

I am directed to inform you that it is the desire of Congress that you would secure the capture until the further order of Congress, and that in the mean time you cause such part of the loading as would otherwise perish, to be disposed of by Sale.[1]

The assistance you gave to Colonel Heard is highly approved.

I am further directed to inform you that in consequence of your recommendation, the congress have agreed that you deliver to Captain Dempster and his Mates, their several adventures which were on board the ship at the Time she was Taken, and that Captain Dempster be Liberated, and he has the permission of Congress to improve an opportunity of returning to England, from such port as shall be most agreeable to him.[2]

Your Several letters are now under the Consideration of a committee, as soon as they Report, and Congress have determined thereupon, I will take the Earliest opportunity of acquainting you with the result.

I have the honor to be, with much Esteem, My Lord, your most obedt. humble servt.,   John Hancock Presidt.

Tr (PHi).
  [1] See *JCC*, 4:100.
  [2] See *JCC*, 4:94–95, 106.

Maryland Delegates to
the Maryland Council of Safety

Gent.,   Phila. 2d February 1776.
Last Night We received your Letters by Maynard, covering the Resolutions of Congress relative to the Plates & Paper for the Provl. Currency.[1] As the furnishing Devices is a Business to which We are

entire Strangers, We have advised with Doctr. B. Franklin & shall with his Assistance set the Engraver to Work in a few Days. As the Convention have ordered [both?] Plates & Paper here, We submit to you, whether it would not be expedient to have the printing also done by Hall & Sellers, of this We are certain, the Business would be done with much greater Expedition but in this shall be governed by your Directions.

With Respect to Cannon, so far as We can form any Opinion from the short Time to make the Enquiry, none can be had here or from any of the Eastern Governments, they are very scarce thro' the whole Continent. A Committee of Congress of which Mr Rogers is a Member, have been appointed to make Enquiry into the Quantity of Cannon on Hand & what will be wanted & where & on what Terms they can be had;[2] No Report is yet made, but a Letter from Mr Chase to Mr Paca mentioning that Hughes in Fredk. had contracted with Convention to supply our province at £32.10.–, being communicated to Congress, the Members of the Committee were immediately very desirous to see Mr Hughes & to know whether he would make the like Contract for supplying the Demands of Congress; this will convince you that a Supply cannot be had from hence & that you must rely on your Resources, by casting them in the Province. Mr Paca purchased from Mr. Morris 12 Guns of 6 pound Ball for £600 by order of Mr Johnson, they would have been sent down, had not the Ice stopped the Navigation.

We are with Respect Gent, yr Hble servants,   R. Alexander

Wm. Paca

P.S. Agreable to your Request, a Pasport was granted Maynard, who proceeded immediately to New York.[3] Mr. Purviance inclosed us Affidavits of two Shippers who had been taken by Ld Dunmore, mentg that a pilot Boat with a Clergyman from Maryld. had arrived at Norfolk, who gave Information of the Outfit of Store & the Provision Vessels. If you have heard of this Business, be pleased to advise us; We are desirous of knowing the Truth, a difficult Task at present.

RC (MdAA). Written by Alexander and signed by Alexander and Paca.

[1] For the council's letter of January 20, see *Md. Archives*, 11:101.

[2] See *JCC*, 4:55.

[3] See *Md. Archives*, 11:108–9. The passport for Maynard was to permit him to take three letters from Gov. Robert Eden to New York for the packet to England. Eden's letters, to his brother William and to Lord Dartmouth, enclosed copies of the Maryland Convention's instructions to its delegates to avoid any course of action in Congress leading to independence. "The [Governor's] Step cannot be productive of an ill effect;" the council asserted, "it may be of the greatest Service; it may possibly bring about some Overture to a general Reconciliation."

Richard Smith's Diary

[February 2, 1776]
Friday 2. Letters from Gen. Washington, Gen. Arnold, Col. Lord Stirling and others particularly from Gen Schuyler containg. a full Accot. of his Proceedings with the Tories in Tryon and of his Treaty with Sir John Johnson and the Scotch People there & with the Neighboring Indians.[1] The Jersey Delegates recd. a Letter from Azariah Dunham Esqr. Second in Command on the Expedition to Queens County containg. a Narrative of Col. Heards Transactions.[2] McKean, myself and Wisner appointed to make out a compleat List of the Captive Officers and privates with their Women and Children & where stationed. Capt. Dempster ordered to be discharged.[3] Prescott allowed to recieve Visits from his Bror. Officers and to have Pen, Ink and Paper. Lewis informd of several Vessels returned to New York from unsuccessful Voyages for Arms & Ammunn. A Comee. was chosen to deliberate upon some of the Letters recd. today. E Rutledge reported the Substance of some Papers about the Southern Indians that they are disposed to live quietly and take no Part on either Side. Ward from a Comee. reported that the Petn. of Keppele and Steinmetz prayg. Compensation for their Ship and Cargo detained by Gen. Howe, ought not to be granted.[4] A Memorial from the Indian Preacher Sampson Occum for establishing Missionaries in the Indian Country was referred to a Committee.[5] Adjorned till Monday Morng.

MS (DLC).
[1] This day Congress received letters and enclosures from Schuyler to Hancock of January 22, 23, and 25, 1776. PCC, item 153, 1:406–11, 414–46, 450–77; and *Am. Archives*, 4th ser. 4:802–5, 818–29, 851–56. Enclosed with Schuyler's January 25 letter were letters from Benedict Arnold to David Wooster of January 5 and 6 and a letter from Wooster to Schuyler of January 14. There is no other record that on this date Congress received any letters from Washington or William Alexander.
[2] For what appears to be the letter and enclosures from Dunham referred to here, see *Am. Archives*, 4th ser. 4:858–61.
[3] See Smith's Diary, January 31, 1776.
[4] Ibid., January 27, 1776, note 2.
[5] For Congress' response on February 5 to this petition from Occum, a Connecticut Mohegan, see *JCC*, 4:111.

Josiah Bartlett to John Langdon

Dear Sir,   Philadelphia Feby 3d 1776.
    Your's of the 22d ultimo I recd the first inst. and am glad to hear you got home well and in good order. I perceive by your letter that our Colony have taken up Govt.; "as you say a Committee of both Houses waited on you" and "that some difficulties had arose which you hoped

could be soon ended." I wish you had been a little more particular, as I am very desirous of knowing how things go on in our Province. I am glad to hear that delegates are like to be soon sent here to relieve me; hope good hearty Sons of Liberty will be appointed. I hope the Gentn you say has the same as he had in the Militia will be taken proper notice of in the appointments. Quere—whether the office of High Sheriff of the County of Rockingham might not be agreeable to him.

I have not been able to procure the draft of the ship till last night, shall send it as soon as possible and shall enclose in this letter some directions about building. I enquired of the Committee concerning the bigness of the masts; they say they know of no stated rule so it must be left to your and the carpenter's discretion. I sent you a contract with the Secret Committee for ten thousand dollars for importing sail cloth, blankets &c which I hope you have rec'd. I have the pleasure to inform you that Mifflin's brig arrived in this river yesterday with sixty tons of salt petre and seven tons and a half of powder on account of the contract and five tons and a half of powder and 1297 complete stands of arms as a private adventure; and this day the Secret Committee have sent down to Reedy Island to land the cargo and bring it up by land as the ice hinders her getting up any further.

While I tarry here I shall expect to hear from you every week and hope you will if you have time be a little more particular, and if it should be in my power to serve you, I shall do it with great pleasure.

Capt Hazzen of Canada who came here with the news of the fate of poor Montgomery is appointed Col of a regiment of Canadians and is returned to raise them.[1] Col Bull's regt. are gone off for Canada; the first company has I hope got to Albany by this time. I hope our Colony will use their utmost to raise and send forward the regt for Canada that Quebec may be taken before the enemy arrives in the Spring.

General Prescot for his conduct with regard to Col Allen is by order of Congress confined in close gaol in this city.

Our men of war fell down the river the fore part of last month but stopping about 30 miles down to take in supplies were stopped by the ice and have not yet sailed.

Col Gadsen is returned home. The draft is so big, I cannot send it by the post. Mr. Hancock will send it with those for their Province in a few days.[2] The dimensions for the Pallas frigate is sent by Govr Hopkins desire; he says it may be of some advantage.

I am your Sincere friend,   Josiah Bartlett

Tr (DLC).

[1] Moses Hazen was appointed a colonel on January 22. *JCC*, 4:78.

[2] When Langdon had not received the plans by the end of February, he informed Bartlett that "we are going on with one of our own Drawing." Langdon to Bartlett, February 26, 1776, quoted in Lawrence S. Mayo, *John Langdon of New Hampshire* (Concord: Rumford Press, 1937), p. 118.

William Livingston to John Hancock

Dr Sir.   Woodbridge 3 Feby 1776
I had the pleasure last Evening to see Collo Herd returning with his Troops from his Queens County Expedition which he has by all Accounts conducted with the greatest Prudence & Zeal for the Cause.[1] This morning he dressed up his Troops & they really made a fine legion. Among his Prisoners are some of the most dangerous Tories in the Country. Having no particular orders here to dispose of his Prisoners, he is resolved to conduct them to Philadelphia unless he meets with the orders of Congress to the Contrary. The party of the continental Troops he had with him, behaved in so disorderly a manner that he was obliged to dismiss them. The Collo. has really great merit in the Conduct of the affair, & I hope will receive the approbation of the Congress. You will excuse the badness of the paper, there being no better to be had here. I am, Sir, your most humble Servt,   Wil Livingston

RC (DNA: PCC, item 68).
[1] For Col. Nathaniel Heard's "Queens County Expedition," see Richard Smith's Diary, January 3, 1776.

Secret Committee Minutes of Proceedings

Phila. Com. Ch[amber]. Feby 3d. 1776
At a meeting of the Com. of Se[crec]y present Saml. Ward, Benj. Franklin, J. Alsop, Josiah Bartlett, Thos. McKean, Jos. Hews, Fras. Lewis. A report being made to the sd. Committee by Col. Saml. Mifflin & Capt. Mason that a certain vessel was at or near Cape May on board of wch. there was a quantity of powder & Saltpetre, belonging to the U[nited] C[olonies], the Comee. directed the sd. Col. Mifflin & Capt Mason immediately to proceed to the sd. Cape or other place where sd. vessel might be & take every proper measure to get the sd. vessel into Morris river, or some other safe place & get her unloaded with all possible dispatch & imploy proper Waggoners to bring the sd. powder & Salt-petre up to this City as soon as possible.[1]

MS (MH).
[1] For more information on the voyage of this vessel, see Caesar Rodney to Thomas Rodney, February 4, 1776, note 3.

Oliver Wolcott to Samuel Lyman

Sir,   Philadelphia 3d Febry. 1776
I do myself the pleasure to let you know I am well and have been so

since I left Home.[1] And as I write to you from this Place I believe you
will expect I shall tell you much more News than I am furnished with—
and if I should do so it would be nothing uncommon in a Story teller
but the News of this day and which may be believed, is, that a Capt.
Mason of this City a private adventurer, has brot into this River
(Delaware) sixty Tons of Salt Petre, Twenty Tons of Gunpowder and
Two Thousand Stands of Arms. This together with the sixty Tons of
Petre before recd will be a small but needfull Supply. The Mills are
constantly at Work—and I wish to hear they may be soon so in Connecticut. The Congress have Resolved that after the first of next March
they will carry on Trade with every Nation and People, except England,
Ireland, the British West India, &c under the Reg[ul]ation of the association—and Subject to Such Other Regulations as Congress shall Ordain
who probably will not alter the Association but in some Very few
particulars.[2] The Ladys I hope will still make themselves contented to
live without Tea for the good of their Country. The News you have in
the publick Prints. It seems the Ministry intend to offer special Pardons
upon the Points of Bayonets, but I think We are not well disposed to
receive their Graces in that Manner. The old Trick of endeavouring
to divide will be probably still practisced but I believe without Effect.
I think the Word Rebel is not made quite so free a use of by their
High Mightinesses of late—but I more fear their Temporary Moderation
than their Arms. Common Sense Operates pritty well, but all Men
have not common Sense.

We hear nothing in special from the westward. Our fleet are still
froze in the River. The Armament lately gone from Boston, I Suspect
go West of Us. New York is perhaps too favorite a Colony to be hurt—
they have had Address enough to prevent General Lee's going forward
as I understand. A Committee of Congress have gone to New York.
Col Harrison, Mr. Lynch and Mr. Allyn. What Advantages will accrue
from it, I am yet to learn. The People of New York say the Men of
War behave Very politely, and if much stirr should be made in Town
they will certainly fire upon it. Upon which Acco. it will be Very
dangerous to erect any defensive Works there. The Repu[l]se at Quebec
I Suspect was pritty necessary for our good, tho I most sincerely regret
the Loss of our brave officers and men. The Exertions of the New England
People would do them great Honour if it had not become so habitual
as to render it less Noticed—but I hope they will persevere; that People
under God are most to be relied on. Two Battalions are ordered from
this Colony for Canada and one from the Jersys, and are going forward,
but I wish the New England People might get Quebec before they get
there.

Young Mr Burr is amongst the News Paper Heros. He behaved
Very bravely and I hope will not get killed—he has an Appointment in
the Army. You See I write just as Matters come into my Mind—but

you will think I have Many Things to attend to. If you should ask me how I like attending Congress, I must tell you I cannot answer that Question yet. I hope I shall do my Duty and have Satisfaction in doing it. I believe there will be no Recess of Congress till Spring, and then it will depend on Circumstances. I should be glad to hear from you and my other Freinds to whom you will please to present my Compliments. Letters put into the Post Office and directed to Me as Member of Congress will come safe. The Union of the Colonies I trust may be relied upon—but the Establishment of these Colonies in Peace and Security will require great Deliberation—but I know of No Time which can be more Necessary and seasonable than the present, to conclude this mighty Affair. To give up any of our Rights will never I hope be done and I imagine Great Britain will never settle with us upon the Terms of Enjoying them, what Consequences these contrarient and fixed Claims must produce will be easily conceived. But I run such a length, that I shall tire you (for I know not what) with my scribble. That America may be happy is my Ardent Wish—and also that you in particular may share in the Blessings of the Almighty. I am Sir, your most humble Servant,   Oliver Wolcott

RC (PHi).

¹ Samuel Lyman (1749–1802), Litchfield, Conn., lawyer and Wolcott's kinsman, served on the Connecticut Committee of the Pay-Table, 1779–84, and was later elected to the Massachusetts legislature. Franklin B. Dexter, *Biographical Sketches of the Graduates of Yale College*, 6 vols. (New York: Henry Holt and Co., 1885–1919), 3:338.

² Wolcott is apparently referring to a decision reached in the committee of the whole on January 17 to open American ports after March 1 under specific restrictions to be recommended by a committee appointed that day. Otherwise his assertion—that "the Congress have resolved"—is in error, for the subject of opening American ports remained under discussion for another two months, and Congress did not formally resolve to open American trade to nations not under British sovereignty until April 6. On the other hand, it is clear from the comments of other delegates that Wolcott's assumption was widely shared, that they had agreed in principle to open the ports on March 1, and that only the specific restrictions under which American trade would operate had yet to be worked out. Hopes that an agreement on those regulations could be reached before March 1 were soon frustrated by the intrusion of the questions of American independence and foreign commercial agreements. As the delegates came to perceive that the opening of American trade would inevitably require commitments on such difficult allied issues, they balked at making an official declaration of policy. Not until the need for imports became even more pressing and the delegates evinced greater concern over preparing the colonies against a major armed attack in 1776, was Congress finally able in April to agree to a decision which in February it was widely assumed would be made before the end of the month. See Richard Smith's Diary, January 17, February 16, 26, and 29; Silas Deane to Thomas Mumford, January 25, 1776, note 3; and *JCC*, 4:62, 257–58. For other references to this issue, see also Richard Smith's Diary, January 12, 1776, note 1.

Thomas Nelson to Thomas Jefferson

Dear Jefferson   Philadelphia. [Fe]by 4th. 1776.
I had written to you soon after the repulse of our Troops at Quebec, giving you, as I thought, a true state of that unfortunate affair; but upon comparing it, (altho I had my information from a person who pretended to know a good deal of the matter) with one that I saw afterwards, I found they differ'd so materially that I burnt my Letter and determin'd to leave you to the News papers for your intelligence.
We have late advices from England, which you will see in the inclos'd papers. I had rather send you a dozen Ledgers and Evening Posts, than transcribe three paragraphs out of them. But I have good News for you, which neither of these papers contains. A Vessel arriv'd two nights ago with 60 Tons of Salt Petre, 13 Tons of Gunpowder and 2000 Stands of Arms and we are in daily expectation of 25 Tons more of Gun powder.
Troops are marching every day from hence to support the remains of our Army before Quebec. The Eastern Governments are raising Men for the same purpose. One Battallion has already march[ed] from Connecticut, so that We are still in hope of reducing the Garrison before it can be reliev'd in the Spring.
General Washington has sent Major General Lee [to] New York at the head of 1200 Volunteers from Connecticut to defend that Province against a detachment sent from Boston, which the General was informed by a deserter, was certainly intended for that place. The Deserter, I fancy, was mistaken, sufficient time having elaps'd since they sail'd for their arriving there, and we have no account of them. The Committee of safety of New York however sent a remonstra[nce] to Lee setting forth the extreme danger the City would be in from the Men of War, should he enter it, and especially as they were apprehensive he intended to make an attack upon the Ships. Lee sent the remonstrance to Congress and wrote the President that he thought it his Duty to carry his Orders into execution, which he was preparing to do with the first division, the rest of the Troops being ready to support him. The Letter and remonstrance being read, a violent debate arose on one side as to the propriety of an armed force from one province, entering another without permission of the civil power of that province, or without express orders of Congress. It was alledged that this was setting up the Military above the Civil. On the other side was urged the absolute necessity of securing that province, the loss of which would cut off all communication between the Northern and Southern Colonies and which if effected would ruin America. The debate ended in the appointment of a Committee of Congress to confer with Lee and the Committee of Safety.[1] Harrison, Lynch and Allen were the Committee and they sat out the next day upon their Ambassy, but what the result has been we

are not inform'd, not having heard from them since they went.

You would be surpriz'd to see with how much dispatch we have done business since Dyer and Gaddesden left us. The former you know was superseeded and the latter was order'd home to take command of his Regiment.

I have much more to say to you but the person who carrys this to you is impatient to set out on his journey. He is one of your County Men by the name of Blane.

You must certainly bring Mrs. Jefferson with you. Mrs. Nelson shall nurse her in the small pox and take all possible care of her. We expect Braxton every day[2] and then I shall beat a march for a few Weeks. I have not time to add more than to desire my Compliments to Mrs. Jefferson and to beg that you will believe me Your sincere friend & hb Sert.,   Thos. Nelson Jr

P.S. I send you a present of 2/ worth of Common Sense. I had like to have omitted to send you a present from the Quakers also.

RC (DLC). Jefferson, *Papers* (Boyd), 1:285–86.
    [1] See *JCC*, 4:94.
    [2] Carter Braxton presented his credentials to Congress on February 23. *JCC*, 4:167–68.

Caesar Rodney to Thomas Rodney

Dr Sir,   Philadelpa Sunday Feby 4th 1776
    The letter you wrote to Collins,[1] and the Copy of the Councils Order I delivered, and Conversed with him on the Subject. Mr. Collins was of opinion with me that it would be more prudent to Employ some person in Philada. who had been accustomed to that kind of Trade, than to Join with the New Castle County people in the Expedition they then had on foot. The applying to a proper person here was left to me. Upon this as soon as I got to town I Spoke to David Beveridge who immediately told me he would undertake it, provided he and the Contractors Could agree, which he had no doubt of, and on Tuesday last, I provided an Express to go to Collins at Willmington and return on the next day, which he did. By this Express Beveridge wrote Collins the outlines of the Bargain, but that they might Confer more particularly desired Collins would meet him as on Thursday last at Chester. When the Express Returned he Shewed me Collins's answer which was that he was oblidged to set out on that day for Kent, that he should be up again in ten or twelve days, would then endeavour to fix the matter, and that from the appearance of the weather he thought it would then be time enough. This is all I now know of the matter, Except that Several other verry good hands have since been with me to get the

Contract, so that you and Collins or either of you may have a Contract whenever you set about it.[2] The night before last Captn. Mason (who went to France in the Service of the Congress) Came to town.[3] He says he Came in a Brigg Commanded by Captain Craige, that they had Seven weeks passage from Bellisle to the Coast off Egg-Harbour, that he then Came on shore and Crossed the Jersey to town, that the Brig stood for our Capes, that she has on bord on account of the Congress fifteen Tons of gunpowder, Sixty Tons of Salt-petre, & thirteen hundred Stand of Excellent fire-arms, and he supposes she is now safe within the Capes. General Arnold is likely to recover. He Expects to be fit to do duty in three week from the date of his letter, which was the fifth of January, and Troops are now on their march for Canada from all the Colonies as far South as Pennsylvania. Genl Wooster sent Arnold 120 men imediately. We are determined (God willing) to have Quebec before the frost Break's up. I intend to set out for Dover on Sunday next. But what Collo. Collins will do with the money (which I hear he has Carried down) in the mean time, I Cannot Say. I hope it will be made safe somewhere.

I understand that the Committee of Inspection & Observation for this City & County have thought themselves Elected but for Six months, and that accordingly they directed a new Election. I therefore Suppose your Committee have ordered a new Choice, and hope that you and your friends will Endeavour to recommend the Choice of such persons as will prudently, but firmly Support the Cause. This is a Critical period, and you all well know how much depends on the County Committee. I am with much love to my relations, and many good wishes for my friends, Your Most Obedient &c,   Caesar Rodney

RC (MeHi).

[1] Thomas Collins (1732–89), Delaware military and political leader, was elected a member of the provincial council in 1776 and served as president of the state, 1786–89. *Appleton's Cyclopaedia of American Biography.*

[2] The Delaware Council of Safety had authorized the county committees of safety on January 13 to "contract with proper Persons to export the Produce of these Colonies to the Foreign West Indies at the joint Risque of the Government agreable to the Recommendation of the Continental Congress of the 26th October last for the Purchase of Arms, Ammunition." Leon De Valinger, Jr., ed. "Council of Safety Minutes," *Delaware History* 1 (January 1946): 77. The proposed enterprise with David Beveridge was apparently later disapproved by the Delaware Council. See also Thomas Rodney's letters to Caesar Rodney of February 3 and 9, 1776, in Clark, *Naval Documents,* 3:1116, 1186.

[3] For information on the origin of Capt. Thomas Mason's voyage, see Clark, *Naval Documents,* 1:1127–28. Writing from Brunswick, N.J., on February 6, Elbridge Gerry reported an account of Mason's voyage that was related to him by John Carey, a member of the New Jersey Convention. "Capt. Mason informed him [Carey] that he had just arrived at Egg Harbour from Port Le Orient in France with *seventy Tons of Gun Powder & 2000 stands of Arms*, & gave him the following circumstantial Account of his Voyage which is somewhat remarkable—Vizt that while he (Capt. Mason) was at Port L'Orient the British Ministry had Information that the

sixty Tons of Salt petre which lately arrived at Philadelphia was provided to be shipped to America; that in Consequence of this they immediately dispatched Intelligence to the Commandant who ordered the Vessel on board of which it was then shipped to be seized, & Capt. Mason (who had the Care of both Vessels while at L'Orient) to be imprisoned; that he obtained his Liberty that Day on Parole of Honor having promised to see the Commandant the Day following & at Night sent the Saltpetre Vessel to Sea; that the Commandant appeared to be highly disgusted at his Conduct but found it was too late to recover the Saltpetre & by the Help of Friends the Matter was accomodated. That he found it impracticable to load on board his other Vessel the 70 Tons Powder & 2000 stands of Arms & agreed with a Dutchman to take them in & deliver them to him at Sea which he accordingly did for a proper Reward; that the Arms belonged to the 4th Regiment of the King of France & were obtained by the Merchants there to send to *Holland*, in which We have a striking Instance of the sincere Freindship subsisting between his sacred Majesty & ever most gracious Sovereign; as well as Attachment of the Dutch to that *virtuous* Prince—further give Leave to inform You that Capt. Mason spoke with Capt. Griffin in Egg Harbour who had just arrived from the West Indies with *eighteen Tons more of gunpowder*, so that We may expect soon to hear of your acting at Cambridge & Roxbury the second Scene of Burgoyn's humourous Farce 'the Blockade of Boston.' " Elbridge Gerry to Unknown, February 6, 1776, MH.

Andrew Allen to Sarah Allen

My dear Sally,   New York Feby 5th 1776
  This Town has been in the greatest Confusion and Distress ever since we arrived; the People had taken it into their Heads that we had come with positive Orders from the Congress to Genl. Lee to attack the Men of War lying here, which would have introduced the Destruction of the Town.[1] In Consequence of this they were all in Motion moving out their Household Goods & Families. With Difficulty we quieted their Apprehensions by Assurances that the Purport of our Journey was directly the Reverse. No sooner was this Matter accomplished than their Fears were revived, and with greater Probability of Reason, by the Arrival of Genl. Clinton, who we had Intelligence, sailed from Boston with some Men of War & 600 Soldiers destined as was supposed for this Town. The Troops which accompanied him are not yet arrived but are supposed to be left behind at Sandy Hook, & we have *every Reason to conclude* are intended to make an Attack on one of [the Southern Co]lonies, most probably Virginia. I cannot [. . . cer]titude upon the comparatively [. . .] at Philadelphia; the continual [. . .] Dangers which threaten this Place must effectually exclude all Tranquillity & agitate their Minds with the most distressing Apprehensions. I assure you that when Mr. Clinton arrived I fully expected that Hostilities would immediately have commenced & the Scene which would then have ensued was sufficient even in Idea to shock my Humanity. Paint to yourself (what indeed would be the Consequence) Women & Children driven at this inclement Season from their Habitations without an Opportunity of taking with

Andrew Allen

them the Necessaries of Life & without a Prospect of finding Shelter for their wretched Heads. Add to this the Number of Sick, the lying in Women, which must be many in so large a Town whose Situation would not admit of a Removal unattended with instant Death, & you may guess my feelings who expected this Picture to be shortly exposed to my View. However Thank God the Storm has at present blown over & the Town begins to recover it's Calmness.

General Lee is arrived & we are just called to a Conference with him which will account for the Hurry which marks this Letter. I hope to set off on Wednesday next at farthest & if I have the Happiness of finding you & my dear Children well I shall think myself amply [. . .] every Distress & Inconvenience [. . .] me to. You can let my Father know [. . .] in this Letter & make my dutiful Re[spects . . .] my dear Sally most affectionately [. . . .]

RC (NN).
[1] For the appointment of the committee (Allen, Harrison, and Lynch) that was directed to confer with General Lee and the New York Committee of Safety about the threat to New York posed by the entry of Lee's troops into the city, see *JCC*, 4:94, and John Hancock to Charles Lee, January 26, 1776.

Lord Drummond's Minutes

Memorm: N. York Sunday Feby. 5th. 1776.
The following was one of the Subjects of Discussion with the Gentlemen of the Deputation from Phila.[1] this forenoon at their Lodgings.

The Question was put by Mr. Lynch, whether on the Supposition of a Negotiation taking Place; a Suspension of Hostilitys woud be agreed to by Genl. Howe. That tho' the Season wou'd not as yet admit of the Opening the Campaign, Partizan work might disturb the present tranquillity and retard a Negotiation.

To this it was replied that if General Howe shoud become convinced of their Sincerity to treat, either by the intended Deputation from the Congress sailing for England, or any other decisive Measure, it was not improbable but General Howe willing to forward so humane a Purpose might take upon himself a Step of this Nature untill he shoud obtain Instructions from England, that it was obvious however that such an Indulgence woud be accompanyd by *Conditions*. Two were apparent. That prepared as he was to take the field so soon as the Season woud permit he woud not think himself justifiable in giving any Indulgence at the Expence of *wasting Provisions* which were transported at such an Expense across the Atlantic. That he woud therefore expect Supplies from America of *fresh* Provisions, and at the Rates payd heretofore.

A Second Condition in all Likelyhood woud be that to prevent any Insults passing between the Outposts of the Armys, and indeed to fullfill

the purposes themselves had now in View, it woud be necessary there
shoud be a neutral Ground of at least a Days March or 25 Miles. That
as Genl. Howes Situation did not admit of his moving further to the
Eastward, it woud be necessary for Genl. Washington to withdraw the
whole Distance.

The above Conditions are acknowledged by these Gentlemen to be
consistent with Reason and to be necessary from Genl. Howe in his
present Situation and as such shall accompany any Propositions that
shall be made to Genl. Howe on this Subject, and which they suggested
shoud be by means of a Deputation from the Congress over Land on the
first appearance of a Negotiation taking place.[2]

MS (Scottish Record Office: Drummond Castle Papers).

[1] That is, Andrew Allen and Thomas Lynch. For their presence in New York at
this time, see Drummond's Notes, January 3–9? 1776. See also Thomas Lynch to
Washington, this date.

[2] The diary of William Smith, a member of the New York Council who was
acquainted with Drummond, contains a lengthy account of a discussion Smith had
with Lynch on February 4 on the subject of Drummond's mission.

"I had a Visit this Morning from Mr. Lynch the S Carolina Delegate. . . . He
asked me whether I had seen Lord Drummond & what his Character was? I told
him I had often & that he was esteemed among us as a Man of Faith and Honor
and that he had conducted himself with more Prudence than common to People of
his Years. What do you think says he of his Accounts concerning the Intentions
of the Ministry? I said that I believed what he reported for it is very natural to
suppose Administration alarmed at the Consequences of the present Quarrel. He
desired to know what he thought of the Congress to which I answered that it gave
me a great Deal of Pleasure to hear that Nothing dropp'd by them had abated his
Prospects of a happy Reconciliation and after causing me to relate what Drummond
said of the Ministers Designs he told me this was what he had communicated at
Philadelphia & more. . . .

"The New Matter of Information I now got from Mr. Lynch was this.

"That they did not dislike the Proposal of a Duty to raise a Revenue for the
common Defence. If we seperate says he from England we shall be obliged to set
up a Republic & that is a form of Government some People are fond of which I think
reads better than it works. It is best in Idea, bad in Experiment.

"He affected says Lynch to deny that he had any Credentials, but being pushed
upon the Points we think essential & the Importance of knowing the Ministers
Sentiments respecting them he pulled out a Paper which under great Caution he
read & laid on the Table as what he had from Lord North. He would not suffer us
to copy it but consented to our abstracting the substance in our own words till we
were satisfied of its meaning.

"The Point of Revenue settled the other Duties in regulating Commerce were to
belong to the Colonies.

"Further Aids pro re nata to be expected by way of Requisition as formerly to
the Assemblies singulatim.

"The Minister did not doubt that the offensive Acts would be repealed.

"Great Britain would for the Revenue renounce the Claim of Taxation.

"Parliament might be prevailed upon if the People of Massachusetts so chose to
restore the Governmt. established by the Charter of King William or the Altering
Act might be amended.

"The greatest Difficulty apprehended respected the Quartering & March of
Troops. The Prerogative of the Crown was concerned here & made it a Matter of

extreme Delicacy.

"To this last Mr. Lynch said Matters might be made easy. Drummond said at first the Colonies must give it up. We said British Troops here were as odious as foreign Troops in Great Britain but we can come to a compromise if they will stint them to a reasonable Number & then divide them among the Provinces. Drummond thought this would go down & the Delegates said that in that Case all Objections would be removed for they should consider them as so many Hostages for the good Behavior of the Mother Country.

"What think you says he of what he much urged our dispatching Commissioners to declare our Minds to the Minister as they have done to us. I suddenly approved the Measure. We says he have Difficulties. We can trust no Body not of the Congress. It is too much to trust even them. Perhaps their Overtures are a Snare. They may hang our Comrs. We must send our best Hands. They are not to be spared. How can we perswade any Man to such a Risk. I wish you would think of this says he and let me know the Result.

"If we don't send soon says he Drummond thinks they will arm at all Points for War. He says Comrs. will come to us, & if our's pass their's it may prevent another Campaigne.

"Upon the whole I found that Congress gave confidence to Lord Drummond and Mr. Elliot and that Mr. Lynch at this Day has no Idea of pushing for the Independency of the Colonies." William Smith, *Historical Memoirs from 16 March 1763 to 9 July 1776 of William Smith . . .*, ed. William H. W. Sabine (New York: Colburn & Tegg, 1956), pp. 261–63. Smith made a copy of this entry in September 1778 for Drummond's use, which is in the Drummond Castle Papers, Scottish Record Office.

William Floyd to
the New York Committee of Safety

Sr   Philadelphia February 5, 1776

I forwarded by Mr Lynch & Mr Allen, a Sum of money to the honourable Committee of Safety with a few lines Advising what that money was Intended for,[1] And by your Letter to us wherein you mention you would forward it to General Schuyler,[2] and the Small Sum to the marine Committee, I fear our Letter must have been Misunderstood.

Therefore I trouble you with this. The forty thousand Dollars was for Mr Lewis, from the Marine Committee; the twelve thousand five hundred Dollars, for the Raising the Battalion for Canada; and the Small Sum of one hundred and Some odd Dollars were Sent to Mr Lewis to pay off Some accounts Charged against the Riffle Companies in passing through our province. I hope it is not yet otherways Disposed of, if it is it may Impeed Mr Lewis's proceding agreeable to his Directions.

I am with the Greatest Respect Sr. your most obedt. humble Servt.

Wm Floyd

P.S. If it is not sent off please to Deliver it to Mr Lewis's Son.

RC (N). Addressed: "To the Honble Congress or Committee of Safety in New York."
[1] See New York Delegates to the New York Committee of Safety, January 27, 1776.

² See the letter from the New York Committee of Safety to the New York Delegates of January 31, 1776, in *Am. Archives*, 4th ser. 4:1094.

Thomas Lynch to George Washington

Dear Sir   New York Feby 5. 1776

You have doubtless heard of my being here on a Come of Congress.[1] The object was to consult with Genl Lee & the People of this Place on the best manner of securing it. God knows there is ample room for it. Every thing is wanting. The strong Apathy that hold Congress in fetters is still more forceable here, however luckily Clinton is come without Force, he has none but the Mercury and one Transport Brig.

I mentioned to you some Time ago some Propositions, which Lord Drummond had been talking to me of.[2] Genl Robinson [Robertson] writes to him by Clinton that he (Clinton) is very desirous of being Instrumental in bringing about the Same End. It is mysterious to me how such a Man shoud be sent on such an Errand. Be it as it may, it will not produce any Remission of our using the present Moment to strengthen ourselves & weaken our Enemies.

Lord Drummond's great Point is to get some Member of Congress to go home, to inform the Cabinet of the real desires and Intentions of that Body respecting the Reestablishment of Peace. To promote this Purpose he has desired me to inclose you a Letter which, after you have read, if you think it can do no harm you will be so kind as to forward to Robinson & to send his answer to his Lordship under your Cover.[3] Robinson will doubtless send it open to you.

Were I to guess at my Lords Motives it woud be that Lord North and his Scottish Friends found that their Places were in danger and that there is no way left to secure them but by restoring the nation to that State in which alone little Minds can rule it, vizt Peace and Quiet. Indeed every Paper I have seen seems tending that way.

My best Compliments attend your Ladies & Family. Dear Sir your most obedt. Serv,   Tho Lynch

RC (DLC).

[1] See Committee of Congress to the New York Committee of Safety, February 1, 1776.

[2] See Lynch to George Washington, January 16, 1776.

[3] Lord Drummond's letter of this date to James Robertson is in *Am. Archives*, 4th ser. 4:943–44. Washington's response to Lynch's request to forward Drummond's letter to General Robertson is discussed in Lord Drummond's Notes, January 3–9? 1776, note 1. See also Richard Smith's Diary, February 29 and March 5; and John Hancock to George Washington, March 6, 1776. In regard to the project for sending a congressional peace delegation to England, Drummond noted sometime around February 5: "In Consequence of an Enquiry at the desire of the Gentn. from Phila. [*i.e.* Andrew Allen and Thomas Lynch] with Regard to the Procuring a Ship to go to Engd. the Ship Rose, Captn. Miller, is found to be a Roomey and fast going

Letter of February 5, 1776, from Thomas Lynch, Sr., to George Washington

Ship and can be got ready for Sea in the Space of a few Days." Lord Drummond's Memorandum, ca. February 5, 1776, Drummond Castle Papers, Scottish Record Office.

Secret Committee Minutes of Proceedings

Comee Ch[amber] Feby. 5th. 1776.

At a meeting of the Com. of Secy. present Saml Ward, Jo Alsop, F. Lewis, Jos. Hewes, Tho. McKean, Josiah Bartlett, Robt. Morris & Robt. Alexander. Resolvd. That it is the opinion of this Come. it wd. be more for the interest of the U[nited] C[olonies] to confine the importat[io]n of Indian goods to one set of gentlemn. than to divide it.[1]

At a meeting of the Come. of Secy. present Saml. Ward, Benjn Franklin, John Alsop, Jos. Hewes, Frans. Lewis & Robt. Alexander. A Contract was enterd into between Willing, Morris & Co. of the City of Phi. Merchts. & sd. Come. That the sd. Willg., M. & Co. shall & will, with the utmost dispatch they can possibly & prudently make procure by themselves or their Agents the quantity of 2000 barrls. good Gunpowder, one thousand stand good Arms & 12 brass feild peices 6 poundrs.[2]

MS (MH).

[1] See Secret Committee Minutes of Proceedings, February 20, 1776.

[2] For an account of transactions pertaining to Willing, Morris & Co.'s agreements with Congress in 1775–76, see Clark, *Naval Documents*, 4:580–82. This contract of February 5, 1776, apparently involved a renewal and revision of their agreement of September 27, 1775, which they had previously been unable to execute. See Secret Committee Minutes of Proceedings, September 27, 1775. For other documents pertaining to the firm's efforts to import powder, see Willing, Morris & Co.'s letters of March 1 to Gregory & Guille, and of March 6, 1776, to Samuel Beall, in Clark, *Naval Documents*, 4:128–29, 199–201.

Richard Smith's Diary

Monday 5 Feb. [1776]

The Minutes read. Dickinson acquainted Congress that Dr. Brian of Trenton a Surgeon on Halfpay had recd. Orders to repair to the Ministerial Army in Boston and desired Leave so to do, this was rejected by all but Dickinson (& perhaps was a Contrivance of Bryan to save his Halfpay).[1] Wyth reported on Gen Schuylers Letters which was passed.[2] Wyth reported on the Rev. Mr. Occum's Proposals. Fowler & Johnson Two Indians intended for Missionaries are to inform upon what Terms they will act in that Capacity.[3] The Compans. from hence (Pennsylva.) already marched to the Northward having very defective Arms, Gen.

Schuyler is directed, after Opposition from Duane & others, to cause an Examination of them & supply the Deficiency with the Arms he lately seized in Tryon County. A Letter recd. from Col. Maxwell giving Notice that he will march one Compy. tomorrow & 3 others directly after.[4] Dr. Cadwallader certifying that Gen. Prescott's Wound (recd. at the Battle of Fontenoy) is bad, his Room in Jail damp and his Case dangerous, he was indulged with Liberty to take Lodgings in the City Tavern under a Guard from the Barracks. Duane presented several Papers from the Convention of N York desiring to know Whether they may admit Two Delegates from Staten Island chosen since the Interdict was laid on that Island, they were canvassed & postponed.[5] A Petition from the City Comee. desiring to know the Determinn. respecting Tea was postponed because Rob. Morris is not present. Gen Schuylers Narrative of his Transactions with Sir John [Johnson] and the Tories was ordd. to be published in the Newspapers. The Foreigner[6] whom Dr. Franklin and St Clair were to examine as to his Proficiency in the Knowledge of Artillery was now recommended to Gen Schuyler for Preferment, tho some Members, Paine and Sherman in particular, did not approve of employing in our Service Foreign Papists. Douglass is our Commodore on the Lakes.[7]

MS (DLC).
[1] For the case of Dr. William Bryant, see the Trenton Committee's letter to Hancock of January 23, 1776, in PCC, item 68, fols. 41–46, and *Am. Archives*, 4th ser. 4:815, where the sender is incorrectly identified as the New Jersey Committee of Safety.
[2] For the letters from General Schuyler in question, see Smith's Diary, February 2, 1776, note 1.
[3] Ibid., note 5.
[4] See Col. William Maxwell's letter to Hancock of February 3, 1776, in PCC, item 78, 15:11–12, 14, and *Am. Archives*, 4th ser. 4:923.
[5] For Congress' action on this issue on February 8, see *JCC*, 4:121. See also New York Delegates to the New York Committee of Safety, February 11, 1776.
[6] Dohickey Arundel. Smith's Diary, January 16, 1776, note 3.
[7] This day Congress appointed Capt. Jacobus Wynkoop to serve under Maj. William Douglas, who had been made a "Commodore" and placed in charge of the American flotilla on Lake Champlain by General Montgomery in November 1775. *JCC*, 4:111; *Am. Archives*, 4th ser. 4:805; and Clark, *Naval Documents*, 2:1100. However, Douglas balked at continuing in this office on the grounds of ill health, and on May 2 Congress authorized Schuyler to replace Douglas with Wynkoop if Douglas declined to serve, which Schuyler did on May 7. *JCC*, 4:237, 322; *Am. Archives*, 4th ser. 5:389, 437, 1378, 1397, 1464, 1478–79; and Clark, *Naval Documents*, 4:1440.

Samuel Chase to Daniel of St. Thomas Jenifer

Dear Sir [1]   Philada. Feby. 6th. 1776
The Congress just now received the Letter from the Council of Safety

of N. York.[2] Pray dispatch Copy to Virginia by the post or if gone by Express to their Convention. A Brig is arrived to Mr. Morris with 15 Tons of Powder & 1500 Stand of Arms—5 Tons & 500 arms belong to our province. Adieu, S Chase
in Congress.

RC (MdAA). Endorsed: "Letter Mr. Chase, Febry. 9th 1776. relative to Arms & Ammun. Importd in Willing & Morris' Brig. Ent[ere]d."
[1] This letter was undoubtedly directed to the president of the Maryland Council of Safety, Daniel of St. Thomas Jenifer (1723–90), who was subsequently president of the Maryland Senate, 1777–79, a delegate to Congress, 1779–81, and Maryland's intendant of finance, 1782–87. *DAB.*
[2] For this February 4 letter of the New York Committee of Safety to the New York delegates announcing the arrival at New York of British ships carrying Gen. Henry Clinton and a force apparently destined "to the southward"—a copy of which, in the hand of Charles Thomson, Chase enclosed to the Maryland Council—see *JCC,* 4:112; and *Am. Archives,* 4th ser. 4:1107. Another copy, which is in Chase's hand and apparently was enclosed in a similar brief letter of February 6 to the Baltimore Committee of Safety, is in the Purviance Papers, MdHi, although the letter itself is in the George Ball Signers Collection, InU. To the Baltimore Committee Chase also sent a copy of "the address of the Commons [to the King]," which he asked them to publish and which subsequently appeared in the February 15 issue of Frederick Green's *Maryland Gazette.* Chase to the Baltimore Committee of Safety, February 6, 1776, InU.

John Hancock to Philip Schuyler

Sir   Philada. Febry 6th. 1776
    Your Letters of the 22d & 25th of last Month, together with the Narrative of your proceedings in Tryon County, & the several inclosures have been duly Receiv'd and Communicated to Congress,[1] in Answer to which I am directed to forward you the inclos'd Resolutions.[2]
    It is with great pleasure I inform you, that the Prudence, Zeal and Temper manifested in your late Expedition met with the warmest Approbation of Congress, tho' at the same time I cannot forbear expressing my Grief for your Relapse, I hope your Exertions in the cause of your Country, will not make you forget the necessary Attention due to your health.
    As the Operations in Canada which are so important in their consequences cannot be carried on without a large supply of Specie, the Congress have Recommended it to the severall Colonies to Employ proper persons for Collecting all the Gold and Silver they can to be Exchang'd for Continental Bills, and have Recommended to you to Encourage Sutlers to attend the Army in Canada, and the Money arising therefrom to be Dispos'd of agreeable to the Resolve inclos'd which mode will be very Advantageous, and Doubt not your Exertions to Effect it.[3]

I must Refer you to the Resolutions of Congress herewith Transmitted, and being pressd for time, cannot Add, but that I am with much Esteem, Sir, Your very huml Servt.

LB (DNA: PCC, item 12A).
¹ The letters were read in Congress and referred to committee on February 2, 1776. See *JCC*, 4:107–8; and Richard Smith's Diary, February 2, 1776, note 1.
² See *JCC*, 4:109–12.
³ See *JCC*, 4:73, 113–14.

Joseph Hewes to Samuel Johnston

Dr Sir   Philada. 6th Feb. 1776
I have but just time to enclose you a Copy of a Letter from the Committee of Safety of New York.¹ Our Accts. from the Camp are that two Regiments in a number of Transports, Men of War, Bomb Vessels &c. are sailed, Supposed for Virga. or the Carolinas, that General Clinton had sail'd with them. I hope Our province will be on their guard, and that You are in great forwardness with your third Regiment.
I have not time to add more. Yours &c.   J. Hewes

RC (NNPM).
¹ See Samuel Chase to Daniel of St. Thomas Jenifer, this date, note 2.

Joseph Hewes to Robert Smith

Dear Sir   Philadelphia 6th Febry 1776
I have received your two favours of the 25th of January from Williamsburg and am a good deal out of Temper at the extraordinary conduct of the Virga. Convention, respecting our Brigg Fanny.¹ The delegates from that Province now here shewed me a Letter to them from Mr Pendleton in which he informed them of the Arival of the Fanny in York River with all circumstances attending it and that the Convention had ordered the Vessel to be returned to me and the Freight paid. This whole matter with every circumstance attending it as far as I know was mentioned to almost every Member of Congress and they all Agreed that the convention of Virga. had done right, what they will now say I know not. I had made a conditional agreement with Mr. Morris as I wrote you last Post, that agreement cannot yet be compleated, it will be sent by next Post, and I shall take care to make it as profitable as I can.² At all events I intend the united Colonies shall insure her against all risques whatever, in which case we may afford to let her go on very reasonable terms. You may depend on it I shall do the best I can. As to

Capt. Cunningham, you must do as you please with him, if he will not do, turn him out and get another that will do better. Mr. Morris wrote to Mr. Harrison to get the Brigg Laden and the papers, Orders &c should be sent in time; I shall get an Order of Congress respecting the Naval Stores and send by next Post, it cannot now be done in time.[3] No Vessel can now get from this Port, all is froze fast & has been for Six weeks past, our fleet are all froze up at Reedy Island. If you can any way put £150 into the North Caro. Treasury I can get so much Continental money here and remit it to Lowther.

If I can get the Guns you mention I will also get a Vessel if possible and send them as soon as the Ice breaks up. I write in Congress room and am affraid I shall lose the Post. Adieu. Yours, &c &c,

Joseph Hewes

RC (NcU).

[1] Hewes' brig *Fanny*, Capt. John Cunningham, master, was captured off Hampton Roads on January 4 and discovered to be carrying a cargo of provisions from Ireland for the British Army in Boston. On January 10 the Virginia Convention ordered the *Fanny's* cargo to be confiscated and sold "for the use of this Colony," and two days later directed that the vessel be returned to Hewes, he being "wholly a stranger to the ill conduct of the Captain in taking the injurious freight from Cork to Boston." *Am. Archives*, 4th ser. 4:114, 117–18; and Clark, *Naval Documents*, 2:1354, 3:662.

[2] See Secret Committee Minutes of Proceedings, February 13, 1776.

[3] See *JCC*, 4:114–15, 131; and Richard Smith's Diary, February 12, 1776.

William Hooper to
Joseph Hewes and John Penn

My dear friends   New York Feby 6t 1776

I leave this early to morrow Morning, I have been detained here all day writing, fishing for intelligence of Gen'l Clinton's destination.[1] What the inclosed conveys I think may be depended upon.[2] Therefore write all your friends to stand forth & to exert themselves. Pray press the matter on Mr Thos Person; urge him to call forth the back Country.

In the letter you write you need not mention my Absence, tho you may if you think it necessary, I care not much about it. You will subscribe my name to any Official letters you may send.

I am affectionately Yrs,   Wm Hooper

RC (NjHi).

[1] Hooper, who had stopped in New York City while on his way to Cambridge, Mass., to visit his mother, was back in Congress by March 6. See Joseph Hewes to Samuel Johnston, February 11; and Richard Smith's Diary, March 6, 1776.

[2] The enclosure in question was probably Hooper's other letter of this date to Hewes and Penn.

William Hooper to

Joseph Hewes and John Penn

My dear friends   [February 6, 1776]
Upon my arrival here I found that the Mercury Man of War with
General Clinton on board, and a Transport under his convoy had come
into this Harbour on Saturday last. This occasioned much Speculation &
late last evening their destination remained a secret. It is now confessed
& it is generally believed, for my own part I have not the least doubt
of the fact that Genl Clinton is on his way to North Carolina. The
particulars as far as we have been able to obtain information of them are
these, that 7 Regiments are to embark on the first day of December
from Great Britain from thence to proceed to Hampton Road there to
wait till Genl Clinton joins them with the small body of troops which
he carries with him from Boston & When with the Advice of Govr
Dunmore they have settled the plan of operations, they are to proceed
to North Carolina to make an impression into that & the adjacent
Colonies. Genl Clinton says that three Transports sailed with him from
Boston having on board 200 light armed Troops, that they left him in
a Snow Storm of[f] Sandy Hook. His object in coming in here is probably
to confer with Govr Tryon & carry off what ordinance stores he can
pillage from hence. We have just received information that the Men of
War have dispatched their Barges to Turtle Bay to possess themselves
of some Cannon Shot which are there. Genl Lee sends a party to oppose
them.[1]
It will immediately occur to you that it is necessary that our Constituents should be informed of this new Maneuvre, that their best
efforts may be exerted to defeat the purposes of it. When I consider the
defenceless State of No. Carolina arising from a want of Arms &
Ammunition, the divided sentiments of the people, the effect it might
have upon the Highlanders & Regulators if Governour Martin supported with a body of Troops should introduce himself amongst them,
I am importunate that no stone should be left unturned to protect in
that province the friends to the American Cause. I need say nothing
to stimulate you to contribute every thing in your power, I do not
affect to dictate, I beg leave to hint to you that it will be prudent
immediately to send off an Express to Edenton with the Intelligence I
herewith afford you, & thereby to recommend to them to call as soon
as may be the Provincial Congress to take such measures under their
Sanction as may prevent the cause of America, so far as N. Carolina is
concerned in support of it, going to total destruction.
I leave to you whether it will not be prudent to assemble in Arms all
the well affected part of the back Country, that they may strive to keep

in order those of contrary sentiments, and may be prepared to march at a moment's warning to any part of the Sea Coast of No. Carolina or Virginia where the enemy may attempt to land. It will answer another good purpose as it will give them some little discipline before they are brought into action. I would not confine this to the back Country. The Inhabitants on the Sea Coast must be put in the same readiness. General Officers must be appointed, one Brigadier General for each district, a General & Lieutent Genl over the whole. I think it a matter of supreme importance that the River of Cape Fear should be obstructed. The Navigation also should be impeded at Newbern. I leave to you the propriety & possibility of effecting it there & elsewhere. Attention ought to be given to providing Cannon—particularly Field pieces. I wish the Gunpowder &c intended to go by the next Waggon were on the way. In a Word I think everything is now at stake with us, & unless the whole force of our province is called forth—farewell to all our Struggles for freedom. We must be satisfied to sit down the Spectators of the Triumphs of our Enemies over our dearest rights & privileges, condemned to abject Slavery, as the reward of our successless virtue. May Heaven avert it.

In the letter to our Provincial Council I hope nothing will be omitted that may work upon their Reason, or affect their passions, You will know the avenues that lead to their Hearts, I am sure you will pursue them attentively. Seven Regiments 680 each with the accession of Tories is a very formidable force, it will require their best abilities to oppose it. A large Sum of Money must be had from the Congress, our Treasury is exhausted, Our Wants upon this occassion will be great & urgent. Pay, subsistance, Warlike Stores must be had—must be answered with money.

By this Time the Troops from England are in Hampton Road, to morrow Genl Clinton sails from this, not a moment ought to be lost in sending off your express—a delay might involve our province in irremediable ruin. I think it would be attended with beneficial consequences that one or more of the delegates of No. Carolina were at home, I cannot take it upon me to urge you or Mr Penn at this disagreeable Season to undertake a Journey home, sure I am much benefit might arise from your presence there & should one or both of you think such a measure necessary I will instantly return to Philadelphia to supply your places as far as I am capable. Or will take that Service upon myself if you think proper to enjoin it.

It is necessary that the whole province of North Carolina be alarmed, therefore direct that your Expresses be published thro the whole of it, & by all means communicated to the Inhabitants of Mecklenb[urg]h County as soon as possible. Adieu, I write this in such a hurry that I cannot answer for its inaccuracies, I have not time to go over it again. Pray forward the inclosed when you send your express. I am my dear friends, Your Affectionate, Wm. Hooper

[*P.S.*] Col. Harrison says the Mercury mounts 26 Guns.

Clinton no doubt gets good information here as to our back Country from Gov Tryon &c.[2] Write me if an Oppty. offers to the Eastward Suddenly. Lord Stirli[n]gs Regt expected here every hour—all in confusion. I have a piti for Duane, My love to him & God have mercy on his *Tory City*. This in Secret.

Will it be necessary to say any thing of drawing home our Troops. Better I think to leave it to this [over?] discretion of the Provincial Council.

Pray urge the Council not to wait for the Provincial Congress before they proceed to take measures for their defence.

RC (NcU: Hayes Collection microfilm).

[1] General Clinton's expedition is discussed in Paul H. Smith, *Loyalists and Red-coats: A Study in British Revolutionary Policy* (Chapel Hill: University of North Carolina Press, 1964), pp. 18–29.

[2] New York governor William Tryon had served as governor of North Carolina from 1765 to 1771.

William Hooper to Samuel Johnston

My dear Sir   [New York] February 6 1776

The express who carries this will inform you by a letter to the Provincial Council of North Carolina addressed by their delegates,[1] that Genl Clinton is at New York in the Mercury of 26 Guns bound to Hampton in Virginia with 3 transports of 200 light troops, there to join 7 Regts from England & from thence proceed to North Carolina, & in all probability to Cape Fear. As they go upon Govr. Martins requisition they will probably proceed immediately to join him. I flatter myself you will prepare for their reception.

Much attention should be paid to prevent our Pilots convoying the ships—to prevent their obtaining fresh provisions. Might not our Rivers be obstructed, Narrow passes secured, bridges taken up, Mud batteries thrown up, Some Cannon placed advantageously. Must not every man a friend to the Cause, and capable of duty turn out with his musquet. Do we not now play a Game, where Slavery or Liberty are the Stakes—but why do I teise you who are much better capacitated to judge of the proper measures to be pursued than I am—but suffer me. Must you not have Brigd Generals, in districts and Superiour Officers over the whole. Must not very large bodies be placed immediately along the Sea Coasts. Were I to advise, the whole force of the Colony should be collected ready for immediate exertion when called upon, & bid adieu to plough shares & pruning hooks till the Sword can find its scabbard with safety & honor to its owner. My first wish is to be free—

My second to be reconciled to GB. God grant that both may soon take place.

Measures must be taken immediately—'er this the Troops of the Enemy are in your Country. May you Stand forth like Men & fight the Cause of *Liberty* the Cause of the living God.

Adieu My dear Friend. When we meet may we meet in peace & happiness, Your's truly, Wm Hooper

[*P.S.*] Lee is in New York with 1000 Connecticut Troops, the Phœnix of 40, Asia of 64, Mercury of 26 Guns lying before the Town. I fear New York will not long have a being.

Pray write Harnet & Maclain concerning the Pilots.

RC (NN).
[1] See North Carolina Delegates to the North Carolina Council of Safety, February 10, 1776.

Secret Committee Minutes of Proceedings

Com. Ch[amber]. Feby. 6. 1776.

At a meetg of the Com. Secy. present S. Ward, J. Alsop, B. Franklin, J. Hewes, J. Bartlett & F. Lewis. A Contract[1] was enterd into between Josiah Hewes of the City of Philadelphia, Mercht. An Attorney in behalf of Nico. & Jo. Brown of Providence Rhode Island, M[erchant]s, by virtue of a power of Attorney to the sd. Josiah of the one part & the sd. Commee. of the other That a voyage or voyages shall be undertaken to some proper port or ports in Europe for the speedy procuring 10,000 good strippd Blankets for Soldiers at 4/6 or 5/ sterg. or near that price for each Blanket, 9000 yds. of 6/4 broad Cloth, the colours brown & blue for Officers & Soldiers uniforms & 800 yds. of 6/4 broad Cloth, of different colours suitable to face them, the greatest part of the Cloths being for Privates to be about 4/stg. per yd., that for the Officers about 6/, 10 tons lead & 250 stand good Arms such as are usd by the Infantry of France, with 50 barls. 100 lb wght each, of good gunpowder &c.

MS (MH).
[1] This contract, and letters from the Browns to Josiah Hewes and to Samuel Ward concerning it, are printed in Clark, *Naval Documents*, 3:878–79, 1153–54. See also Samuel Ward to Henry Ward, December 12, 1775; and Clark, *Naval Documents*, 4:1215–16.

Richard Smith's Diary

Tuesday 6 Feb. [1776]

The Minutes read. Col. Heard attending with 18 Tories from Queens

County, Crane, McKean & E. Rutledge were named to take his Account
of the Expedition, which being reported, the Prisoners are ordered
under Guard to N York to be examined and secured by the Convention
there who are to report thereon to Us. A Comee. of 5 was chosen to get
Naval Stores from N Carolina to our Men of War building in New
England.[1] Letters from Commissary Lowrey & others.[2] A Petition was
presented from 3 Captains in Maxwells Battalion for the Allowance to
the recruitg Officers of 10/ for each Man inlisted, which was granted
for the 2 first Jersey Regts. by 6 Cols. to 2. The last or Dayton's Regt
is already allowed it. Two Subalterns were appointed as recommended
by the Comee. of Lancaster.

MS (DLC).

[1] For the report of this committee, which was submitted to Congress on February 12
and approved the following day, see *JCC*, 4:131; and Smith's Diary, February 12,
1776.

[2] This day Congress received letters of February 4 from the New York Committee
of Safety to the New York delegates and from the Reading Committee of Correspondence to the Pennsylvania delegates. See PCC, item 69, fols. 91–92, 94; and
Am. Archives, 4th ser. 4:937, 1107. No letter from New Jersey commissary Thomas
Lowrey has been found.

Samuel Ward to Henry Ward

Dear Bror.   Philadela. 6th Feby. 1776
    Your Letters of 21st & 23d were very acceptable, I am much obliged
to You for your kind Concern for Sammy; Blessed be God that He has
behaved well and hath escaped even a Wound. I have wrote him twice [1]
& also had the Pleasure of a Letter from him, a Copy of which is inclosed. The Sense which he appears to have of the divine Goodness, of
his Duty to his Country and his Chearful Resolution to do it at every
Hazard, his filial Piety, his ardent affection for his Sisters & Brothers &
that benevolent Wish that they might not be acquainted with the
Danger to which he was about to be exposed give Me the highest
Satisfaction. Be kind enough to let Harry make Copies for my Daughters
Nancy & Kitty & send them by first Opportunity.
    Your Favor by Capt. Grinnel I never received & by your not men-
tioning many of my Letters I imagine they must also have miscarried;
do for the future mention the Dates of such as you receive from Me.
    I am grieved for the People still in Newport. I am sorry such unworthy
Sentiments prevail: Is it not astonishing that any Man living Can be
content to depend upon the Will of a drunken worthless Savage for the
Enjoyment of his Life & Property. I hope every possible Measure will
be taken to prevent those selfish, slavish Sentiments which govern too
many in Newport from spreading in the Colony.[2] I am sensible of the

Justice of your Observations & shall when I can get time take more particular Notice of them, at present I am much fatigued.

As the Gentlemen by whom I write will give you all the News you'l excuse the omission on that Head. In my next you may expect my Sentiments fully upon the present State of public Affairs. I long for an Opportunity. In the mean time it is unnecessary for me to say that the closest Attention & every possible Support in my Power shall be given to the great Cause in which We are engaged.

I have great Hopes that We shall get the two Battalions into continental Pay but if We do I beleive they must be newmodelled: I wonder more Attention was not paid to the continental Establishmt. Our Battalions consist of 8 Companies, these two of 12 which multiplies Officers & consequently Expences, ours contain 728 Men, your[s] 750. I wish I knew who would be agreable for a Brigadier General.

I designed to have done myself the Pleasure & Honor of writing to the Governor, but it is so late I can only desire You to make my most respectful & affectionate Compliments to him, to ackrowledge my obligations for his generous Sympathy with Me on Acct. of my Son and to assure him that I shall Pay the utmost Attention to every Part of his two last Letters[3] & hope to give him an agreable Acct. of our Success.

I designed to have wrote to Messrs. Browns & shall do it soon. At present be kind enough to let them know that I lost not a Moment in getting their Contract finished & doubt not but they will execute it in such a Manner as will do honor to the Colony & their house.[4]

Remember Me to all who love our Country and happen to enquire after Your very affect. Bror.   Sam Ward

P.S. Dr. Franklin upon my mentioning to him a Letter from the Govr. relative to making Powder gave Me a Receipt from some Author which I enclose:[5] the resolve of Congress you'l deliver the Govr. also.[6]

RC (RHi).
[1] The only extant letter which Ward had written to "Sammy" since his capture at Quebec is that of January 21, 1776. See Ward, *Correspondence* (Knollenberg), pp. 175–77.
[2] For an explanation of these references to Newport, see Gov. Nicholas Cooke's January 21 and 30, 1776, letters to the Rhode Island delegates. Ibid., pp. 178–82.
[3] Presumably the letters of Governor Cooke cited in the preceding note.
[4] See Secret Committee Minutes of Proceedings, this date.
[5] See Governor Cooke's November 27, 1775, letter to the Rhode Island delegates in Ward, *Correspondence* (Knollenberg), pp. 129–31.
[6] Presumably Congress' January 30, 1776, resolution requesting New England assemblies to assist Washington in obtaining arms for his troops and thanking them for such assistance as they had already extended. *JCC*, 4:103. On February 6 Ward also wrote a brief personal letter to one of his daughters in which he observed: "As to my Return home Business grows so very important and increases upon Us so fast that I have no Hopes of seeing my dear Family this Winter; I can only recommend You all to God and to each other." Ward, *Correspondence* (Knollenberg), pp. 183–84.

Richard Henry Lee to Samuel Adams

Chantilly the 7th of February 1776. Laments "our illfortune in Canada," but hopes all is not lost there. "The winter is the season for our surest and best exertions, and by wisely availing ourselves of this opportunity the most important points may be secured without much effusion of human blood. I pray you Sir to leave nothing undone that may secure Canada & New York this winter. These are the openings thro which America may, by able fencers, receive the worst wounds. I think our Canada Committee reported there were more important heights on Hudsons river than that which had been fixt on. Let all the very important heights have strong batteries with troops well commanded placed on them, and a strong Camp fixt either at Kings bridge or nearer the City. Has not Tryon, that *great friend to America* something of much moment, as he thinks, in agitation, by his calling an assembly. This man is one of those kind of *friends* that requires the most constant and unremitting watching. What means his Agent in his public summons of the freeholders where he says 'To be representatives of the said city and county to *assist* the *Captain General*, or Commander in chief, in a general Assembly.' This is new language I think and wants explanation.[1] Cant you furnish us with a good general Officer or two from the north-ward to command the 9 battalions raised here? This will be quite necessary should any considerable force be sent to this quarter. We have already done, with the enemy now here, all that can be expected from us. They are driven to seek shelter on board their Ships where they are not furnished with a single carrot, nor suffered to come on shore for water without chastisement. Would our fleet could come this way where a great prize is, and I think attainable without much risk. We learn that the Tory property on float in a number [of] small Vessels amounts to more than £150,000 and it is protected by three ships of war only, the Liverpoole, Otter, & Kingfisher. As for the small Tenders, & Merchantmen badly manned & worse provided by Dunmore, they are of little consequence. Our Convention have not taken up government totidem verbis, but I think totis viribus, because Sheriffs & Judges are appointed by Ordinance, and the Committee of Safety vested with all the Executive powers. This indeed has been indispensable in the present situation of things.

"I hope to see you early in March,[2] and in the meantime shall be extremely glad to hear from you."

RC (NN). Richard Henry Lee, *The Letters of Richard Henry Lee*, ed. James C. Ballagh, 2 vols. (New York: Macmillan Co., 1911–14), 1:167–69.
[1] Governor Tryon had dissolved the New York Assembly in December 1775, hoping that the forces for reconciliation would gain strength in a new assembly, but when the special January elections did not produce a tory majority, Tryon prorogued the legislature and it never met again in the colony. See Bernard Mason,

The Road to Independence (Lexington, Ky.: University of Kentucky Press, 1966), pp. 129–33.
[2] Lee returned to Congress on March 11. See *JCC*, 4:196.

Secret Committee Minutes of Proceedings

Com[mitte]e Ch[amber]. Feby. 7. 1776
At a meetg. of the Come of Secy. Prest. Saml Ward, B. Franklin, Jos. Hewes, Ths. McKean & Robt. Alexander. A Contract was agreed upon, to be enterd into between John Alsop, Francis Lewis, Silas Deane, Philip Livingston & Robt. Morris and sd. Comme. for exportg. the produce of these Colons. to the amount of £40,000 stg. & purchasing with the proceeds such goods as they shall be directed.[1]

A Petition from Piere La Fargue referrd to this Come. was also read & granted under the usual restrictions.[2]

MS (MH).
[1] A list of goods to be imported was agreed to on February 16 and the contract was completed on the 20th. See Secret Committee Minutes of Proceedings, February 16 and 20, 1776.
[2] See *JCC*, 4:117, 119–20.

Richard Smith's Diary

[February 7, 1776]
Wednesday 7.[1] Letters from Ld Stirling and Harrison One of the Delegates gone to N York and from the Comee. at Lancaster.[2] 10,000 Dollars granted to Commissy. Mease on Account & 250,000 to the Army at Cambridge & 20,000 to the Marine Comee. E. Rutledge, myself & Duane were chosen to look over the Journals & prepare a State of the Business before the Congress. 2 Committees were consolidated & desired to have all the Officers prisoners put upon Parole, such of these as are at Trenton to be boarded in that Neighborhood.[3] Accots. reported & allowed & some Subalterns appointd. Several Comees. chosen. A Frenchman who had brought into this Port Ammunition now requested Leave to export Produce therefor, it was referred to the Secret Comee.[4] Duane's Draught of a Resolution about the Deputies from Richmond County was canvassed, altered by Chase and forgot by the Interference of other Matters.[5] A Controversy Whether We have yet determined the Affair of Tea.[6] Some Regulations were presented by Lewis about Suttlers in the Northern Army.

MS (DLC).
[1] This day Robert Treat Paine noted in his diary: "Fair. Heard Genl Clinton &

Genl Lee met at N. York." MHi.

² Col. William Alexander's letters to Hancock of February 2 and 5 and enclosures are in PCC, item 162, 2:402–11; and *Am. Archives*, 4th ser. 4:913–16, 938, where the February 5 letter is misdated February 4. No letters from Benjamin Harrison or the Lancaster Committee have been found. In regard to the latter, however, it is possible that Smith was confused about a letter from the Reading committee which Congress acted upon this day. See *JCC*, 4:113, 116.

³ For the report of this committee, which was submitted to and approved by Congress on February 8, see *JCC*, 4:119.

⁴ See Secret Committee Minutes of Proceedings, this date.

⁵ For other references to this issue, see Smith's Diary, February 5, 1776, note 5.

⁶ Ibid., January 12, 1776, note 2.

Josiah Bartlett to Mary Bartlett

My Dear   Philadelphia Febry 8th 1776

On the 6th Instant I Recd yours of the 19th of last month Enclosing Some letters from the Children, and with pleasure hear you are all well and that Levi is learning to Cypher, I hope you will try to Keep him as much to Learning as Possible till my return. I am now pretty well; the headach which I mentioned to you in my last, held me longer than Common but has now left me. By a letter I Recd from Capt Langdon, I am in hopes I shall soon be relieved by Delegates from our Province agreable to my Request. In a short time after they arrive here, I shall Set out for home; how soon that will be, you will be likely to know Sooner than I, as you will hear when they are Chose & when they Set off for this place.

The 3d Instant a vessel arrived in this River with Sixty Tons of Salt Petre, fifteen Tons of powder & 1297 Compleat firelocks with Bayonets and Accoutrements but by reason of the Ice she Cannot Come up to this City. For 5 or Six Days we have had Some Steady Cold weather here, tho not like our New Hampshire winter weather, we have had no snow of any consequence Except what we had about Christmas which Soon went off. I have wrote to you Every week this year and Shall Continue to write to you weekly. A letter I Sent about a week before George Set off, to inform you of his Coming I find you have not Recd. Remember my love to all the Children and give my Compliments to all friends. I am yours &c,   Josiah Bartlett

RC (NhHi).

John Hancock to John Bull

Sir   Philada. 8 Feby. 1776

The Congress have order'd Two hundred & fifty Thousand Dollars to be Sent to General Washington, & having been inform'd that you was dispos'd to Take Charge of it, they have Agreed, & I am to Acquaint you that the money is Ready, & you will Engage two persons to Accompany you in whom you can Confide, & when you are Ready, please to let me know.[1] I am, Your hume servt,   John Hancock Presidt

RC (NjMoHP).
[1] *JCC*, 4:117. John Bull (1730–1824), Pennsylvania farmer and mill owner, had been colonel of the First Pennsylvania Battalion until his resignation on January 22, 1776. *PMHB* 3 (1879): 197; and *JCC*, 4:78. Hancock later wrote a letter of recommendation for Bull to Washington. Hancock to George Washington, February 12, 1776. NjMoHP.

Richard Smith's Diary

Thursday 8 Feb. [1776]
Votes read. 12,000 Dollars granted for the 4 New York Battals. now raising. 100 Dollars ordered to be presented to the French Artillery Officer to bear his Charges to Albany.[1] A Report from the Secret Comee. in Favor of the Martineco Man was agreed to.[2] Col. Bull offering his Service was employed to guard the Money to Cambridge. The Form of a Parole settled. Morton, Lewis and Wilson elected to contract for Victualling the Battalions in Chester, Cumberland & York Counties. Dickinson moved to advance Money to a Canadian Gentn. Prisoner at Trenton, was opposed and dropt his Motion.[3] Debate on a Report allowing a Vessel at Norwich in Connect. to go out with her Cargo, it was postponed. Conolly allowed to walk the Prison Yard 2 Hours every Day on Report of his Physician Dr. Rush. A Cask of Powder allowed to Col. St Clairs Riflemen to shoot at Marks. A Memorial was read from the Comee of Safety in Pennsa. about Powder Mills and a Motion made by Alexander and others to desire them to manufacture 20 or 30 Ton of our Saltpetre immediately.[4] Duanes Motion was passed, to refer the Acceptance of the Staten Island Deputies and to take off the Interdict, to the N York Conventn.[5]

MS (DLC).
[1] Dohickey Arundel. *JCC*, 4:120.
[2] See Secret Committee Minutes of Proceedings, February 7, 1776.
[3] There is no mention of this action in the journals.
[4] This "Memorial" has not been found, but for its provenance see the proceedings of the Pennsylvania Committee of Safety for this date in *Am. Archives*, 4th ser. 4:1567. On January 12 Congress ordered the Secret Committe to deliver 50 tons of saltpetre to the committee of safety to be manufactured into gunpowder. *JCC*, 4:128.
[5] See Smith's Diary, February 5, 1776, note 5.

John Adams' Memorandum
of Measures to Be Pursued in Congress

[February 9–23? 1776]

Mem.

The Confederation to be taken up in Paragraphs.[1]

An Alliance to be formed with France and Spain.

Embassadors to be sent to both Courts.

Government to be assumed in every Colony.

Coin and Currencies to be regulated.

Forces to be raised and maintained in Canada and New York. St. Lawrence and Hudsons Rivers to be secured.

Hemp to be encouraged and the Manufacture of Duck.[2]

Powder Mills to be built in every Colony, and fresh Efforts to make Salt Petre.[3]

An Address to the Inhabitants of the Colonies.

The Committee for Lead and Salt to be fill'd up, and Sulphur added to their Commission.

Money to be sent to the Paymaster, to pay our Debts, and fullfill our Engagements.

Taxes to be laid, and levied, Funds established. New Notes to be given on Interest, for Bills borrowed.

Treaties of Commerce with F. S. H. D. &c.[4]

Declaration of Independency, Declaration of War with the Nation, Cruising on the British Trade, their East India Ships and Sugar Ships.

Prevent the Exportation of Silver and Gold.

MS (MHi). Although it is impossible to ascertain the exact date of this document, Adams probably composed it soon after he returned to Congress on February 9. For a fuller discussion of the origin and meaning of the document, see Adams, *Diary* (Butterfield), 2:231–33.

[1] Adams also composed a draft resolution about this time, ordering the appointment of "a Committee to prepare a Draught of firm Confederation, to be reported as soon as may be to this Congress, to be considered and digested and recommended to the several Assemblies and Conventions of these united Colonies, to be by them adopted, ratified and confirmed." Ibid, p. 233. But a committee was not appointed until June 12, 1776. *JCC*, 5:433. See also Samuel Adams to John Adams, January 15, and Richard Smith's Diary, January 16, 1776.

[2] Adams later prepared four resolutions for the encouragement of agriculture and manufactures, one of which urged the promotion of "Flax, Hemp, and Cotton and the Growth of Wool in these United Colonies." See Adams' Draft Resolutions for Encouraging Agriculture and Manufactures, March 21? 1776.

[3] On February 23, Adams introduced four resolutions for the promotion of the manufacture of saltpetre, powder, and lead. See Richard Smith's Diary, February 23, 1776; and *JCC*, 4:170–71.

[4] France, Spain, Holland, and Denmark. The opening of America's foreign trade had been debated in a committee of the whole on four occasions during Adams'

absence in Massachusetts, and shortly after his return the issue was again taken up on February 14, 15, and 16. The notes of the debate on February 16 which Adams recorded are testimony to his great interest in the subject, and it was perhaps in the context of these discussions that he wrote in his diary the following sentence, which appears to have been a proposed article for the report of the committee of the whole. "Any Goods or Commodities, except Staves for Sale, may be exported, from the united Colonies to any other Part of the World, not subject to the Crown of G.B." For the evaluation of this document by the editor of Adams' papers, see Adams, *Diary* (Butterfield), 2:234.

Richard Smith's Diary

Friday 9 Feb. [1776]

Minutes read & Letters from Gens. Washn., Schuyler, Wooster & Arnold & from the N Jersey Convention & a Packet of intercepted Letters from England taken by Manley inclosing private Signals of the Men of War and Transports.[1] Copies of these Signals ordered to Admiral Hopkins & to the Delegates of each Colony. The Jersey Convention recommend Elias Dayton for Col., Anthony Waters [Walton] White for Lt. Col. & Francis Barber for Major of the 3d Battalion raising there & they were now chosen unanimy. & their Commissions made out. The Convention also desire Directions about Tea saying that People sell and use it on a supposed Connivance of Congress. The Letters from our Gens. were Com[mitte]d to Comee. of 5. Debates ensued about disposing of the Powder arrived here in Capt. Craig & 2 Tons were allotted to Pennsa. in Part of what has been borrowed, 1 Ton to N Carolina as formerly voted and the rest left for Considn. The Manufacture of the Saltpetre was put under the Direction of our Secret Comee. by a Vote 5 Colonies to 4, the latter wishing that the Pennsa. Comee. of Safety might have Charge of it. Maryland say they have no Gunpowder at present. Mr. Gerry from Massacs. Bay took his Seat.[2] Adjorned till Monday.

MS (DLC).
[1] See *JCC*, 4:123.
[2] Robert Treat Paine had noted in his diary on February 8: "Rainy, Warm. John Adams & Elbridge Gerry Esqrs. arrived." MHi.

Samuel Chase to Daniel of St. Thomas Jenifer

Dear Sir, Philada. Feby. 10th 1776

Inclosed You receive a proposal to furnish our Troops with the new invented Knapsack, and Haversack, & of Cartouch Boxes etc.[1]

The Blockade of Quebec is continued. Arnold has 700 Men with

him—daily Aids are going. He expects to take the Command in Six
Weeks. No News of Consequence. Your obedt. Servant,

Saml Chase

RC (MdAA).
[1] The enclosure, consisting of a sketch and letter to Chase from J. Young, is in
the "Red Books," 4:14, MdAA, and has been printed in *Md. Archives*, 11:150–51.

North Carolina Delegates to
the North Carolina Council of Safety

Honble Gentlemen   Philadelphia 10th Febry 1776
    We had the pleasure of writing to you some time ago by Mr. Goddard
surveyor of the Post Office. We now send by the Waggon that you
directed us to procure (to the care of Saml. Johnston Esquire at Edenton)
the Drums, Colours, Fifes, Pamphlets and a quantity of Powder to
make up the load.[1] We hope you will receive them safe and doubt not
you will cause them to be distributed in such manner as to make them
most usefull. We have searched almost every Book sellers shop in this
City for pamphlets but have made a poor Collection. Few are Written,
none read, since the appeal to Arms.
    You will please to observe that 400 lb of the Powder is the property
of Mr. John Cooper with whom you are to Account. The remainder
and all the other Articles are to be placed to the Credit of the United
Colonies and such of them as are expended in their service you will
charge to their Account. We obtained an Order on the Commissary
for One Ton of Powder which with the Cash we have received is
charged to our Colony.[2] The Waggon can not carry the whole of it
with the other Articles. If no good Opportunity should Offer to send
you what remains we shall take care that the Colony has Credit for it.
If the Accounts and Vouchers for the Several Articles we have purchased
can be had in time they shall be sent herewith. If not, we shall transmit
them by the first safe hand as also an Account of the sums we may
receive from the Public Treasury.
    You have herewith sundry resolutions of Congress (part of which
have been transmitted before). We beg leave to recommend them to
your Serious Attention.
    The Third Regiment which you are raising and the Vessels of War
you are fitting out will enhance your expenses amazingly. The whole
will be too much for your Strength to Accomplish. We therefore take the
liberty to request of you to forward to us as soon as may be an exact
account of your expenditures for the Three Battalions on Continental
pay and for the Indian Treaty with every other charge that you have

Against the United Colonies. We also wish to have an exact State of your Army, a particular Account of your Navy expence, a State of the Strength and disposition of your Minute Men and Militia & what Arms, Amunition and Cannon may be wanted for the defence of the Province.

We have had very lumping Accounts from two or three Colonies. Some of our members have made severe Animadversions thereon and the Congress has ordered them back for explanation. We entreat you to be very particular in making out your public accounts so that it may be seen at one view how and for what the money has been expended. It is necessary to inform you that no draught on the Treasurers of the united Colonies from any Province or public officer whatever is paid 'till Congress has enquired into the matter and directed the President to issue his Order to the Treasurers and a minute of the whole transaction made on the Journal, when if the sum is for a particular Colony, that Colony is charged with it and is accountable for the expenditure. Your own Judgment will point out to you the wisdom of this measure. You will please to direct us what sums of money to apply for and how they shall be remitted.

By the latest Accounts from England down to the 17th of November we have reason to apprehend that our Colony will be attacked in the Spring. We submit it to your consideration whether it would not be prudent to call a meeting of the Provincial Congress earlier than the first of May that you may be the better enabled to Counteract the wicked designs of the ministry by providing against the Armament intended to destroy your liberties. For further particulars respecting News we refer you to the public papers enclosed. It is more than probable that the American seas will be covered with Men of War and cutters in the spring for the purpose of intercepting Vessels and plundering the Shores for provisions. The Sea Coast of our Colony is very extensive and may require your notice and Attention.

We need not urge to you the Necessity of giving all possible encouragment to the recruiting Service 'till your three Regiments are compleat, to the forming independant Companies where the minute establishment is deficient or not approved, and to the making Arms, Salt Petre and Gun powder.

We are with the greatest respect & esteem, Gentlemen, Your mo Obedient, and very huml Servants[3]

FC (NcU: Hayes Collection microfilm). In the hand of Joseph Hewes. Addressed: "Honble Cornelius Harnett Esqr. and the other Members of the Council of Safety of North Carolina."

[1] The North Carolina delegates purchased these supplies and pamphlets in accordance with resolutions adopted by the North Carolina Provincial Council on December 21 and 24, 1775. *Am. Archives*, 4th ser. 4:304, 306.

[2] On January 25 Congress authorized the North Carolina delegates to draw $10,000 from the Continental treasurers and apply it "for the use of the battalions

ordered to be raised" in their province. *JCC*, 4:91.

³ To a large extent this letter is based on an outline which Hooper prepared for
Hewes and Penn just before he left Philadelphia around February 4 to visit his
mother in Massachusetts. This outline, which is also in the Hayes Collection, bears
the endorsement "Memorandum by Wm. Hooper," and reads as follows:

"With the Waggon in which you propose to send the Gunpowder, Drums &
Colours & Pamphlets it will be necessary to write the Provincial Council. I submit
it to your Consideration if it will not be necessary to inform them:

(*"That you have taken an order upon the Continental Treasurer for the sum of 10,000 dollars,
what part of it has been applied & in what manner & what remains in our hands subject to
their further direction.*)

"To urge the necessity of these publick assemblies, to wit the Congress & provincial
Council, meeting more frequently particularly the Congress before the first of May
to provide against the armament intended against them early in. January—& refer
them to the news paper.

(*"To request of them to forward us exact States of their demands against the Continent upon
Account of payments made the Troops enlisted there—& to send us a particular account of their
Navy the expense and Indian expense—what Cannon they want for the province.*)

"To request the distribution of the pamphlets.

"To desire an exact state of their Army.

"To urge forming independent Companies.

"To beg their Attention to the Sea coast.

"To urge most pressingly the necessity of hurrying the recruiting service.

"A Word about Saltpetre & powder Mills.

"Send all the late news papers.

"Sign Mr Hoopers name for him to the Letter.

"Free pamp[h]lets to be had."

Samuel Ward to Catharine Ward Greene

My dearest   Philadelpa. 10th Feby. 1776

I desired Mr. Greene to let you know that I had the Pleasure of your
Letter 9th last Month. You begin by observing that my Letter was a
Pleasure and a Disappointment, a true Picture this of Life in general.
The divine Wisdom has thought best (& I believe it is absolutely
necessary) At the same time that We are surrounded with innumerable
Mercies and Comforts to vary the Scene with Disappointm[ent], Pain,
Sickness & other things which We call Trouble. We are full fond of
this World & too negligent of the next as things. now stand. If there
were no Troubles, Sickness or Distress, but one continued State of
Health, Ease & Pleasure I believe they would be fatal to human nature.
Let us then adore that all gracious Being whose Goodness preserves,
& whose mercies surround us & make life comfortable & who at the
same time by the Shortness & Uncertainty of [. . .] and the various Disappointments attending [. . .] shews us the Insufficiency of temporal
Enjoyment [and] kindly leads Us to look for compleat Happi[ness in]
that World alone which is to come; May We all be prepared for it.

I do not wonder that You [*are*] concerned at my constant application
to Business, I am amazed that I am so well, may this Instance of divine

Goodness encrease my Love & Gratitude & induce Me to live more to his Glory.

Your dear Bror. Sammy, I am much pleased that you could in that beautiful Sentiment of Popes so chearfully commit him to his Maker. May You continue to have such a lively Sense of the divine Wisdom & Goodness as chearfully to resign Yourself & every thing dear to You to his all wise Direction and Government.

I am very glad your Bror. Charles has got a Commission,[1] I hope with you that he may do his Duty, Do write to him as often as you can well and encourage him in the Paths of Religion & Virtue. I design to write to him soon.

The Acct. which you give Me of [Polly, Ray] and other Relations is very acceptable & [I most] devoutly thank God that you are so [happy in] that nearest of all Connections. May you [both have] Wisdom to behave in such a Manner as [that esteem,] Regard & mutual affection may continue [&] encrease to your latest Breath & ever ac[knowledge] that Goodness which hath made You th[us].

I wrote Mr. Greene in great Haste [when I] enclosed him the Contracts to sign;[2] when [he returns] them to Me I wish he would enclose a co[py of my] Letter to him that I may see whether [every thing] I wrote was as I would wish.

We are very happy in the Arrival of about 120 Tons of salt petre & 20 Tons of Powder & 1300 stand of Arms, We shall need them & much more for our Enemies will do their utmost. It is necessary therefore to make all possible Preparation to receive them properly. I hope every thing will [be] done to put your Part of the Colony into a proper Posture of Defence. The Compy. I hope will make all proper[3]

RC (RHi).

[1] For the commission of Ward's eldest son, Charles, see John Adams' second letter of October 25, 1775, to James Warren, note 1.

[2] See Secret Committee to the Rhode Island Committee of Safety, January 29, 1776.

[3] Remainder of MS missing.

Samuel Ward to John Ward

My dear Son [1]   Philadelpa. 10th Feby. 1776

The old Proverb is with You "better late than never." I have some-times been displeased that you have not obeyed my Commands & wrote to Me. I will however forgive you but dont omit for the future to write to Me once a Month at least & let me know all about the Business of the Farm & Stock, how you all do, how you imploy your time, what Progress in learning you make and what Books you read.

Goods you observe are scarce; We must learn to manufacture every thing necessary and to do with out every thing else. When the Enemy has invaded our Lives, Liberty and Property, We must exert every Nerve to defend them; when We have once secured them, let Us turn our Attention to the Conveniences of Life: but without Liberty my dearest there is no safety or enjoyment in Life. Could you read History and see the dreadful Miseries of the unhappy People who have lost their Liberty, young as you are I believe you would consent to give up Goods, Business & ease & every pleasure and chearfully suffer all the Dangers & Hardships of War & even risque your Life in Defence of your Country rather than submit to that horrid State of Oppression, Slavery & Misery which others now groan under & Britain is trying to reduce Us to. The War between the Dutch & the Spaniards, lasted sixty years; should this War last one quarter so long you would be able to take up Arms in Defence of your Country; Cherish therefore the Love of Liberty & your Country which next to the Love of God I have endeavoured to plant in your tender heart that you may be qualified the Moment your Age & Strength allow it bravely to take up Arms in the Defence of your dear Country if necessary.

I am pleased with the Acct. which You give Me of the military Operations in the Colony, I expect We shall suffer much, I hope We shall bear it as becomes Freemen and have no Doubt but Heaven will crown our generous Efforts with Success & that We shall finally expel the Monsters from this Continent & establish the Peace, Welfare & Happiness of our Country upon a lasting Foundation.

Write to Me soon; tell Ray & Dicky that I command them to write to me by first Post. You must all take the best Care which you can of the Business, spend all the time you can in improving your Minds, be sure to avoid every thing mean, base or wicked, keep no bad Compy. & as little that is low as possible. May God preserve my dear Son & his Bros. & Sisters. Your affectionate Father,　　　　　S Ward

[*P.S.*] Give my warmest Love to your dear Sister Betsy, tell her I think much of her & long to see her, do all you can to make her & each other happy.

RC (RHi).
　[1] John Ward (1762–1823) was Ward's second youngest son. Ward, *Correspondence* (Knollenberg), pp. 214, 217.

Oliver Wolcott to Ezekiel Williams

Sir,　　　　　　　　　　　　　　　Philadelphia Febry 10, 1776
　The Congress have decreted a List to be taken of all the Prisoners of War of the United Colonies and transmitted together with the Paroles of the Officers so as to have them lodged on File. You are therefore Sir,

with the Committee requested to send Me the Names, Rank and Parole
of every Officer in Connecticut, also the Number of Non Commission
Officers, privates, Women and Children and to what Regiment they
respectively belong, and the Name and Character of all other Prisoners.[1]
You will also inform in what Towns the Prisoners Reside, and what
Number in each Town. I have enclosed a Copy of Parole approved of
by Congress, which Mutatis Mutandis (as this was adapted to the
Condition of some officers in this City) may be well in future to use as
a Model.[2]

The Pay Table have been wrote to with Regard to their transmitting
the proper Vouchers for their Expenditures, which I hope will be
Authentically done, as such evidence will be required. Govr. Trumbull
has wrote for a Quantity of Money, to be accounted for, but as this
Requisition is but now recd. nothing has yet been done upon it.[3]
Congress before I came here refused to advance any Thing to Rhode
Island for the Bounties given by them to their Soldiers last Spring.
This I think a Very hard Case as We well know the Troops could not
be raised without a Bounty. This is an ill omen upon our Colony, as
our Cases are similar, but We shall try to have it allowed and I wish
the Prospect of Success was fairer.

There has lately been brot into this River about Sixty Tons Salt Petre
for the Colonies, about fifteen Tons Gunpowder, 1300 Stands of Arms.
This together with the Salt Petre before recd. makes more than one
hundred Tons. This you are sensible is not printed News, tho publickly
known here. It is Manufacturing here, Three Mills are going, more are
erecting, and will go soon. I wish to know whether the Powder Mills in
Connecticut are ready and whether the owners would wish to Make up
any of this Petre. They Manufacture it here on Condition of receiving
forty Eight shillings our Currency for every hundred of powder when
delivered. The Manufacturer finds every Thing but the Nitre. I hope
the Salt Petre Business goes on well in the Colony, all but our internal
Resources must be precarious. I want to know whether you have a
sufficiency for present Use of Sulphur, & what Expectations you have
as to this Article. No Sulphur is Manufactured here nor in any of the
Southern Colonies that I hear of. The smelting Lead Ore succeeds it is
said at Middlebouro, and I beleive this is not Manufactured any where
else on the Continent.

Letters of Intelligence and Speculation are Very agreable to us from
our Friends, and I wish they might not be wanting to Us in this respect.
I have Nothing in special to Communicate as to News. An infatuated
Ministry with a self witted inexorable Prince seem determined to goad
us. I wish no one would ever expect any Thing from them but Injury,
as I Veryly beleive they will never deal out any Thing else to us. Mr.
Huntington has been inocculated and has got almost thro with his
Disorder, and is out of all Danger. Mr. Sherman Well. My Complements

to Col Williams, Mr Chester and Mrs. Williams. I am, Sir, your most humble Servant,   Oliver Wolcott

Tr (DLC).
¹ Ezekiel Williams (1729–1818), of Wethersfield, Conn., was appointed by the assembly in May 1775 to a committee to care for prisoners sent to Connecticut, subsequently became commissary of prisoners for the state, and was a member of the committee of the pay-table from April 1775 until the end of the war. From 1767 to 1789 he served as sheriff of Hartford County. Harrison Williams, *The Life, Ancestors and Descendants of Robert Williams of Roxbury* (Washington: W.F. Roberts Co., 1934), pp. 126–27.
² On February 7 Oliver Wolcott was appointed to a committee to oversee the disposition of prisoners, and the form of parole was approved the following day. See *JCC*, 4:115–16, 119.
³ Jonathan Trumbull's letter of February 3, 1776, which was read in Congress on the ninth, is in PCC, item 66, 1:71, and *Am. Archives*, 4th ser. 4:930–31. Connecticut was granted an advance of $100,000 on March 7. See *JCC*, 4:123, 188. For other references to Connecticut accounts, see Wolcott to Thomas Seymour, April 16, 1776.

John Adams to Abigail Adams

My Dear   Philadelphia Feby. 11. 1776
Here I am again. Arrived last Thursday,¹ in good Health, altho I had a cold Journey. The Weather, a great Part of the Way, was very severe, which prevented our making very quick Progress, and by an Accident which happened to one of my Horses, which obliged me to leave her at Brookfield and hire another, was delayed two days. An Horse broke loose in the Barn and corked mine under the foreshoulder. I hope that Bass upon his Return will find her well.
My Companion was agreable and made the Journey much less tedious than it would have been.
I can form no Judgment of the State of public Opinions and Principles here, as yet, nor any Conjectures of what an Hour may bring forth.
Have been to meeting and heard Mr. Duffill from Jer. 2.17. Hast thou not procured this unto thy self, in that thou has forsaken the Lord thy God, when he led thee by the Way? He prayed very earnestly for Boston and New York, supposing the latter to be in Danger of Destruction.
I, however, am not convinced that Vandeput will fire upon that Town—It has too much Tory Property to be destroyed by Tories.
I hope it will be fortified and saved. If not the Q[uestion] may be asked "hast thou not procured this &c?"
Tomorrow, Dr. Smith is to deliver an oration in Honour of the brave Montgomery.² I will send it, as soon as it is out, to you.
There is a deep Anxiety, a kind of thoughtfull Melancholly, and in some a Lowness of Spirits approaching to Despondency, prevailing,

through the southern Colonies, at present, very similar, to what I have often observed in Boston, particularly on the first News of the Port Bill, and last year about this Time or a little later, when the bad News arrived, which dashed their fond Hopes with which they had deluded themselves, thro the Winter. In this, or a similar Condition, We shall remain, I think, untill late in the Spring, When some critical Event will take Place, perhaps sooner. But the Arbiter of Events, the Sovereign of the World only knows, which Way the Torrent will be turned. Judging by Experience, by Probabilities, and by all Appearances, I conclude, it will roll on to Dominion and Glory, tho the Circumstances and Consequences may be bloody.

In such great Changes and Commotions, Individuals are but Atoms. It is scarcly worth while to consider what the Consequences will be to Us. What will be the Effects upon present and future Millions, and Millions of Millions, is a Question very interesting to Benevolence natural and Christian. God grant they may and I firmly believe they will be happy.

RC (MHi). Adams, *Family Correspondence* (Butterfield), 1:345–46.
  ¹ That is, February 8. Adams and Elbridge Gerry had left Watertown on January 25. Adams, *Diary* (Butterfield), 2:227.
  ² Rev. William Smith's oration was delivered on February 19. See Richard Smith's Diary, February 19, 1776.

John Adams to James Warren

Dr Sir   Philadelphia Feb. 11. 1775 [*i.e.* 1776]
  Mr Archibald Buchannan, and Mr Walter Tolley both of Maryland, and hearty Friends of America, introduced to me by my Friend Mr Chace, are bound to the Camp, and Mr Chace requested a Letter from me.
  Chace is a Man of common sense.
  I recd your Packett. I am obliged to you for opening the Letter from our Friend Mr Adams, and if you had opened all the others, you should have been equally welcome, altho I would not give a similar Permission to more than two or three other Persons in the World. I have no Correspondences for private Amusement, or Personal Interest, and therefore most Letters to me, might be seen by any public Man of public Virtue, good Understanding and Common Decency without Danger, Inconvenience, or offence. But as so many Persons who have not all those Qualities, become in the Course of Things public Persons, We cannot be too cautious I find what We write, whom We write to, and how it is conveyed.
  I have Seen the Copy of a Letter. Let the Writers Passions fume away, unnoticed. Peepers often Spy disagreable Objects. Let them pay for

their Peeping. I have Reason to complain of Negligence in one Gentn. and, I fear, of Unkindness in another upon this occasion, but I will not complain. They shall take all Advantages against me that they can get. They cannot hurt me nor you. The only Advantage they have got upon this occasion is to torment themselves, and gratify others. The Gentn. promised me to deliver those Letters into the Hand of Mr. S[amuel] A[dams] but he did not.[1]

I have only this Moment to write. Yours, sincerely

RC (MHi). In Adams' hand, though not signed.

[1] Adams is apparently referring to the angry reaction of Robert Treat Paine to James Warren's December 3 letter to John Adams, which had been delivered to Paine. See Robert Treat Paine's letters to Joseph Hawley, to Joseph Palmer, and to James Warren, January 1, 1776.

Benjamin Franklin to Charles Lee

Dear Sir,   Philada. Feb. 11, 1776.

The Bearer Monsr. Arundel is directed by the Congress to repair to Gen. Schuyler, in order to be employed by him in the Artillery Service.[1] He purposes to wait on you in his way, and has requested me to introduce him by a Line to you. He has been an officer in the French Service, as you will see by his Commissions; and professing a Good Will to our Cause, I hope he may be useful in Instructing our Gunners and Matrosses—Perhaps he may advise in opening the nailed Cannon.

I received the enclosed the other day from an officer, Mr. Newland, who served in the two last wars, and was known by Genl. Gates who spoke well of him to me when I was at Cambridge.[2] He is desirous now of entering into our service. I have advised him to wait upon you at New York.

They still talk big in England, and threaten hard; but their language is somewhat civiler, at least not quite so disrespectful to us. By degrees they may come to their senses, but too late I fancy for their Interest.

We have got in a large quantity of saltpetre 120 Ton, & 30 more expected. Powdermills are now wanting. I believe we must set to work, and make it by hand—but I still wish with you that Pikes could be introduced, and I would add bows and arrows. Those were good weapons not wisely laid aside:

1. Because a Man may shoot as truly with a Bow as with a common Musket.

2. He can discharge 4 arrows in the time of charging and discharging one Bullet.

3. His object is not taken from his view by the smoke of his own side.

4. A Flight of Arrows seen coming upon them terrifies and disturbs the Enemy's Attention to his Business.

5. An Arrow striking in any part of a Man, puts him *hors de combat* 'till 'tis extracted.

6. Bows and Arrows are more easily provided every where than Muskets & Ammunition.

Polydore Virgil speaking in one of our Battles against the French in Edward the 3rds reign mentions the great confusion the Enemy were thrown into, *sagittarum nube*, from the English; and concludes, *Est res profecto dictu mirabilis, ut tantus ac potens Exercitus a solis ferè Anglicis Sagittariis victus fuerit; adeo Anglus est Sagittipotens, &* ID GENUS ARMORUM VALET.

If so much Execution was done by Arrows when Men wore some defensive Armour, how much more might be done now that it is out of use.

I am glad you are come to New York; but I also wish you could be in Canada.

There is a kind of suspense in Men's minds here at present, waiting to see what terms will be offer'd from England. I expect none that we can accept; and when that is generally seen we shall be more unanimous and more decisive—Then your proposed solemn League and Covenant will go better down; and perhaps most of your other strong measures adopted.

I am always glad to hear from you, but I do'nt deserve your Favours being so bad a Correspondent. My Eyes will now hardly serve me to write by Night; and these short days have been all taken up by such a variety of business, that I seldom can sit down three Minutes without Interruption.[3]

God give you Success. I am with the greatest esteem, Yours affectionately,   B. Franklin.

MS not found; reprinted from *NYHS Collections* 4 (1871): 284–86.

[1] See *JCC*, 4:111–12, 120.

[2] The "enclosed" letter of February 5 to Franklin from Trevor Newland is in *NYHS Collections* 4 (1871): 286–92.

[3] The continued pressure of business led Franklin two weeks later to send a letter of resignation to the speaker of the Pennsylvania Assembly, asking both that another member be chosen to the assembly in his stead and that the house "be pleased to dispense with my further Attendance as one of the Committee of Safety." Franklin to John Morton, February 26, 1776, *Pa. Archives*, 8th ser. 8:7410–11. The assembly immediately declared Franklin's seat vacant and ordered steps to be taken for election of a new member. Ibid, p. 7411.

Joseph Hewes to Samuel Johnston

Dear Sir   Philadelphia 11th Feb. 1776

I have got a waggon made, have purchased four good Horses and expected to have sent them of[f . . .] yesterday, but when I went to examine the powder in the Magazine I found to my surprise there was none but cannon powder and that very coarse and ordinary, not fit for musketry. Knowing the greatest part that is wanted for our province ought to be good musket powder I thought it best to detain the waggon till such could be obtained. Seven Tons of such I hear is on a Vessel below and will be up as soon as the Ice will suffer any thing to pass. I hope in a few days to get the waggon away. The Horses came pretty high, two of them £50 each, the other two £35 each, they are all Bays and young.

Our friend Hooper has taken an oppertunity when he could be best spared from Congress to fly to the Camp at Cambrige to see his Mother who has lately got out of Boston. He has been gone about Ten days and will return as soon as possible. He desired me to put his name to any Letters we should write to the provincial Council. I believe he would not wish they should know he was absent. Late last night I received a Letter from him dated at New York the 6th.[1] He seems greatly alarmed at the intelligence he had received there and urged very pressingly the Necessity of sending of[f] an express to you. The substance of the information he gave, what has been received from thence since he left it, you will find in our Letter to the Council which you have herewith.[2] The anxiety of my worthy friend for the Safety, honour & happiness of our province and for his dearest connections there I imagine has induced him to paint things in the Strongest colours to me, however I wish there may not be too much truth in his Suggestions. All Accounts from England seem to agree that we shall have a dreadfull Storm bursting on our heads thro' all America in the Spring. We must not shrink from it, we ought not to shew any simptoms of fear, the nearer it approaches and the greater the sound the more fortitude and calm, steady firmness we ought to possess. If we mean to defend our liberties, our dearest rights and privileges against the power of Britain to the last extremity we ought to bring ourselves to such a temper of mind as to stand unmoved at the bursting of an Earthquake. Altho the storm thickens I feel my self quite composed. I have furnished my self with a good Musket & Bayonet and when I can no longer be usefull in Council I hope I shall be willing to take the field. I think I had rather fall there than be carried off by a lingering illness. In this I am pretty much of the same opinion with the French General, who, confined a long time by sickness to his bed, on hearing the Duke of Berwick was killed by a cannon Ball, exclaimed, Great God, how unfortunate I am, Berwick was always a lucky fellow.[3]

RC (OClWHi).
[1] See William Hooper's letters to Joseph Hewes and John Penn, February 6, 1776.
[2] See North Carolina Delegates to the North Carolina Council of Safety, February 10, 1776.
[3] For the continuation of this letter, see Hewes to Johnston, February 13, 1776.

New York Delegates to
the New York Committee of Safety

Gentlemen   Philad. 11t Feby 1776

Agreeable to your Instructions we have represented to Congress the Case of the Inhabitants of Richmond County. As our Convention might be embarrassed while it seemed doubtful to you whether they ought, without the Intervention of Congress to decide on the propriety of admitting the Deputies elected for that County; it became our Duty to press for a speedy Decision on this Subject. It was readily agreed that the Convention ought to be the sole Judges of their own members; and on this principle the Resolution which we have the honour to enclose was grounded.[1]

We have obtained a Warrant on the continental Treasury for 12000 Dollars to strengthen your Hands in raising, within our Colony, the four Battalions intended for its immediate Protection and Defence. The first oppertunity which presents itself to you, or us, shall be embraced to forward the money.[2]

The great Difficulties with which our Convention was, on a similar Occasion, pressed the last year will, we hope, be avoided by this Expedient; and for which we were the more sollicitous from our Ignorance, whether the State of our provincial Finances would admit of your performing this essential Service, to advantage, without such Aid.

Some time since we were favour'd with an Order of our Convention authorizing us to draw on the provincial Treasurer for the Allowance they were pleased to provide for their Delegates. To such of us as have continued here since the last Recess of Congress, it woud be convenient, and prevent the Risk and Difficulty of double Carriage, should we be directed to deduct out of the money which will pass thro' our Hands agreeably to the above mentioned warrant, our respective Ballances.[3] In that Case the Residue shall be accompanied by our Receipt to the provincial Treasurer as his Voucher.

We expect soon to have the Honour of writing to you again on other Subjects of your Dispatches, on some of which we think it probable you may have consulted the Deputies of Congress[4] who arrived this day from your City.

We are Gentlemen, with great Respect, your most Obedient, humble
Servants,   Jas. Duane   Wm. Floyd

                                   John Alsop   Frans Lewis

RC (N). Written by Duane and signed by Duane, Alsop, Floyd, and Lewis.

[1] On this point, see *JCC*, 4:121; and Richard Smith's Diary, January 5, 1776, note 5.

[2] Congress authorized the appropriation of this money on February 8. *JCC*, 4:120.

[3] The New York Provincial Congress granted this request on February 22. *Am.*

Archives, 4th ser. 5:296.
[4] For these "Deputies," see Committee of Congress to the New York Committee of Safety, February 1, 1776.

Samuel Ward to His Daughter

My dearest   Philadela. 11th Feby. 1776
   I am thankfull to find by yours of 29th last that you are all well except Nancy & that She mends. May Heaven make her easy, chearful & happy in herself and grant the ardent Wish & Prayer of her Soul that She may be enabled to diffuse Happiness all around her. I have often thought that the highest Pleasure which Wealth, Power And all other earthly Possessions afford Us in this World is the godlike Pleasure of doing good; the benevolent Mind feels more true Happiness in relieving the distressed & the Patriot in promoting the Good of his Country than all the Gold that now is or ever was in this World can give the Miser.
   I do not wonder that you feel so much at the Recollection of what your dear Brother has suffered. Ever adored be that gracious Being who supported him, gave him Courage in the severe Action he was engaged in & covered him in the Day of Battle, may this remarkable Instance of divine Protection teach all my dear Children never to distrust the divine Goodness, never to shrink from Danger in a good Cause but bravely to follow where ever their Duty to God & their Country calls them. From the large Reinforcements which We have ordered to Canada (some of which are there before now) & the favourable Disposition of the Canadians I doubt not but We shall soon get Quebec & that your Bror. if he escapes or recovers of the small Pox will soon be released, but do not My dearest depend upon seeing him soon. The small Pox may open the Doors of eternal Bliss to him, if not He will probably make the next Campaign in Canada but in whatever Situation he may be, while you are satisfied that he is either reaping the Rewards of his Virtue or bravely fighting for his Country your Love of Liberty & your Country will notwithstanding your ardent affection for him make you support his Absence with Fortitude.
   The Poem which you mention I gave You: The Monitor I believe (with Polly) might not be so absolutely necessary as my Panegyrick upon Neatness might imply but You know my dearest it is not in my Power to give you all Fortunes. I wish to supply the Place of them by what is infinitely more truly valuable every Virtue, and every useful, agreable & amiable Accomplishment and happy very happy shall I be If I may under the divine Direction be an Instrument in forming the Minds & Manners of my dear Children in such a Manner that they may be worthy & useful Members of Society here and after having sustained with Honor the Posts committed to them until relieved by the all wise Direction of all things be translated to the mansions of Bliss.

I cant give up your writing & cyphering. Dont be discouraged, try to get time to write a little every Day. There is a copper Plate Book of your Bror. Charles's & which you can write after and possibly Nancy can teach you a little cyphering. At least by studying the Books of arithmetic & a little of her help you may learn much. The Oeconomy of a Family requires some Knowledge. I am obliged to your Cousin Celia for her Regards. I hope She has been happy at our House & will enjoy herself with You as long as her good Mamma can spare her.

Tell your dear Aunt Betsy that I cannot say when She will visit Newport again, the Spring will bring on a most vigorous Campaign, it is probable that amidst the general Calamities Newport may be destroyed by one Side or the other every but thing ought to be done for its Defence that can with any Probability of Success be Attempted.

None of You mention the receiving a Pamphlet entitled Common Sense nor a Poem McFingal. I hope my Letters covering them have not miscarried.

I have just received Advice of the Arrival of another Vessel or two with Arms & Ammunition; as our Dangers approach, Providence kindly enables us to meet them. Below is a list of late Arrivals. Remember Me to all my dear Family & Friends.[1] Your very affece. Father

Sam Ward

1 Vessel 57 Tons salt petre now manufacturing into Powder.
2nd do. 60 Tons salt petre, 15 Tons powder & 1300 Stands of Arms.
3rd do. 20 Tons Powder & 500 Stands Arms.
4th do. 30 T[on]s salt petre & 2 1/2 Tons Powder. The three last are very lately arrived.

RC (RHi).
[1] For two other letters Ward wrote this day to members of his family, see Ward, *Correspondence* (Knollenberg), pp. 189–91.

John Alsop to Alexander McDougall

Dr sr,   Philada. 12 Feby 1776

Your favor of the 6 Instant to Mr. Jay & Self have Just recd (Mr. Jay is not yet return'd to Congress) informg of our unanimous ellection as representatives in the Assembly, and that the usual custom in such cases was to give The Sum of £50, for the use of the poor, which I readily agree to, but as I suppose My family is removed out of Town upon the present allarmg Situation of our City, I must request that you'll please to apply to the Committee of Safety or Convention for Said Sum of Fifty pounds, and I will account to them for it in my pay as a delegate, as this must be a Distressing time to the poor. (When you receive it please directly to apply to their relief as you and Mr. Livingston may Judge proper.)

I have not the least doubt but Gen Lee will endeavor [to] preserve The peace and good order of the City with the advice and in Conjunction with our Comittee of Safety, yet I shall take it kind when you pass my house that you'll Turn an eye Towards it, for I have many Valuables in it that are not remov'd, & note the Condition its in, for I think my family have gone out of Town & Shut it up, and when you have leizure shall be glad of a line from you to know the State of our City, and if you are at liberty to give me your Sentiments, about having My effects removed from the City. As I write this in Congress whilst they are debating the fate of our City,[1] you'll excuse its incorrectness, & have only to add that I am Dr sr, yr Very hble Servt.,   John Alsop

P.S. Coll Dickinson of the 1st Battallion of the Associators has this moment offered to go to N York with a Detachment from the four Batts. of this City makeg one Compleat Battallion & Suppose may begin their march Tomorrow & a Batt. of the Jersey Militia or minute men, will be with you soon.

RC (NHi).
[1] On this point, see John Hancock's letters of this date to John Dickinson, to Charles Lee, and to the New Jersey Provincial Convention.

John Hancock to John Dickinson

Sir,   Philada. 12 Feby. 1776 Monday Morng.
I have this moment Rec'd a Letter by Express from General Lee at New York, mentioning the Arrival of some Troops in the Harbour of N York, and Requesting an Augmentation of Troops from this Colony; these Circumstances Render it necessary that there should be a punctual Attendance of the Members of Congress, & as full as possible; I therefore trouble you with this to Request your Attendance at 10 oClock, that we may Avail ourselves of your Advice & Aid.[1]
I have the honour to be, Sir, Your most hum servt.
                                                    John Hancock Prest.

RC (PHi).
[1] When Congress this day ordered reinforcements from New Jersey and Pennsylvania to New York in response to General Lee's letter of February 9, Dickinson volunteered to command the battalion of Philadelphia associators. Before they could march, however, Congress suspended Dickinson's orders when no British troops landed at New York. See *JCC*, 4:127–28, 133, 151; and John Adams to Abigail Adams, February 13, 1776.

John Hancock to Charles Lee

Sir   Philada. Febry. 12. 1776

Your Letter of the 9th Inst. I this morning Rec'd, and immediately laid before Congress, who without delay, paying that Attention to it, which the intelligence therein contain'd Requir'd, Dispatch'd an order to the Convention of New Jersey, and made Application to the Committee of Safety of Pennsylvania requesting them to Send immediately to your Assistance from each of their respective Colonies, Detachments from the Minute Men and Associators equal to a Battalion from each Colony.[1]

The Battalion from New Jersey which lies contiguous will I hope be with you in two or three Days.

A Ton of Powder is also order'd to be Sent forward to you with all possible Expedition.

The four Battalions order'd to be rais'd in Pennsylvania are I understand in great forwardness. The Congress have given orders to have a Return made of those enlisted.

That God may Restore you to health, and Crown your Endeavours in defence of Liberty with Success, is the sincere & ardent prayer, of, Sir, your most hume Servt.,   J H Pt.

[*P.S.*] The Congress will Determine as soon as possible respectg. an hospital, and you shall know the result.

LB (DNA: PCC, item 12A).

[1] General Lee's letter is in PCC, item 158, 1:13–16, and *Am. Archives*, 4th ser. 4:965. For Congress' response, see *JCC*, 4:127–28.

John Hancock to
the New Jersey Provincial Convention

Gentlemen,   Philadelphia 12th Feby 1776

The arrival of Troops at New York, the importance of that place to the Welfare of America, & the Necessity of throwing up a Number of Works to prevent our Enemies from Landing and Taking post there, render it necessary that a Number of Troops should immediately Join General Lee. I am therefore Desir'd to apply to you, and Request you, would with all possible Expedition send Detachments of your Minute Men equal to a Battalion under proper officers, & well Arm'd & Accoutred to New York, there to be under the Command of Genl. Lee.

Your approved Zeal in the Cause of your Country gives me the strongest Assurances that you will with Alacrity embrace this Oppory. of Giving Aid to your Neighbours, and that your People will chearfully

Engage in a Service by which they will not only render a very essential Service to their Country, but also have an Oppory. of Acquiring Military Skill & knowledge in the Construction of Field Works & the Method of Fortifying & retrenching Camps, by which they will be the better able when occasion Calls to Defend their Rights & Liberties.[1]

I am Gentlemen, Your Obedt. hume sevt,   J H Prest.

LB (DNA: PCC, item 12A).

[1] On February 15 the New Jersey Provincial Congress voted "that Detachments of Minute Men, properly accoutrd, equal to a Battalion in the Continental Service, be immediately made, & marched to New-York." *Am. Archives*, 4th ser. 4:1593.

John Hancock to George Washington

Sir,   Philadelphia Febry 12th. 1776
Your Letters of 24th & 30th ulto. have been duly Rec'd, and laid before the Congress, are now with their severall Inclosures under the Consideration of a Committee, as soon as Report is made, I shall do myself the hortour to Transmitt you the Result of Congress thereupon.[1]

I yesterday morng. Rec'd an Express from General Lee, requesting an Augmentation of Troops, Congress immediately directed one Battalion of Minute Men from New Jersey in Addition to Lord Stirling's Battalion, & one Battalion of Associators from this City to proceed to New York & be under the Command of General Lee, the latter Commanded by Coll. Dickinson who very chearfully step'd forth, & both Battalions will immediately March.[2]

RC (MH).

[1] Washington's letters were read in Congress on February 9 and acted upon on February 16. *JCC*, 4:123, 154–55. These letters, with enclosures, are in PCC, item 152, 1:435–64, and *Am. Archives*, 4th ser. 4:840–46, 890–95.

[2] Remainder of MS missing.

Francis Lightfoot Lee to Landon Carter

My dear Colonel   Philadelphia Feb. 12 1776
I intended to have devoted yesterday to answer your kind Letters by last Monday's post; but unexpected business intervened which prevented me, and this day I find my obligation increased by the receipt of yours of the 1st Inst. I must now content myself with assuring you that I am very sensible of your Friendship; and acquainting you with the occurrences in this part of the world; the only return in my power for your kindness. Genl. Washington having intelligence that Genl. Clinton with a body of troops had sailed from Boston & suspecting their intention

was to make a lodgment in N. York; dispatched Genl. Lee to prevent its Lee arrived there last week with 1100 men, & on the same day in pop. Clinton, who had been seperated from his fleet in a snow storm. Finding Lee there, he & Tryon assured the town upon their honor that the troops were not destined for N. York & nothing hostile was intended agst. them. Lee knowing the cue of the Ministry & all their agents, continued to call in more forces. This day he sent us an express that one of the transports full of soldiers was arrived & several others seen at the hook. However as Lee had 4000 men, it is immagined Clinton will comply with part of his *honorable* engagement, & attempt nothing agst. N. York; but proceed to Virga. which place, some Gentlemen (in pretended confidence) were assured, was the original destination of the fleet so that perhaps old bess will not long remain lean. Clinton's pretended rendezvous is at Hampton Road where he is to be joined by a fleet from England with 5 Regiments. His present force is supposed to be 6 or 700 men. I fear your want of Arms & good Genls will make this little army very formidable to you. We have not yet apply'd to Congress for yr. Genl. Officers, nor do we know where they will be got; those that are good for anything seem to have their hands full to the North & Eastward. Whenever they are appointed, you may be assured I will not fail to put in a good word for my young friend Landon.[1] Had we not been deceived in our intelligence respecting the 30 tons of powder, Boston in all probability woud now be in our possession, but alas for want of that necessary, the favorable season has passed away without anything being effected; & now the nest must remain probably till next winter. However we have now in hand 117 tons of saltpetre, 13 of powder & 1300 stand of arms. The utmost dispatch is using to manufacture the Saltpetre which will soon enable us to answer all demands wch are now very great from all quarters; but we expect in the present scramble for the 13 tons, to get one or two for Virga. Our affairs in Canada are in as a good a situation as we coud expect since our unfortunate attempt upon Quebec. We have no doubt of having a sufficient force there to render a good Acct. of Carlton before he can be reinforced. Capt. Manly of the Lee, now of the Hancock, is daily taking some of their supply transports, in return for which two ships loaded by the Congress to procure military stores, have fallen into the Enemy's hand.

I find Ld. D. is endeavouring to persuade the settlers on the Rivers to remain quiet & not remove their stocks & provisions. No doubt till he is enabled to come & ease them of them all. Tis strange that this monster & the rest of his infernal tribe shou'd expect to be credited by a single person, after the innumerable instances of cruelty, rapacity & perfidy, fresh in everyones mind, which they have exhibited in every part of the world. The Ministerial scheme agst Sayre, Lee & others was this. The workmen leaving the docks, demanding higher wages, applying to the American friends to supply them with money to convey them out of the Kingdom, was all under the direction of Ld Sandwich, in order to bring the Americans under the penalty for inveigling the Kings workmen out of the Kingdom. It was about to take effect when one more honest than the rest of his fellows, disclosed the whole affair to the Alderman. This failing, their next plan is, to make one Richardson, a native of this City whom they have made an officer in the Guards, swear away the life of Sayre, & it is apprehended [of] the other also.[2] Is it possible that any one can expect anything good from such abandoned Villains? From them & all their hellish plots Good Lord deliver us. Our best respects to Sabine Hall, & believe me Dear Col. Your afft. friend & very hble Sevt.   Francis Lightfoot Lee

RC (ViHi).
    [1] Carter had asked Lee to recommend his grandson Landon as an aide-de-camp to the commander of the southern department. However, Gen. Charles Lee, who was appointed to head the southern forces on March 1, subsequently retained the aides-de-camp already serving with him. See Landon Carter, *The Diary of Colonel Landon Carter of Sabine Hall, 1752–1778,* ed. Jack P. Greene, 2 vols. (Charlottesville: University Press of Virginia, 1965), 2:1006–7; and Francis Lightfoot Lee to Landon Carter, March 19, 1776.
    [2] For further information about the "next plan" against Stephen Sayre (1736–1818), an American banker and merchant who served as sheriff of London, 1773–74, and was arrested there in October 1775 for allegedly plotting to kidnap the king and seize the Tower of London, see Edmund Burke, *The Correspondence of Edmund Burke,* ed Thomas W. Copeland (Cambridge: At the University Press, 1958–), vol. 3, *July 1774–June 1778,* ed. George H. Guttridge (1961), pp. 233–34; and Horace Walpole, *The Yale Edition of Horace Walpole's Correspondence,* ed. W. S. Lewis (New Haven: Yale University Press, 1937–), 24:138–39. See also *DAB.*

John Penn to Thomas Person

Dear Sir   Philada. Feby. 12th 1776
    I suppose you [1] have heard before now that the Brave and Gallant General Montgomery is no more, he fell in an unsuccessful attack on the Town of Quebec the 31st of Decembr. last, the particulars you will see in a news paper. Our men have been able to keep the field and have continued the blockade as appears by letters of a late date. The Canadians in General are on our side. The People to the Northward have showed great Spirit on this occasion. A number having Immediately marched to Quebec on hearing of our repulse, there will be several thousands before the Town next month so that I hope they will have easy work. From a news paper I learn that Governor Martin has at length obtained his wishes. Administration having agreed to send seven Regiments to North Carolina, they were to have sailed the first of December. General Clinton left Boston about three weeks ago. He

called at New York last week to pay Governor Tryon a visit in order as it's thought to consult him what measures to persue when he gets to No. Carolina and inquire the situation of the Country, as it is supposed he is to command the above force when arrived. I make no doubt but the Southern Provinces will soon be the Scene of action, as our enemies may hope to obtain greater success there than at the Northward. Will it not be necessary for your Committee to do something immediately for puting the Province in a Condition to oppose the designs of our enemies; and to desire the Convention to meet sooner than May in order to consult what steps may be necessary for you to take. The People to the Northward have Spirit and Resolution which I doubt not will carry them victorious through this Contest, I hope we to the South-ward shall act like men determined to be free. It will perhaps be neces-sary for you to aid the recruiting service and to put the Militia in such a situation as to be able to march at an early notice & to keep the Tories under; they have all been disarmed at New York which measure I believe will contribute to the Salvation of that Province. I dont know that a step of that kind could be taken with you, perhaps it would be dangerous. I expect the Waggon with the powder, drums &c. will set off this week, you may depend nothing will be omitted by us to contrive you such necessary articles. Is there any preparation for making Salt petre, gun powder or Guns? The house of Commons have approved of the Kings speech and promised to support him. Should they persevere in their attempts to reduce us to a state of Slavery by carrying on this unatural war with fire and sword, we must determine to act with unanimity and assume every power of Government for the purpose of Legislation, in order to be the better able to defend ourselves. We have obtained an order for 10,000 dollars for the use of our Province, wch. sum is ready when ever you think proper to call for it.[2] I suppose the great expense you are at will oblige you to have some Continental money to prevent making so much Provincial as you will have occasion for, lest it depretiates in value. The great distance we are off and hearing so very seldom gives me some concern lest matters of consequence happen without our hearing of it. One reason for our sending an express to inform you of the above is that I think the expence is nothing com-pared to the advantage it may be of. Please to remember me to my Friends to whom I had not time to write. For God sake my Good Sir encourage our People, animate them to dare even to die for their Country. Our struggle I hope will not continue long. May unanimity and success crown your indeavours is the wish of, Dear Sir, Your mo. obt. Servt., John Penn

[P.S.] I send you some news papers. I have been plagued with a pain in my head that I can hardly [bear. Rem]ember me to yr. Lady. J.P.

RC (Nc-Ar).

[1] Thomas Person (1733–1800), of Granville County, N.C., and once a leading Regulator, was at the time a member of the North Carolina Provincial Congress and the provincial council. Later in 1776 he was instrumental in drafting the instructions which directed the North Carolina delegates to vote for independence and in drawing up North Carolina's first state constitution and bill of rights. *DAB*.

[2] On this point, see North Carolina Delegates to the North Carolina Council of Safety, February 10, 1776, note 2.

Richard Smith's Diary

Monday 12 Feb. [1776]

Our Comee. sent to N York made Report of their Proceedings. A Letter from Gen. Lee by Express, it appears that he will have soon above 5000 Troops & Militia at New York, Debates whether to send Him more Force and from whence. A Motion by the Virginia Delegates for 3 Battalions to be raised there on Continental Pay in Addition to the 6 already on Foot, occasioned a warm Controversy and was at last postponed.[1] Hewes made a Report which was accepted, on the Mode of getting Naval Stores conveyed from N Carolina to the Northern Colonies.[2] Much Time was spent on the Means of Manufacturing Saltpetre & erecting Powder Mills, agreed to put 50 Ton of Saltpetre into the Hands of the Pennsylvania Comee. of Safety & to confirm their Contracts, agreed to send 10 Ton to Massachusetts Bay, 10 Ton to New York and on Vote Whether to send 10 Ton to Connecticut the Colonies were equally divided, consequently it passed in the Negative. In Consequence of Advertisements for that purpose from the Comee. of Safety here, Proposals have been made by 8 or 10 Persons for erectg Powder Mills in Penna. & Jersey. A Motion by McKean to put 250 Stand of Arms just arrived into the Hands of the Companies here and then they will be ready to march for Quebec, was thrust out of Notice by other interfering Matters. A Note was recd. from Dr. Smith about inviting the Gen. Assembly, Corporation, Associators &c. to hear the Oration next Monday, it was given to the Comee. on Gen. Montgomerys Monument.

MS (DLC).

[1] Congress reconsidered and rejected this "Motion" on February 13. See Smith's Diary, February 13; and Benjamin Harrison to Robert Carter Nicholas, February 13, 1776.

[2] A draft copy of this report, in the hand of Hewes, is in NcU: Hayes Collection microfilm. See also Hewes to Robert Smith, February 6, 1776.

John Adams to Abigail Adams

Feby. [13] [1] 1776

Lee is at York,[2] and We have requested a Battalion of Philadelphian

Associators, together with a Regiment of Jersey Minute Men, to march
to his Assistance. Lord Sterling was there before with his Regiment,
so that there will be about 1000 Men with Lee from Connecticutt,
about 600 with Ld. Sterling from the Jerseys, one Battalion of about
720 Minute Men from Jersey and one of the same No. from Philadelphia. We shall soon have four Battalions more raised in Pensilvania,
to march to the same Place and one more in the Jerseys.[3]

Mr. Dickinson, being the first Collonell, and Commander of the
first Battalion too, claimed it, as his Right to march upon this Occasion.
Mr. Reed, formerly Gen. Washingtons Secretary goes his Lt. Coll.
Mr. Dickinsons Alacrity and Spirit upon this occasion, which certainly
becomes his Character and setts a fine Example, is much talk'd of and
applauded. This afternoon, the four Battallions of the Militia were
together, and Mr. Dickinson mounted the Rostrum to harrangue them,
which he did with great Vehemence and Pathos, as it is reported.

I suppose, if I could have made Interest enough to have been chosen
more than a Lt., I should march too upon some such Emergency, and
possibly a Contingency may happen, when it will be proper for me to do
it still, in Rank and File. I will not fail to march if it should.

In the Beginning of a War, in Colonies like this and Virginia, where
the martial Spirit is but just awakened and the People are unaccustomed
to Arms, it may be proper and necessary for such popular Orators as
Henry and Dickenson to assume a military Character. But I really
think them both, better Statesmen than Soldiers, tho I cannot say they
are not very good in the latter Character. Henrys Principles, and Systems, are much more conformable to mine than the others however.

I feel, upon some of these Occasions, a flow of Spirits, and an Effort
of Imagination, very like an Ambition to be engaged in the more
active, gay, and dangerous Scenes. (Dangerous I say but recall that
Word, for there is no Course more dangerous than that which I am
in.) I have felt such Passions all my Lifetime, particularly in the year
1757, when I longed more ardently to be a Soldier than I ever did
to be a Lawyer. But I am too old, and too much worn, with Fatigues
of Study in my youth, and there is too little need in my Province of
such assistance, for me to assume an Uniform. Non tali Auxilio nec
Defensoribus istis Tempus eget.

I believe I must write you soon, Lord Sterlings Character, because
I was vastly pleased with him. For the future I shall draw no Characters but such as I like. Pimps destroy all Freedom of Correspondence.

RC (MHi). Adams, *Family Correspondence* (Butterfield), 1:346–48.
[1] Although Adams omitted the specific date of this letter, his discussion of the
four Philadelphia battalions and John Dickinson's appearance before them is similar
to the references to them in Joseph Hewes' letter to Samuel Johnston this date.
[2] That is, New York City.
[3] See *JCC*, 4:127–28; and John Hancock to Charles Lee, February 12, 1776.

John Adams to John Trumbull

Dr Sir   Philadelphia Feb. [13] [1] 1776
I take this opportunity by Mr Romain to write you one Line more
for the Sake of reminding you of my Existence, and requesting that you
would favour me with authentic Evidence under your Hand of yours,
than any Thing I have to Say.

Politicks are a Labyrinth, without a Clue—to write upon that
Subject would be endless. N. York I think is now in a critical state, but
I hope We Shall Save it. Mr Dickinson is to march at the Head of a
Battallion of Philadelphian associators to the Assistance of Gen Lee &
Lord Sterling. He has this afternoon been harranguing the Battallions
in the State House Yard with the Ardor and Pathos of a Grecian
Commander, as it is reported.

By Intelligence hourly arriving from abroad We are more and more
confirmed, that a Kind of Confederation will be formed among the
Crowned Skulls, and numbskulls of Europe, against Human Nature.

Prussia defended itself last War, against France, Spain, Germany and
Russia, not withstanding its Vicinity to those Empires and Kingdoms.
America will have a Combination not less formidable to resist perhaps,
but We are Three Thousand Miles off. If these Colonies are not as
Powerfull as Prussia what is the Reason?

It will be Said Prussia is an absolute Monarchy, America, a Chaos at
present and it can be at best, but a Republic.

To this I answer, So much the better. For, that a Monarchy absolute
or limited is better for War than a Republic I absolutely deny. Upon the
Contrary look through the whole Wor[ld] and universal History and
you will find that Republics have been invariably the most warlike
Governments, and you will find no Instance of a Republic conquered
by a Monarch, by Arms, nor any other Way but by Corruption and
Division. If therefore the Colonies can be Secured against Corruption
and Division I think with the Blessing of Heaven, they may hope to
defend themselves. In all Events they will try the Experiment. Pray
write me your Connecticut Politicks. You mix the Caution and Jealousy
of Athens with the Valour of Sparta. But dont let your People forget
or neglect to cultivate Harmony and preserve the Union. Your Friend

RC (PPRF). In the hand of Adams, though not signed.
[1] See Adams to Abigail Adams this date, note 1. Adams' reference below to John
Dickinson's appearance before the Philadelphia battalions indicates that both this
and the preceding letter to Abigail were written the same day.

Josiah Bartlett to John Langdon

Dear Sir, Philadelphia Feby 13th 1776

I have rec'd your's of the 29th ulto which is now before me and in answer would inform you that I have last week sent you all the votes of the Committee that you will want that are already passed. The draft goes this day with the money to the Camp at Cambridge.

As to your being further impowered, I have took the opinion of many of the Committee separately (for there has been no meeting since I rec'd yours) and they are all of opinion that you are already authorised to build, rig, equip and fit for sea the ship to be built in our Colony and that you will do it according to your discretion, except where you have particular orders: what orders are sent to you are the same that are sent to the other builders and where any thing cannot be supplied in the Colony they will inform the Committee by a letter to the Chairman.[1] Hemp and cordage you say are high; as to that I would inform you that Mr Lewis has procured a considerable quantity: Russia hemp at 65s and this country do. from 56s to 58s per hundred York money so you will See whether it is best to buy with you or Send to New York.

I expect the Committee will meet tomorrow evening; when they meet I will try to procure an order for more money to be sent you and hope to send it off this week and will enquire concerning the length of cable and weight of anchors. As for cannon I believe a Committee of Congress have contracted for them. By order of Congress a detachment of this City Associators equal to one battalion, is ordered to march to New York. Col Dickinson takes the command; Major Patton goes Major of the detachment and Mr Dean will go; so I shall be left alone at my lodgings. I expect to see Col Whipple here the latter end of this week as you say he was to set out the next week when you wrote. I expect to write to you again in a few days and am, your friend &c,

Josiah Bartlett

Tr (DLC).
[1] Langdon's efforts to build a frigate for the Marine Committee are discussed in Lawrence S. Mayo, *John Langdon of New Hampshire* (Concord: Rumford Press, 1937), pp. 115–28.

John Hancock to Thomas Cushing

My Dear Sir, Philadelphia, 13 Feby., 1776.

Your favor of Jany. 30th I have now before me, am glad to hear the Reception you met with, and have no Doubt but you will ever Acquit your self the honest Man, and be superior to the Arts and Cunning of Designing Men. I am Oblig'd to you for the hints you give respecting the Designs of some against me, and wish in your next [you] would be as particular as possible, and let me know every thing passing in your Quarter, by the State of the Elections neither you or I were much Neglected. I am much oblig'd to the Assembly for their Notice of me in the Militia, etc.[1] I intended writing you a long Letter by this Opportunity, but I am so engag'd, and indeed I trust the next Post will Reach [Cambridge] as soon as Col. Bull who carries this and has Charge of the Money to the General; that I have only Time to Acquaint you that by Col. Bull I have sent you the Two Drafts for the Ships, and beg the closest Attention may be paid to them, and pray hurry them on as fast as possible, Employ as many persons as possible. I have also sent you by Col. Bull Twenty five Thousand Dollars towards the Expence of the Ship, etc. It is pack'd in a Box directed to you, and you will please to send me a Receipt for it; I will send you some more Money by the Person I desir'd you in my last to send, and by him will write you or sooner, more particularly. Inclos'd you have Dimensions, etc. of the Ships for your Guide. Pray inform me in your next how much Hemp, Cordage, etc. you have or can purchase; as to the Iron you must get it on the best Terms you can, as it will be impossible to get it from hence. As to Cannon more in my next upon that head, the Committee have not yet reported on that matter. Let me know in your next how much Duck you will want and it will be sent from New York. Do engage every Article you can and let me know your Success as soon as possible. Let me know your prospect as to Iron. I beg you will be very particular in your next; pray employ as many hands as can possibly be usefull about the Ships, don't be behind any of the Colonies. I Rely much on your Activity. I will send you as much more Money as I can obtain.[2]

The purport of this is only to Inform you of sending the Plans and Money, don't forget to send me a Receipt for the Money, and do let me know how you go on. I have Deliver'd to Col. Bull a Plan for Mr. Langdon of Portsmouth to your Care, do forward it to him. I shall write you more particular by next.

Lord North's Motion of the 20 Novr. bodes no Good, but as you undoubtedly have it, I need not enlarge; the making all our Vessells lawful Prize don't look like a Reconciliation.[3]

Do let me hear from you by all Opportunities. As my next Letter will probably Reach you before this I will not add, save my best Respects to Mrs. Cushing and Family. I hope she has not Taken amiss the Freedoms I used on the Back of your quondam Letters, you know my Disposition and Intentions and you must Reconcile it to her.

I wish you every Blessing and am with solid Friendship, Dear Sir, your's very sincerely

[P.S.] Col. Dickinson marches in a few days at the head of a Battalion of Philadelphia Associators to join Genl. Lee at New York.[4]

Mrs. Hancock begs her Regards to you and Mrs. Cushing.

MS not found; reprinted from *Proceedings of the Massachusetts Historical Society* 60 (January 1927): 102–4.

[1] Hancock had been appointed major general of the Massachusetts militia on February 8. *Am. Archives*, 4th ser. 4:1294.

[2] Cushing's efforts to expedite work on the Continental frigates being built in Massachusetts are described in M. W. Brewington, "The Designs of Our First Frigates," *American Neptune* 8 (1948): 11–25.

[3] The Prohibitory Act, which was a product of this motion, was passed on December 22, 1775. See *Am. Archives*, 4th ser. 6:186, 237.

[4] Congress suspended the march of the Philadelphia Associators on February 15, after receiving news that General Clinton had left New York. *JCC*, 4:151.

Benjamin Harrison to Robert Carter Nicholas

Dear Sir,   Phila Feby 13th. 1776

Have your Favor of the 3d Instant by post. The Paper sent you by Capt Innis was for the Smaller Bills, and you have now on its way 35 1/2 Ream more for the larger which left this place ten Days ago.[1] It was not understood by Mr Jefferson who had your Letters on the Subject, that you wanted Plates for more than the smaller Bills. I confess I understood it as you intended it, but was overruled, he insisting you had only given us the Number of the Different Denominations you wanted, that we might calculate the quantity of Paper it would take, he therefore Orderd no other Plates than those sent you, which for myself I rejoice at as I never saw such Shocking things.

I do not remember ever to have seen a Letter of yours on the Subject of geting Mr. Byrd his money; I have forwarded your letter to the General and will take Care when I get his Answer that the money shall be paid. You have inclosed a Copy of my Acct. with the Public as also an Acct. of the Expenditures of the five hundred Pounds sterling Bills formerly sent. Mr Nelson tells me the Delegates had Recd. whilst I was at N. York my Sons Draft in your Favor on Willing & Morris for five hundred Pounds which had been presented and accepted.

We had to-Day a warm Debate in Congress about takeing the whole Battalions Raised in Virga. into Continental pay. The determination is put off till to-morrow so that you will not get the result by this Post, but I am inclin'd to think they will not take more than the six formerly Voted.[2] Your Delegates will leave no Stone unturnd to Carry the Point, but I wish the Congress had been treated with more Delicacy. Every Country has the same right to judge for themselves that Virginia has, and I really doubt if we should carry our point whither Virga. will not pay more money in the end than she will if we do not, as we must In justice take at least twelve thousand men from the Different Colonies into pay that have been hitherto Refused.

I left New York on Wednesday last.[3] Genl Clinton was then there and I believe on his way to Virga. to meet a fleet which he expected from

England. He gave out that he was to go to the Southward but you must prepare for him, for I think he will most assuredly Stop with you, as he certainly intends to Hampton Road to wait for his Troops which are to rendeavous there. Should he land them God knows what will become of you even if you have your 9 Battalions Raised, for I understand you have not Arms for a Quarter part of them. The Congress have done every thing in their Power to procure them without Effect, and this will forever be the Case as long as we carry on this war and no War, we shall Start at Shadows till we are undone, and shall never see our error till the Shackles Gingle on our Feet and awake us out of our Fatal Lethargy. I could fill a Volume on this Subject but it will avail nothing. The sooner I conclude therefore the better. I will only add one truth more which is that I am, your affct. Servt,　　　Benj Harrison

RC (NNPM).

¹ See Harrison to Robert Carter Nicholas, December 30, 1775.

² Congress resolved on March 25 to assume the pay and expense of three additional Virginia battalions. *JCC*, 4:235.

³ Harrison was a member of the committee sent to confer with General Lee on the defense of New York City. *JCC*, 4:94.

Joseph Hewes to Samuel Johnston

[February] the 13th. [1776]

I mentioned to you some time ago that a Vessel was Arived here with near Sixty Tons of Saltpetre on board and that several quantities of powder had been brought in. A few days Since another Vessel Arived in this River and is now kept below by the Ice. She has Sixty Tons of Saltpetre, 13 Tons of powder and 1300 Muskets on board. Those Supplies appear considerable and yet we find by experience they are quite trifling when compared with our demands. Powder Mills are Scarce, the manufacturing goes on very Slow, and powder wastes exceedingly in a large Army even where little is fired away. Soldiers are careless, their Cartouch boxes get wet, and much is lost in dealing it out in small parcels. Notwithstanding all our Supplies we now find both powder & Arms greatly wanted at our Camp at Cambrige, by our Army in Canada, by the troops in New York, in this Province, Maryland and Virginia. Applications are made every day to Congress for powder and Arms. Give us powder or we perish is the language from all quarters. It is astonishing to think what pains the British Court has been at to prevent every Nation in Europe from Supplying us with these Articles. Several persons who have lately come from France, Spain, Portugal and Holland say every Port, every Town and almost every public house has Spies from England to watch the motions of the Merchants, so that scarsely any thing can be brought away even by a Circuitous Voyage but they find it out. By the ingenuity of some Dutch and French Smugglers a little is sometimes brought away. Americans ought to be more industrious in making those Articles at home, every family should make Salt petre, every Province have powder Mills and every body encourage the making of Arms.

It is hinted in the papers that persons will be sent from England to Negotiate with the Colonies. Many people do not believe it, those who do have but little expectation from it. They are to treat under the influence of a mighty Fleet & Army. What are we to expect from the mouth of a Cannon or the point of a Bayonet. See Lord Norths Motion in the House of Commons the 20th of November,[1] what have we to expect from parliament?

You desire to know when the Additional pay of the officers commenced, it was on the 4th of November last, how I neglected to mention it before I know not.

The only pamphlet that has been published here for a long time I now send you, it is a Curiosity, we have not put up any to go by the Waggon, not knowing how you might relish independency. The Author is not known. Some say Doctor Franklin had a hand in it, he denies it.[2]

General Lee in a Letter to Congress received yesterday says he expects a large number of British Troops will be sent to New York as early as possible.[3] He intends to Fortify the City in the best manner he can, calls for More Troops, and wishes to have a Battalion of the Philadelphia Militia that they might be instructed in Village fortification, Camp duty &c., &c. His desire was immediately made known to the City, the Colonels of the four Battalions instantly applied to Congress for the command of the detachment should one be sent, the Pennsylvania Farmer Mr. Dickinson being the eldest Colonel insisted on his right to command, & is to have it. The four Battalions were this day drawn out when it was proposed that two companies from each should turn out for that service so as to make a compleat battalion from the whole, they did it with great chearfullness. It was diverting enough to see both officers and men Soliciting to be employed in the Service. Some of the Companies will march to morrow, to day I might have said for the watchmen are this moment crying past one OClock, the express calls on me at eight. Hooper being gone, and Penn not very well, I am obliged to write all, I intended to have wrote to Mr Iredell & Mr Jones, am much fatigued and cannot do it, excuse me to them, they have my best wishes.

May the grand dispencer of all good give health and happiness to you and all your dearest connections and protect you and them from all calamity is the Ardent wish of, Dear Sir, your mo Obedt. hum Serv,

Joseph Hewes

RC (OClWHi). A continuation of Hewes to Johnston, February 11, 1776.
[1] See John Hancock to Thomas Cushing, this date, note 3.

² Hewes is doubtless referring here to Thomas Paine's *Common Sense.*
³ See Charles Lee's letter to Hancock of February 9, 1776, in PCC, item 158, 1:13–16; and *Am. Archives,* 4th ser. 4:965.

Maryland Delegates to the Maryland Council of Safety

Gentlemen.   Philada. Febry. 13th. 1776
  Be pleased to pay unto Messrs. Saml. Purviance Junr., William Lux, & David Steward on their Order three hundred pounds Common Money for Value received of them, being so much Money belonging to them & which We received to be applied for the purchase of Guns for the Defence.   Saml. Chase   R. Alexander

                         Wm. Paca   J. Rogers

RC (MdAA). Written by Chase and signed by Chase, Alexander, Paca, and Rogers. Endorsed: "Received the Amount of the Within Order in full, £300. David Stewart."

Thomas Nelson to John Page

My Dear Page   Philada Feby 13th 1776
  I have before me yours of the 3d Instant which came by yesterdays post. It would certainly be prudent to draw off the Troops from Norfolk for what purpose can they serve by being kept before a ruinous Town & my word for it, you will have occasion for them elsewhere ere long. I am not a little uneasy at the situation of Williamsburg for by the intelligence we have here, that City is but in a weak state of defence; & should Clinton proceed shortly to Virga, as is imagined, depend upon it Dunmore will make a violent push to effect 'the destruction of that place.
  We laid the Virginia matters before Congress yesterday & supported them with all our powers; but they met with so strong an opposition from almost every Colony, that altho' they were defer'd till to day as a piece of respect, yet I am almost afraid I know their fate. I do not believe that they will allow a Man more than the Six Battallions formerly voted; nor do I think they will agree that the two Battallions first raisd shall be taken into continental pay from the first of Novr, but from the time the vote past.¹ They say that this will introduce an immense expence, as almost every Colony will have a claim of the same sort. However we shall neglect no step that will serve Virginia.
  I hope to have the pleasure of seeing you during the next Month, for I propose to get leave of absence for a few Weeks, that I may settle

my family & my affairs; the one driven from their place of residence since I left them & the other I had not time to adjust before I left Virginia having but a few days, after I left the service of the Convention at Richmond, before I set off for Philadelphia. My request will not, I think be deem'd unreasonable, after six Months absence, especially as the Colony will be represented & it is not imagin'd that matters of any great moment will come on before April, by which time I propose to return, & our affairs are in such a train now, that if we can but be supplied with Arms & Ammunition, I do not doubt of success in this glorious undertaking. Independance, Confederation & foreign alliance are as formidable to some of the Congress, I fear to a majority, as an apparition to a weak enervated Woman. These subjects have been but gently touch'd upon. Would you think that we have some among us, who still expect honorable proposals from administration? By Heavens I am an infidel in politicks, for I do not believe were you to bid a thousand pound per scruple for Honor at the Court of Britain that you would get as many as would amount to an ounce. If Terms should be propos'd they will savor so much of Despotism that America cannot accept them.

We are carrying on a War & no War, they seize our property wherever they find it, either by Land or by Sea & we hesitate to retaliate, because we have a few friends in England who have Ships. Away with such squeamishness say I, but I cannot do as I would wish. What think you of the Right Revd Fathers in God the Bishops? One of them refus'd to ordain a young Gentleman, who went from America, because he was a rebellious American, so that unless we will submit to Parliamentary oppression, we shall not have the gospel of Christ preach'd among us. As a Member of the Church of England I am sorry for it, but let every Man worship God under his own Fig Tree.

Mrs. Nelson has been gone so long that I have forgotten the length of her foot, but Mr. Young tells me he has a Shoe of Mrs Pages.

You need not answer this Letter as I shall have left Philada before your answer will arrive.[2]

Give my Love to my Cousin Page & the little Folks.

Adieu Dr Page.

[P.S.] Maggies Letters shall be sent safely, Doctr Franklin having undertaken the care of them.

RC (ViW photocopy).
[1] Later this day Congress agreed to assume the expenses of two Virginia battalions retroactively to November 1, 1775. Three additional battalions were placed on Continental pay on March 25. JCC, 4:131–32, 235.
[2] Nelson was apparently still in attendance on February 23, for Congress ordered payment of an account to him that day. Since Carter Braxton arrived that same day, Nelson probably departed soon thereafter. See JCC, 4:167–68; and Nelson to Thomas Jefferson, February 4, 1776.

North Carolina Delegates to
the North Carolina Council of Safety

Honorable Gentlemen   Philadelphia 13th Feby 1776
    We received information from Genl. Washington about ten days ago
that the Mercury Ship of War and several Transports with General
Clinton and a number of Soldiers on board had sail'd out of Boston
harbour, and that he was informed they were bound to New York, in
consequence of this intelligence he had sent of[f] General Lee to take
the Command of such forces as could be immediatly marched into that
City for its defence.[1] General Clinton arrived before the Town in the
Man of War on the same day that General Lee marched into it. We
are this day informed that one of the Transports full of Soldiers has
got into the harbour,[2] it seems to be doubtfull wether Clinton intended
to land in New York had he arrived there in time. Some think he is to
proceed to the southward, his going in there has occasioned much
Speculation, it is generally believed by those who get the best information and we have not the least doubt of the fact, that he is on his way
to North Carolina and that he called at New York to confer and advise
with Governor Tryon respecting the situation of our Colony, the number
& temper of the people, and in what manner he might best attack
them with a probability of success. The particulars as far as we have
been able to obtain information of them are these: that seven Regiments
were to embark from Great Britain about the first of December and
proceed to Hampton Road in Virginia, there wait till Genl. Clinton
joins them with the troops from Boston, settle the plan of opperation
with Lord Dunmore and proceed to make impressions into North
Carolina and the adjacent Colonies in such places and manner as may
best suit their purposes by dividing their forces. We thought it absolutely necessary that you should be informed of these matters that your
best efforts may be exerted to defeat the purposes of them, should
Governor Martin supported by a body of these troops, introduce himself
amongst the highlanders and Regulators the Consequences might prove
fatal to our Colony.
    We Recommend it to your consideration whether it will not be pru-
dent to call a meeting of your Congress early in April or sooner if it
can be done with propriety. Will it not be proper to appoint several
General officers to command the Militia in case large bodies of them
should be called forth? Seven Regiments of 680 men each with the
Accession of Tories and perhaps Negroes will be a very formidable
force and will require your greatest abilities to oppose it.[3] You will see
by Lord Norths Motion in Parliament on the 20th of November what
the Colonies have to expect from that quarter. We earnestly hope our

Colony will stand firm and oppose the Tyranny of that Corrupt Parliament to the last extremity.

We wrote to you three days ago when we expected to have sent of[f] the Waggon, but meeting with a disappointment in the powder (that in the Magazine being all Cannon powder very coarse and Ordinary) we Judged it improper to send any till the best kind can be got.[4] We are obliged to detain the Waggon a few days till a Vessel arrived in the River (with Sixty Tons of Saltpetre, Thirteen Tons of powder and 1300 Arms) gets up to Town. A copy of that Letter with sundry papers therein referred to we now enclose. We shall be glad to know the time you fix upon for the meeting of your Congress, and are with the utmost respect, Honble Gentlemen, your mo. Obedient and very huml. Servants,

FC (NcU: Hayes Collection microfilm). In the hand of John Penn and Joseph Hewes. Addressed: "The honble Corn[eliu]s Harnett Esqr and the other Members of the Council of Safety of No. Carolina."
[1] Washington gave this information in a letter to Hancock of January 14, which Congress received on January 25. *JCC*, 4:90.
[2] This intelligence was contained in General Lee's letter to Hancock of February 9, which Congress received on February 12 not February 13. *JCC*, 4:127.
[3] Remainder of MS in the hand of Hewes.
[4] See North Carolina Delegates to the North Carolina Council of Safety, February 10, 1776.

Secret Committee Minutes of Proceedings

Com[mitte]e Ch[amber]. Feby. 13 1776.
At a meeting of the S[ecret] Come. Present Saml. Ward, J. Alsop, F. Lewis, Robt. Morris & Joseph Hewes. The Come. bought of Jos Donadson 1635 lb. powd. at 25£ Pensa. Cury. per Cwt. £408.15. Gave him an order on the Contl. Treasurer for 1090 dlls in full for the powder. Also a Certificate to the Come. of Inspection & Observtn. for Philada. for the purchase of the same. Granted to Benjn. Harrison junr. Esqr. of Virga. a Permit to load the Brigantine Fanny,———Master, with produce of that Colony & export same.[1]

At a meeting of the Secret C. Present Saml Ward, John Alsop, Rob. Morris, F. Lewis & Ths. McKean.
A Charter party was enterd into between Joseph Hews Esqr. of North Carolina Mercht. & sd. C. for freighting the Brigantine Fanny, ——— Master, for a voyage to be performd by her in the service of the U[nited] C[olonies] from York River, in the Colony of Virginia.[2]

At a meeting of the Come. Present Saml. Ward, J. Alsop, Josiah Bartlett, F. Lewis, Ths. McKean, Jos. Hewes. A Contract was enterd into with Hodges, Bayard & Co. for importg. a number of good arms for the use of the U[nited] C[olonies] For which purpose the sd. S. C. shall advance to the sd. Hodges, Bayard & Co. the sum of 5000£ Stg. in Bills of Exchange on Holland, or in specie.[3]

MS (MH).
[1] This permit has been printed in Clark, *Naval Documents*, 3:1262–63.
[2] Joseph Hewes' contract with the committee, dated February 14, 1776, has been printed, ibid., pp. 1285–87. See also Hewes to Robert Smith, February 6, 1776.
[3] The main points of this contract are summarized in *Pa. Archives*, 1st ser. 4:708. Hodges, Bayard & Co. received an advance of $23,333.30. See Secret Committee Account, September 27, 1775–August 26, 1776.

Richard Smith's Diary

[February 13, 1776]
Tuesday 13. Votes read. The Question Whether the 3 Battals. in Virginia shall be taken into Continental Service passed in the Negative 8 Colonies to 3, & one divided. It was agreed to pay the Two first Battals. there from Novr. last. 30,000 Dollars advanced for the Troops in Virginia and the Field Officers of the 6 Battalions there, were now elected by Ballot which is our Customary Method. A Major Gen. & Adjutant General were asked for by the Virgians and a Comee. of 5 chosen to consider of a Southern Military Department.[1] Letters from the Jersey Convention & from the Field Officers of Daytons Regt. were read and comd. to myself, Bartlett & S. Adams.[2] 600 Dollars advanced to Fairlamb the Commissary in Chester County, & several large sums ordered for sundry Uses. Wilson brought in the Draught of an Address to our Constituents which was very long, badly written & full against Independency.[3] (Wilson percieving the Majority did not relish his Address & Doctrine never thought fit to stir it again.) Chase gave Notice that he would move tomorrow for Orders to Admiral Hopkins to seize all Ships of Great Britain & to recommend to all the Colonies to fit out Privateers.[4] A Direction given that McKean should request the City Comee. to delay publishing the Sellers of Tea in the Papers till further Order. Some Money advanced for Gen Lee's Troops in New York & for Col. John Dickinsons who goes on Thursday with a Detachment of Associators from hence to that City. Agreed to continue the Pay of Capt. Bernard Romans during his Stay in Philada. on public Business.

MS (DLC).
[1] This committee submitted its report to Congress on February 17, and on the basis of it Congress approved the creation of a middle and a southern military department on February 27. *JCC*, 4:157, 174.
[2] For the receipt of these letters and the resolves adopted by Congress on February 15 in response to the report of the committee appointed to consider them, see

JCC, 4:129–30, 150–51.
³ The text of Wilson's address is in *JCC*, 4:134–46. See also John Dickinson's Proposed Resolutions on a Petition to the King, January 9–24? 1776, note; John Dickinson's Draft Address to the Inhabitants of America, January 24? 1776, note 1; and Smith's Diary, January 9, 1776, note 3.
⁴ For the progress of this issue in Congress, which eventually was taken under consideration in response to the receipt of several petitions and letters, and culminated in the adoption on March 23 of a series of resolves authorizing American privateers to prey on British shipping, see *JCC*, 4:180, 200–201, 210, 213–14, 229–33; Oliver Wolcott to Matthew Griswold, March 9, and to Samuel Lyman, March 16; John Adams to James Warren, March 21, and to Horatio Gates, March 23; and Smith's Diary, March 1, 13, 16, 18, and 22, 1776.

John Adams to James Warren

Dear Sir   Philadelphia Feb. 14. 1776

I Shall inclose to a Lady of my Acquaintance all the News Papers which have been printed in this City, Since my arrival, by which you will See, to what Point the Tide of Political Sentiment, Setts. Scarcely a Paper comes out, without a Speculation or two in open Vindication of opinions, which Five Months ago were Said to be unpopular. A vast Majority of the People, indeed, I very well knew Secretly entertained the Same Perswasion then, but injudiciously avoided Speaking out. The Restraint however, is now taken off.

I expect to hear the New England Papers, very soon chiming in, with the Concert.

I have written to Mr Sever that Congress have ordered Ten Tons of Salt Petre to the Council, to be made into Powder and requested him to communicate it to the Court.¹ I hope every Nerve will be exerted with the Utmost Vigour to sett up Powder Mills, compleat them, and procure Persons Skilled in the Manufacture of Powder. I am not without Apprehensions that such Persons will be wanted. I apprehend however, that there are Persons who are possesed of the necessary Knowledge of the Composition and Proportions of Ingredients. Even Mr Reed of Weymouth I conjecture would be able to instruct others. The same Rule, which has made a small Quantity in a Family Mortar, applied to a large Mill will make a larger Quantity. No Expence, No Industry ought to be Spared.

Dont fail, my dear Friend, to inform me, of every Step in the Progress of the Manufactures of Salt Petre and Powder.

Measures are taking to make Cannon both of Brass and Iron. Some Experiments have been made in Maryland, Philadelphia and New York, with success. I will acquaint you with Particulars as fast as I can. I am, your Friend.

[*P.S.*] Shall We be able to get Seamen to man our Navy when our Trade shall be opened? Will they not be all better employed?

RC (M-Ar). In Adams' hand, though not signed.
[1] See *JCC*, 4:129. Adams' letter to William Sever has not been found.

Robert Treat Paine to Robert R. Livingston

Dear Sr.   Philada. Feby. 14th. 1776
    I cannot omit so good an Opportunity of writing to you; the bearer
brings ten Tons of Saltpetre to yr mills for manufacture.[1] I am very
glad to hear yr. mills are repaired, I rely upon it that affectual care
will be taken to prevent a like Accident in future. Mills are wanted to
manufacture the Saltpetre that is imported, I hope your Mills are enlarged as well as rebuilt. I hope also that your neighbourhood will soon
furnish Saltpetre sufficient to keep your Mills at Work. This Manufacture has recd. great improvements lately. Dr. Wm. Whiting of
Massachusetts, & one of a Committee of General Assembly to improve &
promote the manufacture, had reported to sd. Assembly a certain process
the result of Experiment & this process has been published in many
papers. I have had repeated Accounts from many places of the good
Success of this process; I wish you would promote experiments on it.
I am satisfy'd with a little more application we shall make Sufficient
of this valuable Article, but sr. when we have got powder enough, we
then shall want Small Arms & Cannon, the former of wch. we undoubtedly make very good, application only is wanted to exercise
them. As for Cannon, I am of a Comttee to enquire into this matter, &
should be obliged to you if you would inform me if Cannon can be made
at the Furnace in the Mannor & of what size; if they can be made, it
will save the transporting them to many places where they are wanted.
Pray favour me with your Sentiments on these matters as soon as you
can. With Compliments to yr family & Freinds, I am yr most hble
Sevt,   R T Paine

RC (N). Addressed: "To Robert R Livingston Esq at Claremount lower Mannor
of Livingston."
[1] Ordered by Congress on February 12. *JCC*, 4:128–29.

John Penn to Thomas Person

Dear Sir   Philadelphia Feby 14th. 1776
    From a newspaper printed in Ireland which arrived here today I
find that the Parliament there have agreed that 4,000 Troops there
should be imployed against America, and to receive the like number
of Hanoverians in their room. It also appears that Lord North had

moved to bring in a bill to repeal the Boston Port act, their Fishery, and the restraining act which prevents the trade of the Colonies, but to license his Matys armed Vessels to seize the American Ships where ever bound and to make prizes of them and their cargoes. There were 190 odd for the motion 60 against it. It appears that the King and his ministers are determined if possible to subjugate us to the control of a British Parliament. All accounts mention that they intend to send over a large Force against the Spring. It is said seven Battalions are alloted for No. Carolina. Have we any way of opposing them and keeping those under that are Inimical to us; the Virginians I make no doubt will be ready and willing to assist you upon every occasion but may you not suffer before their Troops could get to you. I have the pleasure to assure you that our Province stands high in the opinion of Congress. The readiness with which you marched to Virginia and South Carolina hath done you great credit.[1] It will be necessary to keep up a certain number of Battalions in the Southern Colonies, to be ready to prevent our enemies from landing and penetrating into the Country. Those that are not raised in our Province, will be in Virginia, So. Carolina or Georgia. From our situation it is thought they could easier and sooner assist their Brethren than from any other part. I suspect we shall not be able to do much in the trading way when we open our ports as the British minister has been soliciting all the Powers in Europe to refuse to supply us with Arms & Ammunition or to trade with us at all. They have succeeded in several places so that our ships were obliged to return empty. In such a condition would it not be prudent for you to imploy as many of your People at the expense of the Colonies in general as you can? Will it not be a means of providing for a number who might otherwise suffer, and at the same time making them good Soldiers, the better able to defend their Country when necessarily called upon? Could you raise four or five Battalions in the whole? If you can and approve of the measure let us know immediately, but in this matter exercise your own prudence, you are better Judges than I can be. Our dispute with Britain grows serious indeed. Matters are drawing to a crisis. They seem determined to persevere and are forming alliances agt. us. Must we not do something of the like nature? Can we hope to carry on a war without having trade or commerce some where? Can we ever pay any taxes without it? Will not our paper money depreciate if we go on emitting. These are serious things and require your consideration. The consequence of making aliances is perhaps a total seperation with Britain and without something of that sort we may not be able to procure what is necessary for our defence. My first wish is that America may be free, the second that we may be restored to peace and harmony with Britain upon Just and proper terms. If you find it necessary that the convention should meet sooner than May let us know of it as I wish to return at that time. I have been very sick for two or three days but am getting

well again. I beg you will remember me to my Friends and am Dear Sir,
Your mo: obt. Servt.   John Penn

[*P.S.*] I send you a pamphlet called Common Sense published here abt.
a month ago.

RC (Nc-Ar).
[1] North Carolina's aid to Virginia in opposing Lord Dunmore and to South
Carolina in quelling a Loyalist uprising is described in Hugh F. Rankin, *The North
Carolina Continentals* (Chapel Hill: University of North Carolina Press, 1971), pp. 22–
27. Joseph Hewes also noted the beneficial effect which news of these events had
upon North Carolina's reputation in Congress. "When Hooper & myself arived
here [*in the fall of 1775*]," Hewes observed to an unidentified correspondent in a draft
letter probably written around this time, "the Congress had been seting [for six
weeks?], frequent enquiry had been made after the North Carolina delegates,
people out of doors wondered they did not come, some Tory Scoundrells propagated
a report that the Colony being dissatisfied with the proceedings of Congress and
the conduct of their members would no longer send any, that the inhabitants were
a poor deluded [. . .], disaffected to the common cause of American freedom. Thus
stood the Character of our poor Colony.
"With pleasure I can inform you it is now high in Estimation, it is no longer
abused but spoken of with great veneration," Hewes continued. For upon learning
of the assistance which North Carolina had extended to Virginia and South Carolina,
the common sentiment in Philadelphia was: "its impossible, they must be a brave
people, I wish they were our Neighbours say a Pennsylvanian. I wish you may be
able to retain those honours unblemished." NcU: Hayes Collection microfilm.

Secret Committee Minutes of Proceedings

Com[mitte]e Ch[amber]. Feby. 14 1776
At a meeting of the Come of Secy. Present Saml. Ward, B. Franklin,
Thos. McKean, F. Lewis, Robt. Alexander, Robert Morris, Jos. Hewes.
The Come drew an order in favor of Robt. Irwin wagn. Master upon the
Contl. Treasurers for 266 2/3 dlls. Also an order on Mr. Matlock the
Storekeeper for 10 ton of Saltpetre to be transported to Mr. Livingstons
powder mill in the province of N. Y. A letter to Messrs. Pliarne, Penet &
Co. was read, approvd & signd, by said Com[mitte]e.[1]

MS (MH).
[1] Letter not found, but for other mention of Penet and Pliarne, see Richard
Smith's Diary, December 30, 1775, and January 9, 1776.

Richard Smith's Diary

Wednesday 14 Feb. [1776]
Letters from Schuyler, Wooster and Arnold recd. & committed.
Some Accots. reported. Application was made from the Shipwrights

at this Place in the Continental service praying Interposition of Congress to stop their Servants and Apprentices whom they cannot hinder from going on the Expedition tomorrow to N York; accordingly a Recommendation took place to that Purpose. A Proposition was mentioned for sending Two of our Body to Canada with Charles Carrol Esqr. and John Carol a popish Priest both of Maryland with a View of confirming the Friendship and to induce a Coincidence with our Measures.[1] Most of the Day passed in Grand Comee. on Trade.

MS (DLC).
[1] On February 15 Congress appointed Samuel Chase, Benjamin Franklin, and Charles Carroll of Carrollton a committee "to proceed to Canada, there to pursue such instructions as shall be given them by Congress," and authorized them to persuade John Carroll to join them in this mission. Neither Charles Carroll, a prominent Catholic layman from Maryland, nor John Carroll, a Jesuit priest who later became the first Catholic bishop in the United States, was a member of Congress, but nonetheless they were asked to undertake this mission in order to enhance the committee's influence among their coreligionists in Canada. Congress finally approved the main instructions for this committee on March 20 and some supplementary ones on March 23. *JCC*, 4:151–52, 192–93, 197, 213, 215–19, 233. For the work of this committee, see, in addition to the correspondence of the committee members published in this series, Charles Carroll, *Journal of Charles Carroll of Carrollton, during His Visit to Canada in 1776, as One of the Commissioners from Congress*, ed. Brantz Mayer (Baltimore: Maryland Historical Society, 1876); and Francis F. Beirne, "Mission to Canada, 1776," *Maryland Historical Magazine* 60 (December 1965): 404–20. While traveling on this mission, Charles Carroll also wrote a large number of letters to his father which fall outside the scope of this edition of delegate letters and therefore have not been printed below, but which may be consulted in the Carroll Papers, Mdhi.

South Carolina Delegates to the Pennsylvania Committee of Safety

Gentlemen   Phila. February 14. 1776

Being informed that there is Room sufficient in the Barracks of this City to accommodate a Party of Recruits which have been procured by us for South Carolina, untill the Ice will permit the sailing of the Vessell in which they are to embark, to sail, We take the Liberty to apply to you for Leave to Quarter these Recruits in those Barracks for the little Time they are to stay here.[1]

Gentlemen Your most Hume Servants   Tho Lynch

                                                    Edward Rutledge

RC (PHC). Written by Lynch and signed by Lynch and Rutledge.
[1] There is no indication in the committee of safety's proceedings for February 1776 of its response to this request for assistance. *Am. Archives*, 4th ser. 4:1570–78.

Robert Morris to Robert Herries

Philadelphia 15 Feby 1776

It seems almost too late in the present unhappy dispute to trouble you[1] with political Opinions, especially as the determinations in the Parliament now Sitting will probably fix the whole complexion of the War; but we can assure you thus much, If any terms of reconciliation are offer'd, that the Congress ought to accept, they will be embraced. None but terms fit for Freemen will be thought admissable either by the Congress, Committees or People at large, and should Great Britain prefer the destructive War She has plunged herself & this Country into; for the sake of the Shaddow when She promis'd the Substance, to the idea of doing justice to her Colonial Subjects, we really dread the Consequences to both Countries. In the event She will most undoubtedly lose this Territory, And probably fall a prey hereafter to Some of her powerful Neighbours & Rivals. America has long been charged by her Enemys in England with aiming at Independency. The charge was unjust, but we now plainly see, that the burning of Towns, seizing our Ships, with numerous acts of wanton barbarity & Cruelty perpetrated by the British Forces has prepared Men's minds for an Independency, that were shock'd at the idea a few weeks ago. This you may depend on, and should this Campaign open with furious Acts of Parliament, you may bid adieu to the American Colonies. They will then assuredly declare for Independency, and if they once make such pretensions they have no doubt of being able to support them, even without the assistance of Foreigners; but it can hardly be imagined that the Court of France will refuse assistance & protection to the Trade of America if a pre-emption of that Trade is offer'd as a consideration. Surely the People of England are infatuated, that they permit such Arbitrary & Tyranical Measures to be pursued by their Rulers as must in their consequences destroy their immediate Interests, and in the end ruin the Nation. For our part we do most sincerely pray that such terms of reconciliation may be held out as can be accepted on this side. We are happy to know there is a disposition to receive such, and we believe this to be the only line that can possibly save the two Countries from the most ruinous Consequences.

We have formerly told you early in this dispute that the People of America would sacrifice their Trade & Abandon their Towns sooner than submitt to arbitrary Taxation. Events have proved our opinions to be well founded, and they will persist to the last. They are not dismay'd at the news of 26,000 Men being voted for this Service, but are preparing a warm reception for them.

We have made such preparations for the preservation of this City, that we are pretty confident that neither your Fleet nor Army can ever get before it; however if this & every other City & Town on the Coast of America was destroy'd it would do more injury to Great Britain than America, and would totally put submission, reconciliation, terms & treaties out of the question. In short nothing can save or serve the true Interest of Great Britain but holding out just & equitable Terms before it is too late.

We have often repeated to you that let public matters take what course they might, we should preserve inviolate our private Connection, faith & friendship with you and Others, this we hope has been fully manifested to all our friends. We persevere in the same disposition & ever shall so, hoping however to meet with the like attachment & attention from those we so much esteem. Under this persuasion we cannot help mentioning to you in *confidence*, that we have been much solicited by Gentlemen of Virginia & Maryland to form a Contract for supplying the Farmers General of France with Tobacco; this we have hitherto declined on the supposition & in hopes of reconciliation soon taking place, but as this now seems almost but too doubtfull, and as such a Contract will sooner or later be made, we give you this early hint, that you may think of it, and improve it into such advantages as you can contrive for yourselves. Hitherto we have taken no steps, neither will we whilst there is a hope of that reconciliation we so ardently wish for, but when that is cutt off, we will make immediate application either to contract or to act as Factors, and if we referr them to you for our Characters we flatter Ourselves it will not be to our disadvantage.

Tr (MiU-C). Enclosed in Robert Herries to Lord George Germain, June 27, 1776. Endorsed: "Extract of a Letter from Philadelphia dated 15 Feby 1776." Author identified by Jacob Price, *France and the Chesapeake: A History of the French Tobacco Monopoly, 1674–1791, and of Its Relationship to the British and American Tobacco Trades*, 2 vols. (Ann Arbor: University of Michigan Press, 1973), 2:684. The letter was undoubtedly written in behalf of the firm Willing, Morris & Co.

¹ Sir Robert Herries (1730–1815), a holder of the French tobacco purchasing agency for the farmers-general, 1771–79, and a member of Parliament, 1780–84, tried repeatedly during the early stages of the war with America to obtain "passes" from the British government to permit trade in Chesapeake tobacco for reexport to France. Thus he supplied this letter from Philadelphia in support of his scheme to convince the ministry that otherwise the lucrative trade would go by default to France. Although the warning seems unnecessary, one should note that Price, in a concluding note, conjectured: "It is possible that the letter was a 'plant,' written with the deliberate intention of being shown to those in authority to persuade them to give Herries his passes." Ibid., 2:1065n.17. In any event, such pleas failed to move the government to grant concessions, and Herries himself remained a "strong supporter of Britain's 'iron fist'" in America and ignored Morris' suggestion that he endorse Willing, Morris & Co. as his designated successor. For further information on the ramifications of the Chesapeake tobacco trade and the impact of the war on Britain's reexport trade to France, see ibid., 2:681–727.

Richard Smith's Diary

[February 15, 1776]
Thursday 15. The Votes read. I reported on the Jersey Letters.[1]
30,000 Dollars granted on Accot. to Commissary Lowrey, 5000 Dols.
to the Convention or Comee. of Safety for purchasing Arms, the Long
Island Arms in Heards Hands to Col. Dayton and Half a Ton of Powder
to the Jersey Conventn. or Comee. of Safety. A Letter being recd. from
Gen. Lee the Associators were countermanded going to N York. A
Report was made & agreed to about the Mode of fortifying Hudsons
River. Some Gentn. were selected to go into Canada viz. Dr. Franklin,
Saml. Chase & Charles Carol of Carolton Esqrs. together with the
Rev. John Carol.[2] 150 Arms ordered to Maxwells Troops out of the
Parcel just arrived. 8 Ton of Powder ordered into Canada from hence.
The Comee. of Safety at N York desired to prosecute the Discovery of
the Lead Mine at New Canaan. The Cannon Comee. required to pro-
cure what Brass can be collected for Casting Cannon which may be done
at the Air Furnace in N York, at Faesch's Iron Works near Elizabeth
Town and at other places. 5 Ton of Powder said to be arrived at Egg
Harbor and gone thro Brunswick to New York, a Brimstone Mine is
said to be at a Place called the Roundabout upon the Raritan between
Amboy & Brunswick.

MS (DLC).
[1] See Smith's Diary, February 13, 1776, note 2.
[2] See Smith's Diary, February 14, 1776, note 1.

John Adams' Notes of Debates

1776. Feb. [16][1]
In Committee of the whole.
Cant we oblige B. to keep a Navy on foot the Expence of which will
be double to what they will take from Us. I have heard of Bullion
Sp[anish] Flotas being stopped least they should be taken—But perish-
able Commodities never were stopped. Open your Ports to Foreigners.
Your Trade will become of so much Consequence, that Foreigners will
protect you.[2]
Wilson. A Gentleman from Mass. thinks that a middle Way should
be taken.[3] That Trade should be opened, for some Articles, and to some
Places, but not for all Things and to all Places.
I think the Merchants ought to judge for themselves of the danger
and Risque. We should be blamed if We did not leave it to them.
I differ from the Gentleman of Massachusetts. Trade ought in War
to be carried on with greater Vigour. By what means did B. carry on

their Tryumphs last War? The United Provinces their War vs. Spain. If We determine that our Ports shall not be opened, our Vessells abroad will not return. Our Seamen are all abroad—will not return, unless We open our Trade. I am afraid it will be necessary to invite Foreigners to trade with Us, altho We loose a great Advantage, that of trading in our own Bottoms.

Sherman. I fear We shall maintain the Armies of our Enemies at our own Expence with Provisions. We cant carry on a beneficial Trade, as our Enemies will take our Ships. A Treaty with a foreign Power is necessary, before We open our Trade, to protect it.

Rutledge.[4]

Harrison. We have hobbled on, under a fatal Attachment to G.B. I felt it as much as any Man but I feel a stronger to my Country.

Wythe. The Ports will be open the 1st. March. The Q. is whether We shall shutt em up. Fæce Romuli non Republica Platonis. Americans will hardly live without Trade. It is said our Trade will be of no Advantage to Us, because our Vessells will be taken, our Enemies will be supplied, the W.I. will be supplied at our Expense. This is too true, unless We can provide a Remedy. Our Virginia Convention have resolved, that our Ports be opened to all Nations that will trade with us, except G.B., I. and W.I.[5] If the Inclination of the People, should become universal to trade, We must open our Ports. Merchants will not export our Produce, unless they get a Profit.

We might get some of our Produce to Markett, by authorizing Adventurers to Arm themselves, and giving Letters of Mark—make Reprisals.

2d. by inviting foreign Powers to make Treaties of Commerce with us.

But other Things are to be considered, before such a Measure is adopted. In what Character shall We treat, as subjects of G.B.—as Rebells? Why should We be so fond of calling ourselves dutifull Subjects.

If We should offer our Trade to the Court of France, would they take Notice of it, any more than if Bristol or Liverpool should offer theirs, while We profess to be Subjects. No. We must declare ourselves a free People.

If We were to tell them, that after a Season, We would return to our Subjection to G.B., would not a foreign Court wish to have Something permanent.

We should encourage our Fleet. I am convinced that our Fleet may become as formidable as We wish to make it. Moves a Resolution.[6]

MS (MHi). Adams, *Diary* (Butterfield), 2:229–30.

[1] Congress met on February 16 in a committee of the whole to "take into consideration the propriety of opening the ports, and the restrictions and regulations

of the trade of the colonies." *JCC*, 4:154. Adams' notes can be dated by a comparison with Richard Smith's diary which also records the speeches and resolutions of Harrison and Wythe. Richard Smith's Diary, February 16, 1776.

² Adams did not identify this speaker.

³ Probably either Paine or Hancock. In his retrospective view of debates on foreign alliances, the opening of American ports, and independence during the fall and winter of 1775–76, Adams noted that he was a staunch advocate of strong measures. "I received little Assistance from my Colleagues in all these Contests: three of them [*Cushing, Paine and Hancock*], were either inclined to lean towards Mr. Dickinsons System, or at least chose to be silent, and the fourth [*Samuel Adams*] spoke but rarely in Congress, and never entered into any extensive Arguments, though when he did speak, his Sentiments were clear and pertinent, and neatly expressed." Adams, *Diary* (Butterfield), 3:327–30. Elbridge Gerry, who had replaced Cushing, favored opening American ports. See Gerry to James Warren, March 26, 1776.

⁴ Adams left a blank space of more than half a page, but failed to record Rutledge's comments.

⁵ The Virginia Convention had resolved on January 20 to instruct the Virginia delegates to secure the adoption of measures for "opening our Ports to all persons willing to trade with us, *Great Britain, Ireland*, and the *British West Indies* excepted; . . . so soon as it shall be deemed proper by the said General Congress to permit exportation from *North-America*." *Am. Archives*, 4th ser. 4:130–31.

⁶ For Wythe's resolutions, see Richard Smith's Diary, this date.

Robert Alexander to
the Maryland Council of Safety

Gent.   Phila 16 Feby 1776

I send you inclosed Copies of the Instructions & private Signals of the several Men of Warr & Transports on the American Station. As these may be of essential Service to the different armed Vessels now fitting out in America, Copies by order of Congress have been transmitted to the different Colonies,¹ and I am ordered by Congress to acquaint you, that as they have bound themselves to Secrecy, so it is expected that you will consider yourselves under the like Tie, and the Copy you deliver to the Capt. of your armed Vessel, be under Seal inclosed, to be opened after his sailing.

The publick Papers will communicate all the Intelligence We have, except the Arrival of 20 Tons of Powder and 3000 Stand of small Arms in Connecticut. We shall send forward some Powder & Arms to your Province, but I am sorry to say if We rely on foreign Arms & they are not better than the sample We have, our dependance will be like a broken Reed, as I think if used, they will kill more of our Troops than the Enemy. What those imported for our Province cost I know not; a parcel imported here on a private Adventure, have been purchased by Congress at £3.25. Every thing of this kind is exceeding high, Powder £17.10 Per C[wt]. Much of this Business passes through a Committee of which I am a Member, Patriotism sinks before private Interest and

I find many Men here who rank themselves in that Class, generally exactg. the most from the Necessity of their Country, hence the Publick is plundered. We have sent off 10 6 pounders for the Ship & shall purchase 2 more. Congress have appointed a Delegation to Canada, the Persons are Doctr. Franklin, S. Chase & Mr. Carroll of Carrolton. I wish you would erect a Powder Mill in your Province, I could procure you Salt Petre. Yr Letters of the 1, 8, 9, & 10 Inst. are come to Hand & the Contents shall be observed.[2] I am with Respect, Gent., Yr Hbl. Sevt.

R. Alexander

RC (MdAA).
[1] See *JCC*, 4:124.
[2] The council's letters of February 1 and 8 are in *Md. Archives*, 11:129, 142–43.

John Hancock to Thomas Cushing

Dear Sir   Philadelphia 16 Febry. 1776

I wrote you two days past by Coll Bull, when I Sent you the Plans of the Ships, and Twenty five Thousand Dollars towards the Expence of Building the two Ships for the use of the Continent, which hope will Come safe to your hands, and give Additional Springs to the Exertions of those Employ'd, and Rely on you to promote the wish of the Comittee in Expediting the Completion of the Ships with all possible Dispatch. Iron must be had with you if possible, but if the whole cant be obtain'd, let me know as early as possible, tho' you may Send to Connecticutt or wherever it can be had. I have Engag'd Two hundred pieces of Duck at New York, which I will Send down to you as soon as may be, but as yet I have not been able to meet with small Duck for the light Sails, do let me know whether any of that kind is to be had with you. We have now under Consideration the Mode of furnishing Cannon for the Ships, as soon as Congress have Determin'd on that Subject, you shall know. I shall be Glad to know from you as early as possible, what Quantity of Duck, Hemp, Cordage &c you can Obtain, or in other words, what Articles in the whole, or what Quantities of any of the Articles which are necessary for the Compleating the Ships, will be Expected. I shall supply from hence, the earlier I can be Asscertain'd in this the better; as I would by all means be as forward in the Supplies, & be as Ready with our Ships, as any of the Committee, and this in a great measure depends upon you.

Upon the Arrival of your Messenger I shall have some more Money ready to Send you. I note in Mr Cross's Letter mention of Drawing on me; of this give me Notice, for if I Send down the Amo. of the whole Estimate for our two Ships, & you still Draw upon me, I shall be put to inconvenience. It will be as agreeable to me to pay orders here from you, as to Send the Money down, & whatever orders are Drawn previous to Sending the Remainder of the Money, shall be most punctually paid, the Mode in this Case I Refer to you.

If there be any thing in the way of these Ships that would be Serviceable & Agreeable to my Brother,[1] & he as Capable for it as any other, & he unemploy'd, I shall be glad you will give him the preference; in this, or in any other thing from the Council or House that you could Serve my Brother in, I shall Take it as a very particular favour if you would promote him, & with this I beg to Impress your mind, & pray use your Influence to have him Notic'd. I think I have suffer'd enough in the common Cause to be entitled to some Notice in this Respect & beg you will improve the hint, & let me hear from you on the Subject, and pray Encourage his promotion.

Upon the whole Subject of the Ships in every particular, the wants &c I beg to hear from you by the first opportunity, and as soon as I can have from You the general & full State, I will afford every possible Supply, & hope you will not meet with a Delay for want of any Supplies; I will do my best, & shall at least be on a footing with others of the Committee.

I wish you would give my Brother a hint of what I have wrote Respectg. him, & do Aid him if possible.

Pray Employ as many hands in every Department as may be usefull in Expediting the Completion of the Ship; and be particularly Cautious &c I beg to hear from you by the first opportunity, and as soon as I can the Publick.

I hope soon to hear that things are in forwardness. You shall have every aid from me.

My best Respects to Mrs. Cushing, and I am very truly, Dear Sir, Your Real Friend, & very hum servt.   John Hancock

[*P.S.*] Do let me hear what passes with you; what in the Camp, assembly &c.

RC (MHi).
[1] Ebenezer Hancock (1741–1819), Boston hardware merchant, who was appointed deputy paymaster general for the Eastern District in June 1776, a post he held for three years. See *JCC*, 5:432; and Shipton, *Harvard Graduates*, 14:619–23.

Benjamin Harrison to
the New York Committee of Safety

Sir,[1]   Philada Feby. 16th. 1776
Inclosed you have an order of the Congress for the Two Brass Field pieces made in your City,[2] I have great Reason to suppose they will

soon be wanted in Virginia and must therefore beg the Favor of you to send them to this Place immediately, the urgency of the Case will I hope plead my Excuse for giving you this Trouble. I am, your most Obedt Servt, Benja. Harrison

RC (NHi).
¹ Although this letter is located in the papers of Alexander McDougall, it seems likely that it was directed to the chairman of the New York Committee of Safety, who passed it on to McDougall for action.
² A copy of the resolution of February 14, signed by Charles Thomson and certified by John Hancock. See *JCC*, 4:147.

Robert R. Livingston to James Duane

[*Clermont?*] *February 16th 1776.* Expresses thanks "for your kind condolence on the losses I have sustained" and discusses possible developments in Anglo-American relations. "I can not help thinking from the late advices from England on the increase of our Friends there that we shall before long be enabled to carry our great points and that they are already prepared to give up the *right of taxation* and I can hardly think that they will deem our external government of sufficient consequence to make it the subject of a war. Upon what ground we stand I have been too long absent from Congress to say, or how far our views may be *enlarged*. This I know that another year of war and devastation will confirm me a republican though at present I wish to join hand with a nation which I have been accustomed to respect, yet I am persuaded that the continuance of the war will break my shackles and I shall learn to despise the pusillanimity of our British friends and abhor the cruelty of our foes. But perhaps I feel too much to judge impartially." Discusses the treachery of Duane's servant James Brattle and New York governor William Tryon,¹ and concludes: "And indeed the sudden deaths of three parents and Montgomery have made my attention to the affairs of the family so necessary that I know not how to quit them for any long time—and yet I am ashamed to be useless to the public. It is the opinion of Schuyler and must be of every man who is any way acquainted with the state of our northern army that a committee should be at Albany. He has wrote to the Congress on the Subject.² If such a matter should take place I should wish to be one as I can then divide my attention a little between my private and public concerns."

Tr (NN).
¹ See James Duane to Mary Duane, February 22, 1776, note. In a letter written to John Jay from Clermont on February 15, Livingston dealt with "a story" involving "a suspicion of my having betrayed the secrets of congress to Mr. Tryon." "The report itself gave me no pain," he observed, "because whatever my own character may be the little contemptible resentment which Mr. Tryon discovered

in suspending my father from his office, shews that he did not think he had many friends in this family; nor do I believe that the most credulous could have found any thing in my conduct which should induce them to think that I would belie the acknoledged principles of my father, and two Brothers, both of whom through my means were armed, in defense of those rights which I am not less interested in the defense of, than any other person at congress, or elsewhere. But I am asshamed of having said that much upon the subject, if my conduct needs a justification I should not be trusted. I am only hurt that my friends should be silent on a subject in which I was so deeply interested." Livingston also asked Jay to "draw for my wages for my attendance on Congress 162 days which amounts to 648 dollars." Jay, *Papers* (Morris), 1: 226–29.

² In his letter to President Hancock of January 13, General Schuyler had suggested that Congress should send a committee to Albany. PCC, item 153, 1:396–98; and *Am. Archives*, 4th ser. 4:666–67.

Secret Committee Minutes of Proceedings

Feby. 16, 1776.
At a meetg. of the Com[mitte]e present Sml. Ward, Robt. Morris, Jos. Hewes, Jo. Alsop, F. Lewis & Ths. McKean. A letter to Mr. J. D. Schweighauser at Nantes was read, approvd & Signd by said Come. A list of goods was agreed upon to be shippd by Mr. Schweighauser to said Come. The Come. drew an order on the C[ontinental] Treasurers in favor of Willing, Morris & Co for 23333 dlls. being for bills of Exchange purchased of them for the use of the U[nited] C[olonies]. Granted a Permit to Willing, Morris & Co. to load a vessel or vessels with the produce of these Colonies (hornd Cattle, sheep, hogs & poultry excepted) to the amount of 23333 1/3 dlls for the use of the U[nited] C[olonies]. A list of Goods proposed to be imported by Messrs Livingston, Alsop & Lewis agreed to.¹

At a meeting of the Come. of Secy. Present, Saml. Ward, Ths. McKean, Jo. Alsop, F. Lewis, Jos. Bartlett, Robt. Alexander, Jos. Hewes & Robt. Morris. A list of Goods proposd to be imported by Silas & Barnabas Deane agreed to.² A Contract proposd by Mr. Gary³ to Bilboa, approvd & Contracts orderd to be drawn.

MS (MH).
¹ See Secret Committee Minutes of Proceedings, February 7 and 20, 1776.
² See Secret Committee Minutes of Proceedings, January 11, 1776.
³ Possibly Elbridge Gerry, who had commercial contacts in Bilbao, Spain, with Joseph Gardoqui and Sons. Although no further information on this particular contract has been found, Gerry devoted considerable time in Philadelphia to commercial opportunities, and the following month John Adams' uncle reported that Gerry was attempting to purchase a cargo of fish, which, he believed, was "by the Order of Congress." See Elbridge Gerry to James Warren, March 6, 1776, note 3; and Adams, *Family Correspondence* (Butterfield), 1:364–65, 372–73.

Richard Smith's Diary

Friday 16 Feb. [1776]

After various Subjects were discussed & decided upon 4 or 5 Hours were spent in Grand Comee. on Trade,[1] Harrison offered some Propositions in Lieu of the Report heretofore delivered in from a Comee. on the necessary Regulations, Wyth also offered Propositions whereof the first was that the Colonies have a Right to contract Alliances with Foreign Powers, an Objection being offered that this was Independency there ensued much Argument upon that Ground, a leading Question was given Whether this Proposn. shall be considered by the Comee. it was carried in the Affirmative 7 Colonies to 5. Then it was debated and postponed, afterwards the Regulations of the Trade were handled & finally whether it shall be opened or not and when, upon this Head Chase spoke largely against carrying on Trade at present and Harrison and E Rutledge vehemently for it. There was no Determination.

MS (DLC).

[1] See Smith's Diary, January 12, 1776, note 1; and John Adams' Notes of Debates, this date.

Robert Morris to Charles Lee

Dear Sir,   Phila Febry. 17th, 1776.

I am four letters in your debt, dated 30th January, 6th, 9th, and 14th Instant,[1] and if you have not been able to account for my silence, I am now able to write that I have been half or two-thirds blind for three weeks past, owing to a cold and inflammation in my eyes, which thank God, I have now nearly got the better of, by abstinence, exercise, a few doses of salts and a good deal of patience, probably this cure would have been effected much sooner, but unluckily I was harassed the whole time by much public busyness, of which I do assure you, more than one mans share falls to my lot.

Nothing more need be said about your Memorial.[2] If any circumstance turns up to render such a measure eligible we will take care of you—and in some future letter I will give you my sentiments about independency—Its subject I have thought on, and have partly made up my mind respecting it. When I wrote you respecting Canada, I considered the service in that country as most important of any now agitated. Quebec is possessed by our Enemy's, consequently the navigation of the River St Lawrence, will be theirs unless we dispossess them in time. If they have a free passage into that country, they will no doubt pour in a sufficient force to compel the undetermined Canadians to take up arms against us; the Indians must join them, and the combined force of Brittain, Canada and the Savages of that country will be brought down upon the Frontiers of the Northern and Middle Colonies; a force in my opinion more formidable than that of all the British Troops they can import into America. I have long considered the possession of Canada as essential to the welfare of the United Colonies, and still continue to think so; and after the unfortunate check of our Troops at Quebec attended with so capital a loss as that of Montgomery (whose name is recorded in the annals of Fame, there to stand in conspicuous characters until time shall be no more) I repeatedly revolved in my mind who should be his successor. Your Experience as a Soldier, to say nothing of your Talents, always pointed you out, as the man. Therefore I put the question to you, expecting other Gentn wou'd, *nay must* look to you for that purpose and I wished to know your mind, this day my opinion was verified, it was moved in Congress that you shou'd be appointed to the command in Canada, I took an opportunity to declare the terms of your answer to one on that subject, that you considered it your indispensible duty to go wherever you cou'd be most usefull & not valueing consequences to yourself, you wou'd acquiesce in the desires of Congress, altho' you were apprehensive the last shock your Constitution received by a complicated attack of Gout and Rheumatism, wou'd render you unfit to encounter a Northern Climate, especially as you attributed your present illness to the having been too much exposed to cold already, but as I did not pronounce you absolutely averse to this appointment, and all agreed your abilities were necessary in Canada, where the worst of the winter will be spent before you can get on the spot, they unanimously voted you for that Service, and I hope it will not be long before we are happy enough to hail you the Conqueror of Quebec. You will soon be informed by letter from the President of your appointment, and the force you will have under your command, which I hope and think will be sufficient for the purpose.[3] Whilst I am on this subject let me recommend to you a young Gentleman now in Canada, Mr John White Swift [Smith?], son of John Smith late Collector of this Port; he left Quebec to avoid taking up arms against us, and Carleton has instituted a Suit against him for attempting to send us powder from thence—his Effects are all left behind in that City and I suppose will be seized. He writes me to procure him some Employment, but don't point out what. I will send him a few lines to deliver to you in Canada, which will remind you of him; and if anything offers in which you can consistently, I hope you will readily, serve him. Should any thing offer for him that depends on Congress to appoint, I will do the needful here, and will also mention him to Doctor Franklin and Mr. Chase who are appointed a Committee of Congress to go into Canada.

You are to have two Battalions from Pennsylva. I believe they will prove good soldiers, Col. De Haas, Lt. Col. Irwin, Major Morris, and Capt. Lu Mar of the 1st Battalion I believe are all very deserving men, and some of them have seen service before. I know but few of the other officers of that Battalion. Col. St Clair of the 2nd Battalion has seen much service; was in the King's army a Lieutenant, is a sensible, worthy man, much esteemed in Bedford County, where he is ———— and has acquired considerable property; he is also much esteemed and respected here. Lieut. Col. Wm Allen you know undoubtedly; he is young and inexperienced, and can only be characterized at present by the rank and distinction of his family, the goodness of his own heart and temper. I hope ambition will prompt him to acquire and perform all the duty's of his station, and to gain all the knowledge a Soldier ought to possess, so far as the General can consistently shew attention to a young Field Officer, so far I hope he will experience your superintendency and profit by your lessons and example. Major Wood has not experience as a soldier, but he has strong natural understanding, great spirit and Bravery or I am much mistaken. I have a regard for and wish to serve him, and make no doubt he will recommend himself to you by his activity and zeal in the service. I have given you this account of these officers, both to serve them and you, as I judge it essential for a General to know as much as possible of the characters, circumstances and merits of the officers under his command; and I believe you will find in these two Battalions, the Captains and subalterns pretty generally men of some Education, capable of becoming good officers, willing to do their duty and to support good discipline; but it depends much on their Superiours what discipline is to be established amongst these troops, in my humble opinion the stricter the better; and if the Superiour keep the Inferior Officers under proper command, they from example will keep the Privates so. I hope you will not think me impertinent for intruding my opinions on a subject I am so little acquainted with, but next to the Honour and Interest of the whole United Colonies I am anxious to promote the honour & credit of this Province, and on this score you will excuse me.

You will find enclosed a letter from Mr White, and I shall forward those you sent for him and Mr Nourse, by a private hand going there in a day or two. I think you may totally disregard Mr. Hite and his threats—He certainly is a worthless fellow, or he has great injustice done to him; but the World seldom join in crying down a mans character unless he gives Cause for it.

You will doubtless have heard the various reports of Commissioners coming out to treat with us. I wish it be true, provided they come with proper Powers; but to come limited to terms inconsistent with Freedom will be doing nothing. France is certainly filling her West India Islands with troops, the ostensible reason for doing so is that upon reconciliation between Great Britain and this Country the Great Force introduced into America during the disputes, may be employed to seize their Islands unless well prepared for defence; but I fancy their real design is to be able to take advantage whenever the event of this war, wherever oppor-

tunity offers; and I don't conceive this a proper time for this Country
to make Treaty's with any Foreign Power, we don't want their assistance to defend our Country, it is only protection to our Trade that we
can want from any Country in Europe, the benefit of that trade will
always most readily be admitted as a full compensation for the Protection of it hereafter, altho' the Ministers of Great Britain were not satisfied with it; If we by resistance obtain proper terms, reconciliation and
connection with Great Britain, we want no other protection than hers.
If by our own Force of Conduct, we establish an Independent Empire,
notwithstanding the utmost exertions of Britain, there is not a Nation
in Europe, but will be glad to treat and trade with us on our own terms:
therefore I think it best to persevere in our own measures, and depend
on our strength, which I believe is quite sufficient; and if so, we shall ever
after hold respectable consequence in the World. But notwithstanding
these Notions I am of opinion with you that we shou'd know the sentiments and dispositions of Foreign Nations, of and towards us; and you
cannot doubt but measures have been taken to obtain such knowledge—
a word to the wise.

Genl. Schuyler is to take your Post at New York. I think it a Command also of great importance, and its very likely the utmost exertions
may be called for there in the course of this summer. Our associates
were called upon to furnish a Battalion to join you—Col. Dickinson &
greater numbers than were asked, turned out most cheerfully, but on
Mr Clinton's departure the Congress stopped the march. I don't know
how I have found time to scribble so much, for I am so much employed
and hurried that you must not expect such long letters from me often,
and I have no time to copy this. I will do something for young Mr.
Nourse, and am, Dear General, Your Affectionate Friend,

                                                      Robt Morris.

MS not found; reprinted from *NYHS Collections* 4 (1871): 303–8.
  [1] Lee's letters of January 30, February 9, and 14, 1776, are in *NYHS Collections*
4 (1871): 266–68, 280–81, 295.
  [2] Not found, and apparently never presented; but see Lee's letter to Morris of
January 30. Ibid., p. 266.
  [3] See John Hancock to Charles Lee, February 19, 1776; and *JCC*, 4:157.

Richard Smith's Diary

                                                      Saturday 17 Feb. [1776]
  The Votes read. Wyth made a Report on the Letters from the several
Generals which was gone thro. It was determined that Gen. Lee shall
command in Canada. Some Cannon and Military Stores ordered there
from New York. 35000 Dollars are to be sent by Delegate Floyd to the
N York Convention for the Troops there, Gen Schuyler ordered down

to N York. (An Invitation was sent to the several Delegates to the Funeral of Mrs. John Cadwallader this Afternoon.) Duane reported the State of the Treasury whereupon the followg. Resolutions passed,

Resolved That a standing Committee of Five be appointed for Superintending the Treasury. That it shall be the Business of this Comee. to examine the Accounts of the Treasurers and from Time to Time to report to Congress the State of the Treasury. To employ and instruct proper Persons for liquidating the Public Accounts with the different Paymasters and Commissaries in the Continental Service and the Conventions, Committees of Safety and others who have been or shall be intrusted with the Public Money and from Time to Time to report the State of such Accounts to Congress. To superintend the Emission of Bills of Credit. To obtain from the different Assemblies and Conventions of the United Colonies Accounts of the Number of Inhabitants in each Colony according to the Resolution of Congress on that Subject.

The Members chosen Mr. Duane, Mr. Nelson, Mr. Gerry, Mr. Smith and Mr. Willing. Four Millions of Dollars more voted unany. to be Struck under like Regulations with the former Six Millions & it was agreed to have one Million of them in small Bills and to put the Superintendance under the above Comee. John Halstead was appointed Dep. Commissary in Canada. Some Accots. were reported by Mr. Willing Chairman of the Comee. of Claims. John Adams, Wyth & Sherman were chosen to prepare Instructions and a Commission for the Commissioners going to Canada.[1] A Report brought in for dividing the Colonies into 3 Military Departments & fixing the Arrangements; it was postponed.[2] A Move to suffer Lieut. Felton to go to England on Accot. of Sickness was denied. Mr. Lewis is engaged to procure Shoes for Part of the Army; he has had a Parcel made in Jersey because cheaper than elsewhere. In the Eveng. I attended the Treasury Comee. at the City Tavern.

MS (DLC).
[1] See Smith's Diary, February 14, 1776, note 1.
[2] Ibid., February 13, 1776, note 1.

John Adams to Abigail Adams

My dearest Friend   February 18. 1776
    I sent you from New York a Pamphlet intituled Common Sense, written in Vindication of Doctrines which there is Reason to expect that the further Encroachments of Tyranny and Depredations of Oppression, will soon make the common Faith: unless the cunning Ministry, by proposing Negociations and Terms of Reconciliation, should divert the present Current from its Channell.[1]
    Reconciliation if practicable and Peace if attainable, you very well

know would be as agreable to my Inclinations and as advantageous to my Interest, as to any Man's. But I see no Prospect, no Probability, no Possibility. And I cannot but despise the Understanding, which sincerely expects an honourable Peace, for its Credulity, and detest the hypocritical Heart, which pretends to expect it, when in Truth it does not. The News Papers here are full of free Speculations, the Tendency of which you will easily discover. The Writers reason from Topicks which have been long in Contemplation, and fully understood by the People at large in New England, but have been attended to in the southern Colonies only by Gentlemen of free Spirits and liberal Minds, who are very few. I shall endeavour to inclose to you as many of the Papers and Pamphlets as I can, as long as I stay here. Some will go by this Conveyance.

Dr. Franklin, Mr. Chase, and Mr. Charles Carroll of Carrollton in Maryland, are chosen a Committee to go into Canada.[2] The Characters of the two first you know. The last is not a Member of Congress, but a Gentleman of independant Fortune, perhaps the largest in America, 150 or 200, thousand Pounds sterling, educated in some University in France, tho a Native of America, of great Abilities and Learning, compleat Master of French Language and a Professor of the Roman catholic Religion, yet a warm, a firm, a zealous Supporter of the Rights of America, in whose Cause he has hazarded his all.

Mr. John Carroll of Maryland, a Roman Catholic Priest and a Jesuit, is to go with the Committee. The Priests in Canada having refused Baptism and Absolution to our Friends there.

General Lee is to command in that Country, whose Address, Experience, and Abilities added to his Fluency in the French Language, will give him great Advantages.[3]

The Events of War are uncertain: We cannot insure Success, but We can deserve it. I am happy in this Provision for that important Department, because I think it the best that could be made in our Circumstances. Your Prudence will direct you to communicate the Circumstances of the Priest, the Jesuit and the Romish Religion only to such Persons as can judge of the Measure upon large and generous Principles, and will not indiscreetly divulge it. The Step was necessary, for the Anathema's of the Church are very terrible to our Friends in Canada.

I wish I understood French as well as you. I would have gone to Canada, if I had. I feel the Want of Education every Day—particularly of that Language. I pray My dear, that you would not suffer your Sons or your Daughter, ever to feel a similar Pain. It is in your Power to teach them French, and I every day see more and more that it will become a necessary Accomplishment of an American Gentleman and Lady. Pray write me in your next the Name of the Author of your thin French Grammar, which gives you the Pronunciation of the French

Words in English Letters, i.e. which shews you, how the same Sounds would be signified by English Vowels and Consonants.

Write me as often as you can—tell me all the News. Desire the Children to write to me, and believe me to be theirs and yours.

RC (MHi). Adams, *Family Correspondence* (Butterfield), 1:348–49.

[1] Adams' favorable view of Thomas Paine's *Common Sense* is in marked contrast to his later acerbic comments on the pamphlet and its author. See Adams, *Diary* (Butterfield), 3:331–35.

[2] On February 17 John Adams had been appointed a member of the committee "to prepare instructions for the committee appointed to go to Canada." *JCC*, 4:159. See also Richard Smith's Diary, February 14, 1776, note 1.

[3] Although Charles Lee was ordered to Canada on February 17, his departure was postponed on February 28, and on March 1 Congress placed him in command of the southern department. *JCC*, 4:157, 175, 180–81, 206. See also John Adams to Charles Lee, February 19, 1776.

John Adams to Thomas Crafts, Jr.

Dear sir   Philadelphia Feb. 18. 1776

Since my Arrival in this City and not before, I received your Favour of December the sixteenth.

I am very sorry to learn that you ever was even for a Moment in a State of Scepticism concerning the Existence and Reality of sincere Friendship. Surely there is sincerity, surely there is Friendship among Men, altho it must be confessed that too Many Persons ground it on improper Principles and too easily forget its Feelings. I rejoice, however, that your Faith returned so soon.

You was not forgotten, my dear sir, by any of your Friends here, but alass, it was not in their Power to do more than they did. It was the Wish of your Friends here, that you and Mr Trott should have all those Rewards from your Country which you can desire and it [is] still their earnest Desire, that you and Mr Revere should be provided for.[1] But it is not in their Power to affect it, and whether it ever will be is uncertain. You know the State of Coll Brewer's Case[2]—an experienced and a brave officer, removed from a Regiment and the General Officers thought[3]

FC (MHi).

[1] Thomas Crafts, Jr., had informed Adams of his decision to turn down the offer of a majority in the artillery regiment. See Thomas Crafts, Jr., to John Adams, December 16, 1775, Adams Papers, MHi; and George Washington to John Hancock, December 14, 1775, Washington, *Writings* (Fitzpatrick), 4:161. For Adams' previous efforts to aid Crafts, see John Adams to James Warren, December 3, 1775, note 2.

[2] Apparently Col. David Brewer of the Ninth Massachusetts Regiment, who had been court-martialed and dismissed from the service on October 23, 1775. Washington, *Writings* (Fitzpatrick), 4:39–40.

[3] Remainder of MS missing.

John Adams to William Heath

Dear sir   Philadelphia Feby 18. 1776
    Your Favour of January 22 never reached me, untill my arrival at this City.

    I am much obliged to you for the Information you have given me of the Character and Services of Coll Baldwin, and should be happy to do any Thing in my Power, to obtain Justice for so deserving an officer.[1] Upon shewing your Letter and another from him to some of my Colleagues, they are of opinion that Coll Baldwin will have a better Chance for obtaining an Adequate Establishment, by making a Representation of the Fact to his Excellency Supported by a Line from you, and General Putnam who I perceive has written to my Friend Mr Adams in his favour, and requesting General Washington to represent them to Congress, or to inclose your Representation, than by any Motion that we can make because a suspicion may arise that the motion is made by us, without any Intimation from the General because of some Disquiet that he may have taken at Coll Baldwin, which though it would be a groundless would be a natural Jealousy.

    I dont mean by this, to decline making such a Motion. I will readily do it, but should be glad of the Generals opinion to assist it, and also should be glad to know whether Coll Baldwin has any Command in the Army and what it is, or has any station there besides that of Overseer or Director of the Works and whether he has any Commission or Warrant and what it is—because he informs me, he cannot now receive more than Captains Pay. I should be glad to know what Title he has to that.

    I should also wish to know your opinion of his Qualifications to serve as an Engineer, in Canada in any other Department, and indeed what other Engineers there are in your Army. Engineers are very scarce, rare and dear. We want many, and Seem to have none. I think it high Time We should have an Academy for their Education. Our Country abounds with young Gentlemen of Genius and Learning. It grieves me that so few of them think of turning their Talents to so honourable, so usefull, and so profitable a Branch of service. I am sir, with great Esteem and Respect your very humble servant,   John Adams

RC (MHi).
    [1] Jeduthan Baldwin (1732–88), a member of the Massachusetts Provincial Congress, 1774–75, had helped design the American defenses around Boston. When Baldwin declined an appointment as captain of engineers in March 1776, Washington recommended that he be offered the rank of lieutenant colonel, which Congress accordingly authorized on April 26. See Washington to John Hancock, April 22, 1776, Washington, *Writings* (Fitzpatrick) 4:500–501; *JCC,* 4:312. See also *Appleton's Cyclopaedia of American Biography;* Jeduthan Baldwin to John Adams, January 21, and William Heath to John Adams, January 22, 1776, Adams Papers, MHi.

John Adams to James Warren

My dear Sir   Feby 18. 1776

We have at last hit upon a Plan which promisses fair for Success.

Dr. Franklin, and Mr Chase of Maryland, and Mr Charles Carroll of Carrollton, are chosen a Committee to go to Canada. I must confess I have very great Confidence, in the Abilities and Integrity, the Political Principles and good Disposition of this Committee.

Franklins Character you know. His masterly Acquaintance with the French Language, his extensive Correspondence in France, his great Experience in Life, his Wisdom, Prudence, Caution, his engaging Address, united to his unshaken Firmness in the present American System of Politicks and War, point him out as the fittest Character for this momentous Undertaking.

Chase is in younger Life, under forty; But deeply impress'd with a sense of the Importance of securing Canada, very active, eloquent, spirited, and capable.[1]

Carroll's Name and Character are equally unknown to you. I was introduced to him, about Eighteen Months ago in this City, and was much pleased with his Conversation. He has a Fortune, as I am well informed, which is computed to be worth Two hundred Thousand Pounds Sterling. He is a Native of Maryland, and his Father is still living. He had a liberal Education in France, and is well acquainted with the French Nation. He Speaks their Language as easily as ours— and what is perhaps of more Consequence than all the rest, he was educated in the Roman Catholic Religion, and still continues to worship his Maker according to the Rites of that Church. In the Cause of American Liberty, his Zeal, Fortitude and Perseverance have been so conspicuous that he is Said to be marked out for peculiar Vengeance by the Friends of Administration. But he continues to hazard his all: his immense Fortune, the largest in America, and his Life. This Gentlemans Character, if I foresee aright, will hereafter make a greater Figure in America. His Abilities are very good, his Knowledge and Learning extensive. I have Seen Writings of his which would convince you of this. You may perhaps hear before long more about them.

These three Gentlemen compose a Committee, which I think promisses great Things.

But We have done more. We have impowered the Committee to take with them, another Gentleman of Maryland Mr John Carroll, a Roman Catholic Priest, and a Jesuit, a Gentleman of learning and Abilities. This Gentleman will administer Baptism to the Canadian Children, and bestow Absolution upon Such as have been refused it by the toryfied Priests in Canada. The Anathema's of the Church so terrible to the Canadians, having had a disagreable Effect upon them.

In Addition to the whole General Lee is ordered into Canada, to take upon him the Command of the whole Expedition.[2] His Address, his Fluency in French, his Activity, his great Experience and Skill, We hope will Succeed.

I long to hear from N. England that the three Regiments are marched. It would damp me, very much to hear that our People continue to hesitate about Bounties, and Trifles.

The Unanimous Voice of the Continent is Canada must be ours, Quebec must be taken.

I think the most prudent Measures have now been adopted, and We must leave the Event. If We fail now, I shall be easy because I know of nothing more or better that We can do. I did not feel so well Satisfied, after the News of the Failure at Quebec.

It is true that We want Lee both at Cambridge and New York. But We cannot have him in three armies at once, and Canada Seems to Me, the most dangerous Post, and that there is the greatest Necessity for him there. Schuyler is to command in N. York, with Ld. Stirling under him who is a very good officer.

The Importance of Canada arises from this, and occasions our remarkable Unanimity at present in deciding the Affairs of it. In the Hands of our Enemies, it would enable them to inflame all the Indians upon the Continent, and perhaps induce them to take up the Hatchet, and commit their Robberies and Murders upon the Frontiers of all the southern Colonies as well as to pour down Regulars, Canadians and Indians together upon the Borders of the Northern.

I am, my dear Sir, unfeignedly your Friend

RC (MHi). In Adams' hand, though not signed.

[1] Samuel Chase had demonstrated his enthusiasm for the conquest of Canada in a January 12 letter written from Annapolis to John Adams who was then in Braintree. "The early attention and great Dependance of the Ministry on Canada evince the infinite importance of that Country in the present dispute; to obtain the Possession of that province is an object of the first Consequence. We must at all Events procure and keep Possession of that province. Quebec must at every Hazard be ours. No succours can arrive there before 1st May. I would have a chosen Committee go to Canada as soon as the Lakes are frozen hard enough, let them call a Convention, explain the Views and designs of Congress, and persuade them to send Delegates there. Let a body of 6,000 Canadians and 2000 Colonists be embodied for the defence of that province. I think the Success of the War will, in great Measure, depend on securing Canada to our Confederation. I would earnestly recommend Charles Carroll Esqr. of Carrollton, of this province to be one of your Deputies to Canada. His attachment and zeal to the Cause, his abilities, his Acquaintance with the Language, Manner & Customs of France and his Religion, with the circumstances of a very great Estate, all point him out to that all important Service. My Inclination to serve my Country would induce Me to offer my Services, if I did not esteem Myself unable to discharge the Trust." Chase to Adams, January 12, 1775 [i.e. 1776], Adams Papers, MHi.

[2] See John Adams to Charles Lee, February 19; and John Hancock to Charles Lee, February 19, 1776.

John Adams to Charles Lee

My dear Sir,   Philadelphia Feby. 19, 1776
The Congress have Seen such a Necessity of an able Commander in Canada, as to destine you to that most arduous Service.[1] I tremble for your Health, yet I hope the Campaign will rather promote it than otherwise.

We want you att N. York—We want you at Cambridge—We want you in Virginia—But Canada seems of more Importance than any of those Places. And therefore you are sent there. I wish you as many Laurells as Wolf and Montgomery reaped there, with an happier Fate, Health and long Life, after a glorious Return.

But I am ashamed to go on in such a Strain, when writing to you whose time is so much better employed than in reading it, when I took up my Pen only to introduce to your Acquaintance a Country man of yours and a Citizen of the World, to whom a certain Heretical Pamphlet called Common Sense, is imputed. His Name is Paine. He is travelling to N. York for his Curiosity and wishes to see a Gentl[ema]n, whose Character he so highly respects.

A luckier & happier Expedition than yours to N. York never was projected. The whole Whig World is blessing you for it and none of them more than, your Friend & Sert,   John Adams

RC (Facsimile, Samuel T. Freeman & Co. Catalog, *The Frederick S. Peck Collection of American Historical Autographs*, February 17, 1947, p. 1a).
[1] See John Hancock to Charles Lee, this date.

Josiah Bartlett to Mary Bartlett

My dear   Philadelphia Febry 19th 1776
Yours of the 2nd Inst. I Recd this morning and with pleasure, am informed that you and the family were then well; I think it a great favor, that so large a family Should be Blessed with health, for so long a time, I hope it will Continue till it shall please God, to return me home in health, when that will be I Know not; But if life and health permit, I hope to be at home before the middle of April, for as soon as the going is any thing like, I Design to Come home Even if I should be obliged to return again to this City after a short Stay with you.

When I read at the Close of your letter, an account of the Death of my good friend, John Wadleigh, it very sensibly affected me, as I had received no account of his being worse than when I left home. I had really a great value for him, and think the Town & Especially that part of it, have met with a great loss in his Death. I Cant help Calling to mind the many hours, pleasant Conversation I have had with him, and tho' he had Some Sentiments Different from mine, yet I really Loved & Esteemed him, and I Despise the Bigot, who Can have no Esteem or friendship for any man, whose religious opinions are Different from his own.

This Day Dr Smith of this City Delivered a funeral Oration, to the Memory of General Montgomery and the other Brave men, who fell in the attack on Quebeck; the oration was Delivered in a large and Beautiful & Elegant Dutch Church. The Congress, the General Assembly of this province, the Committes of Safety & inspection, and about 30 Clergymen of the Different Denominations in this City, with other Gentlemen, walked from the Court house, in a Body, to the Church, on Each Side walked three Regiments of the City associators. The musick was very solemn & mournful, and composed with the organs, Bass viol, 8 or 10 violins, German flutes, French horns &c, the whole was Conducted with great order & Decency.[1] The solemnity of the ocassion, with the news of the Death of my friend Wadleigh, or something Else, Seems to have Setled my Spirits at least a peg too low. I know that troubles & Disappointments are the Common lot of all men, and that the Supreme Disposer of all Events, Can, and I really believe, will over rule all things for the best, that is my greatest Comfort when things Seem to look with a Dark and Dismal Countenance, either of a publick or private nature.

I am sorry to hear that the post from Cambridge to Exeter, is not likely to Continue riding, as I fear it will put us under a Difficulty, of gitting Each others letters, but I shall nevertheless Continue to write to you weekly. The weather here has been very pleasant till yesterday, it is now very Cold for this place tho not Equal to Some in New Hampshire.

I am in good health at this time. Remember my love to the Children, and My Regards to all friends.

February 21st. I am now very well and Still Remain your,

Josiah Bartlett

RC (NhHi).

[1] Robert Treat Paine took note of this occasion in his diary this date: "Dr. Smith pronounced an Oration in Memory of Genl. Montgomery at the new Calvinist Meeting house." MHi. Smith's oration was subsequently published as William Smith, *An Oration in Memory of General Montgomery, and of the Officers and Soldiers, who fell with him, December 31, 1775, before Quebec; drawn up (and delivered February 19th 1776) at the Desire of the Honorable Continental Congress* (Philadelphia: John Dunlap, 1776), and widely criticized on account of its tory overtones. See Richard Smith's Diary, February 21, 1776.

A N

O R A T I O N

In MEMORY of

GENERAL MONTGOMERY,

AND OF THE

OFFICERS AND SOLDIERS,

WHO FELL WITH HIM, DECEMBER 31, 1775,

BEFORE

Q U E B E C;

DRAWN UP (AND DELIVERED FEBRUARY 19th, 1776.)

AT THE DESIRE OF THE

HONORABLE CONTINENTAL CONGRESS.

By WILLIAM SMITH, D.D.

PROVOST OF THE COLLEGE AND ACADEMY
OF PHILADELPHIA.

O thou, who bad'st them fall with honor crown'd,
Soon make the bloody pride of war to cease !
May these the only sacrifice be found
To public freedom, and their country's peace.

P H I L A D E L P H I A:

PRINTED BY JOHN DUNLAP, IN MARKET-STREET;

M,DCC,LXXVI.

William Smith's *Oration in Memory of General Montgomery*

Josiah Bartlett to John Langdon

Dear Sir   Philadelphia Febry 19th 1776

Yours of the first Inst. is now before me, and would inform you, that the Marine Committe look on you as fully authorised to Build the ship to be Built in New Hampshire and finish her fit for the Sea; if any thing is wanted that you Cannot procure, they Expect you will Give them timely notice.[1] The Draught is Sent forward & you will no Doubt receive it before this Comes to hand; I Enquired Concerning the length and Bigness of Cables & weight of anchors, but the Committe has not Determined on it; Govr Hopkins Says he told their Contractor that the Cables must be fifteen Inches, & 120 fathoms Long at least, and had Sent them the Dementions of the Pallas frigate as a rule for the masts & yards of the 32 gun Ships; However the Committe advised to apply to the Comissioners for Building the Ships in the City, to know their Determination on those articles which as soon as I can procure I will Send you.

The Marine Committe have given me an order in your favor, for twenty Thousand Dollars, which I was to have Sent by a man who is to take some money for the Ships to be in built in Massachusetts, But as you inform me, you have drawn one and are likely to draw more orders here, I Believe I shall not send the whole by that oppertunity.

In yours of the 29th ulto. you informed me that Col Willm Whipple was to set out for this place the then next week, and in consequence I now look out sharp for him, & hope he will be here this week, as I am Extremely anxious not only for his assistance but to be informed of what nature the Difficulties are which you say have unaccountably turned up in regard of the Civil government of the Colony. What you have hinted, has given me vast uneasiness and could wish you had mentioned the particular Difficulties, for I am greatly at a loss to Guess at them. I am greatly Surprized to hear, that there is Danger, that the poison of Toryism, will spread in the Colony of New Hampshire. If you had informed me of the Danger of the Smallpox or *plague* Spreading, it would not have given me half the Concern, as the one is only temporal, and the other in a sense eternal, for if our rights & priviledges are now given up, they are gone forever.[2] I think it very Strange that the Committe of Safety, nor any one of them, have wrote me a line of the Situations of the affairs of the Colony, nor answered any of my letters for above three months past. What is the reason I know not, how Disagreable it must seem, you know by Experience in some measure, however I hope soon to be informed by my worthy Colleagues.

The Pamphlet *Common Sense* has already had three Editions in this City; in the last there is an apendix and large additions, it has also been reprinted at N. York; by the best information it has had a great Effect on the minds of many here & to the Southward.

General Lee is ordered for Canada & Schuyler to New York; Col Dickinson was Countermanded just as he was on the march, hearing that Clinton had Sailed. The Common opinion here is, that Comissioners are Coming from England to treat with the Congress. I think it not unlikely, but fear no good will accrue to the Colonies from that measure. If no hurt I shall be glad. Dr. Franklin, Mr Chase & one Caryl of Maryland are going as Deputies from the Congress to Canada. As to an agent being appointed in the Several Colonies, I Believe it will be a useful Expedient for the Continent, But as yet nothing is done about it in any of the Colonies. When any thing of that Kind is done by the Congress in any of the Colonies I will take Care that the same be done for us, and make no doubt you will be appointed,[3] But think it not proper to move it till I see a proper time and things ripe for it. At this time I am Sure it would answer no good end.[4]

RC (Capt. J. G. M. Stone, Annapolis, Md., 1973).
    [1] See Bartlett to Langdon, February 13, 1776, note 1.
    [2] For a discussion of the opposition in New Hampshire to the assumption of full governmental powers, see Bartlett to Meshech Weare, March 2, 1776, note 1.
    [3] Ultimately Congress did appoint Langdon as an "agent of Prizes for the Colony of New Hampshire," but not before Langdon agreed to resign from Congress to avoid the holding of "any lucrative office" by a member of Congress. *JCC*, 5:478; William Whipple to John Langdon, April 29, 1776; and Lawrence Mayo, *John Langdon of New Hampshire* (Concord: Rumford Press, 1937), pp. 128–34.
    [4] For the continuation of this letter, see Bartlett to Langdon, February 21, 1776.

Benjamin Franklin to Charles Lee

Dear Sir: Philadelphia, Feb. 19, 1776
    I rejoice that you are going to Canada. I hope the Gout will not have the courage to follow you into that Severe Climate. I believe you will have the Number of Men you wish for: I am told that there will be 2000. more: but there are always Deficiencies.
    The Bearer Mr. Paine has requested a Line of Introduction to you, which I give the more willingly, as I know his Sentiments are not very different from yours. He is the reputed, & I think the Real, Author of Common Sense, a pamphlet that has made great Impression here. I do not enlarge, both because he waits, and because I hope for the pleasure of conferring with you face to face in Canada. I will only add, that we are assured here on the part of France, that the Troops sent to the W. Indies have no inimical Views to us or our Cause. It is thought they intend a War without a previous Declaration. God prosper all your Undertakings, and return you with Health, Honour & Happiness.
    Yours most affectionately,   B. Franklin

[*P.S.*] Martinico & Cape Francois by the last Advices, are now fortifying with immense Diligence & great Expence.

MS not found; reprinted from Samuel T. Freeman & Co. Catalog, *The Frederick S. Peck Collection of American Historical Autographs* (February 17, 1947), pp. 6–7.

John Hancock to Charles Lee

Sir   Philadelphia Febry. 19th. 1776

I have the honor to Inclose you Sundry Resolutions of Congress, by which you will perceive it is the Desire of Congress that you should Repair to Canada and take upon you the Command of the Army of the United Colonies in that Province.[1]

I need not mention the importance of the Trust reposed in you, and the happy Effects it will have in securing the Liberty of America, if you should be so fortunate as to Drive our Enemies, the Enemies of Liberty & the Rights of Mankind out of it, I heartily pray that the Disposer of Events may grant you Success equal to your Merit and Zeal.

As you will want Battering Cannon which are not be be had in that province, you are to apply to the Convention or Committee of Safety of New York, to whom by this opportuy. I Send the Recommendation of Congress to Supply you with Twelve, such as you shall Judge most suitable, and some Mortars, if they have or can procure them, with Balls, Shells & other Necessaries, and also to assist you in forwarding them.[2]

Eight Tons of Powder are now on the way to Albany for the Forces in Canada, and as a very considerable Quantity of Salt Petre is sent to the Mills of Mr Wisner & Mr Livingston,[3] should there be Occasions for more you will be Supplied from thence.

You will readily perceive the necessity of Conferring with General Schuyler, and with him consulting on the best method of having Necessaries convey'd to you across the Lakes.[4] The Congress have a full Confidence that you will Cooperate in securing the Possession of the Lakes and mutually Assisting each other as Occasion may Require, and as far as in your power give mutual Aid in supporting the cause of Freedom & Liberty.

I Expect the Deputies will in a short time be ready to proceed to Canada.[5]

I am with every Sentiment of Esteem, Sir Your most Obedt. Servt.,

J H Presdt.

[*P.S.*] Your favr. respecting the Departure of the Ships from New York, and your Conjectures as to their Designs is just come to hand, & shall be laid before Congress.[6]

LB (DNA: PCC, item 12A).

¹ Although on February 17 Congress ordered Lee to take command of the army in Canada, he was directed on February 28 "not to set out for Canada." On March 1, Congress resolved that Lee should take charge of the Continental forces in the "southern department." *JCC*, 4:157, 175, 180–81. See also Hancock to Charles Lee, February 28, and March 1, 1776.

² See John Hancock to the New York Provincial Convention, February 20, 1776.

³ See Secret Committee to Philip Schuyler, February 21, 1776; and *JCC*, 4:128–29.

⁴ General Schuyler, who was in poor health, had been ordered by Congress to take command of the forces in New York. *JCC*, 4:157; and John Hancock to Philip Schuyler, February 20, 1776.

⁵ Although Benjamin Franklin, Charles Carroll, and Samuel Chase had been appointed by Congress on February 15, they did not leave Philadelphia until late March. See *JCC*, 4:151–52; and William Whipple to Josiah Bartlett, March 24, 1776.

⁶ Lee's letter of February 17 was read in Congress on February 20, 1776. *JCC*, 4:161.

Roger Sherman to Zebulon Butler

Sir   Philadelphia Feb. 19th. 1776

I wrote to You the 19th of January last & enclosed a Newspaper containing Several resolutions of the Congress and an Act of the General Assembly of Connecticut, I now enclose an attested Copy of Said Act. Mr. Gore has been here some time expecting some direction from Governor Trumbull, in consequence of a message You Sent by Mr. Avery.¹ I mentioned the matter to the Governor in a letter soon after Mr. Gore came here and have this Day receiv'd a letter from him, wherein is the following paragraph viz, "I was not made Acquainted with Mr. Gore's going to Congress, and expectations of any thing from me, relative to his Petition from the Committee of Westmoreland. Is there any thing more can be done by this Colony to quiet that contest than is already? It appears to me the Honorable Congress will lay their hand upon it, and do every thing needful that Justice may be done, and any future attacks on our peaceable people at that place prevented."

Mr. Gore has Concluded to leave the Petition and depositions with the President of the Congress, and return home to morrow.² I dont know what further can be done by Congress, unless to recommend to the Assembly or Committee of Safety of this Colony to enquire into the matter and See that the resolutions of Congress already passed be duly observed. When the late attack happened the people in Northumberland County had not been made acquainted with the last resolutions of Congress past about the 20th of December.³ I hope they will desist from further Hostilities, and remain quiet, until the Controversy is decided. I wrote to You before, advising that application be made to the Magistrates or the Sheriff at Sunsbury or both for restitution of the

Goods or effects taken at Warriours Run, and if not restored to complain to Congress. I dont hear of any preparations or intentions to give You further trouble but it is best to keep a good look out. I Shall take the first opportunity to inform what is done in Congress relative to the representation You have Sent by Mr. Gore—or of any future plots of the Land jobbers to disturb you, that may come to my knowledge. I Suppose the Militia with you are furnished with Arms and Ammunition according to Law, for your own & your Country's defence. We have no late news from England but all the accounts that we have had agree that the Ministry design to continue the war against us. We have large reinforcements marching to Canada, & we have accounts of some arriving there. General Lee with about 3000 Troops are in New York for the Defence of that City. I am Sir Your humble Servant

Roger Sherman

RC (InU).

[1] On December 29, 1775, soon after Butler's men had repulsed an attack by Pennsylvanians under William Plunket, the town of Westmoreland agreed to send Christopher Avery to Connecticut to inform Governor Trumbull of their situation and appointed Obadiah Gore, Jr. (1744–1821), to present to Congress their account of "the late invasion made by the tory party of the Pennsylvania people." Charles Miner, *History of Wyoming* (Philadelphia: J. Crissy, 1845), p. 179. See also Sherman to Zebulon Butler, January 19, 1776.

[2] On February 20 the petition was read and referred to a committee, which on March 5 recommended that it be transmitted to the Pennsylvania assembly. See *JCC*, 4:161–62, 184–85

[3] See *JCC*, 3:439–40, 452–53.

Richard Smith's Diary

Monday 19 Feb. [1776]

Some little Business being done, the Congress, attended by the Pennsa. Assembly and other invited Bodies[1] with a vast Crowd of Spectators, proceeded in State to the Dutch Calvinist Church where Dr. Smith pronounced an Oration for Gen. Montgomery, the Band of vocal and Instrumental Music was good but played too low for the Place, the light Infantry and Rifle Rangers walked on both Sides of the Congress going and coming.

MS (DLC).

[1] See Charles Thomson's February 13 invitation to the Pennsylvania Committee of Safety in *Pa. Archives*, 1st ser. 4:714.

Samuel Ward to Henry Ward

Dear Brother   Philadelpa. 19th Feby. 1776

Yours of 6th inst. is now before Me. The Spirit with which Troops have been raised in N. England for the Canadian Service does fresh Honor to our Country, and the Measures of Congress with the divine Blessing must answer all our Expectations; your observations upon the immediate Necessity of a Confederation are clearly conclusive. I am daily in Pursuit of it & never intend to loose sight of it. That unhappy Jealousy which I have more than once mentioned I believe retards it, Dr. Franklin who is full for it advises the four N. England Governments to enter into one themselves & invite the other Colonies to accede to it and let them fall in as they may like. I sometimes think this would be the surest Way to induce the other Cols. to join Us, many important Considerations on both Sides of the Question are to be weighed before We come to a conclusion. I should be very glad of your Opinion & that of such of our Freinds as you may think proper to consult upon the Subject.

Somehow or other my Letters must have miscarryed. To write by every Post is impossible for he sometimes comes in while I am in Congress and goes out in two Hours but I have constantly embraced every Opportunity of writing in my Power & shall continue to do it.

To my ardent Affection for the Town of Newport not only you but Heaven itself is a Witness, there is nothing consistent with the Preservation of the Liberties of America (upon which theirs as well as the general Happiness depends) but what I would do at the Hazard of my Life & Property to serve them, They most certainly mistake their own Interest. When the Ship founders in the midst of the Ocean can Passengers be safe in any part of her? no more can the Town expect when one general Ruin involves the Liberties & Property of All America to be saved from the general Destruction.[1]

I must refer you to my Letter to the Govr. for News,[2] since writing that We have an Acct. of a Sloop arrived in N. York with Powder.

I see no Advertisement in the Providence Paper for reprinting Common Sense; that Pamphlet ought surely to be distributed throughout all the Colonies if it was even at the public Expence. It has done immense Service; I am told by good Judges that two thirds of this City & Colony are now full in his Sentiments; in the Jerseys & Maryland &c they gain ground daily. The Gentn. from that Colony whom in a former Letter I mentioned to You as having made a glorious Speech upon seeing the Kings Proclamation continues firm in those Sentiments; He is the Person going with Dr. Franklin to Canada.[3]

Mr. & Mrs. Hopkins are very well. I was forced to write separately to the Governor or miss the Post.

I designed to have wrote Messrs. Brown this Post but Time will not

admit, be kind enough to let them know that Mr. Cooke del[ivere]d
their Letter to Messrs. Pliarne and Penet to Mr. Hopkins who did not
Deliver it to Me until Messrs. Cooke & Russel were gone out of Town,
they have answered it since and I have put the Letter into the office.[4]

Make my affectionate Compliments to all our Friends. I am, Yours
most affectionately,   Sam Ward

RC (RHi).
    [1] Ward is apparently referring to Newport's decision in January 1776 to supply
provisions to Capt. James Wallace's royal naval squadron—a decision that was
reluctantly approved by the Rhode Island Assembly. Clark, *Naval Documents*, 3:86,
99, 751, 835–36, 861, 901–2, 917, 937–39.
    [2] Ward's latest extant letter to Gov. Nicholás Cooke is that of January 16, 1776.
    [3] Samuel Chase. See Ward to Henry Ward, November 2, 1775.
    [4] The letter from John and Nicholas Brown referred to here has not been found,
but for what was apparently Penet and de Pliarne's reply, see Clark, *Naval Documents*, 3:1176–77.

Oliver Wolcott to Samuel Lyman

Sir   Philadelphia 19 Febry. 1776
    Your letter of the 25th ult came safe in about a dozen days to hand,
& I hope you have rec'd one from me, which I sent you Sometime since.
Your concern for my family demands my sincerest thanks & heartily
wish your kindness in this respect may be continued. Your correspondence is extremely agreable. You say you want to Know the news here.
You may Easily conceive that to be informed of the State, apprehensions, the Views, Designs, fears, and hopes of the people, who sent me
here would be equally agreable to me. I believe the publick prints will
anticipate almost any Thing I can Tell you. You hear it Said in the
prints, that the Port Bill, Fish Bill, and restraining act are repealed, and
that instead thereof, they have ordered all our shipping to be seized;
and that they are about to send over commissioners, to treat with the
Congress. All this news makes no impression on firm whigs. It is considered as an insidious manoeuvre. Clinton has gone from N York,
probably to Virginia. Our small fleet went out this river last sabbath,
and will Stand Some chance of coming across him. Genl Lee is ordered
to Canada. Schyler, if his health permits, to N York. The ports, except
such restraints as the Association laid, would of course open the first
of March. I wrote you that they would not be closed,[1] except so far as
the association Shut them; which would still, in every material matter,
govern—and some further regulation would be made but this is not
completed. You will easily perceive, the business might very naturally
involve in it, many important Questions. But as no decisions have been
passed, can say no more than I did before, that the ports will be open

under Some regulations. The Subject of no undecided matter may be communicated. I mean a Subject of discussion. Our difference with Great Britain has become very great & I imagine but little prospect of a speedy accomodation. The people of the colonies will give up no material point, and a foolish, wicked, court are (I believe) inflexibly determined to support (if possible) an unrighteous authority. What matters will issue in, I cannot Say, but perhaps in a total disseverance from Great Britain. This, I perceive, has got to be a good deal of a popular expectation. I do not perceive but little intimidation, and our union I hope is firm. Since I began my letter, I hear our fleet has not Sailed—what occasions the delay, have not heard. We have no news, but what is in the publick prints. In haste Sir, Your most humble Servant,

Oliver Wolcott

Tr (CtHi).
[1] See Wolcott to Samuel Lyman, February 3, 1776, note 2.

Oliver Wolcott to Laura Wolcott

Philadelphia. 19 Febry 1776. Urges his wife not to be concerned about his well-being and cautions about succumbing to anxieties and family cares. As his return is "Very uncertain," he advises her to proceed with several domestic matters as she sees fit. Continues: "There is news that Commissioners are appointed by the British Court to Treat with America and that the port Bill, Fish Bill and Restraining Act are repealed, but the whole I consider as an insidious Manoeuvre, and no advantage will be derived from it. Orders are given to Seize all our Shipping. Clinton has left N. York. Genl Lee probably prevented his Landing. This Force may have gone to Virginia. Every Thing is ripening to produce a most important Crisis, and I hope Wisdom will be given to those to whom the publick Councells are Committed. An Accommodation with Great Britain I think becomes less and less probable. Wisdom and Firmness are necessary and I hope they will Mark the Lines of publick Conduct."

RC (CtHi).

John Hancock to the New York Provincial Convention

Gentlemen   Philadelphia, 20th Februy. 1776
I have the honour to enclose you sundry Resolutions of Congress, by which you will perceive their determination as to the Works on

Martler's Rock, that no Additions be made, but that those already Effected there be supported and garrisoned. You will please to order the Execution of the Works Recommended by Congress in the Inclos'd Resolves, to which beg leave to Refer you.[1]

The Congress have Directed General Lee to Repair to Canada to conduct the Military Operations in that Quarter; and as battering cannon are much wanted there, they have order'd him to request you to supply him with some suitable pieces, & Mortars if possible, with Shells, Balls &c. I make no doubt but your Zeal will readily lead you to afford the General your Aid in these instances, & also in assisting to forward every Necessary with all Dispatch.[2] I must Refer you to the Resolutions, & have only time to Request yr particular Attention to them.

I am with Esteem, Gentn, your most Obedt. Servant.

John Hancock Prest.

[P.S.] Genl Schuyler is to Repair to New York & Take the Command. I shall Send the Commission by next oppor[tunit]y.

RC (N). *Journals of N.Y. Prov. Cong.* 1:317. RC damaged; missing words supplied from Tr.

[1] See *JCC*, 4:152–53.

[2] See Hancock to Charles Lee, February 19, 1776, note 1.

John Hancock to Philip Schuyler

Sir   Philadelphia Febry. 20th. 1776

I have the Honor of inclosing you sundry Resolutions of Congress, to which Refer you.[1]

I must beg leave to inform you that the Congress hear with great Regret the precarious State of your health and the Return of your Disorder, they are fully Apprized & Sensible of your Services and Abilities, and should have been very happy to have made use of them in Canada; but knowing the importance of your Abilities, the influence and weight you have among the Indian Tribes, the Service you are capable of doing to the common Cause even in the present infirm state of your Health, and at the same time being Apprehensive should you be Sent on so fatiguing a service as that of Canada must be, especially at this inclement Season, your Country might be Depriv'd of the Advantage of your Services which are so much wanted at this critical conjuncture, they have thought it best to Send General Lee to Canada, Reserving to you the Command of the Forces and the Conduct of Military operations in the Colony of New York.

Your known Zeal and warm Attachment to the cause of Liberty assure me that you will Concert with Genl Lee the best means of Securing the Communication of the Lakes, and of facilitating the Transportation of Necessaries for the use of the Army in Canada, and give him all the Aid & assistance in your power for accomplishing the great Ends we all have in View.

Your severall Letters are now under the Consideration of a Committee of Congress, so soon as Report is made and a Determination had in Congress, I will Do my self the honour of Transmitting you their Result.[2]

I Send by this Express a Number of the Articles of War Translated into French which you will please to forward for the use of the Canadian Regiments.

I most sincerely wish to hear the agreeable Tidings of your perfect Restoration to health, and am with the utmost Esteem, Sir, Your most obedt Sevt.   J H Pt.

LB (DNA: PCC, item 12A).
[1] Probably the resolves of February 17 concerning the army in New York and Canada. *JCC*, 4:157–60.
[2] It is unclear which letters are referred to, but Schuyler's letters of January 29, 31, and February 1 were read in Congress on February 9 and referred to a committee whose report of February 16 was laid on the table. In the meantime, on February 14, Congress had received Schuyler's letter of February 7 and committed it to George Wythe, John Adams, and Samuel Chase, three members of the first committee. On February 15 Congress received Schuyler's letter of February 4 and committed it "to the same committee to whom the letters received yesterday were referred," which made its report on February 17, and consequently Congress passed a series of resolves based on "sundry letters" from Schuyler and other general officers concerned with the northern command. Hancock apparently anticipated further recommendations from the committee, which continued to be assigned letters in March, but there is no mention in the journals of further action directly related to letters from Schuyler that had been received by this date. *JCC*, 4:123, 147, 151, 154–55, 157–59, 185, and 188–89. These Schuyler letters are located in PCC, item 153, 1:478–511; and *Am. Archives*, 4th ser. 4:880–81, 898, 906–7, 938–39, and 955–56.

Joseph Hewes to Samuel Johnston

Dear Sir   Philadelphia 20th Feb. 1776

This will be delivered to you by James Thompson and John Crowley who have charge of the Waggon, Horses and sundry Articles that make up the Load, an Inventory of which you will see in the packet directed to the Provincial Council.[1] I have not been able to get in the Accounts for the Horses & Waggon nor for the Articles sent therewith, but shall forward them by Post as soon as I can make a proper state of them. I mentioned to you in my Last[2] per express that we had not sent any copies of the Pamphlet entitled *Common Sense* but finding Brother Penn had a fondness for them have agreed some should be sent, the Council can Judge of the propriety of distributing them. Let me know your

opinion on that head. The Roads being very bad I was advised to put
five horses to the Waggon. I hope they will all be delivered safe to you.
I have put up a large Flag for Edenton on Mr Jones's request. Please
to let me know the time the Waggon arives. I intend to make a charge
of 30/ per day to the Continent and hope to get it allowed or you may
charge it in the Accounts you send. John Crowley who is the driver
is recommended to me as a man very carefull of Horses and used to the
business of driving a Waggon. He can neither read or write and his
old master says should not be trusted with money. Both the men are
to have 3/ per day and all expenses born, if they return here pay them
no more money than Just to bear their expenses. They are to be in pay
till they Arive here, provided they come directly back.
  I am respectfully, Dear Sir, your mo. Obed Servant,

                                                        Joseph Hewes

RC (NN).
  [1] A receipt from John Crowley to the North Carolina delegates, dated "Philada.
Feby. 21. 1776," lists the contents of this wagon as "Seven barrels of Powder, Three
Boxes of Drums, one Do. of Colours and three Boxes of Pamphlets." NcU: Hayes
Collection microfilm.
  [2] See Hewes to Samuel Johnston, February 13, 1776.

Samuel Huntington to Joseph Trumbull

Dear Sr   Philidelphia 20th Feby. 1776
  I receivd your favour of 31st ult. but was then confind with the Smallpox which circumstance beg you to accept as an excuse for delaying
an answer until this. Col Dyer not being continued in Congress was
unexpected & disagreeable to me, but as I am at present Stationed here
Shall be very happy in the favour of your correspondence during my
residence at this place. Have conversed with Mr. J. Adams on the Subject you mentioned & Shall take further oppertunity with him thereon;
you may expect any assistance in my power consonant to the Strictest
Friendship & honor, which I know is all you desire.[1] General Clinton
is gone from N York with his Crew, tis Conjectured to the Southward.
This morning at About Eight o'Clock the Worthy Mr Lynch of South
Carolina was taken with an Appoplectic fit; remains very Ill tho' his
reason is restored & Speech So as to answer questions. May God restore
his health & usefullness. Thro' divine goodness I am restored to health
So as to give constant attendance to business, & remain, Sir with much
esteem, your humble Servant,   Saml Huntington

RC (CtHi).
  [1] Trumbull was apparently interested in having his pay as commissary general
increased. See Eliphalet Dyer to Joseph Trumbull, December 26, 1775, and January 1, 1776.

Secret Committee Minutes of Proceedings

Feby. 20, 1776.

At a meeting of the com[mitte]e. Present Saml. Ward, Benjn. Franklin, Ths. McKean, Jos. Hewes, Josa. Bartlett & Robt. Alexander. A Contract was enterd into with Jo. Alsop, Phil. Livingston, F. Lewis, Robt. Morris & Silas Deane for the importg. such goods, wares or merchandize as the said Come of Secy. shall direct.[1]

At a meeting of the Come. of Secy. Present Saml Ward, J. Alsop, F. Lewis, Jos. Bartlett, Rob. Alexander, Robert Morris, B. Franklin. A Contract was enterd into with J. Langdon of N. Hampshire Esqr. for importg. such woollen or other goods as the said Come. shall direct. Drew an order on the treasurers for 10,000 dlls in favor of Mr. Langdon. Also a permit to export the produce of these Colonies to that amount agreable to the association. A Charter party was enterd into with Saml. Penrose of the City of Phila., Mercht., for freightg. ship Sally, to said Come. A Permit was granted for said Ship to sail, She being loaded by a former Permit of this Come. A Letter to Mr. J. D. Schweighauser of Nantes was read, approvd & signd. Instructions to Ths. Rawlins, Master of ship Sally above, signd by Come.

MS (MH).

[1] On January 27 Congress authorized the Secret Committee to contract for the importation of goods suitable for the Indian trade to a value of £40,000 sterling. *JCC,* 4:96–97. For this contract, which was dated February 19, see John Alsop et al. to Silas Deane, March 1, 1776. See also Robert Morris to Deane, March 30, 1776. A 33-page account (audited by the U.S. Treasury, July 6, 1790) pertaining to transactions under this contract is in Robert Morris Miscellaneous MSS, NHi.

Richard Smith's Diary

[February 20, 1776]

Tuesday 20. Mr. Crane went Home & Mr. Sergeant attended in his Stead by Virtue of the new Appointment in these Words,

In Provincial Congress New Jersey

Brunswick 14 Feb. 1776.

On Motion, Resolved Unanimously That Wm. Livingston, John De Hart, Richd. Smith, John Cooper & Jonatn. Dickinson Sergeant Esqrs. be Delegates to represent this Province in the Continental Congress for the Space of One Year or untill others shall be legally appointed in their Stead and that they or any Three or more of them have full & ample Power to consent and agree to all Measures which such Congress shall deem necessary, And this Province bind themselves to execute to the utmost of their Power all Resolutions which the said Congress may adopt, And further if the said Congress shall think necessary to adjorn we do authorize our said Delegates to represent and act for this Province in any One Congress to be held by Virtue of such Adjornment during their Delegation. A true Copy from the Minutes. Wm. Patterson Secretary

Wm. Livingston was added to the Cannon Comee. & they were authorized to contract for Cannon. Chase drew a Form, which I altered, for disposing of the Ship Blue Mountain Valley and her Cargo, no Judge of the Admiralty being yet appointed in Jersey, this Matter was debated & the Necessity of taking the whole Government from the Kings Substitutes was descanted upon & postponed. Reports of Accots. settled by the Comee. of Claims were made. A Petition and sundry Papers on the Wyoming Dispute were read, spoken to and deferred.[1] A few Arms granted to compleat Maxwells Battalion. A Guard of the Soldiers destined for Canada was ordered to escort the Powder going there. Waynes Battalion was ordered for N York when properly armed. Lewis, Alsop and P. Livingston were directed to forward to Gen Washn. at Cambridge the 5 Tons of Powder now at New Brunswick.

MS (DLC).
[1] See *JCC*, 4:161–62. For the resolves which Congress adopted on March 5 in response to the report submitted by the committee appointed to consider this matter, see *JCC*, 4:184–85.

Josiah Bartlett to John Langdon

Febry 21st [1776]

Febry 21st. Last Evening the Secret Committe met, Signed the Contract &c which I shall Enclose to you.[1] They have likewise drawn an order for the money, which order I have taken and have given my Recept that I have Recd it for you, but how to Conduct the affair I know not, whither the treasurers, if I should Desire it, will be willing to Deliver me the money as I have no order from you to Receive it I know not and if I should Receive it without order, and Send it Down & any mishap befall it, I may bring my self into Difficulty, without any prospect of advantage. How or when I shall have a safe opertunity to send Down So large a Sum as 30,000 Dollars I know not;[2] The man that Mr Hancock Expected is not come and when he Does I am uncertain whither he will be willing to take charge of it. I could wish you had given some more particular orders about the money as I am puzzeled how to Conduct for the best. I shall write you again in a few Days.

Yesterday Mr Lynch was taken with an apoplectick fit and was thought to be near his end, but is something better to Day.

I Believe it is certain the British parliament has ordered all American vessels to be Seized, as you will see by the publick papers. Two of the outward bound vessels fitted out by the Secret Committe, for the purpose of necessaries, are taken and Carried into the West Indies, the master of one has got back. In short we have nothing to Expect from Brittain, but war & Bloodshed, notwithstanding the pretence of sending Commissioners here to treat.

I am this Day informed that a petition to the Congress, is Signing fast by the Inhabitants of this City, for Leave to fit out privateers, and make reprisals on all Brittish vessels, to indemnify them for the Losses they have Sustained by the Depredations of Brittish men of war.[3] Indeed it seems very hard that Brittain is Seizing all American vessels and the Americans are not permitted to return the Compliment. The late measure has I think (*Sub rosa*) much altered the minds of the people here and in the C[ongre]ss too. Give my Compliments to all Enquiring friends & believe me to be, *your* friend,   Josiah Bartlett

P.S. By the latest account it seems the parliament has altered their measure of treating, and the Comisrs. are to treat with Each Colony Seperate, which will Certainly, and unfailingly, Destroy the whole, for I am sure no Colony will, at this time, treat seperately. I think I may venture to Engage for New Hampshire.   J. B.

[*P.S.*] The Invoice of the goods you are to procure with your Contract and the weight of anchors &c I Shall Send in my next.

RC (Capt. J. G. M. Stone, Annapolis, Md., 1973). A continuation of Bartlett to Langdon, February 19, 1776.
   [1] See Secret Committee Minutes of Proceedings, February 20, 1776.
   [2] See Bartlett to Langdon, March 5, 1776.
   [3] For additional references on this issue, see Richard Smith's Diary, February 13, 1776, note 4.

Secret Committee to Philip Schuyler

Sir   Philadela. 21st Feby. 1776
   The Congress having directed the Secret Comee. to Send eight Tons of Powder to Canada with all possible Dispatch,[1] We have sent it forward & directed the Waggon master to deliver it to You or in your Absence to the Commanding Officer of the United Forces at Albany in order to be transported to Canada as soon as possible.[2] I am, in behalf of the Comee., Sir, Your most obedient, hble Servt,
                                        Sam. Ward Chairman

RC (MeHi).
   [1] For Congress' resolve of February 15, see *JCC*, 4:152.

² This day the committee also sent a request to the Pennsylvania Committee of Safety to provide wagons for this shipment, and on February 26 Chairman Ward wrote a letter to wagonmaster Robert Irwin directing him to take "the safest & best Road to Albany" to deliver this shipment to Schuyler. Samuel Ward to the Pennsylvania Committee of Safety, February 21, Society Collection, PHi; and Samuel Ward to Robert Irwin, February 26, 1776, Schuyler Papers, NN. That Irwin was delayed until at least February 26 seems also to be confirmed by the Secret Committee's order of that date to issue $400 "on account of the wagon service." See Secret Committee Minutes of Proceedings, February 26, 1776.

Richard Smith's Diary

Wednesday 21 Feb. [1776]

Letters from Gen. Schuyler & others read and committed to 3 Members. The Papers about the Wyoming Dispute and those about the Limits or proposed temporary Line between Virginia and Pennsa. were referred to Hewes, Wm. Livingston, Paca, Chase and [Rutledge].¹ Duane from the Treasury Comee. made several Reports which were accepted, establishing the Denominations of the 4 Millions. One Million of them is to be in 2/3ds, 1/2, 1/3d, & 1/6th of a Dollar & the other 3 in Bills of One Dollar, 2, 3, 4, 5, 6, 7 & 8 Dollars, but more of the 1 & 2 than of the others. An Office is to be established by the Comee. and Clerks employed and all Assemblies, Conventions, Comees. of Safety, Paymasters & others who have recd. Public Money are to settle their Accounts at this Office &c. Duane was the Author of this Plan. Willing from the Comee. of Claims reported some Accots. Wm. Livingston moved that the Thanks of the Congress be given to Dr. Smith for his Oration on Gen. Montgomery and that he be desired to make it public. This was objected to for several Reasons; the chief was that the Dr. declared the Sentiments of the Congress to continue in a Dependency on G Britain which Doctrine this Congress cannot now approve. Principal Speakers for the Motion Duane, Wilson, Willing; against it Chase, John Adams, Wyth, E. Rutledge, Wolcott, Sherman. At length Mr. Livingston withdrew his Motion.²

MS (DLC).

¹ Although the printed journals indicate that Congress took this action on February 20, the entry in the rough journals raises the possibility that this issue was referred to committee on the 20th but that the committee was not actually appointed until the 21st. See PCC, item 1, fol. 355; and JCC, 4:161–62.

² See Josiah Bartlett to Mary Bartlett, February 19, 1776, note.

James Duane's Notes of Debates

[February 22, 1776.] ¹

1. 2000 men unarmed.

2. Enlistments go on slowly.

3. Want of arms—no prospect of getting them.

3. Two Militia men are paid for one during every relief.

3. General Washington opinion that a bounty ought to be given, but can't say what will answer.

4. Obliged to borrow from Massachusetts.

S. Adams. 1. Never has been proposed to enlist soldiers during the war, never tried.

Moves that we take into consideration the lengthening the time of enlistment.

Paine—nothing.

Geary. 1. Militia have no desire to be called in frequently.

2. Men must engage under officers from other Colonies which they · dislike.

Sherman. 1. Long enlistment is a state of slavery. There ought to be a rotation which is in favor of liberty.

2. Difficulty arises from enlistment being too long neglected by Congress.

3. Taking out of the hands of the Assemblies to nominate officers.

Harrison. 1. For withdrawing our officers & soldiers and leaving it to the New England Governmts. and giving them yearly 3,000,000 dollars.

J. Adams. 1. If General means that none Should enlist but during the war, he is against it—But (says) nothing against any enlisting in that maner who may choose it.

2. People in New England averse to giving large pay to officers.

3. No army but what is mercenary.

4. The high pay of officers only gives them an opportunity of extravagance.

5. People there can't be reconciled to the [2]

6. He has no doubt but many decline enlisting in expectation of a bounty.

7. As much danger from the aristocratic part as in N. E. from the democratic.

8. In favor of the proposition for raising men during the war, but not to depend upon it, as men must be averse to it—war may last 10 years.

Wilson. 1. Difficulties on every side—Question which the least.

2. No troops ever raised in a more glorious cause or more essential to themselves. Liberty, property and safety of their wives and children. Yet our troops the most expensive of any that were ever raised; and not under these circumstances to be had to man the lines.

Something then must be done.

1. The General proposes the enlisting troops during the war.

Objection.

Dangerous to have standing army

Objn. to the giving N. E. a sum for their defence.

1. May be too much or too little.

2. Suppose all the troops to land in N. E. Sum would be too small.

3. If the troops land in the other Colonies the sum may be too little.

4. His expedient is this. [1.] To fix the number of men during the campaign or war.

2. To (ascertain)? the pay at the lowest 5 dollars.

In proportion of the colonies to the [   ] [3] he would settle the quotas.

Chase. 1. Does not agree to give a particular sum to the New England Colonies.

2. The officers threaten to throw up their commissns unless the pay was advanced.

Tr (NN).

[1] Richard Smith's diary clearly demonstrates that the debates which Duane recorded here occurred this day. The debates themselves were sparked by one of Washington's three letters to Hancock of February 9. PCC, item 152, 1:477–80; and Washington, *Writings* (Fitzpatrick), 4:315–18.

[2] Sentence unfinished in MS.

[3] Blank in MS.

James Duane to Mary Duane

Philad. 22d Feb 1776.

I recd, my dearest Polly, your kind Letter dated in the present month. I think you have a Just Claim to set yourself down as a Patriot, since, for the good of your Country, you can consent to be seperated from your Husband. I assure you that your Spirit, upon this Occasion, has reliev'd me from part of the anxiety I sufferd. Our dear Father has also been pleasd to urge me to continue here for the same Reason which you suggest; and assures me he will take all necessary Care of my Family during my absence. I shall therefore endeavour to content myself a little longer. A great Share of Health Contributes to keep me in tolerable spirits, and a constant Scene of Business passes away the time almost imperceptibly, which woud otherwise hang heavily on my hands.

I look upon the City of New York to be at present in no great Danger. The Men of War have fallen down to some distance, & the Commanding Officer, I am well informd, does not wish nor mean to destroy it, so that my Books are safe enough under Dunscomb's Care. I shall however give him a particular Charge about them.

I agree with you that James was a most ungrateful villain, and that his Employers, whoever they were, ought to be detested by all honest Men.[1] No man can guard against the Infidelity of his Domestics. I leave him to the pangs of his own Conscience.

Be assurd that your Postscript gave me very great Pleasure. I entreat you to take the greatest Care of your Health, & to be easy and cheerful that our little Philadelphian may have nothing to discompose or disturb him.

Kiss and bless our little ones for me and present my affectionate Regards to all our Friends. Adieu my Dearest Polly, and believe to be unfeignedly, Your ever faithful & affece Husband,   Jas Duane

RC (NHi).
¹ Early in January 1776 James Brattle, Duane's valet, was detected passing on intelligence to New York governor William Tryon, who had induced him to act as a spy for the British. Brattle managed to escape from Philadelphia before he could be apprehended and tried. See Clark, *Naval Documents*, 3:698–700.

Richard Smith's Diary

[February 22, 1776]

Thursday 22. The minutes read. An Application was made from the Jersey Convention to know Whether the Battalion of Minute Men under Col. Charles Stewart and Lt. Col. Mark Thompson which are getting ready for N York at the Requisition of Gen Lee, shall march or not? and if so, desiring some Arms for them, after Debate the Battalion was countermanded.¹ Letters from Gen. Washington, Ld. Stirling and others were read & referred to a Comee. of the whole, Govr Ward in the Chair.² The General complains that he cannot get Men or Arms enough, that at least 2000 Men in his Camp are without Firelocks & the New England Men are averse to inlisting for a longer Term than One year & not fond of serving under any but Officers of their own choosing. Harison proposed that 3 Millions of Dollars shall be given Annually to the 4 New England Governments and they to carry on the War their own Way. After these Subjects had been argued and sundry Remedies proposed, the Comee. rose without Determination. The Companies of Waynes Regt. ordered to N York as fast as they can be got ready. Leave was given for the Colonels of several Regts. in Penna. to purchase Arms for their Corps & to draw for the Amount on the Comee. of Safety here which was on Motn. of Wilson. Paine and others wished a Comee. to be raised to consider of the speediest Methods of manufactg. Fire Arms in America, deferred.³

MS (DLC).
¹ On this point, see John Hancock to the New Jersey Provincial Convention, February 12, 1776; and *Am. Archives*, 4th ser. 4:1592–93.
² Washington's letters to Hancock of February 9 and enclosures are in PCC, item 152, 1:465–84; and Washington, *Writings* (Fitzpatrick), 4:311–18. Col. William Alexander's letter to Hancock of February 19 and enclosures are in PCC, item 162, 2:412–17; and *Am. Archives*, 4th ser. 4:1199–1200.
³ Congress established such a committee on February 23. *JCC*, 4:169.

Secret Committee Minutes of Proceedings

Com[mitte]e Ch[amber]. Feby. 23d 1776

At a Meeting Prest. Saml Ward, B. Franklin, J. Alsop, Robt. Morris, Jos. Hewes, Josa. Bartlett & Robt. Alexander. A Charter party with Blair McClenachan owner of the ship Hancock & Adams was executed. The Come. signd a letter to Mr. Schweeghauser, Also Instructon. to Capt. Saml. Smith. Orderd that Mr. R. Morris write to Mr. Jonathan Hudson, Baltimore & offer him 6s per bushell for wheat & 15s per 100 for flour on board the ship Molly, Danl. Laurence Mastr. & the Come. to pay him 14d. sterlg. per bushl. freight & 5s 6d per bbl to Cadiz, with customary additions if she goes further & to ensure the ship valued at £500 Cur[renc]y. Col. Roberdau to settle the Charter & value of the vessel he shall employ for the Continent.

At a meeting of the Come. Present Saml. Ward, B. Franklin, Josa. Bartlett, Robt. Morris, Jos. Hewes, & Jo. Alsop. A permit was granted to J. & Peter Chevalier to load the Ship Union with the produce &c (sheep &c) & export the same.

MS (MH).

Richard Smith's Diary

Friday 23 Feb. [1776]

The Votes read. Carter Braxton Esqr. from Virginia took his Seat. A Comee. of one from each Colony, Sergeant for N Jersey, was balloted for to superintend Saltpetre and Lead Matters & a Sett of Recommendations to all the Colonies on those Heads and to erect Powder Mills was passed, these were presented by John Adams and are ordered to be published. Ward Chairman of the Secret Comee. informed Congress that 2 of the Continental Vessels with Merchandize are taken by the British Men of War and desired to know Whether other Two shall be sent which was carried in the Affirmative after Debate. Application was made for the Discharge of 13 Servants inlisted in Capt. Harmans Compy. without Consent of their Masters, a Comee. of 3 was appointed to inquire into it. A Comee. of 5 was elected to encourage the manufacture of small Arms in all the Colonies. £600 in Gold ordered to be collected by the Treasurers for the Expences of our Ambassadors to Canada, J Adams presented a Sett of Instructions for them which were recomd. that some Matter may be added.[1] Debates about the several Powers of the Treasury Comee. and the Comee. of Claims and a Proposal for consolidating them took Rise from Duane's desiring Advice Whether the Public Accots. shall be settled in the Several Colonies by able Accountants employed by the Treasy. Comee. or whether the Accounts shall be sent here, the Members inclined to the latter but it was postponed.[2] The Two Stoves in our Room (the Assembly Room in the State House) were ordered by general Consent to be taken down as affecting the Health and Eyesight of the Members. Adjd. till Monday.

MS (DLC).

[1] See Smith's Diary, February 14, 1776, note 1.

[2] For Congress' resolution of this issue on April 1, see *JCC*, 4:243–46.

James Duane to Alexander McDougall

Sir   Philad. 25t. Feby 1776

I receivd your Favour of the 13th Instant which shoud sooner have been noticed had not other business put it out of my power. What I said to explain the motives of your Conduct was a debt of Justice; which I was bound to discharge both in my private Character as a Gentleman, and my publick one as a Delegate. To suffer the innocent to be misrepresented, when we have the Power of doing him Justice, is to partake, in my Opinion, of the Guilt of the Calumniator; & to cross the first Rule of true morality, which teaches us to do to others what, under the like Circumstances, we woud wish they shoud do to us. As a Representative of the Colony I was peculiarly Called upon to Justify an absent Fellow Citizen, and publick Officer, whose Reputation might have been unjustly sullied. I mention these particulars because I do not wish to claim a merit, where I have barely performed a Duty, incumbent upon every man who has the least pretension to Honour or Integrity. You may be assurd that whenever occasion requires it, I shall make a proper Use of the materials you now furnish. I shall have no Objection, in a personal Interview, to mention the Circumstances which led both to the Reflection and Information, tho' you may in the mean time rest assured that it proceeded from the Subject, & not From malice. The fact was true, but the Reasons which influenced you were unknown to the Speaker to whom I am perswaded you was a Stranger.[1]

Mr. Jay's absence and your Request authorized me to open the Letter directed to him of the same date.

Lieut Obrian's Evolutions were presented to Congress by Col. Morris before I had taken my Seat, which deprivd me of the opportunity of introducing the Treatise in the manner I intended.[2] Nobody seemd to be acquainted with the merit of the Author, and few, if any of us, are capable of Judging of it, was there Leisure to give it a perusal. Whether it will be reprinted at the publick expence Is not determind. Indeed Congress is so much employd in matters of immediate Necessity that there has been no time to give it Consideration.

I communicated your Remarks on the new Frigates to several members of the marine Committee, who assure me, that the models are free from the Objections you make, & that you will be convinced of it by a Recourse to the plan which accompanies Mr. Lewis.

I expected long since to have taken some Recess, as I hinted in my Letter to you; but our Representatives have all along been so slender, and the distance from my Family so great; that I coud not Justify it to myself. I hope When the Season becomes more pleasant, Mr. R. Livingston & Mr. Clinton who are infirm, will be able to attend, and that I shall be indulged with a Relaxation in some proportion to my long Confinement. My private affairs, which are hurrying fast into Ruin, really require some Attention, especially as I am engaged in expensive Buildings and Improvements, which are entirely left to the discretion of my workmen. I am Sir Your most huml Sevt

Jas. Duane

RC (NHi).

[1] For an explanation of Duane's assistance to McDougall, see Duane to McDougall, November 15, 1775, note.

[2] Christopher O'Bryen, *Naval Evolutions: or, A System of Sea-Discipline; Extracted from the Celebrated Treatise of P. L'Hoste, Professor of Mathematics, in the Royal Seminary of Toulon* ... (London: W. Johnston, 1762), a copy of which McDougall had sent to Lewis Morris on February 13. See Alexander McDougall to John Jay, February 13, 1776, in Clark, *Naval Documents*, 3:1257. Congress never authorized a reprinting of this treatise by Lieutenant O'Bryen of the Royal Navy.

James Duane to
the New York Provincial Convention

Gentlemen   Philad. 25 Feby 1776.

I have this moment receivd your favours of the 22d Instant.[1] The post who did not get in till near 7 oClock in the Evning, will be dispatched back so soon that I can have no opportunity, in the Interim, of confering with my Brethren, and one of the Subjects is too important to admit of delay. I therefore beg leave to give you my Sentiments upon it. If any thing further occurs, on a Consultation, it will be transmitted the next Conveyance.

General Schuyler, some time since, proposed to Congress that our second, or Albany Battalion, shoud be recruited for the Service of Canada and recommended the former Field Officers. Of this Congress approvd; and 12500 Dollars were forwarded to you for the dispatch of that Business.[2] The General in a subsequent Letter informd Congress that the money was sent to him, and seems to be uneasy that the Care of raising the Battalion shoud be superadded to the other Burthens of his Command.[3]

He mentions his Intentions of applying to the Committee of Albany for assistance on that Occasion: but what Progress has since been made we do not learn.

The Congress have also declard their Intention of promoting Capt Henry Livingston, who came Express from General Montgomerie with the News of the Surrender of Montreal, when an Opportunity shoud offer: but nothing has yet been done in his favour.[4]

A Resolution has since passed for raising four Battalions in New York for its immediate protection and Defence, of which you have receivd a Copy. It was followed by another that in the Appointment of their officers such as behavd well during the last Campaign shoud be provided for, a Copy of which has likewise been forwarded for your Direction.[5]

As New York was thought to be in a critical State, and no Recommendation had appeard from our Committee of Safety, of the officers for the four Battalions, it occasioned much Surprize and uneasiness; and the Apology I was able to make—vizt—The Expectation of a meeting of the Convention and the Utility of their Advice; which indeed depended on my own Conjecture, did not prove satisfactory. It was said that while every thing was done for New York at the publick Expence that coud be wished or asked, they neglected their own Defences &c. This produced a Resolution that an Enquiry shoud be made into your Progress with respect to those Battalions.[6] These Circumstances, if my memory has not failed, are all that have happend on This Subject, and which will suffice to convince you that there is no Obstruction in the way of your nominating the Field Officers agreeable to the recommendation of Congress.[7]

You will doubtless see the propriety of Dispatch both on Account of your Security, and your Reputation, both of which no Man can have more sincerely at Heart than myself.

Apprehensive that you might be distressed to maintain the Army now in our City Capital, from the lowness of your Finances, we thought it adviseable to obtain a warrant in your favour for 35000 Dollars which Mr Lewis receivd and will deliver you.[8]

I shoud do great Injustice to Congress, if I did not assure you that they are disposed to do every thing which can be reasonably requird for your Protection.

I have the Honour to be with the utmost Regard, Gent., Your most obedient & very humble Servant,   Jas. Duane

RC(N).
  [1] See the New York Provincial Congress' two letters to the New York delegates of February 22 in *Am. Archives*, 4th ser. 5:296, 301.
  [2] See *JCC*, 4:40, 74; and the second letter of the New York Delegates to the New York Committee of Safety dated January 27, 1776. See also General Schuyler's

letters to Hancock of December 8, 14, 21, 26, 1775. *Am. Archives*, 4th ser. 4:219–20, 260–61, 375–76, 463–64.

[3] See Schuyler's letter to Hancock of February 13. *Am. Archives*, 4th ser. 4:1130–32.

[4] On this point, see John Jay to Robert R. Livingston, Jr., December 19, 1775, note; and New York Delegates to the New York Provincial Congress, January 5, 1776, note 1.

[5] Congress approved these resolves on January 19 and February 17. *JCC*, 4:69, 158–59.

[6] See *JCC*, 4:167. The provincial congress described the steps it had taken to raise these four battalions in a letter to Duane of February 28, 1776. *Am. Archives*, 4th ser. 5:318n.

[7] At length the provincial congress submitted a list of nominees for field officers of these four battalions, in a letter to Hancock of February 28, and on March 8 Congress made the appointments on the basis of this list. See *JCC*, 4:182, 190; PCC, item 67, 1:180–86; and *Am. Archives*, 4th ser. 4:1530–31.

[8] Congress approved this appropriation on February 17. *JCC*, 4:159–60.

John Jay to Robert R. Livingston

Eliz. Town 25 Feb. 1776. Expresses concern about Livingston's health and the impact of the recent deaths of four of his close relatives. Goes on to discuss some rumors about certain New York delegates. "The ridiculous Story of your having been concerned in giving intelligence to Governor Tryon, I once or twice heard, but as I Never met with a single Person who gave the least Credit to it, and as it occasioned general Disgust and Indignation, I did not think it worthy of Notice, and therefore treated it with the Contempt it deserved.

"A Report of this Kind relative to Mr. Duane has long been extensive and serious.[1] It has given him much Concern, and tho I believe him to be innocent every Body does not. He told me I was coupled with him, & that the Report was against us both. A few Days Inquiry however made me perfectly easy, for neither myself nor my friends could find the least Trace of such Report respecting me. Mr. Duanes Author for it never appeared. Some of our Delegates & others indeed heard it, but they assured me from no other Person but Mr. Duane. It is natural for men to desire Company in Distress, and it sometimes happens that improper Means are used to gratify that as well as other Desires." Expects to "set off Tomorrow or next Day for Philadelphia."

RC (DLC). Addressed: "To Majr. Robert R. Livingston at Cler Mont."

[1] No other information is available about this allegation against Livingston, but at least one contemporary observer noted that Duane was suspected of complicity in the treachery of his valet, James Brattle. William Smith, *Historical Memoirs from 12 July 1776 to 25 July 1778 of William Smith,* . . . ed. William H. W. Sabine (New York: Colburn & Tegg, 1958), pp. 103–4. See also James Duane to Mary Duane, February 22, 1776, note.

Maryland Delegates to the Maryland Council of Safety

Gent.   Philadelphia 25th February 1776.
Mr. Alexander Ross, a Gentleman of our acquaintance, has applied
to Us to procure for him from Congress, a pasport to Lord Dunmore,
upon whom he says he has a very considerable claim, which he hopes
he shou'd be able to secure, cou'd he have an opportunity of making
a personal demand. From the multiplicity of business now before the
Congress an application of this kind wou'd be attended with great delay,
and as a licence from your Honorable Board will be at least as effectual,
We take the liberty of recommending him to your indulgence, being
well pursuaded he will religiously observe any injunctions you may
think proper to lay him under.[1]
We are Gentlemen, Your most obedt. servants,

J. Rogers

Robt. Alexander

RC (MdAA). Written by Alexander and signed by Alexander and Rogers.
[1] For further information on Ross, whose request was referred by the Maryland
Council of Safety to the Virginia Council of Safety, see *Md. Archives*, 11:185, 207–8,
332, 339, 384–85; and John Hancock to the Baltimore Committee of Safety, April 16,
1776, note.

Samuel Adams to Elizabeth Adams

My Dear   Philada Feby 26 1776
I have been impatiently waiting for a Letter from you. I think your
last was dated the 21st of January—you cannot do me a greater Pleasure
than by writing to me often. It is my Intention to make you a Visit
as soon as the Roads which are now excessively bad shall be settled.
Perhaps it may be not before April. I have tarried through the Winter,
because I thought my self indispensibly obligd so greatly to deny my
self. Some of my Friends here tell me that I ought not to think of leaving
this City at so critical a Season as the Opening of the Spring, but I am
happy in the Return of Mr Adams with Mr Gerry and in being assured
that my Absence from Duty for a short time may be dispensd with and
though I am at present in a good State of Health, the Jaunt may be
necessary for the Preservation of it. Whenever I shall have the pleasure
of seeing you, to me it will be inexpressible, and I dare say our Meeting,
after so long an Absence, will not be disagreeable to you.
I have nothing new to write to you. In one of your Letters you told
me that Dr C [1] had requested that I would sometimes write you on the

Politicks of this place, and that he might see my Letters of that kind. Pay my due Regards to the Doctor when you see him & tell him that I can scarsely find time to write you even a Love Letter. I will however for once give you a political Anecdote. Dr Smith Provost of the College here, by the Invitation of the Continental Congress, lately deliverd a funeral Oration on the gallant General Montgomery who fell at the Walls of Quebec. Certain political Principles were thought to be interwoven with every part of the oration which were displeasing to the Auditory. It was remarked that he could not even keep their Attention. A Circle of Ladies, who had seated themselves in a convenient place on purpose to see as well as hear the orator, that they might take every Advantage for the Indulgence of Griefe on so melancholly an Occasion, were observed to look much disappointed and chagrind. The next day a Motion was made in Congress for requesting a Copy for the Press. The Motion was opposed from every Quarter, and with so many Reasons that the Gentleman who made the Motion desired Leave to withdraw it. Such was the fate of that oration which is celebrated in the *Newspapers* of this City, perhaps by some one of the orators Friends for I will not presume that *he* was privy [*to*] the Compliment paid to it, as "*very animated and pathetick.*"

RC (NN). In Adams' hand, though not signed.
[1] That is, Samuel Cooper.

Josiah Bartlett to Meshech Weare

Sir   Philadelphia Febry 26th 1776
    The Enclosed order of Congress of the 23d inst I am Directed to transmit to our Colony, and I make no Doubt (if they have not already) they will Speedily Comply with the Recommendations.[1]
    The nec[e]ssity of arms & ammunition for our Defence, and the Danger of a Disappointment, Shews the necessity of using our utmost Efforts, to be Supplied as much as may be within our Selves. And tho I can with pleasure inform you, that large Quantities of powder and Salt petre have arrived here, and more is Dayly Expected, yet as we have reason to believe that as soon as the Spring opens, our harbours will be much infested by the Brittish Cruizers, who have orders to Seize all American vessels, and as large Quantities of military Stores will be wanted, for Sea, as well as land Service, I humbly Conceive it will be prudent to Endeavor to Supply our Selves, with the necessaries of life & Defence within our Selves and leave as little to the uncertainty of winds, weather & Enemies as possible, at least for the present.
    You will please Sir to See that the Several orders of our Convention or assembly for manufacturing arms, gunpowder & Salt petre be trans-

mitted to me, and an account of what has been Done in Consequence of such orders; as it is necessary the Congress should know as Soon as may be, the true State of all the Colonies with regard to their Supplying themselves with these necessary articles, and when our assembly meets you will please to lay these resolves before them and in the mean time Communicate them to the Council or Committe of Safety or who ever they have left to transact Business in their Recess. I am your most obedt Servant,   Josiah Bartlett

RC (MeHi).
[1] Undoubtedly the congressional resolutions asking provincial assemblies and conventions to encourage the manufacture of saltpetre, sulphur, and gunpowder. *JCC*, 4:170–71.

Benjamin Franklin's Proposed Resolution

A Motion   [February 26? 1776] [1]
Resolved, That from and after the 20th of July 1776 being one full Year after the Day appointed by a late Act of the Parliament of G. B. for restraining the Trade of the Confederate Colonies, all the Custom Houses in the said Colonies shall be shut up, and all the Officers of the same be discharged from the Execution of their several Functions, and all the Ports of the said Colonies are hereby declared to be thenceforth open [to] the Ships of every State in Europe that will admit our Commerce, and protect it, who may bring in and expose to Sale free of all Duties, their respective Produce & Manufactures, & every kind of Merchandize, excepting Teas, and the Merchandize of Great Britain, Ireland, and the British West India Islands.
Resolved, That we will to the utmost of our Power, maintain and support this Freedom of Commerce for two[2] Years certain, after its Commencement, and as much longer [as] the late Acts of Parliament for restraining the Commerce and Fisheries and altering the Laws & Charters of any of the Colonies shall continue unrepealed.[3]

MS (PPAmP). In the hand of Benjamin Franklin.
[1] This motion—another draft of which in PCC was first submitted July 21, 1775—was probably reintroduced early in 1776 and brought to a vote at this time. See Richard Smith's Diary, this date; Burnett, *Letters*, 1:364; *JCC*, 2:200; and forthcoming volume 22 of Franklin, *Papers* (Willcox), under date July ? 1775.
[2] Franklin first wrote "one," which he deleted in favor of "three" before settling on "two."
[3] The following comments, also in Franklin's hand, are found on the verso of this document. "Ready to receive Irish Woollens whenever they shall ascertain Methods of sending them free of all Imposition.
"Resolve—Not to treat separately.
"Resolve concerning the Power of Parliament to alter Constitutions.
"Difference has been whether we shall give our Money, or have it taken from us by Force, contrary to our Rights."

Secret Committee Minutes of Proceedings

Feby 26th. 1776.

At a meeting of the Come. Present S. Ward, J. Alsop, Josiah Bartlett, Robt. Morris & Jos. Hewes. A Charter party between the Come. & J. Brown & Co. of Philada. Merchts. was signd. Ordered that Mr. Robt. Morris ship a Cargoe of produce on board the Brigane. ———, Capt. Moore, for Carolina, the nett proceeds to be applied towds. the purchase of Rice, Indigo &c wch. he is orderd to ship from thence to Europe. Dr. Franklin afterwards present. An order issued to the Con-[tinenta]l Treasurers in favor of Robt. Irwin for 400 dlls on Acct. of the waggon service.

At a Meeting of the Come. Present Saml Ward, B. Franklin, Josa. Bartlett, J. Alsop, Robt. Morris & Jos. Hewes. A permit was granted to Mr. Jac[ob] Winey of this city Mercht. to load the ship King of Prussia with the produce of these Cols. for the benifit &c & agreeable to the Resolves &c.

MS (MH)

Richard Smith's Diary

Monday 26 Feb. [1776]

The Votes read, and a Letter from Gen Lee informg. that he will set out for Canada in a few Days, and a Letter from the Jersey Convention desiring Two more Battalions and Two Companies of Artillery may be raised there for the immediate Defence of the Province, this was referred to the Comee. on the Gens. Letters. 6000 Dollars advanced to Carpenter Wharton the Commissary. 22000 Dollars ordered to the Maryland Delegates to be exchanged for Gold and Silver in that Colony, £8000 being there offered on Delivery of the Paper Money. An Order passed after long Debate that all the Shipping in the United Colonies now bound to G Britain, Ireland or the British West Indies in Virtue or under Color of a former Resolve allowing Produce to be exported for importing Military Stores, shall be immedy. stopped till further Order & this resolution to be published, & the further Consideration of that Subject & whether the Custom Houses shall be shut up was referred to a Comee. of 5.[1] Agreed to pay a French Printers[2] Expences and to give Him 25 Half Joes to remove Himself, his Family and Types to Canada and there set up a free Press. A Bill from the Pay Master at Cambridge for 80,000 Dollars being presented for Acceptance was postponed.

MS (DLC).

¹ *JCC*, 4:172–73. For the resolves which Congress adopted on March 4 in response to this committee's report, see *JCC*, 4:183.

² Fleury Mesplet, for an account of whom, see Aegidius Fauteux, "Fleury Mesplet: une étude sur les commencements de l'imprimerie dans la ville de Montréal," Bibliographical Society of America, *Papers*, vol. 28, pt. 2 (1934), pp. 164–93.

Robert Alexander to
the Maryland Council of Safety

Gent.   Phila. 27 February 1776.

Your Letter by the Post is received, & on Application to Congress, they have ordered 22000 Dollars equal to £8250 to be advanced, this Money I shall receive & transmit you by the first safe Conveyance.¹ The Cartridge Paper I have purchased, 25 Reams part of the Quantity, shall be sent off by the Stage this Week, the residue will follow next Week, and I shall then furnish you with the Acct. The price is 16/ by the Ream. I called in Mr. Morris to know the Quantity of Arms & Powder imported by him for the Province, he was from home, his Clerk informed me about 400 Stand of Arms & 3500 lbs of Cannon powder. I have directed a Gent of Maryland now in this City to receive them & to forward them by the Stages to Elk from thence to send them in a Boat to Back River in Balt. Coty, with orders for the Skipper of the Boat to proceed to Balt. Town & there take Directions, in what manner to land them. I have taken this Precaution to avoid all Danger for should any Tender or armed Vessel be cruising in Patapsco River, the Boat can proceed to the Head of Back River & land the Arms & powder within five miles of the Town—if no Vessel of the Enemy, she can run round without any great Expence incurred by the Delay. Last night a Ship arrived here from Bristol which she left the 17th of Decr.² She cleared out for Cork to avoid Suspision, notwithstanding which, she was strictly searched & a Letter being discovered, directed to a Mercht in Philadelphia, the Ship was detained but the Letter being meerly on private Business, the Capt on his petition, was discharged & permitted to sail. Some Newspapers & private Letters are brought in. They were stowed away by a Passenger in the Bottom of a Barrel of Bread, which being placed in a careless Manner, as if for the Ships Use, it escaped the Search, one of the Letters was directed to Willing & Morris, without any Signature. It contained a printed Copy of my Lord North's *conciliatory Act* by which all American Vessels found on the Coasts of Great Britain or Ireland are to be seized & confiscated on the first Day of January—all American Vessels sailing into or out of the ports of America after the first of March are to be seized & confiscated—all foreign Vessels trading to America after the first of June to be seized—all Communication between Great Britain or Ireland or the British West Indies with America to be cut off—All Captures made by British Ships of War or by the Officers of the Kings Troops in America adjudged by this Act to be lawfull Prizes and as such Courts of Admiralty to proceed in their Condemnation—all orders for the Regulation of Courts of Admiralty in America, heretofore made by the King in Council or which may hereafter be made, are confirmed. The Boston Port Bill, the Fishery Bill, and the restraining Act are repealed by this Bill, the Colonies being in the like Circumstances & Situation. The last Clause of this more than diabolical Act enables the King to appoint Commissioners to grant Pardons & receive the Submissions of any Province, County, Town or District. I shall make no Comments on this Act, it is only a further Step in that System of Tyranny, hitherto persued by that ——— who under the Influence of a Scotch Junto now disgraces the British Throne. What Measures Congress may persue in Consequence of this Act, I know not; with me every Idea of Reconciliation is precluded by the Conduct of G. Britain, & the only Alternitave, absolute Slavery, or Independancy. The latter I have often repudiated both in publick & private, but am now almost convinced the Measure is right & can be justified by Necessity.[3] The Gent. who inclosed the Bill to W[illing] & M[orris] writes that 26000 Troops are to be employed in America, that a sufft. Body of Men are to defend Boston, while difft. Bodies are to attack New York, Virginia & South Carolina, that Lord Cornwallis is destined for the last Place with 5000 Men & was to sail in January. The Gent. adds the Minority gains Ground, that some of the Bedford Party had defeated Administration, that the Scotch Faction headed by Sr G. Elliot ostensibly, & by Lord Bute & Mansfield privately, directed & influenced the Councils & Measures of the Court.

I make no doubt you have heard Mr Chase is ordered to Canada. He sets off in a few Days. Mr Rogers has Leave of Absence, should he leave Congress, Maryld. will be without Representation. I mention this, to show the Necessity of your requesting Messrs. Johnson & Stone to attend. I wrote Mr Tilghman, but have not any Answer; Altho' my private Business requires my Presence in Maryland, I shall not leave this City, until a sufft number of my Brethren arrive.

I am with Respect Gent, Yr very Hble Servt,   R. Alexander

RC (MdAA).

[1] See the council's February 24 letter to the Maryland delegates, *Md. Archives*, 11:179; and *JCC*, 4:173.

[2] Robert Treat Paine's diary entry for February 26 reads: "Drizley raw Weather. This Evening a Ship arrived from Bristol, & brought the bill for empowering the Navy to Cruize on the Americans &c." MHi.

[3] Alexander's admission that he could almost justify independence on the ground of necessity is particularly interesting in light of the fact that within a few months he withdrew from public affairs and eventually became an avowed loyalist. See Janet B. Johnson, *Robert Alexander, Maryland Loyalist* (New York: G. P. Putnam's Sons, 1942), pp. 84–104.

Committee of Congress to
the Baltimore Committee of Observation

Gentlemen: Philada. Febry. 27th. 1776

We take the earliest Opportunity to send You the enclosed Resolution of Congress,[1] & to request your immediate attention thereto, & that You will inform Us of the Number & Circumstances of the Permits which have been granted & the Destination of the Vessells for Exporting the produce of the Colonies in Consequence of the Importation of Ammunition & warlike Stores. We are appointed to make Enquiry into this Subject.

We are Gent. Your obedt. Servts.   Duane   Levingston

Chase   Wythe

Wilson

P.S. A [. . .] arrived in the River, last Night from Hispaniola, with arms & powder—Qty unknown.

RC (MdHi). In the hand of Samuel Chase, who also added the names of the other delegates on the committee.

[1] For Congress' resolve "that no vessel loaded for Great Britain, Ireland, or the British West Indies, be permitted to sail until the further order of Congress," see *JCC*, 4:172–73.

Secret Committee Minutes of Proceedings

Com[mitte]e Ch[amber]. Feby. 27. 1776

At a meeting of the Come of Secy. Present Saml. Ward, Benj. Franklin, Thos. McKean, Josa. Bartlett, Robert Morris. A Charter party with Jacob Winey of this City, Merht., for the ship King of Prussia, Thos. Dowmen Master, was signd by the Come. A Charter party with Boyce, McIlvaine & Briges of this City, Merchts., for ship Grace, Jas. Irwine, Master, was also signd. Another with Mr. McClanachan & Jackson of [Philadelphia], Merchts., for ship Fame, [Hugh] Lisle Mastr., also signd.[1]

MS (MH).

[1] Robert Morris had been granted a permit to load the ship *Fame* on January 29, and on March 1 the committee issued a sailing permit for Captain Lisle. Journal of the Secret Committee, fols. 28, 40, MH.

Richard Smith's Diary

[February 27, 1776]
Tuesday 27. A Motion by E. Rutledge to countermand Gen. Lee's
Journey to Canada & send Him to command the Southern Colonies
was discussed & postponed till Tomorrow.[1] A report from a Comee.
was confirmed which divides the Country into 3 Military Districts each
to be commanded by some General Officers under the Commander in
Chief viz. the 4 N England Colonies in the Eastern District; N York,
N Jersey, Pennsa., Delaware and Maryland in the Middle District;
and the Colonies South in the Southern District; and it is understood
that Canada composes a 4th or Northern District. Some N England
Delegates urged to have N York in their District sed non Allocatur.
An Order passed requestg the Jersey Convention to secure the Ship
and Cargo at Elizabeth Town till further Direction.[2] Rob. Morris
produced Letters just recd. from Bristol[3] with a Copy of the Ministerial
Bill for seizing all American Ships which were read, One Letter says
their American Army will be about 25000 Strong, Part of it to be directed agt. the Southern Colonies, Part agt. N. York, that the Whigs
are under the Marquis of Rockingham and will desert Us if We aim
at Independency, otherwise not, that Commissioners are certainly
coming out to treat, that the Scotch Regiments in the Dutch Service
are engaged to come here. The Bill is very long & cruel. 100 Dollars
voted to a Canadian for his Assistance to Montgomys Troops and he is
to be recommended to the Commanding Officer in Canada.[4]

MS (DLC).
[1] See John Hancock to Charles Lee, March 1, 1776.
[2] The ship in question was the *Blue Mountain Valley*. See Smith's Diary, January 31,
1776; and Clark, *Naval Documents*, 3:959–60, 1012–14, 1200–1203, 4:140–41.
[3] See also Robert Alexander to the Maryland Council of Safety, this date.
[4] See *JCC*, 4:174.

John Hancock to Charles Lee

Sir   Philada. 28 Febry. 1776
    Your Letter of 22d Inst.[1] has been duly Rec'd & Referr'd to a Com-
mittee of Congress, who have not yet Reported thereupon. As soon as
the Congress have come to a Determination I shall do myself the
pleasure to Communicate the same to you. In the mean while I am
Directed to Desire you not to set out for Canada, untill you Receive
further orders from Congress.[2] I have the honour to be, Sir, Your obedt
hume servt,   J H Prest.

LB (DNA: PCC, item 12A).

¹ This letter was read in Congress on February 26 and is in PCC, item 158, 1:25–28, and *Am. Archives*, 4th ser. 4:1475–76. See *JCC*, 4:172.

² On March 1, Congress placed Lee in command of the southern department. *JCC*, 4:175, 180–81. See also Hancock to Charles Lee, March 1, 1776.

Richard Smith's Diary

Wednesday 28 Feb. [1776]

Votes read. 20,000 Dollars advanced to Commissary Mease. A report was delivered in by J Adams that 5000 Troops be kept up at N York, that 2 more Battalions and 2 Artillery Comps. be raised in Jersey &c, it was put off.¹ A Report made by Wyth on Gen Schuylers Letters was partly agreed to, by one Article of it the Jersey Delegates are desired to send the General a Quantity of Steel. E Rutledge renewed his Motion to send Gen Lee to the Southward; it was postponed but Mr. Lee is to stay his Journey to Canada till further Order. Wilson made a partial Report about the Captives which was confirmed, by Part of it the Comees. of Observation and Inspection where Prisoners are stationed are to oversee them and imprison them if their Behavior deserves it. A Petition from a Frenchman² who has brot. Half a Ton of Powder and the rest of his Cargo in Molasses &c for Leave to export Produce to the Amount of his whole Cargo was argued and the Prayer granted under the Conditions that several other Foreign Vessels have had.

MS (DLC).

¹ Congress rejected this report on March 1. See *JCC*, 4:181n.3; and Smith's Diary, March 1, 1776.

² Anthony Marmajou. *JCC*, 4:176.

Richard Smith's Diary

[February 29, 1776]

Thursday 29. Mr. Whipple of New Hampshire took his Seat. The Minutes read as was a Letter from Gen. Washington inclosing a Letter from Lord John Drummond to Gen. Robertson wherein his Lordship of his own Accord, takes Steps for a Treaty & desires Passports for Commissioners on the Part of the Congress.¹ 4 Hours were spent in Grand Comee. on Trade without any Conclusion,² by a former Resolve Trade opens Tomorrow under the Restrictions of the Association. The Points now agitated were the Expediency & Probability of contracting foreign Commercial Alliances and chiefly with France and Spain,³ and the Advantages and Disadvantages of attempting to carry on Trade in our present Circumstances, much was said about declaring our Independency on G Britain when it appeared that 5 or 6 Colonies have instructed their Delegates not to agree to an Independency till they, the Principals, are consulted, the President (Hancock) moved that Madeira Wine may be imported notwithstanding the Association, he meant to please the Southern Delegates who insist on having Wine, but no Question was put upon it. Hewes had a Petition from a Foreigner who has imported Military Stores, praying Leave to load with Produce but Congress adjorned in the Moment of Presentation.

MS (DLC).
  [1] See Lord Drummond's Notes, January 3–9? 1776, note 1.
  [2] See Smith's Diary, January 12, 1776, note 1.
  [3] On these points, see also John Adams' Notes on Foreign Alliances, March 1, and his Notes on Relations with France, March 4? 1776.

John Adam's Notes on Foreign Alliances

1776 March 1.
   How is the Interest of France and Spain affected, by the dispute between B[ritain] and the C[olonies]?[1] Is it the Interest of France to stand neuter, to join with B. or to join with the C. Is it not her Interest, to dismember the B. Empire? Will her Dominions be safe, if B. and A[merica] remain connected? Can she preserve her Possessions in the W.I? She has in the W.I. Martinico, Guadaloupe, and one half of Hispaniola. In Case a Reconciliation should take Place, between B. and A. and a War should break out between B. and France, would not all her Islands be taken from her in 6 Months?
   The Colonies are now much more warlike and powerfull than they were, during the last War. A martial Spirit has Seized all the Colonies. They are much improved in Skill and Discipline. They have now a large Standing Army. They have many good officers. They abound in Provisions. They are in the Neighbourhood of the W.I. A British Fleet and Army united with an American Fleet and Army and supplied with Provisions and other Necessaries from America, might conquer all the French Islands in the W.I. in six Months, and a little ⟨less⟩ more Time than that would be required, to destroy all their Marine and Commerce.

MS (MHi). Adams, *Diary* (Butterfield), 2:235.
  [1] Adams probably organized these thoughts on foreign alliances in the aftermath of a four-hour debate in Congress on February 29 on "the Expediency and Probability of contracting foreign Commercial Alliances and chiefly with France and Spain, and the Advantages and Disadvantages of attempting to carry on Trade in our present Circumstances." When it became apparent to the delegates that a decision in favor of a foreign alliance would inevitably lead to a declaration of independence, debate in Congress ended because "it appeared that 5 or 6 Colonies have instructed their Delegates not to agree to an Independency till they, the Princi-

pals are consulted." Richard Smith's Diary, February 29, 1776. Subsequently, Adams prepared a resolution, based on the instructions of the Massachusetts Assembly to its delegates in Congress, that would recommend "to the several Assemblies and Conventions of these united Colonies, who have limited the Powers of their Delegates in this Congress, by any express Instructions, that they repeal or suspend those Instructions for a certain Time, that this Congress may have Power, without any unnecessary Obstruction or Embarrassment, to concert, direct and order, such further Measures, as may seem to them necessary for the Defence and Preservation, Support and Establishment of Right and Liberty in these Colonies." *Am. Archives,* 4th ser. 4:1266; and Adams, *Diary* (Butterfield) 2:236–37. See also John Adams' Notes on Relations with France, March 4? 1776.

John Alsop, Philip Livingston, Francis Lewis and Robert Morris to Silas Deane

Sir   Philada. March 1st 1776

We deliver you herewith one part of a Contract made with the Secret Committee of Congress for exporting Produce of these Colonies to Europe & Importing from France Certain Articles suitable for the Indians. The first part of this business we have undertaken and shall accomplish it as soon as possible by Shipping Cargoes to the Markets they are best adapted for & ordering the Consignees to remit the proceeds to the following Houses Vizt Messrs. Saml & J. H. Delap in Bourdeaux, Messrs. Geo. Clifford & Teysett in Amsterdam, Mr. John Hodgshon in Amsterdam.

We think it prudent thus to divide the remittances that none of the Houses may know the Extent of your Commission but each of them will have orders to Account with you for the Amount of what comes into their hands for this purpose & to hold the same Subject to your drafts & orders. On your part you are immediately to repair to France for the Execution of that part of this Contract which by our private agreement you have undertaken.[1] We deliver you herewith Sundry letters of introduction to respectable Houses in France which we hope will place you in the respectable light you deserve to appear & put you on a footing to purchase the Goods wanted on the very best terms. We deliver you herewith an Invoice of the Goods wanted which has been inspected & approved by the Secret Committee. We hope you will readily & expeditiously procure every article wanted, & immediately Shipped in such manner as you judge most likely to answer the purpose of getting them safe landed in some of the United Colonies of North America. You will transmit to the Secret Committee Bills of Loading & invoices for every parcell of Goods you remit & as the Brigt Rachell has been Chartered for the express purpose of Carrying you to France and for bringing back a part of these Goods, We deliver you herewith a letter from the Secret Committee to Capt Isherwood directing him to

obey your orders. Therefore you can deliver it whenever you see proper
to disclose yourself to him. The Vessel is on Monthly pay. Therefore the
sooner you dispatch her back the better & you will give this Captain
and all others suitable directions for approaching this Coast on their
return with circumspection.[2] We are, Sir, Your hble servants,

John Alsop, for Self

Phil Livingston and

Francis Lewis

Robt Morris

P.S. Youl please to supply Capt Isherwood with Money to pay the
Brigt Rachells charges & transmit his receipt for the amount.

ENCLOSURE

Be it remembered that it is agreed by and between John Alsop, Francis
Lewis and Philip Livingston of the City of New York—Merchants and
Silas Deane of the Colony of Connecticut, merchant—and Robert
Morris of the City of Philadelphia, merchant, of the one part, and
Samuel Ward, Benjamin Franklin, Thomas McKean, Joseph Hewes,
Josiah Bartlett and Robert Alexander, Esqrs, members of the Com-
mittee of Secresy appointed by the Hon. Continental Congress of the
thirteen United States of North America, of the other part as follows—
to wit.[3]

That the sum of 200,000 Dollars, continental money now advanced
and paid by the said Committee of Secresy to the said John Alsop,
Francis Lewis, Philip Livingston, Silas Deane and Robert Morris, shall
be laid out by them in the produce of these Colonies and shipped on
board proper vessels, to be by them chartered for that purpose, to some
proper port or ports in Europe (Great Britain and the British Isles excepted) and there disposed of on the best terms. And the neat proceeds
of such cargoes laid out in such goods, wares or merchandise as the said
Committee of Secrecy shall direct and shipped for the said United
Colonies to be landed in some convenient harbor or place within the
same and notice thereof given as soon as conveniently may be to the
said Committee of Secrecy.

For which the said John Alsop, Francis Lewis, Philip Livingston,
Silas Deane and Robert Morris shall be allowed five per. ct. for purchasing the cargo here; and also to such of said contractors as shall go
personally to Europe to execute and superintend this business—exclusive of the charges of selling the produce and manufactures of these
Colonies, to be exported as aforesaid, and for shipping the remittances,
besides the duties, a clear commission of five per. ct. on the original
cost of such remittances in Europe, the said United Colonies running

the whole risk of the said adventure, being for their benefit and advantage, and also insuring such vessels against all British seizures and captures.

Witness our hand this 19th day of February in the year of our Lord, one thousand, seven hundred and seventy six, at Philadelphia—

Witness, John Legg.

John Alsop for self and	Samuel Ward
Philip Livingston	Benjamin Franklin
Francis Lewis	Thomas McKean
Robert Morris	Joseph Hewes
Silas Deane	Josiah Bartlett
	Robert Alexander.

RC (CtHi). In the hand of Robert Morris and signed by Morris and Alsop. The names of Livingston and Lewis were affixed by Alsop. This letter was written to Deane by the signatories in their capacity as fellow contractors for importing Indian trade goods rather than as members of the Secret Committee. Enclosure: reprinted from *NYHS Collections* 19 (1886): 117–18.

[1] For the political aspects of Deane's mission to France, see Committee of Secret Correspondence Minutes of Proceedings, March 2, 1776.

[2] Deane left Philadelphia on March 8, embarking from Chester, Pa., in the brigantine *Rachell* bound for Bordeaux on March 10. After being delayed by head winds, Deane was "running down the [Delaware] Bay" on March 16, but an accident at sea forced him to return to Philadelphia. On March 27 the Secret Committee ordered Robert Morris to dispatch the sloop *Betsey* for Deane's passage to Bermuda. Deane's reembarkation was threatened by the arrival of the *Roebuck*, a 44-gun British warship, at the mouth of the Delaware, but he apparently left Philadelphia in the sloop *Betsey* on April 3, accompanied by a military guard. After being convoyed down the bay by the schooner *Wasp*, the *Betsey* cleared the capes on the 13th and arrived in Bermuda on April 24. After completing his business there, Deane sailed for France on May 3 and arrived at Bordeaux on June 6. See Robert Morris' letters to Deane of March 30, April 4, and 8; John Hancock to the Commanding Officer, April 3, 1776; Clark, *Naval Documents*, 4:367, 802, 1274–79, 1399–1400; and *NYHS Collections* 23 (1890): 245–47.

[3] See Secret Committee Minutes of Proceedings, February 20, 1776.

James Duane to William Alexander

Dear Sir,   Philad. 1 March 1776

I am afraid you will suspect I have been unmindful of your Request when last here, and of your Interest: but I beg you will be assured that Inattention to my Friends is one of the Vices of which I feel myself incapable.

The first opportunity I have embraced to solicit your promotion, in which I was so happy as to be supported by my Friends. Your Lordship is accordingly appointed a Brigadier General for the middle Department comprehending New York, New Jersey, Pensylvania, the lower Counties and Maryland. The Colonies to the Southward; the four Eastern Provinces; and Canada form the other three Departments. It is now determined that General Lee shall command in the Southern Department, where an immediate Attack is expected. The debates of this day did him singular Honour, and evincd the Confidence the Congress place in his Zeal and Abilities. He was given up to the Southern Colonies, as the most exposed, with great Reluctance. General Schuyler with Brigadier General Thompson & yourself are destined for the middle Department. The Commander in Chief for Canada remains to be fixed upon, and is a Subject of some perplexity, as well as of very great Importance.[1] It was the anxious wish, and earnest advice, of our much lamented Friend Montgomerie that he shoud be succeeded by General Lee, but the Situation of our affairs has prevented it. General Schuyler's very precarious State of Health, and the Danger to which his native province is exposed, will, we suppose, make the disposition respecting him very agreeable.[2] Present my respectful Compliments to him and to General Lee and believe me to be with great Regard, My Lord, Your Lordship's Affect. Nephew, & most obedt Sert,

Jas. Duane

RC (NHi).
[1] Congress appointed Gen. John Thomas to this command and promoted him to major-general on March 6. See *JCC*, 4:186; and John Hancock to John Thomas, March 6, 1776.
[2] See *JCC*, 4:157; and John Hancock to Philip Schuyler, February 20, 1776.

John Hancock to William Alexander

My Lord,   Philadelphia March 1t. 1775 [*i.e.* 1776].
I do myself the Honour of enclosing to you a Commission of Brigadier General in the Continental Army.[1] From the high Opinion the Congress entertain of your Zeal and Attachment to the American Cause, they flatter themselves you will do every Thing in your Power to discharge your Duty to your Country on this important Occasion. I have it in Charge from Congress to direct that you continue at New York, until further Orders. I have the Honour to be, My Lord, your Lordship's, most obedt. & very hble Servt.   J.H. Prst.

LB (DNA: PCC, item 12A).
[1] Alexander was one of six brigadier generals appointed by Congress on March 1. *JCC*, 4:181. Hancock wrote letters transmitting commissions to Robert Howe, Andrew Lewis, and James Moore on March 1, and to John Armstrong and William Thompson on March 2. PCC, item 12A.

John Hancock to Charles Lee

Dear Sir   Philadelphia March 1st. 1776

After a warm Contest occasion'd by the high Estimation the Members of Congress have of your worth and Abilities, every one wishing to have you where he had most at Stake, The Congress have at Length Determin'd to Superceed the orders given you to proceed to Canada, and have this day come to a Resolution that you shall take the Command of the Continental Forces in the Southern Departmt. which Comprehends Virginia, North Carolina, South Carolina & Georgia.[1]

The Congress have also Appointed Six new Brigadiers General, Vizt. John Armstrong, William Thompson, Andrew Lewis, James Moore, Lord Stirling and Robert Howe Esqrs. four of whom are to Command under you in the Southern Departmt. and two in the middle.[2] By this Conveyance I have forwarded the Commission for his Lordship. As soon as your Health & the necessary orders you may think proper to give for putting New York in a state of Defence will permitt, I have it in Charge to Direct that you Repair to the Department put under your immediate Command.

In Expectation of Seeing you soon in this place on your way, I need not add; but that I am with every Sentiment of Regard & Esteem, Sir, Your most Obed servt,   J H Prest.

LB (DNA: PCC, item 12A).

[1] Congress had intermittently debated a motion to transfer Lee to the southern command since February 27, 1776. *JCC*, 4:180–81; and Richard Smith's Diary, February 27 and 28, 1776.

[2] Armstrong, Howe, Lewis, and Moore were assigned to General Lee's southern command, while Alexander and Thompson were assigned to the middle department. *JCC*, 4:181.

Joseph Hewes to Samuel Johnston

Dear Sir   Philadelphia 1st March 1776

The Congress have this moment determined that General Lee shall repair to the Southwd. to take upon him the Command of the forces in Virga., North & South Carolina & Georgia which are included in the Southern district. We have also this moment appointed Six Brigadier Generals to rank as they stand below in the Continental Service after the others that have been heretofore appointed. Armstrong is to go to South Carolina, Moore to stay in No. Carolina, Lewis & Howe in Virginia till Gen. Lee shall direct otherwise.[1] Hooper is not yet returned from Boston, I expect him every moment.[2] Penn is now writing to the Council of Safety which Letter I shall sign for Hooper & self.[3]

An express is now waiting, he is sent to So. Carolina by the delegates of that Province to inform them of this days appointments and of the Critical state of Mr. Lynch's health who a few days ago had an apoplectic stroke and is now in great danger. We shall send off another Waggon in a day or two with what Powder the new Waggon left, also drums & Colours for your third Regiment. I am in haste, Dr Sir, Your mo. Obedt Sevt,   Joseph Hewes

John Armstrong ⎫
William Thompson ⎪
Andrew Lewis ⎪
James Moore   ⎬ Brigadier Generals
Lord Stirling   ⎪
Rob. Howe   ⎭

N.B. The new Waggon went of[f] eight days ago. I hear it is now no further than Wilmington, that One of the best Horses cut one of his hind feet very much with his shoe and cannot proceed. I have this day sent a carefull person down to purchase another Horse and bring the lame one back if it should be found Necessary. Never was any person more unfortunate than I have been in executing your Order respecting the Waggon &c. Of this more per next oppty.   J. H.

RC (Nc-Ar).
  [1] See *JCC*, 4:180–81.
  [2] For an explanation of William Hooper's absence from Congress at this time, see his first letter to Joseph Hewes and John Penn of February 6, 1776, note 1.
  [3] Not found.

Richard Smith's Diary

Friday 1 March [1776]

The Votes read & Letters from New Hampshire about a Dispute there on their setting up an Independent Form of Government, these were committed to 3.[1] The Report for raising 2 more Regiments & 2 Artillery Companies in N Jersey was considered & rejected.[2] Some Quæries of Commissary Mease were referred to a Comee. of 3.[3] A Comee. of 3 was appointed to [   ].[4] Six new Brig. Generals were chosen by Ballot viz 1 Armstrong of Pennsa., 2 Thompson of Pennsa. now at Cambridge, 3 Lewis of Virginia, 4 Moore of N Carolina, 5 Ld. Stirling, 6 Howe of N. Carola. and their Stations assigned in the Middle and Southern Departments. Armstrong is to go to Virginia & together with Lewis, Moore & Howe to be under the Direction of Gen. Lee who was now voted to Command to the Southward. Thompson is to join

Ld. Stirling at N. York. An Addition was made to the Salary of Joseph Reed Esq. Secry to Gen. Washington, he had before 66 Dollars per month, it was now made 100 under Pretence that he is obliged to act as Secry. to the Naval Departmt. too, this was on Motion of Harrison. A Chest full of Accots. transmitted from the Assembly or Government of Mass. Bay hither for Settlemt. was referred to the Comee. of Claims, a Person attends from thence to explain them.[5] A Petition was presented but not now acted upon, from a large Number of Philadelphians prayg the Congress to grant Leave for Privateers and Letters of Marque to seize the Ships of G Britain, Ireland and the other British Dominions.[6] Adjd. till Monday.

MS (DLC).
[1] See Josiah Bartlett to Meshech Weare, March 2, 1776, note 2.
[2] See Smith's Diary, February 28, 1776, note 1.
[3] Commissary James Mease's letter to Hancock of February 29 is in PCC, item 78, 15:15–18, and *Am. Archives*, 4th ser. 4:1537. No report by this committee has been found, but for a resolve which Congress adopted on March 18 that may have been related to Mease's letter, see *JCC*, 4:211.
[4] Blank in MS. Doubtless a reference to the committee considering a petition from the people of Falmouth. *JCC*, 4:179.
[5] See Elbridge Gerry to James Warren, March 6, 1776, note 4.
[6] See Smith's Diary, February 13, 1776, note 4.

Josiah Bartlett to Meshech Weare

Sir   Philadelphia March 2nd. 1776
Yours of the 8th ulto per Col. Whipple I Recd the 28th and am glad to be informed of the Spirited behaviour of our Colony in raising a Regiment for Canada without waiting for the order of Congress.[1]
The Several matters relative to our Colony affairs, are according to order laid before Congress, as Soon as a Determination is had I hope to be the bearer of them myself to you.[2]
I am very Sorry for the unhappy Difficulties in our Colony at a time when we have nothing to expect from our inveterate Enemies but war and Bloodshed notwithstanding their hipocritical pretences of treating & Reconcilliation to amuse us. I pray God we may not be taken in the Snare. I am your most obedt Servant,   Josiah Bartlett

P.S. I Should have wrote more largely but the post this minute is Setting off.   J. B.

RC (Nh-Ar).
[1] See Meshech Weare to John Hancock, February 8, 1776. PCC, item 64, fols. 5–6; and *Am. Archives*, 4th ser. 4:964. It was read in Congress on March 4. *JCC*, 4:183.

[2] The assumption of full powers by the revolutionary government in New Hampshire met surprising resistance in January 1776. Opponents secured a January 27 vote in the House to direct the Committee of Safety to petition Congress, lay the plan of government before them, and "Let them Know that a Number of the Members of this House Dissented to & Protested against the same; Supposing it breathed too much of the Spirit of Independence; and to know the judgement of the Congress thereon." *N.H. Provincial Papers*, 8:65. The documents prepared by the Committee of Safety, dated February 10, 1776, are in *Am. Archives*, 4th ser. 4:996–97. These papers were read in Congress on March 1 and referred to a committee of George Wythe, Carter Braxton, and Benjamin Franklin. *JCC*, 4:179. The committee read its report on March 7, but neither the contents of the report nor any further action by Congress is recorded. *JCC*, 4:189. See also William Whipple to Meshech Weare, April 12, 1776. On May 10, 1776, Congress passed a resolution urging all provinces to "adopt such government as shall, in the opinion of the representatives of the people, best conduce to the happiness and safety of their constituents in particular, and America in general." *JCC*, 4:342.

Committee of Secret Correspondence
Minutes of Proceedings

March 2d. 1776

The Committee met, VIZ, Coll Harrison, Mr Dickenson, Mr Morris, Mr Franklin.[1]

Agreed upon the Instructions to Mr Deane, & signed them. Also signed & sealed a Certificate that Mr Deane is authorized by the Committee, which Instrument follows in these words.[2]

We the Underwritten, being the Committee of Congress for secret Correspondence, do hereby certify whom it may concern, that the Bearer Mr Silas Deane is appointed by us to go into France, there to transact such business commercial & political, as we have committed to his Care, in behalf & by Authority of the Congress of the thirteen United Colonies.

In testimony whereof, we have hereunto set our hands & Seals at Philadelphia, this 2d day of March 1776.

Instructions for Silas Deane, Esqr.[3]

On your arrival in France you will for some little Time be engaged in the Business of providing goods for the Indian Trade. This will give good Countenance to your appearing in the Character of a Merchant, which we wish you continually to retain among the French in general, it being probable that the Court of France may not like it should be known publickly, that any Agent from the Colonies is in that Country.

When you come to Paris, by delivering Doctor Franklin's Letters to Monsr Le Roy——— [4] and Monsr Dubourg,[5] you will be introduced to a Set of acquaintance, all Friends to the American Cause.

By conversing with them, you will have a good Opportunity of learning the Parisian French & you will find in Monsr Dubourgh, a Man prudent, faithful, secret, intelligent in Affairs, & capable of giving you very sage advice. It is scarce necessary to pretend any other business at Paris, than the gratifying of that Curiosity which draws Numbers thither yearly, meerly to see so famous a City.

With the Assistance of Monsr Dubourg, who understands English, you will be able to make immediate Application to Monsr De Vergennes, Minister &c[6] either personally or by a Letter, if Monsr Dubourg advises that method, acquainting him, that you are in France upon Business for the American Congress in the Character of a Merchant—That having something to communicate to him that may be mutually beneficial to France & the Colonies, you request an Audience of him, & that he would be pleased to appoint the Time & Place.

At this Audience, if agreed to, it may be well to show him first your Letter of Credence, & then acquaint him, that the Congress finding that in the common course of Commerce, it was not practicable to furnish the Continent of America with the Quantities of Arms & Ammunition necessary for its defence (the Ministry of Great Britain having been extremely industrious to prevent it) you had been dispatched by their Authority to apply to some European Power for a supply.

That France had been pitched upon for the first Application, from an Opinion that if we should (as there is great Appearance we shall), come to a total Seperation from Great Britain, France would be looked upon as the Power, whose Friendship it would be fittest for us to obtain & cultivate—That the Commercial Advantages, Britain had enjoyed with the Colonies had contributed greatly to her late Wealth & Importance.

That it is likely great part of our Commerce will naturally fall to the Share of France, especially if she favors us in this Application, as that will be a means of gaining & securing the friendship of the Colonies— And, that as our Trade rapidly increasing with our Increase of People & in a greater proportion, her part of it will be extremely valuable.

That the supply we at present want is Cloathing & Arms for 25,000 Men, with a suitable Quantity of Ammunition & 100 field pieces—That we mean to pay for the same by Remittances to France, Spain, Portugal & the French Islands, as soon as our Navigation can be protected by ourselves or Friends, & that we shall besides want great Quantities of Linens & Woolens, with other Articles for the Indian Trade, which you are now actually purchasing & for which you ask no Credit; & that the whole (if France should grant the other supplies) would make a Cargoe, which it might be well to secure by a Convoy of two or three Ships of War.

If you should find Monsr De Vergennes reserved & not inclined to enter into free conversation with you, it may be well to shorten your Visit, request him to consider what you have proposed, acquaint him with your place of lodging, that you shall stay yet some time at Paris &

that knowing how precious his Time is, you do not presume to ask another Audience.

But that if he should have any Commands for you, you will upon the least Notice, immediately wait upon him.

If at a future Conference, he should be more free & you find a Disposition to favor the Colonies, it may then be proper to acquaint him, that they must necessarily in your Opinion[7] be anxious to know the disposition of France on certain points, which with his Permission, you would mention—Such as, whether, if the Colonies should[8] form themselves into an Independent State, France would probably acknowledge them as such, receive their Ambassadors, enter into any Treaty or Alliance with them, for Commerce, or defence, or both? If so, on what principal Conditions? Intimating, that you shall speedily have an Opportunity of sending to America, if you do not immediately return.

And that he may be assured of your fidelity & Secrecy in transmitting carefully any thing he would wish conveyed to the Congress on that Subject.

In subsequent Conversations, you may as you find it convenient enlarge on these Topics that have been the Subject of our Conferences with you, to which you may add occasionally, the well known substantial Answers, we usually give to the several Calumnies thrown out against us.

If these Supplies on the Credit of the Congress should be refused, you are then to endeavour obtaining a permission of purchasing & exporting those Articles, or as much of them, as you can find credit for.

You will keep a daily Journal of all your material Transactions & particularly of what passes in your conversation with great personages; and you will by every safe Opportunity furnish us with such Information, as may be important.

When your business in France will admit it, it may be well to go into Holland & visit our Agent there, at Monsr Dumas's, conferring with him on Subjects that may promote our Interests & on the means of Communication.

You will endeavour to procure a Meeting with Mr Bancroft,[9] by writing a Letter to him under cover to Mr ———— [10] & desiring to come over to you in France, or Holland, on the Score of old acquaintance.

From him you may obtain a good deal of Information of what is now going forward in England & settle a mode of continuing a Correspondence.

It may be well to remit him a small Bill for defraying his Expences in coming to you. Avoid all political Matters in your Letter to him.

You will also endeavour to correspond with   [11] Esqr. Agent of the Colonies, in London. You will endeavour to obtain an acquaintance with Monsr Garnier   [12] if now in France, or if returned to England, a Correspondence with him, as a person extremely *intelligent* & friendly to our Cause. From him you may learn many particulars occasionally, that will be useful to us.

Dated at Philadelphia, this second day of March, 1776.

signed
B Franklin	John Dickenson
B Harrison	Robt Morris
John Jay	

Tr (CtY).

¹ John Jay's name was apparently omitted inadvertently, since he signed the two documents agreed upon at this meeting of the committee.

² This "Instrument," in the hand of Jay, and signed and sealed by Jay, Dickinson, Franklin, Harrison, and Morris, is in the Deane Papers, NHi.

³ The following "Instructions" were communicated to Deane in the form of a letter from the committee dated March 3, which has been printed in Jared Sparks, ed., *The Diplomatic Correspondence of the American Revolution*, 12 vols. (Boston: N. Hale & Gray & Bowen, 1829–30), 1:5–9. Variations between the instructions contained in that letter and the committee's minutes are noted below.

⁴ "At the Louvre," in Sparks, 1:6. Jean-Baptiste Le Roy (1720–1800), French physicist and member of the Académie des sciences, with whom Franklin had begun an extended correspondence in 1768 that resulted in a warm friendship during Franklin's later years in France. See Benjamin Franklin, *The Papers of Benjamin Franklin*, ed. Leonard W. Labaree (New Haven: Yale University Press, 1959–), 10:61n, 15:82.

⁵ Jacques Barbeu-Dubourg (1709–79), French physician and intellectual, who had prepared a French edition of Franklin's works in 1773. Alfred O. Aldridge, "Jacques Barbeu-Dubourg, a French Disciple of Benjamin Franklin," *Proceedings of the American Philosophical Society* 95 (1951): 331–92.

⁶ "*Ministre des Affaires Etrangères*" in Sparks, *Diplomatic Correspondence*, 1:6.

⁷ "In your Opinion" deleted in Sparks, 1:8.

⁸ "Be forced to" inserted in Sparks, 1:8.

⁹ Edward Bancroft (1745–1820), American physician and chemist, who since 1767 had been living in London where he had become acquainted with Franklin. Entering the employ of the British secret service in 1776, he subsequently enjoyed a long and successful career spying on American commissioners in Paris, who employed him in various capacities throughout the war. See Julian P. Boyd, "Silas Deane: Death by a Kindly Teacher of Treason?" *WMQ* 16 (1959): 176–87, 319–29ff.

¹⁰ "Griffiths at Turnham Green, near London," inserted in Sparks, 1:9.

¹¹ "Mr. Arthur Lee" in Sparks, 1:9.

¹² "Late *Chargé des Affaires de France en Angleterre*," in Sparks, 1:9. Charles Jean Garnier (1738–83?). See Adams, *Diary* (Butterfield), 2:298n.3.

William Whipple to Meshech Weare

Sir,   Philadelphia, March 2d, 1776.

I arriv'd here the 28th Ulto, the Roads were so extreem bad it was impossible for me to get here sooner. The Papers which Capt. Long gave me sealed up & directed to the President, I delivered on my arrival; they were yesterday read in Congress & referr'd to a Committee.¹

My Colleague talks of leaving in about a fortnight; by that time I hope shall be able to forward the determination of Congress on the Petition for a Battalion.[2] If your delegates could have been furnish'd with an estimate of the Colonial expences they might have improved them to advantage; but you may be assur'd we shall do the best we can without them; but I beg the acct may be sent forward as soon as possible, or if the acct cannot be got ready let me be furnished with an estimate both of the Continental & Provincial charges.

I was much surprised to find there was no instructions among the Papers given me by Capt. Long—not a word about the Purchasing the Flour which was so much talked of when I was last with the Committee. If anything of that sort is to be done I sho'd be glad to be advised of it as soon as possible, for no doubt the Risque increases with the advancement of the season. The Congress have appointed six more Brigadier Generals, four for the Southern and two for the Middle Department. Its probable General Lee will have the command of the Southern Army. I have nothing new that I can communicate; when I have you may be assured I shall be very particular, & I hope shall hear from you often. All the Delegates except from New Hampshire are furnished weekly with all the transactions of their respective Colonies, & really wish to be on a footing with them in that respect.

I shall write to you again shortly. In the mean time give me leave to assure you that I am, With greatest Respect, your most obt & Faithful Servt,   Wm. Whipple.

MS not found; reprinted from *N.H. Provincial Papers*, 8:76–77.

[1] See Josiah Bartlett to Meshech Weare, this date, note 2.

[2] The petition to Congress, which was approved by the New Hampshire House on January 27, 1776, requested the stationing of a battalion of troops in Portsmouth. *N.H. Provincial Papers*, 8:67. This petition was read in Congress on March 1, and committed to a committee, which read its report in Congress on March 7. But Congress took no further action until May 14, when it authorized New Hampshire to raise another battalion that would "be taken into continental pay, so soon as they shall be armed and mustered." *JCC*, 4:179, 189, 357. See also Whipple to Weare, May 16, 1776.

Oliver Wolcott to Laura Wolcott

My Dear   Philadelphia March 2d. 1776
I recd. Mr Lymans favour of the 14 Ult. which I shall give an answer to. In the Mean Time can only Thank him for his Kindness. Was Very sorry to be informed that you was troubled with the Rheumatism. I hope it is not Very Affecting. I wish to know as often as may be the State of your own Health and the Condition of the Family. I wish it might be as particular as needful. I feel much concernd at the Burden

which necessarily devolves upon you. I hope you will make it as light as possible. You may easily believe from the Situation of publick Affairs, that the critical Moment seems Near which will perhaps decide the Fate of this Country and that the Business of Congress is Very Interesting. Yet if any Time can reasonably be allowed for my Return ⟨for a Short Time⟩, shall Think myself justified in doing it. The circumstances of my affairs, in ordinary Demand it—and you will let me know if any Thing besides my Knowledge Shall render it further necessary.

By the Blessing of God I am well, and hope it may be continued to Me. I have wrote to Mr. Champion[1] a little particularly tho Very hastely, which I am obliged to do generally. You will let me know wheather my Letters will probably go more certain from N. Haven or Hartford. I told Oliver to Take them at N Haven but I suspect that was wrong. I have sent Laura a Gown Pattern to Oliver. You'll let Me know wheather tis enough. I hope soon to Write you again. Give my Love to my Children and all Other Acquaintance. In trust I am, your Most affectionately,   Oliver Wolcott

P.S. By My Mentioning the Times being critical and interesting youll not understand there is any special unknown Evil attending Us. Nothing of that kind is Meant. I believe G. Britain will for ever lament its Rashness.

RC (CtHi).
[1] Not found.

William Whipple to Joseph Whipple

Dr Bror.[1]   Philad 3d March 1776
    Just as I sent my letter of this date to the Post (which I was obliged to close in a hurry to save the Conveyence) I received Yours of the 20th Ulto inclosing that notable performance of Mr Sheafs, I think a mind must be weak indeed to be impos'd on by such stuff. I am not able to inform you any thing perticular with regard to the Commissioners. I believe there is no doubt such a set of Animals are coming but its not thot they are to treat with the Congress but with Provincial Assemblies; their coming Will be of but little avail. Genl. Lee is Fortifying N. York. I just heard he has stoptd all communication between that City & the Men of War which was not done when I pass'd thro' that place. The Congress have appointed 4 new Brigadiers General for the Southern Department & two for the Middle. Lee is to Command in the Southern Dept. where hot work is expected. I find my time will be exceedingly taken up, shall therefore Expect to receive several letters from my Friends for every one I write. The Roads were so bad that my journy was very fateaging.

Feby. [*i.e.* March] 4th. A Brig is just come to the Wharf from Holland with 27 1/2 Tons Powder, some salt Petre & 300 stand Arms, several more Vessels are daily expected, with Milatery stores. There has been imported here within 2 months 120 Tons Salt Petre; a vessel hourly expected with [?]0 Tons more. Your Affecte Bror.

W. Whipple

RC (MH).
[1] Joseph Whipple (1737–1816), formerly a Portsmouth merchant operating in partnership with his brother William, settled down to the life of a gentleman farmer after 1773, became a founder of Jefferson, N.H., and sat in the New Hampshire Assembly for several terms during the period 1776–85. Chester B. Jordan, "Col. Joseph Whipple," *Proceedings of the New Hampshire Historical Society* 2 (1888–95): 289–320.

John Adams' Diary

Monday March 4. 1776
Resentment is a Passion, implanted by Nature for the Preservation of the Individual. Injury is the Object which excites it. Injustice, Wrong, Injury excites the Feeling of Resentment, as naturally and necessarily as Frost and Ice excite the feeling of cold, as fire excites heat, and as both excite Pain. A Man may have the Faculty of concealing his Resentment, or suppressing it, but he must and ought to feel it. Nay he ought to indulge it, to cultivate it. It is a Duty. His Person, his Property, his Liberty, his Reputation are not safe without it. He ought, for his own Security and Honour, and for the public good to punish those who injure him, unless they repent, and then he should forgive, having Satisfaction and Compensation. Revenge is unlawfull.

It is the same with Communities. They ought to resent and to punish.

MS (MHi). Adams, *Diary* (Butterfield), 2:236.

John Adams' Notes on Relations with France

[March 4? 1776] [1]
Is any Assistance attainable from F.?
What Connection may We safely form with her?
1st. No Political Connection—Submit to none of her Authority—receive no Governors, or officers from her.
2d. No military Connection—receive no Troops from her.
3d. Only a Commercial Connection, i.e. make a Treaty, to receive her Ships into our Ports. Let her engage to receive our Ships into her Ports—furnish Us with Arms, Cannon, Salt Petre, Powder, Duck, Steel.

MS (MHi). Adams, *Diary* (Butterfield), 2:236.
[1] Although these notes are undated, they follow Adams' March 4 entry in his manuscript diary and apparently represent a summation of his thoughts on an alliance with France. The subject of foreign alliances arose frequently during the following weeks, and it undoubtedly began to receive more attention from the delegates at this time because of the imminent departure of Silas Deane as an agent to France. See John Adams' Notes on Foreign Alliances, March 1; and Committee of Secret Correspondence Minutes of Proceedings, March 2, 1776.

Joseph Hewes to Samuel Johnston

Dear Sir   Philadelphia 4th March 1776
 I have been very unfortunate in executing the Order for a Waggon and Horses a particular acco[unt] of which hereafter.[1] I also overloaded them not expecting the Roads would have been so bad as they proved to be. I have hired another Waggon in which I have put four barrels of Powder containing 926 lb weight, two Boxes contg. eight drums and one Box contg. eight Colours all compleat being for the third Regiment of No. Carolina Troops. This Waggon I expect will overtake the New One at Wilmington and will take out as much of her Load as will make both Loads equal. The Bearer John Powell who has charge of the whole is related to some good families in this City. I have received great civilities from several of them, and wish he may be taken more notice of than his present employment may probably entitle him to. The hired Waggon is at 30/, say four dollars per day till she returns, allowing after her discharge at Edenton 25 Miles per day. Mr. Powel has 6/8 per day, the other two with the New Waggon 3/ each and all expenses borne till they return, allowing a reasonable time for so doing. I am respectfully, D Sir, your very hum Serv,   Joseph Hewes

N.B. I have delivered to Mr. Powell 200 dollars and to James Thompson who set of[f] with the New Waggon 90 Dollars; these sums I hope will [*cover*] all expences.

RC (NNPM).
[1] See North Carolina Delegates to the North Carolina Council of Safety, February 10, note 1; and Hewes to Samuel Johnston, February 20, 1776.

John Jay to Robert R. Livingston

My dear Friend   Pha. 4 March 1776
⟨*The Evening before the last I arrived here after a most disagreable Journey thro intolerable bad Roads.*[1] *I heard by the Way that your Brother had been here & was returning. How we missed each other is a mystery to me. I wish I had seen him. He would have told me twenty things about you that I am anxious to know.*⟩

Fame says you are still much indisposed. I pray God she may on this, as she does on many other occasions, prove a Lyar. I wrote you last week from Elizabeth Town, tell me whether you have recd. that and which other of my Letters. I was in Hopes of finding a Letter from you here for me, & the Disapointmt. is the greater as the State of your Health for some time past has given me much anxiety. The Prospect of being soon deprived of a Father & a Mother whom you know I tenderly love, the unhappy situation of some of my Family added to the Distress I feel for the late misfortunes & Sickness of my Friends have occasioned more gloomy Ideas in my mind than it has ever before been the Subject of. Despondency however ill becomes a man. I hope I shall meet every severe Stroke of Fate with Firmness & Resignation, tho not with sullen Indifference. I[t] gives me Consolation to reflect that the human Race are immortal that my Parents & Friends will be divided from me only by a [. . .] Curtain which will soon be drawn up, and that our great and benevolent Creator will (if I please) be my Guide thro this Vale of Tears to our eternal & blessed Habitation.

Notwithstanding your Letter, I still suspect that your Disorder is to be ascribed more to your Solicitude, than Constitution. I well remember that tho' to appearance not robust, you could endure great fatigue and few of our Contemporaries have enjoyed more Health than yourself. I possess a kind of *Confidence* that Exercise, Temperance & Chearfulness would be as friendly to you as they were to old *Cornaro*. I wish you could get away from Home & pursue no other Objects. Try, if it be only for a month or two, and give up all Kind of Business of what nature so ever. Dont permit any Body to say a word to you about your Causes, your Rents, your Farm, nay for the present avoid even politics—defer joining the Congress, the Assembly or any other Body of Men whose Object is Business. Suppose, when the Season becomes more mild you were to take Lodgings at Bristol? The Waters wd probably be useful to you. They have kept Mr. Verplank alive for some Years past. You wd. see as much & as little Company as you pleased, & I promise to go to Church with you every Sunday. Tell Mrs. Livingston I beg she will join her Persuasions to mine. Such a little Journey would be useful to you both and I should think the middle of April would not be too early for it.

The Committee for Canada was appointed before I reached this Place. It consists of Doctr. Franklin, Mr. Chace & a Mr. Carryl from Maryland. Had I been here I should have proposed you, tho I must confess I think you can employ your Time more to the advantage of your Health in many other ways. Your Country has no Demands upon you till that be reestablished. Let me entreat you therefore to confine your Attention to it.

⟨*Mr. Lynch continues very ill, tho better than he has been.*⟩ Twenty Seven Tons of Powder, some Salt petre & 300 Arms arrived here Yesterday;

& we hear from good Authority that 5 tons of Powder has arrived safe at N Carolina.

This is all the News I have heard since I have been in Town. As to Politics—you know the Letters of Congress People should be silent on that subject in these Times, when Letters often miscarry &c.

God bless you & give you Health. I am &c.

FC (NNC).
[1] According to Jay's account with the New York Provincial Congress, dated July 3, 1776, he received "Ninety Nine Pounds four Shillings" for "attendg the Cont. Congress from 3d March to the 3d May [1776] inclusive being 62 Days." Carson Collection, PP.

Secret Committee Minutes of Proceedings

Com[mitte] Chambr. March 4th. 1776.

At a meeting of the Secret Committee. Present Saml Ward, J. Alsop, Jos. Hewes, Josh. Bartlett & Robt. Morris.

A Contract was enterd into with Mr. Robt. Morris & John Ross of this City, Merchts.[1] A Charter party was likewise entered into with Benjn Gibbs of the same place Mercht. The Comme. determind Mr. York might load his vessel upon the same terms as before on account.[2]

Agreed that if Congress direct the Come. to proceed with their importations, that Mr. Adam Babcock may load a vessel with potash, Oil &c, for Europe to the amount of 10,000 dlls.[3] Gave an Order to Mr. Eve for a ton of Saltpetre.

MS (MH).
[1] Morris and Ross received an advance of $90,000 on this contract. Secret Committee Minutes of Proceedings, March 14, 1776.
[2] On March 8 Thomas Yorke was granted a permit to load the brigantine *Hetty*, but ordered not to sail. The contract and advance were signed on March 16. Journal of the Secret Committee, fols. 43, 45, MH. See also Secret Committee Minutes of Proceedings, June 19, 1776.
[3] See Secret Committee Minutes of Proceedings, March 6, 1776.

Samuel Ward to Henry Ward

Dear Brother   Philadelpa. 4th March 1776

The Post went out so soon after I recd. yours of 18th and 21st that it was not in my Power to write by him.

An Appendix to common Sense you will find enclosed. I wish the Author had gone more largely into the Subject but upon the whole I think it has been in the middle Colonies of immense Service and doubt not but it will [*be*] so with you, Carter can print the Appendix separately to compleat the Work.[1]

The abandoning our Islands must be a very heavy Loss, but great as it may be it is more eligible than continuing the Possession of them at the Hazard of being plundered and perhaps murdered or compelled to furnish our Enemies with Provisions. The Case of Block Island I will consult some of my Friends in Congress upon and if I think I can obtain a Resolve for making it a continental affair as it certainly ought to be I will propose it.[2]

Your Recommendation of Capt. Tompkins interests me much in his Favor, you may rely upon my best Endeavours to serve him and I flatter Myself they will not be ineffectual.[3]

The Arrival of the Powder you mention is very agreable, We have had several small Quantities here amounting to about twelve Tons in the whole & the salt petre mentioned in my late Letters will make 150 Tons. Many Importations are daily expected but these are uncertain and as We shall need vast Quantities I hope every Colony will pursue the manufacturing Salt petre with all possible Attention, there is a late Resolve of Congress upon the Subject which you will find in the Paper inclosed.[4]

There are Letters in Town from N. York which mention the Prussian Nobleman said in your Letter to be arrived, it is reported here that he is an officer of Distinction and an intimate Friend of Genl. Lee's and is come a Volunteer.[5]

We had Letters yesterday from the Generals Schuyler, Wooster & Arnold. The latters were of 12th Feby. About 4 or 500 of the Enemy had sallied out to take Possession of some Cannon which We had near the City, but upon our People's advancing briskly to attack them they retreated very precipitately. The principal Part of the Garrison is Sailors, they are obliged to mount Guard every other Night, some desert, they are at short Allowance for Provisions and are in such Want of Fuel as soon to be obliged to burn the Houses & Ships. About 300 of the Reinforcements lately ordered had joined General Arnold and about the same number had reached Montreal and great Numbers are on their March that I have no Doubt but We shall get the Place before April. The brave Detachment under Colo. Greene who are Prisoners seem doomed to try a second Time the Force of Famine but I hope it will not be long before they will be relieved.

You have long since expected that the Enemy would exert every Nerve to crush us the ensuing Campaign. The Act of Parliament for seizing American Ships &c and compelling the Mariners in them to enter into the Kings Service; for seizing other Vessels coming to or returning from trading with us, giving the Crown & privy Council a Power to give to the Courts of Admiralty any new Rules or Orders for condemning our Property and many other tyrannical Purposes confirm your Opinion. Some of their Troops may be expected very soon. The Congress is taking Measures for the Defence of all Parts of the Continent; N. Yk., N. Jy., Penna., lowr. Counties and Maryland are made a middle Departmt. under General Schuyler; Virginia, No. Carolina, So. Caroa. & Georgia the southern Department under Genl. Lee who will soon be detached there. Six Brigadiers are appointed for these Colonies, Colos. Armstrong & Thompson of this Colony, Col Lewis of Virga., Moore of No. Carolina, Ld. Sterling of the Jersies & Howe of No. Carolina; there are above thirty Battalions raising or raised in these Departments & more can be raised so that I hope the Enemy may meet a proper Reception in any Quarter.

A Comee. is appointed by Congress to contract for the making of Arms,[6] this is a Matter of immense Importance, We have but about 1300 imported here in all one third of which belonged to Maryland, the other two were furnished to the Troops destined for Canada; I think every Colony should make the most exact Scrutiny what Smiths can do any thing towards making Guns or Locks and keep them constantly employed in that Business solely; this Matter deserves the utmost Attention of Government.

This moment a Vessel is arrived from Europe with twenty five Tons of Powder, ten Tons salt petre and five hundred Stands of Arms. How kindly Providence proportions our Supplies to our Wants, let us be thankfull for them, make a wise and brave use of them and at the same time take every proper Measure for procuring further Supplies.

Genl. Lee is fortifying N. York, the Captain of the Enemy's Ships gave out they would fire on the Town, Genl. Lee in Return gave out that if they did he would chain a hundred of their best Friends together and the first House they sat on Fire should be their funeral Pile.[7]

My worthy Friend Dr. Franklin desired Me to give the Bearer Mr. Levy a Letter of Recommendation. He assures me that He has been long acquainted with him and that He is an honest Man, Justice is one of the great Supports of Society and is due to all Mankind; I therefore wish it to Mr. Levy, your Civilities to him I shall consider as a Favor.

Our Friend Dr. Young & Family are very well, his Pen is frequently employed in the common Cause.

You'l observe by a late Paper that all Vessels bound to G. Britain, Ireland or the British W. Indies were ordered to be stopd until further Orders from Congress, these Vessels had imported Arms & Amunition agreable to the Resolve of 15th July & the Importers supposed that they had a Right to export to any Part of the World, this was not the Intention of Congress originally but as the Vessels were loaded & the concerned beleived that they had the Faith of Congress that they should do so, it was resolved that they might be permitted to sail; I think they will be seized especially when it is known that this Permission has been granted only to the Importers of Arms & Ammunition.[8]

Mr. Hopkins & Lady are very well. Present my most affectionate & Respectful Compliments to the Governor.

Let me know how the building the Ships go on, how the Colony is supplied with Arms & Ammunition & every thing else interesting.

I am obliged to you for your congratulations on my Daughters marriage. I think She has a good Prospect. Make my Compliments to all our Friends.

I am, Yours most affectionately,   Sam Ward

P.S. Our worthy Friend John Collins sent his Regards to Me by a Gentn. who saw him lately at Camp and said he was as well as ever and hoped to take the Command of a Ship in the Spring. You'l have the opportunity of conversing with him upon it.

RC (RHi).
[1] See T. R. Adams, *American Independence*, pp. 171–72.
[2] In February 1776, apparently in response to a request from Washington, the Rhode Island Assembly ordered the removal of all surplus cattle from Block Island to prevent them from falling into the hands of the British. John R. Bartlett, ed., *Records of the Colony of Rhode Island and Providence Plantations in New England*, 10 vols. (Providence: A. Crawford Greene, 1856–65), 7:444, 455. Congress never compensated Rhode Island for this act.
[3] On June 6, 1776, Congress appointed Samuel Tompkins of Prudence, R.I., captain of one of the two frigates then ordered to be constructed in that colony. *JCC*, 5:422–23; and Ward, *Correspondence* (Knollenberg), p. 195n.47.
[4] Doubtless the resolve which Congress passed on this subject on February 23. *JCC*, 4:171.
[5] Baron Frederick William de Woedtke. See John Hancock to Baron de Woedtke, March 19, 1776.
[6] This committee was appointed on February 23. *JCC*, 4:169. See also Committee of Congress to Abraham Hunt, March 9, 1776.
[7] For a fuller description of this incident, see Charles Lee's undated letter to Capt. Hyde Parker of the Royal Navy in *NYHS Collections* 4 (1871): 341.
Although Knollenberg printed the remainder of this letter under the conjectural date of March 1, 1776, and to an unidentified recipient, Ward's reference below to the resolution on trade which Congress adopted on March 4 demonstrates that he wrote it on the fourth, and other evidence indicates that the two fragments are parts of the same letter. See Ward, *Correspondence* (Knollenberg), p. 194.
[8] On this point, see Richard Smith's Diary, February 26, 1776, note 1.

William Whipple to John Langdon

My Dear Sir,   Philadelphia 4th March 1776.

Just as I took my pen in hand yesterday to write to you I heard the post was going out; therefore was obliged to close my letter as soon as I began it. Those cursed papers which were enclosed to the President, have given me more uneasiness than the rascal's necks are worth who were the cause of them.[1] Col Bartlett intends to leave me in about a fortnight—by that time shall be able to give you a more particular account of those notable papers and expected to have rec'd a letter from you on my arrival here but was disappointed. Pray let me hear from you oftener. Be very particular; don't let the most trifling occurrence pass unnoticed. I already feel the necessity of knowing all that passes at home. Tell Dr B[rackett] I expect a letter from him before I write him. There has been no mention yet of Agents for any of the Colonies. When there is I shall be mindful of what you mentioned.

A Brig arrived this morning from Holland with 27 1/2 tons gun powder, some salt petre and 300 arms. 10 tons was immediately ordered to the camp.[2] Brigadier General Thomas is advanced to the rank of Major General and ordered to Canada.[3] A committee also set off for that place in a few days. The committee are Dr Franklin, Mr Chace and a Roman Catholic gentleman belonging to Maryland.[4]

I am sincerely yours, Wm Whipple

Tr (DLC).
[1] See Josiah Bartlett to Meshech Weare, March 2, 1776, note 2.
[2] See *JCC*, 4:183.
[3] Congress did not take this action until March 6, 1776. *JCC*, 4:186.
[4] Charles Carroll of Carrollton.

Josiah Bartlett to John Langdon

Dear Sir, Philadelphia March 5 1776

Yours of the 19th ulto is now before me and am very sorry that any person in New Hampshire could pretend to write and print so ridiculous a piece as that you mention. I had the reading of it, being enclosed to Col Whipple. I think your Committee acted wisely in putting a stop to it, though the chief hurt that will arise from the publishing such trifling, inconsistent and puerile pieces is to make the persons and the place producing them mean and ridiculous to every sensible reader. I am extremely sorry that our Colony, who has hitherto stood high in the esteem of the whole Continent, for their manly and spirited exertions in the cause of liberty should by such productions added to some late manoeuvres of Portsmouth and some other towns in regard to taking up govt. fall to the lowest depth of ignominy and contempt, which unless a stop is put it will certainly be the case. The packet containing the whole of the affairs of taking up civil govt we carried in the evening to the President, who opened it while we were present.[1] After reading the whole to himself for some time, he asked us what was the question the Colony wanted to have put to the Congress for their answer as he said he could not find out by reading the papers, and neither Col Whipple nor I could inform him; for the order of Congress to take up civil Govt. in such a manner as the Colony should think proper nobody can deny and that the Colony had taken up such a form as was most agreeable to majority is not disputed; that a number disliked it and protested against it is set forth, but what the Congress can say in the matter I am at a loss to guess, consistent with their constant declaration not to interfere with internal Govt of any of the Colonies, any further than to recommend to them to adopt such forms, as they shall think best calculated, to promote the quiet and peace of the Society, leaving every Colony to take such govt as is most agreeable to the majority, during the present dispute. However as it was directed to the Congress, it was the next day publicly read together with the petition for a regt to be stationed at Portsmouth; the whole was committed to Dr Franklin, Mr Wythe and Mr Braxton, a new member from Virginia; what or when they will report is uncertain, but for the honor of the Province I wish it had been kept at home.

The protestor's insinuation that it was unfairly obtained, I think (and they are not alone in it) reflects highly on the Congress in general as well as the delegates of New Hampshire, which the whole Congress know is illiberal and unjust. According to the best of my remembrance (as well as of some others that I have asked) not more than one Colony voted against it (if one): however I hope the difficulty will soon subside, and by the future good conduct of the Colony, they will regain their former esteem. Their spirit and activity in raising the regt. for Canada is highly commended.[2]

The twenty thousand dollars for which the Marine Committee gave me an order, as mentioned in my last,[3] I have rec'd and have agreed with Mr [Avery] (who is to take some money down for Mr Cushing) to take fifteen thousand dollars for you. I have taken up your order to Mr Dalton for 1333 1/3 dollars, the remaining 3666 2/3 dollars, I shall leave with Col Whipple to answer such orders as you may draw on him, or the Marine Committee.

I enclose you an account of the goods you are to purchase with your contract;[4] the money cannot be sent till you empower somebody to draw it for you.

The order of the Secret Committee (a copy of which I shall enclose) I shall leave with Col Whipple and you will send him a power to draw it for you and to pay it to such persons or send it down to you as you think best. Yesterday a vessel arrived here with twenty seven tons and a half of powder, 5 tons of salt petre, 300 stand of arms.

I expect in 10 or 15 days to set out for New Hampshire to see how affairs go in with you, when I hope to have the pleasure to see you well.[5]

I am, Sir, your friend,   Josiah Bartlett

P.S. This letter goes by the Express: the money will set off this afternoon by Mr Avery and will be sent to the care of Mr Thomas Cushing where you must send for it.   J. B.

Tr (DLC).
[1] See Bartlett to Meshech Weare, March 2, 1776, note 2.

² Reported in Meshech Weare to John Hancock, February 8, 1776, *Am. Archives*, 4th ser. 4:964.

³ See Bartlett to John Langdon, February 21, 1776.

⁴ See Secret Committee Minutes of Proceedings, February 20, 1776.

⁵ Bartlett apparently left Philadelphia on March 18 and arrived in Portsmouth on March 30. In his accounts to the New Hampshire Assembly, Bartlett submitted a claim for "my own time"—which included travel time—"from the 3d of September 1775 to the 30th of March 1776, 209 days." Entries covering his board, his horse, and "expenses for waiters," however, claimed compensation only "to the 18th of March 1776." Nh. In his personal copy of *Poor Wills Pocket Almanack, 1776*, Bartlett made the following pertinent entries: "Mar. 18 Set out from Philad. for New Hampshire," and "Mar. 28 Arrived at my own house in Kingstown." MiU-C.

Richard Smith's Diary

Tuesday 5 March [1776]

Letters from Gens. Schuyler, Wooster and Ld. Stirling,¹ part of one of Schuylers was com[mitte]d to 3. It was concerning a supposed Invitation from Govr. Penn to the 6 Nations to meet Him at Philada. Andrew Allen said he had made particular Inquiry into the Report & assured the Congress it was groundless.² The other Letters were referred to a former Comee. An Order passed to furnish the first & 3d Jersey Regts. with Medicine Chests. The Comee. on the Wyoming Papers recommended that they be referred to the Pennsa. Assembly which was done accordingly. 4 or 5 Hours were spent in Grand Comee. Col Harrison in the Chair, on Lord Drummonds Letter to Gen. Robertson. Wyth offered a Sett of Propos[ition]s importg that no Public Bodies or private Persons other than the Congress or the People at large ought to treat for Peace &c which were negatived 8 colonies to 3 & one not fully represented, a Motion by Wm. Livingston that Ld. Drummond be sent for (from N York) to explain his Conduct non allocatur, Nothing more was done on it than the Letter ordered to remain with our Papers & the President desired to acquaint Gen. Washn. that the Congress agree in Sentiment with him on the Subject.³ The rest of the Gens. Letter was referred to a former Comee. It appeared that Ld. Drummond had conversed with several Delegates as E. Rutledge, Wilson and Duane on the Subject of Pacification and, unauthorized by the Ministry, had thrown out his own Ideas of what the Ministry would concede and expect and had endeavored to draw from those Members what Congress would demand & accede to on their Part.

MS (DLC).

¹ General Schuyler's letters to Hancock of February 26 and 27 and enclosures are in PCC, item 153, 2:19–26, and *Am. Archives*, 4th ser. 4:1499–1500, 1510–11. Enclosed with the former were letters to Schuyler from General Wooster of February 21 and from James Deane of February 24. There is no record in the journals of the reception this day of any letters from General Alexander, although it is possible that

Congress received Alexander's letter to Hancock of March 3. PCC, item 162, 2:428;
and *Am. Archives*, 4th ser. 5:51.
    [2] See Andrew Allen to Philip Schuyler, March 17, 1776.
    [3] See Lord Drummond's Notes, January 3–9?, note 1; and John Hancock to
Washington, March 6, 1776.

Henry Wisner to George Clinton

Sir: Goshen 5th of March 1776.
    Some time after you Left Congress a Resolve past Signefying that the
person to Command the fortifycation in the highlands should Bear the
Rank of Coll, in Consequence of which four persons have Recommended
to wit Capt. Grinnold [Grenell], one Levingston, and two other persons
whoes names I have forgot; however for perticular Reasons they ware
not appointed, But the appointment put of and I Believe they will not
Be appointed, and as Mr. Nicoll has an inclination to Continue in the
Servis if you think proper to Joyn me in a Recommendation of him to
that office,[1]
    Pleas to Draw one and subscribe my name under yours. I am Sir
yours to Serve,   Henry Wisner.

MS not found; reprinted from George Clinton, *Public Papers of George Clinton . . .*,
ed. Hugh Hastings and J. A. Holden, 10 vols. (New York and Albany: Wynkoop
Hallenbeck Crawford Co. et al., 1899–1914), 1:227.
    [1] See New York Delegates to the New York Provincial Congress, January 5, 1776,
note 1.

James Duane to Robert Livingston

Dear & honourd Sir   Philad. [6–11?] [1] March 1776
    I beg you will accept my Thanks for your obliging Favour of the 25th
of February. At this distance and after so long a Separation [an] account
of the Health of My Family [. . .] [2] cannot fail of being very valuable.
God grant that we may all still be indulged with this valuable Blessing,
and be enabled to make of [. . .] [3] it!
    The unnatural War is like to rage this Summer with Violence, and
yet if administration mean to augment their Army now here only to
25,000, one woud conclude that they do not hope to penetrate far into
the Country; much less to take possession of Colonies. New York, Virginia and South Carolina are supposed to be most in danger. For their
better protection two new military Departments are formed: the middle
comprehendg New York, New Jersey, Pensylvania, the lower Counties
and Maryland: the Southern Department including the four Southern
Colonies. Exclusive of 20372 Men voted for the defence of the [five?]
Eastern Governments; & 9023 for the service of Canada, 8000 are raising

for the protection of the middle Colonies and 9500 for the Southern Colonies. General Lee and General Armstrong are to have the Chief command to the Southward & to be assisted by three other Brig. Generals. Major General Thomas & Brig. Genl. Arnold are to direct the Army in Canada. General Schuyler to keep his head Quarters at Albany: that he may have the means of supplying the Canada Army and Managing the Indians &c &c. It being much doubted whether any other Person is qualified to conduct these two important objects.

Brig. Genl Thompson of Pensylvania and Lord Stirling are to command in the middle department; tho if any serious attempt is made on New York it seems to be taken for granted that General Washington will repair to its Assistance. This is the present disposition of the Continental Army founded on the Supposed Plan of the ministry. It must be subject to alterations according to their maneuvres.

This will be deliverd to you by Col. Allen son of the Chief Justice Allen of this City who is going into Canada.[4] I am intimate with this respectable Family, & flatter myself that you will be pleased to shew Civilities to a young Gentn of his Spirit and Connections. Be kind enough to introduce him to Mrs Duane &c. I have no time to write to her by this opportunity but shall do myself that pleasure in a few days by Doctr Franklin, Mr Chase & Mr Carryl who are going into Canada as Deputies [. . . .]

Be pleased to present my dutiful Regards to Mamma; my best Love to my Polly and our dear Children, and the rest of our Friends and believe me to be with the utmost Regard, My dear & hond Sir, your most affect Son & most obedt Sert.   Jas. Duane

RC (NHpR: Livingston-Redmond Collection deposit). Endorsed by Livingston: "A Letter from Son Duane, Recd. 23 March 1776."

[1] This date has been suggested because Duane's letter contains no reference to any action of Congress taken later than March 6 and was carried by Lt. Col. William Allen, who was in New York on March 13. See William Allen to John Hancock, March 13, 1776, *Am. Archives*, 4th ser. 5:204.

[2] MS damaged; approximately three words illegible.

[3] MS damaged; approximately three words illegible.

[4] Lt. Col. William Allen of the Second Pennsylvania Regiment was on his way to Albany with 6 companies of reinforcements for General Schuyler when, having stopped at New York City to secure transportation up the Hudson for his troops, he was ordered by General Alexander on March 13 to remain there to assist in its defense. Evidently Alexander thereupon made arrangements for the delivery of Duane's letter to Livingston as well as other letters which Allen was carrying. Ibid., 5:204, 217–18.

Benjamin Franklin to Daniel Roberdeau

Dear Sir   Wednesday March 6. [17]76
The Congress desire a Return to be made to them of the Powder the

Committee of Safety have lent them, that it may be known how much is due.[1]

I am very respectfully, Dear Sir, Your most obedt huml Servt,

B Franklin

[*P.S.*] A Copy of the Order for Replacing the Arms was given 2 Days since by Mr Thomson to the Commissary Mr Towers.

RC (InU).
[1] See *JCC*, 4:186–87; and *Am. Archives*, 4th ser. 5:720–21.

Elbridge Gerry to James Warren

Dear Sir   Philadelphia March 6. 1776

An Express goes off in a few Hours for the Camp & affords just Time to hint a few Things which I beg You Will communicate to the honorable House.

It is of great Importance that your Militia should be well armed & equipped & Powder is essentially necessary—without it what will be the Distresses of the Sea Coast Frontiers & how can they defend themselves? I have heard of my Vessel in the Service of the Colony & am apprehensive of her being detained at St Antonio in Spain, I saw a Letter from the Master to the Commander of a Ship arrived in this place, & find that Capt Johnson was waiting for his Crew, which had been dispatched from Bilbao by Messrs Guado———[1] ten Days before & ought to have arrived in two or three at most. He was very uneasy & intended to get another Crew if his own did not arrive soon, & I have since heard a Rumour that the Vessel is detained wch. there is Reason to fear. She had on board four hundred & thirty barells Powder, or in other Words twenty one Tons & an half & should she arrive will clear for the Colony seven thousand five hundred Pounds lawful estimating the powder at 5/ per pound which is low—but this a trifling Consideration compared with other Advantages. Five Tons were ordered to Cambridge about a Week since from the Jerseys, since which twenty seven Tons & an half have arrived here wth. about five Tons Salt petre & 300 stand Arms. Ten Tons of this Powder is also ordered to the Camp at Cambridge, but this will not *equip your Militia*. Pray let a petition be immediately press'd for a Return of the Powder Which We have lent the Continent, & I apprehend it can be obtained.[2] I mean the Powder collected from the Towns in the Massachusetts—Mr Hunt can furnish a list of the most of them. I would beg one thing further, that You will not suffer any of your Stocks of Ammunition to be carried out of the Colony or into the Camp without pressing Necessity or the Desire of Congress. News is just arrived of five Tons more Powder imported into

North Carolina, & each Colony looks out for itself as the Times require it.[3]

The Congress have this Day preferred General Thomas & made him a Major General; he is ordered to proceed without Delay to Canada & General Lee is to go to the Southern Colonies.

We are obliged to the hona House for the Journals & Acts of Assembly lately sent here & hope that the other Journals will be forwarded when ready & that one or more Persons will be appointed to transmit weekly the Doings of the Assembly as great Advantages will result to the Colony from this Step. The File of Letters, Memorandums, & Day Books of the Committee of Supplies are much Wanted in adjusting the Colony Accounts. I understand they are left with Deacon Cheever.[4]

I cannot help inculcating the Necessity of attending to Powder & carefully preserving it, for should the Enemy remove & the Army follow them, our Colony may be destitute of this Article & what a Situation will it then be in. One thing further I'll beg leave to hint. The Assembly sometime since passed a Resolve relative to Fire Arms & I cannot learn that any great Number have been yet manufactured. Is it not necessary to enquire into the Cause of it & appoint a Committee to contract with Individuals (who manuf[acture]) for a certain Number in a convenient Time? The Southern Colonies give a higher Incouragement than We have offered & it may be of great Importance to follow their Example; this the Assembly will de[cide].

Pray give my best Respects to Major Hawly, Colo Orne, Mrss Sullivan, Cooper, Freeman & all our other Friends, believing me to be sincerely sir your Friend & very hum sevt,   Elbridge Gerry

[*P.S.*] Pray forward the inclosed Letters.

RC (M-Ar).
[1] Gerry undoubtedly meant the Spanish mercantile firm of Joseph Gardoqui & Sons. For additional information on the fate of Gerry's ship, *Rockingham*, see William Sinclair to Gerry, June 4, 1776, in Clark, *Naval Documents*, 5:369–70.

[2] Gerry's letter was considered in the Massachusetts General Court on March 14, and a committee was appointed "to obtain an account of all the Powder lent by this Colony to the Continental Army." On March 28 another committee was named to present the account to General Washington. *Am. Archives*, 4th ser. 5:1239, 1252. The account, which Washington received on March 28, is in the Washington Papers, DLC. James Otis' letter of May 10 to the Massachusetts delegates, requesting that they "solicit" Congress to replace this powder, is in PCC, item 65, 1:85–86, and *Am. Archives*, 4th ser. 6:419.

[3] From his vantage point in Philadelphia Gerry often acquired commercial news that he was able to pass on to the advantage of his constituents and friends in Massachusetts. In a letter of February 26 to his brother Samuel of Marblehead, for example, Gerry communicated information pertaining to Samuel's business affairs and added the advice that because "the price of Flower is reduced . . . I think You would act prudently to store it at Newbury Port a Month or two, as it must necessarily be higher in a short Time." Gerry to Samuel R. Gerry, February 26, 1776, Gerry Papers, MHi.

⁴ The Massachusetts accounts were assigned to the Committee of Claims on March 1. *JCC*, 4:180. Gerry's hint led the Massachusetts General Court to appoint on March 14 a committee to forward the records of the Committee of Supplies. *Am. Archives*, 4th ser. 5:1239.

John Hancock to Thomas Cushing

Dear Sir,   Philada. March 6th. 1776

I Rec'd your Letter by Mr. Avery, & this Day your's by Mr. Osgood wherein you mention the Rect. of the plans, & express a Surprize at Receivg no Letter. I am to inform you that the Plans were Sent by Coll. Bull, by whom I not only wrote you but Sent you Twenty five Thousand Dollars, & at same time committed to your Care the Plan for the New Hampshire Ship.¹ I am surprized that I have no Accott. of the Rect. of them. I have this Day Rec'd a Letter from Coll Bull Acquainting me of his arrivall, & that he should Deliver his Charge to you the next Morng. I hope however soon to hear from you respecting these matters. I shall dispatch Mr Avery the 8th inst. with some Money, & give you every particular with Respect to Boats, Masts, Cables &c, & every other matter that the Committee Determines upon respectg the Ships. I am waiting for the Committee, I am always Ready, but you know the Mode, & I must Submitt, I have however call'd a meeting of the Committee tomorrow Eveng. when I will have these things Settled, & then Dispatch Mr Avery to you with the Results. In the mean time I must most earnestly entreat and Beg of you that you exert every Nerve in forwarding our two Ships, & that you Employ as many Men in every Department as can possibly work & be of Service in expediting them, in short spare no Expence in forwarding them, for *inter nos* some *here* who are not very friendly to you & I (& of our province you know who) begin publickly to Say that the Massachusetts Ships will be the last finish'd, that they are in no forwardness &c. I want to Counteract them, in order to which you must Exert your self, & I must Repeat to you, that no Emolument to any particular person must prevent the ordering as many people as can possibly attend. Dispatch & not profit is the Object, & pray attend to this Night & Day. Do write me often, & particularly of the Scituation of the Ships that I may have authority to Contradict the Reports of our ——— . And at same time give me an accott. of what is passing with you, all the particulars of the Assembly, & in short every Circumstance of News; how stands the Military Appointmts., how were Mr. P[aine's] Letters Relish'd.² I have order'd the Two hundred pieces of Duck to be Sent you by Land, Mr Avery will inform you further, as I have given him a Letter to New York to Mr Lewis on that Subject.³ I also Refer you to Mr. Avery for some Anecdotes &c, as to Mr A[dams], G[erry] & myself.

With Respect to his allowance to Mr Avery I Leave it to you. I would have him reputably paid, but do justice between him & the publick & Charge it in your Accott. I shall direct your Reimbursemt. of the 50 Dollars you was so kind to advance to Sprigs for me, with Thanks. I wrote you by one of Mr. Mifflin's Deputies, whose name I forget, a few days ago, hope you will Receive. Pray Acknowledge the Receipt of my Letters, and by all means Remember the mention I made of my Brother, pray do something for him.

I See you were to have an Oration on the 5th March. Do Send me one when printed.[4]

I have got to 11 oClock, & must Refer to mine by Mr Avery, for further particulars, in mean time beg my best Respects to your Family, and am, Dear Sir, Your Friend & Servt.   John Hancock

[P.S.] Inclos'd is one of Doctor Smith's Orations.

Inclos'd is a Letter to Mr Sharp of Salem, about Selling my Ship that lies at Salem.[5] It is open for your perusal; Seal it, and I ask your particular Attention to this matter. Do See that the Letter be carefully deliver'd, & aid this for me, & pray Receive the money & forward it to me here as soon as you can or an order on me from Warren. I Rely on your good offices.

The Inclos'd Letters for Mr Lowell & Mr Bant pray let be carefully Deliver'd.[6]

RC (MdAN).
[1] See Hancock to Cushing, February 13, 1776.
[2] Hancock is referring to Robert Treat Paine's critical letters of January 1, 1776, to the Massachusetts Council, to Joseph Hawley, to Joseph Palmer, and to James Warren.
[3] Not found.
[4] The oration delivered by Rev. Peter Thacher at Watertown was quickly printed. Peter Thacher, *An Oration Delivered at Watertown, March 5, 1776, to Commemorate the Bloody Massacre at Boston: Perpetrated March 5, 1770* . . . (Watertown: Benjamin Edes, 1776).
[5] Not found.
[6] Not found.

John Hancock to John Thomas

Sir,   Philada. March 6h. 1776

The Situation of Canada, being at this Juncture an Object of the greatest Importance to the Welfare of the United Colonies, the Congress have been anxious to fix upon some General Officer, whose military Skill, Courage and Capacity will probably insure Success to the Enterprize. In Major General Thomas they flatter themselves they will not be disappointed.[1] Accordingly I do myself the Honour to enclose your

Commission as Major General; and shall only add, that Congress have the firmest Reliance on your exerting yourself to the utmost. I beg Leave to refer you to General Washington for the necessary Instructions on your Expedition, and am, Sir, your most obedt. & very Hble Sert.

John Hancock Presidt.

RC (MHi). In the hand of Jacob Rush and signed by Hancock.

[1] Thomas was promoted to the rank of major general and appointed "to command the forces in Canada" on March 6, 1776. *JCC*, 4:186. For an indication that agreement on this decision had been reached at least two days previously, see William Whipple to John Langdon, March 4, 1776.

John Hancock to George Washington

Sir,   Philada. March 6th. 1776.

Since my last I have had the honour of Receiving your Letters of the 24th and 30th of January, 9th, 14th, 18 and 21st and 26th of February, which were communicated to Congress.[1] On the Settlement and Adjustment of the Accounts, the Congress have not yet come to any Determination; nor have they yet had Time to contrive expedients for remedying the Inconveniences mentioned in that of the 9th which is referred to and will be taken up in a Committee of the whole.

The Congress highly Approve your Care and Attention in stopping Lord Drummond's Letter, and entirely concur with you in Sentiment, with Regard to his Lordship's officious and unwarrantable Zeal.[2]

The Situation of the Middle and Southern Colonies hath engaged the Attention of Congress. These are divided into two Departments, the Middle comprehending New York, New Jersey, Pennsylvania, Delaware and Maryland, under the Command of a Major General and two Brigadier Generals; the Southern comprehending Virginia, North and South Carolina, and Georgia, under the command of a Major General and four Brigadier Generals. As there is Reason to think the Force of our Enemies will be directed against the Colonies in the Southern Department, Major General Lee is appointed to that Command. The Brigadier Generals are John Armstrong, William Thompson, Andrew Lewis, James Moore Esqr., Lord Stirling and Robert How Esquire. Of these gentlemen, Genl. Armstrong is directed to repair to South Carolina, Genl. Lewis and Genl. Howe to Virginia, Genl. Moore to North Carolina, and Genl. Thompson and Lord Stirling to New York. And that our Affairs in Canada may be under the Direction of an able Officer, and General Schuyler's Health not permitting him to go thither, or if he could, as his Presence is so necessary in New York, the Congress have promoted Brigadier General Thomas to the Rank of a Major General, and directed him to repair to Canada and take the Command of the Continental Forces in that Quarter. I have accordingly inclosed his Commission, and am to desire you will give him orders to repair, with all Expedition, to his Post. To enable him to execute the Purposes Congress have in View in Canada, they have ordered twelve Battering Cannon to be sent from New York, and have forwarded ten Tons of Powder. Of this Article, we have lately received several Supplies, and have some Time ago ordered five Tons and a Half to be sent to you, which, if you have not already received, will, I hope, soon reach you. The Congress have also ordered ten Tons more of Powder to be sent you, which will set out tomorrow, or next Day. Besides this, in the Beginning of last Month, they ordered ten Tons of Salt Petre to be sent to Mr. Wisner's Powder Mill in the Colony of New York; and on the 12th of the same Month, ten Tons to Mr Livingston's Mill in the same Colony, and ten Tons to the Council of Massachusetts, with a Desire to have it manufactured into Gun-Powder, with all possible Expedition and sent to you for the Use of the Army under your Command. Besides this, I have the Pleasure to inform you, that the Powder Mills in this Colony are employed and more Mills are building, which will be employed, so that I have strong Hopes we shall soon have a plentiful Supply of that necessary Article.

With Regard to Arms, I am afraid we shall, for a Time, be under some Difficulty. The Importation is now more precarious and dangerous. To remedy this, a Committee is appointed to contract for the making Arms; and as there is a great Number of Gunsmiths in this and the neighbouring Colonies, I flatter myself we shall soon be able to provide ourselves without Risque or Danger.[3] But we must, like other States engaged in the like glorious Struggle, contend with Difficulties. By Perseverance and the Blessing of God, I trust, if we continue to deserve Freedom, we shall be enabled to overcome them. To that Being, in whose Hands is the Fate of Nations, I recommend you and the Army under your Command.

I have the Honour to be with every Sentiment of Esteem, Sir, Your most obedt. hble Sevt.   John Hancock Presidt.

[*P.S.*] The Inclos'd Letter I Request the favr. you will please to order to be Deliver'd to Mr Cushing.

RC (DLC). In the hand of Jacob Rush, with signature and postscript by Hancock.
[1] These letters, with their enclosures, are in PCC, item 152, 1:435–508; and they are printed in Washington, *Writings* (Fitzpatrick), 4:271–75, 286–93, 312–18, 330–32, 335–38, 348–50. Washington's letter of February 21 has not been found and its receipt is not noted in the journals. For the reading and disposition of these letters in Congress, see *JCC*, 4:123, 154–55, 166, 171, 178, 180, 185–87, 200, 214.
[2] Drummond's letter was enclosed in Washington's February 14 letter to Hancock. For a detailed discussion of the Drummond peace mission, see Lord Drummond's Notes, January 3–9? 1776, note 1.
[3] This committee was appointed on February 23, 1776. *JCC*, 4:169. See also Committee of Congress to Abraham Hunt, March 9, 1776.

John Langdon to the New Hampshire Assembly

Portsmouth. 6 March, 1776. Expresses satisfaction that he has had the honor to be appointed a delegate to the Continental Congress. "When I shall have finished the business in which I have the honour to be immediately employed by the Continent, or have it in such forwardness to leave, shall, when my duty calls me, attend in my place, at the Genl Congress, where it will be my greatest Pride to serve (in any way that may be in my power) this COLONY in particular and the CONTINENT in general." [1]

Abstracted from *N.H. Provincial Papers*, 8:77. Addressed: "To the Honble the Speaker, and the Gentlemen of the Assembly for the Colony of New Hampshire."
[1] Langdon resigned from Congress before attending again. See Josiah Bartlett to Langdon, February 19, 1776, note 3.

Robert Treat Paine to Joseph Palmer

Philadelphia, March 6th, 1776.
I have written Mr. Cushing a long letter on cannon foundery, which you will see.[1] I am desirous to have cannon founding set up our way if we have ore.

Thus, my friend, you find a lawyer, whose business is scientific, labouring through a long detail of the mechanism of cannon foundery; let not this surprise you, for if cannon are the ultima ratio, surely a discourse on them must be chopping logic.

In search of true freedom in vain do we roam,
To hold it for ever we must find it at home.

America never can support her freedom till we have a sufficient source of arms and ammunition of all species among ourselves, and the more these sources are distributed among the colonies, the greater the security of external and internal peace. In pursuance of this idea, I am of a committee who are labouring to push saltpetre and gunpowder making through all the colonies,[2] and are also devising methods to establish a regular and extensive manufacture of muskets, and hope soon to exhibit. . . .[3]

When I began, I intended to have answered some of your political observations, but having exerted myself so much on the sine qua non, you will neither doubt my orthodoxy, nor expect my answers, till I have taken breath from writing, and you from reading.

MS not found; reprinted from *New York Review and Atheneum Magazine* 2 (April 1826): 400.
[1] Not found.

² Joseph Palmer had written three letters to Paine about the production of saltpetre and lead in Massachusetts. Palmer to Paine, January 24, 31, and February 24,
1776, Paine Papers, MHi. Palmer's February 24 letter enclosing a report on lead
was read in Congress on March 6 and referred to the committee for encouraging the
production of saltpetre, of which Paine was a member. *JCC*, 4:185–86.
³ Ellipsis in Tr.

George Read to Caesar Rodney

Dear Sir,   6th March 1776.
   The State of the publick business in Congress has been such that I
cou'd not leave this place with Propriety for these two days past tho
truly little has been done in them,¹ particularly the Marine Committee
is so wanting in Attending Members that for 2 Evenings past we could
not procure a sufficient Number to proceed to business. It is proposed
to supply some Vacancies this day if Congress shall be prevailed on to
Attend to it,² and I firmly resolve on leaving this place on the morrow
to attend our House of Assembly to whom I beg you to excuse me.
Whether Mr. McKean will go down I know not, he has not given me
his Answer. We have nothing new here save that the Assembly of this
Province yesterday voted 2 Battalions of 1500 men in the whole to be
raised for the particular defence of the Province. Col. Bedford setting
off this morning unexpectedly to me, must apologize for this Scrawl of
your, very sincerely,   Geo. Read

RC (Facsimile, Samuel T. Freeman & Co. Catalog, *The Frederick S. Peck Collection of
American Historical Autographs*, February 17, 1947, p. 27).
   ¹ Read was probably responding to instructions he had received from the Delaware
Assembly to return to Newcastle "unless Business of the first Importance should
make your Stay in Congress necessary—if so, you are immediately to let the House
know it." Caesar Rodney to George Read and Thomas McKean, March 6, 1776,
Rodney, *Letters* (Ryden), pp. 71–72.
   ² This day Samuel Huntington, Jonathan Dickinson Sergeant, Benjamin Harrison,
and Edward Rutledge were appointed to the Marine Committee, to which William
Whipple was also added on March 19. *JCC*, 4:186, 214.

Secret Committee Minutes of Proceedings

Com[mitte]e Ch[amber]. March 6th. 1776.
   At a meeting of the Come. Present Saml. Ward, B. Franklin, J. Alsop,
Josa. Bartlett, Josh. Hewes & Rob. Alexander.
   An order was drawn on the continentl. Treasurer in favor of Mr.
Irwin for 800 dlls on Acct. of waggon service.
   At a meeting of the Committee Prest. S. Ward, J. Alsop, T. McKean,
R. Morris & J. Bartlett. A charter party with Wm. Smith of this City,

Broker, for the Brigane. Rachel, F. Pilgrim Isherwood, Master, was Executed, also Instructions to said Master signd. Another with Jonathn Hudson of the town of Baltimore, Maryld., Mercht., for Ship Molly, D. Laurence, Master, was likewise sign'd. Mr. Adam Babcock having presented an estimate of a cargoe from Europe amountg. to 20,000 dlls., Agreed that instead of the Contract proposd 4th inst. for 10,000 dlls he might load a vessel or vessels with potash, oil, beeswax &c to the amount of but not exceedg. 20000 dlls & to export the same for the benefit of the U[nited] C[olonies] to Bordeaux in France for wch. he is to receive the usual Commissions for exportg. & importg. his Father being a party with him in the Contract.[1]

MS (MH).
[1] The contract with Joshua and Adam Babcock was signed on March 7. Journal of the Secret Committee, fol. 43, MH. In a letter of January 31, 1776, Joshua Babcock had asked his kinsman Silas Deane to recommend his son Adam for a Secret Committee contract. *Collections of the Connecticut Historical Society* 2 (1870): 355–56. See also Secret Committee Minutes of Proceedings, March 27, 1776.

Richard Smith's Diary

Wednesday 6 March [1776]

The Votes of Yesterday read & some Letters from Gen Washington and others. Some Motions among the King's Troops in Boston indicate that they intend soon to evacuate the place, our Gen. intends to bombard the Town if he can get Powder but a Council of War have determined it not to be expedient at present. The Marine Comee. was filled up (Sergeant for N Jersey). Our Debts of Powder to Pennsa. and N York ordered to be paid and 5 Tons ordered to the Southern Departmt, one Ton to the Lower Counties, one Ton to N Jersey and some to Maryland. The 350 Stand of Arms just arrived, were ordered, some of them to repay Pennsa. & the remainder to Waynes Battaln now going to N York. A motion by E Rutledge to send Major Hausaker to the Southward was carried in the Negative 6 Colonies to 5. On motion of Harrison, Thos. Bullet of Virginia was made Dep Adjutant Gen. with the Rank of Lt Col. Brig. Thomas was voted to command in Canada with the Rank of Major Gen. This was on Motion of E. Rutledge. Hooper just returned from Boston[1] says that Capt. Manley with 5 or 6 privateers are laid up for Want of Powder. (Manly soon got out again.) A Motion to appoint the Field Officers for 4 Battals. in N York was considered and postponed.[2] The Business of finding & smelting Lead was given in Charge to the Salt petre Comee. Willing Chairman of the Comee. of Claims prayed Advice at what Period the Massach[usett]s Bay may begin their Accots. agt the Continent Whether from the Battle of Lexington or some Time before, this Point could not now be settled. Motion by Sherman to examine Thos. Walker & Mr. Price of Montreal before the House on the State of Canada, was opposed as unnecessary and dropt.

MS (DLC).
[1] See William Hooper's first letter to Joseph Hewes and John Penn, February 6, 1776, note 1.
[2] See James Duane to the New York Provincial Convention, February 25, 1776, note 7.

John Adams to John Thomas

Dr Sir   Philadelphia March 7, 1776
The Congress have determined to send you to Canada. They have advanced you one Step, by making you a Major General, and have made an handsome Establishment for a Table.[1]

Your Friends the Delegates from your native Province were much embarrassed, between a Desire to have you promoted and placed in so honourable a Command, on the one Hand, and a Reluctance at loosing your Services at Roxbury or Cambridge on the other. But all agreed that you ought to be placed where you could do the most service, and Canada was thought by all to be very important and by some the most important Post in America.

You will have excellent Advice and assistance in the Committee we are sending Dr Franklin, Mr Chace, Mr Carroll and his Relation.

Mr Walker, Mr Price and Mr Bondfield, will be in Canada too, as soon as you. General Wooster and Arnold will give you the best Information.

The Department to which you are destined has been in Great Confusion, and every Gentleman who has come from thence has given a different account.

General Schuyler, who is an honest Man and a good Patriot, has had a Politeness about him towards Canadian and British Prisoners, which has enabled them and their ministerial Friends to impose upon him in some Instances. This has occasioned some Altercation between him and Wooster. But Wooster has done that in Canada which Schuyler could not have done. He has kept up an Army there through the Winter.

Schuylers head Quarters will be at Albany, I suppose and he will be of vast service, in procuring and forwarding Supplies, and in many other Ways in promoting the service but his Health will not permit him to go into Canada.

I wish I could write you a Volume—for to give you the Characters of Persons in Canada of whom we have heard, and some of whom We have seen, and to explain to you every Thing which has been opened here relative to that Province would fill one. But these Hints must suffice.

Your huml sert,   John Adams

348 MARCH 7, 1776

[*P.S.*] Let me beg of you to write me, if you can Spare the Time. It is of great Importance that the Delegates from New England should be truly informed, of the Course of Things in Canada.

RC (MHi).
¹ See John Hancock to John Thomas, March 6, 1776.

John Hancock to Thomas Cushing

Dear Sir,   Philadelphia March 7th. 1776

I wrote you of yesterday's Date, by an Express, under Cover to General Washington, which informed you every Circumstance that occurred necessary for your Government, as to the Ships. I hope soon to hear of your having received my Letter, and the twenty five Thousand Dollars, as well as the Plans; all which I sent under the Care of Col Bull; and that I shall soon have a Receipt for the Money. I have been obliged to detain Mr. Avery, longer than I intended, owing to the urgent Business of Congress, and the necessary Attendance of the Members in Congress, which has prevented the Meetings of the Marine Committee, and of Consequence retarded their Business, which has delayed Mr. Avery. I now inclose you, the Dimensions of every Thing necessary for your Guidance in Matters respecting the Ships, & other Appurtenances. What further occurs to you necessary, let me know, and the Directions shall be transmitted to you. I now beg you will set every Wheel in Motion. Employ every Man that can be useful in the different Branches. Procure every necessary that can be obtained with you; The Deficiencies acquaint me of, and I will endeavour to supply them from hence. In short, exert every Nerve to promote Dispatch. Let the Heads and Galleries for the Ships, be neatly carved & executed. I leave the Device to you. But, by all Means, let ours be as good, handsome, strong, and as early completed, as any that are building here, or in any of the other Colonies, for your Reputation and mine are at Stake; and there are not wanting those who are fond of prejudicing both. I have ordered two Hundred Pieces of Duck from New York. Set the Sail-Makers to Work. Iron, I hope, you will find with you. If not, let me know, as soon as possible, and I will send some, though, at present, there is none to be purchased in the City, owing to the Badness of the Roads.

I send you by Mr. Avery a further supply of Money in Bills and Dollars. The Bills I took to oblige the Gentlemen. Please to return them immediately to Me, if not honoured; and if paid, send me a Receipt for the whole Sum, and employ the Money in the Service of the Ships, for the publick Account. The Bills and Money are as follows—viz

William Barrel & Jona. Mifflin junr. Bill on
Thomas Mifflin, of this Date for—   Dollars   6000

Will. Barrel on Joseph Barrel Do. Date—	1000
Andrew Cabot on Capt Geo. Dodge of	
Salem, Do. Date—	4000
The above Bills you will find enclosed—	11000
Continental Money delivered to Mr. John Avery—	19000
Dollars	30000

Do be careful to engage good Block-Makers, and let every Article be well executed.

In writing my several Letters to you, previous to this Date, I had not Time to take Copies. I must therefore beg, at your Leisure, you will please to favour me with exact Copies of all; together with the first Instructions delivered to you on your leaving Philada. This as soon as you can.

I was in hopes of being able to Send you the Dimensions of Rigging &c but the Committee are not ready, however if you are Ready before you hear from me do not wait, but Employ the best Judges and follow their Advice. I however Inclose you the Estimate of the Report with respect to Cables & Anchors, the other smaller Cables & Anchors necessary Determine with you, if you do not hear timely from me.

I have nothing New to Communicate. Do write me often and give me every Occurrence. I hope you will Send me my Commission as Major General that I may Appear in Character. I assure you this Appointment pleases me, I think I know a little of the Duty, & on my Return I will Endeavour under the Direction of your Board to put the Militia upon a Respectable footing. I will not be wanting.

My utmost Exertions shall never be witheld for the Good of my Colony, whenever they can be usefull they shall be Employ'd in that Service however Dangerous, and I Defy Malice itself to Contradict the sincerity & uprightness of those Assertions.

I Beg to be Remembered to all Friends. The Inclos'd Letters I Beg you will order to be Deliver'd; that to Mr. Bant is of Consequence, I therefore Request your particular Care of it.

Mrs. Hancock Joines me in best Respects to your good Lady & Family & I am very truly, Dear Sir, Your Real Friend & hum sert,

John Hancock

[*P.S.*] What I wrote you in my last respecting my Ship at Salem, I beg your Attention to. The Congress finding my Business increase so much, desir'd me to appoint a private Secretary wch. I have done, a Bror. of Dr Rush,[1] he Copied the first part of this Letter, but I was oblig'd to call him off, wch. will account for the Diversity of the writing. I am immensely hurried.

New Hampshire should pay part of the Expence, Mr Avery paid Harry's Expences to Fairfield wch. you will Charge & is Right.

I Beg you will Acquaint my good Friend Mr Wm Cooper, that I

Recd his Letter, am much oblig'd to him, will write him fully by next; that my Regard & Friendship for him is not nor cannot be Lessen'd, that I am his Friend & ever the Friend of my Colony.

RC (MHi). First four paragraphs in the hand of Jacob Rush, with remaining paragraphs and signature by Hancock.
[1] Jacob Rush (1747–1820), Pennsylvania lawyer and brother of Dr. Benjamin Rush, served as private secretary to President Hancock from January 1776 to November 7, 1777, when he was appointed deputy secretary of Congress. *JCC*, 9:875; and Benjamin Rush, *The Autobiography of Benjamin Rush*, ed. George W. Corner (Princeton: Published for the American Philosophical Society by Princeton University Press, 1948), p. 28n.22.

John Hancock to Philip Schuyler

Sir   Philadelphia 7 March 1776
    Since my last I have had the honour to Receive your several Letters of the 10th, 13th, 15th, 20th, 21st, 23d, 26th, & 27th Febry. which were immediately Communicated to Congress.[1] I have the pleasure to inform you that the Congress highly Approve the orders you have given to Colo. Warner. They have Directed a quantity of Steel to be purchas'd & forwarded to you by the Delegates of New Jersey, and have order'd an Accott. to be made out and Sent to you of the money paid to the Pennsylvania Troops who have Marched to Canada.[2] Your other Letters are under Consideration, as soon as the Congress come to a Determination thereon, I shall do myself the honour to transmitt to you.
    I am extremely sorry to find you Recover health so slowly, I hope that your Attention to publick Affairs will not make you neglect the Care necessary for perfecting your Recovery. The Congress have the most Anxious Concern for you, knowing the important services you can render to your Country at this critical Conjuncture.
    As there is Reason to Apprehend that our Enemies intend to direct their operations in the ensuing Campaign against the middle & Southern Colonies, the Congress have thought proper in order to prepare for their Defence, to Divide those Colonies into two Departments, one to Comprehend New York, New Jersey, Pennsylvania, Delaware Government & Maryland, under the Command of a Major General and Two Brigadier Generals, and the other, the Colonies to the Southward, under the Command of a Major General & four Brigadr Generals. The Brigadier Generals are John Armstrong, William Thompson, Andrew Lewis, James Moore Esqrs., the Honl. William Earl of Stirling & Robert Howe Esqr. General Armstrong they have Directed to Repair to South Carolina, General Lewis & General Howe to Virginia, Genl Moore to North Carolina, & General Thompson & Lord Stirling to New York. With Regard to Canada, the Congress have superceeded the orders formerly

Given to Genl Lee, & Directed him to take the Command in the Southern Department, and have promoted Brigadr. General Thomas to the Rank of a Major General, & order'd him to Repair to the Province of Canada & Take the Command of the Continental Forces there. But still they Rely greatly on your Efforts for perfecting the work so conspicuously begun & so well Conducted under your orders last Campaign. The Supplies of Provisions, Military Stores &c for the Army in Canada must be procured in these Colonies & Sent across the Lakes. On these Supplies being regularly Sent will depend not only the Success but the existence of the Army in Canada. For this Reason I am directed to inform you it is the Desire of Congress you should for the present or untill you Receive further orders fix your head Quarters at Albany, there without being exposed to the fatigues of the Camp, untill your health is perfectly Restor'd, you will be in a Scituation to direct the proper Arrangements for Supplying the Army in Canada, & to superintend the operations necessary for the Defence of New York & Hudson's River (the Security of which is a matter of the last importance) & also the affairs of the whole middle Department. The Generals under you will Receive & Execute your orders, & in case of Necessity you will be Ready to bring down to their aid the whole force of the Colony.[3] I would just observe that it is the Desire of the Congress that the Soldiers be employ'd in erecting & throwing up the necessary works for Defence both in New York & on Hudson's River. The Commissioners will set out this week, they will Call on you in their way to Canada, and I Expect they will be invested with full powers not only to Settle the Affairs of that province, but to Adjust those matters that have Given you uneasiness.[4]

With sincere & hearty wishes for your health & prosperity, I have the honour to be, with great Esteem, Sir, Your most Obedt sevt, J H Prt.

LB (DNA: PCC, item 12A).

[1] These letters of Schuyler with enclosures are in PCC, item 153, 1:512–65, 2:1–36, and *Am. Archives*, 4th ser. 4:990–91, 1131–32, 1156–57, 1214–17, 1469, 1481–83, 1499, 1510–11. For the reading and disposition of these letters in Congress, see *JCC*, 4:164, 177, 183–84, 187, 190–92.

[2] See *JCC*, 4:177.

[3] See *JCC*, 4:180–81, 186, 191–92; and Hancock's letters to Charles Lee and to William Alexander, March 1, and to John Thomas, March 6, 1776.

[4] Congress did not approve the instructions for the commissioners to Canada until March 20. *JCC*, 4:215–19.

Richard Smith's Diary

Thursday 7 March [1776]
The Votes read and Letters from various Persons. Reports of Accots.

made & agreed to be paid. Harrison informed Congress that Major Isaac Melchior had grossly abused the President & damned Him and the Congress, the President had presented Him with a Captains Commission which was much below Melchiors Expectation (he went a Volunteer from Philada. to Cambridge & from thence with Arnold over to Quebec). After long debates on the Power of the Congress to commit, and on a Motion made by Harrison to declare Him incapable of serving the Continent hereafter, a Resolution drawn by Johnson took Effect which after shortly stating the Offence charged, orders Him to appear before Congress to morrow Morng. at 11 oCloc to answer the same. An Applicatn. made by the Jersey Delegates in Favor of a Demand of Michael Kearney was com[mitte]d to the Comee. on Gen Washingtons Letters. Ld. Stirling had seized Kearneys Shallop and made Use of Her in taking the Blue Mountain Valley. The Shallop being afterwards taken by the Enemy, the Prayer is for Compensation out of the Ship.[1]

The Lt. Col of Thompsons Riflemen was promoted to the Regiment & the Eldest Capt. made Lt. Col.[2] Lt. Col. Wm. Winds of Lord Stirling's was made Col & Matthias Ogden (who was at the Affair of Quebec) Lt Col.[3] These Two were vacant by their Cols. becoming Brigadiers. Arms were ordered for the Powder Guards. 100,000 Dollars advanced to Connecticut in Part of their Demand after much Fault found with them for not settling their Accounts. Hooper says the Eastern Demands agt. Us are vastly great, that some Commissary there employs above Sixty Clerks at our Expence &c.

MS (DLC).
[1] The New Jersey delegates almost certainly made this "Application" in response to Gen. William Alexander's February 25 letter and enclosures to William Livingston; and in consequence of it Congress awarded Kearney $725 on April 9 for the loss of his shallop. See *JCC*, 4:214, 266; and *Am. Archives*, 4th ser. 4:1492–93.
[2] The officers referred to here by Smith are Edward Hand and James Chambers. See *JCC*, 4:188. A letter of this date from John Hancock to Colonel Hand, informing Hand of his promotion, is in PCC, item 12A, and *Am. Archives*, 4th ser. 5:100.
[3] John Hancock's letters of this date to Colonel Winds and Lieutenant Colonel Ogden, informing them of their promotions to these ranks, are in PCC, item 12A, and *Am. Archives*, 4th ser. 5:99.

John Adams to Abigail Adams

My Dear   Philadelphia March 8. 1776
Yesterday by Major Osgood I had the Pleasure of a Letter from Mr. Palmer,[1] in which he kindly informed me of your and the Familys Welfare. This is the first Intelligence I have had from Braintree since I left it—not a Line from you. Am sorry to learn that Braintree People are alarmed—hope they will not be attacked. Want to know the Particulars—how they have been threatned &c.

Thomas is made a Major General and ordered to Canada. The general Expectation here is that the boldest Efforts of our Enemies will be made at Virginia and S. Carolina. I believe no such Thing. Boston, N. York and Quebec will be their Object.

I have sent you, as many Letters as I could, and some Pamphlets and News Papers, and shall continue to do so. I want a servant excessively. Know not what to do for Want of one. So much Company—and so many Things to do.

Write me as often as you can—let me know whether Bass got home without any Accident, and whether your Fathers beautifull Mare is well of her Wound.

God bless you my dear, and all about you, to whom be pleased to remember my most tender Affection.

RC (MHi). Adams, *Family Correspondence* (Butterfield), 1:356–57.
[1] Joseph Palmer's February 19 letter to Adams is in the Adams Papers, MHi.

Samuel Adams to James Warren

My dear sir,   Philada. March 8 1776

I now sit down just to acknowledge the rect of your favor of the 14th of Feby,[1] and to mention to you a Matter which considerd in it self may appear to be of small Moment but in its Effects may possibly be mischievious. I believe I may safely appeal to all the Letters which I have written to my Friends since I have been in this City to vindicate myself in affirming that I have never mentiond Mr C[ushing] nor referrd to his Conduct in any of them, excepting one to my worthy Colleague Mr A[dams] when he was at Watertown a few Weeks ago, in which I informd him of the side Mr C had taken in a very interresting Debate; and then I only observd that he had a Right to give his opinion whenever he thought himself prepard to form one.[2] Yet I have been told it has been industriously reported that Mr A and my self have been secretly writing to his Prejudice and that our Letters have operated to his being superceded. So fully perswaded did some Gentlemen seem to be of the Truth of this Report, and Mr D[uane] of NY in particular whom I have heard express the warmest Affection for Mr C, that he appeard to be surprizd to hear me contradict it. Whether this Report and a Beliefe of it inducd the Friends of Mr C to open a charitable Subscription in Support of his Character I am not able to say.[3] If it was so, they ought in Justice to him to have made themselves certain of the Truth of it; for to offer Aid to the Reputation of a Gentleman without a real Necessity is surely no Advantage to it. A Letter was handed about, addressed Mr C. The Contents I never saw. His Confidential Friends signd it. Other Gentlemen at their Request also set their hands to it,

354 March 8, 1776

perhaps with as much Indifference as a Man of Business would give a Shilling to get rid of the Importunity of a Beggar. I hear it is supposd in Watertown to be a Vote of Thanks of the Congress to Mr C for his eminent Services in which his Recall is mentiond with Regrets; but this is most certainly a Mistake. The Gentlemen signd it in their private Capacity With Submission, should they not have addressd it to another person, or publishd it to the World after the Manner of other Addresses; for if they intended it to recommend Mr C to his own Constituents, was it not hard to oblige him to blow the Trumpet himself which they had prepared to sound his Praise. But Major Osgood is in haste. I must therefore drop this Subject *for the present* and conclude affectionately yours

RC (MHi). In Adams' hand, though not signed.

[1] Warren's February 14 letter is in the Samuel Adams Papers, NN. It does not, however, mention the split between Samuel Adams and Thomas Cushing, which is Adams' main preoccupation in this letter.

[2] Adams had made these comments in his letter of December 22, 1775, to John Adams, who probably told Samuel of the circulation of such accusations in Massachusetts after he returned to Philadelphia on February 8.

[3] Only a fragment of this testimonial letter survives; it is quoted in John Hancock to Thomas Cushing, January 17, 1776, note 2.

Josiah Bartlett to John Langdon

Dear Sir,   Philadelphia March 8th 1776.

I have just now procured the dimensions of masts, yards &c which I enclose to you. The length and bigness of cables and weight of anchors is not determined on but hope to bring it with me in a few days. Yours of the 26th ult is now come to hand enclosing a sketch of the harbor of Portsmouth for which I thank you.[1] I have not any thing new to inform you except that General Clinton with his troops from Boston after tarrying a few days with Lord Dunmore left him and sailed for the Southward. I forget whether I informed you in my last that General Thomas is advanced to the rank of a Major General and ordered to take the command in Canada. General Lee is ordered to the Southern Department and the Brigadier Generals Armstrong, Lewis, Moore and Howe are to command under him. The Brigadier Generals Thompson and Lord Sterling for New York or the middle department.

I am your friend &c,   Josiah Bartlett

P.S. I have sent the 15,000 dollars to the care of Mr Thomas Cushing.
                                                                  J.B.

Tr (DLC).

[1] Langdon's letter of February 26, in which he explained that he was proceeding

with the frigate's construction using plans "of our own Drawing," is printed in Clark, *Naval Documents*, 4:79.

John Hancock to
Michael Hillegas and George Clymer

Gentlemen   Philada. March 8th. 1776

    Please to pay to The Honl. Mr. Paine, Coll. Willson, Mr Huntington, Coll Lee & Coll Morris a Committee for Encouraging the Manufacture of Fire Arms, Ten Thousand Dollars, the said Committee to be Accountable for the Expenditure of said Sum.[1]

    I am Gentn., Your very hum servt,   John Hancock Presidt.

RC (MHi).
[1] Congress authorized this expenditure on this date. *JCC*, 4:192.

Richard Smith's Diary

[March 8, 1776]

    Friday 8. The Minutes read. The Field Officers of 4 N York Battalions were now elected by Ballot as usual. Isaac Melchior sent in a penitential Letter and attending according to Order was called in and acquainted by the President with the Particulars of the Charge agt. Him, he pretended Ignorance of the Words but begged Pardon of the President and of the Congress for his bad Behavior, whereupon he was dismissed without Punishment in Consideration of his late Military Services.[1] A Comee. of 3 viz. Gerry, L Morris and Wolcott appointed to consider of the best Methods of victualling the Canadian Army,[2] a Report was agreed to on this Subject and on the Gens. Letters, by part whereof Peter Zabriskie is to be employed to convey Provisions to Albany, by another Article no Indian is to be employed in our Army without Leave of the Indian Nation in Council and withot. express Leave of Congress (this appeared to me a very absurd and impolitic Regulation).[3] A long Altercation followed on the first Article of a Report made by John Adams for reconciling the Differences between the Generals Schuyler and Wooster, the Article was at last voted out and other Parts of the Report adopted.[4] An Application to make Mr. Price Dep Commissary of Canada was referred to our Gentn. now going there.[5] Accounts transmitted from Canada by Col. Hazen of the Damages done to Him by our Soldiers who had destroyed or damaged his House at St. Johns & killed his Cattle &c were referred to a Comee. of 4 viz. Wyth, Ward, Sherman and S. Adams.[6] Letters read from Gen Lee and others.[7] E.

Rutledge reported That the Comee. had conferred with Govr. Penn on the supposed Message to the 6 Nations who disclaimed any Knowledge of it.[8] Some Order was taken to inform Gen Schuyler hereof & to desire Him to send down the Person who had misinformed Him. An Advance of 10,000 Dollars [. . . .][9]

MS (DLC).

[1] See Smith's Diary, March 7,.1776.

[2] For the resolves which Congress adopted on March 25, 29, and April 15, 1776, in response to the reports of this committee, see *JCC*, 4:221, 236, 240–41, 257, 284.

[3] The foregoing resolves were adopted in response to a report from a committee considering the letters of various Continental generals, not the committee on the supply of the army in Canada. *JCC*, 4:191–92.

[4] For the background of the conflict between Generals Schuyler and Wooster, see Schuyler's letters to Hancock of January 25 and February 20 and to Wooster of January 26. PCC, item 153, 1:450–53, 540–50; and *Am. Archives*, 4th ser. 4:851–52, 1003–4, 1214–16. See also Wooster's letters of February 11 to Hancock and of February 20 to Schuyler. PCC, item 161, 2:265–66; and *Am. Archives*, 4th ser. 4:1001–2, 1007.

[5] Congress appointed James Price to this office on March 29. *JCC*, 4:240–41.

[6] Col. Moses Hazen's letter to Hancock of February 18 and accompanying accounts are in PCC, item 78, 11:17–26, and *Am. Archives*, 4th ser. 4:1186–90. For the report on these accounts which this committee submitted to Congress on March 12, see *JCC*, 4:198–99.

[7] This day Congress received letters to Hancock of March 2 from Connecticut governor Jonathan Trumbull and of March 5 from Gen. Charles Lee. See PCC, item 66, 1:83, 86, item 158, 1:33–36; and *Am. Archives*, 4th ser. 5:46, 74–75.

[8] See Andrew Allen to Philip Schuyler, March 17, 1776.

[9] Remainder of entry missing.

Samuel Ward to His Daughter

My dearest   Philadelpa. 8th March 1776

You know me so well that it is unnecessary for me to say that 'tho' in arranging the various Duties of Life I always consider that which is due to my Country as superior to all others save that due to the supreme Parent of the universe yet while I have a Regard to any thing in this World you & all my Children will ever have a large Share of my Heart, but affectionate as I am the incessant Employ of my public Station denies me the Pleasure of paying that Attention to you all which in a State of public Tranquility my affection, Duty & Inclination would all conspire to induce me to do. I can no more, all gracious Heaven will do the rest for You.

I can't help smiling to think that you expect when your Daddy & Bror. Sammy are at home you shall be compleatly happy notwithstanding "that something still which prompts the eternal Sigh." Heaven wisely did not design this World for a State of perfect Bliss, We have innumerable Mercies daily bestowed upon Us, but the Mind like the wandring Eye no sooner takes in one agreable object than it overlooks it and stretches after another. This Imperfection may be in some degree natural but the mischiefs of it are greatly increased by inattention to the Duties of Religion, by a Want of a thorough Confidence in the Wisdom & Goodness of God, by an ungrateful Heart which is insensible of the innumerable Mercies we enjoy and peevishly frets and worries itself & all around it for want of a thing which perhaps if obtained would make it very unhappy. Let any Person compare what they enjoy with what they may suppose they want and they will find their wants few compared with their Enjoyments, why should a Being who is sure of living but a few moments (for such only is a long Life compared with Eternity) be so anxious about things of very little consequence to an immortal mind, but we want grand Houses & Gardens, gay Clothes, a Chariot & a thousand other such Trifles for what my Dear. Cant the philosophic Mind that places its true Happiness in living according to the Dictates of Reason and Virtue be as happy in a House barely comfortable and convenient, in a good Kitchen Garden which affords a proper Repast for a frugal Table, in plain neat Clothes, in walking or riding a good Horse as in the Possession of ten thousand Superfluities? Most clearly It can, but even Riches my dearest when properly employed by the benevolent Mind afford a most rational Satisfaction, the surest Road to Happiness is to consider what our Duty requires and to do it chearfully leaving all events to Providence or in the Words of your Favorite Pope "What right, what true, what fit we justly call, let that be all my Care for that is all."

I have bought Polly & you each a Gown not of dark purple callico but a light shaped cotton one. I think it pretty & good to wear, I cant find one dark one for Nancy that pleases Me, I shall try once more & take the cleverest I can get. I have bought a piece excellent Lawn off which she shall have an Apron, I have bought four [. . .] handkc. very good, two for her and one for each of you, how I shall get them home I know not at present but shall do it as soon as I can.

Your Bror. Sammy I have not heard from since he was taken Prisoner,[1] poor Child Heaven thinks best to try his Virtue & Fortitude. He is probably once more reduced to a short allowance of Provisions for by the last Letters from Genl. Arnold, the Garrison had sallied out once but our People advancing briskly to attack them, they retreated precipitately and having got neither Provisions or Fuel since he blockaded the Place they were reduced to short Allowance of Provisions & would soon be forced to burn their houses and Vessels. The Prisoners are treated very well & I doubt not will fare as well as the Garrison & your Bror. as well as any one of them; I hope He will make a proper use of his Time, the School of affliction tho for the time it lasts not the most agreable is often the best. Some of the worthiest Characters which have adorned the Scene of human Action were thus educated and thus refined; may Heaven stamp so deeply upon your Bros. Soul the Impressions of every moral, political & Social Virtue that no Temptations may deface them. Dr. Franklin & Mr. Chase are going to Canada; by them I shall inclose your Letter to your Brother.

My last to Polly contained not a Sentiment save about Business I believe, in this you have some other Ideas & no Business; you must make one common Stock of both & divide them equally between you. Want of Time prevents my writing to the little Boys and Betsy; help them all to behave well and to improve their Minds as much as possible; when I shall be with them God only know. Business encreases upon us, and I very soon expect some important Actions both in the North & South.

My very affectionate Regards to your Aunts & cousin Betsy, to all my Family and Friends; write to Me as often as you can; I am, My dearest, Your very affectionate Father,   Sam. Ward

P.S. Dont forget to hold your Head up & dont suffer Betsy or your little Brothers to hold theirs down; keep them all if possible from being awk[w]ard in their Behavior and clownish or vulgar in their Language.

RC (RHi).
[1] See Ward to Samuel Ward, Jr., January 21, 1776, in Ward, *Correspondence* (Knollenberg), pp. 175–77.

Oliver Wolcott to Laura Wolcott

My Dear   Philadelphia March [8] [1] 1776
I Wrote to you a few days ago and let you know I was well. By the Blessing of God I continue So, and it would be a great Satisfaction to Me to know that you and the Family injoyed the same favour, but that is impossible for me at this Moment to know, and it becomes Me to Acquiesce in the divine Government. I hope a mercifull Providence may be your shield and Support. Congress will undouptedly Sit for Some Time and how you will Order the Summer Business I cannot Say. Labour will probably be extremely Scarce, and whether there may be any Profit in hiring much help you must judge. Trade must languish during the present Struggle. Every Thing here is buying up and is Very dear and growing continually More so. Those who Venture in Trade will pay themselves for their Risque. I think it will be well for you to Secure Such Articles as you May want particularly Cloathing especially Linings & Buttons and West Indian Articles, so as to carry thro till next Winter. I wish I had wrote to you earlier on this Head. I wish to know what Articles may be necessary for Me to purchase here. Trade will be carried on perhaps before a great While but in Such an uncertainty of Affairs it will be well to be a little provident. You may not think

it necessary to mention these particulars, as they may Occasion more Speculation than they deserve.

The Association is the only Restraint now on Trade. That may probably continue Materially the same for some Time. The People of this City are peculiarly Attentive to their Interest. The Expence of living at the same Rate or Manner We do at Litchfield is I believe at least six Times as dear. I am in a House hospitable and kind, Neat and Virtuous, accommidations comfortable, but not in the high Way of Life—but am well Suited. Mr. Huntington has had the small Pox but for Near three Weeks has Attended the Congress—And I am happy in my Company. Mr Sherman is well and talks of making a Short Visit home next Week.

Since my last Twenty Seven Tons of G. Powder, one Ton of Salt Petre and 500 Stands of Arms have been bro't in here. Very soon they will be able to Manufacture Several Tons a Week in this Colony, and I wish the like may be done in every Other. The cruel British Administration are I believe fix'd upon our Ruin, but God Reigns and I beleive our Adversarys will be disappointed.

A Convention of this Colony are to meet the Second of April and they will probably alter the Instructions the Assembly gave their Delegates. A Petition from a Considerable Number of Merchants of the City lys before Congress Asking for Letters of Mark and Reprizal. Genl. Thomas is ordered to Canada and Genl. Lee Stands Ordered to the Southward. For further News refer you to the Papers. If I should not be able to Write Soon to Mr. Lyman, present him my Compliments and tell him no part of our [Army] is or ever has been by any Resolution of Congress under a Provincial Direction and I cannot Guess how Such a Story Should arise.[2] As it may be of some gratification to you to have some Account of this City, would inform you, that it is Situated about 150 miles from the Sea, on the West Side of the River Delaware, which runs near N. and South, and is about one mile Wide against the City, and Navigable for Ships of 500 Tons. The Tide rises here several feet. There are a great Number of Short Wharves with slips between them, the whole length of the City to which any Ships may come and unload. The Streets of the City are Streight and intersected, the foot paths paved with Bricks of which their Houses are universally made tho covered all with Shingles, which they say is a much better Security against fire than Slate, as such heavy coverings would make an approach to a House on fire extremely dangerous. I have seen better Houses in N York than any private Houses here, tho' these are generally elegant, and their Houses as well as every thing else is founded on the highest Principles of Economy—Utility and Duration—and indeed there is no Distinction amongst this People but Sick and Poor. Their State House and Churches are elegant, and their Hospital, Bettering House and jail probably much surpass any Thing of the like kind upon the continent. The two Former are spacious, Very Neat and well provided for, every Thing Seems to

be under the finest Regulation. Their jail in Appearance more re-
sembles a Princes Palace than a House of Confinement, yet it affords
the greatest Security. From this House I have not visited the House of
Correction. I have seen the outside of it which looks well enough, but
I will keep myself from being able to inform you how it is within. The
City is Seated much upon a plain (which in my opinion renders it less
beautiful) and is capable of the largest Extention. The inhabitants are
supposed to be about forty five Thousand. About 500 Houses are built
yearly in common Times—and Should no great publick Convulsions or
desolating Calamities retard its growth I believe within 150 years it
will Excell any City in Europe. They have one great Market which it
is a Curiosity to See. It is extreemly fine for everyThing except Fish,
which it is but Very poorly provided with.

There are Many Things here which discover great Ingenuity and
Design, but Nothing Struck my Mind in any Degree like the Amazing
Orrery of Mr Rittenhouse. As I am but little acquainted with astronomy
or Mechanism I could only View it with the strange Wonder of a Bar-
barian for such I could only consider myself when compared to such a
Matchless Genius. The whole Solar System is here represented, the com-
paritive Distances and Magnitude of every Planet and their Satellites,
and all their true Motions made by turning a small crank in the manner
a Man turns a Grind stone, each turn Makes a day. The outer Circle
of this Works on which the Signs are marked which make a retrograde
Rotation once in Twenty five Thousand years, moves so inconceiveably
Slow as to require Nine Million one hundred Twenty five Thousand
Turns to bring this Circle once round. This Work which has a Vast
Number of Wheels and an Infinity of Indentations and Teeth is capable
of representing the Exact Position of every Moon and Planet at any
Period for eighteen hundred years forward. How Such a Complicated
tho't could ever enter into, or be retained by a human Soul, and if retained how Such an Amazing Design could ever be executed, infinitely
exceeds all my Comprehension. I Viewed an Eclipse of the Sun which
will be total if I remember right a little South of this City the Tenth
of June 1776 and what to me was Very wonderful when I first Viewed
the Moon thro the Glass it appeared quite luminous but as it drew more
into a Line with the Sun it grew gradually darker till it became quite
so when it covered the Suns face but this was owing to Reflection. This
Work is calculated to Make an ordinary Genius humble while it leads
to adore that fountain of Wisdom which has darted such a bright Ray
of himself upon any human Soul. I saw Mr Rittenhouse and Viewed
him with great Curiosity, but I saw no other Mark of Genius Stamped
upon him than what is discoverable in an ordinary man. He appeard
extreemly Modest and rather what We call Shamefaced—but he has
erected a Monument which will be admired while learning lasts, or
Man is capable of adoring the Creator.

By my Writing so long a Letter you may Think I have little else to do, but I assure you I am Very Busy but as I cannot See you let me take the pleasure of Writing to you. Upon reveiwing my Letter I wish it was wrote more legibly but it must pass as it is. My Love to my Children and my best Compliments to all my Freinds—and I wish they could think of Me so much, as once in a while to Write Me a Letter. Wishing you all possible Happiness, I am yours with the tenderest affection.

Oliver Wolcott

P.S. There has been two small flights of snow since I have been here. A good deal of cold Weather but the Grass now begins to start. I have not heard how your Winter has been.

RC (CtHi).
[1] The assignment of this date is based on Wolcott's reference (in his March 19 letter to Laura) to a letter of "the 8t instant," and on the similarity of topics Wolcott discussed in this letter and in his letter of March 9 to Matthew Griswold.
[2] On January 2 Congress had granted provincial governmental bodies limited authority to control, within their borders, Continental troops called upon for assistance to deal with civilians inimical to the American cause. Gen. Charles Lee had apparently misunderstood this resolution and had used it to explain his decision to order a Connecticut regiment to return home instead of assisting in the defense of New York City. See *JCC*, 4:20; and *Am. Archives*, 4th ser. 4:954–55.

Committee of Congress to Abraham Hunt

Sr,   Philada March 9th. 1776
    The Congress have appointed a Cmttee to Contract for the making Musketts & bayonetts, in persuance of wch. they have agreed with Ebenezer Cowel to carry on the manufacture of gunlocks for the use of the United Colonies & have advanced him 267 Dollars & he is to be paid weekly for all the good substantial double bridled gunlocks he shall make & deliver.[1] This makes it necessary that there should be some person in Trenton who will receive the said gunlocks as they are made & pay Mr. Cowell the money for them; upon Enquiry it was strongly recommended to us to make application to you to undertake this business. You will please to let us know as soon as may be your inclination in the matter that we may Supply you with a Sum of money for the said purpose.
    I am yr hble Servt,   RTP by order of sd. Cmttee

FC (MHi). In the hand of Robert Treat Paine. Addressed: "To Abraham Hunt Esq. at Trenton."
[1] The committee's letter to Ebenezer Cowell has not been found, but the committee wrote to "Benjamin Yard in Trenton" seeking a contract: "as they have been informed that you are capable of making the barrels they desire you would immediately inform them whether you will undertake in this business, & whether you can

procure bayonetts to be made & all the other parts except the locks, & what your terms are that a Contract may be made if agreable." Robert Treat Paine to Benjamin Yard, March 9, 1776, MHi. See also *JCC*, 4:169.

Thomas Johnson to
the Maryland Council of Safety

Gent.   Phila. 9 March 1776.
    Capt. Tibbett has this Moment arrived. The Vessell he went out in is sold & he is in an armed Vessell;[1] he has only about 2,000 lb of powder, about 6 Tons of Lead, Duck, Ozn[aburg]s, &c. The Vessel is on her way to the City; we shall send forward the Effects as well as the powder borrowed from our province by Virga. which is ordered out of a very scanty Stock to be returned.
    I am Gent. very respectfully, Your most obedt Servt.
                                                              Th Johnson Junr

RC (MdAA).
    [1] Capt. James Tibbett had sold the *Rachel* and purchased the armed brig *Wild Duck* in St. Eustatius for Maryland. On March 13, Congress directed the Marine Committee to purchase the brig, which was subsequently renamed the *Lexington* and placed under the command of Capt. John Barry. Clark, *Naval Documents*, 4:310–11; *JCC*, 4:201; Richard Smith's Diary, March 13; and Maryland Delegates to the Maryland Council, March 19, 1776. For an embellished account of Barry's appointment to this command and his exploits as commander of the *Lexington*, see William Bell Clark, *Gallant John Barry, 1745–1803* (New York: Macmillan Co., 1938), pp 72–81.

William Livingston to Philip Schuyler

Sir   Phil. 9 March 1776
    This will accompany 1000 lb of Steel from Trenton which you desired Congress to order to you or the Commander in Chief at New York for the use of the Black Smith & Armourers who are to go into the Indian Country.[1] I am, Sir, your most obedt Servt,
                                                              Wil. Livingston

RC (NHi).
    [1] See *JCC*, 4:164, 177; and Schuyler to Hancock, February 10, 1776, *Am. Archives*, 4th ser. 4:990–91.

Maryland Delegates to Henry Hollingsworth?

Sir.[1]   Phila. 9 March 1776.

Very soon after your Receit of this, a Ton of powder on it's way to Balt will be at the Head of Elk which pray put into two waggons with fresh Horses and send forward as quick as may be. It may possibly with the utmost Diligence get to Baltimore Town Time enough to be of Service. You'll discharge the waggons which carry the Powder to Elk. You will also very soon receive from Christeen about three Tons of Powder partly imported on our Account & partly borrowed all designed for Balt. Do pray get Waggons prepared and forward it by Land with all possible dispatch.

We are Sr., Your most hble Servts.   Th Johnson junr

                                             R. Alexander

RC (MdAA). Written by Johnson and signed by Johnson and Alexander.

[1] Probably Henry Hollingsworth (1737–1803), of Head of Elk, lieutenant colonel of Maryland militia, whose location at that key point was a factor in his involvement in the shipment of quantities of goods between Maryland and Pennsylvania throughout the war. See Maryland Delegates to the Maryland Council, March 20, 1776.

Maryland Delegates to the Maryland Council of Safety

Gent.   Phila. Sat. Ev. 9 Mar 1776

Immediately on Receit of a Letter from Mr. Purviance by Express advising us of a Man of War being in your Bay, We applied to Congress for one Ton of Powder, which was readily granted. The Delegates of Virga had sent off one Ton in a Waggon, this without Sollicitation they offered us & We excepted & have sent their Order to the Waggoner to proceed to Balt. We had an Order for 1875 due Maryland from Congress & this Day Capt Tibbit arrived from Statia with about one Ton of Powder for our Province. We have dispatched the Powder to Chris[tiana] Bridge as Waggons are not to be had here & have wrote different Gent at the Bridge & Head of Elk to assist in forwarding the powder to Balt. Town.

We are Gent Your very affect friends & Servts.

                                             Th Johnson junr

                                             R. Alexander

RC (MdAA). Written by Alexander and signed by Alexander and Johnson.

Richard Smith's Diary

[March 9, 1776]

[. . . .] [1] Instruc[tions for the Commissioners] going to Canada and [. . .] of them took up 3 or 4 Hours [. . .] that Part recommendg. to them [to] form a Constitution and Governmt. for themselves without Limitation [of] Time which Jay and others said was an Independency & there was much Argumt. on this Ground.

MS (DLC).
  [1] MS damaged; approximately three lines missing.

Oliver Wolcott to Matthew Griswold

Hond. Sir[1]   Philidelphia 9t March 1776.

Your Favour of the 27 Ult. has come safe to Hand, and I return you my Thanks Sir, for the In[te]lligence therein communicated. I am Very sensible the Colony must have been distressed for Want of a Supply of Money. It has been unhappy our Troops did not take their pay, in the continental Way, which I understand they might have done. It would not only have prevented this Trouble—but those Jealousys which Gentlemen this Way, too readily entertain of Sinister Designs in those who go out of the ordinary Course which they have tho't proper to point out. We have tho with Difficulty obtained an advance of One hundred Thousand Dollars,[2] which will be transmitted by Mr. Sherman who intends next Week to make a Short Visit to his Family. About Thirty pay Roalls are now recd. the Rest are I understand Making out as fast as possible. These will be liquidated as soon as the Committee of Claims have examined a great number of Accounts brot in by the Massachusetts. The whole now advanced to our Colony (if I remember right) is £78,000.

All the Bounties given by R Island to their Troops were refused Payment (as I understand) before I came here. Should the same Decision take Place with regard to Connecticut it will make a large Defaulkation from the Account. Our Claim will be made and as I fully believe it is just, I wish the Probability of Obtaining it, was greater. The R Island Demand was I take it Very generally rejected. As the Congress have taken up the Army, should think it not for the Interest of the Colony except upon the most pressing Exigences, to advance Money in future, upon general Services. But as I have no Reason to doupt of the Prudence of the Colony Administration I believe a proper Attention will be had in these Times of Vast Expence to their own particular circumstances, consistent with a Regard to the general Wellfare.

I am glad to hear of the attention given to procure a Marine Strength—it will I beleive be Very usefull. The continental Fleet has been out for some Time. I think We may shortly expect to hear from it. The Manufacturing Arms and G Powder are objects which cannot be too much attended to. If every American was well furnished with the Means of Defence I should think We might be almost a Match for the World. G. Powder is manufacturing here continually. Very soon they will in this Colony make five Tons Weekly. Twenty seven Tons of G. Powder, one of S. Petre and 500 stands of Arms have within a few days arrived. A Petition lies before Congress from a large Number of Merchants of this City requesting Letters of Mark and Reprizal—the Matter has not yet been discussed. The Business of Congress seems continually to encrease so that no Recess is tho't of at this Time. The persevering Cruelty of the British Administration is such that I fear We are to expect no further Benefit from what We have heretofore fondly called the Mother Country. A Convention of this Colony are to Meet the 2d April notwithstanding the Assembly does now Sit. It is said the People are uneasy at the Instructions given their Delegates as well as with other Matters. We seem to be brot. near a most important Period, May God guide the publick Councills of this Land, and carry us safely thro' the severe Conflict of the present unhappy Times. I do not perceive any Dismay. Severity but gives further Energy—and I hope our Union is firm.

The Military Division of the Colonies I believe Sir you must have heard of, and a further Establishment of General officers. Genl. Thomas is ordered to Canada. Genl Lee is going to the Southward. Genl. Clinton it is said has just touched at Virginia but has now left it but I do not tell this for a certainty. Please to present my Compliments to my Sister and your Family, and be assured Sir that your literary favours will be greatly regarded. I am Sir with Esteem, your most obedient and humble Servant,   Oliver Wolcott

RC (CtY).
[1] Matthew Griswold (1714–99), a Lyme, Conn., lawyer, who served as deputy governor and chief justice of Connecticut, 1769–84, and as governor, 1784–86, was married to Wolcott's sister, Ursula. *DAB.*
[2] Congress had approved this advance on March 7. *JCC,* 4:188.

Robert Morris to Silas Deane

Dear sir   Philada. March 10th. 1776
I was sorry to find by your Note of the 8th that you determined to wait at Chester for the Pilot Boat because certain Gentn seem exceedingly anxious that you sho'd be gone & you know well how tedious & troublesome it is to obtain decisive orders on any point wherein Public

Expence is to be incurred. I cou'd not send a Boat without orders unless at my own Expence and altho I obtained such orders yesterday yet I was so harrassed between the assembly & Congress that it was not in my power to dispatch her. I am attempting it this Morning & hope she will depart in time to put this onboard the Brigt and then run down before you. You will find herein a letter from your Brother which Doctr Franklyn & myself thought best to open least it might be of disadvantage to him or you & cause some disapointment about the Money you left for him, but you'l find it is not of Consequence in the way of bussiness. Yesterday arrived about 6 to 8 Tons of Powder by different Vessells from the West Indies. They bring English Papers later than any we had before & the Kings Proclamation for dividing Prize Money by which you will know the Act of Parliament for Cutting of all Trade & intercourse with us is passed and I suppose this will produce some decissive measures on our side.

A Man of Warr & two Tenders were within about 20 Miles of Baltimore and the People there preparing a Warm Reception for them. The Molly, Cap Lawrence, had got back into that Harbour and I think will be defended with others now lying there. Powder, Arms &c are on the way to them and I think no great harm will be done in that quarter. I think you shou'd not loose one Moment, the sooner you are on the Ocean the better chance of arriving safe & of not being interrupted on your Voyage; but the Sea will Swarm with Men of Warr & some Privateers before long.[1] The People in Antigua were applying for Commissions to fit out Privateers against us. I hope they will live to repent it. A report is come up from Virginia that Colo Corbin who went on board Ld. Dummore's Fleet by his LdShips invitation was returned & says he saw Genl Clinton, that Commissioners are Certainly Coming out from England to treat and offer the terms of 1763, but that they can only Treat with the Colonies separately & will have nothing to do with the Congress. If this be the case they may as well stay where they are. However I dont think this intelligence comes quite well authenticated yet.

You'l find the Evening Post herein which Contains all the intelligence. I have just got it & am with the best wishes & most sincere attachment, Dr Sir, Your Affectionate hble sevt,   Robt Morris

P.S. If I have time shall enclose some letters herewith which must be Secreted or destroyed if you are Captured &c.

RC (CtHi).
[1] For an explanation of the delays and difficulties Deane experienced in attempting to embark for France, see John Alsop et al. to Silas Deane, March 1, 1776, note 2.

Benjamin Franklin to Philip Schuyler

Sir   Philade. March 11. 1776

The Congress have appointed three Commissioners to go to Canada, of which Number I have the Honour to be one. We purpose setting out some day this Week. I take the Liberty of mentioning this, as possibly a little previous Notice may enable you more easily to make any Preparation you shall judge necessary to facilitate and expedite our Journey, which I am Sure you will be kindly dispos'd to do for us. A Friend with us will make our Company Four, besides our Servants. We shall either come in Carriages directly to Albany, or by Water, if the River is open, from N York.

Hoping Soon for the Pleasure of seeing you I now only add, that I am, with the sincerest Esteem and Respect, Sir, Your most obedt, humble Servant,   B Franklin

P.S. The Bearer M. Le Jennesse has been considered by the Congress as a Friend to the American Cause, and he is recommended to your Protection in his Return to Canada.[1]

RC (NN).

[1] Prudent LaJeunesse. See *JCC*, 4:148–49, 163.

John Hancock to George Washington

Sir,   Philada. 11 March 1776.

Since my last I have had the honour of receiving your letter of the 9th of Feby.[1] The Congress have not yet come to any resolutions on your former Letters.

The design of this is only to desire you to send Captain Morgan Connor of the riffle Battallion to Philada, the Congress having occasion to employ him in the southern department.[2]

The Congress having promoted Edward Hand Esqr. to be colonel of the riffle batallion in the room of col Thompson whom they advanced to the rank of Brigr. genl. and James Chambers Esqr. to be lieutenant colonel of the same, I have forwarded their commissions accordingly.[3]

I have the Honor to be with much Esteem, Sir, Your most Obedt Servt.   John Hancock Presidt

RC (DLC). In the hand of Charles Thomson and signed by Hancock.

[1] Washington's letter was read in Congress on March 7, 1776. *JCC*, 4:187. The letter is in PCC, item 152, 1:481–84, and Washington, *Writings* (Fitzpatrick), 4:311–12.

[2] *JCC*, 4:192.

[3] See Richard Smith's Diary, March 7, 1776, note 3.

Richard Smith's Diary

[March 11, 1776]

[. . . .] [1] in the Ne[gative.] Letters from Ld. Stirling [and] Gen Lee,[2] the latter being in Town desires to know how & when he may pay his Respects to Congress and recieve their Commands. A Comee. of 3 viz R. H. Lee, E Rutledge & [*William Whipple*] was appointed to inquire of the General the best Methods of defending New York.[3] Sherm[an re]ported an Inquiry into the Cau[se that] brings so many Indians (about [. . .] different Tribes) at present to Philada. They only come, it seems, to see the Governor and recieve Presents from him as usual. Our Secret Comee. of Correspondence, Harrison, Franklin and Dickinson, were asked what they knew of the Disposition of France and other Foreign Powers and say they have not yet had Time to recieve Returns to their Dispatches.

MS (DLC).

[1] MS damaged; approximately six lines missing.

[2] Letters to Hancock of March 8 from Gen. William Alexander and of March 11 from Gen. Charles Lee are in PCC, item 158, 1:37–38, item 162, 2:432, and *Am. Archives*, 4th ser. 5:131–32, 183. Lee's arrival in Philadelphia, which occurred this day, was tardily noted by Robert Treat Paine in his diary for March 12: "Fair. Genl. Lee to town from N York." MHi.

[3] For the report which this committee submitted to Congress on March 14, and the related resolves Congress adopted that day, see *JCC*, 4:201–4.

Samuel Ward to Samuel Ward, Jr.

My dear Son   Philadelpa. 11th March 1776

I wrote You by an Express soon after the Action at Quebec & inclosed my Letter to Genl. Wooster desiring him to forwd it & again by Lt. Colo. Antle by whom I sent you six half Joes with orders to draw upon me for any Sum which should be necessary for your comfortable & decent Subsistence.[1] I enclosed you a Letter of recommendation & credit from a Canadian Gentleman a Prisoner here to his Bror. in Canada a Gentn. of fortune who I doubted not would honored his Bror. Recommendation if in his Power. I hope you have recd. all these; should it be so a Repetition of the leading Sentiments will not be disagreable to wit That the great object of Creation was human Happiness, The Path and the only Path which leads to it Virtue, all History as well as Reason confirms this Truth. I will mention only one Instance out of many. (Your favourite Study) the Roman History, while temperate, frugal, just & virtuous what Wonders did they perform, with what amazing Velocity They rose to Glory and Empire. It is true that after this happy Period their Exertions were vast & their

Empire immensely extended but these Efforts were like the violent throws of a Person in a convulsion & Fits than the steady yet vigorous exertions of a Man of a good constitution in high health & the Empire like the unhappy sick Man after being torn to Pieces by violent Convulsions sunk under them & is no more. Your own Reading will furnish innumerable Instances of this Kind & young as you are you must often have observed the fatal Effects of Vice. Shun therefore my dear Son as inevitable Ruin, Luxury & Vice of every Kind & endeavour to impress deeply upon your Heart the Love of God, of Mankind & of Country, in one Word every moral, social & relative Virtue, next to these endeavour to acquire every useful & amiable Accomplishment; if you spend your Time in this, a truly glorious Employ, it may be very happy for you that you was taken a Prisoner. May the eternal Fountain of Wisdom lead you in the Way in which you should go.

Your Friends in general are well. Your Sister Nancy was married lately to your Friend Capt. Clarke. She is very well; your Sister Greene is so & indeed all our Family.

Dr. Franklin does me the Favor to take Charge of this Letter and very politely tells Me He will with Pleasure serve You. Present my very affece Regards to your Kinsman Colo. Greene & all your fell[ow] Pr[isoner]s. Write to Me by every Opportunity. My dearest Son May the Lord be with You & prosper You.

I am, Your very affece. Father,   Sam Ward

FC (RHi). Endorsed by Ward: "Part of a rough Draught to Sammy. 11th March 1776."

[1] See Ward to Samuel Ward, Jr., January 21, 1776, in Ward, *Correspondence* (Knollenberg), pp. 175–77.

Richard Smith's Diary

Tuesday 12 March [1776]

In Comee. of Claims we agreed to give Timothy Matlack and One Clerk employed by Him £6 per Week for their Services (there are more Clerks employed by the Comee.) [. . .] has had hitherto 15/ per Diem [for] attendg. the Comee. of Claims. In Congress the Votes were read. 20,000 Dollars advanced to Commissary Mease. 4 or 5 Hours were spent on the Instructions to our Canada Commisss. They were gone thro but Chase offered some others in Addition which are to be considered tomorrow.[1] Wyth made a Report on Hazens Demand referring the Facts to be ascertained by the Commissioners which was confirmed.[2]

MS (DLC).
[1] See Smith's Diary, February 14, 1776, note 2.
[2] Ibid., March 8, 1776, note 6.

William Hooper

William Hooper to Samuel Johnston

My dear friend   March 13 1776. Philadelphia
    I had a sight of your last to Mr Hewes. I am glad to find that you
are in the land of the living. Life was never more properly called
transitory than in the present uncertain state of things. He makes a
very wild Wager who bets upon existence for 6 Months to come. I am
happy to hear that my family are well; would to God I was with them.
The Commotions in Carolina are alarming, I wish the Accounts we
have of the success of the friends of Govt against them may be true. I
hope that you will not be lulled by their promises into a delusive security,
the little regard which they have had to their past promises is a bad
earnest for their future punctuality. We are kept in most surprizing
Ignorance of the present state of North Carolina. When we leave the
province, our friends seem to consign us to Oblivion, and give us the
important trust of defending their liberties, without affording us such
Intellgince of their situation as is absolutely necessary to put it in our
power to do it effectually. We anxiously wait the return of Chew the
Express.
    20 Commissioners have sail'd from England to treat with Assemblies—
Counties—Townships in America; in the last instance with the continental Congress when they have tried every other expedient unsuccess-
fully. Amherst & Lord Howe are of the number. The King would not
for a long time consent to treat with the Congress but was at last prevailed upon. They are to contend for much & be content with little.
Their Creed is *divide & impera*, Heaven Grant that America may have
virtues to resist their lures. I most earnestly wish peace & reconciliation
upon terms honourable to America. Heaven forbid that I should submit
to any other.
    The Inclosed will give you the state of the Army in & out of Boston.
Howe is leaving it with his troops & we suppose is bound to New York.
Pray make my best respects to your Lady & family & all my good
friends near you.
    I am, Yours affectionately,   Wm Hooper

N.B. What I say of the Commissioners I have only on report—take it
for so much.

RC (CtY).

William Hooper to Joseph Trumbull

My dear Sir,   February [*i.e.* March] [1] 13th 1776
    I thank you for your very obliging letter by the last post; & deter-

mined that a Correspondence which you have begun, & in the continuance of which I am sincerely interested, should meet no discouragement from any omission of mine, I snatch my pen to answer it.

Your Success in taking possession of Dorchester Hights exceeds the expectations of us all. With the small quantity of powder you had in possession, & the probability that such a measure would bring on a general attack We imagined a delay would have been unavoidable, but—Fortes fortuna privat, to men animated with the glorious cause in which they are engaged, dangers & difficulties are visionary, & their Strength and courage increase in proportion to what they are brought to oppose. I lament the splitting of the mortar called the *Congress.*[2] I hope it augurs no ill to us. To what are we to ascribe the disaster? To a misfortune which all beginners suffer. Inexperience. From our disasters we shall learn Wisdom & we shall not be the first example, if defeats should be the Consequence of our first efforts; of a people learning the arts of War from Enemies & being drubbed into the means of being afterwards successfull.

In the packet which lately arrived at New York came passengers Mr William Temple, late of New Hampshire and Mr Francis Dana of Cambridge. By Mr Temple we learn that a 90 Gun Ship with 20 Commissioners on board, at the head of whom are Lord Howe & Genl Amherst has sailed for the province of Virginia. It is said that they have instructions to bring about a negociation with the several assemblies of the provinces, nay to condescend to treat with Counties, Towns, particular associations but to avoid, if possible any Correspondence with the continental Congress lest by any act of theirs they should recognize the legality of that body. We are told however that rather than return *re infecta* they are to make propositions to the Continental Congress. It is hinted that in the last instance their proffers will be liberal, & that if we resist the allurements which parade, persuasion, venality and Corruption may throw out, the day is our own & that Britain must hold forth by her Commissioners a Carte Blanche to her injured Sons in America. The King objected to treat with the Congress let the consequence be what it would, choosing rather to part with us than hold us upon what he calls an ignominious condition. He was told that matters were too far gone, to suffer punctilioes to delay the carrying the measures into Execution. The haughty monarch relented and the matter & manner are left without limitations to these Ambassadors.

The Congress are employed upon the State of New York and the means necessary to be pursued for the defence of that City, Battalions are ordered from the Jerseys & one from the back of Pennsylvania to that place, & before we rise this day effectual measures, as far as such can be taken with the present scarcity of Arms & warlike stores, will be pursued against the suspected designs of Gen Howe & his Myrmidons.

They have cut out Work for us in the Southern Colonies. Lord Cornwallis with 3000 Men, and a great number of men of War has sailed for Virginia & North Carolina. Govr. Martin is to aid them with his abilities, by exciting disaffection in the back parts of our province among a body of men called regulators, stimulating the Highlanders to support him, & to compleat the motley tribe our negroes are to be armed against us. Martin has so far succeeded that 1100 Highlanders with 600 Regulators under the Command of one McLeod who escaped from the Lexington battle & was sent by Genl Gage to fan a flame which unfortunately existed in our deluded province, the cursed consequence of Tryons expedition,[3] and the pursuit of vengeance against a few who followed his banners.

Your old friend General Thomas is ordered to Canada, You will part with him with reluctance, should the Troops continue to the Eastward. You will miss him but this disposal of him has been unavoidable. Lee goes to So. Carolina or rather to the Seat of War wherever he finds it in the Southern Colonies. Brig. Genl Armstrong is to take the same route. I fancy they will find a spirit prevailing amongst our people which they do not expect. 4000 Militia were in Arms the 23d of Feby to oppose *Martin*.

Adieu my dear Col. I have exhausted my present budget & before this your patience. Remember me respectfly to Col Mifflin & Lady, Genl Putnam & to the many others whose Civilities I experienced when with you & believe me to be Dear Col, with truth & Sincerity, Your most Obed Humble svt,   Wm Hooper

[*P.S.*] I wish you may find leisure to give me a line by every post. Were it only to be informed that you are in the land of the living the Intelligence to me will be always interesting.

RC (CtHi).
[1] Not only is this letter a response to Trumbull's letter to Hooper of March 6, but internal evidence clearly demonstrates that Hooper wrote it in March rather than in February. See Commissary General Joseph Trumbull's letter to Hooper of March 6, 1776, Nc-Ar; and *Am. Archives*, 4th ser. 5:200–201.
[2] On this point, see Washington's letter to Hancock of March 7, 1776, Washington, *Writings* (Fitzpatrick), 4:370–77; and Richard Smith's Diary, March 15, 1776.
[3] An allusion to then North Carolina governor William Tryon's expedition against the regulators in May 1771. Hugh T. Lefler and William S. Powell, *Colonial North Carolina: A History* (New York: Charles Scribner's Sons, 1973), pp. 236–38.

John Jay to Alexander McDougall

Dr. Sir   Philad. 13. March 1776

Had your Letter been sent by the Post it would ere this have come to my Hands.[1] I am now retired to the Lobby to answer it without Delay. I have many things to say to you and upon many Subjects. The enclosed Articles will furnish Answers to the Questions you ask relative to Seamans Wages &c.[2] A Model of a Pike shall be sent you. The Resolution of Congress restraining military officers from offering oaths by Way of Test to the Inhabitants I hope has reached you. I cant account for your Convention's submitting to this usurpation on the Rights of their Constituents. To impose a Test is a sovereign Act of Legislation—and when the army become our Legislators, the People that Moment become Slaves.[3] I must conclude, And am Dr Sr, your friend & hble Servt,   John Jay

RC (NSchU). Addressed: "To Coll. Alexander McDougall in New York."

[1] See McDougall's letter to Jay of March 7 in John Jay, *The Correspondence and Public Papers of John Jay*, ed. Henry P. Johnston, 4 vols. (New York: G. P. Putnam's Sons, 1890–93), 1:46–47.

[2] Jay sent McDougall *Rules for the Regulation of the Navy of the United Colonies of America* (Philadelphia: W. and T. Bradford, 1775). See *JCC*, 3:513.

[3] Congress adopted this resolve on March 9 in reaction to Gen. Charles Lee's order to Isaac Sears, his acting adjutant general, to impose a test oath on certain Long Island tories. *JCC*, 4:195; and Bernard Mason, *The Road to Independence: The Revolutionary Movement in New York, 1773–1777* (Lexington: University of Kentucky Press, 1967), pp. 208–9. See also New York Delegates to the New York Provincial Congress, March 15, 1776, note 3.

Richard Henry Lee to George Washington

Dear Sir,   Philadelphia 13 March 1776

I was in Virga. (from whence I am but just returned) when your favor of the 26th Decr.[1] came here, and now I have but a moment before this Gentleman goes off to thank you for it, and to cover a letter from your brother, with the proceedings and ordinances of our last Convention.[2] Gen. Clinton had left Virginia before I did, and was gone to one, but which we do not know, of the Carolinas. Gen Lee is now here on his way to the Southward where he is to take the direction of our and the Carolina Troops. I shall write you fully in a Post or two, in the mean time beg my compls. to your Lady, Mr. & Mrs. Custis. I am dear Sir Your most affectionate friend.   Richard Henry Lee

RC (DLC).

[1] See Washington, *Writings* (Fitzpatrick), 4:186–87.

[2] The proceedings of the Virginia convention, which convened in Richmond on December 1, 1775, and adjourned at Williamsburg on January 20, 1776, are in *Am. Archives*, 4th ser. 4:75–148.

Richard Smith's Diary

[March 13, 1776]
Wednesday 13. The Votes read. On Motion of Chase a Comee. of 7, Duane at their Head, was chosen to consider of Ways and Means of raising Supplies. R Morris informed Congress that a Tender was sent from New York to cruize at our Capes; whereupon it was agreed that our Marine Comee. should purchase for the Continent a Maryland armed Brig now at Philada. & send her immedy. to fight the Tender & to keep this Matter secret for the present. 5 or 6 Barrels of Powder were allowed to Cecil County Maryland. A Letter read from the Comee. at Eliza. Town desiring some Powder, with other Letters.[1] A Report made and allowed, from the Comee. of Claims for paying the Music at Dr. Smiths late Oration. From 12 oCloc till 4 the Congress was in Comee. Govr. Ward in the Chair, on the Petitions for allowing Privateers to cruize agt. the English, Chase offered a Sett of Propositions & Wyth a preamble, Willing & Johnson were the only Members who spoke directly and clearly agt. the Measure, Jay was for a War against such only of the British Nation as are our Enemies, E. Rutledge was agt. privateering in any Case and for Letters of Marque in this Case, many Delegates were strongly for the Thing but the Determination was left till Tomorrow. Dr. Franklin read some Extracts of Letters to Him from Paris giving a high Character of the Baron Woedtke late a Major Gen of Cavalry in the Prussian Service and Aid du Camp to that King but now in Philada. whither he came last from Paris.[2]

MS (DLC).
[1] Letters to Hancock of March 7 from the Essex, N.J., committee and of March 12 from John Macpherson are in PCC, item 68, fols. 109–12, item 78, 15:23–24, 26, and *Am. Archives*, 4th ser. 5:101, 191–92.
[2] See John Hancock to Baron de Woedtke, March 19, 1776.

Matthew Tilghman to Anna Maria Tilghman

My dear Child,   Phila. Mar. 13. 1776
I somehow or other missed the Oppertunity of last post. Indeed I was told that he did not get away from Hence at the usual time last week & by that means we have no post in Monday as was expected. I have now an Oppy. by Tenny Cox who is going to Baltimore. You have been I fear in much Dread of the Man of War.[1] However it is gone over for the Time very luckily, wish the Affr. mayn't produce something worse. There's a Packet arrived at N York with a great Number of Letters, but none come to Hand. A Mr. Temple who came in her is expected here every Moment—coming, some say from the

Minority. The Comrs. are dayly expected up this River. I have recd. but one Letter & that from C Carroll since I came up. Wish very much to hear you are all well. All well at Dickys the 4th. I have some Comfort in thinking that you[2] are happily placed with yr Sister & that your Mama is in a place of Safety; 'tis all I have except that I am as happy my self as I can be in this City. But the dreadfull prospect of Affrs. deprives me of any other Satisfaction than what I can derive from the above Considerations. The Prospect for peace is as little as possible; yet so pleasing is the Hope that I cant altogether give it up. Let me hear from you my Love I beg, and tell me if you want any thing, 4 pr. Shoes I have at yr Mama's desire bespoke for you. I wish to know what Books you read and whether any wanted that may be got here. I am uneasy that I have not heard from you. Give my Love to Sister. My prayers for you both are frequent & now attend you both with much Anxiety for yr Welfare; dont be much frightned about Men of War. I judge you can if there's occasion get out of their way. I shall not fail writing some of you by every post. Wish you as much Happiness as the times will admit & remain, yr. truly tender & Aft Father,

Mat. Tilghman

RC (Mrs. John Frazer, Philadelphia, Pa., 1973).
    [1] H.M.S. *Otter*, Capt. Matthew Squire, which had been ordered to Baltimore from her station off Norfolk to engage the *Wasp* and the *Hornet*. See Clark, *Naval Documents*, 4:92–93, 203, 242–43, 340–41.
    [2] Undoubtedly his daughter Anna Maria (1755–1843), who was at this time staying with her sister Margaret, the wife of Charles Carroll, Barrister. James Bordley, *The Hollyday and Related Families of the Eastern Shore of Maryland* (Baltimore: Maryland Historical Society, 1962), pp. 259–60.

John Hancock to John Shee, Robert Magaw, William Irvine, and Elias Dayton

Sir   Philadelphia March 14th. 1776
    The State of New York Requiring an immediate Reinforcement, I have it in Command from Congress to direct you immediately to March your Battalion to New York, and put your self under the Commanding Officer of the Continental Troops there.[1] For Expediting your March, you are to Send forward one or Two Companies at a time, & let the Rest follow at the Distance of One Day's March.
    I am Sir, Your most obedt Servt.   J H Prt.

LB (DNA: PCC, item 12A). Addressed: "To Coll. John Shea of the 3d Battan. of Pensyla. Troops, Phila. Coll Robert Magaw of the 5th Ditto—Philada. Coll. William Irvine of the 6th Ditto—At Carlile. Coll. Elias Dayton of the 3d Battan. New Jersey Troops—Eliza. Town."
    [1] See *JCC*, 4:204.

Secret Committee Minutes of Proceedings

March 14, 1776.
At a meetg. of the Secret C[ommittee]. Present S. Ward, J. Alsop, Robt. Alexander & Robt. Morris. Drew an order dated 13 inst. on the Contl. Treasurers in favor of Robt. Morris & John Ross for 90,000 dlls accordg. to Contract made 1st March inst. Do. in favor of Chs. Biddle for 1080 dlls 13/25 for his Commisn. for transactg. business for the U[nited] C[olonies]. Do. in favor of Anthony Marmason for 90 dlls, for the same number of cutlasses bought of him for the U[nited] C[olonies]. Executed a Charter party with John Dorsius & Butler owners of the brigantine Dolphin, W. Moore, master to Bordeaux in France & Do. with Wm. Moore master of a Brigantine for a voyage to S. Carolina.[1] Drew an order on the Treasurers in favor of Graham Oakman, Hoge & Ramsay for 40502 3/3 [sic] dlls in full for arms & ammunition purchasd of them. Also Certificate of the purchase. Granted a permit to Capt. Moore Master of the Brigantine Dolphin af[oresai]d loaded on acct. of the Contt. to depart the port with her cargo.

At a meetg. of the C[ommitte]e of Secy. Present Rob. Morris, B. Franklin, J. Alsop, Jos. Hewes & Jos. Bartlett. The Come. proceeded to the choice of a Chairman, (Mr. Ward the late Chairman being confined with the Small-pox) & unanimously elected Mr. Robt. Morris. Drew an order on Mr. Robt. Towers Commissary to return to the Comme. of safety of this Province the number of muskets borrowd of them for the Continent. Also to return to the sd. Come. 12066 1/2 lb powder likewise borrowd of them. Agreed that Mr. Hudson of Baltimore, who proposes going Supercargo in the ship Molly, Capt. Laurence, loaded on Continl. accot. for Cadiz, if he delivers the sd. Cargoe at Cadiz shall be allowd £50 stg for his care & trouble. Issued an order to Robt. Towers to deliver to the order of Robt. Irwin to be transported in waggons by him provided to N. York & then delivered to the order of the Con[tinental] Com[missary] Officer.

MS (MH).
[1] Robert Morris had been ordered previously to ship a cargo "for Carolina" by Captain Moore. Secret Committee Minutes of Proceedings, February 26, 1776.

Richard Smith's Diary

Thursday 14 March [1776]
The Minutes read. R. H. Lee from a Comee. reported Gen Lees Opinion about fortifying New York which was considered. He recommends 8000 Troops to be kept there which was agreed to & the fol[lowin]g Battals. destined to that City viz Wind's, late Ld Stirlings,

already there & Daytons from N Jersey, Wayne's, Irwin's, Shee's & Magaws from Pennsa., with the 4 N York Regts. now raising, it was moved that Hazletts from New Castle be also sent but this was postponed. Wm. Livingston moved that a Day of General Fasting and Prayer be appointed which was relished & he desired to draw up his Motion.[1] Some Accots. passed. Much Time was spent in a Resolution to disarm the Tories generally, the Thing was not opposed but the Terms of the Resolves were fully discussed. They passed at length and the Delegates of each Colony are to transmit them for Execution. A Letter was read from Brig. Prescot complaing. of a Breach of Capitulation in the Treatment of his Person and Effects. It was referred to the Comee. on Prisoners (myself One of them) to hear & examine the General and report to Congress, the Vote was taken to hear Him before the House but carried in the Negative.[2]

MS (DLC).
 [1] According to the journals, Livingston made this motion on March 13. *JCC*, 4:201. For the text of the fast resolution which Congress adopted on March 16, see *JCC*, 4:208–9.
 [2] No letter from Gen. Richard Prescott has been found, but for the report which the committee on prisoners submitted to Congress on April 6, and which Congress ordered tabled, see *JCC*, 4:261–62.

John Hancock to William Alexander

My Lord,   Philada. March 15th 1776.
 I had the Honour of receiving your Letters of the 12th [*i.e.* 10th] and 13th, which were immediately laid before Congress.[1]

Whatever may be the Designs of General Howe, it appears from all the Intelligence received, more than probable, that the Ministry will make an Effort to gain Possession of New York. It is therefore the Desire of the Congress, by all possible Means, to provide for the Defence of that Place.

They have the Satisfaction to find, by the Report of a Committee appointed to confer with General Lee on that Subject,[2] that though the City of New York cannot easily be made defensible against an Attack by Sea, yet it may be made an advantageous Field of Battle; and that by Works thrown up in proper Places, the Enemy may be prevented from gaining Possession of it, and making it a Place of Arms. It is therefore the Desire of Congress, that you would exert the utmost Dilligence in erecting the Works, and perfecting the Defence agreeable to the Plan he left you.

By the enclosed Resolves you will perceive, the Congress have voted eight Thousand Men for the Defence of the Colony of New York. Three Battalions, & a Company of Rifle-Men from Pennsylvania, and one

Battalion from New Jersey are ordered to join you with all Expedition. Col. Irvine's Battalion and the Rifle Company are said to be compleatly armed. The Rest are not so well provided as could be wished. But by the Resolve for taking the Arms out of the Hands of the disaffected and Non-associators, it is hoped, they may be soon supplied.[3]

As the Tempest approaches and threatens to burst upon them, I flatter myself the Convention of New York will strain every Nerve in speedily raising and arming the four Battalions, ordered to be raised there for the Defence of their Colony.

Until these Battalions can be got ready, the Congress approve your calling some Militia to your Aid; and I am directed to request the Governor of Connecticut, the Conventions of New York and New Jersey, to hold their Militia in Readiness to march in such Numbers, and at such Times, as may be desired by the Commander of the Forces at New York.[4] This large Power I have no Doubt will be exercised with the greatest Discretion, as the Exigince of Affairs may require.

The Congress have a just Sense of the Importance of defending New York. But as they conceive this may be done by the Means pointed out, they would not have the Measures interrupted which are taken for accomplishing their Views in Canada. I have it therefore in Command to direct you, to order the Troops destined for Canada to proceed on their March agreeably to their former Orders.[5]

I have the Honour to be, My Lord, your Lordship's most obedt. & very hble Sevt.   John Hancock Presidt.

[P.S.] The Inclos'd Letter for Govr. Trumbull,[6] I beg the favour you will immediately forward to him by a fresh Express, & Return to me the Man I Send to you, as soon as your Dispatches are ready.

RC (NjP). In the hand of Jacob Rush, with signature and postscript by Hancock.
[1] Alexander's letters of March 10 and 13, which were read in Congress on March 15 (*JCC*, 4:206), are in PCC, item 162, 2:447–48, 451, and *Am. Archives*, 4th ser. 5:175–76, 202.
[2] This committee's report of March 14 is printed in the journals and is followed by Congress' subsequent resolutions pertaining to New York. See *JCC*, 4:201–4, 206–7.
[3] This resolve was adopted by Congress on March 14. *JCC*, 4:205.
[4] See *JCC*, 4:207.
[5] Ibid.
[6] See Hancock to Jonathan Trumbull, Sr., this date.

John Hancock to
the New Jersey Provincial Convention

Gentlemen   Philadelphia March 15th. 1776
From the Intelligence lately Rec'd both from Boston & England,

there is but too much Reason to believe our implacable Enemies are Determin'd to bend their Force against New York & Endeavour to possess themselves of that important post.

The Congress have therefore thought proper to order Coll. Dayton's Battalion thither & Rely that you will exert your most strenuous Endeavours in arming and forwarding them.[1] But lest the Enemy should come before our Troops are prepar'd to Receive them, or in case they should come with a superior force, the Congress have Empower'd the Continental Commander to Call in the Aid of the Militia of that & the Neighbouring Colonies agreeable to the Inclos'd Resolve, and I am Directed to Request you to hold your Militia in Readiness to March in such Numbers & at such times as he may Desire.[2] The Alertness & Zeal you have hitherto shewn, render it unnecessary to use any Arguments to enforce this Request. I Trust by the Blessing of God our United & Spirited exertions, will baffle the Designs of our Enemies, & notwithstanding all their Attempts secure & preserve the Liberties of our Country.

I am with Respect, Gentn., Your most Obed hum sevt,

J H Prt.

LB (DNA: PCC, item 12A).
[1] See Hancock to John Shee et al., March 14, 1776.
[2] See *JCC*, 4:207.

John Hancock to
the New York Provincial Convention

Gentlemen,   Philada. March 15th. 1776.

As it is now apparent, that our Enemies mean to prosecute this cruel and unjust War, with unrelenting Fury; and as every Intelligence assures us, that they mean to bend their Force against your Colony, I would not do you the Injustice to suppose, there will be any Occasion to use Arguments, to stimulate you, to exert your most strenuous Endeavours to expedite the raising and arming the Battalions ordered to be raised in your Colony, for its Defence. Enclosed I send you the Commissions for the Field Officers. If any of them are provided for in Canada, they are to continue there, and others will be elected in their Room. Such of them as are in Canada, and unprovided for, have Orders immediately to repair to their respective Regiments.[1]

Lest our Enemies should come upon you before the Continental Troops can be in Readiness to receive them; or in Case they should come with superiour Force, the Congress have thought proper, to empower the Continental Commander at New York, to call to his

Assistance the Militia of your Colony, and that of Connecticut, and New Jersey, agreeably to the enclosed Resolve: [2] and I have it in Command to request you, to hold your Militia in Readiness, to march in such Numbers, and at such Times, as he may desire.

The Congress have ordered five Tons of Powder for the Use of the Troops employed in your Defence, which will be forwarded with the utmost Expedition.

I have the Honour to be, Gentlemen, your very hble Sevt.

John Hancock Presidt

[*P.S.*] The Col. of the 3d Battalion is not appointed, for Reasons that will be mentioned by your Delegates, to whose Letters I beg Leave to refer you. [3]

RC (DLC photostat). In the hand of Jacob Rush and signed by Hancock.

[1] Congress had appointed the officers on March 8. *JCC*, 4:190, 199.

[2] See *JCC*, 4:207.

[3] See New York Delegates to the New York Provincial Convention, this date, note 7.

John Hancock to Jonathan Trumbull, Sr.

Philada. March 15. 1776. Informs Trumbull that Congress fears an imminent attack on New York City, and in preparation for its defense "they have order'd a Number of Battalions to be Rais'd, but for want of the Supplies expected from abroad, those that are Rais'd are very deficient in Arms. Measures however are taking to procure Arms for them in another way. In the mean time lest an Attack should be made before our Forces are prepar'd to Receive them, or in case the Enemy should Come with a superiour force, the Congress have thought it prudent to Empower the Continental Commander at New York to Call in the Aid of the Militia from that & the Neighbouring Colonies; and I have it in Command to Request you, agreeable to the Inclos'd Resolve, [1] to hold your Militia in Readiness to March in such Numbers and at such times as he may Desire."

LB (DNA: PCC, item 12A). *Am. Archives*, 4th ser. 5:233.

[1] See *JCC*, 4:207.

New York Delegates to
the New York Provincial Convention

Gentlemen   Philad. 1st [*i.e.* 15] March 1776 [1]

We laid before Congress your Representation in favour of Mr. St.

Clair, [Sinclair], which met with their approbation; as you will observe by the Resolution which we have the honour to enclose.[2]

General Lee informed Congress, by Letter, that he had imposed a Test upon the Inhabitants of our Colony, in order to ascertain their political Principles. However salutary such a Measure might be, when grounded on a legal and constitutional Basis; we were much alarmed that it shoud owe it's Authority to any military officer, however distinguished for his Zeal, his Rank, his accomplishments, and Services. We considered it as one of the most solemn and important Acts of Legislation, and a high Encroachment upon your Rights as the Representatives of a free People. We cou'd not therefore be silent upon so momentuous a Point, tho we were not favoured with your Sentiments or Instructions; nor informed of what, or whether any thing, had passed between you and the General respecting the disaffected Inhabitants. We took up the Subject on general Principles. There can be no Liberty where the military is not subordinate to the civil power, in every thing not immediately connected with their Operations. Your House, the natural and proper Tribunal for all civil matters within the Circle of your own Jurisdiction, was assembled: and Congress itself within the General's reach, ready to enforce every reasonable Proposition for the publick safety. To one or other he ought to have applied. A similar Effort in Rhode Island had passed over unnoticed; reiterated Precedents must become dangerous: we therefore conceived it to be our unquestionable Duty to assert The Independance and Superiority of the civil power, and to call the Attention of Congress to this unwarrantable Invasion of it's Rights by one of their Officers. A resolution passed, in Consequence, on the 8t [i.e. 9th] of March, "that no Oath by way of test be imposed upon, exacted, or required of any Inhabitant of these Colonies by any military Officer" and it was ordered to be immediately published.[3]

We flatter ourselves that our Conduct on this Occasion will meet with your Approbation.

This will be presented by Brigadr General Thompson who for the present will command in your Capital; General Schuyler's Residence at Albany being deemed indispensable.[4]

General Thompson is a gallant officer and very much respected in this Province: and we doubt not of your Endeavours to make his Command as agreeable to himself, and as salutary to the Country, as possible; to which nothing can contribute more essentially than Harmony and mutual Confidence between him and the civil Power.

Congress were much perplexed in appointing the Officers to the four New York Battalions not knowing whether a former Resolution directing the English Troops who winterd in Canada to be formed into two Battalions, had been carried into Effect.[5] In that Case a Provision will be made for such of the Gentlemen in that Country as are entitled to

Promotion. However it was not thought Just to expose them to any Uncertainty. It is the Intention of Congress that if any of them should have been promoted in that Department they shall continue there and others be appointed for the new Battalions. If not, that they shall Join those Corpses [Corps].[6]

A Battalion was intended for Col. Ritzema; but some Objections having been Suggested it is left vacant untill he can have an Opportunity of being heard, of which you will be pleased to inform him.[7]

We have the Honour to be with the utmost Regard, Gentlemen, Your most obedent, humble Servants,

Jas Duane John Alsop

John Jay Lewis Morris

P.S. The following battalions are assigned for the defence of New York, besides the four you are raising viz: Pensylvanians— Waine's, Erwines [Irvine's], Shea's, Magaw's; New Jersey—Lord Sterling's & Dayton's. These Troops are raised but not armed. The Want of Arms will, it is thought, be in a great Degree remedied, by executing the Resolution of Congress of the 14t Instant, a Copy of which goes with these dispatches. It is directed to be kept as secret as the Nature of the Service will admit.[8]

For your immediate Defence the General, in your department, is authorized to apply to the Governour of Connecticut, Your Convention, and the Committee of Safety of New Jersey, for so many of the militia as he may Judge necessary, who are to be paid by the Continent at 5 dollars a month for each private.[9] A Resolution passed the 8t [i.e. 6th] Instant for Supplying you with 5 tons of Gun powder, and it was ordered to be immediately forwarded, by the Committee of secrecy.[10] We took it for granted that it had been sent forward accordingly, till Mr Lewis's Letter to Mr Alsop led to an Examination; when the chairman of that Committee reported that it had been detaind for want of Carriages. A Copy of the order for the powder is enclosed. We shall be glad to know how far the Battalion's of last year were compleated; as our Colony is reflected upon for a greater deficiency than we believe to be consistent with Truth. It has also been represented that recruiting, for the present Service, goes on very slowly, which considering your danger & distresses we scarce think credible.

RC (N). Written by Duane and signed by Duane, Alsop, Jay, and Morris.

[1] Duane's reference in the postscript to a resolution passed by Congress this day indicates that he probably completed this letter on March 15. See note 9, below.

[2] Congress' resolution of March 11 permitting Capt. Patrick Sinclair, the lieutenant governor of Michilimackinac, to return to Europe, was adopted in response to a letter of March 7 from the New York Provincial Convention. See *JCC*, 4:196; PCC, item 67, 1:190–92; and *Am. Archives*, 4th ser. 5:101–2.

[3] See JCC, 4:195. For Gen. Charles Lee's imposition of test oaths on Rhode Island and New York tories, see Lee to Robert Morris, January 3, and to John Hancock,

January 22 and March 21, 1776, in *NYHS Collections* 4 (1871): 233–34, 247–51, 360–61; and John Jay to Alexander McDougall, March 13, 1776, note 3.

[4] Gen. William Thompson received this assignment from Congress on March 1. *JCC*, 4:181.

[5] See Congress' resolve of January 8 in *JCC*, 4:40.

[6] See also James Duane to the New York Provincial Convention, February 25, 1776, note 7.

[7] Col. Rudolphus Ritzema was made commander of the Third New York Battalion on March 28. *JCC*, 4:238. Ritzema himself described his appointment to this position in "Journal of Col. Rudolphus Ritzema of the First New York Regiment, August 8 1775 to March 30 1776," *Magazine of American History*, 1 (February 1877): 107.

[8] See *JCC*, 4:204.

[9] Congress approved this resolve on March 15. See *JCC*, 4:207; and John Hancock to the New York Provincial Convention, this date.

[10] See *JCC*, 4:186.

Richard Smith's Diary

[March 15, 1776]

Friday 15. The Votes read & Letters from Gen Washington with a Packet of intercepted Letters, and Two Letters from Arthur Lee to Wm. Temple and brought by Him from England sewed in the Lining of his Cloaths.[1] Our Troops have bombarded Boston with little Effect except that Howe and his Men are about to leave the Town, we burst 5 Mortars. Lee's Letters say· that the Ministry cannot get Russians, France having influenced Sweden to interfere, nor can the King make his Force here 20000 Men this Summer by any Means whatever, that France declares if Foreign Troops are sent She cannot be an idle Spectator, and is really disposed to favor our Cause &c. A Letter from Lt. Col Wm. Allen informing that Ld Stirling has detained his 6 Companies at N York and a Letter from his Lordship explaining his Motives and saying that he has ordered Militia from N York and Jersey to his Assistance.[2] A Letter from Gen. Lee prayg. his Orders.[3] The Congress in Comee. (Col Harrison in the Chair)[4] came to several Resols. importing that Nelsons Comp[an]y of Riflemen shall march immedy. to N York, that the Troops detained by Ld. Stirling shall proceed on their Destination to Canada, that the Colonies of Connecticut, N York & N Jersey shall be directed to hold their Militia in Readiness to march on the Requisition of the Commandg. Officer at N York, that the Pay of such Militia shall be 5 Doll[ar]s per Month &c. The last occasioned great Debate the N England and Southern Pay being 50/ this Currency. J. Adams moved that the Baron de Woedtke be made a Brig. Gen. and stationed at N York. This was recd. favorably but not now Settled.[5] Agreed in Congress on motion of R H Lee that all General Officers travelling on the Public Service shall make a Charge of their Horses Keeping, the same Thing passed, on Motion of Harrison, some Days ago with respect to Aids du Camp.[6] Lee & Franklin were desired to wait on Gen. Lee and request Him to repair from hence forthwith to his Southern Department. The Massachusetts raised (as is said by one of their Delegates) 18000 Men in the Beginning of this War, whereof 16000 were taken into Continental Pay & Service. An Order took place for arming the Guard which sets off this Eveng. with the Powder for Virginia.

MS (DLC).

[1] Washington's letter to Hancock of March 7 and enclosures are in PCC, item 152, 1:509–20, and *Am. Archives*, 4th ser. 5:106–9. The letters from Arthur Lee have not been found.

[2] The letters from William Allen and from William Alexander to Hancock are in PCC, item 78, 1:1, item 162, 2:451, and *Am. Archives*, 4th ser. 5:202, 204.

[3] Possibly Gen. Charles Lee's letter to Hancock of March 11, which Congress received the same day. PCC, item 158, 1:37–38; *Am. Archives*, 4th ser. 5:183; and Smith's Diary, March 11, 1776.

[4] See John Adams' pungent autobiographical account of the circumstances surrounding Benjamin Harrison's assumption of the chairmanship of the committee of the whole, in Adams, *Diary* (Butterfield), 3:370–71.

[5] See John Hancock to Baron de Woedtke, March 19, 1776.

[6] See Congress' March 13 resolution on aides-de-camp in *JCC*, 4:201.

John Hancock to William Alexander

My Lord   Philadelphia March 16th. 1776

I had the honour of writing to you this Morning.[1] Since the Express set off I have Rec'd your Letter of the 14th which was immediately Communicated to Congress.[2] In Consequence of which I have it in Command to Direct you to send forward the Powder Destin'd for Cambridge, unless you have Rec'd express Advice from General Washington that the Enemy's Fleet & Army have quitted Boston and Sailed out of that harbour. The five Tons of Powder which I mention'd in my Letter of this Morng. to be intended for the Troops under your Command will be sent forward with all possible Dispatch.

I have the honour to be, my Lord, Your Lordship's obedt huml servt.

J H Prt.

LB (DNA: PCC, item 12A).

[1] Not found.

[2] For Congress' action on General Alexander's letter see *JCC*, 4:207–8. The letter is in PCC, item 162, 2:455–66; and it is printed with enclosures in *Am. Archives*, 4th ser. 5:217–21.

John Hancock to Duncan Campbell

Sir,   Philada. March 16th. 1776.

It having been represented to Congress that Mrs. Campbell is arrived in this City, and so much indisposed as not [to] be able to pursue her Designs of visting you at Reading, and being desirous of seeing you, I am directed by the Congress to inform you, that you have their Permission to repair to this City, and remain with Mrs. Campbell during the Continuance of her Illness, and until she is able to attend you on a Journey to Reading.[1]

I am Sir yours &c,   John Hancock Prest.

LB (DNA: PCC, item 12A).

[1] Subsequently Capt. Duncan Campbell, who had been imprisoned in late October 1775, was permitted by Congress "to reside with his wife and family in the city of Burlington, in the western division of New Jersey." *JCC*, 4:264. For further information on Campbell's arrest, see *JCC*, 3:305–6, 309; and Hancock to the New York Provincial Congress, October 26, 1775, note 1.

John Hancock to

the Reading Committee of Inspection

Gentlemen,   Philada. March 16th. 1776.

I take the Freedom to inclose a Letter for Capt John Nelson of a Company of Rifle-men who was to call on you for seven Hundred Dollars transmitted you some Time ago.[1] If he has not yet reached you, I beg you to Keep the inclosed and deliver him on his Arrival with you; But if he has passed you, I am earnestly to desire you to take a fresh Express and send the Letter with all Expedition that it may reach him as early as possible, it being of Consequence.

I am Gentlemen, your most obedt. Serv.

John Hancock Prst.

[*P.S.*] The Express I send to you is bound to Carlisle.

LB (DNA: PCC, item 12A).

[1] Hancock's March 16 letter to John Nelson ordered him "to repair with the Company of Rifle-Men under your Command with all Possible Expedition to New York, and put yourself under the orders of the Officer commanding the Continental Forces in that Department." PCC, item 12A; and *Am. Archives*, 4th ser. 5:244.

Robert Treat Paine's Diary

[March 16, 1776]

Fair. Wrote to the Assembly of N Hampshire, Massachusetts & Connecticutt[1] & also to Col Palmer by Col Butler. Mr. Francis Dana to town from London.[2]

MS (MHi).

[1] Paine wrote these letters, the first three of at least eight such letters he sent during the next three weeks, in his capacity as chairman of the committee for "promoting and encouraging the manufactures of salt petre, sulphur and powder." For a discussion of Paine's letter-writing campaign, and the fullest surviving text of these letters, see Committee of Congress to the Maryland Convention, March 28, 1776.

[2] Francis Dana (1743–1811), a Boston lawyer who had sailed to England in April 1775 to settle his father's estate, was soon elected to the Massachusetts Council, 1776–80, and served as a delegate to the Continental Congress, 1777–78, and 1784. Shipton, *Harvard Graduates*, 15:204–17; and *DAB*.

Richard Smith's Diary

Saturday 16 March [1776]

The Minutes read and sundry public Letters. Wm. Livingston brought in the Draught of an Order for a General Fast which was agreed to and ordered to be published. The Baron de Woedtke was unanimy elected a Brig. Gen. and ordered to N York for the present and to go with the Commissioners to Canada.[1] Congress resolved itself into a Comee. on authorising Privateers, Jay offered his Propositions, he and others contended for discriminating Foes from Friends. Dr. Franklin thought a Declaration of War ought to precede this Business, there was no Determination. A Note of Hand from Gen Wooster to Thos. Walker of Montreal Esqr. for 50 Half Joes with Interest, was presented for Payment, Chase and others objected to paying Interest as our Officers might run Us into an enormous Debt, it was postponed.[2] The Accounts of Mr. Price of Montreal were offered for Adjustment and referred to the Comee. of Claims, this Gentn. & his Partner Mr. Haywood have lent great sums to our Army there.[3] Carpenter Wharton the Commissary was authorized to continue victualling the Penna. Troops after their Arrival in N York.

MS (DLC).

[1] See John Hancock to Baron de Woedtke, March 19, 1776.

[2] Congress ordered the payment of the principal, but not the interest, of this note on March 23. *JCC*, 4:233.

[3] For Congress' action on James Price's accounts, see *JCC*, 4:274–75, 288, 297, 303.

Richard Smith to Samuel Tucker

Dr Sir   Philada. Saturday March 16. 1776
   This Morning I was favored with Yours of Yesterday. The Business
of the Prisoners at Trenton and elsewhere rests with a Comee. of which
I am a Member, & I should be glad of your Opinion where we shall re-
move them & whether the County of Morris is not a cheap & proper
Country.[1] Mrs. Stelle's Accounts were allowed Yesterday. Our Presidt.
sent you this Morning by Mr. Serjeant a Resolution which least you
should not receive I Inclose You the rough Copy marked N.J. You ask
for News & I will give you Such Matters as occur at present to my
Memory. The Congress have this Day appointed a Day of General
Fasting, Humiliation and Prayer which you will See in the next Papers.
Our Countryman & Acquaintance Dr. Sonmans is to be interred this
Afternoon. John Cooper declines accepting the Delegateship & John
DeHart has never yet attended the Congress tho he has passed this
Town on a Journey to some Place below.
   An Express arrived Yesterday from General Washington with a
Packet of intercepted Letters from England, and One Wm. Temple
also came to Town with Letters to the Congress from a Person of Note
in London whose Name I am not at Liberty to Mention.[2] The following
Particulars, Part of these Dispatches, are supposed to be authentic viz.
That France had instigated Sweden to interpose & thro this Channel
had actually frustrated the Treaty for sending Russians to America.
The ostensible Reason given by Russia for Refusal was that no Cartel
being settled here, all their Prisoners would be liable to be massacred
by the Provincials—that the French Ambassador at St. James's had
declared that his Master did not mean to interfere while British Subjects alone were concerned, but if Foreigners were employed he could
not remain an idle Spectator—that all the Efforts of the Ministry
cannot get 20,000 effective Men here this Summer & even the Highlanders were averse to the Service & inlisted slowly—that France
secretly favors our Cause (this is confirmed by the Baron de Woedtke
late aid du Camp to the King of Prussia & a Major Gen. of his Cavalry,
but came last from Paris and who this afternoon was unanimously
Elected by the Congress a Brig. Gen. of their Forces).
   Temple is a high Whig & says He is certain Two Thirds of the Nation
are for Us & that he is confident there will be a Revolution shortly in
England, & the King has been heard to declare Let what will happen
he has a safe Asylum in Hanover.
   Gen. Washington has bombarded Boston, with what Effect is not
yet precisely known—he split 5 Mortars. Howe & his Troops are said to
be on the move either to Halifax or N York. Congress have voted 8000
Men for the Defence of N York & the followg Regiments are ordered
there Viz, Wind's late Ld. Sterling's (already there) & Daytons from

our Province, Wayne's, Irwin's, Shee's and Magaw's from Pennsylvanis & the 4 Battals. now raising in N. York. A Report is current that our New England Piccaroons have just taken 5 Store Ships out of 8 & were in Pursuit of the other 3.

I remain Yours,   Richd. Smith

[P.S.] Your Name Sake Dean Tucker has published another Pamphlet[3] to persuade the People of G Britain that they ought to acknowledge Us & treat With Us as an Independant Power. The Piece is arrived here & it is confidently said that Tucker is employed by the Ministry to inculcate this Doctrine.

RC (NN).
    [1] See JCC, 4:115, 213, 220.
    [2] Arthur Lee.
    [3] Presumably Josiah Tucker, *The Respective Pleas and Arguments of the Mother Country and of the Colonies Distinctly Set Forth; And the Impossibility of a Compromise of Differences or a Mutual Concession of Rights Plainly Demonstrated with a Brief Epistle to the Plenipotentiaries of the late Congress at Philadelphia* (Gloucester: R. Raikes, 1775).

Matthew Tilghman to the Maryland Council of Safety

Gent   Phila. 16 Mar. 1776
    I Inclose you a resolution of Congress which I am directed to forward to you, and as I recollect was ordered not to be made public.[1]
    I am Gent, Yr mo. obedt Servant,   Mat. Tilghman

Reprinted from *Md. Archives*, 11:256–57.
    [1] The resolution of March 14 for disarming the "notoriously disaffected." Despite Tilghman's recollection, the resolution was printed in the *Pennsylvania Gazette* on March 20, as was a follow-up resolution on the confiscation of arms that was published on March 27. See JCC, 4:205, 220–21.

Oliver Wolcott to Samuel Lyman

Sir,   Philadelphia 16t. March 1776
    Your favour of the 14 Ult. came safe to Hand. I have been expecting by every Post to have recd. Letters from Home but none comes. I have heard nothing from my Family since I recd your Letter. Perhaps it might be easier to Send Letters to Mr. Ellerys office than to N Haven. I have ordered Oliver to forward mine, but perhaps he is an improper Person for this Service as his Acquaintance is only with the College.
    I Notice your Observations on the little Pamphlet I sent you. It has

had a Surprizing run, which is an Evidence it falls in with the general Sentiments of the People. Court Measures may necessitate the Colonies to realise these Sentiments in general. What has been done of a publick Nature since my last is a Recommendation to the Assemblys and Conventions to disarm all such as will not associate to defend the American Rights by Arms.[1] A Petition lyes before Congress from a Number of Merchants of this City requesting Letters of Mark against the British Trade. The Result will douptless be a general License for that Purpose. By the late pirating Act the Colonies are intirely cast out of the King's Protection, in an explicit manner. It behoves us therefore to take Care of ourselves. As to Commissioners coming over, I believe it is Very certain that their Powers are only to receive the Submissions of the Colonies—and I am Very confident they will not therefore be ever Able to Execute their Trust. A proclamation for a fast has issued to be kept the 17t. May but no particular Notice is taken of the British Court but only as they fall under the general Denomination of Enemies. As to Matters of internal Police which you mention they are not at present the Objects of Attention, but in the Course of Affairs they may become so. The Business of Congress is Very Various and extensive. We have but a Very little spare Time; the Vast Number of Applications calls for a constant Attention. I want to hear the Result of the Cannonading of Boston. God grant that it may be happy. No News of consequence from the Westward since my last to Mrs. Wolcott. We hear of some Piracy committed upon our Trade, I believe but few Merchants will choose to Venture their Property Abroad at present, We must Avail ourselves of Armed Ships to cruize upon the British Trade.

I have observed in a N Haven Paper the doings of their County Committee,[2] and as I tho't they proceeded upon Very mistaken Principles and such as must be attended with Very mischeivous Effects, the Other evening I Sat down and Scketched some thots upon the Subject with an Intention to Send to you. Your own Prudence will dictate how farr it may be proper that they Should pass for Mine.[3] It is impossible sometimes to combat with any Advantage Opinions never so erronious, and I believe none could be worse founded than those of this Committee. Such a Conduct if we are debarred Trade will insure our Ruin—for it discourages every kind of home Manufacture—which wheither We have Warr or Peace We ought to our Utmost to improve. I hope that false Policy will not spread into Litchfield County. The Soldiers I understand are not paid in the Colony; it is unhappy it was not taken in the continental Way. A few of the pay Rools are come to hand—which with other Accounts will I suppose be Sent as soon as they can be made out—and it will take some time to have them liquidated. We have with difficulty obtained an advance of Thirty Thousand pounds, which will be Sent.[4] R Island was refused Payment for the Bounties they advanced to their Soldiers before I came here; and I suppose Connecticut upon the same Principle must share the same Fate. I set down Matters as they come into my mind, I must write without much Method. I heartily wish you would write to me, it certainly will be a Satisfaction to Me if I can Read yr Letters. My best compliments to all my Friends as tho particularly Named. I am sir with Regard your assured Freind and most humble Servant,   O Wolcott

RC (MdBJ-G).
¹ See *JCC*, 4:205.
² The minutes of the February 19 meeting of the New Haven County committees of inspection, which were published in the *Connecticut Journal*, February 28, 1776, urged strict adherence to the Association and recommended, among other measures, that raw material for home manufactures, including leather, wool, and flax, be sold at 1774 prices.
³ Lyman apparently extracted Wolcott's sketch and submitted it for publication in the *Connecticut Journal*. The following unidentified piece, entitled "Observations on the price of Wool and Flax" and introduced as the "reflections" of "one ——— ———, of my sensible and learned correspondents," appeared in the April 24, 1776 issue.
"Every people who have not necessary supplies of diet and cloathing within themselves, must depend upon others for their very existence, or procure those supplies by the chance of war. To such a people every accident renders their condition very insecure; to obtain perminent independency and consequently freedom, they must carefully attend to, and if possible obtain internal supplies of these two necessary articles. Diet, by the blessing of God, this country produces plenty of; cloathing is what we are very deficient in, but which by a proper attention to our own affairs, may be obtained in as great plenty as the former. Those therefore who can raise the raw materials, Wool and Flax, ought to have the greatest encouragement. This can be done no other way than by allowing a good price for those articles. This encouragement naturally arises out of public want; for scarcity or want is the foundation of price, and in its consequences of plenty; for a high price naturally prompts men to industry, in raising that which will certainly procure for them an advantageous sale. Plenty is the natural consequence of an encrease of manufactures. Scarcity and plenty will almost inevitably produce each other, and from the most obvious causes. Therefore in a time of scarcity, to restrain the price of necessary articles, which may be internally procured, is the greatest absurdity, as it necessarily precludes every hope of plenty. Temporary inconveniencies naturally accrue to the poor by an advanced price of necessaries, and this is undeniable; but it is certain, that this high price (unless prevented by unnatural management) will terminate to their advantage by giving them plenty. The allowance of a high price, is more especially necessary, when further knowledge in manufacturing ought to be obtained. History informs us, that the wisest states have often designedly produced this scarcity, by laying large duties upon imported articles, which a people might internally obtain. This prudent conduct has in a thousand instances, procured for a people the greatest affluence and independency."
At this point the contributor—Lyman—observed that, if the "mode of reasoning" of "my ingenious correspondent" is true, the committees of New Haven County should give bounties to encourage production rather than restrict prices, since "it would afford ten times more probability of plenty than any restrictions could possibly do."
"To imagine that internal plenty may be had by reducing price," the "Observations" continued, "is to imagine, that the system of nature may be best preserved by that which has the greatest tendency to its subversion. If by an act of power

wheat was reduced to 2s a bushel, famine would be the consequence. The Association, which directs that no advantages shall be taken as to the price of wool, flax,
and internal manufactures, but that the same shall be sold reasonably, can mean
only to prevent monopolising and forestalling, (a practice in its nature truly detestable) but can never mean to regard a price as to internal productions, which
price naturally arises out of the condition and state of the country; for what does in
every article of our own growth, constitute a reasonable price, but the public demand?
If such was the plenty of linens and woolens, that the whole people were amply
supplied, and no vend could be had for those articles, the reasonable price of flax,
&c might be a penny a pound. In a word, public exigencies constitute price, and
those exegencies alone must effect the lowering of price, which it will infallibly do.
Skillful political physicians will carefully attend the system of nature, and help her
in her own operations, but will never counteract the natural exertions upon which
the cure of every political evil depends."
    Wolcott's interest in encouraging the cultivation of flax and wool was shared by
a majority of his colleagues in Congress, who adopted several resolutions on March 21
aimed at promoting agriculture and manufactures. See *JCC*, 4:224.
    [4] See *JCC*, 4:188. For additional references to Connecticut accounts, see Wolcott
to Thomas Seymour, April 16, 1776.

John Adams to Abigail Adams

My dearest Friend   March 17. 1776
    Our worthy Friend Frank Dana arrived here last Evening from N.
York, to which Place he came lately from England in the Packet. In
Company with him, is a Gentleman by the Name of Wrixon, who has
been a Field Officer in the British Army, served all the last War in
Germany, and has seen service in every Part of Europe. He left the
Army some time ago, and studied Law in the Temple, in which Science
he made a great Proficiency. He wrote lately a Pamphlet under the
Title of the Rights of Britons, which he has brought over with him. He
is a Friend of Liberty and thinks justly of the American Question. He
has great Abilities as well as Experience in the military Science, and is
an able Engineer. I hope We shall employ him.[1]
    The Baron De Woedke, We have made a Brigadier General, and
ordered him to Canada. The Testimonials in his favour I shall inclose
to you.[2]
    Mr. Danas Account, with which Mr. Wrixons agrees, ought to ex-
tinguish in every Mind all Hopes of Reconciliation with G. Britain.
This delusive Hope has done us great Injuries, and if ever We are
ruined, will be the cause of our Fall. A Hankuring after the Leeks of
Egypt, makes us forget the Cruelty of her Task Masters.
    I shall suffer many severe Pains, on your Account for some Days.
By a Vessell from Salem a Cannonade was heard from Dark till one
O Clock, last night was a Week ago. Your Vicinity to such scenes of
Carnage and Desolation, as I fear are now to be seen in Boston and
its Environs, will throw you into much Distress, but I believe in my

Conscience I feel more here than you do. The sound of Cannon, was not so terrible when I was at Braintree as it is here, tho I hear it at four hundred Miles Distance.

You cant imagine what a Mortification I sustain in not having received a single Line, from you since We parted. I suspect some Villany, in Conveyance.

By the Relation of Mr. Dana, Mr. Wrixon and Mr. Temple, Mr. Hutchinson, Mr. Sewall, and their Associates are in great Disgrace in England. Persons are ashamed to be seen to speak to them. They look dejected and sunk.

I shall inclose an Extract of a Letter from Monsr. Dubourg in Paris and a Testimonial in favour of our Prussian General.

Adieu.

RC (MHi). Adams, *Family Correspondence* (Butterfield), 1:361–62.

[1] After much debate Elias Wrixon, a German, was offered a colonelcy and the post of "a chief Engineer, in the continental Army in Canada," but he declined the post and later returned to Europe. *JCC*, 4:219–20, 242, 275, 316; Elias Wrixon to John Hancock, April 28, in PCC, item 78, 23:273–74, and *Am. Archives*, 4th ser. 5:1110; John Adams to Horatio Gates, April 27, and to Francis Dana, August 16, 1776. See also Adams, *Diary* (Butterfield), 3:382.

[2] The testimonials are printed in *Am. Archives*, 4th ser. 5:410–11.

Andrew Allen to Philip Schuyler

My dear Sir,   Philada March 17th 1776

Give me leave to introduce to your Notice the Bearer Col. De Haas of the first Battalion of the Pennsylvania Forces in your Department. He is now on his Way to join his Regt and will I hope be of considerable Service, as he is an Officer of Experience & well accquainted with military Discipline and the Ettiquettes of an Army and is besides a worthy honest Man.

You have no doubt been informed by the Presidt according to Order of Congress that the Information Transmitted to you by Mr. Dean & inclosed in yours to Congress respecting Mr. Penn's Inviting the Six Nations to a Treaty at Philada. has been reported void of Foundation by the Commee.[1] I well knew it was a scandalous falsehood before Inquiry made, as Mr. Penn never Entertained such an Idea & it would be preposterous in him if he meant such a Thing to propose Philade. as the Place of holding the Treaty directly under the Nose of the Congress. I can readily guess the Quiver from whence the Shaft came, and the Object it had in view. The Means were scandalous & the Cause diabolical. My long Friendship with you emboldens me to open myself & my Suspicions to you without Disguise. In short I have the greatest Reason to think it a deep laid Plot of your Eastern Neighbours directed to favor the Designs of the Colony of Connecticut in their Dispute with Mr. Penn, and also to blow up the Constitution and Government of this Province which has hitherto been a Barrier against their dark designs. Shall I take the Liberty to intreat you to fathom this cursed Scheme (I suspect Dean) and endeavour to get this pretended Message of Mr. Penn's which if in Writing I am sure is a forgery into your Hands. Your Friendship & the sacred Regard I know you bear to the Honor of every Gentleman will excuse this Trouble. You will be intitled to the grateful Thanks of the Gentleman struck at & everlastingly oblige Your affectionate & obedient Friend & Servt.   Andw Allen

RC (NN).

¹ This issue came before Congress on March 5 when Schuyler's letter enclosing James Deane's letter of February 24 was read and referred to a committee. According to Richard Smith's diary (the journals are silent on the point), the committee reported on March 8 and an "Order was taken to inform Gen Schuyler hereof and to desire Him to send down the Person who had misinformed Him." Although Allen assumed that President Hancock had already informed Schuyler of the committee's report, no such letter had been sent (perhaps Hancock intended to send it by the commissioners to Canada, who were originally expected to leave Philadelphia the week of March 11), and it was not until April 25 that the journals record a resolution directing that the report be sent to Schuyler. The reintroduction of the issue before Congress at that time suggests that the failure to send the report to Schuyler had been an oversight, a surmise consistent with the additional curious fact that there are two slightly variant copies of the committee's report in PCC. See *JCC*, 4:184, 308–9; PCC, item 19, 2:29–32; Richard Smith's Diary, March 8, 1776; and *Am. Archives*, 4th ser. 4:1499–1500.

Richard Henry Lee to Samuel Purviance, Jr.

Dear Sir,   Philadelphia 17 March 1776

I received your account of the retaking Husdons ship¹ and the flight of the enemy with great pleasure. I hope you will make wise use of the opportunity to render the avenews to yr. flourishing Town inaccessible to the enemy. I think you have the means of doing this most effectually, and sure it ought not to be neglected. I suppose the Defence and her Tender will now be employed in keeping your Bay Coast as far as Potomac clear of Sloops and Tenders from our Enemies. I am sure Capt. Squires will not interrupt your Trade so long as he knows Capt. Nicholson is with you, and as for larger Ships, if they should come, which is not very probable, it will be no difficult matter to get out of their way by retiring to shallow waters. I expect this will be delivered you by General Lee who is on his way to his Southern command. I am in no doubt of the worthy General meeting with those civilities from you that prove so agreable to every body else. It is of great importance that Gen. Lee should quickly get to the place of his destination, and therefore, if he should want either horses or Guides for this purpose, I know your patriotic Committee will furnish them. I need not trouble you with news, as the General can give you any that prevails here.

I am, with much esteem, Sir your obliged and obedient servt.

Richard Henry Lee

RC (MdHi). Addressed: "Samuel Purveyance Jun Esqr. Chairman of the Committee of Baltimore. Favored by General Lee."

[1] A reference to the prize taken by the British sloop *Otter*, Capt. Matthew Squire, on March 6, which was retaken by the Maryland ship *Defence*, Capt. James Nicholson, on March 9. Clark, *Naval Documents*, 4:286.

William Whipple to Joshua Brackett

My Dear Sir [1]   Philadelphia 17th March 1776

I am now going to give you some accot of affairs in this part of the world. Every warlike Preparation is making at N. York, two Brigadier Generals viz Thompson, & Lord Sterling, are there, 8,000 men are order'd there, & requisitions to Conecticut, New York, & New Jersey, to hold their Militia in readiness to go to the assistance of York, if needful—13 Regiments for Vergania & Carolinas, Major Genl. Lee & four Brigadiers Genl. in that department. Commissioners are to set off for Canada in a few days; they have with them two Roman Catholick Gentn. of Merriland warm Friends to the American Cause, one of them an Ecleseastick;[2] there is no doubt in my Opinion but that Province will be secured to the United Colonies. Baron De Woedlke who is taken into the Continental service is also going there; this Gentleman is recommended in the Strongest terms by some of the first Carecters in France, both for his love of Liberty & Military knowledge, those who recommend him are well known to some Gentn here. He is well acquainted with the French Language & I suppose has a long string of titles which will please them People. Before this reaches you, You'll hear of the arrival of the Packet at N. York. Some Passengers are come in her, among them is a Mr. Dana & Mr. W. Temple, the lat[t]er is now here in a very bad state of health. Our Friends in England recommend Firmness in the strongest terms. Its fully expected that the late acts of Parliment (Justifing the Pirates in seizing & destroying American Property & confiscating all American Property whereever to be found) will cause a final seperation, in short administration themselves can think no other as is evident from their seting scriblers to work to shew that the Colonies are of but very little consequence to Britain. It may be depended on that no assistance can be obtain'd from Russia, it is also an undoubted fact that 20,000 men is the utmost they will be able to get to America this summer, including those already here & this you may be assur'd of inter Nos that France stands ready to assist us whenever we ask her. Now Sir what have we to fear? Powder is almost daily arriving in small Quantities & there is the greatest prospect of an ample supply of all military stores; shall we in these circumstances Bow the knee to B? God forbid. We have perticular accots. from Cambrige up to the 8th inst. I am anxious to hear what has happend since. Shod the Royals Brutes, Buchers & Pirates evacuate Boston & that Harbour (which I dont believe tho' many do) I suppose you'll think yourselves tolerable safe at Portsmouth. I hope I have some letters from you on the Road. Pray write often & be very perticular. I suppose my B——r [Joseph Whipple] will expect a letter from me by this conveyence but when I write to you I suppose I am at the same time writing to him & besides my avertion to writing I have but little time & expect less when my Colleague is gone. Tell Mrs. B. [Hannah Whipple Brackett] I expect some of her Female Politicks & in return I shall give her some accot of the fine Country as soon as I have opportunity to take a view of it. Remember me Dutifully to My Mother, who I wish to hear from. Tell Mrs. Trail that Mr. Temple saw her son in London & speaks well of him, he also saw her *Dearee* Mr. R——[3] &c at Falmouth. Mr. T[emple] is or seems to be a high whig; he Damns King, Lords, & Commons, without reserve and at the same time talks much of his acquaintence with the Great. The Ostensible cause that Russia will not assist Britain, is that there is no Carttel settled between Britain, & America, but the real cause is France's interposition thro Sweeden. These Gentn that came in the Packet left London the 23 Decr. & Falmouth 7th Jany. They saw Col. Allen in Pendeniss's Castle in Irons but before they left Falmouth he was sent on Board a man of war to do duty as a common Sailor; this ship is coming to America. Can there be an American so lost to Humanity as to wish a connection with a set of Barbarians. I have sent some news papers to Mr. Langdon, remember me kindly to all friends & be assured I am with Great Sincerity, Yours,

W Whipple

RC (Paul Francis Webster, Beverly Hills, Calif., 1974).

[1] Joshua Brackett (1733–1802), Portsmouth, N.H., physician and brother-in-law of William Whipple, was a member of the New Hampshire Provincial Congress and was appointed judge of the New Hampshire Admiralty Court in 1776. Shipton, *Harvard Graduates*, 13:197–201.

[2] Charles Carroll of Carrollton and John Carroll.

[3] Probably Robert Trail, Portsmouth, N.H., merchant and brewer, and husband of Whipple's sister, Mary Whipple Trail. Charles W. Brewster, *Rambles About Portsmouth*. First series (Portsmouth, N.H.: C. W. Brewster & Son, 1859), p. 150.

William Whipple to John Langdon

Dear Sir,   Philadelphia 17. March 1776.
Since my last I have had the pleasure of receiving your two favors
viz. 26 ult and 3d inst. Must refer you to Col Bartlett for an account of
transactions up to this time. What happens after this, shall inform you
of particularly. I think it will be a good way for you to forward a particular list of such articles as will be wanted for the ship that cannot be
procured there and I will do my endeavors to have them sent you as soon
as possible. It would give me great pleasure to hear that the New Hampshire is the first ship at sea. The committee of this Province met and
determined to call a Convention which has given the Assembly a considerable start.[1] They have called in a larger representation, voted 3
battalions and it is supposed will give new instructions to their delegates. This will satisfy the people without a convention. I must refer
you as above for the last news from London and am with respect, Yours,
                                                            Wm Whipple

Tr (DLC).
[1] For further information on this issue, see John Adams to James Warren,
March 21, 1776, note 2.

Richard Smith's Diary

                                              Monday 18 March [1776]
The Votes read. 20,000 Dollars advanced to Commissary Mease.
Some Promotions made in One of the Virginia Regts. in Consequence
of Col. Henry's Resignation. The Congress was again in Comee. on the
privateering Business, several Resoluts. were come to after an able
Debate. By the first, Leave is to be given to commission Privateers and
Letters of Marque to cruize on British Property. The Vote stood thus,
For the Resolution New Hampshire, Massachusetts, Rhode Island,
Connecticut, N York, Virginia and North Carolina, against it Pennsa.
and Maryland, the other Colonies not sufficiently represented to vote.
Ireland was excepted & the other British Domins. with the Consent of
all but Chase & myself (it appearing to me very absurd to make War
upon Part only of the Subjects & especially after the Irish Parlt. had
declared decisively agt. Us).[1] Leave for the Comee. to sit again on the
same Affair.[2] R H Lee moved to take Monsr. Arundel and another
Frenchman into the Southern Departmt. which was opposed by Dr.
Franklin and referred to our Comee. for considerg. the Application of
Foreigners.[3]

MS (DLC).

¹ In November 1775 the Irish Parliament had approved the king's request for the transfer to America of 4,000 British troops then stationed in Ireland. *Am. Archives*, 4th ser. 3:1641–48.

² For additional references to this issue, see Smith's Diary, February 13, 1776, note 4.

³ According to the journals, this day Dohickey Arundel was ordered to the southern department for service with Gen. Charles Lee, and the following day was appointed captain of artillery in the Continental Army. *JCC*, 4:211, 212. See also Smith's Diary, January 16, 1776, note 3. The other "Frenchman" has not been identified, although it is possible that Smith was referring to the chevalier de St. Aulaire, who was authorized by Congress on March 21 to raise a company of rangers in Canada. *JCC*, 4:223.

John Adams to Abigail Adams

March 19. 1776

Yesterday I had the long expected and much wish'd Pleasure of a Letter from you, of various Dates from the 2d. to the 10 March. This is the first Line I have received since I left you. I wrote you from Watertown I believe, relating my Feast at the Quarter Master General with the Coghnawaga Indians, and from Framingham, an Account of the ordnance there, and from New York I sent you a Pamphlet—hope you received these.

Since my arrival here, I have written to you as often as I could.

I am much pleased with your Caution, in your Letter, in avoiding Names both of Persons and Places, or any other Circumstances, which might designate to Strangers, the Writer, or the Person written to, or the Persons mentioned. Characters and Descriptions will do as well.

The Lye, which you say occasioned such Disputes at the Tavern, was curious enough.¹ Who could make and spread it? Am much obliged to an Unkle, for his Friendship: my worthy fellow Citizens may be easy about me. I never can forsake what I take to be their Interests. My own have never been considered by me, in Competition with theirs. My Ease, my domestic Happiness, my rural Pleasures, my Little Property, my personal Liberty, my Reputation, my Life, have little Weight and ever had, in my own Estimation, in Comparison of the great Object of my Country. I can say of it with great Sincerity, as Horace says of Virtue— to America only and her Friends a Friend.

You ask, what is thought of Common sense. Sensible Men think there are some Whims, some Sophisms, some artfull Addresses to superstitious Notions, some keen attempts upon the Passions, in this Pamphlet. But all agree there is a great deal of good sense, delivered in a clear, simple, concise and nervous Style.

His Sentiments of the Abilities of America, and of the Difficulty of a Reconciliation with G.B. are generally approved. But his Notions, and Plans of Continental Government are not much applauded. Indeed this Writer has a better Hand at pulling down than building.

It has been very generally propagated through the Continent that I wrote this Pamphlet. But altho I could not have written any Thing in so manly and striking a style, I flatter myself I should have made a more respectable Figure as an Architect, if I had undertaken such a Work. This Writer seems to have very inadequate Ideas of what is proper and necessary to be done, in order to form Constitutions for single Colonies, as well as a great Model of Union for the whole.[2]

Your Distresses which you have painted in such lively Colours, I feel in every Line as I read. I dare not write all that I think upon this Occasion. I wish our People had taken Possession of Nook Hill, at the same Time when they got the other Heights, and before the Militia were dismissed.

Poor Cousin![3] I pitty him. How much soever he may lament certain Letters I dont lament. I never repent of what was no sin. Misfortunes may be born without Whining. But if I can believe Mr. Dana, those Letters were much admired in England. I cant help laughing when I write it, because they were really such hasty crude Scraps. If I could have foreseen their Fate, they should have been fit to be seen and worth all the Noise they have made. Mr. Dana says they were considered in England as containing a comprehensive Idea of what was necessary to be done, and as shewing Resolution enough to do it. Wretched Stuff as they really were, (according to him) they have contributed somewhat towards making certain Persons' to be thought the greatest Statesmen in the World. So much for Vanity.

My Love, Duty, Respects, and Compliments, wherever they belong.

Virginia will be well defended, so will N.Y., so will S. Car. America will err long, raise her Voice aloud, and assume a bolder Air.

RC (MHi). Adams, *Family Correspondence* (Butterfield), 1:362–64.

[1] In her letter of March 2–10 Abigail had told John of a report "that you and your President had gone on board a Man of War from N—y and saild for England." Adams, *Family Correspondence* (Butterfield), 1:352.

[2] Adams gradually formed a less favorable opinion of Thomas Paine's *Common Sense*. Adams to Abigail Adams, February 18, 1776, note 1. Adams' own views on a constitution for a republican government are explicitly set forth in Adams to John Penn, March 19–27? 1776.

[3] Isaac Smith, Jr., whose sentiments Abigail had discussed in her letter of March 2–10 to John. Adams, *Family Correspondence* (Butterfield), 1:354.

John Adams to John Penn

Dear Sir   [March 19–27? 1776][1]

If I was possess'd of Abilities equal to the great Task you have imposed upon me, which is to Sketch out the outlines of a Constitution for a Colony, I should think myself the happiest of Men in complying with your Desire; because as Politicks is the Art of Securing human Happiness, and the Prosperity of Societies depends upon the Constitution of Government, under which they live, there cannot be a more agreable Employment to a benevolent Mind than the Study of the best Kinds of Governments.[2]

It has been the Will of Heaven, that We should be thrown into Existence at a Period, when the greatest Philosophers and Lawgivers of Antiquity would have wished to have lived: a Period, when a Coincidence of Circumstances, without Example, has afforded to thirteen Colonies at once an opportunity, of beginning Government anew from the Foundation and building as they choose. How few of the human Race, have ever had an opportunity of choosing a System of Government for themselves and their Children? How few have ever had any Thing more of Choice in Government, than in Climate? These Colonies have now their Election and it is much to be wish'd that it may not prove to be like a Prise in the Hands of a Man who has no Heart to improve it.

In order to determine which is the best Form of Government, it is necessary to determine what is the End of Government? and I Suppose that in this enlightened Age, there will be no dispute, in Speculation, that the Happiness of the People, the great End of Man, is the End of Government, and therefore, that Form of government, which will produce the greatest Quantity of Happiness, is the best.

All Sober Enquirers after Truth, ancient and modern, Divines, Moralists and Philosophers, have agreed that the Happiness of Mankind, as well as the real Dignity of human Nature, consists in Virtue. If there is a Form of Government then, whose Principle and Foundation is Virtue will not every wise Man acknowledge it more likely to promote the general Happiness than any other.

Fear, which is Said by Montesquieu and all other political Writers to be the Foundation of some Governments, is so sordid and brutal a Passion that it cannot properly be called a Principle, and will hardly be thought in America a proper Basis of Government.

Honour is a Principle which ought to be Sacred: But the Grecians and Romans, pagan as well as Christian, will inform Us that Honour at most is but a Part of Virtue, and therefore a feebler Basis of Government.

A Man must be indifferent to Sneer and Ridicule, in some Companies to mention the Names of Sidney, Harrington, Lock, Milton, Nedham, Neville, Burnet, Hoadley; for the Lines of John Milton in one of his Sonnetts, will bear an application, even in this Country, upon Some occasions

"I did but teach the Age, to quit their Cloggs
by the plain Rules of ancient Liberty,

THOUGHTS

ON

GOVERNMENT:

APPLICABLE TO

THE PRESENT STATE

OF THE

AMERICAN COLONIES.

In a LETTER from a GENTLEMAN
To his FRIEND.

*By John Adams of Massachusets.
to George Wythe of Virginia.*

PHILADELPHIA:
PRINTED BY JOHN DUNLAP.

M,DCC,LXXVI.

John Adams' *Thoughts on Government*

When lo! a barbarous Noise surrounded me
Of owls and Cuckoo's, Asses, Apes and Dogs."
These great Writers however, will convince any Man who has the
Fortitude to read them, that all good Government is Republican: that
the only valuable Part of the British Constitution is so; for the true Idea
of a Republic, is "An Empire of Laws and not of Men": and therefore
as a Republic is the best of Governments, so that particular combination of Power, which is best continued for a faithfull Execution of the
of the Laws, is the best of Republics.

There is a great Variety of Republics, because the arrangements
of the Powers of Society are capable of many Variations.

As a good Government is an Empire of Laws, the first Question is,
how Shall the Laws be made?

In a Community consisting of large Numbers, inhabiting an extensive Country, it is not possible that the whole should assemble, to make
Laws. The most natural Substitute for an Assembly of the whole, is a
Delegation of Power, from the Many, to a few of the most wise and
virtuous. In the first Place then establish Rules for the Choice of Representatives: Agree upon the Number of Persons who shall have the Priviledge of choosing one. As the Representative Assembly should be an
exact Portrait, in Miniature, of the People at large, as it should think,
feel, reason and act like them great Care should be taken in the formation of it, to prevent unfair, partial and corrupt Elections. That it may
be the Interest of this assembly to do equal Right, and Strict Justice
upon all occasions, it should be an equal Representation of their Constituents, or in other words equal Interests among the People, Should
have equal Interests in the Representative Body.

That the Representatives may often mix with their Constituents,
and frequently render to them an account of their Stewardship, Elections ought to be frequent
Like Bubbles on the Sea of Matter borne
They rise, they break and to that Sea return.
These Elections may be Septennial or triennial, but for my own Part
I think they ought to be annual, for there is not in all science a Maxim
more infallible than this "where Annual Elections End, there Slavery
begins."

But all necessary Regulations for the Method of constituting this
Assembly, may be better made in Times of more Quiet than the present,
and they will suggest themselves naturally, when the Powers of Government shall be in the Hands of the Peoples Friends. For the present it
will be safest to go on in the usual way.

But We have as yet advanced only one Step in the Formation of a
Government. Having obtained a Representative assembly, what is to
be done next? Shall We leave all the Powers of Government in this
assembly? Shall they make and execute, and interpret Laws too? I

answer no—a People cannot be long free, and never can be happy, whose Laws are made, executed and interpreted by one assembly. My Reasons for this opinion are these.

1. A Single Assembly is liable to all the Vices, Follies, and Frailities, of an Individual—Subject to fits of Humour, Transports of Passion, Partialities of Prejudice: and from these and other Causes apt to make hasty Results and absurd Judgments: all which Errors ought to be corrected, and Inconveniences guarded against by some controuling Power.

2. A Single Assembly is apt to grow avaricious, and in Time would not Scruple to exempt itself from Burdens, which it would lay upon its Constituents, without Sympathy.

3. A Single Assembly will become ambitious, and after Some Time will vote itself perpetual. This was found in the Case of the long Parliament: but more remarkably in the case of Holland whose assembly first voted that they should hold their Seats for seven years, then for Life—and after some Time, that they would fill up Vacancies as they should happen without applying to their Constituents at all.

4. The Executive Power cannot be well managed by a Representative Assembly for want of two essential Qualities, Secrecy and Dispatch.

5. Such an assembly is still less qualified to exercise the judicial Power because it is too numerous, too slow, and generally too little Skill'd in the Laws.

But shall the whole Legislative Power, be left in the Hands of such an Assembly? The three first, at least of the foregoing Reasons, will shew that the Legislative Power ought not to be wholly intrusted to one assembly.

Let the Representative Body then elect, from among themselves or their Constituents, or both, a distinct assembly, which We will call a Council. It may consist of any Number you please, say twenty or thirty. To this assembly should be given a free and independent Exercise of its Judgment, upon all Acts of Legislation, that it may be able to check and correct the errors, of the other.

But there ought to be a third Branch of the Legislature: and wherever the Executive Power of the State is placed, their the third Branch of the Legislature ought to be found.

Let the two Houses then, by joint Ballott, choose a Governor. Let him be chosen annually. Divest him, of most of those Badges of slavery called Prerogatives, and give him a Negative upon the Legislature. This I know is liable to some Objections—to obviate which you may make him in a Legislative Capacity only President of the Council. But if he is annually elective, you need not scruple to give him a free and independent Exercise of his Judgment, for he will have so great an affection for the People, the Representatives, and Council that he would Seldom exercise his Right, except in Cases, the public utility of which would soon be manifest, and some such Cases would happen.

In the present Exigency of American Affairs, when by an Act of Parliament We are put out of all Royal Protection, and consequently discharged from all obligations of Allegiance; and when it has become necessary to assume governments for immediate Security, the Governor, Lieut. Governor, Secretary, Treasurer, Attorney General should be chosen by joint Ballot of both Houses.

The governor, by and with and not without the Advice and Consent of Council, should appoint all Judges, Justices, and all other officers civil and military, who should have Commissions signed by the Governor and under the Seal of the Colony.

Sheriffs should be chosen by the Freeholders of the Counties.

If you chose to have a Government more popular all officers may be chosen by one House of Assembly subject to the Negative of the other.

The Stability of Government, in all its Branches, the Morals of the People and every other Blessing of Society, and social Institutions depend so much upon an able and impartial Administration of Justice, that the judicial Power should be Seperated from the Legislative and Executive, and independent upon both; the Judges should be Men of Experience in the Laws, of exemplary Morals, invincible Patience, unruffled Calmness, and indefatigable application; their Minds should not be distracted with complicated jarring Interests—they should not be dependent on any Man or Body of Men—they should lean to none, be subservient to none, nor more complaisant to one than another. To this End they should hold Estates for Life in their offices, or in other Words their Commissions should be during good Behaviour, and their Salaries ascertained and established by Law. If accused of Misbehaviour, by the Representative Body, before the Governor and Council, and if found guilty after having an opportunity to make their Defence, they should [be] removed from their offices and Subjected to such other Punishment as their offences deserve.

A Rotation of Offices, in the Legislative and Executive Departments has many Advocates and if practicable might have many good Effects. A Law may be made that no Man shall be Governor, Lt Governor, Secretary, Treasurer, Counciller, or Representative more than three years at a Time, nor be again eligible untill after an Interval of three Years.

A Constitution like this, of which the foregoing is a very imperfect Plan naturally introduces generally Knowledge into the Community and inspires the People with a conscious Dignity, becoming Freemen. A general Desire of Reputation and Importance among their Neighbours, which cannot be obtained without some Government of their Passions, some good Humour, good Manners and good Morals, takes Place in the Minds of Men, and naturally causes general Virtue and

Civility. That Pride which is introduced by such a Government among the People, makes them brave and enterprising. That ambition which is introduced into every Rank makes them sober, industrious and frugal. You will find among them some Elegance, but more Solidity, a little Politeness but a great deal of Civility—some Pleasure, but much Business.

Let Commissions run thus "Colony of North Carolina to A. B. Greeting" &c and be tested by the Governor.

Let Writs run "The Colony of &c to the sherriff" &c.

Let Indictments conclude "against the Peace of the Colony of North Carolina, and the Dignity of the same," or if you please against the Peace of the thirteen united Colonies.

We have heard much of a Continental Constitution. I see no occasion for any But a Congress. Let that be made an equal and fair Representative of the Colonies, and let its authority be confined to three cases, War, Trade, and Controversies between Colony and Colony. If a Confederation was formed, agreed on in Congress, and ratified by the assemblies, These Colonies under such Terms of Government and such a Confederation would be unconquerable by all the Monarchies of Europe.

This Plan of a Government for a Colony you see is intended as a temporary Expedient under the present Pressure of affairs. The Government once formed, and having settled its authority will have Leisure enough to make any Alterations that Time and Experience, and more mature deliberation may dictate. Particularly, a Plan may be devised perhaps and be thought expedient, for giving the Choice of the Governor to the People at large, and of the Councillers to the Freeholders of the Counties. But be these Things as they may. Two Things are indispensibly to be attended to—one is some Regulation for securing forever an equitable Choice of Representatives—another is the Education of Youth both in Literature and Morals.

I wish, my dear sir, that I had Time to think of these Things more at Leisure, and to write more correctly. But you must take these Hints rough as they run. Your own Reflections assisted by the Patriots of North Carolina will improve upon every Part of them.

As you brought upon yourself the Trouble of reading these crude Thoughts, you cant blame, your Friend

RC (MHi). Adams, *Works* (Adams), 4:203–9. RC damaged; missing words supplied from Tr.

¹ Although this manuscript, which ultimately became Adams' pamphlet *Thoughts on Government*, cannot be precisely dated, it was certainly written before March 27, when John Penn left Philadelphia to return to North Carolina, and it was probably written after March 19, when Adams wrote to his wife criticizing Thomas Paine for "very inadequate Ideas of what is proper and necessary to be done in order to form Constitutions" and asserting that he himself would have made "a more respectable Figure as an Architect" had he undertaken such a work. The implication

seems inescapable that Adams had not yet begun to draft such a plan of government. See Joseph Hewes to Robert Smith, March 27, note 3; and Adams to Abigail Adams, March 19, 1776.

[2] Adams prepared this essay on a constitution for a republican government at the request of William Hooper and John Penn who were about to return home to attend North Carolina's constitutional convention. Apparently Adams prepared two manuscript drafts in letter form for Penn and Hooper but failed to retain a copy himself. Adams is known to have written at least two other versions of this document for George Wythe of Virginia and Jonathan Dickinson Sergeant of New Jersey. Faced with a further request for a copy from Richard Henry Lee of Virginia, Adams showed him the manuscript prepared for Wythe. Lee then had the Wythe version published as *Thoughts on Government: Applicable to the Present State of the American Colonies. In a Letter from a Gentleman to his Friend* (Philadelphia: John Dunlap, 1776). For Adams' contemporary explanation of the evolution of the variant texts, see Adams to James Warren, April 20, 1776. For a fuller discussion of the provenance of this document, see Adams, *Diary* (Butterfield), 3:331–332n. See also Adams to Richard Henry Lee, November 15, 1775.

John Hancock to Baron de Woedtke

Sir   Philadelphia 19th March 1776

In Consequence of the warm Recommendations in your favour, & in hopes, by your emminent Abilities, you will be able to Render essential service to the cause of Liberty, the Congress have thought proper to Appoint you a Brigadier General in the Army of the United Colonies, and I have the honour to Inclose you their Commission.[1]

The Desire of Congress is that you Repair to New York as soon as you can with convenience, and there wait the Arrival of the Commissioners going to Canada, and that you Accompany them to that Province, where you will put yourself under the Command and Receive the orders of the Commander in Chief in that Department.

I have the honour to be, Sir, Your most Obedt hum Servt.

J. H. Prt.

LB (DNA: PCC, item 12A). Addressed: "To Frederick William Baron De Woedtke Knight of Malta &c &c & at Philada."

[1] Frederic William, baron de Woedtke (d. 1776), former Prussian cavalry general, was appointed a brigadier general on March 16. *JCC*, 4:209–10. For "the Warm Recommendations in your favour," see *Am. Archives*, 4th ser. 5:410–11.

Samuel Huntington to Jabez Huntington

Sir   Philadelphia 19th March 1776

I am favoured with yours of the 27th Febry. by Mr Hooper, as also the former Letter therein mentioned. We have obtained thirty thousand pound from the Continental Treasury[1] which is now Setting out for

Hartford & will be there in about ten days. I hope this Sum will answer present necessity, & that all the accounts of our Colony against the Continent may be forwarded as Soon as possible & no further advances for Continental Service by the Colony if possible to avoid them. The Congress have appointed a General fast the 17th of May: also granted Liberty for Privateers & armed vessels against Great Brittain, that is only vessels & Cargos belonging to the Inhabitants of that Iland.[2] Am not able to find any Manufacturers of Oznabrigs in this City. Remain Sir, with much Esteem, your humble Servt, Saml Huntington

RC (CtHi).

[1] An advance of $100,000 was approved on March 7. *JCC*, 4:188.

[2] The resolutions concerning privateering, which were entered in the journals on March 23 along with a declaration approved that day, were embodied in a report of the committee of the whole that was approved by Congress on the 19th. See *JCC*, 4:213–14, 229–32.

Francis Lightfoot Lee to Landon Carter

My dear Col.   Philadelphia March 19. 1776 [1]

Before this I suppose you have recd. a Copy of common sense which I sent you some time ago; if not, I now send a parcel to Col. Tayloe of whome you may have one.

Our late King & his Parliament having declared us Rebels & Enemies, confiscated our property, as far as they were likely to lay hands on it; have effectually decided the question for us, whether or no we shou'd be independant. All we have now to do, is to endeavour to reconcile ourselves to the state, it has pleased Providence to put us into; and indeed upon taking a near & full look at the thing, it does not frighten so much, as when view'd at a distance. I cant think we shall be injured by having a free trade to all the world, instead of its being confined to one place, whose riches might allways be used to our ruin. Nor does it appear to me that we shall suffer any disadvantage, by having our Legislatures uncontrouled by a power so far removed for us, that our circumstances cant be known; whose interest is often directly contrary to ours; and over which we have no manner of controul. Indeed great part of that power being at present lodged in the hands of a most gracious Prince, whose tender mercies we have often experienced; it must wring the heart of all good men to part; but I hope we shall have christian fortitude enough to bear with patience, & even chearfullness the decrees of a really most gracious King. The danger of Anarchy & confusion, I think altogether chimerical, the good behaviour of the Americans with no Government at all proves them very capable of good Government. But my dear Col, I am so fond of peace that I wish to see an end of these distractions upon terms that will secure America from future outrages, but from all our intelligence I really despair. There is such an inveteracy in the ——— & his advisers, that we need not expect any other alternative, than slavery or seperation. Is it not prudent therefore, to fit our minds to the state that is inevitable. Virginia it seems is consider'd at home, as most liable to deception & seduction; & therefore the Commissioners are to bend their cheif force that way, backed by a considerable detachment of the Army. I hope it will turn to the honor of my Country as it will afford an opportunity of shewing their Virtue & good sense. Col. Tayloe has the news. I wrote yesterday to my friend Col. R. Carter by the post [2] letting him know that Genl. Lee, who has the Southern command, was furnished with the two aid de Camps paid by Congress, before my application; but agreed to take your Grandson, as a supernumerary Aid he bearing his own expences. If this is agreeable you will perhaps see the Genl. as he had some thots of passing thro' Richmond. Best respects to Sabine Hall.

    Adieu my dear friend.   Francis Lightfoot Lee

P.S. I forgot to mention to Col. Carter that I desired Mr. R. Colston to carry with him Mrs. Carter's cotton cards & always understood he had done so. When I recd. Col. Carter's Letter, there was not a pair in this City. I have sent to New York, if I get any from thence, will send them by the first opportunity.

RC (MH).
[1] On this day also Richard Henry Lee wrote from Philadelphia to John Page: "It gives me pleasure to find the mutinous spirit of our Soldiery so well subdued, and I hope the character and weight of our General Officers will prevent the like irregularities for the future. As the putrid fever rages so much in the Norfolk fleet, 'tis pity but Dunmore and his people could be forced into their Ships to partake the ruin of that distemper . . . I hope and wish that both the Committee of Safety and Convention would immediately establish public works for making common Salt. We have no Chance for importation, and the want of this Necessary will produce universal riot and convulsion . . . I find it gives concern in our Country that the Continentall Troops are not under Colonial direction." Extract of autograph letter signed, printed in *The Collector* 61 (August 1948): item M1586.
[2] Not found, but see Francis Lightfoot Lee to Landon Carter, February 12, 1776, note 1.

Maryland Delegates to the Maryland Council of Safety

Gent.   Phila. 19 March 1776.
    Capt Tibbit in a Brig from Statia, purchased & loaded by Abraham Vanbibber for our Province, arrived here last Week, the Capt applied

to Us for Orders agreable to Directions, he had received for that purpose from Vanbibber; We order'd the Cargo to be landed & stored, and the Hands to be discharged. A few Days since Application was made to Us, for the Sale of the Brig to the Congress, which We agreed to, and have delivered her up with the Guns, Stores, &c.[1] The Accts. relative to her, will be settled in a few Days, & shall be transmitted. You have inclosed a List of the Goods imported, all of which will be forwarded by the Stages, except the Duck. We have retained this, 'till your Orders, it is an Article very scarce & dear in this City, if you do not want the whole Quantity, We can sell it, at a Price that will leave a considerable Profit. Congress have advanced 22000 Dollars, to be exchanged for Gold & Silver in your Province, this Money would have been sent you had any convenient Oppertunity offered. R. A. who intended for Maryland last Sunday, prevented our Writing, by the Saturdays Post as he proposed going to Annapolis, and could give you fuller Information of the State of Affairs, than can be contained within the Compass of a Letter. We make no doubt you have heard various Reports relative to a Mr. Temple, who came passenger in the Packet & is now in this City. Before his Arrival here it was asserted, that he was charged with Dispatches from the Minority to Congress, that Commissioners were appointed with full Powers, and that if on their Arrival in America, the different Assemblies refused to treat, they were to treat with Congress. Temple on his Arrival, delivered his Budget, which was truly farsical, being only a Button of his Coat, in which was contained a Scrawl from Arthur Lee informing Congress, that Troops were to sail from Ireland & for the particulars, referring to Temple who could give Information, as he Lee had acquainted him with the State of Affairs & the Designs of Administration. We have never seen Temple, it is said, he is sick, some say he is mad, from his Conduct in taking this Journey to deliver such a trifling Letter, if this is his sole Business, the latter Opinion seems well founded. The Packet Letters are put on Board the Asia Man of War, the Post Master, it is reported has refused to deliver any Letters, unless the Postage of the whole is paid. We are in Expectation of an Express from Boston; Genl. Washington took Possession of Dorchester Poi[nt wh]ich commands South Boston, it is said by the [Genl. in a] Letter to Congress, that Howe was embarqueing his Artillery, Stores, &c in the greatest Confusion.

We are with Respect, Gent, Yr Hble Servants,

The Delegates of Maryland

RC (MdAA). In the hand of Robert Alexander. Endorsed: "R. Alexander Letter, & other Deputies, 19th March 1776, relative to a Brig named Wicked Dick [*Wild Duck*] sold Congress, &c."

[1] See Thomas Johnson to the Maryland Council, March 9, 1776.

Maryland Delegates to
the Pennsylvania Committee of Safety

Gent.   Phila. March 19. 1776.
    The Convention of Maryland voted a considerable Sum of Money
to defend the Harbour of Baltimore Town the most considerable place
of our Trade. Fortifications & Batteries are now erecting and every
Means in our Power to procure Cannon have failed. If your Colony [1]
can spare us four eighteen Pounders or eight Twelves or eight Nines,
which shall be returned as soon as others can be procured, they will be
of infinite Service in defending a Boom now or very nearly ready to be
laid across the River.
    We are Gent., Your most obedt. Servts.   Th Johnson Junr

                                                Saml. Chase

                                                Wm. Paca

RC (PHi). Written by Johnson and signed by Johnson, Chase, and Paca.
    [1] An identical letter was sent to the New York Committee of Safety. Emmet
Collection, NN. See New York Delegates to the New York Provincial Convention,
this date.

New York Delegates to
the New York Provincial Convention

Gentlemen   Philad. 19 March 1776
    We beg leave to recommend to your particular Attention the enclosed
Request from the Delegates of Maryland. We are not sufficiently acquainted with the State of our Artillery to judge whether it will be in
your Power to oblige a Sister Colony on this pressing Occasion. We can
only say that it will give us great pleasure if you can consistently contribute to the Safety of Maryland: from whose Delegates our Colony
has always received a uniform and zealous Support.[1] Their Friendship
in procuring an Instruction from their Convention, expressly directing
them to move & use their Endeavours for procuring Relief to our Colony
in the Article of Tea, and their generous offer to supply us with a Ton
of their scanty Stock of powder, some months ago, deserve our grateful
Acknowledgments, and the Esteem of our Constituents. We cou'd not
indeed avail ourselves of the last Favour: because the Interposition of
Congress was necessary, and we had Reason to be apprehensive that
the Powder woud have been sent another way, where it was then
thought more necessary.

We have the Honour to be, with the greatest Respect, Gentlemen, Your most Obedient, humble Servants,

Jas. Duane   John Jay

John Alsop   Lewis Morris

RC (N). Written by Duane and signed by Duane, Alsop, Jay, and Morris. Endorsed: "Letter from N York Delegates at Continental Congress accompanying a Letter from Th. Johnson &c. of the Maryland Convention requestg. the loan of Cannon."
  [1] Apart from an order to its secretary to draft replies to the letters from the Maryland and New York delegates (which replies are no longer extant), there is no record of the response to the Maryland request for cannon by the New York Committee of Safety, which was the first to receive it, or by the Provincial Convention, which did not reconvene until May 1776. *Am. Archives*, 4th ser. 5:1389, 1491–1507. See also Maryland Delegates to the Pennsylvania Committee of Safety, this date.

Secret Committee Minutes of Proceedings

March 19. 1776.

At a meetg. of the Come. Present Robt. Morris, B. Franklin, J. Alsop, Jos. Hewes & Richd. Henry Lee appointed one of the Committee of Secrecy by Congress this day. Issued an order on Robt. Towers Com[missar]y to deliver to the Commissioners for buildg. the Frigates 1 ton powdr. agreable to a resolve of C[ongress] of this date. Issued an order on the Treasurers in favor of Mr. Saml. Meredith & Capt. Mason for 92 dlls. for services done the Cols. in looking after the Cargoe of the Brige. Chance. Issued an order in favor of Mr. Samuel Mifflin for [   ]370 dlls for freight of the Brige. Chance &c & other expences bore by him in looking after the Cargo of the sd. Brige. Do. on Mr. Towers Comy. to deliver to Capt. Blanchard of the Jersey light horse, 1 ton of powdr. agreable to a Resolve of Cong. of the 6th inst. for delivery of that quantity to the Jersey Delegates. The Come. was pleasd this day to appoint Mr Brown an assistant Secy. Executed a Charter party with Mr. Ross & Co for Ship Lion.

MS (MH).

Richard Smith's Diary

[March 19, 1776]

Tuesday 19. Minutes read. 250,000 Dollars advanced to Gen Washington and 50,000 to Gen Schuyler. The Comee. of the whole went thro the Articles on Privateers and they were referred to Wyth and Two others to prepare a Preamble. Vacancies in several Committees were filled up. A Captain of Artillerys Commission ordered to Monsr. Arundel. Wyth made a Report for the Appointment of a Commissary of Prisoners which was recommitted[1] and for recompensing Michael Kearney for the Loss of his Boat which was confirmed.[2] A Ton of Powder was ordered for the Vessel of War here & ready to go down to guard Delaware Bay. Sundry public Letters read & some of them Commitd. Johnson threw out for Consideration the Propriety of establishing a Board of Treasury, a War Office, a Board of Public Accounts and other Boards to consist of Gentn. not Members of Congress. The Draught of a Commission to Dr. Franklin, Chase and Carrol was brot. in & some additional Instructions.[3] In the Eveng. S. Adams, Wilson & myself spent an Hour with Gen Prescott at the new Tavern, he was open & free, endeavored to justify every Thing by the Commands of Carlton & explained at large his Complaints.[4]

MS (DLC).
  [1] Not until October 7, 1776, did Congress recommend that each state appoint a commissary of prisoners. *JCC*, 4:361, 5:850.
  [2] On this point, see Smith's Diary, March 7, 1776, note 1.
  [3] See also Smith's Diary, February 14, 1776, note 1.
  [4] Ibid., March 14, 1776.

Oliver Wolcott to Laura Wolcott

My Dear   Philadelphia 19 March 1776
    I Wrote you a Letter the 8t instant which I hope you have by this Time recd. I have heard nothing from you since I recd. a Letter from the D[eputy] Govr. from Fairfield. I imagine I must have some Letters upon the Road and hope I may soon have the Satisfaction to hear from you. I continue by the Blessing of God, well. I have found it necessary as I can have but little Exercise to Observe some Discipline in living, especially to avoid Supper, which you may easily conceive is Very unnecessary, as We generally dine about five. A pritty light Breakfast of Swetened Water and Milk with some Toast with a pritty hearty dinner I find Suits Me and without losing Flesh. I was sorry to hear that you was troubled with the Rheumatism. I hope you are now well of it. My own Wishes are not gratified in living from my Family, but as in an important Circumstance of Life which has since lead me much from Home, I hope I committed the future allotments of Life to the Disposal of divine Providence. I humbly hope it may please God to bless me with his Guidance and take Care of and Protect those who are most dear to me, tho I am unworthy of his favours. Your own Cares must be many. I earnestly Wish you may injoy Health and fortitude of mind. Mr. Sherman is going to make a short Visit to his Family[1]—when I may do so is uncertain. The publick Trust is Very important and a hasty recess

from it will not be justified but for urgent Reasons. I mean to con-
tinue to Write one in about a Week or Ten days,[2] but the Transmittance
of Letters out of the Post Road across the Country I suppose is pritty
Uncertain. I have wrote to Mr. Lyman to let me know wheither my
Letters shall be sent to N. Haven or to Mr Ellerys office at Hartford.
The weekly Post might carry them from thence.

I have bo't a sett of Shakespeares Works Price 8 dollars for Mariana,
as I heard she was fond of them. I shall Send them to Oliver first Oppertunity. Have Sent to Oliver and Frederice Dr Smith's Oration on the
Death of Genl Montgomery. Dr Smith has too much covertly introduced his own political Sentiments of the Times and defamed Col Enos
without any Authority.[3] Dr. Smith's character is not I take it the most
unexceptionable and being a Wioming Claimer is peculiarly inimicial
to our Colony and N England in general. He was desired by Congress to
deliver this Oration but has not Obtained their Thanks for so doing.
Neither is it printed at their Desire. There are Strokes in it of Sublime
Oratory—but I think he meant rather to gratify himself than to do
Honour to the Memory of anyone, but this by the bye. I am affectionaly
yrs.   O Wolcott

P.S. My kindest Love to my Children and Freinds.

RC (CtHi).
[1] Roger Sherman may have left Philadelphia this day, since the $100,000 con-
gressional advance for Connecticut, which Wolcott had earlier indicated would be
transmitted by Sherman, left Philadelphia on March 19. See Wolcott to Matthew
Griswold, March 9; and Samuel Huntington to Jabez Huntington, March 19, 1776.
Although the date of Sherman's departure is not definitely known, the notes and
accounts he recorded in his 1776 almanac document his return to Philadelphia on
April 10. Sherman Papers, DLC.
[2] Wolcott wrote a brief note to his wife on March 22 reporting that he was sending
home presents for the family. Etting Collection, PHi.
[3] Roger Enos, a Connecticut officer commanding the rear division of Arnold's
expedition to Canada, had returned with his men to Cambridge in response to
complaints over shortages of provisions. Although Enos had been acquitted by a
court-martial of the charge of returning home without Arnold's permission, Smith
implied in his address that those who returned were deserters. The proceedings of
the court-martial and Smith's oration are printed in Am. Archives, 4th ser. 4:238–40,
1675–84. For congressional reaction to Smith's oration, see Richard Smith's Diary,
February 21; and Samuel Adams to Elizabeth Adams, February 26, 1776.

James Duane to Robert R. Livingston

Philad. 20th March 1776
I have been favour, my dear Sir, with your Letter of the 15t of
February.[1] As it only notices the Receipt of one of mine I conclude that
a second miscarried which woud alone be sufficient to deter me from

writing to you with Freedom on political Subjects. Indeed at present it woud be unnecessary as my Friend Chase who with Doctor Franklin and Mr Carrol of Maryland are employd on a Deputation from Congress to Canada, has promised me to call on you at Clermount. He will with pleasure communicate everything worth your Knowledge. You will find that his Usual warmth is not abated and that tho' closely attached to his Friends he still keeps the Start of them in his political System. The social Intercourse which was formed amongst the Delegates of the five middle Colonies and North Carolina has suffered no Diminution, and I am perswaded they woud all combine to give you Pleasure. But as nothing has transpird from General Schuyler for fixing Residents at Albany, and the Deputation for Canada was agreed upon before your Inclinations were communicated, your Plan[2] cannot take place for the present. If it shoud hereafter be judged necessary, you may take it for granted that your Services will be most acceptable, and that you will be appointed Whether I am here to remind our Friends of you or not.

When I first wrote to you I expected soon to have visited my Family a Happiness of which I have too long been deprived! But such is the critical State of my dear native Country, and so slender has been our own Representation, that I coud not reconcile it to my Ideas of the important Trust of which I partake. Whether we shall be reconciled to Great Britain, or seperated from her perhaps forever? is a question which a few weeks may probably decide, and on which the Happiness of millions may depend. I wish for Peace if it can be accompanied by Liberty and Safety. I expect little from the Justice and less from the Generosity of Administration; but I am not without Hopes that the Interest of Great Britain will compel her ministers to offer us reasonable Terms. I am unwilling that while Commissioners are daily looked for, we shoud by any irrevocable Measure tie up our Hands, and put it out of our power to terminate this destructive War. I do not think this Line of Conduct incompatible with the most vigorous Efforts for our Defence in the ensuing Campaign. I believe it to be agreeable to the Sense of our Constituents, a Consideration which woud alone be decisive with me. Under these Impressions I wait for the expected Propositions with painful anxiety. If they shoud prove oppressive or frivolous you will be at no Loss to form a judgment of the Consequences.

I cannot think with patience of the Infidelity of my favorite & ungrateful Servant; and much less of the baseness and Treachery of his Employer:[3] but thankful for the seasonable detection, I leave them to that Remorse of Conscience which must one day prove their punishment. To the Circumstance, respecting your Father, hinted at in your Letter, I am a stranger. I congratulate you on your Election, as you had it at heart and it is a further Evidence of the respect of your Country and the more so for being unsolicited. But I am much more pleased at the Reestablishment of your Health which will enable you, after settling your Family affairs, to resume your Seat in Congress, where, without a Compliment, you can be very serviceable.

I am much obliged to you for your Attention to my wife & Daughter who I fear spend their Time very solitarily; not for want of a very agreeable Neighbourhood; but from an Indisposition to visit which prevails at the Manshion. I hope however that you and Mr Patterson will be able to effect some Alterations.

Our Friend Hooper is just returnd from Cambridge where he has been on a Visit to his Mother. This Circumstance will prevent your condemning him for a supposed Negligence, provided he now makes you amends, which he promises to do.

Your Brother Henry is appointed Lieut. Colonel of one of the four Battals. raising in our Colony.[4] Our Convention were pleased to set him down towards the Bottom of the List of Majors; & to recommend Henry G. Livingston as Lieut Colonel.[5] I did not comprehend the wisdom of this Arrangement nor the Reasons upon which it is founded. Congress were heartily disposed to promote your Brother, and all the officers who served the last Campaign, in preferrence to Gentlemen who expected a Regiment or Lieut Colonelcy as the very first step. Indeed they so far controuled our Convention as to pass an order that in the Recommendation of the Field officers, the officers who served in Canada shoud be provided for; which was a fortunate precaution.[6] A Battalion is left open till Col. Ritzma can be heard.[7] If he does not succeed to it, it will lie between Col Yates and Col. Courtlandt. The former I do not Know and what is worse I never heard any thing of him. Pray let me have your Sentiments. If Clinton shoud be provided for in Canada, where two Regiments are orderd to be formed out of the English Troops, there will be room for Mr Yates and Courtlandt both. Mr Chase will furnish you with further particulars on this subject. The uncertainty with respect to the Gent. now in Canada perplexed Congress not a little. It was however thought prudent to secure such of them as coud any way be provided for in the new Battalions, at all Events.

If time permits I shall write to Cousin Harry and acquaint him of his promotion. But least I shoud be disappointed, I beg you'l present my Compliments to him with the Intelligence. I am not sure it will answer *his* Expectations, but I flatter myself that you will think it a suitable provision. For my own part I thought the Issue, considering the Arrangement of our Convention, not unfavourable, tho' perfectly just.

My Letter is running to an enormous Length, tho' it is not very interesting. It however serves as a substantial proof of the earnest desire I have to do you a pleasure.

Present my respectful Compliments to your Lady, Mamma, & Mrs. Montgomerie and the rest of our Friends at both Houses and believe me to be with the greatest Esteem, My dear Sir, Your Affect. Kinsman & most obed huml Sert,   Jas Duane

[*P.S.*] The Deputies are so long detaind here that I have concluded to
, send this Letter forward by Col Dehass [John deHaas] of the Pensylvanians who is on his way to Canada. He is a Gent. of great Merit and
as such permit me to recommend him to your Attention.

RC (NHi).
  ¹ Internal evidence strongly suggests that in fact Duane was referring to Livingston's letter to him of February 16. Whether Duane had misread the date or whether
this was done by the 19th-century transcriber who made the only extant copy of
Livingston's letter cannot be determined now. See Robert R. Livingston to Duane,
February 16, 1776.
  ² Presumably Livingston's proposal that he be appointed to serve on a congressional committee to confer with General Schuyler at Albany—a committee whose
creation was originally urged by Schuyler himself in January 1776. Ibid.
  ³ These references are to James Brattle and New York governor William Tryon.
See Duane to Mary Duane, February 22, 1776, note.
  ⁴ Henry Beekman Livingston. See *JCC*, 4:190; and New York Delegates to the
New York Provincial Congress, January 5, 1776, note 1.
  ⁵ See *Am. Archives*, 4th ser. 4:1530–32; and Duane to the New York Provincial
Convention, February 25, 1776, note 7.
  ⁶ This resolve was approved by Congress on February 17. *JCC*, 4:158–59.
  ⁷ See New York Delegates to the New York Provincial Congress, March 15, 1776,
note 7.

Joseph Hewes to Samuel Johnston

Dear Sir,   Philadelphia 20th March 1776.
  I have received your favour of the 23rd of Feb'y, and also one from
Mr. Hogg at Hillsborough of the 20th, I am exceedingly anxious for
the safety of our Province. We sent an express to you about five weeks
ago, since which I have not heard anything of him, I wait his return
with impatience. The act of Parliament prohibiting all Trade & Commerce between Great Britain and the Colonies has been lately brought
here by a Mr. Temple from London, it makes all American property
found on the Sea liable to Seizure & confiscation and I fear it will make
the Breach between the two Countries so wide as never more to be reconciled. We have heard much talk of Commissioners to be sent to treat
with us, I do not expect any, the act of Parliament empowers the King
to appoint Commissioners to receive submissions and grant pardons
but no futher. Doctor Franklin told me last evening he had a Letter
from London dated the 25th December, no Commissioners were then
appointed, parliament was prorogued to 25th of January. I see no
prospect of a reconciliation, nothing is left now but to fight it out, and
for this we are not well provided, having but little ammunition, no
Arms no money, nor are we unanimous in our Councils. We do not
treat each other with that decency and respect that was observed heretofore. Jealousies, ill natured observations and recriminations take

place of reason and Argument, our Tempers are sound, some among us urge strongly for Independency and eternal separation, others wish to wait a little longer and to have the opinion of their Constituents on that subject, you must give us the sentiment of your province when your Convention meets.[1] Several Merchants and others have petitioned the Congress for leave to fit out privatiers to Cruize against British Vessels, it was granted yesterday, the Restrictions are not yet completed or I would have sent you a copy of them.[2] I send you the last News paper enclosed to which refer for news.

My Compliments to all. I am Sir, Your most obedt Servt.

Jos. Hewes.

MS not found; reprinted from *N.C. Colonial Records*, 11:288–89.

[1] On April 12, 1776, the North Carolina Provincial Congress unanimously resolved to authorize the North Carolina delegates "to concur with the delegates of the other Colonies in declaring Independency, and forming foreign alliances." *N.C. Colonial Records*, 10:512.

[2] See Richard Smith's Diary, March 19, 1776.

Francis Lewis to William Livingston

Dr. Sir, New York 20 March 1776

I have been favored with your Letter of the 15 Inst [1] & pursuant thereto have agreed with Mr. John Griffiths proprietor of Orange Iron Works for the several Articles specified at foot.[2] He this day complaind to me that by information from one Cox & others who had contracted with the Committee [3] at Phila. that they had much higher prices than those Stipulated for by him, hopes to be considered tho' will not fall back from his agreemt. By this youl see how necessary it is for Committees of Congress to be circumspect or they will be imposed upon.

Mr. Erskine of Ringwood Iron Works [is now?] in Town & to give me his proposalls for Cannon [Sh]ot tomorrow, but is apprehensive cannot cast Cannon larger than 9 pounders, but can furnish shot of any size & Quantity of both which let me know the extent you would have engaged, by next Post.[4]

I am, Dr. Sir, your very Humbl Servt, Fra. Lewis

Engaged with Mr. John Griffiths for
150 Tons Pig Iron for Ballast @ £8 per Ton d[elivere]d at the ships
 30 Tons of 12 pd shott⎫
 20 Tons of 9 pd do ⎬ @ £15 per Ton dd where ordered
 4 Tons of 4 pd do ⎭
 6 Tons of Grape shot @ £20 per Ton dd the same
 20, 9 pd Cannon finished @ £28 per Ton proved and dd any where
  on Hudsons River by the End of May

Francis Lewis

RC (MHi). Addressed: "To William Livingston Esqr Elizabeth Town."
  ¹ Not found.
  ² Lewis, a member of the Naval Committee, contracted for these "Articles" in connection with the construction of the Continental frigates *Congress* and *Montgomery* at Poughkeepsie, N.Y., under a congressional resolution of December 13, 1775. *JCC*, 3:425–26; Clark, *Naval Documents*, 3:90n.2, 4:119, 233–34; and Lewis to Robert Treat Paine, May 20, 1776.
  ³ Doubtless the "Committee on the ways and means of procuring cannons," of which William Livingston was a member, created by Congress on February 20. *JCC*, 4:55, 153, 154, 155.
  ⁴ For some of Lewis' previous dealings with Robert Erskine, see Clark, *Naval Documents*, 4:119.

Maryland Delegates to the Maryland Council of Safety

Gent.   Phila. 20 March 1776

On the Arrival of Capt Tibbit, we engaged a Boat, on Board of which was shipped the Powder & Arms, together with one Ton of Powder advanced by Congress & 1875 lbs returned by Congress for the Quantity borrowed by Col Harrison. This Boat went to Christiana Bridge, from whence the powder was sent to Balt. in Waggons.¹ Of this Transaction, We advised you by the Return of the Express, that brought the Intelligence of the Otter & her Tenders arrival in Patapsco. The Qty of Powder that was private Property in Tibbit, was very small, part of it was owned by a Gent. in Accomack County in Virginia, the Residue about 6 or 8 q[uarte]r Casks, Mr Bowley informs us, is the Property of Gentn. in Balt. to whom it was sent. Powder is an Article, that cannot be purchased in this City. Mr. Johnson had a Sum of Money lodged in his Hands by Col Hollingsworth of Cecil County, to purchase a small Qty of powder for that County, the Money being raised by Subscription for that Purpose. This he could not accomplish; and at the pressing Instance of that City We procured from Congress 5 Barrels, which is sent down. The Demand from the Eastward being very great, and our Magazine almost empty, prevents our making any further Application.

We are with Respect, Gent., Yr. Hble Servts,
                              R. Alexander for self & Colleagues

RC (MdAA). In the hand of Robert Alexander.
¹ See Maryland Delegates to Henry Hollingsworth, March 9, 1776.

Richard Smith's Diary

Wednesday 20 March [1776]

The Minutes of yesterday were read with Letters from Ld. Stirling and others.[1] The Commission and Instructions to the Canada Commissioners were canvassed & finished, by One Clause any Two of them are allowed to abate Fortifications and to construct any so as not to exceed 100,000 Dollars.[2] Some Comees. were filled up. Major Brixon [Wrixon] lately from England being recommendd. for the Service in Canada in Quality of an Engineer a Comee. was raised to consider the Application.[3] Several Accots. allowed. E Rutledge moved that Magaws Regiment may be furnished with Pikes they having no Guns, it was desired also for several other Regts. The Matter was debated & left for further Consideration.[4] On like Motion Col Magaw was allowed 3000 Dollars on Accot. to purchase Arms with. S. Adams reported about the Prisoners at Trenton.

MS (DLC).
   [1] Gen. William Alexander's letter to Hancock of March 16 is in PCC, item 162, 2:466–68, and *Am. Archives*, 4th ser. 5:247–48.
   [2] For further references to this issue, see Smith's Diary, February 14, 1776, note 1.
   [3] See John Adams to Abigail Adams, March 17, 1776, note 1.
   [4] See *JCC*, 4:215, 224.

John Adams' Draft Resolutions
for Encouraging Agriculture and Manufactures

[March 21? 1776][1]

Resolved, That it be recommended to the several Assemblies, Conventions, Councils of Safety and Committees of Correspondence and Inspection, that they use their utmost Endeavours, by all reasonable Means to promote the Culture of Flax, Hemp, and Cotton and the Growth of Wool in these united Colonies.[2]

Resolved That it be recommended to the Assemblies, Conventions, and Councils of Safety, that they take the earliest Measures for erecting in each and every Colony a Society for the Encouragement of Agriculture, Arts, Manufactures and Commerce, and that a Correspondence be maintained between such Societies, that the numerous natural Advantages of this Country for supporting its Inhabitants may not be neglected.

Resolved that it be recommended to the said Assemblies, Conventions and Councils of Safety that they consider of Ways and Means of introducing the Manufactures of Duck and Sail Cloth into such Colonies where they are not now understood and of increasing and promoting them where they are.

Resolved that   be a Committee, to receive all Plans and Proposals for encouraging and improving the Agriculture, Arts, Manufactures and Commerce both foreign and domestic of America, to correspond with the several Assemblies, Conventions, Councils and Committees of Safety, Committees of Correspondence and of Observation in these united Colonies upon these interesting Subjects.[3]

That these be published.

MS (MHi). Adams, *Diary* (Butterfield), 2:234–35.

[1] Adams may have drafted these resolutions considerably earlier than March 21, but it seems likely that they were written shortly before they were adopted by Congress this day. Richard Smith said that Adams reported them from a committee, but there is no mention of such a committee in the journals. Richard Smith's Diary, March 21, 1776; and *JCC*, 4:224.

[2] For the amended text of the first three resolutions adopted by Congress, see *JCC*, 4:224.

[3] This final proposal was rejected by Congress. Richard Smith's Diary, March 21, 1776.

John Adams to James Warren

My dear sir   March 21. 1776

I have not recd more than one Letter from you since I left you and that was a very Short one.[1] I have written as often as I could. If you get a Sight of the New York and Philadelphia News Papers you will see what a mighty Question is before the Tribunal of the Public. The Decision is yet in suspence, but a Guess may be formed what it will be.

The Day before yesterday the Committee of Observation of this City, a virtuous, brave and patriotic Body of Men 100 in Number, voted with only one dissentient Voice, to petition their Assembly now sitting, to repeal their deadly Instruction to their Delegates in Congress. This assembly, a few days ago upon a Peti[ti]on from the Same Committee and some other Bodies, has voted seventeen additional Members, in order to make the Representation of this Province more adequate.[2]

You will soon see a sett of Resolutions, which will please you. The Continental Vessells, the Provincial Vessells, and Letters of Marque and Privateers will be let loose upon British Trade.[3]

I hope and believe it will not be long before, Trade will be open.[4] Foreign Nations, all the World I hope will be invited to come here, and our People permitted to go to all the World except the Dominion of him, who is adjudged to be Nerone Neronior.

I think the Utmost Encouragement must be given to Trade—and therefore We must lay no Duties at present upon Exports and Imports— nor attempt to confine our Trade to our own Bottoms, or our own seamen. This for the present.

We have so much Work to do, by sea and Land, and so few Hands to do it, that We shall not be under any Necessity nor will it be good Policy, I think, to attempt such Restrictions as yet.

The Act of Assembly here for Seventeen additional Representatives,

will give a finishing Blow to the Quaker Interest in this City—at least
to its ascendency. It will strip it of all that unjust and unequal Power,
which it formerly had over the Ballance of the Province. The Tories
here, attribute this Maneuvre to your Friends to whom you are sometimes so partial. If the Charge is true the Posterity of Pensylvania will
have cause to bless your Friends from Generation to Generation. You
cant think how much I am flattered with it. As I have the Pleasure of a
particular Acquaintance, and frequent friendly Conversations with
several Gentlemen of this City belonging to the Committee of Observation, I am inclined to hope, that a small Portion of this Merit, is due to
me. But I would not be too vain and proud of it.

RC (MHi). In Adams' hand, though not signed.

[1] Warren's March 7 letter to Adams is in *Warren-Adams Letters*, 1:209–10.

[2] In February Philadelphia radicals had temporarily outmaneuvered the moderates who dominated the Pennsylvania Assembly. After winning control of the
Philadelphia Committee of Inspection and Observation in a February 16 election,
they engineered the committee's petition to the assembly calling for a provincial
convention to take "into consideration the present state of the province." Critics
were certain that this was a New England inspired plan designed to compel changes
in the Pennsylvania government and its congressional delegation and to reverse
Pennsylvania's opposition to independence.

A group of Philadelphians who were members of both the assembly and the
committee, among them Joseph Reed and John Dickinson, worked out a compromise,
which the assembly accepted on March 8, calling for an enlargement of the assembly's
membership by 17 seats—four going to the city of Philadelphia and 13 to the back
counties. Although the radicals believed that they would easily capture the new
seats in a May 1 election and thus gain control of the assembly, the moderates
ultimately won enough seats to retain their power. The radicals, temporarily
thwarted, were thus forced to devise more daring maneuvers in May and June.
David Hawke, *In the Midst of a Revolution* (Philadelphia: University of Pennsylvania
Press, 1961), pp. 13–31. On the May 1 election, see also Caesar Rodney to Thomas
Rodney, May 1, 1776, note 2.

The full story of the Pennsylvania radicals' connections with the New Englanders,
particularly John and Samuel Adams, is more difficult to assess, although there is
no reason to doubt the influence of "the Cunning Men of the East," as they were
described by Edward Shippen. Beyond the repeated testimony of John Adams, it
is known that Philadelphia firebrands such as Benjamin Rush and Thomas Young,
a former member of the Boston Sons of Liberty, were close friends of the Adamses.
Christopher Marshall, another radical leader, often consulted with the Adamses,
and on the evidence of his diary he made at least four visits to their lodgings during
the critical 12 days between the February 16 election and the February 28 call for
a provincial convention. Furthermore, the election defeat of May 1 did not deter
them from continuing their behind-the-scenes efforts to advance the cause of independence by overthrowing the proprietary government of Pennsylvania. See John
Adams to John Winthrop, May 12, to James Warren, May 15 and 20, to Abigail
Adams, May 17, and to Patrick Henry, June 3, 1776; Samuel Adams to Thomas
Young, October 17? 1774; Adams, *Diary* (Butterfield), 2:115n.5; and Hawke, *In the
Midst of a Revolution*, pp. 20, 111–64.

[3] Congress passed several resolutions authorizing privateering on March 23, but
basic agreement on them had been reached in the committee of the whole on
March 19. *JCC*, 4:213–14, 229–32.

⁴ Congress opened American ports to trade with all countries except Great Britain and her dependencies on April 6. *JCC*, 4:257–59.

James Duane to
the New York Provincial Convention

Gentlemen   Philad. 21st March 1776
    The Bearer Mr Carpenter Wharton is Commissary for the Pensylvania Troops.¹ He supplies them by Contract at seven pence per Ration. He will probably make the same offer for the rest of the Army in the middle Department; and unless others will be equally reasonable must be entitled to a preference, it being the Intention of Congress to have their Armies supplied on the easiest Terms. He supports a very fair Character in this place & is well connected.²

    I have the Honour to be Gentlemen, with the utmost Regard, Your most Obedient, huml servt,   Jas. Duane

RC (N). *Journals of the N.Y. Prov. Cong.*, 2:148–49. RC damaged; date supplied from Tr.
¹ See *JCC*, 4:210.
² The New York Committee of Safety, which received Duane's letter while the provincial congress was in adjournment, promptly informed Congress that it could not take advantage of Commissary Wharton's services because the provincial congress had recently granted a contract for victualling troops employed in the defense of New York to Abraham Livingston, whom deputy commissary Walter Livingston had appointed as assistant deputy commissary of stores and provisions. See New York Committee of Safety to John Hancock, March 26, 1776, PCC, item 67, 1:198–206; and *Am. Archives*, 4th ser. 5:1406–7. See also *Am. Archives*, 4th ser. 5:222, 380, 384. Congress confirmed Livingston's contract with the provincial congress on April 6, but soon thereafter he began to experience so many difficulties in implementing this contract that he resigned it early in May—an act for which he earned a resolution of thanks from Congress on May 10. See Abraham Livingston to John Hancock, May 8, 1776, PCC, item 78, 14:71–72; and *Am. Archives*, 4th ser. 5:1236. See also *JCC*, 4:338, 346; and *Am. Archives*, 4th ser. 5:989–90.

John Hancock to George Washington

Sir,   Philadelphia 21st March 1776
                                        Thursday Eveng.
    I am this Moment honour'd with your favr. of 13th. by Express which I shall lay before Congress in the Morning;¹ I expect immediately to be order'd to Dispatch the first Fessenden to you, when I shall have the honour to write you very particularly.

    This is only to Inform you that I have Sent Two hundred & Fifty Thousand Dollars for the use of the Army under your Command, to the Care of Thomas Hanson, John Donaldson & Moses Franks Esqrs. Gentlemen of Character, who I am Confident will meet your Notice.[2]

I am with the fullest Sentiments of Esteem, Sir, Your very hume sevt,

John Hancock Presidt

RC (PHi).

[1] Washington's letter, which was read in Congress on March 22, is in PCC, item 152, 1:521–30, and Washington, *Writings* (Fitzpatrick), 4:390–94. See *JCC*, 4:225.

[2] Hancock also wrote letters this day to Paymaster General James Warren, informing him of the shipment of this money, and to Thomas Hanson, John Donaldson, and Moses Franks, instructing them on procedures for delivering the funds. PCC, item 12A; and *Am. Archives*, 4th ser. 5:447.

John Hancock to Thomas Wolverton

Sir,   Philada. March 21t. 1776.

I am to inform you, that the Congress have agreed to take your Company into the Service of the Continent, and as soon as they are mustered and properly armed, and accoutred, they are to enter into Pay, which being effected, I am commanded by Congress to direct, that you proceed with your Company with all Expedition to the City of New York and put yourself under the Orders of the Officer commanding the Continental Troops there.[1]

I have deliverd Col. Charles Stuart the Commissions for your Officers, and yours as Captain I delivered to you. I have also paid into the Hands of Col. Stuart, Money, 600 Dollars, to defray the necessary Expences of your Company previous to their March, to whom you will please to apply.[2]

I wish you Success, and am Sir, your most hble Servt.

J. H. Presidt.

LB (DNA: PCC, item 12A). Addressed: "To Capt. Thomas Woolverton of a Company of 76 Men in Continental Service."

[1] See *JCC*, 4:212, 223.

[2] Charles Stewart affixed his signature to the following statement which Hancock wrote in his letterbook at the bottom of this letter: "Rec'd the above Six hundred Dollars for the sd purposes, for wch. I am to Account."

John Jay to Alexander McDougall

Dr. Sir   21 March 1776

I have at Length procured a Pike for you which will be sent by the Stage. Your fitting out an armed Vessel on the Colony Account does you Honor. I am at Liberty to inform you that the Congress have passed a Vote for privateering, by which I hope the hopes of some of our Friends will be repaired. It is expected that vigorous Measures will be taken in preventing such as may be inimical to the cause from injuring its friends. Future Subscriptions to associations must be ridiculous and was inserted in the Resolve of Congress merely to accommodate it to those Colonies who have hitherto had no associations among them. Fear & motives of Interest & Convenience would doubtless induce many to sign it who are our Enemies in there Hearts & whose uniform Conduct has hitherto been very suspicious if not unfriendly.

This Subject recalls to my Mind a little Report which I am told some Tories on Long Island were pleased to form and propagate respecting me—Vzt. That I should have said they were misrepresented to Congress. This Is not true, & to be ranked with many other false Reports which there is Reason to believe originated with that order of Men.

Would it not be well to remove such as are notoriously disaffected to Places where their arts and Influence will do us no Harm. Where are your Accounts?

It is suspected that certain People on Staten Island daily afford Supplies to the Enemy! Ought not the watering Place to be guarded and would not the troops which might be designed for that Purpose be useful in other Respects. I should think your Army sufficiently numerous to admit of such a Detachment.

I hope you are careful of provincial Powder. The Continent are able to supply a Sufficiency of that article for continental Purposes. This Colony takes Care to keep there own Stock good & I think act wisely. I wish your Convention would pass a Place Bill & direct their Delegates to promote such a Measure here. One or two other Colonies have done it and it would redound much to your Honor to patronize such a Measure. Adieu for the present. I am your Friend,   John Jay

RC (NHi).

Richard Smith's Diary

[March 21, 1776]

Thursday 21. The Votes read. Col Charles Stewart of Hunterdon directed to muster Capt. Woolvertons Compy who offer themselves for the Service and 600 Dollars were allowed the Col for their Use.[1] John Adams from a Comee. reported some Resolutions which were amended and passed recommending to the Colonies to encorage the Culture of Flax, Hemp, Cotton and the Increase of Wool, to form a Society in each Colony for the Encoragement of Arts, Manufactures, Agriculture and Commerce &c.[2] These were ordered to be published, a Clause was erased for a standing Comee. of Congress to correspond with and assist these Societies. A Comee. of 3 was appointed to superintend and hasten the Printing of the Journal. Some Letters and Papers from N Carolina were read giving an Accot. of the Defeat of the Tories by Col. Caswell, Brig. Gen Donald McDonald is taken Prisoner, Capt. MacLeod & other Officers killed.[3] Harrison moved that Gen Washington do discharge all the unarmed Men in his Camp when he has used his Endeavors without Success to arm them, which was carried after some Opposition. Monsr. le Chevalier de St. Hillaire [Aulaire] was made Capt. of an Independent Compy. & ordered to Canada.

MS (DLC).
    [1] See John Hancock to Thomas Wolverton, this date.
    [2] See John Adams' Draft Resolutions for Encouraging Agriculture and Manufactures, March 21? 1776.
    [3] For a detailed account of the crushing defeat sustained by North Carolina loyalists at the battle of Moore's Creek Bridge on February 27, 1776, see Hugh F. Rankin, *The North Carolina Continentals* (Chapel Hill: University of North Carolina Press, 1971), chap. 2.

Benjamin Franklin to
Charles William Frederic Dumas

Dear Sir,   Philadelphia, March 22, 1776.
    I wrote to you lately by Mr. Story, and since by another conveyance.[1] This line will be delivered to you by Mr. Deane, who goes over on business of the Congress, and with whom you may freely converse on the affairs committed to you in behalf of that body. I recommend him warmly to your civilities. Mess'rs. Vaillant and Pechard continue close at their new business, and are already able to subsist by it: as they grow more expert, they will be able to make more money.
    Mr. Deane will inform you of every thing here, and I need not add more, than that I am, with esteem and respect, Dear Sir, Your most obedient, And most humble servant,   B. Franklin.

MS not found; reprinted from *Port Folio*, 3 (July 2, 1803): 214.
    [1] For the letter delivered by Mr. Thomas Story, see Franklin to Charles William Frederic Dumas, December 9, 1775. The other letter has not been found.

Richard Smith's Diary

                                            Friday 22 March [1776]
    Votes read & Letters from Gen Washn., Ld. Stirling and others.

Dr. Franklin moved that 750 Doll[ar]s be advanced to the Baron de Woedtke out of his Pay & this was agreed to, he moved also to present the Baron with 250 Dollars to bear his Expences in coming over Sea & to buy Horses &c. Lee and others supported the Motion which was opposed by Duane & al. & carried in the Negative. Wyth reported the Preamble about Privateering, he and Lee moved an Amendt. wherein the King was made the Author of our Miseries instead of the Ministry, was opposed on Supposition that this was effectually severing the King from Us forever and ably debated for 4 Hours when Maryland interposed its Veto and put it off till Tomorrow, Chief Speakers for the Amendt. Lee, Chase, Serjeant, Harrison, against it Jay, Wilson, Johnson. Willing presented Heard's Accounts and asked Whether Congress would allow Pay to the Minute Men who went on the late Expedition to Queens County, this was denied and the Accot. amounting to £2300 and upwards docked to £800 and odd, the Feriages being above £60 were allowed, Willing moved for a Standing Rule that only Half Ferriage shall be hereafter taken for Soldiers, but other Business intervened. A Petition from a Sufferer in the Disputes at Wyoming was committed to 3, after Objection that it was improper for our Cognizance.[1] Agreed to grant Commissions to Capt. Wm. Shippen & his Officers who are about to cruize in a Privateer on or out of Chesapeak Bay, agreed also to sell Him lb 300 of Powder.[2]

MS (DLC).
[1] Concerning the petition which Congress received this day from John Secord, see *JCC*, 4:225, 273, 283; and *Am. Archives*, 4th ser. 5:687, 689, 695.
[2] Beneath this entry, Smith wrote the following for March 23: "Saturday I was not present but inter alia 30,000 Dollars were advanced to Commissary Lowrey."

Oliver Wolcott to Andrew Adams

Sir [1]   Philidelphia 22d March 1776
Your kind favour of the 9 inst. came safe to hand, your other Letter which you mention I have not been so happy as to receive, this failure I hope will not discourage you from Writing to Me, as your literary correspondence will be extreemly agreable, and gratefully Acknowledged. I thank you for your Inteligence, tho' some parts of it, the Death of our Acquaintance, is Meloncholly. The Prussian Gentleman You Mention was an officer of distinction in the King of Prussias Service, and a favourite of that capricious Despot, but undeservedly disgraced by him, but as his Recommendations were Very good, he is made a Brigadier Genl. in the American Army and will soon go into Canada.[2]
Am glad to hear of the progress of the Salt Petre Works, every Supply that can be internally obtained, I hope will be *sedulously* attended to. This will procure us an Indepen[den]cy on which We may rely. The

Canadians have not Sent Delegates as you mention, this can hardly be expected before the Reduction of Quebec. Dr. Franklin and Mr Chaice Members of Congress and a Mr. Carrol of Virginia [Maryland] go forward in a Very few days into that Country with full and conciliatory Powers for Effecting a Union.

We have just recd. News from N Carolina that there has been a battle there between the American Regulars and the Regulators, who upon an old Grudge are become Torys, in which the Latter were defeated, their Genl. taken Prisoner, the second in Command killed, together with a Number of their followers, and the rest dispersed.[3] These People became inimical on Acct. of former Resentments against the lower Countys during the Administration of Govr. Tryon, which Story you well remember—but as a Vast force is up in that Colony they will douptless reduce the Insurgents to order; for other News refer you to the Papers. The last Resolution passed in Congress of a much interesting Nature is permitting Privateers to Cruize upon the British Trade. This will be published as soon as a proper preamble or Declaration of Grounds on which &c is settled.[4] The inhuman pirating Act calls forth every Exertion, and I hope We may in Time be able with tolerable Success to Combat G Britain upon that Eliment which She boasts herself the Mistriss of—but still We shall be oblidged to remember that Rome was not built in a day, tho' she finally became mistriss of the World. The World We shall not covet but so much of America as may be needfull for us, I hope We shall injoy without any earthly controul.

You mention the Efficacy of common sence, the leading Sentiment which it dictates I am sensible Very greatly prevails. Some People Still please themselves with the delusive Phanptom of Commissioners coming over, with the Proffers of Peace—but I beleive it is Very certain they have nothing in their Hands but Pardons for Rebells. As these will not be accepted of, their Embassy will be fruitless—indeed I consider the whole as a most idle Whim. The British Court mean only to have America under their feet, and I fancy will hardly Attempt even to disguise their Intention. When that is once known the little hesitancy which still remains, I imagine will Vanish. The colonies will enter into no Seperate Nigotiation, and the Congress will not yeild any essential Claim. The important Crisis which must Stamp the Character of America must be Near—and I do not perceive that its approach produces but Very few sad faces.

The Business of the Colonies is Very interesting as well as Various and extensive. May God carry us thro the severe Conflict, guide the American Councills and give us Peace safe and honorable. My Compliments to Mrs Adams whose Health I wish restored—and also my Compliments to Mr Champion (to whom I lately wrote) and my other Friends—and be assured that I am Sir, your most Obedient, humble Servant,   Oliver Wolcott

RC (InU).

¹ Andrew Adams (1736–97), a Litchfield, Conn., lawyer, was a member of the Connecticut General Assembly, 1776–81, and served briefly as a delegate to Congress in 1778. *Bio. Dir. Cong.*

² Undoubtedly a reference to Frederic William de Woedtke, who was appointed a brigadier general on March 16, *JCC*, 4:209.

³ The battle of Moore's Creek Bridge. See Richard Smith's Diary, March 21, 1776, note 3.

⁴ See *JCC*, 4:213–14, 229–32.

John Adams to Horatio Gates

Dear Sir   Philadelphia March 23. 1776

I had the Pleasure, a few days ago, of your Favour of 8th Instant,¹ for which I esteem myself under great obligations to you.

We rejoice here at the Prospect there is of your driving the Enemy from Boston. If you should Succeed in this I hope effectual Measures will be taken to fortify the Harbour, that the Navy may never enter it again. I think the Narrows may be so obstructed that large Ships will not be able to pass—and the Channell between Long Island and the Moon may be commanded by Batteries upon each of these Islands in such a manner that Boston may be Safe from Men of War. I hope my Countrymen will hesitate at no Expence to attain this End, if in order to accomplish it, they should be obliged to remove the rocky Mountains of my Town of Braintree into the Harbour.

But I cannot yet clearly Satisfy myself that they will leave Boston. It will be a greater Disgrace to the British Arms than to be taken Prisoners in the Town in a Body. If they should abandon the Persons and Property of their dear Friends the Tories in Boston, will any other Tories in any other Part of the Continent ever trust to their Protection? It will be considered as such Impotence, or such Infidelity that I am inclined to think few Professors of Toryism would ever afterwards be found anywhere.

I agree with you, that in Politicks the Middle Way is none at all. If we finally fail in this great and glorious Contest, it will be by bewildering ourselves in groping after this middle way. We have hitherto conducted half a War, acted upon the Line of Defence &c &c. But you will See by tomorrows Paper, that for the future We are likely to wage three Quarters of a War. The Continental ships of War, and Provincial ships of War, and Letters of Mark and Privateers are permitted to cruise upon British Property, wherever found on the Ocean.² This is not Independency you know, nothing like it.

If a Post or two more should bring you unlimited Latitude of Trade to all Nations, and a polite Invitation to all Nations to trade with you, take care that you dont call it, or think it Independency.³ No such

IN CONGRESS,

MARCH 23, 1776.

WHEREAS the Petitions of thefe United Colonies to the King, for the Redrefs of great and manifeft Grievances, have not only been rejected, but treated with Scorn and Contempt; and the Oppofition to De-figns evidently formed to reduce them to a State of fervile Subjection, and their neceffary Defence againft hoftile Forces actually employed to fubdue them, declared Rebellion: And Whereas an unjuft War hath been com-menced againft them, which the Commanders of the Britifh Fleets and Armies have profecuted and ftill continue to profecute with their utmoft Vigour and in a cruel Manner; wafting, fpoiling and deftroying the Country, burning Houfes and defencelefs Towns, and expofing the helplefs Inhabitants to every mifery from the Inclemency of the Win-ter, and not only urging Savages to invade the Country, but inftigating Negroes to murder their Mafters: And Whereas the Parliament of Great-Britain hath lately paffed an Act, affirming thefe Colonies to be in open Rebellion; forbidding all Trade and Commerce with the Inhabitants thereof, until they fhall accept Pardons and fubmit to defpotic Rule; declaring their Property, wherever found upon the Water, liable to Seizure and Confifcation; and enacting that what had been done there, by Virtue of the Royal Authority, were juft and lawful Acts and fhall be fo deemed: From all which it is manifeft, that the iniquitous Scheme, concerted to deprive them of the Liberty they have a right to by the Laws of Nature and the Englifh Conftitution, will be pertinacioufly purfued. It being, therefore, neceffary to pro-vide for their Defence and Security, and juftifiable to make Reprifals upon their Enemies and otherwife to annoy them, according to the Laws and Ufages of Nations; the CONGRESS, trufting that fuch of their Friends in Great-Bri-tain (of whom it is confeffed there are many intitled to Applaufe and Gratitude for their Patriotifm and Benevolence, and in whofe Favor a Difcrimination of Property cannot be made) as fhall fuffer by Captures, will impute it to the Au-thors of our common Calamities, DO DECLARE AND RESOLVE as followeth, *to wit,*

RESOLVED, That the Inhabitants of thefe Colonies be permitted to fit out Armed Veffels to cruife on the Enemies of thefe United Colonies.

RESOLVED, That all Ships and other Veffels, their Tackle, Apparel, and Furniture, and all Goods, Wares and Merchandizes belonging to any Inhabitant or Inhabitants of Great-Britain, taken on the high Seas, or between high and low water-Mark, by any Armed Veffel fitted out by any private Perfon or Perfons to whom Commiffions fhall be granted, and being libelled and profecuted in any Court erected for the Trial of Maritime Affairs in any of thefe Colonies, fhall be deemed and adjudged to be lawful Prize, and after deducting and paying the Wages the Seamen and Mariners on board of fuch Captures as are Merchant Ships and Veffels fhall be intitled to according to the Terms of their Contracts until the Time of Adjudication, fhall be condemned to and for the Ufe of the Owner or Owners, and the Officers, Ma-rines and Mariners of fuch Armed Veffel, according to fuch Rules and Proportions as they fhall agree on. *Provided Always,* That this Refolution fhall not extend, or be conftrued to extend, to any Veffel bringing Settlers, Arms, Ammunition, or Warlike Stores to and for the Ufe of thefe Colonies, or any of the Inhabitants thereof who are Friends to the American Caufe, or to fuch Warlike Stores, or to the Effects of fuch Settlers.

RESOLVED, That all Ships or Veffels with their Tackle, Apparel and Furniture, Goods, Wares and Merchandizes belonging to any Inhabitant of Great-Britain, as aforefaid, which fhall be taken by any of the Veffels of War of thefe United Colonies, fhall be deemed forfeited, one third after deducting and paying the Wages of Seamen and Mariners, as aforefaid, to the Officers and Men on board, and two thirds to the ufe of the United Colonies.

RESOLVED, That all Ships or Veffels with their Tackle, Apparel and Furniture, Goods, Wares and Merchandi-zes belonging to any Inhabitants of Great-Britain as aforefaid, which fhall be taken by any Veffel of War fitted out by and at the Expence of any of the United Colonies fhall be deemed forfeited, and divided, after deducting and paying the Wages of Seamen and Mariners as aforefaid, in fuch Manner and Proportions as the Affembly or Convention of fuch Co-lony fhall direct.

RESOLVED, That all Veffels, their Tackle, Apparel and Furniture, and Cargoes belonging to Inhabitants of Great-Britain, as aforefaid, and all Veffels which may be employed in carrying Supplies to the Minifterial Armies, which fhall happen to be taken near the Shores of any of thefe Colonies, by the People of the Country or Detachments from the Army, fhall be deemed lawful Prize, and the Court of Admiralty within the faid Colony is required, on Condemnation thereof, to adjudge that all Charges and Expences which may attend the Capture and Trial be firft paid out of the Monies arifing from the Sales of the Prize, and the Remainder equally divided among all thofe who fhall have been actually engaged and employed in taking the faid Prize. *Provided,* That where any Detachments of the Army fhall have been employed as aforefaid, their Part of the Prize-money fhall be diftributed among them in Proportion to the Pay of the Officers and Soldiers fo employed.

Extract from the Minutes,

CHARLES THOMSON, SECRETARY.

PHILADELPHIA: Printed by JOHN DUNLAP.

Resolves on Privateering, March 23, 1776

Matter. Independency is an Hobgoblin, of so frightfull Mein, that it would throw a delicate Person into Fits to look it in the Face.[4]

I know not whether you have seen the Act of Parliament call'd the restraining Act, or prohibitory Act, or piratical Act, or plundering Act, or Act of Independency, for by all these Titles is it called. I think the most apposite is the Act of Independency, for King, Lords and Commons have united in Sundering this Country and that I think forever. It is a compleat Dismemberment of the British Empire. It throws thirteen Colonies out of the Royal Protection, levels all Distinctions and makes us independent in Spight of all our supplications and Entreaties.

It may be fortunate that the Act of Independency should come from the British Parliament, rather than the American Congress: But it is very odd that Americans should hesitate at accepting Such a Gift from them.

However, my dear Friend Gates, all our Misfortunes arise from a Single Source, the Reluctance of the Southern Colonies to Republican Government. The success of this War depends upon a Skillfull Steerage of the political vessel. The Difficulty lies in forming Constitutions for particular Colonies, and a Continental Constitution for the whole. Each Colony should establish its own Government, and then a League should be formed, between them all. This can be done only on popular Principles and Maxims which are so abhorrent to the Inclinations of the Barons of the South, and the Proprietary Interests in the Middle Colonies, as well as to that avarice of Land, which has made upon this Continent so many Votaries to Mammon that I Sometimes dread the Consequences. However Patience, Fortitude and Perseverance, with the Help of Time will get us over these obstructions.

Thirteen Colonies under Such a Form of Government as that of Connecticutt, or one not quite so popular leagued together in a faithfull Confederacy might bid Defiance to all the Potentates of Europe if united against them.

Pray continue to make me happy with your Favours, accept of my most cordial Wishes for your safety, Happiness and Honour, make my most respectfull Compliments to the General and the Ladies, and the whole Family, and believe me to be with great Respect your affectionate Friend & servant,   John Adams

RC (NHi).
[1] Gates' March 8 letter describes the military maneuvers that subsequently forced the British into a hurried withdrawal from Boston. The letter, which is at MHi, is printed in Bernhard Knollenberg, ed., "The Correspondence of John Adams and Horatio Gates," *Proceedings of the Massachusetts Historical Society* 67 (March 1942): 137–38.
[2] For the resolutions concerning privateering passed by Congress this day, see *JCC*, 4:229–32.
[3] Resolutions loosening the restrictions on American trade were passed on April 6. *JCC*, 4:257–59.

⁴ Adams later accused opponents of independence of suppressing several resolutions offered in Congress this day by not recording them in the journals. *JCC*, 4:233. Adams wrote: "Here is an Instance, in addition to many others, of an extraordinary Liberty taken by the Secretary, I suppose at the Instigation of the Party against Independence, to suppress, by omitting on the Journals the many Motions that were made disagreable to that sett. These motions ought to have been inserted verbatim on the Journals, with the names of those who made them." Adams, *Diary* (Butterfield), 3:375. For other instances of complaints about Charles Thomson's omissions from the journals, see also ibid., 3:365n.4.

John Hancock to
the New Jersey Committee of Safety

Gentlemen,   Philada. March 23d. 1776.
   Your several Letters have been duely received, and laid before Congress.¹ I beg Leave to acquaint you, they are at this Time under Consideration, and that as soon as any Determination is made thereon, you may expect to have it communicated to you.
   The Necessity of the Thing has induced the Congress to come to the inclosed Resolution, which I am directed to request you will carry into immediate Execution.²
   I am Gent your most obedt. & hble Sert.   J. H. Prest.

LB (DNA: PCC, item 12A).
   ¹ It cannot be determined to which letters Hancock is referring.
   ² On March 20 Congress had resolved "that the committee of safety of the colony of New Jersey be desired to remove the prisoners from Trenton." *JCC*, 4:220. Samuel Tucker replied for the committee of safety on March 23 that the prisoners were being removed from Trenton to Mount Holly. PCC, item 68:118–19; and *Am. Archives*, 4th ser. 5:474.

John Hancock to Philip Schuyler

Sir   Philadelphia 23d March 1776.
   The Bearer Mr. Cole is charg'd with some hard Money for the Use of the Troops in Canada;¹ should he request a Guard or any assistance to further his passage over the Lakes you will be pleased to furnish him.
   I wish your Notice to Mr. Cole, as he is a Gentlemen of Boston and known to me. I am Dear Sir, Your most humble Servant.
                                                       John Hancock

Tr (NN).
   ¹ See *JCC*, 4:228–29.

John Jay to Alexander McDougall

Dear Collonel   Philadelphia March 23. 1776
   When the Clerk of the Congress gave me the printed Papers which
I enclosed you,[1] he told me they contained the Navy Establishment.
Whatever Deficiencies there may be in them as to that Matter will I
hope be supplied by the Extract now inclosed.
   As to continental Colors, the Congress have made no order as yet
respecting them, and I believe the Captains of their armed Vessels have
in that particular been directed by their own fancies and Inclinations.
I remember to have seen a flag designed for one of them on which was
extremely well painted a Rattle Snake rearing his Crest and shaking
his Rattles, with this Motto *"Dont tread on me"*. But whether this Device
was generally adopted by the fleet, I am not able to say. I rather think
it was not.
   The Inlet you allude to certainly deserves Attention,[2] and the Hints
you gave me respecting it have not been forgotten. Something of that
Kind is now under Consideration. A Distinction however will always
be made between continental & provincial objects, and how far this
may affect that Matter is as yet uncertain.
   I am by no Means without my apprehensions of Danger from that
Licentiousness which in your Situation is not uncommon. Nothing will
contribute more to its Suppression than a vigorous Exertion of the
Powers vested in your Convention & Committee of Safety, at least till
more regular forms can be introduced. The Tenderness shewn to some
wild People on Account of their supposed attachment to the Cause has
been of Disservice. Their eccentric Behaviour has by passing unreproved
gained Countenance, lessened your Authority and diminished that
Dignity so essential to give weight and Respect [to] your ordinances.
Some of your own People are daily (if not employed) yet instigated to
calumniate and abuse the whole Province and misrepresent all their
actions and Intentions. One in particular has had the Impudence to
intimate to certain Persons that your Regiments last Campaign were
not half full and that Van Schaacks Regimt. had more officers than
Privates. Others insinuate that you have all along supplied the Men
of War with whatever they pleased to have, and thro' them, our Enemies
in Boston. By Tales like these they pay their Court to People who have
more ostensible Consequence than real Honesty, and more Cunning
than Wisdom.
   I am happy to find that our intermedling in the affair of the Test is
agreable to You.[3] For Gods Sake resist all such attempts for the future.
   Your own Discernment has pointed out to you the Principle of Ld.
Sterlings advancement. Had the age of a Colls. Commission been a
proper Rule, it would have determined in favor of some Coll. at Cambridge, many of whose Commissions were prior in Date to any in New

York. The Spirit you betray on this occassion becomes a Soldier.

The inclosed Copy of a Resolve of Congress will I hope settle all Doubts relative to Rank, which may arise from your new Commission.[4] The Consequence you drew from that Circumstance was more ingenious than solid, for I can assure You that the Congress were not disposed to do anything wrong or uncivil—and I can also add that your not having joined your Regimt. last Summer has been explained to their Satisfaction as far as I am able to judge.[5] With Respect to this however as well as some other Matters I shall defer particulars till we meet. In a word with some Men in these as in other Times, a Man must either be their Tool and be despised, or act a firm disinterested Part and be abused. The latter has in one or two Matters been your fate as well as that of many other good Men. The Attack was insidious not open or effectual. Adieu. I am dear Sir, your Friend,   John Jay

RC (NHi).

[1] See Jay to Alexander McDougall, March 13, 1776, note 2.

[2] A reference to McDougall's reflections on the security of Egg Harbor, which he made in his letter of March 20 to Jay. See Jay, *Papers* (Morris), 1:237.

[3] See Jay to Alexander McDougall, March 13, 1776, note 3.

[4] See the resolution on the ranking of officers, passed by Congress this day, in *JCC*, 4:226. The copy of this resolution which was transmitted to the New York Provincial Convention contains the following note. "N.B. This passed to settle a dispute between officers of the same rank, where one who was prior by the date of his first commission was put posterior to another in the new appointment both still holding the same rank. But was not to have any affect in cases of promotion, Congress having reserved and exercised the power of promoting merit without regarding prior Rank." *Journals of N.Y. Prov. Cong.*, 2:412.

[5] On this point, see James Duane to Alexander McDougall, November 15, 1775, note.

Marine Committee to
the Pennsylvania Committee of Safety

                                        Marine Committee March 23. 1776
Resolved

That application be made to the Committee of Safety requesting them to lend to this Committee at least thirty good Arms (to be repaid with the first Arms which arrive) that number being absolutely necessary to the fitting out of the Brigantine Lexington intended for the protection of the Trade on this Coast.[1]

By Direction of the Marine Com[mitte]e,

                                        John Hancock Chairman

Colo. Roberdeaux is earnestly requested to gratify the Committee in this request, the Vessell waiting only for the Arms.   J. H.

Tr (PHarH).
[1] For the response of the committee of safety, which on March 25 directed commissary Robert Towers "to deliver said number of Arms to Captain Barry," see *Am. Archives*, 4th ser. 5:730.

Benjamin Franklin to James Bowdoin

My dear Friend,   Philada. Mar. 24. 1776
Inclos'd is an Answer to the Request from the Inhabitants of Dartmouth. I have comply'd with it upon your Recommendation, and ordered a Post accordingly.[1]

I have put into Mr Adam's Hands directed for you, the new Edition of Vattel. When you have perus'd it, please to place it in your College Library.[2]

I am just setting out for Canada, and have only time to add my best Wishes of Health & Happiness to you & all yours. Permit me to say my Love to Mrs Bowdoin, & believe me ever, with sincere & great Esteem, Yours most affectionately   B Franklin

RC (MHi).
[1] Not found. Apparently the inhabitants of the town of Dartmouth, Bristol County, Mass., had directed to Postmaster General Franklin a request for the establishment of a Post.
[2] Bowdoin's letter of August 19, 1776, reporting that he was sending "Vattel's Droit des Gens" to the Harvard College Library in accordance with Franklin's instructions, is in "The Bowdoin and Temple Papers," *Collections of the Massachusetts Historical Society*, 6th ser. 9 (1897): 400–402.

William Whipple to Josiah Bartlett

Dear Sir   Philadelphia 24th March 1776
Inclos'd you have invoice & Bill Loading of five Barrels flouer. The man who ship'd it made a mistake & ship'd fine instead of common. It was too late to change it before I knew it, the difference in the price is only 1/9 per Ct., common wod have cost 14/3. If you shod prefer Common flouer no doubt you may have it chang'd at Newbury to advantage.

We have gone on since you left us much as Usual. Have at last finish'd the Privateer Business after spending two days on the Preamble; the whole was compleated Yesterday & order'd to be printed. I shall forward them to you as soon as they come from the press.[1]

Some pleasing accots. from North Carolina have arriv'd since you left this place which you may [see] in the inclos'd papers.[2] I have twice mov'd to have the N. Hampshire matter finish'd without success but hope shall get it done this week.[3] The Brig. Lexington drops down today.

Govr. Ward is shockingly paid off. I believe he'll be thoroughly purged
both of Original Sin & actual Transgression. The Doctrs. say he is not
dangerous. The Canada Commissioners are to set out tomorrow.[4] A
schooner arriv'd Yesterday from France but have not yet heard what
she brings. It's a French Vessel. I suppose the Genl. Court is now setting.
Please to give my respects to all friends & be sure write every weak &
settele matters at home as soon as possible for I find I shall soon want you
here. Its my private opinion the Grand Question will soon be debated.
The time I think cannot be far off. I am, with great sincerity, Yours,

                                                    Wm Whipple

10 O'Clock in the eveng. I have just heard from Govr Ward. He is
extream Ill, the Chance much against him.

RC (NhD).
  [1] See *JCC*, 4:229–32.
  [2] See Richard Smith's Diary, March 21, 1776.
  [3] See Josiah Bartlett to Meshech Weare, March 2, 1776, note 2.
  [4] Robert Treat Paine noted both the death of Ward and the departure of the
commissioners in his March 26 diary entry: "Last night Govr. Ward died of the
Small pox & Congress adjourned to 4. This Day the Committee sett out for Canada.
Wrote to Wife & Dr. Cobb & Mr. Cushing by Fessenden Express." MHi.

William Whipple to Joseph Whipple

My Dear Bror.,   Philadelphia 24th March 1776
    I received Yours of the 9th inst. Am much obliged for the perticular
accot. you gave me of the brush at the camp, it seems they soon after
had another. By all accots. it seems the enemy are going, but I cannot
yet bring myself to believe it.[1] You'll see by the papers that the provincials in North-Carolina have defeted a large party under the command of Genl. McDonald & taken him Prisoner; these were all Scotch
men who lately came over and have been treated with great kindness
by the People of that Country but ingratitude is the true Carecteristick
of that nation. I hope the Continent will be soon clear of them. I understand there are but few left in Vergenia where they were very Numerous.
If you can keep on with you[r] plantation till the war is at an end no
doubt you'll make something clever of it. In this Country they give the
setlers seven Years improvment & oblige them to clear a certain Quantity Yearly; thats all the encouragment given to Emigrants from the
old Countries but we are not to expect setlers to the Northward on so
good terms as they have them here but when the war is over shall have
them on much better terms then now. I shall soon send you direction
for raising & cureing hemp which I immagine well worth your attention. Its now almost 12; must therefore bid you a good night. Your
affecte. Bror.   Wm. Whipple

RC (MH).

[1] Robert Treat Paine noted in his diary this day: "Heard that the Ministerial Troops had evacuated Boston & that Genl Washington had taken possession of it last Monday." MHi.

John Hancock to William Alexander

Sir   Philadelphia 25th March 1776

Capt James Young of this City having by Letter Represented to Congress that his Son John Young in Januy last Elop'd from him and got on board the Phœnix Man of War at New York;[1] from whence he was proceeding to Boston & on his passage was Cast away on Long Island, & that he is now *fortunately* a Prisoner at New York; & Desiring that he may be permitted to be a Prisoner on his Parole at the Estate of his late Grandfather Doctor Greame; In Consequence of which I have it in Charge to Direct that the said John Young be allow'd to Reside at the house of the late Dr Greame. You will therefore please to order him to be Deliver'd to his Father, first Taking his Parole which he must Subscribe, & you will forward it to me.

Capt James Young is a Gentleman exceedingly friendly to our Cause, I therefore beg leave to Recommend him to your Notice.

I have the honour to be, Sir, Your most hume Servt,

J H Prt.

LB (DNA: PCC, item 12A). Addressed: "To the Officer Commandg. the Continental Troops at New York."

[1] Young's letter is in PCC, item 78, 24:651, and *Am. Archives*, 4th ser. 5:464–65. See also *JCC*, 4:227.

John Hancock to George Washington

Sir,   Philadelphia March 25th 1776.

I had the Honour of receiving, yesterday, yours of the 13th [*i.e.* 19th] containing the agreeable Information of the ministerial Troops having abandoned Boston.[1] The partial Victory, we have obtained over them in that Quarter, I hope will turn out a happy Presage of a more general one. Whatever Place may be the Object of their Destination, it must certainly give a sincere Pleasure to every Friend of this Country, to see the most diligent Preparations every where making to receive them. What may be their Views, it is indeed impossible to tell with any Degree of Exactness. We have all the Reason however, from the Rage of Disappointment & Revenge, to expect the worst. Nor have I any Doubt, that as far as their Power extends, they will inflict every Species of

Calamity upon us. The same Providence, that has baffled their Attempt against the Province of Massachusetts Bay, will, I trust, defeat the deep laid Scheme, they are now meditating against some other Part of our Country.

The Intelligence that our Army had got Possession of Boston, you will readily suppose, gave me heart-felt Pleasure. I beg, Sir, you will be pleased to accept my warmest Thanks for the Attention you have shewed to my Property in that Town. I have only to request, that Capt. Cazeneau will continue to look after it, and take Care That it be no Ways destroyed or damaged.[2]

This Success of our Arms naturally calls upon me to congratulate you, Sir, to whose Wisdom and Conduct, it has been owing. Permit me to add, that if a constant Discharge of the most important Duties, and the Fame attending thereon, can afford genuine Satisfaction, the Pleasures you feel, must be the most rational and exalted.

I have it in Charge from Congress to direct, that you send an Account of the Troops in your Camp, who are deficient in Arms, to the several Assemblies or Conventions of the Colonies to which those Men belong, and request them to send a sufficient Number of Arms for the Men coming from the respective Colonies; and that if Arms cannot be procured, that such as have not Arms, be dismissed the Service.[3]

The Congress being of opinion, that the Reduction of Quebec, and the general Security of the Province of Canada, are Objects of great Concern, I am commanded to direct, that you detach four Battalions into Canada from the Army under your Command, as soon as you shall be of opinion, that the safety of New York, and the Eastern Service, will permit.[4]

Your several Letters are, at this Time, under the Consideration of a Committee. As soon as any Determination is made thereon, I will immediately forward it to you.

I have the Honour to be, with the greatest Esteem, Sir, your most obedt. & very hble Sevt.   John Hancock Presidt.

RC (DLC). In the hand of Jacob Rush, and signed by John Hancock.

[1] Washington's March 19 letter, which is in PCC, item 152, 1:537–40, and Washington, *Writings* (Fitzpatrick), 4:403–5, was read in Congress on March 25. As a result of the news, Congress authorized a letter of thanks to General Washington and the troops under his command and ordered the preparation of a commemorative medal for presentation to Washington. *JCC*, 4:234. The letter of thanks, which was approved by Congress and sent over Hancock's signature on April 2, is printed in *JCC*, 4:248–49.

[2] Isaac Cazneau's report of damages to Hancock's extensive Boston property is extracted in Herbert S. Allan, *John Hancock, Patriot in Purple* (New York:. Macmillan Co., 1948), pp. 218–19.

[3] See *JCC*, 4:223.

[4] See *JCC*, 4:236; and Richard Henry Lee to Charles Lee, March 25, 1776.

Richard Henry Lee to Charles Lee

My Dear Friend,   [Philadelphia, March 25, 1776]
I have just received your letter from Baltimore covering one for Mr. Hancock.[1] My Brother who was present in Congress when the Resolve you allude to passed, says that every Gentleman acknowledged the necessity under which you acted, and approved the measure. The precedent alone they feared, when less judgment was used. They endeavored therefore to guard against pointing at you by directing their Resolve to future occasions.[2] As then there was no design to reflect on you, so we have concluded that the better way will be not to present the letter, but content ourselves with informing Congress of your having taken the Engineers and getting their approbation.[3] Gen. Washington entered Boston this day sennight, the Enemy having quitted it with some precipitation, and apparent apprehension of being disturbed in their retreat. To prevent this, they left their works undemolished, and placed images large as life representing Soldiers on guard as usual on Bunker Hill—Our friend Sullivan first discovered the cheat. They have left 30 of their light Horse behind them almost famished, and stores to the amount of 25 or 30,000 pounds. Where they will go next, heaven knows, but we must endeavour to be prepared at all points. I this day moved in Congress and succeeded, to send an order for four battalions to be detached for Canada from Gen. Washington's Army.[4] I am afraid we shall loose poor Govr. Ward, who now lies dangerously ill with the small pox taken in the natural way. The Eastern Army will all be at N. Y. presently.[5]
I sincerely wish you happy and successful because I am with great affection Yours.   Richard Henry Lee

MS not found; reprinted from *NYHS Collections* 4 (1871): 362–63.
[1] Charles Lee's March 21 letter to John Hancock is in *NYHS Collections* 4 (1871): 360–61.
[2] A resolution forbidding military officers from imposing test oaths was passed on March 9, in reaction to General Lee's administration of such an oath to certain New York inhabitants. See *JCC*, 4:195; and New York Delegates to the New York Provincial Convention, March 15, 1776.
[3] Two engineers were elected for the southern department on March 30. *JCC*, 4:241.
[4] See *JCC*, 4:236.
[5] Three days later Richard Henry wrote a brief note to the general introducing his brother-in-law, William Aylett. "Give me leave to introduce my friend and relation Colonel William Aylett to your acquaintance and friendship. You will find Colo. Ayletts worth deserving your esteem, and his connection with me, will, I am sure not lessen it.
"No news since my last, we know not yet where the Boston fugitives are gone." Richard Henry Lee to Charles Lee, March 28, 1776. RPJCB.

Richard Smith's Diary

Monday 25 March [1776]

Votes read & Letters from Gen Washn., President Tucker and many more. Howes Troops have abandoned Boston and our People are in Possession. John Adams moved that the Thanks of the Congress be given to the Officers there for their good Conduct and that a Gold Medal be struck with a proper Device & presented to Mr. Washington, accordingly J. Adams & 2 more were appointed a Comee. for those Purposes.[1] S. Adams from a Comee. reported Major Brixon [Wrixon] as fit to be Adjutant General in Canada with the Rank of Brigadier, this was objected to, by Allen particularly, & the Report recommitted.[2] R. H. Lee moved that Gen Washn. be directed to detach from his Army 4 Battals. to Canada if the Service will admit, he was supported by Johnson & Duane and strongly opposed by Harrison but the Motion passed in the Affirmative. A Report for appointing a Commissary General in Canada was much agitated, Mr. Price was proposed but it appeared that one Halstead was in Possession at Quebec, by Consent of Congress & that Walter Livingston had been appointed, the Report was negatived,[3] an incidental Question was debated Whether Schuyler or Thomas was to have the chief Command and whether Canada was a distinct Department. 20,000 Dollars advanced to the Virginia Troops. Johnson made a Report inter alia, that 2 Battalions now on Foot in South Carolina & 3 in Virginia should be put upon Continental Pay & Establisht. which passed without any Negative but my own.

MS (DLC).
[1] On this point, see John Adams to George Washington, April 1, and to Abigail Adams, August 14, 1776. For Adams' autobiographical account of this motion, see also Adams, *Diary* (Butterfield), 3:375–76.
[2] See John Adams to Abigail Adams, March 17, 1776, note 1.
[3] See Smith's Diary, March 8, 1776, note 5.

Elbridge Gerry to James Warren

Dear sir   Philadelphia March 26. 1776

I received with great Pleasure your Favour of the 7th Instant,[1] & two Days ago the agreable News of the Reduction of Boston reached this place, on which happy Event give me Leave to congratulate You.

What an Occurrence is this to be known in Europe? How are parliamentary pretensions to be reconciled to Facts? "Eight or ten thousand *British Troops* are sufficient to pervade America" & yet that Number of their best Veterans, posted in Boston—a Peninsula fortified by Nature—defended by Works which are the product of two Years Industry—surrounded by navigable Water & supported by Ships of War—& Commanded by their best Generals—have done what? Wonders? No, but what is truly wonderful they are driven out of Boston by about the thirtieth Part of the Power of America, scattered in Lines of nearly fifteen Miles Extent & unable to bring more than four thousand Men to Action at a Time. Surely the invincible Veterans laboured under some great Disadvantages from Want of Provisions, military Stores &c which the Americans were amply supplyed with? Directly the Reverse is the Fact. They had Ammunition, Muskets & Accoutrements for every Man, & a peice of ordnance for every ten or fifteen, while the Americans were almost destitute of any & after twelve Months Collection had only a sufficiency of the former to tune their Cannon about six or eight Days & accomplish this Business. I am at a Loss to know how Great Britain is to recover from this Disgrace, & reestablish her Fame & the Glory of her Arms in Europe. I am certain that her Conquests in America never will do it. The Congress have voted Thanks to the General, & all the Officers & Soldiers of Army for their Valour on this Occasion & ordered a Medal of Gold With a suitable Device to be presented the former. I hope however that this will not abate your Exertions to obtain by your own Manufactures sufficient Resources of military Stores, for on this & the Discipline of your Militia depend your Liberty. I am also glad to find that Care is taking to prevent the spreading of the small pox & that such Troops only as have had the Distemper are sent into the Town; surely it ought immediately to be cleansed & all Intercourse stopped for the present.

You are desirous to know whether Capital Measures are to be expected? Give me Leave to refer You to Colo Orne for what is done relative to privateering[2] & I hope soon that all your Ports will be opened and a free Trade allowed to all Nations, but this latter is not yet done. All this does not satisfie your soreing independent Faculties & I hope nothing less will accomplish it than a Determination of America to hold her Rank in the Creation & give Law to herself. I doubt not that this will soon take place, & am certain that N England will never be satisfied with less since not only the Government of Great Britain but the Collective Body of the people are corrupt & totally destitute of Virtue. I sincerely wish that You would originate Instructions expressed with decent Firmness (your natural Style) & give your Sentiments as a Count in Favour of Independency. I Am certain It would turn many doubtful Minds & produce a Reversion of the contrary Instructions adopted by some assemblies. To accomplish such a Reversion the Committee of Inspection of this City have preferred to the Assembly a petition for that purpose; & since some timid Minds are terrified at the Word Independency It may be well to give the Thing another Name. America has gone such Lengths that she cannot recede, & I am persuaded that a few Weeks or Months will convince her of the Fact; but the Fruit must have Time to ripen a little in the Southern Colonies, notwithstanding in N England the Hot Bed of Sedition, as North impudently Called Boston, It has come to Maturity. Would it not be good Policy for the N E Governments to think on this Matter & adopt similar Measures? Perhaps a Circular Letter & the publication of your Instructions would accomplish it.[3]

We have been so unfortunate as to loose Governor Ward; he dyed this Morning of the small pox which he took the natural Way. He was a firm Friend to America.

Four Battalions of your Army at Cambridge are order'd to Canada, & the Commissioners with Baron de Woedke who is a continental Brigadier are gone this Morning.

The Destination of the Fleet is only known to the marine Committee "the Lords of the Admiralty" & nothing has transpired relative to them since their sailing.

I thank You for a Recommendation to Matrimony, & am certain You have had the best Experience in this Garden of pleasure. When providence shall kindly place me in a Soil so happy, I will endeavour to follow your worthy Example & do it equal Justice in the Cultivation.

Your Information relative to the Militia & the armed Vessels was very acceptable, the more so as our Friends in general supposing We have the power of Divination, neglect to relate Things of Importance as they occur, in your Government—& as to the Commissioners I am at a Loss to determine whether they deserve to be received.[4]

Is it not curious that the British ministry should know so little of our feelings or character that after seizing our property, burning our towns and destroying their inhabitants, they should make an act to interdict our trade, and suppose that towns, counties and colonies will bury in oblivion all former abuses, and subscribe themselves slaves in order to be rescued from the severities of this commercial tyranny? This is an instance of the wisdom and policy of the British ministry! Have they not yet ascertained that we know our rights, or at least that we think we know them? Have they not learned that we can defend them too?

I remain your friend,   E. Gerry

RC (DLC). In Gerry's hand, but at least one page with the signature is missing.

[1] Warren's March 7 letter to Gerry is in C. Harvey Gardiner, ed., *A Study in Dissent: The Warren-Gerry Correspondence, 1776–1792* (Carbondale: Southern Illinois University Press, 1968), pp. 8–10.

[2] Congress had adopted resolutions authorizing and regulating privateering on March 23. *JCC*, 4:229–32. Gerry's letter to Azor Orne has not been found.

[3] The Massachusetts House, of which James Warren was speaker, did not vote to ascertain its constituents' sentiments on independence until May 10, and then the council refused to concur, forcing the radicals to utilize the newspapers to ask town meetings "to instruct" their representatives in the general court. When the assembly met in early June the towns had overwhelmingly instructed their representatives that they favored independence. James Warren to Elbridge Gerry, June 12, 1776,

in Gardiner, *A Study in Dissent*, p. 31; and Stephen E. Patterson, *Political Parties in Revolutionary Massachusetts* (Madison: University of Wisconsin Press, 1973), pp. 139–48.

[4] Remainder of MS missing. The following paragraph is taken from a variant copy of this letter, now also missing but perhaps Gerry's retained copy, which was first published in Austin, *Life of Gerry*, 1:174–75.

Joseph Hewes to Samuel Johnston

Dear Sir   Philadelphia 26 March 1776

Our Express has returned and brought me your favours of the 3d and 10th instant. I am very glad to find the Regulators & Highlanders have been put to the Rout, I hope they will not be able to appear again in the field. I wrote to you some time ago that Congress had divided the Colonies into districts; that Virga, North & South Carolina and Georgia composed the Southern district; that Majer General Lee was to command the forces there. We sent Five Tons of Powder a few days ago by Land to Virga. for the use of that district; you must apply there for what you may want.[1] We cannot get any Small Arms, many are expected, and a considerable quantity are manufactured but the call for them has been so great as to put it out of our power to get any, hope soon to be able to furnish you. I had purchased 12 very pretty double fortified four pounders and had got them well fitted, they would have done for a Vessel or for Field pieces. I waited only for an oppertunity to send them, but Congress being informed that two or three Cutters were cruizing on this Coast and had taken several Vessels, and being apprehensive if they were suffered to stay there they would fall in with some of our Vessels returning with powder & arms, purchased a fine Bermudian Brigg which they fitted out with 16 Guns & 90 Men and she sailed in a Week.[2] They took my Guns for this Vessel not having it in their power to get any other suitable, I am endeavouring to get more, they are now become very scarce, if I find any good ones shall have them properly fitted & sent, this is now become doubtfull. No Vessel can be had to carry them should they be procured unless I will ensure her against Captures. They ask me 33 1/3 per Cent for insurance to Edenton. This will not do, I might as well purchase a Vessel at once. I have not the means, shall I purchase a small one on the province account, will you not suffer greatly for want of salt and will not that cause insurrections. I wish my Salt that was thrown into the River had been stored and given to the poor. You must make Salt or you will be undone. You must also make Salt Petre & powder if you mean to defend your liberties to the last extremity. If you mean to have your province represented in Congress you must add one or two more delegates so that they may take it by turns, no man can attend constantly. You know my Constitution and how it is affected by a constant attention to business. We set till four, some times five oClock and I attend some Committee every night and frequently in the morning before Congress meets, I find myself declining. I Am willing to spend the last remains of life in Our Cause in any way I can be most usefully employed. The expence of living here is very great; our allowance will not bring about the year. I must suffer greatly in my private concerns, by being so long absent. If it should be thought proper to increase the pay of your delegates I hope it will have retrospect. Dont let the New hands be on a better footing than your old Servants. The last convention put our friend Penn on a much better than their former Servants had received, I cannot think it was right.[3]

An exact return should be made of your Regiments with the names of all the Officers according to their rank that Commissions might be made out & Sent to them. You should enlist your Soldiers during the War or at least for three years, subject to be discharged at any time by Congress, on giving them a months pay. You must take up some kind of Government, otherwise your people will get too licentious. I send you a short Sketch of the Government of Connecticut. I have heard you speak much of it. I hate republicks and would almost prefer the Government of Turkey to live under, however I expect I must Submit to it for I see no prospect of a reconciliation. If the people can be made happy I shall endeavour to be content. I will get the shoes you mention soon as possible. My Compliments to all friends.[4] Adieu & believe me to be with great Sincerity, Dear Sir, Your mo. Obedt. hum Servt,

Joseph Hewes

RC (MeHi).

[1] See *JCC*, 4:186–87.

[2] See Thomas Johnson to the Maryland Council of Safety, March 9, 1776, note.

[3] On May 1, 1776, the North Carolina Provincial Congress, ignoring Hewes' advice to enlarge the colony's delegation in Congress, simply reappointed Hewes, William Hooper, and John Penn to serve another term. At the same time, however, the provincial congress approved an additional allowance of $666 for each of the delegates to help pay for the expenses they had incurred after their election in September 1775, and changed their salaries from £500 "proclamation money" to $2,000 for their new term in Congress. *N.C. Colonial Records*, 10:190, 204, 553.

[4] In a letter written this day to James Iredell, and otherwise dealing chiefly with personal matters, Hewes observed: "As I imagine you will be at Halifax, and will there see my friend Hooper, who will be able to give you all the news and politics, I shall not trouble you with any thing in that way; as to myself, I am ashamed to be always complaining, yet I must say I think myself declining fast; such close attention to business every day in Congress till three, four and sometimes five o'clock, and on committee almost every evening, and frequently in the morning before Congress meets, is too much for my constitution—however, my country is entitled to my services, and I shall not shrink from her cause, even though it should cost me my life. I send you enclosed the locket you desired me to get made for Mrs. Iredell; the jeweller was a long time about it, and has not pleased me in the execution; the letters are not plain enough. In these times, when every mechanic is employed in learning how to kill Englishmen, it is impossible to get any thing done right." Griffith J. McRee, *The Life and Correspondence of James Iredell, one of the Associate Justices of the Supreme Court of the United States*, 2 vols. (New York: D. Appleton and Co., 1857–58), 1:274–75.

Samuel Huntington to Joseph Trumbull

Sir   Philadelphia 26th March 1776
   Your favour of the 6th Instant have duly receivd. Be assured Sir
that I understood the Sentence in your former letter in the same sense
as you explain it in this, & shall never be inclind to put any unfavourable
Construction on any of yours that I may be favour'd with. Your agreeable Intelligence of the taking possession of Dorchester Hills, & the
various prudent Maneuvers for that end, were Entertaining;[1] the Consequence of which we have Since receivd that the Troops are gone from
Boston. Let me Congratulate you on this happy event which appears
to me of great Importance. If this Letter finds you in Boston or elsewhere please to Inform me what is become of Master Lovell, in particular, & any other of the Inhabitants of that Town you Shall think proper
to mention. Have the pleasure to acquaint that Mr Lynch is Some
Better, but alas! the Worthy Govr Ward is gone. This morning about
Two he died of the Smallpox which he had Insensibly taken. By the
public papers you will receive what further Intelligence I might be
able to add at this time. Remain Sir with much Esteem, your Humble
Servt,   Saml Huntington

RC (CtHi).
   [1] Joseph Trumbull's letter of March 6 describing this action to his father and
Governor Trumbull's cover letter of March 10 forwarding it to the Connecticut
delegates are in *A Historical Collection, From Official Records, Files, &c., of the Part
Sustained by Connecticut, during the War of the Revolution,* comp. Royal R. Hinman
(Hartford: E. Gleason, 1842), pp. 556–58.

Maryland Delegates to
the Maryland Council of Safety

Gent.   Phila. 26 March 1776.
   The inclosed contains a State of the powder and Arms we have sent
from hence.[1] Willing and Morris still assure us they daily expect an
Arrival of powder to enable them to furnish us with the Quantity they
contracted for. They were but partly interested in the Salt petre which
arrived & had not the Management of it nor was it in their power to
procure any of it to be manufactured for us the Congress having immediately on the Arrival of the Salt petre taken up all the powder Mills.
If you think it necessary we have no Doubt but that we can borrow a
Ton of powder more as it begins now to come in from the Mills. We
should be inclined to borrow & forward it but that we think the additional Expence and Risk cannot be justified but by necessity. We

should have got a Return of the Musquets furnished the Hornet & Wasp with the powder but the Congress have it not in their power. Mr. Rittenhouse has been pressed to get the plates done. He has been lately chose into the Assembly which has been sitting a good while past. He promises to let us have plates to begin, enough for one sheet, next Week; the paper was to be finished about this Time.[2]

Inclosed you have the pay in the Marine Service and for the 3 independent Companies. You'll be pleased to attend to the Memorandum at Bottom.

There is no getting Camp Kettles or Canteens on any Terms or at least such Terms as you could submitt to. Instead of Canteens the Congress has been obliged to substitute little Keggs. There's no Arrival here of any Tin. The price of Duck & indeed every Kind of Linnen exceeds here what it does with you. Any Thing of the Kind cannot be got at scarce any price nor could it when T. J. got to Phila. wherefore no Attempt was made to get Knapsacks & Haversacks. Hoping proper Materials might arrive in Poto. or from Vanbibber Time enough, we hope what was sent down of Vanbibbers Cargo will answer for these purposes & for Tents. The Duck is too heavy for any Use about our Troops. We have sold the Holland Duck at 8.10. & the Russian at 7.10 a piece. The Sale was to the Congress for the use of the frigates and to the Virginians for their armed Vessels.

Immediately on T. Js. coming to Phila. he & R. A. mentioned the Defence to the Marine Committee either to sell or have insured. They seemed not very fond of taking her off our Hands. Before the Matter was totally given up Capt Squires Expedition was defeated.[3] T J confirms our Opinion that if any Depredations should take place after we had parted from the Vessell it would be imputed to the Sale of her and there's no Idea of the Congress taking her off our hands but on subjecting her to the uncontrolled Orders of the Congress. We have therefore thought it best to let this Matter rest till the Convention. Mr R. A. has received of the Congress £8250 to exchange for Gold, of which on S. Cs. Orders he let him draw 105. The rest Mr Buchanan carries down; the Change for the Money T. J. brot up & for Majr. Jenifers 1/2 Joes is put up seperately. Would it not be well that some person in Balt Town should be specially appointed to take Charge & keep accounts of all things sent there for the public Use. We congratulate you on the Evacuation of Boston. We have not yet received any account of the Course the forces went. Some think they are destined for N York, others for the Southward but most for Hallifax.

We are Gent, with the greatest Respect, Your most obedt. Servts.

Th Johnson junr

R. Alexander

[*P.S.*] The enclosed Letter for Mr Calvert We believe is from Mrs Custis.

RC (MdAA). Written by Johnson and signed by Johnson and Alexander.

¹ This letter is a response to requests contained in the council's letters to the Maryland delegates of March 17 and 23, 1776. See *Md. Archives*, 11:255, 277–78.

² On April 9 the Maryland delegates dispatched 51 reams of paper to Annapolis and reported that "Mr. Rittenhouse now promises [the plates] shall be done by next Saturday [April 13]. Ibid., p. 319.

³ For information on the operations of Maryland's armed ship the *Defence*, Capt. James Nicholson, see Clark, *Naval Documents*, 4:220, 241–42, 269–72, 340–41, 457–58.

William Paca, Thomas Johnson, and Stephen Hopkins to the Amboy Committee

Gentlemen: Philada. March 26th, 1776.

The bearer hereof is Mr. Pots, a gentleman who some years past left England and resided in Maryland. He is now on his return and proposes to embark from Amboy. He brings with him several letters from gentlemen of Maryland for their correspondent in London. We believe these letters are not upon political subjects but if any doubts should be entertained, he is ready to submit them to inspection. We are personally acquainted with Mr. Pots and know that he is not unfriendly to America.

The gentleman who accompanys Mr. Pots is Mr. Thomas a native of Maryland and a friend to America.

Your humble servant,   Wm. Paca

Th. Johnson, Jr.

Stephen Hopkins

MS not found; reprinted from George C. Thomas, ed., *Autograph Letters and Autographs of the Signers of the Declaration of Independence* (Philadelphia: Privately printed, 1908), no pagination. Addressed: "To The Committee of Observation at Amboy."

Secret Committee Minutes of Proceedings

March 26. 1776.

Upon a Letter being produced from the Sub Comme. of Inspection in this City certifying that it was their opinion Mr. J. Winey shoud pay all expence of putting the arms into proper order (lately purchased of him by this C[ommittee]), Res[olve]d that the Chairman shoud speak & settle the matter with Mr. Winey. Another letter from sd. S[ub] C[ommitte]e being likewise producd giving informatn. of the arrival of 1 bar. gunpdr. & 27 muskets in the Schooner Marrion, Capt [Novaue?].

Resd. that the Chairmn. direct the C[ommissar]y Mr. Towers to examine the arms & ammunitn. & purchase the same on the best terms. A Charter party with J. & Peter Chevalier for the Ship Union, Jo. Harvey Master, was signd by a quorum of the Come. A Charter P[art]y with Blair Mcclanachan for the ship Hope, G. Curwin Master, signed by a Quorum.[1] Do. with Josh. Wallace for Brige. Polly, McFadden Masr., signd by a Quorum.[2]

The Chairman dispatched an order to all masters of vessels &c to repair immediately within the Cheveaux de frize on certain intelligence of a man of war[3] & a tender being arrivd in our capes. A letter from Mr. Langdon being produced & read, Orderd that the Chairmn. answer it.[4]

MS (MH).

[1] Regarding the departure of the ships *Hope* and *Union*, see Secret Committee to the Pennsylvania Committee of Safety, April 29, 1776.

[2] For information on the fate of the brig *Polly*, see Secret Committee to Philip Lacey, May 14, 1776, note.

[3] H.M.S. *Roebuck.* Clark, *Naval Documents*, 4:510, 529.

[4] For the committee's response, see Secret Committee to John Langdon, April 4, 1776.

Richard Smith's Diary

[March 26, 1776]

Tuesday 26. A Comee. of 3 viz Hopkins, S. Adams and Wolcott named to take Order about the Funeral of Govr. Ward who died last Night of the Small Pox and to invite the Rev. Mr. Stillman to preach a Sermon, the Congress agreed to attend the Funeral as Mourners, to wear Mourning for a Month, to invite the Gen Assembly and other Public Bodies and to do no Business till the Funeral is over, only Hooper going Home desired that North Carolina may, if they think it necessary raise Two more Battals. upon Continental Pay & Establishment which was granted, no Man but myself dissenting. The Pay of the Maryland Minutemen who lately went to Virginia settled at 50/. Commodore Douglass ordered to his Command on the Lakes. Adjd. till Thursday 10 O Cloc.

MS (DLC).

Virginia Delegates to Robert C. Nicholas

Dr Sir,   March 26th. 1776.

I was yesterday reminded by the Presidt of the Congress that the

Virga. Delegates stood Charged with an order Deliver'd them Drawn on you for a hundred Pounds Virga. Currency by Mr Mathews, I sometime ago transmitted a Copy of this order to you,[1] but have never been favour'd with your an[swe]r whether you would pay it or not, you'l please to Inform us by the next Post.

We advanced Mr Jonston Smith 600 Dollars of the Continental Money put into our Hands for the use of the Committee of Safety of Virga. for which we have his Note to Acct. with you at the rate of six shillings Virga Currency per Dollar, he was out of Cash and would have lost the purchase of 50 muskets if we had not done this, you'l please to Acct. with the Comme. for the money.

I saw a Letter of yours to my Son in answer to one he wrote you, in which you tell him you had made Ample Remittance to your Delegates to enable them to pay Capt. Innis's Balance; as you never had said a Word to us that I know of, no orders had been given to W[illing] & Morris about it, but it is now placed to our debit, and is upwards of seven hundred Pounds. Mr Nelson inform'd me you some time ago (when I was at Baltimore) sent £500 which he had paid those Gentn. If I can get a State of their acct. with us you shall have it inclosed, by it you will find we shall soon want money.

The Order of the Salt Petre maker is come to hand and accepted, when paid it shall be placed to the Credit. of the Country.

I am Dr Sir, your most obedt Servt,

Benj Harrison

for Self and Colleagues [2]

RC (PHi). In the hand of Benjamin Harrison.

[1] See Benjamin Harrison to Nicholas, January 17, 1776.

[2] The following brief note, in the hand of George Wythe, signed by Wythe "for himself & his brethren," and bearing the dateline "Philadelphia, 26 March 1776," was probably also directed to Nicholas. "Mr. Rubsamen's order for one hundred pounds, of Virginia currency, hath been presented to the persons upon whom it was drawn; and they have agreed to accept it." Signers of the Declaration, NNPM. No other information on Jacob Rubsamen's dealings with the Virginia delegates has been found, but see Henry Wisner to Benjamin Towne, December 21, 1775, note 2, for his interest in the manufacture of gunpowder.

Benjamin Franklin to William Alexander

My dear Lord   Brunswick, March Wedny. 27. 1776

I received your obliging Letter some Days since at Philada. but our Departure from thence being uncertain, I could not till now acquaint your Lordship when we expected to be at New York. We move but slowly, and think we shall scarce reach farther than Newark to-morrow, so that we cannot have the Pleasure of seeing you before Friday. Being myself from long Absence as much a Stranger in N York as the other Gentlemen, We join in requesting you would be so good as to cause Lodgings to be provided for us, and a Sloop engaged to carry us to Albany. There are five of us, and we propose staying in New York two Nights at least. With great and Sincere Esteem & Respect, I have the Honour to be, My Lord, Your Lordship's most obedient & most humble Servant,   B Franklin

RC (NHi).

Joseph Hewes to Robert Smith

Dear Sir   Philadelphia 27th March 1776
   I wrote to you yesterday by Post[1] but least that should Miscarry I will endeavour to give you the substance of it as near as I can recollect for I keep no Copies. I am sorry to find by yours brought me by the return express that you could not get any Vessel to bring Naval Stores, a Vessel Arived some days ago from Newbern and sold Turpentine 35/, Pitch 25/, Tar 20/ per barrel, a good Profit. Mr. Rob. Morris has loaded sundry Vessels lately for Acct. of the Continent some of which are bound to France & other foreign Countries in order to import such articles as will be most wanted for the Army & Navy, our Brig Fanny is one of these. I proposed to him that I thought a Vessel or two might be laden in North Carolina with Tobacco, that they might probably get out of Occacock at almost any time as that inlet would not be so narrowly watched by Cutters as many other places. He has agreed that you should purchase 200 or 300 hhds of Tobacco if to [be] had. If you can get either of these quanti[ti]es in and about Halafax and get them down to Daylys I would have you enter upon it immediately; can it be done? Can you get a Vessel or Vessels to Charter to carry it to France or any other country in Europe. The Charter party I sent you for the Fanny will be a guide to you;[2] get them either by the Month or Ton, the Vessels to be ensured against British Captures by the Congress; five Cent will be allowed as a Commission for purchasing and continental Money or Virga. money will be sent you to pay for the whole; let me have your answer fully on this matter as early as possible, and if any thing can be done I will send you the money, or if I can get away will bring it my self, but unless Hooper or Penn should return I cannot leave the Congress,[3] I dare not leave our Province unrepresented, or perhaps you might get some trusty person to come express in the service of the Province in case they should think such a thing Necessary to bring any particular information; in that case the money might be sent to you without expence, or if you could draw for it to any advantage & get money for your Bills it would do just as well; would not such a sum of money

passing thro' your hands be of service exclusive of the Commission. Proper Certificates shall be sent from Congress to the Committees to let such Vessels pass. If the Tobo. could not all be got in Carolina could not some be had in Virginia & brought down Notaway & Black Water Rivers to Edenton. Care must be taken not to Value the Vessels too high, it would be well to have them Valued by indifferent persons, and that Valuation under the hands of those Persons sent here, as the Vessels might be obliged to go to several Ports it would be best to Charter them by the month. Let me have your Sentiments fully. Hooper & Penn will tell you all the News.[4] I am Dr. Sir, Yours Sincerely,

Joseph Hewes

RC (NcU).

[1] Not found.

[2] See Secret Committee Minutes of Proceedings, February 13, 1776; and Clark, *Naval Documents*, 3:1285–87.

[3] Hooper and Penn returned to North Carolina at this time to attend its provincial convention, which met from April 4 through May 14. *N.C. Colonial Records*, 10:499–590.

[4] Hewes also wrote a letter this day to Samuel Johnston in which, after describing his efforts to send two wagonloads of gunpowder and drums to North Carolina, he observed: "I have been put on so many Committees, some of a Commercial kind, that I [have] a much harder time of it than either of my brethren. I envy them both the pleasure of travelling [. . . .] Penn, I believe, would not choose to stay at any rate from the Convention. Hooper & myself thought it right that one of us should go also.

"I think he will be most useful in Convention. If the Commissioners we have heard so much of [come?] here I shall [send?] off an express & you must in that case send them both back, or some other in their stead. I must not in that case have the weight of the whole province on my shoulders. Why cannot you come yourself ?" Edmund C. Burnett Transcripts, DLC.

Stephen Hopkins to Henry Ward

Sir   Philadelphia 27th March 1776

I am very sorry to be under the necessity of writing so disagreable News, as the death of your brother the honorable Samuel Ward Esqr. must be. He first found himself a little out of order, on Wednesday the 13th of March, and on that and the two following days, he attended Congress, but on the last of them he was so poorly as to be obliged to leave it before it rose, and on Saturday the 16th in the morning the small pox appeard plainly and very full upon him. To this time, and for some days after, the Symptoms appeared favourable, and the doctors Young and Bond, who attended him, thought not at all dangerous—Tho' I confess for myself, I was apprehensive of danger much sooner than they. The Symptoms from this time began to grow more and more malignant every day, until Friday the 22nd, when the Doctors themselves began to be much alarmed. His face was now excessively swelled, his breathing difficult, and his throat much obstructed by Phlegm. He continued, with the bad Symptoms rather increasing, until yesterday morning about two o'clock, when he expired without a groan or Struggle. He appeared to have retained his senses quite thro' his whole disorder, even to the last.

His Funeral is to be attended, this day at three o'clock, by the Congress as Mourners—by the General Assembly of the Province of Pennsylvania—by the Mayor and Corporation of the city of Philadelphia— the Committee of safety of the Province, and the Committee of inspection of the city and liberties—The Clergy of all denominations preceeding the Corpse—Six very respectable Gentlemen of this city being Pallbearers. He will be carried into the Great Presbiterian Meeting house in Arch Street, where a Funeral discourse will be delivered by the revd. Mr. Stillman. The Corpse will from thence be carried to the Baptist burying ground in this city & there interred.[1]

As to such papers and other things as your brother has left behind him, I shall take the most exact care, that, after a particular account being taken of them, they shall be duly packed up, preserved, and sent to his Family. I shall also take care to settle such accounts as he may have open here, and transmit to you an exact account of what I have done in the whole matter.

His servantman Cudgo, who is now under inoculation, as soon as he is sufficiently recovered, I shall send home with the horses and every other thing which he may be able to carry.

I sincerely condole with you on this melancholly occasion—and am, Your very affectionate Friend,   Step Hopkins

RC (RHi). In a clerical hand, and signed by Hopkins.
[1] Robert Treat Paine noted in his diary this day: "Raw cold. Govr. Ward buried. Congress attended the funeral. A Sermon preach'd at Arch Street meeting house by Revd. Mr. Stillman. Dind Mr. Duane." MHi.

John Jay to Alexander McDougall

Dear Sir   Philadelphia 27 March 1776
As Mr. Willet leaves this Place in the morning, I shall commit these few Lines to his Care, and tho they contain nothing important will nevertheless tend to manifest my constant Attention to the Province as well as to the Person for whom they are designed. I am sorry no Provision has been made for Mr. Willet, from everything I can learn, he has merit, and I hope when we shall be informed of the Arrangemt. in Canada, that a Place will be found for him.

How do your People like the Design of privateering. In the Year 1757 they had thirty nine Sail & no less than 4060 Men employed in that Business. I feel so much for the Honor of our calumniated Colony, that it would give me Pleasure to see them distinguished by vigourous Exertion. Indeed had it not been for the Slanders of some of our own Citizens Fame would have done us Justice—however she has been detected in so many dirty Misrepresentations to vilify New York that I can assure you the Province stands well with the Congress & has at least its due Weight. It gives me great Satisfaction that your military Appointment will probably admit of your continuing in the City, where I cant but think your Presence extremely necessary—and the more so as many among you observe no medium, and are either all Flame or all Frost.

It is said Boyd has not fulfilled his Contract and has only delivered six or seven Musquets. I suspect all is not right in this Business, and that there are more Reasons for the Delay than ostensible ones. If so he ought to feel the Indignation of the Public.[1]

That no salt Petre is making in the Province is a sad Tale. I wish we could contradict it. A work at public Expense should be erected, if it were only for the Honor of the Colony. I hear you have emitted more Money.[2] Will you never think of Taxes? The Ice must be broken, the sooner it is begun & more insensibly performed the better. I tremble for this Delay. There is much Money in the Province, the Produce of the Country retains its Price & a moderate Tax would be born without Murmur especially & the Payment can be enforced and the necessity obvious.

The Tories at Boston are left to the Mercy of their incensed Countrymen. I hope our wise ones will draw proper Inferences from this Circumstance, and not seek for Protection from those who never think of their Friends longer that [than] Interest may dictate attention. Mr. Willet is waiting.[3] Adieu. I am yr Frd.   John Jay

RC (NHi).
[1] For Robert Boyd's difficulties in fulfilling his contract with the New York Provincial Congress for the manufacture of gun barrels, see *Am. Archives*, 4th ser. 2:1302, 5:253, 319.
[2] The New York Provincial Congress had approved the emission of bills of credit to the amount of £55,000 on March 5. Ibid., 4:1025, 5:295, 321–22, 334, 337–39.
[3] Four days later Jay wrote to his wife inquiring about her health and the health of their two-month-old son, Peter Augustus. Jay to Sarah Jay, March 31, 1776, Jay, *Papers* (Morris), 1:246.

Secret Committee Minutes of Proceedings

March 27 [1776]

At a meeting of the Come. this day, Present, R. Morris, R. H. Lee, Ph. Livingston, J. Alsop, Th. McKean & J. Hewes. The Chairman produced a letter from Josh. Babcock Esqr. dated Westerly 20th March, engaging to be security for his son's contract.[1] Also an order from Adam Babcock Esqr. on this C[ommitte]e for 20000 dlls stipulatd to be pd. him by his Contract. In consequence of which issued an order on the Continentl. Treasurers for the above sum in favor of Adam Helme for Acct. of sd. Babcock as per his receit of this date. Orderd that Mr. Morris dispatch the Sloop Betsey, Capt. Tucker, directly with a cargoe of Provisions for Bermuda in order to send Silas Deane Esqr. on that Island,[2] that he may from thence obtain a safe passage to Europe in order to execute with dispatch the contract for Indian goods.

MS (MH).
   [1] For this contract, see Secret Committee Minutes of Proceedings, March 6, 1776.
   [2] See Robert Morris to Silas Deane, March 30, 1776.

Oliver Wolcott to Samuel Lyman

Sir,   Philadelphia 27 March 1776
   Your favour of the 9th inst I recd. with Pleasure. I had hereby not only the Benefit of Your Correspondence personally but an Acco. of the Health and Condition of my Family. You mention it as a matter of publick Concern, that the Commissioners might perhaps delude the Colonies. I hope there is no danger of an Event of this Nature. G. Britain will proceed douptless upon their usual Governmental Maxims— Violence and Corruption—but neither I hope will succeed against America. Folly has hitherto Marked her Councills and I think they will continue distinguished with that disgracefull Characteristic. Some few Americans may wish to support a Monarchy which is lavish in its Bountys, hoping to Share in the oppressions of Power—some may be timid and fearfull of entring upon untried Scenes and others who have supported the Distinctions of an Aristocracy may fear the Prevalency of a Republican Spirit—but God has evidently Appeared to Vindicate the Rights of this People, and I beleive they will be taken Care of but not by their own Wisdom nor Power. The Expulsion of the Troops from Boston is a great Event, it has bro't a Disgrace on the British Arms which they had not so such a Degree suffered for a long Time. I wish they might not desolate the eastern Coast. It is rather conjectured by Many that they will go for Hallifax but the certainty of their Destination will be known long before this reaches you and so no conjecture ought not to have been mentioned. I have sent you a few Papers which will give you the present News. My compliments to my Freinds, particularly to Mr Morrice I am sir with regard, your most humble Servt.
                                                        Oliver Wolcott

RC (PHi).

Committee of Congress to
the Maryland Convention

Gentlemen,   Philadelphia March 28th. 1776.[1]

The Congress taking into consideration the urgent importance to the safety, freedom & wealth of the united Colonies, that the manufacture of salt petre & gun powder should be established in all of them, in addition to their former resolves on that subject, have passed those herewith transmitted & appointed the Committee therein mentioned.[2] In persuance of this trust the Committee inclose you the resolves, & being deeply impressed with their importance to our Common Cause, think themselves in duty bound to urge upon you the immediate & vigorous execution of them.[3]

The erecting public works as mentioned in the resolves, will be the first step to promote this useful business, if prosecuted with skill & diligence it will ensure the making saltpetre in large quantities & will also afford the best method for suitable persons to learn the process & from thence be sent abroad to teach those who have not opportunity of learning from these public works; for it is thought an object of the greatest concern that private families should be induced to make it; the inconsiderable expence attending the making it in families, when the method is once understood, & the quantities that each family may make, should remove all Objections to their putting it in immediate practice.

When we consider the great consumption of Saltpetre, used in medicine, in preserving meat, & in gunpowder, even in times of peace, it should seem a sufficient inducement to private families to learn & practice this art, but most of all when so large quantities are wanted for our necessary defence, & when it will in a great measure supply the want of salt which the rage of our enemies may render Scarce, it should not reasonably be supposed, that any true American will neglect it.

As there can be no doubt but that every Colony may produce saltpetre enough at least for their own consumption, it is necessary that powder mills be erected & skillful persons provided to manufacture gunpowder, & proper regulations established for preventing their explosion.

It is supposed that Sulphur may be found in many Colonies, & it is necessary that it should be collected, tryals may be made at places supposed to contain it at no great expence.

It must afford great pleasure to find that some Colonies have already in a measure anticipated the design of these resolves, from the good effect of which it is clearly evinced, that we can never want the most abundant Supply of ammunition from our own manufacture, but through inattention and neglect.

We doubt not you will consider these proceedings as designed to promote the best welfare of the Colonies, & that you will as soon as may be & from time to time inform the Congress of the state of these manufactures in your Colony, of the quantity of Saltpetre already made, the preparation for & prospects of encreasing it, what quantity of gunpowder is already made, & the state of your powder mills, & also what discovery is made of sulphur mines & the progress in working them.

Supposing the most approved method of making saltpetre may not have reached you, we have inclosed such as experience in some Colonies has recommended.

The laying together suitable composts either in fences or beds in order to collect nitrous matter, seems necessary to be immediately attended to, as the earth from under old buildings may soon be exhausted.

It is hoped this effort of the Congress will have the desired effect, without which we have reason to fear, it will ere long be said of us, that we are become Slaves because we were not industrious enough to be free.

By order of the Committee I Subscribe, your humble Servant,

Rob Treat Paine

P.S. I take the liberty herewith to send an extract from Dr. Brownriggs treatise of making *Salt*.[4] The climate is so suitable, & there are So many places on our sea coasts where neither Men of War nor Cutters can come, where salt may be made in plenty, that it is hoped some persons of sufficient judgment & application will immediately undertake it. The extract was made for the benefit of those who are unacquainted with the original, to which recourse may be had by those who are disposed to manufacture *white salt*. Any Account of your success in these undertakings must give great pleasure to all lovers of America.   RTP

RC (NN). Written and signed by Paine for the committee for "promoting and encouraging the manufactures of salt petre, sulphur and powder." Addressed: "Circular. To the honble. Convention or Council of Safety of the Colony of Maryland."

[1] Although this letter is clearly dated March 28, Paine may have sent it on April 2. His diary entry for April 2 reads: "Wrote Col. Palmer & Comitte of Safety Maryland abt. Saltpetre & Salt dated 28th ulto. & Majr. Hawley." MHi.

[2] These resolves, passed by Congress on February 23, 1776, are in *JCC*, 4:170–71.

[3] Paine, as chairman of the committee for "promoting and encouraging the manufactures of salt petre, sulphur and powder," sent copies of this circular letter to at least eight provinces in addition to the copy to Maryland printed here. On March 16, Paine sent nearly identical copies, without the postscript appearing here, to New Hampshire, Massachusetts, and Connecticut. Robert Treat Paine's Diary, March 16, 1776. MHi. The Massachusetts copy is at M-Ar, and the New Hampshire copy is at MeHi and printed in *Am. Archives*, 4th ser. 5:245. On March 28, Paine also noted in his diary: "Sent Letters to Convention of Georgia, So. Carolina, No. Carolina & Virginia. Wrote 26th instant, with the process of Saltpetre making & also Bay Salt; sent them by Mr. Hooper & Penn." A MS fragment of this March 28 letter is at CtY; and a copy dated April 4, 1776, but with no designated addressee, is among Paine's papers at MHi. He apparently sent another copy to the New York Committee of Safety on April 6, although it was dated March 28, 1776. See Paine's

Diary, April 6, 1776; and *Am. Archives*, 4th ser. 5:528–29.

Paine also wrote a brief letter to John B. Bordley (1727–1804), merchant of Queen Anne's County, Md., inquiring about the "easiest & most practical method" for extracting sulphur from pyrite, probably during this same period. Paine's undated FC of the letter to Bordley is in the Paine Papers, MHi.

⁴ William Brownrigg, *The Art of Making Common Salt, as Now Practicesed in Most Parts of the World: with Several Improvements Proposed in that Art, for the Use of the British Dominions* (London: C. Davis, 1748). See also Robert Treat Paine to the Massachusetts General Court, April 15, 1776, note 1.

John Hancock to Thomas Dewees

Sir,   Philada. March 28th. 1776.

I have it in Command from the Congress to desire you immediately to confine in seperate Apartments Mr. Conally, Mr. Smith, & Mr. Kirkland, who were some Time past committed to your Custody by Order of Congress: and I am further to direct, that you suffer no Person whatever to visit or converse with either of the above named Persons without an Order from me in Writing.[1]

I am, Sir, your most obedt. Servt.   J. H. Prsidt.

LB (DNA: PCC, item 12A). Addressed: "To Mr. Dewees Keeper of the Philada. Prison."

[1] Congress issued this order following the receipt of information "that some prisoners in the gaol of this city have meditated an escape, and are near carrying their plan into execution." *JCC*, 4:239. Notwithstanding this directive to the keeper of the Philadelphia prison, Connolly's friends apparently continued efforts to communicate with the prisoners, and as a result of further intelligence on the subject Congress on April 2 came to the following resolve, which Secretary Thomson failed to enter on the journals. "Resolved, that the enclosed be delivered by Mr. Wilson to the Com'ee of Safety of Pensylvania, & request them to take such steps as they think best for the public Service." Both the resolve and the "Intelligence" printed below are taken from the *Pa. Archives*, 1st ser. 4:728–29.

"Mr. Samuel Sample, an Inhabitant of Pittsburgh, and nearly Related to Mr. John Connolly, came to this City about a week ago. The day he arrived he went to the Jail, and was permitted to see and Converse with Mr. Connolly freely, as well as with others in the like Situation, and was in several of their Appartments. A plann for a general escape of the State or Tory prisoners, It now appears, had been in contemplation among these prisoners sometime before. It happened, the day after Mr. Samples admission, that their whole scheme of escape was discovered; Upon this such Orders were given; that tho' he applied to different members of Congress for leave, he cou'd not be allowed to a second interview, which seemed to vex him a good deal. These circumstances, and his connection with Mr. Connolly, being known to several gentlemen now in Town, some of them from a regard of their Countrys safety, could not refrain from observing as follows.

"That a Stout full faced boy, about 14 or 15 years of age, has frequently, every day since an Intercourse was denied, waited on Mr. Sample, at his Lodgings, with letters or messages from the Jail. Mr. Sample has several times been questioned about the boy and his business with him, and has as often declared that he knew nothing about the boy, but that he is going up to Carlisle with him; notwithstanding his professed ignorance of the boy, it is known that he has engaged a horse to carry him, and to deliver the horse safe at Carlisle. The boy being asked if he was going along with Mr. Sample, said he was going to Carlisle with him; being asked if he wou'd go any farther, he answered with some hesitation, he believed he would go to Pittsburgh with him.

"It is well known that Mr. Connolly's great hopes of strength & support in his Designs are on the River and waters of the Ohio. It is humbley submitted to superior Judgment, whether letters from him to that country might not yet have a bad effect; whether it might not be safer to send letters by a boy travelling with, or some distance before or behind a particular friend, than by the friend; whether upon some farther enquirey into the matter, It might not be proper to direct that both friend and boy should be very narrowly searched at some proper distance from the City. If these hints should tend in the smallest degree to promote the safety of the country, the writter of them gains his only aim.

"Mr. Sample setts off this day, April 2d."

For the response of the Pennsylvania Committee of Safety, see *Minutes of the Provincial Council of Pennsylvania from the Organization to the Termination of the Proprietary Government*, 10 vols. (Philadelphia: Jo. Severns & Co.; Harrisburg: Theo. Fenn & Co., 1851–53), 10:533.

John Hancock to
the New Jersey Committee of Safety

Sirs   Philadelphia 28th March 1776

Your two Letters of the 27th being Rec'd by Express were Communicated to Congress, and I have their orders to inform you that the Congress see no Reason to Change their Requisition of the 15th.[1] I have it therefore in Command to Request you to Exert your utmost Endeavours in Expediting the March of the Troops to New York agreeable to the Requisition of the Commanding officer.

I am Sir, Your most obedt Servt.   J H Prt.

LB (DNA: PCC, item 12A). Addressed: "Honl Saml Tucker Esqr., & Gentlemen of Committee of Safety of New Jersey, at Trenton."

[1] See *JCC*, 4:238; and John Hancock to the New Jersey Convention, March 15, 1776. Tucker's letters are in PCC, item 68, fols. 117–24, and *Am. Archives*, 4th ser. 5:517–18.

Richard Smith's Diary

Thursday 28 March [1776]

The Votes read and Letters from Prest. Tucker & others. Our Colony has raised on their own Bottom 4 Companies to be stationed in Middx. & Monmouth & our Militia are marching to N York or Staten Isld. under their Brigadiers Dickenson & Wm. Livingston. McKean informed Congress that the Tory Prisoners in Philada. Goal have attempted an Escape & have provided Implements and a Ladder to escape this Night whereupon Mr. McKean is to direct the Sheriff to confine Conolly, Smith and Kirkland seperately & get a sufficient Guard from the Barracks.[1] 20,000 Dollars advanced to Commissary Mease & 1000 to Fairlamb Commissary to Waynes Battalion. R. H. Lee moved sundry Resols. which were negatived as for a Dep. Commissary General to be established in Virginia and for Aids du Camp to the Brigadier (Armstrong) commandg there, he moved also for Two Engineers there which passed.[2] Dugan of Canada presented with 1000 Dollars for his past Services and created a Major with the Rank of Lt. Col. He is to have the Command of 3 Companies of Rangers in Canada & to name all his Officers. This was in Consequence of a Report made by Harrison from a Committee. R. Morris moved to purchase another Ship on Continental Accot. in this Harbor to be fitted out for the Protection of Delaware Bay which was granted. A Petition from Thos. Walker of Montreal setting forth his Sufferings from Prescott & Carlton and praying Redress was considered and left undetermined, Mr. Walker soon after returned to Montreal without Redress & his Case on Oath was published in Bradfords Paper about 1 May.[3] Ritzma elected Col. of a N York Battaln.[4]

MS (DLC).
[1] See John Hancock to Thomas Dewees, this date.
[2] See also Richard Henry Lee to Charles Lee, March 25 and April 1, 1776.
[3] Thomas Walker's "Statement" of his case is in *Am. Archives*, 4th ser. 4:1176–78, under the date April 24, 1776.
[4] See also New York Delegates to the New York Provincial Congress, March 15, 1776, note 7.

William Whipple to Josiah Bartlett

Dear Sir   Philadelphia 28th March 1776

I am just return'd from attending the remains of our worthy Friend Govr. Ward to the place appointed for all the Humain race.[1] His better part took its flight to world of Spirits on Tuesday morning, this loss will be felt by Congress, and no doubt greatly laimented by the Colony he so faithfully represented. The Corps[e] was first carried to the meeting house in Arch Street, where an excellent Sermon well suited to the Maloncoly occation was deliverd by Mr. Stilman, from thence to Mr. Stilmans Meeting house where it was depossited.

My last was by Express to Cambridge inclosing Bill Loading & invoice of your flouer,[2] which I wish safe to hand, but am somthing doubtful of it as the coast is much infested with pirates. Its reported that a 40 Gun ship is at the Capes. The Lexington is gone down. The M[arine] C[ommittee] have bot another ship which will be ready to sail in a week.

The Battery goes down to her station to morrow & the Province ship will follow her in a few days. We have a report that Our fleet is at South Carolina, but no certain advice of it. I suppose you visited Boston in you[r] way, pray give me a perticular accot. how you found matters there. I have not yet received a line from any body concernd in publick affairs in N. Hampshire. I shall be glad to know what I have done to deserve such neglect, however I shall expect better things of you while you tarry, which I hope will not be long. Settle your affairs as soon as possible and come away, for I expect them Devils from the other side the water very soon. Its said they will certainly be here by the middle of April.

There is nothing new in papers; however I send you one. Congress have not yet had time to take up the report on New Hampshire matters.

I am, with great Respect Your real Friend & Humle Sert,

Wm Whipple

RC (PHi).
[1] Samuel Ward was buried on March 27.
[2] See Whipple to Bartlett, March 24, 1776.

John Adams to Abigail Adams

March 29. 1776

I give you Joy of Boston and Charlestown, once more the Habitations of Americans. Am waiting with great Impatience for Letters from you, which I know will contain many Particulars.

We are taking Precautions to defend every Place that is in Danger—The Carolinas, Virginia, N. York, Canada.

I can think of nothing but fortifying Boston Harbour. I want more Cannon than are to be had, I want a Fortification upon Point Alderton [Allerton], one upon Lovells Island, one upon Georges Island, several upon Long Island, one upon the Moon, one upon Squantum.

I want to hear of half a Dozen Fire ships and two or three hundred Fire Rafts prepared. I want to hear of Row Gallies, floating Batteries Built, and Booms laid across the Channell in the Narrows and Vesseaux de Frize, sunk in it. I wish to hear, that you are translating Braintree Commons into the Channell.

No Efforts, No Expence are too extravagant for me to wish for to fortify that Harbour so as to make it impregnable. I hope every Body will join and work untill it is done.

We have this Week lost a very valuable Friend of the Colonies, in Governor Ward of Rhode Island, by the small Pox in the natural Way. He never would hearken to his Friends who have been constantly advising him to be inoculated ever since the first Congress began. But he would not be perswaded. Numbers, who have been inoculated, have gone through the Distemper, without any Danger, or even Confinement, but nothing would do. He must take it in the natural Way and die.

He was an amiable and a sensible Man, a stedfast Friend to his Country upon very pure Principles.

His Funeral was attended with the same Solemnities as Mr. Randolphs. Mr. Stillman being the Anabaptist Minister here, of which Perswasion was the Governor, was desired by Congress to preach a sermon, which he did with great Applause.

Remember me as you ought.[1]

RC (MHi). Adams, *Family Correspondence* (Butterfield), 1:366.

[1] Adams wrote a similar letter this day to Cotton Tufts. Adams, *Family Correspondence* (Butterfield), 1:367–68.

John Adams to James Warren

March 29. 1776

Since the joyfull News of the Reduction of Boston by the Forces of the united Colonies, my Mind has been constantly engaged with Plans and Schemes for the Fortification of the Islands and Channells in Boston Harbour.

I think that if Cannon and Ammunition, in the necessary Quantities can possibly be obtained, Fortifications ought to be erected upon Point Alderten, Lovells Island, Georges Island, Castle Island and Governers Island, Long Island and Moon Island, and Squantum, the Heights of Dorchester and Charlestown, and Noddles Island.

The Expence of the Quantities of Cannon necessary to make this Harbour impregnable, will be very great. But this must not be regarded.

Cannot Vesseaux de Frize be placed in the Channell—cannot Hulks be Sunk—cannot Booms be laid across—nay cannot the Channell be filled up, or at least Obstructed with Stone.

Cannot Fire be employed as a Defence. I mean Fire Ships, and Fire Rafts. Cannot Gallies or floating Batteries be used to Advantage.

We Suppose that the Fleet and Army, under General How are gone to Hallifax with Design to go up the River of Saint Lawrence, as early as possible in the Spring. They may go up the River, early in May, if not the latter End of April.

We are taking Measures to give them such a Reception as they ought to have.

The Baron de Woedke is gone to Canada, a Brigadier. A Lady at Braintree can furnish you with his Credentials which are very good.[1]

He is a great officer.

Pray appoint a Committee to look for suphur in our Colony—and let me know what Progress Salt Petre makes.

RC (MHi). In Adams' hand, though not signed.

[1] Shortly after baron de Woedtke's March 16 appointment as a brigadier general, Adams had sent his wife testimonial letters highly laudatory of Woedtke. See *JCC*, 4:209–10; and Adams to Abigail Adams, March 17, 1776, note 2.

Benjamin Franklin to Anthony Todd

Dear Sir,   New York. March 29. 1776

Being here in my Way to Canada and understanding that your Packet[1] sails to morrow, I take the Opportunity of sending a Line or two to some Friends;[2] among the rest give me leave to salute you with my warmest Wishes for your Health & Prosperity.

I shall write Politicks to none of them, but to you. How long will the *Insanity* on your side the Water continue? Every Day's Plundering of our Property & Burning our Habitations, serves but to exasperate & unite us the more. The Breach between you & us grows daily wider and more difficult to heal. Britain without us can grow no stronger. Without her we shall become a tenfold greater and mightier people. Do you chuse to have so increasing a Nation of Enemies? Do you think it prudent by your Barbarities to fix us in a rooted Hatred of your Nation, and make all our innumerable Posterity detest you? Yet this is the Way in which you are now proceeding. Our Primers begin to be printed with Cuts of the Burnings of Charlestown, of Falmouth, of James Town, of Norfolk with the Flight of Women & Children from those defenceless Places, some Falling by Shot in their Flight. Allen & his People, with Lovell, an amiable Character & a Man of Letters! all in *Chains* on board your Ships. Is any body among you weak enough to imagine that these Mischiefs are neither to be paid for nor be revenged, while we treat your People that are our Prisoners with the utmost Kindness & Humanity? Your Ministers may imagine that we shall soon be tired of this, and submit. But they are mistaken, as you may recollect they have been hitherto in every Instance in which I told you at the time that they were mistaken. And I now venture to tell you, that tho' this War may be a long one (and I think it will probably last beyond my Time) we shall with God's Help finally get the better of you; The Consequences I leave to your Imagination.

I hope your dear little Girl is well, and that you continue happy. Pray present my most affectionate Respects to my good Lord Le Despencer: & my Love to Mrs & Mr Jackson. With sincere Esteem & Regard, I am ever, Dear Sir, Your most obedient, humble Servant,

B Franklin

P.S. Since writing the above I have been riding round the Skirts of this Town to view the Works; they are but lately begun, but prodigiously forward, all Ranks of People working at them as Volunteers with the greatest Alacrity, & without Pay, to have them ready for the Reception of Gen. Howe, who having finish'd his Visit to Boston is daily expected here.

What will you do with this Spirit? You can have no Conception of Merchants & Gentlemen working with Spades & Wheelbarrows among Porters & Negroes. I suppose you will scarce believe it.

I do not trouble you with the enclos'd in order to frank them. Be so good as to wafer, charge and forward them: By that means they will go safe.

RC (PRO: C.O. 5, 7).
[1] Anthony Todd (1717–98) was secretary of the British post office from 1762 until his death (except for a brief term) and had also been associated with Franklin as a member of the Grand Ohio or Walpole Company, formed in 1769 to acquire a large tract of western land in America. See Benjamin Franklin, *The Papers of Benjamin Franklin*, ed. Leonard W. Labaree (New Haven: Yale University Press, 1959–), 10:217n.
[2] Franklin's brief letter of this date to his grandnephew Jonathan Williams, Jr., whom Franklin questioned about his intentions of returning to America from London, is at PPAmP.

Richard Smith's Diary

Friday 29 March [1776]

Votes read & Letters from the Comee. of Safety at New York, from Gen Schuyler, Gen Wooster & a Letter from Vice president Fisher of New Jersey praying Congress to reconsider Heards Accots. and grant Pay to his Minute Men.[1] On Motion of Lee a Report was taken up on Canadian Affairs and after Debate Mr. Price was elected Deputy Commissary with a Salary of 60 Dollars per Month. Trumbull the Commissary General has 80 Dollars per month. Mr. Price is to have the Canadian Department, some Articles of the Report were expunged. (Our Comee. of Safety have ordered £200 for the Use of their Delegates here.) The Modes of supplying the Treasury were considered.[2]

MS (DLC).
[1] General Schuyler's letters to Hancock of March 19 and 21 are in PCC, item 152, 2:57–70, and *Am. Archives*, 4th ser. 5:415–17, 452. Enclosed with the former were letters to Schuyler from General Wooster of March 5 and 13. Allen MacDonnell's letter to Hancock of March 25 is in PCC, item 78, 7:27–29, and *Am. Archives*, 4th ser. 5:495; that from the New York Committee of Safety (identified in the journals as the provincial convention) of March 26 is in PCC, item 67, 1:198–206, and *Am. Archives*, 4th ser. 5:509–11; and that from the New Jersey Committee of Safety of March 28 is in PCC, item 68, fols. 125–28, and *Am. Archives*, 4th ser. 5:533.

[2] Smith's diary entry for March 30, the last one that he made, reads: "I was not present but among other Things ut audivi, Heards Accots. were reconsidered & the whole Demand allowed.

"I went Home to Burlington on Sunday having suffered in my Health by a close Attendance on Congress."

John Adams to Norton Quincy

Dear Sir [1]   Philadelphia March 30th. 1776

The Acquisition of Boston, and its Harbour is of Such vast Importance to the Province of Massachusetts Bay and New England in general, and indeed to all the confederated Colonies; that the Utmost Wisdom and public Spirit of our Countrymen ought to [be] employed in order to preserve it by Such Fortifications as will make it impregnable for the future by any hostile Fleet.

There is not in the whole World perhaps an Harbour, whose Channell is commanded by so many Eminencies, both upon Islands and the Main: But in order to avail ourselves of the full Benefit of these natural Advantages many heavy Cannon and much Powder will be wanted. I hope that Measures will be fallen upon to procure a supply of both.

I think that the Militia of every Town which lies around Boston Harbour, ought to be formed into Matrosses or Artillery Men, that so they may be ready upon occasion to go down to the Garrisons in the Harbour, and there officiate for the Defence of their Country.

It is now Twelve Days, since our Army entered Boston, and We have heard no Particulars. I wish you would be kind enough to put your Pen to Paper, now and then, for the Edification, Comfort, Information &c of your Friend,   John Adams

[P.S.] Remember me to all.

RC (MH).

[1] Norton Quincy (1716–1801), retired Boston merchant and Braintree gentleman farmer, and uncle of Abigail Adams, became chairman of the Braintree Committee of Correspondence in 1774. Shipton, *Harvard Graduates*, 10:75–78.

Samuel Huntington to James Cogswell

Honrd Sir,   Philadelphia 30th March 1776

I take this Opportunity to pay my respects to you,[1] altho have nothing of news to communicate relative to public affairs more than you will receive in the public prints. On Sunday morning the 17th Inst my attention from my Chamber window was Suddenly called to behold a mightly Cavalcade of Plebeians marching thro' the Street with drums beating and at every Small distance they halted & gave three Huzzas. I was apprehensive Some outrage was about to be Committed, but Soon perceived my mistaken apprehentions & that it was a Religious exercise of the Sons of Saint Patrick, it being the anniversary of that Saint the morning Exercise was ushered in with the ceremony above describd. However Sir Should I leave you to Judge of the Religion of this City from the above Story only; it would not be Just, there are devout pious people in this City, a number of pious & Excellent preachers, & he who does not lead a virtuous & religious life here must accuse himself. Every man has Liberty to persue the dictates of his own Conscience.

My Business is very arduous as well as Important. We commonly Set from Ten in the morning until between four & five in the afternoon Intent on business without any refreshment. It was very tedious at first but by usage is become Tolerable. I have by divine blessing enjoyd a very good State of Health ever since my recovery from the Small Pox. I cannot forget my native Country; & prize Connecticutt higher than ever I did before. It is disagreable to be So long removed from my famaly & Freinds, however I must chearfully obey the calls & dictates of Providence with out refuising. I herewith send you a Resolve of Congress for a general Fast tho it may likely appear in the public papers.[2]

Please to present my Duty to Madam, my kind Respects to Mr Justice Devotion; & let me request an Interest in your prayers that I may be enabled faithfully to perform the Trust reposed in me, & in due time be returnd to my famaly & native Land in peace.

Am Sir with due respect, your Humble Servant,

Saml Huntington

RC (PHi).

[1] James Cogswell (1720–1807), minister of Windham, Conn. Franklin B. Dexter, *Biographical Sketches of the Graduates of Yale College*, 6 vols. (New York: Henry Holt and Co., 1885–1919), 1:101–4.

[2] A resolution of March 16 recommended that May 17 be observed as a "day of humiliation, fasting, and prayer." *JCC*, 4:208–9.

Samuel Huntington to Joseph Trumbull

Dear Sir   Philadelphia 30th March 1776

This day receivd yours of the 26th Instt and note the Contents. Some material occurrences which I am not at Liberty now to communicate, I hope hereafter to relate in Some Social hour when I may have the pleasure to be honord with your Company. May only Say at present that your favour of the 27th which was receivd before the above mentioned, came to hand most opportunely in a lucky moment & will I trust have beneficial effects.

I wrote you the 26th Instt, as at Cambridge but was then doubtful where my Letter might find you, hope it fell into your hands at N. Yorke.[1] Have nothing new of Importance to Communicate. We are anxious to hear which way the fleet & army are gone from Nantaskett road. I Shall be happy to receive from you the earliest Intelligences of any material occurrences to the northward & Eastward during your residence at N. Yorke. Interim, Am, Sir, with due Respect, your humble Servant,   Sam. Huntington

RC (CtHi).

[1] Huntington had written a brief note to Trumbull on March 28 as follows: "Yours of yesterday per post have this moment receivd & note the Contents, the other you mention by private hand have not recivd. I wrote you the 26th Instant, as at Cambridge by the post, tho' was uncertain where my Letter would find you. Hope your Timely arrival at N. York may be Servicable to your Self & the public." CtHi.

Robert Morris to Silas Deane

Dear Sir   Philada. March 30th. 1776

You will find herein an Invoice & bill of Loading for Sundry Merchandize I have Shipped on board the Sloop Betsey, Capt John Tucker, which is Consigned to you & is intended for Sale in the Island of Bermuda provided the Sloop can be admitted to land the Same with Safety there and I think there is not much reason to doubt of your being able to accomplish that point, as the Island will probably be in want of the Cargo which is also cleared out from the Jerseys previous to the 25th March, consequently does not come within the late Prohibitory Act of Parliament, however Capt Tucker will put in at the West End of the Island where there is no Custom House & he will directly apply to Henry Tucker Esqr to whom I have given him & you letters. This Gentn I expect will be able to inform you of every thing you wou'd wish to know respecting that Island, and I flatter myself he will be willing to afford you all the assistance & advice you can stand in need of. One grand point to be accomplished is to procure a New Register for the Sloop Betsey which I hope may be obtained by pleading that her first Register is lost, and as she was built and originally Registered in the Custom House in Bermuda and it does not appear in that office that ever the property was changed I think they can have little objection to reviewing that Register from the Record, perhaps the former owner may be willing to lend his Name or if that cannot be Ventured on Capt Tucker must have her Registered in his Name as a Resident in that Island which will effectually Cover the property.

If you succeed in obtaining a Register for her which must be dated before the 1st Jany. 1776, but the farther back the better, I think you had in that case best to make the remainder of your Passage in her, but here I must observe that I have pointed out some business for Capt Tucker to execute which if he can accomplish will oblige him to leave the Sloop. In that case you & he can either appoint the Mate or procure another good Master to go in her. I think the latter wou'd be best and that if you go in her you shou'd take a New Master, Mate & hands clearing her out from Bermuda for London and making them believe you are bound there (except the Master who shoud know better). Capt Tucker will very soon know whether he can execute the business I have pointed out to him and if he cannot do that he will stick by the Sloop. He is directed to be governed entirely by your orders so long as he sticks by her and is with you or has your orders in writing, and if she is Registered in his Name and he leaves her you will then see that he signs proper instructions as owner to the New Master. If on your arrival at Bermuda you find there is no safety or protection there for either yourself, the Sloop or Cargo you will doubtless proceed on, direct for your destined Port in Europe without loss of time, only in such case I wou'd wish Capt Tucker to remain in Bermuda if he can do the intended business, and another good Captain can be immediately got, if not he must go on; but if you find safety and protection for yourself, Vessell & Cargo I think you had best in such case to Land & make sale of the Cargo or put it into proper hands for Sale. None can be properer than Mr Tucker if he will Act therein and procure as much Money or good bills of Exchange to be advanced you thereon as you possibly can. I immagine this Cargo will sell directly for ready Money and that you may receive the whole in hard Money or bills. Whatever you do receive must be put to the Credit of the Indian Contract and if you leave any part unsettled you'l direct the same to be accounted for to me hereafter. I have also written Mr. Tucker to pay you in hard Money or good bills, a ballance due to me on a former Cargo of provisions I Sent thither and whatever you Receive on this Account please to give Mr. Tucker a draft on Messrs. Alsop, Livingston, Lewis & myself for that Amount you Crediting the Indn Contract for the Same. These points Settled, if you cannot get the Betsy a Bermuda Register or if you determine not to proceed further in her, order the Captain of her to proceed from Bermuda for Hamburg and there put himself under the care of Mr John Parish untill he receives further orders from me or from Willing, Morris & Co. but if you do obtain for this Sloop a Bermudas Register I think you cannot do better in that case then to proceed in her from that Island to Bourdeaux clearing her out for London as already mentioned for by doing this you save the trouble and expence of Chartering any other Vessell and her Register. Clearance for London with orders suitable from the Ostensible Owner named in the Register will make her as Safe a Conveyance as any can be. Shoud you proceed in this manner you will not have Occasion for this Sloop at Bourdeaux as I shall send you others to Answer your purpose, therefore I wish you to order her from thence to

Hamburg as already mentioned to wait my further orders or those of my House, as we have the public Service to attend to in that quarter, but shou'd you find it necessary to detain her & not send her to Hamburg inform Mr John Parish thereof by a few lines to prevent disapointmt. Shou'd you find it necessary to Charter a Vessell in Bermuda to carry you to Bourdeaux you are Authorized to do so by the Secret Committee and your Contract will be made good by them. Mr Tucker will assist you to do this on the most reasonable terms, but I hope it will not be necessary. If you transact any business in Bermuda I think you will do well to establish a Correspondance with some Gentn. there on whom entire dependance can be had, who wou'd undertake to keep a look out for such Vessells as you may order to Call at the West end of the Island for advice and as I shall occasionally be sending small Boats there let him write me by the first that Calls and I shall then lodge such intelligence for the Captains as I may then think most likely to bring them safe into Port, but at all events I think you had best establish this matter & let them Call there, particularly the Sloop Betsey if you send her back from France, and if she goes to Hamburg I shall take care of that because Tucker must there resume the Command.

I do not recollect any thing more that is necessary for me to add at this time except to assure you that I am Dear sir, Your very Obedt hble servt,   Robt Morris

RC (CtHi).

John Adams to George Washington

Dear Sir   Philadelphia April 1. 1776
The Bearer of this Letter Francis Dana Esqr of Cambridge, is a Gentleman of Family, Fortune and Education, returned in the last Packett from London where he has been about a Year. He has ever maintained an excellent Character in his Country, and a warm Friendship for the American Cause. He returns to share with his Friends in their Dangers, and their Triumphs. I have done my self the Honour to give him this Letter, for the Sake of introducing him to your Acquaintance, as he has frequently expressed to me a Desire to embrace the first opportunity of paying his Respects to a Character, so highly esteemed, and so justly admired throughout all Europe, as well as America.

Mr Dana will Satisfy you, that We have no Reason to expect Peace from Britain.

I congratulate you, Sir, as well as all the Friends of Mankind on the Reduction of Boston, an Event which appeared to me of so great and decisive Importance, that the next Morning after the Arrival of the News, I did myself the Honour to move, for the Thanks of Congress to your Excellency and that a Medal of Gold should be Struck, in Commemoration of it. Congress have been pleasd to appoint me, with two other Gentlemen to prepare a Device. I should be very happy to have your Excellencys Sentiments concerning a proper one.[1] I have the Honour to be, with very great Respect, sir, your most obedient and affectionate Servant   John Adams

RC (DLC).
[1] For Congress' action, see *JCC*, 4:234. Washington's April 15 response left the design of the medal to the committee of Congress. "What ever Device may be determined upon, by the respectable committee they have chosen for that purpose will be highly agreeable to me." Washington, *Writings* (Fitzpatrick), 4:483–84.

John Hancock to Charles Lee

Sir,   Philada. April 1t. 1776
     The Congress having appointed Mr. Dohicky Arundel Captain of an Artillery Company in the Continental Service, and directed him to repair to the Southern Department, and there to put himself under your Command, I have it in Charge from that Body to inform you, that you are directed to set in Foot the raising a Company of Artillery.[1] This you will endeavour to accomplish as early as possible, being sensible the Service calls for such a Company, that we may be the better enabled to defend ourselves, and annoy our Enemies.
     The Convention or Comee of Safety of Virginia (to whom I write by this Conveyance) are requested to appoint the other officers of the said Company.[2]
     I have the Honor to be, Sir, your most obedt. & very hble Sert.
                                                                           J. H. Prest.

[P.S.] I have paid Capt. Arundel sixty Dollars which you will please to have stopped out of his Pay.

LB (DNA: PCC, item 12A).
[1] Congress had taken these actions on March 18 and 19. *JCC*, 4:211–12.
[2] For Lee's response, see his letter to Hancock of April 19, 1776, in PCC, item 158, 1:45–48, and *Am. Archives*, 4th ser. 5:981–82.

John Hancock to the Virginia Convention

Gentlemen,   Philadelphia April 1t. 1776.
     Mr. Dohicky Arundel being appointed a Captain of an Artillery Company in the Continental Service, and directed to repair to the Southern Department, to put himself under the Command of Genl Lee,

who is directed to set on Foot the raising such a Company, I have it in Charge from Congress to inform you, that it is recommended to you to appoint the other Officers in the said Artillery Company.[1]

I have the Honor to be, Gent, your most obed. & very hble Ser.

J. H. Prst.

LB (DNA: PCC, item 12A). Addressed: "The Honble Convention or Commee. of Safety of Virginia."
[1] See *JCC*, 4:211–12.

Richard Henry Lee to Landon Carter

Dear Sir   Philadelphia 1st April 1776

It hurts me exceedingly that you should attribute to declining friendship what realy arose from the necessity of my situation. After an absence of many months, I had obtained leave to pay a short visit to my family, where I had been but a few days when the public business called me to Williamsburg and Mrs. Lees illness occasioned a summons from thence. She was but just recovered before I was compelled to return to this place. This situation of my affairs will very sufficiently account for my not gratifying myself by visiting Sabine Hall, without imputing it to want of regard. You will have heard no doubt of our enemies shameful flight from Boston, where they left behind them many marks of apprehention and hurry, altho they took time to remove with them all the American prisoners (they had made) in chains, while they left to the resentment of an injured country, many Tories, to whom they had promised protection. Where these hostes humani generis will go next, we can only guess, and havg. already strengthened N. York, we are preparing with 10,000 men well commanded, to meet them in Canada, the Capital of which Country still continues besieged by the Continental forces. It is curious to observe that whilst people here are disputing and hesitating about independancy, the Court by one bold Act of Parliament, and by a conduct the most extensively hostile, have already put the two Countries asunder—They think forever, and are therefore preparing the minds of the people of England for this event, by having hired Dean Tucker to prove the measure an eligible one.[1] As well, dear Sir, might a person expect to wash an Ethiopian white, as to remove the taint of despotism from the British Court. The vicious principle has pervaded every heart, perverted every head, and will govern every movement of that Body. The measure of British crimes is running over, and the barbarous spoliation of the East is crying to Heaven for vengeance against the Destroyers of the Human Race. Out of 8 Vessels from Whitehaven with provisions for their army, 7 have been taken and the 8th driven on shore. They are disgraced in the East and the North, and their friends beaten in the South. Were it not for their present Marine superiority, I do verily believe that N. America could give law to that proud imperious Island. Be so kind as give my compliments to your Son and inform him that I, as well as my brother, applied to Gen. Lee to receive Squire Landon as an Aid de Camp, but the General was already provided with two, Mr. Byrd & Mr. Morris, and two only were allowed by the Continent; but the General is willing to receive Mr. Carter into his family if he chooses to attend on his own expence as an Aid de Camp.[2] I wish you healthy and happy dear Sir for I am sincerely your affectionate friend,

Richard Henry Lee

P.S. If Mr. Carter chooses to go as above mentioned I shall be ready to furnish him with a letter to General Lee.

RC (MeHi).
  [1] See Richard Smith to Samuel Tucker, March 16, 1776, note 3.
  [2] See Francis Lightfoot Lee to Landon Carter, February 12, 1776, note 1.

Richard Henry Lee to Charles Lee

My Dear Friend,   Philadelphia, 1st April, 1776.
    I hope my former reasons for not delivering your letter to the President will meet your approbation.[1] Since I wrote you last, the Congress has appointed two Engineers for the Southern department, Mr John Stadler, now in Virginia, and the young German Massenbach whom you took with you from Baltimore.[2] They have also appointed Monsr Dohicky Arundel (who I expect will deliver you this) a Captain of Artillery in the Continental service with the following resolve, "That General Lee be directed to set on foot the raising a Company of Artillery, and that it be recommended to the Convention or Committee of Safety of Virginia to appoint the other officers of said Company of Artillery."[3] The better opinion now is, that Gen. Howe will rest awhile at Halifax, and embrace the first opportunity of pushing up to the relief of Quebec, and we are making ready to meet him there. I think the number of men already ordered for that country amounts to more than 10,000. We are informed that General Howe carried off all his American prisoners with him in chains. The people of New-York have collected and burnt publickly every copy they could find of Plain Truth,[4] and they have treated the Effigies of Tryon in the same manner. The arrival of 10 tons of powder and a considerable quantity of sail cloth to the Eastward, is all the news we have here. Farewell my dear friend, I wish you happy, healthy, and successful.   Richard Henry Lee

[P.S.] Cato still continues to write nonsense,[5] and the other Tories to forge lies about the Commissioners.

MS not found; reprinted from *NYHS Collections*, 4(1871): 367–68.
  [1] See Richard Henry Lee to Charles Lee, March 25, 1776.
  [2] See *JCC*, 4:241. For the identity of Massenbach (Felix Lewis Maussenbaugh), see *Md. Archives*, 11:173, 274.
  [3] See *JCC*, 4:212.
  [4] *Plain Truth: Addressed To The Inhabitants of America, Containing Remarks on a Late Pamphlet, entitled Common Sense . . . By Candidus . . .* (Philadelphia: R. Bell, 1776). For James Chalmers' authorship of this pamphlet, see T. R. Adams, *American Independence*, p. 152.
  [5] Rev. William Smith, provost of the College of Philadelphia, was the author of the "Cato" letters, which appeared in the Pennsylvania newspapers during March and April 1776 and are in *Am. Archives*, 4th ser. 5:125–27, 188–90, 443–46, 514–17, 542–46, 839–43, 850–53, and 1049–51. See also John Adams to Abigail Adams, April 28, 1776.

John Adams to Joseph Palmer

Dear sir   Philadelphia April 2d. 1776
  This will go by my worthy Brother Dana who is returned, as he went, a very good Whigg and much more abundantly.
  I hope he will be appointed a Judge or Attorney General immediately, as he is extreamly well qualified for Either.
  Since my return to this Place, I have lived in tolerable good Humour with our old Friend, notwithstanding the rash Anger he expressed in certain Letters.[1]
  I have had two Conversations between him and me concerning his seat upon a certain Bench. He has not said positively, but perhaps, if the Place should be left open till his Return, which probably will not be very long for a Visit at least, he may be induced to accept. For my own Part I wish he might. I have ever lived in Friendship with him, untill in the Month of August last he was pleased to quarrell with me, chiefly on Account of some Important Points of Rank, I suppose. But these Seem to be blown over.
  The Evacuation of Boston is a great Event, and if wisely improved will be a decisive one. But We must fortify the Harbour. I must intreat you to let me know, with what Quantities of Powder you are likely to be Supplied and what Cannon you have, or can get, or what you want.
  Perhaps we might obtain some assistance from the Continent in fortifying that Harbour, if We knew what assistance you would want. Let Us know and We will try.
  The Tories, I think will never loose Sight of that Town; if they can possibly, prevail on the Ministry to set on foot another Expedition against it, they will. They will pursue it with a Bitterness and Severity, inexpressible.

Fortify, Fortify, and never let them get in again.

We continue Still between Hawk and Buzzard. Some People yet expect Commissioners to treat with Congress—and to offer a Chart blanc. All declare if they do not come impowered to treat with Us, and grant Us our Bill of Rights, in every Iota, they will hesitate no longer.

I wish I could enter into an unreserved Detail—But I dare not. I think We shall do pretty well. The Conventions are now about meeting every where, and We expect assistance from them.

In great Haste Adieu.

[*P.S.*] Pray let Us know how much Powder you have furnished to the Continental Army, from the Magazines of the Province, or of Town stocks. Because if We knew how much, We would endeavour to have it reimbursed to you. We must get those Town stocks replaced and the Colonial Magazine replenished.[2]

RC (Sol Feinstone, Washington Crossing, Pa., 1974). In Adams' hand, though not signed.

[1] For additional details on the feud between Adams and Robert Treat Paine, see Paine to Joseph Hawley, January 1, notes 1 and 2; and Paine to the Massachusetts Council, January 1, 1776, note 2.

[2] The Massachusetts General Court had already prepared and forwarded such an account to General Washington. Elbridge Gerry to James Warren, March 6, 1776, note 2.

Samuel Adams to Joseph Palmer

My Dear sir,   Philad April 2 1776

I am yet indebted to you for the obliging Letter I receivd from you some Months ago.[1] The Subject of it was principally concerning a young Gentleman whom I personally know, and whose Merit in my opinion intitles him to singular Notice from his Country. This may seem like Flattery—you may be assured it is not—nor indeed do I know how to flatter. Words however are oftentimes, though spoken in Sincerity, but Wind. If I had had it in my Power substantially to have servd that young Gentleman you would have long ago heard from me. The Want of that Opportunity caused me to lay down my Pen diverse times after I had even begun to write to you. You will not therefore, I hope, construe my long Delay to the least Want of due Respect for you.

Some Advantages arose to our Colony by the Congress adopting the Army raisd in New England the last Spring; but among other Circumstances attending it, this was one, namely, that it being now a continental Army, the Gentlemen of all Colonies had a Right to and put in for a Share in behalf of their Friends in filling up the various Offices. By this Means, it was thought, that military Knowledge & Experience as well as the military Spirit would spread through the Colonies; and

APRIL 2, 1776

besides, that they would all consider themselves the more interrested in the Success of our Army, and in providing for its Support. But then there was less Room for Persons belonging to the Colonies which had first raisd the Army, who were well worthy of Notice. Many of our Friends were discontented who did not advert to this as the true Cause why they were not promoted. When the Quartermaster was appointed, I question whether any of your Friends knew, I am sure I did not know it, that the Gentleman I have referred to had sustaind that office; there was therefore no designd Neglect of him here. Mr M[ifflin]s Character stood so high that no Gentleman could hesitate to put him into a place which was understood to be vacant & which he was so well qualified to fill. The Truth is, we have never had that Information from our Friends at Watertown of the State of things which we have thought we had good reason to expect from them. I do assure you I have often been made acquainted with the State of Affairs in our Colony, as well as I could from Letters shown to me by Gentlemen of other Colonies. I do not mention this without duly considering that the Attention of our Friends must have been turnd to a great Variety of Business.

I heartily congratulate you upon the sudden and important Change of our Affairs, in the Removal of the Barbarians from the Capital. We owe our grateful Acknowledgments to him who is, as he is frequently stiled in sacred Writ, "The Lord of Hosts." We have not yet been informd with Certainty what Course the Enemy have steerd. I hope we shall be upon our Guard against future Attempts. Will not Care be immediately taken to fortify the Harbour, and thereby prevent the Entrance of Ships of War ever hereafter? But I am called off and must conclude abruptly.

Adieu my Friend, and be assured I am affectionately, yours,

S Adams

RC (MeHi). FC (NN). RC damaged; missing portions supplied from FC.
¹ Not found.

Maryland Delegates to the Maryland Council of Safety

Gent.   Phila. 2d April 1776.

Mr Arch. Buchanan could not take the Money as he expected & promised. Mr Ringgold collected & brought up here 160.17.6. It has been delivered into the Treasury; besides the Charge for that Sum we have delivered 4000 Dollars to Mr Ringgold. W P sets out in a few Days. He will take with him the rest of the Money and we hope the plates & that the paper may be sent off about the same Time. We have nothing that can be depended on as to the extent of the powers the Committees are to be invested with. Whilst we are in Suspense on this Head we think no Step of Consequence could be prudently taken and therefore do not expect our Convention will continue long or go fully into Business. We could wish if agreeable to them that there might be an Adjournmt. till about the 20th of May with a Continuance of the present existing powers if they think proper. We shall be obliged to you if you will cause Affidavits to be made and transmitted to us of the Time of the Capture and recapture of Hudson's Ship[1] that we may get the Salvage, the Quantum of which depends on the Time she was in possession of the Tender, ascertained and paid. We were desired to let the Claim which we made of Salvage rest till the Event of another Effect was known. We hope the Ship is now out of the Bay.

We are Gent., Your most obedt. Servts.

Ths. Johnson Junr,	Wm. Paca
R. Alexander	T. Stone

RC (MdAA). Written by Johnson and signed by Johnson, Alexander, Paca, and Stone.

[1] For information on the "Capture & Recapture of [Jonathan] Hudson's Ship" by the *Defence*, Capt. James Nicholson, see Maryland Delegates to the Maryland Council of Safety, March 26, 1776, note.

Robert Treat Paine to Joseph Palmer

Philadelphia, April 2d, 1776.

The evacuation of Boston by the king's troops, and the repossession of it by the right owners, agitates my mind with a thousand queries and calculations. As yet we know so little of the state in which they have left the town in general, or the possessions of individuals in particular, that I do not consider myself as yet come to my feelings about the matter; amidst all the joys there must be many scenes of distressing wo. I have not the least reason to doubt the general court will direct many circumstances relating to this occurrence with wisdom and expedition; if, therefore, I mention some matters that occur to me, I trust you will attribute it rather to my desire to help in the common cause, than to an inclination to direct. Would it not be serviceable to appoint some honest, skilful persons, to take an account of all damage done to the houses, furniture, goods, merchandise, and property of every kind, and by whom done, as near as may be; this may be applied to two uses at least, first, to make a fair representation to the world of the injury done us; (what use this may be applied to we do not yet know;) and also sufferers may expect and receive, perhaps, some compensation, which, without such an early estimate, may be very unequally distributed.

I wish, also, that those persons who have tarried in town through the whole siege, who are most capable, might be called upon to draw up as correct a narrative of the whole proceedings of the enemy, and the distress of the inhabitants, and particularly the behaviour of the tories, collectively and individually, as may be. I should think it by no means advisable to destroy our lines as yet; if it be in the power of the exiled tories to cause the town to be again attacked they will effect it; I doubt not there will be great consultations to fortify the harbour against men-of-war; if we have cannon enough it may be done. I wish much to know what is become of the cannon that belonged to the castle; I fear they are carried off or destroyed. Those cannon which they have spiked up may easily be bored out [. . . .] [1]

The scene of action is only changed; the efforts of the enemy will be more vigorous elsewhere. I mention this, because I can easily conceive, that people who have been long harassed are too apt to sink into ease when immediate danger seems to be withdrawn. Canada and New-York are now grand objects of attention, and very interesting to New-England.

Pray be kind enough to send me as particular an account of the state of affairs in Boston as you conveniently can; who of the tories are left behind; how they behave, and what they say for themselves? Whether Master Lowel [2] and other prisoners were carried off? whether they have taken away the bells? whether any quantity of merchandise is left? any sulphur or other matters that we want? any cash? are the records of the province, superior and inferior and probate courts, left? Have they carried off the lifeless carcase of the charter, as one of *their own party* that was slain, or have they left it putrefying to contaminate the air? These, and such other matters as you may think worthy of note, will be very agreeable to me, not merely as matters of curiosity, which in this case I think is very natural, but as facts which may be of service to know; the place they have gone to is a material fact.

MS not found; reprinted from *New York Review and Atheneum Magazine* 2 (April 1826): 400–402.
  [1] Ellipsis in Tr.
  [2] James Lovell.

Robert Treat Paine to Philip Schuyler

My dear Sr,   Philadelphia April 2d. 1776
Every since the receipt of your kind letter in Jany.[1] I have been determined to write you in special refferrence to your [. . .]scious paragraph on the dear Dulcinea, [but] innumerable intervening objects have

susp[ended] the execution of it till Time the destro[yer of] all earthly affairs has deprived me of my Subject. Alass the vestal Virgin is no more! The Nuptial Alter has received the Sacrifice & the being to whom it is offered I dare say, smells a sweet savour, the Keys are delivered up & the sweet Casket may not be opened but by him who possesses them. What you will do for a toast I dont know. I sincerely commisserate you. I believe it must be to her memory.

Salt petre, Sulphur, lead, cannon, musketts, like our dayly bread should never be out of our attention; the success in making Salt petre in Massachusetts & Connetticut is exceeding all expectation. We have likewise exceeding good amounts from Virginia. Other Colonies are also begginning. It is very clear, if we once induce farmers & private families to make it as they do in New England we shall have enough very soon to expend gun powder as freely as we please. I take the freedom to send you some newspapers which contain the successful Method of making it in New England. I doubt not you will distribute them with your authoritative injunctions to put it into immediate & vigorous execution. Please to present my Compliments to Mr. Dewar & furnish him with [. . . .] I suppose a tea drawn from a mixture of Ashes & Stone Lime will answer the purpose mentioned in the discription. Some say that Lime water only will do, & some say that the stone lime may be put into the nitrous water & let settle. I mention these matters because I Suppose Lime stone is very plenty near Mr. Dewar's & it may be easily tryed & in some places may be cheaper & more easily got than ashes.

We are like to suffer for want of Sulphur. If it lays in your way to have Brimstone Hill near Cherry Valley examined it might be serviceable.

I hope these will find you & your good family in health & happiness. Please to make my best Respects to them.

The evacuation of Boston will doubtless open a new scene, but where, as yet we don't conjecture. Our business is to be armed at all points. No. Carolina has surprised us with their heroism.[2] I believe every Colony will give a good account of their political Faith.

I hope in the revolution of human affairs we may at Sometime meet in peace & joy, but should so desired an event be denied me, when the trials of human affairs are ended, may we meet in the land of Heroes.

That felicity may Surround & never leave you is the wish of yr friend & hble Servt, R T Paine

RC (NN)
[1] Schuyler's letter of January 24 is in the Paine Papers at MHi.
[2] Paine is undoubtedly referring to the victory of North Carolina troops over a loyalist force at Moore's Creek Bridge on February 27. See Richard Smith's Diary, March 21, 1776.

Secret Committee Minutes of Proceedings

April 2d. 1776

At a meeting of the C[ommitte]e of Secy. Present Robt. Morris, Ths. McKean, J. Alsop, P. Livingston, R. H. Lee, Jos. Hewes & Robt. Alexander. A letter from Nich Browne & John Brown dated Providence March 20th [1] being producd & read, Orderd that the Chairman answer it, expressg. that the Come are glad to hear of the arrival of the goods mentioned therein. When the Marine Come. determine, a disposition of it will be orderd, in the mean time they may send us an Invoice of the cost &c. Linens are ordered Otherwise. A letter from Mr. J. Langdon was read dated Portsmouth 19 March. Orderd that the Chairman answer it,[2] informg. Mr. Langdon that if the Genl. gives orders for the Powder, it is to be deliverd, if not, to wait the orders of this Come. Issued an order on R[ober]t Towers Com[missar]y to deliver Messr Wm. Henry & Co. 15 lb powdr. to prove some Muskets agreable to a Res. of C[ongress] 29th March. R. Towers Comy. having deliverd our late Chairman Saml. Ward Esqr. (when sick) 5 returns of powder & arms dated from 10th to 30th March they did not appear to the Come. before this day, but are now in our possession.

The Commissary has made us the followg. return of Powder in the Magazine dated the 31st of March

Lushes 2 q[uarte]r Casks		50 lb
Bayard & Co. 89 h[alf] bar.		4628
Hazlehurts 5 qr Casks		135
Eves 8 brrl., 13 ha. brrs., 14 qr. barrs.		1800 lb
	Total	6613.

A Charter Party with J. Tucker Master of the Sloop Betsey for sd. Sloop was signd by a Quorum.[3]

MS (MH).
[1] This letter is in Clark, *Naval Documents*, 4:419–20. For the committee's reply, see Secret Committee to Nicholas Brown and John Brown, April 3, 1776.
[2] See Secret Committee to John Langdon, April 4, 1776.
[3] See Secret Committee Minutes of Proceedings, March 27; and Robert Morris to Silas Deane, March 30, 1776.

William Whipple to John Langdon

My Dear Sir,   Philadelphia 2d April 1776.

Your favor of the 19th March I rec'd yesterday. I heartily rejoice at the arrival of the two powder vessels, but you don't tell me where they are from, what news they bring, what is become of the other vessels &c. What think you of the retreat of the Barbarians from Boston—it will be a pretty story to tell their master. What's the general opinion with you of the notable commissioners that are coming over. I hope either Col. Bartlett, or you will be here to receive their Low Mightenesses. Some people here (I mean out of doors) are for shutting them up the moment they land. However, I hope they will be treated with civility and sent back with a flea in the ear, for I cannot possibly think they are commissioned for any good, nor can I yet realize their coming. There is a forty gun ship now laying at the Capes; the brig Lexington went down before we heard of her being there. We have now a ship fitting out that will go down in a few days. These vessels were intended to clear the coast of the tenders that are so troublesome. Admiral Hopkins was at New Providence the 4th inst. where he finds a great number of cannon, say 200 and a large quantity of ball, but they had sent off all their powder except 14 barrels; he'll take all the military stores.[1] The North Carolina people have taken 1800 stand of arms from the rebels there and found a chest of money in a stable, said to contain £15,000 sterg. I hope Hopkins will give a good account of Dunmore, Campbell, or Martin, or all of them before he returns. I hope you'll be able to get your anchors at Boston. Don't know where the guns will come from, but suppose from Providence where they are casting cannon with success. Just heard of the arrival of a considerable quantity of duck at Rhode Island; the ships building there and at Newbury are supplied, so I imagine you may be supplied from thence. There is about 4 1/2 tons powder lately arrived at Rhode Island and about the same quantity in Virginia. The mills going on briskly so I hope we shall be well supplied with that article. Several large quantities which were expected, it's to be feared have fallen into the enemy's hands. Tell Dr Brackett to write to me and let me know how the politics of Portsmouth stand. Can they yet reconcile themselves to that illustrious stranger that was so much feared.[2] Common Sense has made all the Southern Colonies his friend, and I hope the Northern Colonies will soon open their arms to receive him. It's my opinion *under the rose* that the salvation of America depends on him. More of that hereafter.

Your assured friend &c,   Wm. Whipple

Tr (DLC). RC (Ronald von Klaussen, state of Florida, 1976).
[1] The New Providence expedition is discussed in Nathan Miller, *Sea of Glory, the Continental Navy Fights for Independence, 1775–1783* (New York: David McKay Co., 1974), pp. 107–15.
[2] "That illustrious stranger" was undoubtedly the idea of American independence.

John Adams to James Warren

Dear sir   April 3. 1776
    As foreign Affairs become every day more interesting to Us no Point

should be Spared to acquire a thorough Knowledge of them, and as the inclosed Extract contains some Observations which are new to me, I thought it might not be uninteresting to you.

Howe has put 3000 Troops on board of Transports, which lie or at least lay last Saturday at Staten Island. Whether this is a Feint, or a Serious Maneuvre, with Intention to go to the Eastern shore of Cheasapeak Bay, as they give out I dont know, or whether they Aim at this City. I rather Suspect they mean another Course, i.e., up Hudsons River but Time will discover.

For Gods Sake and the Lands Sake send along your Troops. They are wanted very much, I hope General Washington has informed you how much. Troops are now coming from North Carolina, Virginia and Maryland. If they come here We shall have a scuffle for this City. The Languor of New England surprizes me. If there had been half the Energy in those Governments that there was two years ago, Howe would now have been in Another World or the most miserable Man in this.

RC (MHi). In Adams' hand, though not signed.

Samuel Adams to Samuel Cooper

My dear Friend   Philade April 3 1776
I lately recd a very obliging Letter from you for which I now return you my hearty Thanks. I wish your Leisure would admit of your frequently favoring me with your Thoughts of our publick Affairs. I do assure you I shall make use of them, as far as my Ability shall extend, to the Advantage of our Country. If you please, I will employ a few Minutes in giving you my own Ideas, grounded on the best Intelligence I have been able to obtain.

Notwithstanding Shame and Loss attended the Measures of the British Court the last Summer and Fall, yet by the latest Accounts recd from our Friends in that Country, it appears that they are determined to persevere. They then reckond (in December) upon having 20,000 Troops in America for the next Campaign. Their Estimate was thus. 6000 in Boston—7000 to go from Ireland—3000 Highlanders raising under General Fraizer and the rest to be in Recruits. Of the 7000 from Ireland, we are told that 3000 were to sail for Virginia and North Carolina & were expected to be in that Coast in March or the Begining of April. It is probable then that the Ministry have not quitted the Plan which they had agreed upon above a twelvemonth ago; which was, to take Possession of New York—make themselves Masters of Hudsons River & the Lakes, thereby securing Canada and the Indians—cut off all Communication between the Colonies Northward & Southward of Hudsons River, and thus to subdue the former in hopes by instigating the Negroes to make the others an easy Prey. Our Success, a great Part of which they had not then heard of, it is to be hoped has rendered this Plan impracticable; yet it is probable that the main Body of these Troops is designd to carry it into Execution, while the rest are to make a Diversion in the Southern Colonies. Those Colonies, I think, are sufficiently provided for. Our Safety very much depends upon our Vigilance & Success in N York & Canada. Our Enemies did not neglect Hudsons River the last year. We know that one of their Transports arrivd at N York, but Gage, seizd with a Panick orderd that & the other Transports destind for that Place, to Boston. I have ever thought it to be their favorite Plan; not only because it appeard to me to be dictated by sound Policy, but because from good Intelligence which I receivd from England the last Winter, they revivd it after it had been broken in upon by Gage, and sent Tryon to New York to remove every obstacle in the Way of landing the Troops there, and to cooperate with Carleton in The Execution of it.

The Kings Troops have now abandoned Boston, on which I sincerely congratulate you. We have not yet heard what Course they have steerd. I judge for Hallifax. They may return if they hear that you are off your Guard—or probably they may go up St Lawrence River as early as the Season will admit of it. Does it not behove N England to secure herself from future Invasions, while the Attention of Congress is turnd to N York & Canada. We seem to have the Game in our own hands; if we do not play it well, Misfortune will be the Effect of our Negligence and Folly.

The British Court sollicited the Assistance of Russia; but we are informd that they faild of it through the Interposition of France by the Means of Sweden. The ostensible Reason on the Part of Russia was, that there was no Cartel settled between Great Britain and America; the Want of which will make every Power reluctant in lending their Troops. France is attentive to this Struggle and wishes for a Seperation of the two Countries. I am in no Doubt that she would with Chearfulness, openly lend her Aid to promote it, if America would declare herself free and independant; for I think it is easy to see what great though different Effects it would have in both those Nations. Britain would no longer have it in her Power to oppress.

Is not America already independent? Why then not declare it? Upon whom was she ever supposd to be dependent, but upon that Nation whose most barbarous Usage of her, & that in multiplied Instances and for a long time has renderd it absurd ever to put Confidence in it, & with which she is at this time in open War. Can Nations at War be said to be dependent either upon the other? I ask then again, why not declare for Independence? Because say some, it will forever shut the Door of Reconciliation. Upon what Terms will Britain be reconciled with America? If we may take the confiscating Act of Parliamt or the Kings last Proclamation for our Rule to judge by, she will be reconciled upon

IN CONGRESS,

APRIL 3, 1776.

RESOLVED, That every Perfon intending to fet forth and fit out a Private Ship or Veffel of War, and applying for a Commiffion or Letters of Marque and Reprifal for that Purpofe, fhall produce a Writing, fubfcribed by him, containing the Name, and Tonnage or Burthen of the Ship or Veffel, the Number of her Guns, with their Weight of Metal, the Name and Place of Refidence of the Owner or Owners, the Names of the Commander and other Officers, the Number of the Crew, and the Quantity of Provifions and Warlike Stores; which Writing fhall be delivered to the Secretary of Congrefs, or to the Clerk of the Houfe of Reprefentatives, Convention or Council or Committee of Safety of the Colony in which the Ship or Veffel fhall be, to be tranfmitted to the faid Secretary, and fhall be regiftered by him. And that the Commander of the Ship or Veffel, before the Commiffion or Letters of Marque and Reprifal may be granted, fhall, together with fufficient Sureties, feal and deliver a Bond, in the Penalty of Five Thoufand Dollars, if the Veffel be of One Hundred Tons, or under, or Ten Thoufand Dollars, if of greater Burthen, payable to the PRESIDENT of the CONGRESS in Truft for the Ufe of the United Colonies, with Condition in the Form following, *to wit*,

" The Condition of this Obligation is fuch, That if the above-
" bounden   who is Commander of the
" called   belonging to
" of   in the Colony of   mounting
"   Carriage Guns, and navigated by   Men,
" and who hath applied for a Commiffion or Letters of Marque
" and Reprifal, to arm, equip and fet forth to Sea the faid
" as a Private Ship of War, and to make Captures of Britifh Vef-
" fels and Cargoes, fhall not exceed or tranfgrefs the Powers and
" Authorities which fhall be contained in the faid Commiffion, but
" fhall in all Things obferve and conduct himfelf and govern his
" Crew by and according to the fame, and certain Inftructions
" therewith to be delivered, and fuch other Inftructions as may
" hereafter be given to him; and fhall make Reparation for all
" Damages fuftained by any Mifconduct or unwarrantable Pro-
" ceedings of himfelf, or the Officers or Crew of the faid
" Then this Obligation fhall be void, or elfe remain in Force.
" *Sealed and Delivered*
" *in Prefence of* "

Which Bond fhall be lodged with the faid Secretary of Congrefs.

By Order of Congrefs,

John Hancock PRESIDENT.

Privateer Commission—April 3, 1776, Resolve of Congress

our abjectly submitting to Tyranny, and asking and receiving Pardon for resisting it. Will this redound to the Honor or the Safety of America? Surely no. By such a Reconciliation she would not only in the most shameful Manner acknowledge the Tyranny, but most wickedly, as far as would be in her Power, prevent her Posterity from ever hereafter resisting it. But the Express now waits for this Letter. I must therefore break off. I will write to you again by another opportunity. Pay my Respects to the Speaker pro Temp. [William Cooper] and tell him that I have never received a Line from him since I have been in this City. My Respects are also due to Mr S P S [Samuel P. Savage], from whom I yesterday receivd a kind Letter, which I shall duly acknowledge to him when I have Leisure to write. Give me Leave to assure you that I am with the most friendly Regards for your Lady & Family very affectionately yours   S A

FC (NN).

John Hancock to the Commanding Officer

Sir,   Philadelphia April 3d. 1776.
    I have it in Command from Congress to direct, that upon the Application of Silas Deane Esqr you furnish him with a Guard of twenty Men under a proper Officer, to proceed with him to the Capes, from thence to be returned.[1] You will therefore comply with this Requisition, immediately on his Application.[2]
    I am, Sir, your most obed Sevt.   J. H. Prst.

LB (DNA: PCC, item 12A). Addressed: "To the officer commanding the Continental Troops or the officer commanding where this Letter shall be produced."
    [1] For information on Deane's mission, see John Alsop et al. to Silas Deane, March 1, 1776.
    [2] This day Hancock also directed "The officer Commanding the Battalion of Continental Troops in Delaware Government" to order "two Companies of the Continental Troops under your Command to March to Lewis Town, there to do Duty & promote the Service of the Continent untill the further order of Congress." See PCC, item 12A; Am. Archives, 4th ser. 5:774; and JCC, 4:251.

John Hancock to Thomas Cushing

Dear Sir   Philadelphia 3d April 1776.
    Your favr. of 18th March I duly Rec'd; Congratulate you on Possessing Boston, and that your House is in good order and Additions made to your Furniture. Am Glad to hear the Ships go on so well,

pray Continue your Exertions to the uttermost. I have an Accott. of the Arrival of some Duck at Providence in Capt. Comstock, what you want to make up the proper Quantity you can purchase there.[1] Let me know every Deficiency & as far as it may be had here it shall be Sent you. I want much to be with you, but I cannot with propriety request Leave at present, I must therefore Submit. I hope you have Dispos'd of my Ship at Salem, do be attentive to it for me. I think General Washington & the Army have great merit; Inclos'd I Send you Copy of the Letter of Thanks I am Commanded to Transmit him by this Express.[2] General Heath is Arriv'd at New York. We have no Accott. of the Destination of the Troops. Do give me a very particular Accott. of the State of Boston, the Tories &c, & what you are doing at the Assembly. How stands the Militia Bill? The Inclos'd for Capt. Cazneau please to Cause to be deliver'd him. I have my hands full of Business, I must Dispatch the Express.

Adieu. Mrs. Hancock joines me in best Regards to you, your Lady & Family, and I am, Dr Sir, Your very hum sevt,

                                                           John Hancock

[*P.S.*] I wish you would write me every Post.

5 oClock Tolls. A French Vessell is just Arriv'd with Twelve hundred Barrells of Powder.

RC (MHi).
    [1] For this account of the arrival at Howlands Ferry of assorted naval stores, including "193 Bolts Roushie Duck," see Nicholas Brown to the Secret Committee, March 20, 1776, in Clark, *Naval Documents*, 4:419–20. See also Secret Committee to Nicholas Brown and John Brown, this date.
    [2] Hancock's April 2 letter to Washington is printed in *JCC*, 4:248–49.

Massachusetts Delegates to
the President of the Massachusetts Council

Sir   Philadelphia April 3d 1776
    The Congress being Inform'd by a Letter from Genl. Washington, that two Thousand of the Continental Troops at Cambridge & Roxbury are deficient in Fire Arms, & that he has not been able to Purchase the Same from the Inhabitants or obtain them from the Assemblies of the New England Colonies, have Directed the General to make Returns to the Assemblies of the Numbers of men Inlisted from their Respective Colonies that are destitute of Arms, & to Dismiss from the service such of them as cannot be thus supplied.[1]
    In Consequence of this, the Delegates from Massachusetts Bay think it their Duty to write to your Honour on the subject, & thro you to

Inform the Honl. Assembly, that for the better Regulating the army & Promoting the Means of Defence, the United Colonies are divided into Districts or Departments, and are to supply with Fire Arms the Continental Troops that shall be Rais'd by them Respectively & be in Want thereof.[2]

The eastern District Consists of the N E Colonies, who during the whole of this Conflict have discover'd the firmest Attachment to American Liberty & the warmest Zeal & Ardor in it's Defence. Should they at any Time fail in this, or Nelgect to Supply their Quota's of Men & Arms they must in Consequence hereof be the greatest Sufferers & may infer on themselves the Censure of the rest of the Continent.

We are fully Sensible that the late Difficulties of Raising Men & Procuring Arms in the Eastern District are justly Chargeable on the Mode adopted for Establishing the Army at Cambridge, but We hope for a Different Regulation in future, & shall use our utmost Endeavours that in any New Levies of Men the General Assemblies may have the Direction of the same subject to the Controul of Congress.

We think it necessary to Inform the Honl. Assembly that in some of the Colonies all Persons whatever are Prohibited from Purchasing or selling Fire Arms to be carried from the same. The safety of the Eastern district may Possibly require the like Precaution.

We rejoice at the Success Attending the Measures of Massa. Bay for promoting the Manufactg of Military Stores & think that a steady perseverance in the same Plan is the wisest Mode that the Colonies can Adopt for a permanent Establishment of their Rights & Liberties. We therefore hope that diligent Enquiry will be made for all the Manufactorers of Fire Arms in the Colony, Who from Want of Means or other Circumstances are unemploy'd in this Business, & that Publick Works will be Erected for them with suitable Encouragement to engage them in the Service.

We sincerely Congratulate the honorable Assembly on the happy Recovery of Boston from our Enemies & are fully Assured that this Opportunity of fortifying the Harbour will be successfully Improv'd & thereby an Assylum secured for the Ships of War & other Navigation of the Continent.[3] We presume that Genl. Washington will see the Necessity of such a Measure & order some of the Cannon brought from Ticonderoga to be Appropriated to this Purpose, but should it otherwise happen we think there can be no Objection to the Assemblys taking such of the Cannon & Carriages at Cambridge as they have supplied & deducting from their Accounts against the Continent the charge of any Part thereof which they may have made in said Accounts; more especially as New York is better supplied with Cannon than New England, And the Reason there is to Expect another Vissit from the Enemy in that Quarter, Renders every Precaution & preparation Necessary to Receive them.

We have the Honor to be Sir with great Respect your most Obedt. &
very Huml. Servants,   John Hancock   Rob T Paine

                                Samuel Adams   Elbridge Gerry

                                John Adams

RC (M-Ar). In a clerical hand, and signed by John Adams, Samuel Adams, Gerry,
Hancock, and Paine. Endorsed by John Lowell, deputy secretary of the Massachusetts Council: "In Council Apr. 15th. 1776 Read & Sent down."

    [1] For Congress' March 21 decision to send this directive to Washington, see *JCC*,
4:223. Washington's February 9 letter to Hancock explaining his arms shortages
and his February 10 appeal to the Massachusetts General Court are in Washington,
Writings (Fitzpatrick), 4:314, 326–27.
    [2] For congressional action on the creation of military districts, see *JCC*, 4:132–33,
157, 174.
    [3] The Massachusetts General Court had already appointed a committee to study
the defense of Boston Harbor, which made a preliminary report on April 3. Two
days later another committee was appointed to direct the fortification of the harbor.
Am. Archives, 4th ser. 5:1260–62, 1270.

Robert Treat Paine to William Whiting

Dear Sir,   Philada. April 3d. 1776
    I should have gratified my self in corresponding with you on the sub-
ject of saltpetre making, but that I have always been uncertain whether
my Letters would reach you. But as you have now got the works in a
good way, I may expect this will find you at General Court; I am exceeding happy to find your great success, & have laboured abundantly
to promote the same in all the Colonies. I trust my labours have not been
in vain. I have lately caused your method to be reprinted & have sent
it to all the Colonies where I supposed it was not known,[1] & procured
a great number of Copies to send to private persons, as I made an
Introduction I send you one for your inspection. I have been all winter
sending to particular persons other methods which I was possessed of,
& I delayed a republication of yours in order to have one matter explained, I wrote to somebody our way to enquire of you but have had
no answer. It is this Vizt. all earth that contains Saltpetre, more or less
contains marine Salts; all methods of making Saltpetre beside yours
take notice of the method of seperating it; if the fermentation occasioned
by mixing the lyes produces this effect, I wish it had been mentioned;
in yr first letter to me you mention the using allum to promote the refining, but you do not mention it in your proposed process; in short Sr.
I republished it upon the credit of its great Success presuming the
Marine Salt would seperate though you do not say how; I wish to know
of you what is the true proof that there is no marine Salt adhering to the
Petre. If it deflagrates without crackling, is that a sure sign? Suppose

your ashes lye is made with a portion of Stone or other lime, will it answer? It is said that some have substituted lime water intirely, & that some have put Stone lime into the nitrous lye to good effect, this may be advantagious where lime is more plenty than ashes. For the good of the Common Cause I wish to have a particular answer to these querys.

I think my Freind it must be matter of great pleasure to us (who had so hard work to set this manufacture a going in the begginning of it, in our Colony) to observe our prodigous success, I reflect upon my labours with great satisfaction, & the world knows your merit.

I hope these will find you in health & happiness, I doubt not you'll use your endeavour to have the Saltpetre manufacture so established as that we may never more be disposed to import gunpowder.

Pray write me what Success there is in working nitre beds or Walls, some judgment should be formed of the time they take to impregnate.

I hope to hear soon from you; mean while I am yr freind & Servt,

R T Paine

RC (MHi).
[1] Paine apparently enclosed instructions for Whitings' method of making saltpetre in the several letters that he sent to the provincial governments in March and April. See Committee of Congress to the Maryland Convention, March 28, 1776. See also Paine to William Whiting, November 6, 1775.

Secret Committee to
Nicholas Brown and John Brown

Gentn.   Philada. April 3d. 1776

We have received your letter of the 20th Ulto. directed to the late chairman of this Committee[1] & are well pleased to learn thereby, that the Sloop you first dispatched to the West Indies In Consequence of your Contract[2] with the Continent was returned and has brought in 193 Bolts of Russia Duck, 43 p[iece]s Russia Sheeting, one pair of Swivell Guns, 14 Small Arms, 12 Ct of Powder & 30 Ct Ball, all which we hope you have long since got safe Landed, and you will please to keep the same in your Possession untill the Marine Committee shall determine how the same are to be disposed of, when You will receive directions from them or us. We desire you will furnish us with Invoices & bills of Loading for the cargoes you export on Account of the Continent, Acct Sales when you receive them, also Invoices of the return Cargoes & the Acct Current with those that transact the business abroad that we may in due time have the whole transactions regularly before us.[3] We have not yet heard of the arrival of the Rich Jews Brigt. which you mention, but if such a one sailed we hope she may soon appear. We thank you for the Account of the arrival of Arms & Ammunition which we suppose is on Private account as you do not say they are for the Public.

Linens have been ordered from different parts in Virtue of other Contracts & we have no orders from Congress to Import Hemp; therefore you had best Confine your Importations to the Articles you Contracted for, unless you find a surplus of Money arise abroad on the Sale of your Cargoes & in that case you may increase the quantity of Goods or order such Surplus in Arms & Ammunition. We are sirs, your hble Servants. By order of the Secret Committee,

Robt Morris, Chair Man

RC (RPJCB). Written and signed by Morris.

[1] See Secret Committee Minutes of Proceedings, April 2, 1776, note 1.

[2] This was the contract made with John Brown on December 26, 1775. Nicholas Brown bought a one third interest on January 20, 1776. See Secret Committee Minutes of Proceedings, December 26, 1775; and Clark, *Naval Documents*, 3:879–80.

[3] The Browns' response of July 15, 1776, is in Clark, *Naval Documents*, 5:1083–84.

John Hancock to Philip Schuyler

Dear Sir   Philadelphia 4th April 1776.

I have now only Time to forward the inclosed Resolves;[1] & to request that You will send an Account of the Lead at Ticonderoga,[2] that Article being Much wanted here, am in Hopes that You will be able to spare some.

I take the Freedom to mention to You Capt. Romans the Bearer of this. He is appointed Capt. of an Artillery Company but in the Opinion of Many his Abilities are not fully Call'd forth, he is said to be well skilled in the Engineering Branch of which on Conversation, You will be the best Judge, & I dare say, from my Knowledge of Your Disposition, so far as You find him Capable that You will be ready to recommend him & promote him. You will excuse this Mention.

I shall write You fully in a few Days, & am with Every Wish in Your Favor, Dear Sir Your very Humble Servant.

John Hancock Pt.

Tr (NN).

[1] These resolves, dealing with various features of military operations in Canada, were approved by Congress on March 25, 28, and 29. *JCC*, 4:236, 239, 240–41.

[2] See *JCC*, 4:246. Schuyler replied to this inquiry in a letter to Hancock of May 3, 1776. See PCC, item 153, 2:129–32; and *Am. Archives*, 4th ser. 5:1181–82.

Robert Morris to Silas Deane

Dr sir   Philada. 4 April 1776

I recd your Note at the State House[1] and on coming down here find your Conjecture about the Schooner is right. She is one that Collo Harrison fitted out in Maryland but I cannot find the Captain. Other People tell me she is leaky & sickly, however I will have her fitted quick as possible and sent down with particular orders to attend you if she gets down in time.

This however is uncertain and You must determine for yourself whether to wait for her or proceed without. You know how hard it will be to get the People on bd again but all the dispatch that is possible shall be made. I am most truely Yours &c,   Robt Morris

RC (CtHi).
[1] An extract of Deane's letter to Morris of this date, in which he speculates on the identity of the schooner *Wasp* just spotted and concludes that "We shall go from hence, the next Tide, if the Wind Moderates," is in Clark, *Naval Documents*, 4:665.

Secret Committee to John Langdon

Sir   Philada. April 4th. 1776

Your letters of the 14 [*and*] 19th Ulto directed to the late Saml. Ward Esqr. are now before me & have been read to the Secret Committee by whose order I now answer them.[1] We are sorry for the loss of the Brigt, Cap Shockford, but as things now stand we must expect many more losses of the same kind & think ourselves happy if a sufficient number does but return to keep the Continent supplyed with Arms, Ammunition & necessary Cloathing.

We rejoice however to find by your Second letter that Cap Peverly was returned with 6 to 7000 lb of Powder, which you were lodging in the magazine. Shoud the General give any orders for this Powder or any part of it, you will transmit us a Copy of his order & the receipt of those you deliver it to, in Virtue of such orders and observe the same Method with any other parcels you may receive on Continental Account. Shou'd the Genl. not give any orders the Powder must remain for the future orders of this Committee. We also desire to be furnished in due time with the Invoices of the outward & homeward Cargoes and with all the Accounts & Documents relative to the Contracts.[2] This is mentioned at present only to remind you that such will be wanted when the transactions are wound up.

You will find before this gets to hand, that the Congress have met your Wishes and granted Licenses for Privateering on our Enemys[3] but they have stopped rather short of the Mark, by not including West

India Property. We shall be glad to hear of the Success of the other Vessells you have dispatched & are to dispatch to fullfill the Contract, & thanking you for the other intelligence contained in Your letters remain sir Your Obedt hble Servants, By order of the Committee.

Robt Morris, Chair Man

RC (Capt. J. G. M. Stone, Annapolis, Md., 1973). Written and signed by Morris.

[1] See Secret Committee Minutes of Proceedings, March 26 and April 2, 1776.

[2] Langdon had made contracts with the Secret Committee on November 8, 1775, and February 20, 1776.

[3] See *JCC*, 4:229–33.

Commissioners to Canada to Israel Putnam

Sir,[1]   Off Constitution fort April 5th 1776
                                               On board The Rhode Island packett

We this Evening arrived here, and from Curiosity Mr Chase & Mr Carroll went ashore, and found the State of the fort as follows—3 Companies of Minute Men, Captain Moffats, Capt. Raymonds, & Capt. Wesners, Consisting of 5 Lieutenants, 6 Serjeants, 8 Corporals, 2 Drummers, a fifer and 102 privates. Mr Seth Marin 1st Lieutenant of Capt. Moffats Company has now the Command. On the South Bastion are 13, 6- & 1 9-pounder mounted. On the East Bastion are 7, 9- & 1 6-pounder mounted. There are 81 Quarter Barrells & 1 whole Barrell of powder. About one half of the privates are armed & about 60 Bayonets among them. In the block House are 8 double fortified 4-pounders mounted. The Fort on the Land Side is intirely open. There is not one Gunner or Artillery Man in the fort. Nothing but pork, Beef & flour, no Vegetables. No Barrack Master. The Minute Men work about 6 Hours in the Day & that with great Reluctance.[2]

We are informed by Capt. [Bendloe?] that at Pooplopens Kill there are 180 Troops under the Command of Lieutent. Lee—that 6 32-pounders, and all other Necessaries for Cannon, except powder, arrived there the 3rd Inst.

The fortifications directed by Congress 15 Feby, and laid out by Mr Smith, remain wholy neglected.

Hearing of the Arrival of part of the fleet at the Hook we thought it proper to give You this Information by Express. You will be pleased to communicate the Substance of the above to Congress.

We are Sir, Your obedt. Servants,   B Franklin

Saml. Chase

Ch. Carroll of Carrollton

RC (DNA: PCC, item 159). Written by Chase and signed by Chase, Franklin, and Carroll. Endorsed by Charles Thomson: "Letter from Franklin, Chase & Carrol, enclosed in general Putnams of the 7th April. 1776."

¹ Israel Putnam (1718–90), major general of the Continental Army, had just taken command of the American forces preparing the defenses of New York City. His letter to Congress of April 7, in which the commissioners' letter was enclosed, is in PCC, item 159, 1:3–4, and *Am. Archives*, 4th ser. 5:811.

² In contrast to this appraisal of conditions at Fort Constitution (later renamed Fort Lee), see Franklin's letter to his English correspondent Anthony Todd describing the vigorous activities underway to complete the defensive works around New York City. Benjamin Franklin to Anthony Todd, March 29, 1776.

William Whipple to Josiah Bartlett

My Dear Sir   Philadelphia 5th Apl 1776

I hope this days post will advise me of your arrival 'tho I don't fully depend on it but shall the next.¹ By the time this reaches you I hope You'll be preparing to set out. Have not yet got the New Hampshire matters pass'd in Congress. Have been ever since your departure on the Privateering business, & Regulation of Trade. The latter was finish'd Yesterday.² Shall send them to you next post. I have given over all thots. of hearing from any body concerned in the Legislature of New Hampshire. I have been now near two months from thence & have not received a single line 'tho the Genl. Court has been seting almost a month.

A schooner arrived this week from Guardalupe with 1200 cask Powder but they are small the whole containing no more than 7 or 8 Tons. The Wasp arrived the 3d inst. She parted from the fleet about 12 days ago off Bermudas where they had been cruising for the transports from the West Indies. They have on board 90 or 100 Cannon from 18 to 42 pounders, a large Quantity of shot & one Ton Powder taken from New Providence. Have also Brot off the Gov., Lieut Gov. & an officer belonging to Pensacola.³ The Capt of the Wasp says the fleet are bound to New England; suppose that if so you'll hear of them before I shall. A Piolet Boat which was taken sometime ago by the Roebuck (now Laying at the Cape) was a few days ago retaken near Lewistown with a Leiut. & 3 or 4 men belonging to the Roebuck. No late news from Canada.

I am with great Esteem, Yours,   Wm. Whipple

RC (NhD).

¹ Bartlett did not arrive in Philadelphia until May 17. See Whipple to Meshech Weare, May 17–18, 1776.

² New trade regulations were approved in the committee of the whole on April 4, but Congress did not actually pass resolutions opening American ports until April 6. No action was taken on April 5 because "Congress did not Sett being good Friday." Robert Treat Paine's Diary, April 5, 1776, MHi; and *JCC*, 4:256–59.

³ John Brown, acting governor of New Providence, reported the capture by the Americans of Gov. Montfort Browne, Lt. James Babbidge, secretary of the province, and Thomas Irving, former customs collector in South Carolina. Clark, *Naval Documents*, 4:463.

William Whipple to John Langdon

My Dear Sir,   Philadelphia 5th April 1776
    We have at last heard of Admiral Hopkins. The Wasp arrived here
the day before yesterday leaky. She parted from him about a fortnight
ago off Bermuda where he had been cruising some time, to intercept
the transports from the West Indies. He has been at New Providence
and taken from thence between 90 and 100 cannon, from 18 to 42 pounders, a large quantity of shot and one ton powder. It's supposed he is
gone to Rhode Island—if so you'll hear of him before I shall. A schooner
arrived the 2d inst from Guadaloupe with 1200 casks powder, but it
seems they are small; the whole contained no more than 7, or 8 tons.
The Marine Committee begin to talk of the officers for the new frigates;
those for the ship you are building must be taken from there; send me
a list of those you think of. Will Thompson take the command. I think
Follet would make a good officer—there are many good men that I
cannot recollect. I hope we shall have such as will do honor to the service;
there must be three Lieutenants. I have mentioned Agents in the Committee; They agree its necessary there should be one in every seaport.
I expect to advise you by the next post of their appointment.[1] Hopkins
has brought off the Govr. and Lt Govr. of Providence and an officer
belonging to Pensacola. In haste yours,   W Whipple

Tr (DLC).
[1] See Whipple to John Langdon, April 29, 1776, note 1.

John Adams to Abigail Adams

[April 6, 1776] [1]
    As to coming home, I have no Thoughts of it—shall stay here till the
Year is out, for what I know. Affairs are in a critical state and important
Steps are now taking every day, so that I could not reconcile it to my
own Mind to be absent from this Place at present.
    Nothing is expected from the Commissioners, yet We are waiting
for them, in some Respects. The Tories, and Timids pretend to expect
great Things from them. But the Generality expect nothing but more
Insults and Affronts. Privateering is licensed and the Ports are wide
open. As soon as the Resolves are printed, which will be tomorrow, I'le
send them.[2]
    I have had a long Conversation with   .[3] He seems to be in a
better Temper, and I live on Terms of Decency and Civility with him
and he with me. And I am determined to live so. Have lived in more
Decency with him and another, since my last Return than ever, at

least than since last August when the sin of Precedence was committed. Theres the Rub. But what cant be cured must be endured.

RC (MHi). In the hand of John Adams.
¹ This fragment of a letter was mistakenly placed with Adams' letter to Abigail of December 3, 1775, by Charles Francis Adams when he was preparing their correspondence for publication, and it was printed as a part of that letter both in his compilation and in the modern edition of Adams' papers. See Charles Francis Adams, ed., *Familiar Letters of John Adams and His Wife Abigail Adams, during the Revolution* (New York: Hurd and Houghton, 1875), pp. 126–28; and Adams, *Family Correspondence* (Butterfield), 1:331–32. It is clear, however, from the physical evidence of Adams' letters, from John's endorsement on Abigail's letter to him of March 16, 1776, and from the content of this document, that the manuscript is actually the last page of a missing letter of this date.
The sheet of paper on which this fragment is written is unlike the paper Adams was using in December 1775 but is from the stock that he was using for his letters in March and April 1776. John's endorsement on Abigail's letter to him of March 16, 1776, containing an inquiry about "the Expectation of Commissioners," reads: "answed April 6th. 1776." See Adams, *Family Correspondence* (Butterfield), 1:359–60. And several passages from these three concluding paragraphs support an April rather than December date. Thus not only did Adams on December 8 ask leave to return home, a fact difficult to square with his assertion here that he had "no Thoughts" of returning, but Congress did not license privateering and open the ports until March 23 and April 6, 1776, respectively. Furthermore, the person with whom he had recently conversed but whose name he left blank was undoubtedly Robert Treat Paine, who was not in Philadelphia in December 1775, and his reference to "my last Return" was undoubtedly to his absence from Philadelphia December 9, 1775–February 9, 1776.
² The April 6 resolves opening the American ports to trade were published in the *Pennsylvania Gazette*, April 10, 1776.
³ Adams is undoubtedly referring to Robert Treat Paine, with whom mutual recriminations had mounted following Adams' appointment as chief justice of the Massachusetts Superior Court of Judicature. See John Adams to Abigail Adams, November 18, 1775.

Elbridge Gerry to James Warren

Dr. sir,   Philadelphia April 6th 1776.
I have just Time to send You by the post a News Paper in which is inserted the Resolves of Congress for opening the American Ports to all Nations excepting such as are subjects to the King of Great Britain.¹
As it is a Matter of Importance that these Resolves should be published in all the papers & sent to every Part of Europe & the West Indies not inimical to the Colonies, I doubt not the Committees of Correspondence or other Suitable persons will be desired by the honble Court to attend to such a Measure & cause the same to [be] republished in foreign Papers. I hope by the next Post to send some Blank Commissions & Instructions for Letters of Marque & the Resolves of Congress relative thereto, they being now in the press.²
I remain sir respectfully your very huml serv,   Elb Gerry

RC (M–Ar). Addressed: "Hona. James Warren, Esqr. or in his Absence William Cooper, Esqr." Endorsed by Warren: "In the House of Representatives April 18th. 1776. Recd & committed to the Committee on the State of the Colony. Sent up for Concurrence. Js Warren Spkr."

¹ Probably the *Pennsylvania Ledger*, which printed the resolves on this day. See *JCC*, 4:257–59.

² The form of commissions and the instructions to privateer commanders were approved by Congress on April 2 and 3. *JCC*, 4:247–48, 251–54.

John Hancock to Philip Schuyler

Dear Sir   Philadelphia, April 6. 1776

Major Zedwitz has just delivered me Your Favour.¹ I have now only time to beg Leave to introduce to Your Notice Coll. St. Clair of the Second Pennsa. Battalion, a Gentleman of Reputation, & a Good Officer, he served many Years a Captain in the Regular Army.

I know Your Goodness will excuse my frequent Applications of this Kind, & from the same benevolent Motive You will be Induced to extend Your Civilities to Coll. St. Clair, which will be Esteemed as done to, sir, Your very humble Servt,   John Hancock

Tr (NN).

¹ Schuyler's letter to Hancock of March 26, enclosing a letter to Congress from Gen. David Wooster of March 6, is in *Am. Archives*, 4th ser. 5:511.

Robert Morris to Horatio Gates

Dear Sir,   Philada. April 6th. 1776

I have been long in debt for your favour of the 20th Feby which you'l probably think the more inexcusable as it is a letter of business. The order it contained for four hundred & twenty four Dollars has been paid & is at your Credit.

Was ever the British Arms so disgraced as by Mr. How's Inglorious retreat from Boston. This woud at any other time or in any other Cause have been a most Mortifying Reflection both to you & me, but as things are now Circumstanced I do most sincerely Congratulate you on that important Event, and altho my Scenes of Action are in another line, I almost envy every one of You that share the Glory of driving them from their den. You may depend that infinite pains has been taken & is still Continued to obtain ample supplys of Arms & Ammunition but our Enemies were before hand with us & have so guarded all avenues that it is with the utmost hazard & difficulty we succeed, many attempts have totally failed. However nothing will be left undone in this respect that can be done, the rest must be left to Fate.

I suppose you know that Doctr Franklin, Chase & two Mr. Carrols are gone to Canada and I hope a sufficient Force will be there to put Quebec under their direction for I jump in oppinion with you, that Country must be ours at all Events. Should it fall into the hands of The Enemy they will soon raise a Nest of Hornets on our backs that will Sting us to the quick.

We are plagued for hard Money to Support the Warr in that Country and must by some Means or other bring them to take our paper.

Our Friend Lee has taken possession of the Palace at Wmsburg which I fancy will not be much approved of by the Gentn of that Country, however he will soon be called for No. Carolina if it be true that Clinton has effected a Landing with 1500 Men at Wilmington and thrown up entrenchments there. In short the Scene thickens and if our Enemies can find Men we may expect to be attacked in all quarters, but to do this they must Certainly have recourse to Foreigners as they cannot meet success in the Recruiting Service in any of the three Kingdoms. Where the plague are these Commissioners, if they are to come what is it that detains them; it is time we shoud be on a Certainty & know positively whether the Libertys of America can be established & Secured by reconciliation, or whether we must totally renounce Connection with Great Britain & fight our way to a total Independance. Whilst we Continue thus firmly United amongst ourselves theres no doubt but either of these points may be carried, but it seems to me, We shall quarrell about which of these roads is best to pursue unless the Commissioners appear soon and lead us into the first path. Therefore I wish them to Come, dreading nothing so much as even an appearance of division amongst ourselves.

I hear Mrs. Gates is returned to N York & thence Conclude that you will soon follow. May happiness & Success attend you is the sincere Wish of Dr sir, Your Obedt Servt.   Robt Morris

RC (NHi).

Jonathan Dickinson Sergeant to John Adams

Dear Sir   6 Apl. 1776.
    I arrived here[1] last Evening in a very indifferent State of Health & shall return or not return according as I have Reason to believe I may be more useful here or there.

So then! I am told You have a Report that Cato's Commissioners[2] are coming at last, 46,000 strong. Mr.————, I suppose, will tell us that he never expected the Commissioners to come without a strong Force to back them. O for the just Vengeance of Heaven on the Heads of those who have laboured so assiduously to fetter our Hands these six Months past! If we fall I must ascribe it to our fatal Mismanagement. We have backened the Zeal of our People, discouraged our warmest Friends, strengthened the Hands of our Enemies open & concealed, consumed our Time, wasted our Strength; but I hope we shall yet awake & at least not fall unrevenged.

How does this Report work with You? I hope it will rouze, not intimidate. We can if we are in Earnest cope with all this power & with the Assistance of Heaven may defeat them. If this is done I should hope, like the Defeat of the Spanish Armada, it will forever break the Force of our Enemies. I think You should neither exaggerate nor attempt to conceal such News if it be true or even probable; but let it work. If the People do not kindle at it, if they do not resolve now to exert themselves, they would do yet worse if it should come unexpectedly upon them. They should be solemnly appealed to, they should be called upon to make the last Effort of their Strength and I trust we may yet be delivered. I wish they had never been lulled into a Sort of Security from that State of Expectation of strong Attempts against us which they were in before the Talk of Commissioners.

You see I am rather in the Dumps; but You must ascribe part of it to my Disorder & part to a Reflection wch. has some Time haunted me, that there is a Tide in these Matters which I fear we have suffered to ebb.

I should be much obliged to You for one of your anonymous Epistles upon this Subject informing me whether You will have it in your power to secure me an Asylum in the Land of my Forefathers after the Rest of the Colonies shall have submitted; for I have strong Faith still in New England. Let me know too how it works in Philadelphia, how in Congress &c. We have Resources if we have the Virtue to use them. The Crown lands, the Quit-rents, the Tories; but alas! Quos Deus vult perdere. Could not we bid as high for Hessians & Hanoverians in the Article of Lands & Estates as our Enemies? My Head achs & my Heart achs. I tremble for the Timidity of our Counsels. Adieu! You know my Hand & imitating your Caution will at least do no Harm.

RC (MHi). In Sergeant's hand, though not signed. Endorsed by Adams: "Intell. Mr. Sergeant."

[1] Princeton. Sergeant was back in Congress by April 23. See Marine Committee to Esek Hopkins, April 23, 1776.

[2] On March 12, "Cato," in the second of eight letters "To the People of Pennsylvania" published in various Pennsylvania newspapers during March and April 1776, had forcefully argued that the colonies should enter into negotiations with peace commissioners being sent by Great Britain. See *Am. Archives*, 4th ser. 5:188–90.

John Hancock to Israel Putnam

Sir   Philadelphia April 8th. 1776

On Saturday I Rec'd a Letter from General Heath requesting that some Money might be Sent to New York for the use of the Troops, which I immediately laid before Congress, & was Authorized to forward One hundred Thousand Dollars, which I have accordingly Sent by Capt. Nathaniel Faulkner, and as I am uninform'd whether the Paymaster is arriv'd at New York, I have Directed Mr. Faulkner to Deliver the Money to you.[1] If the Paymaster is with you please to order it to his Care for the Use of the Troops, if not, you will order the Money to be improv'd for the payment of the Troops under your Command. Please to Acquaint General Heath that I Rec'd his Letter, but have not Time to write him now. You will please to forward me a Receipt for the Money.

Last Eveng. I had the honour of yr Letter by Major Sherburne desiring that Three hundred Thousand Dollars may be Sent for the use of the Troops. As the Congress does not meet this Day,[2] I have judg'd it best to Detain Major Sherburne here, untill I know the Determination of Congress, which I shall know to morrow and whatever further Sums they order I will Dispatch by Major Sherburne, in the meantime I have thought it most proper to Send forward by Capt. Faulkner the One hundred Thousand Dollars as that Sum may be improv'd untill the other Arrives.[3]

I have the honour to be with Sentiments of Esteem, Sir, Your most Obedt servt.   J H Prt.

LB (DNA: PCC, item 12A). Addressed: "To Major General Putnam Commandg. the Continental Troops at New York."

[1] Gen. William Heath's letter to Hancock of April 3 is in PCC, item 157, fols. 3–5; and *Am. Archives*, 4th ser. 5:775–76. Congress approved this appropriation of $100,000 on April 6. *JCC*, 4:261.

[2] This day Robert Treat Paine noted in his diary: "Being Easter Monday Congress did not set. Rainy raw Day." MHi.

[3] See Israel Putnam to Hancock, April 4, 1776, in *Am. Archives*, 4th ser. 5:787. On April 9 Congress appropriated an additional $200,000 for the use of the Continental Army at New York. *JCC*, 4:263; and Hancock to Putnam, April 10, 1776.

Marine Committee to John Barry

Sir   Philada. April 8th 1776

We received your Letter by Mr. Scott and approve of your Conduct in Sending in the St. Croix Sloop. Altho she does not prove to be a prize, yet as the circumstances attending her appeared Suspicious you did right.

Should this be delivered to you by Capt. Hallock at or about Cape
May he will also put on board your Lieutt. of Marines and some men.
If he does not see you he will land them at Cape May, and as Lieut.
Scott takes a Copy of it to Egg Harbour, you will by this means learn
that you will have either to take them of[f] from the Cape or him from
Egg Harbour. We wish Capt Hallock may fall in with you before he
parts with Mr. Deane on board the Sloop Betsey, Capt John Tucker,
and in that case We desire that you will take that Sloop under your
Convoy and see her Two, three or four days Run of the Coast, until
you and Mr Deane shall think her out of danger of the Enemies Tenders
and Cutters.[1] Wishing you Success, We are your friends,

Robt Morris   John Hancock

Richard Henry Lee   Step Hopkins

Joseph Hewes   Wm. Whipple

John Alsop

RC (NHi). In the hand of Morris, and signed by Morris, Alsop, Hancock, Hewes,
Hopkins, Lee, and Whipple.
[1] Capt. John Barry of the Continental brig *Lexington* had just taken the British
tender *Edward* and was apparently in Egg Harbor when Capt. William Hallock of
the *Wasp* arrived at the capes. After escorting the *Betsey* out to sea on April 13
Hallock left Barry's men at Cape May on the 15th. See Clark, *Naval Documents*,
4:790, 802, 839; Robert Morris to Silas Deane, April 8; and Marine Committee to
Barry, April 11, 1776.

Robert Morris to Silas Deane

Dear Sir   Philada. April 8th. 1776
I wrote you a few lines this morning[1] by the return of your Express
to whom I paid 40s. in full of All demands for his Journey. Since his
departure I procured a Meeting of the Marine Committee and orders
to send down the Schooner soon as possible, therefore I hope you will
receive this from Capt Hallock who is orderd to Consult with you the
best & Safest Method of getting out to Sea and to follow such orders as
you may give him from time to time untill your departure; when he is
to return.
He has a letter for Capt Barry[2] & shoud you be lucky enough to fall
in with him he is directed to see you three or four days run off the Coast
untill you & he may think the dangers of Tenders & Cutters is over.
If you dont find Barry at the Capes you had best take the letter from
Hallock as you may fall in with Barry afterwards. I have ordered the
Brigt Polly Capt McFadden to embrace this Convoy & go down in
Compy with you and most sincerely do I hope both of you may get
clear. The 2d bills for £1200 Stg are on bd her, and her Cargo Cost

near £3000 Curry. Therefore you'l have an Eye to her security as well as your own.

I am now at the 9th & yesterday wrote a Note to Mr Jay[3] desiring him to furnish you with News and to send his letter to me, as yet it is not come, however there is little news to inform you of. The troops keep filing off from Boston for New York where Men of Warr & some People on shore have had a little firing. I dont mean at the City, but in some part of that Bay our People took their Boats Crew prisoner, wounded some men & obliged the ship to [slip] her Cable & anchor which our Folks [have] since weighed and got. The report is that two or three Men of Warr are arrived at the Hook, so we may expect the Campaigne will open in that quarter before long. Nothing New from the Southward by the last Post.

I have just heard that Capt Barry was at Cape May last Friday & Convoyed out some New England Men. I hope you'l meet him. We find difficulty to get Men to go down in the Schooner as they have a Notion they will catch the distemper she brought in with her but we must get the better of this oppinion and perhaps I may write to you again if any delay happens which however I will endeavour to prevent, being most truly, Dr Sir, Yours &c,   Robt Morris

P.S. If you cou'd clear of Cape May in the night it might do well.

RC (CtHi).
[1] This letter, dealing with the preparations being made to get Deane safely out to sea, is in Clark, *Naval Documents*, 4:726–27.
[2] See Marine Committee to John Barry, this date.
[3] Not found.

Joseph Hewes to Samuel Johnston

Dear Sir,   Philadelphia 9th April 1776

I enclose you a Letter for Doctor Haslen, also a draught on him for £42.10, which if he pays put into the Treasury and direct me to pay a like sum to Mr. Geo. Scott in this City, I have agreed to this measure to oblige a very worthy friend of your Name, a delegate from Maryland.[1]

You will have heard ere this reaches you that the Kings Troops have left Boston. It is reported and generally believed that they are bound to some port, South of the one which they lately Abandond. A Centinal at Newport in hasy weather counted 23 large Ships which were soon after covered by Fog, he alarmed the whole Country, expresses were sent to Gen. Washington who ordered a Brigade to march that way. The Fog cleared up in the afternoon and discovered the Fleet to be only Trees on a point of Land at a distance.[2] A Ship of War Arived two days ago in the River below New York and is said to be one of the Fleet from Boston. I believe the whole force is expected at New York, great preparations are making there to defend the City and to prevent the Enemy from landing. Generals Putnam, Heath, Thompson & Lord Sterling are now there with near Ten thousand Men, the Generals Sullivan & Green are on their March with their Brigades and are expected at New York in a day or two, General Washington was soon to Follow and may be expected there next week, two or three Regiments only are left at Boston to fortifie it. A Forty four Gun Ship lies in this Bay near the Cape and has taken Several Vessels. Congress has agreed to open the Trade as you will See by the enclosed paper.[3] Some other resolutions I am told are preparing by some Members respecting trade in which I expect will be inserted something looking towards independancy, as I have not seen them I can say nothing further of them. A Violent head which follows me perpetually obliges me to lay down my pen. If the Bearer Mr Stevens should not go to morrow I may probably add something, as we expect by every Post something new from the Eastward.[4]

RC (PHi).
[1] Thomas Johnson.
[2] For further information about this incident, see Washington, *Writings* (Fitzpatrick), 4:456–59, 470–71; and Clark, *Naval Documents*, 4:593, 611.
[3] See *JCC*, 4:257–59.
[4] For the continuation of this letter, see Hewes to Johnston, April 11, 1776.

Francis Lightfoot Lee to Landon Carter

Dear Colonel,   Philadelphia Apl. 9th. 1776
The assurances of friendship in your Letter of the 30 of March, give me very great pleasure. I hope it will always continue, as a compensation for the many disquietudes, unavoidable in this Life. Who in the name of Heaven, coud tell you, that Independancy had been 3 times thrown out of Congress? You may be assured, the Question has never been before the Congress, and it is probable they will wait till the people brings it before them; which event is not far off, from the best accounts, from the different parts of the Continent; for your information, with respect to the disposition of the northern people is as erroneous as the other. Of this I am very cohfident, having made it my business to be informed. It is not improbable but that even the Colony of N. York will step foremost in this great Question.
It makes me uneasy to find from yr. Letr. that licentiousness begins to prevail in Virga.; tho' I have always expected it, from the mismanagement of the Gentlemen. The old Government being dissolved,

& no new one substituted in its stead; Anarchy must be the consequence. The Congress foresaw this, & therefore recommended it to Virga. & the Southd. Colonies to establish such Government as wou'd best secure their peace & happiness.[1] I anxiously hope this will be done, the next convention, or I dread the consequences.[2] Rhode Island & Connecticut having Governments of ther own everything has been carried on with order & quiet. New Hampshire & Massachusetts Bay, whose Governors & other officers were appointed by the Crown, were getting into the utmost disorder; but upon their assuming Government, by the advice of Congress, they are restored to perfect harmony & regularity. The Southern Colonies by delaying the remedy, will I fear, have violent symptoms to encounter.

I feel myself deeply interested in the security & happiness of America; compared with which, the interests of Britain, is as a feather in the scale. Let us my dear friend do the best we can for the good of our Country, & leave the event to fate. I take it for granted that all our friends at Sabine Hall & in Richmond are well. God grant they may long continue so. My better half & myself are well. Col. Tayloe has the papers. There is very little news. I forgot to tell you that a Pamphlet written against Common sense,[3] was burnt in the temperate City of N. York by a vast majority of its inhabitants. Farewell my dear Sir,

Francis Lightfoot Lee

RC (MeHi).
    [1] See the resolutions of December 4, 1775. *JCC*, 3:403–4.
    [2] The Virginia Convention took the initial step in forming a new government on May 15, 1776, when it appointed a committee to prepare a declaration of rights and a plan of government. See its proceedings in *Am. Archives*, 4th ser. 6:1524.
    [3] James Chalmers' *Plain Truth*.

Secret Committee Minutes of Proceedings

April 9th. 1776.

At a Meetg. Prest. R. Morris, J. Alsop, Jos Hewes, Rob Alexander, Th. McKean & R. H. Lee. Issued an order on the Treasurers in favor of Saml. Meredith & Ths. Mason for 48 dlls part expences attendg. their looking after Brigante. Chance's Cargo.[1] Do. of J. & Peter Chevalier for 70840 dlls being the amount insurd on the Ship Two Brothers, Capt. Johnston [James Johnson], laden by us for Ferrol & taken on her passage 26 Decr. last by the Experimt. man of war, Capt. Robt. Keeler,[2] & since condemnd as a prize as appears by Capt. Jonstons protest before Mathew Clarkson, Not. Pub., of 4th Inst. Do. in favor of S. Mifflin Esqr. for dlls 6270 being the amount insurd on Ship Peggy, Capt. Davidson, loaden by us for Cadiz & taken on her passage the 8th

Decr. last by the Viper Sloop of war,[3] Capt. Sl. Graves, & since condemnd as a prize as appears by Capt. Davidsons protest before M.
Clarkson, N.P., dated 28th March last. Do. for 1244 dlls 7/9 in favor
of S. Mifflin, G. Clymer & S. Meredith, being the balance of their
Acct. dated in Sepr. 1775.

MS (MH).
   [1] Capt. Thomas Mason had arrived in February with a cargo of powder and arms.
See Secret Committee Minutes of Proceedings, February 3; and Caesar Rodney to
Thomas Rodney, February 4, 1776.
   [2] See Secret Committee Minutes of Proceedings, December 5, 1775; and Clark,
Naval Documents, 3:1121.
   [3] For Samuel Mifflin's December 2 instructions to Samuel Davidson, and the
Viper's account of the *Peggy*'s capture on December 9, 1775, see Clark, *Naval Documents*, 2:1236, 3:38–39.

John Hancock to Israel Putnam

Sir,   Philadelphia April 10th 1776.
   In Consequence of your Letter, I laid the Application before the Congress; who were pleased, in Addition to the one Hundred Thousand
Dollars sent by Capt. Faulkner on Monday last, to order two Hundred
Thousand more, which I have the Pleasure of forwarding by Major
Sherburne.[1] Should the Paymaster be at New York, please to order it
to his Care for the Use of the Troops. If not, you will order the Money
to be improved for the same Purpose, and send a Receipt for it. I have
the Honour to be, Sir, your most obedt. & very hble Sevt.
                                     John Hancock Presidt

R C (DLC). In the hand of Jacob Rush and signed by Hancock.
   [1] See Hancock to Israel Putnam, April 8, 1776, note 3.

Oliver Wolcott to Laura Wolcott

My Dear,   Philidelpa. 10th April 1776
   I wrote to you the 27t. last which I hope you have recd; nothing in
special since has occurred to Write to you upon. Merciful Providence
still continues my Health to Me. Thro Various Scenes of Life God has
Sustained me. May he ever be my unfailing Freind, May his Love
cherish my Soul, May my Heart with Gratitude Acknowledge his
Goodness and may my Desires be to him and to the Remembrance of
his Name. Vanity by the Wisest of men has been inscribed on every
Thing Mortal and no Experience has ever contradicted this Declaration. May We then turn our Eyes to the bright Objects above, and may

God give us Strength to travel the upward Road. May the divine Redeemer conduct us to that Seat of Bliss which he himself has prepared for his Freinds; at the Approach of which every Sorrow shall Vanish from the human heart, and endless scenes of Glory Open upon the enraptured Eye. There our Love to God and each other will grow stronger, and our Pleasures never be damp'd by the Fear of future Seperation. How indifferent will it then be to us wheither We obtained Felicity by travelling the thorny or the agreable Paths of Life, wheither We arived at our Rest by passing thro the envied and unfragrant Road of Greatness or Sustained Hardship and unmeritted Reproach in our Journey; Gods Providence and Support thro the perilous perplexing Labyrinths of human Life, will then forever excite our Astonishment and Love. May a Happiness be granted to those I most tenderly Love which shall continue and increase thro an endless Existence. Your Cares and Burdens must be Many and great, but put your Trust in that God who has hitherto supported you and me, he will not fail to take Care of those who put their Trust in him.

As to News inclose you a Paper in which the latest most material Resolves of Congress are inserted. The Tea now in the Country will undouptedly in a Very few days (by Resolve of Congress) be permitted to be consumed. The general Complexion of Affairs gives little ground to expect an Accomenedation with Great Britain on former Terms. Nothing as I hear of has happened of Consequence since my last in the Southern Colonies. There is a great Ardor amongst the People this Way in support of American Rights. The low Torys under the Mark of Patriotism are converting every Measure to perplex the Whig Interest. They are sensible that Things must soon make an absolute Crisis and they are now making their last Struggles, but they will be ineffectual. It is most evident that this Land is under the Protection of the Almighty, and that We shall be Saved, not by our Wisdom nor by our might, but by the Lord of Host who is wonderfull in Councill and Almighty in all his Operations.

Letters from Home are extreamly agreable to Me and hope my Freinds will not forget Me. Present my best Regards to them, particularly to my Children, and be assured that I am with the tenderest Affection yours,   Oliver Wolcott

P.S. Commodore Hopkins has been to N Providence and bro't from thence about Two hundred Cannon and Warlike Stores.[1] You may perhaps hear this News more parti[cu]larly before this reaches you as he may perhaps put in to the eastward.

RC (CtHi).
[1] See William Whipple to John Langdon, April 2; and John Hancock to Esek Hopkins, April 17, 1776.

John Hancock to
Michael Hillegas and George Clymer

Gentlemen   Philadela. April 11th 1776

    Please to pay to the Honble Elipt Dyer & Wm Williams Esqrs, one hundred sixty six thousand & six hundred sixty six & two thirds Dollars, on Account of Advances made by the Colony of Connecticut for the service of the Continent, the said Colony to account for said sum in the settlement of their Accounts.[1]

    I am Gentlemen Your most humble Servant,

                                    John Hancock Presidt.

Tr (CtHi). In the hand of William Williams, and endorsed by him: "Recd. the Contents 12 Apl." "Congress' order for the £50,000 recd by Col Dyer & me, 11 April 76. Copy." "72 Dols. in a Sheet. 25 sheets to Quire. 1800 Dol. in a Quire. 8 Quire in a Bundle. 14,400 Dols in a bundle. 11 whole Bundles is 158400 Dols. 14 sheets more is 1008 Dol. A broken sheet 58 Dol. & 2/3 in Change." Notation in unidentified hand: "100 Sheets, 72 Dollars."

  [1] See *JCC*, 4:272; and Oliver Wolcott to Thomas Seymour, April 16, 1776, note 2.

Joseph Hewes to Samuel Johnston

The 11th, [April 1776]

    The above was written in Congress, where I am obliged to write most of my Letters unless I break in upon the hours of Sleep, as I am doing at this moment. Advice is Just received from New York that Comodore Hopkins with two Ships, two Brigs & a Sloop under his Command fell in with the Glasgow man of War of 20 Guns, a Bomb Briga and three Tenders off the east end of Long Island when a smart engagement ensued in which the Bomb Brigg & three Tenders were taken, the Glasgow got off by out sailing our Ships, the Commodore has got safe into New London in Connecticut with his little Fleet and Prizes.[1] This Morning arived here a Prize Sloop taken by Capt. Barry of the Brig. Lexington a Vessel lately Fitted out by Congress. The Sloop was Commanded by a Lieutenant of the Liverpool, had Six Carriage & Six Swivel Guns & 35 Men. See Barrys Letter in the News paper enclosed to Mr Hooper.[2] The bearer Mr Stevens has been warmly recommended to me; if it falls in your way to render him any Services it will oblige me. My Complemts. to all my friends, you have always the best wishes of, Dr Sir, Your mo. Obed Servant,   Joseph Hewes

RC (PHi). A continuation of Hewes to Johnston, April 9, 1776.

  [1] For more detailed descriptions of this engagement, see Clark, *Naval Documents*, 4:679–81, 697, 735–36.

[2] Capt. John Barry described his capture of the sloop *Edward* in a letter to the Marine Committee of April 7, which was published in the *Pennsylvania Evening Post* on April 11. Ibid., p. 702.

John Jay to Alexander McDougall

Dear Colonel   Philad. 11 Apr. 1776

Whether my last Letter has reached you or not is uncertain. From your Silence I sometimes suspect it has not. However as I know you must be perpetually engaged in Matters of more Consequence, I cannot expect to hear from you so often as when you enjoyed more Leizure.

I would wish to be informed of the number of Troops now employed in New York, how your Levies go on, & whether there is a Prospect of our Battalions soon being compleated.[1]

From a late York Paper there is reason to apprehend a disagreable Dispute between some of the Citizens & the Convention relative to the Mode of appointing Delegates to the Congress. I esteem every Controversey of this kind as a misfortune to the Colony & cannot but think the mode proposed by the Mechanicks useless as well as unseasonable. All the Delegates who now compose this Congress were chosen either by provincial Assemblies or Conventions & I really can see no good Reason for deviating from it in one Colony.

As it is intended that the next Convention should be expressly authorized by their Constituents to appoint Delegates I cannot perceive how the Right of Election will be injured by their exerting a Power so publickly & openly given them by the People, from whom I readily admit all civil Authority must originate.[2]

The making of Gun Locks, Arms & Salt petre goes on rapidly in this Colony, & from the Accounts recd. lately from Virginia they will soon manufacture as much Powder as they may want.

A very rich mine of Sulphur lying just under the Surface of the Earth has been discovered in Jersey, & a Man who understands preparing or refining the Ore has been found & employed—so that in all Probability we shall never after this Year be indebted to foreigners for ammunition.

As the Sound is now pretty well secured against the Incursion of the Enemy, would it not be prudent for the Convention to cause Salt Works to be erected. I fear the Scarcity of that Commodity will in the Course of another Year distress our People exceedingly.

I hope to see you sometime next Month unless the arrival of the Commissioners or some other extraordinary Event should detain me.[3] As to those Gentlemen, I sometimes think their coming questionable, and should they arrive, I suspect their Powers will be too limited, to promise us much from Negotiations.

From the present Appearance of Things it is natural to suppose that the Sword must decide the Controversey—and with a View to that object our measures should in a great Degree be taken. The first Thing therefore in my opinion to be done is to erect good & well ordered Governments in all the Colonies, and thereby exclude that Anarchy which already too much prevails. This is a Step which it is probable will not be taken by the Conventions till the Business of the Commissioners is over, but it is a Matter which ought nevertheless to be attended to, and inculcated. I am Dr. Sir, Your Friend & hble Servt,

John Jay

RC (NHi).

[1] The next two paragraphs of this letter were printed in New York on April 16 as a broadside entitled *Extract of a Letter from John Jay, Esq., a Delegate at the Continental Congress, to a Gentleman of this City*, Charles Evans, *American Bibliography*, 12 vols. (Chicago: Privately printed, 1903–34), no. 14813.

[2] For a discussion of the complex issues in the April 1776 election in New York for a new provincial congress, see Carl L. Becker, *The History of Political Parties in the Province of New York, 1760–1776*, Bulletin of the University of Wisconsin no. 286 (Madison, 1909), pp. 256–60.

[3] Jay left Philadelphia at the beginning of May to visit his family and attend the New York Provincial Congress.

Marine Committee to John Barry

In Marine Committee
Sir   Philadelphia April 11th. 1776

We have received your Letter of the 7th instant per the Prize Sloop Edward which shall be immediately Libelled in the Court of admiralty of this Colony,[1] and when Condemned a fair Sale or valuation of the vessel, her Stores and Materials will be made. The Share thereof belonging to you, the officers and Crew shall be deposited in the hands of your Agents and in every respect the utmost Justice shall be done to all concerned.

We send down the prize Master and Men to Little Egg Harbour where you propose to Call for them, and our letter by Lieut. Scott wou'd inform you that Capt. Boys with four or five Marines went down to Cape May in the Schooner Wasp, where they were to Land if you did not fall in with them; consequently you will take them off.[2] As the Men of Warr in Virginia, Delaware and New York will undoubtedly hear of you they will probably lay some plans to surprize or decoy you, but we dare say a continued vigilance will enable you to avoid the Snares and power of those that are too strong for you, as well as to send us some more of those that are not an over match for the Lexington. We repeat our approbation of your Conduct, and beg you may signify to your officers and Men that the Marine Committee of Congress highly ap-

plaud their Zeal and bravery. With the best wishes, We are Sir, Your
Friends,   Joseph Hewes   John Hancock

                              Geo. Read   Robt Morris

                              Wm. Whipple   John Alsop

                              Step Hopkins   Richard Henry Lee

RC (NHi). In a clerical hand and signed by Alsop, Hancock, Hewes, Hopkins, Lee, Morris, Read, and Whipple.
   [1] Barry's letter is in Clark, *Naval Documents*, 4:702. For the condemnation proceedings against the *Edward*, see pp. 801–2, 1334–41.
   [2] See Marine Committee to John Barry, April 8, 1776. Capt. Abraham Boyce and his marines from the *Lexington* were left at Cape May by Capt. William Hallock on April 15.

Jonathan Dickinson Sergeant to John Adams

Dear Sir   Princeton. 11 Apl. 1776.
   Your late worthy Governor Hutchinson used to mark some of his Letters *confidential*. You will give me Leave to use this Hint & at the same Time to take the Liberty of adding that, I believe, You know pretty well whom I can *confide* in, among our Acquaintance in Congress.
   The Jersey-Delegates (will You believe it) are not in the sweetest Disposition with one another. Mr. D'Hart has gone home with an avowed Determination not to return without General Livingston & at the same Time has declared that he will offer himself as a Candidate for the Provincial Convention thinking that a more important post, in Order that he may control the mad Fellows who now compose that Body. He has signified the dangerous Disposition of Mr. Smyth & another of his Colleagues; and all the great & the mightly ones in the Colony are preparing to make their last Stand against the Principle of levelling which prevails in it. Mr. Smith's Health it seems will not admit of his Attendance, at least not very steadily. In the mean Time I have engaged to return when ever called upon by General Livingston & Mr. D'Hart; but rather believe they will not call upon me, tho I have wrote to them requesting it, in Order that the Colony may not be *unrepresented*; tho I fear it will be *misrepresented* if we attend.
   Whether to return without them is a Matter of some Doubt with me, especially since I have been told that some very pious People are circulating a Rumour that I have left Congress in Disgust at the Doctrines of Independency which are there advanced. Whether I may not do more good at home considering all things I am at a Loss to determine. If my Colleagues should go into the Provincial Convention I should be glad to meet them there; and I know the old Leven of Unrighteousness will strive hard to poison that Body by pushing in every Creature that can

lisp against Independence, which in other Words, in my Opinion, is every Creature who would wish to give up the Quarrel. In Congress, if I am to be alone, it will avail little; if with my Colleagues less still. Here I can & will preach up the Necessity of a new Government.

From this State of the Case I should be much obliged by your Opinion. If You will let me have that & inclose the Copy of a Paper I spoke with You about the Evening before I left Town by the Saturday's post I shall take it as a Favour. By Sunday I must determine one Way or the other if possible.[1]

You will be good enough to excuse this Trouble & deliver the inclosed packet with my Compliments to Mr. Hewes & beg him to forward it for a Friend of mine here & believe me to be, with great Respect & Esteem, Your Friend & most hble Servt.   Jona D Sergeant

12 Apl. 1776.

P.S. I have been disappointed in the Conveyance by which I proposed to have forwarded this Letter & have therefore broke open the Packet to add this Postscript.

If I could receive your Answer by the Return of the Post I should be glad, & that you wd. inform me how Matters go among You. Doctor Rush has sent me an Evening-Post containing a Dialogue on Government said by him to have been wrote by an Author to whom he pays high Compliments.[2] The Pennsylvania Assembly have resolved to stick by their Instructions he tells me.[3] What do their Constituents think of them? The grand Difficulty here is that People seem to expect Congress should take the first Step *by declaring Independence*, as they phrase it. And *Cimon* has endeavoured to have a piece printed in New York & Philadelphia, calculated to lead them into a Method of doing the Business; and I believe the People of some of our Eastern Counties will be likely to revolt against the old Government at the first Hint. But if a single Stroke will not do they must be repeated: and I wish People universally could have their Attention fixed to the Question of new & old Government instead of waiting for Deliverance from Congress. There is a Tide in Human things & I fear if we miss the present Occasion we may have it turn upon us. I declare boldly to People Congress will not declare Independence in Form; they are independent; every Act is that of Independence and all we have to do is to establish Order & Government in each Colony that we may support them in it. Could not this Idea be substituted in the place of Independence in the Controversy, which, as it is treated, is no determinate Object, brings nothing to an Issue. Meantime the Catos (Cato You know is the common name of a Negroo-Slave in modern Times) will keep us in play talking about it & about it 'till the Spirit of the People will evaporate or these blessed Commissioners will have Time to play their pranks. God bless us. I wish Quebec was taken! What think You of all this? Adieu, Yours,   JDS.

RC (MHi).
¹ This is doubtless the request which led Adams to supply Sergeant with one of the earliest texts of what subsequently appeared as the pamphlet *Thoughts on Government*. See John Adams to John Penn, March 19–27? 1776, note 2.
² Presumably the dialogue of "A Friend to Government by Assembly," which appeared in the April 4 issue of the *Pennsylvania Evening Post*.
³ On April 6 the Pennsylvania Assembly rejected a petition from the Philadelphia Committee of Inspection and Observation for the repeal of the assembly's November 9, 1775, instructions to the Pennsylvania delegates to oppose "any Propositions . . . that may cause, or lead to, a Separation from our Mother Country, or a change of the Form of this Government." See *Pa. Archives*, 8th ser. 8:7352–53, 7513; *Am. Archives*, 4th ser. 5:434–35; and John Dickinson's Proposed Instructions, November 9? 1775.

William Whipple to Joshua Brackett

My Dear Sir   Apl. 11 1776
   I received your favor of the 26 Ulto. You put a hard Question viz whether I am *Thoroughly* aquainted with the Members & important Business of Congress. I can only answer that I have made myself as well acquainted as the time & my small capacity admits of. You'll see by the late resolves of Congress how we go on, & that we are every day drawing nearer the important Question. You see trade is open to all foreign countries except *Great Britain & its dependencies*. One step more & the point is settled.¹ I congratulate you on the success of our small fleet.² I have but an imperfect accot of the matter, but no doubt you have the particulars ere now as they arriv'd at New-London. One of our cruisers (after an hours engagement) took a tender Mounting six Carriage Guns & 35 picked men commanded by the first Leiutt of the Liverpool.³ Some men were killd & wounded on both sides. We have several small cruisers out & going out which I hope will give a good accot of the petty Pirates that infest the coast. The men of war at New York are not suffer'd to land on any pretence whatever, so they will be obliged to go as far as Vigenia for water. A 40 Gun ship laying at the Capes of Delawar is in the same scituation. One of her Lieutts is a prisoner & now on his way to this City. I hope the late act of the British Parliament will reconcile every body to an eternal seperation from a People abandoned to every vice & whose Rulers make cruelty & injustice the Guide of all their actions. Lord Mansfields Speech points out what we are to expect from such Barbarians;⁴ for my part I see no alternative but Freedom or Slavery. Providence has kindly offerd us our choice & shall we Hesitate which to accept I hope not. God forbid that an American shod be animated with so Base a Soul as not to embrace the former with Eagerness. The People of South-Carolina look on the late act of Parliament as a declaration of war and have seized a ship put in there to refit, bound from the West Indies to London. This was done before they knew

of the Resolves of Congress respecting that matter.

Pray write often and let me know every thing that passes. How goes on your town Meetings, Committees &c. Tell Mrs Br[acket]t she must write to me. I have wrote you a letter of some length but my present Hurry won't permit me to look over it.

Your very affte Friend Sr,   Wm. Whipple

[*P.S.*] My Duty to Mother. Let me Know how she does.

RC (MHi).
    [1] Apparently Whipple interpreted the resolutions opening American trade to all foreign countries as only one step short of independence.
    Robert Treat Paine noted this report in his diary this day: "Fair. Heard of Comodore Hopkins Engagement & Success in taking a Bomb Ketch & 3 Tenders off East end of Block Island." MHi. For Hopkins' official report of the action, see Esek Hopkins to John Hancock, April 9, 1776, Clark, *Naval Documents*, 4:735–36.
    [3] A reference to the capture of the tender *Edward* by the Continental brig *Lexington*. Clark, *Naval Documents*, 4:772–73.
    [4] Undoubtedly a reference to Mansfield's speech in the House of Lords on December 20, 1775, supporting passage of the Prohibitory Act and urging vigorous prosecution of the war. *Am. Archives*, 4th ser. 6:233–34.

William Whipple to John Langdon

Dear Sir   Philadelphia 11th April 1776
    I rec'd your favor of the 24th ult. Col Bartlett took with him the Marine money, you mention. The 10.000 dollars from the Secret Committee shall send by the first opportunity which I expect will be in about a week by Mr Jos. Henderson who is here in a carriage and will set out about that time.[1] I find you are going to Boston and shall expect from you a particular account of the situation that town was left in by the Barbarians, also what Tories are left behind &c &c. There are several contracts for guns—if your ship cannot be supplied nearer home they must be sent from here.

    I congratulate you on Admiral Hopkin's success, the particulars of which no doubt you have before now. Yesterday arrived here a sloop— she was a tender fitted out by the Liverpool with 6 carriage guns and 35 picked men commanded by the first Lieutenant of the Liverpool. She was sent in by the Lexington whom she engaged an hour and killed two of his men and wounded two. The sloop had one man killed and 5 or 6 wounded. There are several more of these small fellows on the coast, which I expect the Lexington will give a good account of. The army have converted all the Yankees. I expect the statue of the Royal Brute now standing in Bowling Green will soon be demolished. In my last,

I mentioned the officers for the ship you are building. I shall be glad if you'll also think of proper persons for Marine officers. I suppose there must be a Captain and two Lieutenants; the officers for all the ships will soon be appointed. The day is set for appointing Agents, so expect my next will enclose your commission.[2] I suppose the late Act of Parliament declaring all American rebels has reached you before now; I should have sent you a copy had I have been able to obtain one but it has not yet been printed here. On the arrival of that Act in South Carolina, the Convention there seized a ship loaded with sugars bound from the West Indies to London (and had put in there to repair some damages she had rec'd and was then ready to sail), ordered ship and cargo to be sold and the money lodged in the Treasury and have sent to Congress for approbation. Their conduct no doubt is justified by some late Resolves which I now enclose you. Refer you to the papers for news.

Yours sincerely,   Wm Whipple

Tr (DLC).
   [1] Whipple did forward the money a few days later. See Whipple to Langdon, April 15, 1776.
   [2] See Whipple to Langdon, April 29, 1776.

John Adams to Abigail Adams

April 12. 1776

Inclose a few Sheets of Paper, and will send more as fast as Opportunities present.

Chesterfields Letters are a chequered sett. You would not choose to have them in your Library, they are like Congreeves Plays, stained with libertine Morals and base Principles.[1]

You will see by the Papers, the News, the Speculations and the Political Plans of the Day.

The Ports are opened wide enough at last, and Privateers are allowed to prey upon British Trade. This is not Independency you know. What is? Why Government in every Colony, a Confederation among them all, and Treaties with foreign Nations, to acknowledge Us a Sovereign State, and all that. When these Things will be done, or any of them, Time must discover. Perhaps the Time is near, perhaps a great Way off.

RC (MHi). Adams, *Family Correspondence* (Butterfield), 1:376–77.
   [1] Abigail had asked John to purchase a copy of the earl of Chesterfield's *Letters to His Son.* Adams, *Family Correspondence* (Butterfield), 1:359.

John Adams to Joseph Palmer

April 12. 1776

We begin to make some little Figure here in the Naval Way. Captn. Barry was fitted out here a few days ago in a sixteen Gun Brig, and put to Sea by the Roebuck Man of War which lies in Delaware River, and after he got without the Capes fell in with a Tender belonging to the Liverpool Man of War, and took her after an Engagement of two Glasses. She had 8 Carriage Guns and a number of Swivells. One Thing remarkable is that four of her guns are marked Liverpool which shews that guns are not very plenty with them; otherwise the Liverpool would not have Spared any Part of hers.

I long to hear what Fortifications are preparing for Boston Harbour. I cant but Think that Row Gallies would be of excellent Use. They might dodge about behind the Islands in that Harbour and into shoal Water, in such a Manner, that the Weight of their Metal, and the Certainty of their Shots, and the Place, between Wind & Water, at which They would be levell'd, would render them terrible to large ships. Fire, carried upon Rafts and in Small Vessells, I should think would be very troublesome to these Gentry. I cannot bear the Thought of their ever getting into Boston again, or into that Harbour. I would willingly contribute my share, that indeed would be but little, towards any Expence, nay I would willingly go and work myself upon the Fortifications if that was necessary.

Where will the Cloud burst next? Are they gone to Hallifax? Will they divide their Force? Can they do that with safety? Will they attempt Quebec? Or will they come to N. York? Or will they come to Philadelphia, or go further South, to Virginia, or one of the Carolinas? Or, which I sometimes Suspect is more probable than any other Supposition, will they linger out the Summer in Hallifax, like Lord Loudoun and themselves, fighting Mock Battles and acting Grubstreet Plays. I should dread this, more than their whole Force applied to any Port of the Continent. I really think this would be the best Game they can play with such a Hand as they have for upon my Word I am almost enough elated to boast that We have high, low, & Jack in our Hands, and We must be bad Gamesters indeed if We loose the Game.

You and the rest of my Friends are so busy I presume in purifying Boston of small Pox, and another Infection which is much more malignant, I mean Toryism and I hope in fortifying the Harbour, that I have reconciled myself, to that State of Ignorance, in which I still remain of all the Particulars, discoverd in Boston.

Am very desirous of knowing if I could, what Quantities of Salt Petre came in, and what Progress is made in the Manufacture of it, and of Cannons & Musquitts and especially the Powder Mills. Have you Persons who understand the Art of making Powder?

RC (MeHi). In Adams' hand, though not signed.

John Adams to William Tudor

April 12. 1776

I wish you Joy, sir, of your new Abode. I hope you found the Houses, Wharves &c, &c, in the Town of Boston which are hereafter to contribute to your Satisfaction in Life, in good order.

I Should be very happy to learn the Condition in which the Town appeared, the situation of the Buildings and the State and History of the Inhabitants, during the Seige, what Tories are left, and what is to be done with them. Very few Particulars have reached Philadelphia. I suppose my Friends have been so busily employed, that they could not Spare the Time to write. I commend them for devoting their whole Time to the Care of the Town and the Fortifications of the Harbour. But as Soon as they can snatch a little Leisure, I hope they will write to me.

You talk about Common Sense and Say it has been attributed to me. But I am as innocent of it as a Babe.

The most atrocious literary sins have been imputed to me these twelve years

"Poor harmless I! and can I choose but Smile

"When every Coxcomb knows me by my Style."

I could not reach the Strength and Brevity of his Style, nor his elegant Symplicity, nor his piercing Pathos. But I really think in other Respects, the Pamphlet would do no Honour even to me. The old Testament Reasoning against Monarchy would have never come from me. The Attempt to frame a Continental Constitution, is feeble indeed—it is poor and despicable. Yet this is a very meritorious Production.

In Point of argument there is nothing new. I believe every one that is in it, had been hackneyd in every Conversation public and private, before that Pamphlet was written.

You desire me to send you an oration, but I wont. I have too much Contempt and Indignation, at that insolent Performance to meddle with it.[1]

The Ports are open you see, and Privateering is allowd. Is this Independency?

I wish you would let me know whether the Courts sit, and whether Business is done.

I am Sure it is Time that a certain Name & style was discarded. Commissions, Writs, & Indictments Should run in another Form.

The Colony of &c to the Sherriff.

The Colony of to A. B.

Against the Peace of the Colony of &c
This must be the Style.

RC (MHi). In Adams' hand, though not signed.
[1] Tudor had requested a copy of William Smith's oration commemorating the
death of Gen. Richard Montgomery. William Tudor to John Adams, February 29,
1776, Adams Papers, MHi. See also Josiah Bartlett to Mary Bartlett, February 19,
note; and Richard Smith's Diary, February 21, 1776.

John Hancock to Certain Colonies

Gentlemen,   Philadelphia April 12th. 1776
   While the British Ministry are taking every Step, that Cruelty and
Revenge can dictate, for the Destruction of American Liberty, it is incumbent on these United Colonies, to exert their utmost Efforts to defeat them. Happily for our Country, their military operations have not
been attended with that Success which they so sanguinely expected.
This Circumstance however, far from abating their Rage against us,
has had the Effect, constantly produced by disappointed Passions. It
has roused them to make new Exertions of Power against Us; and we
now behold American Property, by a late Act of Parliament, made
legal Plunder.[1] Such a Strain of Rapine and Violence can be equalled
only by the Spirit, with which it is likely to be executed. Having authorized the Seizure of Vessels belonging to these Colonies, where-ever
found upon the High Seas, there is too much Reason to apprehend, the
Execution of the Edict (which we may expect in its greatest Extent)
will, for a Time, prove a severe Clog to the Trade of America. Under
these Circumstances The Congress, in Hopes of checking, in some Degree, an Evil, which they cannot at present remove, and acting on the
same Principles of Self Preservation, and Retaliation which they have
hitherto adopted, have been induced to come into sundry Resolutions
relative to the fitting out Letters of Marque & Reprizal. The Trade of
America is an object of so much Consequence, and the Protection of it
so necessary, that I make no Doubt of your giving all the Encouragement in your Power to any Measures that may be deemed expedient
for its Security & Existence. I herewith transmit Bonds, Commissions,
and Instructions, which the Congress has thought proper to request the
several Assemblies, Conventions, & Committees of Safety, to make Use
of on the Occasion.[2]
   I have the Honour to be, Gent., Your most obedt. & very hbl ser.
                                             J. H. Presidt.

LB (DNA: PCC, item 12A). Addressed: "To Hon. Assembly of New Hamsphire.
To the Honble the Assembly of Massachusetts Bay. Assembly of Rhode Island.
Assembly of Connecticut. Convention of Virginia."

¹ A reference to the Prohibitory Act.

² See *JCC*, 4:247–48, 251–53. Hancock had already sent these forms to the New York Provincial Congress, enclosed in a letter of April 10. PCC, item 12A; and *Am. Archives*, 4th ser. 5:843–44. Hancock also sent a brief letter to the Massachusetts Assembly on April 13, enclosing a resolution of April 11 encouraging the colonies to send to foreign nations news of Congress' resolves on trade, and one of April 12 relative to the treatment of prisoners of war. M-Ar. See also *JCC*, 4:273–74, 275.

Samuel Huntington to Jabez Huntington

Sir   Philadelphia 12th April 1776

I had the Honour to write you the 19th March per Capt Tracy, Since which am favour'd with yours of the 16th per Col. Williams. Have acquainted the Delegates from Rhode Island & Massachusetts of the save [safe] arrival of the 400 bolts Duck to your care. The Congress have been exceeding busy, commonly Set from ten in the morning until between 4 & 5 in the afternoon without any refreshment. It is needless at this time to be particular on the head of News as Col Williams the bearer will be able to Inform every thing which I am at Liberty to comminicate. Hope we Shall be able to obtain for N London harbour a number of the heavy cannon brot. in there by Commadore Hopkins. We are Endeavouring to obtain some Assistance from Congress to fortify that Harbour as an assylum for the Continental fleet.¹ With Compliments to all enquiring Friends, I remain sir with much regard your humble Servt,   Saml Huntington

RC (Paul Francis Webster, Beverly Hills, Calif., 1974).

¹ See *JCC*, 4:283, 289. In his response of May 7, a draft of which is on the verso of this document, Jabez congratulated Samuel "on the Success of Canon for N London Harbour & the prospect of having Assistance from Congress to fortify there as I am Clearly of Opinion that no Harbour in any of the United Colonies is so well by Nature Situated & Formd to Serve the Continentall Fleet as that. Much is done already & Could wish to have more to make it Sufficiently Strong." He also reported that a number of sick seamen from the Continental fleet were in New London hospitals and noted that should a military hospital be established there, Dr. Turner "would be willing to be appd. to some Department for that Hospital. From his Experience in the Army & known Skill in Surgery Should think he would serve the Continent to Satisfaction & if any proper opening for him, Could heartily Recommend him." Philip Turner, physician and surgeon to Connecticut troops, was appointed surgeon general of the hospital in the eastern department on April 11, 1777. *JCC*, 7:254.

Maryland Delegates to the Maryland Council

Gentlemen.   Phila. April 12th. 1776. [9] OClock night.

Yours of the 9th Inst. was delivered to Us this day at twelve O'Clock, and we immediately handed the Packet inclosed to the President.[1] It contained the Act of Parliament for restraining the Trade of the Colonies passed in December last, and which was received here in the Begining of February. Our friends in South Carolina supposed we might not have received the Act and therefore sent the first Copy they received. There having been an Arrival of Powder lately on Account of the Congress, We just before the Rec[eip]t of your Letter borrowed a Ton and shall send it to Chester Town to wait your Order in the Distribution thereof. Every other Colony has been supplied from the Continental Magazine & this was spared to Us without Hesitation.

We are Gent., Yr most humb. Sevts,   Th Johnson junr

T. Stone

RC (MdAA). Written by Johnson and signed by Johnson and Stone.

[1] The Maryland Council had forwarded a packet for President Hancock, which they had received on April 9 from the Virginia Committee of Safety. See *Md. Archives*, 11:317.

William Whipple to Meshech Weare

Sir   Philadelphia 12th Apl 1776

Inclos'd you have some papers contg the late Resolutions of Congress.[1] Blank Commissions &c will be forwarded by the President. I hope Col. Bartlett will soon be here. I Expect he will be set out before this reaches you. If the accots can not be got ready, a Petition from the Genl Court or if they are not seting from the Committee representing the exertions of the Colony in the Common Cause and the disadvantages of emiting such large sums in Colonial Bills, will have a very good effect, & I am inclin'd to think wod. obtain a Grant of about two thirds the sum the Colony is in advance.[2]

Congress have been so exceeding ingaged I have not been able to call their attention to the Report of the Committee on the application of your Committee but hope shall very soon be able to transmit their determination. I am, with Great Respect & Esteem, Sir, Your Most Obt. Sert.   Wm. Whipple

RC (PPRF).

[1] Probably the resolutions authorizing privateering and opening American ports. *JCC*, 4:229–32, 251–54, 257–59.

[2] New Hampshire ultimately received an advance of $60,000 from Congress on August 8, 1776. *JCC*, 5:637.

Oliver Wolcott to Philip Schuyler

Sir, Philidelpa. 12 April 1776

I have Enclosed to you some Resolves of Congress respecting the Indian Affairs in the Northern Department,[1] and Am Sir, your most Obedient and humble Servant, Oliver Wolcott

RC (MH).
[1] Probably the resolves of April 10. See *JCC*, 4:266–68.

Benjamin Franklin to John Hancock

Sir Saratogo, April 13. 1776

We have been here some Days waiting for General Schuyler's Orders to proceed, which we have just received, and shall accordingly leave this Place to morrow.[1] Tho' by the Advices from Canada communicated by him to us, and as we suppose sent forward to you, I am afraid we shall be able to effect but little there. We had a heavy Snow here yesterday and the Waters are so out, as to make Travelling difficult by Land, and there is a strong Fresh in the River against the Boats, but we shall endeavour to get on as well as we can. We join in Respects to the Congress, and to yourself in particular. I have the Honour to be, Sir, Your most obedt huml Servt, B Franklin

RC (DNA: PCC, item 78).
[1] Taking advantage of the opportunity of the "Express" carrying Franklin's letter to Congress, Samuel Chase explained their delay at Saratoga in a brief letter sent to his wife this date. "We at this place are waiting for the breaking up the Lakes which is daily expected." Adams Papers, MHi.

Maryland Delegates to the Maryland Council of Safety

Gent. Phila. April 13th. 1776

There is not an Ell of light Duck in this City or We should have bought some agreable to your Request.[1] We advised with persons here who understand what Articles are fit for Tents and they inform Us that the Cruger sent by Mr Bowley from hence is very proper for that purpose. We wish to know if you have received the Cruger and other Linens imported in the Wild Dick: We directed them to be lodged at Baltimore for your Order And expect they are arrived before this. Inclosed You have a Memorandum of the several per[son]s. Be pleased

[*to*] inform Us if you have heard from Vanbeber. No important Occurance since We last wrote You.

We are, Yr most Obt Serts.   Th. Johnson Junr

                                                          T. Stone

                                                          R. Alexander

[*P.S.*] We wish to be informed if in your Opinion the Cruger is proper for Tents.

RC (MdAA). Written by Johnson and signed by Johnson, Stone, and Alexander.
[1] See the council's letter of April 5 to the Maryland delegates. *Md. Archives*, 11:314.

Thomas McKean to Philip Schuyler

Sir,   Philadelphia April 13th. 1776.

I had the pleasure of your Letter of the 21st of February last and have since made all the inquiry I could respecting the real Situation of Allen McDonell and the Highlanders, but cannot arrive at perfect satisfaction. Mr. McDonell has been here these three weeks soliciting liberty to return or that the families of the Scotch prisoners may be supported. The latter he seems most desirous of, but upon the whole the Congress have directed the Committee on prisoners of which I am one to take your opinion, "whether the said Allen McDonell and the other hostages taken in Tryon county may, consistent with the public safety, be permitted to return to their respective homes on their parole." [1] As [the] Continent has been at considerable expence for these people already, and must add to it by maintaining their respective families unless they return, the Congress expect your answer as soon as possible.

Mr. Hamar was at Trenton; on the 23d Novemr. last it was agreed he might reside at Mr. Duers near Saratoga and at his desire; on the 17th January he was permitted to reside at Mr. Stainforth's near Princetown, where I have heard he purposed to bring Mrs. Hamar as soon as the weather was suitable for her to travel. [2] If he should incline to remove to any other place, please to let me know, and I shall render him, or any other friend of yours, all the services in my power. I congratulate you on the Evacuation of Boston by the British forces, on the reduction & conquest of the Tories, & Partisans of Governor Martin, in North Carolina, and on the success of the American Navy. We have heard nothing lately about the much talked of Commissioners, but are determined to be prepared at all points. I am, Sir, with much esteem, Your most obedient servant,   Tho McKean

RC (NN).
[1] *JCC*, 4:264. See also McKean to Schuyler, January 30, 1776.
[2] See John Jay to Ibbetson Hamar, November 22, 1775; and *JCC*, 4:62.

John Adams to Abigail Adams

Ap. 14. 1776

You justly complain of my short Letters, but the critical State of Things and the Multiplicity of Avocations must plead my Excuse. You ask where the Fleet is. The inclosed Papers will inform you. You ask what Sort of Defence Virginia can make. I believe they will make an able Defence. Their Militia and minute Men have been some time employed in training them selves, and they have Nine Battallions of regulars as they call them, maintained among them, under good Officers, at the Continental Expence. They have set up a Number of Manufactories of Fire Arms, which are busily employed. They are tolerably supplied with Powder, and are successfull and assiduous, in making Salt Petre. Their neighbouring Sister or rather Daughter Colony of North Carolina, which is a warlike Colony, and has several Battallions at the Continental Expence, as well as a pretty good Militia, are ready to assist them, and they are in very good Spirits, and seem determined to make a brave Resistance. The Gentry are very rich, and the common People very poor. This Inequality of Property, gives an Aristocratical Turn to all their Proceedings, and occasions a strong Aversion in their Patricians, to Common Sense. But the Spirit of these Barons, is coming down, and it must submit.

It is very true, as you observe they have been duped by Dunmore. But this is a Common Case. All the Colonies are duped, more or less, at one Time and another. A more egregious Bubble was never blown up, than the Story of Commissioners coming to treat with the Congress. Yet it has gained Credit like a Charm, not only without but against the clearest Evidence. I never shall forget the Delusion, which seized our best and most sagacious Friends the dear Inhabitants of Boston, the Winter before last. Credulity and the Want of Foresight, are Imperfections in the human Character, that no Politician can sufficiently guard against.

You have given me some Pleasure, by your Account of a certain House in Queen Street. I had burned it, long ago, in Imagination. It rises now to my View like a Phœnix. What shall I say of the Solicitor General? [1] I pity his pretty Children, I pity his Father, and his sisters. I wish I could be clear that it is no moral Evil to pity him and his Lady. Upon Repentance they will certainly have a large Share in the Compassions of many. But let Us take Warning and give it to our Children. Whenever Vanity, and Gaiety, a Love of Pomp and Dress, Furniture, Equipage, Buildings, great Company, expensive Diversions, and elegant Entertainments get the better of the Principles and Judgments of Men or Women there is no knowing where they will stop, nor into what Evils, natural, moral, or political, they will lead us.

Your Description of your own Gaiety de Coeur, charms me. Thanks be to God you have just Cause to rejoice—and may the bright Prospect be obscured by no Cloud.

As to Declarations of Independency, be patient. Read our Privateering Laws, and our Commercial Laws. What signifies a Word.

As to your extraordinary Code of Laws, I cannot but laugh.[2] We have been told that our Struggle has loosened the bands of Government every where. That Children and Apprentices were disobedient—that schools and Colledges were grown turbulent—that Indians slighted their Guardians and Negroes grew insolent to their Masters. But your Letter was the first Intimation that another Tribe more numerous and powerfull than all the rest were grown discontented. This is rather too coarse a Compliment but you are so saucy, I wont blot it out.

Depend upon it, We know better than to repeal our Masculine systems. Altho they are in full Force, you know they are little more than Theory. We dare not exert our Power in its full Latitude. We are obliged to go fair, and softly, and in Practice you know We are the subjects. We have only the Name of Masters, and rather than give up this, which would compleatly subject Us to the Despotism of the Peticoat, I hope General Washington, and all our brave Heroes would fight. I am sure every good Politician would plot, as long as he would against Despotism, Empire, Monarchy, Aristocracy, Oligarchy, or Ochlocracy. A fine Story indeed. I begin to think the Ministry as deep as they are wicked. After stirring up Tories, Landjobbers, Trimmers, Bigots, Canadians, Indians, Negroes, Hanoverians, Hessians, Russians, Irish Roman Catholicks, Scotch Renegadoes, at last they have stimulated the   to demand new Priviledges and threaten to rebell.

RC (MHi). Adams, *Family Correspondence* (Butterfield), 1:381–83.

[1] Jonathan Sewall.

[2] In her March 31 letter, Abigail had urged John to "Remember the Ladies" when preparing a new code of laws and to "be more generous and favourable to them than your ancestors." She warned him that "If perticuliar care and attention is not paid to the Laidies we are determined to foment a Rebelion and will not hold ourselves bound by any Laws in which we have no voice, or Representation." Adams, *Family Correspondence* (Butterfield), 1:370. For a further glimpse into Adams' views on government and the rights of women, see John Adams to James Sullivan, May 26, 1776.

Carter Braxton to Landon Carter

Dear Sir,[1]   Philada April 14 1776.

In this much elevated Station to which I fear I was improperly called by my Country, it has been my desire to seek the Advice and opinions of my friends that I might with better Judgment determine on the important matters that daily occur. In this number Nature gave me a right

A N

A D D R E S S

TO THE

C O N V E N T I O N

OF THE

COLONY AND ANCIENT DOMINION OF

V I R G I N I A;

ON THE

Subject of Government in general, and recommending
a particular Form to their Confideration.

By a N A T I V E of that COLONY.

P H I L A D E L P H I A:
PRINTED BY JOHN DUNLAP, IN MARKET-STREET.

M,DCC,LXXVI.

Carter Braxton's Pamphlet *An Address to the Convention of the Colony and Ancient Dominion
of Virginia*

to rank you, & my knowledge taught me to expect your Wisdom & Experience would be a luminary in the present maze of Politicks, the intricacies and windings of which I own often puzzles my Understanding. To assist in finding a Clue by which my Country may be safely & honourably directed thro this labyrinth shall be my peculiar Study & Attention. If in this pursuit I differ in Sentiment with some of my Countrymen I flatter my self their Charity will prevent any injurious imputations on the motives that influence my Actions.

Independency & total Seperation from Great Britain are the interesting Subjects of all ranks of Men & often agitate our Body. It is in truth a delusive Bait which Men inconsiderately catch at without knowing the hook to which it is affixed. It is an Object to be wished for by every American; when it can be obtained with Safety & Honor. That this is not the moment I will prove by Arguments that to me are decisive & which exist with certainty. Your refined notion of our publick Honor being engaged to await the terms to be offered by Commissioners operates strongly with me & many others & makes the first reason I would offer. My next is that America is in too defenseless a State for the declaration having no Alliance with a naval Power nor as yet any Fleet of Consequence of her own to protect that trade which is so essential to the prosecution of the War & without which I know we cannot go on much longer. It is said by the Advocates for Seperation that France will undoubtedly assist us after we have asserted the State, and therefore they urge us to make the experiment.

Would such a blind, precipitate measure as this be justified by Prudence, first to throw off our Connexion with G. Britain and then give ourselves up to the Arms of France. Would not this Court so famous for Intrigues & Deception avail herself of our Situation & from it exact much severer terms than if we were to treat with *her* before hand & settle the terms of any future alliance. Surely she would, but the truth of the matter is, there are some who are affraid to await the Arrival of Commissioners, lest the dispute should be accomodated much agt their Will even upon the Admission of our own terms. For however strange it may appear I am satisfied that the eastern Colonies do not mean to have a Reconciliation and in this I am justified by publick & private Reasons.

To illustrate my Opinion I will beg leave to mention them. Two of the new England Colonies enjoy a Government purely democratical the Nature & Principle of which both civil & religious are so totally incompatible with Monarchy that they have ever lived in a restless State under it. The other two tho not so popular in their frame bordered so near upon it that Monarchical Influence hung very heavy on them. The best opportunity in the World being now offered them to throw off all Subjection & embrace their darling Democracy, they are determined to accept it.

These are aided by those of a private Nature but not less cogent. The Colonies of Massachusetts & Connecticut who rule the other two have Claims on the Province of Pensylvania in the whole for near one third of the Land within their Provincial Bounds & indeed the Claim extended to its full extent comes within four Miles of this City. This dispute was carried to the King & Council & with them it now lies. The eastern Colonies unwilling they should now be the Arbiters have exerted their Claim by force & have at this time eight hundred Men in Arms upon the upper part of this Land called Wyoming, where they are peaceble at present only thro the Influence of the Congress.[2] There naturally then arises a heart burning & Jealousy between these People & they must have two very different Objects in View.

The Province of New York is not without her Fears & apprehensions from the Temper of her Neighbours, their great Swarms & small Territory.

Even Virginia is not free from Claims on Pennsylvania nor Maryland from those on Virginia.

Some of the delegates from our Colony carry their Ideas of right to Lands so far to the eastward that the middle Colonies dread their being swallowed up between the Claims of them & those from the East. And yet without any Adjustment of their disputes & a variety of other matters, some are for lugging us into Independence. But so long as these remain unsettled & Men act upon the Principles they ever have done, you may rely no such thing will be generally agreed on. Upon viewing the secret movements of Men & things I am convinced the Assertion of Independence is far off. If it was to be now asserted, the Continent would be torn in pieces by intestine Wars & Convulsions.

Previous to Independence all disputes must be healed & Harmony prevail. A grand Continental League must be formed & a superintending Power also. When these necessary Steps are taken & I see a Coalition formed sufficient to withstand the Power of Britain or any other, then am I for an independent State & all its Consequences, as then I think they will produce Happiness to America. It is a true saying of a Wit— We must hang together or seperately. I will not beg yr pardon for intruding this long Letter upon yr old age which I judged necessary in my Situation & to conclude by assuring you I am with great regard, your affect Nephew, Carter Braxton

[P.S.] If any of our News papers will be agreable say so in yr next.

RC (MeHi).
[1] Apparently Landon Carter, who was the brother of Braxton's mother.
[2] See *JCC*, 3:439–40, 4:283.

John Adams to Abigail Adams

April 15. 1776

I send you every News Paper, that comes out, and I send you now
and then a few sheets of Paper but this Article is as scarce here, as with
you. I would send a Quire, if I could get a Conveyance. I write you,
now and then a Line, as often as I can, but I can tell you no News, but
what I send in the public Papers.

We are Waiting it is said for Commissioners, a Messiah that will
never come. This Story of Commissioners is as arrant an Illusion as
ever was hatched in the Brain of an Enthusiast, a Politician, or a
Maniac. I have laugh'd at it—scolded at it—griev'd at it—and I dont
know but I may at an unguarded Moment have rip'd [1] at it—but it is
vain to Reason against such Delusions. I was very sorry to see in a
Letter from the General that he had been bubbled with it, and still
more to see in a Letter from my sagacious Friend W[arren] at Plymouth, that he was taken in too. [2]

My Opinion is that the Commissioners and the Commission have
been here, I mean in America, these two Months. The Governors,
Mandamus Councillors, Collectors and Comptrollers, and Comman-
ders of the Army and Navy, I conjecture compose the List and their
Power is to receive Submissions. But We are not in a very submissive
Mood. They will get no Advantage of Us.

We shall go on, to Perfection I believe. I have been very busy for
some time—have written about Ten sheets of Paper with my own Hand,
about some trifling Affairs, which I may mention some time or other—
not now for fear of Accidents. [3]

What will come of this Labour Time will discover. I shall get nothing by it, I believe, because I never get any Thing by any Thing that I
do. I am sure the Public or Posterity ought to get Something. I believe
my Children will think I might as well have thought and laboured,
a little, night and Day for their Benefit. . . . [4] But I will not bear the
Reproaches of my Children. I will tell them that I studied and laboured
to procure a free Constitution of Government for them to solace themselves under, and if they do not prefer this to ample Fortune, to Ease
and Elegance, they are not my Children, and I care not what becomes
of them. They shall live upon thin Diet, wear mean Cloaths, and work
hard, with Chearfull Hearts and free Spirits or they may be the Children of the Earth or of no one, for me.

John has Genius and so has Charles. Take Care that they dont go
astray. Cultivate their Minds, inspire their little Hearts, raise their
Wishes. Fix their Attention upon great and glorious Objects, root out
every little Thing, weed out every Meanness, make them great and
manly. Teach them to scorn Injustice, Ingratitude, Cowardice, and
Falshood. Let them revere nothing but Religion, Morality and Liberty.

Nabby and Tommy are not forgotten by me alto I did not mention them before. The first by Reason of her sex, requires a Different Education from the two I have mentioned. Of this you are the only judge. I want to send each of my little pretty flock, some present or other. I have walked over this City twenty Times and gaped at every shop like a Countryman to find something, but could not. Ask every one of them what they would choose to have and write it to me in your next Letter. From this I shall judge of their Taste and Fancy and Discretion.

RC (MHi). Adams, *Family Correspondence* (Butterfield), 1:383–85.
¹ For Adams' meaning in his use of the verb *rip*, see Adams, *Diary* (Butterfield), 1:97.
² See George Washington to John Hancock, March 24, 1776, in Washington, *Writings* (Fitzpatrick), 4:427–28; and James Warren to John Adams, March 7, 1776, in *Warren-Adams Letters*, 1:209–10.
³ Adams is undoubtedly referring to his constitutional essay which was soon published as *Thoughts on Government*. See Adams to John Penn, March 19–27, 1776.
⁴ Suspension points in text.

John Adams to William Heath

Dear sir   Philadelphia April 15. 1776

Altho I never had the Pleasure and the Honour of so intimate an Acquaintance with you as I wished yet I have a long Time been sufficiently acquainted with your Character, to have the utmost Confidence in your Patriotism and your Judgment of the true Interest of our Country.

The critical State of the Colonies, at this Time, is the Cause of my writing you, because Providence has now placed you in a situation where you have an opportunity of serving your Country in a civil and political Capacity no less essentially than in a military one.[1]

There is nothing of more indispensible Importance in the Conduct of this great Contention, than that New York should go Hand in Hand with the rest of the Colonies both in Politicks and War. The Number of the Tories, the Wick[ed]ness and Credulity of some People, & the Treachery of others, have hitherto prevented that Colony from exerting herself in this mighty Struggle in Proportion to her Strength and Weight.

If you compare the Exertions of Connecticutt with those of New York you will easily see the Importance of having all the Powers of Government in the Hands of the Friends of the People.

It is now perhaps the most critical Moment that America ever saw. There is a Tide in the affairs of Men—and Consequences of infinite Moment depend upon the Colonies assuming Government at this Time.

So convenient an opportunity may never again present itself as the present, while a powerfull Army is there sufficient to overcome any turbulent opposition, and prevent every danger of Convulsion.

To exercise a Government under a King, who has published such a Proclamation and Signed such an Act of Parliament, to pray for his Salvation, temporal I mean—to take oaths of allegiance—to swear to keep his secrets—to swear to try Issues between our sovereign Lord the King and any Criminal at this Time, is such an Absurdity, such Immorality, such Irreligion that I am amazed it can be endured in any one Spot in America.

Governments must be assumed or Anarchy reign, and God knows the Consequences.

I must beg of you therefore, to endeavour to convince the Citizens of New York and the Inhabitants of the Province as opportunity presents, of the Necessity of this Measure. Depend upon it, you cannot do your Country a more important, a more essential Service.

I am well informed that Mr William Smith, Mr. P[hilip] L[ivingston] and I fear Coll McDougal will retard and obstruct this Measure. I hope they will be perswaded to the Contrary, if they have not they may have hereafter the pleasing Reflection that they destroyed their Country.

You must have seen the happy Fruits of this Measure in your own Province, so clearly, as to render it impertinent in me to point out the Benefits of it.

If Nine Months ago the Colonies had assumed Governments, they would have been infinitely better armed, trained, furnished with Ammunition, Salt Petre, Powder Works—they would have been rid of the Plague of Toryism—&c.

I have Time only to hint, and that is enough to you. If you are at a Loss to know me, ask General Sullivan. I am your Friend & most obedient servant

RC (MHi). In Adams' hand, though not signed.
[1] General Heath had been sent to New York by Washington as the commander of the advance brigade of Continental troops. See Heath's "Instructions and Orders" of March 19, 1776, in Washington, *Writings* (Fitzpatrick), 4:408–9.

Samuel Adams to Joseph Hawley

My dear Sir   Philade April 15 1776
Your obliging Letter of the 1st Inst came duly to my hand.[1] So early as the last Winter was a twelve month ⟨past⟩ I was informd by a worthy and very intelligent Friend in London, that the Subduction of the New England Colonies was the *first* Object of our Enemies.[2] This was to be effected, in a Manner coincident with your Ideas, by establishing themselves on Hudsons River. They were thereby at once to secure Canada and the Indians, give Support and Protection to the numerous Tories in New York, supply their Army at Boston with Provisions from that

Colony and intirely prevent the southern from affording any Aid to those invaded Colonies. This Plan was in my opinion undoubtedly dictated by sound Policy; and it would have been put in Execution the last Summer, had not the Necessities to which Gage was reducd & by Apprehensions from our having a formidable Army before Boston, obligd him to break in upon it. They did not neglect Hudsons River the last year; for we know that two of their Transports actually arrivd at New York. But these were immediately orderd by Gage, together with the rest of the Fleet to Boston. My Friend in London whose Intelligence I have never yet found to fail, informd me the last Fall, that our Enemies did not quit this Plan. Upon hearing that it had been thus interrupted, they revivd it, and sent Tryon to New York to keep the People there in good Humour and cooperate with Carleton in the Execution of it. They reckond the last Winter upon having 20,000 Troops in America for the ensuing Campaign, of which 3000 were to go to Virginia or one of the Carolinas. These last I suppose are designd for a Diversion, while the main Body of all the Troops they will be able to send, will be employd in executing their original & favorite Plan. Thus, my Friend, I am yet happy in concurring with you in Sentiments; and I shall persevere in using the small Influence I have here, agreable to your repeated Advice, "to prevent the Enemies establishing themselves & making Advances on Hudson & St Laurence Rivers."

The Mercenary Troops have at length abandond Boston on which, I perceive, you will not allow me *yet* to give you Joy. May I not however advise, that the favorable opportunity which this important Event, added to the Season of the year has offerd, be improvd in fortifying the Harbour so as to render it impracticable for the Enemies Ships to enter it hereafter. I hope this fortunate Change of Affairs has not put you off your Guard. Should you not immediately prepare against future Invasions, which may be made upon you before you are aware? Your Sea Coasts must still be defended. We shall soon realize the Destination of the Enemies Forces. Those under the Command of General Howe will probably remain at Hallifax till the Season of the Year will admit of their going up St Laurence river; The Troops coming from Ireland may be destind to New York & will expect to get Possession there. At least they will attempt it. A Failure may lead their Views back to Boston; for I am in no Apprehensions that they will think of subduing the Southern Colonies till they shall have first subdued those of the North. The Southern Colonies, I think, are sufficiently provided for, to enable them to repell any Force that may come against them the ensuing Summer. Our Safety therefore much depends upon the Care which New England shall take for her own Preservation and our Vigilance and Success in New York and Canada. There are Forces enough already *orderd* to answer all our Purposes. Our Business is, to imitate our Enemies in Zeal, Application & Perseverence in carrying our own Plans into Execution.

I am perfectly satisfied with the Reasons you offer to show the Necessity of a publick & explicit Declaration of Independency. I cannot conceive what good Reason can be assignd against it. Will it widen the Breach? This would be a strange Question after we have raised Armies and fought Battles with the British Troops, set up an American Navy, permitted the Inhabitants of these Colonies to fit out armed Vessels to cruize on all Ships &c belonging to any of the Inhabitants of Great Britain, declaring them the Enemies of the united Colonies, and torn into Shivers their Acts of Trade, by allowing Commerce subject to Regulation to be made by *ourselves* with the People of all Countries but such as are Subjects of the British King. It cannot surely after all this be imagind that we consider ourselves or mean to be considerd by others in any State but that of Independance. But moderate Whigs are disgusted with our mentioning the Word! Sensible Tories are better Politicians. *They* know, that no foreign Power can consistently yeild Comfort to Rebels, or enter into any kind of Treaty with these Colonies till they declare themselves free and independent. They are in hopes that by our protracting this decisive Step we shall grow weary of War; and that for want of foreign Connections and Assistance we shall be driven to the Necessity of acknowledging the Tyrant and submitting to the Tyranny. These are the Hopes and Expectations of Tories, while moderate Gentlemen are flattering themselves with the Prospect of Reconciliation when the Commissioners that are talked of shall arrive. A mere Amusement indeed! When are these Commissioners to arrive? Or what Terms of Reconciliation are we to expect from them that will be acceptable to the People of America? Will the King of Great Britain empower his Commissioners even to promise the Repeal of all or any of their obnoxious and oppressive Acts? Can he do it? Or if he could, has he ever yet discoverd a Disposition which shews the least Degree of that princely Virtue, Clemency? I scruple not to affirm it as my Opinion that his heart is more obdurate, and his Disposition towards the People of America is more unrelenting and malignant than was that of Pharaoh towards the Israelites in Egypt.[3] But let us not be impatient. It requires Time to convince the doubting and inspire the timid. Many great Events have taken place "since the stopping the Courts in Berkshire"—Events at that time unforeseen—Whether we shall ever see the Commissioners is Matter of Uncertainty. I do not & never did expect them. If they do come the Budget must open and it will be soon known to all whether Reconciliation is practicable or not. If they do not come speedily, the hopes which some Men entertain of reconciliation must vanish. I am my dear Sir very respectfully, yours,

SA

FC (NN).

[1] Joseph Hawley's letter of April 1 is in the Samuel Adams Papers, NN.

[2] See Arthur Lee's letters to Adams of February 21 and 24, 1775. Ibid.

[3] In this FC Adams lined out three sentences which were probably not included in the letter sent to Hawley. "His Ministers and Task Masters have possessed the same cruel Spirit. Why then should any be fond of continuing subject to a Tyrant? Or being politically or at all connected with a Nation which has in multiplied Instances and for a long time suffered and enabled him thus to act the Tyrant over us."

Benjamin Franklin to Josiah Quincy

Dear Sir,   Saratoga, April 15. 1776

I am here on my Way to Canada, detain'd by the present State of the Lakes, in which the unthaw'd Ice obstructs Navigation. I begin to apprehend that I have undertaken a Fatigue that at my Time of Life may prove too much for me, so I sit down to write to a few Friends by way of Farewell.

I congratulate you on the Departure of your late troublesome Neighbours. I hope your Country will now for some time have Rest, and that Care will be taken so to fortify Boston, as that no Force shall be able again to get Footing there.

Your very kind Letter of Nov. 13, inclosing Lord Chatham's Speech & Lord Camden's, I duly receiv'd. I think no one can be more sensible than I am of the Favours of corresponding Friends, but I find it impracticable to answer as I ought. At present I think you will deem me inexcusable, and therefore I will not attempt an Apology. But if you should ever happen to be at the same time oppress'd with Years & Business, you may then extenuate a Little for your old Friend.

The Notes of the Speeches taken by your Son (whose Loss I shall ever deplore with you) are exceedingly valuable, as being by much the best Account preserv'd of that Day's Debate.[1]

You ask, "When is the Continental Congress by general Consent to be formed into a supreme Legislative, Alliances defensive & offensive formed, our Ports opened, and a formidable naval Force established at the Public Charge?" I can only answer at present that nothing seems wanting but that general Consent. The Novelty' of the Thing deters some, the Doubt of Success others, the vain Hope of Reconciliation many. But our Enemies take continually every proper Measure to remove these Obstacles, and their Endeavours are attended with Success, since every Day furnishes us with new Causes of increasing Enmity, and new Reasons for wishing an eternal Separation; so that there is a rapid Increase of the formerly small Party who were for an independent Government.

Your Epigram on Lord Chatham's Remark has amply repaid me for the Song. Accept my Thanks for it; and for the charming Extract of a Lady's Letter contain'd in your Favour of Jan 22d.

I thought when I sat down to have written by this Opportunity to Dr Cooper, Mr Bowdoin and Dr Winthrop; but I am interrupted. Be so good as to present my affectionate Respects to them, and to your good Ladies. Adieu, my dear Friend, and believe me ever, Yours most affectionately,   B Franklin

RC (PHi).

[1] A reference to notes by Josiah Quincy, Jr., of speeches made by Chatham and Camden in the House of Lords on January 20, 1775, when Franklin and Quincy had attended debates on "the present American quarrel" as the guests of Chatham. A few days later Quincy contracted an illness from which he never fully recovered, and of which he died on his return voyage to Boston in April 1775. See Josiah Quincy, *Memoir of the Life of Josiah Quincy Jun. of Massachusetts*, ed. Josiah Quincy (Boston: Cummings, Hilliard, & Co., 1825), pp. 318–35.

John Jay's Proposed Resolutions

[April 15–May 3? 1776] [1]

Whereas it is unjust as well as impolitic that Americans should afford aid to the Enemies of their Country, and particularly in the Seizure of Vessels or other Property belonging to Inhabitants of these Colonies or by purchasing of the Enemy any of their Property so seized.

Resolved That all Americans who shall be guilty of the said Offences ought to be liable for the Damages which the Persons injured by such Seizure may sustain thereby.

Resolved therefore that it be recommended to all the Legislatures and Conventions in these united Colonies to enact Laws or Ordinances for the Purposes aforesaid where Courts competent to the Cognizance of such Cause, do not already exist to erect them and to the End That the said Laws or Ordinances in the different Colonies may the better correspond, and their objects obtained with the greater Facility and Justice.

Resolved That the Party injured as af[oresai]d ought to commence his Action against the offender who ought to be entitled to Bail in the Court so erected or to be erected in the Colony where the Offender ⟨shall happen, be committed, and where the same shall happen on the high Seas then in these Colonies next that he may think proper⟩ can or shall be taken, and that the Proceedings in the said Action ought to be according to the Modes of Proceeding used in the said Colony in Civil Causes. And that appeals ought to be admitted and prosecuted as in other civil action, except in Colonies where the Governors or others appointed by the King were heretofore Judges in Error, In which Colonies the Conventions ought to appoint proper persons to recieve and determine such Appeals provided the Parties demanding the same shall and give reasonable Security for prosecuting the same in which all further Proceedings ought to be stayed till the said Appeal be determined.

And whereas it may happen that the Estate or Effects of the Def[endan]t may not be in the Colony in which such Cause may be tryed but in some other whereby in case Judgment should pass against the Def[endan]t the Damages cannot be levied Resolved that in all such Cases a Transcript of the Record certified by the Judge or Judges of the said Court ought on the Request of the Plt[Plaintiff] to be transmitted to the Judge or Judges of the Court erected or to be erected as af[oresai]d in the Colony where the Estate or Effects of such Def[endan]t may be which Judge or Judges on Reciept thereof ought to award and cause Execution of the said Judgment to be had.

Resolved further that Costs agreable to the Laws and usage of the Colony in which such Actions may be commenced and prosecuted ought to be allowed in these as in other civil actions.

And the better to prevent any vexatious Suits being commenced under Color of the said Laws or Ordinances Resolved that the Plt[Plaintiff] ought previous to the commencement of the said action to make Aff[idavi]t of the Cause of Action and file the same with the Clerk of the Court, and further give Bond with Security to the said Clerk to prosecute the said Action to Judgment and in Case Judgment should pass on the appeal (in case there should be one *determination*) against him to pay the Def[endan]t his Costs, and such Clerk ought in Case the said Action should be finally determined against the Plt[Plaintiff] to assign the said Bond to the Def[endan]t.

MS (NNC). In Jay's hand and endorsed by him: "Dr. Resolutions in Congress agt. purchasg. the Enemy's Prizes &c."

[1] On April 15 Congress appointed Jay, Carter Braxton, and George Wythe as a committee "to bring in a Resolution, whereby persons resident, having property in America, who assist any of the enemies of these United Colonies in the captures of vessels or goods, may be made liable to make good the damages to the sufferers." *JCC*, 4:284. Jay undoubtedly drafted these resolutions sometime after his appointment to the committee but before his departure from Philadelphia on May 3. The journals contain no information on whether they were ever submitted to Congress, and no formal action was ever taken on the basic issue that had been referred to the committee. As the most recent editor of Jay's papers explained, "the debates on independence placed supporters of the British cause in a legal position different from that envisioned by [Jay's] proposed statutes." Jay, *Papers* (Morris), 1:256n. For Jay's attendance at Congress in the spring of 1776, see Jay to Robert R. Livingston, March 4, 1776, note 3.

Richard Henry Lee to Charles Lee

Dear Sir,   Philadelphia, 15th April, 1776.

I have but a moment to acknowledge your last favor[1] which gave me the pleasure of knowing you were well arrived at Williamsburg. It would seem as if Gen. Howe was yet floating on the Ocean incertum quo fata ferant, because the greatest part of his fleet sailed southward from Boston, and because a sloop of war came into N. York and carried Tryon out to sea, to consult we suppose. The riflemen have had a fair engagement with a small man of war for the watering place at N. York, when the former drove the latter off, and have since fortified the spring, so that they must go some where else for water. If it be true as reported here that Sr Peter Parker is arrived in Virginia with Troops we must look to you for news in future, and I make no doubt but we shall have good news.

Our old Commodore Hopkins has actually beaten the Glasgow in a fair fight, and Wallace with his Squadron have fled from the Rhode Island station.[2] Capt. Barry in an armed Brig from hence has taken off the Capes of Virga and sent her in here, a cutter,[3] with 8 carriage Guns belonging to the Liverpool, with one of that ships Lieutenants commanding her. He fought his tender well, not submitting until he was near sinking.

Farewell my dear friend. May you be healthy, happy, and successful.

Richard Henry Lee

[*P.S.*] Gen. Ward has resign'd his command in the Continental Army.[4]

MS not found; reprinted from *NYHS Collections* 4 (1871): 421.

[1] Probably General Lee's letter of April 5, which is in *NYHS Collections* 4 (1871): 378–80.

[2] For variant accounts of the April 6 engagement between the Continental fleet and the *Glasgow*, as well as of the departure of Capt. James Wallace's squadron from Newport harbor, see Clark, *Naval Documents*, 4:679–82, 697, 708–10.

[3] The sloop *Edward* was captured April 7. See Marine Committee to John Barry, April 11, 1776.

[4] See John Hancock to Artemas Ward, April 24, 1776, note 1.

Robert Treat Paine to the Massachusetts General Court

Philada. April 15th. 1776

The Congress at their last Sessions considering the importance to American liberty that all Necessarys of life & defence Should be produced by the Inhabitants of the united Colonies among other things directed an enquiry to be made of the most practicable method of making Salt. As I have the honour to be of that Comttee, I applied some Attention to it & having met with a learned Treatise of Dr. Brownigg on the Subject I extracted the practical part of it & adding a few observations I caused it to be inserted in the Pensylvania Magazine[1] & a great no. of Copies to be detached & have sent them to all the Colonies as far as Georgia.[2] I now do my self the honor to inclose some of them for your Consideration to be disposed of as in your wisdom you may deem best.[3] I can but think there are many parts of our Colony where these works may be profitably erected, in the Southern parts more especially. It must afford great happiness to every lover of the American united Colonies to defeat the cruel designs of their Enemies in any respect, & it will gratify me to have attempted it, tho unfortunately it should not succeed.

Hoping Success to this & every undertaking to promote the welfare of our Colony I Subscribe my self with great Respect yr Honours hble Sevt,   R P

FC (MHi).

[1] Extracts from William Brownrigg's treatise on making salt appeared in the *Pennsylvania Magazine: or American Monthly Museum* 2 (March 1776): 128–33. The same issue contained a brief article, "The Process of making Boiled Salt," accompanied by the editorial note: "The above Account was handed to us by a member of the hon. Continental Congress." Ibid., p. 146. See also Committee of Congress to the Maryland Convention, March 28, 1776, note 4.

[2] Paine's diary entry for April 17 reads: "Wrote Assembly of Connecticut inclosing the Essay on *Salt*, & sent by Col. Dyre." MHi.

[3] The Massachusetts General Court responded by urging the production of salt in the seacoast towns, printing and distributing 150 copies of the article on salt-making that Paine forwarded. *Am. Archives*, 4th ser. 5:1297–98.

William Whipple to John Langdon

Dear Sir,   Philadelphia 15th April 1776.

This goes by Mr Jos. Henderson accompanying the 10,000 dollars from the Secret Committee. I have desired him to forward the letter to you and keep the money for your orders. The Marine Committee have assigned this evening for the appointment of officers for the ships but I shall get the appointment for your ship put off till I hear from you.[1] I have wrote you several times on this subject and hope soon to have a long list and that it will contain something more than is necessary, that I may have a hand in the choice; enclosed you have the numbers of the Bills that in case of any accident they may be advertised. I have agreed to give Mr Henderson twenty dollars for his care of the money; therefore if you send for it, you'll give directions that whoever receives it will pay him that sum—I have his receipt. Mr Henderson declined taking any thing at first, but I could not with any face ask him for a receipt unless he was paid for the carriage. I proposed the sum and think it low compared with the charges I every day see here. I think if you had been here, and I had visited Boston, I should have given you some particular account of the situation of that place, also any little anecdotes that I might have heard of our *Tory Friends* who, I suppose have skulked off.

Yours with great Sincerity,   Wm Whipple

Tr (DLC).

[1] See Whipple to Langdon, April 20, 1776.

John Adams to Joseph Ward

Dear Sir,   Philadelphia, April 16, 1776.

Upon the receipt of your favor of the third of April,[1] I shewed your recommendation of Capt. Fellows to several gentlemen; but it had been previously determined that Captain Manley and Captain Cazneau should have the command of the two ships building in the Massachusetts.[2]

If you should be thrown out of the service by the resignation of General Ward, and there should be any place in particular that you have an inclination for, if you will give me a hint of it I will do you all the service in my power, consistent with the public good, and I doubt not my colleagues will do the same. But I presume that General Ward will now continue in the service, unless his health should be worse. I hope the duty will be less severe than it has been.

As far as I am capable of judging, I am perfectly of General Ward's opinion, that the five regiments are too small a force to be left in Boston.

It is a great work to fortify Boston harbour, and will require many men—But however, I am not sufficiently informed to judge of the propriety of this measure. If there is the least reason to expect that Howe's army will return to Boston, it was wrong to remove so many men so soon, but it is hard to believe that that army will very suddenly return to that place. The Militia of that Province are tremendous to the enemy, and well they may be, for I believe they don't know of such another.

I am much obliged to you for the intelligence you have given me, and wish a continuance of your correspondence. I should be glad to know of every movement in and about Boston.

Every motive of self-preservation, of honour, profit, and glory, call upon our people to fortify the harbour so as to be impregnable. It will make a rendezvous for men of war and privateers, and a mart of trade.

My most respectful compliments to Gen. Ward and best wishes for the restoration of his health.

You seem to wish for independence. Do the resolves for privateering and opening the ports satisfy you, if not let me know what will? Will nothing do, but a positive declaration that we never will be reconciled upon any terms?

It requires time to bring the Colonies all of one mind, but time will do it.

MS not found; reprinted from *Literary World* 11 (September 1852): 179.

[1] Ward's April 3 letter to Adams is in the Adams Papers, MHi; and an extract is printed in Clark, *Naval Documents*, 4:641–42.

[2] These appointments may have been "previously determined" by the Marine Committee, because Congress did not appoint John Manley and Isaac Cazneau to command the Massachusetts frigates until April 17. *JCC*, 4:290.

John Adams to James Warren

Dear Sir   April 16. 1776

I agree with you, in yours of the 30 March,[1] in opinion that five Regiments are too Small a Force to be left with you, considering the Necessity of fortifying the Harbour, and the Danger there is that the Enemy may renew their Designs upon our Province. Am happy to learn that you have Sent a Committee to view the Harbour of Boston and report the best Method of Securing it. When this Report is made I beg it may be transmitted to me.[2] I wish you could transmit to me, a good Plan of the Harbour at the Same Time, for I want to convince this Congress, that that Harbour may be made as strong and impregnable as Gibralter, that they may be inducd to contribute Somewhat to the Fortification of it. I have a great opinion of the Efficacy of Fire, both in Rafts And Ships, for the Defense of that Harbour, among the numerous Shoals and Narrows, and the Multitudes of Islands. Will not Row Gallies be very usefull? would not they dodge about among those Islands, and hide themselves at one Time and make themselves dangerous to a Ship at another?

Batteries must not be omitted, upon the Heights on the Islands. Nor must We forget to obstruct the Channell. I am a miserable Engineer I believe, but I will not Scruple to expose my own Ignorance in this usefull service for the Sake of throwing out any broken Hints for refreshing the Memories of others who know more. If I was to write a Letter to my little Tom, I should say something to him about fortifying Boston Harbour.

Your Letter to the President, I have shewn to My Friends Mr Adams and Mr Gerry. It has puzzled me a little what to do with it. But We are all of opinion upon the whole that it will be most for your Honour to deliver it—and indeed for your Interest, for there will be too much Risque in trusting this office to any one you can employ at a Distance from you.[3]

You inform me that the Council have appointed and   Judges.[4] What, Sir, do you think must be my Feelings upon this occasion? I wish you would acquaint me whether Mr Reed has accepted—and what the Court intends to do, about the Commissions and Salaries of the Judges—Whether they are to lie at the Mercy of Coll Thompson, Coll Bowers and Mr Brown of Abington?

This is a great Constitutional Point, in which the Lives, Liberties,
Estates and Reputations of the People are concernd, as well as the Order
and Firmness of Government in all its Branches and the Morals of the
People besides. I may be suspected of sinister and interested Views in
this, but I will give any Man a Pension out of my own private Fortune
to take my Place. It is upon Principle, and from this Principle let Major
Hawley think of it as he may, I cannot depart.

You will learn the Exploits of our Fleet, before you get this. They
have behaved as all our Forces behave by Sea and Land. Every day
convinces us that our People are equal to every Service of War or
Peace by Sea or Land.

You Say the Sighhs for Independence are universal. You say too,
what I can scarcely believe that *Moderation* and Timidity are at an End.
How is this possible? Is Cunning at an End too—and Reserve—and
hinting against a Measure that a Man dare not oppose directly or disapprove openly. Is trimming at an End too? and Duplicity? and Hy-
pocricy? If they are I give you Joy sir of a group of Tyrants gone. But
I have not yet Faith in all this. You deal in the Marvellous like a Travel-
ler. As to the Sighs, what are they after? Independence? Have we not
been independent these twelve Months, wanting three days?

Have you Seen the Privateering Resolves? Are not these Independence
enough for my beloved Constituents? Have you seen the Resolves for
opening our Ports to all Nations? Are these Independence enough? What
more would you have? Why Methinks I hear you say we want to compleat our Form and Plan of Government. Why dont you petition Congress then for Leave to establish such a Form as shall be most conducive
to the Happiness of the People? But you say why dont the Southern
Colonies Seize upon the Government? That I cant answer. But by all We
can learn, they are about it, every where. We want a confederation you
will say. True. This must be obtained. But we are united now they say—
and the difference between Union and confederation is only the same
with that between an express and implied Contract.

But we ought to form alliances. With Whom? What alliances? You
dont mean to exchange British for French Tyranny. No, you dont mean
to ask the Protection of French Armies. No, We had better depend upon
our own. We only Want commercial Treaties. Try the experiment
without them. But France and England will part the Continent between them. Perhaps so. But both will have good Luck to get it.

But you will say what is your own opinion of these Things. I answer
I would not tell you all that I have Said, and written and done in this
Business for a shilling, because Letters are now a days pimp'd after.
Why dont your Honours of the General Court, if you are so unanimous
in this, give positive Instructions to your own Delegates, to promote
Independency? Dont blame your Delegates untill they have dissobeyed
your Instructions in favour of Independency.[5] The S. Colonies say you

are afraid.

RC (MHi). In Adams' hand, though not signed.

¹ Warren's letter is in *Warren-Adams Letters*, 1:217–20.

² A preliminary report was delivered to the Massachusetts General Court on April 3, and a committee was subsequently appointed on April 5 to "give directions for the fortifying Boston Harbour." *Am. Archives*, 4th ser. 5:1260–62.

³ Warren's March 30 letter of resignation as paymaster general of the Continental Army was read in Congress on April 18, and the request was accepted the next day. *JCC*, 4:291, 296. The letter is in PCC, item 78, 23:269–72, and *Am. Archives*, 4th ser. 5:551. See also John Jay to William Alexander, April 17, 1776.

⁴ Warren had reported that Jedediah Foster and James Sullivan had been appointed judges of the Massachusetts Superior Court. *Warren-Adams Letters*, 1:219.

⁵ For further references to Massachusetts' instructions on independence, see Elbridge Gerry to James Warren, March 26, 1776, note 3.

John Adams to Mercy Warren

Madam   April 16. 1776

Not untill Yesterdays Post, did your agreable Favour of March the Tenth, come to my Hands.¹ It gave me great Pleasure and altho in the distracted Kind of Life, I am obliged to lead, I cannot promise to deserve a Continuance of so excellent a Correspondence yet I am determined by Scribbling Something or other, be it what it may, to provoke it.

The Ladies I think are the greatest Politicians, that I have the Honour to be acquainted with, not only because they act upon the Sublimest of all the Principles of Policy, vizt the [that] Honesty is the best Policy, but because they consider Questions more coolly, than those who are heated with Party Zeal, and inflamed with the bitter Contentions of active public Life.²

I know of no Researches in any of the sciences more ingenious than those which have been made after the best Forms of Government nor can there be a more agreable Employment to a benevolent Heart. The Time is now approaching, when the Colonies will find themselves under a Necessity of engaging in Earnest in this great and indispensible Work. I have ever Thought it the most difficult and dangerous Part of the Business Americans have to do, in this mighty Contest, to continue some Method for the Colonies to glide insensibly, from under the old Government, into a peaceable and contented Submission to new ones. It is a long Time since this opinion was conceivd, and it has never been out of my Mind, my constant Endeavour has been to convince Gentlemen of the Necessity of turning their Thoughts to these Subjects. At present the sense of this Necessity seems to be general, and Measures are taking which must terminate in a compleat Revolution. There is Danger of Convulsions. But I hope, not great ones.

The Form of Government, which you admire, when its Principles are pure is admirable indeed. It is productive of every Thing, which is great and excellent among Men. But its Principles are as easily destroyed, as human Nature is corrupted. Such a Government is only to be supported by pure Religion, or Austere Morals. Public Virtue cannot exist in a Nation without private, and public Virtue is the only Foundation of Republics. There must be a possitive Passion for the public good, the public Interest, Honour, Power, and Glory, established in the Minds of the People, or there can be no Republican Government, nor any real Liberty. And this public Passion must be superiour to all private Passions. Men must be ready, they must pride themselves, and be happy to sacrifice their private Pleasures, Passions, and Interests, nay their private Friendships and dearest Connections, when they Stand in Competition with the Right of Society.

Is there in the World a Nation, which deserves this Character. There have been several, but they are no more. Our dear Americans perhaps have as much of it as any Nation now existing, and New England perhaps has more than the rest of America. But I have seen all along my Life, Such Selfishness, and Littleness even in New England, that I sometimes tremble to think that, altho We are engaged in the best Cause that ever employed the Human Heart, yet the Prospect of success is doubtfull not for Want of Power or of Wisdom, but of Virtue.

The Spirit of Commerce, Madam, which even insinuates itself into Families, and influences holy Matrimony, and thereby corrupts the Morals of Families as well as destroys their Happiness, it is much to be feared is incompatible with that purity of Heart, and Greatness of soul which is necessary for an happy Republic. This Same Spirit of Commerce is as rampant in New England as in any Part of the World. Trade is as well understood and as passionately loved there as any where. Even the Farmers, and Tradesmen are addicted to Commerce. And it is too true, that Property is generally the standard of Respect there as much as any where. While this is the Case there is great Danger that a Republican Government would be very factious and turbulent there. Divisions in Elections are much to be dreaded. Every Man must sincerely set himself to root out his Passions, Prejudices and Attachments, and to get the better of his private Interest. The only reputable Principle and Doctrine must be that all Things must give Way to the public.

This is very grave and Solemn Discourse to a Lady. True, and I thank God, that his Providence has made me Acquainted with two Ladies at least, who can bear it.

I think Madam, that the Union of the Colonies, will continue and be more firmly cemented. But We must move slowly. Patience, Patience, Patience! I am obliged to invoke this every Morning of my Life, every Noon, and every Evening.

It is Surprising to me that any among you should flatter themselves with an Accommodation. Every Appearance is against it, to an Attentive observer. The Story of Commissioners is a Bubble. Their real Errant is an Insult. But popular Passions and Fancies will have their Course, you may as well reason down a Gale of Wind.

You expect, if a certain Bargain Should be complied with, to be made acquainted with noble and Royal Characters. But in this you will be disappointed. Your Correspondent has neither Principles, nor Address, nor Abilities, for such Scenes. And others are as sensible of it, I assure you as he is. They must be Persons of more Complaisance and Ductility of Temper as well as better Accomplishments for such great Things.

He wishes for nothing less. He wishes for nothing more than to retire from all public Stages, and public Characters, great and Small, to his Farm and his Attorneys office. And to both these he must return.

RC (MHi). In Adams' hand, though not signed.
[1] Mercy Otis Warren's March 10 letter to John Adams, which discusses plans for a republican form of government and the need for independence, is in the Adams Papers, MHi.
[2] For additional insight into Adams' views on women's role in government, see also Adams to Abigail Adams, April 14, and to James Sullivan, May 26, 1776.

Samuel Adams to James Warren

My dear Sir,   Philadelphia April 16 1776
I have not yet congratulated you on the unexpected and happy Change of our Affairs in the removal of the Rebel Army from Boston. Our worthy Friend Major H[awley] in his Letter to me declines giving me Joy on this Occasion—He thinks it best to put off the Ceremony till the Congress shall proclaim Independency.[1] In my opinion however, it becomes us to rejoyce and religiously to acknowledge the Goodness of the supreme Being who in this Instance hath signally appeard for us. Our Countrymen are too wise to suffer this favorable Event to put them off their Guard. They will fortify the Harbour of Boston, still defend the Sea Coasts and keep the military Spirit universally alive. I perfectly agree with the Major in his opinion of the Necessity of proclaiming Independency. The Salvation of this Country depends upon its being done speedily. I am anxious to have it done. Every Days Delay trys my Patience. I can give you not the least Color of a Reason why it is not done. We are told that Commissioners are coming out to offer us such Terms of Reconciliation as we may with Safety accept of. Why then should we shut the Door. This is all Amusement. I am exceedingly disgusted when I hear it mentiond. Experience should teach us to pay no Regard to it. We know that it has been the constant Practice of the King & his Junto ever since this Struggle began to endeavor to make us beleive their Designs were pacifick while they have been meditating the most destructive Plans, & they insult our understand-

ings by attempting thus to impose upon us even while they are putting these Plans into Execution. Can the King repeal or dispense with Acts of Parliament? Would he repeal the detestable Acts which we have complaind of if it was in his Power? Did he ever shew a Disposition to do Acts of Justice and redress the Greivances of his Subjects? Why then do Gentlemen expect it? They do not scruple to own that he is a Tyrant; Are they then willing to be his Slaves and dependent upon a Nation so lost to all Sense of Liberty and Virtue as to enable and encourage him to act the Tyrant. This has been done by the British Nation against the Remonstrances of common Honesty and common Sense. They are now doing it and will continue to do it, until we break the Band of Connection and publickly avow an Independence. It is Folly for us to suffer our selves any longer to be amusd. Reconciliation upon reasonable Terms is no Part of their Plan; The only Alternative is Independence or Slavery. Their Designs still are as they ever have been to subjugate us. Our unalterable Resolution should be to be free. They have attempted to subdue us by Forces but God be praisd! in vain. Their Arts may be more dangerous than their Arms. Let us then renounce all Treaty with them upon any Score but that of total Seperation, and under God trust our Cause to our Swords. One of our moderate prudent Whigs wd be startled at what I now write. I do not correspond with such kind of Men—you know I never overmuch admired them. *Their* Moderation has brought us to this Pass, and if they were to be regarded, they would continue the Conflict a Century. There are such moderate Men here, but their Principles are daily going out of Fashion. The Child Independence is now struggling for Birth. I trust that in a short time it will be brought forth, and in Spite of Pharaoh all America shall hail the dignified Stranger.

RC (MHi). In Adams' hand, though not signed.
   [1] See Samuel Adams' response to Joseph Hawley, April 15, 1776.

John Hancock to
the Baltimore Committee of Safety

Gentlemen,   Philada. April 16th. 1776.
   I received, & immediately communicated to Congress, your Letter of the 14th, with the important Papers enclosed. In Consequence of which, the Congress have resolved, that the Person and Papers of Governour Eden be immediately seized by the Committee of Safety, to whom I write by this Opportunity. The Person mentioned in the inclosed Resolution (Mr. Alexander Ross) is represented as a dangerous Partizan of Administration, who has lately been with Lord Dunmore,

and, it is suggested, is on his Way to the Indian Country to execute the execrable Designs of our Enemies. I have no Doubt, but you will exert your utmost Endeavours in seizing & securing him.[1] I am with Respect, Gentlemen, your most obed.   John Hancock Presidt.

[P.S.] You will please not to make public mention of the Resolution respectg Gφvr. Eden, untill the Come. of Safety have executed it.

RC (MdHi). In the hand of Jacob Rush, with signature and postscript by Hancock.

[1] The Baltimore committee's letter to Hancock of April 14 and enclosures (including two letters of December 23, 1775, from Colonial Secretary George Germain to Maryland governor Robert Eden) are in PCC, item 70, fols. 13–24, and *Am. Archives*, 4th ser. 5:928–30. Germain's letters to Eden, which were susceptible to the interpretation that the Maryland governor had urged the North ministry to take strong measures against the revolutionary party in his province, were originally taken from Alexander Ross, a merchant on an unauthorized visit to Lord Dunmore in Virginia, and sent to Gen. Charles Lee and the Virginia Committee of Safety. While the Virginia committee forwarded these letters to the Baltimore committee, Lee wrote to Samuel Purviance, Jr., the chairman of the latter body, and urged him to arrest Eden. The Baltimore committee sent the letters to Congress and simultaneously set on foot a plan to seize Eden. But this plan was frustrated by the Maryland Council of Safety, which, learning of Germain's letters on April 15 (the day before Congress passed the resolves about Eden and Ross referred to in the text above), examined the governor and satisfied itself that he had made no recommendations adverse to the province and was not planning to leave it. As a result, the council, incensed at the challenges to its authority posed by the actions of both the Baltimore committee and Congress, subsequently refused to carry out Congress' resolves about Eden, although it did apprehend Ross. See *JCC*, 4:285–86; *Am. Archives*, 4th ser. 5:800–801, 810, 1146–47; and *Md. Archives*, 11:333–93. See also Thomas Johnson to the Maryland Council of Safety, April 17, and to Daniel of St. Thomas Jenifer, April 23; Maryland Delegates to the Maryland Council of Safety, April 18 and 25; Thomas Stone to Daniel of St. Thomas Jenifer, April 24; and Richard Henry Lee to Samuel Purviance, Jr., May 1 and 6, 1776. For fuller accounts of this episode in the context of the political situation in Maryland, see Bernard C. Steiner, *Life and Administration of Sir Robert Eden*, Johns Hopkins University Studies in Historical and Political Science, ser. 16, no. 7 (Baltimore, 1898), pp. 105–28; and Ronald Hoffman, *A Spirit of Dissension: Economics, Politics, and the Revolution in Maryland* (Baltimore: Johns Hopkins University Press, 1973), pp. 157–63.

John Hancock to
the Maryland Committee of Safety

Gentlemen,   Philadelphia April 16th. 1776.

By the Letters of Lord Germaine to your Governour, Copies of which you have enclosed, it evidently appears, that Mr. Eden has been carrying on a dangerous Correspondence with the Ministry of Great Britain, who seem desperately bent on the Destruction of America. The Congress therefore have come to a Resolution that the Person and Papers of Governour Eden be immediately seized, from which there is Reason to believe, we may not only learn, but probably defeat, the Designs of our Enemies.[1]

The Congress also being informed, that there is one Alexander Ross in your Colony, who has lately been with Lord Dunmore, and is represented as a dangerous Partizan of the British Administration, him also the Congress are desirous of apprehending, and for that Purpose, have passed a Resolution, which you have enclosed with the other.

The Congress, relying on your Zeal, confide that you will exert your best Endeavours in executing said Resolutions.

I have the Honour to be, Gentlemen, your most obedt. hbl Ser.

John Hancock Presidt.

RC (MdAA). In the hand of Jacob Rush and signed by Hancock.
[1] See *JCC*, 4:285–86.

John Hancock to Israel Putnam

Sir,   Philadelphia April 16th. 1776.

Congress, finding by Intelligence from Genl. Washington,[1] that the greatest Part of the Troops that were before Boston, are either on their March to New York, or actually arrived there, judge it improper to keep a larger Body of Men together than is called for in that Place. I am therefore commanded by the Congress to direct that you discharge the whole, or such Part of the Militias of New York & Connecticut, now in the Pay of the Continent, as the public Service will permit; and also that you discharge the whole of the Militia of New Jersey.[2] I have the Honour to be, Sir, your most obedt. and very hble Servt.

John Hancock Presidt

RC (DLC). In the hand of Jacob Rush and signed by Hancock.
[1] See Washington to Hancock, March 27, 1776, in PCC, item 152, 1:563–66, and Washington, *Writings* (Fitzpatrick), 4:436–38.
[2] Congress ordered the discharge of these militia units on April 11. *JCC*, 4:272.

Maryland Delegates to the Maryland Council of Safety

Gent   Phila 16 Apl 1776

We this morning sent off in a Waggon one Ton of Powder for Chester Town, which is directed to the care of Messrs Smyth & Hands if absent to be delivered to the Committee of observation.[1] We have wrote these Gent to receive the powder to await yr orders for the Distribution, this powder We obtained on application from Congress, who grant Supplies to the difft provinces, as the Circumstances & situation of them make it necessary, knowing the exposed & defenceless state of the Eastern Shore. We have sent off this supply which we expect, will meet your Approbation, you will observe Cecil County has been supplyed by us from hence with 500 lbs. We mention this, to prevent any part of the Ton being sent that County. We send you by the post 8 of the Plates with the Devices for the Money. Rittenhouse says the remg 4 will be finished in 10 or 12 Days. We are with respect Gent, Yr Hble Servts,

R. Alexander.

T. Stone.

RC (MdAA). Written by Alexander and signed by Alexander and Stone.

[1] For the brief letter which the Maryland delegates sent with that wagonload of powder, see *Md. Archives*, 11:335.

Secret Committee Minutes of Proceedings

April 16. 1776.

At a meetg. of Come. present Rob. Morris, J. Alsop, Tho McKean, Jo. Hewes, R. H. Lee, & Rob. Alexander. A charter party for ship Sally, S[amue]l Howell Owner, was read & signd.[1] Do. for Brigt. Patty, R. Brige [Robert Bridges?] Owner, was read & signd.[2] Do. for Brigt. Jaimaicia Packet, J. Maxwell Nesbit & Co. Owners, was read & signd.

Issued an order on the Contl. Treasurers in favor of Capt. Ths. Mason for Dlls 128 1/4 being the amt. of his acct. for two double fortifyd cannon with carriages put on board the Schooner Peace at Port L'Orient together with 2 pr Swivels deliverd sd vessel & 340 gun flints deliverd Tim. Matlack as per receit.[3] Issued an order on R. Towers Com[missar]y in favor of Laurence on acct. of the Inhabitants of Monmonth C[ount]y N. Jersey, for 300 lb powdr. for wch. the Chairman receivd the cash £75. Do. on Tim Matlack in favor of the above Laurence for 500 flints for wch. he is to pay Mr. Matlack who is to acct. with this Come. for the same.[4] Do. on the Com[missar]y to deliver Lt. Col. Hartley 4 q[uar]ter cask Gpowder to repay so much borrowed by him for the use of the Continent. Res[olve]d that Mr Morris charter & load a small vessel[5] with about 5 or 600 brrs. flour for Martinique to be consignd Messrs. Rd. Harrison & M. Lemaitre on continentl. acct., returns to be made in arms & ammunition & that Mr. Lemaitre have liberty to ship the value of £200 curry. in produce by sd. vessl. on his own Acct.

MS (MH).

[1] On April 30 the Pennsylvania Committee of Safety issued a permit to the ship *Sally*, Capt. John Osman, to take a pilot. Secret Committee to the Pennsylvania Committee of Safety, April 29, 1776, note 2.

[2] The brig *Patty*, Capt. McIvers, was one of several vessels that sailed under convoy of the schooner *Wasp* on April 24. See Secret Committee to the Pennsylvania Committee of Safety, April 23, 1776.

[3] For details of Mason's voyage to France to procure powder and arms, see Caesar Rodney to Thomas Rodney, February 4, 1776, note 3.

[4] See *JCC*, 4:283, 288.

[5] The sloop *Fanny*, Capt. William Briton. See Secret Committee to the Pennsylvania Committee of Safety, April 29; and Secret Committee Minutes of Proceedings, May 2, 1776.

Oliver Wolcott to Thomas Seymour

Sir [1]   Philidelpa. 16 April 1776

Your favour, together with the Lexington Alarm pay Rools have come safe to hand. These Accounts together with those bro't by Messrs. Dyer and Williams will soon be presented to Congress for Liquidation. [2] I observe with regard to the expences incur'd by the Riflemen, no Original Vouchers are Sent. This has been (since I have been here) invariably required, but We shall Endeavour to get the Acco. pass'd as it is, and if the Vouchers must be had, shall Write for them.

You tell Me Sir that you are about Making out the Prisoners Acco. In doing so, I should think it might be well to draw a general Account of what is due to every Person for supplying the Prisoners with Diet, Medicine and Cloathing, and have it noted thereon by the Committee of Prisoners that they have examined the Accounts and are of opinion that they are just and reasonable; by this Means these Expences will not be bro't into the Colony Acco. with which they have no Relation, and thereby keep down and confine the Colony Acco. and so not have the Money advanced for this Purpose out of the Money [*that*] has been now recd. If the Committee has recd Money of the Colony Treasrs. for these Purposes and paid some of the People, it must be considered as Money lent them, and as soon as the committee receive pay, they can replace it. In future the Govr and Committee of safety will draw on the President of Congress for support of Prisoners. This Resolution with some others will in a day be published and sent into the Colony. [3] You will Sir when you Send the Prisoners Acco. Send the Vouchers also.

To go thro and settle the Colony Accounts I am sensible must be a tedious Service, and I doupt not but you Sedulously Attend upon it and indeed the Interest of the Colony requires it. As I before wrote to Col Pitkin and Mr. Sheriff Williams, I am still of Opinion that the sooner the Colony Accounts are settled the better, in every respect—and I think as little Money should be advanced on a continental Acco. as the Nature of the Service will admit of. If Militia Men March or supplys of any kind are afforded at a continental Requisition, if the pay is made immediate by Warrant from the General or Commanding Officer, who has a Right to draw on the Pay Master, it will save all the intermediate Trouble of liquidating the Accounts of this kind in the colony and here,

which now are Very great. This Mode will secure the Colony against
Loss and the Money May be as soon paid to those to whom it is due this
Way as any other. The Rools Sent down by Col Dyer and Col Williams
have enabled us confidently to tell Congress that We were now able to
Shew that there was a large Sum due to the Colony. A grant has been
made tho not without some Opposition, of fifty Thousand pounds, out
of which I beleive you will have to pay Col. Hinmans and Waterbury
Regiments as the Matter of Bounties, Equipments and Allowance to the
officers for paying their Men, is what Genl. Schuyler will chose to decline passing any Opinion upon. This with Other Reasons, will I
imagine cause these Troops to be turned upon the Colony for Payment.
I Very well know that a great deal of Money must be advanced for continental Purposes by the Colony, the Necessities of publick Services require it, I mean no more than that when it can be avoided, I think it
would be best secure the Colony Interest. For News refer you to the
publick Papers. The Regulations of Trade which you will have before
this reaches you, is an Object of great Importance, both in a Commercial
and political Veiw. In Consequence thereof We have permitted the
Ladys to drink what Indian Tea there is in the country, they paying
3/4 dollar per pound therefore. The Steady Progression of our publick
Affairs and the Changes consequent thereon ought to be attended to,
by those who regulate the Social Conduct of the People, least by a too
Sedulous regard to literal Constructions of Congress, which might much
better be admitted of, a year ago, they attempt to fix a Changing Scene,
which is impossible to be absolutely fix'd, and so undesignedly do a
material publick and private Wrong—for no Necessary Exertions ought
not to lye under a discouragement, which will totally impede them,
and to require an Authoritative fixedness to objects continually and
necessarily Changing is to Demand impossibilities. But the good sense
and Virtue of my Countrymen I beleive will guard them against any
Material Mistake and I hope and beleive Things will before long acquire
such an Establishment, by the total Confusion of British Councills, and
the Blessing of God on the most laudable and prudent Exertions of this
People, as will free every one from those Embarrassments which this
Very peculiar kind of War has bro't us into. I hope this Country will
Exhibit the most glorious Displays of Civil and Religious Liberty (rendered certain to the people of it by Constitutions, permanent, rational,
and just) that the World ever beheld, and that these Colonys injoying
every necessary, particular Colonial Authority, may by fraternal Union
strengthened by every Thing necessary therefor possess that internal
Peace and Security which is Necessary for their Happiness, and by
Confederated Power be able to repel whatever Attempts to Disturb
them. Excuse a long, hasty, unrevised Sc[r]ibble, and present my best
Compliments to my Freinds. I Am Sir, with Esteem, your most Obedient,
and humble Servant,   Oliver Wolcott

RC (Ct).

[1] Thomas Seymour (1735–1829), Hartford representative in the Connecticut Assembly, 1774–93, and mayor, 1784–1812, served as head of the committee of the pay-table from April 1775 until the end of the war. Franklin B. Dexter, *Biographical Sketches of the Graduates of Yale College*, 6 vols. (New York: Henry Holt and Co., 1885–1919), 2:378–79.

[2] The settling of the colony accounts had been a concern of the Connecticut delegates for some time. The efforts of Connecticut officials to raise troops and collect supplies for the common defense placed a continual strain on their treasury, and the scale of their contributions delayed the preparation of their accounts. In December 1775 Silas Deane had questioned the propriety of certain charges against the continent and requested clarification of other accounts that had been forwarded to the delegates in late November. Governor Trumbull's repeated requests for advances were first rejected in January 1776 because of the lack of supporting accounts and then only partially satisfied by a £30,000 advance on March 7. This money probably had not been received when the Connecticut Council of Safety voted on March 22 to send Eliphalet Dyer and William Williams to Philadelphia to seek additional funds and information on the state of the colonies. Dyer reported to Joseph Trumbull that they were received "rather Cooley" by Oliver Wolcott and Samuel Huntington, who were "some alarmd att our appearance," and that their inquiries about Congress "were answered rather with demure looks than expressive Words." Wolcott was undoubtedly sensitive to the opposition in Congress to requests for advances. Nevertheless, Dyer's and Williams' memorial was read in Congress on April 11, summarizing Connecticut's expenditures for the continent in excess of £100,000, explaining their temporary inability to submit complete accounts, and requesting that their exhausted treasury be replenished by an advance of at least £50,000 in order to continue their exertions on behalf of the continent. On the basis of this petition and the partial accounts accompanying it, Congress immediately approved an additional advance of £50,000. *JCC*, 4:188, 272; J. H. Trumbull and Charles J. Hoadly, eds., *The Public Records of the Colony of Connecticut . . .*, 15 vols. (Hartford: Case, Lockwood & Brainard Co., 1850–90), 15:253–54; Eliphalet Dyer to Joseph Trumbull, April 11, 1776, Joseph Trumbull Papers, CtHi; and Memorial of Eliphalet Dyer and William Williams, April 1776, William Williams Papers, CtHi. For further references to Connecticut accounts, see Connecticut Delegates to Jonathan Trumbull, December 5, 1775; Richard Smith's Diary, January 13; Wolcott to Ezekiel Williams, February 10; Wolcott to Matthew Griswold, March 9; John Hancock to Michael Hillegas and George Clymer, April 11; and Wolcott to the Connecticut Committee of the Pay-Table, May 4, 1776.

[3] See the resolves of April 9. *JCC*, 4:264–65. See also Wolcott to Thomas Seymour, April 17, 1776.

Committee on Fortifying Ports to
George Washington

Sir,   Philad. Apr. 17th. 1776.

We are appointed by the Congress a Committee[1] to examine into and report to them the Properest Places for the Building Forts for the Protection of our Trade, our Cruisers, and their Prizes, and we have permission from them to request of you to send some Person in whose judgment you can confide to take an exact Plan of the Harbours of

Cape Ann and New London, and the fortifications now erected at those Places, with the Number and Size of the Cannon in them, and give us his Opinion what more is necessary to be done to put them in such a State of Defence as will answer the above purposes, with an estimate of the Expense.[2] We also wish to be inform'd the Distance of each of those Ports from the sea, what Difficulties attend the geting into, or out of them, or whether they may be easily block'd up by the Enemy, in short we would gladly be inform'd of every advantage and disadvantage attending them, and hope you will order as full a Report as possible.

We Congratulate you on your safe arrival at New-York and are, your most obedt Servts, Benj Harrison

John Adams

Wm Whipple

RC (DLC). Written by Harrison and signed by Harrison, Adams, and Whipple.

[1] This committee, which in addition to the signatories also included Joseph Hewes and Robert Morris, was appointed March 23. *JCC*, 4:233.

[2] See *JCC*, 4:283. In his response of April 22, Washington named Col. Richard Gridley and Col. Henry Knox to undertake this task. PCC, item 152, 1:603–6; and Washington, *Writings* (Fitzpatrick), 4:504.

James Duane to Walter Livingston

Dear Sir Philad. 17th April 1776

I have your favour on the Subject of the Commissary General's office. The unexpected removal of the regular Troops, I mean the ministerialists, from Boston, has produced a Circumstance which was not forseen as in Consequence of that Event The Commander in Chief, his Suite, & the Commissy. General have taken up their Quarters in New York. No Conclusion can however be formed from past Incidents. The weight of the war may fall to the Southward which will call for fresh dispositions. In the mean time Albany must remain a Post of Importance and cannot indeed be otherwise till there's an End of War. You woud therefore be sure of holding your Employment if it was an Object worthy of your Attention.

I suppose as you coud not wish to have gone into Canada, the Appointment of Price cannot be an Injury to you.[1] He is to consult with General Schuyler on the Supply of the Canada Army. Everything except bread must I suppose be drawn from Albany as usual; nor will it be easy to supply even that unless our Continental Bills attain a Currency in that Country. If General Schuyler & Price think it best that the provisions to be bought up for the Canada Army in our Government shoud be supplied By Contract at a fixed Price, & will recommend such a Measure as advances of the publick Interest & Service, there can be no doubt but it will meet with the Approbation of Congress who mean to use Œconomy in all their Conduct, and indeed there is sufficient Occasion for it. My Colleagues write you by this opportunity so that I need not be more particular.[2] Mr Chace has misapprehended the Order of Congress authorizing the New York Convention to enter into a Contract for supplying the Troops with provisions, if he supposed it extended to Canada, for it was certainly confined to the army raised for the defence of New York. There is the same Reason for a Contract In every Quarter if it will be a Means of saving publick money.[3]

Present my affectionate Regards to my sister and friends and believe me to be most sincerely, Dear Sir, Your affectionate Brother, & very huml sevt,   Jas. Duane

[P.S.] Let me know whether the money sent General Schuyler by Mr Chace is not applied to the support of your department.[4] I take it for granted; & have therefore movd for none on your account. I have lent your Express who had the misfortune of loosing his Horse four dollars. Be so good as to see that he pays it to my Friend Mr John Stevenson on whom I have drawn.

RC (NN).
[1] James Price had been appointed deputy commissary for the American army in Canada on March 29. *JCC*, 4:240–41.
[2] See New York Delegates to Walter Livingston, this date.
[3] See *JCC*, 4:133, 150, 159–60; and Duane to the New York Provincial Convention, March 21, 1776, note 2.
[4] Congress had appropriated $50,000 for General Schuyler's army on March 19. *JCC*, 4:213.

John Hancock to Esek Hopkins

Sir,   Philada. April 17th. 1776
Your Letter of the 9th of March [*i.e.* April], with the Enclosure, was duely received and laid before Congress; in whose Name, I beg Leave to congratulate you on the Success of your Expedition.[1] Your Account of the Spirit and Bravery shewn by the Men, affords them the greatest Satisfaction; and encourages them to expect similar Exertions of Courage on every future Occasion. Though it is to be regretted, that the Glascow Man of War made her Escape, yet as it was not thro any Misconduct, the Praise due to You and the other Officers, is undoubtedly the same.

I have it in Charge from Congress to direct, that you send a compleat List and State of the Stores taken and brought from Providence with the Sizes &c and that the Cannon, and such other of the Stores as are not necessary for the Fleet, be landed and left at New London.[2]

The following Extract of a Letter from Antigua, I hope will be of

Service to you. With that View I send it.

"Antigua March 26th. 1776. The third Division of Transports will leave Antigua in a few Days it is said for New York, under Convoy of an old East India Ship, mounting 16 Guns. There will be six in Number."

Wishing you the greatest Success and Happiness, I am, Sir, your most obedt. & very hble Sert.[3]   John Hancock Presidt

RC (RHi). In the hand of Jacob Rush and signed by Hancock. Addressed: "Commodore Hopkins at New London."

[1] Hopkins' letter to Hancock and an inventory of the stores which he captured on his New Providence expedition are in PCC, item 78, 11:33–37, and *Am. Archives*, 4th ser. 5:823–24. See also William Whipple to John Langdon, April 2, 1776, note 1.

[2] See *JCC*, 4:289.

[3] This day Hancock also wrote to Washington, directing him to order "that Two Companies of Coll Dayton's Battalion of New Jersey Troops be Station'd at Cape May for the protection of the Property and Navigation in that Quarter." *Am. Archives*, 4th ser. 5:967. See also *JCC*, 4:284–85, 291.

John Jay to William Alexander

My Lord: Philadelphia, 17th April, 1776.

Your Lordship's letter of the 15th instant was delivered to me on yesterday. Should the present paymaster resign his appointment, your Lordship may rely on my paying great respect to your recommendation on this, as well as every other occasion.

Mr. Palfrey's character is known to many gentlemen of the Congress; and your Lordship's testimony in his favor will tend, not a little, to confirm the opinion they entertain of his merit.[1]

We are informed that the fortifications in New York are nearly completed. The activity and spirit both of the troops and inhabitants, does them honor; and I have the pleasure to assure you, that your Lordship's attention to the service, while in Chief command there, was very satisfactory and agreeable to the Congress.

I am, my Lord, Your Lordship's most obedient Servant,

                                                    John Jay

MS not found; reprinted from *American Historical Record* 1 (September 1872): 420.

[1] Congress accepted James Warren's resignation as paymaster general of the Continental Army on April 19 and chose William Palfrey to succeed him on April 27. See *JCC*, 4:291, 296, 315; and John Adams to James Warren, April 16, 1776, note 3. See also John Hancock's letters to Palfrey of April 20, to Warren of April 26, and to Washington of April 30, 1776.

Thomas Johnson to
the Maryland Council of Safety

Gentlemen.   Philadelphia 17 April 1776.

Yesterday Morning just before the Meeting of Congress the Letters from Balt. which occasioned the Resolution of Yesterday came to the Hand of the President.[1] By the same Express, and as I believe under the same Cover, came an Anonymous Letter referring to a Copy therein inclosed from Genl. Lee to Mr. Samuel Purveiance. I saw and read the Copy which was in Purveiances Hand Writing; Lee strongly urged the immediate seizing and securing of the Govr. After the Minutes of the preceeding Day were read the President began reading the Anonymous Letter, but he had not proceeded far before he came to a part desiring that it might not be made known to the Congress but, as I think to such only as the President might think proper to trust with the Contents. The President hesitated, for he had not before read the Letter, and seemed desirous of running his Eye over it but on being desired to read out he did so: from the Inclosure above mentioned as well as many Expressions in the Letter and Mr. Purveiances being the Heroe of the Tale which was told in the first person I had not the least Doubt but that Purveiance was the Author and Mr. Andrew Allen who saw the Letter and is acquainted with Purveiances Hand writing says it was his.

The Letter informs that the writer of it had impressed on Genl Lee, in his way to Virga., an Idea that the Council of Safety was timorous and inactive and represents the Council of Safety and Convention too as being afraid to execute the Duties of their Stations. His own and the Conduct of the Convention on an Affair that you must remember he contrasts to the Disadvantage of the Latter whose inaction he imputes to want of Spirit. He speaks of the Orders he gave Capt. Nicholson on the late Alarm and how the Council of Safety was alarmed and frightened at the Spirit and boldness of them—represents himself as an Object against whom the Intentions of the Council of Safety are levelled and in proof writes a Conversation with, or saying of one of them to the Effect that he was a warm Man or a hot headed Man whose power must be pulled down or he would throw things into Confusion. As I heard the Letter read but once I cannot undertake to repeat Expressions with exactness, but I think I have preserved the Sentiments and have not exaggerated in any Thing and on the whole I esteem it a vile injureous Calumny calculated like his Conversation with Genl Lee to spread Suspicion and Distrust of the only executive in our province. If I am not mistaken the Letter mentions further that some Gent were sent from Balt as were by him proposed to be sent to Annapolis, who should engage the Officer commanding the Troops there to Secrecy under Oath and then endeavour to get his Assistance to execute what you are requested o do by the Resolution; this I suppose may be easily traced.

As soon as the Letter was read a Motion was made to send the original or a Copy of it to you which was warmly supported but it was put off ill today to make Way for the Consideration of the Subject of the Express and in the mean Time all was ordered to be secret. Messrs. Stone and Alexander, who had been delayed in writing Letters for the post, came into the Congress in this Stage of the Affair and are, as well as myself, privy to the after Transactions.

I am Gent., Your mo. obed. Servant,   Th Johnson Junr

RC (MdAA).
[1] See John Hancock to the Baltimore Committee of Safety, April 16, 1776, note.

New York Delegates to Walter Livingston

Sir,   Philadelphia 17th Apl. 1776.

We received your Favour of the 8th Instt. The Office of Commissary is extreamly embarassed. The Commissary Genl (who it was expected woud have continued in the Eastern Department) is now (by the Removal of the Army from Boston) in New York—tho it was originally intended (as we understood) that you as Deputy Commissary General shoud have the sole Managemt of that Office in the Northern Department. The Provincial Congress of New York by the Directions of this Congress entered into a Contract with Mr. Abm. Livingston to supply the Army stationed at New York with Provissions at the Price you mention per Ration. When the Pensylvania Batallions were raised (Part of which are now at New York) a certain Mr Wharton was appointed by Congress Commissary for those Levies who contracted to supply them at the Rate of 7d. Pensylvania Currency per Ration; which you will perceive interferes with Mr. Abraham Livingston's Contract; but it is probable Mr. Wharton who was lately at New York & is returned here will relinquish his Contract.[1] The Congress have lately appointed Mr. Price Commissary for the Troops in Canada but have not made any particular Contract with him for furnishing the Provissions for that Part of the Army. He is to consult General Schuyler as to the Mode of supplying those Troops and is to be furnished With Money by Congress for that Purpose. Flour & Bread he expects to procure in Canada; but no other Part of the Provissions.

These being the Facts we have but little if any Prospect of procuring any Contract or Appointments for you that we think may be worth your accepting. It is not thought that any of the above Contracts interfere with your Office of Deputy Commissary General which it is likely will continue to be a necessary Office in Albany. Perhaps on Mr. Price's consulting with Genl. Schuyler on the most proper Method of supplyign the Army in Canada something may turn up worth your Attention;

shoud this be the Case be assured we will not forget you as we consider you as having served the Public in your present Office without an adequate Compensation for your extraordinary Trouble. We are your Most Obedt. Servts.   John Alsop   Geo Clinton

                                                          John Jay   Lewis Morris

RC (NHi). Written by Clinton and signed by Clinton, Alsop, Jay, and Morris.
   [1] See James Duane to the New York Provincial Convention, March 21, 1776, note 2.

Oliver Wolcott to Samuel Lyman

Sir,   Philadelphia 17t April 1776
   Your kind favour of the 3d and 9t of April recd. yesterday. The day before that, one from you and one from Mr. Adams of the 21 and 22d Febry. came safe. Your Correspondence is Very agreable and you will easily believe much increased, as I have by you News of my Family, whom you will observe are most dear to Me. I heartily rejoice that a merciful God gives them his Protection and that my Freinds are kind to them. Nothing can excite more Strongly my Gratitude than those clear Evidences of their Freindship.
   I am much oblidged to you for home Intelligence, as I feel much Interested in whatsoever happens to my Freinds. Your observations upon my Strictures on Agriculture &c I notice.[1] It is in Vain to fix a changing Scene, you may as well Arrest the Shadows that fly over a Corn Feild. A new scene is opening. The Regulations on Trade which you by this Time have likely seen, will of Course, together with other operating Causes, do away imperceptibly the Material Parts of the association, and the Prudence of Committees must necessarily lead them to observe the Varying Scene—but this to you and by the by.
   I observe the Instructions given Litchfield Deputys.[2] The Probity of my Countrymen is not to be doupted of, and their Love of a rational Liberty and the Constitution of the Colony are great & Commendable, and I dare say nothing would give them a greater Alarm, than the introducing political Maxims which would effectually sap the Constitution of the Colony. Is it not one material Part of the Continental Members Duty to guard the Constitution of the Colony, ought they not therefore to be Ameniable to the Jurisdiction of the Colony, and liable to be called to an Account or displaced by them whenever they Please? If the continental Delegates are Chosen by the People at large (which I have no objection to if it does not in its Consequences absolutely destroy the Colony jurisdiction) can they ever be called to acco. by the assembly or be displaced or receive any Instructions or advice from them more than from so many Individuals and would not the Colony be absolutely Bound (or rather I may say the People living within the

present Lines of the Colony, for upon this Idea they could hardly be called a Colony as they would have no seperate Jurisdiction) by every Act their Delegates should do, as they would have all the Authority absolutely and independently which the People could give them, as fully and compleatly as any of the present Members of Parliament have, and if they should (being thus Appointed) concurr in Adopting any Maxims intrenching never so much on the Colony Constitution, would not the People be absolutely Bound by their own Act? In a Word, would not the Consequences (if attended to) reduce in a few years the Colony Jurisdiction as low as the present Powers of our Selectmen—unless Imperium in Imperio can Exist? This Principle or mode of Choice as simple as it may appear, and advance of the Libertys of the People, I much Suspect will have a Very different Effect, and is pregnant with Ten Thousand consequences.[3] Indeed all the natural, moral and Political Phenomena originate from a Very few simple Principles—Principles which will invariably operate, for they are if I may so say the Maxims of the divine Goverment. Political Principles are as certain in their Operation as those we called Natural, and their Energy will never fail without a miracle. A Physician may as well hope to cure sickness by counteracting every Effort of the human Constitution—as a political Physician to maintain a Sound political constitution by not regulating himself by political Cause. The Laws of Commerce are equally fix'd and indeed every Thing else, all are operating Causes established by God himself. They are the Ordo Rerum, which none but God Almighty can controul. Would not such seperate Authoritys keep up an everlasting (or till one had destroyed the Other) Strife and contention in the Colony. I beleive no Colony but what means to Maintain a Colonial and seperate Jurisdiction. I certainly never Shall consent to any Thing otherwise and I believe not a single Member of Congress intends any thing else, when Goverment shall be set up anew in each Colony which must be the case—for I consider an Accommodation with G. Britain upon former Terms as being impossible—but you know my Opinion always was not to make speculative opinion a Principle, but let Principles be adapted to and established upon human Occasions and Exigences, and then Experience, Nature's sure hand maid, will guide us right. I hope and beleive that future Congresses will be as Wise and good as the present (I speak not thus in derogation of the present Congress) but We shall do our Duty, if We become the happy means of defending this Country from external Violence, secure (while in Place) by our Recommendations and advice, and neither ourselves nor advise others to introduce Principles which by Reason of their Rigidity or Laxity, will produce unhappiness. Indeed if We Maintain and secure the Liberty, Peace and Safety of the Country while in Place and do not introduce false Maxims, We shall do well. One great unhappiness which has almost always attended Civil Contentions is that those engaged in them have hastily and while the human Passions were up either adopted tyrannical Maxims without consideration, or in their Passion drove every Thing Amiable out of the World and but pretty rarely have gained half the good they fought for. While Passion is awake, Wisdom sleeps. Let it not be so in Connecticut, amongst a People who have been famed for their Wisdom. May they listen only to the Voice of Reason, never take a hasty step. Many Men and Communities have been ruined by it. I have Very hastily wrote you almost a Sheet of Paper and I must look it over and see what it is, but have not Time to mend it let it be what it may. I am sir, with esteem, your humble and obedient Servant,

Oliver Wolcott

P.S. I trust my hasty Observations with you, your Prudence will be sufficient to stifle them or communicate them to particular Freinds as you may think may be best for me and others.

RC (PHi).
[1] See Wolcott to Samuel Lyman, March 16, 1776, note 3.
[2] Not found.
[3] In spite of Wolcott's opposition to the direct election of delegates to Congress the idea continued to appeal to many in Litchfield County, and at the May 15 meeting of the county committees of inspection it was recommended that "the members of the Congress be annually elected by the impartial, unbiased, uncorrupted voice of the freemen at large." *Am. Archives*, 4th ser. 6:471–72.

Oliver Wolcott to Thomas Seymour

Sir,   Philadelpa. 17t April 1776
By my Letter of yesterday I acknowledged your favour and the Lexington Alarm Rools which came safe. I wrote you Sir, upon the Colony Acco. and advised to send the Vochers for dieting, Cloathing and Medicene for the Prisoners. This has been usually and indeed so far as I know invariably required, but considering what Trouble it must be to you, I have applyed to the Committee of Claims, to know wheither your own Attestation of having Examined and Approved the Accounts would not be satisfactory, which they have agreed to Accept. You need do more therefore than draw an Acco. generally of the Sums due to each Person, and distinguish the Accounts wheither for Diet, Cloathing, Medicene &c. and note your Approbation, and if there has been any Extra Cases you will note them properly in the Accò.—and shall Endeavour to have the Monies Advanced to you as Committee of Prisoners under which Signature you will transmit the Acco.—and if the Colony has advanced Money on this Acco. it now may be replaced by you.[1] By this Means no Money will be taken out of or Charged rather against the Colony for Money already advanced by Congress, as I dare say

you will have occasion before your Accounts are liquidated for the whole already advanced by the Congress. I am Sir, your most obedient and humble Servant,   Oliver Wolcott

P.S. The ordinary Allowance for privates will be a Dollar a Week— that is the Sum Allowed here for those at Board at Farmers Houses— but you will Send yr. Acco. as they are, noting the Time they have been Boarded.

RC (Ct).
[1] See Wolcott to the Connecticut Committee of the Pay-Table, May 4, 1776.

Oliver Wolcott to Laura Wolcott

Philidelpa. 17 April 1776. Discusses family matters and continues: "Nothing Very special has occurred since my last. I have cut out of a Newspaper a Resolution allowing the Consumption of India Tea.[1] The Ideal Phamton of Commissioners coming over to settle our Disputes has almost Vanished, indeed I do not know any one could be serious in such an Expectation. A final Seperation between the Countrys I consider as unavoidable. What the scenes of War will be this Summer cannot be known. About seven Regiments of British Troops will prob- ably be sent into the Southern Colonies. I do not think the King of England will be able to Send any large land force into this Country. The Warr he carrys on is infamous to his Troops. A Prize has been lately bro't in here, and libelled in the Provincial Admiralty office as the Property of George the Third King of G. Britain and will be ad- judicated under that Description. The Prize was a Man of War's Tender."

RC (CtHi).
[1] See *JCC*, 4:278.

John Adams to John Quincy Adams

My dear Son   Philadelphia April 18. 1776
I thank you for your agreable Letter of the Twenty fourth of March.
I rejoice with you that our Friends are once more in Possession of the Town of Boston, and am glad to hear that so little damage is done to our House.
I hope you and your Sister and Brothers will take proper Notice of these great Events, and remember under whose wise and kind Provi- dence they are all conducted. Not a Sparrow falls, nor a Hair is lost, but by the Direction of infinite Wisdom. Much less are Cities conquered

and evacuated. I hope that you will all remember, how many Losses, Dangers, and Inconveniences have been borne by your Parents, and the Inhabitants of Boston in general for the Sake of preserving Freedom for you, and yours—and I hope you will all follow the virtuous Example if, in any future Time, your Countrys Liberties should be in Danger, and suffer every human Evil, rather than Give them up. My Love to your Mamma, your Sister and Brothers, and all the Family.[1] I am your affectionate Father,   John Adams

RC (MHi). Adams, *Family Correspondence* (Butterfield), 1:388.
   [1] John Adams also wrote to his daughter Abigail this day. After teasing Abigail about spending time learning Greek and Latin, he urged her to study French— "French, my dear, French is the language, next to English—this I hope your mamma will teach you." Adams, *Family Correspondence* (Butterfield), 1:387–88.

Samuel Chase to John Adams

My Dear Sir,   Fort George. April 18th. 1776.
   I left Saratoga last Tuesday & arrived at this place the same Afternoon.[1] I expected to find the Lake open but am disappointed.
   General Thomas left this yesterday Morning and intended to break his Way. On this Day about 40 Batteaus went off with the same Intention, with about 500 Men. The Residue of the Troops here, about 300, & the Cannon, 4.32, 4.24, 4.18 & some 9 pounders, wth. 8 Ton of Powder go off in the Morning, & I expect to sett off some time tomorrow, or on the next Day. The Batteaus which went away today, we just hear, are above 12 Miles. Colo. Sinclear's Regiment is at Fort Edward, & are ordered here tomorrow. I am told above 100 of that Battalion have deserted. Ought not Desertion to be punished with above 39 Lashes? The Inhabitants buy their Arms, pray declare some severe punishment for such infamous Conduct. On this Day arrived here, with their Interpreter Mr Dean, The Delegates from the seven Tribes of Indians in Canada, from the Congress of the Six Nations lately held at Onandago. I was introduced to & had the Honor to take them by the Hand. Their Warriors are to stay at Home till their Return & to wait the Result of their Counsils. I beleive they will wait on Us in Montreal for the purpose of professing Friendship and extorting presents, what are we to do without the Means? Mr. Dean says the Indian Congress have resolved to observe a strict Neutrality, & have appointed Deputies to attend our Indian Commissioners at Albany & they may be daily expected there. I have seen Mr. Deans Notes of the proceedings of the Onandago Congress. The Oneidas, Tuscoraras, the Deputies from Canada, & some other small Tribe appear to be our firm Friends, but the Senecas, Mohawks & the others seem to me to be very unfriendly, & I am satisfied are ready from Inclination to act agt. Us. I beleive one

Colo. Butler has been using his Influence wth. those people. They have agreed, i.e. the Six Nations, a majority of them, to apply to You for their Trade as usual, & to open the Path to them by Fort Stanwix, and from Quebec, & threaten if not granted. In Truth they have never been supplied from Quebec, or very triffling. I hope our Commissioners will be very civil & give them good Words & some presents but very firm & resolute.

I beg to hear from you, & shall, with pleasure communicate to you any Thing which may be worthy of your Notice.

You will be pleased to make Me remembered with every Sentiment of Respect and Regard to our worthy president & his Lady, to my Friend Mr. Adams & Mr. Paine & Mr. Gerry. Adieu. Your Affectionate Friend and Obedient Servant, Saml. Chase

RC (MHi).
[1] The commissioners to Canada had spent a week enjoying General Schuyler's hospitality at Saratoga but had resumed their journey northward on April 16. Chase had accompanied Schuyler in pressing directly ahead to Fort George, while the rest of the party spent the night of April 17 at Wing's tavern halfway between Fort Edward and Fort George. *Journal of Charles Carroll*, pp. 58–62. Benjamin Franklin's letter of April 17 to Schuyler, written "At Mr Wyng's" and reporting their immediate travel plans, is in the Schuyler Papers, NN.

Maryland Delegates to
the Maryland Council of Safety

Gent. Phila. Thursday. 18 April 1776.

We moved yesterday in Congress, that the Letter referred to by Mr. Johnson should be immediately transmitted to you, that you might have an Opportunity of vindicating your Honour against the malitious Charges made by the Writer, this produced a Warm Debate which lasted for several Hours.[1] We insisted (and were supported by several Gentlemen) that the Letter containing the most severe reflections upon you as a publick Body ought not to be concealed; that it was absolutely necessary in the present State of our Affairs that the Dignity of the Executives of every province should be supported if properly conducted and if there rested a Suspicion that any publick Body either from Weakness or want of Integrity omitted or refused to execute the Trust committed to them it ought to be made known to their Constituents that the power might be placed in more safe Hands. That the Exertions of the Letter Writer had already produced in part of the Council of Virginia Distrust and Suspicion of you. That we had the most convincing Proofs upon all Occasions of your Integrity, Vigilance and Activity in the Common Cause and therefore esteemed it our Duty to insist that Justice might be done to your injured Character. It was argued against

the Motion that the Letter was confidential, that it had raised no
Suspicions in the Congress of your Zeal or Integrity, because they had
reposed the highest Confidence in You immediately afterwards by the
Recommendation sent by the Return of the Express, And that the
Mischief which would be produced by communicating the Letters
would be greater than any Benefit which could be expected from it.
And that the President was not obliged to produce the Letter for the
Congress to take Order thereon, Altho it had been read in the House.
Upon the Question whether the President should be requested to lay
the Letter before Congress five Colonies voted in the Neg., three in the
Affirma. and one divided. We conceived this Treatment to You & our
Province to be cruel and injurous to the last Degree, the Obligation to
Secrecy expired yesterday and We immediately determined to give you
such a State of this Transaction as our Memories supply Us with, and
Mr. Johnson committed to writing what passed on the first Day. We
this Morning waited on Mr Hancock to demand the Letter, but he
refused to see Us. Thus the Affair rests at present, & as we cannot delay
communicating it to you longer, we have ordered an Express immediately to set out for Annapolis and have not the least Doubt but you will
take the proper Steps to vindicate your Honour against the foul Calumny
of Mr Purvyance who has dared to detract from your Patriotism &
Spirit. We are determined at all hazards to support you, And tho very
sorry for the Occasion hope you have complied with the Recommendation of Congress, by securing Mr. Eden and his papers. If he has conducted himself fairly, an Examination will do him Credit, if otherwise
we ought to know it and guard against his unfriendly Endeavours. We
shall write you by the Post, and are, Gent., Yr most Ob. Sevts,

                                                          Th Johnson Junr

                                                          T. Stone

                                                          R. Alexander

RC (MdAA). Written by Stone and signed by Stone, Alexander, and Johnson.
[1] There is no mention of this debate in the journals, but see John Hancock to
the Baltimore Committee of Safety, April 16; and Thomas Johnson to the Maryland
Council of Safety, April 17, 1776.

John Adams to James Warren

                                                          April 20th. 1776
    Last Evening, a Letter was received, by a Friend of yours, from Mr
John Penn,[1] one of the Delegates from North Carolina, lately returned
home to attend the Convention of that Colony, in which he informs,
that he heard nothing praised in the Course of his Journey, but Common
sense and Independence. That this was the Cry, throughout Virginia.

That North Carolina were making great Preparations for War, and were determined to die poor and to die hard, if they must die, in Defence of their Liberties. That they had repealed, or should repeal their Instructions to their Delegates against Independence. That South Carolina had assumed a Government, chosen a Council, and John Rutledge Esqr, President of that Council with all the Powers of a Governor, that they have appointed Judges and that Drayton is Chief Justice. "In short, sir," says this Letter, "The Vehemence of the southern Colonies is such, as will require the Coolness of the Northern Colonies, to restrain them from running to Excess."

Inclosed you have a little Pamphlet, the Rise and Progress of which you shall be told.[2]

Mr Hooper and Mr Pen of North Carolina, received from their Friends in that Colony, very pressing Instances to return home and attend the Convention, and at the Same Time to bring with them every Hint they could collect, concerning Government.

Mr Hooper applied to a certain Gentleman, acquainted him with the Tenor of his Letters and requested that Gentleman to give him his sentiments upon the subject. Soon afterwards Mr Pen applied to the Same Gentleman, and acquainted him with the Contents of his letters, and requested the same Favour.

The Time was very short. However the Gentleman thinking it an oppertunity, providentially thrown in his Way, of communicating Some Hints upon a subject, which seems not to have been sufficiently considered in the southern Colonies, and so of turning the Thoughts of Gentlemen that way, concluded to borrow a little Time from his sleep and accordingly wrote with his own Hand, a Sketch, which he copied, giving the original to Mr Hooper and the Copy to Mr Penn, which they carried with them to Carolina. Mr Wythe getting a sight of it, desired a Copy which the Gentleman made out from his Memory as nearly as he could. Afterwards Mr Sergeant of New Jersey, requested another, which the gentleman made out again from Memory, and in this he enlarged and amplified a good deal, and sent it to Princetown. After this Coll Lee requested the same Favour. But the Gentleman, having written amidst all his Engagements five Copies, or rather five sketches—for no one of them was a Copy of the other, which amounted to Ten sheets of Paper, pretty full and in a fine Hand was quite weary of the office. To avoid the Trouble of writing any more he borrowed Mr Wythes Copy and lent it to Coll Lee, who has put it under Types and thrown it into the shape you see. It is a Pity it had not been Mr. Serjeant's Copy, for that is larger and more compleat, perhaps more correct. This is very incorrect, and not truly printed. The Design however is to mark out a Path, and putt Men upon thinking. I would not have this Matter communicated.

I think, by all the Intelligence We have that North Carolina, Vir-

ginia, Maryland, and New Jersey will erect Governments, before the
Month of June expires. And, if New York should do so too Pensylvania
will not neglect it. At least I think so.

There is a particular Circumstance relative to Maryland, which you
will learn eer long, but am not at Liberty to mention at present, but will
produce important Consequences in our favour, I think.

But, after Governments shall be assumed, and a Confederation formed
we shall have a long, obstinate and bloody war to go through and all
the Arts, and Intrigues of our Enemies as well as the Weakness and
Credulity of our Friends to guard against.

A Mind as vast as the ocean, or Atmosphere is necessary to penetrate
and comprehend all the intricate and complicated Interests which compose the Machine of the Confederate Colonies. It requires all the Philosophy I am Master of and more than all, at Times to preserve that
serenity of Mind and Steadiness of Heart, which is necessary to watch
the Motions, of Friends and Enemies, of the Violent and the Timid, the
Credulous and the dull, as well as the Wicked.

But if I can contribute ever so little towards preserving the Principles
of Virtue and Freedom in the World, my Time and Life will be not ill
spent.

A Man must have a wider Expansion of Genius than has fallen to my
share to see to the End of these great Commotions. But, on such a full
sea are We now afloat, that we must be content to trust, to Winds and
Currents, with the best skill We have, under a kind Providence to land
us in a Port of Peace, Liberty & Safety.

RC (MHi). In Adams' hand, though not signed.

[1] The earliest extant letter written by John Penn after his return to North Carolina
was that to John Adams of April 17, 1776, which Adams received on April 28, 1776.
It is abstracted in Adams to Penn, April 28, 1776, note 1.

[2] See John Adams to John Penn, March 19–27? 1776, note 2.

John Hancock to Thomas Lowrey

Sir,   Philada. April 20th. 1776.
    I have it in Charge from Congress to direct your immediate Attention
to the inclosed Resolve of Congress for the Purchase of two Thousand
Barrels of Pork, which when purchased, or Part thereof, you will forward
in the most expeditious Manner to General Schuyler at Albany; as it is
of great Importance the Army in Canada should be well supplied, you
will exert yourself to affect this Purchase speedily.[1]

Whenever you send or draw for the Money, your Bill on me shall
meet due Honour for twenty Thousand Dollars.

My Respects to Mrs. Lowry. I hope I shall soon have Time to write

& thank you & Mrs. Lowry for your Politeness. I am Sir, your most hble Ser.   J. H. Prsid.

LB (DNA: PCC, item 12A).
[1] See *JCC*, 4:297.

John Hancock to William Palfrey

Dear Palfrey   Philadelphia Apr. 20. 1776

I Rec'd your very short Letter of 15 from New York. I beleive you forgot the Print for me. I had thoughts to have Set out on Monday for Fairfield, & had made a proposition to Congress, but this moment hearing that my Aunt had Determin'd to Come to this place, suspends the Execution of my Design for a time. I have mention'd to the General my wish to See you here for a day or two, if he could consistently Dispense with your Absence for a few days, which I dare Say if possible he will Gratify me in.[1] I have Rec'd a Letter of Resignation from Coll Warren, & laid it before Congress, which they have Accepted, & Monday next is Assign'd for the Appointmt. of a Successor;[2] Coll. Harrison's Son was lately Appointed Depy Pay Masr. & now Acts in the Southern Departmt.[3] If he can hold the birth of Pay Masr Genl. & remain in Virginia, I beleive he will have it, but as I Judge that will not be permitted, as the Principal should be at Head Quarters; but in either case it is my opinion you will be brought into View, & either of which would be reputable, for if you be the Depy Pay Mr Genl. you will Reside with the General at New York. I shall do my best; & I think you may Depend on being promoted, you stand well, and any Additions of mine will not be wanting.

I thought I had known heretofore what it was to be hurried in Business, but really my Department, tho' exceedingly honorary, is a Department of great Business & constant Attention. Night & Day have I a Levee, I determine to persevere, tho' it is really hurtfull to my health.

I am going to move into the most Airy Elegant house in the City, havg. had the Offer of it, ready furnished by the Owners, & in a way I could never have Expected, in short, a polite offer to use the House, Furnishg., Gardens, Stables &c at will, & the Compliment of the Use.

I am hurried, many to Attend to; Congress, Marine Come. & others, that I can't Add but expectg to see you. Close wishing you well. My Mrs Hancock is not very well, but Time must be the Physician. Yours,

    J Hancock

RC (MH). Addressed: "To Major Palfrey Aid De Camp to General Washington. New York."
[1] Hancock's letter of this date to Washington, asking him to allow Palfrey "to pass two or three Days with me in this City, on Business of importance to me," is in

Am. Archives, 4th ser. 5:996.

[2] See John Jay to William Alexander, April 17, 1776, note.

[3] Benjamin Harrison, Jr., had been appointed to this office on February 15, 1776.
JCC, 4:151.

John Hancock to Philip Schuyler

Sir,   Philada. April 20th. 1776.

I do myself the Honour of transmitting herewith the Resolutions of Congress, under the Hand of the Secretary, as far as they relate to your own Conduct.[1] You will perceive they have ordered four Battalions to Quebec; and by Letter from Genl. Washington, I understand, they are preparing to march with the greatest Expedition.[2] I expect very soon to do myself the Pleasure of writing more fully. In the mean Time, I have the Honor to be with every Sentiment of Regard, yours &c.

J. H. Prst.

LB (DNA: PCC, item 12A).

[1] Congress passed a variety of resolutions relating to General Schuyler's army on April 6, 9, 11, 12, 15, and 17. See *JCC*, 4:260, 264, 271, 275, 282–84, 297.

[2] For the troops Congress directed Washington to detach to Canada, by a resolution of March 25, see *JCC*, 4:236; and Washington to Hancock, April 4, 1776, Washington, *Writings* (Fitzpatrick), 4:470–73.

John Hancock to George Washington

Sir,   Philadelphia. April 20th. 1776.

Your several Letters of the 24th and 27th of March, the 1st, 4th and 15th Inst. I had the Honour of receiving in the Order of their Dates, by the last of which I learn with Pleasure, that you had safely arrived at New York.[1] The Dispositions you made to expedite the Embarkation of the Troops, were highly proper and judicious.

Too much Dispatch cannot be used in sending the Battalions to Quebec; as it frequently happens in conducting such important affairs, that a Week, a Day, even an Hour, proves decisive, and the greatest Advantages are thereby either gained or lossed for Ever.

The Resolutions of Congress as far as they relate to yourself, or those Parts of your Letters that have hitherto come under their Consideration, I do myself the Honour to transmit herewith,[2] and am, Sir, with every Sentiment of Esteem & Regard, your most obed. and very hble Servt,   John Hancock Presidt

RC (DLC). In the hand of Jacob Rush and signed by Hancock.

[1] These letters from Washington to Hancock are in PCC, item 152, 1:541–44,

563-66, 571-74, 577-84, 587-90, and Washington, *Writings* (Fitzpatrick), 4:424-28, 436-38, 456-57, 470-73, 479-81.

[2] These resolves concerned the disposition of the cannon captured by Commodore Esek Hopkins on his New Providence expedition and the resignation of Paymaster General James Warren and were passed by Congress on April 16 and 19. *JCC*, 4:289, 295-96.

Richard Henry Lee to Patrick Henry

Dear Sir,   Philadelphia 20th April 1776

Having done myself the pleasure of writing to you by General Lee, I must now refer you to that letter,[1] and at present invite your attention to the most important concern of our approaching Convention.[2] Ages yet unborn, and millions existing at present, may rue or bless that Assembly, on which their happiness or misery will so eminently depend. Virginia has hitherto taken the lead in great affairs, and many now look to her with anxious expectation, hoping that the spirit, wisdom, and energy of her councils, will rouse America from the fatal lethargy into which the feebleness, folly, and interested views of the Proprietary governments, with the aid of Tory machinations, have thrown her most unhappily. The 12 years experience we have had of the perfidy and despotic intentions of the British Court, is still further demonstrated by the Kings speech, by the express declaration of every Ministerial Man in both houses of Parliament, by their infamous retrospective robbery Act, and by the intercepted letter from the Secretary of State to Governor Eden. All join in proving the design of the British Court to subdue at every event, and to enslave America after having destroyed its best Members. The Act of Parliament has to every legal intent and purpose dissolved our government, uncommissioned every magistrate, and placed us in the high road to Anarchy. In Virginia, we have certainly no Magistrate lawfully qualified to hang a Murderer, or any other Villain offending ever so attrociously against the State. We cannot be Rebels excluded from the Kings protection, and Magistrates acting under his authority at the same time. This proves the indispensable necessity of our taking up government immediately, for the preservation of Society, to effect the purpose of applying with vigor the strength of the Country to its present critical state; and above all, to set an example which N. Carolina, Maryland, Pennsylvania, and N. York will most assuredly, in my opinion, follow; and which will effectually remove the baneful influence of Proprietary interests from the councils of America. When this is done, give peremptory instructions to your Delegates to take every effectual step to secure America from the despotic aims of the British Court by Treaties of Alliance with foreign States, or by any means that shall be thought most conducive to that end. A slight attention to the late proceedings of many European Courts will sufficiently evince the spirit of partition, and the assumed right of disposing of Men & Countries like live Stock on a Farm, that distinguishes this corrupt age. St. Domingo, Louisiana, Corsica, & Poland indisputably prove this. Now Sir, I leave it with you to judge, whether, whilst we are hesitating about forming Alliance, Great Britain may not, and probably will not, seal our ruin by signing a Treaty of partition with two or three ambitious powers that may aid in conquering us[3]—Upon principles of interest and revenge they surely will. When G. B. finds she cannot conquer us alone, and that the whole must be lost, will she not rather choose a part than have none, certainly she will, and to gain the necessary aid give up a part, and thus involve us, unaided, unassisted, in a very unequal destructive contest with three or 4 of the greatest States in Europe. Nothing in this world is more certain than that the present Court of London wd. rather rule despotically a single rod of earth, than govern the World under legal limitations. All this danger however, may be prevented by a timely alliance with proper and willing powers in Europe. Indeed we are a singular instance in Modern times, of a people engaged in war with a powerful Nation, without taking any steps to secure the friendship or even neutrality of foreign States—Leaving to our enemies the full opportunity of ingaging all. And we know with certainty that every maritime State in Europe has been interceeded with not to supply us with military Stores, and many States have been applied to for Troops to destroy us, as Russia, Hesse, Hanover & Holland. Is it not the most dreadful infatuation in us to remain quiet in this way and stir not until it is too late—But no State in Europe will either Treat or Trade with us so long as we consider ourselves Subjects of G. B. Honor, dignity, and the custom of States forbid them until we take rank as an independant people. The war cannot long be prosecuted without Trade, nor can Taxes be paid until we are enabled to sell our produce, which cannot be the case, without the help of foreign Ships, whilst our enemies Navy is so superior to ours. A contraband Sloop or so may come from foreign parts, but no authorized & consequently sufficiently extensive Trade will be carried on with us whilst we remain in our present undefined unmeaning condition. Our clearest interest therefore, our very existance as freemen requires that we take decisive steps now, whilst we may, for the security of America. It is most fortunate for us that the present quitrent revenue, with the impost on Tobo. & Tonnage will do more than defray all our expences of Civil government witht. fresh Taxes on the people, and the unappropriated lands will pay the expences of the war. The inclosed pamphlet on Government is the production of our friend John Adams.[4] It is sensible and shews the virtue of the Man, at the same time that it proves the business of framing government not to be so difficult a thing as most people imagine. The small scheme printed in hand bill I had written before I saw this work of Mr. Adams,[5] and he agrees that the Council of State had better be a distinct body from the Upper house of Assembly, meaning the Upper house, their duration indeed may be too long, but it should be for a longer term than the lower house, in order to answer the purpose of an independant middle power. The sheriffs had better I think be appointed as now in Virginia, as by choice of the freeholders in each County.

The recommendation of Congress about taking Government is, as you see, of old date,[6] and therefore it is said during the continuance of the present disputes. But it matters not much, for the Government taken up ought to be the best, whither it be for this, that, or another term of years. This I take to be the time & thing meant by Shakespeare when he says "There is a Tide in the Affairs of Men which taken at the Flood leads on to fortune—That omitted, we are ever after bound in Shallows" &c. Let us therefore, quitting every other consideration heartily unit in leading our countrymen to embrace the[7] present flowing tide, which promises fair to waft us into the harbor of safety, happiness, liberty and virtue.

Perhaps some may endeavour to injure you on account of your concurrence in opinion with Mr. Glyn and others, relative to the right derived to the company of Wharton and others from their Indian grant of lands within the colony; but as I consider it meant only to say, that unappropriated lands had better be purchased from the Indians or prime occupants, not denying the propriety of paying dues accustomed to the colony in which such lands lie, and complying with its laws: the objection against such an opinion loses its force.

I am well pleased to hear that you are going into Convention, and I hope your powers will be fully exerted in securing the peace and happiness of our country, by the adoption of a wise and free government. I shall be impatient to know your thoughts on these great subjects, and hope you will inform me as early as possible.

Excuse the length of this letter, And believe me sincerely Yours,

RC (Vi). Richard Henry Lee, *The Letters of Richard Henry Lee*, ed. James C. Ballagh, 2 vols. (New York: Macmillan Co., 1911–14), 1:176–80. RC damaged; missing words supplied from Tr.

[1] Not found.

[2] Henry represented Hanover County at the Virginia Convention that convened at Williamsburg on May 6.

[3] Similar arguments, perhaps the product of Lee's pen, were set forth in "Serious Questions addressed to the Congress, and all other Legislative Bodies in America," published in the *Pennsylvania Evening Post*, April 16, and reprinted in the *Virginia Gazette* (Dixon and Hunter), May 11, 1776. For a discussion of the possible effect fear of a partition treaty had on the timing of a formal declaration of independence, see James H. Hutson, "The Partition Treaty and the Declaration of American Independence," *Journal of American History* 58 (March 1972): 877–96.

[4] *Thoughts on Government*. See John Adams to John Penn, March 19–27? 1776.

[5] Lee's "small scheme" has not been found.

[6] The resolutions of December 4, 1775. *JCC*, 3:403–4.

[7] Remainder of letter supplied from Tr.

William Whipple to John Langdon

Dear Sir,   Philadelphia April 20th 1776
  My last accompanied the 10,000 doll[ar]s by Mr Henderson which
I wish safe to hand in due time. I hope cannon may be obtained at New
London or Rhode Island, if not I know of no resource at present but
this place and if they must come from here it will be some time before
you can have them as they are yet to be made. I am continually teazing
the Marine Committee about the canvass but have got nothing yet determined, nor have you wrote me how much you shall want. The Committee determined last evening on the nomination of Agents which will
be reported to Congress to morrow. I expect my next will advise you
of the appointment. I have got the nomination of officers for your ship
put off: it is not now as it was when the other ships were fitting out—
then there was a scarcity of officers, but now an abundance of applications. As that is the case the Committee are very critical in examining
the characters, so if you recommend any that I am not well acquainted
with, you must furnish me with a history of them, whether they have
been in ships of war, if their courage has been tried, their political
principles &c.[1] I think New Hampshire can officer one ship very well.
We must be very careful that no consideration but real merit influence
our recommendations. I have just heard South Carolina has taken up
Govt., chosen a Council and it's said a Governor—shall be able to inform you more particularly in my next.[2] It's expected North Carolina
and Virginia will soon follow the example. Private letters from Virginia
mention Lord Dunmore's having published in his camp a declaration
of war, which he lately rec'd from England; how does this agree with the
Olive Branch to be brought by the Commissioners.
  I have not heard a word of nor rec'd a single line from a member
of the Legislature of New Hampshire since I left that Colony. Am much
better acquainted with what's doing in any other Colony than in that
I have the honor to represent—what can be the meaning of all this.
Mr Hancock talks of setting out for Boston in a few days—it's probable
he'll be there about the last of this month. I think it would be worth
while for you to see him as you would have an opportunity of conferring with him about your ship—his stay will be very short. I suppose
Br. Bartlett will have set out before this reaches you, if not send my best
regards to him and tell him bear a hand.
  I am with great respect, yours,   Wm Whipple

Tr (DLC).
  [1] The *Raleigh's* officers were not appointed until July 22, 1776. *JCC*, 5:601. However, Langdon wrote many letters recommending officers for service on the *Raleigh*,
among which are letters to Whipple of May 20, 27, and June 16, and to Josiah
Bartlett of June 3, August 13, and September 14, 1776, in Clark, *Naval Documents*,
5:159–60, 264–65, 355–56, 559–61, 6:161–62, 816–17.

² The South Carolina Provincial Congress had adopted a new constitution on March 26. *Am. Archives*, 4th ser. 5:608–14.

Samuel Chase to John Adams

My Dear Sir,

Landing at North End of Lake George.
April. 21st. 1776. Sunday Afternoon

I left Fort George on last Fryday afternoon and arrived at this place yesterday Evening. I have just seen a Gentleman, who left Quebec on the 6th Inst. General Worster arrived there on the 1st. On the 3rd we opened a four Gun Battery of 9 pounders on Point Levy, another was erecting on the plains of Abraham, and a third on Passage [   ] ¹ which would be finished in a few Days. We on the 6th had before Quebec 2500, of which about 800 are in the Hospital (the far greater part of the small Pox) and about 1000 whose Enlistment expired the 15th. In the late Skirmish there were 7 Canadians killed, 4 wounded, 2 since dead, & 30 taken prisoners. The rest dispersed, & delivered up Carltons Letter which induced them to take up arms. We have here 800 Troops, & Sinclears Regimt. will reach this on Tuesday. I am informed of Warner's Regiment of green Mountain Boys, there were only 90 fit for Duty.

I have been at Ticonderoga, and am satisfied it would not be proper to repair it. The Expence would be great, it is commanded on each Side, & would be releived with great Difficulty. The Schooner, Royal Savage pierced for 16 Guns of 4, 6 & 9-pounders & another Schooner of 6 4-pounders taken at Saint Johns, are repairing, but they gave no Guns. They would secure the Command of Lake Champlain against any force which could be brought there this Summer, if we should be so unfortunate as to lose the Possession of Canada. Pray have the Guns returned. These were sent to Cambridge.

If there is no Rule of Congress that no officer should sell to or supply their soldiers, it is high Time. The Expence of convoying their Bagage is very great. Pray attend to this. I beleive there is a Resolve agt. *Suttling*. This is evaded. ²

I thus drop you a Line as any Intelligence or any defect in our Regulations occur without any Regard to Accuracy or precision.

Remember me to all my Friends. Your Affectionate, Obedt. Servant,

Saml Chase

RC (MHi).
¹ MS blank.
² According to Richard Smith, "Some Regulations were presented by Lewis about Suttlers in the Northern Army" on February 7, 1776, but there is no indication in the journals that any such regulations were instituted until Congress adopted new Articles of War on September 20, 1776. See *JCC*, 4:113, 158, 5:794, 6:935, 937; and Richard Smith's Diary, February 7, 1776.

John Hancock to Charles Thomson

Sir,   Sunday Morng 21st Aprl. 1776
    I last Eveng Rec'd Dispatches by Express of such a Nature as to
induce me to Summon a Meeting of Congress this Morng. at half past
8 oClock, and am to request your Attendance at that time.[1] I Beg you
will Acquaint Mr. Dickinson of it, that if he can conveniently he will
please to attend.
    I am in haste, Sir, Your very huml sevt,   John Hancock Pt.

RC (PHi).
    [1] Robert Treat Paine noted in his diary for this date: "Fair. Express from Canada.
Congress call'd together for an hour or two. Raind. P.M. Heard Mr. Stillman."
MHi. This unusual Sunday session of Congress, which was not recorded in the
journals, was occasioned by the arrival of an April 12 letter from General Schuyler
enclosing dispatches about the alarming situation of the army in Canada from Gen.
David Wooster, Col. Moses Hazen, and Capt. William Goforth. See PCC, item
153, 2:101–20; and Am. Archives, 4th ser. 5:868–71. These dispatches, discussing the
low morale of American troops, shortages in money and supplies, a sudden upsurge
of Canadian hostility against the American invaders, and the spectre of large-scale
Indian attacks on American forces at Montreal and Quebec, led Congress to adopt
a series of remedial resolves on April 23 and 24. See JCC, 4:301–5. See also Hancock's letters to Washington, April 23, to Moses Hazen, April 24, to Philip Schuyler,
April 26, and to the Commissioners in Canada, April 26, 1776.

William Whipple to Joshua Brackett

    Philadelphia, Apr. 21. 1776. "By the Inclos'd paper You'll see the Dis-
position of the Southern Colonies, with Regard to Independence. I
need not tell you the Disposition of the Northern Colonies. When you
are sure there is a weight somewhere, & find the Ends are free, it will
not require a Newtonian head to determine the weight must be in the
Middle. However there is no doubt with me but these difficulties will
soon be remov'd. The first of next month there will be a considerable
addition to the Assembly of this Colony which will greatly affect the
Political wheels of this & the Neighboring Colonies . . . the two most
Southern Colonies have not been represented in congress since I've been
here, but their delegates are now on their way & daily Expected." [1]

MS not found; reprinted from extract in *The Collector* 61 (May 1948): item M790.
    [1] The credentials of the South Carolina delegates were presented on April 24,
and the Georgia delegation appeared in Congress on May 20. JCC, 4:305–6, 367.

John Adams to James Warren

April 22. 1776

The Management of so complicated and mighty a Machine, as the United Colonies, requires the Meekness of Moses, the Patience of Job and the Wisdom of Solomon, added to the Valour of Daniel.

They are advancing by slow but sure Steps, to that mighty Revolution, which You and I have expected for Some Time. Forced Attempts to accellerate their Motions, would have been attended with Discontent and perhaps Convulsions.

The News from South Carolina, has aroused and animated all the Continent.[1] It has Spread a visible Joy, and if North Carolina and Virginia should follow the Example, it will Spread through all the rest of the Colonies like Electric Fire.

The Royal Proclamation, and the late Act of Parliament, have convinced the doubting and confirmed the timorous and wavering. The two Proprietary Colonies only, are still cool. But I hope a few Weeks will alter their Temper.

I think it is now the precise Point of Time for our Council and House of Representatives, either to proceed to make such Alterations in our Constitution as they may judge proper, or to Send a Petition to Philadelphia for the Consent of Congress to do it. It will be considered as fresh Evidence of our Spirit and Vigour, and will give Life and Activity and Energy to all the other Colonies. Four Months ago, or indeed at any Time Since you assumed a Government, it might have been disagreable and perhaps dangerous. But it is quite otherwise now.

Another Thing, if you are so unanimous, in the Measure of Independency and wish for a Declaration of it, now is the proper Time for you to instruct your Delegates to that Effect. It would have been productive of Jealousies perhaps and animosities, a few Months ago, but would have a contrary Tendency now. The Colonies are all at this Moment turning their Eyes, that Way. Vast Majorities in all the Colonies now see the Propriety and Necessity of taking the decisive Steps, and those who are averse to it are afraid to Say much against it. And therefore Such an Instruction at this Time would comfort and cheer the Spirits of your Friends, and would discourage and dishearten your Enemies.

Coll Whipples Letters from New Hampshire, are nearly in the Same Strain with yours to me, vizt that all are now united in the great Question. His Letters inform him that even of the Protesters there is now but one left, who is not zealous for Independency.

I lament the Loss of Governor Ward exceedingly because he had many Correspondents in Rhode Island, whose Letters were of service to Us, an Advantage which is now entirely lost.

After all, My Friend, I do not att all wonder, that so much Reluctance has been Shewn to the Measure of Independency. All great Changes are irksome to the human Mind, especially those which are attended with great Dangers, and uncertain Effects. No Man living can foresee the Consequences of such a Measure. And therefore I think it ought not to have been undertaken, untill the Design of Providence, by a series of great Events, had so plainly marked out the Necessity of it that he that runs might read.

We may feel a Sanguine Confidence of our Strength: yet in a few years it may be put to the Tryal.

We may please ourselves with the prospect of free and popular Governments. But there is great Danger, that these Governments will not make us happy. God grant they may. But I fear, that in every assembly, Members will obtain an Influence, by Noise not sense—By Meanness, not Greatness—By Ignorance not Learning—By contracted Hearts not large souls. I fear too, that it will be impossible to convince and perswade People to establish wise Regulations.

There is one Thing, my dear sir, that must be attempted and most Sacredly observed or We are all undone. There must be a Decency and Respect, and Veneration introduced for Persons in Authority, of every Rank, or We are undone. In a popular Government, this is the only Way of Supporting order. And in our Circumstances, as our People have been So long without any Government att all, it is more necessary than in any other. The United Provinces were So sensible of this that they carried it to a burlesque Extream.

I hope your Election in May will be the most solemn and joyfull that ever took Place in the Province. I hope every Body will attend. Clergy and Laity should go to Boston. Every Body should be gratefully pious & happy. It should be conducted with a solemnity that may make an Impression on the whole People.

RC (MHi). In Adams' hand, though not signed.
[1] On March 26 the South Carolina Provincial Congress had adopted a new constitution. *Am. Archives*, 4th ser. 5:608–14.

Richard Henry Lee to Charles Lee

My Dear Friend,   Philadelphia, 22nd April, 1776.
I thank you heartily for your obliging favors by this and the last Post,[1] they have made me very happy by the good opinion you have of our officers and troops. I have no doubt they will verify upon the Enemy, when they come, your opinion of them. It always gave me much pleasure to reflect on your appointment to the Southern Department, well knowing the signal benefit and security that would result to my country therefrom. Your measures are in my opinion extremely wise and well

adapted to the ends you have in view. I am sure your water manœuvres will give great security to our rivers and confidence to the people thereon, at the same time that it will distress the enemy by preventing their getting provisions. The idea entertained by some that the battalions were to be stationed here and there to defend against Cutters was very absurd, and if executed would have rendered the Regiments useless for that and for every other purpose, unless we could have prevailed on the enemy to go there only to maraude where the troops were fixed. It was certainly the idea of Congress, and it is so expressed in their resolve,[2] that you should raise a Company of Artillery for Monsr. Arundel, and the Convention or Committee of Safety to appoint the inferior Officers— Capt. Innis's company it was never proposed to affect in any degree by this new raised Company. You will hear more of this hereafter. Your desire is complied with by a Resolve of Congress directing letters to Generals commanding in separate detachments to go post free.[3] The pay of an Engineer under the chief is no more than twenty dollars a month, and as yet no rank is settled. Your letter to Congress concerning shoes and blankets has been considered, and a very good man is ordered to procure and forward immediately to Williamsburg 5000 blankets and as many shoes for the Troops in Virginia.[4] Three tons of powder are likewise ordered. You may expect these ere long. The want of discipline among our Troops in Canada this winter has occasioned some disturbances in that country where a small engagement has actually happened between the country people and a party of our men in which the former were defeated. We are taking all the means in our power to compose these unhappy differences, and hope it will be effected by our Committee, better discipline, and the large body of troops going thither. We know not yet where the mercenaries from Boston are gone unless it be to Halifax. Manly has taken one of their Transports with two capital Tories and Tory goods imported from G. B. valued at £35,000. sterlg. 2 of their Transports with provisions from England for Boston have been lately taken. You have no doubt heard how Commodore Hopkins has drubbed the Glasgow and would certainly have taken her, if he had not been so heavy with Providence stores—A Bomb Brig & 3 Tenders he did take and carry into N. London—Wallace & his little Squardon have fled from the Rhode Island Station, and left it to our Fleet. The Commodore we expect is now out on another cruise. When Sir you find anything whatever deficient about the troops, a letter from you to Congress thro' the President will be the quickest and surest way to obtain it, as happened the other day when you applied for powder, blankets, and shoes. You ask me why we hesitate in Congress. I'll tell you my friend, because we are heavily clogged with instructions from these shamefully interested Proprietary people, and this will continue until Virga. sets the example of taking up Government, and sending peremptory Orders to their delegates to pursue the most effectual measures for the Security of America. It is most certain that the people in these Proprietary Colonies will then force the same measure, after which Adieu to Proprietary influence and timid senseless politics. You have enclosed a sensible little pamphlet on government written by Mr John Adams. 'Tis well fitted for the times, shewing that to be easy and necessary, which the unthinking people have supposed to be unnecessary and difficult. We have an account in Town that the Court of London has demanded from that of Portugal all the American property in the Portugese dominions, and 'tis supposed this will be complied with. Every days experience still confirms the most diabolical wickedness and violence of that execrable Court. I do most heartily wish it were in my power to attend our Convention at their coming Session—But it is impossible to leave this place, and you would think it quite improper if you were here.

Your affectionate friend, Richard Henry Lee

[*P.S.*] I am so hurried that I scarcely know what I write.

MS not found; reprinted from *NYHS Collections* 4 (1871): 440–43.

[1] Charles Lee's letters of April 5 and 12 are in *NYHS Collections* 4 (1871): 378–80, 416–17.

[2] See *JCC*, 4:212.

[3] See *JCC*, 4:294.

[4] In response to Charles Lee's April 6 letter to Congress, which is in PCC, item 158, fols. 41–42, and *NYHS Collections*, 4 (1871): 382–83, Ephraim Blaine was appointed to procure blankets and shoes for the Virginia troops. See *JCC*, 4:296–97.

John Adams to Abigail Adams

April 23d. 1776. "This is St. Georges Day, a Festival celebrated by the English, as Saint Patricks is by the Irish, St. Davids by the Welch, and St. Andrews by the Scotch. The Natives of old England in this City heretofore formed a Society, which they called Saint Georges Clubb, or Saint Georges Society. Upon the Twenty third of April annually, they had a great Feast. But the Times and Politicks have made a schism in the society so that one Part of them are to meet and dine at the City Tavern, and the other att the Bunch of Grapes, Israel Jacobs's, and a third Party go out of Town.

"One sett are staunch Americans, another staunch Britons I suppose, and a Third half Way Men, Neutral Beings, moderate Men, prudent Folks—for such is the Division among Men upon all Occasions and every Question. This is the Account, which I have from my Barber, who is one of the Society and zealous on the side of America, and one of the Philadelphia Associators." Continues with an account of his barber, John Byrne, and apologizes for writing "so trifling a Letter upon so

uninteresting a subject, at a Time, when my Country is fighting Pro
Aris et Focis."

RC (MHi). Adams, *Family Correspondence* (Butterfield), 1:391–93.

John Hancock to Nathaniel Shaw, Jr.

Greeting,   [April 23, 1776]
You being Appointed by Congress Agent for Continental Prizes in
the Colony of Connecticutt, I do hereby Authorize & Impower you
to Act in said Office, and to Appoint one or more Deputies under you
as you may Judge necessary, & do Require you to be carefull in the
Execution of said Trust, & strickly to Conform to the orders & Directions herewith Transmitted you, & to such further Directions as you
shall from time to time Receive from Congress, or the Marine Board
touching your said Office.[1]
Given under my hand at Philadelphia this Twenty third Day of April
1776. By order of Congress,   John Hancock Presidt

RC (CtNlHi). Addressed: "The Delegates of the Thirteen United Colonies to
Nathaniel Shaw, Jur. Esqr."
[1] For a list of the other prize officers appointed by Congress this day, see *JCC*,
4:301. This letter must have taken an unusually long time to reach Shaw for as
late as June 19, 1776, he complained that he still had received no word from Congress about his appointment. Clark, *Naval Documents*, 5:625–26. At least one other
prize agent experienced comparable difficulties. John Bradford, chosen this day as
prize agent for Massachusetts, did not receive his commission until August 1776.
Ibid., 4:1216n.2.

John Hancock to George Washington

Sir,   Philadelphia April 23d. 1776.
I am to acknowledge the Receipt of your Favour of the 19th of April
enclosing several Papers: all which were immediately laid before Congress.[1]
The important Intelligence they contain, makes it necessary that the
most vigorous Measures should be adopted, as well to defend our Troops
against the Canadians themselves, as to ensure Success to the Expedition.
The Congress being determined on the Reduction of Quebec and the
Security of that Country, for Reasons too obvious to be mentioned,
have left Nothing undone, which can any Ways contribute to that End.
Whatever may be the Causes of the late Insurrection, good Policy requires, that while we endeavour to prevent every Thing of the Kind
for the future, we should also make Provision, in Case it should happen.
Accordingly Congress have come into sundry Resolutions calculated to

quiet the Minds of the Canadians and to remove the Sources of their Uneasiness & Discontent. They have likewise ordered six more Battalions to be sent into Canada from the Army at New York as you will see by the enclosed Resolves.[2] Whether any further additional Forces will be wanted there is a Matter of some Uncertainty with Congress. Should you, from your Knowledge of Facts, the State of Canada, the Possibility that Genl. Howe will attempt to relieve Genl. Carlton, and comparing all Circumstances together, be of opinion that an additional Force is still necessary, you will please to signify it to Congress; and at the same Time inform them whether in that Case, such additional Force can be spared from the Army now at New York.[3]

I transmit herewith sundry Resolves of Congress for your Direction, and have the Honour to be, Sir, your most obedt. and very hble Serv,

John Hancock Presidt.

[*P.S.*] The Inclos'd Letter for Commodore Hopkins,[4] I leave unseal'd for your perusal *only,* after which I beg the favour of you to Seal & forward by Fessenden, or a fresh Express.

I have paid Mr Fessenden Twelve Dollars, which you will please to Note on Settlement with him. J H

RC (DLC). In the hand of Jacob Rush, with signature and postscript by Hancock.
[1] Washington's letter to Hancock is in PCC, item 152, 1:595–98; and Washington, *Writings* (Fitzpatrick), 4:492–94. The "several Papers" enclosed therein were copies of General Schuyler's letter to Hancock of April 12 and accompanying enclosures. See Hancock to Charles Thomson, April 21, 1776, note. See also Washington to Schuyler, April 19, 1776, in Washington, *Writings* (Fitzpatrick), 4:495–97.
[2] For these resolves, which Congress adopted this day, see *JCC,* 4:301–2.
[3] Washington opposed sending any more reinforcements to Canada from the troops deployed for the defense of New York. See Washington to Hancock, April 25, 1776. PCC, item 152, 1:619–30; and Washington, *Writings* (Fitzpatrick), 4:515–21.
[4] See Marine Committee to Esek Hopkins, this date.

Thomas Johnson to
Daniel of St. Thomas Jenifer

Dr. sr. Phila. 23d April 1776.

Mr. Wallace & Mr. Green set off Tomorrow Morning by one of whom we intend to write you fully but as the post may possibly be in before these Gent. we think it necessary to advise you that all your Deputies here from Maryland approve the Conduct of the Council of Safety and resolve to support it.[1] The Letter to the president gave high Offence to some of the very hot Gent. No Resolution is yet formed on it but probably will to day. R. A. & T. S.[2] join in Respects to you & yr. Brethern.

I am dr. sr., Your very affect Servt. Th Johnson Junr

RC (MdAA).

[1] For the Maryland Council of Safety's account of their response to the receipt of John Hancock's letter of April 16, see their letters to the Maryland Delegates of April [19] and 22, 1776, in *Md. Archives*, 11:354–56, 368–70.

[2] Robert Alexander and Thomas Stone.

Marine Committee to Esek Hopkins

Sir   In Marine Committee. Philada. April [23] 1776.[1]

As it is essentially necessary for promoting the Service that full & speedy Information of the State & Condition of the Enemies' Fleets in the different parts of America should be communicated to You from whence You may be the better enabled to act with Vigour & Success in your Naval Department, we therefore write to acquaint You that from the best Information the Force in Virginia at this Time consists of the Liverpool Frigate Capt. Bellew of 28 Guns, the Otter Sloop Capt. Squires of 16 Guns, the William an armed Ship of 10 Guns with Lord Dunmore, the Eilbeck a large Store-ship with some small Guns. It is said & believed that both the Liverpool & Otter are exceedingly weak from the Want of Hands, their Men being chiefly employed on Board a Number of small Tenders fitted out by Lord Dunmore to distress the Trade on the Coast of Virginia & Bay of Chesepeak. His Lordship has now between 100 & 150 Sail of Vessels great & small the most of which are Prizes & many of them valuable. These, so far from being any Addition in point of Strength, will rather weaken the Men of War, whose Hands are employed in the small Vessels. The Force at Wilmington in North Carolina You will observe by the inclosed Extracts of Letters.

Whether You have formed any Expedition or not, the Execution of which will interfere with an Attempt upon either or both of the above Fleets we cannot determine; but if that should not be the Case, there is no Service, from the present Appearance of things in which You could better promote the Interest of your Country than by the Destruction of the Enemies' Fleet in North Carolina or Virginia; for as the Seat of War will most probably be transferred in the ensuing Campaign to the Southern Colonies, such a Maneuvre attended with Success will disconcert or at least retard their Military Operations for a Length of Time, give Spirits to our Friends & afford them an oppurtunity of improving their Preparations for Resistance. These Reasons, Sir, added to your known Spirit & Inclination to Serve America, will, we make no Doubt, sufficiently weigh with You to undertake that Service.[2] The Roebuck Capt. Hammond of 40 Guns is now in Lewis Town Road. You will observe by the Papers that Capt. Barry in the Brigantine Lexington has taken an armed Tender with 25 picked Men commanded by a Lieutenant of the Liverpool wch is a Loss, as they cannot easily provide for the Want of Men. Should You come to the Southward &

determine to go into Chesepeak, advise us of the Time of your sailing, that Orders may be given to the different armed Vessels on the Coast as also to those in Chesepeak & the Commander in chief in Virginia to co-operate with You in the Attack. As You were directed by a former Instruction,[3] in Case You determined to proceed into Chesepeak Bay, "that You should Dispatch a swift sailing Vessel to reconnoitre the Coast & gain Intelligence of the Strength of the Enemy" we now remind You of that Instruction & desire You would send a Vessel for that Purpose from the Fleet. Wishing You Success, We are Sir with Esteem, Your most Obedt Servts,   John Hancock   Geo. Read

Step. Hopkins   Richard Henry Lee

Joseph Hewes   Saml. Huntington

R. Alexander   Jona D Sergeant

RC (CSmH). Written by Sergeant and signed by Sergeant, Alexander, Hancock, Hewes, Hopkins, Huntington, Lee, and Read.

[1] The assignment of this date is based on the postscript to Hancock's letter to Washington of this date, requesting that the "Inclos'd letter for Commodore Hopkins" be forwarded by express.

[2] In his response of May 1, Hopkins described the state of his ships, intimating that, with his forces weakened by an outbreak of fever and divided by personnel conflicts, the fleet was not ready to undertake a major expedition. See Clark, *Naval Documents*, 4:1358–60.

[3] Hopkins' cruising orders, dated January 5, 1776, are printed in *JCC*, 4:335–36.

Robert Morris to Charles Lee

Dear sir   Philada. April 23d. 1776

I had the pleasure to receive Yours of the 10th yesterday.[1] Your professions of attachment are flattering to my Vanity and pleasing to my Heart, but dont talk of obligations, when it is in my power to render you Services Command them freely, I have as much pleasure in doing them as you cou'd wish. I am sorry to tell you the two bills for £1500 St[erlin]g each are Noted for Non Acceptance & expected to come back; therefore it is lucky I did not Negotiate them. The Securitys lie safe in England and I still think your Estate may be drawn from thence by & by. Mr James Nourse has drawn a bill on me for two hundred & fifty Pounds this Curr[ence]y which I had accepted before Your letter came & am pleased to find I did right therein and Congratulate you on the favourable Accounts he gives of your purchase.

I see clearly the many difficultys You have to encounter in your new Command & think with you that the Force is inadequate. However we have an amazing Army on foot, the Expence will be enormous and nothing but necessity can justify any increase of it. The People of Virginia are a Noble Spirited People and I have no doubt when danger approaches them but they will exert & Strain every Nerve in defence of their Country. I think you shou'd make a point to Cultivate their good oppinion; it will be usefull to you. Their Convention, Committee of Safety & other Public Bodys Consist of respectable Men that Consider themselves as the present Civil Authority which ought to have Controul over the Military and if they are not respected in that light by the Military Commanders I fancy disputes will soon ensue, the Service will become disagreeable, Ill Consequences will arise & God knows where they may End. But a Contrary Conduct will gain their Confidence & Esteem, they will render the Service easy & agreable and in short every happy & Good Consequence may be expected from it. You must excuse me, if you think these hints unnecessary. I only offer them as hints from a Friend that entertains the best wishes for your happiness & glory. I read Your letter to Colo Lee respecting Mr Yates but I think he said a promise in favour of another had Escaped him.[2]

The Post is near departure & having much to do & write I must bid adieu being, Dr sir, Your affectte. Friend & Servt.

Robt Morris

RC (DLC: photostat). Addressed: "To Majr. General Charles Lee at Head Quarters, Wiliamsburgh."

[1] Lee's letter to Morris, which is printed under the date April 16, 1776, in *NYHS Collections* 4 (1871): 424–26, is at DFo.

[2] General Lee had reported to Morris that Edmund Randolph, who had been appointed deputy muster-master general for the southern department on March 25, 1776, "has declined but begs leave to recommend in his place a Mr. Yates his relation. Will you mention the affair to Colonel Lee in my name? they say Mr. Yates is very capable." Ibid., p. 426. Congress accepted Randolph's resignation on April 26 and appointed William Yates in his place on the 27th. *JCC*, 4:236, 311, 315.

Secret Committee to
the Pennsylvania Committee of Safety

Gentlemn.   April 23d 1776.

The Secret Come. of Cong. have directed the Brige. Polly, Capt. McFadden, & Brige. Patty, Capt. McIvers, to be dispatchd under convoy of the Wasp Schooner,[1] & by their order I apply to you to licence two proper pilots to carry down those two vessels by Cape May Chanl. The Wasp has orders to bring the pilots up again, unless they chuse to land at the Cape. I am Gentlen. respectfully, yr. very humb. Servt.   Robt Morris, Chairman of the Sect. Come.

Tr (MH).

[1] The Secret Committee had signed contracts with the owners of the brigs *Polly*

and *Patty* on March 26 and April 16. See Secret Committee Minutes of Proceedings, March 26 and April 16, 1776.

John Adams to William Tudor

Dr sir   April 24. 1776

Your Favour by Mr Palfrey, I recd this Evening, and it was the more agreable because it resolved a Question I had often asked and never before could obtain an answer, vizt whether the Judge Advocate was come with the Army to N. York.[1]

Am very Sorry to hear that Boston is in so defenceless a Condition. That Harbour must be made impenetrable at all Events. I think our People will exert themselves—But I could have wished that more Troops had been left there at least for a Time.

It gives me Pleasure to learn that N. York is put in so good a Posture of Defence. But I wish I could hear that the Inhabitants were better pleased with their military Visitants.

There is one Event, which I think would essentially alter the political Character and Conduct of those People, and that is the Institution of a new Government.

This Point must be accomplished, in that, and every other Colony. South Carolina has nobly led the Way, and I hope, and from the best Intelligence believe, that North Carolina and Virginia will follow the Example, with equal Wisdom and Magnanimity. The Jerseys too have the Same Thing in Contemplation. This Province and Maryland will be the last—But not the least resolute when they do adopt the Measure.

I wish you would make this a Subject of Conversation as much as you can, both among the Gentlemen of the Army and the Citizens, and convince all, of the Expediency, Practicability and Necessity of this Measure. Believe me there is nothing upon which the Salvation of America more depends.

When this Step is taken, the new Legislatures would exert themselves with tenfold alacrity in every warlike Preparation by Sea and Land. They would study and labour to better Purpose, in manufacturing, Salt Petre, Powder, Arms, Cloathing and every Thing they want.

Besides it would cement the Whiggs and discourage the Tories.

It would introduce order in the Place of Confusion.

In short the Advantages are innumerable and the Disadvantages, none.

How it is possible for People to hear the Crier of a Court pronounce G—d Save the King, and for Jurors to Swear well and truly to try an Issue between our Soverign Lord the King, and a Prisoner, or to keep his Majestys Secrets, in these days I can't conceive. Dont the Clergy pray that he may vanquish, and over come all his Enemies, yet? Who do they mean by his Enemies? Your Army? Have People no Consciences, or do they look upon all oaths to be Custom house oaths?

You must not mention my Name. You know the Reason. It will do more good to come from your self.

The New York Congress has done very well, in their Resolutions about Salt Petre and Powder, and their Council of Safety I think have done very well.

The Friends of Liberty in that City and Colony have great Merit. They have struggled with many Embarrassments. They ought to be treated with great Respect. And indeed the Lukewarm, the moderate, the Timid, and even the Trimmers and Tories should be gained by gentle Treatment, where that will do.

I wish to know if Major Austin and Mr Price are at N. York—and also to know What Regiments are left in Boston. Who are the Colonells.

Write me by every Post. Dont omit one.

RC (MHi). In Adams' hand, though not signed.
[1] William Tudor, the American army's judge advocate general, had written to Adams from New York. Tudor to Adams, April 21, 1776, Adams Papers, MHi.

John Hancock to Moses Hazen

Sir   Philada. April 24th. 1776

It affords me great Pleasure to have it in Charge from Congress to convey to you their approbation of your Letter to Genl. Schuyler, as well as your Attention to the Public Good.[1] Tho it appears that some of the continental Troops have behaved in an imprudent Manner towards the Canadians, yet I trust the Evil is not incurable. It is only by cultivating a friendly Intercourse with them, and restraining by exemplary Punishment the ⟨Outrages⟩ Irregularities of the Soldiery, that their Affections can be ever regained. To accomplish This most important Purpose, the Congress have enjoined the Commanding officer in Canada to be very attentive to military Discipline, & to punish severely every Violation thereof.[2] To this must be added all the Acts of Insinuation & Address, which I make no Doubt, you in particular, & the Rest of the officers, will exert to the utmost of your abilities. I have the Honour to be, Sir, your most obedt. & very hble Servt.

J. H. Prest.

LB (DNA: PCC, item 12A). Addressed: "Col. Hazen, Montreal."
[1] See Hazen to Philip Schuyler, April 1, *Am. Archives*, 4th ser. 5:869–70; and Hancock to Charles Thomson, April 21, 1776, note.
[2] See *JCC*, 4:302.

Secret Committee to Philip Schuyler

Philadelphia, April 24, 1776. "We are directed by Congress[1] to fo[rward] Five Tons powder from the Mills of Mr. Wisner & Mr. Livingston to you for the Continental Service in Canada and in obedience to that order we have this day wrote Messrs. Wisner & Livingston to forward that quantity of Powder to you for which proper receipts will no doubt be granted to them. We think it necessary to inform you of this transaction that you may write those Gentlemen if you find it delayed or that your interference is necessary and when you receive this or any other p[owder] to for[ward it] under direction of. . . ."[2]

RC (NN). In a clerical hand; signed "By order of the Secret Committee, Robert Morris, Chairman."
   [1] See *JCC*, 4:304.
   [2] MS damaged; most of the remainder indecipherable.

Thomas Stone to Daniel of St. Thomas Jenifer

My Dear Sir   Phila. April. 24. 1776. Wednesday
   Mr. Johnson wrote to You yesterday by Post and I wrote to Mr Hall.[1] Nothing is done since in Consequence of your Letter and resolution to the Presidt. We have been very much engaged for some days in attending to the affairs of Canada, having recd. late Intelligence from that Quarter. I presume the Canada Department, its Connections and Dependancies will ingross our Attention for a few days, And then some Ans[we]r will probably be given to your Letter.[2] What it will be I can't guess, with any Degree of Certainty but I am inclined to think every thing will be left to the Convention. We shall attend the Meeting of that Assembly. Gov. Eden's Letter is published in one of the Papers here and various are the Comments on it. Independant of every thing else it is very suspicious; but taking Mr Eden's Conduct, the Letters from his Brother, who must know his Sentiments, into Consideration I think lessens greatly the Charge which the intercepted Letter would of itself import. If the Commissioners do not arrive shortly and conduct themselves with great Candor and Uprightness to effect a reconciliation, a Seperation will most undoubtedly take place as then all Governors & officers must quit their Posts and new men must be placed in the Saddle of Power. I wish to conduct affairs so that a just & honourable reconciliation should take place, or that we should be pretty unanimous in a resolution to fight it out for Independance, the proper way to effect this is not to move too quick. But then we must take Care to do every thing which is necessary for our Security and Defence, not suffer ourselves to be lulled or wheedled by any deceptions, Declarations or Giv-

ings out. You know my Heart wishes for a Peace upon Terms of Security and Justice to America. But War, any thing is preferable to a Surrender of our Rights. You may rely on my friendship on all Occasions. My Brothers are all Steady friends to your Council. And we have not the least Doubt but when your Conduct comes to be tried by your Country you will receive it's thanks for your great Attention to the publick Good. You have been steady, firm and determined in the p[resent] Opposition to ministerial Tyranny and I hope will persevere to the End, bearing all Blasts with unshaken Constancy and resolution. Nothing new here. I shall set out on Saturday or Sunday next to meet my wife. Be pleased [to] shew this to your Brothers in Council to whom I present my most respectfull regards.

I am, Dr Sir, Yr most obliged & aff Friend,   T. Stone

RC (MdAA).
  [1] Stone's letter to John Hall, not found.
  [2] That is Jenifer's letter to Hancock of April 19, "By Order and on Behalf of the Council of Safety of the Province of Maryland," which was read in Congress on April 22 and is in PCC, item 70, fols. 5–8. Jenifer had explained the council's refusal to arrest Governor Eden, since they were satisfied that his continuance in office posed no threat to the colonies. Congress, unable to agree on an appropriate response, never sent the "Answer" Stone anticipated.

John Hancock to George Washington

Sir   Philadelphia 25th April 1776
    I have Deliver'd in Charge to Mr Hanson & Cox Three Hundred Thousand Dollars for the Service of the Army in Canada, & have directed them by order of Congress to Deliver the same to you, and am to Request you will please to order it to be Sent to General Schuyler at Albany under the Care of an Officer & some of the Troops destin'd for Canada to be Deliver'd [to] General Schuyler.[1]
    Your Favrs. of 22d & 23d Inst. I last Night Rec'd. by Major Palfrey & are now under the Consideration of a Committee.[2]
    I Beg leave to Recommend Mr Hanson & Cox to your Notice, & am with Esteem, Sir, Your very hume Servt.

                                            John Hancock Presidt

[P.S.] The 300,000 Dollars are Pack'd in three Boxes.

RC (DLC):
  [1] Hancock also wrote a brief note to General Schuyler this date, informing him of this transmittal, which Congress had approved on April 23. See JCC, 4:301; PCC, item 12A; and Am. Archives, 4th ser. 5:1067.
  [2] These letters from Washington to Hancock are in PCC, item 152, 1:603–6, 611–14, and Washington, Writings (Fitzpatrick), 4:500–507. For the resolves which

Congress adopted on April 26 in response to the report of the committee to which these letters were committed, see *JCC*, 4:311–12.

Maryland Delegates to
the Maryland Council of Safety

Gent.   Phila. 25 April 1776.

We this Day about 12 oClock received your Letter of the 22d by the Return of our Express.[1] No further proceeding in Congress on Mr Edens Affair. King came in on Sunday about 3 oClock and is but just now discharged. We think proper to mention it that you may not think him blameable.[2] If Mr. Rogers is able we wish his attendance here that as many of us as might be should be at the Convention.[3] We do not think the province ought to be left unrepresented here.

We are Gent., Your most obedt. Servts.   Mat. Tilghman

Ths. Johnson Junr

T. Stone

RC (MdAA). Written by Johnson and signed by Johnson, Stone, and Tilghman.

[1] See *Md. Archives*, 11:368–70.

[2] Apparently John King, a messenger employed by the council. Ibid., p. 301.

[3] The council immediately sent a request to John Rogers to attend Congress, to which he replied on April 28: "I am just recovering from a severe attack of the Gout, and find myself much relaxed and weaken'd, but I am in hopes of being able to set off on Wednesday next, and of getting to Philadelphia time enough for such of the Maryland Gentlemen as intend to be at the Convention, to attend the first day of its Meeting." Ibid., p. 393.

John Hancock to the Commissioners to Canada

Gentlemen,   Philada. April 26th. 1776.

The late Disturbances in Canada, owing to an Insurrection of a Number of the Inhabitants, have, for some Time, occupied the most serious Attention of Congress.[1] In Persuance of which they have come into sundry Resolves calculated both to increase our military Force in that Country, and to allay the Fears & Apprehensions of the People. Of this latter Kind is the Resolve I herewith transmit by order of Congress to you.[2] In Addition to the four Battalions now on their March to Canada, the Congress have, since the Receipt of Genl. Schuyler's last Letter, ordered six more to be sent there as soon as possible. With sincere wishes for your Health, and Success, in your important Engagements I have the Honour to be, with every Sentmt. of Esteem & Regard, Gent., your most obed. & very hble Sevr.   J. H. Prest.

LB (DNA: PCC, item 12A).
  [1] See Hancock to Charles Thomson, April 21, 1776, note.
  [2] On April 23 Congress approved an instruction to the commissioners directing them to prepare an address to the people of Canada offering to redress their grievances against the American army. *JCC*, 4:301–2.

John Hancock to Philip Schuyler

Sir,   Philada. April 26th. 1776
  The Intelligence contained in your last Letter and the Papers transmitted therewith, being of the utmost Importance, the Congress have paid them the Attention which they deserved.[1] It is indeed to be lamented that the Misconduct of our Troops should have given Occasion to the Canadians to proceed such Lengths as to commence Hostilities. New raised Recruits, such as those of the United Colonies, cannot immediately be bro't to submit to exact Discipline & Subordination. Without having Recourse to that Love of Liberty & Aversion to military Restraint, which are natural to Freemen, to account for this, it is sufficient to observe, that to make Men Soldiers, is the Work of Time & Labour, even in Countries where the genius of the Government, has prepared Men for that Kind of Despotism, which is indispensibly necessary in an Army. Tho it is much to be wished that the subaltern Officers in Canada had exerted themselves more in keeping the Troops in Order, yet I am apt to think, the utmost Vigilance could not have totally prevented all Irregularities.[2] But we were compelled unprepared hastily to take up the Weapons of Self Preservation, and have consequently had numberless Difficulties to struggle with; of which the Expedition into Canada has been a continued Scene. This is the true source of all our Misfortunes with which you are too well acquainted to make it necessary for me to repeat them. I cannot help suspected [suspecting] that the Defection of the Canadians is more the Result of Policy than Inclination; not that I beleive they have any more Inclination for one Side than the other. But finding the Force of the United Colonies in Canada fall much Short of Expectation, they naturally throw themselves into the Scale which they believe begins to preponderate. It is not however material at present what are the Causes of the late Insurrection, any further than to provide a Remedy agt. the Evil. Congress have accordingly passed sundry Resolves, adapted both to conciliate the affections of the Canadians, and to operate on their Apprehensions as to the Strength of the Colonies. Having ordered ten Battalions into that Country, & given Directions to Mr. Trumbul, and Mr. Lowry to forward to you four Thousand Barrels of Pork, they have also directed 10,000 Pair of Shoes, & 10,000 Pair of Stockings to be sent to you for the Use of the Continental Army in Canady. I have it in Charge from Congress to desire you to pursue the best Means for furnishing such other

Necessary Articles as may be wanted for the Army in Canada, having
Regard to such of them as the Commissary in that Province can supply,
and also that you inform them what Quantity of Gun-Powder, you have
received for Canada since the first of Jany. last; and that you go on to
give the earliest Notice to Congress of the Occasion for the Supplies of
such Necessaries, as it may not be in your Power to procure.[3]

I transmit herewith sundry Resolves of Congress under the Hand
of the Secretary, for your future Directions & Conduct, and have the
Honour to be, Sir, your most obed. & very hble Sevt.

                                                                      J.H. Prest.

LB (DNA: *PCC*, item 12A).
   [1] See Hancock to Charles Thomson, April 21, 1776, note.
   [2] At this point the following sentence was deleted from the LB: "Had it been in
the Power of the Continent fully to have ⟨adopted⟩ executed those Measures which a
Regard to their Country evidently pointed out, I flatter myself Nothing of the
Kind would have happened in Canada."
   [3] See *JCC*, 4:297, 303–4.

John Hancock to Joseph Trumbull

Sir,   Philadelphia April 26th. 1776.
   I have it in Charge from Congress to direct your immediate Attention
to the enclosed Resolve, for the Purchase of two Thousand Barrels of
Pork; which when purchased, you will forward, in the most expeditious
Manner, to Genl. Schuyler.[1]

   As it is of great Importance the Army in Canada should be well
supplied, you will exert yourself to effect this Purchase as speedily as
possible.

   Whenever you send or draw for the Money, your Bills on me for
twenty Thousand Dollars, shall meet with due Honour.
   I am, Sir, your most obed. & very hble Servt.

                                                            John Hancock Presidt

RC (Ct). In the hand of Jacob Rush and signed by Hancock. Addressed: "Mr.
Trumbull, Com[missar]y Gen[era]l."
   [1] See *JCC*, 4:303.

John Hancock to Artemas Ward

Sir,   Philadelphia April 26th. 1776.[1]
   I am commanded by Congress to acquaint you, that your Letter of
Resignation of the 12th Inst. was this Day laid before them, and that
they have been pleased to accept of the same.[2]

The Motives which first induced the Congress to appoint you a Major General in the Continental Service, would naturally make them regret your retiring from the Army. But when it is considered, that in the Course of your Duty in that high Rank, you have acquitted yourself with Honour and Reputation, I am persuaded, the Reluctance they feel at your retiring, is much increased.

The Congress in a Letter to Genl. Washington of the 2d Inst. have declared the Thanks of these United Colonies to be due to the brave Officers under his Command, and have requested him to communicate to them this distinguishing Mark of the Approbation of their Country. I mention this, as the Letter did not reach the General until he arrived at New York. With the sincerest Wishes for a Restoration of your Health, and for your future Happiness, I have the Honour to be, Sir, your most obedt. & very hble Servt.[3]   John Hancock Presidt

RC (MHi). In the hand of Jacob Rush and signed by Hancock. Addressed: "To The Honble Artemas Ward Esqr. Major General & Commander of the Forces of the United Colonies &c At Boston."

[1] Since Congress read and acted upon Ward's letter of resignation on April 23, Hancock's letter was probably composed on that date. *JCC*, 4:300. The LB of Hancock's letter is dated April 24. PCC, item 12A; and *Am. Archives*, 4th ser. 5:1048.

[2] Ward's letter of resignation is in PCC, item 159, fol. 360, and *Am. Archives*, 4th ser. 5:872. Notwithstanding Congress' acceptance of his resignation, Ward continued to serve in the Continental Army until March 1777. See Charles Martyn, *The Life of Artemas Ward, the First Commander-in-Chief of the American Army* (New York: Artemas Ward, 1921), pp. 216–18, 222–23, 238–40. Congress' August 21, 1776, resolution authorizing Ward to continue his command "until farther orders" is in *JCC*, 5:694.

[3] On April 24 Hancock wrote a letter to Gen. Joseph Frye signifying Congress' acceptance of his resignation from the Continental Army. PCC, item 12A. Frye's letter of resignation, addressed to Washington and dated March 18, is in *Am. Archives*, 4th ser. 5:489. Congress had formally accepted Frye's resignation on April 23. *JCC*, 4:300.

John Hancock to James Warren

Sir,   Philada. April 26th. 1776.

I have it in Charge from Congress to acquaint you that they have been pleased to accept your Resignation as Pay Master Genl. of the Army, and that there are Superintendants of the Treasury appointed, to whom you are to render your Accounts & Vouchers which I will do myself the Pleasure of putting into their Hands, if you think proper to forward them to me for that Purpose.[1]

I have the Honour to be, Sir, your most obed. & very hble Servt.

    J. H. Prst.

LB (DNA: PCC, item 12A).

[1] See John Adams to James Warren, April 16, note 3; and John Jay to William Alexander, April 17, 1776, note.

John Adams to Horatio Gates

Dear Sir   Philadelphia April 27 1776

Your Favour of the Twenty third, I received Yesterday, and it put me into a good Humour, the benefit of which I feel to this Moment, and shall continue to experience a long Time.[1]

Was you idle enough to read the Tales in the London Papers and Magazines, a few years ago concerning the Cock Lane Ghost, and the others concerning a Man of six-feet high who leaped into a Quart Bottle and corked himself up? Do you remember that a great Part of the Nation, perhaps a Majority, believed these marvellous stories to be true? If you recollect these Things, you will not wonder that the Tales of Commissioners to treat with Congress should have gained Credit with many in America nor will you wonder that many pretend to believe them who do not.

I think with you, that it requires a Faith, which can remove Mountains, to believe that Liberty and Safety can ever hereafter be injoyd by America, in any Subjection to the Government of Great Britain. Dependence and Subordination to Great Britain, always indeterminate and nonsensical Expressions, if they mean any Thing must now mean perpetual Animosity, Discord, Civil War, Encroachment and Usurpations on one side, and Discontent, Mutiny, Sedition, Riot and Resistance on the other. Hense it terminates in downright submission, and that beyond all doubt would be followed with Persecution and Imprisonment, Scorn & Insult, Blocks, Halters, Gibbetts.

Your opinion of Indians, and the best Policy, in our Management of them, may be right for any Thing that I know. But as I know very little of them, I always leave the Measures relating to them to gentlemen who know a great deal. It is Said they are very expensive and troublesome Confederates in war, besides the Incivity and Inhumanity of employing Such Savages with their cruel, bloody dispositions, against any Enemy whatever.

Nevertheless, Such have been the Extravagances of British Barbarity in prosecuting the War against Us, that I think We need not be So delicate as to refuse the assistance of Indians, provided We cannot keep them neutral. I Should not hesitate a Moment in this Case.

That we have been a little tardy in providing for Canada is true. Owing to innummerable difficulties, however We have been roused at last, and I hope have done pretty well. If you think We have not, let me know it, and whatever you may think further necessary, if it is not done it shall not be my Fault.

I am grieved to find the least Intimation of Languor, among my Countrymen in fortifying Boston and its Harbour. I have not written a Letter since We recd the News of your Success, in driving the Enemy from that Town without stuffing it with Exhortations, as well as Plans for the Fortification of that Harbour. Warren writes me, that they have Sent a Commi[ttee] to fortify the Harbour So that I hope it will be done. G[eneral] Ward's Resignation is accepted, but We must have a General officer in Boston. I hope General Washington will send one. Your opinions of the Difficulties General How will meet with, in attempting to get up the St. Lawrence early, gives me great Comfort. God Send him Wind and Ice enough. Am Sorry to Learn that there are so many Tories where you are. They must be watched. But there is one Measure, which I think would lessen the Number of them. If the Provincial Congress and Committee of Safety could be convinced of the Propriety, Utility and Necessity of following the virtuous and glorious Example of South Carolina, in instituting a compleat Government in that Colony I think there would be a great Revolution of Sentiment in the City and through the whole Province, and most of their Divisions and Distractions removed. The Tories will have a pernicious Influence, and will be indefatigable in their Intrigues, Insinuations and Cabals, in every Colony while anyone of them holds an office under a King. When "Thrones, Dominations, Princedoms, Powers," in the Language of Milton, are excluded from their Ideas of Government, Toryism will be disarmed of its Sting.

You ask me what you are to think of Robt. Morris? I will tell you what I think of him. I think he has a masterly Understanding, an open Temper and an honest Heart: and if he does not always vote for what You and I should think proper, it is because he thinks that a large Body of People remains, who are not yet of his Mind. He has vast designs in the mercantile Way. And no doubt pursues mercantile Ends, which are always gain; but he is an excellent Member of our Body.

Pray continue to write me, for a Letter from you Cures me of all Anxiety and ill Humour, for two or three Days, at least, and, besides that, leaves me better informed in many Things and confirmed in my good Resolutions, for my whole Life. Yours without Disguise

John Adams

[P.S.] There is a Major Wrixon here—a fine, Sensible Fellow—a Field Officer in Germany last War—a Man of Letters, sense and spirit—the best Principles. I wish you was a Major General and He Adjutant General, what say you to it?

RC (NHi).
[1] Gates strongly advocated American independence, warned against the powerful influence of tories in New York, and recommended employing the Indians in Canada, reinforcing the Canadian army, and strengthening Boston's fortifications. Gates to Adams, April 23, 1776, MHi; and Bernhard Knollenberg, ed., "The Correspondence of John Adams and Horatio Gates," *Proceedings of the Massachusetts Historical Society* 67 (March 1942): 140–41.

John Hancock to Thomas Cushing

Dear Sir   Philada. 27th April 1776

Many Oppors. & Posts without even a Line from you. I did not think that *you* would have so soon fallen in with the common mode, of which we all us'd to Complain.

I have not time to write Capt Manly & Cazneau, but if you have Oppory. do Acquaint them from me that they are appointed Commanders of our two Frigates, & pray them to Send me their Answers.[1]

Inclos'd you have a List of the Officers &c determin'd for each Ship. I wish you & Capt Bradford, with such others as you chuse to advise with would immediately Recommend proper persons to me for Lieutenants, you will observe there are three for each Ship, & also Recommend proper Persons for Capts. & Lieuts. of Marines. With Respect to the other Officers Say, Masters & all other inferior ones, I leave their Appointments to you and Capt Bradford, & I beg it be immediately done, & their Names Transmitted to me that Warrants may be made out, pray let them be good Men &c I have not time to Enlarge. I don't know but I shall be with you by & by, but keep writing me till you hear further.

Capt Bradford is appointed Agent for Prizes, with Power to Appoint Deputies where he Judges necessary.[2] As I have not time to write him, do inform him & beg his Answer, if he Accepts I will Send his Commissn. & Instructions, he must Excuse my not writing him now, as I am closely Engaged.

Do write me all the News &c. I shall send you every Necessary paper Relative to the Engaging Men &c, & by next will Send you the Names of the two Frig[ate]s.

Remember me to all Friends. I am in great haste, your Friend,

                                                                John Hancock

RC (MHi).
 [1] See *JCC*, 4:290.
 [2] See *JCC*, 4:301.

John Hancock to Benjamin Harrison, Jr.

Sir,   Philada. April 27th. 1776.

The Congress having ordered two Hundred and fifty Thousand Dollars to be sent to you for the Use of the Continental Troops, I do myself the Pleasure of forwarding the same herewith.[1]

By the inclosed Receipt you will perceive I have paid Messrs. Willing & Morris of this City forty Thousand Dollars, which you will consider as Part of the two Hundred & fifty Thousand.

The Money is packed up in three Boxes, and committed to the Charge of Capt. West.

I have the Honour to be, Sir, your most obedt. & very hble Ser.

J. H. Prest.

[*P.S.*] I have also forwarded by this opportunity to the Come. of Safety of your Colony fifty Thousand Dollars to be exchanged for Specie. Should they be so successful as to get more [*than*] that Sum in Specie, I have requested them by order of Congress to draw on you for all they can procure above it, in which Case you will take Care that their Drafts are duely honord.

LB (DNA: PCC, item 12A). Addressed: "To Benja. Harrison Junr. Esqr. of Berkley, Charles County Virginia."
   [1] See *JCC*, 4:310. Benjamin Harrison, Jr. (d. 1799), son of Virginia delegate Benjamin Harrison, had been appointed paymaster "for the troops in Virginia" by Congress on February 15, 1776. "Harrison of James River," *Virginia Magazine of History and Biography* 35 (January 1927): 89–92; and *JCC*, 4:151.

John Hancock to
the Virginia Committee of Safety

Gentlemen,   Philada. April 27th. 1776.

You will receive herewith the Sum of fifty Thousand Dollars, which I am commanded by Congress to request you will use your utmost Endeavours to exchange into Specie in order to remit it to the Continental Treasurers.[1] I beg however you will not confine yourselves to that Sum, but exert yourselves to procure all the Specie in your Power. Shd. you be so successful as to get more than 50,000 Dollars in Specie you will please to draw for all such Sums on the Paymaster in Virginia, who has orders to pay such Drafts. Your zealous & uniform attachment to the Cause of America makes it unnecessary to use any Arguments to call your particular Attention to this Request of Congress.

I have the Honor to be Gent. Your most obed. & very hble Servt.

J. H. Prst.

P.S. Please to deliver the inclosed Commissions to the Commissary & Muster Master.[2]

LB (DNA: PCC, item 12A).
   [1] See *JCC*, 4:310.
   [2] William Aylett and William Yates. *JCC*, 4:315.

John Hancock to George Washington

Sir,   Philadelphia April 27th. 1776.
The enclosed Resolve of Congress respecting the Rifle Battalions
and independant Rifle Companies, would have been transmitted sooner,
had it not been omitted, through a Mistake.[1]
I do myself the Pleasure of forwarding at this Time several Resolves
of Congress relative to such Parts of your Letters as have hitherto come
under Consideration.[2]
I propose writing more fully by Mr. Palfrey who will set out for New
York on Monday.[3] In the mean Time, I have the Honour to be, Sir,
your most obedt. & very hble Servt.   John Hancock Presidt

RC (DLC). In the hand of Jacob Rush and signed by Hancock.
[1] See Congress' April 15 resolution on this issue in *JCC*, 4:284.
[2] See *JCC*, 4:311–12.
[3] See Hancock to Washington, April 30, 1776.

John Jay to Alexander McDougall

Dear Collonel   Philad. 27 Ap 1776
Accept my Thanks for your friendly Letter of the 16th Inst.[1] and its
Inclosures, which contain useful as well as agreable Information. I am
glad to see New York doing something in the naval Way, & think the
Encouragement given by the Convention to the Manufacture of arms,
Powder, Salt Petre and Sea Salt, does them Honor.
Many of the Reasons you alledge for delaying Taxation are weighty,
& I confess did not occur to me. It is certainly unreasonable to impose
on the City, in its present Circumstances, so great a Share of the public
Expences.
The late Election, so far as it respects yourself, has taken a Turn I
did not expect, & am at a Loss to account for; except on the Principles
of your holding a military Commission, or of that mutability which
from various Causes, often strongly marks popular opinions of men &
measures in Times like These. But whatever may have been the Reason,
I am persuaded that the Zeal you have shewn & the Sacrifices you have
made in this great Cause, will always afford You the most pleasing Reflections, and will one Day, not only merit, but receive the Gratitude
of your Fellow Citizens. Posterity you know always does Justice. Let no
circumstance of this Kind diminish your Ardor, but by persevering in
a firm uniform Course of Conduct, silence Detraction & compel Approbation.
I am much obliged to You for your kind Attention to my House, &

be assured that I shall omit no opportunity of evincing the Esteem and
Sincerity with which, I am your Friend & h'ble Servt,

John Jay

RC (NHi).
[1] McDougall's letter to Jay is in Jay, *Papers* (Morris), 1:256–57.

John Jay to the New York Committee of Safety

Gentlemen   Philadelphia 27 April 1776
    The Congress having been informed of a very extraordinary oath
ordered by Govr. Tryon to be administered to Passengers in the late
packet, whereby they bound themselves not to disclose any Thing relative to American affairs except to the Ministry, have appointed a Committee (of which I am one) to ascertain this Fact.
    I must therefore request of you Gentlemen, to appoint proper Persons
to examine into this Matter, and if possible, ascertain the Truth of the
Report, by affidavits taken before the Mayor, or one of the Judges of
the Supr. Court.[1]
    I have the Honor to be Gentlemen, Your most obedt. Servt.

John Jay

RC (N). *Journals of N. Y. Prov. Cong.*, 1:428. RC damaged; missing words supplied
from Tr.
[1] Congress had appointed Jay, James Wilson, and George Wythe as a committee
to investigate this matter on April 11. *JCC*, 4:273. How Congress received this
"Report" that Tryon was exacting an oath is not apparent, but the "Report" itself
seems to have been unfounded. The Committee of Safety appointed a committee to
look into this matter on May 1, but evidently it never submitted a formal report.
Am. Archives, 4th ser. 5:1482.

John Jay to Marinus Willett

Sir,[1]   Phila. 27 Ap. 1776.
    It is much to be regretted that all human affairs are liable to errors
and imperfections, and that real as well as imaginary evils are so widely
spread thro the world.
    The subject of your letter deserves attention; it is however unneces-
sary for me to repeat what I have already said relative to it, except
again to assure you that my endeavours shall not be wanting to obtain
for you an appointment equal to your merit. General Schuyler's letter
does you honor, & had it been made known to the members of Congress
a few months sooner, I am confident it would have had all the influence
you would have wished.

I hope care will be taken of the officers you allude to; men who deserve well of the country are entitled to its regard, and in my opinion no opportunity of distinguishing and rewarding merit ought to be omitted.

I am glad your indisposition is removed, and hope it will not be long before an occasion of again calling you to the service of your country will present itself.

I am Sir, Your very h'ble Servt,   John Jay.

Reprinted from John Jay, *The Correspondence and Public Papers of John Jay*, ed. Henry P. Johnston, 4 vols. (New York: G. P. Putnam's Sons, 1890–93), 1:56–57.

[1] Marinus Willett (1740–1830), a New York merchant, had served as a captain of the First New York Regiment during the Canadian campaign. After Congress ordered four new battalions to be raised in New York on January 19, the New York Provincial Congress had nominated eight men, including Willett, for the four majorities in these units, but on March 8 Congress passed over Willett in favor of Joseph Benedict, a captain with less seniority. *JCC*, 4:60, 190; *Am. Archives*, 4th ser. 4:317–18; and Jay, *Papers* (Morris), 1:245n.1, 262n.1. Willett's indignant, undated letter to Jay, complaining "how it came to pass that I should be superceeded by Captain Benidect is truly strange to me," is in Jay, *Papers* (Morris), 1:260–62. Schuyler's February 27 letter of recommendation for Willett to the New York Provincial Congress, a copy of which Willett enclosed in his letter to Jay, is in *Journals of the N. Y. Prov. Cong.*, 2:121.

John Adams to Abigail Adams

April 28. 1776

Yesterday, I received two Letters from you from the 7th. to the 14. of April. I believe I have received all your Letters, and I am not certain I wrote one from Framingham. The one I mean contains an Account of my dining with the Indians at Mr. Mifflins.

It gives me Concern to think of the many Cares you must have upon your Mind. Am glad you have taken [*Belcher*] [1] into Pay, and that Isaac is well before now I hope.

Your Reputation, as a Farmer, or any Thing else you undertake I dare answer for. . . . [2] Your Partners Character as a Statesman is much more problematical.

As to my Return, I have not a Thought of it. Journeys of such a Length are tedious, and expensive both of Time and Money neither of which are my own. I hope to spend the next Christmas, where I did the last, and after that I hope to be relieved for by that Time I shall have taken a pretty good Trick att Helm whether the Vessell has been well steer'd or not. But if My Countrymen should insist upon my serving them another Year, they must let me bring my whole Family with me. Indeed I could keep House here, with my Partner, four children and two servants, as cheap as I maintain my self here with two

Horses and a servant at Lodgings.

Instead of domestic Felicity, I am destined to public Contentions. Instead of rural Felicity, I must reconcile myself to the Smoke and Noise of a city. In the Place of private Peace, I must be distracted with the Vexation of developing the deep Intrigues of Politicians and must assist in conducting the arduous Operations of War. And think myself, well rewarded, if my private Pleasure and Interest are sacrificed as they ever have been and will be, to the Happiness of others.

You tell me, our Jurors refuse to serve, because the Writs are issued in the Kings Name. I am very glad to hear, that they discover so much Sense and Spirit. I learn from another Letter that the General Court have left out of their Bills the Year of his Reign, and that they are making a Law, that the same Name shall be left out of all Writs, Commissions, and all Law Proscesses. This is good News too. The same will be the Case in all the Colonies, very soon.

You ask me how I have done the Winter past. I have not enjoyed so good Health as last Fall. But I have done complaining of any Thing. Of ill Health I have no Right to complain because it is given me by Heaven. Of Meanness, of Envy, of Littleness, of—of—of—of—I have Reason and Right to complain, but I have too much Contempt, to use that Right.

There is such a Mixture of Folly, Littleness, and Knavery in this World that, I am weary of it, and altho I behold it with unutterable Contempt and Indignation, yet the public Good requires that I should take no Notice of it, by Word or by Letter. And to this public Good I will conform.

You will see an Account of the Fleet in some of the Papers I have sent you. Give you Joy of the Admirals Success. I have Vanity enough to take to myself, a share in the Merit of the American Navy. It was always a Measure that my Heart was much engaged in, and I pursued it, for a long Time, against the Wind and Tide. But at last obtained it.

Is there no Way for two friendly Souls, to converse together, altho the Bodies are 400 Miles off? Yes by Letter. But I want a better Communication. I want to hear you think, or to see your Thoughts.

The Conclusion of your Letter makes my Heart throb, more than a Cannonade would. You bid me burn your Letters. But I must forget you first.

In yours of April 14. you say you miss our Friend in the Conveyance of your Letters. Dont hesitate to write by the Post. Seal well. Dont miss a single Post.

You take it for granted that I have particular Intelligence of every Thing from others. But I have not. If any one wants a Vote for a Commission, he vouchsafes me a Letter, but tells me very little News. I have more particulars from you than any one else. Pray keep me constantly informed, what ships are in the Harbour and what Fortifications are going on.

I am quite impatient to hear of more vigorous Measures for fortifying Boston Harbour. Not a Moment should be neglected. Every Man ought to go down as they did after the Battle of Lexington and work untill it is done. I would willingly pay half a Dozen Hands my self, and subsist them, rather than it should not be done immediately. It is of more importance than to raise Corn.

You say inclosed is a Prologue and a Parody, but neither was inclosed. If you did not forget it, the letter has been opened and the Inclosures taken out.

If the Small Pox spreads, run me in debt. I received a Post or two past a Letter from your Unkle at Salem,[3] containing a most friendly and obliging Invitation to you and yours to go, and have the Distemper at his House if it should spread. He has one or two in family to have it.

The Writer of Common Sense, and the Forrester, is the same Person. His Name is Payne, a Gentleman, about two Years ago from England, a Man who G[eneral] Lee says has Genius in his Eyes. The Writer of Cassandra is said to be Mr. James Cannon a Tutor, in the Philadelphia Colledge. Cato is reported here to be Dr. Smith—a Match for Brattle. The oration was an insolent Performance. . . . A Motion was made to Thank the orator and ask a Copy—But opposed with great Spirit, and Vivacity from every Part of the Room, and at last withdrawn, lest it should be rejected as it certainly would have been with Indignation. The orator then printed it himself, after leaving out or altering some offensive Passages.

This is one of the many irregular, and extravagant Characters of the Age. I never heard one single person speak well of any Thing about him but his Abilities, which are generally allowed to be good. The Appointment of him to make the oration, was a great oversight, and Mistake.

The late Act of Parliament, has made so deep an Impression upon Peoples Minds throughout the Colonies, it is looked upon as the last Stretch of Oppression, that We are hastening rapidly to great Events. Governments will be up every where before Midsummer, and an End to Royal style, Titles and Authority. Such mighty Revolutions make a deep Impression on the Minds of Men and sett many violent Passions at Work. Hope, Fear, Joy, Sorrow, Love, Hatred, Malice, Envy, Revenge, Jealousy, Ambition, Avarice, Resentment, Gratitude, and every other Passion, Feeling, Sentiment, Principle and Imagination, were never in more lively Exercise than they are now, from Florida to Canada inclusively. May God in his Providence overrule the whole, for the good of Mankind. It requires more Serenity of Temper, a deeper Understanding and more Courage than fell to the Lott of Marlborough, to ride in this Whirlwind.

RC (MHi). Adams, *Family Correspondence* (Butterfield), 1:398–401.

[1] Blank in MS, but Belcher's identity is clear from Abigail's letter of April 7–11 to John. Adams, *Family Correspondence* (Butterfield), 1:375.

[2] Suspension points in MS, here and below.

[3] Isaac Smith to Adams, April 6–8, 1776, ibid., pp. 372–73.

John Adams to John Penn

Dear Sir   Philadelphia April 28. 1776
     This Morning I had the Pleasure of receiving yours of April 17th for which I think my self much obliged to you.[1]

The account you give of the Temper and Sentiments of the People in Virginia and Carolina, and their general Inclination to those Measures which will be absolutely necessary for the Preservation of their Liberties is very encouraging.

I cannot Sufficiently admire the Spirit and Valour of the Gentlemen of North Carolina. May Heaven reward them for their Magnanimity, by establishing a free Constitution, for their Children—and I know of no greater Reward in this Life.[2]

Cornwallis and Clinton will receive their Deserts from your Climate, in due Time, if you only block them up. Boston was a better Place to live in, upon Salt Provisions without Vegetables, than Carolina or Virginia. Crush them however, at once, if you can.

The Baseness and Cruelty of your Enemies dont Surprise me. They are all alike, in general, at least, through the Continent abandoned to a reprobate Sense.

You tell me that all Fondness for the King and Nation is gone. This is the Effect of the late Act of Parliament every where.

In a Letter from my own Colony I am told, that "the Jurors refuse to Serve, because the Writs are in the Kings Name," [3] and in another, from the Speaker of the House in these Words "We are at present engaged in forming a Bill for disusing the Kings Name in all Acts, Commissions, and Law Proscesses." [4]

You know Sir, that I have but a Single Vote, but you may always depend upon that, for affording your Colony all the Assistance, She can reasonably desire, according to your Request.

Rejoice to hear that you are forming a Constitution, but it is whispered here that, altho you are unanimous for instituting a Government, you are divided about the Form. For Gods Sake teach one another Patience, and Forbearance. The Majority must govern in Committees and Assemblies. There is—there can be no other Rule. And when a Measure is carried, it becomes the Duty of the Minority, not only to acquiese, but heartily to join in promoting it.

I hope that all the Colonies will make the Judges independent—but Governers should be chosen now and then—for their good as well as that of the People.

You Say I may expect a popular Form of Government: But the Degrees of Popularity in a Government are so various that I can form no probable Conjecture, what it will be from this Expression. It is much to be wished that the Elections of Representatives, in every Colony might be annual. Those of Councillors, Governors, and other great officers of State may be trienniel or septennial. But the Representatives ought to account for their Conduct, once a year.

I have great Expectations from the Wisdom, Virtue, and Valour of North Carolina, and beg to be informed minutely of your Constitution as soon as it is formed.

Mr Long may depend upon my Vote, from your and Mr Hewes's Recommendation, if there is no just Objection in the Way which I am not aware of.[5]

My respectfull Compliments to my Countryman Mr Hooper. Tell him, I am very sorry for his Misfortune. But in Such a Time as this, Losses, which at another would be vexatious, are Trifles, and rather animate a Man to his Duty, and indeed gratify his Pride. You know too well the Avocations and Interruptions We have here, to need any Apology for this scroll.

Believe me to be with much Respect, Sir, your very humble Servant,

John Adams

RC (MHi).

[1] In his April 17 letter Penn provided Adams with his soundings of Virginia's and North Carolina's attitudes toward independence. "As I came through Virginia I found the inhabitants desirous to be Independant from Britain, however they were willing to submit their opinion on the subject to whatever the General Congress should determine. North Carolina by far exceeds them occasioned by the great fatigue trouble and danger the People here have undergone, for some time past; Gentn. of the first fortunes in this Province have marched as common Soldiers and to incourage & give spirit to the men have footed it the whole time. Lord Cornwallis with seven Regiments are expected to visit us every day, Clinton is now in Cape Fear with Govr. Martin who has about 40 sail of vessels armed and unarmed waiting his arrival; the Highlanders & Regulators are not to be trusted; Govr. Martin has coaxed a number of Slaves to leave their masters in the lower parts, every thing base and wicked are practised by him; these things have totally changed the Temper and disposition of the Inhabitants that are Friends to liberty, all regard or fondness for the King or the nation of Britain, is gone, a total seperation is what they want. Independance is the word most used, they ask if it is possible that any Colony after what has passed can wish for a Reconciliation, the Convention have tried to get the opinion of the People at large, I am told that in many Counties there were not one dissenting voice. . . . We are endeavouring to form a Constitution as it is thought necessary to exert all the powers of Government, you may expect it will be a popular one." Adams Papers, MHi.

[2] Adams' congratulations proved to be premature. Not until November 1776, and then only after protracted debates over the form of government, did North Carolina adopt a new constitution. Elisha P. Douglass, *Rebels and Democrats; the Struggle for Equal Political Rights and Majority Rule during the American Revolution* (Chapel Hill: University of North Carolina Press, 1955), pp. 119–35.

[3] Abigail Adams to John Adams, April 7–11, 1776. Adams, *Family Correspondence* (Butterfield), 1:376.

[4] James Warren to Elbridge Gerry, April 15, 1776. C. Harvey Gardiner, ed., *A Study in Dissent: The Warren-Gerry Correspondence, 1776–1792* (Carbondale: Southern Illinois University Press, 1968), p. 18.

[5] Nicholas Long, whom Penn had recommended in his letter of April 17, was appointed "deputy quarter master general for the southern department to be employed in North Carolina" on May 7, 1776. *JCC*, 4:332.

Samuel Chase to John Adams

My Dear Sir   Saint Johns April. 28th. 1776
I left Ticonderoga last Wednesday and arrived at this Fort yesterday Afternoon. Our Troops were to come off the next Day, & twenty four Batteaus have already passed, and the Wind blows a fair and fresh Gale. I am afraid all our Efforts to take Quebec will prove fruitless. We met on the Lake the Letter from General Arnold to General Schuyler. I hope You will attend to every Quarter of America, and not neglect *Us*, for I now esteem Myself a Canadian, and not spend your precious Time in Debates about our Independancy. In my Judgment You have no alternative between Independancy and Slavery, and what American can hesitate in the Choice; but don't harrangue about it, act as if we were. Make every preparation for War, take all prudent Measures to procure Success to our Arms, and the Consequence is obvious. Get Money & Arms, and as a fund immediately seize & appropriate all the Crown Lands. I am called on for my Letter, therefore adieu. Remember Me to all & write to, Your Friend & Servt,[1]   Saml. Chase

RC (MHi).
[1] Charles Carroll wrote a letter to General Schuyler this day conveying the thanks of the commissioners for "the polite & friendly reception" given them at Saratoga, and reporting that "Carpenters are much wanted here [St. Johns] to build row gallies to prevent the enemy's vessels from coming up the St. Lawrence," a concern expressed to them by Col. Moses Hazen. Charles Carroll of Carrollton to Philip Schuyler, April 28, 1776, Sparks Manuscripts, MH.

John Adams to James Otis, Sr.

Sir,   Philadelphia, 29 April, 1776.
As the day of the general election draws nigh, I think it my duty to express my grateful acknowledgments to the honorable electors of the last year, for the honor they did me in choosing me into the council. My station in the continental Congress has made it impossible for me to attend my duty at the honorable board; and as the same cause must prevent my attendance during a great part of the ensuing year, and the dangers and distresses of the times will require the assistance of the whole

number, I cannot think it becoming in me to deprive the colony of the advice of a counsellor, for the sake of keeping open a seat for me. I must therefore beg the favor of you, to make my resignation known to the two honorable Houses, and request them to choose another gentleman to that honorable seat, who will be able to discharge the duties of it.[1]

I am, with great respect to the two honorable Houses, Sir, your most obedient and very humble servant,   John Adams.

MS not found; reprinted from Adams, *Works* (Adams), 9:374.

[1] Adams resigned from the Massachusetts Council in the midst of rising complaints about plural officeholding by members of Congress. He also considered resigning as the chief justice of the Massachusetts Superior Court, but he retained this post until February 10, 1777. The antipluralism campaign was apparently spearheaded by the Maryland delegates, who had been instructed in January by their provincial convention to seek a resolve in Congress "that no person who holds any military command in the Continental, or any Provincial regular forces, or marine service, nor any person who holds or enjoys any office of profit under the Continental Congress, or any Government assumed since the present controversy with Great Britain began, or which shall hereafter be assumed, or who directly or indirectly receives the profits of such command or office, shall, during the time of his holding or receiving the same, be eligible to sit in Congress." *Am. Archives*, 4th ser. 4:654. William Whipple stated that, when he sought to have Congress appoint fellow New Hampshire delegate John Langdon to the post of prize agent, a motion was introduced (by a delegate whom Adams, in a letter to Samuel Chase, later identified as a Marylander) to bar members of Congress from holding a Continental office of profit. Adams, believing the action was directed at him, successfully defeated the resolution, which consequently was not entered in the journals. Adams, *Diary* (Butterfield), 3:360–63; John Adams to James Warren, May 12; John Adams to Samuel Chase, June 14; and William Whipple to John Langdon, April 29, 1776. Neither Adams nor his fellow delegates and Massachusetts councillors—Samuel Adams, John Hancock, and Robert Treat Paine—were reelected to the Massachusetts Council in May 1776. Ellen Brennan, *Plural Office-Holding in Massachusetts, 1760–1780* (Chapel Hill: University of North Carolina Press, 1945), p. 116.

Secret Committee to
the Pennsylvania Committee of Safety

Gentn,   Philada. April 29th. 1776

The following Vessells being loaden on Acct of the Continent it is now intended to dispatch them under the protection of the Ships of Warr going down,[1] therefore you are requested to grant the Owners permission to take Pilots on board as they may respectively apply for the same.[2] By order of the Secret Committee,

Robt Morris, Chairman

Ship Union, Capt Harvey
Ship Hope, Capt Curwin
Ship Sally, Capt Osman

Brigt Rachell, Capt Pitt
Brigt Jamaica Packet, Capt Benjn. Wickes
Sloop Fanny, Capt. Briton

RC (NN).
    [1] Probably the Pennsylvania ship *Montgomery* and the Continental ship *Reprisal*, which were under orders to proceed down Delaware Bay and capture H.M.S. *Roebuck*, aground on Brandywine Shoal. Clark, *Naval Documents*, 4:1315, 1342, and 1363. Also on this day the Secret Committee ordered the commissary to deliver to Lambert Wickes, commander of the *Reprisal*, "1 ton powdr. 5 swivel guns & all the Muskts. in his possession." Journal of the Secret Committee, fol. 60, MH.
    [2] On April 30 the Pennsylvania Committee of Safety issued identical permits for the ships *Union, Hope,* and *Sally* and the sloop *Fanny* "to pass the Chevaux de Frize, and to go down the River & Bay of Delaware with a pilot." Clark, *Naval Documents*, 4:1342.

William Whipple to John Langdon

Dear Sir,   Philadelphia 29th April 1776.
    I rec'd your's of the 15th inst by which I find some of my letters respecting guns, canvass &c has not come to hand. I am doing every thing in my power to forward these matters and flatter myself shall be able to obtain an order for the canvass (by this post) to be forwarded from Providence or New London. I can say nothing about the guns, but what I have already wrote you. The colors has thirteen Stripes red and white for the field and a union. As to the Agency I wrote you that I had nominated you in Committee, where there was no objection, nor did I imagine there would be in Congress, but I was mistaken, for when the nomination came before Congress, there was objections from every part of the room on account of your being a member. It was proposed to be put off which I did not object to, finding I should not be able to carry it at that time. There has since been a motion that no Member of Congress shall hold any lucrative office; if this should not obtain I shall make another attempt. You say you'll resign your seat in Congress rather than not have the Agency; if my advice can have any weight with you, you certainly will not.[1] Such a step would have an avaricious appearance and on the other hand there cannot be a greater evidence of patriotism, than preferring the public good, to one's private interest. I should be very sorry that any person who has stood forth in the glorious cause of liberty should take a step that will in any measure destroy the lustre of so glorious a character as that of a true Patriot. I heartily wish to see every place of public trust filled by such persons as will best serve the public interest for which reason I should be exceeding glad if your present desire might be gratified, but I by no means can advise to your resigning your seat in Congress; if the nomination of another person should be urged, I shall be much at a loss who to propose. It should be

a person of great integrity, a good accountant, a Staunch friend to the cause and one who will give close attention to the business, but I hope shall have the assistance of a Colleague in this matter, if I can't get you appointed which I really don't expect.

Pray send a list of proper persons for officers for the ship; Thompson I think is a very good man; there must be three Lieutenants, a Captain and two Lieutenants of Marines; the Master must be a very good man. I hope we shall have such men as will do honor to the Colony. There has been no mention of Flaggs, nor do I imagine there will be any appointment for some time; if there should, you may be assured I shall not be unmindful of my friend. The Committee have promised me an order to morrow morning for the canvass to be forwarded from Providence—that is the heavy canvass—as for light canvass, I don't know where it is to come from. I shall send you the name of the ship next post and hope you will have the canvass soon after this reaches you. I am with great sincerity, yours, Wm Whipple

Tr (DLC).

[1] See John Adams to James Otis, Sr., this date, note. Langdon ultimately ignored Whipple's advice and resigned from Congress in order to be appointed prize agent, an appointment Congress made on June 25, 1776. *JCC*, 5:478.

Samuel Adams to Samuel Cooper

My dear Sir   Philada April 30 1776

I am to acknowledge the Receipt of your Favour of the 18th Instant by the Post.[1] The Ideas of Independence Spread far and wide among the Colonies. Many of the leading Men see the absurdity of supposing that Alligience is due to a Sovereign who has already thrown us out of his Protection. South Carolina has lately assumd a new Government. The Convention of North Carolina have unanimously agreed to do the same & appointd a Committee to prepare & lay before them a proper Form. They have also revokd certain Instructions which tied the Hands of their Delegates here. Virginia whose Convention is to meet on the third of next month will follow the lead. The Body of the People of Maryland are firm. Some of the principal Members of their Convention, I am inclind to believe, are timid or lukewarm but an occurrence has lately fallen out in that Colony which will probably give an agreable Turn to their Affairs. Of this I will inform you at a future time when I may be more particularly instructed concerning it. The lower Counties on Delaware are a small People but well affected to the Common Cause. In this populous and wealthy Colony political Parties run high. The Newspapers are full of the Matter but I think I may assure you that Common Sense prevails among the people. A Law has lately passed in the Assembly here for increasing the Number of Representatives and tomorrow they are to come to a Choice in this City & divers of the Counties. By this Means it is said the representation of the Colony will be more equal. I am told that a very popular Gentleman who is a Candidate for one of the back Counties has been in danger of losing his Election because it was reported among the Electors that he had declared his Mind in this City against Independence. I know the political Creed of that Gentleman. It is, so far as relates to a Right of the British Parliament to make Laws binding the Colonies in any Case whatever, exactly correspondent with your own. I mention this Anecdote to give you an Idea of the Jealousy of the People & their Attention to this Point. The Jerseys are agitating the great Question. It is with them rather a Matter of Prudence whether to determine till some others have done it before them. A Gentleman of that Colony tells me that at least one half of them have N. Engd. Blood running in their Veins. Be this as it may their Sentiments & Manners are I believe similar to those of N England. I forbear to say any thing of New York, for I confess I am not able to form any opinion of them. I lately recd a Letter from a Friend in that Colony informing me that they woud soon come to a Question of the Expediency of taking up Government; but to me it is uncertain what they will do. I think they are at least as unenlightened in the Nature & Importance of our political Disputes as any one of the united Colonies. I have not mentioned our little Sister Georgia; but I believe she is as warmly engagd in the Cause as any of us, & will do as much as can be reasonably expected of her. I was very sollicitous the last Fall to have Governments set up by the people in every Colony. It appeard to me necessary for many reasons. When this is done, and I am inclind to think it will be soon, the Colonies will feel their Independence. The way will be prepared for Confederation, and one Government may be formd with the Consent of the whole—a distinct State composd of all the Colonies with a common Legislature for great & General Purposes. This I was in hopes would have been the work of the last Winter. I am disappointed but I bear it tollerably well. I am disposd to believe that every thing is orderd for the best, and if I do not find my self chargeable with Neglect I am not greatly chagrind when things do not go on exactly according to my mind. Indeed I have the Happiness of believing that what I most earnestly wish for will in due time be effected. We cannot make Events. Our Business is merely to improve them. There has been much to do to confirm doubting Friends & fortify the Timid. It requires time to bring honest Men to think & determine alike even in important Matters. Mankind are governd more by their feelings than by reason. Events which excite those feelings will produce wonderful Effects. The Boston Port bill suddenly wrought a union of the Colonies which could not be brot about by the Industry of years in reasoning on the necessity of it for the Common Safety. Since the memorable 19th of April one Event has brot another on, till Boston sees her Deliverance from those more than savage Troops upon which the execrable Tyrant so much relyed for the Completion of his horrid Conspiracys and America has furnished herself with more than seventy Battalions for her Defence. The burning of Norfolk & the Hostilities committed in North Carolina have kindled the Resentment of our Southern Brethern who once thought their Eastern Friends hot headed & rash; now indeed the Tone is alterd & it is said that the Coolness & Moderation of the one is necessary to allay the heat of the other. There is a reason that wd induce one even to wish for the speedy arrival of the British Troops that are expected at the Southward. I think our friends are well prepared for them, & one Battle would do more towards a Declaration of Independency than a long chain of conclusive Arguments in a provincial Convention or the Continental Congress. I am very affectionately yours,   S A

P.S. I am much concernd at the present defenceless State of Boston, & indeed the whole Eastern District which comprehends New England. We have applied for and obtain a Com[mitte]e of Congress to consider the State of that District. In the mean time I hope the General Assembly and the Town are exerting themselves for their Security. Our grateful Acknowledgments are due to the Supreme Being who has not been regardless of the multiplied oppressions which they have sufferd. They have endured the severe Conflict with that Magnanimity which will be recorded in History to their immortal Honor. But the American Contest is not yet ended. I earnestly wish they may now have some Respite. This however is uncertain. By their eminent Exertions for the preservation of publick Liberty they have renderd themselves particularly obnoxious to the Vengeance of the British Tyrant. They will therefore be upon their Guard. I long to meet my fellow Citizens in our Faneuil Hall but my Duty Still detains me here. They are restored to their Habitations & the Privileges of Citizens. I hope they will recover ancient Principle and [2]

FC (NN).
   [1] In his April 18 letter to Adams, which is in the Samuel Adams Papers at NN, Cooper reported: "People here almost universally agree with you ... that the Moment we determin'd to defend ourselves by Arms against the most injurious Violence of Britain we declar'd for Independence."
   [2] Remainder of MS missing.

Samuel Adams to John Scollay

My dear Sir   Philadelphia Apr 30 1776
   While I was sitting down to write you a friendly Letter I had the pleasure of receiving your Favor of the 22 Instant by the Post.[1] My In-

tention was to congratulate you and your Brethren the Selectmen, upon the precipitate Flight of the British Army & its Adherents from the Town of Boston and to urge on you the Necessity of fortifying the Harbour so as that the Enemies Ships might never approach it hereafter. Our grateful Acknowledgments are due to the supreme Being who has not been regardless of the multiplied Oppressions which the Inhabitants of that City have sufferd under the Hand of an execrable Tyrant. Their Magnanimity & Perseverance during the severe Conflict has afforded a great Example to the World, and will be recorded by the impartial Historian to their immortal Honor. They are now restored to their Habitations & Privileges; and as they are purgd of those Wretches a Part of whose Policy has been to corrupt the Morals of the People, I am perswaded they will improve the happy opportunity of reestablishing ancient Principles and Purity of Manners. I mention this in the first place because I fully agree in Opinion with a very celebrated Author, that "Freedom or Slavery will prevail in a (City or) Country according as the Disposition & Manners of the People render them fit for the one or the other;" and I have long been convincd that our Enemies have made it an Object, to eradicate from the Minds of the People in general a Sense of true Religion & Virtue, in hopes thereby the more easily to carry their Point of enslaving them. Indeed my Freind, this is a Subject so important in my Mind, that I know not how to leave it. Revelation assures us that "Righteousness exalteth a Nation." Communities are dealt with in this World by the wise and just Ruler of the Universe. He rewards or punishes them according to their general Character. The diminution of publick Virtue is usually attended with that of publick Happiness, and the publick Liberty will not long survive the total Extinction of Morals. "The Roman Empire," says the Historian, "*must* have sunk, though the Goths had not invaded it. Why? Because the Roman Virtue was sunk." Could I be assured that America would remain virtuous, I would venture to defy the utmost Efforts of Enemies to subjugate her. You will allow me to remind you, that the Morals of that City which has born so great a Share in the American Contest, depend much upon the Vigilance of the respectable Body of Magistrates of which you are Member.

I am greatly concernd at the present defenceless State of Boston, & indeed of the whole Eastern District which comprehends New England. We have applied for and obtain a Committee of Congress to consider the State of that District.[2] In the mean time I hope the General Assembly and the Town are exerting themselves for the Security of the Harbour. I could indeed earnestly wish that the inhabitants of Boston, who have so long born the Heat & Burden of the Day might now have some Respite—But this is uncertain. Their generous Exertions in the American Cause, have rendered them particularly obnoxious to the Vengeance of the British Tyrant. It is therefore incumbent on them to be on their

Guard, and to use the utmost Activity in putting themselves in a Posture of Defence.

I trust their Spirits are not depressed by the Injuries they have sustaind. The large Experience they have had of military Tyranny should rather heighten their Ideas of the Blessings of civil Liberty and a free Government. While *their own* Troops are posted among them for their Protection, they surely will not lose the Feelings and resign the Honor of Citizens to the military; but remember always that standing Armies are formidable Bodies in civil Society, & the Suffering them to exist at any time is from Necessity, & ought never to be of Choice.

It is with heartfelt Pleasure that I recollect the Meetings I have had with my much esteemd Fellow Citizens in Faneuil Hall, and I am animated with the Prospect of seeing them again in that Place which has long been sacred to Freedom. There I have seen the Cause of Liberty & of Mankind warmly espousd & ably vindicated; and that, at Times when to speak with Freedom had become so dangerous, that other Citizens possessed of less Ardour, would have thought themselves excuseable in not speaking at all.

Be so kind as to pay my due Respects to my Friends & be assured that I am with the most friendly Regards for Mrs Scollay and Family, very affectionately yours,   S A

FC (NN).
¹ John Scollay (1711–90), Boston brazier and merchant, was a political ally of Samuel Adams and perennial selectman in Boston. Shipton, *Harvard Graduates*, 16:90, 520. His letter of April 22 is in the Samuel Adams Papers, NN.
² A committee 'to take into consideration the state of the eastern department" was appointed on April 26, and its report was read on May 10. Several related resolves were passed on May 11, 14, and 16. *JCC*, 4:311, 344–45, 347–49, 355–56, 359–60.

John Hancock to Certain Colonies

Gentlemen,   Philada. April 30th. 1776.

In order to give Success to the Expedition into Canada, Nothing is so much wanted at this Juncture, as a Supply of Specie. Genl. Schuyler says it is absolutely necessary, and the Congress have received from him the most pressing Letter on that Head.¹

Should the Army be compelled to evacuate Canada, it is impossible to say what will be the Consequences, or where the Mischief may end. It becomes us therefore as we regard our Country and its best Interests, to exert every Nerve to guard agt. so fatal an Event. For this Purpose, & as a Step of the utmost Importance, I am commanded by Congress earnestly to request you to take the most speedy & effectual Measures to collect as much hard Money as possible, and to send the same to General

Schuyler.[2] Whatever Sum you may collect for this Use, you will please to draw on me for the Amount, and the Bills shall be honored.

The unprepared State of the Colonies on the Commencement of the War, and the almost total Want of every Thing necessary to carry it on, are the true Sources from whence all our Difficulties have proceeded. This Fact however furnishes a most striking Proof of the Weakness or Wickedness of those, who charge them with an *original* Intention of withdrawing from the Government of Great Britain, and erecting an independant Empire. Had such a Scheme been formed, the most warlike Preparations would have been necessary to effect it.

From the distinguished Ardour & Zeal of the Colony of Massachusetts Bay[3] in the American Cause, I am persuaded you will pay all the Attention to this Request of Congress, which the Importance of it demands. I have the Honour to be, Gent. your most obedt. & very hble Servt.[4]

J. H. Prest.

LB (DNA: PCC, item 12A). Addressed: "Council of Massachusetts Bay. New Hampshire. Gov. Trumbul of Connecticut. Govr. Cooke of Rhode Island."

[1] See Schuyler's letters to Hancock of January 29 and March 6, PCC, item 153, 1:478–84, 2:37–40; and *Am. Archives*, 4th ser. 4:880–81, 5:91.

[2] See *JCC*, 4:318–19.

[3] Or "New Hampshire," "Connecticut," or "Rhode Island," according to addressee.

[4] The RC of this letter sent to the Massachusetts Council contains the following postscript: "I inclose a Resolve just pass'd respectg the Vessels left in Boston, to which beg leave to Refer you." M-Ar. This resolve is in *JCC*, 4:320–21.

John Hancock to Philip Schuyler

Sir   Philadelphia April 30. 1776

I do Myself the Honor of transmitting Herewith, the Resolution of Congress, under the Hand of the Secretary, as far as they relate to Your own Conduct.[1] You will perceive they have Ordered four Battallions to Quebec; & by Letter from General Washington[2] I understand they are preparing to March with the Greatest Expedition. I expect Very soon to do Myself the Pleasure of Writing more fully. In the mean Time, I have the Honor to be, with Every Sentiment of Regard, Your most Obedt. & Very Humble servt.   John Hancock Presidt.

Tr (NN).

[1] Although these resolutions cannot be identified with certainty, they probably included those concerning General Schuyler's army which Congress approved on March 25 and April 25, 28, 29, 1776. *JCC*, 4:236, 308, 312–14, 318–19.

[2] See Washington to Hancock, April 4, 1776, in Washington, *Writings* (Fitzpatrick), 4:470–73.

John Hancock to George Washington

Sir,   Philadelphia April 30th. 1776.
The Congress having accepted the Resignation of the honorable
James Warren as Paymaster General have been pleased to appoint
William Palfrey Esqr to succeed him in that Department. I have wrote
to Mr. Warren to acquaint him that there are Superintendants of the
Treasury appointed to whom he is to render his Accounts and Vouchers.[1]
I have also directed Mr. Winthrop to deliver to Mr. Palfrey all the
Cash and Papers in his Possession belonging to the office.[2]
Your several Letters have been duely received, and as soon as Con-
gress shall have come to a Determination thereon, I will do myself the
Pleasure of forwarding the same, at which Time I shall write more
fully. In the Interim, I have the Honour to be, Sir, your most obedt. &
very hble Sevt.   John Hancock Presidt

RC (DLC). In the hand of Jacob Rush and signed by Hancock.
   [1] See Hancock to James Warren, April 26, 1776.
   [2] Hancock's brief letter of this date to William Winthrop, directing this delivery,
is in PCC, item 12A, and *Am. Archives*, 4th ser. 5:1139–40.

Joseph Hewes to Samuel Johnston

Dear Sir   Philadelphia 30th April 1776
I have received your favours of the 15th & 17th instant and am exceedingly Anxious for the Safety of North Carolina.[1] It is not in my
power to get any Muskets or Cannon, many of our Soldiers at New
York and in this Province are without Arms, the Congress cannot find
ways & means to supply them. Many Vessels have been sent to Foreign
Ports in Europe & the West Indies for Arms; few, very few are yet
arived. There are so many Men of War & Cruisers on the Coast that I
fear should any be procured abroad they will be lost on our own Sea
Coasts. The Cannon I had purchased for your Vessel at Edenton, I
informed you were put on board a Continental Armed Vessel. I cannot
get them replaced, there are none to be sold. I have agreed with a person
to Cast 24 four pounders, it will be some time before they can be got
ready, if I could get them in any reasonable time part of them would do
for your Vessel and the others for Field pieces, I have no expectation
of geting them till June. The Bills you drew in favor of Mr Cracket will
be paid. By our Regulations of the Army we have but one Quarter
Master General for all America, he attends the General, each Seperate
department has a deputy Quarter Master General. That office in the
Southern department has been filled some weeks ago by one Mr. Finnie
of Virginia & I am exceedingly sorry it so happened; had there been a

Vacancy I would have done my utmost to have got Col. Long appointed.[2] I will look over the Journals and if there should be any Vacancy with his Acceptance I will exert my self to the uttermost to get the appointment for him. The recommendation for Field Officers shall be laid before Congress as soon as I can get a proper opportunity. A Committee is already appointed to take the several papers & Information from North Carolina under consideration. I shall transmit you such Resolutions as Congress may agree to respecting them.[3] My Compliments to all friends & be assured that I am with respect, Dear Sir, your mo Obed huml sert,   Joseph Hewes

RC (CtY).

[1] An extract from Johnston's letter of the 15th is in Clark, *Naval Documents*, 4:841–42.

[2] Although William Finney had been appointed deputy quartermaster in the southern department on March 28, Hewes managed to secure the appointment of Col. Nicholas Long as deputy quartermaster for North Carolina on May 7. See *JCC*, 4:239, 332; and John Adams to John Penn, April 28, 1776, note 5.

[3] On April 27 Congress appointed a committee to consider a letter from Samuel Johnston to the North Carolina delegates enclosing North Carolina Provincial Congress resolves of April 9, 10, and 13 concerning the raising of six battalions there. See *JCC*, 4:314–15; and *N.C. Colonial Records*, 10:494–95, 506, 508–9, 513–14. This committee submitted its report to Congress on May 2, on the basis of which Congress adopted a number of resolutions about officers and supplies for these battalions on May 7. See *JCC*, 4:323, 331–33; and Hewes' letters to Johnston of May 15 and 16 1776.

Richard Henry Lee to Robert Carter Nicholas

Dear Sir,   Philadelphia 30th April 1776

I thank you for your kind favor by last Post, and I am well pleased to hear that Gen. Lee is exerting himself for the security of our country. His military talents are considerable, and his zeal in the American cause equal to his martial accomplishments. His plan for securing our rivers with armed boats, from piratical ravage, is very wise, and I hope it will meet the countenance and support of our convention. The manner of making common salt, as practised in France, and well described in a pamphlet we sent the Committee of Safety, seems to deserve the most serious attention of the public.[1] Our water is more salt & our sun hotter than in France, nor are they much less subject to rains, but from this interruption we need not fear much inconvenience, where the evaporation from the suns heat is so great as in Virginia. I realy think that revenue as well as supply of the commodity may be obtained from public works of this kind. Salt petre too, is an object of great consequence, but I incline to believe that bounties to encourage the making this in private families will more certainly produce it in large quantities than any other plan. We are told that Massachusetts Government alone, will in this way furnish 100 Tons by midsummer. But Sir, do you not see the indispensable necessity of establishing a Government this Convention? How long popular commotions may be suppressed without it, and Anarchy be prevented, deserves intense consideration. A wise and free government may now be formed, and the sensible advantages soon derived from it, will, added to the Magistrates authority, effectually prevent the numerous evils to be apprehended from popular rage & licence whenever they find the bonds of government removed, as is certainly the case, by the last wicked Act of Parliament. We cannot be in rebellion, and without the Kings protection; and Magistrates acting under his authority at the same time. Would not the President act as Governor, if chosen by the Convention? I sent you a small pamphlet by Squire Lee, written here by a very sensible Gentleman on the subject of Government. His plan, with some variation, would in fact, be nearly the form we have been used to.

Our enemies are at this time holding a treaty with the Indians at Detroit, and propose another at Niagara the 1st of May, to persuade these Savages to join them in the war against us. This mischief will forever attend us whilst one of the Forts are suffered to remain in possession of the enemy in that Country. However, I expect an expedition will soon be sett on foot that will effectually oust them. Gen Howe is certainly gone to Hallifax to refresh his dispirited, fugitive army, but his distress there must be considerable, as the climate is bad, and the scarcity of provisions considerable. We conclude here that Quebec and Hudsons river will be their great objects this Campaign, and we are preparing to give them a proper reception both in Canada and New York. I think Ld. Germains intercepted letter shews us pretty clearly that the 7 regiments under Cornwallis are all that are intended for the Southern Colonies this year, and their insufficiency is very apparent. But this is one good consequence arising from Ld. Dunmores vain boasting of his own prowess, and what he could do in Virga. with a few troops, He has led his friends into another scrape. We have sent 8 Gallies & 2 Ships of war down after the Roebuck as she is reported to be on Shore near the Capes of Delaware. Should this prove true, it will be a fine acquisition.[2]

Colo. Harrison told me you desired the account of each Delegate to be sent you. I have accordingly inclosed you mine.[3] The general Account of the disposition of the money obtained from the bills you have sent here, will likewise be transmitted. I had, in my last account sent you when in Virga., stated our allowance at half a joe per day because I was informed that was the sense of Convention. But since the Ordinance mentions forty five shillings we must abide the loss. The Congress has sent 250,000 dollars to the Paymaster in Virga. & 50,000 to the Committee of Safety to get changed for specie to support the Troops in Canada. From this quantity of Continental money in Virginia you will have no difficulty hereafter I suppose Sir [in] procuring as much as will pay our wages.

[You]r goodness will, I am sure, pardon the length [of] this letter.

I am dear Sir your affec[tionate] and obedient servant,

Richard Henry Lee

[*P.S.*] Mr. Ro. Morris purchased the bills you sent by me and the exchange was 77 1/2.

RC (MHi). Addressed: "Robert Carter Nicholas Esqr., Treasurer of Virginia at Williamsburg."

[1] In his April 20 letter to Richard Henry Lee, Edmund Pendleton, chairman of the committee of safety, had endorsed the construction of public saltworks and requested information on the "approved method of making it." Edmund Pendleton, *The Letters and Papers of Edmund Pendleton 1734–1803*, ed. David J. Mays, 2 vols. (Charlottesville: University Press of Virginia, 1967), 1:163–65. See also Robert Treat Paine to the Massachusetts General Court, April 15, 1776.

[2] Lee discussed similar topics in his letter of this date to John Page, which is extracted in *Stan V. Henkels Catalog*, no. 712 (December 14, 1893), item 30.

[3] Lee's copy of his account, endorsed "R. H. Lee's Accot. with Treasury Virga., 30 April 1776," includes a charge for 145 days of service as a delegate for the period September 1775 through April 1776. Lee Family Papers, ViU.

Roger Sherman to David Waterbury

Sir   Philadelphia 30th April 1776

The Congress passed an order last Summer,[1] that a number of blank Commissions Should be Signed by the President and Sent to proper persons to be filled up and delivered to the officers then in the Army, who had been appointed by the Several Colonies, and it has been reported here that the officers of the Troops raised in Connecticut which were in the New York and Canada departments had refused to receive sd Commissions under the Congress, and it has likewise been asserted, that no Such Commissions were offered them and that they knew nothing of the matter.[2] A few lines from You informing me whether any Such Commission was offered to You & refused, also what You know relative to their being refused by the other Connecticut officers, will oblige me and May be of Service in the common Cause.

The Congress has ordered that authentic Muster rolls of the Militia that Served in New York and accounts of their expences be transmitted to Congress that they may be paid.[3] I Suppose the President has transmitted a Copy of the resolution to the Governor. We have no news here remarkable. I am Sir with Esteem Your humble Servant.

Roger Sherman

RC (CtY).

Samuel Chase

¹ Probably the resolve of September 14, 1775. See *JCC*, 2:249.

² David Waterbury (1722–1801), Stamford, Conn., soldier who had served as colonel of a Connecticut regiment in the Canadian expedition in 1775, had apparently informed Eliphalet Dyer of his disappointment at not being offered a Continental commission. While in Philadelphia on colony business, Dyer tried to obtain a postdated commission for Waterbury, but only succeeded in initiating a congressional investigation of the distribution of blank commissions by General Schuyler and the New York Committee of Safety in 1775. Dyer was also able to lay the groundwork for what resulted in an offer to Waterbury to command a regiment formerly headed by Benedict Arnold, which Waterbury declined. He finally accepted a Connecticut commission as brigadier general of militia, and during the summer of 1776 he commanded the post at Skenesboro, N.Y., where a fleet was being built for the Lake Champlain campaign. See *JCC*, 4:317; John Hancock to Philip Schuyler, May 4, 1776; Eliphalet Dyer to David Waterbury, April 25, 1776, Waterbury Family Collection, CtY; *Am. Archives*, 4th ser. 5:1001–2, 1133, and 6:436, 871; and *Appleton's Cyclopaedia of American Biography*.

³ Waterbury's accounts were received on June 15 and referred to the claims committee. See *JCC*, 5:444.

Commissioners to Canada to John Hancock

Sir,   Montreal 1st May 1776 ¹

After some difficulty & delay in getting thro' the ice of Lake George, we arrived here on Monday last, and were very politely received by General Arnold who at present commands in this Post.²

It is impossible to give you a just idea of the lowness of the Continental credit here from the want of hard money, and the prejudice it is to our affairs. Not the most trifling service can be procured without an assurance of instant pay in silver or gold. The Express we sent from St. John's to inform the General of our arrival there, and to request carriages for La Prairie, was stopt at the ferry, till a friend passing changed a Dollar for him into silver, and we are obliged to that friend (Mr. M'Cartney) for his engagement to pay the Caleches, or they would not have come for us. The general apprehension, that we shall be driven out of the Province as soon as the King's troops can arrive, concurs, with the frequent breaches of promise the Inhabitants have experienced, in determining them to trust our people no farther. Therefore the utmost dispatch should be used in forwarding a large sum hither (we believe twenty thousand pounds will be necessary); otherwise it will be impossible to continue the war in this Country, or to expect the continuance of our interest with the people here, who begin to consider the Congress as bankrupt and their cause as desperate. Therefore till the arrival of money, it seems improper to propose the federal union of this Province with the others, as the few friends we have here, will scarce venture to exert themselves in promoting it, till they see our credit recoverd, & a sufficient army arrived to secure the possession of the Country.

Yesterday we attended a Council of war, the minutes of which we inclose.[3] The places proposed are proper to prevent the further progress of the Enemy, in case they should oblige us to raise the siege of Quebeck. The plank & timber for the Gondolas is all prepared and ready at Fort Chamblee, & some of the Carpenters are arrived from New York; others are to be engaged here, and as hard money is necessary for these, we have agreed to advance some out of what the Congress put into our hands for our own subsistance; to be replaced when cash shall arrive.

We understand that the Troops now before Qubeck have not ten days provision; but hope, as the lakes are now open, supplies will soon reach them.

We have directed the opening of the Indian Trade, & granting passports to all, who shall enter into certain engagements to do nothing in the upper Country prejudicial to the Continental interests.

We hope to morrow to obtain an account of our debts, that ought instantly to be paid. If besides what is necessary for that purpose, we had a sum to manage by opening a bank for exchanging continental bills, it is supposed that we might thereby give a circulation to those bills. The twenty thousand pounds above mentioned will, we think, answer both these purposes.

We are told that not less than the eight thousand orderd by Congress will be a sufficient army for this quarter. As yet there are but about three thousand, including those now passing down to Quebeck, who are just come over the lakes. The small pox is in the army, & General Thomas has unfortunately never had it.[4]

With great respect to yourself & Congress, we have the honour to be, Sir, Your most obedient humble Servts.,

B Franklin

Samuel Chase

Ch. Carroll of Carrollton

RC (DNA: PCC, item 166). In a clerical hand and signed by Carroll, Chase, and Franklin.

[1] For the disposition of this letter, which was read in Congress on May 16 and referred to a committee consisting of John Adams, Thomas Jefferson, and William Livingston, see *JCC*, 4:358–59; and Jefferson, *Papers* (Boyd), 1:295–96. The letter was sent via General Schuyler at Albany, who forwarded it with his letter to Congress of May 10, 1776. An extract of the commissioners' letter of May 1 to Schuyler accompanying their letter to Hancock is in *Kenneth W. Rendell Catalog*, no. 75 (June 1972), p. 10. "We arrived here on Monday last and have proceeded to business, as you will see by the enclosed letter to Congress, which we leave open for your perusal, and request you will seal and forward it. We are deeply impressed with a sense of the many civilities we received from you and your good family, and your kind attention to everything that might render our passage over the lakes as convenient . . . as possible. Accept our thankful acknowledgements, and make them acceptable to Mrs. Schuyler."

An extract of another letter of this date, written to an unknown recipient by John Carroll, the fourth member of the party Congress directed to Canada, is in

Am. Archives, 4th ser. 5:1167–68.
² For an account of the conditions the commissioners encountered when they reached Montreal, see Justin H. Smith, *Our Struggle for the Fourteenth Colony: Canada and the American Revolution*, 2 vols. (New York: G. P. Putnam's Sons, 1907), 2:334–56.
³ See *Am. Archives*, 4th ser. 5:1166–67.
⁴ John Thomas died of smallpox at Sorel on June 2, 1776.

Elbridge Gerry to James Warren

My Dear Sir,   Philadelphia, May 1, 1776.

I am exceedingly desirous that measures of defence should be first attended to, and have place of every other undertaking, and shall be most happy to hear that the capital, and its valuable harbour is well fortified, and something done for the other seaports; that your powder mills are at work; that manufactures of lead and sulphur are attended to, and preparation made for casting cannon; that the committees of correspondence throughout the colony are ordered to make returns of the manufactures of fire-arms, employed or unemployed, and that measures are taken to erect public works; that the established forces, whether continental or colonial, are well armed, equipped and ready for action. When this is done, and I think with a little assiduity it may be accomplished, the colony will be in a situation to receive the enemy; and they being informed thereof, as they generally are of our weakness or strength, will carefully avoid another visit.

I think it may be demonstrated that the eastern district alone is able of itself to declare independency. The colony of South Carolina have behaved nobly in taking up government, choosing a governour, &c.;[1] and the convention of North Carolina have unanimously voted to follow their example.[2]

Virginia is always to be depended upon; and so fine a spirit prevails among them, that unless you send some of your cool patriots among them, they may be for declaring independency before congress is ready.

I am glad you approve the proposal for instructions, and can with pleasure inform you that North Carolina has taken off from their delegates the restriction relative to this matter, and as I am informed, has left them at liberty to vote for a final separation from Great Britain.[3]

Your friend as ever,   E. Gerry.

MS not found; reprinted from Austin, *Life of Gerry*, 1:177–78.
¹ See John Adams to James Warren, April 20, 1776. The South Carolina Constitution is in *Am. Archives*, 4th ser. 5:609–14.
² See John Adams to John Penn, April 28, 1776, note 1.
³ This North Carolina Provincial Congress resolution of April 12 is in *Am. Archives*, 4th ser. 5:860.

Richard Henry Lee to Samuel Purviance, Jr.

Dear Sir,   Philadelphia 1st May 1776
I thank you for your favor of the 23d of April which I should have answered before now if I had not been prevented by much business. If zeal in a good cause may not cover small irregularities or deviations from the strict line of Office, and regard for the public safety be chained to the letter of business, I fear such pedantic politics will ruin America, as they must fatally injure every country where they prevail. The public of America is a generous public, and when appealed to will readily distinguish things dictated by the General good tho irregularly executed, from such as are evil in their nature and merely the suggestions [of] folly [and] wickedness.[1] I am sure a generous Community will not su[ffer any] person to be persecuted for the former, nor would I scruple in such a case to say as of old Provoco ad Populum, and then look the proudest connections in the face, trusting to the wisdom of the Object & the integrity of design, notwithstanding the manner might be something unusual.

I find Capt. Nicholsons merit is well understood here, and therefore I hope he will succeed in his desires.[2]

You have my congratulations Sir on your marriage, for I am truly your friend and obliged humble servant,   Richard Henry Lee

RC (MdHi). Addressed: "Samuel Purveyance Junr. Esqr. of Baltimore in Maryland. Favored by Doctor Bankhead."

[1] The Maryland Council of Safety had condemned Purviance for his conduct in the proposed seizure of Governor Eden and had ordered him to appear before the Maryland Convention to answer for usurping the authority of the council and the convention. *Md. Archives*, 11:372–82, 388. For information on Purviance's role in the Eden affair, see John Hancock to the Baltimore Committee, April 16, note; and Thomas Johnson to the Maryland Council of Safety, April 17, 1776. See also Lee to Purviance, May 6, 1776.

In the midst of this incident, Daniel of St. Thomas Jenifer, the president of the Maryland Council of Safety, made a mysterious trip to Philadelphia, and in a letter of April 30 to Charles Carroll, Barrister, vice president of the council, he offered a partial explanation of his activities. "I have been present at two meetings of our Delegates, (the last I am but this moment returned from,) to consult upon the principal points to be discussed in Convention, and the Delegates to attend. There will be another meeting this evening or to-morrow, when they will be finished and agreed upon. I believe Mr. *Goldsborough* and Mr. *Johnson* will be the Delegates. The points as to the Governour's staying, and representation, will be determined, I think, as you and my brethren would wish, with the latitude of being varied by the Convention, as circumstances may cast up. . . . I have, I think, almost brought *R.H.L.* to shame. He has the impudence and assurance of the devil. He at first justified *Purviance*, and denied that General *Lee* had directed the Governour to be seized; and brought his brother *Frank* to pledge his honour that the fact was not so. I concealed from them that I had a copy of the General's letter in my pocket, nor do they yet know I have it. I shall this day show it to some gentlemen that were present when they roundly asserted and assured me that I had been misinformed.

Colonel *Harrison* has written to his friends in the Committee of Safety of *Virginia*, that they must apologize to our Council for the insult. We are highly applauded, in this city, for our spirited conduct in the late conspiracy, for such I must term it." *Am. Archives*, 4th ser. 5:1146–47. For a discussion of Jenifer's visit to Philadelphia and efforts to obtain information for use in the case against Purviance, see Ronald Hoffman, *A Spirit of Dissension: Economics, Politics, and the Revolution in Maryland* (Baltimore: Johns Hopkins University Press, 1973), pp. 160–63.

² Probably a reference to James Nicholson (1736–1804), who on June 6 was appointed captain of the Continental frigate *Virginia*, which was being built in Maryland. *JCC*, 5:422–23.

Robert Treat Paine's Diary

[May 1, 1776]
Congress did not Set, the State room being taken up by the Election in choice of Burgesses.¹ Raw, Cold.

MS (MHi).
¹ For further information on the elections for the Pennsylvania Assembly, see Caesar Rodney to Thomas Rodney, May 1, 1776, note 2.

Caesar Rodney to Thomas Rodney

Sir,   Philada. May the 1st. 1776
I have Obtained and Sent you herewith A Commission for Mr. Thomas Holland the Adjutant, appointing him a second Lieutenant in the Delaware Battalion; And Also a Commission for Mr. John Corse appointing him an Ensign, vacant by the promotion of Mr. Holland. Be pleased to deliver them (with my Complimts.) to those Gentlemen.

Your Mention of Mr. Gordon¹ with My knowledge of, and long Acquaintance with the Man, Will induce me to make use of my influence to Serve him, Whenever I Can do it with propriety, as in this Case, And Should have verry little doubt of Obtaining it for him, But am apt to think no paymaster will be appointed: as there is no instance of the like to any other of the Battalions, Unless when Joined the Army, where there is a pay-master-general.

You Say the negroes are much avers'd to being Sold, which I don't doubt, and Agree with you and Billey that it will be a verry disagreable Task, Tho. from their past Vile Misbehaviour, they have no right to Expect any favour, or partiallity for them at my hands. They have done me so much Damage and behaved so Wickedly, That I have lost all Confidence in, and almost all Affection or feeling for them, And Am Apprehensive that the plantations will not procure Such additional Rent with Negroes on them, as Will be Adequate to the Interest of So much Money, the Risque of their lives and the Certain Expence of Doctor's Bills &c.

I have thought proper to Suggest these things; But upon the Whole, Shall leave it to Billy and You Either to Lett, or Sell them, as You both Shall incline. If you Should think proper to Lett the Negroes with the places, whither it will not Also be Necessary to divide And let the Stock with them.

I Could wish that all the places were Contracted for, and Leases Entered into, as soon as possible to Commence from the first day of January Next, that I might be the better Assured of the part I have to Act in the mean time with respect to the Negroes, Stock, farming &c. This will lay upon you to do, as I Shall be Seldom there, and when I am, but verry little time to attend to it.

I have Recd a Sample of my Wheat, Think it verry good, and have had some talk with John Brown, Who Says he will Endeavour to Sell it for me. If he doth to my likeing, I Shall Send you Orders for haveing it brought up.

You have hitherto made no mention to me Whether Manlove has as Yet been up to Dover with the public Money—or what was done with it.

No News Except that Yesterday a Court of Admiralty was held on the Tender-Prize When She with her Tackle &c. &c. was Condemned, And that this day is like to produce as warm if not the warmest Election that ever was held in this City.[2] The Forms for the parties are Whigg & Tory—dependence & Independence. I am with much love &c &c., yours &c,   Cæsar Rodney

RC (PHi).
  [1] In an April 26 letter to Caesar Rodney, Thomas Rodney had recommended John Gordon as paymaster of the Delaware battalion, an office to which John Yates was appointed on August 9. See Rodney, *Letters* (Ryden), p. 73; and *JCC*, 5:640.
  [2] This day Rodney's fellow delegate George Read discussed the election for the Pennsylvania Assembly in a letter to his wife. "This day is their election for additional members of Assembly. Great strife is expected. Their fixed candidates are not known. One side talk of Thomas Willing, Andrew Allen, Alexander Wilcox, and Samuel Howell, against independency; the other, Daniel Roberdeau, George Clymer, Mark Kuhl, and a fourth I don't recollect; but it is thought other persons would be put up." William T. Read, *Life and Correspondence of George Read, a signer of the Declaration of Independence* . . . (Philadelphia: J. B. Lippincott & Co., 1870), p. 157. For a detailed analysis of the election, see David Hawke, *In the Midst of a Revolution* (Philadelphia: University of Pennsylvania Press, 1961), pp. 13–86.

Secret Committee to
Nicholas Brown and John Brown

Gentn.   Philada. May 1st. 1776

We wrote you the 3d Inst. to which referr,[1] the present being to request that you will immediately send forward, One hundred pieces of Russia Duck (part of that imported by you in the Sloop Commanded by Capt B. Comstock) to John Langdon Esqr at Portsmouth, New Hampshire for the use of the Continental Frigate building there, and you'l obtain his receipt for the Same to serve as a Voucher of the delivery when your accounts are adjusted with this Committee.

We are sir Your obed Servants. By order of the Secret Committee.

Robt Morris Chair Man

RC (RPJCB). Written and signed by Morris.

[1] See Secret Committee to Nicholas Brown and John Brown, April 3, 1776.

Secret Committee to Thomas Mumford

Sir   Philada. May 1st. 1776

We have received your favour of the 17th Ulto. & learn thereby the safe arrival of two of your Vessells with Powder, Sulphur & Salt, all which you have landed & deposited at Norwich as a place of Safety.[1] The Cost of this Powder is very reasonable & it will give us pleasure if you are equally Successful in procuring the remainder.

Capt Champlin has certainly acquitted himself Well[2] & we will lay your letter before the Marine Committee that it may operate in favour of the appointment you recommend. It is a pity your Friends were disapointed of the Powder they expected from Ireland, but such disapointments have been too Common in Europe. We hope however they will Succeed better elsewhere as no Articles are so much wanted as Powder, good Muskets & Gunlocks; either of the latter wou'd now be as acceptable as the former.

There can be no objection to your being repaid the Powder you lent Genl. Washington but if that Powder was your private property we had rather pay for it in Money, especially as your Colony have applyed for a return of some Powder they lent the General, which probably may be the same you mention, but this you'l explain hereafter and mention whether a payment in money will be equally acceptable or not. In the mean time you'l keep the Powder waiting our further orders. With respect to the Sulphur we request you will forward Nineteen barrells thereof to Mr. Henry Wisner's Powder Mill & Ten barrells to Mr.

618MAY 1, 1776

Livingstons Powder Mill.[3] Both these Mills are in New York Government and if you are at any loss for the means of sending the Sulphur to them, you may forward it down to Francis Lewis & Philip Livingston & Jno Alsop Esqrs., Members of this Committee now at New York, with a Copy of the above paragraph requesting them to forward it soon as they can to the Mills. Be pleased to send with the Sulphur an Invoice of its weight & a Copy to us. The Salt may remain for further orders or you may sell it to the Inhabitants if they are in Want. If not, it had best remain untill the Sale of it will relieve some distress.

The Owners of the Ship Liberty refuse to sell her for 700 half Johannes's; therefore your Friends Messrs. Burch & Co must not Consider that Sale as Valid, and the Ship must remain on pay according to Charter party. We shall be very glad to hear of your receiving more Powder as we want to repay your Colony what they lent Genl. Washington as well as for a quantity of theirs now in our possession.

We are sir, Your Obedt Servants. By order of the Secret Committee,
Robt Morris, Chair Man

RC (Robert J. Sudderth, Jr., Lookout Mountain, Tenn., 1973). Written and signed by Morris.

[1] For the contract that Mumford had made with the committee, see the Secret Committee Minutes of Proceedings, November 28, 1775.

[2] Probably Samuel Champlin, who had arrived in New London on April 6 with a quantity of powder from St. Eustatia after twice evading pursuing British tenders. Clark, *Naval Documents*, 4:784.

[3] According to the committee journal, this request was formally authorized the following day. See Secret Committee Minutes of Proceedings, May 2, 1776.

John Hancock to the
Commanding Officer of the Delaware Battalion

Sir,   May 2d. 1776.
You are hereby directed to station thirty five Men with a proper officer of your Battalion at the False Cape to protect the Navigation & do Duty there until further Orders.[1]

I am, Sir, your very hble Ser.,   J. H. Prest.

LB (DNA: PCC, item 12A). Addressed: "To the officer commanding the Battalion of Continental Troops in Delaware Government."

[1] Congress authorized Hancock to issue this order in response to a May 1 letter from Maj. Henry Fisher to the Pennsylvania Committee of Safety in which Fisher urged the committee to persuade Congress to station a detachment of Continental troops "at the False Cape to cover the Landing of any Cargo that may arrive, as that is a Place where any of your Vessels may run there Jib Boom for the Sand and save there Cargoes if they should be Chased." See *JCC*, 4:322; and Clark *Naval Documents*, 4:1367–68.

Francis Lewis to Roger Sherman

Sir: New-York, May 2, 1776.
I have been favoured with your letter of the 25th ultimo, which should
have answered sooner, but waited for an opportunity of consulting
Colonel *Mifflin*, Quartermaster-General, on the subject of shoes, who
informs me that the full quantity, (say ten thousand pair,) ordered by
Congress, will be wanted for the Army.[1] I have therefore directed Mr.
Ogden to continue the shoemakers at work in *Jersey*, and have also employed others here. Stockings are not to be procured in this city; they
must be got at *Philadelphia*, and money must be sent here to pay for the
shoes.
    Enclosed you have a return of shoes already delivered here. Hempen
and yarn stockings will be the most suitable.
    As our election for Delegates is to be on the 14th instant, I shall defer
my return to *Philadelphia* till that is over. I am, sir, your very humble
servant,   Francis Lewis

MS not found; reprinted from *Am. Archives*, 4th ser. 5:1174–75.
    [1] Sherman's letter of April 25 has not been found, but judging from the content
of this letter it must have informed Lewis that John Alsop, Lewis, and Sherman had
been appointed by Congress on April 24 as a committee to purchase 10,000 pairs of
shoes and stockings for General Schuyler's army. See *JCC,* 4:304.

Secret Committee Minutes of Proceedings

                                                      May 2d 1776
    Order on Tim. Matlack in favor of G. Losch for two Casks Saltpetre.
At a meetg. of the Come. present Robt. Morris, Ths. McKean, Jos.
Hewes, R. H. Lee & Robt. Alexander. A letter to Messrs. Rd. Harrison
& Adrian Lemaitre Merchts., Martinique was wrote, read & approved.[1]
Order on the Treasurers in favor of George Mead Esqr. & Co. for
2413 1/2 Dollars amount of an Invoice of Sundries purchased by them
& shippd by this Come. on board the sloop *Fanny*, Capt. Wilm. Briton,
for Martinico consignd to Messrs Ricd. Harrison & Adrian Lemaitre
of that Island returns to be made in good Soldiers muskets, double
bridled gun locks & good Cannon & pistol powdr.[2] A letter wrote to
Mr. John Ross was read & approvd of.[3] A letter from Ths. Mumford
dated Groton April 17th was producd, to which the Chairman was desird to write an Ansr. requestg Mr. Mumford to forward nineteen brrls
Sulphur to Mr. Wisners powdr. mill & 10 barrls to Mr. Livingstons
Mill N. York province.[4] An Affidavit of Ths. Higgins & Js. McClary
agt. Ths. Genn Master of the Brige. Cornelia was producd & read & is
put up with the charter party.[5] Issued an order on the Contl Treasurers

in favor of Oswell Eve for 533 1/3 [dollars] in part payment for powder manufactured by him.

MS (MH).
 ¹ Not found.
² For a contract with Mead & Co. for the *Fanny*, see Secret Committee Minutes of Proceedings, May 26, 1776. For disposition of the net proceeds of the *Fanny*'s cargo, see Secret Committee to Adrien Le Maitre and Richard Harrison, June 3, 1776.
³ Not found.
⁴ See Secret Committee to Thomas Mumford, May 1, 1776.
⁵ See Secret Committee Contract, February 1; and Secret Committee Minutes of Proceedings, June 13, 1776.

Commissioners to Canada to Philip Schuyler

Sir   Montreal May 4th 1776
    Having orders from Congress¹ to enquire into the case of John Fraser Esqr. now prisoner at Œsopus, we have thought proper to direct the Commanding Officer there to allow him to repair hither, on his parole to present himself before us immediately on his arrival. We desire you to give the necessary orders for this purpose. We are with great regard, Sir, Your most obedt. humble Servts,
                                                                              B Franklin

                                                            Charles Carroll of Carrollton

                                                            Saml. Chase

RC (CtY). In a clerical hand and signed by Carroll, Chase, and Franklin.
¹ See the instructions of Congress to the commissioners, *JCC*, 4:217–18.

John Hancock to Philip Schuyler

Sir,   May 4th. 1776
    Since writing the foregoing¹ I have it further in Charge from Congress to desire you to inform them whether the Continental Commissions sent to you for the Officers of the Troops raised by Connecticut the last Campaign, were delivered or offered to them or any, and which of them, and whether any & which of them accepted or refused the same, and particularly whether Commissions were offered to Col. Waterbury & Col. Easton, and whether they refused accepting them,² and also to desire you in Case Major Douglass declines to take the Command of the Vessels on the Lakes that you appoint Capt. Wynkoop to that Command, & inform Congress thereof by the first opportunity.³
                                                                              J. H. Prst.

LB (DNA: PCC, item 12A). Addressed: "Major Genl. Schuyler at Albany."
  [1] At this point in the MS an asterisk was inserted to refer to Hancock's letter to Schuyler of April 26, 1776.
  [2] For further information on this issue, see Roger Sherman to David Waterbury, April 30, 1776, note 2. This day Hancock also wrote a similar letter to the New York Committee of Safety inquiring about the officers for the Connecticut troops. See PCC, item 12A; and *Am. Archives*, 4th ser. 5:1188–89.
  [3] For a discussion of Douglass and Wynkoop, see Richard Smith's Diary, February 5, 1776, note 7.

John Hancock to George Washington

Sir,   Philadelphia May 4. 1776
  A vacancy having happened in the first New Jersey batallion by the promotion of lieutenant Colonel Winds, the Congress thought proper to elect Mr Ogden to supply his place.[1]
  Lord Sterling in his letter of the 18th of March last, among other things informed the Congress, that by this appointment Major de Hart and the batallion considered themselves "exceedingly hurt" and enclosing a memorial from Major de Hart and the officers of that regiment he strongly hinted & expressed a hope that the Congress would supersede Mr Ogden & appoint Major de Hart or some other officer of the batallion in his stead.
  This letter with the memorials enclosed having been committed & a report made thereon the Congress came to sundry resolutions which I have the honour to enclose,[2] and am, Sr., Your most obedt servt.
                                                        John Hancock Presidt

[*P.S.*] You will please to order Colo Ogden to Join his Regimt.

RC (DLC). In the hand of Charles Thomson, with signature and postscript by Hancock.
  [1] Congress made this appointment on March 7, 1776. *JCC*, 4:188.
  [2] Gen. William Alexander's letter to Hancock of March 18 and enclosures are in PCC, item 162, 2:471–76, and *Am. Archives*, 4th ser. 5:403–4. Congress' resolution of May 3 reaffirming Ogden's appointment as lieutenant colonel of the First New Jersey Battalion and two other resolutions of that date pertaining to the Continental Army are in *JCC*, 4:324–25.

Samuel Huntington to Jabez Huntington

Sir   Philadelphia 4th May 1776
  I am happy in receiving your favour of the 19th ulto. It brings the latest Intelligence which I have had from my famaly. Hope the last Supply of money by Colonels Dyer & Williams may be of Special Service to the Colony.[1] The Congress have Some time since ordered

their Journals to be printed, that the Colonies may See their whole proceedings, but by one accident or other they are not yet finished.[2] Hope the Impressions will be out soon, Shall not fail to forward Some to Connecticut first opportunity. They have on mature deliberation taking of [taken off] the restrictions for regulating the price of goods except the article of Teas, as trade is now open to all foreign ports.[3] It is a Long time Since we have had any news from England, & nothing late from Quebec. Please to make my Compliments acceptable to your Lady, & be assured I am with Esteem your humble Sert,

                                                           Saml Huntington

RC (CtY).

    [1] See *JCC*, 4:272.

    [2] See *JCC*, 4:224; 5:822, 829; 6:1128. The *Journals of the Proceedings of Congress, from January to May 1776*, was published and advertised for sale by Robert Aitken in the *Pennsylvania Gazette*, October 9, 1776.

    [3] See *JCC*, 4:277–78, 320.

Samuel Huntington to Nathaniel Shaw, Jr.

Sir   Philadelphia 4th May 1776
    I am favoured with yours of the 24th April, note the contents, but before it came to hand, I had the pleasure of procuring you to be appointed Agent, being the most Suitable person I could think of. The Resolution of Congress appointing you will doubtless come to hand before this reaches you.[1] We have obtaind an order of Congress to exchange your powder in this City for continental powder in New London, the Committee will Soon give you particular directions on that Subject. Hope the harbour of New London will Soon be Sufficiently fortified as I make no doubt Ships of force will Soon be in there if it be not made Secure.[2]
    Am Sir your humble Servt   Saml Huntington

RC (CtY)

    [1] See John Hancock to Nathaniel Shaw, Jr., April 23, 1776.

    [2] This day Congress received Shaw's April 25 letter to Gov. Jonathan Trumbull enclosing an invoice of the cannon received at New London from Commodore Esek Hopkins. See PCC, item 66, 1:165–66; and Clark, *Naval Documents*, 4:1250–51.

Oliver Wolcott to
the Connecticut Committee of the Pay-Table

Gentlemen   Philidelpa. 4t May 1776
    Your Favour of the 22 Ult. with the Paroles, Lists of Prisoners and

Acco. of their Expences except Col. Gay's came safe.[1] The Acco. of Col
Gay's was not inclosed with the Rest, instead thereof came Two Accts.
of Dr. Phelps and D Barbur respecting their Care of one D Jenkins
which as it is not Marked so I suppose does not belong to those other
Accounts.

By a Resolution of Congress gone forward by Col Williams you will
perceive that another mode of settling these Accounts has been adopted
but the Accounts as sent will be offered to Congress.[2] I perceive their
is a difference from 5s to 7s in the Charges, probably for good Reasons.
I am most heartily glad the rest of the Prisinors are to be settled in the
Colony. I was in hopes a Code abstracted from a Variety of particular
Resolutions respecting Prisoners would have been published before now
but it is not accomplished, by Reason of the Variety of other Business.
It would undoubtedly be well to let the Prisoners Labor for their support but not give them Liberty to depart, but have them under the
Inspection of the Committees. To suffer them to go out of the Colony
has I perceive been practised. This Circumstance if known Would make
a deep Impression on the Congress, which together with the List not
being certified by the Committee of Prisoners will require Consideration
wheither it will be best to present it. The Congress have ordered the
Accts. and Militia Rools of those who served in N York to be paid
there. This was in Consequence of a Letter from Genl. Washington,
who Wrote those Inconveniences might arise on Acco. of their going
away unpaid.[3] No Time has yet been had of putting in the Colony
Accts. but it will be done in a few days.[4] If any special Dificulties
should [arise] you will be advised of it. Upon so Novel a System and
Accots. arising out of sudden Emergincies, and where no fix'd Rules
have been established it is not possible to Say with absolute certainty
what will be required, but I hope no Dificulty will attend them. The
Case of R Island I before mentioned, I beleive, to you.

My Inducement to Mention to you, the having Accts. paid immediately by the Continent, was to prevent the great Inconveniency arising
from an exhausted Treasury—and the double Labor in closing these
Accts. but I am sensible my opinion in that Case was unnecessary as
you are much more able to judge of the particular Exigences of the
Colony than I am. Your Assiduity in setling the Colony Accts. I do not
doupt of. I easily perceive it must be attended with great Labor and
dificulty in almost every respect—and no small Share may fall to the
Lot of us who are here. We shall attend to this Matter as well as We are
able, and I hope the Business in time may be happily closed.

For News refer you to the Papers, as nothing Very special has occurred. The Modle of Governmt erected by S Carolina is not yet come
here. I understand the House of Assembly which is much enlarged by
this establishment, chose a Council of Thirteen, then both the Houses
chose the Govr. or President and Vice President. Govr., Council and

Assembly constitute distinct Branches of Legislative Authority. The Executive Department is established by an Act of the whole Legislative Authority. The Govr has a privy Council chosen by the Council and Assembly, three by each House, to assist him in the Business of Government, the Govr, council and Assembly to be biennally elected, according to this Institution. I am with Esteem, Gentlemen, your Most Obedient and humble Servant,[5]   Oliver Wolcott

RC (Ct).
[1] See Oliver Wolcott to Ezekiel Williams, February 10, and to Thomas Seymour, April 16 and 17, 1776.
[2] JCC, 4:264–65.
[3] JCC, 4:312. Washington's April 22 letter is in Washington, *Writings* (Fitzpatrick), 4:500–502.
[4] For other references to Connecticut accounts, see Wolcott to Thomas Seymour, April 16, 1776, note 2.
[5] Wolcott also wrote a brief note this day to his wife apologizing for having toc little time to write. Oliver Wolcott to Laura Wolcott, May 4, 1776, Signers of th Declaration, NNPM.

John Jay to Philip Schuyler

Dear Sir   Eliz. Town, 5th May 1776
    This Letter will be delivered to you by Henry Brockholst Livingston, my Brother in Law, whom I take the Liberty of introducing to your Acquaintance. He intends engaging in the Service as a Volunteer, and for that Purpose will embark with Coll. Daytons Battalion.[1]
    I can with great Truth assure You, that this young Gentlemans Conduct has hitherto been very satisfactory to his Family & Friends, and if he perseveres in it, I flatter myself he will receive from you every Mark of that Attention, which, as a General, you so readily extend to [. . .] and as a Friend, to your most obedt. Servt,   John Jay

RC (NN). Addressed: "Majr. General Schuyler at Albany."
[1] Henry Brockholst Livingston (1757–1823), son of Jay's father-in-law, New Jersey delegate William Livingston, soon became an aide-de-camp to Schuyler. *Am. Archives*, 4th ser. 6:416. On May 6, 1776, Robert R. Livingston, then in New York preparatory to returning to Philadelphia, also wrote a letter of introduction to Schuyler for young Livingston, in the course of which he reported: "We have just recd an account of the arrival of the Commissioners in Nantasket road together with seventy transports so that the poor Bostonians have had but a short respite. I dont however imagine they will land, but as we have no particulars, the express not yet being come in |and] the acct we have being by water from Rhode Island we can only conjecture their force & destination." Schuyler Papers, NN.
    A letter from William Livingston to Schuyler of May 2, 1776, introducing Col. Elias Dayton of the Third New Jersey Battalion, is also in the Schuyler Papers, NN.

New York Delegates to
the New York Committee of Safety

Gentlemen   Philad. 5 May 1776
  Agreeable to your Directions communicated in your Letter of the
23rd of March respecting the Command in the marine Department on
the Lakes, we immediately introduced the Subject to Congress and a
Resolution passed that Mr Douglass shoud forthwith repair to his
Station. As this was in the military Line the Resolution was forwarded
to General Schuyler: and we did not think it necessary to trouble you
with a Copy.
  We again applied to Congress, on Receipt of your favour of the 29th
of April last from which we learn that Douglass had not yet proceeded
to the Lakes. This occasioned the further Resolution of which we have
the Honour to enclose you a Copy.[1] It will bring the point to an immediate determination; and we hope fully answer your Expectations.
  Major Tuthill is appointed to succeed Benedict. We sincerely wish for
an Opportunity of promoting Mr Willet. His Merit is with us unquestionable: but as Major Tuthill sustains a good Character, and has the
advantage of priority, Congress has given him the Preference. The
Commission will be forwarded by the next Conveyance.[2]
  We have the Honour to be, with the greatest Respect, Gentlemen,
Your most Obedt. hume Servant,   Jas. Duane

                                                  Lewis Morris

                                                  Wm. Floyd

P.S. We have obtaind and enclose the Commission for Major Tuthill.

RC (N) damaged; reprinted from Burnett, *Letters*, 1:439.
  [1] On May 2 Congress authorized General Schuyler "in case Major [William]
Douglass declines to take the command of the vessels on the lakes . . . [*to*] appoint
Captain [Jacobus] Wynkoop to that command." *JCC*, 4:322. For some account of
the events leading up to the adoption of this resolution, see Richard Smith's Diary,
February 5, 1776, note 7. The committee of safety's letters of March 23 and April 29
are in PCC, item 67, 1:208–11, and *Am. Archives*, 4th ser. 5:1123–24, 1397.
  [2] See *JCC*, 4:326. In its April 29 letter to the New York delegates, the committee
of safety nominated Maj. Barnabas Tuthill and Capt. Marinus Willett as candidates
to succeed Joseph Benedict, who had just resigned from the majority of the First
New York Battalion to which Congress had appointed him on March 8, 1776. *JCC*,
4:190; and *Am. Archives*, 4th ser. 5:1124. See also John Jay to Marinus Willett,
April 27, 1776, note.

Robert Treat Paine's Diary

                                                  [May 5, 1776]
  Cool. P.M. Mr. Stillmans; arrivd Capt. Young from Port l'Orient

brings a Dublin Paper of [*March 2*] containing an Acct. of 45000 men half foreigners destined for America.[1]

MS (MHi).
[1] For further information on Capt. John Young's account of the imminent arrival of foreign troops, see Clark, *Naval Documents*, 4:1415, 1441.

John Adams to John Winthrop

Dear Sir   May 6 1776
Your Letter by your son I have not received, but I hope to have that Pleasure soon together with that of waiting upon him here.[1]

Your Brothers Right to the office you mention cannot be questioned, but whether the Court will appoint two, and who they will be I can form no Conjecture, having never had any Conversation with any Gentleman upon that Subject. An Application was indeed made to me, in Favour of Mr Henshaw when I was at Watertown, but I could give no opinion concerning it. Whether I shall have any Voice in the appointment I know not, I rather think I shall not, because it must soon be made I suppose, and I shall not be soon in the Colony. But if I should your son, sir, will be more likely than any one I know of at present to have it. But in such Cases every Candidate has a Right to have his Pretentions examined and impartially weighed, and therefore it would be improper for me to make any Promises.

It gives me Pleasure to learn that our People are at last in Earnest to fortify the Harbour. Believe me, my dear Sir, it is of the last Importance. I am very far from being certain that the Armament, at Hallifax, with a large Reinforcement will not return to Boston. Nothing will prevent it, but the vigorous Exertion of our Government to render the Town inaccessible. There is not in the World, an Harbour, better fitted by Nature to be rendered impregnable by Fortifications than that is. I wish I was with you that I might be able to Satisfy myself. Is there no such Thing as getting upon Lovells Island, or Georges Island, and driving away the Men of War, which lie in Nantaskett Road. Can nothing be done at Hull or Point Aldertin? I am afraid you are as destitute of active and capable Engineers as in Spirited Commanding officers.

As to the Cannon taken by Hopkins, I fear that none of them can be Spared you. The Continent have so many demands for Cannon, for their Ships, and a Variety of Service by Sea and Land that I am afraid We shall not be able to obtain any of them. Congress have given our Colony all that belonged to it, and the King.

Am extreamly disappointed in the Experiment at Providence. I hope it is not certain and settled that We have not ore, in the Northern Colonies, which is fit for the Manufacture of Cannon.

You rejoice me very much by acquainting me, that there is Plenty of Materials for making Sulphur, in the Country. Wish to be informed in greater detail, what these Materials are, where and when they were found and whether the Art of Sublimating it, is understood, among our People. There is a sulphur ore, in New Jersey, and We hear of it, in other Places. We have a Committee for Salt Petre, Sulphur, Powder, Cannon, Musquetts &c but I dont hear so much from it as I wish.

Our People, you say are impatiently waiting for the Congress to declare off from Great Britain. What my own sentiments are upon this Question, is not material. But others ask to what Purpose should we declare off? Our Privateers are at Liberty, our Trade is open, the Colonies are Sliding into New Governments, a Confederation may be formed, but why should We declare We never will be reconciled to Great Britain, again, upon any Terms whatsoever. You ask how it would be relished by the Congress, if our Colony should declare off. I am happy to hear that our Colony is disusing a certain Name in all Commissions, Acts, and Law Proscesses,[2] and I should like very well if they would choose a Governor, or at least ask leave of Congress to do it. But I cannot advise them to make any public Declarations, Seperate from our Sister Colonies. The Union is our Defense, and that must be most tenderly cherished. If our Colony has an Inclination to instruct their Delegates in Congress, no reasonable objection can be made to this.[3] They may if they think proper, instruct their servants, never to vote for any subjection to Parliament in any Case whatsoever, never to vote for submitting to any Crown officer, Whether Governor, Mandamus Counciller, secretary, Judge of Admiralty, Commissioner or Custom House officer &c &c if this is their Sentiment, or never to vote for acknowledging any allegiance, or subjection to the Crown of Great Britain, or King of Great Britain. But if they do all this I hope you will allow us to make Peace as an independent State.

It is my opinion, sir, that We shall have but little Difference of Sentiment among the Colonies upon these great Questions in a few Weeks. I am with great Respect, &c.

RC (MHi). In Adams' hand, though not signed.
[1] Winthrop had solicited Adams' aid in securing appointments as clerks to the Massachusetts Superior Court for both his brother Samuel and his son William. Winthrop to Adams, April 5 and 30, 1776, Adams Papers, MHi.
[2] The Massachusetts General Court at its session ending May 10, 1776, passed a bill for changing the form and style of commissions, writs, etc., which in effect eliminated the use of the king's name from all legal documents. *Am. Archives*, 4th ser. 5:1283, 1285–86, 1315.
[3] See Elbridge Gerry to James Warren, March 26, 1776, note 3.

Samuel Chase to John Thomas?

Dear Sir [1]   Montreal May 6th. 1776

I am sorry to hear, that General Wooster has appointed Doctor Nicholson[2] as his Aid de Camp: I am convinced he is not worthy of so great a Trust. It is said here, that he passes as a Native of the province of Maryland. I hope, Sir, You will take Care to place no Confidence, in Mr. Nicholson, and I really think it would be proper, if it can be done without giving him Alarm, to send him to this City. I am afraid he has so far gained an Influence with General Wooster, that he might trust Nicholson with the Contents of this Letter. I think the public Service requires his instant Removal from Camp: If he should come here, I should wish to send him out of the Colony.

I wish you Health and Success, and am, Sir, with Respect, Your obedt. Servt.   Saml. Chase

RC (MeHi).

[1] Apparently Gen. John Thomas, who at this time was commanding the army encamped near Quebec, where Gen. David Wooster was also.

[2] Maj. George Nicholson. For papers relating to an investigation of his conduct in handling supplies at Montreal in March 1776, see PCC, item 19, 1:317–24.

Commissioners to Canada to John Hancock

Sir   Montreal May 6th. 1776

In our letter of the 1st instant, we informed you of the lowness of the Continental credit in this Province, and the necessity of a speedy supply of hard money. Unless this very essential article arrives soon, our forces will suffer exceedingly from the want of many necessaries, particularly flour, which might be laid in much cheaper here, than it could be supplied from New York, provided gold or silver could be procured to purchase it. It is very difficult to keep Soldiers under proper disciplin without paying them regularly. This difficulty increases in proportion to the distance the troops are removed from their own country. The want of money frequently constrains the Commanders to have recourse to violences in providing the army with carriages, and other conveniencies, which indispose and irritate the minds of the people. We have reason to conclude that the change of sentiments, which we understand has taken place in this colony, is owing to the above mentioned cause, and to other arbitrary proceedings. If hard money cannot be procured and forwarded with dispatch to Canada, it would be adviseable, in our opinion, to withdraw our army & fortify the passes on the lakes to prevent the enemy, & the Canadians, if so inclined, from making irruptions into & depredations on our frontiers. We have given orders for

the return of Mr. Frazer to this city, and we now have under consideration the confinement of the other Gentlemen particularised in our
instructions.[1]

At Fort George we had an interview with the Deputies of the seven
Indian tribes of Canada to the great council at Onondaga. They were
on their return home from this council. They informed us that the result of their deliberations was to maintain a perfect neutrality during the
present contest: that they had received the hatchet from Colonel Guy
Johnson, but being a sharp weapon and liable to wound their bosoms,
they were resolved no longer to keep it, but to deliver it up to us. Since
our arrival in this city, we have had another conference with the same
Deputies, which terminated in a confirmation of their former promises
not yet complied with, but delayed only to give time for the assembling
of all their tribes, that the hatchet may be given up with the consent of
the whole, and with greater solemnity. We judge it expedient to make
them a small present, and we think it will be necessary to make them
another more considerable when the hatchet is deliverd up.

We are informed that our debts in this Colony amount to ten thousand
pounds, exclusive of what is due to Mr. Price. We have hitherto obtained
a list amounting only to between three & four thousand. It will be
necessary to appoint persons to settle these accounts.

With great respect to Yourself & the Congress we have the honour
to be, Sir, Your most obedient humble Servants,

B Franklin

Samuel Chase

Charles Carroll of Carrollton

RC (DNA: PCC, item 166). In a clerical hand and signed by Carroll, Chase, and
Franklin. Endorsed: "Read May 18. Referred to Mr W Livingston, Mr Jefferson, &c."
[1] See Commissioners to Canada to Philip Schuyler, May 4, 1776.

Commissioners to Canada to Moses Hazen

Dr. Sr.[1]   Montreal 6 May 1776.

To enable you the better to Attend Your Command of St. John's &
Chambly (the first of which we think demands your immediate notice
and ought instantly to be put into some state of Defence) and that you
may afford us your Advice here, we have thought proper to appoint
your friend Mr. M'Cartney[2] to Execute the office of Deputy Quarter
Master 'till the pleasure of Congress be known.

We shall be glad to know your opinion on the propriety of Establishing 3 Magazines of Provisions at St. John's, Chambly & St. Dennis, the
first to be the principal. We wish to see you as soon as your present

Multiplicity of Business will permit. Make our respectful Compliments
to Mrs. Hazen.[3] We are, Dr. Sir, Yr. Most Obedt. Hum. Servt.

Saml. Chase

Cha. Carrol of Carrollton

Tr (NHi).

[1] Moses Hazen (1733–1803), former British officer who had retired in 1773 at
St. Johns, Quebec, had joined General Montgomery in the autumn of 1775 and
was appointed by Congress on January 22, 1776, colonel of the Second Canadian
Regiment, which he was to recruit from Canadian inhabitants and refuges. Upon
General Arnold's arrival at Montreal in late April, Hazen had been sent to take
command of Chambly and St. Johns. *DAB*; and *Am. Archives*, 4th ser. 5:1155.

[2] William McCarty, whose appointment apparently was not confirmed by Congress. See also Commissioners to Canada to John Hancock, May 17, 1776.

[3] For the commissioners' stay at the Hazen home April 27–28, see the *Journal of Charles Carroll*, pp. 90–91.

Commissioners to Canada to Philip Schuyler

Dr. Sir   Montreal May 6th. 1776.

General Arnold thinking the publick interest would be better promoted by appointing Colonel Hazen to command at St. John's and
Chambly, in the room of Colonel Buel, has ordered the latter to repair
to the Camp before Quebeck, where the General is of opinion his services
will be more wanted. Colonel Hazen speaking the French language, and
having a considerable influence over the people in the neighbourhood
of S. John's & Chambly, and being as active and zealous in the service,
and as intelligent as Colonel Buel, induced us to concur with Genl.
Arnold in approving the appointment of Colonel Hazen. As we are
convinced that you wish only, and seek how best to promote the publick
service, so are we satisfied that this arrangement will meet with your
approbation. We are informed by General Arnold that the army before
Quebeck is only victualled up to the 15th or 20th inst. at farthest. We
need not point out to you the necessity of keeping our forces in this
country well supplied with provisions, as, excepting flower, none can be
procured here, and that not without hard money. The army is entirely
without surgeons: Dr. Stringer receives 30s a day. His assistance is much
wanted at the Camp & the Congress, no doubt, expects, when they pay
for services, to have them performed. We desire to be respectfully remembered to your family, and are with great esteem, Dr. Sir, Yr. most
obedt. humble servants,   B Franklin

Samuel Chase

Ch. Carroll of Carrollton

RC (NN). In a clerical hand and signed by Carroll, Chase, and Franklin.

James Duane to
the New York Provincial Congress

Gentlemen   [c. May 6, 1776] [1]
We are really concern'd at the Contents of your favour of the 24t
Instant. Ever since the Emission of Continental money we had it in
our power to keep our Convention fully supplied with money to answer
every Service which might be requested from them by Congress. Nothing
was expected, on their part, but to render their accounts in reasonable
periods, & it is to be lamented that from their Extensiveness this difficulty
has hitherto proved insurmountable. The Congress conceive it an indispensable Duty to adjust the publick Accounts, and to call upon all
who have been intrusted with the Expenditure of the continental money.
Massachusetts and Connecticut have brought in theirs but not till after
a Neglect had been complaind of or rather become the Subject of Ani-
madversion, on which occasion the Remisness of our own Colony was
not forgotten. You are not however to ascribe such Reflections to a
Spirit of Jealousy or Distrust; but to a Desire that the publick Accounts
may not run into Confusion, and a Settlement of them be attended with
insuperable Difficulties. Under these Circumstances we dare not venture to ask for a further Advance to our Convention untill we receive
their Accounts of the past Expenditures. Especially as it is not long since
that a similar Request in behalf óf Connecticut was rejected, and the
payment deferred till the Accounts were produced. [2]
We hope these matters were fully explain by Mr Clinton in his
way home; and only repeat them least by some Incident he may have
been deprived of the pleasure of seeing you.
300,000 Dollars have been sent to General Washington since the
Army arrived at New York. We shoud suppose that he woud repay you
what you have advanced for these Troops. General Schuyler has likewise receivd a Remittance from Congress of the like Sum to support
the Army in Canada; and We presume he woud reimburse what you
may have furnished for that service. [3] The Production of the Accounts
woud however be the shortest Road to the money. The Congress have
established a Board of Treasury under the direction of three Superintendents who are instructed to call upon all publick Bodies & officers
as well as private persons who have been Entrusted with publick money
to settle their Accounts. Your Convention will hear from them soon as
circular Letters are now preparing at the office. [4]
I am for Mr Jay & self, Gent., Your most Obedient, huml Servt.,
                                                Jas. Duane

FC (NHi).
[1] This date has been conjectured because the first of the circular letters "now

preparing" at the Board of Treasury, to which Duane refers at the conclusion of this letter, was sent on May 7. It seems improbable that this letter was written in April, although Duane does identify the provincial congress' letter of April 24, now lost, as "your favour of the 24t Instant."

[2] On this point, see *JCC*, 4:180, 188, 272; Richard Smith's Diary, January 13, note 2; and Oliver Wolcott to Thomas Seymour, April 16, 1776, note 2.

[3] For the appropriation of these sums to Schuyler and Washington, see *JCC*, 4:261, 263, 301.

[4] See Board of Treasury to Certain Colonies, May 7, 1776.

Richard Henry Lee to Samuel Purviance, Jr.

Dear Sir,   Philadelphia May 6th 1776

I received yesterday your favor of the 2d instant, and in answer to that part of it desiring to know if Mr. Hancock gave a copy of your letter to any person I must say that I do not know whether or not, but I am inclined to think he has not.[1] This business appears to me thus. When Mr. Hancock received the dispatches from Baltimore, he proceeded to read the whole in Congress, and among others, a letter containing observations on the Council of Safety of Maryland, relative to the timidity of their Councils; which it appears he had not previously read in private, because, when he came to that part of it which mentioned its being written in confidence, he stopt, and observed it was private, and proposed it should be so considered; but as he had read so much of it, he went on but read no name at the bottom, & in the debate consequent upon it 'twas supposed to be anonymous, and it was conjecture alone that fixed you as the Author. I should have certainly informed you of this if I had then found myself at liberty to do it, and when I heard from you of your summons before the Council, it was too late for a letter to reach you before your appearance at that board. But the idea of drawing from the mouth of a person accused his own condemnation is reprobated by English jurisprudence, and is the practise only of inquisitorial or Star chamber Tyranny. I should incline to think that this persecution will be carried no further; at least I am sure the time is quickly coming when violence from without will render absolutely necessary a perfect union within. A late arrival from Port L'Orient with 13 tons of powder & 30 of Salt petre brings us a Cork paper near the middle of March, by which we learn that more than 40,000 men would sail from Portsmouth & Grenoch about the 1st of April for N. America. They consist of Hessians, Hanoverians, Mechlenburghers, Scotch Hollanders, & Scotch Highlanders, with some British Regiments. Their destination not certain, but said to be N. York, New England, Canada, & 2 expeditions more South. Should the persecution go on against you, I would advise answering no interrogatories, but plainly detail my conduct, acknowledge such parts as were without the strict line of duty, and lay it to the account of my zeal for the cause of America, which I hoped a generous community would pardon and forget.

My time and attention is so taken up with public business, that I must now conclude with referring you to my letter by Dr. Bankhead.[2]

I am, with regard, Sir your friend and obedient servant,

Richard Henry Lee

RC (MdHi).
[1] See John Hancock to the Baltimore Committee, April 16, 1776, note.
[2] See Lee to Purviance, May 1, 1776.

William Whipple to Joseph Whipple

My Dear Bror.   Philadelphia 6th May 1776

I have received Yours of 9th, also of the 20 Ulto. You'll excuse my not writing oftener for besides my great dislike to writing, I have but very little time. There has been no opportunity of shiping any thing for any part of New-England, for some time past, if there had been the articles you mention are near as high here as with you & no insurance to be obtain'd. There has been a 40 Gun ship at the cape, for 6 weeks past and lately join'd by two other men of war who take many homeward bound vessels, however many vessels do go out espetially the arm'd vessels of which there is several besides the Continental vessels. Of the latter there is a very fast sailing Brig. of 16 4 Pounders cruising between the Capes of Vergeinia & N. York has taken only one prize yet a ship of 16 six pounders & 120 men now in the river outward bound. One sloop of 10 Guns, another of 8 & a schooner of 6 will be ready to sail in a day or two, these small vessels are to clear the coast of the paratical tenders. In order to clear up your doubts about these vessels geting out I will endeavor to discribe the scituation of Delaware Bay. The two Capes viz Cape May & Cape Henlopen are 7 leagues apart, between these two Capes, is a shoal that will take up a very small vessel; the ship Chanel is between this shoal & Cape Henlopen; there is also a chanel under Cape May, where our vessels go in & out; in this chanel is only 10 or 12 feet Water. The British Man of Warr boats are not suffered to land on any pretence whatever, the shores being well guarded & the People spirited.

You mention the appointment of B. De Woodlke. I think your observation very just with regard to Strangers. To satisfy you as to this Gentn, He is a Prussion, has had a distinguished Command in that monack's service but on some occation has fallen out with Royalty, Retired from his own country to France, from whence he comes highly recommended by Gentn. of distinguishd Characters, & known integrity.

He understands the French & other languages, is therefore sent to Canada with the Command of Brigadier Genl.

I don't wonder at your anxiety to know the disposition of Congress Respecting the most important Question before them. I shod be happy was it in my power to satisfy you on this head, but it is not. Thus much I'll tell you *under the Rose*. The four Northern Colonies are perfectly united, South Carolina have taken a form of Government, North Carolina are doing the same (the Convention of the latter have unanimously declard for Independency), I dayly expect to hear Verginia has done the same, New-Jersey will undoubtedly follow the example, there is but very little doubt of N. York, The Propriety Colos are coming over with great Rapidity. From this state of matters you may judge the day is not far distant when there will be such a Power, as the *free & Independent states of America*. You'll say delays are dangerous, I acknowledge they are big with many evils, and that the continent have been 6 months too late in all their movements, but there is now a fair prospect of surmounting every difficulty; our affairs in Canada have not been so successful as I cod. wish, this is owing to delay! However that expedition is now going on with more spirit. 10 Regiments have been order'd from N. York, 4 of which have been gone about a fortnight; the remaining 6 are by this time on their march. These ten Regiments in addition to what was before order'd there, will make a very Formidable Army in that Country.[1] Genl. Thomas is at Quebeck before this time with a number of Heavy Cannon and a full supply of Amunition of which they have been in great want. The Commissioners are also there e'er now. The southern Department in all probability will be the seat of war this summer, this plan will be consistant with the wisdom of the British Court, that is: consistant with all their other plans respecting America. The Climate will no doubt kill more then the sword. May the supreme director of all events ever afford them a Hushai to direct their Counsels.

I shall endeavor to follow your directions respecting the Cooper, Miller, &c, but think it will be difficult at this time to engage laborers of any sort, as every body seems ingaged in the war. I am glad you turn your attention to the Culture of Hemp & flax, those articles must certainly be in great demand. Flax is sold here at 2/6 & no doubt those articles must be very high during the war & will always be in demand, I know of nothing you can raise will bare the expence of transportation so well. If I can't engage you a man for this season shall endeavor to get one for the next. You dont tel me how you found matters at Dartmo. but you intimate you shall carry Mrs. W[hipple] up, I shall long to hear from you perticularly after she gets there. I intend to take a Ride when my Colleague returns & shall make the inqueiries you mention.

Several parcels of Powder have arrivd within a month & we have great reason to fear, many vessels with powder, have been taken, some we know have, however there is no danger of wanting that article. The Mills are at work. I have visited one about 5 miles from this city that makes 22 hundred weight per week. There are two other mills in this Province, several in N. York, some in Connecticut &c. Cannon we are also making. I make no doubt we shall be able to supply foreign states with those articles in a short time, that is, in a few years. News is this minute Brot. me the Brig. Lexington is come up having sprung her foremast. She was chas'd by two Frigates this day week in Latitude 34. They were part of a fleet of 17 sail who by the Course they stear'd were bound for Verginia or Carolina; suppose have on board the troops that have been some time expected from Europe or those that were in the West Indies but there is no certainty. I this moment hear of the arrival of a vessel from France; must go out to learn the perticulars.[2]

She is from port Le Oreint in 5 weeks with 13 Tons Powder & 20 Tons Salt Petre for accot. of the United Colonies. She brings a paper from Ireland of the 2d March which I have not yet seen, some extracts from it will be immediately publish'd in a hand Bill which I shall inclose if I can get it seasonably. There is a report that the three ships that have been some time at the Cape are coming up the River. I Heartily wish it may be true.

Your very affte Bror, Wm. Whipple

RC (MH).
[1] Oliver Wolcott also commented on the reinforcements ordered to Canada in a letter written this day from Philadelphia, which he probably addressed to Andrew Adams. The following extracts and summary of the letter were printed in a sale catalog of autograph manuscripts. " '*The Evacuation of Boston by the British Troops was an important Event. I wish they might not be equally troublesome in Canada. Ten Batallions from G. Washington's Army are going into that Country. I pray God they may be poss'd of Quebec before the British Troops get there.*' After discussing various measures before Congress, he comments on conditions in Philadelphia and New York, and proceeds: '*Carolina has, you perceive a Modle of Government, the form has not come here. I understand their Assembly is much incensed, etc. The heterogeneous carrying on in the Statehouse in this City will give you an Idea of this Colony, a House of Assembly seting and by themselves raising Men, Arming Vessels and, in short, laying themselves out large in providing defence against British Troops—this same Assembly so far approv'd of by the Gov'r that he gives his Assent to their Bills except in matters of Warr which are not offered him, a Judge of Admiralty condemning the King's Ships; an Executive Court carrying on all business in the King's name—N. York is much the same,*' etc." George D. Smith Catalogue of Autographs, no. 172 (1912–13), item 498.
[2] A sloop, fitted out at Continental expense by Francis Lewis and John Alsop and commanded by Capt. John Young of New York, arrived in Philadelphia on May 5. JCC, 4:328. See also Clark, Naval Documents, 4:1415, 1441.

Board of Treasury to Certain Colonies

Treasury Office Philadelphia May 7th. 1776

Honourable Gentlemen.

We inclose to you the resolutions of Congress passed the 26th De-

cember 1775 and 17th February following, and have to request your
Honourable House will cause the number of Inhabitants of your Colony
to be taken and transmitted to this Office, conformable to the directions
laid down in the first mentioned resolve.[1]

I have the Honour to be in the Name of the superintendants of the
Treasury, Honourable Gentlemen, Your most Obedient, Humble
servant,   Jas. Duane, Chairman

RC (DLC). In a clerical hand and signed by Duane. Addressed: "To the Honble
the Convention of New Hampshire." This day Duane also sent the same letter to
the conventions of Maryland, New Jersey, and New York as well as to the assembly
of Rhode Island, texts of which are located respectively in Red Books, MdAA;
Myers Collection, NN; *Journals of N. Y. Prov. Cong.*, 1:451; and Red Series, R-Ar.
On May 9 he sent out additional copies of this letter in circular form, addressed
"To the Assembly of . . ." and presumably intended for the provinces which he had
not written to on May 7. *Am. Archives*, 4th ser. 6:395.

[1] The resolution of December 26 called upon each colony to provide Congress
with an accurate census of its population so that Congress could determine its share
of Continental bills of credit; those of February 17 set forth the duties of the Board
of Treasury. *JCC*, 3:458, 4:156. For the background and subsequent history of this
board, see Jennings B. Sanders, *Evolution of the Executive Departments of the Continental
Congress, 1774–1789* (Chapel Hill: University of North Carolina Press, 1935), pp.
50–64; and Edward Forbes Robinson, "Continental Treasury Administration, 1775–
1781: A Study in the Financial History of the American Revolution" (Ph.D. diss.,
University of Wisconsin, 1969), pp. 45–65, 121–26.

Board of Treasury to
the Colonies, Commissaries, and Paymasters

Sir.   Treasury Office Philadelphia May 7th. 1776.
The Congress having on the 17th February last appointed a standing
Committee for superintending the Treasury, and on the first April
following among other things Resolved "That all Assemblies, Conventions, Councils and Committees of safety, Commissaries, Paymasters
and others intrusted with public Monies, should within a reasonable
time after being called upon for that purpose by the Committee of the
Treasury, produce their Accounts and Vouchers at the Treasury Office,
in order to their being settled and adjusted," We are in pursuance of the
said Regulations to request that you Sir will be pleased to render an
account of the expenditure of the Continental Monies, which by the
Acts of Congress have passed through your hands, with the proper
Vouchers, that the same may be settled and adjusted here, and reported
for the final allowance of Congress.[1] I am in the Names of the superintendants of the Treasury, Sir, Your most humble servant.
                                             Jas. Duane, Chairman

RC (R-Ar). In a clerical hand and signed by Duane. Addressed: "To the Honble. the General Assembly of Rhode Island." Texts of the same letter, addressed to the Massachusetts Assembly, the New Hampshire and New York conventions, Connecticut governor Jonathan Trumbull, Sr., and to Commissary General Joseph Trumbull, are located respectively in Revolutionary Letters, M-Ar; Force Papers, DLC; *Journals of N.Y. Prov. Cong.*, 1:451; and Jonathan Trumbull Papers and Joseph Trumbull Papers, CtHi.

[1] See *JCC*, 4:245.

Board of Treasury to
the New York Committee of Safety

Treasury Office, Philadelphia, May 7th, 1776.

Honourable Gentlemen,

Captn. Heman Allen's account of disbursements as captain of a company in Colonel Warren's [Warner's] battalion,[1] is now under examination in this office. He informs us that he could not settle it with your honourable body to his satisfaction, nor are we able without some information to state it in a clear light to Congress. We, therefore, request that you will be pleased to let us know what allowances you have made to the New-York battalions, and the reason why Captain Allen's claim was in part rejected.[2]

I have the honour to be, in the name of the superintendents of the treasury, Honourable gentlemen, Your most obedient humble servant,

Jas. Duane, Chairman.

MS not found; reprinted from *Journals of N.Y. Prov. Cong.*, 1:452.

[1] Heman Allen, brother of Ethan Allen and a captain in Seth Warner's battalion of Green Mountain Boys, appears in volumes four and five of the journals of Congress as Herman Allen.

[2] Captain Allen's memorial having been read in Congress and referred to the committee on claims on May 6, Congress decided on May 24 to allow Allen "for sundry disbursements for the use of his company . . . three hundred and sixty dollars, over and above the account allowed by the New York convention, amounting to two hundred and forty pounds eighteen shillings, New York money." *JCC*, 4:328, 339, 385. The New York Provincial Congress, which received this letter instead of the committee of safety, referred it to its "pay table committee," but the committee's action was not recorded in the journals of the congress. *Journals of N.Y. Prov. Cong.*, 1:452.

John Hancock to Esek Hopkins

Sir,   In Congress May 7. 1776

The Congress having by the foregoing resolve[1] agreed to lend twenty of the heaviest cannon taken at Providence & carried to Rhode Island,

638 MAY 7, 1776

to the Committee of safety of Pensylvania for the defence of this City I have to desire you will immediately deliver the same to the person or persons whom the sd. Committee sent to receive & bring them hither.[2]

I am, Sr, Your humble servt,[3]   John Hancock, Presidt

RC (CSmH). In the hand of Charles Thomson and signed by Hancock. Addressed: "To Commodore Es. Hopkins, or in his Absence, to Daniel Tillinghast Esqr."

[1] Thomson wrote this letter underneath a resolve extracted from the minutes of Congress for this day. See *JCC*, 4:333.

[2] On May 11 the Pennsylvania Committee of Safety appointed Levi Hollingsworth and Thomas Richardson to go to New London or to Newport for these cannon. Hollingsworth and Richardson informed Commodore Hopkins of their mission, which Hopkins explained to the Rhode Island Assembly and Council on May 20. The Rhode Islanders responded by sending Congress a memorial stating that the cannon were needed for the defense of Newport and claiming that since Hopkins had delivered more cannon to New London than was required for its defense perhaps Connecticut could send spare cannon to Pennsylvania. This memorial, supported by a May 22 letter to Hancock from Hopkins, himself a native of Rhode Island, led Congress on May 30 to direct that six heavy cannon from Newport and fourteen from New London be sent to Philadelphia. In the meantime, however, Hopkins had sent Hollingsworth and Richardson to Connecticut's governor Jonathan Trumbull with an order to provide 20 heavy cannon. Trumbull indignantly refused to comply with it because of his conviction that these cannon were necessary for the defense of New London as well as because Samuel Huntington, then "Passing thro this Town [*Hartford*] from Congress," advised him that Hopkins was under instructions to send the cannon at Newport. In response to Congress' May 30 resolution, however, Trumbull reluctantly agreed to send six heavy cannon to Philadelphia, while Rhode Island, for its part, also sent six. See *JCC*, 4:406; and Clark, *Naval Documents*, 5:50–51, 165–67, 185–86, 199, 270–71, 320, 510, 527, 587–89, 707–8, 1056–57.

[3] This day Hancock also wrote brief letters to Washington and to the Massachusetts Council, merely for the purpose of enclosing a resolution of Congress. PCC, item 12A; and *Am. Archives*, 4th ser. 5:1227–28. Although not identified, it was probably the resolution of May 4 concerning the disposition of "cannon, and other stores" in Boston. *JCC*, 4:327.

William Whipple to John Langdon

My Dear Sir,   Philadelphia 7th May 1776

Yours of 22 ulto is now before me, the greatest part of which is answered in my last. I dont much admire the nomination of the first Lieutenant—I think him too unsteady to be depended on. I shall expect a list from you by next post agreeable to my request which I suppose you must have rec'd some time ago. I now enclose you the Resolves of Congress respecting Privateers, captures &c.—they did not come out till to day.[1] You'll find the pay of the officers in the Navy—but in that there will be considerable alterations. The petty officers will I believe be considerably lowered and I shall do my endeavors to raise the Captain—that is, for the new frigates; there is a Committee chosen by the Marine Committee for that purpose. If you should engage any petty or warrant officer, it will be best not to mention their pay till you hear farther. You will have the appointment of all except the Capt, Lieuts, Master, Surgeon, Capt & Lt of Marines; these must be recommended to congress. No doubt you must have English colors for the ship. Your ship is a forward of those building here. The Lexington returned yesterday from a cruise having sprung her foremast; a week ago she fell in with a fleet of 17 sail, was chased by two frigates from the fleet; it's supposed they were bound for Virginia or Carolina but it's altogether uncertain—they may be the fleet from the West Indies bound to Boston. Yesterday also arrived a vessel from France at Egg Harbor with 13 tons powder and 20 of salt petre. The enclosed from Capt Flagg was left in a tavern in the State you now find it. It's of so old a date that I suppose it will afford you no information. The vessel above mentioned from France brings a Dublin paper of the 2d March—extracts of which you have enclosed. In haste, yours,   Wm Whipple

Tr (DLC).
¹ See *JCC*, 6:1119–20.

Commissioners to Canada to John Hancock

Sir   Montreal May 8th 1776

With this You will receive Copies of our two preceding Letters. We find Ourselves obliged to repeat the Necessity of sending immediately the Supply of hard Money therein mentioned. We have tried in vain to borrow some here for the immediate Occasions of the Army, either on the public or our own private Credit. We cannot even sell Sterling Bills of Exchange which some of Us have offered to draw. It seems it had been expected, and given out by our Friends, that We should bring Money with Us. The Disappointment has discouraged every Body, and established an Opinion that none is to be had, or that the Congress has not Credit enough in their own Colonies to procure it. Many of our Friends are drained dry, others say they are so, fearing perhaps We shall never be able to re-imburse them. They show Us long Accounts, no part of which we are able to discharge, of the Supplies they have furnished to our Army, and declare that they have borrowed and taken up on Credit so long for our Services that they can now be trusted no longer even for what they want themselves. The Tories will not trust Us a Farthing, and some who perhaps wish Us well, conceiving that we shall thro' our own poverty, or from superior Force be soon obliged to abandon the Country, are afraid to have any Dealings with Us, least they should hereafter be called to Account for Abetting our Cause.

Our Enemies take the advantage of this Distress, to make Us look contemptible in the Eyes of the Canadians, who have been provoked by the Violences of our Military in Exacting provisions and services from them, without Pay; a Conduct towards a people, who suffered Us to enter their Country as Friends, that the most urgent Necessity can scarce excuse, since it has contributed much to the Changing their good Dispositions towards Us into Enmity, makes them wish our Departure; and accordingly we have daily Intimations of Plots hatching and Insurrections intended for Expelling Us, on the first News of the Arrival of a British Army. You will see from hence that your Commissioners themselves are in a critical and most irksome Situation, pestered hourly with Demands great and small that they cannot answer, in a place where our Cause has a Majority of Enemies, the Garrison weak, and a greater would, without Money, increase our Difficulties. In short, if Money cannot be had to support your Army here with Honor, so as to be respected instead of being hated by the people, We repeat it as our firm and unanimous Opinion, that it is better immediately to withdraw it. The Fact before your Eyes, that the powerful British Nation cannot keep an Army in a Country where the Inhabitants are become Enemies, must convince You of the Necessity of Enabling Us immediately to make this People our Friends. Exclusive of a Sum of Money to discharge the Debts already contracted, which General Arnold informs Us amounts to 14,000 besides the Account laid before Congress by Mr. Price, a further Sum of hard Money not less than Six thousand pounds, will be necessary to re-establish our Credit in this Colony; with this Supply, and a little Success, it may be possible to regain the Affections of the People, to attach them firmly to our Cause, and induce them to accept a free Government, perhaps to enter into the Union, in which Case the Currency of our Paper Money, will We think follow as a certain Consequence.

With great Respect to Yourself and the Congress We have the Honor to be, Sir, Your Most obedt. Servants,

B Franklin

Samuel Chase

Charles Carroll of Carrollton

RC (DNA: PCC, item 166). Written by Chase and signed by Chase, Carroll, and Franklin. Received and read in Congress on May 18. *JCC*, 4:362.

Marine Committee to John Barry

Sir   Philada. May 8th. 1776
You are hereby directed to Collect your officers & Men and repair

down to the Provincial Armed Ship, Capt Reed, and Supply him with as many of your People as he may want to completely Man that Ship fit for Immediate action.[1] You will also Spare any of them that may be wanted onboard the Floating Battery, or onboard the Ship Reprisal and in short We expect the utmost exertions from you, your officers & Men in defending the Pass at Fort Island, and to prevent their coming up to this City, also that you will assist in taking, Sinking, & destroying the Enemy if it is thought adviseable to pursue them of which the Committee of this Board[2] now down the River will judge.

By order of the Marine Committee   Robt Morris, Vice Prest

P.S. You may go down in the Sloop Hornet, Capt Hallock.[3] Capt Thos Read by Special Commission is the Commander at the Chevaux de Frize.

RC (PHC). Written and signed by Morris.

[1] Pennsylvania's provincial fleet, commanded by Capt. Thomas Read, was preparing to engage the *Roebuck* and its flotilla, reportedly sailing up the Delaware toward Philadelphia. Barry's orders probably were given in response to Read's desperate requests for additional men and ammunition. Clark, *Naval Documents*, 4:1465. For contemporary accounts of the ensuing naval encounter that took place near Wilmington on May 8 and 9, see *Naval Documents*, 4:1466–71; 5:13–19, 36–37, 53–55. See also John W. Jackson, *The Pennsylvania Navy, 1775–1781* (New Brunswick, N.J.: Rutgers University Press, 1974), pp. 39–57.

[2] Apparently a careless and confusing reference to the Pennsylvania Committee of Safety, of which Morris was a member and which had on May 7 dispatched a subcommittee downriver to oversee activities of the provincial navy of Pennsylvania. Morris, who operated in many different capacities, was certainly writing this letter for the Marine Committee of Congress, which was the only body that could have issued such a directive to Continental Navy captain John Barry, commander of the then disabled brig *Lexington*. For the committee of safety's appointment of a subcommittee to direct operations against the *Roebuck*, see Clark, *Naval Documents*, 4:1444–45.

[3] Two days later Morris wrote a brief note on behalf of the Marine Committee to Capt. William Hallock of the *Hornet* in reply to his request for permission to return upriver for supplies. "As we don't imagine your services will now be wanted, you had best come up in order to be properly fitted, &c., but keep your people on board." Hallock's letter to the Marine Committee and the committee's response, May 10, 1776, are in *Pa. Archives*, 1st ser. 4:751–52.

Robert Morris to John Bradford

Sir.[1]   Philada. May 8th. 1776

A Committee of Congress of which I am a Member have requested me to purchase a small fast sailing Vessell of about 80 to 100 Tons Burthen, either at Boston, Salem, Marblehead or Cape-Ann, whichever there is least danger of her being blocked up at, by our Enemies Cruizers; and Our Worthy President Mr Hancock having recommended you as a proper person to be employed in this business, It is with pleasure I embrace the Occasion of telling you that my own personal knowledge of you in Jamaica [. . .] 1757 has also added weight to the recommendation as I had then some little opportunity of knowing your merit. Therefore on receipt of this letter I request you will look out for the fastest sailing Vessell you can hear of, about the Burthen of 80 to 100 Tons. She is intended to Cross the Atlantic and of course a double Deck'd Brigt would be the best, but if such cannot be had, you must get the most suitable you can find. We dont on this occasion seek for a Vessell of Burthen, it is a fast sailer we want as the principal object is to go & come safe. I know you are an excellent Judge and have no doubt you will procure one to our wishes. You will doubtless purchase her on the best terms in your power, let her have a clean bottom, be well fitted and sound, particularly with plenty of good Sails, this done you'l please to buy on the best terms in your power as much good dry Cod Fish Oil, Whale Bone, Pott Ash, Bees Wax or any other Articles suitable for the markets in the Bay of Biscay as will put said Vessell in a good Set of Ballast but no more. The more the Cargo is assorted the better and the more valueable the better, provided the Goods are well bought and good in quality. You will please to employ a Sprightly, Active, Sensible Man that is faithfully attached to the Interest of America to go Master of this Vessell, a Man of Spirit he shoud be because we shall direct her to be .armed on the other side the Water. This business must be performed with all possible expedition and you'l please to furnish me as soon as you can with the Cost & outfit of the Vessell, an Invo & bill of Loading for the Cargo, the Masters Name and all other Circumstances that ought to be made known to the Committee. You'l please to Call this Vessell The Dispatch & keep her in readiness to sail in a few hours after orders arrive from the Committee for her to depart. I shall then also give you directions for addressing the Cargo &c. As you have Occasion for Money to carry this Order into Execution draw upon me and your drafts shall be punctually paid or if that cannot be Conveniently done I will send you Money on the first Notice & remain, sir, Your obedt hble s[ervant],[2]   Robt Morris

RC (DLC). Addressed: "To Capt John Bradford, Agent for the Continental Navy, Boston."

[1] John Bradford (1718?–1784), who had been appointed Continental prize agent at Boston on April 23, 1776. *JCC*, 4:300–301. His activities in 1776, which led to a dispute that required arbitration the following year, have been discussed at length in William Bell Clark, *George Washington's Navy* (Baton Rouge: Louisiana State University Press, 1960), pp. 151, 170–79, 203–7, 219–24. See also Adams, *Family Correspondence* (Butterfield), 2:181, 202–3.

[2] Bradford's May 30 reply, reporting his success in obtaining a suitable brig (one recently captured by Capt. John Manley) and describing goods available to make up a cargo, is in Clark, *Naval Documents*, 5:304–5.

Caesar Rodney to Thomas Rodney

Sir,   Philadelphia May the 8th 1776

I am much pleased to hear that my Battalion behaved so Well,[1] both as to their assembling and the discharge of their Duty when Met. As to those Turbulent Spirits Who would Endeavour to render the Instruments of those wise and Necessary Regulations Obnoxious to the people and would Even Sacrafice the Most Virtuous Cause any Body of men ever were Engaged in to gratifie themselves with a Seat in the House, I Detest them and their wicked designs and make no doubt but you and all real friends to Liberty will take the hint in time and by an Active persevering part disappoint them and Save Your Country from the government of All such Courtly Tyrants. If you Set about the work and are Industrious, I make no doubt of your Success.

As to Advertising the places in the papers, I Imagine it Can answer no very good purpose, as those Who are best acquainted with the Land and the advantages they have from Scituation will be likely to give most, and Such will be Sufficiently noticed without taking that Step.

Yesterday afternoon We were informed by letter from General McKenly that the Rhobuck and Nautilus Men of War then lay at New Castle, and at 3 O Clock the Same afternoon all the Gondola's left the fort and went down to Attack them, Especially if they can get them Seperate.[2] I have Sent down to Sally a pound of what is recommended to me for the best Green-Tea in the City, it Comes at 35/ beside the Canister. Tell Betsey to taste it, and if She likes it, I will Send her a pound by the next post. I Shall procure ten or twelve pounds if not more Good Bohea Tea, but must wait an opportunity by water to send that down. I Should be glad to know how Your family and mine are now Circumstanced as to that article.

I have no News of importance Except what You will find in the papers, by which you will see that our (Much Talk'd of) Comissioners are turned into Men of War and foreign Troops.

I am with much love and desire to see You all [. . . .] Yours &c.,

                            Caesar Rodney

RC (Sol Feinstone, Washington Crossing, Pa., 1976).

[1] See Thomas Rodney to Caesar Rodney, May 5, 1776, in Rodney, *Letters* (Ryden), p. 74.

[2] Robert Treat Paine noted in his diary for May 8: "The Roebuck & Liverpool being come up the River as far as Christian Creek, the Committee of Safety sent down the Gondolas to attack them & all this P.M. was firing." MHi.

William Floyd to John McKesson

Dear Sr,   [May 9, 1776] [1]
    I have this morning Recd. a letter from Thomas Everit acquainting
that he was offering to his Creditors the payment of one half Down
provided he Could have letter of licence for two years and half, if there
is no better Chance and the Creditors in General agree to it, I believe
you had as good Do it in my behalf. But I leave the matter wholly with
you to Conduct it as you would your own, and I shall be Content. Two
Men of War yesterday came up the River with some tenders and prize
vessels with them. Between Wilmington and Chester they were met by
13 Roe galleys of this place when a Battle Ensued which lasted most
all the afternoon, with very heavy firing on Both Sides. I have not
heard the Galleys have suffered any Dammage, the Roe Buck which is
the largest Ship was Obliged to Stop the Bullet holes Round her Side
and at highwater Ran aground; while the man of War was Engaged,
our vessel the (Wasp) went out of Wilmington River and Retook one
of the prize vessels. The provence Ship mounting 16 or 18 guns full
maned is gone to the Assistance of the Galleys, we have no news this
morning from them But expect every moment to hear.
    The preparations which are making By our Enemies on the other
side the water from the Intelligence we have, appeare to be very Considerable, which makes it Necessary that all the Collonies Should be in
a Situation best Calculated to Exert its whole Strength. I think it Cannot
be long before our provencial Congress will think it necessary to take
up Some more Stable form of Government than what is now Exercised
in that provence. The two Carolina's have done it, and Virginea I expect will Soon Do the Same. As to Commissioners Coming to treat of
peace we have little or no hopes of it, therefore we ought to be in a
Situation to preserve our Liberties another way. My Complements to
all friends. I am Sr. your most obedt.,   Wm Floyd

RC (MeHi).
    [1] Floyd's description of the naval engagement "yesterday. . . . Between Wilmington
and Chester" indicates that he wrote this letter on this day. See Marine Committee
to John Barry, May 8, 1776, note 1.

John Hancock to Walter Stewart

Sir,   Philadelphia, May 9th, 1776.
    The Congress having granted a passport for Mrs. Bellew to land from
the Liverpool Frigate and come up to this city under your Escort you
are hereby authorized to repair on board said Frigate with a Flagg,
and produce to Capt. Bellew the paper given you herewith and if the

permission be accepted you are to conduct the Lady to such lodgings in this city as she may desire.[1] We doubt not she will be perfectly satisfied with that politeness and attention she will meet with from you and all other persons you meet on the Journey, when it is known this is done under proper authority.

By order of Congress.   John Hancock, Presidt.

MS not found; reprinted from *The Historical Magazine*, 1st ser. 1 (August 1857): 231. Addressed: "To Capt. Walter Stewart of the 3d Battalion of Continental Troops."

[1] On or about May 9 Capt. Henry Bellew, commander of H.M.S. *Liverpool*, then cruising in Delaware Bay near Newcastle, sent a letter to Congress asking permission for one of his officers imprisoned in Pennsylvania to escort Mrs. Bellew to Marblehead, Mass., to visit relatives. Instead, Congress granted Mrs. Bellew leave on May 9 to come to Philadelphia and wait there for the arrival of some friends from Marblehead. When Captain Stewart went aboard the *Liverpool* on May 10 and informed Captain Bellew of this resolution, Bellew denounced the arrangement and refused to accept it. See Bellew's letter to Congress and Stewart's narrative of his interview with the British naval officer, ibid., pp. 231–32. See also *JCC*, 4:338–40; and Clark, *Naval Documents*, 5:242. The following month, however, Mrs. Bellew finally left for Marblehead. As John Hancock explained in a letter to his brother: "The Bearer Capt [William] Budden of this City, having been lately taken by the men of War in this River & Exchang'd, carries down to Marblehead Mrs. Belew, the wife of one of the Capts. of the Men of War, & proposes to Visit Boston. I Recommend him to your Notice and Civilities he being a Stranger; & Desire you will make his Stay in Boston as agreeable as you can." John Hancock to Ebenezer Hancock, June 18, 1776, "Copied from the original then in the possession of Mr. Stan V. Henkels," Burnett Papers, DLC.

Commissioners to Canada to John Hancock

Sir   Montreal May 10th 1776

By Col. Campbell, who arrived here early this morning from Quebeck we are informed that two men of war, two Frigates & one Tender arrived there early on Monday the 6th inst. About eleven o clock the enemy sailed out, to the number, as is supposed, of one thousand men. Our forces were so dispersed at different posts, that not more than two hundred could be collected together at Head Qrs; this small force could not resist the enemy; all our cannon, five hundred muskets, & about two hundred sick unable to come off have fallen into their hands. The retreat, or rather flight was made with the utmost precipitation and confusion; however Col. Campbell informs us, that he imagines we have lost very few men except the sick above mentioned. Genl. Thomas was last Thursday evening at De Chambeau; at a Council of war it was determined by eleven to three to retreat to the mouth of the Sorel. This day Genl. Arnold goes down here; and if he can get information of the enemy's real strength, and it should be found inconsiderable, perhaps a council of war on reconsideration, may think proper to march the army back to Dechambeau, which is now strengthened by Col. Gratton's, Burrels, & Sinclair's regiments. Besides the above losses, one batteau loaded with powder, supposed to contain thirty barrels, and an armed vessel, which the Crew were obliged to abandon, were intercepted by one of the enemy's frigates. We are afraid it will not be in our power to render our Country any farther services in this Colony. If an army should maintain possession of any considerable part of this country, it will be absolutely necessary to keep some power to controul the military.

With our respects to yourself & the Congress, we have the honour to be, Sir, Yr. most obedt. humble Servts,

B Franklin

Samuel Chase

Charles Carroll of Carrollton

RC (DNA: PCC, item 166). In a clerical hand and signed by Carroll, Chase, and Franklin. Received and read in Congress on May 18. *JCC*, 4:362.

Commissioners to Canada to Philip Schuyler

Dear Sir   Montreal May 10th, 1776 [1]
Colo. Campbell arrived here early this morning from Quebeck; he informs that five ships of war arrived there last Monday the 6th about sunrise, viz. two large ships, two frigates & a Tender. The enemy made a sally on Monday between 10 & 11 o'clock, in a body supposed not to be less than a thousand. Our forces were so dispersed that not more than two hundred could be collected at Head Quarters. In this situation a retreat was inevitable and made in the utmost precipitation & confusion with the loss of our cannon on the batteries, provisions, five hundred stand of small Arms, and a batteau load of powder going down with Colo. Allen. Colo. Campbell believes the loss of men inconsiderable, except the sick in the respective Hospitals, amounting in the whole to about two hundred so ill, as not to be removed, who have fallen into the Enemy's hand.

Our army are now on their way to the mouth of the Sorel, where they propose to make a stand. Colo. Gratton's battallion is arrived there, & we expect the residue of the Brigade under the command of Genl. Thompson is arrived before this at St. Johns. From the present appearance of things, it is very probable we shall be under the necessity of abandoning Canada, at least all, except that part which lies on the Sorel. We may certainly keep possession of St. John's till the Enemy can bring up against that post a superior force, & an artillery to besiege it.

A farther reinforcement will only increase our distress; an immediate supply of provisions from over the lakes is absolutely necessary for the preservation of the troops already in this province. As we shall be obliged to evacuate all this country, except that part of it already mentioned, no provisions can be drawn from Canada; the subsistence therefore of our army will entirely depend on the supplies it can receive, & that immediately, from Ticonderoga.

We need not mention the propriety of immediately fitting out the vessels at that place to bring over provisions & the sending off batteaus, & constructing more for drawing the troops out of Canada, should we be constrained by superior force to take that measure; and in the interim to bring them provisions. It is probable a considerable part of the batteaus now on the S. Laurence will be destroyed, or fall into the Enemy's hands. We mention this circumstance to shew the necessity of constructing more.

We can form no opinion of the force brought into Quebeck by the enemy. Col. Campbell mentions that the information received at our camp before Quebeck was that fifteen sail of ships were in the river, tho' only five were come up, as before mentioned.

We received your Favour of the 2d Instant directed to BF. We are with great respect & regard, Dear Sir, Yr. most obedt. hum. Servts.

> B Franklin
>
> Samuel Chase
>
> Ch. Carroll of Carrollton

RC (NN). In a clerical hand and signed by Carroll, Chase, and Franklin.

[1] This day Chase also directed another letter to Schuyler stating their plans to leave Canada. "Our Letter communicates to You all our Intelligence. As We can render our Country no further Services in this Colony, I beleive We shall leave this City in a little Time. I hope You will direct whether We had better go by Wood-Creek, and as We would wish to make Haste to Congress I hope Carriages will be ready. Drop a Line at Ticonderoga." Schuyler Papers, NN.

John Hancock to George Washington

Sir,   Philadelphia May 10th. 1776.

I am to acknowledge the Receipt of your several Favours of the 5th and 7th Inst. which I had the Honour of laying before Congress.[1]

By the enclosed Resolves you will perceive the Sense of Congress upon some Parts of your Letters.[2] The others are under the Consideration of different Committees. As soon as I am authorized, I will do myself the Pleasure of immediately transmitting the Result.

Congress have been pleased to appoint Col. Tuthill Major of the first New York Battalion in the Room of Major Benedict who has resigned. I have sent him his Commission.[3]

The Account of the Powder sent to the Eastward shall be forwarded agreeably to Mr. Palfrey's Application, as soon as the Secret Committee can furnish me with it.

I have thought proper to detain the Express that I may be able to inform you, whether any Arms can be procured from the Committee of Safety in this Place. The Committee, to whom that Business was referred, I expect will make their Report this Morning.

The Particulars of the Engagement in the River below this City, tho at present it is over, are so variously reported, that it is impossible to give any consistent Representation of it. It is certain however that the King's Ships have quitted their Stations, and have fallen down the River as low as Reedy Island. When the Gondolas began the Attack, they were almost as high up as Chester.

The 400,000 Dollars for the Use of the Army under your Command, shall be forwarded on Monday. I have the Honour to be, Sir, your most obedt. and very hble Serv.[4]   John Hancock Presidt.

RC (DLC). In the hand of Jacob Rush and signed by Hancock.

[1] Washington's two letters to Hancock of May 5 and one of May 7 are in PCC, item 152, 1:639–44, 657–60, 663–66; and Washington, *Writings* (Fitzpatrick), 5:13–20, 22–23.

[2] These included one resolve of May 6 concerning the treatment to be accorded British peace commissioners and several resolves of May 10 on various matters pertaining to the Continental Army. See *JCC*, 4:328, 341–42.

[3] See *JCC*, 4:326.

[4] This day Hancock also wrote a brief letter to the Massachusetts Assembly transmitting "enclosed resolutions." PCC, item 12A. Although Hancock did not describe these resolves, they were probably those of May 7 concerning the purchase of stockings for the American Army in Canada and the use of cannon from Ticonderoga in Boston. See *JCC*, 4:333–34.

Marine Committee to Esek Hopkins

Sir,   In Marine Committee Philada. 10th May 1776

You will perceive by the foregoing that Congress have order'd Twenty of the Cannon you brought from Providence to be improv'd in Philadelphia,[1] and in order that the Benefit of that order may be Realiz'd as soon as possible, we direct that you order the said Twenty Cannon to be put on board the Fly or any one other of your Vessells & Carried to New York & direct the Commander of the Vessell to Call on General Washington for his further proceeding to whom we shall write on the Subject.[2] This to be Effected in the best manner you can, but by no means to be done to the Prejudice of more essential Service. The Cannon however must be sent as speedy as possible by some Conveyance that shall be Judg'd best.

We are, Your very huml serts,

John Hancock	Joseph Hewes
Robt Morris	Saml. Huntington
R. Alexander	

RC (RHi). Written by Hancock and signed by Hancock, Alexander, Hewes, Huntington, and Morris.
[1] See John Hancock to Esek Hopkins, May 7, 1776.
[2] No letter from the committee to Washington on this subject has been found.

Commissioners to Canada to Benjamin Franklin

Dr. Sir,[1]   Montreal May 11t. 1776 [2]
    We are fully sensible of the great Risk of taking post at Dechambeau. We have suggested in Writing the Difficulties and Reasons which have occurred to us against that Measure to Genl. Arnold. Our army's remaining at Dechambeau will depend in great Measure on the Strength of the Enemy's Land Forces and their activity and Diligence in following up the Blow they have already given our small and shattered army. Before this, no Doubt General Thomas has received some Information of the Enemy's Numbers and of their Motions. We are inclined to think a Retreat will be made first to St. John's and then to the Isle aux Noix. Our Letter to General Schuyler[3] will give you all the Information we have in our power to give respecting the possibility of subsisting our army in Canada.
    We are of opinion that General Sullivan's Brigade ought to be stopped at Fort George, till General Schuyler can send over with them a sufficient Supply of pork not only for the Subsistence of that Brigade but of the Rest of the army in Canada. Flour we are in Hopes of procuring in Sufficient Quantities to support the army, at least for four Months, provided we can keep possession of the Country adjacent to the River Sorrel for the Space of three Weeks. We sincerely wish the perfect Reestablishment of your Health. Our Stay at this place is uncertain; we shall be cautious to retreat in Time to St. Johns. We understand there is but a very small garrison there and exceedingly negligent. No Centries posted in the Night. This Information we had from Mr. Price who was an Eye witness of this Negligence. Do speak to Col. Hazen about it. We are with great Esteem, Dr Sir, Your affec. humble Servants,
                                    Ch. Carroll of Carroll-Ton

                                    Samuel Chase

Tr (DLC). Apparently written in response to a letter of this date from Franklin. See Franklin to Philip Schuyler, May 12, 1776. Enclosed by Philip Schuyler in his letter of May 16 to George Washington.

¹ Franklin's separation from Chase and Carroll is explained by Carroll in his journal entry of this date. "Dr. Franklin left Montreal to-day to go to St. John's, and from thence to congress. The doctor's declining state of health, and the bad prospect of our affairs in Canada, made him take this resolution." In his entry of May 12 Carroll added: "Mr. John Carroll went to join Dr. Franklin at St. John's, from whence they sailed the 13th." *Journal of Charles Carroll*, pp. 93–94.

² Another letter of this date, directed to an unknown recipient and requesting protection for Mrs. Thomas Walker of Montreal on her trip to Philadelphia, bears the signatures of all three commissioners. It may have been written earlier in the day before Franklin left Montreal, but it seems more likely that Franklin simply added his signature after the letter reached him at St. Johns, since he was the last to sign it. Significantly, Franklin's signature appears first on all the other May 1776 letters signed by all three commissioners. Samuel Chase, Charles Carroll of Carrollton, and Benjamin Franklin to Unknown, May 11, 1776, Château de Ramezay Museum, Montreal.

³ See Commissioners to Canada to Philip Schuyler, this date.

Commissioners to Canada to Philip Schuyler

Dear Sir,   Montreal 11th May 1776

The inclosed intelligence came to hand at 2 o'clock this morning. It is impossible to procure any pork in this colony; there is none but what came over the lakes. A Schooner sails this afternoon for De Chambeau with 350 barrels of flour, and about Ten Barrels of Pork, which is the whole to be procured here. After the arrival of the Brigade under Genl. Thompson, we compute there will be about 5,000 troops in Canada. We understand this Brigade brings only ten days provision with them.

Mr. Price thinks he can procure a sufficient quantity of wheat with the bills of exchange (£ st. 3000) lodged with him by Congress; & Mr. Bondfield, with specie lent us by that Company, will endeavour to purchase some beef, but the quantity is very uncertain, and the quality will be very indifferent. Some peas may be bought, but no other vegetables of any kind can be expected.

Genl. Arnold leaves us this afternoon to go down to De Chambeau. We cannot flatter ourselves with the keeping possession of that post; the cannon which you sent, & our powder (about five tons) are at the mouth of the Sorel. We think it impracticable, indeed without maintaining our ground at Jacques Cartier, we believe it impossible. If the enemies frigates should pass the falls of Richlieu and a fair wind alone is necessary, Our army will be cut off from provisions, and a retreat by water. Retreat by land will not only be very difficult, but very dangerous, if pursued by the enemy. We are unable to express our apprehensions of the distress our army must soon be reduced to from the want of provisions and the small pox. If further reinforcements are sent without pork to victual the whole army, our Soldiers must perish, or feed on each other. Even plunder, the last resource of strong necessity, will not relieve their wants. We do not see the propriety of sending more troops, before you hear from us. We have undoubtedly a sufficient number to maintain S. John's & the Isle aux Noix. You will be pleased to communicate the present situation of our affairs, & forward the inclosed papers to Congress.[1]

We wish you a speedy restoration of your health, & every blessing of this life & remain with the most perfect esteem & regard, Dr. Sr., Yr. very affectionate & obedt. servts,   Saml Chase

Ch Carroll of Carrollton

RC (NN). In a clerical hand and signed by Carroll and Chase. Addressed to Schuyler "at Fort George."

[1] For a critical appraisal of the commissioners' impact on command decisions and American morale during the crucial days of the American retreat from Quebec in the face of the British advance of May 1776, see Justin H. Smith, *Our Struggle for the Fourteenth Colony: Canada and the American Revolution*, 2 vols. (New York: G. P. Putnam's Sons, 1907), 2:354–56; and Thomas Walker to Samuel Adams, May 30, 1776, Samuel Adams Papers, NN.

Committee for Indian Affairs to George Morgan

Sir,[1]   Philadelphia, 11th April [*i.e.* May] 1776

The congress have directed you, as you may see by the inclosed resolve,[2] to purchase, upon the best terms you can, the indian goods which they have been informed are at Fort Pitt, for the use of the colonies. The goods are designed to be distributed amongst the indians, when they come to treat with the comissioners. We doubt not you will transact this business, as well as every other belonging to your department in a proper manner. It being thought necessary to have treaty on the 20th day of July, you will be pleased to give the indians the earliest notice you can of it,[3] and make provision for their reception, and in the meantime to the utmost of your power endeavour to keep them in good temper, and prevent any hostilities on their part, assuring them of the pacific disposition of congress towards them. We wish to hear from you by every opportunity, or, if the matter be important, by express. The indian goods are supposed to be in the hands of Messrs Gratz and Symonds. We shall forward a ton of gunpowder for the use of the indians. We are, Sir, your humble servants   G. Wythe

Lewis Morris

Oliver Wolcott

RC (DLC). Written by Wythe and signed by Wythe, Morris, and Wolcott. Endorsed by Morgan: "Philada April 11th. 1776. Orders from the Commissn. Recd May 26th. 1776—this ought to have been dated May 11th. GM."

[1] George Morgan (1743–1810), Philadelphia merchant and speculator in western lands, was Indian agent for the middle department, 1776–79. *DAB.*

[2] See *JCC*, 4:346–47.

[3] See *JCC*, 4:347–48. On August 19 Congress resolved to let the commissioners of the middle department postpone the conference "to such time as they think best." *JCC*, 5:668.

James Duane to John Jay

Philad. 11 May 1776

I received, my dear Sir, your favour of the 8t Instant[1] and really feel for you in the double distress which attends you. I sincerely wish that in both Instances you may be speedily relievd by the Recovery of Persons so near and dear to you.

The Report you mention of the Arrival of Commissioners is not founded on any Authority nor Credited.[2] A Resolution has passed a Committee of the whole Congress recommending it to the Colonies to assume All the powers of Government. It waits only for a preface and will then be usherd into the world. This in Confidence as *res infecta.*[3]

A Business of still greater moment is on the Carpet.[4] You may Judge of my Situation when our Representation is so Slender. I hope my Friend Rob[5] is on the way. I will do the best I can.

The enclosd Note[6] I have just receivd from Mr Lynch. It speaks his sentiments fully with respect to the horse or rather Mare he wishes you to purchase.

The enclosd Letter I have taken up for you. I wish you'd send the Note enclosd to Mr Jones; it relates to a Sum of money he owes our Friend Dick Peters for Land.

I am with great Regard, your affect & most Obet Serv,

Jas. Duane

RC (Windsor Castle: The Royal Archives). Endorsed by Jay: "Res of Cong. recommends Colonies resume all the powers of gov."

[1] Not found.

[2] Doubtless the same "Report" as that mentioned by Robert R. Livingston in his letter of May 6 to Philip Schuyler and quoted in John Jay to Philip Schuyler, May 5, 1776, note.

[3] Congress approved a preamble drafted by John Adams for this resolution on May 15 and then ordered both to be published. See *JCC*, 4:342, 357–58; and John Adams to James Warren, May 15, 1776.

[4] Doubtless the question of independence.

[5] Robert R. Livingston.

[6] Not found.

Elbridge Gerry to William Heath

Dear sir,   Philadelphia May 11th 1776
   I have only Time to desire You (by Express now waiting) to inform
me with the Number of Cannon left at the Lines in Cambridge &c, of
those that were brot from Ticonderoga, & also of the Number brot to
New York from the Camp aforesd which were supplied by the N England
Colonies. The first if there are any left, are given by Congress to the
Colony & the latter not being charged belong to it.
   I suppose You have e'er this heard of the Repulse which the Roebuck
& another Frigate have met with by the Row Gallies in this River;[1]
nothing new Occurs excepting that Congress have passed a Resolve
recommending it to all the Colonies not having Governments competent to their exigent Circumstances to take up the same[2] & that
10 Tons of Powder are ordered from Egg Harbour to New York.[3]
10 3/4 Tons lately arrived in a Vessel belonging to Newbury Port at
Kennebeck, 18 pieces Cannon, 1/2 Ton steel, & 5 1/4 Tons Brimstone.
I hope We shall soon have agreable News from Canada & remain
sincerely sir, your Friend & very huml serv,   Elbridge Gerry

RC (MHi).
   [1] See Marine Committee to John Barry, May 8, 1776, note 1.
   [2] This resolve was passed on May 10, but its publication was delayed pending
preparation of a preamble which was passed on May 15. See *JCC*, 4:342, 357–58;
and John Adams to James Warren, May 15, 1776.
   [3] *JCC*, 4:342.

John Hancock to Joseph Trumbull

Sir   Philada. 11th May 1776
   I Rec'd your favour, and have only Time to inform you that the
Intention of Congress is to have the whole Quantity of Pork order'd
to Genl. Schuyler & Sent as fast as possible, that you will please to
pursue the purchases untill you have Compleated the whole including
the Two Thousand Barrells I lately sent you an order to purchase.[1]
Mr Livingston has wrote to Congress a Letter which does him honour,
& he will certainly have the Notice of Congress in future, he offer'd
to Resign his Contract if any Advantage would Redound to the Publick,
& Congress have Accepted his Resignation.[2] I have paid your Bill for
Ten Thousand Dollars.[3]
   I shall be ready to render you any Service, & when I may be usefull,
it will give me much pleasure to promote your Interests.
   I want from Genl Putnam or from you a particular State of the Services perform'd by the Revd Mr Leonard, I mean when he Officiated

for several Regiments previous to the Regular Establishment. When I am possess'd of that he will be recompensed.[4]

I am Sir, Your very hume Servt.   John Hancock Presidt

RC (Ct).

[1] Hancock's letter to Commissary General Joseph Trumbull of April 26, 1776, enclosing a resolution of April 24 authorizing Trumbull to purchase 2,000 barrels of pork for General Schuyler, had led Trumbull to inform Hancock on April 28 that he had already bought 4,000 barrels in accordance with an earlier order issued by Gen. Charles Lee and to request confirmation of Congress' intention to acquire an additional 2,000 barrels. See Joseph Trumbull to Hancock, April 28, 1776, in PCC, item 78, 22:21–22, and *Am. Archives*, 4th ser. 5:1112. See also Hancock to Joseph Trumbull, April 26, 1776.

[2] See Abraham Livingston to Hancock, May 8, 1776, in PCC, item 78, 14:21–22, and *Am. Archives*, 4th ser. 5:1236. For a discussion of the background of Livingston's resignation of his victualling contract with the New York Provincial Congress, see James Duane to the New York Provincial Convention, March 21, 1776, note 2.

[3] See Joseph Trumbull to Hancock, May 6, 1776, in PCC, item 78, 22:25, and *Am. Archives*, 4th ser. 5:1212.

[4] Congress voted $300 for the Rev. Abiel Leonard on August 16, 1776, "as a reward for his services." *JCC*, 5:661.

Richard Henry Lee to Charles Lee

My Dear Friend,   Philadelphia 11th May 1776.

Since I wrote you last nothing of consequence hath happened, unless it be, that the Roebuck & Liverpoole coming up the river Delaware, were met a few miles above New Castle by the 13 Gondolas of this city, and after a cannonade of 3 hours each day for two successive days, the ships returned down the river, and the Gallies to their former Station— The latter unhurt, and the former repulsed after being pretty well pepper'd with shot from 18 to 32 pounders.[1] My friendship for you is so strong, and the sense I have of the obligations America is under to you so high, that I shall ever pray the liberty of being full and free on every subject that materially concerns you. I find a spirit prevailing here, which leads its possessors to regard with a jealous eye, every instance of deviation (in a military or naval Commander) from the line of instructions, and every undertaking productive of expense which is not warranted by express order of Congress. Thus animated, I find some Gentlemen expressing dissatisfaction at your having promised forage and rations to such Cavalry as might be assembled in Virginia, & likewise because of the boats you had ordered to be built for the security of the Rivers.[2] You know my friend that the spirit of liberty is a jealous spirit, and that Senators are not always wise and candid,[3] but that frequently they are governed by envy, enmity, and a great variety of bad passions—Upon these considerations, may it not be prudent when it can be done, without danger, to the common cause previously to obtain the Consent of Congress, where much deviation from the usual routine of business is requisite, and especially where expence is created thereby. Such is the opinion entertained of you, that when you press a thing as necessary, if it is in the power of Congress, I am inclined to think a majority of that Body will readily adopt the measure. What I hear and see has induced me to say thus much—I am satisfied that *verbum sapienti sat est*—some still continue to gape for Commissioners, altho' there is no more reason to expect any than to look for virtue from a Tory, or wisdom from a fool. I fancy the Hessian, Hanoverian, & Highland Commissioners, will shortly give us a different kind of treaty from the one that has been expected. We have no very late authentic accounts from Canada, but those we have, do not remove all hope of Quebec being ours before assistance can reach it.

The Proprietary Colonies do certainly obstruct and perplex the American Machine—Those who wish delay, and want nothing done, say, let the people in the Colonies begin, we must not go before them—Tho' they well know the language in the Country to be, Let the Congress advise. In fact, the other Colonies must do what is right, and on giving proper and positive orders to their Servants in Congress, the Proprietary men will be obliged to pursue the right road. Before this reaches you I suppose the powder and medicines will be arrived, and the Blankets and shoes will quickly follow.[4] We have had 23 Tons of powder, and a good deal of Saltpetre arrived within these 10 days. Since writing the above, a french Gentleman, who appears sensible and clever, has been with us.[5] His letter is enclosed. He has been bred to Cavalry, and wishes to serve in Virginia. As a Committee of Congress has already reported against having Continental Cavalry in North Carolina, I suppose the same opinion will prevail respecting Virginia.[6] But the measure is so wise and necessary for the defence of our Colony, that I wish and hope a few squadrons will be formed on Colonial expence, in which case, this Gentleman wd answer well as an Instructor & Commander.

Farewell my dear friend,   Richard Henry Lee.

Reprinted from *NYHS Collections* 5 (1872): 24–26.

[1] See Marine Committee to John Barry, May 8, 1776, note 1.

[2] General Lee's April 19 letter to Congress and his proposal for recruiting volunteer cavalry are in *NYHS Collections* 4 (1871): 432–36. For the official response of Congress to his requests, see the resolutions of May 18, *JCC*, 4:363–65. A fragment of General Lee's response to Richard Henry and his July 1 comments to Washington on the urgency of raising cavalry are in *NYHS Collections* 5 (1872): 99–100, 102–3. A Continental cavalry regiment was not authorized until December 1776. *JCC*, 6:1025, 1045.

[3] An incomplete draft of this letter is in the Lee-Ludwell Papers, VHi, and was printed in Richard Henry Lee, *The Letters of Richard Henry Lee*, ed. James C. Ballagh, 2 vols. (New York: Macmillan Co., 1911–14), 1:189–90. At this point Lee apparently changed his mind about how to continue and therefore omitted most of the following passage from the letter he sent to General Lee. "Upon this consideration, will it

not be prudent to put it out of the power of any person to complain with justice, by a timely representation of such things as are necessary, and unless in great and most urgent cases, not to let the adoption precede the Congressional order of any measure. I am very sufficiently conscious of the thousand occasions in which the service must suffer immensely if Commanders at a distance are not to accommodate conduct to circumstances—But I know also that all men are not candid, not wise; and that some are governed frequently by envy, by enmity, and by evil designs. I would therefore carefully avoid furnishing such men with the opportunity of cavil, by obtaining the proper sanction for all such things as were extraneous to the immediate line of duty, unless, as I have before mentioned, in cases where the Distance, time and public good would not admit of delay."

[4] See *JCC*, 4:296–97, 324.
[5] Probably Caunier de la Berthaudure. See *JCC*, 4:348.
[6] See Joseph Hewes to Samuel Johnston, May 16, 1776.

Robert Treat Paine to Joseph Palmer

Philadelphia, May 11, 1776.

Not having heard from you so long, nor seen your name mentioned in a gubernatorial capacity, I am led to think either that you are unwell, or on public business abroad. I have wrote you several long letters, particularly March 7th, 16th, and April 2d and 14th,[1] some of which I fear you have not received, as they were on such practical subjects as I think you would have taken some notice of. I have laboured exceedingly to establish certain important manufactures, without which speculation would be a phantom. I think we shall not want cannon— four furnaces make them good, as large as 18 pounders; and 24 pounders have been made, but have not as yet stood proof; the manufacturers say they are sure of success. Exceeding good muskets are made here, and I suppose with you, but what comes of them I can't find out, for it is certain that a great many of our troops are unarmed, and we are not able to get arms for them. I have made great inquiries about this matter, and have been always told that every man who could work at the business was employed. I wish to know if that be the case with you, and what the price of muskets is. Our musket committee have been able to make but two contracts for making muskets, but I hope our endeavours have set others a going. The congress was appointed to promote the good of the whole, but this can't be done without knowing the circumstances of all the parts; but as I wish the salvation of my country, I know nothing of our colony but what I find out by accident. I write letters of inquiry in vain. I hope we shall be more regular in doing business for the future, or we shall need leading-strings again.

MS not found; reprinted from *New York Review and Atheneum Magazine* 2 (May 1826): 447–48.
[1] Only a portion of Paine's April 2 letter to Palmer, printed above, has been found.

Secret Committee to George Washington

Sir   Philada. May 11th. 1776

In Complyance with an order of Congress passed Yesterday,[1] We forward by the bearer hereof[2] Ten Tons of Gun Powder which Your Excellency will cause the proper officers to receive and upon this & every similar Occasion We beg the favour of a line from You or the Commissary, acknowledging the receipt of such Powder or other stores as We may send to your department.[3] We have The Honor to be, Your Excellencys Most obedt hble servts.

By Order of the Secret Committee of Congress.

Robt Morris Chair Man

RC (DLC). Written and signed by Morris.

[1] See JCC, 4:342.

[2] On behalf of the committee, Morris also wrote a brief note to Pennsylvania commissary Robert Towers this day, requesting that he "deliver to Robt. Irwin, waggon Master on order 10 tons G. Powdr. to be forwarded to his Excelly. Genl. Washington." Journal of the Secret Committee, fol. 64, MH.

[3] Washington's May 20 letter to Morris acknowledging receipt of the powder is in Washington, *Writings* (Fitzpatrick), 5:63–64.

William Whipple to John Langdon

Dear Sir   Philadelphia 11th May 1776.

Your favor of the 29th Ulto came duely to hand. I have nothing new to tell you save that there has been a little Brush here with the men of war viz. the Roebuck of 44 & the Liverpool of 28 Guns.[1] They came up as far as Wilmington last Monday & stole a pasell of Cattle from the Jersey shore. On Wednesday the 13 Gallies attack't them but keep at too great a distance. On Thursday they renew'd the attack with more vigour, & is suppos'd did the ships considerable damage. The Gallies receiv'd very little, which is very surprising as they were in reach of Grape shot several hours. They follow'd the ships as far as New Castle. These Gallies have one Gun each one of them a 32 Pounder, three 24, the rest 18. There were many Spectators from this City who all agree the Gallies behav'd with great Spirit & Resolution the second day. Its probable shall hear what damage is done the ships soon as there is a Flag gone on board to exchange some prisoners.

In great hast, Yours,   Wm. Whipple

RC (Ronald von Klaussen, state of Florida, 1975).

[1] See Marine Committee to John Barry, May 8, 1776, note 1.

William Whipple to Meshech Weare

Sir   11th May [1776]
    The Resolution of Congress respecting the Cannon that were left
in Boston by the enemy I thot necessary to transmitt to you, that if any
of those which were taken from fort William & Mary last winter are to
be found among them, they may be return'd for the security of our
Harbour.[1] I shall be exceeding glad to be inform'd what state our fortifications are in, also when the General Court setts. I have not received
a line from any body concern'd in Public affairs in New-Hampshire
since I left that Colony which is near three months. I take the Liberty
to inclose a Pamphlet intitled Thots. on Government which may afford
some useful hints.[2] You may soon Expect to hear that all the colonies
except Pensilvania & Maryland have taken up Government, & they
notwithstandg the influence of the proprietors will not be able to hold
out long. ⟨A Confederation of the Colonies is absolutely necessary to enable Congress to Conclude foreign alliances.⟩ I flatter my self shall have the Pleasure
next post of transmitting you some intresting Resolutions. In the mean
time am &c

FC (Capt. J. G. M. Stone, Annapolis, Md., 1973).
    [1] On May 4 Congress resolved to allow Massachusetts and New Hampshire to
reclaim the cannon and stores, originally purchased and provided by them, that
the British had left in Boston. JCC, 4:327.
    [2] That is, John Adams, Thoughts on Government: Applicable to the Present State of the
American Colonies (Philadelphia: John Dunlap, 1776).

Oliver Wolcott to Laura Wolcott

My Dear,   Philidelpa 11 May 1776
    I Write to you much oftner than I hear from you, but it is true my
Oppertunity of forwarding Letters are more frequent than you have.
I have had no Letter from Home since the 9t last, but I always hope
that the next post will bring one. The Natural World opens upon us with
great Beautty, while the political one is all Convulsed. When will Tyrant
Worms cease to disturb human Happiness. We may soon expect to hear
of further Arrivals of the Enimy. Your news from the Eastward is that
they are on their Way. But this can be no surprize to any one. We know
they Mean to prosecute the War. In such tempestuous Times no one
can say what the Events of Things May be. Tho I have no Apprehension
that G Britain can subjugate this Country, to give us much trouble is
douptless in her Power to do. The Enimy may Endeavour to possess
themselves of Hudsons River, if they Should Succeed in it the Post will
be less regular. I mention these Things as Possibilities and to advice

you to give yourself No Concern about them. We may Expect the Events of War will be probably Various—and a People engaged in War must not always Expect Prosperity in all their Undertakings. God has indeed in a Wonderful Manner hitherto granted us his Protection and I hope he will continue it. Possess your own Mind in Peace. Fortitude not only enables us to bear Evils, but prevents oftentimes those which would otherwise befal us. The Roman and Grecian Matrons not only bore with Magninimity the Suspentions of Fortune, but Various kinds of Adversity, with amazing Constancy. An American Lady instructed in sublimer Principles I hope will never be outdone by any of these illustrious Examples if she should be called to the Exercise of the greatest female Heroism. I do not mean that you should suppose I apprehend any personal Danger. I do not, and if I did I hope I shall never betray that Baseness as to Shrink from it, but I do think it is not unlikely We may have a trouble some summer and if so, let every one bear his part of the publick Calamity with Fortitude. By the Blessing of God I am Well. Oliver I suppose is at home. You will tell him that I have sent Homes Elements to N Haven by Mr. Jeremiah Atwater. My Love to My Children and Freinds whom may God preserve and Bless. I am with the tenderest Affection, yrs.   Oliver Wolcott

P.S. I most heartily Wished that you could have Breakfasted with Me this Morning upon some Very fine Radishes. In hast.

RC (CtHi).

John Adams to Abigail Adams

May 12. 1776

Yours of April 21. came to Hand yesterday. I send you regularly every Newspaper, and write as often as I can—but I feel more skittish about writing than I did, because since the Removal of Head Quarters to New York, We have no Expresses, and very few Individual Travellers, and the Post I am not quite confident in. However I shall write as I can.

What shall I do with my Office—I want to resign it for a Thousand Reasons.[1] Would you advise me?

There has been a gallant Battle, in Delaware River between the Gallies and two Men of War, the Roebuck and Liverpool, in which the Men of War came off second best—which has diminished, in the Minds of the People, on both sides the River, the Terror of a Man of War.

I long to hear a little of my private Affairs, yet I dread it too, because I know you must be perplexed and distress'd. I wish it was in my Power to relieve you.

It gives me great Pleasure to learn that our Rulers are at last doing something, towards the Fortification of Boston. But I am inexpressibly chagrin'd to find that the Enemy is fortifying on Georges Island. I never shall be easy untill they are compleatly driven out of that Harbour and effectually prevented from ever getting in again. As you are a Politician, and now elected into an important Office, that of Judgess of the Tory Ladies, which will give you naturally an Influence with your sex, I hope you will be instant, in season and out of season, in exhorting them to use their Influence with the Gentlemen, to fortify upon Georges Island, Lovells, Petticks [Peddocks], Long, or wherever else it is proper. Send down Fire ships and Rafts and burn to Ashes those Pirates.

I am out of all Patience with the languid, lethargic Councils of the Province, at such a critical, important Moment, puzzling their Heads about Two penny fees and Confession Bills and what not, when the Harbour of Boston was defenceless. If I was there I should storm and thunder, like Demonsthenes, or scold like a Tooth drawer.

Do ask Mr. Wybirt and Mr. Welld, and Mr. Taft to preach about it. I am ashamed, vex'd, angry to the last degree! Our People by their Torpitude have invited the Enemy to come to Boston again—and I fear they will have the Civility and Politeness to accept the Invitation.

Your Uncle has never answered my Letter.[2] Thank the Doctor. He has written me a most charming Letter, full of Intelligence, and very sensible and usefull Remarks.[3] I will pay the Debt as far as my Circumstances will admit, and as soon. But I hope my friends will not wait for regular Returns from me. I have not yet left off "pitying the fifty or sixty Men" and if My Friends knew all that I do, they would pity too.

Betcy Smith, Lazy Huzzy, has not written me a Line, a great While. I wish she was married—then she would have some Excuse. Duty to Pa. Love to all. How is the Family over against the Church?

RC (MHi); Adams, *Family Correspondence* (Butterfield), 1:406–7.

[1] Adams is undoubtedly referring to his position as chief justice of the Massachusetts Superior Court of Judicature. He had just resigned his seat on the Massachusetts Council. John Adams to James Otis, April 29, 1776.

[2] John Adams to Norton Quincy, March 30, 1776.

[3] Cotton Tufts to John Adams, April 26, 1776, printed in Adams, *Family Correspondence* (Butterfield), 1:393–96.

John Adams to James Warren

My dear Friend   May 12. 1776

Yours of Ap. 30 was handed me yesterday.[1] My Writing so seldom to you, proceeds from Necessity not Choice, I assure you. I can Sympathise with you in your ill health, because I am always unwell myself. Frail as I am, at best, I am feebler in this Climate than at home. The Air here has no Spring, and My Mind is overborn with Burdens. Many Things are to be done here and many more to think upon by day and by night. Cares come from Boston, from Canada, from twelve other Colonies, from innumerable Indian Tribes, from all Parts of Europe and the West Indies. Cares arise in this City, and in the most illustrious assembly—and Cares Spring from Colleagues. Cares enough! Dont you pity me. It would be some Comfort to be pitied. But I will Scatter them all—avaunt ye Dæmons!

An address to the Convention of Virginia has been published here as an antidote to the popular Poison in "Thoughts on Government." [2] Read it, and see the Difference of Sentiment. In New England, the "Thoughts on Government" will be disdained, because they are not popular enough. In the Southern Colonies, they will be despised and detested, because too popular.

But my Friend, between you and me, there is one Point, that I cannot give up. You must establish your Judges Salaries—as well as Commissions. Otherwise Justice will be a Proteus. Your Liberties, Lives and Fortunes will be the Sport of Winds.

I dont expect, nor indeed desire that it should be attempted to give the Governor a Negative, in our Colony—make him President, with a casting voice. Let the Militia Act remain as it is. But I hope you will make a Governor, or President in May. Congress have passed a Vote, with remarkable Unanimity for assuming Govt. in all the Colonies, which remains only for a Preamble. [3] You will see it in a few days.

It is the Fate of Men and things which do great good that they always do great Evil too. Common Sense by his crude, ignorant Notion of a Government by one assembly, will do more Mischief, in dividing the Friends of Liberty, than all the Tory Writings together. He is a keen Writer, but very ignorant of the Science of Government. I see a Writer in one of your Papers, who proposes to make an Hotch Potch of the Council and House. If this is attempted, farewell.

Who will be your Governor, or President, Bowdoin or Winthrop, or Warren. [4] Dont divide. Let the Choice be unanimous, I beg. If you divide you will Split the Province into Factions. For Gods Sake Caucass it, before Hand and agree unanimously to push for the same Man. Bowdoins splendid fortune would be a great advantage, at the Beginning. How are his Nerves and his Heart? If they will do, his Head and Fortune ought to decide in his favour.

The office of Governor of the Massachusetts Bay, surrounded as it will be with Difficulties, Perplexities, and Dangers, of every Kind, and on every side will require the clearest and coolest Head, and the firmest Steadyest Heart, the most immoveable Temper and the Profoundest Judgment, which you can find any where in the Province. He ought to have a Fortune too, and extensive Connections. I hope that Mr Bowdoins Health is such, that he will do. If not you must dispense with Fortune, and fix upon Winthrop I think. I know not where to go, for a better—unless the Major General for the old Colony,[5] can be agreed on with equal Unanimity whom I should prefer to both of the other, provided an equal Number would agree to it. For I confess, my Rule should be to vote for the Man upon whom the Majority run that the Choice might be as unanimous and respectable as possible. I dread the consequences of Electing Governors, and would avoid every appearance of and Tendency towards Party and Division, as the greatest Evil.

I have sent down a Resignation of my Seat at the Board, because this is not a Time, if ever there was or can be one for Sinecures.[6] Fill up every Place. They ought to be full. I believe I must resign the office, which the Board have assigned me for the same Reason.[7] But I shall think a little more about that and take Advice.

RC (MHi). In Adams' hand, though not signed.

[1] This letter is printed in *Warren-Adams Letters*, 1:236–38.

[2] Carter Braxton, *An Address to the Convention of the Colony and Ancient Dominion of Virginia: on the Subject of Government in general, and recommending a particular Form to their Consideration*. (Philadelphia: John Dunlap, 1776).

[3] See John Adams to James Warren, May 15, 1776.

[4] Massachusetts did not elect a governor until 1780.

[5] That is, James Warren, who lived in Plymouth.

[6] For Adams' resignation from the Massachusetts Council, see Adams to James Otis, April 29, 1776.

[7] Adams did not resign as chief justice of Massachusetts until February 10, 1777. John Adams to the Massachusetts Council, February 10, 1777.

John Adams to John Winthrop

Dear sir   May 12 [1776].

I am favoured with yours by your son, who has arrived here in good Health. I wish he may be provided for in one of the Ways you mention, because I esteem him deserving of it.[1]

The Question of Independence is so vast a Field that I have not Time to enter it, and go any Way in it. Many previous steps are necessary. The Colonies should all assume the Powers of Government in all its Branches first. They should confederate with each other, and define the Powers of Congress next. They should then, endeavour to form an alliance with some foreign State. When this is all done, a public Declaration might be made. Such a Declaration may be necessary, in order to obtain a foreign Alliance—and it should be made for that End. But Some are fearfull of making it public, if they should agree to make it.

A Recommendation has pass'd to all the Colonies to institute Governments, which will be published in a few days.[2] A Confederation will

soon be thought of.[3] Instructions against Independence and Confederation are all repealed, excepting Pensylvania and theirs will be soon.
The Colonies are about assuming Governments, and most Gentlemen
are now sensible of the Necessity of Confederation.

It is a great Satisfaction to my own Mind that it was not my fault,
that all these Things were not done Eleven Months ago. If My Country
had not suffered so severely by the Neglect, I should enjoy a Tryumph,
when I see Gentlemen every day converted to those sentiments and
Measures which I supported ten Months ago with all my poor Endeavours and they opposed with all their great Abilities. But so it is.
Mr. Dickinson himself is now an Advocate for Colony Governments,
and Continental Confederation.

I was pleased to learn by your Letter that our Colony abounded with
Materials for making Sulphur. Shǫuld be happy to know where and
what they are and how it is manufactured. Our Province must bring
this and every Thing else to perfection.

I want to know the Reason that our Courts of Justice, have not proceeded. I fear there is a disagreable Spirit among the People, but cannot
learn any particulars. I heard it hinted that the Justices had been inte-
rupted by Force in Taunten, Hampshire and Berkshire—Hope it is not
true. If it is should be glad to know the Complaints.

RC (MHi). In Adams' hand, though not signed.
    [1] See John Adams to John Winthrop, May 6, 1776, note 1.
    [2] Publication of the May 10 resolve on instituting new governments was delayed
until the adoption of a preamble, which was drafted by Adams and passed on
May 15. *JCC*, 4:342, 357–58.
    [3] A committee to prepare articles of confederation was appointed on June 12.
JCC, 5:433.

Samuel Adams to James Warren

My dear sir,   Philada May 12 1776
    I had the pleasure of receiving your very friendly Letter of the 2d
Instant by a Mr Park.[1] I can readily excuse your not writing to me so
often as I wish to receive your Letters, when I consider how much you
are engagd in the publick Affairs; and so you must be, while your Life
is spared to your Country.

I am exceedingly concernd to find by your Letter as well as those of
my other Friends, that so little Attention has been given to an Affair
of such weight, as the fortifying the Harbour of Boston. To what can
this be attributed? Is it not wise to prevent the Enemies making Use of
every Avenue, especially those which lead into the Capital of our Country. I hope that no little party Animosities can even exist much less prevail in our Councils to obstruct so necessary a Measure. Such Conten-

tions you well remember, that Fiend Hutchinson and his Confederates made it their constant Study to stir up between the Friends of the Colony in different parts of it in order to prevent their joynt Exertions for the Common Good. Let us with great Care avoid such Snares as our Enemies have heretofore laid for our Ruin, and which we have found by former Experience have provd too successfull to their wicked purposes. This will, I think, be an important Summer. I confide therefore in the Wisdom of our Colony; and that they will lay aside the Consideration of smaller Matters for the present, & bend their whole Attention to the necessary Means for the Common Safety. I hope the late Scituation of Boston since the Enemy left it, is by this time very much alterd for the better. If not, it must needs be a strong Inducement to them to reenter it; and whether we ought not by all means in our power to endeavor to prevent this, I will leave to you and others to judge.

Yesterday the Congress resolvd into a Committee of the whole to take under Consideration the Report of a former Committee appointed to consider the state of the Eastern District, which comprehends New England. It was then agreed that the Troops in Boston should be augmented to 6000. The Question now lies before Congress and will be considerd tomorrow.[2] I am inclind to think the Vote will obtain But what will avail the ordering additional Battalions if men will not inlist? Do our Countrymen want Animation at a Time when all is at Stake! Your Presses have too long been silent. What are your Committees of Correspondence about? I hear Nothing of *Circular Letters*—of *joynt Committees* &c &c. Such Methods have in times passd raisd the Spirits of the People, drawn off their Attention from *picking up pins* and directed their Views to great objects. But not having had timely Notice of the Return of this Express, I must conclude (earnestly praying for the Recovery of your Health) very affectionately, Your   S A

[*P.S.*] Congress have orderd 400,000 Dollars to be sent to the Paymaster Genl at N. Y. for the Use of the Troops there & in Massachusetts Bay.[3]

RC (MHi).
  [1] Warren's May 2 letter to Adams is in the Samuel Adams Papers, NN.
  [2] A committee to consider the "state of the eastern department" had been appointed on April 26. Its report was presented to Congress on May 10 and discussed in the committee of the whole. Congress then passed several resolutions to strengthen its forces in the eastern department on May 11, 14, and 16. *JCC*, 4:311, 344–45, 347–49, 355–56, 359–60.
  [3] See *JCC*, 4:342.

Commissioners to Canada to Benedict Arnold?

Sir,[1]   At Colo. Livingstone's, Sunday noon 12th May 1776.
We shall order the two Batteaus immediately back to Montreal, and

We desire that one of them may be at the Service of Colo. Livingston & Mr. Vanderheyden for the Conveyance of their Families to Longueil or La Prairie.

We recommend to You to take into possession, and keep under a strict Guard, all the Batteaus, & Canoes, You can lay your Hands on.

If the Inhabitants of Montreal should break their Capitulation, & molest the Garrison or any of our Friends, We wish You would instantly seize the principal Citizens, and keep them as Hostages, and if necessary convey them to the commanding officer at Laprairie. We desire You to communicate any Intelligence You may receive to Us or the officer at Longuile & Laprairie.[2]

We are Sir, Your obedt. Servts.　　Saml. Chase

Ch. Carroll of Carrollton

RC (PHi). Written by Chase and signed by Chase and Carroll.
[1] Apparently Benedict Arnold, who was at this time in command of the American forces at Montreal.
[2] For Arnold's letters to the commissioners of May 15 and 17, see *Am. Archives,* 4th ser. 6:579–81, 592–93.

Commissioners to Canada to John Thomas

Dear sir　　　　LaPrairie,[1] May 12th. 1776. 6 o'Clock P.M.

We are informed by Mr. Price that there is not water enough in Lake St. Pierre for a frigate to pass over with her Gunns & Stores. He says that there is not, even at this season of the Year when the water is highest, more than between 14 & 15 feet in the channel, which is very narrow. If this representation be just, our Gondoloe now at the Mouth of the Sorrell may perhaps prevent the enemies ships of War from coming higher up the River St Lawrence than Lake St Pierre. Fresh Provisions and Flour Mr. Price says may be had for Specie, if Authority should be exercised over those who having such provisions should refuse to part with them on the tender of a reasonable price in hard money. Mr. Price is also firmly of opinion that provisions of the aforesaid sort may be had in the Country above the Sorrell sufficient to support an Army of fifteen thousand Men above six Months. You Sir are the best Judge whether a stand may be made at the Sorrell and must certainly be well informed of the quantity of Gun powder, we now have in Canada. If our Military Stores are adequate to the defence of the part of the Country above the Sorel, and our forces should be judged capable of opposing the Enemy, of whose numbers we hope you are by this time pretty well informed, we are clearly of Opinion that the present difficulty arising from the want of Provisions may be surmounted by the Specie now in the hands of Mr. Price, or by using force if a reasonable price should be refused; We think force regulated by a proper Authority, not only justifiable in this case, but that it will prevent the horrors arising from the Licentiousness of a Starving, & of course an uncontroullable Soldiery.

It has been suggested to us by Mr. Price, that if we abandon Montreal and that side of the River from Berthier upwards, that it will be extreamly difficult to keep possession of the Country adjacent to the [Sorel] & between that river & the St Laurence even if we should [have] ten thousand Men to defend it. Mr. Price recommends the little River Berthier as the properest post to be taken on the North Side of the St. Laurence to prevent the Enemy from coming up on that side. The above intelligence and observations appear to us so material, that we have thought it adviseable to send off an express with this letter, to which we request your Answer as soon as possible.[2]

We are with great Respect, Dear sir, Your most Obt humble Servants,

Samuel Chase

Ch. Carroll of Carrollton

P.S. The Depth of water in Lake St Pierre may be ascertained by Sounding.

RC (NN). In a clerical hand and signed by Carroll and Chase.

[1] For information on the commissioners' movements on May 12–14, 1776, see *Journal of Charles Carroll*, pp. 94–96.

[2] For Thomas' response of May 15 to this letter, see *Am. Archives*, 4th ser. 6:588–89.

Benjamin Franklin to Philip Schuyler

Dear Sir   St. John's. May 12. 1776.

The enclosed from the other two Commissioners to me[1] is in answer to a few Lines I wrote them[2] from the Ferry after I had taken leave of them, and had in the meantime conversed with Mr Price, who told me the other Regiments coming into Canada brought with them 10 Days Provisions. Col. Paterson's I left at La Prairie, no boats to take them over. It was with the utmost Difficulty I got a Conveyance here, the [Canadians] being all afraid to be known to [provide us carriages?]. You will see the absolute [necessity by] the other Papers of forwarding Provisions hither. [Otherwise?] the Army must starve, plunder or surrender. I open'd the Letters to you being refer'd to them by that to me. I proceed to day having waited here 36 Hours, & now seeing no probability of the others joining me since I understand they intend only to retire when the Garrison does. With the greatest Respect I am, Dear Sir, Your most obedt hum Servt,   B Franklin

RC (NN).

[1] See Commissioners to Canada to Benjamin Franklin, May 11, 1776.

[2] Not found.

Richard Henry Lee to Edmund Pendleton

Dear Sir,   Philadelphia 12th May 1776
    Before this reaches you I hope much progress will have been made
towards the establishment of a wise and free government, without which,
neither publick or private happiness or security can long be expected.
I make no doubt but you have seen a small pamphlet published here
with the Title of "An address to the Convention of the Colony & Ancient
Dominion of Virga. on the Subject of Government &c." [1] This contemptible little Tract betrays the little Knot or Junto from whence it
proceeded. Confusion of ideas, aristocratic pride, contradictory reasoning with evident ill design, put it out of danger of doing harm, and
therefore I quit it. The difficulty we have to encounter in constructing
this fabric from whence so great good or evil may result, consists certainly in blending the three simple forms of Government in such manner
as to prevent the inordinate views of either from unduly affecting the
others, which has never been the case in Engd altho it was the professed
aim of that system. But there a fine design was spoiled in the execution.
The perogative of making Peers & Boroughs effectually destroyed the
equepoise, and presented an opportunity of applying that corruption
which has now swallowed up everything but the forms of freedom in
G.B. However imperfect the English plan was, yet our late government
in Virginia was infinitely worse. With us, 2 thirds of the Legislative, all
the executive & judiciary powers were in the same hands. In truth it
was very near a Tyranny, altho the mildness with which it was executed
under whig direction, made the evil little felt. Abridged duration, temperate revenue, and every unnecessary power withheld are potent
means of preserving integrity in public men and for securing the Community from the dangerous ambition that too often governs the human
mind. But why need I mention these things to a gentleman who knows
them so well. I have only to wish your health may enable you to attend
to this arduous business with the closeness it deserves. [2] If you consider
the nature of the funds with which the war has been hitherto carried
on, the great & growing expence of this contest and the probable prospect of its continuing for sometime longer, I suppose until G. B. has
lost all hope of regaining us, it must be evident beyond a doubt that
foreign Alliance is indispensible, and should be immediately sought.
Our Trade must be opened, which cannot be done until we get protection for our property on the water, and can induce some competent
power to undertake to trade with us. About this no time is to be lost,
and therefore I wish positive instructions on this head may be sent your
Servants in Congress soon as possible. [3] Would it not be well to appoint
Mr. President Nelson the first Governor if he wd. accept, since he possesses knowledge, experience, and has already been in a dignified
station?

The Roebuck & Liverpoole were lately met Coming up the Delaware by 13 Gondolas from this City, when after 2 engagements on two following days, of 3 hours each time, The Ships returned down the river well bored with large Cannon Shot.

We have had upwards of 20 Tons of powder & more Salt petre with several brass pieces, arrived within the last 10 days and we dayly expect to hear of the arrival of the Hessian, Hanoverian & Highl. Commissioners. I hope my Countrymen will push the Articles of Common Salt, Salt Petre, & Arms; and that all possible encouragement will be given to manufactures of every useful kind. Let a wire Mill be set up for the purpose of making "Wool & Cotton" Cord. I am inclined to think there is no better way to produce a spirit of manufactures than by offering very encouraging public rewards for the 1st, 2d & so on largest quantity of Linnen or Woolen Cloths.

FC (ViU).

¹ Written by Carter Braxton and printed by John Dunlap in Philadelphia, the pamphlet was reprinted in the *Virginia Gazette* (Dixon and Hunter), June 8 and 15, 1776. See T. R. Adams, *American Independence*, p. 151.

² Lee's interest in the formation of a new provincial government in Virginia is also indicated by an earlier Pendleton letter to him, acknowledging the receipt of *Thoughts on Government*. "From your brother Colonel Thos. L. Lee, I received by your Favor a Pamphlet on American Government for which I am much Obliged to you, as every help to the Judgment on that important Subject, is acceptable at this time, when it must be discussed." Pendleton to Lee, May 7, 1776. Edmund Pendleton, *The Letters and Papers of Edmund Pendleton, 1734–1803*, ed. David J. Mays, 2 vols. (Charlottesville: University Press of Virginia, 1967), 1:176.

³ On May 15 the Virginia Convention approved resolutions instructing their congressional delegates to propose that Congress declare the united colonies independent states and authorizing them to support measures for forming foreign alliances and establishing a confederation. *Am. Archives*, 4th ser. 6:1524. For evidence that these resolutions were the work of Pendleton, the president of the Virginia Convention, see David J. Mays, *Edmund Pendleton, 1721–1803, a Biography*, 2 vols. (Cambridge: Harvard University Press, 1952), 2:106–10. For the resolutions Richard Henry Lee introduced in Congress on June 7 in accordance with these instructions, see *JCC*, 5:425–26; and Thomas Jefferson's Notes of Debate, June 7–28, 1776.

John Adams' Notes of Debates

[May 13–15, 1776] ¹

Mr. Duane moves that the Delegation from N. York might be read.²

When We were invited by Mass. Bay to the first Congress an Objection was made to binding ourselves by Votes of Congress.

Congress ought not to determine a Point of this Sort, about instituting Government. What is it to Congress, how Justice is administered. You have no Right to pass the Resolution—any more than Parliament has.

How does it appear that no favourable Answer is likely to be given to our Petitions? Every Account of foreign Aid, is accompanied with an Account of Commissioners.

Why all this Haste? Why this Urging? Why this driving? Disputes about Independence are in all the Colonies. What is this owing to, but our Indiscretion?

I shall take the Liberty of informing my Constituents that I have not been guilty of a Breach of Trust. I do protest vs. this Piece of Mechanism, this Preamble.

If the Facts in this Preamble should prove to be true, there will not be one Voice vs. Independence.

I suppose the Votes have been numbered and there is to be a Majority.[3]

McKean. Construes the Instructions from N. York as Mr. Sherman does, and thinks this Measure the best to produce Harmony with G. Britain. There are now 2 Governments in direct Opposition to each other. Dont doubt that foreign Mercenaries are coming to destroy Us. I do think We shall loose our Liberties, Properties and Lives too, if We do not take this Step.

S. Adams. We have been favoured with a Reading of the Instructions from N. York. I am glad of it. The first Object of that Colony is no doubt the Establishment of their Rights. Our Petitions have not been heard—yet answered with Fleets and Armies and are to be answered with Mirmidons from abroad. The Gentleman from N. York, Mr. Duane, has not objected to the Preamble, but this—he has not a Right to vote for it. We cant go upon stronger Reasons, than that the King has thrown us out of his Protection. Why should We support Governments under his Authority? I wonder the People have conducted so well as they have.

Mr. Wilson. Was not present in Congress when the Resolution pass'd, to which this Preamble is proposed. I was present and one of the Committee, who reported the Advice to Mass. Bay. New Hampshire, Carolina and Virginia, had the same Advice, and with my hearty Concurrence.

The Claims of Parliament will meet with Resistance to the last Extremity. Those Colonies were Royal Governments. They could not subsist without some Government.

A Maxim, that all Government originates from the People. We are the Servants of the People sent here to act under a delegated Authority. If we exceed it, voluntarily, We deserve neither Excuse nor Justification.

Some have been put under Restraints by their Constituents. They cannot vote, without transgressing this Line. Suppose they should hereafter be called to an Account for it. This Province has not by any public Act, authorized us to vote upon this Question. This Province has done much and asked little from this Congress. The Assembly, largely increased, will [not] meet till next Monday. Will the Cause suffer much, if this Preamble is not published at this Time? If the Resolve is published without the Preamble. The Preamble contains a Reflection upon the Conduct of some People in America. It was equally irreconcileable to good Conscience Nine Months ago, to take the Oaths of Allegiance, as it is now. Two respectable Members last February, took the Oath of Allegiance in our Assembly. Why should We expose any Gentlemen to such an invidious Reflection?

In Magna Charta, there is a Clause, which authorises the People to seize the K[ing]'s Castles, and opposes his Arms when he exceeds his duty.

In this Province if that Preamble passes there will be an immediate Dissolution of every Kind of Authority. The People will be instantly in a State of Nature. Why then precipitate this Measure. Before We are prepared to build the new House, why should We pull down the old one, and expose ourselves to all the Inclemencies of the Season. [4]

R. H. Lee. Most of the Arguments apply to the Resolve and not to the Preamble.

MS (MHi); Adams, *Diary* (Butterfield), 2:238–41.

[1] Although the journals of Congress contain no reference to such debates on May 13 or 14, Adams undoubtedly made these notes after the May 13 reading of his draft preamble to the May 10 resolve for instituting new governments but before the adoption of the preamble on May 15. Assignment of these specific dates to the debates therefore rests primarily upon references to them contained in letters written by Carter Braxton and Thomas Stone a few days later. "When the Preamble was reported," Braxton noted "much heat and debate did ensue for two or three Days." See Carter Braxton to Landon Carter, May 17; and Thomas Stone to James Holly-day?, May 20, 1776. See also *JCC*, 4:342, 351, 357–58; and John Adams to James Warren, May 15, 1776.

[2] Duane's motion involved a reading of the New York delegates' credentials, adopted by the New York Convention on April 12, 1775, which instructed them to determine measures "for the restoration of harmony between Great Britain and the Colonies." See *JCC*, 2:15–16. See also James Duane to John Jay, May 16, 1776.

[3] See Carter Braxton to Landon Carter, May 17, 1776, note 3.

[4] Wilson's assertion was soon borne out by the course of events, since Congress' resolution calling for the colonies to establish new governments led to formation of a new government in Pennsylvania to replace proprietary authority, one of the primary objectives of the independents in pressing for this action in Congress. See David Hawke, *In the Midst of a Revolution* (Philadelphia: University of Pennsylvania Press, 1961), pp. 130–64; and J. Paul Selsam, *The Pennsylvania Constitution of 1776* (Philadelphia: University of Pennsylvania Press, 1936), pp. 94–145.

John Hancock to William Palfrey

Sir,   Philadelphia May 13th. 1776.
    I transmit herewith four Hundred Thousand Dollars for the Use of the Troops in New York and Massachusetts Bay, which you will please to apply accordingly. But the particular Disposition of it with Regard

to the latter of those Colonies, I am not able at present to ascertain. I will therefore lay the Matter before Congress this Day, and shall inform you by tomorrow's Post of the Result.[1]

The Money is contained in six Boxes, five large ones, and one of a smaller Size. I have committed it to the Care & Charge of Captn. Lenox and Mr. Becker, Officers in the Pennsylvania Forces in Continental Service, whom I beg Leave to recommend to your Notice and Attention.

You will please to forward me a Rect. for the Money.

I have the Honour to be, Sir, your most obedt. & very hble Sevt.

John Hancock Presidt.

[P.S.] Pray let me know whether Coll. Henry B Livingston is now at New York.

RC (MH). In the hand of Jacob Rush, with signature and postscript by Hancock.

[1] See *JCC*, 4:342. Apparently Hancock never brought up in Congress the question of the "particular Disposition" of this money. See paymaster general William Palfrey's letters to Hancock of May 19 and June 3, 1776, in *Am. Archives*, 4th ser. 6:508, 692.

John Hancock to George Washington

Sir,   Philadelphia May 13th. 1776.

I have delivered in Charge to Captn. Lenox and Co. four Hundred Thousand Dollars, contained in six Boxes, for the Use of the Troops in New York and Massachusetts Bay. The particular Disposition of it with Regard to the latter of these Colonies, I cannot at present ascertain. I will therefore lay the Matter before Congress this Day, and inform you by tomorrow's Post of the Result.

The Secret Committee have been so extremely engaged by a Multiplicity of Business, that they have not yet furnished me with the State of the Powder sent to the Eastward. In a few Days, I expect a Report will be made upon the whole of your Letters under the Consideration of Congress.[1]

The Success of the application to the Committee of Safety of this Colony for Arms, is still unknown, as no Report has been made.[2]

As soon as I have it in my Power, I shall, with the greatest Pleasure, transmit you the Resolutions of Congress upon this and all other Occasions.

I have the Honour to be, Sir, your most obedt. & very hble Servt.

John Hancock President

[P.S.] The Powder goes forward this Morning.

RC (DLC). In the hand of Jacob Rush, with signature and postscript by Hancock.

[1] See Hancock to Washington, May 16, 1776, note 1.

[2] Washington had written to Hancock on May 5 asking Congress to supply arms for his troops by borrowing from the Pennsylvania Committee of Safety and reporting that he was considering the appointment of an agent to purchase arms from private persons in the middle colonies. Congress responded on May 14 by authorizing Washington to employ such an agent but took no action on his request for arms from the committee of safety. The minutes of the committee of safety contain no mention of this subject. See *JCC*, 4:354; PCC, item 152, 1:657–60; Washington, *Writings* (Fitzpatrick), 5:18–20; and *Am. Archives*, 4th ser. 6:651–70, 1277–1300, *passim*.

Committee for Indian Affairs to George Morgan

Sir,   Philadelphia, 14 May, 1776

This day your letter of the 3d instant to the commissioners came to hand. The resolution of congress, by which you were appointed agent, and of which we doubt not you carried a copy with you, was in itself a supersedeas of captain Butler's commission. We hope he is by this time, or will soon be satisfied in the matter; colonel Wilson having written to him upon the subject.[1] The procurement of proper interpreters is referred to you. Mr John Gibson is thought to be skilful in the Delaware dialect. Accounts of your disbursements, with the vouchers, and the approbation of the commissioners, when that can be obtained, should be sent, from time to time, to congress, that they may be examined, and repaid. Wampum shall be sent by the bearer, if it can be procured in time.[2] Powder is already forwarded. A minister, school-master and gunsmith shall be provided as soon as possible.[3] In the mean time we wish you to look out for the two latter, and let us know whether they will be employed, and upon what terms. You may see by the inclosed order upon what fund and how far you may draw for the money you expend. We are, Sir, Your humble servants.

G. Wythe   Oliver Wolcott

James Wilson   Jas. Duane

RC (DLC). Written by Wythe and signed by Wythe, Duane, Wilson, and Wolcott.

[1] Wilson's letter to Richard Butler has not been found.

[2] On the cover of this letter George Wythe added the following: "Mr Morgan is desired to let the committee know if he can procure silver trinkets for the indians at Pittsburg or what of those things shall be got here."

[3] The remainder of the letter appears to have been written at a later date. Its physical appearance and content suggest that Wythe completed the letter on May 16, which was the day Morgan was authorized to draw up to $6,000 from the Indian Commissioners' account, as well as the day James Duane was appointed to the committee. *JCC*, 4:359.

Lewis Morris to Ephraim Blaine

Dear Sir   Phia. May 14th 1776

The Bearer of this will Deliver you one Ton of Powder which you will forward to Capt George Morgan at fort Pitt,[1] the wagoner Says he will take it along to Pittsburgh to Capt Morgan, you are the best judge whether it should go in a waggon or with horses, if he takes it he thinks it would be best to take out at Carlisle 300 wt, as the roads are so much worse from there. My best compliments to Mrs Blain and all friends. Your friend, and Most Hume,   Lewis Morris

RC (DLC).

[1] Ephraim Blaine (1741–1804), Pennsylvania farmer and merchant, served during 1776 as commissary to the Eighth Pennsylvania Regiment stationed in the vicinity of Carlisle, as deputy commissary general for the middle department, 1777–79, and as commissary general, 1780–82. George N. Mackenzie, ed., *Colonial Families of the United States of America . . .*, 7 vols. (1907–20; reprint ed., Baltimore: Genealogical Publishing Co., 1966), 4:49–50. For some of the difficulties encountered in delivering this powder to Pittsburgh, see John Hancock to the Cumberland County Committee, June 13, 1776, note.

Caesar Rodney to John Haslet

D Sir,   Philadelphia May the 14th 1776

I am much oblidged by the Letter received from you[1] since your departure, I happened to be dining at Mr. Hancocks in a large Company when it Came to hand Who were all much pleased to find such Attention paid by the Troops and people in General there to the Movements of the Enemy.

You will find published in the next paper of tomorrow a Matter of such importance as ought and No doubt will, Command Your serious Attention. It is no less than a Resolution of Congress Recommending it to the Assemblys or Conventions of all those Colonies (Who have not already done it) to assume Regular Government,[2] that the several Colonies may be Competent to the opposition now making, and which may tend to the good Order and well being of the people. In Short, the Absurdity of a Governor and Magistrate holding their Authority under our principal Enemy must be Evident to every one.

The Reasons, if duly weighed, must inforce the Necessaty of immediately laying the foundation of a new Government, (which may be with us similar at present to the one we now have Except as to the derivation of Authority).[3] Nothing will tend more to Ensure Success in the prosecution of the war; because there is nothing so conducive to vigour, Expedition, secrecy, and every thing advantagious in War, as a well regulated Government. Much inconvenience and detriment have been already Sustained, from the want of a proper distribution of the Civil powers. Confusion and perplexity accompany us, in almost every department; which is hurtfull to us in general, but particularly injurious to our Warlike operations. We Stand in need of a Good Executive, and may Expect our undertakings will go on much more prosperously, if we Speedily provide one.

It is impossible to tell how long the War may last; And no prudent man would choose to Trust himself long, without the Security of a regular Established Government. The Civil and Municipal Laws, for want of proper Authority to Execute them, will grow into disuse and Contempt. All the Evils of anarchy may then prevail, and the most wanton depredations be Committed. To correct these Mischiefs, and for want of Laws and Magistrates, Whose Authority is Acknowledged and Respected, recourse may be had to Military power; fatal (perhaps) to the Liberty and Safety of the people. When the people are accustomed to Irregular Government, it is Exceedingly difficult to recover them to the love of order and Obedience to those Laws which are the Essential bands of Society. Bad habits in the political, as well as the Natural Body, are Verry Easy to be acquired and verry hard to be Eradicated.

Many Arbitrary Exertions of Authority are Every day to be seen among us, which tho Justified by the present Necessaty, are Nevertheless Much to be Regretted, so far as they tend to Exhibit bad precedents, and to introduce a disorderly Spirit in the State. These things to men of penetration wear a Serious aspect, and seem Urgently to demand a speedy remedy, which is only to be found in the Establishment of a Regular Constitution. The Continuing to Swear Allegience to the power that is Cutting our throats, and attesting Jurors to keep the Secrets and try offenders against the peace of our Sovereign Lord the King, &c is Certainly absurd. However as I know all these things to be familiar to you, Shall dwell no longer on the Utility of the Measure, and turn my thoughts a little to what may (perhaps) be necessary to bring it about. In the first place will not the assembly to whom this Recommendation is, be apt to say at their next meeting, We ought to know the Sense of our Constituents? If so, would it not be best the people should make known their desire by petitions to the house Signed by them previous to the Sessions of Assembly, to prevent delay which in this Case is dangerous? Will it not be better that the Petition be fully drawn, and prefaced with the Recommend[at]ion of Congress? Will it not be Expedient for proper persons who are friends to the Cause, To Set about that work as soon as the Recommendation appears in the public papers least those who are unfriendly Should give opposition by the Same mode? Will not Doctr. Tilton who we know to be an Active patriot be one of those proper persons? I leave all those things to your Mature Consideration, but think it would be improper for those who are presently members of the Assembly to be Openly Active in the Matter; and for this Reason as I am a Member of both Congress and Assembly, hope You will nòt Communicate this to any Except my brother Tommy, Mr. Killen and Doct Tilton, or Such other person in whom you may have the fullest Confidence, not to mention it.

The Resolution before mentioned has Actually passed Congress, and as it is a Matter of the first importance think it would not be Amiss for you, Mr. Killen, Tommy & the Doctr. Tilton to have a Short private Council Composed of your four Selves only, held soon on the Occasion—Else The weaker part of mankind may be led astray by the designing. Therefore it is that I Give you this timely Notice, Tho Nothing Relative to your plans ought to transpire or be put in Execution till you see the Resolution published in the News-paper; However your usual prudence will dictate to you those and many more things.

The Colony of Rhode-Island has passed an Act Repealing an Act (which had been long Since passed) securing to the King the Allegiance of the people of that Colony. Massachusetts has done the Same.

Coll. J Mifflin[4] Came to town last night from New-York. We have no News that I think verry Matterial, out of the line of News-papers, but when there is any worth your attention it Shall be Carefully Communicated by Sir, Your Most Obedt., Humble Servt.   C

RC (MiU-C). In Rodney's hand, though not signed. The recipient is identified from references in Haslet's letter to Rodney of May 7 and in Thomas Rodney's letter of May 26. See Rodney, *Letters* (Ryden), pp. 74–75, 79–81, 84, where the letter to Haslet printed here appears under the date May 17, 1776.

[1] The May 7 letter of John Haslet (d. 1777), who had been appointed colonel of the Delaware Battalion on January 19, 1776 (*JCC*, 4:69), is in Rodney, *Letters* (Ryden), pp. 74–75.

[2] See *JCC*, 4:342, 357–58; and John Adams to James Warren, May 15, 1776.

[3] For the reaction in Delaware to the call for forming new provincial governments, see John Haslet to Caesar Rodney, May 1776, and Thomas Rodney to Caesar Rodney, May 26, 1776, in Rodney, *Letters* (Ryden), pp. 83–84, 86–88. Delaware suspended its government on June 15 and adopted a new constitution in September 1776. John A Munroe, *Federalist Delaware, 1775–1815* (New Brunswick: Rutgers University Press, 1954), p. 83.

[4] Thomas Mifflin, who, according to Christopher Marshall, "in company with his wife and attendants, arrived in town, from New York" during the afternoon of May 13. Christopher Marshall, *Extracts from the Diary of Christopher Marshall, Kept in Philadelphia and Lancaster during the American Revolution, 1774–1781*, ed. William Duane (Albany: Joel Munsell, 1877), p. 70.

Secret Committee to Philip Lacey

Sir   Philada. May 14th. 1776.

You are to put yourself under the Command of the Continental Fleet now going down the Bay and proceed down in Company with them Agreeable to such orders and Signals as they may think proper to give you.[1] You must most carefully avoid the Enemys Ships, Tenders, Boats &c. and be particularly carefull to send your Pilot or put him on board one of the Continental Armed Vessells for he must not get into the hands of our Enemys on any Account. You will take the first fair Opportunity of getting out to Sea, and then make the best of your way in the due prosecution of your Voyage Agreeable to the orders already given you.

I am, Sir, Your hble Servt. By order of the Secret Committee,

Robt Morris, Chair Man

RC (PRO: H.C.A. 32, 424). In a clerical hand and signed by Morris.

[1] Philip Lacey had recently replaced William McFadden as master of the brig *Polly*, chartered by the Secret Committee on March 26. After some delay in procuring provisions and crewmen, Lacey finally made the capes, only to be captured by the *Orpheus* on July 3. See Secret Committee Minutes of Proceedings, March 26; Robert Morris to Silas Deane, April 8 and June 6, 1776; and Clark, *Naval Documents*, 5:153–54, 901.

John Adams to Abigail Adams

May 15. 1776

Mr. Church setts off, tomorrow Morning. I have sent this Morning by Mr. William Winthrop, about half a dozen Letters containing Papers &c. Have nothing new to write.

We have been very busily engaged for 4 or 5 days in procuring Assistance for Boston.[1] Congress has at last voted three Additional Battallions for Boston and that the five old ones be filled up, and We shall send you a Major General and a Brigadier General—Gates and Mifflin I hope but cant promise.[2]

With much Pleasure I learn that, the People of Town and Country as well as the Troops are at length aroused and active to fortify Boston Harbour. I hope they will learn to make and use Fire ships and Fire Rafts.

RC (MHi). Adams, *Family Correspondence* (Butterfield), 1:409–10.

[1] See Samuel Adams to James Warren, May 12, 1776, note 2.

[2] Horatio Gates was elected major general and Thomas Mifflin brigadier general on May 16, 1776. *JCC*, 4:359. For Adams' interpretation of the significance of his support for Gates, see Adams, *Diary* (Butterfield), 3:335, 386–87.

John Adams to James Warren

May 15th. 1776

This Day the Congress has passed the most important Resolution, that ever was taken in America.[1] It is, as nearly as I can repeat it, from Memory, in these Words.

IN CONGRESS,

MAY 15, 1776.

WHEREAS his Britannic Majesty, in conjunction with the Lords and Commons of Great-Britain, has, by a late Act of Parliament, excluded the inhabitants of these United Colonies from the protection of his Crown: And whereas no answer whatever to the humble petitions of the Colonies for redress of grievances, and reconciliation with Great-Britain has been or is likely to be given; but the whole force of that kingdom, aided by foreign mercenaries, is to be exerted for the destruction of the good people of these Colonies: And whereas it appears absolutely irreconcileable to reason and good conscience, for the people of these Colonies now to take the oaths and affirmations necessary for the support of any government under the Crown of Great-Britain; and it is necessary that the exercise of every kind of authority under the said Crown should be totally suppressed, and all the powers of government exerted under the authority of the people of the Colonies for the preservation of internal peace, virtue, and good order, as well as for the defence of their lives, liberties and properties, against the hostile invasions and cruel depredations of their enemies: Therefore

RESOLVED, That it be recommended to the respective Assemblies and Conventions of the United Colonies, where no Government sufficient to the exigencies of their affairs has been hitherto established, to adopt such Government as shall in the opinion of the Representatives of the People best conduce to the happiness and safety of their Constituents in particular, and America in general.   *Extract from the Minutes,*

CHARLES THOMSON, SECRETARY.

PHILADELPHIA: Printed by JOHN DUNLAP.

Resolve on New Governments, May 10 and 15, 1776

"Whereas his Britannic Majesty, in Conjunction with the Lords and Commons of Great Britain, has, by a late Act of Parliament, excluded the Inhabitants of these united Colonies from the Protection of his Crown and Whereas No Answer whatever has been given or is likely to be given to the humble Petitions of the Colonies for Redress of their Grievances and Reconciliation with Great Britain: but on the Contrary, the whole Force of the Kingdom, aided by foreign Mercenaries, is to be exerted for our Destruction,

"And Whereas it is irreconciliable to Reason and good Conscience, for the People of these Colonies to take the oaths and affirmations, necessary for the support of any Government under the Crown of Great Britain and it is necessary that the Exercise of every Kind of Authority under the Said Crown should be totally Suppressed, and all the Powers of Government under the Authority of the People of the Colonies, exerted for the Preservation of internal Peace, Virtue and good order, as well as to defend our Lives, Liberties, and Properties, from the hostile Invasions, and cruel Depredations of our Enemies, therefore,

"Resolved that it be recommended to the several assemblies and Conventions, to institute such Forms of Government as to them shall appear necessary, to promote the Happiness of the People."

This Preamble and Resolution are ordered to be printed, and you will see them immediately in all the News Papers upon the Continent.

I Shall make no Comments, upon this important and decisive Resolution.

There remains however a great deal of Work to be done besides the Defence of the Country. A Confederation must be now pushed with all the Address, Assiduity, Prudence, Caution, and yet Fortitude and Perseverance, which those who think it necessary are possessed of. It is the most intricate, the most important, the most dangerous, and delicate Business of all. It will require Time. We must be patient.

Two or three days, We have Spent in Considering the State of the Massachusetts Bay.[2] Congress have at last voted, that the Five Battallions now in that Province be recruited to their full Complement and that three Battallions more be forthwith raised. The Province has raised one, lately as I am informed. You will have nothing to do, but return the Names of the Field officers to Congress and have continental Commissions for them. The other two Battallions may be raised in Mass. Bay, Connecticutt and New Hampshire, in what Proportions is not determined. Congress have voted that a Major General and a Brigadier General be sent to Boston. Who they will be know not—Gates and Mifflin I hope but cant promise.[3]

This Letter you may communicate if you think it necessary. I am, sir your affectionate Friend.

RC (MHi). In Adams' hand, though not signed.

[1] The resolve that Adams paraphrased in his third paragraph below was actually adopted on May 10. The preamble, which was the product of Adams' own pen, was subjected to greater criticism and passed only after vigorous, intermittent debates that probably took place on May 13, 14, and 15. See *JCC*, 4:342, 357–58; and John Adams' Notes of Debates, May 13–15, 1776. For Adams' autobiographical account of the maneuvering associated with securing adoption of this resolution and preamble, designed in part to create pressures within Pennsylvania, Maryland, and New York in behalf of independence, see Adams, *Diary* (Butterfield), 3:382–86. See also John Adams to James Warren, March 21, 1776, note 2.

[2] See Samuel Adams to James Warren, May 12, 1776, note 2.

[3] See Massachusetts Delegates to George Washington, May 16, 1776.

Samuel Adams to George Washington

Sir,   Philada. May 15 1776

It was not till the Begining of this Month that I had the Honor of receiving your Favor of the 22d of March, respecting a Proposition of Coll Baillie [Jacob Bailey] for opening a Road from Connecticutt River to Montreal. The President, soon after, laid before Congress your Letter of the 5th, a Paragraph of which referrs to the same Subject. The Resolution of Congress thereon has, I presume, before this Time been transmitted to you by him; by which it appears that they have fully concurrd with you in opinion of the Utility of the Measure proposd.[1]

I beg Leave by this opportunity to acquaint your Excellency, that the Letters I have receivd from some Gentlemen of the Colony of Massachusetts Bay express great Concern at the present defenceless State of the Town of Boston, while they are not without Apprehension of another Visit from the Enemy. They thought themselves extremely happy in your Presence there, and regretted very much the Necessity of your Departure, to which Nothing reconciles them, but their earnest Desire that the general Service may be promoted. Congress have resolvd that the five Battalions in that Colony be filled up, and new ones raisd for the Defence of the Eastern District. As two General Officers will be sent thither, it would, I am perswaded, give great Satisfaction to the People, if Generals Gates and Mifflin might be fixed upon.[2] This however, I chearfully submit to your Excellencys Judgment and Determination; being well assurd, that the Safety of that distressed City will have as full a Share of your Attention as shall be consistent with the good of the whole. I have the Honor to be, with very great Esteem and Affection, Your Excellencys most humbe servt.   Samuel Adams

FC (DLC).

[1] Congress' resolution supporting Washington's recommendation to build a road between Newbury, Vt., and Canada was passed on May 10. *JCC*, 4:342. Washington's letters of March 22 to Samuel Adams and of May 5, 1776, to John Hancock are in Washington, *Writings* (Fitzpatrick), 4:419–20, 5:14–15.

[2] See Massachusetts Delegates to George Washington, May 16, 1776.

Commissioners to Canada to John Thomas

Dear sir,   Montreal May 15th. 1776. Wednesday Noon
    We are authorized by Congress to sit and Vote as Members of Councils of War in directing fortifications & Defences to be made in this Colony, and to draw Monies to defray the Expences of the Works. General Arnold inclosed You the Opinions of a Council of War held in this City. We still retain our Opinion as to the great Importance of Jacques Cartier & De Chambault and will most chearfully concur in any Measures for securing those important posts. General Thompson and Colo. Sinclair agree with us in sentiments and We much wish that you would direct those Gentlemen to exert the utmost of their Skill and Abilities to defend those passes to the last Extreamity. We hope no Event has happened to prevent our endeavouring to maintain Possession of both those passes.
    There are very few of Colo. Sinclairs & Colo. Dehaas' Regiments who have not had the small pox and we conceive it would be most adviseable to Station those Troops and such others as have had that Disorder at the posts nearest the Enemy. We submit to You, the propriety of immediately innoculating all our Troops.
    We cannot but concur with General Arnold that by such a measure our Army in a few Weeks would be stronger and more Effective than at present.
    We cannot account for your Distress for powder. Eight Tons came with us, & We are informed that not a Ton of that powder fell into the Enemies Hands. We are sir greatly concerned for your Health; It will be almost impossible for you to escape catching the small pox & therefore wish you would immediately innoculate.
    We are favoured with your letter and immediately transmitted the Contents to Congress.[1]
    We shall always be ready to render You, our Officers and Soldiers, every Assistance in our power and we are, Dear sir, with Esteem & Respect, Your Most Obedt. servants,

                                          Ch. Carroll of Carrollton

                                          Saml. Chase

RC (MdHi). In a clerical hand and signed by Carroll and Chase.
    [1] Thomas' letter to the commissioners of May 7, which they apparently transmitted to Congress with their letter to Hancock of May 10, 1776, is in *Am. Archives*, 4th ser. 6:451–52.

Joseph Hewes to Samuel Johnston

Dear Sir   Philadelphia 15th May 1776

Having obtained a Resolution of Congress for three Tons of Powder for the use of the Continental Troops in North Carolina I now send the same in three Waggons, and enclose the receipts for it.[1] I have given the Waggoners Orders to deliver it at Halifax but if it should be found Necessary, they will proceed to any other place, they have received part of their pay here and are to have the balance when they return so that you will have nothing to pay them, unless some accident should make it Necessary. In that case please to inform me of the sum that it may be deducted when they call for the balance of their wages. I am Dear Sir, your most Obedt. hume Servant,   Joseph Hewes

N.B. The Commissary has not sent me the receipts. The powder is put into Twenty five pork barrels and contains in the whole 6052 lb, whereof 691 lb is Cannon Powder.   J. H.

RC (WHi). Addressed: "Samuel Johnston Esqr. Halifax or in his Absence to Allen Jones Esqr."
[1] This authorization had been obtained on May 7. See *JCC*, 4:332.

Stephen Hopkins to Nicholas Cooke

Sir   Philadelphia 15th May 1776.

Your favour of the 7th May I have received, and the papers inclosed in it. I observe that you have avoided giving me a direct answer to my Queries concerning Dependance or independance, however the copy of the Act of Assembly which you have sent me, together with our instructions leave me little room to doubt what is the opinion of the Colony I came from.[1] I suppose that it will not be long before the Congress will throw off all connection as well in name as in substance with Great Britain, as one thing after another seem gradually to lead them to such a step, they having, within a few days, past a resolve earnestly to recommend to all the Colonies who at present are not under a perfect form of Government to take up and form such, each Colony for themselves which I make no Doubt most of them will very soon do.

I have now the pleasure to inform you that Congress on Saturday last past a resolve for taking into Continental pay the two Rhode-Island Batallions which resolve I herewith inclose.[2]

A Letter from General Washington to Congress warmly recommending it to them to take this step respecting the Colony of Rhode-Island had great influence in procuring it to be done.[3] I could therefore wish the Colony in a handsome manner to acknowledge this favour and to return thanks to the General for his good offices in their behalf.

The affair which you mention respecting Block Island I shall take the first opportunity to lay before Congress and obtain their directions concerning it.[4] I am very glad you have given me a Colleague and am well pleased with the Gentleman whom you have appointed.[5] I am very glad to hear that the colony appeared so very unanimous in the late election, congratulate You in your choice to the office of Government and wish that every part of the Colony would forget and totally banish every kind of jealousy and discord from amongst them. This is a time when the very great danger that all America is exposed to should make every body sensible that the most firm Union in all its parts should be carefully studied and effected. I herewith send you Commissions for all the officers in your two regiments which I hope you will cause to be filled up so as to give the greatest satisfaction. As the Field Officers will be appointed or at least approved by Congress I could wish that you will transmit to me the names of such Gentlemen as you may think most capable to fill those Offices.[6]

I am with great respect, Yours and the Colony's very humble servant,

Step Hopkins

RC (R-Ar). In a clerical hand and signed by Hopkins.

[1] An extract of Rhode Island governor Nicholas Cooke's May 7 letter to Hopkins is in William R. Staples, *Rhode Island in the Continental Congress, 1765–1790* (Providence: Providence Press Co., 1870), p. 68. Enclosed with this letter was an act of the Rhode Island Assembly—"discharging the inhabitants of the Colony from allegiance to the British King," in the words of Governor Cooke—which is in John R. Bartlett, ed., *Records of the Colony of Rhode Island and Providence Plantations in New England*, 10 vols. (Providence: A. Crawford Greene, 1856–65), 7:522–26. The assembly's May 4, 1776, instructions to the Rhode Island delegates are in *JCC*, 4:353–54. Hopkins' "Queries" about independence were contained in an April 8, 1776, letter to Cooke which has not been found.

[2] See *JCC*, 4:347.

[3] See Washington's April 30 letter to Hancock, enclosing a January 15, 1776, memorial of the Rhode Island Assembly to Congress setting forth the various military and naval contributions of that province to the American war effort. PCC, item 152, 1:631–37, and *Am. Archives*, 4th ser. 5:1147–50. Governor Cooke originally sent Washington this memorial in January 1776. Washington took so long in forwarding his copy to Congress because he assumed that Cooke had already sent Congress a copy. *Am. Archives*, 4th ser. 4:797–98, 5:1147–48.

[4] On this point see Samuel Ward to Henry Ward, March 4, 1776, note 2.

[5] William Ellery, whom the Rhode Island Assembly had elected on May 4, 1776, to take the place of Samuel Ward. *JCC*, 4:353–54.

[6] The Rhode Island Assembly did not recommend field officers for these two regiments until August, and Congress did not confirm them until September 7, 1776. See Nicholas Cooke to the Rhode Island delegates, August 13 and 27, 1776, in Staples, *Rhode Island in the Continental Congress*, pp. 81–82; and *JCC*, 5:742.

Caesar Rodney to Thomas Rodney

Sir,   May the 15th 1776

I have sent you inclosed, Extracts from the Journals of the Congress Relative to the Capture and Condemnation of Prizes, and the fitting out Privateers;[1] Also the Art of making Common Salt.[2] Yrs.

Caesar Rodney

RC (NN).

[1] Probably resolutions passed on March 23 and April 2–3, 1776. See *JCC*, 4:229–32, 247–48, 251–53; 6:1119–20.

[2] See Robert Treat Paine to the Massachusetts General Court, April 15, 1776, note 1.

Secret Committee Minutes of Proceedings

May 15 [1776]

Order on the Commissary for 500 lb powder to the Delegates of the lower Counties as above.[1]

Order on Col. Tim. Matlack for one ton Saltpetre to be manufactur'd into Gunpowder at the Contl. mill under the direction of Clem Biddle.

The Chairman wrote to Messrs. Alsop, Livingston & Lewis of N. York to deliver Col. J. Ford Jr. nine bbs. Sulphr. & send us an Invoice thereof.[2] Manifest of the Salt petre & Powdr. on board the sloop Catharine, Capt. Young, as deliverd by him to the Chairman, 42048 lb Salt-Petre, 4000 muskt. powder, 21265 Cannon powder.

MS (MH).

[1] See *JCC*, 4:349.

[2] The committee's letter has not been found, but see *JCC*, 4:355.

INDEX

In this index descriptive subentries are arranged chronologically and in ascending order of the initial page reference. They may be preceded, however, by the subentry "identified" and by document subentries arranged alphabetically—diary entries, letters, notes, resolutions, and speeches. An ornament (☆) separates the subentry "identified" and document subentries from descriptive subentries. Inclusive page references are supplied for descriptive subentries; for a document, only the page on which it begins is given. Eighteenth-century printed works are indexed both by author and by short title. Other printed works are indexed when they have been cited to document a substantive point discussed in the notes, but not when cited merely as the location of a document mentioned. Delegates who attended Congress during the period covered by this volume appear in **boldface type.**

Abel, James, identified, 40

Accommodation; *see* Reconciliation

Accounts: colony, 6, 16, 90, 96, 221–22, 225, 319, 340, 346, 352, 365, 390–91, 406–7, 504, 516, 544–46, 554–55, 622–23, 631, 636; miscellaneous, 20–21, 27–28, 31, 72, 98, 150–51, 160–62, 200, 260, 342, 355, 387, 427, 463–64, 623, 636–37; mode of settlement discussed, 299; delegate, 329, 335, 608–9

Acts of trade, 67, 70, 75

Adams, Abigail Smith (Mrs. John), letters to, 226, 240, 271, 352, 392, 398, 460, 492, 511, 519, 524, 556, 572, 592, 659, 676

Adams, Andrew: identified, 429; letters to, 427, 635

Adams, Charles Francis, ed., *Familiar Letters of John Adams*, 493

Adams, Elizabeth Wells (Mrs. Samuel), letter to, 303

Adams, John: diary, 326; letters from, 55, 226, 227, 240, 242, 253, 271, 273, 274, 275, 276, 277, 347, 352, 392, 398, 399, 421, 429, 460, 461, 464, 468, 472, 479, 484, 492, 511, 512, 513, 519, 524, 525, 534, 535, 537, 546, 555, 556, 558, 569, 572, 578, 586, 592, 595, 597, 626, 659, 660, 662, 676; letters to, 93, 495, 507, 556, 567, 596, 597; memorandum, 218; notes, 260, 312, 326, 668; resolutions, 313, 420; ☆ elected to Congress, xviii; attends Congress, xviii; returns home, 6; criticized by Robert Treat Paine, 6–8, 10–12; appointed chief justice, 7, 10; supports Continental Navy, 55; resented by Silas Deane, 92; prepares draft resolutions, 218–19; arrives in Philadelphia, 219, 226; reflects on soldiering, 241; compares martial qualities of monarchies and republics, 242; encourages manufacture of military supplies, 253; prepares instructions for commissioners to Canada, 271, 298; on *Common Sense*, 271, 273, 398–99, 512; on reconciliation, 271–72, 392, 473, 538–39, 586; encourages study of French language, 272–73, 556; proposes engineering academy, 274; on importance of securing Canada, 276; praises Gen. Lee, 277; opposes motion to thank William Smith, 294; debates state of Continental Army, 295;

694 INDEX

Commissary, northern military department, jurisdiction discussed, 547, 551
Commissary general: allowance, 3, 95; pay, 4, 463; moves to New York, 547; relations with Walter Livingston, 547, 551
Commissioners to Canada: letters from, 490, 611, 612, 620, 628, 629, 630, 639, 645, 646, 649, 650, 664, 665, 680; letter to, 582; ☆ appointed, 257, 260, 263; instructions for, 271, 298, 364, 369, 412, 420, 582–83; specie for, 298; request Gen. Schuyler's assistance, 367; commission for, 412, 420; journey to Canada, 436, 442, 449–50, 517; describe Fort Constitution (Fort Lee, N.J.), 490; arrive in Montreal, 611–12; attend council of war, 611–12; on need for specie, 611, 628, 639–40; open Indian trade, 612; propose creation of bank, 612; investigate John Frazer, 620, 628–29; on need for flour, 628; on American indebtedness, 629, 640; appoint William McCarty deputy quartermaster general, 629; meet with Indians, 629; concur in Moses Hazen's appointment, 630; on futility of mission, 646; oppose sending new reinforcements, 646, 651; on need to abandon Canada, 646; ask Gen. Schuyler for supplies, 646–47, 650–51; on military strategy, 680; recommend smallpox inoculations, 680; mentioned, xxviii, 268, 272, 275, 281, 282, 285, 328, 333, 337, 347, 351, 358, 387, 395, 406, 414, 428, 495, 529, 556, 557, 567, 597, 634
Committee for Indian affairs, letters from, 651, 672
Committee of claims: members appointed, 21, 116; recommends release of Leonard Snowden, 126; mentioned, 20, 27, 28, 31, 72, 80, 83, 86, 98, 161, 162, 292, 294, 299, 319, 346, 364, 369, 375, 387
Committee of secret correspondence: minutes, 320; ☆ Robert Morris added to, 172; appoints Silas Deane Continental agent to France, 320; instructs Silas Deane, 320–23; asked by Congress about attitudes of foreign powers, 368
Committee on arms and ammunition, letter from, 3
Committee on firearms: letter from, 361; ☆ appointed, 297, 299; contracts for muskets, 656; mentioned, 343, 355
Committee on fortifying ports: letter from, 546; ☆ appointed, 547
Committee on Gen. Montgomery, report, 149
Committee on New York: letter from, 181; ☆ appointed, 155–56, 157, 159, 164, 193–94; confers with New York Committee of Safety, 156, 181–82; calms New York inhabitants, 196; confers with Gen. Lee, 198; mentioned, 183, 191, 201, 306
Committee on saltpetre: letter from, 455; ☆ appointed, 298; mentioned, 346
Committee on trade permits, letter from, 309
Committee to the northward: attends Albany conference, 10; report committed, 20; mentioned, 12, 13, 78
Common Sense (Thomas Paine); see Paine, Thomas, Common Sense
Comstock, Benjamin, 484, 617
Confederation, articles of: discussed, 52–53, 405, 431, 523, 678; support for, 52–53, 94, 285, 602, 668; consideration by Congress rejected, 103; need for, 658; mentioned, 218, 249, 536, 662–63
Congress: chronology of, xiii–xv; colony representation, 3, 174–75, 182, 308; orders loyalists disarmed, 3, 27, 378, 390; orders British supplies seized, 3; prepares journals for publication, 13, 426; recommends expedition against St. Augustine, 13; debates disarming loyalists, 13; publishes resolution on deserters, 14; attendance, 21; publishes resolves on treatment of loyalists, 21; sectional alignments, 22; rejects export exemption, 27–28; debates New York defenses, 31, 37, 90; rejects loan to New York, 36–37; considers state of Canada, 50; sends reinforcements to Canada, 59–60, 78–79, 85–86, 95–96, 99, 105, 117–18, 125, 268–69, 438–40, 562, 582–83, 605, 634–35; recess committee, 63; attitude toward independence, 72, 252, 294; committee on Continental Army, 80; committee on recruiting, 83; debates report on paper currency, 83; debates opening American ports, 86–87, 108, 260–62, 267; committee on Gov. Franklin, 98; forbids sale of tea, 98; permits enlistment of free blacks, 102; rejects consideration of articles of

Government (*continued*)
  Congress, 292, 668–70; assumption of by colonies urged by Congress, 320, 500–501, 652–53, 661–62, 668–70, 673, 676, 678, 681; John Adams' plan of, 399–405; assumption of by South Carolina, 559, 566, 570, 595–96; 600, 623–24, 634–35; *see also* Confederation, articles of
Grafton, 3d duke of (Augustus Henry Fitzroy), 168
Gratz, Bernard, 651
Gratz, Michael, 651
Graves, Samuel, 502
Gravier, Charles, comte de Vergennes, 321
Gray, Ebenezer, identified, 4–5
Great Britain: employs mercenaries, 29, 33, 254, 496, 564, 625–26, 632; acts of trade, 67, 70, 75; obstructs American trade, 246–47, 255; war with France predicted, 281; political situation described, 308; fails to obtain Russian aid, 384, 388, 396, 481; revolution in predicted, 388; denounced, 454, 462, 470, 563; asks Portugal to seize American property, 572; *see also* British army; British navy; George III; North, Frederick (Lord); Parliament; Peace commissioners, British; Prohibitory Act
Greaton, John, 646
Green, Frederick, 574
Green Mountain Boys, 567, 637
Greene, Catharine Ward (Mrs. Christopher): letter to, 222; mentioned, 128, 369
Greene, Christopher: identified, 128; mentioned, 155, 330, 369
Greene, Jack P., ed., *Diary of Colonel Landon Carter*, 238
Greene, Nathanael, 5, 223, 500
Greene (Nathanael) & Co., contracts with secret committee, 166
Grenell, John, examined on Highlands' defense, 38
Grenell, Thomas, recommended as commander of Highlands, 336
Gridley, Richard: continued as chief engineer, 102; mentioned, 547
Griffin, Capt., 196
Griffiths, John, contracts with Francis Lewis, 417
Griswold, Matthew: identified, 365; letter to, 364
Gruber, Ira D., *The Howe Brothers*, 26
Gunpowder; *see* Powder
Gurney, Francis, 111
Guttridge, G. H., ed., *Correspondence of Edmund Burke*, 238
Gwinnett, Button, elected to Congress, xvii

Hall, Lyman, elected to Congress, xvii
Hall & Sellers, 187
Hallock, William: letter to, 641; mentioned, 49, 498
Halsey, Jeremiah, court-martial ordered, 73, 78, 79
Halstead, John: appointed deputy commissary in Canada, 271; mentioned, 440
Hamar, Ibbetson, 121, 518
Hancock, Dorothy Quincy (Mrs. John), 106, 484
Hancock, Ebenezer, identified, 264
Hancock, John: letters from, 6, 16, 17, 27, 40, 77, 80, 85, 98, 104, 110, 111, 119, 120, 121, 122, 123, 127, 129, 146, 152, 153, 155, 162, 163, 174, 182, 186, 205, 216, 234, 235, 236, 243, 263, 282, 287, 288, 310, 316, 317, 340, 341, 342, 348, 350, 355, 367, 376, 378, 379, 380, 381, 385, 386, 406, 423, 424, 432, 434, 437, 448, 457, 458, 469, 483, 484, 488, 494, 497, 502, 504, 506, 514, 540, 541, 542, 548, 549, 558, 560, 561, 562, 568, 573, 575, 579, 581, 582, 583, 584, 585, 588, 589, 590, 604, 605, 606, 618, 620, 621, 637, 644, 645, 647, 648, 653, 670, 671; letters to,

Lee, Francis Lightfoot *(continued)*
Drummond peace mission, 58–59; on foreign affairs, 130; on independence, 130, 407–8, 500; on reconciliation, 168–69; on Gen. Clinton's southern expedition, 237; committee on firearms, 355; criticizes George III, 407–8; on forbidding military officers to impose oaths, 439; mentioned, 614
Lee, Richard, 608
Lee, Richard Henry: letters from, 214, 374, 394, 408, 439, 470, 471, 497, 506, 531, 563, 570, 575, 607, 614, 632, 654, 667; letter to, 58; ☆ elected to Congress, xxii; attends Congress, xxii; on invasion of Canada, 214; on defense of New York, 214; criticizes Gov. Tryon, 214; plans return to Congress, 214; committee on defense of New York, 368, 377; motion on officers' traveling expenses, 384; motion on foreign officers, 397; secures publication of John Adams' *Thoughts on Government*, 406, 559, 564–65; encourages saltmaking, 408, 607; secret committee, 411, 453, 478, 501, 543, 619; motion to send reinforcements to Canada, 439–40; on British corruption, 470; on independence, 470; denounces British tyranny, 563; urges assumption of civil government in Virginia, 563–65, 608; fears partition treaty, 563–64; requests authority to seek foreign alliances, 563–64; plan of government printed, 564; on John Adams' *Thoughts on Government*, 572; accounts, 608–9; counsels Samuel Purviance, 614, 632; defends Samuel Purviance, 614; criticizes Carter Braxton's *Address to the Convention of . . . Virginia*, 667; on government, 667; debates preamble to resolution on assuming government, 670; mentioned, xxix, 48, 385, 459, 577
Lee, Thomas, 490
Lee, Thomas Ludwell, 668
Lee, William, 237
Lee, 237
Le Fargue, Pierre, petition to export produce approved, 215
Legge, William; *see* Dartmouth, 2d earl of
Le Maitre, Adrian: supplies arms, 543; mentioned, 619
Lennox, David, 671
Leonard, Abiel, 653, 654
Le Roy, Jean-Baptiste: identified, 323; ☆ introduced to Silas Deane, 320–21
Leslie, Samuel, 30, 31
Letter to the Inhabitants of Canada: illustrated, xxiv, 147; approved, 148
Levy, Mr., 331
Lewis, Andrew: appointed brig. gen., 317–19, 331, 342, 350, 354; mentioned, 316
Lewis, Francis: letters from, 97, 108, 231, 313, 417, 619; letter to, 162; ☆ elected to Congress, xix; attends Congress, xix; illustrated, xxvi, 418; accounts, 160, 162, 200; sent money by marine committee, 162; secret committee, 190, 203, 211, 251, 256, 266, 291; contracts with secret committee, 215, 266, 291, 314–15; proposes regulation of sutlers, 215; victualing committee, 217; procures shoes for army, 271; delivers money to New York, 301; contracts for naval supplies, 417, 419; committee on shoes and stockings, 619; mentioned, 103, 110, 188, 300, 340, 383, 467, 618, 635, 683
Lewis, W. S., ed., *Horace Walpole's Correspondence*, 238
Lexington (Continental brig), 362, 434, 435, 459, 479, 498, 504, 575, 635, 639, 641
Liberty, 618
Linen: price, 80; importation, 488; mentioned, 517
Lisle, Hugh, 309
Litchfield County, Conn., favors popular election of congressional delegates, 554
Liverpool (H.M.S.), 214, 509, 510, 575, 643, 654, 657, 659
Livestock, exportation forbidden, 171
Livingston, Abraham: victuals troops in New York, 423, 551; resigns victualing contract, 653
Livingston, Gilbert: recommended as commander of highlands, 336; mentioned, 415

Montgomery, Richard (*continued*)
    jected, 112–13; funeral oration for, 150, 154, 157, 173, 226, 240, 278, 284, 294, 304, 594; mentioned, xxiv, xxv, 10, 17, 18, 50, 59, 64, 78, 98, 122, 125, 126, 128, 130, 142, 165, 167, 172, 181, 238, 268, 277, 316, 413
Montgomery, 599
Montreal, Indian conference, 629
Moore, James: appointed brig. gen., 317–19, 331, 342, 350, 354; mentioned, 316
Moore, William, contracts with secret committee, 377
Moore, Capt., 306
Moore's Creek Bridge, N.C., Battle of, 426, 428, 436
Morgan, George: identified, 652; letter to, 651; ☆ sent powder for Indians, 651, 672–73
Morgan, John, appointed lieutenant of Pennsylvania Troops, 90
Morgan, John (Dr.): letter to, 5; ☆ needs medical supplies, 5–6
Morgan, Mary Hopkinson (Mrs. John), 5
Morris, Anthony James, 268
Morris, Jacob, appointed aide-de-camp to Gen. Lee, 471
Morris, Joseph, 80
Morris, Lewis: letters from, 381, 410, 551, 625, 651, 673; ☆ elected to Congress, xx; attends Congress, xx; presents Christopher O'Bryen's *Naval Evolutions* to Congress, 299; committee on firearms, 355; committee on victualing army in Canada, 355
Morris, Richard B., ed., *John Jay*, 592
Morris, Robert: letters from, 166, 170, 258, 267, 313, 320, 365, 466, 487, 489, 494, 497, 498, 506, 576, 598, 617, 640, 641, 648, 657, 675; ☆ elected to Congress, xx; attends Congress, xx; opposes arrest of Lord Drummond and Andrew Elliot, 22; secret committee, 59, 82, 184–85, 203, 251, 256, 266, 291, 298, 306, 309, 329, 345, 377, 411, 447–48, 453, 478, 501, 543, 619, 683; authorized to export produce, 82; committee of secret correspondence, 172, 320; contracts with secret committee, 215, 291, 314–15, 329, 377, 543; on reconciliation, 258–59, 269–70, 495; on independence, 258, 270, 495; on alliance with France, 258; on tobacco contract, 259; health, 267; on invasion of Canada, 267–68, 495; on foreign alliances, 269–70; presents copy of Prohibitory Act to Congress, 310; on British peace commissioners, 366; commercial transactions, 450; provides ship for Silas Deane, 454; instructs Silas Deane, 466–68; described, 587; purchases brig, 641–42; mentioned, 107, 151, 165, 187, 204, 205, 206, 207, 307, 375, 459, 609; *see also* Willing, Morris & Co.
Morton, John: letter from, 106; ☆ elected to Congress, xx; attends Congress, xx; victualing committee, 217; mentioned, 172
Morton, Perez, 7, 8, 16
Motte, Edward, 20, 27
Moylan, Stephen, 5, 101
Mumford, Thomas: letters to, 15, 150, 151, 617; mentioned, 619
Murray, John; *see* Dunmore, 4th earl of
Murray, William; *see* Mansfield, 1st earl of

Nagle, George, appointed major of Pennsylvania troops, 31
Nantucket, R.I., trade, 21
Nautilus (H.M. Sloop), 643
Naval Committee: letters from, 34, 48, 79, 111; ☆ orders to Esek Hopkins, 34–36; sends instructions to Samuel Purviance, 48–49; reports rules for distributing prize money, 50; sends orders to William Stone, 79; sends intelligence to Esek Hopkins, 111–12
Naval Evolutions (Christopher O'Bryen), 299, 300

716

Nedham, Marchamont, 400
Nelson, John: letter to, 386; ☆ ordered to New York, 384, 386; mentioned, 167, 172
Nelson, Lucy Grymes (Mrs. Thomas), 194, 249
Nelson, Thomas: letters from, 30, 193, 248; ☆ elected to Congress, xxii; attends Congress, xxii; on American naval preparations, 30; plans to return home, 248–49; on independence, 249; on articles of confederation, 249; on foreign alliances, 249; on reconciliation, 249; board of treasury, 271; mentioned, 245, 449, 667
Nesbitt, John Maxwell: identified, 40; ☆ reports on merchant support for reconciliation, 40
Neville, Henry, 400
New Hampshire: representation in Congress, 3; Continental troops, 14, 88–89, 117, 119–20, 324, 678; appoints delegates, 56; opposition to new government, 85, 88, 93, 318–20, 333–34; military bounties, 117; advanced funds, 118, 131–32; Continental officers, 126; Continental frigate constructed in, 189, 243, 280, 354; disaffection in, 280; accounts, 516
New Hampshire Assembly, letters to, 344, 514
New Hampshire Committee of Safety, letters to, 88, 117, 131
New Hampshire Convention, letters to, 62, 119, 635
New Hampshire Council, letter to, 604
New Hampshire delegates, election, 56
New Haven, Conn., Committee: criticized by Oliver Wolcott, 390–92; urges adherence to Association, 390–91
New Jersey: loyalists in, 13; Continental troops, 80, 120–21, 318; Continental officers, 219, 352, 621; militia, 235–36, 240–41, 297, 379–81, 383–84, 395, 542; powder for, 346, 411
New Jersey Assembly, petition to king, 23
New Jersey Committee of Safety: letters to, 120, 432, 458; ☆ advanced money, 31, 32, 260; requested to purchase arms for Col. Maxwell, 154; requested to provide wagons, 154; sent powder, 260; transfers prisoners, 432; sends money to delegates, 463; mentioned, 127
New Jersey delegates: ordered to execute resolves on loyalists, 38; elected to Congress, 291–92; quorum requirements fixed, 291–92; send steel to Gen. Schuyler, 311, 350, 362; favor compensation for Michael Kearney, 352; sent money, 463; divisions among, 507
New Jersey Provincial Congress: seeks advice on sale of tea, 219; recommends officers to Congress, 219; elects delegates, 291–92; fixes quorum requirements for delegates, 291–92
New Jersey Provincial Convention: letters to, 235, 379, 635; ☆ advanced money, 260; sent powder, 260; inquires about reinforcements for Gen. Lee, 297; ordered to secure *Blue Mountain Valley*, 310; prepares reinforcements for New York, 379–80
New London, Conn., fortification, 515, 546–47, 622
New Providence, Bahamas: assaulted by Continental Navy, 479, 491–92; military supplies captured, 479, 491–92; prisoners taken, 491–92
New York: loyalists in, 3, 27, 37–38, 50, 80, 155–56, 182, 188, 190, 211–12, 374, 382; defenses debated in Congress, 31; loan request rejected, 36–37; Continental troops, 80, 102–3, 117, 231, 300–301, 380; powder supplies, 97, 110; defection feared, 105; Continental frigates constructed in, 108, 417, 419; Continental officers, 122, 300–301, 355, 380–84, 415, 459, 625, 647; advanced money, 231, 300–301; poor relief, 233–34; sent saltpetre, 240; defense, 301, 368, 378–80, 500, 542; included in middle military department, 310; delegates' remuneration, 329; sent powder, 346, 381, 383; reinforcements sent to, 372, 376–79, 380, 383–84, 388, 395, 458; militia, 379–81, 383–84, 395, 542; military efforts criticized, 383; popular licentiousness criticized, 433; criticized, 453; emits currency, 453; disputes selection

718

North Carolina delegates: letters from, 18, 220, 250; ☆ send Presbyterian ministers to North Carolina, 28–29, 42, 58; on Gen. Clinton's southern expedition, 250; on defense of North Carolina, 250; authorized to support independence and foreign alliances, 417, 600, 613; remuneration, 443–44

North Carolina Provincial Congress, authorizes delegates to support independence and foreign alliances, 417, 600, 613

North Ministry: conciliatory proposal (1775), 69, 71; proposes Prohibitory Act, 244, 247, 250–51, 254–55

Northern military department: supplies for, 46, 355; strength, 337; status debated, 440; mentioned, 17, 146; *see also* Canada, American invasion of

Nourse, James, 576

Nourse, Joseph, 270

Novaue, Capt., 447

Oakman, Graham, advanced money by secret committee, 377

Oaths of allegiance: military officers forbidden to impose, 374, 382; imposed on New York loyalists, 374, 382; imposed on Rhode Island loyalists, 382; reportedly administered by Gov. Tryon, 591; mentioned, 439, 670

O'Bryen, Christopher, *Naval Evolutions*, 299, 300

Occum, Sampson, petitions on behalf of Indians, 188, 203

Ogden, Matthias: appointed lt. col. of New Jersey troops, 352, 621; promotion criticized, 621; promotion reaffirmed, 621; mentioned, 619

Ohio Indians, trade, 162

Oneida Indians, friendly to Americans, 556

Onondaga, Indian conference, 629

Orange Iron Works, 417

Oration (David Rittenhouse), presented to Congress, 14

Oration (Rev. William Smith), illustrated, xxv, 279

Oration (Peter Thacher), 341

Orne, Azor, 441

Osgood, Samuel, 340, 352, 354

Osman, John, 543, 598

Osnaburg: importation, 362; mentioned, 407

Otis, James, Sr., letter to, 597

Otis, James, Jr., xxv

Otter (H.M. Sloop), 214, 395, 419, 575

Paca, William: letters from, 186, 248, 410, 447, 474; ☆ elected to Congress, xviii; attends Congress, xviii; mentioned, 187, 294, 474

Paddock, Seth, petition to import flour rejected, 21

Page, John, letters to, 168, 248, 408

Page, Mann, letter to, 30

Paine, Robert Treat: diary, 16, 49, 60, 278, 308, 368, 387, 436, 437, 456, 491, 497, 510, 533, 568, 615, 625, 643; letters from, 6, 8, 9, 11, 19, 156, 254, 344, 361, 455, 457, 475, 476, 484, 486, 532, 656; ☆ elected to Congress, xviii; attends Congress, xviii; arrives in Philadelphia, 6; criticizes James Warren, 6–8, 10–13; criticizes John Adams, 6–8, 10–12; resigns as Massachusetts judge, 8–10; committee to the northward, 9–10, 12–13, 20; opposed in Massachusetts, 106; opposes employment of Roman Catholic officers, 204; cannon committee, 254; on manufacture of powder, 254; committee on firearms, 297, 344, 355; on need for manufacturing military supplies, 344; committee on saltpetre, 344, 455–56; encourages manufac-

Privateering (*continued*)
428–29, 514; mentioned, 62, 103, 261, 346, 366, 390, 435, 441, 452, 459, 489, 490, 492, 494, 511
Prize agents, Continental: nominated by marine committee, 566; appointed by Congress, 573; John Langdon's appointment proposed, 599–600; mentioned, 588 622
Prizes, distribution of shares, 50, 506, 555
Prohibitory Act: proposed by Lord North, 244, 247, 250–51, 254–55; copy presented to Congress, 307, 310; criticized, 395, 416, 442, 509, 514; increases support for independence, 431; mentioned, 286, 293, 330, 331, 466, 511, 515, 516
Providence (Continental sloop), 36, 57
Purviance, Robert, 165
Purviance, Samuel, Jr.: letters to, 48, 164, 394, 614, 632; ☆ instructions from naval committee, 48–49; constructs Continental frigate in Maryland, 164–65; letter read in Congress, 550–51, 574, 632; criticized, 550–51, 557–58; letter debated in Congress, 557–58; condemned by Maryland Council of Safety, 614, 632; defended by Richard Henry Lee, 614, 632; mentioned, 248, 363, 541
Putnam, Israel: identified, 491; letters to, 490, 497, 502, 542; ☆ appointed maj. gen., 90; requests money, 497; sent money, 502; ordered to discharge militia, 542; mentioned, 5, 151, 274, 373, 500

Quakers, 40, 422
Quebec; *see* Canada, American invasion of
Quebec Act, 69
Queens County, N.Y., loyalists disarmed, 27
Quincy, Josiah, letter to, 529
Quincy, Josiah, Jr., 529, 530
Quincy, Josiah, *Memoir of Josiah Quincy Jun.*, 530
Quincy, Norton: identified, 464; letter to, 464
Quorum requirements: New York, 37; South Carolina, 98, 105; New Jersey, 291–92

Race, Henry, *Sketch of Col. Thomas Lowrey*, 152
Rachell, 313, 315, 346, 362, 599
Raleigh (Continental frigate), 88, 566
Ramsay, Mr., advanced money by secret committee, 377
Randolph, Benjamin, petition rejected, 103
Randolph, Edmund, resigns as deputy muster-master general, 577
Rankin, Hugh F., *North Carolina Continentals*, 19
Rawlins, Thomas, instructions from secret committee, 291
Raymond, James, 490
Read, George: letters from, 106, 115, 345, 506, 575, 616; letter to, 115; ☆ elected to Congress, xvii; attends Congress, xvii; illustrated, xxiii, 114; urged to return to Congress, 115; marine committee, 345; instructions from Delaware Assembly, 345; mentioned, 138
Read, Gertrude Ross (Mrs. George), letter to, 616
Read, Thomas, 641
Read, William, 7
Reading, Pa., Committee of Inspection, letter to, 386
Rebecca and Francis, 110
Reconciliation: Drummond peace mission, 22–27, 32–34, 39–40, 42–43, 69–71, 74–75, 91–93, 101–2, 198–201, 335; proposals for, 63–68, 132–34; opposition to, 94–95, 308, 319, 392, 495–96, 539–40, 586; prospects for, 95, 130, 168–69, 229, 244, 258–59, 265, 287, 414, 416, 427–8, 444, 473, 503, 528–29; effect on France dis-

Thoughts on Government (John Adams): illustrated, xxvi, 401; genesis, 405–6, 559; publication, 405–6; discussed, 564–65; reply to, 661; mentioned, xxvii, 508, 509, 525, 572, 658
Tibbett, James, 362, 363, 408, 419
Ticonderoga, N.Y.: defense, 148, 567; mentioned, 146, 488
Tilghman, Anna Maria: identified, 376; letter to, 375
Tilghman, Matthew: letters from, 375, 389, 582; ☆ elected to Congress, xviii; attends Congress, xviii; on reconciliation, 376; mentioned, 71, 308
Tilley (Tylee) Edward, exchange, 38, 81, 83
Tilley (Tylee), Mrs. Edward, 38
Tilton, James, 675
Timothy, Peter, 76, 98
Tin, 446
Tobacco: proposed contract for, 259; mentioned, 62, 450, 451
Todd, Anthony: identified, 463; letter to, 462
Tolly, Walter, 227
Tompkin, Samuel, appointed Continental Navy captain, 330, 332
Towers, Robert: orders from secret committee, 377, 411, 448, 478, 543, 657; advanced money by secret committee, 411; mentioned, 338, 435
Tracy, Jared, 149
Tracy, Nathaniel, 56
Trade: role in reconciliation, 23–25, 67, 70–71, 75, 101–2, 258–59; for military supplies, 27–28, 43–44; in Philadelphia, 45; foreign, 52, 58–60, 72–73, 82, 194–95, 218–19, 269–70, 311–13, 320–23, 536; opening of American ports, 86–87, 108, 151, 191–92, 260–62, 267, 286–87, 305, 421, 423, 429, 431, 492–93, 509; proposed duties on, 102; with Ohio Indians, 162; commercial treaties considered, 218–19, 311–13, 326; obstructed by Great Britain, 246–47, 255, 366; considered in Congress, 257, 267, 311–13; role in foreign affairs, 261; restricted by Congress, 306, 331; committee on exportation of produce for arms, 309; importation of Indian trade goods, 313–15, 320–21; proposals to encourage, 425–26; with Bermuda, 466–68; mentioned, 107, 171, 358, 359, 390, 391, 392, 410, 434, 450, 491, 500, 514, 515, 522, 538, 546, 552, 564; *see also* Nonexportation; Prohibitory Act; Secret committee
Trail, Mary Whipple (Mrs. Robert), 396
Trail, Robert, identified, 396
Treasury; *see* Board of treasury
Treasury committee, 299
Trenton, N. J., 32, 86
Trenton, N.J., Committee: letters to, 129, 153; ☆ requested to supply Col. Maxwell, 153; requested to provide wagons for prisoners' baggage, 153–54; advanced funds, 159
Trott, George, 273
Trumbull, John (1750–1831), letter to, 242
Trumbull, John (1750–1831), *M'Fingal*, 233
Trumbull, John (1756–1843), *The Declaration of Independence*, xxvi
Trumbull, Jonathan, Sr.: letters to, 85, 381, 604; ☆ on Connecticut-Pennsylvania boundary dispute, 283–84; sends cannon to Philadelphia, 638; mentioned, 36, 90, 97, 120, 225, 546
Trumbull, Jonathan, Jr.: paymaster funds authorized, 102; mentioned, 99
Trumbull, Joseph: letters to, 4, 95, 290, 371, 445, 465, 466, 584, 653; ☆ pay as commissary general, 4, 463; commissary general's allowance, 95; moves to New York, 547; relations with Walter Livingston, 547, 551; ordered to send provisions to Canada, 583–84, 653; mentioned, 546

Advisory Committee

Library of Congress American Revolution Bicentennial Program

John R. Alden
James B. Duke Professor of History Emeritus, Duke University

Julian P. Boyd
Editor of The Papers of Thomas Jefferson, *Princeton University*

Lyman H. Butterfield
Editor in Chief Emeritus of The Adams Papers, *Massachusetts Historical Society*

Jack P. Greene
Andrew W. Mellon Professor in the Humanities, The Johns Hopkins University

Merrill Jensen
Editor of The Documentary History of the Ratification of the Constitution

Cecelia M. Kenyon
Charles N. Clark Professor of Government, Smith College

Aubrey C. Land
University Research Professor, University of Georgia

Edmund S. Morgan
Sterling Professor of History, Yale University

Richard B. Morris
Gouverneur Morris Professor of History Emeritus, Columbia University

George C. Rogers, Jr.
Yates Snowden Professor of American History, University of South Carolina

☆ U.S. GOVERNMENT PRINTING OFFICE: 1978 O—214–772